A COMPANION TO GR
POLITICAL THOUGHT

BLACKWELL COMPANIONS TO THE ANCIENT WORLD

This series provides sophisticated and authoritative overviews of periods of ancient history, genres of classical literature, and the most important themes in ancient culture. Each volume comprises approximately twenty-five and forty concise essays written by individual scholars within their area of specialization. The essays are written in a clear, provocative, and lively manner, designed for an international audience of scholars, students, and general readers.

ANCIENT HISTORY

Published

A Companion to the Roman Army
Edited by Paul Erdkamp

A Companion to the Roman Republic
Edited by Nathan Rosenstein and Robert Morstein-Marx

A Companion to the Roman Empire
Edited by David S. Potter

A Companion to the Classical Greek World
Edited by Konrad H. Kinzl

A Companion to the Ancient Near East
Edited by Daniel C. Snell

A Companion to the Hellenistic World
Edited by Andrew Erskine

A Companion to Late Antiquity
Edited by Philip Rousseau

A Companion to Ancient History
Edited by Andrew Erskine

A Companion to Archaic Greece
Edited by Kurt A. Raaflaub and Hans van Wees

A Companion to Julius Caesar
Edited by Miriam Griffin

A Companion to Byzantium
Edited by Liz James

A Companion to Ancient Egypt
Edited by Alan B. Lloyd

A Companion to Ancient Macedonia
Edited by Joseph Roisman and Ian Worthington

A Companion to the Punic Wars
Edited by Dexter Hoyos

A Companion to Augustine
Edited by Mark Vessey

A Companion to Marcus Aurelius
Edited by Marcel van Ackeren

A Companion to Ancient Greek Government
Edited by Hans Beck

LITERATURE AND CULTURE

Published

A Companion to Classical Receptions
Edited by Lorna Hardwick and Christopher Stray

A Companion to Greek and Roman Historiography
Edited by John Marincola

A Companion to Catullus
Edited by Marilyn B. Skinner

A Companion to Roman Religion
Edited by Jörg Rüpke

A Companion to Greek Religion
Edited by Daniel Ogden

A Companion to the Classical Tradition
Edited by Craig W. Kallendorf

A Companion to Roman Rhetoric
Edited by William Dominik and Jon Hall

A Companion to Greek Rhetoric
Edited by Ian Worthington

A Companion to Ancient Epic
Edited by John Miles Foley

A Companion to Greek Tragedy
Edited by Justina Gregory

A Companion to Latin Literature
Edited by Stephen Harrison

A Companion to Greek and Roman Political Thought
Edited by Ryan K. Balot

A Companion to Ovid
Edited by Peter E. Knox

A Companion to the Ancient Greek Language
Edited by Egbert Bakker

A Companion to Hellenistic Literature
Edited by Martine Cuypers and James J. Clauss

A Companion to Vergil's *Aeneid* and its Tradition
Edited by Joseph Farrell and Michael C. J. Putnam

A Companion to Horace
Edited by Gregson Davis

A Companion to Families in the Greek and Roman Worlds
Edited by Beryl Rawson

A Companion to Greek Mythology
Edited by Ken Dowden and Niall Livingstone

A Companion to the Latin Language
Edited by James Clackson

A Companion to Tacitus
Edited by Victoria Emma Pagán
A Companion to Women in the Ancient World
Edited by Sharon L. James and Sheila Dillon
Edited by Kirk Ormand

A Companion to the Archaeology of the Ancient Near East
Edited by Daniel Potts

A Companion to Roman Love Elegy
Edited by Barbara K. Gold

A Companion to Greek Art
Edited by Tyler Jo Smith and Dimitris Plantzos

A Companion to Persius and Juvenal
Edited by Susanna Braund and Josiah Osgood

A COMPANION
TO GREEK
AND ROMAN
POLITICAL
THOUGHT

Edited by

Ryan K. Balot

A John Wiley & Sons, Ltd., Publication

Registered Office
John Wiley & Sons, Ltd, The Atrium, Southern Gate, Chichester, West Sussex, PO19 8SQ, UK

Editorial Offices
350 Main Street, Malden, MA 02148-5020, USA
9600 Garsington Road, Oxford, OX4 2DQ, UK
The Atrium, Southern Gate, Chichester, West Sussex, PO19 8SQ, UK

For details of our global editorial offices, for customer services, and for information about how to apply for permission to reuse the copyright material in this book please see our website at www.wiley.com/wiley-blackwell.

Library of Congress Cataloging-in-Publication Data

A companion to Greek and Roman political thought / edited by Ryan K. Balot.
   p.   cm. – (Blackwell companions to the ancient world. Literature and culture)
  Includes bibliographical references and index.
  ISBN 978-1-4051-5143-6 (hardcover : alk. paper) 978-1-118-45135-9 (pbk. : alk. paper)
1. Political science–Greece–History.   2. Political science–Rome–History. I. Balot, Ryan K. (Ryan Krieger), 1969–
  JC73.C67 2009
  320.0938–dc22

                                         2008035574

A catalogue record for this book is available from the British Library.

Cover image: The forum, Rome, 2002. Photo © Stuart Franklin / Magnum Photos.
Cover design by Workhaus

Set in 10/12.5pt Galliard by SPi Publisher Services, Pondicherry, India
Printed in Malaysia by Ho Printing (M) Sdn Bhd

1   2013

To My Teachers at Jesuit High School of New Orleans

Contents

Notes on Contributors

Ryan K. Balot is Associate Professor of Political Science at the University of Toronto. The author of *Greed and Injustice in Classical Athens* (2001) and *Greek Political Thought* (2006), he specializes in the history of political thought. He received his doctorate in Classics at Princeton and his BA degrees in Classics from the University of North Carolina-Chapel Hill and Corpus Christi College, Oxford, where he studied as a Rhodes Scholar. Balot is currently at work on *Courage and Its Critics in Democratic Athens*, from which he has published articles in the *American Journal of Philology, Classical Quarterly, Ancient Philosophy,* and *Social Research.*

Todd Breyfogle is Director of Seminars for the Aspen Institute. He studied at Colorado College and Corpus Christi College, Oxford (as a Rhodes Scholar) before earning his PhD from the Committee on Social Thought at the University of Chicago. He is coeditor of a five-volume commentary on Augustine's *City of God* (forthcoming from Oxford University Press) and edited *Literary Imagination, Ancient and Modern: Essays in Honor of*

David Grene (1999). He has authored numerous articles on subjects ranging from Augustine, to J. S. Bach, to contemporary political theory.

Eric Brown is Associate Professor of Philosophy at Washington University in St Louis, and the author of several articles on Greek and Roman philosophy, and of *Stoic Cosmopolitanism* (forthcoming). Before moving to St Louis, he studied Classics and Philosophy at the universities of Cambridge, Pittsburgh, and Chicago.

Paul Cartledge is A. G. Leventis Professor of Greek Culture within the Faculty of Classics at the University of Cambridge and a Fellow of Clare College; he also holds the visiting position of Hellenic Parliament Global Distinguished Professor in the Theory and History of Democracy at New York University. His latest book is *Ancient Greek Political Thought in Practice* (2009).

Craige B. Champion is Associate Professor of Ancient History and Classics and Chair of the History Department in the Maxwell School of Citizenship and

Public Affairs at Syracuse University. In 2004, he won the Daniel Patrick Moynihan Award in recognition of scholarly productivity, teaching excellence, and community service. His scholarly interests lie in the history of the hellenistic world and the Middle Roman Republic, and Greek and Roman historiography. He has had an enduring interest in the ancient Greek historian Polybius. He is the author of *Cultural Politics in Polybius's Histories* (2004), editor of *Roman Imperialism: Readings and Sources* (2004), and coeditor, with Arthur M. Eckstein, of a new, annotated, two-volume English-language edition of Polybius, *The Landmark Edition of Polybius' Histories* (forthcoming). He has published numerous articles and review essays on ancient Greek and Roman history and historiography.

Timothy Chappell is Professor of Philosophy at The Open University, Milton Keynes, England, and Director of the Open University Ethics Centre. His books are *Values and Virtues: Aristotelianism in Contemporary Ethics* (2007); *The Inescapable Self* (2005); *Reading Plato's Theaetetus* (2004); *Human Values: New Essays in Ethics and Natural Law* (edited with David Oderberg, 2004); *Understanding Human Goods* (1998); *Philosophy of the Environment* (1997); *The Plato Reader* (1996); and *Aristotle and Augustine on Freedom* (1995).

David J. Depew is Professor in the Department of Communication Studies and the interdisciplinary Project on the Rhetoric of Inquiry (POROI) at the University of Iowa. He writes on the philosophy, history, and rhetoric of biology and its relation to culture in ancient and modern times, with special attention to Aristotle and Darwinism. He is coauthor with Marjorie Grene of *Philosophy*

of Biology: An Episodic History (2004). Recent publications include "Consequence Etiology and Biological Teleology in Aristotle and Darwin," (2008).

Arthur M. Eckstein is Professor of History at the University of Maryland, and a specialist in the history of the hellenistic world and Roman imperialism under the Republic. He has published four books, a coedited book, and 50 major scholarly articles. His two most recent books, *Mediterranean Anarchy, Interstate War, and the Rise of Rome* (2006) and *Rome Enters the Greek East: From Anarchy to Hierarchy in the Hellenistic Mediterranean, 230–170 BC* (2008), are pioneering efforts at combining modern international-systems theory with ancient history.

Matt Edge has recently completed his PhD at the University of Cambridge, on the notion of individual freedom in classical Athens and its modern equivalent, and is in the process of submitting this for publication as a number of articles. His main interests are in political and moral philosophy, particularly the concepts of liberty, cosmopolitanism, and socialism.

Sara Forsdyke is Associate Professor in the Department of Classical Studies at the University of Michigan. She is the author of *Exile, Ostracism, and Democracy: The Politics of Expulsion in Ancient Greece* (2005) and numerous articles on Greek history, Herodotus, and Greek political thought.

John Gibert is Associate Professor of Classics at the University of Colorado at Boulder. He is the author of *Change of Mind in Greek Tragedy* (1995), coauthor (with C. Collard and M. J. Cropp) of *Euripides: Selected Fragmentary Plays II* (2004), and has written articles, chapters, and reviews on Greek drama, religion, and philosophy (including "The Sophists," in the *Blackwell Guide to Ancient Philosophy*). His current project is an edition with commentary of Euripides' *Ion*.

David E. Hahm is Professor of Greek and Latin at the Ohio State University, Columbus. He is the author of *The Origins of Stoic Cosmology*, as well as articles on Plato, Aristotle, hellenistic philosophy and science, and the historiography of philosophy in antiquity. His current projects include Polybius' political theory and Greek physical philosophy.

Dean Hammer is the John W. Wetzel Professor of Classics and Professor of Government at Franklin and Marshall College. He is the author of *The Iliad as Politics: The Performance of Political Thought* (2002), as well as articles on ancient and modern political thought in the *American Journal of Philology, Historia, Political Theory, Classical Journal, Arethusa,* and *Phoenix.* His book *Roman Political Thought and the Return to the World* (2008) explores the relationship between Roman and modern political thought.

Charles W. Hedrick, Jr has taught at the University of California at Santa Cruz since 1990, and he is currently Professor in the History Department there. He is the author of articles, chapters, and books. His principal publications include *The Decrees of the Demotionidai* (1990); *History and Silence: Purge and Rehabilitation of Memory in Late Antiquity* (2000); and *Ancient History: Monuments and Documents* (2006). He is also joint editor of *Demokratia: A Conversation on Democracies, Ancient and Modern* (1996) and of the exhibition catalog *The Birth of Democracy: An Exhibition* (1993).

Zena Hitz is Assistant Professor of Philosophy at the University of Maryland, Baltimore County. She received her degree in 2005 from Princeton University's classical philosophy program and specializes in ancient political philosophy. She has written essays on Plato's critique of democracy and on Aristotle on friendship, and is currently working on the philosophical origins of the ideal of the rule of law.

Rachana Kamtekar is Assistant Professor of Philosophy at the University of Arizona. She is a co-editor (with Sara Ahbel-Rappe) of *A Companion to Socrates* (2006) and the author of several articles on Plato, Stoicism, and moral psychology. She is currently writing a book on Plato's psychology entitled *The Powers of Plato's Psychology.*

Robert A. Kaster is Professor of Classics and Kennedy Foundation Professor of Latin Language and Literature at Princeton University. He is the author of *Guardians of Language: The Grammarian and Society in Late Antiquity* (1988); *Emotion, Restraint, and Community in Ancient Rome* (2005); commentaries on Suetonius' *De Grammaticis et Rhetoribus* (1995) and Cicero's *Pro Sestio* (2006); and articles on Roman literature and culture.

David Konstan is the John Rowe Workman Professor of Classics and the Humanistic Tradition, and Professor of Comparative Literature, at Brown University. His most recent books are *The Emotions of the Ancient Greeks* (2006); a translation of Aspasius' commentary on Aristotle's *Nicomachean Ethics* (2006); *Terms for Eternity* (with Ilaria Ramelli, 2007); and *Lucrezio e la psicologia epicurea* (trans. Ilaria Ramelli, 2007; in English as *A Life Worthy of the Gods: The Materialist Psychology of Epicurus,* 2008). He was president of the American Philological Association in 1999.

Peter Liddel is Lecturer in Ancient History at the University of Manchester. His research is related to Greek political history, ancient Greek historiography, Greek epigraphy, and modern historiography (particularly histories of Greece). He is the author of *Civic Obligation and Individual Liberty in Ancient Athens* (2007), and has edited a republication of Connop Thirlwall's history of Greece: *Bishop Thirlwall's History of Greece* (2007). Currently he is working on articles related to the appearance of inscriptions and other documents in Greek literary texts, and studies of non-Athenian epigraphical habits.

Paul W. Ludwig is a Tutor at St John's College in Annapolis, Maryland. He is the author of *Eros and Polis: Desire and Community in Greek Political Theory* (2002). His articles have appeared in the *American Journal of Philology* and in the *American Political Science Review.* He is currently working on a book on civic friendship, as well as a volume for the Cambridge series Key Themes in Ancient Philosophy on love, friendship, and the family.

Christopher Nadon teaches courses in political philosophy for the Government Department at Claremont McKenna College and is currently at work on a study of the separation of church and state. He is the author of *Xenophon's Prince: Republic and Empire in the Cyropaedia* (2001).

Debra Nails is Professor of Philosophy at Michigan State University, and is the author of *The People of Plato: A Prosopography of Plato and Other Socratics* (2002); *Agora, Academy, and the Conduct of Philosophy* (1995); and articles in ancient and modern philosophy. With J. H. Lesher and Frisbee Sheffield, she

edited *Plato's Symposium: Issues in Interpretation and Reception* (2006).

Carlos F. Noreña is Assistant Professor of History at the University of California at Berkeley. He works primarily on the history of the Roman Empire, especially the political and cultural history of the first two centuries AD. He is currently completing a book, *The Circulation of Imperial Ideals in the Roman West,* that examines the figure of the Roman emperor as a unifying symbol for the western empire.

Josiah Ober is the Constantine Mitsotakis Professor of Political Science and Classics at Stanford University. His books include *Mass and Elite in Democratic Athens* (1989), *Political Dissent in Democratic Athens* (1998), and *Democracy and Knowledge* (2008). His current research projects concern public action and the organization of information in democracies, and the emergence of dispersed authority in extensive ecologies of states. Before coming to Stanford in 2006, he taught at Princeton and Montana State universities.

Robin Osborne is Professor of Ancient History at the University of Cambridge and a Fellow of King's College. He has published widely in Greek history and archaeology, including *Greece in the Making 1200–479 BC* (1996), *Archaic and Classical Greek Art* (1998), and *Greek History* (2004). With P. J. Rhodes he edited *Greek Historical Inscriptions 404–323 BC* (2003). He is a Fellow of the British Academy.

Kurt A. Raaflaub is David Herlihy University Professor in Classics and History and Director of the Program in Ancient Studies at Brown University. His research interests have focused on the social, political, military, and intellectual history of archaic and classical Greece and republican Rome, and on the comparative history of the ancient world. Recent books include *The Discovery of Freedom in Ancient Greece* (2004), winner of the James Henry Breasted Prize of the American Historical Association, *Origins of Democracy in Ancient Greece* (coauthored, 2007), and *War and Peace in the Ancient World* (edited, 2007).

P. J. Rhodes studied at Oxford, and has been working at the University of Durham since 1965: he became Professor of Ancient History in 1983, and since his retirement in 2005 has been Honorary Professor and Emeritus Professor. He is a specialist in Greek history, and particularly in politics and political institutions: his *History of the Classical Greek World* was published in 2005, and most recently he has written the Introduction and Notes to Thucydides, *The Peloponnesian War*, trans. Martin Hammond (2009).

Arlene W. Saxonhouse is the Caroline Robbins Collegiate Professor of Political Science and Women's Studies and Adjunct Professor of Classics at the University of Michigan. She is the author of *Women in the History of Political Thought: Ancient Greece to Machiavelli* (1985); *Fear of Diversity: The Birth of Political Science in Ancient Greek Thought* (1992); coeditor of *Hobbes's Three Discourses: A Modern, Critical Edition of Newly Identified Works by the Young Thomas Hobbes* (1995); *Athenian Democracy: Modern Mythmakers and Ancient Theorists* (1996); and *Free Speech and Democracy in Ancient Athens* (2006).

Malcolm Schofield is Professor of Ancient Philosophy, University of Cambridge, where he has taught in the Faculty of Classics since 1972. He was editor of *Phronesis* from 1987 to 1992.

He is coauthor (with G. S. Kirk and J. E. Raven) of *The Presocratic Philosophers* (2nd edn 1983). Of the many collected volumes he has helped to edit the most recent to appear is *The Cambridge History of Greek and Roman Political Thought* (2000), which he coedited with Christopher Rowe. His other writings on ancient political philosophy include *The Stoic Idea of the City* (1991), *Saving the City* (1999), and *Plato: Political Philosophy* (2006).

Giulia Sissa is a Professor of Classics and Political Science at the University of California at Los Angeles. She has been a researcher at the CNRS in Paris, and Professor of Classics and head of department at the Johns Hopkins University. She is the author of numerous books and articles, including, *Greek Virginity* (1997), *The Daily Life of the Greek Gods* (with Marcel Detienne, 2000), *Le Plaisir et le mal. Philosophie de la drogue* (1997), *L'âme est un corps de femme* (2000), and *Sex and Sensuality in the Ancient World* (2008). She is currently working on politics and the passions and on the pursuit of pleasure from Athens to Utopia.

Philip A. Stadter is Falk Professor in the Humanities Emeritus in the Classics Department of the University of North Carolina at Chapel Hill. His books include *Arrian of Nicomedia* (1980), *A Commentary on Plutarch's Pericles* (1989), and introductions and notes to Plutarch, *Nine Greek Lives* (1998) and Plutarch, *Eight Roman Lives* (1999). He has also edited *Plutarch and the Historical Tradition* (1992) and, with L. Van der Stockt, *Sage and Emperor* (2002).

W. Jeffrey Tatum is Associate Professor of Ancient History at the University of Sydney. He is the author of *The Patrician Tribune: Publius Clodius Pulcher* (1999) and *Always I am Caesar* (2008), as well as numerous papers on Roman history and Latin literature. He is currently writing a commentary on the *Commentariolum Petitionis* attributed to Quintus Cicero.

Robert W. Wallace is Professor of Classics at Northwestern University. He is the author of *The Areopagos Council, to 307 BC* (1989) and *Reconstructing Damon: Music, Wisdom Teaching, and Politics in Democratic Athens* (forthcoming). He coauthored *The Origins of Greek Democracy* (2007) and has coedited four volumes on Greek law, Greek music and performance, and hellenistic political history. He has published widely in the fields of Greek history, law, music theory, numismatics, and literature.

Catherine H. Zuckert is a Nancy Reeves Dreux Professor of Political Science at the University of Notre Dame and editor of *The Review of Politics*. Her books include *Natural Right and the American Imagination: Political Philosophy in Novel Form* (1990); *Postmodern Platos: Nietzsche, Heidegger, Gadamer, Strauss, Derrida* (1996); and *Plato's Philosophers* (2009). She coauthored *The Truth about Leo Strauss* (2006) with her husband Michael, and edited *Understanding the Political Spirit: From Socrates to Nietzsche* (1988).

Acknowledgments

This *Companion* brings together classicists, ancient historians, political scientists, and philosophers in an attempt to offer fresh perspectives on classical political thought. The primary aim of the volume is to reconsider our relationship to the ancient Greeks and Romans, with a view to deepening our understanding of political life as such. The editor and contributors are deeply grateful to Al Bertrand for help, encouragement, and advice throughout the process, and to the production staff at Blackwell/Wiley, including Barbara Duke and Ben Thatcher. Ann Bone has been an outstanding copy-editor. The editor also gratefully acknowledges permission to reprint chapters 21 and 22 from *A Companion to Socrates*, edited by Sara Ahbel-Rappe and Rachana Kamtekar (Blackwell, 2006).

At the beginning of the project, my colleagues George Pepe, Andrew Rehfeld, and Eric Brown of Washington University in St Louis were invariably stimulating inter-locutors. In the midst of working on this volume, I joined the Department of Political Science at the University of Toronto. For their support as I migrated from Classics to Political Science, and from the United States to Canada, I would like to thank George Pepe, Brad Inwood, Kurt Raaflaub, Arlene Saxonhouse, Jill Frank, Steve Salkever, Sara Forsdyke, and Josh Ober. In Toronto, I have been immensely grateful for the companionship and encouragement of my new colleagues, especially Clifford Orwin, Brad Inwood, Edward Andrew, Ronald Beiner, Simone Chambers, Victoria Wohl, and Neil Nevitte. The volume has also benefited from the hard work of my research assistant, Larissa Atkison.

My wife, Carroll, provided invaluable support throughout my work on this project. I would not have been able to finish the collection without her friendship and encouragement. Our daughters, Julia and Corinne, have, as always, given me great joy from start to finish.

I dedicate this volume to four teachers who first taught me Latin and Greek and first introduced me to the Homeric epics, Plato's *Republic*, and Ciceronian oratory: Rev. Claude P. Boudreaux, S.J.; Dr Stephen Pearce; Mr Grégoire C. Richard; and Rev. Wayne Roca, S.J.

Note on Translations

All translations in this volume were done by the authors themselves, unless otherwise indicated. Bibliographic information on the translations used can be found in the List of References and occasionally in the List of Abbreviations.

Abbreviations

This is a list of abbreviations of ancient authors, texts, and editions of fragmentary source material occurring in the chapters. With several exceptions, this list follows that of the *Oxford Classical Dictionary*, 3rd edition, edited by Simon Hornblower and Antony Spawforth (Oxford: Oxford University Press, 1996). In the case of familiar titles, I have tended, by contrast with Hornblower and Spawforth, to use the standard English equivalents rather than the Latin translations (e.g. Pl. *Resp.* = Plato, *Republic*, rather than Plato, *Respublica*).

ABD	*The Anchor Bible Dictionary*
Ael.	Aelianus
VH	*Varia Historia*
Aen.	*Aeneid*
Aesch.	Aeschylus
Pers.	*Persians*
Sept.	*Seven against Thebes*
Aeschin.	Aeschines
Amm. Marc.	Ammianus Marcellinus
Andoc.	Andocides
App.	Appian
B Civ.	*Bella civilia*
Syr.	*Syriakē*

Ar.	Aristophanes
Ach.	*Acharnians*
Eccl.	*Ecclesiazusae*
Lys.	*Lysistrata*
Plut.	*Wealth*
Thesm.	*Thesmophoriazusae*
Arch.	Archytas
Archil.	Archilochus
Arist.	Aristotle
de An.	*De anima*
Ath. Pol.	*Athēnaiōn Politeia*
Cael.	*De caelo*
Eth. Eud.	*Eudemian Ethics*
Eth. Nic.	*Nicomachean Ethics*
Gen. an.	*De generatione animalium*
Hist. an.	*Historia animalium*
Part. an.	*De partibus animalium*
Pol.	*Politics*
Rhet.	*Rhetoric*
Aristid. *Or.*	Aristides, *Orationes*
Arr.	Arrian
Anab.	*Anabasis*
Asc. . . . Cl.	Asconius, ed. A. C. Clark (Oxford Classical Text, 1907)
Athen.	Athenaeus
August.	Augustine
b. conjug.	*De bono coniugali*
c. Faustum	*Contra Faustum Manicheum*
Conf.	*Confessions*
De civ. D.	*De civitate Dei* (*City of God*)
En. Ps.	*Enarrationes in Psalmos*

Ep.	*Epistulae*
Gn. litt.	*De Genesi ad litteram*
lib. arb.	*De libero arbitrio*
nat. et gr.	*De natura et gratia*
Serm.	*Sermones*
trin.	*De trinitate*
[Aur. Vict.] *De vir. ill.*	[Aurelius Victor], *De viris illustribus*
Caes.	Caesar
B Afr.	*Bellum Africum*
B Civ.	*Bellum Civile*
Cass. Dio	Cassius Dio
CH	*Codex Hammurabi*
Cic.	Cicero
Acad. post.	*Academica posteriora*
Amic.	*De amicitia*
Att.	*Epistulae ad Atticum*
Balb.	*Pro Balbo*
Cael.	*Pro Caelio*
Cat.	*In Catilinam*
Clu.	*Pro Cluentio*
De or.	*De oratore*
Deiot.	*Pro rege Deiotaro*
Div.	*De divinatione*
Dom.	*De domo sua*
Fam.	*Epistulae ad familiares*
Fin.	*De finibus*
Har. resp.	*De haruspicum responso*
Leg.	*De legibus*
Leg. agr.	*De lege agraria*
Lig.	*Pro Ligario*

Marcell.	*Pro Marcello*
Mil.	*Pro Milone*
Mur.	*Pro Murena*
Nat. D.	*De natura Deorum*
Off.	*De officiis*
Part. or.	*Partitiones oratoriae*
Phil.	*Philippics*
Pis.	*In Pisonem*
Planc.	*Pro Plancio*
Prov. cons.	*De provinciis consularibus*
Q Fr.	*Epistulae ad Quintum fratrem*
Q Rosc.	*Pro Roscio comoedo*
Quinct.	*Pro Quinctio*
Red. pop.	*Post reditum ad populum*
Red. sen.	*Post reditum in senatu*
Rep.	*De republica (Republic)*
Scaur.	*Pro Scauro*
Sest.	*Pro Sestio*
Sull.	*Pro Sulla*
Tusc.	*Tusculanae disputationes*
Verr.	*In Verrem*
CIL	*Corpus Inscriptionum Latinarum*
Clem. Al.	Clemens Alexandrinus
Strom.	*Stromateis*
Dem.	Demosthenes
Meid.	*Against Meidias*
Din.	Dinarchus
Dio *Or.*	Dio of Prusa (Dio Chrysostomus), *Orationes*
Diod. Sic.	Diodorus Siculus
Diog. Laert.	Diogenes Laertius

Dion. Hal.	Dionysius Halicarnassensis
Ant. Rom.	*Antiquitates Romanae*
Diotog.	Diotogenes
DK	H. Diels and W. Kranz (eds), *Die Fragmente der Vorsokratiker*, 2 vols, 6th edn (Berlin: Weidmann, 1951–2)
DNP	*Der neue Pauly*, 18 vols (Stuttgart: J. B. Metzler, 1996–2003)
Ecph.	Ecphantus
Enn. *Ann.*	Ennius, *Annales*
Ephor.	Ephorus
Epict.	Epictetus
Diss.	*Discourses*
Epicurus	
RS	*Ratae sententiae*
Sent. Vat.	*Vatican Sayings* = *Gnomologium Vaticanum*
Epit.	*Epitome*
Eur.	Euripides
Heracl.	*Heraclidae*
Hipp.	*Hippolytus*
IA	*Iphigenia Aulidensis*
Supp.	*Supplices* (*Suppliants* or *Suppliant Women*)
FGrH	F. Jacoby (ed.), *Die Fragmente der griechischen Historiker* (Berlin: Weidmann; Leiden: Brill, 1923–64)
Flor.	L. Annaeus Florus
fr.	fragment
frr.	fragments
Gai. *Inst*	Gaius, *Institutiones*
Hdt.	Herodotus
Hes.	Hesiod
Op.	*Opera et dies* (*Works and Days*)
Theog.	*Theogony*

Hippoc.	Hippocrates
Aer.	*De aera, aquis, locis* (*On Airs, Waters, Places*)
Hom.	Homer
Il.	*Iliad*
Od.	*Odyssey*
Hyp.	Hyperides
IG	*Inscriptiones Graecae* (1873–)
ILS	H. Dessau, *Inscriptiones Latinae Selectae* (1892–1916)
Isoc.	Isocrates
Antid.	*Antidosis*
Areop.	*Areopagiticus*
C. soph.	*Contra sophistas*
Panath.	*Panathenaicus*
LdÄ	W. Helck, E. Otto, and W. Westendorf (eds), *Lexicon der Ägyptologie* (1975–86)
LIMC	*Lexicon Iconographicum Mythologiae Classicae* (1981–)
Liv.	Livy
Livy, *Epit.*	Livy, *Epitomae*
Lobel-Page	E. Lobel and D. Page, *Poetarum Lesbiorum Fragmenta* (Oxford: Oxford University Press, 1955)
Lucian, *Alex.*	Lucian, *Alexander*
Lyc.	Lycurgus
Lys.	Lysias
M. Aur. *Med.*	Marcus Aurelius, *Meditations*
Men. *Dys*	Menander, *Dyskolos*
Men. Rhet.	Menander Rhetor
ML	R. Meiggs and D. Lewis (eds), *A Selection of Greek Historical Inscriptions to the End of the Fifth Century* BC, rev. edn (1988)
MW	R. Merkelbach and M. L. West (eds), *Fragmenta Hesiodea* (Oxford: Oxford University Press, 1967)
Nic.	Nicander

OGIS	*Orientis Graeci Inscriptiones Selectae*
ORF	H. Malcovati (ed.), *Oratorum Romanorum Fragmenta* (2nd edn 1955; 4th edn 1967)
Ov. *Fast.*	Ovid, *Fasti*
Page	D. L. Page (ed.), *Poetae Melici Graeci* (Oxford: Clarendon Press, 1962)
Pan. Lat.	XII *Panegyrici Latini*
Paul	
Col.	St Paul, *Epistle to the Colossians*
Gal.	St Paul, *Epistle to the Galatians*
Philo, *Mos.*	Philo, *De vita Mosis* (*Life of Moses*)
Philoch.	Philochorus
Phld.	Philodemus
Pindar, *Pyth.*	Pindar, *Pythian*
Pl.	Plato
Ap.	*Apology*
Cleit.	*Cleitophon*
Cri.	*Crito*
Eu. or *Euthphr.*	*Euthyphro*
Euthd.	*Euthydemus*
Grg.	*Gorgias*
La.	*Laches*
Leg.	*Leges* (*Laws*)
Lys.	*Lysis*
Menex.	*Menexenus*
Phd.	*Phaedo*
Phlb.	*Philebus*
Plt.	*Politicus* (*Statesman*)
Prt.	*Protagoras*
Resp.	*Republic*
Sph.	*Sophist*

Symp.	*Symposium*
Tht.	*Theaetetus*
Tim.	*Timaeus*
Plin. *NH*	Pliny (the Elder), *Naturalis historia*
Plin. *Pan.*	Pliny (the Younger), *Panegyricus*
Pliny, *Ep.*	Pliny (the Younger), *Epistulae*
Plut.	Plutarch
Mor.	*Moralia*
Adv. Col	*Adversus Coloten* (*Against Colotes*)
an virt. doc. possit	*An virtus doceri possit* (*Whether virtue can be taught*)
comp. Dem. et Cic.	*Comparatio Demosthenis et Ciceronis*
De Alex. fort.	*De fortuna Alexandri*
De Stoic. rep.	*De Stoicorum repugnantiis* (*On the contradictions of the Stoics*)
De tranq. anim.	*De tranquillitate animi* (*On the tranquility of the mind*)
De Virt. mor.	*De virtute morali* (*On Moral Virtue*)
Vit.	*Vitae parallelae* (*Parallel Lives*)
Alc.	*Alcibiades*
Alex.	*Alexander*
Arat.	*Aratus*
Arist.	*Aristides*
Caes.	*Caesar*
Cam.	*Camillus*
Cic.	*Cicero*
Dem.	*Demosthenes*
Demetr.	*Demetrius*
Lyc.	*Lycurgus*
Per.	*Pericles*
Pomp.	*Pompeius*
Pyrrh.	*Pyrrhus*
Rom.	*Romulus*

Sol.	*Solon*
Ti. Gracch.	*Tiberius Gracchus*
Tim.	*Timoleon*
Polyb.	Polybius
Porphyry *Abst.*	Porphyry, *De abstinentia*
Powell	J. G. F. Powell (ed.), *M. Tulli Ciceronis De re publica, De legibus, Cato Maior De senectute, Laelius De amicitia* (Oxford: Oxford University Press, 2006)
P Oxy	*Oxyrhynchus Papyri* (1898–)
Ps-Xen. *Ath. pol.*	Pseudo-Xenophon, *Respublica Atheniensium* (*Constitution of the Athenians*)
Q. Cic. *Comm. Pet.*	Quintus Cicero, *Commentariolum petitionis*
Quint.	Quintilian
RAC	*Reallexikon für Antike und Christentum* (Stuttgart, 1941–)
RdA	*Reallexikon der Assyriologie*
Sall.	Sallust
Cat.	*Bellum Catilinae* or *De Catilinae coniuratione*
Hist.	*Historiae*
Iug.	*Bellum Iugurthinum*
schol.	scholiast or scholia
SEG	*Supplementum epigraphicum Graecum* (1923–)
Sen.	Seneca (the Younger)
Apoc.	*Apocolocyntosis*
Ben.	*De beneficiis*
Clem.	*De clementia*
Dial.	*Dialogi*
Ep.	*Epistulae*
Sen. *Suas.*	Seneca (the Elder), *Suasoriae*
Sext. Emp. *Math.*	Sextus Empiricus, *Adversus mathematicos*
Stob.	Stobaeus
Stob. *Ecl.*	Stobeus, *Eclogae*

Suda	Greek Lexicon formerly known as *Suidas*
Suet.	Suetonius
Aug.	*Divus Augustus*
Calig.	*Caligula*
Dom.	*Domitianus*
Vesp.	*Divus Vespasianus*
Vit.	*Vitellius*
SVF	H. von Arnim, *Stoicorum Veterum Fragmenta* (1903–)
*Syll.*³	W. Dittenberger et al. (eds), *Sylloge Inscriptionum Graecarum*, 3rd edn (Leipzig: Hirzel, 1915–24)
Tac.	Tacitus
Agr.	*Agricola*
Ann.	*Annals*
Hist.	*Histories*
Thuc.	Thucydides
TGF	A. Nauck (ed.), *Tragicorum Graecorum Fragmenta*, 2nd edn (1889); suppl. B. Snell (1964)
TrGF	B. Snell, R. Kannicht, and S. Radt (eds), *Tragicorum Graecorum Fragmenta*, 4 vols (1971–85); vol. 1, 2nd edn (1986).
Tyrt.	Tyrtaeus
Ulpian, *Dig.*	Ulpian, *Digest*
Usener	H. Usener, *Epicurea* (Leipzig: Teubner, 1887; repr. Stuttgart: Teubner, 1966)
Val. Max.	Valerius Maximus
Weissenborn	W. Weissenborn (ed.), *Titi Livi Ab urbe condita libri*, vol. 5, 2nd edn (Leipzig, 1894)
West	M. L. West (ed.), *Iambi et elegi Graeci ante Alexandrum cantati*, 2 vols, 2nd edn (Oxford: Oxford University Press, 1989–92)
Xen.	Xenophon
Ages.	*Agesilaus*
Anab.	*Anabasis*

Cyr.	*Cyropaedia*
Hell.	*Hellenica*
Lac.	*Respublica Lacedaemoniorum (Spartan Constitution)*
Mem.	*Memorabilia*
Oec.	*Oeconomicus*
Symp.	*Symposium*

PART I

The Broad View

CHAPTER 1

Introduction: Rethinking the History of Greek and Roman Political Thought

Ryan K. Balot

The present *Companion* is designed to introduce the central concepts of Greek and Roman political thought to students and teachers of political science, classics, philosophy, and history. Over the past 20 years, scholars in these distinct fields have begun to communicate with one another intensively across traditional disciplinary lines. This cross-fertilization has led to a significantly deeper understanding of ancient political thought as a product of, and response to, the political world of classical antiquity. More important, perhaps, scholars have also come to recognize that classical political thought provides unique resources for helping us grapple anew with the permanent questions of political life. The time is right, therefore, to integrate these scholarly developments into a comprehensive vision of classical political thought and to ask where we should go from here.

The present volume aims to provide such a vision by incorporating the best recent work on Greek and Roman political thought from a wide variety of disciplinary and methodological perspectives. Yet contributors to this volume have ambitions that go well beyond the work of consolidation and survey. While providing helpful introductions for the uninitiated, they also ask fresh questions. Their essays illustrate the ways in which ancient political thought can inspire us to challenge the conventional political wisdom of late modernity. Contributors to the present volume share the belief that classical political thought constitutes a powerful, if internally diverse, tradition that is capable, even now, of opening us to novel political possibilities. In order to deepen our political understanding, and to expand our political imagination, the authors of the following essays have creatively transgressed their traditional disciplinary boundaries. In doing so, they have begun to delineate the contours of ancient Greek and Roman political thought as a new and distinct subfield – one that draws on traditional frames of reference in classics, history, and ancient philosophy, but also brings ancient political texts into contact

A Companion to Greek and Roman Political Thought, First Edition. Edited by Ryan K. Balot.
© 2013 Blackwell Publishing Ltd. Published 2013 by Blackwell Publishing Ltd.

with broader currents of political theory and an enlarged understanding of political life.

Ancient Greek and Roman Distinctiveness

If the following essays do indeed point toward a new subfield, then they begin to accomplish this goal by uncovering the distinctiveness of ancient Greek and Roman political thought. The Greeks and Romans already stood out within the ancient Mediterranean world, because, unlike their Mediterranean neighbors, they gave a specifically political interpretation to ideals such as freedom and "law and order" (Raaflaub, chapter 3). What is important, however, is not any triumphal claim that the Greeks originated the political, but rather the exploration of why communal political activity became special or even primary for Greeks and Romans. By contrast with other ancient Mediterranean peoples, as Raaflaub shows, the Greeks and Romans erected their conception of the political on the basis of egalitarian practices of political power (to be sure: among the citizenry, not universally) and a concern with collective aims such as justice, well-being, law and order, freedom, and equality. Their political practices came to light as the most useful responses to the Greek experience of life in small-scale, independent, nonhierarchical, and materially and militarily struggling Mediterranean communities.

Even if the Greeks and Romans created newly political ideals, they never settled on immutable and determinate understandings of what politics was *for*, or what constituted its central activities. Dean Hammer's essay (chapter 2) is an exemplary exploration of these points. Through examining the most important modern treatments of ancient politics, Hammer illustrates that ancient Greco-Roman politics should not be reduced to institutional functioning or any Weberian "monopoly of legitimate force" (cf. Herman 2006). (This is one area where the anachronistic importation of modern terminology or concepts can be particularly misleading.) Instead, as Hammer shows, the Greeks and Romans recognized coercive state authority while also understanding individual citizens, including their bodies, as penetrated by the multifarious workings of power. Hammer's clear-minded interpretation of the ancient political experience through the lens of postmodern social theory pays particular dividends for students of politics as they struggle with the inevitably fuzzy dimensions and chaotic landscapes of political life. At all events, Hammer demonstrates more clearly than ever before that the political must be understood contextually, as a feature of the particular times and places in which politics was recognized and practiced. Yet in doing so Hammer also shows that his emphasis on historical particularity can make certain unfamiliar, and perhaps disquieting, political ideas available for our consideration and use.

Ancient and Modern

Initially, at least, those who boldly assert the importance of classical political thought might be greeted with either skepticism or revulsion or both. Skepticism, because our contemporaries will naturally wonder whether the highly particular, remote, and often alien Greco-Roman political experience can shed light on modern political life and thought. How should scholars and citizens "locate" classical political thought within the contemporary world of technological progress, religious pluralism, universal human rights, and multiculturalism? Revulsion, because virtually all ancient Greek and Roman writers were politically intolerant, illiberal slave-owners who would have scoffed at the idea of universal human rights. They would have failed to understand why they should tolerate, much less respect, the diverse standards of different cultural traditions. What relationship do we now bear, or *want* to bear, to the highly particular ancient Mediterranean political world?[1]

Modern political thought can neither ignore nor simply embrace Greek and Roman political analysis. On the one hand, we study classical political thought in the shadow of early modern efforts to reject the claims of antiquity. The seventeenth century founders of modern liberalism, such as Bacon, Descartes, Hobbes, Spinoza, and Locke, aspired to create an utterly new, even utopian, vision of political order and human freedom. Their sanguine attitudes toward modern progress were based as much on faith in scientific and technological advancement as on the creation of new and supposedly more realistic political ideals. As noble as their ambitions may have been, however, the goal of "routing the ancients," of eliminating classical political thought from the theoretical road map of modernity, is not a wise option. Whatever their shortcomings or mistakes, the ancient thinkers captured central truths about political psychology and about the social character of human beings. Even now, the ancient thinkers offer us theoretical and imaginative opportunities to improve our political understanding. We can take advantage of these opportunities without endorsing every feature of the classical thinkers' outlook.

On the other hand, the act of recovering ancient voices or ideas should not be enlisted in the conservative project of establishing orthodoxies that have no real place in the modern world. Political hierarchy, gender inequality, unreflective respect for certain traditions combined with neglect or contempt of others, and the anti-individualistic emphasis on "community" – these are not attractive possibilities for our time. At all events, such projects, if based on claims to the cultural authority of classical antiquity, represent only partial and incomplete recoveries of classical political thought. They do not do justice to the traditions of merciless self-criticism practiced by many of the authors of ancient Greek and Roman political texts (see below, "The Provocation to Self-Criticism").

Without lapsing into either form of extremism, this collection reflects upon the best ways to understand and perhaps reappropriate classical political thought. Our responses derive from the ethical commitment to making our academic work meaningful to inhabitants of the post-enlightenment nation-state. We hope to have addressed the issues in ways that people should care about. In accordance with this commitment, I asked contributors to adopt a self-consciously two-tiered outlook on the ancient material. At least as an initial goal, contributors have located ancient political ideas in their particular historical contexts. This emphasis on historical context grows out of the belief that ancient thinkers offered creative responses to political conventions that they regarded as useless, stultifying, or harmful. These responses were "local." They were particularly meaningful, and perhaps unsettling, to contemporaries familiar with the urgent questions of ancient political life. Yet ancient political writers were not prisoners of particular historical contingencies. Nor did they understand themselves as unshakably entrenched in particular historical moments. Instead, both systematic philosophers and unsystematic thinkers typically regarded themselves as exponents of what they took to be a natural or unchanging order, an order that was not historically contingent but satisfied the basic requirements of our human nature. As the following essays amply illustrate, contributors to the present volume understand that the ancients' ambitions in this regard are worthy of careful consideration and intellectual respect.

Particular and General

Yet one might wonder how, if at all, these two modes of analysis – which might be called "particular" and "general," or sometimes "historical" and "philosophical" – work together. At first glance, the historical emphasis on particularity appears to conflict with any effort to elicit generalized teachings from classical political thought. Is it realistic to think that the gap between particular and general can be bridged by imaginative reflection? Can we avoid mistaking "is" for "ought" in making the transition from history to theory? Is it responsible for scholars and thinkers to put classical political thought to use in the vastly different conditions of late modernity?

To each question, our answer is a resounding yes. Despite the apparent tensions between particular and general, it will emerge that these approaches can cooperate successfully and so produce illuminating results. Study of the ancient city implies neither nostalgia for classical antiquity nor envy of the political lives of ancient citizens. Instead, the ubiquitously rich and deeply alien world of classical antiquity can be recovered as a repository of imaginative and theoretical resources. Recovering the deep history of political thought will remind us of forgotten dimensions of political experience and challenge us knowingly to resist the tyranny of our modern preconceptions. In undertaking such a project of recovery, the difficulty is to avoid either ham-fistedly wrenching classical ideas from their roots in their own native soil or gazing worshipfully on ancient ideas as the wondrous products of a definitively superior era. The appropriate metaphor is rather that of transplanting a healthy tree, with its roots intact, to an alien environment, where it can flower for us to enjoy or perhaps even bear fruit.

To understand why a two-tiered framework of analysis is helpful, consider the fruitlessness, if not impossibility, of writing the history of political thought without employing both analytical modes. On the one hand, purely general and abstract discussions of ancient texts, unanchored in historical understanding, run the risk of anachronism. We can easily distort the ancients' own political vocabulary and outlook. Such distortions inevitably blunt the force of any theoretical challenges or provocations offered by the ancients. This happens all too frequently, as when scholars have anachronistically imported the modern language of sovereignty or social contract theory into study of ancient political ideas or ideology. More specifically, politically central ancient concepts such as *hubris* (arrogance), *aidōs* (shame), or *pietas* (duty) cannot be simply or easily "translated" into the modern political vocabulary. They cannot be communicated to modern audiences apart from historical investigation of the particular communities of meaning in which those concepts played a decisive role.

On the other hand, purely contextual analyses, uninformed by larger questions about political life as such, often result in either meaningless dead ends or reverential "appreciation." Either form of antiquarianism runs the moral and political risk of promoting doctrinaire claims to cultural authority that ignore the elements of self-criticism in Greek and Roman political thought. Such risks can be accentuated if antiquarian history is reinforced by the naive idea that classical antiquity provides uncontaminated moments of origin for later political developments. One and all, the present contributors heed Nietzsche's warnings against simplistic notions of uncorrupted or innocent "starting-points" (*On the Genealogy of Morals* (Nietzsche 1967); cf. Foucault 1977).

Instead of segregating historical and philosophical, or particular and general, approaches, it is most productive to synthesize these modes of analysis. If we envision them as mutually supportive and dialectical, then each approach might teach the other. Neither will have to remain ancillary. In the first instance, our understanding of the history of ancient Greek and Roman political thought can be immeasurably improved if we learn to ask the right questions – questions motivated by broad awareness of political thought and practice in other geographic regions and chronological periods, including European modernity. Modern students of comparative politics have repeatedly illustrated the epistemological value of studying both like and unlike cases, in all their diversity, and they have shed light on how to examine historical *comparanda* with methodological sophistication and self-consciousness (e.g., Katznelson 1997; Lichbach 1997; Landman 2000: 27–32; for an application in ancient history, Pritchard 2007: 349–52). I discern three ways in which our understanding of classical political thought, specifically, can be improved through conducting comparative studies of political thought and political life in other regions and periods.

First, doing comparisons between different periods and regions helps to render visible certain frequently unacknowledged features of the classical political experience. Consider, for example, our understanding of the relationship between Greco-Roman polytheism and classical political life. Despite their theological beliefs and symbols (Osborne, chapter 8), the Greeks regarded their political practices and ideals as human constructs dependent on human effort. In particular, by contrast with political life in other ancient Mediterranean regions, the Greeks and Romans did not, in general, view the political world as a divinely controlled world, nor did they invest their political leaders with transcendent religious authority (see Raaflaub, chapter 3; cf. Lincoln 2007). Authority in Greek and Roman politics derived from the communal power of citizens.

By contrast with politics in early modern Europe, moreover, Greek and Roman citizens were not subject to politically independent and frequently coercive clerical authority. Greeks and Romans had no need of the great modern theorists of toleration, such as Locke; they had no need to be liberated from religious orthodoxy by a Spinozistic *Theological-Political Treatise*. To the contrary, as Robin Osborne (chapter 8) demonstrates, Greek and Roman religion was subject to the authority of politics. Greek and Roman polytheism had no systematic orthodoxy or dogma; Greek and Roman political life was free of the religious controversies that so beset early modern political life. To put the point most provocatively, Greek, and to a lesser extent Roman, religion did not obstruct political rationality.[2] Many of these features of ancient religion, and generally of ancient political life, would be invisible without the points of reference provided by far-ranging scholarly "time travel."

Second, by using analytical vocabularies developed in modern social science, political theory, and philosophy, we can inform our understanding of the classical political experience with a more useful set of interpretative tools (cf. Morley 2004; Ober 2008). In this belief, for example, certain contributors have utilized the vocabularies of modern political science and modern feminism to excellent effect. Josiah Ober (chapter 5) and Craige Champion (chapter 6) use the social-scientific language of collective action theory and international relations theory to explore uncharted territory in the ancient political experience (for other recent examples, see Low 2007; Eckstein 2006; Ober 1998). These chapters successfully defamiliarize certain scholarly commonplaces and make the ancients' political discourse available to us for the improvement of our own political understanding. In a similar vein, Giulia Sissa (chapter 7) uses the conceptual tools of modern feminism to shed light on the distinctive ways in which the classical political experience was "gendered." Sissa (chapters 7 and 18) and Champion, in particular, provide frameworks within which we can understand and evaluate the relationship between Greco-Roman "manliness" and ancient bellicosity, against the background of ancient Mediterranean culture at large.

Third, we improve our historiographic self-consciousness through becoming increasingly aware of our own location within histories of political life and thought. To be sure, we risk anachronism if we allow our interpretative lenses to be clouded with inappropriate terminology (cf. Rhodes 2003a). Yet our modern reconstructions of past practices and discourses are inevitably, though often undetectably, shaped by our twenty-first century vantage-points. If we are not conscious of the impact of our own highly contingent positions as late-modern observers, then we will not be able to take a properly self-critical perspective on our own ways of writing the history of classical political thought (cf. Osborne 2006: 14–28; Herman 2006: 85–101).

If our study of specifically classical political ideas can be improved through awareness of the broader currents of modern political thought, and through comparative study of other chronological periods and geographic regions, then the converse is also true: the larger educational value of studying ancient Greek and Roman politics depends on our sensitivity to historical particularity. Our awareness of historical particularity enables the ancient texts to speak on their own terms to permanent problems of political life, as those problems were interpreted and experienced in classical antiquity. As the following essays demonstrate, classical political life and thought are foreign and thus potentially challenging for us. Yet the ancient Greeks and Romans, even now, are not incomprehensibly remote in such a way as to render stimulating "conversation" impossible.

Like us, for example, the ancient Greeks and Romans confronted the universal problems of human neediness and ignorance, of disputes over scarce resources, of conflicts between the individual and the community, and of the frequently destructive human passions and appetites. They confronted such problems by employing concepts and language that we immediately recognize – justice, equality, freedom, virtue, and governance by law. But the ancient Greeks and Romans managed these problems, and used this familiar language, in an unfamiliar way, and within a life-world that differed from our own in many obvious ways, such as the near-universal acceptance of polytheistic religion, the size of the state, the difference between direct participation and representative government, the exclusion of women from citizenship, the practice of slavery, etc. This combination of similarity with difference means that the ancients have something new to offer, especially to modern citizens who also think in the language of justice, equality, freedom, virtue, and governance by law. By understanding the ancient past in a properly historical way, as I have described it, we might go beyond simply "appreciating" classical authors and political forms in an antiquarian or monumentalizing spirit.

Instead, we begin to render classical ideas and ideologies meaningful in arguments that we should care about. Within this framework, the historian of political thought becomes a creative mediator or umpire who judges the usefulness of historical theories and redeploys them in current political controversies. Thus, if we have tried to heed Nietzsche's strictures against naive historicism, then we also give due consideration to his view that history should be used for the sake of "life." Our goal is to arrive at the advantageous position of being able to make use of historical thinkers and practices, to "put them into play," so to speak, as we strive to ask the recurrent questions of political life. It is in this way that contributors to the present volume have strived not only to formulate the outlook of a newly distinct subfield, but also to uncover the extraordinary resources offered by study of classical political thought.

Politics, Ethics, Citizenship

The ancient Greeks and Romans had a particular way of understanding the relationship between the political and the ethical, which illustrates the larger educational significance of studying classical political thought with attention to its particularity. Ancient Greeks and Romans maintained that political institutions and practices ought to provide an education to virtue. In itself this belief is not distinctive, since virtually all societies have sought to develop functional excellences of character, that is, virtues that are relative to, and instrumentally useful for achieving, particular goals of specific cultures. By contrast with later Christian or commercial virtues, however, the ancient Greeks and Romans emphasized the political virtues and the deliberative prudence of active, self-governing citizens. By contrast with many others, including the "moderns" of Europe and North America, they also laid particular stress on human excellence or nobility, as opposed to the gentler or more peaceful virtues of tolerance, decency, and civility. And, finally, rather than adopting a strictly functional or instrumental conception of virtue, they typically envisioned virtue as an excellence of character whose active exercise was intrinsically good for the virtuous agent.

For the sake of comparison and contrast, it will help to sketch certain later, and perhaps equally distinctive, conceptions of virtue and its relation to political life. By contrast with the fundamentally civic concerns of most ancient polytheists, Christian thinkers, for example, always granted primacy to charity and humility as the chief virtues enabling human beings to fulfill their natural human vocations. The Christian virtues provided a way for the dutiful and observant to win their ultimate reward in the afterlife, that is, a proper place in the heavenly city. As Todd Breyfogle shows (chapter 32), Augustine adapted the polytheistic civic models to a new metaphysical narrative in which our sojourn on earth, even if virtuous or humanly excellent, could only ever have an educative function orienting us to the more important concerns of another type of "city." In Eric Brown's view (chapter 31), this late antique and medieval norm was developed out of a much earlier countercultural stance: already in the fourth century BC, Plato's Socrates had begun to develop private, nonpolitical virtues as an act of political criticism and defiance. Adapting the earlier Socratic model, the Christian virtues constituted an explicit rejection of the polytheists' way of relating the ethical to the political.

When we turn to the early modern founders of liberalism, the situation is of course entirely different. Despite recent liberal aspirations to separate politics and "morality" (e.g. Rawls 1971), the classical liberals, such as Hobbes, Locke, Kant, and Mill, did not shy away from using political authority to help educate citizens to function virtuously in diverse spheres such as commerce and civic life (Berkowitz 2000). In his *Report to the Board of Trade* (1697), for example, John Locke recommended, like many others of his day, the use of work-houses, child labor, and whippings for beggars, in order to cure the poor of their indolence and to promote industry and self-discipline (Tully 1993: 234–41). In the eighteenth century, as J. G. A. Pocock has shown, a newly "commercial humanism" redefined the ancient, austere, and predominantly civic virtues with the aid of the novel concept of "manners," so as to produce a more peaceful and socially diverse expression of the citizen's proper and virtuous functioning (Pocock 1985: ch. 2; cf. Rahe 1992). More recently, in their political practices and practical ideologies, contemporary nation-states have also used political authority to show disapproval of, and even to outlaw, behaviors which were seen to be immoral or intolerable, such as sodomy, bigamy, or blasphemy. Neoconservatives in the United States see a state role for enforcing "family values" and patriotic virtues (Berns 2001; cf. Nussbaum and Cohen 2002), while "communitarians" and liberals alike have argued for the social and political benefits of cultivating virtues of character (Bellah et al. 1985; Dagger 1997). The foregoing examples represent merely a few of the diverse functions to which virtue has been put in modern European and North American theory and practice. Obviously, the horizon of this discussion could be vastly extended if we should turn to the history of Asian or Middle Eastern practices of virtue.

Against this necessarily schematic outline, we can come to understand the highly particular role played by conceptions of ethical and intellectual excellence in classical political thought. In their political theories and ideologies, the ancient Greeks and

Romans emphasized the specifically civic virtues of character such as justice, loyalty to the community, piety, civic friendship, self-control, and courage. Even more importantly, they emphasized civic prudence – that is, the citizens' capacity to deliberate effectively on the city's momentous concerns, such as war and peace, awards of citizenship, the maintenance of sacred land, and the use of collective material resources for public building-projects and festivals. Ancient political thought thereby asserted the importance of the citizens' intellectual faculties – not, of course, their philosophical capacities, but rather the ordinary prudence that enabled citizens to recognize and pursue their own self-interests as members of small-scale political communities. This constitution of the ancient citizen as an active deliberator points to a more actively and robustly civic conception of virtue than those found in the patristic literature, or again in the teachings of early modern liberals such as Hobbes, Spinoza, and Locke, or, finally, in the particular brand of contemporary liberalism associated with figures such as John Rawls, Robert Nozick, and Judith Shklar.

As a counterpart to their concern with virtue, the ancients also meticulously explored the vices that corrupt political life, such as cowardice, greed, dishonesty, self-indulgence, and lack of discretion. In virtually every case, ancient Greek and Roman thinkers and citizens used the language of vice to criticize members of the body politic who failed to make an adequate contribution to civic vibrancy and health. In the distinctive Greek and Roman political environment, the modern commercial virtues would have appeared narrowly self-interested and calculating. They would have been ranged among the vices, above all as greed (*pleonexia* or *avaritia*) or self-indulgence (*akolasia*), but more generally as selfishness that diverted a citizen's attention from the common good. In the mostly small, mostly egalitarian political communities of the Greek and Roman world, the civic orientation of the citizenry was central to the ancient city's material prosperity, military security, and general well-being.[3]

Political thinkers and citizens of classical antiquity *in general* viewed their political lives from within the framework of virtue and vice. As we discover in the essays of Malcolm Schofield, Charles Hedrick, and Philip Stadter, along with the contributors to part III ("The Virtues and Vices of One-Man Rule"), Aristotle and his philosophical forbears did not originate this emphasis on the interconnections between politics and civic virtue. It wasn't only in the philosophers' imaginary utopias that political thinkers envisioned political power as capable of helping citizens achieve a good life through educating them to justice, civic friendship, and prudence. Rather, from its earliest appearances onward, Greek and Roman political reflection emphasized the character development of citizens as the key ingredient in both individual and civic flourishing. This is as obvious from reading the Roman historian Livy as it is from reading Homer, Herodotus, and the Athenian orators. Contrary to a frequently expressed view, the ancient philosophers did not construct utopian cities of virtue and reason in a vacuum; rather, they developed preexisting lines of thought and intervened in contemporary debates.

The ancients' concern with citizenly character, of course, presupposes the all-important category of citizenship itself. It is with the category of citizenship that we can begin to move from identifying the ancients' distinctive concerns to exploring their larger theoretical significance. As P. J. Rhodes illustrates in chapter 4, citizenship and civic ideology were central to the ancient understanding and experience of politics. Given the traditions of civic humanism developed in the Italian city-states, revived by the American Founders, and again rejuvenated by modern theorists of citizenship (e.g., Arendt 1958; cf. T. Pangle 1988; Oldfield 1990; Zuckert, chapter 34), it would be misguided to assert that ideals of active, excellent, and intrinsically worthwhile civic virtues were the unique prerogative of ancient Greeks and Romans. As Christopher Nadon shows in chapter 33, citizenship has constituted a central theoretical and practical category wherever republican forms of political organization have prevailed, such as Renaissance Italy or the colonial United States. More broadly, in fact, the continental tradition of modern political philosophy – including Montesquieu, Rousseau, and Hegel – has built upon and extended the ancient theories of citizenship and civic virtue. Even though such figures often transfigured ancient theories, they tended to agree that the classical experience of citizenship was one of the most fruitful sources of inquiry into this critical political idea. The reason is, roughly, that the egalitarian ancient city-state expected and often demanded from its citizens an extraordinary degree of civic participation and interest. Such demands led to an exceptional degree of reflection upon the nature of civic virtue and vice and on the broad questions of moral psychology and political agency that such reflection usually inspired.

Contemporary political philosophers have increasingly acknowledged the political and ethical importance of virtuous citizenship, and the ancient Greeks and Romans have continued to provide a language for helping them articulate and defend their views. In political philosophy, republican theorists such as Ronald Beiner (1992), as well as liberal perfectionists such as Stephen Salkever (1990; cf. Collins 2006), have turned to the ancients in order to find an appropriate vocabulary and understanding of civic, deliberative virtue; and theorists have begun to talk seriously about democratic virtue (Euben, Wallach, and Ober 1994b; Wallach 1994; Zuckert, chapter 34). Among other things, these theorists are concerned with cultivating prudence, with overcoming apathy, and often with encouraging contemporary citizens to put substantive ideas about human goodness onto the common table of public, democratic deliberation. Guided by the political reflections of the ancients, these theorists explore how we might elevate the modern citizenry's understanding and experience of politics to a level commensurate with its democratic power. The present volume puts on display, among much else, the rich and theoretically well-informed vocabulary of political virtue that the world of classical antiquity has to offer theorists interested in improving the quality of our civic discourse. At all events, classical political life and thought help us to raise additional questions about the distinctively Rawlsian brand of liberalism that remains suspicious of any public conversations based on comprehensive or substantive conceptions of human goodness.

Even if the particular ancient experience has broad philosophical appeal for modern theorists, however, it is worth entering at least one caveat. By contrast with the ancient polis, modern states are large-scale, socially differentiated, and pluralistic political entities. Hence, any efforts to adapt ancient theories or ideologies of virtue to the modern context must contend with these formidable practical differences.

The modern interest in ancient citizenship and citizenly virtue should not lead to calls for wholesale importation of the ancient models into modern nation-states. At least since the publication of Benjamin Constant's "The Liberty of the Ancients Compared with that of the Moderns" in 1819 (Constant 1988; cf. Holmes 1979), and recently since the reinvention of this distinction by Isaiah Berlin (Berlin 1958), political theorists have been all too familiar with the dangers of utilizing political power to inculcate virtue, particularly in modern conditions. As a result, contemporary theorists tend not to commit themselves so strongly to a program of virtue cultivation as Rousseau did in his *Letter to d'Alembert*. Yet, as we have just seen, the contemporary turn to virtue, among liberal, republican, and conservative theorists, is substantial and increasingly important. The thought behind this "characterological turn" is that there must be middle ground between the individualistic, libertarian outlook (cf. Kateb 1992; Nozick 1974) and the insanely demanding standards of virtue-oriented organizations of power such as (say) the Iranian theocracy.

Our particular understanding of that middle ground must both respect modern ideals of freedom and autonomy and adequately educate modern citizens to eschew unreflective relativism and naive conformity to present standards. Classical political thought might prove especially helpful and challenging to modern theorists as we struggle to find such a middle ground. The essays in the present volume indicate just how rich, complex, and diverse the Greek and Roman understanding of civic virtue and deliberative prudence could be. It is hoped that the present collection will provide an interpretative and philosophical basis for supplementing and enriching recent efforts, for challenging contemporary orthodoxies, and for stimulating further reflection upon the political possibilities of virtue politics in modernity.

Supplementing Contemporary Theory

From the perspective of understanding classical political thought as both a supplement and a challenge to contemporary theory, it is worth observing that contemporary theorists of citizenship have paid less attention than they might to two important features of classical political thought. First, human excellence or nobility. The great modern ideal of equality has tended to reduce contemporary interest in human excellence or nobility, as opposed to the peaceful virtues suitable to commercial or liberal republics (Rahe 1992; Pettit 1997). However, certain theorists have redirected attention to intellectual and political nobility by referring to the ancient example. Leo Strauss and Thomas Pangle, for example, aspire to "ennoble" liberalism by offering a more aristocratic interpretation of its key principles and possibilities (Strauss 1968; T. Pangle 1992; Lutz 1998). Their goal is to reassert a nonrelative understanding of the perfectibility of human nature, so as to combat the perceived inadequacies of the contemporary liberal world, including relativism, conformism, and the lack of spiritual fulfillment. Often this political aspiration has been coupled with an appreciation of Plato and Aristotle's belief that political life is incomplete by comparison with the philosophical life. Only philosophy, in the ancient philosophical view, provides the highest fulfillment of human nature and the deepest satisfaction of human longing. Translating such views into a more contemporary idiom, such theorists articulate and defend a principled intellectual life as the best human life altogether, in the spirit of Platonic political philosophy.

Second, the intrinsic worth of the active exercise of political virtue. Although Arendt (1958) and Sandel (1996, 1998) emphasize the intrinsic worth of civic activity, it is possible to discern in classical political thought an even more profound concern with intrinsic goodness than these theorists have recognized. Developing the citizens' character and prudence, and thus providing citizens with an opportunity for a good life per se, was seen to be an essential task of the ancient political regime (cf. Diamond 1977; Licht 1978). Speaking roughly, at least, the ancient polis existed in order to make citizens good, in the belief that both individual lives and the community as a whole would flourish most fully by this means. In other words, the ancient "politics of virtue" should be understood as "eudaimonistic" – that is, as directed toward the cultivation of virtues of character and intellect as a perfection of human nature. The cultivation of virtues which are good for their own sake enables individuals themselves to lead good, flourishing human lives, even as they contribute in functionally excellent ways to the city. This conception of virtue politics envisions civic virtue as an intrinsically worthwhile (i.e., as a "final" or "telic") constituent of human well-being, as well as an instrumentally useful capacity enabling individuals to coexist in just and stable polities. Seen in this light, the classical politics of virtue strives to bridge the gap between individual self-interest and the demands of the larger political society. This volume as a whole shows that the well-known Socratic, Platonic, Aristotelian, and Stoic versions of eudaimonism grew out of, and were developments of, a long, diverse, and exceptionally well-developed Greco-Roman tradition of political thought. This tradition was particularly concerned with understanding how and why the political cultivation of civic virtues and deliberative prudence contributed to the good lives of individual citizens.

This line of interpretation suggests that the classical political philosophy and ideology of civic virtue can be connected to what is now called "virtue ethics." This is true particularly for the Greek traditions of civic virtue. In ethical philosophy, Elizabeth Anscombe (1958), Rosalind Hursthouse (1999), and Gabriele Taylor (2006), among others, have drawn on ancient, and particularly Aristotelian, thinking about virtue and vice in order to remedy apparent shortcomings in the prevailing Kantian and utilitarian theories. As David Depew shows in chapter 26, however, these neo-Aristotelian philosophers should also take account of virtue and vice as *political* phenomena, in the spirit of the ancients' own understanding of the virtues and of *eudaimonia*. Aristotle, most obviously, perceived ethics as a particular branch of politics, and he regarded his *Nicomachean Ethics* as the essential preliminary study for his *Politics*. Again, however, this way of relating ethics to politics was characteristic of classical political ideas and ideologies as a whole. As the essays in this volume indicate, study of ancient Greek and Roman political thought helps to provide a political framework for modern reappropriations of ancient ethics.

Much the same could be said about the resurgence of interest in the political passions. If ancient politics was particularly concerned with citizenly character, then the ancient thinkers were especially well positioned to reflect upon questions of moral and political psychology. Ancient reflections upon the role of the passions in political life have proved to be a fruitful basis for the modern reconsideration of political psychology in all its forms. Contemporary theorists such as Martha Nussbaum (2001), Jon Elster (1999), and Michael Walzer (2004) have taken up with gusto the study of emotion and its political applications, typically in ways that are explicitly and deeply indebted to the Greeks and Romans. The diverse essays by Sissa, Ludwig, Kaster, and Gibert illustrate, among other things, the special importance of Greek and Roman political thought for the study of political emotion and show how broad and pervasive, both chronologically and generically, the ancient interest in political passions came to be. By deepening the conversation (though not, perhaps, the "quarrel") between the ancients and the moderns, these essays strengthen the ancient contribution to our understanding of central, but traditionally neglected, facets of our political experience.

Significant Editorial Choices

With a view to illustrating the challenges posed by classical political thought to contemporary political ideas and ideologies, I have chosen to adopt a topical approach in this volume. By comparison to a conventional author-by-author and chronological approach, the topical approach is far better suited to bringing out both the historical specificity of classical political thought, and its potential to be fruitfully set into dialogue with modern political practices, ideologies, and theories. As a result, this volume will best serve readers with significant interests in real political questions, such as whether the ancient Greeks and Romans had a concept of "rights" (see Cartledge and Edge, chapter 10), whether private freedoms existed in the ancient republics (see Wallace, chapter 11, and part III, "The Virtues and Vices of One-Man Rule"), and whether ancient democratic practice and ideology differed from those of modern democracy (see Liddel, chapter 9). This volume will also be useful to those who come to the ancient material hoping to explore different perspectives on topics they have investigated chiefly with reference to modernity – e.g., the problem of collective action (see Ober, chapter 5), the ideal of cosmopolitanism (see Konstan, chapter 30), and the question of "civil religion" (see Osborne, chapter 8).

To make the same point more audaciously, the topical approach reflects our belief that the continuing importance of classical political thought should never be simply assumed. Traditional chronological and author-based surveys appear to make just such an assumption. Our view is that arguments are needed to show that classical political thought is still meaningful, useful, and interesting in modernity. For, as Bernard Williams has effectively demonstrated, "It is too late to assume that the Greek past must be interesting just because it is 'ours' " (1993: 3). That is exactly right, because, as Williams says, channeling Nietzsche's concern with "untimely meditations," "We, now, should try to understand how our ideas are related to the Greeks' because, if we do so, this can specially help us to see ways in which our ideas may be wrong" (1993: 4).

The essays in this volume might be regarded as providing particular case-studies of "untimely meditations." They begin to address the invitations offered by Nietzsche, Williams, and others of similar outlook, precisely by exploring the ancients' historical particularity within an enlarged framework of philosophical speculation and interest.

Such commitments help our *Companion* to extend the contributions of other collections that have focused specifically on the usefulness of particular ancient thinkers (e.g., Aristotle, as in Tessitore 2002) or particular political regimes (e.g., Athenian democracy, as in Euben, Wallach, and Ober 1994a). But this *Companion* is the first general survey of the field that takes such ambitions seriously. Even 20 years ago, the questions we pursue were not squarely in the center of most scholars' active research programs, despite certain notable exceptions (e.g., Euben 1990; Finley 1985a; MacIntyre 1984; Saxonhouse 1985). The surveys that have traditionally served students and teachers (e.g., Barker 1918; T. Sinclair 1951), and even newer handbooks (Rowe and Schofield 2000), have failed genuinely to address the issue of how best to reappropriate classical political thought within the framework of contemporary political thought and life. New questions have become more generally available through the work of interdisciplinary scholars and theorists who have returned to classical political thought because of their increasing dissatisfaction with contemporary liberal theory and the political cultures based on it (e.g., Douglass, Mara, and Richardson 1990).

Nevertheless, despite our confidence in the freshness and importance of the questions we explore, the present collection does not presume to give authoritative answers to these questions. To the contrary: our own "untimely meditations" are intended as open-ended stimuli to further study of classical antiquity in the same deeply interrogative spirit. It is hoped that readers will finish the volume with a fresh sense of the possibilities for further research and the opportunities offered to us by ancient political thought. From this vantage-point, we are cautiously optimistic that this volume will be of interest not only to students, but also to professional scholars striving to advance our collective understanding. Accordingly, in order to maintain the volume's open-endedness, I have not made any effort to iron out substantive disagreements among my fellow contributors (see, for example, the essays of Chappell and Depew in chapters 25 and 26, respectively). In this sense, I have been guided by Socrates' disconcerting insistence that everyone must think through the most important problems for himself or herself in the aporetic world of political discourse. Readers will hopefully find sources of guidance in these essays, yes, but they should not be tempted to seek any kind of ultimate resolution. Our goal is to enrich our understanding of permanent questions and problems without misleadingly suggesting that we offer unassailable or definitive answers.

As readers will have gathered, we understand "ancient political thought" to include political ideas and ideologies of all stripes, as they emerge from diverse genres of evidence, including drama, material culture, historiography, and oratory, as well as the works of the canonical philosophers. Greek and Roman political thought began with the earliest Greek poets (on which see Raaflaub, chapter 3, and Forsdyke, chapter 15), whose political interventions consisted in developing models of political virtue and critiques of civic vice. Questions of periodization will always be controversial with respect to end-points. I have focused attention on the most important early Christian writers (see Brown, chapter 31, and Breyfogle, chapter 32), in order to illustrate both their continuities with and departures from the earlier traditions of classical political thought. Augustine, in particular, should be understood as intervening in his own right, and all anew, in the central philosophical and political controversies of his day.

Yet, despite the volume's wide range, our center of gravity is still the canonical philosophers, in particular Plato and Aristotle. These two figures are unique in receiving their own dedicated section (part V, "The Athens of Socrates, Plato, and Aristotle"), and their influence is felt widely in other chapters (see, e.g., Hahm, chapter 12; Hedrick, chapter 27; and Nadon, chapter 33). Naturally, these figures, among others, deserve more scrutiny than is possible in any such collection. But our goal of addressing the central topics and questions of political life, and thus our adoption of a topical approach, is most appropriate for explaining why the thought of these and other figures should be important to our contemporary thinking about political life. The ancients' truly "untimely" qualities emerge most forcefully from asking real questions about politics and political theory, rather than from simply assuming that "we" should continue to study the "classics" because they are the (ancient) "greats" or because they are "ours."

The Provocation to Self-Criticism

As readers of this volume will soon discover, the ancient Greeks and Romans themselves should inspire us to recognize the very challenges that they themselves present. Classical political thought inaugurated an extraordinary tradition of self-criticism which it practiced ruthlessly and well (see, e.g., Ober 1998). The Greek and Roman tradition of self-criticism, exemplified by figures as diverse as Homer, Sophocles, Socrates, Cicero, and Seneca, is particularly useful, because it renders self-destructive, even self-refuting, any traditional claims to authority based on the "Classics." Those who seek to understand classical political thought should be inspired by the ancients' spirit of ceaseless inquiry and self-interrogation. They should be inspired, in particular, to interrogate their own conventions without envisioning classical political thought as a straightforward substitute. The greatness of the classical tradition lies, in fact, in provoking us to face our own problems resolutely in the recognition that the problems faced by modernity, and thus the solutions to those problems, can only ever be our own.

Even though the ancients tended, as a whole, to view the political world as an outgrowth of human nature – rather than as an artificial construct such as a social contract – they were also convinced, and distinctively so (cf. Raaflaub, chapter 3), that the political world could be improved, and even transformed, through human efforts. This is self-evidently the premise of Aristotle's *Politics* (on which see the chapters by Depew and Chappell); this premise lies behind Plato's most provocative and ambitious political texts, the *Republic* and *Laws* (on which see the chapters by Saxonhouse and Hitz); and this premise, finally, guided all of Greek thinking about politics as a means of decision-making, of educating citizens to virtue, and of providing security, prosperity, and happiness for all inhabitants of the Greco-Roman world.

Greco-Roman self-interrogation comes to sight most deeply in the question of whether politics itself was necessary, useful, or good. If the ancients tended to view political life as "natural," then particular individuals and movements were forced to contest the ancient "primacy of politics" (Rahe 1984) on the equally fundamental plane of naturalism. As David Konstan, Eric Brown, and Todd Breyfogle demonstrate, withdrawal from and even hostility toward conventional political life took on a variety of forms under the naturalistic banner. Taking inspiration from the critique of conventional political forms, ancient cosmopolitans oriented themselves toward a world-community of the virtuous and rational and toward proper understandings of "living according to nature" (Konstan, chapter 30). Even if unrealizable in practice, anyway, the ancient cosmopolitan utopias provoked contemporaries – and still provoke us – to ask what precisely is wrong with politics-as-usual. Can political life be significantly improved, given the limits of human nature? What might the possibilities for human fulfillment within political life amount to? Yet another type of parallel politics, originating in the Athenian democratic experience, is the Socratic political art, which most fully, perhaps, expresses the turn from actual political realities to a fully ethical understanding of "the political" (compare Brown, chapter 31, with Kamtekar, chapter 22). Given the Platonic interpretation of Socrates' life and death within Athens (Nails, chapter 21), it is understandable why Plato would have presented his distinctive and compelling portrait of the apolitical Socrates as he did (cf. Balot 2006, 2008).

Conclusion

It is fitting to point forward to the essays in this collection by invoking Socrates and his various mysteries, aporias (*aporiai*), and masks (cf. Nehamas 1998). For Socrates, above all, symbolizes not only the spirit of relentless self-interrogation promoted by this volume, but also the belief that speculative inquiry into ethical and political life is intrinsically worthwhile. Whether or not the historical Socrates was a model of good democratic citizenship, certainly Socrates' boldly interrogative and critical outlook, suitably adapted, can provide appropriate models for us (cf. Villa 2001). If Socrates' model proves at all attractive to readers, then they will find that classical political thought provides an unparalleled opportunity to unsettle, provoke, and educate the "moderns" in the spirit of profound Socratic self-examination.

NOTES

For their help, suggestions, and encouragement, I would like to thank Edward Andrew, Bob Connor, Sara Forsdyke, Robin Osborne, David Pritchard, and Victoria Wohl.

1   Before we congratulate ourselves too quickly, however, it is worth asking whether the "master/slave dialectic" is truly a product of bygone ages, considering that the North American and European labor forces are increasingly composed of nonunionized and stateless workers. How much of a difference is there between the terrible conditions of most ancient slaves (who, barring mining slaves, had legal protections against abuse) and the terrible conditions of modern "wage-slaves"? Classical political thought should not be dismissed out of hand because of the self-congratulatory thought that we have made outstanding moral progress since ancient times.

2   I have added the qualifier to Roman religion because of the common tendency of the Roman elite to manipulate religion for political purposes. Although Greek religion (e.g. the Delphic oracle) also admitted of such manipulation by members of the elite, the Greeks tended rather to subject religious interpretation to communal debate, as in the Athenians' famous public discussion of "wooden walls" by which, as Delphi predicted, they would be saved during the Persian assault (Hdt. 7.140–4).

3   The same ethical sensibility held fast even when larger political organizations, such as the Hellenistic kingdoms, or the Roman Empire, assumed primacy of place in the eastern Mediterranean. In those cases, as Arthur Eckstein (chapter 16) and Carlos Noreña (chapter 17) show, the language of virtue and vice was specially adapted to the rulers and other powerful figures on the increasingly unified Greco-Roman political stage.

CHAPTER 2

What is Politics in the Ancient World?

Dean Hammer

In his Preface to *Politics in the Ancient World*, M. I. Finley observed that "The English word 'politics' has a semantic range that differs somewhat from that of its synonyms in other western languages," referring less to "policy" and more to "the implication of the ways, informal as much as formal, in which government is conducted and governmental decisions are arrived at, and of the accompanying ideology" (1983: vii). Finley's sense of the range of meanings of "politics" was certainly correct, but even he could not have anticipated the contending conceptual vocabularies by which politics in the ancient world has come to be understood. My interest in this essay is threefold: to introduce the reader to these different frameworks; to show how each approach provides a different answer to the question, "What is politics in the ancient world?"; and to suggest some of the contributions and limitations of each perspective.

I plan to focus on six different (though overlapping) views of politics, each progressively more expansive in terms of the activities that constitute politics and who is considered a participant in these activities. The views are as follows: politics as formalized processes and institutional arrangements; politics as the instrument of informal group interest and power; politics as the site of class interest and conflict; politics as actions of the state backed by legitimate force; politics as inscribed relations of power; and finally politics as public performance. If we can use the analogy of a body, the trajectory of these conceptual frameworks moves from an analysis of the bones of a political system, to an increasing attention to the sinews that connect and give movement to those bones, to an attempt to grapple with the relationships (healthy and unhealthy) between the parts of the body, to the body as itself inscribed by its surroundings, and finally to a focus on the meaning of the body in movement. In the conclusion, I look at how ancient politics contributes to a reflection on the meaning of the body as political as ancient political writers ask for what purpose and to what end we come together as a community.

A Companion to Greek and Roman Political Thought, First Edition. Edited by Ryan K. Balot.
© 2013 Blackwell Publishing Ltd. Published 2013 by Blackwell Publishing Ltd.

Politics as Formalized Institutions

Perhaps the most conventional, and seemingly the most intuitively defensible, approach to politics is to locate it in a set of constitutional and institutional arrangements that allow a community to allocate resources, enforce values, and adjudicate disputes. By any other name, these formalized institutional arrangements are called governments. Finley, for example, contends that "political decisions" must be "binding on the society" and "political units" must have a "governmental apparatus" (1983: 9). This understanding of ancient politics would be informed largely by two separate traditions: a German legal tradition (which would guide the study of Roman politics and, to a lesser degree, Greek politics); and a twentieth century Anglo and French anthropological tradition (which would be most important in the study of early Greek politics).

Rechtsstaat

The German legal tradition is perhaps best known by way of Theodor Mommsen, whose *Römisches Staatsrecht* can be read as an attempt to construct the unwritten constitutional arrangements, limitations, and functions of Roman political institutions. Although the ancient world may no longer be viewed through the rational eyes of a Prussian jurist, the formalized relationships of ancient governments continue to be fertile ground for scholars. Through the study of political structures, two questions tend to be asked of ancient politics. First, what is the procedural basis by which formalized relationships between different offices are established and sustained? In short, if politics is understood procedurally, then by what procedures is the political system formed? Lintott asks of Roman political development, for example, "what was the authority which sanctioned a given constitutional practice" (1999a: 2)? And Ehrenberg struggles mightily to explain how Cleisthenes could enact sweeping changes in the Athenian constitution when he had no "official position," and how he could implement democratic changes in a seemingly undemocratic way (1950: 542; also 1967: 87–8).

The second political question is a functional one: how, as Jones asks in the title to his article, does the system work (see A. Jones 1960; also Rhodes 1972 and Rhodes, this volume, chapter 4)? How are offices composed and organized, and what are their powers? By what procedures are laws passed and enforced? What is the relationship of these different offices or functions to particular groups or interests in society? At times scholars have sought to answer these questions by interpreting the functioning of politics – the assemblies, councils, law courts, magistrates, and electoral procedures – by way of modern constitutional forms, such as the rule of law, separation and balance of powers, a mixed constitution, or an independent judiciary (Hignett 1952; de Laix 1973; Sealey 1987; Stockton 1990). Understanding the operation of politics by way of a system encounters an explanatory limit: faced with the absence of clear constitutional processes, Hignett, for example, could only ascribe the workings of Athenian democracy vaguely to the "peculiar qualities" of the people (Hignett 1952: 250). More recent scholarship has sought to avoid what Finley describes as the "constitutional-law trap" (1983: 56) and has sought to place these institutions in their broader social, ideological, and comparative context.

One value of such approaches is that they can tell us something about the constraints operating on political behavior. Laws, procedures, and institutions guide how arguments can be proffered, interests advanced, and binding judgments made (see Hansen 1989a). Furthermore, the evolution of constitutional structures can serve as a record of the various economic, social, and political challenges to the perpetuation of rule, such as administrative problems of raising revenue or of incorporating new groups. And the study of formalized processes can be helpful in providing a comparative basis for analyzing political development (Eder 1986: 1991).

The emphasis on process and function imparts a particular perspective, though, in which politics tends to appear continuous, change as incremental, and political life as normal (or normalized). For Crook, for example, Roman law, whatever its flaws, provided a diverse people with a "legal framework in which orderly lives could be led" (1967: 284; see also Johnston 1999). In his exhaustive study of senatorial procedures in imperial Rome, Talbert points to a much slower decline in the corporate significance of the senate under the Principate than we might expect (1984: 4, 490–1). And Lintott uses as his starting point Polybius' organic metaphor of the Roman constitution as a "product of natural growth" that changed through "slow, piecemeal development" (Lintott 1999a: 26, 38; see also Lintott 1993: 188, 192–3).

Structure and function: Greece

One of the problems of constitutional approaches is that they are decidedly unhelpful in understanding what politics looked like in societies lacking formalized institutions. Scholars, particularly those interested in Archaic and Dark Age societies, thus had to look to other models. Perhaps most influential in identifying not only what counts as politics, but also the nature of the evolution of political forms, was the structural-functional anthropology of Radcliffe-Brown, Fortes, and Evans-Pritchard, and the evolutionary approaches of Service, Sahlins, Fried, and Cohen. Although these schools differed in important ways, they shared an attempt to identify and classify politics in structural and functional terms. Informed by this anthropological tradition, classicists, led importantly by Finley (1977, 1981) and Donlan (1989, 1993, 1997), approached the study of politics by first identifying formal institutions or groups within a society and then determining the distinct functions they performed. Politics, from this perspective, came to be identified with the emergence of an autonomous polis and a set of differentiated institutionalized roles and relationships between rulers and citizens within that polis (discussed in Hammer 2002: 19–26 and Hölkeskamp 2002).

One of the virtues of this approach is that it meshed nicely with Aristotle's identification of the typical form of the polis as autonomous, suggestive of the development of sufficient political structures for both internal control of the people and external protection of the territory from others. But the approach often carried with it the assumption that institutions were political although the preinstitutional activity of forming these institutions was not. This posed a significant problem for understanding the politics of early Greece since, as Raaflaub points out, "Institutions and constitutions and the corresponding terminology had to be newly created, and the political sphere itself had to be discovered and gradually penetrated by thought, understanding, and explanation" (1989b: 5).

Group Politics:
Prosopography, Social Power, and Social History

One problem with the study of political structures is that even if we can reassemble the bones and trace their growth, we may still have no idea how the political body actually moved. As W. R. Connor remarks, in his important discussion of the rise of a new type of political leader in Athens, the demagogue, "the formal structure of the state is but the skeleton of her politics. The nerves, the tendons, the musculature of the body politic is to be found in the organization of forces and often of interest groups within it" (1971: 4–5). Seeking to explain how social and political systems could survive for so long without a written constitution, scholars focused on groups that operated behind and between governmental institutions.

I want to look initially at two related approaches. The first is prosopography, an unwieldy term for a historical methodology, pioneered by Matthias Gelzer and Friedrich Münzer, that viewed history and politics through a careful, often empirical, study of the "formation, duration, and dissolution" of influential families and groups that comprised the governing class (Broughton 1972: 251). These groups cultivated networks of personal relationships and support that extended into the law courts and political institutions, and were organized by shared interests, social and economic class, family connection, and political friendships.

We can identify a second approach, which shares some of the same assumptions with, and often finds evidentiary sustenance in, prosopography. That framework, which has its roots in the work of Anton von Premerstein, views politics as a function of social power. Where prosopography often saw relations of power as contingent and separately negotiated, social power (or transactional) approaches attempt to explain these relations of power as a more system-wide phenomenon. Politics and political questions, though, all but disappear in the shadow of the "realities of power" (MacMullen 1988: 116): a whole network of extralegal and extrainstitutional relations or transactions that were organized by the ability to influence (through wealth, patronage and position) and the ability to coerce (through fear).

There are three political questions at the heart of these group approaches: Who really rules? How do they do it? And why do they do it? The answers given to each of these questions resonate with similar debates within political science and sociology between the pluralist school reflected in the work of Arthur Bentley, David Truman, and Robert Dahl, on the one hand, and elite power approaches, reflected in the pioneering work of the Lynds in the 1920s and 1930s and articulated, theoretically, by Gaetano Mosco, Vilfredo Pareto, and Robert Michels, on the other hand. How one appraises group influence, whether oligarchic or democratic, depends to a large extent on the evaluation of the extent to which the informal relations are seen as open, fluid, competitive, or transparent. Connor, for example, following Bentley, views these informal relationships as the stuff of democracy, consisting of small, fluid, and often competitive groups who had to continually cultivate broader support to survive (1971). But Connor is more the exception. The decision to study families and connections between families (whether of marriage or political friendships), and to exclude from prosopographical collections "lower orders" of public officials, all but assumes an answer to the first question, who really rules, since the method can tap only the most elite sectors of the population whose names would be recorded (Barnish 1994: 171; see Badian 1968: 81).

In answering the second question, how do these groups maintain power, informal group approaches look elsewhere than constitutional forms. Precisely because neither Greece nor Rome was a *Rechtsstaat*, institutions and processes did not have power aside from the individuals who could control them. Prosopography and social power approaches thus emphasize the remarkable cohesion of oligarchy, which was created and reinforced through particular "weapons" (Syme 1939: 12): family, which was strengthened through marriage and adoption; money to entertain the populace through games and shows, to bribe voters and jurors, and to support allies; political alliances to build a following among different orders of society; and the ability to manipulate symbols to create both solidarity and affirm elite rule. Not surprisingly, a methodology that identifies names and connections is going to locate the movement of politics in the actions of and connections between particular individuals (as opposed to larger structural or systemic issues in society). Thus Gruen attributes the decline of the Roman Republic not to "underlying causes" but to "accident and irrationality, stubbornness and miscalculations" among the elite (1974: 4). And Perlman sees much of the "stability and preservation of Athenian democracy in the fourth century" as resulting from the influence and activities of the informal (and largely "closed") network of political leaders who dominated Athenian politics (1963: 355, 340).

As for the third question, the motivation for political action seems largely reducible to ambition: raw and naked in its operation, but often veiled in a self-image and ideology of the rightness and responsibility of that group to rule. Group power approaches ultimately end up with "power" as an explanatory variable: the desire for power explains the motivations for action and the possession of power explains the success. As Badian states in his opening to *Roman Imperialism*, the longing for power is so rooted in what we are as humans that it "does not call for explanation" (1968: 5).

At times, prosopographical and social power approaches evince the swagger of an unconscious positivism; not only politics, but also the "conceptual world of a society in the past," can be understood by "subordinat[ing]" oneself "to the evidence" and by avoiding using concepts that would have "contaminated the presentation of the evidence" (Millar 1977: xii; Badian 1996: 189). Yet, these approaches often end up telling us more about their own assumptions about human nature and social life than about the different motivations that may underlie ancient political life. Political institutions and procedures appear as a "sham" or a "bitter joke" (Syme 1939: 15; MacMullen 1988: 90). Ideas – whether as ideologies, common aspirations, particular principles and beliefs, or human yearnings – are, as Momigliano (1940) long ago pointed out, read out of politics (L. Taylor 1949: 8; Paterson 1985: 22; Mouritsen

2001: 117). And those over whom power is exercised all but vanish as people are turned into "mice" who "must simply accept their place in the great scheme of things" (MacMullen 1988: 106). How and why transactions break down – or why the mice sometimes squeak – is less explicable.

There is a third group approach – social history – that sees politics (and political development) as a fairly complex interplay between social groups in their response to each other and to larger structural issues and events, such as demographic changes, famines, debt, and war (see Further Reading below). Social historical approaches have been particularly important in exploring the processes by which groups make claims to a share of the community's material resources and to a part in the political process. Politics, from this perspective, is about social integration. On what basis do particular groups, such as an aristocratic elite, a new plebeian elite, provincial elites, or the people, become conscious of themselves as groups and make claims on a community (or resist claims by the community)? And what are the factors, such as ongoing strife, military needs, elite competition, elite cohesiveness, or tyrants and reformers, that explain why these groups are either successfully or unsuccessfully integrated? In these group interaction approaches, unlike many prosopographical and social power approaches, power is negotiable and politics embodies both material concerns and broader questions of community identity and purpose.

Politics as the Site of Class Relations

Informal group interest approaches have been criticized variously for reducing the motivations for political action to material interest, for viewing the formation and operation of groups in ad hoc or historically contingent terms, and for oversimplifying the operation of power as a possession wielded over others. But if group power approaches spend less time theorizing about their own assumptions concerning the operation of power and politics, then Marxian-influenced approaches head in the opposite direction. Friends and foes alike find themselves subject to exhaustive (and often exhausting) elaborations, distinctions, and criticisms of definitions, concepts, and theoretical applications of Marx. Even Marx cannot escape being labeled a "proto-Marxist" at times (Rose 1999: 27).

It is a shame, though, that Marx has not figured more prominently in classical scholarship. One can employ Marxian insights without being a Marxist (which is why I have chosen to refer to the approach as "Marxian" rather than "Marxist"). Marxian approaches can be helpful in clarifying and challenging how one understands (or what one even looks for in) the operation of power and politics. Marx guides the scholar to focus on the economic production process, which is the critical factor in dividing individuals into classes, defining the terms of class struggle and the basis of power, and providing the foundation (and impetus) for the creation of political, religious, and ideological structures supportive of the economic relations of a society. Most importantly, Marxian approaches emphasize the relational character of economic, social, and political existence: classes become conscious of themselves as they enter into conflict with other groups over the means and relations of production, and over the distribution of the outcomes of production. Politics thus encompasses a broad set of relationships that direct our attention not just to the elites, but to marginal, and previously unstudied, groups (the "mice" in social power analysis): women, laborers, slaves, and communities in the periphery.

The story that Marxian analysis tells of ancient politics is twofold: on the one hand, Marx (particularly in his early work) saw in ancient (especially Athenian) politics the possibility of human emancipation and self-determination (see Marx 1975: 201; Mewes 1976); on the other hand, ancient politics was part of a process of the enslavement – and separation from politics – of increasing portions of the population (Vernant 1976: 68–9). Marxian approaches have lent themselves well to analyses of the economic forces that moved Rome toward a slave (and increasingly enslaved peasant) economy (de Ste Croix 1981; Hindess and Hirst 1975; Carandini 1988). They have posited how we can read the increasing division and conflict in early Greece between an exploitative aristocracy and an exploited, but increasingly resistant, demos (Wood and Wood 1978; de Ste Croix 1981; Bintliff 1982; Tandy 1997; Rose 1997; Thalmann 1998). And others have employed Marx to hypothesize about the structural contradictions around a land tenure system that underlay Spartan society (Cartledge 1975, 2002b).

But Athenian democracy is more perplexing. Both the inclusiveness of political relations among the body of citizens and the difficulty of defining the form of economic relations have confounded Marxian attempts to carve out a distinctive contribution to understanding Athenian politics, specifically, and the emergence of democracy, generally (see Hindess and Hirst 1975: 82; Wood 1988: 51–80). In seeking to address the peculiarity of Athens, several scholars, including Vernant and Godelier, have modified Marx to suggest that politics may have assumed the "functions of relations of production" since the appropriation and distribution of surplus was "mediated via political status" (Godelier 1977: 36; Vernant 1976: 76; 1980: 10; also Hindess and Hirst 1975: 82–91).

Such reconceptualizations, though, have not been uniformly applauded. For some, the elevation of the political over the economic does not explain "the *dynamics* of ancient society" (McKeown 1999: 112). That is to say, it takes the economic engine out of political change. Rose paints a picture of ongoing exploitation of the "peasant masses" in order to support Athens, and of Athenian imperialism as a way of exploiting labor abroad in order to purchase "political accommodation" at home (1999: 26, 36). And though recognizing the "astonishing development of real democracy" in Athens, de Ste Croix insists somewhat unpersuasively that the "basic economic situation asserted itself in the long run, as it always does" (1981: 97).

It is around class approaches to the study of politics that "ideology" has assumed recent theoretical prominence. Whether accurately or (as often) inaccurately ascribed to Marx (or Antonio Gramsci, Louis Althusser, Fredric Jameson, Pierre Macherey, or Raymond Williams), the focus on ideology is meant to identify the systems of belief by which groups (in this case, classes) understood themselves in their relationship to each other (see Rose 2006). The study of ideology has been used to describe the emerging consciousness of the plebeians and demos (Hahn 1975). But ideological approaches have more often identified the ways in which a dominant system of beliefs is able to perpetuate itself. That is, ideological approaches explore how governments exact compliance (particularly from exploited groups) without continual shows of force. To this end, scholars, even those expressly non-Marxian, have employed some version of Althusser's notion of an "ideological state apparatus": how institutions such as education, religion, and media, as well as patronage networks, serve as ways to enforce, through persuasion, the views of the elite (de Ste Croix 1981: 342–3; also Hindess and Hirst 1975: 93; Rose 1999: 31; Ando 2000: 41; Morstein-Marx 2004: 15–16). And fashionable, as well, has been the use of Marxian approaches to view literary texts as sites of ideological conflict and resolution. As Kurke writes, in employing Macherey (a student of Althusser's), "literary text does the work of ideology" by "transforming the 'raw materials' of ideological values in complex ways. Because these values suppress certain possibilities, because they are incomplete and contradictory, the text incorporates those suppressions, inadequacies, and con-tradictions" (Kurke 1999: 24). More than anything else, these approaches have added considerable sophistication to oversimplified views of ideology as perpetuated by propaganda used to manipulate mass belief.

Politics and Legitimate Domination

Weberian approaches, like Marxian approaches, seek to systematically define the rela-tionship between social structure, human motivation, and political action. Setting aside the intricacies of specific Weberian analyses of the ancient world, much of which takes us far outside the scope of politics, I want to highlight one salient difference between Weberian and Marxian approaches that may help us appreciate their distinctive contri-butions to how we analyze ancient politics. Marxian views, by focusing on structural contradictions, draw attention to why systems ultimately fall apart. Weber's political analysis, in contrast, lies in the effort to categorize and make intelligible the subjective basis of human action (how individuals understand and make sense of their world). Weberian approaches, thus, tend more to identify what holds a system together.

One can see the emphasis on the subjective basis of human action and understand-ing in several aspects of Weber's thought. For example, where class is for Marx an economic classification defined by one's relation to production (and the correspond-ing nature and extent of exploitation), status for Weber is defined (however ambigu-ously, at times) by a consciousness of a style of life, each style with its own forms of consumption, economic interests, types of honor, and orientation to others. Weber also broadens the question of motivations for social action from issues of force and economic interest to values, affective ties, and traditional relationships. And perhaps most famously, Weber provides a conceptual scheme to help identify the salient elements of belief systems that underlie the most stable and enduring forms of rule, those forms that have legitimacy or a belief in the rightness of rule.

One should not understate Weberian explorations of the complex interplay of institutions and structural conditions: family, law, politics, economics, the military, religion, geography, resources, population size, etc. These explorations can overlap with, and bear similarity to, social historical approaches, as one sees in scholarship on the ancient city and the ancient economy. Weberian approaches differ in their exploration of the sociological and psychological bases on which political action, as orderly domination, is accepted as legitimate (Weber 1958: 77; 1978: 901–4).

Weber's idea of legitimacy has received considerable attention in classical scholarship recently, more so in the study of Rome than Greece. Finley, for example, who began his career influenced by Marx, has explored Weber's own classification of the Athenian polis as a form of charisma derived from the will of the ruled, a notion of "plebiscitary democracy" that can be more helpfully applied to archaic Greece (Finley 1974; Hammer 2005. Other applications: Finley 1982a; Donlan 1997). More enticing are attempts to identify the basis of Roman political authority by way of Weberian categories of charisma, tradition, and bureaucratic rationality (Loewenstein 1973; Deininger 1985; Meier 1988; 1994; Hatscher 2000: 24-37; Hölscher 2000; Ando 2000).

Two works suggest the distinctive contributions of a Weberian approach. Hatscher uses Weber to negotiate between the structural-historical interpretation of the late republic (as a "crisis without an alternative") and the importance of historical actors in effecting change (2000: 9–15; "crisis" coined by Meier 1980: xliii–liii, 201–5; also 1990). Hatscher argues that out of the crisis of the late republic emerged the figures of Sulla and then Caesar, who both drew upon charismatic strands in the Roman past and consolidated their own charismatic authority around loyal troops (2000: 17; also Hölscher 2000).

And Ando's massive work on Roman administration asks, in true Weberian form, not why the empire fell, but why it lasted so long. Ando's answer is that although the empire was acquired by force, it was not sustained by it but by a "slowly realized consensus regarding Rome's right to maintain social order and to establish a normative political culture" (2000: xi). Ando actually points to three different notions of legitimacy, each operative in different groups. The emperor appealed to charismatic authority in relationship with the people, rational and bureaucratic authority in his relationship to the senate, and traditional authority in relationships with the army. Murky, indeed, is how these distinct forms of legitimacy managed to find their intended target and maintain their distinct streams of authority. What deserves emphasis, though, and points to a more expansive notion of politics, is how Ando focuses on the everyday lives of the people to understand how they participated in rituals and ceremonies – not just religious ceremonies, but the creation and production of imperial documents – that actively engaged the people in establishing and confirming the legitimacy of the emperor.

Politics as Inscribed Relations of Power: From Structure to Poststructure

The trajectory of my argument has been to address conceptual approaches that provide an increasingly expansive understanding of the extent to which, and the ways in which, broader segments of the community are viewed as political actors. I look now at what can be described broadly (though not always helpfully) as poststructural approaches to politics, represented most significantly in classical scholarship by the works of Pierre Bourdieu and Michel Foucault. Suggestive of the overlap and trajectory of the different conceptual approaches described here, Bourdieu's and Foucault's own positions evolved from an intellectual affinity with Marxism and structuralism in their earlier work to an increasing emphasis on how groups and subgroups are engaged in practices that are structured by, and in turn alter, particular historical discourses.

Bourdieu

In many ways, the intersection of classical interests and Bourdieu's work should come as no surprise (on Bourdieu and the classics, see Hammer 2006). Bourdieu's early fieldwork in Kabylia, for example, supplemented a growing interest by classicists in using comparative anthropological data to shed light on the operation of ancient societies. "The Berber house" took as its starting point a description of the arrangement of social space: the house. These arrangements, as Bourdieu suggested, could not be explained completely by "technical imperatives or functional requirements" (1970: 153). Rather, employing a structural approach, one could identify in the household a whole series of symbolically mediated "homologous oppositions": dark and light, nature and culture, animal and human, raw and cooked, and lower and higher, all of which are organized around the complementary opposition of female and male (1970: 157). Like much of structural analysis, these oppositions become political as they are seen as the organizing principles for the society (Bourdieu 1970: 157; also Detienne 1977; Segal 1986; Loraux 1986, 1993; and Vernant and Vidal-Naquet 1988).

   The attention to the organization of space was of interest to classicists because it provided a way to interpret the structures of social spaces from the scant archaeological record (see Gould 1980: 47–8; I. Morris 1999, 2000: 280–6). The problem is, as Morris himself would recognize, that it becomes nearly impossible to untangle whether the structural system of binary oppositions was an artifact of the archaeological record or an artifact of the anthropologist's imagination (Morris 1999: 11). Bourdieu would later revise his structuralism by seeing the categories and boundaries of social and political interaction, including those of Kabyle society, as ambiguous and fluid, subject to manipulation, negotiation, interpretation, and innovation (Bourdieu 1977: 10; see also 1990 and revised interpretations by D. Cohen 1989: 9; Foxhall 1989: 22–4).

   One of the most innovative aspects of Bourdieu's work is his attempt to show how the political order – a field in which agents struggle to assert their vision of how to perceive and express the social world (1991a: 172) – is transferred to and inscribed in our inner expressions and outward conduct. That is, politics is not just about a struggle between groups; that struggle is translated into bodily dispositions, or a "bodily hexis" that is a repository of a "durable way of standing, speaking, walking, and thereby of feeling and thinking" (1990: 69–70). Read into the ancient world, Bourdieu's notion of bodily *hexis* provided a powerful conceptual tool for interpreting the body as the site in which gender and power relations are enacted: how broader social and political structures not only produce the interests, motivations, and practices of individuals and groups, but also how these dispositions may be modified as they confront and are adapted to new situations and experiences (Gleason 1995; Stewart 1997; Steiner 1998; Gunderson 1998, 2000).

Bourdieu's approach allowed not just for an understanding of how the political is inscribed in the body but also, in turn, for a way to interpret the operation of differential relations of power in a society without reducing the determinants of these relations to economic class. Bourdieu extended considerably the insights into the activity of gift exchange, developed most influentially by Marcel Mauss, to understand a variety of social interactions (Bourdieu 1977: 183–6). Social relationships are determined (or at least substantially influenced) by the distribution of different forms of what Bourdieu referred to as "capital": economic capital (material resources), social capital (relationships with key people), cultural capital (possession of culturally valued items, such as knowledge), and symbolic capital (such as prestige) (1991b: 230; 1977: 171–97). Bourdieu offered a way, as well, to interpret hidden strategies of domination. This hiddenness, which Bourdieu refers to as "symbolic violence," occurs as "misrecognized" domination (1977: 192): an acceptance of the legitimacy of differential relations that are maintained through the accumulation of different forms of capital and inscribed in our bodily habits and mental perceptions (or what Bourdieu refers to as "habitus").

Bourdieu's approach, as applied to the ancient world, allowed for a sophisticated way of interpreting the political without reducing it to either objective forces or subjective intentions. Price, for example, uses Bourdieu's model of gift exchange to understand the establishment of the Roman imperial cult in Greece (Price 1984). Habinek focuses on how the "symbolic capital of literature augments the common property of the Roman elites," functioning both to preserve them against autocracy and exclude others from access to elite privilege (Habinek 1998: 66; also Leach 2003). And perhaps most ambitiously, Kurke sees herself as doing for the archaic Greek world what Bourdieu did in *Distinction*: offer a richly textured exploration of the "material symbols that identify and reproduce different class fractions" (Kurke 1999: xi; also D. Cohen 1991 on moral structures; Griffith 1995 on Athens; Alden 2000 on Homer).

Foucault

In many ways, Foucault's work followed the same trajectory as Bourdieu's. In his earlier writings, Foucault emphasized the role of structures, or what he referred to as discursive practices, in constituting individuals as subjects. Discourses could be best understood as regimes of truth, organized around networks of power and institutional arrangements, that defined both the values by which we try to live and the practices that help us live that way.

In his later work, Foucault turned toward identifying what he described as a specifically modern, scientific discourse of sexuality that allowed (and still allows) society to exercise increasing scrutiny and control over the desires of the subject. Foucault's interest in the genealogy of this modern discourse of sexuality pushed him back further and further into the ancient world where he identified a much different discourse organized around the care of the self. Foucault's work has served as an impetus (both as embrace and critique) for many explorations of the social and historical construction of sexuality and gender in the ancient world. The political significance of these analyses lies in the ways that sexuality and gender emerge as sites in which relations of power are both inscribed and contested.

In classical Greece, as Foucault suggests, the care of the self emphasized self-mastery and was organized around, and used to reinforce, the differential power relationships of active citizen and passive noncitizen. A slightly different story is told of Rome. With the disintegration of the city-state and the traditional relationship between "one's status, one's functions, one's activities, and one's obligations," the emphasis of the care of the self turned toward defining a "principle of a relation to self that will make it possible to set the forms and conditions in which political action, participation in the offices of power, the exercise of a function, will be possible or not possible, acceptable or necessary" (Foucault 1990b: 85–6). Extending Foucault's argument, Skinner suggests that we might understand Roman sexuality as serving as "an ordered semantic system for articulating social anxieties" about maintaining authority and honor in an imperial society with increasing constraints (M. Skinner 1997: 5).

Foucault has drawn considerable scholarly fire for his ambitious interpretation of the ancient world. Feminists have criticized Foucault's project because it tended to discount (or outright ignore) the active role and experiences of women in their own sexuality (Richlin 1991; 1992: xiv–xvii; 1998; Foxhall 1998) or of groups outside the narrow elite that Foucault identifies (Edwards 1993: 56–7). In fact, as Richlin reminds us, the notion of the body as constituted by the organizing principles of political life had a long feminist pedigree that preceded Foucault (Richlin 1991: 174; also 1992; Rabinowitz and Richlin 1993). Others have criticized Foucault for failing to recognize the degree of difference and conflict in beliefs and values that may lie within a particular historical period (P. Miller 1998). And significant criticism has come from those responding to his claim that the ancient mode of "subjectivation" (or way of making oneself an ethical being) involved a set of practices that treated and transformed the self as a work of art (Foucault 1990a: 29; 1988). Critics charge Foucault with slipping into a fundamental (and for some, a dangerous) error by making aesthetics itself, and not living according to a universal, rational, and natural order, as the end of self-fashioning. Absent the goal of living in truth (or with the realization that living in truth is living in a constructed discourse of truth), self-fashioning for the sake of self-fashioning is seen as taking on a certain modern feel – a form of "dandyism," in Hadot's oft-quoted words (1992: 230).

Although one can find much with which to quarrel in the historical sweep of Foucault's generalizations, his work broadens considerably the complex interplay between structures of power and the ways we become ethical and political subjects. As Foucault notes, the "practices" by which a "subject constitutes itself" are "not something invented by the individual himself. They are models that he finds in his culture and are proposed, suggested, imposed upon him by his culture, his society, and his social group" (Foucault 1997: 291). This certainly has importance for the historical constitution of sexualities, but it also may provide a framework for exploring the ways in which individuals locate themselves in, and reinterpret, their political context. Edwards, for example, notes how Seneca's *Epistles* can be understood as exercises in self-scrutiny and self-transformation in which the "activities of Roman public life – law-courts, games, elections" were used as "metaphors and images for articulating relationships *within* the self" (Edwards 1997: 36). And one can approach Foucault's care of the self as a form of "looking" or a "conversion of the gaze" in which individuals become the makers of themselves as monuments, the outlines of the self (and what the self stands for) brought into relief so that, as Seneca writes, we may live "in plain sight of all men" (Foucault 2005: 10, 217; Sen. *Ep.* 83.1, trans. Gummere 1996; Hammer 2008).

Politics as Cultural Performance

The final conceptual approach is organized around images of performance. Performance approaches place considerable emphasis on bodies in motion – the ways in which individuals and groups are engaged in negotiation about cultural meanings and practices. "Rituals and religious ceremonies," as Dougherty and Kurke write in their introduction to a volume on *Cultural Poetics*, "are inseparable from what we now call politics, subject to negotiation from above and below" (1998: 5; also Goldhill 1999). There is overlap between performance approaches and the work of Foucault, as suggested by the Foucauldian inspired edited volume *Before Sexuality* that seeks to explore the "cultural poetics" of sexuality (Halperin, Winkler, and Zeitlin 1990: 4). I would describe performance approaches as a more general rubric inspired variously by cultural anthropology (e.g. Victor Turner), sociology (e.g. Erving Goffman), semiotics (e.g. Mikhail Bakhtin), linguistics (J. L. Austin), phenomenology (e.g. Hannah Arendt), philosophy (e.g. Nietzsche), literary analytic approaches of New Historicism and cultural poetics (e.g. Stephen Greenblatt), and feminist theory (e.g. Judith Butler). Common to performance approaches are theatrical metaphors of social and political drama, the political stage, and political performance that remind us "that any drama includes an audience that participates in the action and so forces us to look beyond the elite, the powerful, those on stage" (Dougherty and Kurke 1998: 5). Instead of the Weberian focus on politics as the exercise by the state of legitimate domination, politics is more local, contextual, and appears in a variety of guises: burial and cult sites, myths, festivals, art, monuments, landscapes, economic exchange, crowds and public assemblies, literary and historiographic texts, conduct, and the theater itself (see Gibert, this volume, chapter 28, and Further Reading below). This evidence emerges as an artifact of material culture that is structured by, and in turn serves as "a force in informing social behaviour and in negotiating relations of power and dominance" (Alcock, Gates, and Rempel 2003: 358).

   If there is a common tone to these works, it is of political processes that, for contemporaneous participants, are much less determinant, more open to interpretation and misinterpretation, and more fluid. The politics of prestate societies, such as the Homeric world, take on new complexity when we identify politics not by way of a particular set of institutional attributes tied to specific functions but as a field in which questions of community organization are raised, determined, and implemented (Hammer 2002). Interpretations of the ancient economy focus less on stripping away the distortions of the evidence in order to "figure out how the economy 'really' worked" than on viewing the distortions themselves as giving insight into the "economy" as "a category of representation" in which actors are "manipulating evocative symbols within specific performance contexts" (I. Morris 1994: 356, 351). Even tyranny is reinterpreted. Rather than viewing rituals and ceremonies as propaganda manufactured and controlled by leaders, one can interpret rituals, such as the procession of Peisistratus, as forms of two-way communication in which the people are "alert, even sophisticated actors in a ritual drama" (Connor 1987: 46; also McGlew 1993; Sinos 1998; Raaflaub 2003b; Ober 2003; Morgan 2003: ix on tyranny as a "conceptual force" rather than its "historical instances").

In Roman studies, we move from the careful scrutinizing of law and procedure to, as Millar writes, the "open-air" where the people assemble, listen to speeches, and respond (1998: 1; also Millar 1984, 1986). The conception of the Roman political system itself changes from a "tightly controlled, 'top-down' system" to one in which "rival conceptions of state and society, and rival policies as regards both internal structures and external relations, were openly debated before the crowd in the Forum" (Millar 1998: 6–7). A whole new brand of scholarship has begun exploring spectacle – "the visible component of all rituals and public acts" – as a way in which the people participate in, and experience, the political and cultural world (Feldherr 1998: 13; see Kraus 1994; Slater 1996; Chaplin 2000; Kraus and Woodman 1997; M. Jaeger 1997; Leigh 1997; Boyle 2003). As Potter writes, in arguing against de Ste Croix's view that the decline of democratic institutions in Rome spelled the end of popular power, "The exercise of authority in the ancient world was highly theatrical, and for the performance of power to succeed, it was necessary for the audience to be drawn into the act, to be made to feel a part of the action" (Potter 1996: 131).

The point is not to deny that there are differentials of formal and informal power, or even that elites seek to control the meanings of the spectacles. In fact, scholars have demonstrated how such spectacles and performances transmitted authority (as the authority relations are reenacted) (Feldherr 1998), how orators sought to shape the meanings that were interpreted (Vasaly 1993), how such spectacles were used for elite representation (Hölkeskamp 1995), and how such performances were structured by ideology and limited to competition among "alternative rhetorical personae" (Morstein-Marx 2004: 15, 276–7). The point is that these meanings can never be controlled once and for all because there is always an audience engaged in interpretation. The effect of the audience can be to shape and alter what is actually said (as the actor anticipates and adjusts to the audience), to come up with interpretations that are themselves unintended by the actors, and to form a collective identity (and some power) in the role as interpreter.

Not surprisingly, such approaches provide a more expansive understanding of ways different groups, such as women, may have participated in politics, whether through protests, legal advocacy, political networks and elections, the succession and the transmission of legitimacy, poetic and theatrical performance, and day-to-day interactions (see Sissa, this volume, chapter 7; Hallett 1984; Bauman 1992; Savunen

1995; Corbier 1995; Stehle 1997; Katz 1999; essays in Fraschetti 2001). Perhaps some of the excitement of employing these performance approaches points to their weakness; one can too easily read fluidity, freedom, and indeterminance where there are, in fact, profound structural constraints to action. As Richlin comments, in responding to the tendency of New Historicists to see subversion in everything, "Political gains have been made by means of confrontation, not by inverted commas" (Richlin 1992: xxvi). We come full circle in the contributions of different approaches to politics: bodies in motion must ultimately have backbones.

Ancient Politics as Reflection

Thus far, I have used the metaphor of the body to explore increasingly expansive understandings of what we mean by the political. But to understand ancient politics, one must also pay attention to what is perhaps its most enduring and distinctive contribution: its self-conscious commitment to critical inquiry about the ideals and purposes of community life (see part V, "The Athens of Socrates, Plato, and Aristotle," this volume). Socrates' politics of the agora is a form of political inquiry that places itself in the noisy swirl of contending political ideas, beliefs, and systems and takes on all comers, seeking both to make an argument about and to impart a particular ethical orientation on the community. Ancient politics, in short, gave reflectivity to the political self by seeking to cultivate the virtues of citizenship and to guide one in the practice of the good life.

This reflection on the ends of political life is the basis both of ancient texts and of our thinking about those texts. At its worst, ancient politics reemerges as a romanticizing gesture that cannot help but disappoint. At its most practical, it may provide, as Livy and Thucydides hoped, lessons and warnings (Neustadt and May 1986; Chaplin 2000; Matthes 2000). But our engagement with ancient political thought stimulates a broader inquiry into how we see ourselves as political beings. It may invite us to think about politics as something more than the instrument of interest (Arendt 1958 and Zuckert, this volume, chapter 34), or about the possibilities and limits of participatory and deliberative forms of democracy (see Further Reading below). An inquiry into ancient politics may point to traditions that form a part of who we are (Pocock 1975; MacIntyre 1984; Millar 2002a; Connolly 2007) or the ambivalent legacy on which those traditions have been constructed (Richlin 1992; Saxonhouse 1992; Roberts 1994). It may alert us to the "political and ideological mystifications" of our own age (Habinek 1998: 5) or truths that are hidden or lost (L. Strauss 1953, 1964). It may provide a model of political inquiry (Kraut 1984; Vlastos 1991, 1994a). Or it may prompt a deeper reflection on oneself as an ethical being (Nussbaum 1986, 1990b, 1994; Hadot 1992; Foucault 1997; Balot 2006).

Politics is not one thing. Whether we enter the jail with Socrates, cast a glance back to the earth in Scipio's dream, or roam the recesses of the inner self with Seneca, politics comes into relief by the types of questions we ask, and the stance we assume. I have sought to show how our own inquiry into ancient politics necessarily occurs in a conceptual context that reveals as much as it conceals. The legacy of ancient politics, and the feature of this volume, is to encounter these other stances so that our own thoughts do not simply become reflexes costumed as political argument, but critical and self-conscious reflections on the possibilities of political life.

FURTHER READING

Those interested in further exploring some of the contributions and critiques of new conceptual approaches to studying ancient politics should consult Felson-Rubin 1983; Benjamin 1988; Rabinowitz and Richlin 1993; de Jong and Sullivan 1994; Meier 1994b; McManus 1997; Peradotto 1997; Morley 1999; Fowler 2000; S. Harrison 2001; Bracht Branham 2002; Wiseman 2002; Hammer 2004, 2006.

For further contributions to constitutional understandings of Greek and Roman society, see Bleicken 1990, 1994; Hansen 1989b, 1991; Gagarin 1986; R. Sinclair 1988; Kunkel and Wittman 1995; Sandberg 2000; and Rhodes 2003a: 34–44. See Berent 1996, 2000b and Hansen 2002b for a recent debate about constitutional and anthropological approaches to understanding the ancient *polis*.

Additional prosopographical studies include Badian 1958; A. Jones 1964; Davies 1971; Gruen 1991, 1996; C. Cox 1998; assessments by Carney 1973 and North 1990. Social power approaches appear in MacKendrick 1969; Scullard 1973; Saller 1982; MacMullen 1988; Vishnia 1996; Lendon 1997; and C. Kelly 2004.

Social historical approaches are developed in Brunt 1971; Stein-Hölkeskamp 1989; Raaflaub 1986a, 1986b, 1993a, 1993b, 1997a, 1997b; Ober 1993; essays in Jehne 1995; I. Morris 1996; Hanson 1996; Kienast 1999; Balot 2001a; Hölkeskamp 2004. On tyrants and reformers, see Kolb 1977; Snodgrass 1980; Stahl 1987; Stein-Hölkeskamp 1989; Shapiro 1989; Manville 1990; Eder 1992; McGlew 1993; Raaflaub 1997a, 2003b; and G. Anderson 2003.

Further Weberian inspired debates about the ancient city and ancient economy can be found in Finley 1973, 1982b, 1985b; Lowry 1979; Garnsey, Hopkins, and Whittaker 1983; Breuer 1985; Deininger 1989; Snodgrass 1990; Molho, Raaflaub, and Emlen 1991; Love 1991; E. Cohen 1992; Burke 1992; J. Martin 1994; Nippel 1994; Salmon 1999; and Berent 2000b.

On Marx and the ancients, see Lekas 1988 and McCarthy 2003. Marxian-inspired interpretations of literary texts have been made by Konstan 1983, 1995; Rose 1992, 1997, 1999; Tandy 1997; Thalmann 1998; Habinek 1998; Haynes 2003.

Applications of Foucault's ideas can be found in Halperin, Winkler, and Zeitlin 1990; Winkler 1990; Halperin 1990, 1995; Konstan 1994; Hallett and Skinner 1997; Larmour, Miller, and Platter 1998; Nussbaum and Sihvola 2002; Rabinowitz, Sorkin, and Auanger 2002. Critiques are made by Thornton 1991; Thacker 1993; O'Leary 2002; Detel 2005; and Porter 2005.

Additional contributions employing performance approaches include Zanker 1988; Ober 1989; Sourvinou-Inwood 1990; Nicolet 1990; Euben 1990; Kurke 1991; Dougherty 1993; Edwards 1993; Bartsch 1994; Morris 1994; D. Cohen 1995; von Reden 1995; essays in Slater 1996; K. Galinsky 1996; Stehle 1997; J. Davidson 1997; Habinek 1998; essays in Dougherty and Kurke 1998; Malkin 1998; Yakobson 1999; Goldhill and Osborne 1999; I. Morris 2000; essays in Köhne, Ewigleben, and Jackson 2000; Wray 2001; G. Rowe 2002; Hammer 2002; Slater 2002; Champion 2004a; Calame 2005; Williamson 2005; and Farenga 2006. There has been an explosion of work on propaganda and forms of representation that incorporate a variety of different approaches. See Eck 1984 and essays in G. Weber and Zimmermann 2003 and De Blois et al. 2003.

On the use of ancient politics to explore contemporary democracy, see Euben 1997, 2003; Schofield 1995; Hansen 1996; Ober 1993, 1998; Wallach 2001; Wolin 2004; Samons 2004; Fontana, Nederman, and Remer 2004; Kraut and Skultety 2005; and Frank 2005.

NOTE

My thanks to Amy Miller for her invaluable research assistance on this project and to Kerry Whiteside and Shawn O'Bryhim for reading and commenting on an earlier draft.

CHAPTER 3

Early Greek Political Thought in Its Mediterranean Context

Kurt A. Raaflaub

In the "orientalizing" period, archaic Greek culture was shaped in many ways by a wide range of outside influences.[1] In discussing the emergence of Greek political thought, however, with few exceptions (e.g. Vernant 1982), scholars have failed to look beyond the Greek world. Yet, why should this part of Greek culture alone have remained untouched by foreign ideas – especially when, as Walter Burkert (1992, 2004), Martin West (1971, 1997), and others have amply demonstrated, Greek intellectual achievements, from epic poetry to the beginnings of philosophy and science, integrated multiple impulses from the ancient Near East?[2] How, then, do we identify such impulses? Where exactly did they come from, how did they reach the Greeks, and what was their impact?

Such questions pose formidable challenges. Ultimately they can be answered only through intensive and focused collaboration among specialists in many fields. I myself have tried to stimulate discussion across disciplinary boundaries (Raaflaub and Müller-Luckner 1993) and conducted a series of case studies (Raaflaub 2004a, 2004c, 2008, forthcoming a). The present chapter summarizes some of the results reached so far and presents two additional case studies that are particularly important in the context of early Greek political thought. The result, though preliminary, will be that in the sphere of lawgiving and legal thought outside influences seem to have been substantial but were adapted profoundly to fit the specific needs of Greek communities. In the sphere of political values, such influences are unlikely or nonexistent. The explanation, sketched in the concluding section of this chapter, is that early Greek political thought was too closely tied to the structures and identities of the emerging Greek polis societies to permit the integration of more than partial impulses.

A Companion to Greek and Roman Political Thought, First Edition. Edited by Ryan K. Balot.
© 2013 Blackwell Publishing Ltd. Published 2013 by Blackwell Publishing Ltd.

"Influence": Thoughts on Methodology

Ultimately, it is not very useful, as was done in the recent "culture war" fought between Martin Bernal (1987–2006, 2001) and his opponents (e.g., Lefkowitz 1996; Lefkowitz and Rogers 1996; see also Marchand and Grafton 1997; Berlinerblau 1999), to focus on the question of whether Greek culture was independent or derivative: it was both. The issues that are vital here concern the process of culture transfer and exchange in the ancient world (Humphreys 1993). An influential trend in recent scholarship (represented especially by Burkert and West, mentioned above) not only tries to explain many Greek cultural achievements through influences from the ancient Near East but, to say it pointedly, imagines dissemination as a one-way road and integration as a construction project that uses foreign bricks to enhance the structures of the receiving culture. Yet we are dealing here with complex processes that cannot be grasped sufficiently through simplistic concepts such as "influence" or "import."

What looks on the surface like "foreign influence" can be explained in several ways (Raaflaub forthcoming a, with detailed references). Two of these seem relatively easy: direct borrowing (exemplified by the griffons, sirens, and sphinxes populating archaic Greek sites; e.g. Kreutz 2004) or indirect borrowing through a cultural *koinē*, that is, a pool of ideas and knowledge that emerged from intense interaction among various cultures in the eastern Mediterranean. Seybold and Ungern-Sternberg (1993 and in Burckhardt, Seybold, and Ungern-Sternberg 2007) use this model to explain analogies in the thoughts of Hesiod and the prophet Amos or in the reforms of Solon and King Josiah of Judah (see also Yamauchi 1980). Typological analogies can also result from independent parallel developments in the context of common social or cultural phenomena. An example is debt bondage, widespread in West Asia, Greece, and Rome (Finley 1982b: 150–66), and, like other statuses "between free and slave" (Finley 1982b: 116–49; O. Patterson 1991: 9–44; Weiler 2004), typical of many early societies. Social conflicts resulting from its abuse, the enactment of pertinent reforms, and the justification of such measures by the need to protect the weak from the oppression of the strong – these were logical consequences, documented in many places, that can have occurred independently in various societies (*DNP* 11: 257–63 with bibliog.; Yaron 1993; Irani and Silver 1995). Furthermore, as we shall see, superficial analogies can prompt false assumptions of external influence when tradition has falsified the objects of comparison, that is, when in the extant sources the description of both the supposed external model and the Greek "import" are shaped by the same Greek conceptions. In such cases, the model appears as such only because Greek thought has created or interpreted it to fit the assumption. Many of the Greek cultural imports from Egypt postulated by Herodotus (Lloyd 1975–88) and Diodorus (Burton 1972) fall into this category, even if scholars often accept them uncritically.

Furthermore, in assessing "foreign influences," we need to consider the issues of interaction and integration. By interaction I mean that impulse and counterimpulse, import and export are interdependent even if they are not always balanced. It is thus important to ask how the Greeks "paid" for their cultural imports, both concretely and metaphorically, in the spheres of material culture and ideas, and who were the carriers of such interaction.[3] Traders and itinerant specialists (*dēmiourgoi*) were suitable intermediaries for certain types of cultural goods (Burkert 1992). When it came to social or political issues, I suggest, free farmers or elite leaders in emerging poleis might not have listened to socially low-ranking outsiders, while they may have taken seriously what fellow nobles had to tell who returned from long journeys or foreign service, covered with glory and wealth (Raaflaub 2004a).[4] The other aspect, integration, has largely been neglected in recent research (exceptions include S. Morris 1992: 95; Hoffman 1997: 2 n5). Here too we need to differentiate: the more complex the foreign "object," the more complex the process of integrating it into the receiving culture. It is especially likely that customs or institutions that affected the community as a whole would have been adapted and transformed thoroughly to fit the new conditions.

Assyriologists and Egyptologists, few in number and confronted with the daunting task of publishing and interpreting enormous quantities of primary sources, have been slow in developing an active interdisciplinary discourse and rarely taken the time to tackle broad issues of the type classicists with their much more limited and mostly well-published source base have long taken for granted. Specifically, partial exceptions notwithstanding,[5] comprehensive discussions of Mesopotamian or Egyptian political thought simply do not exist.

The only effective way to tackle all these challenges is intensified and persistent collaboration across disciplinary boundaries. In this chapter, I use two opposed approaches. One focuses on cases of probable foreign impulses and examines the impact and transformation of such impulses in the process of their integration into Greek culture. As an example, I will discuss the monumental inscription of laws and legal texts. The other approach focuses on those themes that were important in early Greek political thought, and looks for analogies in Near Eastern cultures, expecting that a comparison will help answer the question of foreign influence. As examples, I will briefly consider the concepts of good order and freedom.

Distorted Greek Views of Cultural Imports: Importing Egyptian Laws

Sadly, in dealing with the issue of cultural exchange, the Greeks were rather naive. They believed in the principle that each cultural item was invented only once and thus had only one identifiable "first discoverer" (*prōtos heuretēs*). They admired ancient cultures, especially that of Egypt, found in them many phenomena that looked similar to their own, and essentially assumed that their ancestors had discovered these on their travels and brought them back home (Lloyd 1975–88: 1.56, cf. 2.220–1; Zhmud 1996: 65–9). Even more sadly, modern scholars, both outsiders and insiders, have been equally naive in accepting these views. In order to illustrate how cautious one needs to be in this respect, I discuss here one example in some detail. It concerns early Greek lawgiving and is thus directly relevant for one of this chapter's main topics.

According to Herodotus, Solon went abroad for ten years to prevent any change of his laws (1.29–30). In Egypt he learned of a useful regulation enacted by the pharaoh Amasis:

> Amasis established an admirable law, which Solon borrowed and introduced at Athens where it is still preserved because it is excellent; this was that every man once a year should declare before the Nomarch, or provincial governor, the source of his livelihood; failure to do this, or inability to prove that the source was an honest one, was punishable by death. (2.177.2; trans. de Sélincourt and Marincola 1996, modified)

Diodorus claims that Solon's laws prohibiting lending on a person's security and abolishing debt bondage were inspired by laws of the pharaoh Bocchoris/Bakenranef (1.79.3–5). I omit here the thorny problem of the historicity of Solon's travels and focus on that of his borrowing of Egyptian laws.[6]

Diodorus prompts suspicion by grouping Solon together with mythical figures like Orpheus and Daedalus. The "testimony" of Egyptian priests he cites leads to the Serapeum in Memphis, an early Ptolemaic foundation, and suggests a Hellenistic context (Diod. Sic. 1.96.1–3; cf. Burton 1972 *ad loc*). The rationale he gives for Bocchoris' laws on debt unmistakably reflects Greek thought and polis culture. No independent evidence exists for such laws, particularly not in Egypt: apparently, debt bondage played a negligible role in prehellenistic pharaonic legislation (*LdÄ* 1: 993 s.v. "Darlehn"; cf. Burton 1972: 232). Worse, Bocchoris himself is a shadowy figure. He ruled only briefly during the turbulent Third Intermediate Period (around 715 BCE), hardly prevailed over local dynasts, and left minimal traces in Egyptian sources. His elevation to a major legislator clearly is a product of Greek invention (*LdÄ* 1: 846; Burton 1972: 193–4; Kitchen 1995: 141–2, 376–7). Hecataeus of Abdera, probably Diodorus' main source, was a historicizing philosopher under Ptolemy I and wrote books about the Egyptians and Hyperboreans(!). Felix Jacoby characterizes these as "ethnographic utopias" that combined historical and ethnographic material, travel reports, philosophy, and pure invention in discussing conceptions of ideal states and other philosophical ideas supposedly realized in "historical" or mythological societies (Burton 1972: 1–34; Spoerri 1988: 279–82, with ref. to Jacoby). Xenophon's *Cyropaedia* is an early example of this genre (Tatum 1989). Undoubtedly, therefore, Hecataeus generously imported Greek ideas into Egyptian contexts. This remains true even if recent scholarship assesses his work in a more differentiated way, allowing for the possibility that he "recognized the convergence" of Greek and Egyptian ideas and that in his utopias "Egyptian and Greek culture ... could interpenetrate and interpret the other in meaningful ways" (Dillery 1998: 260, 275). Hence here the object of comparison with Greek phenomena is massively distorted; Diodorus is useless as a source for Solon's legal borrowings from Egypt.

Nor is it likely that Solon imported from Egypt the law on income declaration mentioned by Herodotus. On both sides, these kinds of regulations were embedded in specific social contexts that gave them legitimacy and guaranteed their effectiveness. Since these social contexts differed greatly, a simple transfer of relevant laws from one to the other is a priori unlikely. Indeed, a law concerning annual income declaration is well attested and makes perfect sense in the Egyptian tax system: the state depended on this income, honesty in such declarations was essential, and violations were considered serious offenses (Lloyd 1975–88: 1.56 with bibliog. in n227). In Athens, two different laws have been considered (Ruschenbusch 1966: 99–100, frr. 78a–c with comm.). The census classes (*telē*) of Solon's timocracy, however, were connected with taxes only in the fourth century What counted In Solon's time was primarily the citizens' military capacity, based on economic capacity and social status; if agrarian income was already defined in exact quantities – an issue much debated recently – the principle was self-declaration enforced by peer pressure (de Ste Croix 2004: 5–72; Raaflaub 2006: 404–23; van Wees 2006). The *nomos argias* (prohibition of idleness, also attributed to Peisistratus) possibly served two purposes: to safeguard social harmony by protecting the weak or to prevent neglect of one's farm – an understandable concern in a community with insufficient agrarian resources (Todd 1993: 112, 245; Schmitz 2004: 190–202). Overall, then, despite superficial similarities, these laws have very little in common with their Egyptian model suggested by Herodotus. The conclusion seems inevitable: Solon's legal imports from Egypt are a phantom of later Greek imagination.

Greek and Near Eastern Laws, "Law Codes," and Monumental Inscriptions with Legal Texts

I now turn to my first case study. In all Near Eastern societies jurisdiction and the maintenance of law and order were a central function of those who ruled. Ideologies of power emphasized the rulers' responsibility, based on divine sanction, for justice and the protection of the weak from oppression by the strong (e.g. Irani and Silver 1995).[7] In archaic Greece too, justice and good order were primary communal values, leaders and officials served as judges, and concepts of social justice protected the weak from the transgressions by the powerful. Correspondences or similarities have caused some scholars to assume Near Eastern influences in this area as well (Mühl 1933). But next to undeniable analogies we find basic differences, and these are no less important to understand the issues involved.

Legislation, jurisdiction, and conflict resolution require experience, authority, and intellectual capacity. In Greece all these acts took place in public, in the agora; they concerned the communal well-being and were thus political acts, testimonies for political thought. The same is true for Near Eastern states. For example, the Mesopotamian law codes are important sources for the prevailing legal culture. (Although these are not, strictly speaking, "law codes" that represent a "codification of law," the convenient term is still commonly used: *RdA* III.4: 256; Bottéro 1992: 161; Hölkeskamp 1999: 11–21.) The over-lifesize stela of Hammurabi, now in the Louvre, is the best-preserved example; copies stood in the main temples of major cities in Hammurabi's empire, and comparable law codes are attested from other periods (Roth 1995; see generally Westbrook 2003). Although most of the extant evidence comes from copies on clay tablets, it was apparently customary in Mesopotamia to engrave legal texts on monuments and thus to make them public. (Epigraphic remains so far confirm this only for law codes, not for individual laws or small groups of laws: see below.) This habit prevailed in Greece, too, beginning in the seventh century, first with individual laws, later with groups or even large collections of laws, such as those of Solon in Athens and those in Gortyn; the Roman *Twelve Tables* are closely comparable.[8]

To fix laws in writing and to publish them by inscription on stone or bronze was in Greece an unprecedented and, given the still very limited use of writing and restricted literacy (W. Harris 1989; Whitley 1998), far from obvious innovation. Its social, political, and institutional conditions have been illuminated by recent research (Gagarin 1986, 2008; Hölkeskamp 1994; Gehrke 2000). The idea underlying this innovation is often attributed to an impulse coming from the Near East and most likely reaching the Greeks through Phoenician intermediaries, be it in the Levant, on Crete, or in the western Mediterranean, that is, Sicily or southern Italy (e.g., Camassa 1994: 106; Gehrke 2000: 144). Assuming, even if we lack supporting Phoenician evidence, that this was the case, what can we learn from a comparison?

In Mesopotamia the epigraphic publication of law codes was initiated by the king. In the prolog, Hammurabi boasts of his conquests and the establishment of laws and justice:

> When the august god Anu ... and the god Enlil ... allotted supreme power over all peoples to the god Marduk, ... at that time, the gods Anu and Enlil, for the enhancement of the well-being of the people, named me by my name: Hammurabi, the pious prince, who venerates the gods, to make justice prevail in the land, to abolish the wicked and the evil, to prevent the strong from oppressing the weak ... (*CH* i.1–49 sel., trans. Roth 1995: 76)

There follow some 280 clauses, formulated in conditional sentences: "If a man accuses another man and charges him with homicide but cannot bring proof against him, his accuser shall be killed" (no. 1, *CH* v.26–32, trans. Roth 1995: 81). The epilogue explains the monument's function:

> These are the just decisions which Hammurabi, the able king, has established and thereby has directed the land along the course of truth and the correct way of life ... In order that the mighty not wrong the weak, to provide just ways for the waif and the widow, I have inscribed my precious pronouncements upon my stela and set it up before the statue of me, the king of justice, ... in order to render the judgments of the land, to give the verdicts of the land, and to provide just ways for the wronged ... Let any wronged man who has a lawsuit come before the statue of me, the king of justice, and let him have my inscribed stela read aloud to him, thus may he hear my precious pronouncements and let my stela reveal the lawsuit for him; may he examine his case, may he calm his (troubled) heart, (and may he praise me) ... (*CH* xlvii.1–8, 59–78; xlviii.3–19, trans. Roth 1995: 133–4).

The establishment of a firm legal order is thus part of Hammurabi's good rule. The stela is part of a monument, a memorial stone that, together with his statue, eternalizes his fame as "king of justice." The examples of crime and retribution inscribed on the stela prove that in Hammurabi's empire offenses are punished and victims receive justice. The subject seeking justice will have the words on the stela read to him and be encouraged. Overall, then, the stela's main purpose is the self-presentation of the king as an ideal and just ruler.

What about the 280 clauses? Their interpretation has been much debated. Initially they were considered normative laws, like those of the Hittites, in the Hebrew Bible, in Gortyn, and in the *Twelve Tables*, formulated equally in conditional sentences. But important arguments speak against this interpretation. Most of all, Hammurabi himself calls them "pronouncements," "verdicts," and "judgments." Hence this is a collection of legal decisions; although they could serve as precedents and thus have normative impact, they are not laws.[9]

Moreover, apparently Mesopotamian legal thought sticks to individual cases and past experience, reluctant to commit itself to normative generalizations. Hammurabi's collection is based not on abstractly formulated categories but on specific cases that are varied by subdivision. In content, they mostly refer to royal rule and administration. In form and method, they resemble other collections, such as those of omens or medical diagnoses. All this is typical of the working of Mesopotamian schools which were more than scribal training centers: they were the universities of the ancient Near East where literature and sciences were cultivated on a high level of achievement (Landsberger 1939; Bottéro 1992; Westbrook 1989; *DNP* 10: 813–14 with more bibliog.).

Hence, according to the most plausible interpretation, the clauses in Hammurabi's code, whatever their origin (in earlier codes, in royal decrees, in contemporaneous lawsuits, and in the large pool of unwritten customary law), were reformulated and generalized, homogenized, and systematized in the scribal schools. Their purpose is descriptive, not prescriptive, that is, they describe applications of justice but do not set law. They are primarily a literary and scientific product, not a collection of laws (see also Kienast 1994; Renger 1994). Illustrating the king's accomplishments in the sphere of justice, they stand beside his feats in war and building and serve to eternalize his fame.

In addition, despite the expectation expressed in the text, major obstacles prevented general access: reading ability was extremely limited, the text uses an antiquated and solemn style, and its arrangement on the stela lacks subdivisions (Driver and Miles 1955: 286; Charpin 2005: 100–1). The stela and inscription as such thus were primary, the content secondary; their purpose was emphasized already by the crowning pictorial relief (showing the king in front of the seated Sungod Shamash). The closing protective clauses and curses, too, therefore concerned more the monument than its content. The "monumental" nature of these texts perhaps explains as well why apparently only large-scale law codes but not individual laws were inscribed on stone (see below).

In archaic Greece, too, inscribed laws, as we saw, were not generally accessible. As James Whitley (1998: 313–17) observes, however, generalizations are dangerous. In some areas, for instance Attica, from the seventh century writing was used increasingly in a variety of ways and by a variety of persons (including craftsmen). Draco's and Solon's laws, however they were initially inscribed, were displayed publicly

(Stroud 1979) and thus could be read. The question is whether the uses of writing people were normally engaged in (mostly brief names or commemorating phrases) prepared them to read long and sometimes complex legal regulations. On the other hand, especially on Crete, "epigraphic evidence for the widespread production of written law and for its gradual codification sits uneasily with other evidence indicating an otherwise very restricted use of alphabetic literacy" (Whitley 1998: 313). For example, the code of Gortyn presented itself in a beautiful, seamlessly continuing wall of letters (illustrated in Willetts 1967), while the famous "Spensithios decree," a contract between a town and an official, was inscribed on both sides of a bronze abdominal guard (Whitley 1998: 321). Both inscriptions can be read by a schooled eye but understanding was surely limited to a small group of well-educated persons: specialists and aristocrats or, perhaps more precisely, specialists among the aristocrats. At least Spensithios, one of the few among these that we can identify, the "remembrancer" (*mnāmōn*) and "scribe" (*poinikastas*, lit. "specialist in Phoenician letters") of his community, was part of the local ruling aristocracy (van Effenterre and Ruzé 1994–5: 1, no. 22; Whitley 1998: 321). Moreover, Spensithios' office was to be hereditary, and he was to have a monopoly in public writing. Whitley concludes that Crete "was a region where 'scribal literacy' prevailed: that is, where literacy is virtually confined to a small specialist group" (1998: 322).

Why, then, were legal inscriptions set up? Presumably, their mere presence, enhanced by religious connotations, made an important statement (R. Thomas 1996). What Whitley concludes about the code of Gortyn perhaps applies more broadly: it "should be seen first and foremost as a monument, and not a text. It was there to represent the majesty of the law to a population that was largely illiterate. It was designed to present the particular regulations and practices of a small city state as eternal and immutable – permanent and beyond criticism" (1998: 322–3).

The monumental function of such inscribed legal texts, as we saw above, corresponds to Near Eastern features. So does the custom of setting such inscriptions up in sanctuaries and thus placing them under divine protection. In both areas literacy, beyond a minimal level, was limited to educated circles or even to scribes. Other features remind us of this connection, for example, the habit to begin public inscriptions with an invocation of the god or gods (Pounder 1984). Legal texts are usually formulated in conditional sentences (if … then …). Occasionally it is possible to explain difficult clauses through analogies in content (Westbrook 1988: 103–18, concerning the *Twelve Tables*). According to Raymond Westbrook, such analogies in content are, in fact, much more numerous than scholars have noted so far (written communication). The Greek formulary for international treaties too shows correspondences with Near Eastern models (Karavites 1992; Rollinger 2004b).

In the sphere we are examining here, external influences are therefore beyond doubt. This raises important questions. Not least: how far or deep did such influences reach? Westbrook goes even farther: in his view, the law codes from Mesopotamia through Israel to Greece and Rome have so many common characteristics, both in form and content, that they must belong to a single genre. They are connected not merely by copying or emulation but by a "much deeper underlying intellectual tradition." The Greek law codes, just as the *Twelve Tables*, stand on the very edge of the Near Eastern tradition and on the cusp of an intellectual paradigm shift that was to transform the concept and function of a law code. The predominantly casuistic Bronze Age codes of Mesopotamia belonged to the realm of scientific inquiry, while legislation was a separate genre, in the form of predominantly apodictic decrees and edicts. The Iron Age codes of the Mediterranean, Hebrew, Roman, and Greek, begin to combine the two, until the codes themselves become a legislative instrument. (Westbrook forthcoming)

Were one unaware of their provenance, then one would have no hesitation in assigning the Twelve Tables, with their casuistic style and their lack of any abstract categories or definitions, to the same literary genre as the ancient Near Eastern law codes ... [Given that Rome lay on the periphery of Mesopotamian civilization and close contacts with Phoenicians and Carthaginians are well attested,] we submit that the Twelve Tables were a product of that same Mesopotamian scientific tradition ... The Twelve Tables were initially a scientific treatise on law, that is to say, it was descriptive, not prescriptive. It was not legislation in the classical sense, and certainly not a reform measure called into being by particular historical events. (Westbrook 1988: 101)

Only from hindsight, under the influence of Greek philosophical concepts and separated by a wide gulf in time and intellectual development from archaic conditions, the Roman jurists understood the *Twelve Tables* differently, as a collection of prescriptive law that evolved gradually into the law that was valid in their own time (Westbrook 1988: 119). Westbrook's reinterpretation of the early Greek and Roman law codes presents a formidable challenge.[10] Presented, as it is, by one of the few experts fluent in Near Eastern and Greco-Roman law, it must be taken seriously. Can it be correct?

Let us look at the characteristics of early Greek legislation. First, lawgivers were supposedly active in various poleis, but most of them are shadowy, mythical rather than historical, cult or founder figures (such as Lycurgus of Sparta or Diocles of Syracuse), who served as magnets for a wide range of constitutive acts (Sealey 1994: 25–30; Hölkeskamp 1999). Authentic sources for comprehensive legislation are rare. Individual laws or small, thematically focused clusters of laws seem to have prevailed; these dominate in the epigraphical record as well (Koerner 1993; van Effenterre and Ruzé 1994–5). By contrast, it seems, epigraphical evidence for the inscription of individual or small clusters of laws is lacking in Mesopotamia; stelai were reserved for the large codes discussed above (Westbrook 2003 passim; Veenhof 1995).

Second, most of these laws were procedural, in many cases intended to limit the power of officeholders and thus level the competition among elite families (Gagarin 1986). Even when this is not the case, such laws usually seem to have been prescriptive and motivated by concrete crises or challenges. Their purpose was to resolve problems that threatened to destabilize the community. Draco's homicide law is a case in point (ML 86; trans. Fornara 1983: 18–20; Gagarin 1981): it was clearly designed to limit revenge killings (vendettas), especially but not only among elite families, because these could have far-reaching repercussions endangering the entire polis. It seems natural to assume that it was motivated, like so many other archaic Greek laws, by a specific experience or emergency, whether or not we feel justified in identifying this emergency with the crisis caused by Cylon's coup a few years earlier (Andrewes 1982: 368–70; Humphreys 1991; *contra*: Westbrook forthcoming). However they were formulated, these laws were unquestionably normative, not descriptions of cases or judgments. Nor were they always short, apodictic regulations. The earliest extant polis-law, from Dreros on Crete, prescribing an interval of ten years for repeating the important office of *kosmos,* offers a good example (ML 2; van Effenterre and Ruzé 1994–5: 1, no. 81; trans. Fornara 1983: 14).

   Third, the authority behind such laws was not a king, not an aristocratic council of elders, but the community, the assembly of citizens, the polis (see also Forsdyke, this volume, chapter 15). *Had' ewade poli,* "this was decided by the polis," says the law of Dreros. Elsewhere, demos or assembly appear as the acting and deciding subject (Hölkeskamp 1994; see also Raaflaub and Wallace 2007). This is true even when, as in Solon's case, a lawgiver writes the laws, for he is installed and endowed with extraordinary powers by the people, and his laws are accepted and made permanent through oaths and protective clauses by the people. The laws are embedded in the community, and they are often set up or engraved in the communal sanctuary, under the protection of the tutelary deity (Hölkeskamp 1994). This too gives them permanence.

   Fourth, already at the time of their earliest preserved laws, the Greeks used a differentiated terminology (Gehrke 2000: 145–6) and conception of law (Hirzel 1907; Latte 1946) that varied from *rhētra* (the pronouncement) and *thesmos* (what is set, *Gesetz, Satzung*) to *graphos* ("the writ") and from orally transmitted customary and divinely inspired law (*themis:* de Vos 1956) to written law (*nomos:* Ostwald 1969); they thought about justice (Gagarin 1974; Havelock 1978) and the divinely inspired function and responsibility of judges. In a predominantly oral society, the functions of *mnāmōn* (remembrancer) or *histōr* ("knower," mentioned in an arbitration scene in *Il.* 18.501), distinguished from that of the *poinikastas* (scribe, mentioned above), were greatly important. Moreover, despite dependence on the gods (Zeus and Dike) as protectors of justice, because human society does not yet have sufficiently powerful agents to assume this function, authors from Homer to Solon leave no doubt that the responsibility for realizing justice and for the consequences of its violation rests entirely among the humans, whether high or low (*Od.* 1.32–46; Hes. *Op.* passim; Solon fr. 4.1–4 West; Raaflaub 2005: 255–63; see also Osborne, this volume, chapter 8). From this perspective, too, law and justice are thoroughly embedded in the community. Those who are most vocal in emphasizing the crucial importance of this issue are not least the powerless: the Homeric bard, a *dēmiourgos,* itinerant specialist and outsider (e.g., *Od.* 17.383–5; Finley 1977: 36–7, 56), and his Hesiodic successor who presents himself as a simple farmer (Lamberton 1988: 1–11; see Nagy 1990a: 36–82 for a different view).

   Fifth, most of this is valid as well for the Greek law collections in Athens and Gortyn – despite analogies in form and content with Near Eastern law codes mentioned above. Greek law distinguished early between areas covered by statutory law and those left open, the gaps, in which the judge's common sense and concern for justice had to decide. The oath sworn by the Athenian judges (heliasts) in the mass courts of the fourth century is but a late echo of long-established principles: "I will cast my vote in consonance with the laws and with the decrees passed by the Assembly and by the Council, but, if there is no law, in consonance with my sense of what is most just, without favour or enmity" (as quoted by Hansen 1999: 182; see Sealey 1994: 51–5). Casuistic variation occurs in these collections but, I suggest, not as an academic exercise and for its own sake but where it is socially relevant, for example, concerning persons with varying social status. All problems covered are important to prevent or resolve conflicts in the community. In the law collections, too, the law is statute and thus normative.

Differences between these characteristics of inscribed Greek law and those of inscribed Mesopotamian legal texts are thus strong and obvious. These differences stand in tension with the important correspondences we mentioned before. Overall, I think, the basic task of analyzing and comparing content, form, and function of laws and legal texts on both sides has so far been undertaken only partially. Important questions remain, and I pose these as a challenge to specialists in the comparative history of ancient law. For example, should we really explain the typical formulation of early Greek or Roman laws (be they individual or part of larger collections) in conditional sentences ("if ... then ...") as the result of foreign influence? Was it due to a cultural *koinē*, or is this one of the cases of independent parallel development, mentioned before? How else could laws have been formulated? How frequent, precise, and significant are correspondences in form and content between Near Eastern law codes and Greek or Roman laws, and can we define differences even more precisely? True, we know of individual specialized scribes and, at least on Crete, a scribal culture that, however, may have been limited to individual families (Whitley 1998: 322); we know, in large parts of the Greek world around the Aegean, of a highly developed culture of political thought and action, culminating in a group of widely respected "sages" and lawgivers (Meier 1990b: 29–52; R. Martin 1993; Wallace forthcoming). Still, so far we have no evidence in the Greek world for anything corresponding to Near Eastern scribal schools or for the type of academic and intellectual exercises underlying the Near Eastern codes, and in the archaic Roman world it seems difficult even to think of such developed intellectual traditions or political thought as were common in contemporaneous Greece. Furthermore, how, when, and where would traditions of the complexity and sophistication typical of Near Eastern legal thought have been transmitted? Who were the carriers? Is it sufficient that Phoenicians lived and traded in Crete and Carthaginians in Rome (e.g., Hoffman 1997; Stampolidis and Kotsonas 2006; Westbrook 1988: 97–101; R. Palmer 1997)? Should we think rather of the great sanctuaries that emerged in archaic Greece and were visited my non-Greeks as well? If so, what would the equivalent be in archaic Italy and how could direct Phoenician influence on early Roman legal texts be distinguished from indirect influence via southern Greek legal traditions? Finally, do we know enough about Phoenician and Carthaginian legal traditions to have confidence in the Phoenicians as transmitters of older Mesopotamian traditions? If not, what other routes of transmission might we consider?

Finally, what about the contribution of political thought to the development of early Greek law? Clearly, this contribution did not have to wait for the emergence of written law. Homer's and Hesiod's epics, probably written but composed at the end of a long tradition of oral poetry, reflect strong concern for the observation of justice as a crucial condition for communal well-being (see above). The same epics are our earliest witnesses for political thinking (Raaflaub 2000: 27–37). Solon presented his political ideas in elegies and iambics that were performed at aristocratic symposia and, perhaps, also in public (Raaflaub 1996c: 1038–42; Mülke 2002: 11–12). Popular wisdom in poetic form reinforced communal norms (Schmitz 2004: ch. 4), and even early laws apparently were "sung," that is, recited publicly (R. Thomas 1996: 14–16). Awareness of the importance of justice, the formulation in various forms and media of norms and laws, and political thought developed in a culture of "oral performance," in an interactive process, and in the context of the emerging polis. Politics, too, was based on performance (Hammer 2002); hence the importance of speech and persuasion among the leaders' qualities in Homer (e.g., *Il.* 2.139; 9.440–3). The sages and mediators who developed a "third position" above and between the poleis with their internal and external conflicts certainly also operated orally, before they wrote their laws on stone or wooden beams (Meier 1990b: 40–52, esp. 44 ff.; Wallace forthcoming).

All this suggests that in Greece there emerged early on a "political thrust" in a much broader intellectual movement that produced the masterworks of early Greek literature, thought, and art (Kirk 1988; Raaflaub 2009a). This political thrust was represented by poets, leaders, and sages but based on a broad foundation of popular support. It aimed at resolving fundamental problems of communal life and realizing a widespread ideal of good order (*eunomia*: see below). In Sparta and Athens, in periods of severe domestic crisis, first attempts at introducing constitutional regulations and/or broad legislation were placed under this ideal of *eunomia* (Raaflaub 2006: 392–403). The challenge now is to define more precisely the contribution of external impulses to the development of this political thrust. As far as external contributions to Greek law, its formulation, and its fixation in writing are concerned, the Greeks picked up from traditions that ultimately originated in early second millennium Babylonia if not third millennium Sumer not only the idea of inscribing legal texts on stone, but also an as yet undetermined but apparently substantial amount of details both in form and content (see above). Yet in the use and function of what they adopted and engraved they went their own ways, embedding it in their own social contexts and meeting the specific needs of their communities. In the end, Greek law, despite many correspondences, differs greatly from Near Eastern law. I suspect that a comparison of Greek and Near Eastern concepts of justice would yield a similar result.

Since Greek polis communities differed greatly from Near Eastern city-states (Raaflaub 2004c) and even more vastly from the monarchies that produced the law codes, we should hardly be surprised. This result confirms what I have been finding in other case studies as well: when it came to social and political thought, issues, and institutions, external influence on Greek developments was rather limited, and where the Greeks did incorporate foreign impulses, they transformed and adapted them thoroughly to fit their own conditions and needs. A selective examination of political values will offer further confirmation (see below). All this requires further investigation and explanation, and it does not mean that there were no political areas where the Greeks were eager learners. I suggest that this was especially the case where the Greeks had no previous experiences of their own (empire and imperial administration would offer one example: Raaflaub 2009b).

Near Eastern Origins of Greek Political Values?

The value concept of *eunomia*, mentioned above, introduces the last part of my present investigation. Here I will move in the other direction, from Greece back to the Near East. In the archaic period, Greek political thought focused on justice, order, the conditions that fostered communal well-being, and the qualities needed for successful leadership; by contrast, on aristocratic abuse of power and tyranny; more generally, on individual and collective responsibility for the common weal; finally on equality, dependence or servitude, and freedom. The question is whether such political ideas, values, and concepts might have had analogs in the older civilizations of West Asia and Egypt and, if this was the case, whether these might have influenced Greek developments. I focus here on two examples: good order and freedom.

In the archaic Greek world, *eunomia* describes the ideal of a well-ordered community (Ostwald 1969: 62–95; Meier 1990b: 160–2, and bibliog. in Raaflaub 2004b: 55 nn164–6). According to recent suggestions (Fadinger 1996; see also Bernal 1993; for critical discussion, see Barta 2006), Solon was inspired during his travels by the Egyptian concept of *ma'at* and realized it in Athens in his version of *eunomia*. That Solon imported laws from Egypt, we saw earlier, is highly implausible. Here an effort is made to derive from Egyptian models not only a law but a political concept that played a crucial role in archaic political thought. How plausible is this?

To be sure, Solon could have known, directly or indirectly, about Egyptian concepts of order. But does the extant evidence support this? *Ma'at* is an ancient, comprehensive, and very complex concept, that is imagined as divinely sanctioned from the beginning of creation, represented by a deity, and contrasted with *isfet*, its exact opposite and negation (Assmann 1990, 1993; Quirke 1994; Morschauser 1995). It is insufficiently defined by terms like truth, justice, or order.

> *Ma'at* defined the divine ordinances by which the universe was originally set into motion and properly maintained … In the immanent realm, *ma'at* fixed the parameters of Egyptian society itself, setting out the limits for the proper and discretionary exercise of power by those who ruled toward those over whom they had authority. *Ma'at* encompassed specific ethical requirements, characterized as both the official and personal responsibilities of the socially advantaged toward their inferiors, as well as the obligations of subjects toward the state – which was embodied by the figure of the king … While social roles and expectations may have varied according to position, the concept of *ma'at*, nevertheless, provided a moral standard, by which every member of society, king and commoner, could be evaluated and judged … [Moreover, *ma'at*] was *the* ultimate determinant of an individual's ability to achieve a meaningful existence beyond death. (Morschauser 1995: 101–2)

Ma'at described the place of the individual in society, of society in the pharaonic state, and of the state in the cosmic, divine order (Assmann 1990: 17–18).

By contrast, *eunomia*, derived from *eunomos* (having, observing good customs), was much more limited and modest. In the archaic period it was a communal concept; when it described individual behavior (as probably in *Od.* 17.487), such behavior was appraised in a communal context. Even if, for example, Hesiod may have believed in the divinity of Eunomia, making her, like Dike (Justice) and Eirene (Peace) one of the three Horai (goddesses of the seasons, of growth and fertility: *Theog.* 901–3; see Hanfmann 1951: 1. 94–103; *LIMC* 3: 700 s.v. "Eirene") and linking her genealogically to Zeus, such deities differed in nature from the major gods. Essentially, Eunomia appears in early Greek thought as a personified value, enhanced by being inserted into divine hierarchy. It is recognized as central for communal well-being already in Hesiod (above) and thus long before Solon, and in Sparta (Alcman 64 Campbell 1982; Tyrt. 1–4 West; Andrewes 1938) as well as Athens (Solon 4 West). Hence it was one of the earliest and most important Greek value terms with panhellenic significance. Solon's use and hymnic celebration of *eunomia* can be explained sufficiently in a Greek context and by his intertextual discussion with Hesiod (Raaflaub 2000: 40–1).[11]

Furthermore, "vertical solidarity" typical of *ma'at* (that is, the responsibility of the strong and powerful for the well-being of the weak and powerless: Assmann 1993) is less important in Solon's thought and reforms than "horizontal solidarity" in the community (that is, the citizens' responsibility for each other). The latter is realized, for example, in legislation that establishes security of and equality before the law, in the introduction of a special assembly (*hēliaia*) serving as a court of appeals and/or primary court in communally important cases, and in the right of every citizen who wanted (*ho boulomenos*) to take legal action on behalf of an injured third party, presumably in cases where this party was unable to act or was the community itself (Hansen 1999: 30). Finally, those aspects of *ma'at* that most easily lend themselves to a comparison with *eunomia* in fact lost their importance in Egyptian thought and religion at least 400 years before Solon's time (Assmann 1990: 259).

For all these reasons, direct Egyptian influence on Solon's concept of *eunomia* is unlikely. Even if it is possible to observe a number of analogies (Barta 2006) and even if Solon was sufficiently familiar with Egyptian concepts of order to justify the assumption of external influence on his thought and action, this impulse was not specific but vague and general; it showed a direction and did not provide detailed instructions; it was adapted thoroughly to the conditions in and needs of Solon's society (so too Fadinger 1996: 209–10) – and thus transformed so profoundly that it is virtually unrecognizable.

What about liberty? In a social context, liberty denoted free status in contrast to that of the slave and other dependents, and freedom from obligations or taxes. In this sense, liberty probably was recognized as a value wherever slavery and power structures imposing obligations and other forms of dependencies existed, even if its role and significance may have been rather modest (O. Patterson 1991). In this sense, too, liberty is well attested in the earliest written documents of Greek civilization, the Bronze Age Linear B tablets and archaic epics (Raaflaub 2004b: 19–45). At least in the Greek and Roman worlds, however, the observation and experience of such obligations and of slavery apparently was insufficient to cause awareness of liberty as a *political* value and the creation of a corresponding political terminology (Raaflaub 2003a: 175–83; 2004b: 42–4; *contra*: O. Patterson 1991, 2003). Rather, the emergence of political uses of liberty was prompted by incisive political changes: in Greece these included the oppression ("enslavement") of citizens by a tyrant (Forsdyke, this volume, chapter 15; mentioned explicitly for the first time in Solon's poems: 4.18;

9.3–4 West) and the threat of a community's loss of liberty through subjection by an outside power. It was this threat, which they succeeded in overcoming, against all odds, in the Persian Wars, that prompted the Greeks to forge a new word for the abstract notion of "freedom": *eleutheria*. Earlier, they had not needed a noun for this concept! (Raaflaub 2004b: ch. 3; see also Wallace, this volume, chapter 11; for Rome, see Wirszubski 1950; Raaflaub 1984)

It appears that this last step, toward a politicization of the concept of liberty, was not taken in ancient societies outside the Greco-Roman world, neither in China (Raaflaub 2004b: 284 n17) nor in the ancient Near East. In Egypt, as Siegfried Morenz states, "the concept of freedom does not exist" (1973: 314 n1); in the earlier German edition, he adds: "therefore we must resist searching for … political-social freedom" (1960: 144 n1). Indeed, as far as I can see, efforts to deduce such a concept from extant texts do not lead beyond individual freedom of action, decision, and will, individual initiative, freedom of movement, or freedom from obligations and taxes (Morenz 1973: ch. 4 and 137–8; *LdÄ* 2: 298–304). In Mesopotamia, too, freedom is used exclusively for exemption from obligations, taxes, or deliveries in kind, and for personal freedom which is realized by manumission or the flight of slaves (Szlechter 1952; *RdA* 3.2: 110–11; Snell 2001). No one will underestimate the human suffering caused by slavery or the significance of corresponding patterns of behavior and statements in extant documents, but these have nothing to do with political freedom. Finally, the Hebrew Bible

> knows of freedom almost exclusively only as a social state: The free stands in opposition to the slave. Thus the Hebrew terms for "free" and "freedom" …, which are not witnessed very frequently, often occur in discussions of slavery and manumission … Though the redemption of Israel from slavery in Egypt is cited in support for the manumission of Hebrew slaves in the seventh year …, the OT [Old Testament] does not develop a theology of freedom on the basis of the Exodus. Rather, Israel was ransomed in order to be God's servants …, and the language used to describe this event is primarily that of "redemption," not of "freedom." (*ABD* 2: 855)

Hence the *Septuagint* too uses *eleutheria* and related terms exclusively in connection with slavery. A political concept of freedom emerges, under Hellenistic influence, for the first time in *Maccabees* (D. Nestle 1972: 288; Ostwald 1995: 43).

Overall, then, in the realm of social freedom, Greece shares a range of concepts and ideas with the ancient Near East, although, as explained earlier, it is perhaps more plausible to think here of parallel developments rather than terminological or conceptual dependence. In the realm of political freedom, no path leads from the Near East to Greece: here the Greeks made their own discovery, with long-lasting consequences for western thought and ideology (O. Patterson 1991; Raaflaub 2004b; see also Wallace, this volume, chapter 11).

Conclusion

There is no doubt that the Greeks in the archaic age absorbed a wide range of cultural influences from the east and south of the Mediterranean. But scholars have been more interested in identifying possible models than in tracking their adaptation and transformation in Greek culture. All too often they accept simplistic Greek concepts of cultural borrowing and analyze such borrowings on a far too simple level, looking for similarities and ignoring the differences, thinking only of borrowing and not of interaction, and failing to consider the possibilities and limitations of cultural transfer. Moreover, both on the Near Eastern and Greek sides we need to differentiate more carefully between various periods and regions, and we need to think about the carriers and paths or places of cultural transmission. All these shortcomings are especially serious when we are dealing with social and political concepts, values, and institutions.

External impulses in the political realm could reach the Greeks even if, for example, Greek lawgivers never traveled themselves to Egypt or Mesopotamia – just as the members of the Roman commission (decemvirate) charged with writing laws in the mid-fifth century (resulting in the *Twelve Tables*) did not need to send an embassy to Athens to learn about existing Greek laws and codes (Liv. 3.31.8; cf. Crifò 1972: 124–7). There was no lack of contacts and opportunities for transmission, from West Asia and the Levant to Crete and the Aegean and to the western Mediterranean. For example, valuable information could be passed along in places where Greeks and Phoenicians met routinely or even lived together, or during informal visits among "guestfriends" (*xenoi*); it could be learned from knowledgeable priests or hosts abroad or in one of the panhellenic sanctuaries that were visited by foreigners as well (such as Apollo's oracle in Delphi, Zeus' sanctuary in Olympia, or the Heraion in Samos: Malkin 1987: 17–91; Shipley 1987: 54–65; Rosenberger 2003; Kreutz 2004); or it could be picked up during larger gatherings of elite Greeks at panhellenic festivals. Members of the Greek upper class at the time roamed the Mediterranean and spent time in Egypt or Mesopotamia (Raaflaub 2004a). Returning home, they might be able to share useful knowledge. Even vague and third-hand information could spark the thinking of lawgivers who, like Solon, were wrestling with the problem of how to overcome *stasis* and social-economic crisis.

Political values, it seems, developed in Greece independently: Greek concepts of order or freedom do not have analogs or antecedents in Near Eastern civilizations. The same is probably true for equality.[12] The concept of justice, of fundamental concern to every society, requires a closer look: a comparative study might reveal direct or indirect connections, similar to those resulting from the comparative analysis, conducted in this chapter, of inscribed laws and legal texts. Analogies in form, content, and function of such texts as well as the "epigraphic habit" itself suggest that the Greeks were substantially influenced by Near Eastern models, even if important questions concerning the range and significance of such influences as well as the carriers, ways, and places of transmission still need to be answered. Yet, despite such analogies, such texts also served in Greece very different purposes and were embedded in different social contexts, meeting the specific needs of societies that differed greatly from Near Eastern ones. The comparative study of inscribed legal texts in Mesopotamia and Greece (or Rome) thus illustrates what was said at the beginning of this chapter: we need to identify external models and sources that influenced Greek cultural development but it is equally important to pay attention to what the Greeks made of such models: how they adapted and transformed them to make them part of their own specifically Greek culture.

Important further questions loom. Given such differences in dealing with similar issues, what do we learn from them about social and political conditions, basic attitudes, and worldviews, about structures, hierarchies, relationships, openness and lack thereof in the societies involved? More specifically, if the conclusions reached above prove correct, why do we find in the sphere of Greek political thought relatively little foreign influence and relatively high Greek independence? To answer this question, we need to consider, however briefly, differences in structures and priorities in a sphere that concerns the core of Greek community and identity.

In the ancient Near East we find not only centralized and hierarchically structured states ruled by divinely sanctioned absolute kings but also various forms of tribal organizations. These fostered different values and relationships as well as forms of collective government and decision making (Fleming 2004). Yet, however important these may have been locally or even regionally, the great cultural achievements and the bulk of the extant written evidence were produced by the centralized palace and temple states. In the latter's worldview and value system, the individual's ability to fit in the right place in the hierarchy was a primary concern. What was required was obedience, not freedom or independence (Jacobsen 1946: 202–7). As a result, for example, in the Babylonian state of the early second millennium free citizens "were sometimes referred to as slaves of the king … In particular, royal courtiers were referred to in this way: 'the gentlemen, slaves of the king'… Even the term 'slave of the palace' … might sometimes refer to a free man who was merely in the service of the king" (Westbrook 2003: 1.380). The Greeks were confronted with this system in Persian forms of vassalage (*bandakā*) which required certain rituals of reverence and subordination (for example, "prostration") and which they interpreted, typically but incorrectly, as slavery *stricto sensu* (e.g., Hdt. 7.134–6; ML no. 12 = Fornara 1983: no. 35; Briant 2002: 324–6, 491; Raaflaub 2004b: 313 n189). Not that political thought was lacking, but such thought was practiced at the top, among those who ruled and their closest advisers, and it focused on preserving and expanding the power of the rulers (e.g., Machinist 1993; Röllig 1993; see also Larsen 1979). Care for the well-being of the subjects was not to be neglected but it was also, and perhaps largely, a means to the end of maintaining power and stability. Moreover, in a world dominated by divinely sanctioned kingship, in which priests and temples played a powerful role, political thought, too, must have been influenced strongly by religious concerns.

Conditions in archaic Greece were markedly different (Snodgrass 1980; R. Osborne 1996; J. Hall 2007). Small communities crystallized in the tenth to eighth centuries from rural villages and tribal structures. In the emerging poleis ("citizen states" rather than "city states": Hansen 1993), the citizens who owned land and were capable of equipping themselves with arms and armor were a decisive element, despite ongoing efforts of the elite to monopolize power and establish economic, social, and ideological boundaries. The citizen army and assembly appear as crucial elements of the community already in Homer's epics (Raaflaub 1997a). The Greek polis was thus founded in essential ways on citizen equality, which does not mean, of course, that all were equal or that these structures were already democratic (I. Morris 2000: ch. 4). Claims of elite and community often collided – and in the long term, the community won. A few decades after Homer the law of Dreros, mentioned above, states: "This was decided by the polis!" Prompted by this productive tension, Homer and Hesiod integrated in their heroic and didactic epics problems and dilemmas that were important to their panhellenic audiences, helping them to understand their own difficulties and cope with (Raaflaub 2000: 27–37). The personae of these poets, as presented in their poems, did not belong among the aristocracy; on the contrary, the Homeric bard is a *dēmiourgos*, an itinerant specialist and thus outsider (above), while Hesiod in *Works and Days* (passim) talks of himself as a farmer, grappling with economic challenges and elite injustice (above). Political thinking in Greece therefore happened not only at the top (as in the cases of Solon, Pittakos, and the other "Seven Sages" mentioned earlier) but also on lower levels of society, "from below." Moreover, early Greek political reflection was remarkably free of religious concerns: gods like Zeus and Dike, the goddess of Justice, were important as enforcers of justice, particularly in a time that lacked sufficiently powerful human agencies, but the cause of human suffering was sought early on in human actions, not divine caprice, and responsibility for avoiding such suffering was placed squarely on human shoulders (Raaflaub 2001: 87–93; 2005; see also Osborne, this volume, chapter 8).

These communal structures permitted the integration of many elements that were inspired by outside influences, even if only after thorough transformation, but not of entire and alien systems of values, norms, and institutions. In other words, the polis or lawgiving could be inspired and enriched by knowhow and specific ideas that came from the outside, but they could not, as a whole, be imported, and even the parts that were integrated needed to be adapted first. What exactly these parts were, however, still awaits further investigation.

A long time ago, Martin West claimed that Greek literature was essentially Near Eastern literature (1966: 31; cf. Haubold 2002). This seems to me vastly exaggerated and far too general. In the sphere of Greek political thought, I suspect, this would be true only to a very limited extent.

FURTHER READING

O. Murray 1993 and Osborne 1996 offer surveys of archaic Greek history, Kuhrt 1995, van de Mieroop 2004, and Snell 2005 of the ancient Near East. On Greek cultural imports from the ancient Near East, see West 1971, 1997; Burkert 1992, 2004; S. Morris 1992. Contributions in Irani and Morris 1995 discuss concepts of social justice fostered by various Mediterranean societies; those in Westbrook 2003 the history of ancient Near Eastern law. Driver and Miles 1952 and Roth 1995 offer translations of Mesopotamian legal texts, including those of Hammurabi; Westbrook 1989 and Bottéro 1992 discuss the latter, van de Mieroop 2005 the life and significance of Hammurabi himself. Greek legal texts are collected, with a French translation, in van Effenterre and Ruzé 1994–5; the law code of Gortyn in Willetts 1967 (with English trans.); Solon's laws in Ruschenbusch 1966 (without trans.); the Roman Twelve Tables in Crawford 1996 (with English trans.). Gagarin 1986, 2008, Hölkeskamp 1992a, 1992b, 1999, and Sealey 1994 are important for early Greek law; Watson 1975, Wieacker 1988, and Cornell 1995 for early Roman law. On early Greek political thought, see Meier 1990b; Raaflaub 2000, 2001, 2005; Hammer 2002; for political values Raaflaub 2004b.

NOTES

An earlier and, in parts, more detailed version of this chapter will be published in German (Raaflaub forthcoming b). I thank the editors for their generous permission. Some issues are also part of the argument in Raaflaub forthcoming a. This is an essay in comparative history. I am aware that I am trespassing into fields in which I am not properly trained. I ask the specialists for understanding, gentle assistance in correcting mistakes, and willingness to engage in a constructive dialogue. I am most grateful to Raymond Westbrook for patient answers to my questions and for promising further thought and publications on some of the issues I raise in this chapter. I also thank R. Ross Holloway, Saul Olyan, James Allen, and Ryan Balot for generous comments and useful suggestions.

1   See bibliographies in Raaflaub and Müller-Luckner 1993: xvii–xix, and in individual chapters of that volume; Burkert 2004.
2   I use "Near East" here broadly, to include Anatolia, the Levant, Mesopotamia, and Egypt.
3   We should think here, on the one hand, of silver, wool, and other raw materials, and on the other, of skills, for example, of mercenaries, shipwrights, architects, sculptors, etc.: see Raaflaub 2004a, and documentation in Persian sources, e.g., reliefs (Sancisi-Weerdenburg 2001: 326) and building inscriptions in Susa (Steve 1974: 146, 155–7). Some of the observations of Wiesehöfer 2004; Rollinger 2006 on early Achaemenid Persia are valid as well for earlier periods from the late eighth century. I omit here discussion of the possibility that many "imports" (especially in myth, religion, ideas, etc.) could have reached the Greeks in the Bronze Age – a period of well-documented intensive exchange between Greece and the Near East (Dickinson 1994: ch. 7) – and then "filtered down" through the Dark Ages into the Archaic Age.
4   Ross Holloway (written communication) emphasizes the importance in this process of common language, bilingual persons, mixed marriages, and cohabitation on fairly equal terms of Greeks and non-Greeks. By contrast, Raymond Westbrook (written communication) thinks that "ideas travel light, along with any kind of contact, whether conquest, trade, or diplomacy." He sees legal traditions as "amorphous, anonymous – an aspect of wisdom. It is therefore easily penetrable by foreign ideas."
5   Such as Hornung 1971; Helck 1986; Assmann 1990; Wilcke 1993; Starke 2005–6.
6   On the historicity of Solon's travels to Egypt (Plut. *Sol.* 26.1 with Solon fr. 28 West), see, e.g., Lloyd 1975–88: 1.57 n233; Szegedy-Maszak 1978; Rhodes 1981a: 169–70; Wallace 1983: 87–8. On Solon's laws, Arist. *Ath. Pol.* 6.1 with Rhodes 1981a: 125–8; Plut. *Sol.* 15.
7   I will focus here on Mesopotamia. For Egyptian concepts of law, see, e.g., Théodoridès 1967, 1971, and, generally, 1995; Allam 1987.
8   Solon: Ruschenbusch 1966; on the technical details, Stroud 1979 (with illustrations); on the social and political context, Wallace 2007. Gortyn: Willetts 1967; social context, Willetts 1955, 1965. Rome: Crawford 1996: 2.555–721; social context, Wieacker 1967, 1988; Cornell 1995: ch. 11. Individual Greek laws are collected in Koerner 1993; van Effenterre and Ruzé 1994–5. For interpretation, see Hölkeskamp 1999 (with ample bibliog.). See also, generally, important discussions in Farenga 2006 and now Gargarin 2008.
9   More recently, Westbrook 1989; Bottéro 1992; Greengus 1995; van de Mieroop 2005: ch. 8; Wells 2005; see further relevant chapters in Gehrke 1994; Lévy 2000.
10 It resumes, and elaborates upon, a perspective that has been much debated for centuries and even more so since the great Mesopotamian law codes were discovered; Volterra

1937: ch. 1 offers a survey, while himself insisting adamantly on the absolute autonomy of
early Roman law (ch. 2).

11 *Eunomia* was also from the beginning a concept that was linked to an aristocratic order. In
this sense it is still used in the first half of the fifth century by Pindar and Bacchylides.
Logically, it then became, in contrast to *isonomia* (political equality) with its affinity to
democracy, a catchword for oligarchy (Grossmann 1950: 30–89; Ehrenberg 1965 with
references). This development is reflected, in the late fifth and early fourth centuries, in a
rather sudden proliferation of identifiable representations on vases and in a cult in Athens,
together with Eukleia (Hampe 1955; Metzler 1980; Shapiro 1993: 79–85; see also *LIMC*
4.1: 62–5).

12 *DNP, LdÄ, RdA, ABD* have no entry on "equality." Concerning "order," it might be
useful to examine the Greek concept of *kosmos* as well, but what *RAC* 21: 616–17 or *DNP*
6: 769 say about it does not look promising; see also Diller 1956; Kerschensteiner 1962.

CHAPTER 4

Civic Ideology and Citizenship

P. J. Rhodes

Greek city-states (*poleis*, sing. *polis*) and states of other kinds were communities of citizens (*politai*, sing. *politēs*).[1] Except when a "tyrant" had usurped power and ruled (as some but not all tyrants did) not through the regular institutions but autocratically, these citizens were entitled and expected to play a part in the running of the state. At the beginning of book 3 of his *Politics* Aristotle asks, "What is the polis?" and he proceeds to say that "the polis is a body of citizens, so we must investigate who ought to be called a citizen and what a citizen is." After disposing of complications, some of which we shall return to, he concludes that "a citizen in the straightforward sense is defined by nothing else so much as participation in judging [in the law courts] and ruling" (Arist. *Pol.* 3.1274b–1275a). There is a degree of equality, though not total equality, among citizens, so, since not everybody can hold office simultaneously, a citizen must be capable both of ruling and of being ruled (Arist. *Pol.* 3.1277a–b; cf. 6.1317a–b, where this is said to be an aspect of freedom and characteristically democratic). In Euripides' *Supplices* it is said of the "democratic monarchy" of Athens under the legendary king Theseus that "the people rule through annual succession" (406–7), and Xenophon praised his hero, the Spartan king Agesilaus, as choosing not to be supreme in Asia but in accordance with the law to rule and be ruled at home (Xen. *Ages.* 2.16).

In the Bronze Age of the second millennium Greece seems to have been divided into a number of substantial kingdoms, but the Greece which emerged from the dark age of the late second and early first millennium was organized in a large number of small communities, either poleis, particularly toward the south and east, or looser regional units, sometimes called "tribes" (*ethnē*, sing. *ethnos*), comprising a number of local communities, particularly toward the north and west. When Greeks founded colonies around the Mediterranean and the Black Sea, from the eighth century onward, these commonly took the form of poleis with their own politai; often later

A Companion to Greek and Roman Political Thought, First Edition. Edited by Ryan K. Balot.
© 2013 Blackwell Publishing Ltd. Published 2013 by Blackwell Publishing Ltd.

contingents of settlers would be granted land and citizenship too (cf. Hdt. 4.159.1–4 on the enlargement of the colony at Cyrene in the third generation). Athens in the fifth century and again in the fourth established settlements of a new kind, for which cleruchy (*klērouchia*: "allotment-holding") came to be a technical term: here Athenians were given land abroad, sometimes in a new community which had to run its own affairs, sometimes land confiscated from the citizens of a city which continued to exist, but even when they formed a new community that was considered to be an Athenian possession and they retained their Athenian citizenship (e.g. *IG* xii.8 688, a decree of "the Athenians settled in Scyros"). The three north Aegean islands of Imbros, Lemnos, and Scyros belonged to Athens for most but not all of the time from the early fifth century onward: presumably the same men were at some times members of their cleruchy and citizens of Athens, at other times citizens of an independent city (but might still have been accepted as citizens of Athens if they had returned there) (on these settlements see Brunt 1993).

The Homeric poems, though ostensibly about events of the late Bronze Age, were written probably in the eighth century and in many respects reflect what we can believe to be the world of the late dark age, not much earlier than the time of writing. The "catalogue of ships" from Greece said to have taken part in the war against Troy lists contingents in regional groups but from a total of nearly 180 communities (Hom. *Il.* 2.494–760). In the *Odyssey* communities are represented as embryonic poleis, with (far from grand) kings, councils of leading men and assemblies of "all the people" (*pantes laoi*) (e.g. Hom. *Od.* 2.1–259; *pantes laoi* 13), and in the *Iliad* the Greek force at Troy functions as a kind of ad hoc polis, with the overall commander Agamemnon playing the part of the king and the regional commanders forming the council of leading men (e.g. Hom. *Il.* 2.48–399). This was a world with constitutional understandings rather than constitutional rules: assemblies of the "people" were called, to make and to announce major decisions; it is clear from the assembly in *Iliad* 2 that ordinary members were expected to shout their approval or to show silent disapproval, but not to play an active part and speak as Thersites did; and (artificially, for the sake of the plot) Ithaca in the absence of Odysseus had no assembly for 20 years (Hom. *Od.* 2.26–7). The word *polites* is used occasionally, once to refer to a city's contingent of warriors (Hom. *Il.* 2.806), otherwise to refer generally to its inhabitants (e.g. Hom. *Od.* 7.131).

From beginnings which were probably not unlike that there developed a pattern in which a typical Greek state had annually appointed officials (supplanting the king if originally there had been one), a council, and the "people" (most commonly *demos*), who for major decisions could be summoned to an assembly. One of the earliest Greek public inscriptions, from Drerus on Crete in the second half of the seventh century, records a regulation enacted by the "city" (polis) about tenure of the principal office of *kosmos* (ML 2 / Fornara 11). Within the basic pattern there was room for variation over the relative powers of officials, council and people, and over who counted as members of the people; but from an early date it seems to have been accepted that the people, in some sense of that word, had some part to play in the running of their states. As in *Iliad* 2, that was not immediately an active part. In Sparta, probably early in the seventh century, a tantalizing document known as the "great rhetra" provided for meetings of the *gerousia* (council of elders) and assembly, so that the people had in some sense the final right of decision but were expected not to "speak crookedly" (Plut. *Lyc.* 6 quotes and tries to elucidate). Solon in Athens at the beginning of the sixth century created a new council to prepare business for the Assembly (Arist. *Ath. Pol.* 8.4; Plut. *Sol.* 19.1–2), and he wrote in one of his poems, "This is how the people will best follow their leaders, if they are neither let loose too much nor constrained" (Solon fr. 6.1–2 West, quoted by *Ath. Pol.* 12.2).

By the end of the sixth century, probably in most states the "people" in a political sense included all native men who were rich enough to fight as "hoplites" (heavy infantry) in the state's army, and they were involved at least in the making of major decisions in the state's assembly. It was in Athens in the first half of the fifth century, when the city's growing naval power gave to the poorer men who rowed the ships an importance which the hoplites had traditionally claimed, that it was self-consciously decided that even the poorest native men were to be taken seriously as members of the people (though even in Athens the poorest citizens remained excluded from officeholding until the fourth century: cf. below). The word democracy (*dēmo-kratia*, "people-power") was coined for that kind of regime, and in reaction oligarchy (*olig-archia*, "few-rule") was coined for regimes which, deliberately once the alternative possibility had been raised, denied political rights to the poorest members of the community. Aristotle acknowledged that in some kinds of democracy low-grade workers were included among the citizens, but he did not approve of that (Arist. *Pol.* 3.1277b–1278a, 7.1328b–1329a).

Because Greek states were small, and resisted attempts by powerful neighbors to incorporate them (cf. below), a body of citizens was thought of as the body of full members of a local community. In the fifth century Athens extended active membership to the poorest men, but it limited citizenship to men with an Athenian mother as well as an Athenian father (cf. below). At that time Athens had a league of allies, the Delian League, which became increasingly an Athenian empire; but, except when after a rebellion the inhabitants were expelled or killed, the member states remained theoretically separate states with their own citizens, and they would have considered it a form of oppression to be incorporated in the Athenian state even as citizens of Athens. By contrast, we shall see below that Rome in the course of expansion used grants of citizenship as a reward for favored non-Roman communities or members of them, so that citizenship came to be divorced from membership of the local community, and a goal to aim for rather than a sign of oppression (cf. Champion, this volume, chapter 6).

"The citizen is not defined by residence in a place (for metics and slaves share in residence)" (Arist. *Pol.* 3.1275a). In the modern world immigrants who have moved from one state to another are not granted citizenship automatically, and different states show different degrees of generosity in allowing immigrants to become citizens after residing for some time. In the Greek world, and the ancient world generally, there were slaves, often acquired as prisoners of war or by purchase from some less developed people. These belonged to their owners and had minimal rights, and Aristotle in his attempt to justify slavery claimed that those who were "by nature" slaves were those who did not have the ability to participate in ruling (though he had to admit that some men were slaves in terms of their current status but were not slaves by nature) (Arist. *Pol.* 2.1252a–b, 1253b–1255b). There were also free men and women who were migrants, referred to by that term ("metics": *metoikoi*, sing. *metoikos*) in Athens and elsewhere and by Aristotle. Except when a state was actively trying to enlarge its citizen body (cf. below, on Dyme), it was much harder for immigrants to acquire citizenship in their new homes than in the modern world. The citizens might choose to grant them certain rights in the law courts and to impose on them certain duties in terms of military service and taxation; Athens gave additional rights – for instance, to own land and houses, normally permitted only to citizens – to those whom it wished to raise to a privileged status (e.g. Rhodes & Osborne 77.24–8); but full citizenship tended to be conferred only in exceptional cases (e.g. Rhodes & Osborne 33.30–6, as an honor for men not resident in Athens, *IG* ii² 222 / Osborne, *Naturalization*, D 22, for an exile from Delos welcomed in Athens).

"In different ways the free rules the slave and the male rules the female and the man rules the child. All have the parts of the soul, but they have them differently: for the slave does not have the deliberative part at all, the female has it but it is not authoritative, the child has it but it is undeveloped" (Arist. *Pol.* 1.1260a). In the modern world as in ancient Greece children are excluded from political rights, and there is room for disagreement over the age at which political rights should be given: in classical Athens the basic rights and duties were given at 18, but the right to sit on juries and to hold office only at 30 (*Ath. Pol.* 42.1 basic rights; 63.3 juries; 30.2 with Rhodes 1981a: 389–90 office). Aristotle also considered the possibility of a retired status for the oldest citizens, "for there is an old age of the mind, as there is of the body" (Arist. *Pol.* 2.1270b cf. 3.1275a). There is hardly any evidence that that was practiced, but the Malians allowed men over military age to remain citizens but not to hold office (Arist. *Pol.* 4.1297b), whereas in Sparta 60 was the lower age limit for membership of the *gerousia* (cf. below). What has been judged shocking in our time is that women were excluded from political rights; but this was universal until the end of the nineteenth century (the first country to give women voting rights was New Zealand in 1893) and there are still some countries where women do not have full rights. Aristophanes could joke on the subject (Ar. *Eccl.*, cf. *Lys.*, *Thesm.*); Plato accepted in principle that some women might be qualified to hold the highest rank, that of guardian, in his Republic (Pl. *Resp.* 5.454–5); Aristotle, as in the case of slavery, realized that the practice needed to be justified – but the practice was universal, and there is no evidence that anybody seriously thought it ought not to be. (On women cf. Sissa, this volume, chapter 7.)

In an extended sense the children and wives of adult male citizens were a part of the citizen body, because the male children would grow up to become full citizens and the wives would give birth to the next generation of full citizens. In Athens (probably) and elsewhere, legitimate birth from a lawfully wedded wife was a formal requirement for citizenship (cf. Rhodes 1981a: 496–7); and in Athens after 451/0 and again after 403 (setting aside a relaxation during the Peloponnesian War) the wife had to be an Athenian, that is, the daughter of a male citizen: citizenship was considered to be a valuable benefit, which should be enjoyed only by those who deserved it through being true members of the community in question.

Aristotle in his *Politics* and the author of the *Athenian Constitution* sometimes write of citizenship as "having a share in" or "being a partner in" the city, or the citizenship or constitution (*metechein / koinōnein tēs poleōs / tēs politeias*). Equivalent expressions also used are "having a share in" or "being masters (*kyrioi*) of" rule / offices / honors (*archē / archai / timai*). These are ways of referring to holding office and taking part in the activities expected of a citizen: in particular, when discussing the ideal constitution of Hippodamus of Miletus, in which soldiers, farmers and craftsmen would all be citizens, Aristotle first objects to the inclusion of farmers and craftsmen, but then distinguishes between farmers who contribute to the state by providing maintenance for the soldiers and those who farm simply for their own benefit, who can be regarded as residents in but not members of the community (Arist. *Pol.* 2.1268a).

The city was its citizens. The citizens were thought of as men who had a stake in the city, and that is why the ideal citizen was a man who owned some land in the city's territory and who had sons to continue his family's commitment to the city, and why metics unless specially privileged were not allowed to own land. The territory of the state, and the sanctuaries within it, were important (cf. the training program instituted for young Athenians in the 330s: *Ath. Pol.* 42.3); but the polis was primarily a body of politai, which could continue to exist even if removed from its territory. When the Persians conquered Asia Minor in the 540s, of the Greek communities on the Aegean coast the Phocaeans (or many of them) migrated to the western Mediterranean, the Teans migrated to Abdera in Thrace, and it was proposed but not accepted that all the Ionian Greeks should migrate to Sardinia (Hdt. 1.164–70). The Athenians evacuated their city and the whole of Attica when the Persians invaded in 480–479 (Hdt. 8.40–1, 9.3), and they evacuated the countryside and gathered in the fortified area of the city and Piraeus when the Spartans invaded in the Peloponnesian War of 431–404 (Thuc. 2.13.2, 14–17).

There could be gradations within the citizen body. Certain rights might be dependent on age (an Athenian example above, a Spartan example below), or on wealth (from 594/3 the Athenians were divided into four property classes, some offices were reserved for members of the higher classes, and members of the lowest class were not eligible for any offices, but in the fourth century after losses from a plague and the Peloponnesian War those rules were no longer enforced: inference from *Ath. Pol.* 7.3–8.1, 26.2, 47.1), or on family (in Sparta, within a citizen body which was itself a small minority of the whole population, only men over 60 years old who belonged to certain families served in the *gerousia*, the council of elders: inference from Arist. *Pol.* 4.1294b). And we have seen that there could be a distinction between ordinary metics and those who ad hominem had been granted enhanced privileges. However, the most fundamental distinction in a Greek state was that between citizens with their families and noncitizens.

Nevertheless, it must be added that there were places, about which we are frustratingly ill informed, where that fundamental distinction was problematic. In oligarchic states where there was a property qualification for full citizenship, there were men of native descent who were excluded from citizenship simply because they did not satisfy that property qualification. Worse, in states which sometimes had a democratic constitution and sometimes an oligarchic, there were men who sometimes counted as citizens and sometimes did not. How were such men thought of, by themselves and by those who did satisfy the property qualification? What rights and duties did they have, with regard for instance to access to the law courts and military service, when they were excluded from the citizen body? The problem was alluded to by Aristotle (*Pol.* 3. 1277b).

The first instances of this in Athens occurred in revolutionary situations, and were short-lived. In 411 (when a large proportion of the poorer citizens were serving in the navy and were away from Athens) a regime was instituted which was to be based on a council of 400 and a citizen body comprising men "able to serve with their money and their bodies," that is, those able to fight as hoplites, expected to number 5,000. The process of registering the 5,000 was begun, and one registrar claimed to have proposed as many as 9,000 names, but the 400 ruled without convening any meetings of the larger body. After a few months the 400 were deposed, and succeeded by an intermediate regime based on that larger body: we do not know whether the register was now completed or those who claimed to be qualified were simply accepted as qualified (Thuc. 8.45–98, *Ath. Pol.* 29–33; 9,000 names Lys. 20.13). In 410 the full democracy was restored. Then in 404, after the defeat of Athens in the Peloponnesian War, an oligarchic regime based on a council of 30 was established under pressure from the Spartan Lysander. Some time after taking office, the 30 drew up a list of 3,000 men who were to have basic rights, and those not on the list were first disarmed and later expelled from the city. Many fled into exile from Attica, but a growing number of them formed a force which fought its way back against the oligarchs. In 403 the democracy was restored; one proposal made but rejected was that citizenship should be limited to those who owned some land, which allegedly would have excluded about 5,000 men out of perhaps 30,000 (accounts which mention the 3,000 Xen. *Hell.* 2.3.11–4.43, *Ath. Pol.* 34.2–40; proposal to exclude the landless attacked in Lys. 34, *Ancestral Constitution*).

In the late fourth century Athens had two longer lasting regimes based on a property qualification. In 321, after the defeat of a rising against Macedon, a requirement of 2,000 drachmae was imposed: 9,000 men met the requirement and (probably) 22,000 did not; those who were excluded were offered a new home in Thrace, but it is not clear how many went there, how many fled elsewhere, and how many remained without citizenship in Attica. In 318 the democracy was briefly restored. From 317 to 307 there was a regime presided over by the philosopher Demetrius of Phalerum, with a property qualification of 1,000 drachmae. After that the democracy was restored again; and, although upheavals continued for another 45 years, there was as far as we know no other time when the poorest Athenians were excluded from citizenship. We hear no more of the settlement in Thrace; many Athenians must have moved out of and into Attica during the period of instability.

In Sparta the Spartans were a privileged minority among a population of Laconia and (until 370/69) Messenia which also contained *perioikoi* ("those living around": free men living in and administering their own communities but subject to Sparta in foreign policy) and helots ("captives": a body of serfs who farmed the land for the Spartans who owned it). There was an exceptionally strong communal element in the lives of the Spartans, and from the fourth century onward we find the full citizens referred to as *homoioi* ("equals"). In fact it was always the case that some Spartans were richer than others, and to qualify for citizenship a man had to be accepted unanimously as a member of one of the messes at which the citizens dined, and to be able to contribute the prescribed quantities of produce to his mess (Plut. *Lyc.* 12). At the beginning of the fourth century an unsuccessful attempt to unite all classes of noncitizens against the citizens was made by a man called Cinadon, who was one of the *hypomeiones* ("inferiors," contrasted with the "equals"), and it is thought that this was a class of men downgraded from full citizenship owing to inability to make their mess contributions (cf. Arist. *Pol.* 2.1271a).

Most poleis were small, many of them very small, in area, in citizen numbers, and in total population. According to a recent estimate, about 60 percent had a territory of not more than 100 square kilometers / 39 square miles, and only 10 percent had more than 500 square kilometers / 193 square miles. The largest in mainland Greece were Athens and Sparta, which because they had become the political centers of whole regions had about 2,600 square kilometers / 1,000 square miles and 8,400 square kilometers / 3,250 square miles respectively (Hansen, in Hansen and Nielsen 2004: 70–3). For most states numbers of inhabitants can only be guessed at: an exercise on the Aegean islands (which perhaps errs on the low side) suggests that many cities there had under 1,000 adult males and none had over 5,000 (Ruschenbusch 1985). Sparta's privileged minority of citizens numbered about 8,000 at the beginning of the fifth century but declined drastically to 1,000 or fewer by the middle of the fourth (e.g. de Ste. Croix 1972: 331–2). Athens, which accepted as citizens all the native men of the region of Attica, may have had about 60,000 adult male citizens before the Peloponnesian War of the late fifth century and about 30,000 after (Hansen 1988: 14–28, Rhodes 1988: 271–7 (fifth century); Hansen 1986 (fourth century)).

It is plausibly suggested that, the smaller the polis, the higher the proportion of its inhabitants likely to live in the urban center and to go out from there day by day if they worked in the country (Hansen 2004). The dynamics of interaction between the citizens will have been very different in those small cities and in the few large cities. Most cities will have been "face-to-face" communities in which the members lived in close proximity to one another and many of them knew many of the others. But the large Athens was not like that (Osborne 1985a: 64–5, 89, against Finley 1985a: 17). Sheer numbers apart, the population was dispersed in local settlements throughout Attica ("demes": a particular use of *demoi*, sing. *demos*), and the remotest demes were 50 kilometers / 30 miles from the city. When the philosophers contemplated an ideal city they did not contemplate a large city such as Athens. Plato's Republic began as something small and healthy, though it expanded more and more to meet its inhabitants' desire for luxuries (Pl. *Resp.* 2.369b–374d); and the Magnesia of his *Laws* was to have 5,040 citizens (Pl. *Leg.* 5.737c–745e: that particular figure chosen for mathematical reasons, but the order of magnitude is significant), and the aim of its foundation was that the citizens "shall be as happy as possible, and as much as possible friends of one another" (Pl. *Leg.* 5.743c). Aristotle concluded,

> This also is clear from the facts, that it is difficult, and perhaps impossible, for a polis which is too populous to be in a good legal condition. ... A polis of too few men is not self-sufficient (and the polis is something self-sufficient), while one of too many men is

self-sufficient in necessities, but like an ethnos, not a polis: it is not easy for it to have a
constitution [*politeia*]; for who will be general of so greatly excessive a body, or who will
be herald [to make proclamations at a mass meeting] except a man like Stentor?" (Arist.
Pol. 7.1326a–b; Stentor was the bronze-voiced shouter of Hom. *Il.* 7.785–6).

He considered Plato's 5,040 citizens too many (Arist. *Pol.* 2.1265a).

In the largest cities such as Athens, each citizen was a member of one of a number of
small local units, which had their own affairs to manage and their own assemblies and
other institutions, and which provided the kind of intimate community which the large
city could not. In Athens these local units were the 139 demes. An Athenian was a
citizen of Athens and a demesman (*demotes*) of his deme – and also a member of his *phyle*
("tribe") and *trittys* ("third" of a tribe), entities intermediate between the city and the
deme, and of various other social/religious associations within the citizen body.
Membership of the demes was hereditary, so eventually – particularly after the unsettling effect of the times during the Peloponnesian War when the countryside was
abandoned – there were some members of a deme who no longer lived there and may
not have felt closely involved in its affairs. Another way of organizing a region with many
centers of habitation is found in Boeotia, to the north of Attica. For most of the time
from the late sixth century there was a Boeotian federation, which controlled foreign
policy; but the federation was made up of a number of principal cities, which were run
on the same general lines as one another but had a greater degree of independence than
the Athenian demes; and there were in addition some lesser cities, dependent on one of
the principal cities and not directly represented in the institutions of the federation. An
Athenian was, say, a citizen of Athens and a demesman of Marathon, and he would be
identified as a Marathonian within Athens and as an Athenian in the wider Greek world;
a Boeotian was, say, a citizen of Tanagra and a Boeotian.

There was an ongoing tendency for Greeks to remain attached to their individual
cities and to try to retain as much independence for their cities as they could, but there
was also a tendency for powerful cities to try to extend their power and incorporate
weaker neighbors. By a procedure known as synoecism (*synoikismos*, "coming to live
together") small communities could amalgamate to form a single larger community,
which might involve the movement of some of the inhabitants to an existing or a newly
built urban center. In Arcadia, Mantinea, already existing as some kind of entity, was
further united out of four or five villages perhaps in the 470s; it was split into its
component villages by Sparta in 385; it reunited in 370 when Sparta was no longer
strong enough to prevent that (Strabo 337: 8.3.2; Xen. *Hell.* 5.2.1; Diod. Sic. 15.5.4,
12.2; Xen. *Hell.* 6.5.3–5). Early in the fourth century the polis of Helisson, to the
southwest of Mantinea, was absorbed into Mantinea in such a way that it became a
kome ("village") of the polis of Mantinea but for some religious purposes was still
regarded as a distinct community (Rhodes & Osborne 14). One of the proposals said
to have been considered but rejected by the Ionian Greeks when the Persians conquered Asia Minor was that they should undergo a synoecism to make Teos their one
political center and their other cities demes of the single state (Hdt. 1.170.3).

Participation by the citizens in running the affairs of the state was not merely a
right but, if not an obligation, at any rate a strong expectation: citizens met en masse

in their assembly to make decisions, they took turns in holding offices to carry out decisions, and they manned law courts to dispense justice (these are Aristotle's three main categories of political activity: *Pol.* 3.1274a, 4.1297b–1301a). In these ways they "ruled and were ruled"; and states of varying complexions, not only democracies, had limits on reappointment to prevent the emergence of a ruling clique within the body of citizens entitled to hold office.

Athenian oligarchs in 411 alleged that attendance at the Assembly never exceeded 5,000, out of a citizen body which by then was nearer to the postwar figure of ca. 30,000 than to the prewar figure of ca. 60,000 (Thuc. 8.72.1); but there is no sign that in the fourth century the quorum of 6,000 required for some decisions ever failed to be achieved. Not all registered jurors were required every day, but it appears that every year 6,000 men were registered for jury service (late fifth century *Ath. Pol.* 24.3; fourth century not attested but probable), and jurors had to have reached the age of 30. Athens had a large number of annual offices, and an annually appointed council of 500: most civilian officials were appointed by lot and could hold each office only once, but men could serve in the council twice, presumably because without that concession not enough councillors could be found (*Ath. Pol.* 62.3; on the implications of this for fourth century figures see Hansen 2006b: 22–33). There were also offices to be held and assemblies to be attended in the various subsidiary units of the citizen body. The frequency with which the law courts met, even in the fourth century when private suits reached a court only on appeal (*Ath. Pol.* 53), estimated at 175–225 days a year, shows that prosecuting and being prosecuted was not an activity limited to an elite minority (Hansen 1999: 186). Under the system of liturgies (*leitourgiai*, literally "works for the people") the richest citizens were required when called on (and if anxious to build up a reputation for public service might volunteer even when not called on) to supervise and pay for a team performing in a festival or to command and pay some of the running costs of a ship in the navy. To make it work, this system required a high degree of willingness to participate, and we know that it did work.

There will, of course, have been degrees of participation and nonparticipation. Even with stipends for the performance of civilian duties (beginning with service on juries, probably in the 450s, and culminating in attendance at the Assembly, ca. 400: *Ath. Pol.* 27.3–4, 41.3), it was easier for rich men than for poor to devote large amounts of time to public affairs, while their families and slaves attended to the household's livelihood; and it was easier for men living in or near the city than for men in the farthest corners of Attica to take part in public affairs in the city. The Assembly will surely have had a core of regular members and a penumbra of men who attended when it was convenient for them to go to Athens or when a matter which particularly interested them was on the agenda; and we know that there was a small number of men who spoke and made proposals frequently and a much larger number who spoke and made proposals occasionally (Hansen 1999: 144, 272). Those who registered for jury service will not have been exactly the same 6,000 men every year, and not all 6,000 will have presented themselves for service each day. Some men will have been active rarely if at all in city matters but will have played a leading part in their deme or some other organization. And there must have been some "quiet

Athenians" (cf. Carter 1986), who were too busy with their farm or workshop to have much time for public affairs (though farmers tended to be busy at some times during the year but not at others), or who traveled away from Athens for trading or other purposes, or who were nongregarious men like the comedian Menander's Grumpy Man (Men. *Dys.* 1–34), or who preferred athletics or philosophy to the workaday world. Plato represents the philosopher Socrates as claiming that he never appeared in a law court until the trial which resulted in his condemnation, did not speak in the Assembly, and never held any office – but he did serve in the council in 406/5 (Pl. *Ap.* 17d, 31c, 32b).

Nevertheless, as far as we know most forms of political activity were not obligatory: it cannot be proved but seems likely that candidates for office were men who had volunteered (sometimes, no doubt, under pressure from fellow citizens), and so too were the men who registered year by year for jury service. Service in the army, for those rich enough to be conscripted as hoplites, was compulsory (those who were physically unfit could presumably declare that on oath: cf. *Ath. Pol.* 49.2, on the cavalry), but the navy's oarsmen seem usually to have been citizen and noncitizen volunteers. The performance of liturgies by the richest men was compulsory, but ambitious men would volunteer when not compelled (cf. above). And it appears that in the late fifth century devices to move men from the agora to the Assembly's meeting place included the use of a rope dipped in red dye, and any marked by the rope but absent from the Assembly were fined, on the grounds that they easily could have attended (Ar. *Ach.* 22 with schol.). It remains true that a large number of Athenian citizens must have been active reasonably often in some of the ways available to them; and Thucydides represents Pericles as saying that the Athenians alone regard men who do not take part not as noninterfering but as useless, and that such men are in fact parasitic on those who are active (Thuc. 2.40.2, 63.2–3).

How far did other cities resemble Athens in this respect? As all too often, evidence is in short supply and we must make reasonable conjectures. Other cities did not have such elaborate mechanisms or so many offices and meetings, but (particularly if they were oligarchic and excluded the poor) they did not have so large a citizen body, and we may well suppose that peer pressure would make it more difficult to opt out of participation in a small, face-to-face society than in a large one. As noted above, it was not only democratic states which limited reappointment to offices: seventh century Drerus forbade reappointment to the office of *kosmos* within ten years (ML 2 / Fornara 11). The principal annual officials of Sparta were the five ephors (*ephoroi*, sing. *ephoros*: "overseers"). It is not directly attested but is generally accepted that no man could be ephor more than once, and it can be calculated that by the middle of the fourth century, when Sparta's citizen numbers had fallen to 1,000 or fewer, about one in three or four citizens will have had to serve (Rhodes 1981b). Public life was particularly important and private life particularly unimportant in Sparta, and we may assume that there pressure to participate, in officeholding and in attending the assembly (though ordinary citizens seem not to have been able to speak there) was particularly strong. Figures for attendance at cities' assemblies, which we might compare with estimated citizen numbers for the fifth century (Ruschenbusch 1983), are few and mostly of the hellenistic and Roman periods, but when we have them they suggest that a very high proportion of the citizen body, much higher than in Athens, might attend: Iasus, in Caria, for which 800 adult males have been suggested, has produced hellenistic decrees with 858 and 841 citizens voting (*SEG* xli 929, 932).

The conquest of the Persian empire by Alexander the Great made the Greeks part of a new, larger world, but it did not result in the end of the Greek cities and of Greek citizenship. Rival kingdoms emerged in different parts of Alexander's empire, and for the Greek cities maneuvering between these was not unlike maneuvering between the leading cities of the classical period. Kings would sometimes issue orders to the cities, and expected to be flattered by them, but usually they did not interfere directly in the cities' running of their affairs. New cities were founded by the kings, particularly in Asia, and, apart from a greater degree of royal intervention, what is most notable about them is that, somewhat in the manner of earlier colonial foundations in less developed areas, these cities and their citizens formed a privileged stratum within the total population, with the indigenous inhabitants and the land they farmed sometimes subject directly to a king, sometimes made dependent on the nearest Greek city.

The process by which larger cities tended to absorb smaller continued: for this period modern scholars use the term *sympoliteia* ("joint citizenship") rather than *synoikismos* (*Syll.*[3] 647 / Austin 1981: 134 = Austin 2006: 154 uses this, but in fact ancient texts use a variety of terms). In a slight weakening of the traditional particularism of Greek cities, we often find one city granting the rights of citizenship to citizens of a second when they visit or migrate to the first (*Syll.*[3] 472 uses *isopoliteia*, which modern scholars use as a technical term, but again ancient usage is more varied). Early in the fourth century there was a short-lived union of Corinth and Argos, as a device to strengthen an anti-Spartan party in Corinth, and this may have been based on *isopoliteia* (Xen. *Hell.* 4.1.1–13, 4.14–5.9, Diod. Sic. 14.86, 91.2–92.2, Andoc. 3. *Peace* 24–7, 32). The Aetolian League, a league of allies based in northwestern Greece, used *isopoliteia*, either with one member state or with the whole League, to attach to it states outside its own region. Meanwhile in cities which were short of citizens citizenship could be bought: Dyme in Achaea offered citizenship to *epoikoi* (the local term for metics) at a price of 1 talent, to be paid in two installments (*Syll.*[3] 531).

Finally, it will be instructive to contrast the Greek cities with Rome, which began as a city state but, as it extended its power throughout Italy and the Mediterranean and beyond, developed the concept of the state and of citizenship in very un-Greek ways.

Roman citizenship was far more hierarchic than Greek. In the early days of the Roman state there was a formal distinction between the aristocratic patricians and the plebeians; and, although other distinctions later came to be more important, there remained some offices which were open only to patricians and others which were open only to plebeians. Senators were not merely members of a council (to which they normally belonged for life) but formed a privileged class within the state; *equites* ("horsemen"), originally the cavalry of the army, came in the late republic to form a second level of the upper class, then not holding offices and in the Principate holding offices which were not open to senators. While Greek assemblies were organized on the basis of one man one vote (whether the result was arrived at by precise counting or by some other means), Roman assemblies used block voting so that some men's votes were worth more than others'. In the centuriate assembly, based on the organization of the army in early times, men were categorized by age and by wealth, and a century of richer men contained fewer men than a century of poorer, a century of older men fewer than a century of younger. The tribal assembly was based on 35 topographical tribes: the urban poor, who were likely to attend in the largest numbers, were confined to four of the tribes, and the voting was biased in favor of those who were registered in the rural tribes and were able and willing to attend. (On the powers of the Roman People cf. Tatum, this volume, chapter 14.)

Throughout its territorial expansion, Rome retained a city-state form of government, but more and more of its citizens lived at such a distance from Rome that they could not normally attend assemblies, vote in elections, or provide juries for law courts. Rome began as one of a number of Latin states, and had to negotiate with them and with the Etruscans. Already in the third century there were colonies of citizens at some distance from Rome, and during the second century colonies began to be founded in Cisalpine Gaul (northern Italy, then regarded as distinct from Italy proper) and outside Italy altogether. Processes were developed, first in "Latin colonies" (where originally there were reciprocal rights with Rome, later officials were given Roman citizenship), by which men who were not citizens by birth could gain citizenship: all free men in Italy (without Cisalpine Gaul) became citizens after the Social War at the beginning of the first century BC, and the extension of citizenship to individuals and communities deemed worthy of it continued until in AD 212 the emperor Caracalla made virtually all free inhabitants of the empire citizens – but by then a new distinction between *honestiores* and *humiliores* was developing, with some of the former rights of citizens limited to the *honestiores*. As particular instances of the spread of Roman citizenship, soldiers who enlisted as noncitizen auxiliaries were granted citizenship on discharge, and freed slaves of citizens became citizens (whereas in Greece they obtained metic or comparable status, unless rewarded for supporting the citizens in a major crisis: *Ath. Pol.* 40.2 reports an unsuccessful proposal to give Athenian citizenship to all noncitizens who fought on the democratic side in 403). By being given to more and more men who were unable to exercise their political rights in Rome, Roman citizenship was increasingly divorced from the right to participate in the running of the state, and instead became a matter of status and rights at law (cf. Champion, this volume, chapter 6).

While a Greek city was a local community and its citizens were the full members of that community, Rome was the political center and the religious center of the Roman state, but it was not a local community anxious to maintain its distinctness from neighboring local communities. It was a community of men who belonged together and who belonged to Rome, but it included men who did not live in Rome, and it accepted new members from outside the community, as long as they became Roman in allegiance, in religion and in way of life. The Roman world was full of cities: in the early centuries, in addition to citizen and Latin colonies, there were allied cities which had treaties of various kinds with Rome but in practice were all subordinate to Rome; later the principal categories were the colony and the *municipium*. One could be a member of one's colony or *municipium* and at the same time a citizen of Rome. Cicero (from Arpinum, southeast of Rome, which had obtained full citizenship in 188), wrote:

I judge that all members of *municipia* have two fatherlands, one by nature and one by the state. ... We must give priority in affection to that which is called the commonwealth (*res publica*) and the whole state, for which we must be willing to die, to which we must give up ourselves wholly and in which we must place and as it were consecrate all that is ours. But that which gave us birth is not much less sweet than that which received us. (Cic. *Leg.* 2.2.5)

As the Greeks were brought into this world, from the second century onward, their cities were incorporated into this network and continued to have their own citizen bodies and to administer their domestic affairs, whether as ordinary *municipia* or with a higher status which brought honorific more than practical benefits. But it was a world in which Roman citizens could never occupy an inferior position, and so we sometimes find that Roman citizens active in a Greek city, though not themselves citizens of that city, joined with the citizens in the enactment of a decree (e.g. Assus, in the Troad, *Syll.*³ 797).

FURTHER READING

Aristotle's *Politics*, written in the third quarter of the fourth century by a non-Athenian living in Athens, is the most useful presentation of Greek thinking on the matters discussed here; Athens in the fifth and fourth centuries provides the best-documented example of Greek practice, and a particularly useful source of detailed information is the *Athēnaiōn Politeia* (*Athenian Constitution*) written in Aristotle's school. For annotated translations of the *Politics* see Saunders 1981 and Stalley 1995b; for an account of Athenian constitutional practice in the fourth century (the period for which the evidence is most plentiful) see Hansen 1999; for an annotated translation of the *Athenian Constitution* see Rhodes 1984b.

Hansen and Nielsen 2004 contains an extended introduction on various aspects of the Greek poleis, followed by studies of individual states, region by region and polis by polis. On Athenian citizenship see Manville 1990, and on descent and other possible criteria for Athenian citizenship see Davies 1977–8. On Sparta Michell 1952 gives a topic-by-topic account; Hodkinson 2000 modifies that account in important respects; Cartledge 2001 is a stimulating collection of essays. On Greek cities in the hellenistic period see Billows 2003, where more detailed studies are cited.

On Roman citizenship Sherwin-White 1973 is fundamental; a recent book, Howarth 2006, argues that early Rome should be seen as part of the Latin federal system rather than as a single city state. Cicero in imitation of Plato wrote *De republica* ("on the commonwealth") and *De legibus* ("on the laws").

NOTE

1 Inscriptions are cited from the following collections (those marked * contain Greek texts, those marked † contain English translations): † Austin = Austin 1981/Austin 2006; † Fornara = Fornara 1983; * Osborne, *Naturalization* = M. J. Osborne 1981–3; *† Rhodes & Osborne = Rhodes and Osborne 2003. For other abbreviations, readers should consult the list at the front of this volume.

CHAPTER 5

Public Action and Rational Choice in Classical Greek Political Theory

Josiah Ober

As several of the chapters in this volume point out (especially Depew and Ludwig), Thomas Hobbes's bleak view of humans as naturally solitary and motivated by fear of death was not shared by classical Greek theorists. Yet joint action at scale remained a problem. How could a large and diverse "public" come into being? How could a public perform actions with substantial effects? These were difficult questions because Greek theorists regarded human beings not only as social (group-forming) and communicative (language-using) animals, but also as rationally self-interested and strategic. Individuals are capable of distinguishing what is good for themselves from what may be good for others, and acting strategically on that knowledge. Recognizing that humans were sometimes, although not invariably, motivated by expected utility maximization, Greek theorists sought to specify the conditions under which people might be expected to act more or less selfishly.[1]

Public Action: Incentives, Nature, and Knowledge

Social problems that emerge because of rational self-interest can be grouped under the rubrics of collective action (modeled in game theory by the Prisoner's Dilemma), common pool resources (modeled by the "tragedy of the commons"), and credible commitment (modeled by "Odysseus bound to the mast"). Since an action that maximizes expected individual utility may not be the most cooperative (social utility maximizing) choice, human communities must solve incentive problems: How can likely rewards and punishments, attached to particular courses of action, be institutionalized such that individuals consistently choose more cooperative courses of action? The solution to the complex "game" (that is, the situation in which no one

A Companion to Greek and Roman Political Thought, First Edition. Edited by Ryan K. Balot.
© 2013 Blackwell Publishing Ltd. Published 2013 by Blackwell Publishing Ltd.

has a better strategic move, given his knowledge of the moves others are likely to make in response) that emerges in an environment of social institutions constitutes a social equilibrium which may be more or less stable and more or less productive. Groups with incentive systems yielding high and stable rates of return to cooperation are, all other things being equal, more productive. In the competitive environment of the Greek poleis, in which rival states competed for resources and weak competitors were eliminated, there was strong pressure for each polis to seek competitive advantage by devising good incentives. This chapter argues that Greek theorists were well aware of the issue. Although, in contrast to early modern contract theory, strategic self-interest was not the primary motor driving Greek political theory, problems of incentives and self-interest are an important, and relatively overlooked, facet of classical political thought.

Incentive problems come to the fore with the emergence of democracy. As opposed to monarchy or closely held oligarchy (see Forsdyke, this volume, chapter 15), where an individual or small corporate body can speak and act for "everyone," in a complex democratic state like Athens, the public is a demos: a large body of persons, socially diverse, and with diverse interests and preferences. How can that diverse public make decisions or carry them out? Democratic decision and execution require institutional mechanisms, including voting and deliberation, which are potentially vulnerable to strategic manipulation. By allowing diverse individuals to make free choices, democracy creates space for free riding, and the size and diversity of the public raises questions of how that public's commitments can be made credible. Moreover, when the polis is the "collective possession" of a demos, common pool resource issues loom: If each of the many "shareholders" of the polis chooses to take more from the common pool than he gives back to it, the polis will collapse in a "commons tragedy."[2]

In a democracy, each member of the demos has interests somewhat different from those of every other member, and no one has authority to decide whose interests should be paramount. Deliberations over policy may be protracted (thus wasting valuable time) or cut short, leaving people unsatisfied and prone to defect. Interest-sharing subgroups may seek to advance particularistic agendas by taking strategic advantage of voting and deliberations. All of this serves to push up the costs of group action, and thus would seem to degrade the competitive advantage of democracies relative to their more hierarchical rivals. Yet in classical Greece, democracies (and other republican forms of political organization) often did very well in competitive environments.

The puzzles of why democracies (especially Athens) did well, and how nondemocratic communities might do better, stimulated the development of Greek political thought. In the later fifth and fourth centuries, Greek political theorists gained the descriptive and analytic tools necessary to explain public action problems. Classical theorists addressed the puzzle of how democratic communities became and remained productive despite their costly processes for decision making and execution. Their answers centered around the organization of knowledge and, with Aristotle, human nature: Democracies did better than would otherwise be expected because democratic political culture and institutions promoted the aggregation of useful knowledge dispersed across a diverse citizenry. Moreover, democracies gave citizens incentives to cooperate by providing cooperators with access to goods they wanted, including association in public decisions.[3]

Incentive Problems in Greek Literature

Greek literature had been concerned with incentive problems long before the classical era. According to a tradition recorded in the *Ehoiai* (Hesiod frr. 196–204 MW; cf. Eur. *IA* 75 ff.), the suitors of Helen bound themselves by an oath to act in concert in the interests of Helen's husband if Helen were abducted. By this act of self-binding, the Achaean leaders had cut off the option of staying home. The oath, by providing a credible precommitment to a particular line of joint action, solved the coordination problem ("I won't act until you do") necessary to begin the Trojan War. Yet once they arrived at Troy, sustained joint action required that each hero have an incentive to stay: the plot of Homer's *Iliad* is driven by the incentives of fairly shared booty and honors: When Agamemnon seized Briseis, Achilles lost his incentive to cooperate. The *Iliad* explores the consequences of Achilles' rationally self-interested defection, and the difficulties attending Achilles' eventual return, in the context of a culture that included personal honor, friendship, and fame, as well as material goods in the calculation of utility. The *Odyssey* is also much concerned with incentives: Odysseus' act of binding himself to the mast in order to listen to the Sirens has become a standard trope in the contemporary literature on precommitment (Elster 1979, 2000). Odysseus solves his problem (his desire to hear the Sirens, without losing his life) by eliminating in advance his option of acting on the new desires that will be stimulated by the Siren's song. His precommitment (self-binding and orders to the crew not to release him) prevented him from acting on reformed, self-destructive, preferences.

Many other works of Greek literature address aspects of incentive problems: Hesiod's didactic poetry is informed by a worldview that takes for granted the tendency of rational individuals to defect from cooperative behavior when it will advance their own interests. The *Works and Days* is motivated by Hesiod's brother Perseus' defection from the cooperative order of family land distribution and his strategic use of a corrupt legal order (the bribe-swallowing *basileis*) to carry out his plan. Hesiod urges avoidance of public space and great care in lending and borrowing. Yet his enjoyment of trade goods (wine from Byblos) shows that he participates in a system of exchange in which interpersonal and intercommunity cooperation underwrites his way of life: Hesiod is far from a Hobbesian solitary. Aristophanes' characters tend to defect from cooperative public behavior when they perceive that others are not acting cooperatively; an example is Dikaiopolis' private market in *Acharnians*. The "skeptic scene" in *Ecclesiazusae* (770–806) is a pointed case of the difficulty of coordination in the absence of credible precommitment: the skeptic character refuses to donate his private goods to a common store established by the new women rulers of Athens until he sees others doing likewise. Obviously, if no one is willing to go first, the women's revolutionary scheme will not get off the ground. Pseudo-Xenophon (2.17) links the problem of commitment directly to the institutions of democracy, claiming that in an oligarchy, the state's commitments are guaranteed by the names of the rulers, whereas in a democracy, treaties are underwritten only by the impersonal collectivity "demos" – to which no personal responsibility can attach. Lycurgus' case, in his law court speech *Against Leocrates*, revolves around the conception of the polis as a common possession and the looming danger of a commons tragedy: If the jurors acquit Leocrates, the democracy's commitment to sanction malefactors will be proven hollow. If and when that commitment ceases to be credible, other individuals will rationally choose defection over self-sacrificing cooperation. And thus Athens will be more vulnerable to its enemies.

The two preceding paragraphs are *exempli gratia*; cases of Greek authors addressing incentive problems could easily be multiplied. Of course, it is absurd to think that classical literature can be reduced to a meditation on incentives; the point is only that Greek authors recognized choice problems as a rich source of narrative. The remainder of this chapter looks at how the baseline concern with rationality and incentives developed into sophisticated treatments of public action by Herodotus, Thucydides, Plato, and Aristotle.

Herodotus on Utilities and Knowledge Aggregation

Aristophanes, Ps-Xenophon, and Lycurgus each suggested that finding the right incentives to achieve productive cooperation is difficult in democratic communities. Herodotus addresses the question of how a democratic public could come into existence and act effectively by contrasting monarchies with democracies (see further, Forsdyke, chapter 15). The contrast comes through clearly in his stories of King Croesus of Lydia and his account of Athenian decision-making before Salamis.

Rationally self-interested choices are made by calculating expected utility. The social problem of collective action is solved when utilities arise from and are aligned with cooperative choices. For Herodotus, this is a matter of ethics, as emerges from Croesus' request that Solon name the happiest man ever to have lived. According to Herodotus' Solon, the happiest man was Tellus of Athens, who

> was from a prosperous city, and his children were good and noble. He saw children born to them all, and all of these survived. His life was prosperous by our standards, and his death was most glorious: when the Athenians were fighting their neighbors in Eleusis, he came to help, routed the enemy, and died very finely. The Athenians buried him at public expense on the spot where he fell and gave him much honor. (Hdt. 1.30.4–5, trans. Godley 1920)

In the cultural environment evoked by Herodotus' Solon, there is no conflict between individual and community interests: Tellus gave aid to his countrymen, died in battle, and was rewarded with a grave monument. Because archaic Athenian ethical norms defined posthumous public honors as a utility, Tellus' response to a common danger was a rational choice. The community's offer of honors in response to heroism could be anticipated and therefore provided an incentive to take risks in battle for a man whose posterity was already guaranteed by fine children and grandchildren.[4]

Along with the claim that no living man can be judged happy (since he may yet suffer misfortune), "happy Tellus" taught a lesson about expected utility. Herodotus' fifth century readers learned that in the past, a life of optimum utility had been defined by kinship (children and grandchildren), duty (fighting the community's enemies), and moderation (adequate prosperity rather than great riches). Solon's follow-up story, about the Argive brothers, Cleobis and Biton, has similar import. The choices of the three men regarded by Herodotus' Solon as happiest were rational, in their historical and cultural context, not only because each chose to maximize his culturally-defined utility but also because each made his choices under conditions approaching complete social information. Herodotus emphasizes that all mortals were subject to misfortune, yet Solon's happy exemplars had been able to make life-choices with confidence, based on their own inductive knowledge of the unwritten rules of their societies. Maximizing utility through rationally chosen courses of action did not conflict with the good of their communities because their desires were moderate and their ambitions could be realized within the frame of cooperative choices and actions.

The traditional morality expounded by Herodotus' Solon, based on full social information and limited horizons of desire, contrasts sharply with the moral universe of the ambitious eastern monarch. Croesus' utility function is centered on displaying luxury goods and unlimited accumulation of imperial possessions. Although his scope of action is much greater than that of Solon's happy men, Croesus' ambitions are ill-aligned with his choices. Unlike Tellus, Cleobis, and Biton, Croesus cannot accurately foretell the likely consequences of his acts because his decisions are not framed by a comprehensible system of culturally defined incentives and sanctions. Croesus is not a candidate for Solon's happiest man, not only because he is still alive, but because his position as an autocratic ruler makes it difficult for Croesus to choose well in his own or his country's interest (see further, Forsdyke, chapter 15).

Herodotus' fifth century Athenian readers inhabited neither Croesus' world nor that of Tellus. They might look back upon "Tellus' world" with nostalgia, but their lives were lived in different circumstances and according to different plans: As a result of structural changes in fifth century Athenian society, the traditional Greek under-standing of individual utility came under pressure. The transformation of Athens, from "the world of Tellus" to "the world of Themistocles, Pericles, and Alcibiades" – from a relatively simple and directly comprehensible traditional society in which rationally self-interested and socially cooperative choice-making were aligned, to a complex and even "modern" society accessible only by organized knowledge – was a product of the emergence of Athenian democracy, the growth of an Athenian empire, and the burgeoning of an Athens-centered exchange economy. Among the questions Herodotus and his audience confronted was how the "modern" Athenian public came to be reconstituted, such that it was capable of acting as a collectivity in the face

of the substantially increased potential for rational choices to diverge from cooperative choices. One answer was provided by contrasting the behavior of the Athenian
demos with that of Croesus.[5]

A monarch can make his decisions and act upon them without directly confronting
public action problems. Yet a monarch faces difficulties in gaining the right information for effective decision-making. Lacking Tellus' inductive knowledge of a stable
social system to frame his choices, Croesus required *external* sources of information,
both to gain more wealth and to confirm the value of his current holdings: ergo his
conversation with Solon and his consultation of the Delphic oracle. Upon being told
by the oracle that if he were to attack his eastern rival, a great empire would be
overthrown, Croesus invaded Persian-held territory and his army was crushed in a
Persian counterattack. Croesus' failure shows that monarchical decision-making,
while avoiding the costs associated with public action, may not yield competitive
advantage in the absence of the right sort of knowledge. Croesus lost his kingdom
because he confused oracular *information*, which could be bought, with *knowledge* of
how best to act, which was not a readily purchased commodity. In his intertwined
stories of Croesus, Solon, and Delphi, Herodotus' connects expected utility and
social choice-making with knowledge-seeking. Taken together, these stories expose
the gap between gaining information and acting appropriately, based on knowledge:
The point is that information gained outside a social context like that of "Tellus'
world," outside a context of full social information and inductive knowledge,
becomes valuable only if it is properly aggregated and analyzed. The question,
then, is how the Athenian public could aggregate information and analyze it once
the Athenians had left Tellus' world behind.

Among the major themes of Herodotus' sprawling history is Athens' emergence as
a power substantial enough to tip the balance in the Greeks' favor in the Greco-
Persian wars of 490–78 BC. In seeking to explain Athenian success, Herodotus links a
sudden growth in national military capacity with the birth of democracy by emphasizing the value of *isēgoria*: equality in respect to public speech (5.78: quoted by
Forsdyke, chapter 15). In explaining why the Greeks won, Herodotus pointedly
emphasizes Athens' role (Hdt. 7.139). Herodotus argues that the key moment for
the Greek war effort came when the Athenians decided not to abandon their homeland and flee from Greece, even though confronted by apparently dire oracles from
Delphi. The Athenians had an extraordinarily large navy that had been built, as
Herodotus explains (7.144.1–2), through a cooperative and forward-looking public
decision to treat silver revenues as a common pool resource, rather than choosing per
capita distribution. The Athenians might have chosen abandoning Greece over staying to fight. Had they done so, in Herodotus' view, the Persians would have won.
The Athenian decision-making process leading to Salamis therefore becomes the
linchpin in the Greek victory in the Persian Wars – and equally decisive in establishing
Athens' dominant place in the postwar world. In his account of Athenian decision-
making before Salamis, Herodotus shows his readers how the internally diverse
Athenian demos acted as a public, by employing *isēgoria* in choosing, rationally and
cooperatively, to fight the Persians at sea. At the heart of the process is an institutionalized capacity to aggregate and to analyze useful knowledge.

In Herodotus' narrative (7.140–4) the Athenians, like Croesus, first sought oracular information. But rather than simply acting on that information, they gathered
in a deliberative decision-making assembly to decide what to do about it. Each citizen
at that open assembly possessed certain social and technical information; the public
constituted by the assembly potentially had access to a great deal of information that
would otherwise be widely dispersed. The process of deliberating about the meaning
of oracular information was open; multiple opinions (*gnōmai pollai*) were offered.
Elders and experts in oracle interpretation were consulted, but their interpretation
did not adequately account for what many others in the assembly knew and so failed
to carry the day. Eventually, Themistocles offered a policy that aligned oracular
information with what many individual assemblymen knew about emergent Athenian
naval capacity. Herodotus' account of Athenian decision-making at this all-important
juncture ignores the moment of voting. Instead, it directs our attention to the value
of social knowledge: the Athenian's common conviction that the fate of the community could be entrusted to the thousands of men who would row the recently
constructed warships. The inherently costly process of publicly deliberating had
the effect of reinforcing the Athenians sense of themselves as a public. It helped to
better align diverse individual interests with a high-risk, high-payoff public choice by
aggregating and analyzing both the technical and the social knowledge necessary to
make a decision that proved to be a good one. Herodotus knew that a democratic
public would not *always* make decisions better than those made by an individual
(5.97.2–3), but his narrative helped his readers to grasp how democratic decision-
making could be correlated with the polis' success.

Thucydides on Innovation and Learning

Thucydides was deeply concerned with public action and especially with the problem
of the free rider, that is, the defector who rationally seeks to share in the benefits
of others' social cooperation without assuming any of the costs. Thucydides saw
that free riding was likely in a large and prosperous democracy: By expanding the
range of choices available to free citizens, and by eliminating social sanctions typical
of intimate and traditional Greek communities, Athenian-style democracy also
expanded free riders' opportunities. The relationship between political regime and
the organization of useful knowledge is, for Thucydides, integrally related to the
problem of collective political action. Thucydides shows his readers how Athens'
distinctive knowledge regime helped it do well in competition with rivals. If Herodotus' account focuses our attention on public formation and knowledge aggregation,
Thucydides' analysis suggests that outstanding democratic performance was due to
conjoining productive technical innovations with a sustained capacity for reaping
benefits associated with social learning. If innovation and learning were brought
into balance, the returns to social cooperation would more than make up for losses
to free riders – especially if democratic culture identified and sanctioned free riding
and if democratic institutions prevented known free riders from taking an undeserved

share of social goods. The key problem, as he also shows, is that balancing innovation and learning is difficult.

In his assessment of Pericles at 2.65, Thucydides offers a retrospective of the Peloponnesian War and emphasizes the greatness of Athenian resources on the eve of the war. Thucydides is at pains to show that Athens could have won: Pericles was rightly confident that Athens could prevail by avoiding foolish strategic errors, given Athens' superiority in human and material resources – resources that Thucydides shows to be the product of reaping the benefits of internal social cooperation, and reinvesting them in an empire that enriched each individual Athenian (to the extent that he cooperated with his fellows) and the Athenian state. The empire was sustained by the rational preference of weaker states for a hegemonic state that would protect them (in its own interest) from pirates and other powerful states (1.7–8). These points are reinforced in Pericles' two assembly speeches in Thucydides' text (1.40–4, 2.60–4), which focus on the correlation between Athenian resources and social cohesion: on the key importance of remaining a public rather than devolving into interest subgroups concerned only with strategic bargaining. Much of Thucydides' history recounts how Athens' extraordinary resources were subsequently squandered by inferior post-Periclean leaders, who proved incapable of managing a willful demos. That failure of leadership was exacerbated, he suggests, first because the high level of rational social cooperation that had characterized Athens in the expansive prewar years was not fully sustained under the pressure of war, and second because Athens' opponents adopted Athenian habits of innovation and social learning.[6]

In Thucydides' history, political culture and institutions provide the keys to explaining rationally cooperative social behavior. In the funeral oration (2.35–46) Pericles asserts that Athens is characterized by a culture of open access and describes Athens' participatory decision-making process. His argument bears directly on the integration of rational choices with useful knowledge: Rather than depending on a homogenizing Spartan-style ideology of mandatory sameness, Athenians are diverse in their interests and capacities and free to make choices accordingly. Unlike the secretive, discipline-obsessed Spartans, Athenians enjoy an equal opportunity to learn from all those public sources that render the city an "openly shared common possession" (2.39.1), as well as an equal opportunity to share the fruits of cooperation. Pericles celebrates the fact that there is no standard Athenian civic curriculum nor specialized institutions for teaching courage; free citizens freely choose to fight when necessary as a result of living in a free city. There are no preestablished criteria for assuming the role of public innovator; anyone might be capable of demonstrating excellence in some domain – by possessing political skills and sharing what he knows, each citizen could benefit himself and his society.

The burden of Pericles' speech is that democratic Athens is distinctively merito-cratic, distinctively free and open, and therefore distinctively great. Pericles describes Athens as a community of responsibly self-interested individuals. He asserts that politically relevant knowledge is indeed widespread among Athenian citizens – even among those who focus primarily upon their own affairs. He explains the role of mutual instruction and deliberative rhetoric in democratic decision-making. Pericles' Athenians recognize that only some people will actually serve as public speakers. But *all* citizens are expected to participate in making decisions as responsive members of the judging audience of voters. This means that voters are not passive recipients of public speakers' rhetorical performances; rather they are active judges in their own and the public interest, and fully capable of dismissing incompetents. Pericles acknowledges the possibility that some may seek to free ride by sharing in the public goods produced by the political activity of others: Those who do *not* engage in the give and take of mutual instruction, those concerned only with their private ends, are not just "apolitical" but "useless": contemptible and deserving of being sanctioned as such (2.40).[7]

According to Thucydides' Pericles, it is a conjunction of a unique form of government with a unique public culture that fosters the integration of public and private interests. This in turn facilitates a unique Athenian capacity to conjoin bold and decisive action with thoughtful public deliberations. Deliberation over policy becomes a public process of teaching and learning by accessing openly available information and judging reasoned arguments. Thucydides' Pericles describes the democratic collectivity as a public of choice-making individuals, each freely striving to improve his personal position. Pericles overtly contrasts this Athenian "public action based" understanding of the cooperative group that emerges from an equilibrium among the rational individual choices made by free agents, with the Spartans' compulsory approach to community and hostility to any expression of individual difference. Pericles' funeral speech culminates in his vision of Athens as an education to its own citizen and as a model that other states might fruitfully seek to emulate. Exactly how this emulation will manage to coexist with sustained Athenian uniqueness, he does not say; Thucydides' subsequent narrative shows it will be a formidable task under the ever-changing conditions of total war.

Plato on Rational Choice in the Ideal State

While Plato scorned the sources of Athenian wealth (*Grg.* 517a–19b), he readily admitted the value of material flourishing to choice-making individuals. Plato's *Republic* shows that he was also well aware of the close association of material flourishing with a community's capacity to reap the social benefits of cooperation. The project of the *Republic* is the design of an ideal city by Socrates and his interlocutors. They seek to understand the role of justice in the individual soul and the community. The project begins with Socrates' claim that organized communities originally emerged *because* individuals rationally desired to gain for themselves the material benefits of cooperation: Every person needs many things and no one is self-sufficiently capable of providing those things for himself. People thus require "partners and helpers" if they are to live truly human lives, and they "share things with one another, giving and taking, ... *because each believes that this is better for himself*" (369b–c, emphasis added). To be effective, this sharing must be systematic, and thus it requires the institutions of marketplace, currency, and retail trade (371c–d). With these premises established, and the institutions of rational exchange in mind, Socrates sketches a small interdependent community, a modest "first polis." Because the desires of the inhabitants are limited to the basics of reproduction, nourishment, and shelter, they need no elaborate systems of wealth-getting. Nor need they provide for the organized defense of their community, since their simple possessions are insufficient to attract the rapacious attention of outsiders. The level of social cooperation demanded is minimal; few incentives or sanctions are called for, so institutions can remain vestigial.

This first polis is praised by Socrates as healthy, but Glaucon berates it as fit only for pigs and demands a community provided with delectable food and real furniture (372a–d). After the first polis is abandoned, the ideal state that is the subject of the thought experiment of the *Republic* is presumed to be composed of individuals with Glaucon's more expansive conception of individual utility: The expansion of the desires of the citizens to include luxury goods leads inexorably to an expanded institutional infrastructure to support and to defend them. As the polis grows in complexity, it must also occupy an expanded physical territory and gains a larger and more diverse population (372e–373d). The expansion of the imagined ideal polis sharpens the issue of public action. Socrates' interlocutors in the *Republic* had previously agreed upon the "Unique Aptitude Doctrine" – this fundamental principle asserts that because true expertise can only be developed in a single realm of endeavor, each individual must engage in only a single occupation.[8] Because the polis contains desirable luxury goods, it will excite the cupidity of outsiders and must be able to defend its members and their property from attack. The farmers, craftsmen, and traders who are the polis' first members are forbidden by the Unique Aptitude Doctrine from serving as warriors. The ideal state's population must therefore include a specialized military class, the Guardians (373e–374e).

What will prevent these fierce-spirited specialists in violence, with their internal monopoly of organized force, from acting violently toward one another, thus catapulting the polis into civil war, and from cooperating with one another in forcibly seizing the goods of the unarmed producing classes, thus institutionalizing piracy (375b–c, 416a–c)? Absent the right sanctions and incentives, Plato assumes that the members of the military class will choose, like Homer's Agamemnon or the possessor of the famous invisibility-producing "ring of Gyges" (359c–360d), to maximize their own utility by taking the goods of others. There is no "human nature based" altruism (inherent concern for others' interests) built into the foundation of Plato's ideal state; it faces the incentive problems confronted by every complex society.

The ultimate goal of the dialogue is to demonstrate the utility of justice as an end in itself, that is, that actually being just (which includes not seizing the goods of others even if there is no chance of being caught) is more beneficial to the individual (i.e. maximizes his *true* utility) than is acting unjustly (by maximizing *apparent* utility) while appearing to be just. Yet the long dialogue also shows that genuinely grasping the true utility of justice is a difficult undertaking – perhaps achievable only by a very few specially talented individuals who have completed a long and rigorous philosophical education. Given Plato's theory of knowledge, it is not open for him to resort to the democratic forms of knowledge aggregation and innovation discussed by Herodotus and Thucydides. Plato's solution is to resort to the sort of strong ideology that Thucydides' Pericles had proudly rejected and to a highly specialized form of monarchy that elides the problem exposed by Croesus' analytic failure and consequent incapacity to fulfill his wants.

The problem is that the unarmed members of Callipolis own private property, but they will have no incentive to develop that property in economically productive ways if it is subject to arbitrary seizure by the Guardians. Plato recognized that, in the absence of secure property rights on the part of the unmilitarized classes, the society will not produce substantial returns to social cooperation and will fail. That recognition demands specialized institutions: an elaborate system of education for the Guardians, and ideological indoctrination for all citizens. The Guardians are trained from childhood to treat productive insiders as friends, rapacious outsiders as enemies. Each Guardian's acquisitive tendencies and Tellus-like concern with posterity are, moreover, finessed by communal ownership of property, including wives and children. Specialized education and communal property in turn provide the springboard for developing the conjoined moral and metaphysical argument of the dialogue. Solving the public action problems that necessarily arise with the abandonment of the modest "first polis" eventually pays out in the theory of Forms, and the rule of philosopher-kings who have apprehended the Form of the Good. Thinking about rational choice and public action segues naturally to Plato's highly distinctive conjunction of politics, metaphysics, and epistemology.

Aristotle's Rational Political Animals

Like Plato, Aristotle was concerned with the emergence of communities, the challenge of cooperation, and the tendency of communities to devolve into mistrustful factions each strategically seeking its own partisan advantage. Aristotle's *Politics* book 1 explains the emergence of the polis as a natural phenomenon (see further, Depew, this volume, chapter 26). In moving from the choice-making individual to the complex political community, Aristotle describes a series of developmental steps: First is the family as a natural unit for biological reproduction: the baseline Tellus-like human concern for posterity makes the family a rational as well as natural unit. Next comes the village, as families choose to join forces in order to gain two basic goods: better security against hostile natural forces and the conditions of justice. By conditions of justice, Aristotle means the benefits of social cooperation: Aristotle's two primary definitions of justice in the *Politics* are "acting in the common interest" and "acting fairly in respect to the distribution of goods." Yet, like the simple "first polis" in Plato's *Republic*, the Aristotelian village proves unable to secure for its residents material goods adequate to assure their autarkic existence as an independent community. The final developmental stage is the polis, which conjoins villages into a political whole. Aristotle's natural polis represents balances of extremes of scale: It is the smallest community capable of gaining autarky and the largest community capable of maintaining an adequate level of mutual moral knowledge among its citizens.

These considerations lead directly to Aristotle's famous claim that humans are political animals. As David Depew's chapter demonstrates, the distinctive feature of Aristotle's argument is its naturalism: Humans are, for Aristotle, characterized by a natural tendency to live in groups. Moreover, humans are among the "political" subset of group-dwelling animals – that is to say creatures that, by their nature, are prone to work cooperatively toward common ends. This active work for the good of the whole is in contrast to the passive advantages attributable to baseline coordination (e.g. better chances of noticing the presence of predators) experienced by apolitical herd animals, like schooling fish. Aristotle recognizes that humans are not the only animals whose sociability leads them to act cooperatively in seeking common ends, but as group members, humans act somewhat differently from other political animals (such as bees), inter alia because humans can identify individual as well as collective interests. Humans are, according to Aristotle, more political than bees, indeed "the most political" of animals (*Pol.* 1253a). If we were to take "being political" to mean simply "working cooperatively for the good of the whole," and thus "most political" as "most inherently cooperative," we would have to suppose, counterfactually, that Aristotle's political theory broke radically with earlier Greek writers who, as we have seen, accepted individuals as rationally self-interested and were therefore concerned with incentive problems and public action. In fact, "being most political" means, for Aristotle, something quite different from "being most cooperative."

Aristotle associates the hypertrophy of human "political nature" directly with our linguistic ability: Being "most political" is correlated with our distinctively human capacity to communicate effectively with one another about what is advantageous and harmful, right and wrong, good and evil. Humans are unique among the "political animals" in that we use speech to communicate complex information and seek our ends. Speech furthers the potential for high returns to cooperation through exchange of information regarding what is jointly or severally advantageous. Moreover, by enabling us to deliberate about justice, it potentially furthers the ultimate human end of moral flourishing under conditions of justice. Yet Aristotle knew that speech could also be used deceptively, to further individual ends that were contrary to common ends, as he demonstrates repeatedly in his *Rhetoric*. By describing humans as especially political and capable of cooperation, Aristotle was not seeking to paper over problems of public action.

In his discussion of what makes humans the most political of animals, Aristotle suggests that communication about advantage, relevant to joint and several material flourishing, cannot be separated from moral considerations relevant to justice. The arguments developed in Aristotle's *Politics* seek to demonstrate that the genuinely flourishing human community will be one that is strong in a material sense *and* moral: well supplied with the practical means to survival *and* with the conditions of justice. The flip side of this assumption is, however, that every human community contains the seeds of its own potential failure. Aristotle's humans are "the most political" of animals not because they invariably act most justly and thus cooperatively in sharing knowledge but because they have the greatest range of possible choices. They may choose to use speech strategically, to advance plans that are unjust: against the common interest or unfair in respect to distribution. The potential for strategic manipulation is built into the base of Aristotle's conception of human beings as especially political animals. Much of the *Politics* (notably book 5) is devoted to analyzing how things go wrong in polis communities. Aristotle proposes institutional incentives and sanctions that might counteract the tendency of individuals and subgroups to act in their own selfish advantage in ways that lowered returns to social cooperation and thereby undermined the moral end of living the best possible life: *mutatis mutandis*, Aristotle's concerns map those of Herodotus' Solon in the story of Tellus.

According to the logic of Aristotle's argument in the *Politics*, all "complete humans" (i.e. adult males who are not slaves by nature: see again, Depew, chapter 26) are "political animals" possessing an innate impulse (1253a30: *phusei ... hē hormē*) to form a community, in order to achieve the material and moral ends that can only be realized via political communication. In terms of governance, this means that each citizen should not only be willing to, but should want to participate in governance. The proper form of this participation is "ruling over others and being ruled by them, in turn." In Aristotle's theory all adult males are, in the first instance, left in the picture as participants in the work of politics, work that is predicated, as we have seen, on inherent capacity and the material value of mutual instruction: Human nature includes an innate predisposition to deliberate with one another on how best to achieve ends. That disposition is, as Aristotle makes clear in his treatment of civil conflict arising from disenfranchisement of free natives (in tyrannies and narrow oligarchies), grounded in baseline assumptions about utility: For Aristotle, complete humans naturally take political participation, in the sense of "association in decision," as an intrinsic part of their utility.[9]

In order to achieve (or even pursue) *eudaimonia*, people require an adequacy of both material and political goods. Different people may value the political good of association in decision differently, but those with "healthy souls" will assign deliberation a relatively high value.[10] Justice, as fair distribution, requires that participation rights, as well as material goods, be fairly distributed. Yet there are many forms of participatory turn-taking. Aristotle has no need of the implausible notions that everyone should take a turn at every political role or that all need to be associated in every decision. Aristotle's conception of human nature allows for a wide range of individual human characters and their associated behaviors (detailed in *Nicomachean Ethics* and *Rhetoric*, and see Ludwig, this volume, chapter 19). In any regime, some ambitious individuals will seek positions of leadership. Others will require only that leaders gain their positions legitimately, consult with others appropriately before making decisions, announce decisions publicly, and remain appropriately accountable. The scope of participation is broad, but given the prominence of political activity in Aristotelian utility, not infinitely so.

Among the notable aspects of Aristotle's rational naturalism is the expansiveness of the body of citizens it implies. Unlike quotidian Greek aristocratic assumptions about intrinsic human worth, or Callipolis' foundational "noble lie," Aristotle's initial description of human capacity and motivation offers no intrinsic grounds for excluding any "complete human" from ruling in his turn – indeed exclusions come at a high cost, since they necessarily reduce the utility of those excluded and lead to concerted efforts to change the regime in the direction of inclusiveness. Aristotle's "natural polis" is congruent with (although certainly not identical to) Thucydides' Pericles' vision of democratic Athens as a society whose success emerges from an equality of participatory opportunity. Aristotle is, however, far from a Periclean democrat: as Depew shows, the "polis of our prayers" adds special features, to ensure that the native adult male population (the demos) is also a leisured elite.

By building an inherent and rational desire for association in decision into baseline human utility, Aristotle diverged not only from his successors: the early modern social contract theorists – but also from his predecessors: earlier Greek political theorists. Aristotle's naturalism enabled rational choice-making by utility-maximizing individuals to be a *motor for cooperative political action*, as well as (via free riding) *a threat to cooperation*. I have argued elsewhere that one implication of Aristotle's argument about political animals (although he never states it in these terms) is that deliberative, participatory democracy emerges as the best form of governance for the human community. If this argument is right, Aristotle unexpectedly provides a perfectionist explanation for democratic flourishing: Democracy leverages our innate human capacities by enabling each of us to do certain things that we naturally want to do. But unlike overoptimistic modern communitarians, Aristotle recognized that in the real world, aligning rational self-interest with natural sociability required considerable institutional machinery. As a result, the middle books of the *Politics* are devoted to complex incentive schemes meant to give people good reasons for choosing to act in cooperative ways that were in fact in their own deepest interests.[11]

FURTHER READING

Studying the relationship between the choices made by rational agents in political regimes (especially democracy) and the organization of useful knowledge is a relatively recent development within the fields of social epistemology and political science. This chapter is a condensation of a book in progress on the subject of how Greek writers approached the question. See, meanwhile, Ober 2008.

The emerging field of social epistemology explores the relationship between forms of knowledge, judgment, and social contexts, without resorting to the strong postmodern conclusion that knowledge is simply a function of social relations. Fundamental work in the area includes Searle 1995 and Goldman 1999. For an introduction to rational choice theory as it is employed by political scientists, see Elster 1986, updated in Elster 2007; the field is surveyed in detail in Mueller 2003. For uses of choice theory to explain aspects of ancient Greek democracy, see, for example, Schwartzberg 2007 and Kaiser 2007.

Choice theorists are often pessimistic about the potential of participatory democracy. Hardin 2002 is a succinct statement of the problems. Mackie 2003 has, however, argued that democracies operating in the real world are less vulnerable to public choice than choice theorists have claimed. The problems associated with preference aggregation are in any event less pressing when we reconceive democracy as a method of aggregating, coordinating and codifying useful knowledge. J. S. Mill in the mid-nineteenth century and John Dewey in the mid-twentieth century helped to define the relationship between democracy and knowledge. Urbinati 2002 demonstrates that Mill turned to Athenian practice when developing his theory of democracy as a form of active civic education that would, over time, increase the "intelligence" of society. E. Anderson 2006 develops Dewey's concept of democratic experimentalism with reference to F. A. Hayek's mid-twentieth century work on the social uses of knowledge.

NOTES

1 Survey of rational choice and public action problems: Mueller 2003.
2 Collective action: Olson 1965; R. Hardin 1982. Precommitment: Elster 1979, 2000. Commons tragedy: G. Hardin 1968. Polis politics as share-holding: Ostwald 1996. Mackie 2003 argues that democracies are less vulnerable to strategic manipulation than choice theorists have claimed.
3 Explaining the outstanding performance of democratic Athens, in the face of the high costs of democratic decision-making, is the burden of Ober 2008. Greek political thought as a response to democratic success: Ober 1998.
4 On the cultural context of the story (Solon in Lydia) and its relevance for how Herodotus' original readers might have taken it, see Kurke 1999. On the Eleusinian context of Tellus' burial and the contrast with fifth-century Athenian practice: L'Homme-Wéry 1999, 114–18. I owe much to B. King 1997, a thoughtful exploration of how the Tellus narrative defines Herodotus' ethical thought.
5 "Modernity" of classical Athens: Ober 2006.
6 See, further, Ober 1998: ch. 2; Kallet 2001.
7 Cf. Manville 1997; Brennan and Pettit 204.
8 Unique Aptitude Doctrine: *Resp.* 369e–370c; 374a–e; with Reeve 1988: 172–7.
9 Civil conflicts: Ober 2000; "association in decision": Ober 2007.
10 Aristotle on wealth-getting: Meikle 1995, with literature cited.
11 See further Ober 2005a.

CHAPTER 6

Imperial Ideologies, Citizenship Myths, and Legal Disputes in Classical Athens and Republican Rome

Craige B. Champion

Current events make seemingly overworked questions about the nature of empire and citizenship once again relevant. A tenuous American global hegemony resulting from the demise of the Soviet Union, terrorist attacks on the World Trade Center, an American military involvement in Iraq, and massive population movements throughout the world all demand that historians and political scientists redirect their scholarly energies toward these topics. Some neoconservative political theorists have written about America's current global position, arguing that unilateral action and preemptive war in national interests have ample precedents in American history (Gaddis 2004), debating whether the United States is, or should become, a world empire of unparalleled magnitude (Mead 2004; Mandelbaum 2005: 1–30, 75–8, 161–2), and in one case even maintaining that the basic international problem today is America's failure to admit to and shoulder its imperial responsibilities (Ferguson 2004; see Harvey 2003 for another view). In terms of citizenship, some have argued for open borders and global citizen-workers (Hardt and Negri 2004). Others have warned that the influx of *Gastarbeiter* and illegal laborers throughout the European Union and United States – fostered by liberal immigration/naturalization policies – poses a grave threat to national identities and national cohesion (for America, see Huntington 2004, 1996; cf. D. Miller 1999: 119–54 for a more balanced and temperate view, emphasizing integration rather than assimilation). Such concerns over demographic shifts and requirements for citizenship status have been recurrent in the postcolonial world since the dissolution of formal empires.

Studying the ways in which ancient Greeks and Romans addressed these issues may help us to understand them in our own time, since these ancient civilizations have

A Companion to Greek and Roman Political Thought, First Edition. Edited by Ryan K. Balot.
© 2013 Blackwell Publishing Ltd. Published 2013 by Blackwell Publishing Ltd.

profoundly influenced western conceptions of empire and citizenship. After all, even the words for these ideas originated in the classical world: "imperialism" is formed from the Latin *imperium*, while "citizen" is derived from the Latin *civis*. Unfortunately, generalizations about the nature of empire and citizenship derived from classical antiquity invite anachronistic distortions when applied to the present – however, we can learn as much from differences as from similarities between ancient Greece and Rome and today's societies.

With due regard to historical specificities, this chapter argues that uncovering attitudes toward citizenship is crucial to understanding imperial development, both in ancient Greece and Rome and, *mutatis mutandis*, in today's world. Myths of state formation and citizenship give access to these attitudes and reflect imperial practices; legal disputes can show how the deployment of myth reveals political ideology operating in everyday life. For these reasons, the following concentrates on interrelationships between imperial ideologies, citizenship myths, and legal disputes in classical Athens and republican Rome.

Before proceeding further, I must explain my rather casual use of the word "myth" in what follows. "Myth" defies easy definition, though many of course have made the attempt to pin it down (for example, see Kirk 1970 on Greek myth). Some scholars make distinctions between "myth" (an entirely fictitious, frequently etiological tale), "legend" (a tale with some putative basis in historical events), and "folktale" (a common, usually orally transmitted traditional story, without reference to any specific ritual practice). These kinds of differences are important primarily in understanding the creation of a traditional tale. This is not my concern – I am interested in how traditional stories function in particular historical configurations. As Walter Burkert has noted, "to understand myth ... knowledge of historical levels is required. There are at least two levels, the more general tale and the more specific application; both are subject to the forces of history" (1979: 28). My approach therefore concerns the teller rather than the tale; representations of traditional stories in their historical, ideological, and political contexts rather than their origins (cf. collected essays in Tully 1988). Consequently, I use the words "myth," "stories," and "legend" interchangeably.

While my subject of study allows me to use the word "myth" rather loosely, the conceptions of "imperialism" and "citizenship" are themselves another matter. These terms are of crucial importance for the purposes of this essay, and they therefore require as precise articulation as possible. As analytical terms, both "imperialism" and "citizenship" are highly problematic and nearly intractable, since their meanings have been subject to seemingly endless reformulations. The section on "Problematic Analytical Terms" deals with this difficulty and provides working definitions for "imperialism" and "citizenship." With that definitional ground having been cleared, the designation "imperial citizen" can serve as a concise label for the Athenian or Roman who had the political power to have some direct influence on the administration of empire.

The following section considers Athenian and Roman citizenship myths in relation to historical developments of their imperialisms. Both states used mythologies in legitimating imperial rule: while a series of supernatural events marked out Rome as

caput imperii, or "head of empire," Athens devised mythological charters establishing it as the metropole of all Ionian Greeks. In contrast, Athenian and Roman
citizenship myths were strikingly divergent. Athenian citizenship stories presented
an exclusionary strain, revolving around the theme of autochthony; that is, the
conceit that Athenians had sprung from the very soil of Attica. Roman citizenship
legends, on the other hand, proudly proclaimed an expansive heterogeneity; an
inclusive world empire arising from humble, mongrel beginnings.

Citizenship myths found parallels with historical developments in Athens and
Rome. In Athens, state policy regarding the citizen franchise was relatively exclusive
and restrictive, while overall Roman policy was more inclusive and far-reaching. In
both cases, however, imperial citizenship was of premium value for those citizens
residing in the imperial capital, where they could fully enjoy the perquisites citizenship afforded. The stakes, in political, economic, social, legal, and cultural terms,
would have been high in lawsuits concerning a citizen's status. I shall argue that those
stakes involved substantive political powers in the administration of empire much
more in Athens than at Rome, where we should understand the advantages of
citizenship primarily in legal, social, and cultural terms (cf. Rhodes, this volume,
chapter 4).

After that, a section on "Citizenship Myths at Work in Athens and Rome" studies
two such cases, Ps-Demosthenes' *Against Neaira* and Cicero's *Pro Balbo*. These texts
reveal how both Athenian and Roman ideologies of citizenship reflected and helped
to maintain normative citizenship practices. The speeches are aligned with the broad
contours of both Athenian and Roman citizenship myths and actual Athenian and
Roman citizenship policies. In the case of Ps-Demosthenes, the thrust of the
argument is to challenge and deny rights to citizenship, while in the case of Cicero's
speech on behalf of Balbus, the rhetorical goal is to establish more open criteria for
citizenship rights. The speeches offer glimpses of intersections between myths of
"imperial citizenship" and realities of everyday, pragmatic politics.

Problematic Analytical Terms:
"Imperialism" and "Citizenship"

Imperialism is an overused term among historians and social scientists, having taken
on multiple meanings in modern usage. Familiar articulations become particularly
problematic in understanding ancient empires, since Greek and Latin words and
phrases used for one political community's domination of another, such as *archē,
dunasteia,* or *kratos* in the case of the Greek, and *arx omnium gentium, principium
imperii,* or *imperium sine finibus* in the case of the Roman, do not accurately map onto
modern conceptions of imperialism (Finley 1978; Lintott 1981; Richardson 1991).

The term imperialism today usually carries the force of moral condemnation, but
that has not always been the case. Some nineteenth century political commentators
understood imperialism in racist terms, as a moral imperative for the improvement of
the "inferior races," most famously expressed in Rudyard Kipling's poem of 1899

"The White Man's Burden." For a less renowned example, *The Spectator*, a British Liberal journal, stated in 1868 that imperialism "in its best sense" was "a binding duty to perform highly irksome or offensive tasks" (Koebner and Schmidt 1964: 28–9).

Others maintained that the term was strange and unfamiliar. In 1878 Henry Howard Molyneux Herbert, Fourth Earl of Carnarvon and the Conservative Prime Minister Disraeli's estranged Colonial Secretary, said, perhaps somewhat disingenuously, that it was a neologism to him, and as late as 1900 the senior A. E. Stevenson, Democratic candidate for vice-president, stated that imperialism was a "new word in American politics" (Koebner and Schmidt 1964: 95, 153–5, 241). As these examples indicate, imperialism's connotations have been many and varied. The term can therefore easily confuse more than it clarifies, inviting anachronistic interpretations of the ancient Mediterranean world (Champion and Eckstein 2004; cf. Raaflaub 1996a: 274–5).

Two of imperialism's most influential theorists, J. A. Hobson and V. I. Lenin, viewed it as a phenomenon of the nineteenth and twentieth centuries, fueled by the capitalist mode of production (cf. collected essays in Chilcote 2000). According to Hobson and Lenin, capitalism at its most highly developed stage demanded new territories for products and new fields for investment. Both men saw imperialism as an interaction between developed industrialized nation-states and their colonized peripheries, and they lamented the fact that governments of the western powers supported these pernicious and exploitative ventures.

Imperialism as defined by Hobson and Lenin cannot therefore be productively applied to the ancient world without radical modification. Ancient Mediterranean economies, after all, were overwhelmingly agrarian and precapitalist. By modern standards, there were few industrial products in need of distant markets and little available capital for investment.

Postmodernist theories of empire and imperialism are even less helpful than the classical theories of Hobson and Lenin. According to some recent formulations, empire and imperialism are transnational, postcolonial, immanent, globalized, and cybernetic phenomena. Empire is seen as an all-pervasive force, with no apparent center, whose tentacles, assisted by ever more powerful technologies, penetrate everywhere (e.g., Hardt and Negri 2000, 2004, with critical essays in Balakrishnan 2003 and in Passavant and Dean 2004). Such post-Foucauldian, neo-Marxist critiques make for fascinating meditation on the early twenty-first century predicament, but they are useless when applied to ancient Greece and Rome.

Another towering figure in the modern study of imperialism, the economist J. A. Schumpeter, formulated a definition of imperialism that is more applicable to classical antiquity. In sharp contrast to Hobson and Lenin, Schumpeter believed modern imperialism was an atavistic survival of aggressive, militarized social structures of preindustrial times, which capitalism and modernity would ultimately eradicate. In a celebrated phrase, he described imperialism as "the objectless disposition on the part of a state to unlimited forcible expansion" (Schumpeter 1951: 7).

Schumpeter's formulation is more promising for purposes of this essay than the ideas of Hobson and Lenin, insofar as it is compatible with the basic fact that polities of the ancient world were militaristic and aggressive (Hanson 1989; Rich and Shipley

1993; Hamilton and Krentz 1997; W. Harris 1979; Eckstein, this volume, chapter 16). But his definition remains vague; surely we need greater specificity in order to discuss ancient imperialism in any meaningful way. Moses Finley provided this with his six-point typology for characteristic, concrete forms of domination of imperial states over their subjects, which I will take as the definitional components of imperialism:

> (1) restriction on freedom of action in inter-state relations; (2) political, administrative and/or judicial interference in internal affairs; (3) compulsory military and/or naval service; (4) payment of tribute in some form, whether in the narrow sense of a regular lump sum or as a land tax or in some other way; (5) confiscation of land, with or without subsequent emigration of settlers from the imperial state; and (6) other forms of economic subordination or exploitation, ranging from control of the seas and Navigation Acts to compulsory delivery of goods at prices below the prevailing market price and the like. (Finley 1982b: 45; cf. Finley 1978: 6)

The reader is invited to consult general histories of ancient Greek and Roman civilization in order to find Athenian and Roman examples for each of Finley's six points, and to contemplate how useful these criteria may be for understanding the present, tasks beyond the scope of this essay. It will suffice here to say that according to Finley's criteria, both classical Athens and republican Rome qualify as empires.

Next let us turn our attention to the idea of citizenship. After several attempts, Aristotle ultimately settles for defining the citizen (*politēs*) as "he who enjoys the right of sharing in deliberative and judicial office" (*Pol.* 1275b19–20). On this definition, the *archē*, or office, comprises both specific magistracies with limited tenure and indeterminate offices, such as participation in political assemblies and jury courts, with no restrictions on tenure. On the basis of this passage, we might think of formal (officeholding) and informal (untenured, participatory) aspects of citizenship. But Aristotle also seems to recognize that even those who do not belong to either of these two groups (such as women, slaves, resident aliens, and children) are essential (*Pol.* 1277a5–12), in part because the household unit, or *oikos*, including its women, slaves, and children, is necessary as the basic building block of the state (Ober 1996: 161–87). Moreover, even noncitizens possessed some legal rights. In Athens, for example, noncitizen women, children, and even slaves had certain rights against *hybris*, or violent assault and outrage against their persons (see, for example, Dem. 21.46–8).

Following Aristotle's line of thought on the teleological progression from *oikos* to polis, we begin to get an idea of an even more informal criterion for citizenship. Accordingly, we might view Athenian and Roman citizenship in terms of what Manville (1994: 24) calls the "premodern and organic" paradigm. On such a view, citizenship recedes from the more or less formal political arena to the social realm; from the public to the private sphere. Pursuing this idea invites us to consider shadowy places between citizen and noncitizen status. We might even expand upon Moses Finley's idea that various political and social differentiations constituted a "spectrum of statuses" in ancient Greece and Rome (Finley 1982b, esp. chs 7–9).

Since my concern in this study is with interrelationships between citizenship and imperial development, I define citizenship minimally as the right to participate directly in political processes in formal political assemblies, the *ekklēsia* in Athens, and the comitial assemblies in republican Rome. These were the political arenas where citizens could, at least according to formal constitutional arrangements, have had influence in the exercise of the powers outlined in Finley's six-point typology of empire. In effect, of course, this delimitation means that our focus will be primarily upon adult male Athenians and Romans.

Imperial citizens resident in Athens and Rome certainly had some degree of ability to administer their empires, since their popular assemblies elected imperial magistrates, approved or rejected legislative proposals bearing upon imperial subjects, and ultimately controlled foreign policy. Scholars have long recognized this in studies of democratic Athens (e.g. Ober 1989), and in recent decades Fergus Millar (1984, 1986, 1989, 1998) has drawn attention to popular powers in the Roman Republic (but see Champion 1997; cf. Morstein-Marx 2004). Relationships between elites and masses and the locus of political power in classical Athens and republican Rome are likely to remain matters of intense scholarly debate, but constraints of space do not allow for further examination of these problems here. Clearly citizen status was highly desirable in both Athens and Rome, but my working hypothesis in what follows is that in Athens, though legal and cultural aspects were important, citizenship was primarily valued for its political dimension; whereas at Rome legal and cultural perquisites of citizenship were paramount. The following consideration of citizenship myths and legal disputes at Athens and Rome supports such a hypothesis.

Citizenship Myths and Historical Realities of Imperial Expansion

Athenians jealously guarded admission to citizen status. It is true that Aristotle relates that, at the time of his political reforms at Athens after the overthrow of the Pisistratid tyranny, Cleisthenes "enrolled in his tribes many resident aliens who had been foreigners or slaves" (*Pol.* 1275b35–7). But this passage may well reflect exaggerated accounts on the part of Cleisthenes' political enemies. Aristotle states that in the immediate aftermath of the fall of the Pisistratids, many of the common people whom the tyranny had supported were disenfranchised in a revision of the citizenship rolls at Athens (*Ath. Pol.* 13.5). Cleisthenes, therefore, may have simply restored citizenship rights to some of those who had been dispossessed (cf. Ober 1996: 32–52). In any event, at the height of Athenian imperial power in the mid-fifth century BCE, the Athenian statesman Pericles had a law passed restricting citizenship to those who were born of Athenian citizen parents (Arist. *Ath. Pol.* 26.4; Plut. *Per.* 37.3; Ael. *VH* 6.10; *Suda*, s.v. "*dēmopoiētos*"). Some five years after Pericles' law, the Athenians purged their citizen rolls, if we can trust a scholiast's note on Aristophanes *Wasps* 718 (Philoch. *FGrH* 328 F 119; cf. Plut. *Per.* 37.3–4).

By the time of Pericles' restrictive citizenship law in 451/50 BCE, Athens had built an extensive naval empire, and the city itself had become a cosmopolitan, imperial center of commerce and culture (Meiggs 1972: 273–90). Athenian ideological justification for empire largely rested on Athens' role in the Persian Wars (cf. Thuc.

5.89). In 477 BCE, Athens formed an alliance of Greek states, whose ostensible purpose was to continue the fight against the Persians. In the following decades the Persian threat evaporated and this alliance, which modern historians often call the "Delian League," became essentially an Athenian empire. Athenian cultural productions, most famously Aeschylus' *Persians* (produced in 472 BCE), celebrated the city as the savior of Greece from Persian subjection (cf. Hdt. 7.139), and invented the barbarian as the perennial, common enemy, which served to justify the Athenian empire's existence (see Pollitt 1972; E. Hall 1989; M. Miller 1997).

Along with Persian War heroics, Athenians also used myth in legitimating their empire. The Athenian mythological character Ion served as eponymous ancestor of all Ionian Greeks. According to its self-representation, Athens was the metropolis, or "mother city," of Ionia. With this view, Athens posed as the liberator of Ionian Greek states along the coast of Asia Minor, which had previously been subjected to the Persians (cf. Aesch. *Pers.* 584–97). The foundation of the "Delian League" took place in a ceremony pregnant with politico-cultural symbolism on the island of Delos, mythological birthplace of the god Apollo, Ion's father and protector of the Ionians (Arist. *Ath. Pol.* 23.5; Plut. *Arist.* 25.1). Even Thucydides (1.2.5–6), ever eager to debunk commonplace assumptions, confirms that Athens had provided a haven for refugees, some of whom ultimately would colonize Ionia, in the aftermath of the collapse of what modern scholars call the Bronze Age (cf. Hdt. 7.94; 8.44). Yet the tradition of an Ionian migration may simply represent an Athenian legitimizing fiction of inchoate Athenian imperialism around the time of the Persian Wars (Osborne 1996: 32–7).

Euripides' *Ion* (produced in 410 BCE) celebrates the city's imperial destiny and provides evidence for the myth of Athens as "mother city" of the Ionian Greeks. Near the play's end, Euripides has the goddess Athena proclaim its imperial future:

> When the appointed time comes children born of these shall come to dwell in the island cities of the Cyclades and the coastal cities of the mainland, which will give strength to my land. They shall dwell in the plains in two continents on either side of the dividing sea, Asia and Europe. They shall be called Ionians after this boy and win glory. (Eur. *Ion*, lines 1581–8, trans. Kovacs 1999, cf. 74, 1356)

This is cultural imperialism indeed, as in this passage Euripides modifies the earlier mythological tradition, going on to state that the Athenian Creusa, Ion's long-lost mother, and her husband, the foreign-born Xuthus, will produce two children, Dorus and Achaeus, who will establish cities in the Peloponnesus (cf. Bickermann 1952; Momigliano 1987: 9–23; J. Hall 1997, 2001; C. Jones 1999). The play also repeatedly invokes the myth of Athenian autochthony; that is, the notion that Athenians were "born from the earth," a pure and unadulterated people of Attica (see lines 29, 267, 543, 589–90, 737, 1000, 1057–60, 1466).

Certainly Euripides introduces a good deal of irony into his representation of the autochthony myth (Saxonhouse 1986), by stressing that Ion's stepfather, Xuthus, is an alien (lines 63, 290, 293), playing on etymological derivation of the name Ion from the Greek verb for coming and going (lines 661–3, 802, 830–1), and, through a series of misrecognitions, referring in turns to Ion (lines 673–5, 721–4) and Creusa (lines 514, 607, 654) as "foreigners." Euripides' well-known iconoclasm can account for these aspects of *Ion*. In the long run, he only strengthened a myth already embedded in Athenian culture (Loraux 2000). The popular stress on Athens as leader of Ionian Greeks seems to have been particularly salient during the Peloponnesian War (Alty 1982).

Plato's *Menexenus* mocks the state funeral eulogies given at Athens for those who fell in battle in service of the polis (Loraux 1986). The most famous example of these eulogies at Athens is of course Pericles' Funeral Oration, as represented by Thucydides (2.35–46). In this speech Pericles touched upon the autochthony theme, stating that "in this land of ours there have always been the same people living from generation to generation up till now" (Thuc. 2.36.1, trans. Warner 1971). In *Menexenus*, Plato carries the notion to absurd length:

> For there cohabit with us none of the type of Pelops, or Cadmus, or Aegyptus or Danaus, and numerous others of the kind, who are naturally barbarians though nominally Greeks; but our people are pure Greeks and not a barbarian blend; and so it happens that our city is imbued with a whole-hearted hatred of aliens. (245d, trans. Bury 2005; cf. 237b–c)

The ironic treatment of the Athenian autochthony myth in Euripides' *Ion* and its exaggeration in Plato's *Menexenus* notwithstanding, the notion that Athenians were "born of the earth" pervades much of Athenian literature. For example, it is represented in Aristophanes' *Wasps* (1071–8), and in Athenian orators: Lysias (*Funeral Oration*, 17), Hyperides (*Funeral Oration*, 7), and Demosthenes (*Funeral Oration*, 4; *On the Embassy*, 261). We also find the theme in Herodotus (7.161). The myth gave ideological support to Athens' restrictive and exclusionary citizenship practices. It hardly needs to be said that the notion of Athenian autochthony provided a mythological/ideological foundation for a gendered political discourse that subordinated citizen women in Athenian society (see Sissa, this volume, chapter 7).

In contrast, Romans prided themselves on their open citizenship policies. From the time of its foundation, Rome – at a crossroads of the Tiber river and in the agriculturally rich plain of Latium, with valuable salt marshes and iron deposits nearby – attracted would-be usurpers. Incessant conflict with Latins, Etruscans, Sabines, Aequi, Volsci, Hernici, Gauls, and Samnites characterized the city's early centuries. However, by roughly 300 BCE, Rome emerged triumphant, leading a military and political alliance nearly coextensive with peninsular Italy (Cornell 1995: 345–68). This system incorporated in varying degrees subjected peoples throughout Italy into an extended Roman state, with a range of political statuses, from allies (*socii*) to fully fledged Roman citizens, *cives optimo iure* – unparalleled among ancient Mediterranean states (Sherwin-White 1973).

As did Athens, Rome too devised mythological justifications for empire. According to Roman foundation myths, divine signs marked out the city's imperial destiny. Romulus himself foretold that Rome would become the imperial world capital (Liv. 1.16.6–8). Livy (1.55.1–6; cf. 5.54.7) relates that when King Tarquinius Superbus was building the temple to Jupiter Capitolinus, the god Terminus refused to have his shrine moved, indicating the permanence of Roman power. This was followed by another omen: builders discovered a human head, ordaining the spot as the future seat of a vast empire (cf. Dion. Hal. *Ant. Rom.* 4.61.2; Plut. *Cam.* 31.4; Flor. 1.7.9; [Aur. Vict.] *De vir. ill.* 8.4; Brunt 2004: 164–7 on divinely mandated Roman imperial might).

If Roman foundation legends found parallels with those of Athens as imperial charters, Roman citizenship myths differed markedly from Athenian notions of autochthony. They presented the city as a hybrid, multiethnic political community. In the first place, the legendary founders, Aeneas and Romulus, were wanderers and exiles. The senator Q. Fabius Pictor recorded (in Greek) Rome's earliest history (Frier 1999), apparently revealing a composite of Greek, native Italian, and Trojan influences on its foundation: Herakles, Lanoios, Aeneas, Ascanius, Romulus and Remus (*SEG* 26.1123, fr. III, col. A, lines 5–14). Livy (1.33.1–2; cf. 1.30.1–3, Alba Longa) preserved an ancient tradition that the legendary king Ancus Marcius transferred the entire population of Politorium to Rome, "adopting the plan of former kings, who had enlarged the state by making its enemies citizens." He stressed the inclusive, incorporative nature of the polity in the stories of the rape of the Sabine women (1.13.4–8; cf. Dion. Hal. *Ant. Rom.* 2.46.2–3; Plut. *Rom.* 19.7), a story already known to Fabius Pictor (*FGrH* 805 F-5), and the rise of Attus Clausus in the early Roman senate (2.16.4–6). The myth of the rape of the Sabine women, it must be said, along with the story of the rape of Lucretia (Liv. 1.57.6–58.12; cf. Ov. *Fast.* 2.720–58), authorizes the political subordination of women, much like the myth of Athenian autochthony: Roman women, even at their most heroic moments, ultimately display their virtue in the domestic sphere and must submit to the political authority of men. Tacitus later echoed the idea of Roman political (male) inclusiveness in his representation of the speech of the emperor Claudius, who endorsed admission of Gallic nobility to the Curia (*Ann.* 11.24; cf. *ILS* 212). Juxtaposition of passages from Livy and Sallust highlights this theme in Roman citizenship myths:

Aeneas, that he might win the goodwill of the Aborigines to confront such a formidable prospect of war, and that all might possess not only the same rights but the same name, called both peoples Latins; and from that time on the Aborigines were no less ready and faithful than the Trojans to King Aeneas. (Liv. 1.2.4–5, trans. Foster 2002)

The city of Rome, according to my understanding, was at the outset founded and inhabited by Trojans, who were wandering about in exile under the leadership of Aeneas and had no fixed abode; they were joined by the Aborigines, a rustic folk, without laws or government, free and unrestrained. After these two peoples, different in race, unlike in speech and mode of life, were united within the same walls, they were merged into one with incredible facility, so quickly did harmony change a heterogeneous and roving band into a commonwealth. (Sall. *Cat.* 6.1–3, trans. Rolfe 2005)

Next, so that his large city should not be empty, Romulus turned to a plan for increasing the population which had long been used by founders of cities, who gather about them an obscure and lowly multitude and pretend that the earth has raised up sons to them. In the place which is now enclosed, between the two groves as you go up the Capitoline hill,

he opened a sanctuary. A miscellaneous rabble, without distinction of bond or free, but
eager for a new start, fled to this place from the surrounding peoples. These constituted
the first advance in power towards that greatness at which Romulus aimed. (Liv. 1.8.5–7,
trans. Foster 2002, with slight modifications)

While Roman foundation narratives were clearly influenced by Greek *ktiseis*
legends, or legends of eponymous founders (Wiseman 1995: 43–62), it is nevertheless significant that mythological traditions – though sometimes acknowledging
autochthony themes, as in the case of Livy (1.8.5) – unabashedly announced the
city's heterogeneous, lowly peasant origins. As Nicholas Horsfall has observed, Rome
was "a society which preserved vigorously and unconcealed its peasant origins in
language, in proverbs, in riddles, in superstitions, in folk-medicine, in animal-fables"
(Bremmer and Horsfall 1987: 2). Legend even had it that Servius Tullius, penultimate king of Rome, was an outsider, since his mother – though admittedly of noble
lineage – had been an enslaved war-captive from Corniculum (Liv. 1.39.6; Thomsen
1980: 57–67).

Myths of Roman heterogeneous origins afforded a politico-cultural flexibility in
international relations, by which Romans could include or exclude non-Roman
peoples as immediate political circumstances required (Gruen 1992: 6–51; Dench
1995). Athenian autochthony myths, on the other hand, would seem to have been
inimical to such politico-cultural/diplomatic flexibility. What is most important for
the question of imperial citizenship is the fact that the polarized ideologies of
Athenian autochthony and Roman heterogeneity corresponded in general terms to
state policies regarding admission to imperial citizenship – exclusive and restrictive in
the case of Athens; relatively inclusive and incorporative in the case of Rome.

Citizenship Myths at Work in Athens and Rome

Athenian and Roman imperial citizens would have had to reside in or near the capital
in order to attend political assemblies and thereby influence imperial administration.
This was the case simply because neither Athens nor Rome developed the kinds of
representative political institutions familiar in modern times. If the Athenians were
serious about citizen self-government and citizen imperial administration, their
restrictive citizenship policies made sense. Apart from Athenian citizen colonies
abroad, or cleruchies, most Athenian citizens resided in Attica and therefore did
not face insurmountable spatial obstacles to political participation. Even in the case
of cleruchies, Athenian citizen-beneficiaries may have continued to reside in Attica
and acted as rentiers of their properties abroad (A. Jones 1957: 168–74; Brunt 1966;
Erxleben 1975; cf. Rhodes, this volume, chapter 4). Moreover, restrictive Athenian
citizenship laws kept immigrants from unduly swelling the citizen registers and overwhelming the sites of Athenian law courts and political and legislative assemblies.

Roman citizen colonies arose at a considerable distance from Rome as early as
the third century BCE, and in the second century these colonies were established

in Cisalpine Gaul and even outside of Italy itself. Liberal citizenship policies and enfranchised communities far from the capital indicate that, unlike Athens, Rome did not put a premium on substantive duties and powers of Roman citizens in the administration of the affairs of either the city or the empire. It would have been difficult for a nonelite Roman citizen with permanent residence in, let us say, Herdonia to come to Rome for political and legislative assemblies on any sort of regular basis. Generally speaking, admission to citizen status was much easier in Rome than at Athens, largely because Roman citizenship had more to do with legal status and cultural identity than active imperial citizenship. An upper limit on Roman citizen census figures and spatial proximity of Roman citizens to the imperial capital were not therefore issues of primary importance in Roman citizenship policy. In cases at law involving the question of citizenship, we should therefore expect to find imperial ideologies of relative restrictiveness at Athens and relative liberality at Rome.

I suggest that these conditions are reflected in two texts, Ps-Demosthenes' *Against Neaira* and Cicero's *Pro Balbo*, which reveal dominant ideologies of imperial citizenship at play in specific instances of pragmatic politics. The case of *Against Neaira* probably occurred sometime between 373 and 339 BCE. In this public lawsuit, the prosecutors Apollodorus and Theomnestus charged that an alien woman, Neaira, was living as lawful wife to Stephanus, an old personal and political enemy. Athenian law stipulated that if convicted Neaira should be sold into slavery, and that Stephanus should be fined 1,000 drachmae (§16). The prosecution maintained that Neaira was a former slave and prostitute (§49), and that Stephanus had pretended that her children were his own (§38). Moreover, Stephanus had given Neaira's two daughters in marriage to Athenian citizens. Stephanus therefore deceived the bridegrooms into believing that Neaira was herself an Athenian citizen woman. Neaira's legal status was of crucial importance, since according to Pericles' citizenship law, she must be an Athenian citizen woman in order for offspring from these marriages to become legitimate citizens. Perhaps most serious of all was the fact that one of the deceived husbands was Theogenes, the king-archon, whose wife was entrusted with important ritual duties on behalf of the state (§§72–3; cf. C. Patterson 1994; E. Cohen 2000).

Apollodorus, the principal prosecutor, was the son of a naturalized former slave, the wealthy banker Pasion (§2). He clearly was conscious that his own claims to citizenship could be questioned, as he asked his audience to overlook that he was prosecutor and that the supporters of the defendant were Athenian citizens (§115). Apollodorus stressed that Athenian citizenship was a precious gift bestowed only on those who had performed signal services for the Athenians.

> For the civic body of Athens, although it has supreme authority over all things in the state, and it is in its power to do whatsoever it pleases, yet regarded the gift of citizenship as so honorable and so sacred a thing that it enacted in its own restraint laws to which it must conform, when it wishes to create a citizen. (§§88–9, trans. A. Murray 2001)

Apollodorus went on to argue that those granted Athenian citizenship were ineligible for the archonship and were prohibited from holding any of the priesthoods. Their descendants were eligible for these privileges, but only under the condition that they were born from an Athenian woman in a legally recognized marriage (§92). The prosecutor next expounded upon the heroic services of the Plataeans on Athens' behalf, concluding with the observation that even in their case these strictures regarding the citizen franchise still applied (§§94–106).

In the course of his indictment, Apollodorus touched upon the theme of Athenian autochthony, which is in itself remarkable in light of the fact that Apollodorus was a second-generation Athenian whose father had once been a slave. Indeed, his brother-in-law Theomnestus felt compelled in his deposition to relay Apollodorus' past actions, in which he demonstrated his brother-in-law's patriotism and civic-mindedness, clearly in order to remove any doubts as to Apollodorus' right, as an Athenian citizen, to prosecute the case (§§2–5). In any event, Apollodorus recalled how Stephanus had maliciously and unjustly indicted a certain Xenocleides, who ultimately was stripped of his citizenship. He went on to add:

> And yet you do not count it a monstrous thing that this Stephanus has taken the right of free speech from those who are native-born citizens [*tous men phusei politas*] and are lawful members of our commonwealth, and in defiance of all the laws forces upon you as Athenians those who have no such right? (§28, trans. A. Murray 2001)

Later in his speech, Apollodorus noted that in ancient times, the era of Theseus and kingship at Athens, rulers were all-powerful on account of their being born of the earth (§74, *dia to autochthonas einai*), therefore employing the myth of Athenian autochthony to make his case. This reliance upon mythology once again stressed citizenship as a jealously guarded and exclusive privilege.

L. Cornelius Balbus was born around 100 BCE into an influential family of Spanish Gades, a city tied to Rome by treaty for more than a century (*civitas foederata*). Balbus performed conspicuous services for the Roman cause in the war against Sertorius, and was rewarded with a grant of Roman citizenship by Pompey. His Roman citizenship was ratified by the *lex Gellia Cornelia* of 72 BCE (Cic. *Balb.* 19). He later found favor with Caesar, serving as his subordinate officer in Further Spain (§63). After Balbus had taken up residence at Rome and acquired the Roman citizenship his former fellow citizens, the Gaditani, appointed him as their *patronus*, or guestfriend in Rome (§§41–3). He was clearly at the center of high Roman politics, having helped to broker the political alliance among Pompey, Caesar, and Crassus, which modern historians call the First Triumvirate (Cic. *Att.* 2.3.3).

In late summer or early autumn of 56 BCE, however, Balbus faced a challenge to his status as Roman citizen – as had the Greek poet Archias, whom Cicero defended some six years earlier. In the case of Archias, the case was an indirect political attack on the powerful Roman general and statesman L. Lucullus, Archias' patron. Likewise in the case of Balbus, the prosecution was undoubtedly driven by political enmity against Balbus' friends and supporters, Pompey and Caesar (cf. §§58–9, 65). As for the legal substance of the case, Balbus was prosecuted under the same law as Archias had been charged, the *lex Papia* of 64 BCE, which enabled the eviction of noncitizen residents from Rome.

In his defense of Balbus, Cicero followed the speeches of the defendant's supporters, Crassus and Pompey. He began with a lengthy introduction on the great achievements, sound character, and moral probity of Pompey, who had granted Balbus the Roman citizenship (§§1–17). Cicero next moved on to the defendant's own impeccable character, and then to a discussion of the ease and flexibility of Roman citizenship practices: ample precedents for citizenship grants to both individuals and communities, the ability of Roman citizens to change their citizenship by moving to other states, and the imperial logic of rewarding Roman citizenship to those allies who had imperiled themselves fighting on behalf of Rome's empire. The only restriction was that no one could be a citizen of Rome and another state at the same time (§28). Throughout this part of his oration, Cicero repeatedly stressed Rome's open citizenship policies:

> For we are aware that citizenship has been conferred upon many members of tributary states in Africa, Sicily, Sardinia, and the other provinces, and we know that enemies who have gone over to our commanders and rendered our state great services have been honored with the citizenship; and, lastly, we are aware that slaves, whose legal rights, fortune, and status are the lowest, are very often, for having deserved well of the state, publicly presented with freedom, that is, with citizenship. (§24, trans. Gardner 2005, with slight modification; cf. §41)

> For since from every state there is a road open to ours, and since a way is open to our citizens to other states, then indeed the more closely each state is bound to us by alliance, friendship, contract, agreement, treaty, the more closely I think it is associated with us by sharing our privileges, rewards, and citizenship. (§29, trans. Gardner 2005)

Cicero went on to emphasize the incorporative nature of Roman citizenship practices with examples from the earliest Republic (§§53, 55), and he reached back even further into mythical times and the foundation of Romulus.

> But what undoubtedly has done most to establish our Empire and to increase the renown of the Roman People, is that Romulus, that first founder of this city, taught us by the treaty which he made with the Sabines, that this state ought to be enlarged by the admission even of enemies as citizens. Through his authority and example our forefathers never ceased to grant and to bestow citizenship. And so, many members of Latin towns, the inhabitants of Tusculum and of Lanuvium, for instance, and from other stocks whole peoples, such as the Sabines, the Volscians and the Hernicians, were admitted to citizenship. (§31, trans. Gardner 2005)

The remainder of the speech consisted in discussion of the nature of the treaty between Gades and Rome, its irrelevance to the question of Balbus' Roman citizenship, the authority of Roman commanders to grant Roman citizenship and the many precedents for the practice, and the prosecution of Balbus as a political attack on Pompey and Caesar. Cicero drew upon the myth of Roman inclusive heterogeneity, throughout discussing Roman citizenship practices as open and incorporative. It is difficult to imagine an Athenian advocate employing a similar line of argument.

Conclusion

In this chapter I have approached Greek and Roman political thought obliquely through consideration of imperial ideologies, citizenship myths, and legal contestations over citizenship status in classical Athens and republican Rome. From a comparative perspective, in terms of both ideology and actual political practice, classical Athens has emerged as relatively restrictive and exclusionary with regard to the citizen franchise; republican Rome as inclusive and incorporative.

Exceptions are of course ready at hand. Athenians granted citizenship *en bloc* to both Plataeans and Samians for extraordinary services to their state (Osborne 1981–3: 1: 28, 33–7); Romans fought a civil war before granting citizenship to the Italians, and they periodically expelled undesirables from the city and revised their citizen rolls, as in the case of the *lex Papia* of 64 BCE (cf. Balsdon 1979). Moreover, while the legal speeches studied here employed arguments conforming to citizenship myths of unadulterated Athenian autochthony and hybrid Roman political inclusion, it is important to recognize that the speeches were produced in highly rhetorical cultures. We have to believe that in legal trials political and rhetorical needs of the moment could easily have modified or perhaps even subverted citizenship myths.

Against Neaira and *Pro Balbo* nevertheless illustrate persistent themes in Athenian and Roman ideologies, which both reflected and shaped citizenship practices in their respective cities. In Athens, to the best of our knowledge, Pericles' restrictive citizenship law remained in force throughout the classical period, except for a brief time near the end of the fifth century BCE (de Ste Croix 2004: 239–40). In stark contrast the Italian states of Fundi, Formiae, and Arpinum gained full Roman citizenship as early as 188 BCE (Liv. 38.36.7–8), and Caesar conferred citizenship upon all of Balbus' compatriots at Gades a little more than a decade after Cicero's speech (Liv. *Epit.* 110; Cass. Dio 41.24.1; Plin. *NH* 4.119). The extension of Roman citizenship accelerated under Caesar and Augustus (MacMullen 2000), culminating in a virtual blanket grant of Roman citizenship to all free inhabitants of the empire with the *constitutio Antoniniana* of 212 CE.

I opened this chapter with some reflections on current international relations and crises of citizen identities, suggesting that study of empire and citizenship in ancient Greece and Rome may provide useful insights into present-day concerns regarding those issues. The contrast of Athenian exclusivity and Roman inclusiveness could hardly be more salient than in the context of contemporary tensions between the splintering isolationism of renascent, substate nationalisms and xenophobic ethnic militias on the one hand, and on the other hand technological, demographic, financial, and entrepreneurial forces of integrative globalization.

Aspects of Athenian and Roman imperial citizenship discussed in this chapter hardly exhaust the valuable insights into contemporary issues that the study of classical antiquity might offer. For example, another relevant question, resonating with the predicament of the twenty-first century citizen and only briefly touched upon in this essay, concerns the impact of exclusive or inclusive citizenship policies upon citizens' actual capacities to participate meaningfully in political processes.

This is an important question, and it draws attention to a crucial difference between the classical city-state and the modern democratic nation-state. As we have seen, since the former had no well-developed political institutions for representative government, the citizen's ability to influence imperial administration in both classical Athens and republican Rome was related directly to his spatial proximity to the imperial metropole. In the empire of the Roman Republic, the extension of Roman citizenship to distant parts of Italy, and *a fortiori* extra-Italian citizenship grants, created what we might call paper citizens, who could not directly impact the administration of the empire. Athenian cleruchies may have created such paper citizens as well, albeit on a much smaller scale. And so, for quite different historical reasons, we must confront the question of the alienation of the citizen's actual political power in both the classical and twenty-first century worlds (cf. Wood 1994, 1996). But that is a story for another time.

FURTHER READING

For modern theories of imperialism, see Koebner and Schmidt 1964; Owen and Sutcliffe 1972; Waltz 1979; more recently Doyle 1986; Chilcote 2000. For wide-ranging studies of imperialism in the ancient world, see collected essays in Garnsey and Whittaker 1978. On ubiquitous warfare in ancient Greece and Rome, in addition to works cited in the text, see van Wees 2000, 2004; Rosenstein 2004; Chaniotis 2005; Lendon 2005; Eckstein 2006. Meiggs 1972 is fundamental for study of Athenian imperialism; cf. Finley 1982b: 41–61; collected essays in Boedeker and Raaflaub 1998. For an interesting comparative study of Athenian imperialism, which employs historical contrafactuals, see I. Morris 2005. See Badian 1958, 1968; Gruen 1984; Morstein-Marx 1995; W. Harris 1979 for Roman imperialism; also collected essays in Champion 2004b. For modern theories of citizenship, see collected essays in Beiner 1995. The reader can consult two speeches in the Demosthenic corpus for methods of establishing Athenian citizenship: *Macartatus* (43) and *Eubulides* (57). Osborne 1981–3 provides a detailed examination of grants of Athenian citizenship and naturalization, but is intended for the specialist, with reading knowledge of classical Greek. C. Patterson 1981 is a book-length study of Pericles' citizenship law, but must be used with caution. Her thesis that before Pericles' citizenship law Athenian citizenship, based on demes, was unrestricted has not gained many adherents; cf. Boegehold 1994; de Ste Croix 2004: 233–53. On Athenian citizenship, see further collected essays in Boegehold and Scafuro 1994, and bibliography assembled at de Ste Croix 2004: 253. Hamel 2003 provides a recent narrative account of the trial involving Neaira. Henry 2007 provides a new biography of Neaira. The definitive study of Roman citizenship remains Sherwin-White 1973. For Athenian citizenship myths, see Loraux 1986, 1993, 2000. For Roman foundation legends, see collected essays in Bremmer and Horsfall 1987; Wiseman 1995, 2004; D. Braund and Gill 2003; Dench 2005. The legend of Aeneas as Trojan exile of course figures prominently in Roman foundation stories, on which see Galinsky 1969; Horsfall in Bremmer and Horsfall 1987: 12–24; Gruen 1992: 6–51; Erskine 2001. For interrelationships between state size and citizen effectiveness, the idea broached at the end of this chapter, see Dahl and Tufte 1973.

CHAPTER 7

Gendered Politics, or the Self-Praise of *Andres Agathoi*

Giulia Sissa

There is no space, in ancient cultures, for gender blindness. Bodies, habits, and rights, the necessary components of a definition of "gender," are either masculine or feminine. Politics is no exception: on the contrary, politics is the most important sphere of activity that belongs to men and excludes women. Men – one, a few, or many – govern; men deliberate and speak in public; men produce decrees and laws that they enforce; men theorize about politics. From the warriors and kings of the Homeric world to the excellent men, *andres agathoi*, of Athenian democracy, and to the highly individualized empire of the young Alexander, ancient Greek politics comes sometimes in the singular and sometimes in the plural, but always in the masculine. If a woman's voice can be heard in the arena of government, dissent, or advice, this occurs only in a representation that distorts, either genuinely or in jest, existing mores and policies.

Gender in Theory

No political theorist seems to have anticipated Plato, or taken him seriously, in that famous, passing argument on the social or moral irrelevance of gender, a difference which, Socrates claims, matters only for procreation. Such an argument – that engendering children is the only human activity in which sexual dimorphism creates a natural division of labor – was gingerly made in the *Republic*, when Socrates tried to justify a common education for men and women. But it remained confined to Callipolis, a City of Beauty – a fantasy in heaven. Outside Plato's hypothetical construct, gender did matter socially and morally, in theory as well as in practice, and it did so because masculinity defined the conditions of political intelligence, political responsibility, and political action. Politics required manliness, and was for men only. Women were unfit and merely accessory.

A Companion to Greek and Roman Political Thought, First Edition. Edited by Ryan K. Balot.
© 2013 Blackwell Publishing Ltd. Published 2013 by Blackwell Publishing Ltd.

The male monopoly of politics is, I will argue, a multifaceted aspect of how ancient Greeks and Romans created, made work, and understood their political world. Politics was an activity, a performance or, as a French scholar would still say, a "*pratique*": a form of doing, organizing, managing, commanding, enforcing – as much as it was a permanent thinking and speaking, arguing and persuading. This pragmatic definition blends the competing visions of Greco-Roman politics that Dean Hammer examines in this book, from constitutional rules to crude power. Politics was a domain of strong values and compelling norms, but also a domain where the adjustment to rules and principles was to be negotiated all the time. Politics was above all the sphere of debate, deliberation, decision, agency, compliance or dissent: a turbulent mixture of words and deeds, of thoughts and emotions.

The key word that would encompass this turbulence is, of course, "power." Politics was a matter of power for the very first theorists who tried to classify *politeiai*, political orders, on the basis of who would rule: one man, an elite, or the many. But the content of this concept – power – is precisely that endlessly shifting experience of planning, commanding, discussing, disagreeing, convincing, obeying, disobeying or cooperating which depended on characters, intelligence, and passions. Given the perceived differences between a woman and a man in these respects, we cannot be surprised to find that gender distinctions are prominent in political action and discourse, wisdom and affect.

Woman, Plato tells us in the *Timaeus*, came into existence as a punitive metamorphosis of the first generation of men, when some of those original males, because of their cowardice (*deilia*), were reborn as females: from the outset, woman is therefore the very embodiment of that character flaw which is the opposite of *andreia* (*Tim.* 94b). And *andreia*, manliness, I will argue, is the crucial political virtue: the propensity to fight, characteristic of men, *andres*, underpins citizenship as a gendered status. The military and political deeds of men will always display their virility.

Feminine character is softer (*malakoteros*), easier to domesticate, and less spirited (*athumoteros*); and yet all female animals, and above all women, are ready to cause offense and to punch. They are also inclined to discouragement and despair, they are deceitful but gullible, and also envious and resentful, whiny, shameful, and idle. This unflattering portrait, in which only a superior ability to feel pity could be construed as praise, was sketched by Aristotle, in his *History of Animals* (609a21–b18). In the context of a description of habits and lifestyles, this fastidious passage is striking for its emphasis on sociability. The world is in a permanent state of nature – but not a Hobbesian war of all against all, so much as a natural community. Animals, Aristotle observes, are more or less gregarious, organized, cooperative, and warlike. And within each species, males are always more spirited, *thumodestera*, and brutish, *agriotera*, simpler and less cunning; whereas the females, with the exception of the she-bear and the panther, are less endowed with *thumos*, and are all *athumotera*.

Now *thumos*, the source of courage as well as of anger, is the emotional and moral equipment of the political animal. In excessive, insufficient or temperate doses, *thumos* is responsible for peoples' varying disposition to politics. Northern Europeans have too much of it, Asians too little, and the Hellenes, from Miletus to Marseilles, have just the right amount. But females, across the animal world, will always be comparatively deficient. The male is more helpful (*boēthētikōteron*) and more manly (*andreiōteron*), as even the mollusks can demonstrate: if you ever hit a female squid with your trident, the male will rush to her aid, whereas, if you hurt a male, the female will dash away. The cowardly, ungrateful *sepia* is obviously a paradigm of female behavior (609b10).

The consideration of the natural propensity of females to nurture their offspring offers a positive counterpart to all these negative characteristics. Softness makes cuddlier mothers. But the coherence of Aristotelian ethology rests upon a binary set of patterns: on the female side, we have a few skills and dispositions related to procreating, feeding and training a progeny, accompanied by a string of rather unsavory and antisocial behaviors – such as envy, idle contentiousness, instability, pusillanimity and resentment; on the male side, we can see the ample spectrum of agency related to defense, competition, cooperation, solidarity, bravery, self-control, therefore to the sphere of politics.[1] Manliness, a noble ferociousness, provides a way for the gallant mollusk to approximate to the valiant hoplite – and to the active citizen, because courage is, for Aristotle, the quality of those infantry men who tend to rebel against monarchies and establish polities, thus inventing the egalitarian self-government of the best citizens (*Pol.* 3.1279a–b).

Woman, Aristotle argues in the opening pages of his *Politics*, has the same parts of the soul as a man, and is as capable of deliberation as a man (and contrary to a slave), but she is unable to sustain that decision with authority, since her deliberative capacity is *akuros*. And authoritative, responsible deliberation is, as we shall see, the substance of politics. A woman's soul is adjusted to her natural function, which is to be obedient to a man at all times (Arist. *Pol.* 1260a9–14. cf. 1254b13–16), within the confined space of the household, not outside in the arena of assertive decision-making.

Before Aristotle's anthropology, Athenian popular culture pushes to the caricature the same enduring assumptions about the female as a nonpolitical animal. Woman, Aristophanes' comedies take pleasure in displaying, is so obsessed with sex that, were she to meddle in politics, she would recur to nothing but her seductive power as a means of negotiating. This is the plot of *Lysistrata*, a play about an Athenian woman organizing a panhellenic erotic strike, in the hope of putting an end to the Peloponnesian War. The women will save Greece, their leader claims, in the comfort of their cozy interiors, and by using their most distinctive panoply, such as slippers, and saffron diaphanous tunics (*Lys.* 42–8). But even to implement this attractive plan, Lysistrata will have to overcome the resistance of Myrrhina and her friends, when they understand what it requires: to abstain from sex. Tell us! What should we do? We are ready to die for this! Myrrhina enthuses. And Lysistrata, solemnly: "We must refrain from ... the pea! But what? Why are you turning your back? Where are you going?"[2] One word – and the heroic conspirators are gone.

Woman cannot emerge from the universe of sensuality. In another play, the *Ecclesiazusae*, another resourceful Athenian lady, Praxagora, succeeds in making the assembly vote a daring decree that will bring women into power, in order, this time, to save Athens. But here again the new rulers think domestically and sexually, not politically. Their notion of equality culminates with the egalitarian distribution of erotic objects. Praxagora sets her priorities: "I shall begin by making land, money, everything that is private property, common to all. Then we shall live on this common wealth, which we shall take care to administer with wise thrift" (*Eccl.* 597–600). Communism will extend to sexual partners: all women will be held in common and, vice versa, all men will be shared among women. But beauty and youth, what causes spontaneous attraction, are not naturally equal, after all! From now on, however, they will be made equal by political fiat, Praxagora declares: "The ugly will follow the handsomest into the public places after supper and see to it that the law, which forbids the women to sleep with the big, handsome men before having satisfied the ugly and the small, is complied with."[3] With the women in power, the polis will be turned into one, large house, with dining rooms under the porches – for an uninterrupted enjoyment of life. Woman cannot extricate herself from the horizon of comfortable domesticity. Aristophanes' satire makes the thought of a city of women as absurd as a city of birds, up in the clouds.

Always in the open space of democratic Athens, but in public rhetoric, the same idiom shapes successful arguments. If a man was accused of political unfitness for being a prostitute, as was the case for Timarchos in a famous speech by Aeschines, the attack on a consistently shameful and profligate life will culminate in the mention of Timarchos' use of his body, which was male, in manners that are not only transgressive acts (*hamartēmata*), but more precisely "worthy of a woman" (*gunaikeia*).[4] To abdicate maleness disqualifies a citizen from the exercise of his basic civic rights.

In the cultural fabric of the ancient polis, therefore, the template of gender credits femininity with a nonpolitical, or even an antipolitical, agency. But, if we want to map the complex ramifications of gender, we need more than a binary set of patterns. We have to set those patterns in motion. Firstly, we have to remember that normative knowledge circulates in a society; therefore it inspires civility, justifies practices, and shapes institutions. Secondly, we have to identify the conceptual distinctions between, and yet the constant intertwinement of, three dimensions of individual identity: rights, habits, and bodies. I use the language of rights in a sense which is close to the definition given in this book by Paul Cartledge and Matt Edge (chapter 10): as a set of rules that protect negative freedom and ensure a condition of nonslavery. A thoughtful definition of gender must comprise legal constructions, cultural patterns, and the physical inscription of sex difference.

Gender in Practice

A culture is made of a dense, constant flowing of words, which find solid incarnations in institutions and sustain, or rationalize, deeds. Meaning infuses social life. In ancient societies women did not participate in war, did not join meetings of the assembly or the council, and did not take part in civic deliberations; they neither elected magistrates nor could be elected to magistracies; they did not even bring their own cases to the courts. Their only involvement in official functions was limited to priesthood.

This absence from the political arena established a glaring contrast between women and men, especially in the context of ancient democracy, which was characterized by generalized participation, eligibility, and self-defense. But why did ancient citizens maintain such sharp gender discriminations in the conduct of their political life?

Women's marginality makes sense only because it resonates with generally shared beliefs about their competence, entitlement, or propriety. Women do and don't, because they allegedly can or cannot; they actually must or must not. On the reasons why, the arguments abound, we have just seen, and soon they touch upon moral aptitudes: women are born incompetent, they are congenitally cowardly, they lack initiative, they stay at home and care for the family, and, should they step out and try to govern a city, they would put forward their usual priorities: sex and pleasure.

These ideas, principles, and theories are not to be found in inscriptions planted in the pavement of the agora, or in regulations put on display on the Pnyx. They can be found, as just mentioned, in the *Hippocratic Corpus*, the Platonic dialogues, Aristophanes' comedies, the speeches by Demosthenes and Aeschines, or Aristotle's biological and political works. But the textual provenance of these arguments does not imply that they exist in a vacuum, or remain confined to an esoteric intellectual community. On the contrary, normative knowledge spills out, surges, and percolates in the common sense of ordinary people. Ideas find an institutional embodiment in laws and mores, which the orators quote or comment upon. They materialize – reiterated and emphasized – in the actual performance of politics, especially the speech acts of democratic decision-making. Pericles' wish that women should go unobserved, in contrast with male imperishable *kleos*, crowns his funeral oration as an obvious winning point (Thuc. 2.45.2). Aeschines' claims about Timarchos' effeminacy (1.185) would not make sense if they were not supposed to find a successful echo in the audience's set of values.

Principles circulate, via teaching and therapeutic instruction, in the authoritative milieus of medical practice and philosophical schools. The dogma of feminine softness reverberates from the *Hippocratic Corpus* to Aristotle. When Socrates challenges the common sense of women's unfitness for politics, with his suggestions that they should be trained exactly like men in order to become warriors and rulers, he is acutely aware of the paradox. It is so outrageous that, of course, everyone will laugh! (*Resp.* 5.452a–453a)

Theories resound on stage, for the merriment or the pity of the audience, in the devastating predicaments of tragedy or the delirious masquerades of comedy.

Rights, Habits, and Bodies

From the texts of written laws to the rhetoric of the law courts, from the speeches in political assemblies to the lessons in the schools, from the prescriptions of doctors to the spectacular representations of the theatre, ideas, principles, and theories of gender resound everywhere.

But gender is the social construction *of* something: it is the construction of a certain use of the body. The power of gender norms ultimately derives from that: from a body supposed to work in ways that are allegedly intangible and natural, and, crucially, interconnected. *Andreia*, courage, depends on *thumos*, spiritedness, but the actual performance of *thumos* depends on vital heat: that physical quality which, from its source in the heart,[5] travels in the blood that nourishes the flesh, and finally transforms blood into sperm.

The virility of a manly man in bed depends on the abundance of his semen, a frothy fluid full of hot air, *pneuma*, and the product of the perfect concoction of his blood. Blood can change into semen only thanks to a great deal of vital heat (which female bodies fail to provide).[6] The virility of a manly man on the battlefield, in a political meeting or in a law court depends on his ability to get excited, in anger or in nerve, for or against something. This excitement originates, again, from his blood, when it starts to boil and overheat, in the region of his heart.[7] Ill-endowed with animal heat – as their failure to produce sperm and the regular overflowing of menstrual blood demonstrate – women will be more liable to the chills of fear, cowardice or, as *History of Animals* 9 describes, futile contentiousness.

Sexually and politically, manliness irradiates from a man's heart, seat of his *thumos*, it flows into his ebullient blood, it waters his dense, warm, strong muscles, and, finally, it animates his bubbly semen. The predominance of heat over cold generates a complete gendered identity, psychosomatic as well as social. Once again, Aristotle's profile of the young man, compared to the adult and the elderly, offers the most eloquent compendium of such naturalistic views of masculinity. Young men are hot and humid, full of fluids as well as of vital heat: this is why they are erotically passionate, but also courageous and irascible, disinterested and hopeful. Take it as a portrait of, say, Alcibiades. An old man, on the contrary, is still warm, but dry: greedy, uncertain about everything, reluctant to fight, disenchanted. A moody skeptic. A man in his prime will merge the virtues of both (Arist. *Rhet.* 2.10).

Characters are consistent with bodies. Women are cowardly because they are cold and moist; they are unmanly because they are soft, above all in a material sense. Their flesh is watery, spongy, phlegmatic (they are *hugrosarkotera*: *Hist. an.* 4.11);[8] they are prone to dysentery and to that physiological hemorrhage which is menstruation.[9] In societies in which mild weather and a comfortable environment make men soft (like the women), the natural dimorphism of the sexes tends to fade: all individuals look like each other, and share the same tame, peaceful character (Hippoc. *Aer.* 10, 19–20). In such a climate, they all become submissive.

A gendered individual, in sum, is a cluster of anatomy, physiology, and behavior. A body, and a set of habits that relate to his character.[10] This is what we have to reconcile with the normative voice of exclusions and rights. Even from the most skeptical standpoint, can we reckon that in ancient societies, as in our own cultural circumstances, words and thoughts about sex extended far beyond people's erotic lives, and prescribed their movements, limited their activity, dictated their dress code, influenced their diet, impregnated their language. Political fitness is only a sample of the multilayered associations of thoughts, mostly organized by binary oppositions (be they made of open or implicit connections), that define womanly and manly characters.

It would be a mistake to isolate the factoids of gendered politics from a larger picture of gendered life, as much as it would be misleading to minimize the ramifications of sex. Those ramifications created a disorder, a noise, that we have to explain, not ignore. Gender affected people's lives in so many details, I will argue, because arguments about sex in its physical understanding (and its many complicated consequences) created a permanent muddling of the three levels I have mentioned: rights, habits, and bodies. This confusion was constraining for everyone, but for women it was crippling.

Our job is to unravel that confusion. And this for two orders of reasons. The first order of reasons is intellectual. Rights, habits, and bodies: this is a heuristic model because, in the most variously intricate combinations, these three things make up a human life for any individual living in society. They are inseparable. When we try to understand the texture of a culture, we can't fail to see their intertwining. And only if we take the whole picture, from laws to mores to anatomy, can we make sense of how a society thinks – and make people live. For instance: women can't vote because they are soft. Is softness relevant to politics? Well, this is exactly what we have to recognize: that a given society did establish that knot of relevance.

But if we think that softness *should* have nothing to do with political fitness, then it means that, for us, we must keep those three loops clearly distinct. We must consider them as well-defined dimensions of a complex fact, for instance gender, and we have to sort out the universal claims of human rights, the local reasons of culture, and the pleasures and pains of singular bodies. Better than a knot, we may think of a system of mental checks and balances. I cannot forget rights when I consider cultural patterns, because those patterns might be exploitative or humiliating; I cannot forget cultural norms when I look at rights, because this might make me insensitive and provincial; I can never forget the body, because this is what ultimately suffers the consequences of discrimination. This is why the second order of reasons for using this heuristic model is ethical.

I am writing this chapter from the standpoint of our sense of equality and emancipation. I think that we should be careful not to conflate human rights, cultural habits, and corporeal experience, as citizens (because that conflation is the matrix of prejudices) but also as scholars (because the same conflation might lead us to underestimate pain, on behalf of culture; or to extol rights with no attention to mores). It is now unsavory, for instance, to claim that women are soft *and* craven *and* made for domestic life – but only because we finally think that the right to vote is compatible with, say, breast-feeding; because we know that the ability to manage a household does not prevent a person from being an effective president; because we see that one can make tough decisions and wear pearls, etc. We must not underestimate the intricateness of that knot: we have to understand how it worked.

Manly Men

In ancient Greece, politics was, above all, power, governance, and leadership. Even citizenship can be defined as the entitlement to have access to office or, at least, to contribute to effective decisions. In its first incarnations this supremacy entailed a military component. Although the exercise of political responsibility is technically distinct from war, the kings from the remotest past, say Agamemnon and Priam, as well as Darius or Xerxes, were still, in the first place, commanders in chief and were raised as warriors. The authority of words and mind could not be disconnected from the training of a fighting body, and the ability to control and lead an army

The process of democratization, through which, in the sixth century BCE, Athens came to be governed by the citizens themselves (through a general assembly, a council, elected generals and magistrates, but no kings at all), changed profoundly the experience of political affairs. Democracy, however, did not bring women into the arena of shared and rotating power. Why? The answer is that these newly empowered citizens were, precisely, soldiers. Generals, knights, hoplites, and sailors: the city was to remain their business. As Aristotle would later theorize in the design of his ideal *politeia* – the proper government of the many, literally a "city of citizens" – it was the martial virtue of the young man that led to the political prerogative of the mature citizen.

The sheer aggressiveness of power always remained associated with the exercise of governance, even when the *kratos* was offered to the multitude and "placed in the middle," when it was neutralized and diluted through the rotation of charges. Democracy is made of *isonomia*, equality before the law, and *isēgoria*, equal right to free speech, but also of *isokratia* (Hdt. 5.92.a): equal distribution of power, *kratos* – as the very word *dēmokratia*, power of the people, strongly suggests. In the assembly or in the council, and by means of different offices, the many were in charge, without the equivalent of a chief executive, whose presence would have reintroduced a monarchical element. But above the masses, and elected by the popular assembly, stood the highest officials: the ten *stratēgoi*, ten generals who held the most visible and influential political authority. If Pericles and Cleon, Nicias and Alcibiades could be charismatic orators and popular figures, it was because of their military credibility and strategic vision. They could mobilize a body of citizens, always prepared to take the field.

From the outset, radical democracy was associated with warlike endeavors. For Herodotus, freedom and free speech brought Athens to her prosperity and leadership among the Greeks. This particular polis grew more and more powerful, he recounts, thanks to Cleisthenes and his reforms (508), supported by the demos (Hdt. 5.66–78). After those changes, he claims:

> Athens went from strength to strength [*auxanein*], and proved, if proof were needed, how noble a thing equality is [*isēgoria*], not in one respect only, but in all [*pantachē*]; for while they were oppressed under tyrants, they had no better success in war than any of their neighbors, yet, once the yoke was flung off, they proved the finest [*prōtoi*] fighters in the world. This clearly shows that, so long as they were held down by authority, they deliberately shirked their duty in the field, as slaves shirk working for their masters; but when freedom was won, then every man [*hekastos*] amongst them was interested in his own cause. (Hdt. 5.78, trans. de Sélincourt and Marincola 1996, slightly adapted)

Isēgoria is "a worthy thing," *chrēma spoudaion*, because it includes not only justice, but also the *noblest* value of all: heroism. Whereas the slave is the paradigm of the bad soldier, the one who fights for a master thus unwillingly, a first-class warrior,

Herodotus argues, has to be the citizen of a "free" city (like Sparta), where the law is the only master, or, even better, that of a democratic city (like Athens). He is a man who has a lot at stake, personally, individually, *hekastos*, on the battlefield. This individual motivation translates into eagerness and commitment, *prothumia*. That is the beauty of equality.

Herodotus' recollection of the history of Athens establishes this basic principle: freedom (itself won through the military power of the demos) brings, first of all, military power to the people. This train of thought is crucial for our understanding of democracy in its gendered fabric. Democracy requires a novel image of *hoi polloi*: they are not any longer the uneducated, incompetent, irrational, and wicked mob, for whom excellence remains inaccessible. To be trusted as a self-governing group and a reliable army, the majority has to be held reasonable and, above all, courageous. A gentrification of the crowd, so to speak, has to occur in political discourse. This takes place in the fifth century, finally to culminate with the language of autochthony, nobility and patriotism, in the most ideological genre of public rhetoric, the funeral orations.

Prowess on the battlefield is the virtue that best connects the Athenian hoplites, and even the humbler sailors, to the warriors from the aristocratic past. It is the excellence of the intrepid Homeric hero that is now rethought, in the plural. When, in 431, Pericles claims that the Athenians need no Homer to compose the panegyric of their dead, he seals that reenactment: a democratic general is the only Homer they need. It will come as no surprise that this kind of praise, tailored on manliness, sanctions the irrelevance of women. For them, as Pericles famously put it, the best eulogy is silence.

But there is more to the exclusionary strategy of democratic discourse. Pericles had used a well-established *topos* in the rhetoric of the funeral oration: autochthony. The Athenians represent their origin as a spontaneous generation from the soil of Attica. They are natives, and the only natives (they say) in the Greek world. Pericles starts from there (Thuc. 2.36). In the *Funeral Oration* traditionally attributed to the orator Lysias, this opening generates a self-loving, complacent history in which the people are nothing but heroic. In the baroque words of Lysias: "They had not been collected like most people, from every quarter, and had not settled in a foreign land after driving out its people; they were born of the soil, and possessed in one and the same country their mother and their fatherland" (Lys. 2.17, trans. Lamb 1930, slightly adapted).

A unique beginning creates a privileged status for the Athenians taken as a *genos*, a line of descent, originating from one father, Erechtheus, child of Hephaistos, and two mothers: the virgin Athena and Earth. As a dynasty linked to the gods and rooted in their own land, they stand apart from the many, *hoi polloi*, those populations which are but a collection of disparate peoples. As citizens of a uniquely pure and legitimate city, they were all well-born, *eugeneis*. Now, their exceptional birth sets the stage for an exceptional history. The Athenians *become* worthy men, *andres agathoi*, because as children they are first trained in the goodness (*agatha*) of their ancestors, as young men they preserve that ancient fame intact and, finally, they come to display their own excellence, *aretē* (Lys. 2.69). It is only then, when they come to show the result of both their background and their training, in their collective prowess, that they can be considered excellent. And *that* is the mark of true nobility.

In the language of democracy, *aretē* is first of all military, but not in a generic sense. It is the exceptional quality that allows for a special kind of war: the fight for freedom, justice, and democracy itself, a fight that is intrinsically loyal and generously helpful toward others, allies and friends. From the foundational event of the democratic revolution, justice and freedom are profoundly connected to the power of the many. The Athenians, Lysias claims, never expelled previous occupants from their land, but were capable of throwing out their own archaic rulers, *dunasteiai*, from their own city. They were the *first* and *only* people in that time to do so. And they did it out of an anthropological conviction and a highly dignified vision of themselves within humankind: they thought that what defined humanity was obedience to law and reason, as opposed to the beasts who submit to each other by violence (Lys. 2.19). Their superlative excellence culminates with the invention of democracy, because democracy is the political transposition of that nobility.

Again, this montage of arguments requires the systematic removal of anything feminine from the action of politics and war. The Athenians benefit from their mythical origin, as children of Athena as well as Earth: in that way they can consider themselves all siblings, and they can share a twice imaginary origin – a birth from a virgin as well as from the soil – that bypasses the feminine body.[11] From then, their glorious past is a sequence of just wars, against their own tyrants, against the barbarians, against foreign despots, and, most significantly, against a fabulous society of women warriors: the Amazons. The Athenians, Lysias argues, were the first men manly enough to prevail over those unconventional females: by defeating them utterly, they finally exposed their femininity (Lys. 2.15). The fabrication of a diachronic fantasy, intended to underpin a political identity, starts from a maternal background, extols triumph after triumph, and, with the memory of those routed strangers, corroborates the genealogy of the *andres agathoi*. Men so excellent that they embody the highest achievement of humanity. The history of democracy is a history of triumphant masculinity. The success of Athens is the victory of Athenian virility.

Public rhetoric displays the narrative of democratic manliness, but we owe to Aristotle, the most insightful anthropologist of hellenic culture, a normative theory of self-governance (that "city of the citizens" of which democracy is a corrupted version), centered on heroic group-excellence. For Aristotle, kingships come to an end when there is a sufficient number of noblemen who cannot endure any longer the permanent rule of one leader, and impose themselves as a governing elite, an aristocracy (Arist. *Pol.* 3.1286b). And the self-government of the many, in what Aristotle calls "polities," depends upon a critical mass of hoplites willing to take the city in their own hands. All these political actors are indeed excellent, at least in one respect: bravery in combat.

> When the multitude governs the state with a view to what is useful to all, it is called by the name common to all the political orders that is: "*politeia*," a city of citizens. And this comes about reasonably, since although it is possible for one man or a few to excel in virtue, when the number is larger it becomes difficult for them to possess perfect

excellence in respect of every form of virtue, but they can best excel in military valor, for
this is found in a multitude (*plethos*); and therefore with this form of constitution the
class that fights for the state in war is the most powerful, and it is those who possess arms
who are admitted to the government. (Arist. *Pol.* 3.1279a37–b4, trans. Rackham 1944,
slightly modified)

Whereas the other forms of *aretē* are uncommon and exclusive, the virtues of
courage, spiritedness, and solidarity can be found in a large population. Now, Aristotle
does not see *demokratia* in a sufficiently positive light as to celebrate its revolutionary
origin: on the contrary for him, the power of the people remains an altered form
of polity, and merely derives from tyranny (Arist. *Pol.* 3.1286b). The best practical
possibility is the government of the hoplite-citizens, in which the disenfranchised poor
dedicate their trivial lives to trade, farming, and any other manual work. Although
notoriously critical of popular rule, therefore, Aristotle offers a most insightful theory
of collective excellence: military valor can exist in the plural, polities are made of many
men who take turns in governing themselves, and therefore military valor is the virtue
to be found in polities. I also insist on this point in chapter 18 of this volume.

From Aristotle's praise of a *politeia*, we can extrapolate a conclusion, appropriate to
Athenian culture as we have seen it exposed in the funeral orations: in their historical,
ideological memory, the Athenians citizens could come to see themselves as the heirs
to the noble warriors from the Homeric world, because they were, first of all, and all
of them, warriors. They shared the same virtue, because they had in common the
same moral and political experience: war. And, for once, here is a virtue that is not
impossibly rare.

The very idea of a foundational revolution and of a citizenry always ready to take up
arms, presupposes – and brings to the forefront of political discourse – the qualities,
the emotions, the agency *and the gender* of the finest fighters from the most remote,
mythical, and heroic ancient times. Those Homeric times were a usable past for all
hellenic cities. The deeply ingrained amalgamation of democracy and manliness, let
me insist, has to be understood in this context. Ancient democracy sees itself emerging not from a bourgeois revolution, but from the political self-empowerment of an
army, forever mindful of another one, most antique and glorious. An army of males,
who had left mothers and spouses at home, were accustomed to take captives for
erotic enjoyment, and, of course, were fighting to rescue an unfaithful wife, and to
restore the honor of a prince. Beyond the temporal distance, Homer looms large in
Athens, because of the Trojan War.[12]

Democratic Athens chose to infuse the Homeric poems, those aristocratic, foundational "scriptures," into the tender souls of her children, and to have them
reenacted in the infinite variations of so many tragic plots. Even more theatrically,
Athens reperformed the *Iliad* and the *Odyssey* during the most solemn of its civic
festivals, the Panathenaia, against the background of the muscular young men in the
nude who were sculpted on the frieze of the Parthenon.

That sense of martial value was a bridge connecting the present to the right past.
This novel form of government, the rule of many, needed that past. In a culture
where the ordinary citizens – and the commons in the position of ruling – could

be disparaged as ugly, inferior, irrational, vulgar, wicked, it was as vital as it was daring to state and restate the only indisputable quality of the *plēthos*, one that happens to be the most venerable virtue of the demigods from the *Iliad*. Against the repertoire of derogatory and contemptuous characterizations of the plural, the language of *arête* conveys in a transparent fashion (because Homer was so much part of the popular culture) the praise of a multitude that, at the very least, knows how to be manly.

The Gender of Politics

War and citizenship, therefore politics and manliness: we ought to take this train of thought, however, not as a simple causation, but as the focal point of tightly woven, more intricate correlations. The male monopoly of politics seems pervasive in the classical world, but in order to be upheld and widely accepted by all social actors, including philosophers, poets, and women themselves, it must have been corroborated by thicker cultural circumstances.

First, the ancient Greeks came to conceptualize the notion of natural norms, but not that of *universal* human rights. The failure to think inclusively, as a matter of principle, set the stage for a selective limitation of individual entitlements. One cannot even begin to make a compelling argument in favor of women's equality without the explicit, or even implicit, claim to the access of *all* human beings to freedom and parity – including the equally shared liberty to participate in ruling and being ruled. The actual existence of slavery, the exclusion of women from political activity, be it office or advice or vote, their legal minority: these positive facts, largely unchallenged in classical antiquity, presuppose and concur to ratify the idea that human beings insofar as they happen to be dissimilar, can also be held unequal. Aristotle argues that political equality ought to replicate a preexisting sameness, instead of being something a person has an unconditional claim to. This is at the antipodes of the logic of human rights. Equality, for us, must be recognized as applying to individuals, *notwithstanding* and *against* any previous difference.

The exclusionary nature of the liberty and equality of the ancient Greeks can be seen in the process of democratization in Athens. If we read Aristotle and Plutarch on the reforms of Solon, in 594, we can see how his famous cancellation of debts and the abolition of enslavement creates a new social status, that of the free citizen. All those born in the territory of Attica are now endowed with an inalienable condition of freedom, a right that is actually a privilege for the Athenians. Liberty is those citizens' right, that is, but not a human right. They, as Athenians, become all equally invulnerable to bondage, and, as a consequence, masters of slaves imported from outside. This crucially relates to the status of women. With Solon, Athenian women became equally protected from enslavement, but they did not become equally entitled to political responsibility. There is no argument in favor of their political emancipation, as much as there is no argument in favor of a general abolition of slavery. Athens, the progressive polis, went as far as to enforce equal freedom for its native men only.

To ignore human rights creates a predictable, conventional, and rarely challenged legitimation of unfairness. Unchecked by transcultural rights, local norms will prevail in shaping social life. Women should raise children, stay at home, and care for the household, for instance. And Nature will come to support such mores. Feminine bodies are intended for procreation, they are weak and soft. Naturalistic justifications of inequality never encounter a serious limit in social habits, because habits can be easily adjusted to the reasons of Nature. Between *nomos* and *phusis*, gender asymmetry can only flourish. This brings us to the second order of circumstances, contributing to that lopsidedness. The forms of knowledge that offer arguments in matters of sex, such as medicine and philosophy, reinforced the assumption that bodies determine characters; that characters and bodies respond to the environment; that habits are natural and tend to remain stable.

The naturalistic essentialism of philosophy culminates in Aristotle's conception of the political animal. From Plato's narrative of the irruption of women in the world, caused by the occasional *deilia* of the first men, to Aristotle's repeated claim that *andreia* is the basic virtue of a citizen, but all females are innately colder, thus wanting in *thumos*, therefore unable to fight, a persistent train of thought associates femininity with softness, immobility, and sensuality. The she-bear and the panther are exceptions; the spineless female squid shows the rule, together with the human female, always paradigmatic of extreme dimorphism. We have examined those associations. Let us now take the measure of their coherence, at the core of Aristotle's theory of politics.

Nature is the foundation of sociability; nature commands the creation of self-sufficient communities, where individuals can attain happiness and a good life. In a polis a human being becomes a *politēs*. A *politēs* can be defined as someone who takes turns in ruling and being ruled: this rotation of charges, this alternation of passivity and activity, is the key to "citizenship." Now, in a perfect *politeia*, citizens are well-educated *rentiers* who serve as soldiers in their youth, and take political responsibilities in their prime. Courage is their predominant virtue in war; practical intelligence, *phronēsis*, in politics (Arist. *Pol.* 1329a1–25). Now courage, *andreia*, is built in their masculinity, in their being *andres*. It is, literally, manliness. Women cannot be manly. A female, Aristotle, insists, may show some bravery, but it would be of an inferior kind: courage cannot be the same in females and males (Arist. *Pol.* 1260a21–2), and a valorous woman would be the equivalent of a cowardly man (Arist. *Pol.* 1277b20–3). As for the prudence of a mature citizen, one in charge of deliberating (*bouleutikon*) about matters of policy and justice, this quality too appears to be deficient in women: women are capable of deliberation (*bouleutikon*), we have seen, but they lack authority. They are capable of making decisions, but not of carrying them out. They are not born to rule. They are made to hold all the time, *aiei*, without interruption, the same passive position: to be ruled by their husbands.[13] They fall short of becoming part of the army, as much as they fail to meet the requirements of the deliberative class. They are citizens, but cannot rotate as the male *politai* do. In his essay on Aristotelian "naturalism" in this volume (chapter 25), Timothy Chappell argues that Aristotle anchors politics to *phusis* in a way that is much more nuanced than is usually claimed; ultimately justified in view of a specifically human end, happiness; and, as I also argue in "Political Animals: Pathetic Animals," chapter 18 of this volume, in a constant interplay of nature and habituation. Gender, however, seems to be a particularly naturalistic domain, where both difference and inequality remain stable.

Before Aristotle, we can find a similar discourse in the *Hippocratic Corpus*. Unwarlikeness means indifference to the conquest of freedom, thus compliance before tyranny. Certain peoples present such a character, therefore are less endowed with *andreia*, manliness, which is, again, the basic virtue of hellenic politics. The most eloquent theorist of this gendered ethnography is the author of *On Airs, Waters, and Places*, (supposedly) Hippocrates:

> And with regard to the pusillanimity and cowardice of the inhabitants, the principal reason the Asiatics are more unwarlike and of gentler disposition than the Europeans is the nature of the seasons, which do not undergo any great changes either to heat or cold, or the like; for there is neither excitement of the understanding nor any strong change of the body whereby the temper might be ruffled and they be roused to inconsiderate emotion and passion, rather than living as they do always in the state. It is changes of all kinds which arouse understanding of mankind, and do not allow them to get into a torpid condition. For these reasons, it appears to me, the Asiatic race is feeble.[14]

This ethnic profile is indeed heavily gendered, because these people lack manliness. This is the root of their patterns of behavior, consistently marked by softness, cowardice, and sensuality. As Hippocrates writes: "Manliness (*andreia*), endurance of suffering, laborious enterprise, and high spirit, could not be produced in such a state of things either among the native inhabitants or those from a different country, for there pleasure necessarily reigns" (Hippoc. *Aer.* 12).

Among the Europeans, but because of their mild environment, the nomadic inhabitants of Scythia are particularly moist, sagging, flabby, and fleshy, with feeble joints – therefore inclined to idleness. In their exceedingly even weather, one just cannot find the energy to pitch a spear. Fat and hairless, "their shapes resemble one another, the males being all alike, and so also with the women" (Hippoc. *Aer.* 19). However, they remedy this unfortunate condition by surgery: men cauterize their shoulders, in order to dry up, reinforce their joints and become able to ride and throw the javelin. Counteracting nature, the Scythians modify their bodies, naturally unfit for war, transforming themselves into very effective fighters (Hippoc. *Aer.* 20).

The Rhetoric of Gender

These two powerful ideas – the exclusive extension of liberty and equality to *men*; and a naturalistic essentialism – contributed to lock for ever the correlation of war and citizenship, thus manliness and affairs of state. To the synergy of warlike citizenship, selective rights and corporeal essentialism in order to consolidate the calling of politics as a natural male ability, we have now to add, more generally, the binary logic of gender. The feminine variation of the species is always inferior, weaker, always imperfect, always an accident, always late, and not an improvement. Women were not meant to be. The world has been "genderized," (as we might now say: "tenderized") by mistake. This is the meaning of the myths of the invention of the first woman, such as the fabrication of a beautiful evil, *kalon kakon*, in Hesiod's *Theogony*, and Pandora in his *Works and Days*, or the metamorphosis of the first cowardly males in the *Timaeus*.

Now, let us go back to a dissonant voice from the choral claim that politics must be an exclusively male business. I mentioned the exception of Socrates in Plato's *Republic*, and his tentative argument that gender does not matter, except in procreation. It does not matter in education, in morality, and therefore in the ability to care for the city. In all these domains, women can do exactly as men do, because here their corporeal difference is not relevant. It does not make any difference, however, only to the extent that men do everything better.

This statement, which brings Socrates' audacious imagination back to conventional wisdom, offers an interesting standpoint for a final consideration. Not even Socrates, not even the man who is inventing the most daring, novel, and counterintuitive *politeia*, can resist the power of common sense. Women are to be blamed – statutorily, collectively. Why? Why give in?

The answer has to do with the allotment of praise and blame, a profoundly ingrained mode of thinking and speaking in Athenian culture.

To eulogize or to criticize is perhaps the most elementary dilemma for any discourse, first of all in the poetic tradition, from epics to lyric, but also in public rhetoric, especially political speeches and funeral orations. Now, when it comes to the distribution of value to women *versus* men, any speaker inevitably will make judgments that affect the group to which he belongs, thus himself; and the group to which the audience belongs, the *andres athēnaioi*. Because they happen to be the gendered actors of politics, men only are in the position of thinking highly or badly about women. They monopolize, therefore, the poetic and rhetorical discourse about them. But there is more to their speaking power: because of the binary opposition of two, and only two genders, whenever they talk about women they are already talking, comparatively, by an implicit contrast, about themselves. In appreciating or diminishing women, they lower or enhance themselves. Women's weakness is men's force; women's cowardice is men's strength. As it appears in Pericles' claim on women's silent glory, in contrast with the magniloquent panegyric of the warriors, or in Lysias' mention of the Amazons: women are the *faire valoir* of real men. They are the contrasting, enhancing mirror of a self-loving representation.

What is at stake in the estimate of anything feminine is the auto-evaluation of the speaker and, through him, of the audience. A nonwoman speaks to (mostly) nonwomen. This is a compelling cultural paradigm that brings together the epideictic conventions of political rhetoric, the authority of those who are exclusively entitled to use that rhetoric, and the constraints of the binary logic of two mutually defined genders.

The reflection of male self-praise through the disparagement of women is so effortless and pervasive, as a manner of speaking, that even Socrates, we have seen, yields to its inviting simplicity: women do everything less well. Men are saved. There is a limit to Socratic *eirōneia*.

Conclusion, or the Hair-and-Clothes Issue

Gender is not merely a social construction or a performance, it is also a challenge. Anatomy is not only a destiny, it is also a social project. Human beings are rational, narrative, self-interpreting, and political animals: but they are all of the above by negotiating incessantly their gender fitness. This is still true.

In our own, late-modern awareness of who we are, what we can expect, what we can do: could we honestly claim that gender does not have any bearing on our choices, even in a cosmopolitan, sophisticated, liberal society, where universal human rights have become a sacrosanct value? Gender makes a massive difference everywhere: to fit or not to fit the norm of manliness or womanliness is an arduous dilemma for the self-fashioning of any person, because the self is always, in some way, gendered.

Women's emancipation, and our slow recognition as political actors, voters, activists, volunteers, members of parliament, presidential candidates or successful leaders, have failed to eradicate the persistent trains of thought that associate manliness with credible leadership and reliable command. Take the "hair and clothes" issue in Hillary Rodham Clinton's campaign to be US presidential candidate, or the refrain in French politics about the nurturing vocation of Ségolène Royal, joined to her alleged incompetence in the realpolitik of international relations. And her legendary white suits. Why should physical appearance, domestic skills, maternal characteristics have anything to do with drive, self-discipline, competitiveness, vision, ambition, consistency, authority? Because bodies, habits, and rights are still exceedingly intermingled, in the public opinion; they are yet to be unstitched and reorganized in new, less illiberal, constellations.

FURTHER READING

The warlike underpinnings of Greek political forms, including democracy, are receiving more and more scholarly attention. See, for example, Ober 1996 and Forsdyke 2001. Against this background, and on the asymmetrical connection of courage, *andreia*, and masculinity, see Saxonhouse 1980; Gay 1988; Salkever 1991; Balot 2004. On Aristotle's theories of gendered bodies and habits, see Sissa 1990; Koziak 2000; Nichols 2002; Mayhew 2004. For the long history of ideas about sex difference in biology and medicine, before and beyond Aristotle, see Laqueur 1990; King 1999; Mansfield 2006; Sissa 2008. R. Thomas 2000 sketches the epistemological context of Hippocrates' system of humoral and climatic oppositions. Loraux 1993 remains a helpful introduction to the political myths of gender divisions in Athens.

NOTES

1   The disposition to care for the young characterizes the female, as much as an anatomical equipment to attack and defend themselves, such as horns, nails, beak, is allotted to male

bodies. Aristotle's discussion of the gender of bees offers an example of this binary logic, see: *Gen. an.* 3.10.759b1–7.

2   Ar. *Lys.* 123–5. *Peos*, pea, is a current metaphor for the penis.

3   Ar. *Eccl.* 626–9. The same system of priorities will be applied to women, in their egalitarian attribution of desirable males: the law forbids a young man to sleep with a young, sexy girl before having pleased an older, unsavory woman (690–700). Quotations from *Ecclesiazusae* trans. O'Neill 1938.

4   Aeschin. 1.185: "Such, then, was the judgment of your fathers concerning things shameful and things honorable; and shall their sons let Timarchus go free, a man chargeable with the most shameful practices, *a man and a male in the body, but who has committed womanly offences* [ton andra men ka'arrena to soma, gunaikeia d'hamarteka]? In that case, who of you will punish a woman if he finds her in wrong doing? Or what man will not be regarded as lacking intelligence who is angry with her who errs by an impulse of nature, while he treats as adviser the man who in despite of nature has sinned against his own body?" (trans. Adams 1919, adapted). I have discussed the rhetorical strategy of this speech in Sissa 2000.

5   For discussions of *thumos*, see Gay 1988; Freeland 1998; Koziak 2000. My reading of Aristotle's theory of *thumos* is connected to his biological theory of the heart. The shape and texture of the heart are responsible for the character of different animals. Animals with a soft heart are more sensitive; those with a firm muscle are dull. A small heart makes you courageous, because the vital heat remains concentrated and does not get cold; a large heart makes you timorous and cowardly, because your natural heat gets dispersed and chills out. The hare, the deer, the mouse, the hyena, the leopard, the ass, the weasel, all have a wide heart. *Part. an.* 3.667a13–19.

6   Aristotle's theory of the semen can be found in *Gen. an.* 2. See also *Movement of Animals*, 11 for his account of erection. Aristotle establishes an analogy between heart and penis, on the basis of their involuntary movements. Both organs contain vital moisture, blood, and semen; each in a sense is a separate animal.

7   Arist. *de An.* 403a25–32 on the physical definition of anger as the boiling of blood and the region surrounding the heart. Courage and anger are not, of course, only a physical event, they are the response to an attack, but the ability to feel these emotions depends on a certain quantity and quality of blood, available in the body. This is why animals can be more or less prone to passion, and why, for instance, those whose blood is "watery" are fearful. See also *Part. an.* 2.4.650b30 on watery (thus colder) blood conducive to fear, as opposed to dense, more fibrous (thus fiery) blood, making certain animals, such as bulls and boars, notoriously irascible and passionate. "The fibers therefore, being earthy and solid, are turned into so many embers in the blood and cause ebullition in the fits of passion" (*Part. an.* 651a1–3).

8   On the asymmetry of gendered bodies, and in particular on their elementary composition, see Sissa 1990, 1997; King 1999: 19–20, 39; Mayhew 2004: 63–8.

9   Arist. *Gen. an.* 1.20: "Now a boy is like a woman in form, and the woman is as it were an impotent male, for it is through a certain incapacity that the female is female, being incapable of concocting the nutriment in its last stage into semen (and this is either blood or that which is analogous to it in animals which are bloodless owing to the coldness of their nature). As then diarrhoea is caused in the bowels by the insufficient concoction of the blood, so caused in the blood-vessels all discharges of blood, including that of the menstruation, for this also is such a discharge, only it is natural whereas the others are morbid" (trans. Platt 1910).

10 Just a sample of this materialistic view, so indebted to a "hemo-cardio-centric" theory of life: *Part. an.* 651a13–17: "The character of the blood affects both the temperament and

the sensory faculties of animals in many ways. This is indeed what might reasonably be expected, seeing that the blood is the material of which the whole body is made. For nutriment supplies the material and the blood is the ultimate nutriment. It makes then a considerable difference whether the blood be hot or cold, thin or thick, turbid or clear" (trans. Ogle 1882).

11 For Loraux 1993, this is actually the point of autochthony.

12 An eloquent example of the conflation of autochthony and the Trojan War can be found in the rhetoric of the Athenian envoys sent to Syracuse in 481 in the hope of involving Gelon in a coalition against Xerxes' invasion. "Are we not Athenians, the most ancient of all Greek peoples, the only nation never to have left the soil from which it sprang? Did not the poet Homer say that we sent to Troy the best man for ordering and marshalling the army?" (Hdt. 7.161; cf. Hom. *Il.* 2.550–6).

13 Arist. *Pol.* 1260a13. Nichols 1992 offers a much more moderate interpretation of Aristotle's arguments and comes to the conclusion that fundamentally men and women are able to cooperate and better each other, in the household as well as in the city.

14 Hippoc. *Aer.* 16; quotations from Hippocrates from Adams 1849. The passage continues: "and further, owing to their laws for monarchy prevails in the greater part of Asia … Thus, then, if any one be naturally warlike and courageous, his disposition will be changed by the institutions. As a strong proof of all this, such Greeks or barbarians in Asia as are not under a despotic form of government, but are independent, and enjoy the fruits of their own labors, are of all others the most warlike; for these encounter dangers on their own account, bear the prizes of their own valor, and in like manner endure the punishment of their own cowardice."

CHAPTER 8

The Religious Contexts
of Ancient Political Thought

Robin Osborne

This chapter aims to do two things. It asks whether the theological assumptions made
by Greeks and Romans had an influence upon the ways in which political practice and
theory were conducted; and it asks whether the ways in which the worship of the gods
was organized impinged upon the world of politics and the way in which that world
was thought about (on more general issues of religion and politics see Hammer, this
volume, chapter 2).

It is fundamental to these discussions that there was not a single religion in
Greece and Rome but many different religious cults (as recent commentators have
emphasized: Beard, North, and Price 1998; Price 1999). Although many of these
cults shared basic theological assumptions and organizational practice, any general
discussion is bound to introduce a spurious sense of uniformity. I have attempted to
indicate some of the range, but the emphasis inevitably falls upon the directly state-
sanctioned cults of the Greek polis and of the city of Rome. It is important therefore
to emphasize that not only were these state-sanctioned cults not the only cults, but
the sanctioning which they received from the state was very largely a matter of
permission for, and in some cases funding of, particular cult rituals. Greek cities and
the Roman state might appoint particular religious officials, but no collective authority lay with those officials or with the body of worshippers of any particular cult or
group of cults. The existence of the church as an authoritative body alongside and in
some sense against the state has no parallel in antiquity prior to the fourth century AD
and Constantine's adoption of Christianity.

Not only was there no single voice with religious authority, but there was no
separate sphere of "religious" matters held to be outside the authority of the
state. In the modern western world religious convictions are held to be fundamentally a private matter and in the liberal state religion provides the key example of a
private matter in which political interference is regarded as inappropriate. In both
Greece and Rome religious life was public life and religious behavior as proper for

A Companion to Greek and Roman Political Thought, First Edition. Edited by Ryan K. Balot.
© 2013 Blackwell Publishing Ltd. Published 2013 by Blackwell Publishing Ltd.

political control as any other form of behavior. As Nock long ago argued, it was not religious cults but philosophical sects which imposed rules of life upon their adherents and provided the closest that the ancient world comes to fundamentalism (Nock 1933).

Theology

Until a Christian Roman Empire sought to prevent it, the Greek and Roman world worshiped many gods. The earliest Greek literature, the epics of Homer and the didactic poetry of Hesiod, dating in the form we have them from around 700 BC, was reckoned by Herodotus (2.53), writing in the later part of the fifth century, to be the source from which the Greeks learned about the gods. The Homeric epics, the *Iliad* and the *Odyssey*, describe the gods as a family, where Zeus is the most powerful but where other gods can act independently of, and to some extent contrary to, his will (Taplin 1992: ch. 5). Hesiod imagines a past where the gods were originally not in the form of men – "Chaos came to be first, and then broad-chested Earth" (*Theog.* 116–17) – but the children of Earth include some who are in human form, even though others are monsters with a hundred arms and fifty heads, and the subsequent generation, the generation of Zeus and the other Olympian gods, is entirely anthropomorphic.

The Homeric picture was variously reflected in later Greek and Roman literature, but the basic assumptions of plural sources of divine authority incompletely coordinated, of gods who both experience the emotions and reactions of humans and intervene directly in individual human lives but whose own behavior is not constrained by moral rules, and of gods who may be, but cannot certainly be, influenced by human words and actions, continue to lie behind most literary pictures of the gods through Greek tragedy to Virgilian and Ovidian epic and beyond. It was with this literary picture that those concerned to come to a closer understanding of the divine engaged critically, concerned with its plurality, with the relationship between god and man which it laid claim to, and with its immorality.

There is a close correlation between the world of the gods presented in Homeric epic and the political world which that epic portrays (compare Raaflaub, this volume, chapter 3). The multiple sources of authority on Olympus parallel the multiple sources of authority in the Greek camp at Troy in the *Iliad*, where although Agamemnon is recognized as leader, other Greek chiefs may act independently or in defiance of him. The uncertain claim which seniority gives is further reflected in the *Odyssey*, where in the absence of Odysseus, his son Telemachus cannot automatically expect to assume power, even when he comes of age. The behavior of political leaders at Troy and in Ithaca directly impinges on the lives of others, who have some, but uncertain, chances of influencing their own fate, and the political leaders' actions are unconstrained by, although they may be influenced by, moral considerations. When in *Iliad* 16 Zeus contemplates intervening to save his own son Sarpedon from death,

Hera points out to him that he could do so but that it would set a precedent for other deities. Similarly issues of precedent, and of the effect on relationships between leaders that extraordinary acts create, are at the heart of the *Iliad*'s exploration of the working of power in the human world.

But the human world and political organization of the Homeric epics is no simple mirror image of the divine world and its power structure. One notion which is repeatedly explored in explanation of the relationship between Agamemnon and the people at Troy has no parallel in descriptions of the relationship between Zeus and the other gods or Zeus and humankind. This is the image of Agamemnon (and to a less extent other paramount chiefs) as "shepherd of the people" (Haubold 2002: 17–32). By contrast to the Judaic tradition, in which the king's role as shepherd derives from god's role as shepherd (Philo, *Mos.* 1.150 f, 2.9), the Homeric king's shepherding role derives from man's shepherding of beasts, not god's shepherding of man. The metaphor of the shepherd implies that the chief has the responsibility for ensuring the safety of the people, but imposes no responsibilities or obligations upon the people toward their leader. When the people perish this is because the leader has failed in his shepherding role. By contrast, the destruction of the people is one of the means by which Zeus achieves his will – answering the prayer of Achilles to protect the honor which Agamemnon has slighted by giving the Trojans the upper hand over the Achaeans (Haubold 2002: 75–8). But if Zeus restores Achilles' honor he does not answer his every prayer, for despite Achilles' express request he does not preserve his closest companion, Patroclus, from the more general destruction.

Both the parallelism between the gods and mortal rulers and the limits to that parallelism are important. Neither the gods nor the "shepherd of the people" act in direct response to the actions of those over whom they rule. The shepherd's responsibilities are regardless of the folly or malice of the flock, and whereas men who receive gifts are obliged to reciprocate appropriately to the giver, the gods' actions are neither constrained by prayers and offerings nor governed by any sense of proportion. Notoriously, in the *Odyssey*, when Poseidon is unable to destroy Odysseus in revenge for his having blinded Poseidon's son, the Cyclops, he instead turns to stone the ship and crew in which the hospitable Phaeacians kindly returned Odysseus to his homeland. Not only are political relationships in Homeric epic not based on moral claims, but in a world where "double motivation" is the norm ("since I suffered madness, *and* Zeus took away my wits," *Il.* 19.137, emphasis added) no actor is ever in a position to refer his own actions or sufferings exclusively to the gods: "It is a remarkable paradox that nearly every important event in the *Iliad* is the doing of a god, and that one can give a clear account of the poem's entire action with no reference to the gods at all" (Janko 1992: 4). The poet of the *Iliad* once (16.384–92) claims that Zeus punishes those who pass unjust judgments, and individual characters express the expectation that oath-breakers, offenders against the laws of hospitality, and so on, will be punished by the gods (Rutherford 1996: 45). This idea that the wicked are finally punished (see Raaflaub, chapter 3) recurs elsewhere in Greek literature (cf. Hes. *Op.* 24–47), but often, as in the *Iliad*, the gods themselves are represented as unmoved by such considerations. The way that, in the short term at least, securing justice depends upon human action is nicely illustrated by the award, by men to men, of the prize for "straight judgment" in the scene of a homicide trial on the shield that Hephaestus makes for Achilles (18.497–508).

The basic theology of the *Iliad* was certainly traditional, and much can be traced back to Near Eastern roots. But the particular working out of the relationship between gods and men, and the particular presentation both of divine power and of human relations with the gods, are in various ways particular to this poem and this poet (Kirk 1990: 1–14). The poet of the *Iliad* tends to exclude the miraculous and the monstrous, and deemphasizes the gods' appetites – their enjoyment of the savor of burnt sacrifices – although retaining the idea that they enjoy sexual desire both for each other and for humans (Griffin 1977). The particular slant of the *Iliad* had considerable influence on subsequent thought, and some of the criticism of traditional beliefs about the gods simply makes explicit what is implicit already in the *Iliad*'s treatment. These criticisms reveal the extent to which the political arrangements of the Greek city-state and republican Rome were built upon the traditional theology.

Criticisms of traditional theology come in two basic forms: that it was simply what men were bound to say about the gods, and, in particular, served the interest of rulers in justifying particular patterns of human behavior; and that it failed to embody the sorts of standards which the absolute must properly embody. So, in the early fifth century, Xenophanes observed that the Ethiopians say that the gods are snub-nosed and black, and that Homer and Hesiod attributed to the gods all men's vices. A character in Critias' *Sisyphus*, written in the late fifth century, suggests that the gods are merely an invention of men to justify human demands. Plato rejects the Homeric picture of the gods, and insists instead, in book 10 of *Laws*, upon gods who care for the world and cannot be deflected from justice by anything that humans offer them.

If Xenophanes' and Critias' criticisms underline the way in which traditional theology corresponded to, and allowed space for, traditional political arrangements, Plato's reformed theology goes with a very different political order. For Plato the central religious doctrines are that soul is immortal and controls the whole world under the dictates of reason (*Leg.* 967d5–e2). The commitment of his gods to absolute values is in accord with Plato's idealist epistemology and the basis for his view that political power should be restricted to those who have proper insight into these absolute values. In book 4 of *Laws* the connection between divine and human patterns of rule is made explicit, as the fiction of the reign of Cronos becomes part of the means of persuading men of the best political organization for the state. Plato's version of the reign of Cronos holds that Cronos was aware that humans cannot rule over each other without falling into arrogance and injustice, and he therefore set nonhuman spirits as rulers of humans. From this Plato draws the conclusion that "we should run our public and our private life, our homes and our cities, in obedience to what little spark of immortality lies in us, and dignify these edicts of reason with the name of 'law'" (*Leg.* 713e8–714a2, trans. Saunders 1984). The essence of *Laws* is that the laws, not humans, should govern a state, and highest office should be given "to the man who is best at obeying the established laws" (*Leg.* 715c2).

Plato's theology provided the foundation on which later philosophical theology was built. The theology of both Epicureans and Stoics can be seen to start from

Plato's questions, and their crucial difference lies in whether or not they agree with Plato that gods care for the world. For the Epicureans gods exist but not only can they not be influenced by men but they have not a care for the world. In consequence, for Epicurus and his followers justice is simply a matter of contract between men, and potentially what is just will vary from society to society (cf. Epicurus, *Key Doctrines* 33); law is simply provided because men are not able to be mindful of utility (cf. Porphyry *Abst.* 1.7.4). The Stoics, by contrast, agree with Plato on all three counts, and for the Stoic Chrysippus, "It is not possible to discover any other source of justice nor any other origin than from Zeus and from universal nature" (Plut. *Mor.* 1035c), while according to the *Letter of Aristeas to Philocrates* gods intervene to secure virtual action (230, 265, 272). Plato thus stands at the head of the tradition of "natural law" which, developed further by Aquinas, will play so important a part in postclassical political theory.

The development of philosophical theology alongside traditional theology led to the invention in the hellenistic period of the doctrine of the "three theologies." (Feeney 1998: 15–17). Augustine in *City of God* 4.27 records that Scaevola "argued that there were three kinds of gods in the Roman tradition; one strand of tradition coming through the poets, another through the philosophers, the third through the statesmen" (trans. Bettenson 1972), and in 6.5 he has an extensive discussion of Varro's exposition of a parallel distinction between "mythical," "physical" (natural), and "civil" theology (see also Raaflaub, chapter 3). For Augustine "mythical" and "civil" theologies do not merit the name theology, since they are necessarily false, but Roman writers show an ability to sustain the three theologies in a subtle and productive way.

Virgil's gods in the *Aeneid* "are inescapably the gods of Homer, set in the same fundamental laws of epic action" (Feeney 1991: 141). Venus says of Jupiter that he rules "the affairs of men and gods with eternal commands" and terrifies them with thunderbolts (*Aen.* 1.229–30), but he is also the god who rapes both boys and women (e.g. *Aen.* 1.29), and stirs up Mezentius to battle; the morally questionable as well as the morally good is involved in his relationship to the world. But the gods of the *Aeneid* are not simply part of the epic baggage taken over from Homer, along with elaborate similes and the dactylic hexameter. Jupiter's particular concern in the poem for the well-being of the Roman state links the epic god to Jupiter Optimus Maximus of the triad of gods worshipped on the Roman Capitol. When at the very end of the poem the question is raised of Jupiter's responsibility for the fact that things are other than as they should be, this is a question not about how the gods of epic poetry act but about theodicy: "did it please you, Jupiter, that peoples who would live together in eternal peace should collide with such vast upheaval?" (*Aen.* 12.503–4).

"The manifestations of a god are necessarily local and contingent" (Feeney 1998: 104). Philosophical arguments to prove the existence of divinity, that the divine cares or does not care about humankind, or that the divine can or cannot be influenced by men, provide no practical guidance on how divine care might be bestowed or how men and gods can relate. Epicurean denial of divine interest in man leaves the world to be ruled according to principles of utility, but the Platonic and Stoic traditions leave most men in a world where they cannot comprehend the god's actions. Plato notoriously resorts to fictions to reconcile men to this lot, offering myths designed keep ordinary people satisfied and obedient to rule by the few who are enlightened. But, as Cicero observed to Atticus (*Att.* 2.1.8), the real world was the "faex Romuli," rather than Plato's *Republic*, and it was the stuff of myth, rather than the theory of the philosophers, that engaged more directly with the local and contingent. The *Aeneid* uses the tropes of prophecy, borrowed from *Odyssey* 11, and of presentation of scenes of life on armor, borrowed from *Iliad* 18, to present an ecphrasis which is also a history, an allegory which turns out to be an identity parade, as the Story of Rome from Aeneas to Augustus is put on display. The template for the working out of divine power in the world becomes the past of Rome itself, as history is turned into part of a grand plan which both establishes and justifies Rome's particular position within the world.

Christians were very ready to join in the ridicule of "mythical" religion. The very notion of a multiplicity of gods, or of gods who took a particular interest in one aspect of life, was absurd to those for whom it was a necessary assumption that divine power and knowledge was unbounded (cf. August. *De civ. D.* 6.9 for criticism, 12.19 for divine omniscience). Augustine exploits the criticism of "mythical" and "civic" religion by Varro and Seneca (*De civ. D.* 4.31, 6.10), only then himself also to criticize "natural" theology (*De civ. D.* 8), insisting that there has to be contact between men and gods (*De civ. D.* 9.16). That insistence on the existence of a mediator between God and man, together with the insistence that man was made in God's image, in fact made Christianity in important ways like "mythical" religion, albeit inverted. Augustine himself observed that "The Romans made Romulus a god because they loved him: the Church loved Christ because it believed him to be God." Virgil's investment of past Roman history with the force of destiny is closely parallel to the way in which Christians turned the Old Testament into the story of man's salvation history working up to the moment when God saves his people through his Incarnation. But where Virgil's history climaxes with Roman world rule, Christ is the end of a history of personal salvation. But if the end of Christianity is personal rather than political, with Christ as man's "only mediator and advocate" and peace, not power, the good (*De civ. D.* 19), the structure of the church, developed to protect that possibility of personal salvation, came to provide, through the specialization of priestly and episcopal mediation, both a theology and a framework for the maintenance of Roman imperial power that quite transformed the relations of politics and religion.

Cult Practice

As Augustine saw, religion as practiced in the city, Varro's "civic" religion, acted out the claims of the religion of the poets, Varro's "mythical" religion (*De civ. D.* 6.7). Just as the mythical religion of Homer and Hesiod is very closely related to that of Virgil and Ovid, so the structures of public cult in the Roman world closely resemble those in the Greek world. Sacrifice – the ritualized slaughter of domestic animals and the pouring of offerings of wine – is the central ritual for both Greeks and Romans, and for both sacrifice is surrounded by an apparatus of prayer and dedication, of temples and altars, and of priests and priestesses. But behind this checklist of cult practices lie significant institutionalized differences between Greek and Roman cult practice that beg for a political explanation.

In Greek cities priests and other religious officials were of negligible political account (Parker 2005: ch. 5). Cities might listen especially to what priests and other religious officials, such as seers, had to say on religious matters. The plot of the *Iliad* turns on Agamemnon's refusal to return the daughter of the priest Chryses and Apollo's sending of a plague which afflicts the Achaean camp in order to make Agamemnon concede, and much of the tension of Sophocles' *Oedipus Tyrannus* stems from the power of the insights of the seer Teiresias into the Theban plague, insights which Oedipus both does and does not want to hear. In Athenian history, too, we find religious officials bringing to the Assembly matters that relate to cult (as a public statement by Euthydemus, the priest of Asclepius, results in a proposal to the Athenian Assembly about using the rents from a quarry to pay for sacrifices (*IG* ii^2 47), and the Athenian seer Lampon moves amendments to a decree about the offering of first-fruits at Eleusis (*IG* i^3 78)). But priests and seers were only two of multiple sources of religious authority, and we never hear of anyone ever coveting either priesthood or the position of seer for the political influence that it gave. The important fourth century Athenian politician Lycurgus of Boutadai was a member of the family which filled two important priesthoods at Athens, and he himself was priest of Poseidon Erechtheus, but although his religious interests may be manifested in some of his policies and initiatives (granting land for a temple to Citian merchants, overhauling the dedications at a number of prominent temples, making new sacred vessels for the Panathenaea; see Humphreys 2004: ch. 3), there is no reason to believe that his religious position significantly promoted his political career. The two Spartan kings held the priesthoods of Zeus Ouranios and Zeus Lacedaimon (Hdt. 6.56.1), but this religious position was only one of the many sources of royal charismatic authority at Sparta (others of which included double portions at dinner and priority in religious rituals, whether or not either Zeus cult is involved).

Spartan kingship was hereditary – although various devices could be employed to ensure the succession of one royal offspring rather than another. So too many priests in Athens came from particular families (*genē*) and served for life. But in the fifth century some new priesthoods, at least, were chosen, as were most secular magistrates, by lot – even though priesthoods were individual and not a matter of joining a board of ten. Although women were not eligible for allotment to civil magistracies, the principle of allotment was extended to the priestess of Athena Nike established in the third quarter of the fifth century (*IG* i^3 35–6). Various priestly families seem to have gone over to the use of the lot to select among their own members (Parker 1996: 292–3). Selection by lot from a preselected list enabled potential manipulation greater than was possible with a pure inheritance or pure lottery system, but there was no way that even the scion of a *genos* could ever ensure that they would succeed to a priesthood. The holding of office for life distinguished priestly from secular officeholders, and the randomness with which vacancies occurred in priesthoods further contributed to the impossibility of banking on the acquisition of priestly office.

In Greek Asia Minor, from the fourth century onward, the situation was different: priesthoods were sold (Dignas 2002: 251–71). Sometimes the sale was restricted to members of a priestly family, sometimes it was for life, but increasingly priesthoods were sold on an annual basis. Such annual priesthoods, accessible to those who could bid the highest, were much closer to secular magistracies than were the priesthoods of classical Athens – especially since magistracies too could involve shouldering financial as well as administrative burdens. These were cities in a different position to the autonomous city-states of classical Greece. They were subordinate to major powers – hellenistic kings (for whom see Eckstein, this volume, chapter 16 for religion aspects) and then to Rome – and wealth became increasingly the main route to political influence as wealthy men served as ambassadors and bought favor for their cities.

By contrast, in the Roman Republic, although once more sources of religious authority were highly diffuse, there was considerable political competition to hold a priesthood, and the position of "chief priest" (*pontifex maximus*), in particular, came to be coveted by ambitious politicians and could be the basis for political influence and manipulation. Like magistracies, after the "struggle of the orders" the colleges of priests had a minimum number of plebeian members stipulated (by the *lex Ogulnia* of 300 BC), and as with magistracies, the number in the priestly colleges was raised over the years, and in particular by Sulla (Beard 1990: 35). Popular election was brought in as the method of choosing the *pontifex maximus* in the third century BC, and in 104 BC the *lex Domitia* was passed which established that in future new augurs, *pontifices*, *XVviri* and *VIIviri* would be chosen by popular election, albeit from a shortlist chosen by the existing priests themselves (Beard 1990: 23). This both ensured future political importance for these priests and reflected the political nature of the role that they already enjoyed. Priests were expected to acquire and deploy expert religious knowledge, but that knowledge gave them an authority which could be transferred into the political realm.

The differences between Greece and Rome come out clearly if we consider the sources of advice on ritual matters. Plato's dialogue *Euthyphro*, an investigation into piety, frames itself around the actions of Euthyphro, who is bringing an action against his own father for manslaughter after the father has left a murderer in a ditch where he has died. The murderer died while Euthyphro's father was seeking advice on what he should do with him from an *exegetes*, that is, an expounder of religious law. *Exegetai* are somewhat mysterious, and were important enough for Plato to make special, and obscure, arrangements for their appointment in his *Laws* (679d), but their exposition never becomes a political matter. On major religious issues the ultimate source of authority was the oracle at Delphi. By contrast, giving advice on ritual matters was at Rome the duty of the college of *pontifices*, and their intervention to determine matters of burial and family religion, as well as of the proper procedure for establishing temples and sacrifices, gave them a political role, bridging, as their name suggested, between the ultimate source of authority on these matters, the senate, and the people (Beard 1990: 39).

The political significance of priestly office and of religious authority comes out clearly from three incidents in the period during which Caesar, Pompey, and Crassus allied to form the "First Triumvirate" and dominate Roman politics. The first is Caesar's seeking and achieving election in 63 BC to the position of *pontifex maximus*. His campaign for this office seems to have involved not only electoral bribery of the special tribal assembly responsible for the election, but the invention of the tradition that Iulus, mythical founder of the Iulii, had been *pontifex maximus* at Alba Longa (L. Taylor 1949: 43). The second is the use by Bibulus, consul with Caesar in 59 BC, of the device of watching for omens in an attempt to prevent Caesar passing legislation. The third is Cicero's writing to Atticus and suggesting that one thing that would make him support the triumvirs would be the offer of a place in the college of the augurs (*Att.* 2.5.2).

Both the causes and the consequences of the Roman republican expectation that religious office should have a political impact deserve consideration. Given the essentially parallel mythical theology in the Greek city-state and in Rome, and given the acceptance by Roman scholars writing in the late republic that Roman civic religion was quite separate from the "natural" religion of the philosophers, the very different position of religious officials with regard to politics demands explanation. Part of what separates Rome from classical Athens is the commitment of Rome to popular election. Athens selected all bar its military and its highest financial magistrates by lot, relying on boards of ten magistrates in every office to guarantee that the lot could provide sufficient competence. Rome did not employ the lot as a mechanism of selection, but from bottom to top elected its magistrates by various sorts of popular election. Just how "democratic" Roman electoral procedures were has been much debated (see most recently Mouritsen 2001), but the important fact for the current question is that those who held office had been selected by a process that involved weighing capacities against criteria. Those elected to civil magistracies might not be the most expert in the relevant capacities, since there were limits on age and reelection, but they would at least be the best of those available. The Athenian lot enabled no such judgment to be made – rather it was itself made possible by the assumption, most clearly articulated in the myth told by Protagoras in Plato's homonymous dialogue, that all citizens had the relevant minimum of qualifications. In consequence the Athenians had no expectation that those who held office had peculiar virtues that demanded special respect. Like the Romans, the Athenians came to select their priests by processes parallel to, if not identical with, the processes by which they selected their civil magistrates, but with diametrically opposite effects.

Neat though this parallel is, it cannot entirely account for the difference between Greek and Roman practice. For there seems to be no expectation that priestly office was a route to political authority in *any* Greek city, and many Greek cities *did* elect their magistrates, as Sparta elected its ephors. A further factor lies in the strong Roman identification of particular gods with particular places. Greek cities had their own poliad deities, and in every city there was a main cult. But not only did many cities share worship of Athena Polias as their main deity, but the distinction between, say, Athena Polias at Athens and Athena Chalkioikos at Sparta seems never to be stressed. Local heroes might come to a city's assistance at a particular place, as the hero Ekhetlaos was said to have appeared to help the Athenians on the battlefield at Marathon (Pausanias 1.32.4), but it is rare for anything to be made of capturing the gods or heroes of another city. When Herodotus (5.82–6) tells the story of Athens trying to seize the statues of Damia and Auxesia from Aegina, the motivation he gives is that Aegina had refused to offer the annual sacrifice to Athena Polias and Erechtheus which had been the price which the Epidaurians, from whom the Aeginetans had themselves acquired the statues, had been accustomed to pay for the original use of Athenian olive wood for the statues. In marked contrast stands the Roman ritual of *evocatio*, the ritual summoning out of the enemy city of its god. The most famous instance of this is the evocation from Veii of Juno Regina in 396 BC (Livy 5.21 ff.), but a form of this ritual seems to have been operated in the first century BC, to judge by the inscriptional evidence from Isaura Vetus in modern Turkey. This belief that the gods could, and should, be recruited is related to another Roman ritual with no parallel in Greece: the ritual operated by the priestly college of the *fetiales* when the Romans declared war, whereby the war was proclaimed to be just. This ritual involved the public declaration of the Roman grievance which Jupiter was called upon to witness, a period of 33 days when the enemy could concede the claim, and then a symbolic casting of a spear into enemy territory.

As to what lay at the root of this thorough politicizing of the gods at Rome, we can only speculate. Although various Greek cities traced back their origin to particular mythical figures, and made those mythical figures the basis of claims to political friendship (C. Jones 1999), and although the Athenians literally regarded themselves as a "race apart" in claiming to be autochthonous (cf. Loraux 1986, 1993), Rome constructed itself as distinct from the other people of Italy in a much stronger way. This is reflected in the Roman claims to descent from immigrant Trojan refugees from the sack of Troy (Erskine 2001), which seem to have been well formed by the end of the third century BC. Whereas Greek cities recognized cult as one of the things that they had in common – Herodotus 8.144.2 has the Athenians cite common cult places and cult practices as one reason why they would never go over to Persia – Rome was inclined to treat the peoples of Italy as barbarians until such time as they were incorporated into the Roman state, and to stress contrasts in their religious life rather than what they had in common (Dench 1995: ch. 4). Panhellenism was something which various Greek politicians and political thinkers from time to time sought to promote. They had at best limited and temporary success, and that only at moments, such as opposing the Persians, when falling apart was clearly the only alternative to standing together, but the thought that Greeks *ought* to be united was never seriously opposed. By contrast, the only comparable movement with regard to Italy was the combination of Italian peoples against Rome in the Social War at the beginning of the first century BC, and there is only occasional and faint trace, as perhaps in the misohellene Cato's decision as to how to structure his *Origines*, of any conviction that Italy *should* form a unit.

One particular incident deserves attention in this context. In the early second century BC the Romans became worried by activities that were going on in various places in Italy in connection with the cult of Bacchus/Dionysus. The senate passed a resolution which severely restricted the cult, and sent out copies of the resolution to be posted in various parts of Italy. The survival of one copy (*CIL* 1^2.581) from Tiriolo in Calabria, and a long account in Livy 39.8–19 enable us to see both what was done in 186 BC and what Roman tradition made of the affair. In one sense the suppression of the cult was entirely within the tradition of suspicion and hostility toward the god Dionysus. Such hostility is variously embodied in Greek myth, but most famously in Pentheus' attempt to keep Dionysus out of Thebes, as staged in Euripides' *Bacchae*. Cult activity which involved women (only) engaging in rituals not in temples but in the wild countryside and in which the women came to perceive the world differently, and in particular to relate differently to wild nature, is presented in these myths as in tension with the order of the Greek city. But the Roman acting out of the myths to destroy existing cult places, to require future cult activity to happen only with the express permission of the *praetor urbanus* and the Roman senate, and to limit future groups to not more than three men and two women, is quite unlike any intervention in cult activity by any historic Greek city.

The consequences of Roman politicization of priestly office and cult practice extend well beyond the manipulation of matters of cult in relation to the peoples of Italy. In 12 BC Augustus became *pontifex maximus*, and from that point on that office was held by every emperor. The imagery of the emperor sacrificing became both one of the most prevalent imperial iconographies and the dominant sacrificial iconography (Ryberg 1955), with the forging of an artificial scene which fused together different moments in the ritual and transferred the focus from the victim to the sacrificer (Gordon 1990a: 203–5). Imperial domination of the priesthood, both in terms of the office of *pontifex maximus* and in terms of the iconography, inevitably diminished the role of the priestly colleges. Consultation of the colleges became rare, the political significance of the priesthood was concentrated entirely on the one figure of the emperor, and the political desirability of belonging to one of the colleges came to rest on the manifestation of imperial favor and the proximity to the emperor which being made a member signified. The particular Roman construction of the priestly role became in this way a tool of imperial rule.

If the imperial monopoly of the chief priesthood by the emperor led to the emasculation of the priestly colleges, the senate retained its religious authority. It came, indeed, to exercise that authority in an important new way. For it was the senate whose decree had "set Caesar among the stars" and which proceeded to turn approved emperors into gods on their death (Gradel 2002: chs 3 and 12). The emperor, who in life, as *pontifex maximus*, had mediated between senate and people, on death could come to mediate between man and god – whether or not he did so depended precisely on how satisfied the senate was that he had in life performed his mediation between themselves and the people to its satisfaction. For all that emperors might protest their humanity in their lifetime, and intellectuals might mock the rituals of deification after an emperor's death, as Seneca does in his *Apocolocyntosis*, the recognition of the supreme political agent as also divine was simply the operation of the logic of Roman religious cult (Feeney 1998: 108–14).

The politics of cult was also instrumental in Roman rule over its empire in ways that did not centrally involve the emperor. Just as issues of cult had been at the center of Rome's differentiation from the peoples of Italy, so it remained at the center of

Rome's differentiation from the peoples of the empire (Gordon 1990a: 207). It continued to be the case that cults from elsewhere were adopted in Rome and by the citizens of Rome, but those cults were measured against the sacrificial system over which the emperor as *pontifex maximus* presided. In some senses, the cults that develop in the empire do so against the pattern of Roman civic cult, renegotiating sacrifice, establishing alternative criteria for priesthood (cf. the grades of Mithraic initiation), and establishing goals that were personal rather than civic. While the Romans did not automatically move to suppress all cults that fell outside the framework of its civic religion, the potential for conflict was ever present. We see this in the relationship of the Romans to Judaism, which was problematic because of its own strong identification of religious and political leadership. Roman attempts to capitalize on this by making the high priest a Roman political appointment met limited success (Gordon 1990b: 244–5).

While the Romans tried to incorporate Judaism by transforming it into another civic cult, they attempted to reject Christianity as not a religion at all but, like the practices of some of the people of central Italy in earlier centuries, *superstitiones*. Christians neither accepted animal sacrifice nor integrated themselves into the civic structure. The other-worldly goals of early Christianity, admired by some non-Christians as approaching the condition of the philosophers (so Galen *Summary of Plato's Republic* 3), rejected entirely the linking of political and religious elites and set up a quite alternative structure of charismatic authority. As the second century *Epistle to Diognetus* says of Christians:

> while they dwell in Greek or barbarian cities according as each man's lot has been cast, and follow the customs of the land in clothing and food, and other matters of daily life, yet the condition of citizenship which they exhibit is wonderful, and admittedly strange. They live in countries not their own, but simply as sojourners; they share the life of citizens, they endure the lot of foreigners; every foreign land is to them a fatherland, and every fatherland a foreign land … They spend their existence upon earth, but their citizenship is in heaven. (5.4–5, 9, trans. Stevenson 1989 after Radford)

Ironically, that alternative lifestyle and authority structure, politicized by the very persecution which sought to destroy it, came to prove irresistibly attractive to the Emperor Constantine, who saw in the church a network of power more strongly integrated than the discrete local networks formed by traditional Greco-Roman religion.

The practices and institutions of the religions in the Greco-Roman world were inevitably in conversation with the practices and institutions of political organization in that world. There is little doubt that the development of Christianity to be cosmopolitan, and not tied to a chosen people, along with the ambitious claims to universal dominion of the Christian God, by contrast to the particularist interests of both Olympian deities and the god of Judaic tradition, were enabled by the very existence of the Roman Empire. Worship of the emperor conveniently aligned the interests of the deity with those of the overarching political unit, something which worship of none of the parochially defined manifestations of Olympian religion could offer. Worship of the Christian god offered, and would continue to offer, the advantage of not even respecting the boundary of the political empire.

Philosophical ("natural") religion gave little or no purchase on the political world. Christianity, for all that it was built on an inversion of conventional values, respected, as it reflected, the political world. As we move from considering the gods of the city to considering the *City of God*, the theological and cultic construction of the world remains a most important context within which to view political thought.

FURTHER READING

Scholars have been much more ready to discuss institutional aspects of Greek and Roman religion than to discuss its theology. The best introduction to Greco-Roman theological questions is Feeney 1998. For the Homeric gods see Griffin 1980: chs 5 and 6.

Bremmer 1999 provides an excellent general introduction to Greek religion and to modern scholarship. Price 1999 is an alternative, wide-ranging, guide. For an in-depth study of religion in classical Athens see Parker 1996 and 2005. None of these pays much attention to the archaeological evidence, for different aspects of which see van Straten 1992 and 1995 and Spawforth 2006, and in particular the volumes of *Thesaurus Cultorum Rituum Antiquorum*, which have just begun to appear. Issues of Roman religion are well introduced by Feeney 1998. Beard, North, and Price 1998 provides both a thorough history of religions at Rome and a wealth of illustrative textual and archaeological material. For issues of priesthood, in the ancient world in general, but particularly at Rome, see Beard and North 1990. On imperial cult see Price 1984, Gradel 2002.

PART II

Democracies and Republics

CHAPTER 9

Democracy Ancient and Modern

Peter Liddel

Introduction

Forms of democratic self-governance emerged in many of the Greek poleis (city-states) of the archaic and classical period (Hansen and Nielsen 2004: 1338–40). The most famous democratic polis was Athens, but institutions that gave the people some role in decision-making are attested in other poleis from the late seventh century BC onward and in Near Eastern societies before then (Robinson 1997: 16–25). Democracy flourished on the level of the polis in the classical period and appears to have continued in many states even in the hellenistic period (O'Neill 1995: 103–20; cf. Rhodes with Lewis 1997: 531–6). Subpolis organizations such as the Athenian demes functioned as democracies (Osborne 1985a: 64–92); at the other end of the scale, interpolis confederacies such as the Achaian League (O'Neill 1995: 121–33) possessed a popular assembly without power being in the hands of a popular body. According to some interpretations, certain, albeit not many, aspects of the Roman political system may be deemed democratic (see Tatum, this volume, chapter 14).

The fundamental sense in which ancient Greek government was democratic was the centrality of adult male citizens, regardless of their economic status, in individual, corporative, and collective capacities, to the judicial, executive, and legislative workings of government. Democracy was "people power": democracies held the principle that all citizens, including the poor, had equal political power by law. Mechanisms such as the use of lot and election for the filling of magistracies were also important, but the fact that these were employed in organizations (such as the late fourth century Hellenic League of the Antigonid monarchs: see Austin 2006: no. 50) where the mass of citizens did not possess political power suggests that they were not defining. I shall open this contribution with an exploration of the context and content of democratic values that circulated in Greek literature, highlighting the notion of equality and the debate about the value and extent of popular participation, and observing congruencies with, and differences from, modern thought. After

A Companion to Greek and Roman Political Thought, First Edition. Edited by Ryan K. Balot.
© 2013 Blackwell Publishing Ltd. Published 2013 by Blackwell Publishing Ltd.

demonstrating the ways in which the institutions of the ancient Athenian form of democracy made popular participation a possibility, in the fourth part of this essay I shall assess the extent to which the reality of democratic political activity lived up to the ideals of inclusivity and empowerment suggested in its values and institutions. An outline of some of the key differences between ancient and modern democracies will lead to an examination of what the study of ancient Greek democracy might offer to the democratic societies of the modern world.

Democratic Values

In contrast to the modern world, which, since Alexis de Tocqueville's *Democracy in America* (first published 1835–40), has produced a huge and varied corpus of democratic theory (see Blaug and Schwarzmantel 2001), no ancient Greek political thinker composed a fully articulated statement or justification of democratic values. It may be the case that, in Athens, the everyday reality of such a system, combined with the prevailing orality of democratic practice, would have made the prospect of such a treatise appear mundane or self-defeating (Brock 1991: 169). But ancient Greek literature, and in particular the corpus of Attic oratory, contains a wealth of references to debates about democracy and democratic values, indicating that there was indeed discussion and contention about the ideals, merits, and problems of democracy in fifth and fourth century Greece. Indeed, some modern historians have attempted to reconstruct an impression of democratic ideologies (see Raaflaub 1989a; Ober 1989; Brock 1991).

One of the earliest extant statements of democratic values is that which appears in an extraordinary section of Herodotus' *Histories*, a work written in the second half of the fifth century BC. Herodotus put into the mouths of three Persian nobles arguments about what form of government the Persians should establish (Hdt. 3.80–3; cf. 6.43.3; Pelling 2002). The first speaker, Otanes, made a case for popular government by reference to the inclination of monarchical power to become corrupt, inconsistent, and irresponsible. Democracy, on the other hand, was said to feature *isonomia* (equality before the law), the appointment of accountable magistrates by lot, and the discussion among the people of all public resolutions (*bouleumata*) (3.80). The debate was hypothetical: Herodotus probably fabricated the speakers' words, referring to slogans and institutions with which his Greek readers would have been familiar. Nevertheless, two important points emerge from this text: first that the Greeks were, by the 420s BC, thinking about how to distinguish democracy from other systems and to demonstrate its superiority; second, that descriptions of democratic ideas would draw upon the institutional bases of democracy. Significantly, it appears to be the case that democratic ideologies, which justified and explained the democratic system, developed long after the emergence of democratic institutions and practices.

Further justifications of the democratic system appear in Athenian texts, some of which were pronounced on public occasions before audiences consisting of Athenian male (and perhaps female) citizens. One of the most oft-cited Athenian justifications of democracy is that of Pericles' funeral speech for the war dead at the end of the first year of the Peloponnesian War, preserved in Thucydides' history of that war (Thuc. 2.36–46; see Loraux 1986; cf. Samons 2004: 55–7, 187–95). Pericles spoke of equality before the law, of the inclusion of the poor in political processes, of freedom from interference, but also of respect for magistrates, laws and customs (Thuc. 2.37). In a tragedy, *The Suppliant Women*, staged in Athens at the time of the Peloponnesian War (most likely between 426 and 416 BC: see Morwood 2007), Euripides made the legendary Athenian king Theseus a spokesperson for Athenian democratic values. Athens was said to be free because the people (*demos*) rule, taking turns in annual rotation, allowing the wealthy no precedence: in this sense there was equality of political privileges (on the issue of political rights, see Cartledge and Edge, this volume, chapter 10) and access to justice which was guaranteed by the rule of law (Eur. *Supp*. 404–7, 433–7). Freedom was said to consist of the privilege of making a spoken proposal at the assembly (438–41). By enunciating a justification of democracy on the tragic stage, Euripides appeared to embrace the democratic culture which offered political freedoms to his audience (on tragedy and democracy see Henderson 2007; D. Carter 2007).

But *The Suppliant Women* reminds us of a phenomenon suggested in Herodotus' constitutional debates: the fact that justifications of democratic practice often emerge during the course of polemical encounters with opponents of democracy. As we shall see below (in the final section), modern advocates of deliberative democracy praise Athenian democracy because it appears to have encouraged debate and discussion. Euripides' Theseus' words are spoken in response to those of a herald from Thebes, who claimed that democratic political organizations were prone both to the selfish rhetoric of a demagogue, and the caprice of the mob (*ochlos*) (Eur. *Supp*. 411–20). This is reminiscent of Otanes' opponent Megabyzus, who spoke of the brutality and thoughtlessness of the people, carrying a policy like a rushing torrent (Hdt. 3.81.2), or the words of Darius, who claimed that democracy gives rise to political cliques and demagogues (Hdt. 3.82.4). Comparable criticisms of Athenian democracy emerge from the extensive evidence for antidemocratic thinkers (Roberts 1994: 48–92; Ober 1998) but also those without a specific agenda (E. Harris 2005). Plato's philosophy has recently been interpreted as deeply engaged in the Athenian democratic culture in which he lived (Monoson 2000; Wallach 2001), but in the *Republic*, he presented democracy as an anarchic but agreeable form of society, in which there was an excess of liberty (*Resp*. 557a–d, 562a–d). Aristotle's interpretation of democracy centered on the idea of equality: democracies apply numerical equality rather than proportionate equality, which meant that supremacy rested with the majority rather than with an elite minority distinguished by birth, wealth, or education (*Pol*. 1317a40–1318a10). Ideas about equality also emerged in the Athenian law courts: Aeschines (1 *Against Timarchus* 5) reminded the jurors that their government was based on "equality and law" as a way of demanding that they punish his opponent.

The picture that emerges suggests that a handful of closely knit concepts cropped up frequently in ancient Athenian formulations of democratic values: liberty (in both positive and negative manifestations: see Wallace, this volume, chapter 11), the rule of law, accountability and incorruptibility, the significance of popular initiative and participation in political activity, and the notion of equality. Ian Morris has recently argued that the notion of equality has its origins in a challenge, which emerged across

Greece in the archaic period, posed toward aristocratic elitism by a set of "middling" ideologies; this conflict made possible the emergence of a broader democratic equality in the classical period (I. Morris 1996). The idea of citizen equality is attested in classical Sparta (a city which made use of a combination of democratic, oligarchic, and kingly institutions: see Cartledge 2001: 55–67), where citizens were called *homoioi* ("equals"), but it is hard to find evidence for the practice of political egalitarianism in that city (Cartledge 2001: 72–3). In Athens, on the other hand, there is particularly strong evidence for a notion of equality of political privileges (Raaflaub 1996b). In addition to the idea of *isonomia* (see above; Lévy 2005), important to the Athenians were ideas of *isēgoria* ("equal rights of speech"), and *isogonia* (equality of birth), a quality bolstered by the Athenian claim that all her citizens possessed a common ancestor (Hansen 1999: 81–5; Loraux 1986: 193–4; Rosivach 1987). One Athenian orator of the fourth century BC claimed that law and equality were bases of Athenian democracy that made it distinct from oligarchy (Aeschines 1.5). As Balot has suggested, the Athenian conception of equality was sometimes founded on the claim that all citizens were naturally qualified to contribute to the running of democracy (Balot 2006: 78–84; cf. Hansen 1999: 81–5): as we shall see, this claim was contentious in antiquity.

Democratic slogans like equality, liberty, and the rule of law suggest that there is considerable overlap between ancient and modern democratic values (Hansen 2005a), though close scrutiny of these values highlights important distinctions (Hansen 1996; 1999: 81–5; Roberts 1996; Ober and Hedrick 1996). Important strands of modern liberal democratic values are absent from Athenian thinking: these include the concern for religious tolerance (freedom of religious practice was not an issue in the ancient Greek city-states), minimizing the effects of socioeconomic inequality, and the question of how best to address inequalities emerging from gendered and ethnic difference (Rawls 2001: 64–6; Blaug and Schwarzmantel 2001: 120–41). Whereas ancient Athenian democracy was a slave-holding society which gave equal political privileges only to Athenian citizens, modern interpretations of equality tend to emphasize human equality (Hansen 1999: 81–2; Blaug and Schwarzmantel 2001: 132–41; Balot 2006: 78–84). Marxist critiques of liberal democracy suggest that its notion of political equality is undermined by the social and economic inequalities that emerge in a capitalist class-based economy (Blaug and Schwarzmantel 2001: 232–9); the Athenians, on the other hand, did not think that economic redistribution was a prerequisite for political equality (or, for that matter, liberty). Pericles, for instance, insisted that equality of political privileges was unimpeded by poverty (Thuc. 2.37.1). It is clear, therefore, that ancient democratic thought was concerned with political equality but not socioeconomic equality. Liberal historians of Greece (George Grote in the nineteenth century and Josiah Ober in the twentieth) have gone further, suggesting, quite plausibly, that the Athenians, by empowering the masses, instead sought political solutions to socioeconomic tensions (Grote 1906: 6.6–15; Ober 1989; fourth century Syracuse, where redistribution was on the political agenda, was exceptional: see Consolo Langher 2005).

Both modern and ancient interpretations of equality share an absence of consensus in the debate about the desirability and extent of popular participation in government. Elitist forms of democratic theory, such as that of Joseph Schumpeter, propose restricting the role of the people to selecting a government and delegating leadership and decision-making to them (Blaug and Schwarzmantel 2001: 92–4). On the other hand, theorists such as J. S. Mill have urged that democracy might be revived by raising levels of participation through decentralization and the reinforcement of arenas for public debate (Blaug and Schwarzmantel 2001: 542–50). There was no theory of elitist democracy in the ancient Greek world, but there was debate about the value of popular and expert contributions to democratic politics: the most famous statement of the valuation of male citizen participation is that which Pericles proposes in the first half of his funeral speech: "we alone believe the man who does not participate not as a man who minds his own business [*apragmon*], but we believe he is useless [*achreios*]" (Thuc. 2.40.2). The clauses which follow these words, in which the speaker insists upon the complementarity of action and deliberation, evoke the idea that the Athenians alone are able to perform bravely in battle because they have collectively pooled their ideas in order to calculate the best possible action. This passage is the strongest surviving statement of a social obligation on Athenian citizens to contribute toward public decision-making. Given Thucydides' tendency to reinterpret and report political discourse in his own terms, we cannot assume that the ideas that emerge in his work are a fair reflection of contemporary discussions of political activity. However, given the fact that the presentation of political activity as a virtuous contribution is a theme that emerges in other evidence for the discourse of Athenian politics (Liddel 2007: 228–56), it is likely that Thucydides' words reflect a contemporary discussion about the value and necessity of popular participation.

The potential contribution of the people to the political process was given philosophical and allegorical elaboration in Plato's *Protagoras*. In that dialogue, Plato put a so-called Great Speech into the mouth of Protagoras, a fifth century philosopher and itinerant teacher of rhetoric (a sophist: see Kerferd 1981). Protagoras claimed that Zeus, when he realized that man was without adequate means to protect himself from wild animals, sent Hermes to bestow upon all men the arts of respect for others and justice, so that there would be order in their communities. Political virtue arises from these qualities: this is the reason, says Protagoras, that the Athenians allow their citizens to deliberate about questions concerning political excellence (Pl. *Prt.* 322d–323c). This allegory may be read as a justification of mass participation in political deliberation and the idea that all citizens might use their own initiative to contribute to the workings of a community: it may be an expression of Protagoras' own views (Rosen 1994; Ostwald 2005). Protagoras, however, does not rule out the possibility that some men have more aptitude for politics than others; indeed, in the lines that follow this passage, he suggests that a teacher can help to improve a student's level of political virtue (323c–324d).

The value of popular participation and its relation to leadership appears to have been fiercely contended in popular arenas, and at points it appears that there was an ongoing debate about the question of how central good leadership was to effective decision-making. Athenagoras was reported by Thucydides to have claimed, at a meeting of the Syracusan assembly, that the masses were the best at listening to different arguments and judging between them (Thuc. 6.39.1). Cleon, an Athenian said by Thucydides to have been "most persuasive" (3.36.6) among the people in the

420s BC, in an assembly debate over the treatment of rebellious allies of Athens, felt the need to challenge the elitist argument that learned and wise men were better at the administration of the city (3.37.3–4). Demosthenes, in his defence speech *On the Crown*, emphasized instead the contribution of the individual statesman (Dem. 18.173). For this fourth-century statesman, the value of open political participation was that it allowed political experts to offer advice, make speeches, and enact laws and decrees (Dem. 18.320–2). Another Athenian, the fourth century exile Xenophon, envisaged a central political role for a *prostatēs tēs poleōs* (protector of the city) in the improvement of his state's finances (Xen. *Mem.* 3.6). Indeed, when we look at the evidence for the institutions and the actual workings of the Athenian polis, these parallel discourses about the desirability of broad participation are reproduced in the existence of an inclusive, egalitarian framework which made room for people power alongside a political elite (Ober 1989; see below, "The Practices of Democracy"). Greek democracy had the capacity to foster the emergence of a bipolar system of values; but also, as we shall see in the following two sections, in terms of institutions and practices.

Democratic Institutions

So far this discussion has focused upon expressions of democratic values (with particular emphasis on equality and the extent of popular participation) in a general Greek context. Owing to the fact that the best-attested form of Greek democracy is that which existed in Athens during the fifth and fourth centuries, the following discussion of Greek democratic institutions will draw exclusively on the testimonia for democratic Athens: it should be pointed out, however, that democratic practices elsewhere, in places such as Erythrai, Kos, Rhodes, Iasos or the cities of Sicily were quite different (see O'Neill 1995). Given that comprehensive overviews of Athenian democratic institutions already exist (Hansen 1987, 1999; Rhodes 1972, 1981a), this section will focus on the ways in which Athens' political institutions encouraged political equality by promoting wide popular participation in governance.

The exclusion of noncitizens (metics, foreigners, and slaves) from the workings of democracy was a product of the polis centeredness of its organization. Participation, of course, was envisaged by the Athenians not as a human right but as a privilege of male citizens of the Athenian polis, who, from 451 BC, were legally defined as those who were born of a citizen father and mother (Arist. *Ath. Pol.* 26; Davies 2004). Women too were excluded from all political privileges; they were not permitted to represent even their own cases in the courts (Just 1989: 26–39).

The extent to which the institutions of Athenian democracy set in place absolutely equal privileges of participation for all citizens is unclear. Among the reforms connected with Solon was the division of the citizen body on the basis of agricultural productivity into four socioeconomic classes (*Ath. Pol.* 7). At the time of Solon, the lowest class, known as the *thetes*, were deemed ineligible for magistracies, and this restriction was probably never repealed, though, in all likelihood, it was ignored by the second half of the fourth century (Rhodes 1981a: 145–6). *Thetes* however appear to have possessed the right to attend, vote, speak, and propose legislation at the *ekklēsia* (Assembly) and to initiate prosecutions at the law courts.

The history of Athenian democratic institutions to the end of the fifth century BC is narrated in the fourth century *Athēnaiōn Politeia* (this is the *Constitution of Athens* attributed to Aristotle: see Rhodes 1981a: 58–63). Over the course of the sixth and fifth centuries, political participation was extended to an expanding proportion of the citizen body (Hansen 1999: 27–54; Sinclair 1988: 13–23). Solon, the traditional date for whose reforms is 594 BC, was connected with the right of all Athenian citizens to bring grievances (either their own or those of a fellow citizen) to the courts (*Ath. Pol.* 9) and the selection of magistrates by lot (*Ath. Pol.* 8). Cleisthenes appears to have overseen the enlargement to 500 members of the Athenian *boulē* (council), the body which prepared the agenda of the *ekklēsia* (Robinson 2004: 95–122); he is accredited also with the introduction of a system by which members of that council were drawn from the 139 demes, the subpolis institutions which were the main form of civic organization across the territory of Athens (*Ath. Pol.* 21). The establishment of demes as political entities (with their own magistrates and decision-making bodies) was a vital step in the introduction of political activity to a wide spectrum of citizens (see the next section). Pericles is accredited with introducing payment for jury service in the courts (*Ath. Pol.* 27); he may well also have been responsible for introducing payment for councilors and the other magistrates (Hansen 1999: 37–8). The introduction of payment for attending the *ekklēsia* in the early fourth century (*Ath. Pol.* 41.3, 62.1) marked the zenith of institutional encouragement to popular participation in the decision-making process.

Ideas about popular political intervention were expressed in Athenian laws and decrees, and in particular those which aimed to guard against tyranny. In the aftermath of a short nondemocratic period of government, in 410 the Athenians passed a decree which said that all citizens were to take an oath to assassinate anyone plotting to overthrow democracy (Lyc. 1.127). While such institutional impositions of political participation were far from the norm in democratic Athens, it is likely that institutional pressure was exerted on Athenian citizens to fill offices when there were too few volunteers (Rhodes 1981a: 511–12). In addition to the discussion about the value and necessity of popular participation, and the social expectation that prominent politicians would make a contribution to a debate (see the second section above), the fact that the debate of the first item on every assembly's agenda was introduced with the question "Who wishes to speak?" (Hansen 1987: 91) suggests that contribution to political activity could also be construed as an opportunity or a privilege.

Popular participation and initiative were central to the working of Athenian democracy. The Assembly was at the heart of direct democracy inasmuch as it offered opportunities for the male citizen to get involved in the decisions made on behalf of his city. This was the body which made decrees (*psephismata*), though these usually followed the general guidance or the specific recommendation of the *boule* (R. Sinclair 1988: 88–101). The workings of the Assembly were reliant on both individual initiative and participation: some decisions required ratification by a quorum of 6,000 (Hansen 1987: 15). But at the same time it is quite unlikely that the Pnyx, the auditorium at which the Assembly usually met, could ever have accommodated even the fourth century Athenian male citizen population of 30,000 (Hansen 1987: 17). In the fourth century, the statute-making mechanisms of the Athenian state were divided between a number of institutions also reliant on volunteerism: laws (*nomoi*) proposed by Athenian citizens were passed to the *nomothetai*, a board which was drawn from the pool of 6,000 volunteer jurors, who decided whether the law was to be enacted or not (Rhodes 2003b). The law courts themselves were important institutions for the functioning of Athenian politics: in the fourth century Athenian citizens were able, by the process known as *graphē paranomōn*, to prosecute a proposer of a law or decree for making an illegal proposal. If the prosecution was successful, the proposal was annulled (Hansen 1974). Accordingly, both in the law courts and in the Assembly there was room for an individual citizen to make a political impact. The council (*boulē*) was the other important organ of popular government: it prepared the agenda of the Assembly and took responsibility for the everyday affairs of the polis. Citizens, selected probably by lot, sat on the council for a year at a time and were forbidden from holding a seat either for more than one year consecutively or more than twice in a lifetime (Rhodes 1972). The fact that councilors were drawn from the whole territory of Attica and from the across the board of socioeconomic classes meant that its consistency and interests, in all likelihood, would have replicated that of the whole community of citizens. Councilors would have represented the interests of their fellow demesmen (Osborne 1985a: 92); in this sense the council acted as a representative force in Athenian democracy. The institutions of Athenian democracy, therefore, made room for a high degree of political participation; in fact the legislative and judicial workings of Athens were reliant upon popular initiative, participation, and debate. As will become clear in the next section, the existence of elected offices (principally the generalship) and the premium placed on the power of persuasion meant that political expertise was at the same time highly valued.

The Practices of Democracy

To some degree, the practices of democracy in Athens followed the pattern of inclusiveness set by its values and institutions. Allowing the people to propose or to make decisions by majority vote is one way of solving the problem of how the theory of popular rule might be translated into a legitimate democratic reality. Indeed, the people were so powerful in their collective decision-making capacity that in 411 BC, they were able to abolish their own democracy when perceived external pressures made it appear expedient to do so (Thuc. 8.69). Important judicio-political decisions, such as the execution of Socrates or the acquittal of Demosthenes, were also made by the panels of popular jurors, who possessed no expertise other than that which they would have developed as citizens of the Athenian polis. The history of events gives us an example of a case where people power was supreme in Athenian democracy. In 406 BC, the Athenians castigated their generals for failing to rescue men shipwrecked after a battle off the Arginusai islands (Xen. *Hell.* 1.6–7). The council passed a proposal to the Assembly that the generals be tried as a board rather than as individuals. An intervention against this proposal, claiming that such a trial was unconstitutional, was rejected violently in the Assembly, with the "great mass shouting out that it was an intolerable thing if the people was not allowed to do what it wanted" (Xen. *Hell.* 1.7.12). The generals were executed; the people soon regretted their actions (Xen. *Hell.* 1.7.35); Kallixenos, proposer of the motion, was shunned and starved to death. Such imposition of popular power has led to the claim that Athenian democracy in the fifth century was particularly radical or extreme. Indeed, for the author known to modern scholars as the "Old Oligarch," the impact of democracy was to give more power to the poor than the rich (Ps-Xen. *Ath. Pol.* 1.4). However, the partisan view of Athenian democracy as a class struggle was not universally accepted: the Syracusan politician Athenagoras, for instance, defined democracy as that form which gives both rich and poor a share in political rights (Thuc. 6.39.1).

The openness of the democratic system enabled certain citizens to win ascendancy and influence over their fellow citizens so that they became politicians or leaders in a modern sense (Rhodes 2000; on the selection of magistrates see the next section). Although the authority of all magistracies was limited by the powers of the courts and the Assembly, power was accrued by persuasion: expert knowledge, charisma and skill were key qualities, but a politician's standing was as secure as his last speech (Finley 1985a: 38–75). In the fifth century, the most prominent and influential politicians were, for the most part, the generals who were elected to their office (to which they could be reelected without restriction): Pericles, who was elected general continuously for 15 years from 443 BC, is the prime example (Plut. *Per.* 16.3; Thuc. 2.65.10); in the fourth century, politicians rose to positions of prominence through oratorical power in the law courts and Assembly. Often it was the case that these politicians deployed democratic institutions to serve their own interests. The *graphē paranomōn*, for instance, was used by politicians who wanted to build their reputation or to challenge another's ascendancy. Aeschines' prosecution of Ctesiphon in 330, for proposing an unconstitutional and undeserved crowning of Demosthenes, led to a showdown between the prosecutor and Demosthenes: the verdict of the jury drew his political career to a close (Aeschines 3 *Against Ctesiphon*). There were no fixed party groupings in ancient Greece (Anastasiadis 1999; B. Strauss 1986: 9–41), and individuals were free to appeal to as broad a spectrum as possible; however, it is highly likely that individual politicians were able to rally family members, friends and those with shared interests in coalitions known as *hetaireiai* (Connor 1971).

Some modern scholarly research has emphasized the significance of individuals or ruling elites in Athenian politics. While selection by lot of officials appears to have encouraged participation from a wider section of society, those registered as citizens of city-demes were disproportionately well represented in elected magistracies such as the generalship (C. Taylor 2007a). In the judicial sphere, it is clear also that wealth was a very useful tool in political self-promotion. Wealthy citizens would boast of their contributions to public levies in their speeches (Millett 1998); they would have been less deterred by the threat of fines imposed on those who brought unsuccessful public prosecutions, and for this reason they would have been able to take advantage of the procedural flexibility of the Athenian legal system (Osborne 1985b). The wealthy would have been able to make effective use of bribery to buy off would-be prosecutors (C. Taylor 2001). Despite the ideology of political equality enunciated in Athenian public discourse, it is widely recognized that in Athens there was no institutional attempt to eradicate inequality of opportunity, social status, or education. Although jury and assembly pay may have been enough for citizens to support themselves and dependents, and allowed Athenian citizens the leisure to participate (Markle 1985), it is likely that seasonal demand for agricultural labor may have determined the makeup of such meetings (Todd 1990).

While Athenian democracy enabled the existence of "people power," socioeconomic inequalities meant that the rich and the well-born always had a significant presence in Athenian politics. The skill of rhetoric was undoubtedly a significant factor in pursuing a political career (it was a skill which sophists, in exchange for a fee, may have been able to cultivate), and expenditure remained an important factor in raising one's profile. Furthermore, prosopographical studies suggest that some sort of elite (consisting of the wealthy of those citizens whose family origins lay in the city center) played a large part in decree-making and elected officeholding. A disproportionately large number of proposers of decrees came from the wealthiest 4 percent of the population (Hansen 1987: 65). Despite the fact that there is epigraphical evidence to suggest that the dominance of the wealthy in elected offices was less extreme in the fourth century than it was in the fifth, it was still the case that the wealthy played a disproportionately large role in city politics (Osborne 1985a: 71; C. Taylor 2007b). On the other hand, the picture of politics on a local scale, in the demes, is more egalitarian: Osborne's survey of the holders of the locally powerful office of demarch suggests that for the most part, the holders of that office were not men of high socioeconomic status (Osborne 1985a: 85).

While the wealthy and privileged dominated the foremost political roles, there were opportunities for the masses to participate in less prominent roles. Ober has suggested that the effect of popular participation in the fourth century BC was to make the de facto political leadership adapt an agenda which was amenable to the interests of the poor (Ober 1989). The frustrations of antidemocratic authors like the Old Oligarch (see above) appear to reflect this priority of popular interests. While it is impossible to be certain about the proportion of citizens attending the Assembly, it is likely that in the classical period, just fewer than 25 percent of male citizens eligible (those over the age of 30) would have served in the *boule* in any ten-year period (Sinclair 1988: 196). This means that a significant proportion of those with political privileges would have dealt closely with the financial, military and political administration of the city and would have been involved in debate and decision-making on behalf of their city. This may well have given rise to a very high level of political and bureaucratic awareness (Ober 2005b: 27–42); participation in political activity in the demes (Osborne 1985a: 88–92) would have raised political education to a higher degree and may, as J. S. Mill hoped, have stimulated and raised the political awareness of individual citizens (Blaug and Schwarzmantel 2001: 59–67).

What emerges therefore is that the bipolarity apparent in theories about democracy (which allowed for coexisting discourses about the value of mass and elite political activity) appears to have been reproduced by the institutions and practices of Athenian democracy: expert leaders and politicians coexisted with wide and meaningful popular participation. But the Athenian ideal of participation extended far beyond the limits of political deliberation and decision-making. Athenian citizens were highly involved in public activities that did not pertain to the political administration of their city. In many senses, participation was expressed as a way of life as much as it was a political system. The Athenians encouraged their wealthy citizens, by a range of institutional and social pressures, to contribute to a range of financial levies perceived by the citizens to be in the public interest (Liddel 2007: 109–209, 262–93). Activities such as participation in festivals (Connor 1996), public dining (Schmitt-Pantel 1990), attending the theater (which activity the Athenians may well have subsidized in the fourth century (Rhodes 1981a: 514)), and religious activity (such as participation in shared sacrifices) were a central part of citizenship. Contributing to the well-being of the city in a range of ways was all highly valued, and the predominant discourse of Athenian inscriptions, the law courts and the Assembly constructed a theoretical compatibility between civic activity and the notion of free citizenship. To identify participation as the phenomenon at the heart of Athenian democracy is to suggest that that democratic "politics" is a concept that extends deeply into the realm of cultural activity (cf. Scafuro 1994).

Ancient and Modern Democratic Practice and Institutions Compared

In the modern era, the term "democracy," until the early nineteenth century, was used in political thought and practice to refer to Athenian-style direct democracy (though in the hellenistic world, democracy was used sometimes to refer simply to constitutional government (Rhodes with Lewis 1997: 531–6)). Historians and political thinkers alike tended to view democracy as an anarchic form of government; the Athenian experience of government was held up as an example which was to be avoided (Roberts 1994: 156–207). Only after the French revolution did the terms "democrat" and "democracy" start to become universally accepted political slogans (Dunn 2005: 16–17, 71–147). De Tocqueville's *Democracy in America* appears to have been the first text to use the term democracy to describe the modern form of representative government: it was used in this way in an analysis of the American constitution which, until that point, had been described as a republican form of government (Samons 2004: 1). In the mid-nineteenth century, as the word "democracy" came to be one that was increasingly used to describe a set of political institutions and ideals, some liberal historians and political thinkers began to use the history of Athenian democracy as a way of making points about modern democracy (Roberts 1994: 229–55; Turner 1981: 187–363; Urbinati 2002).

But significant discrepancies between the institutions and practices of ancient and modern democracy have made the transcultural significance of Greek democracy difficult to grasp. Greek democracy was significantly different in terms of scale and eligibility (Cartledge 1999). Modern democracy, particularly in powerful states, is most consequential at the level of the nation-state; contrarily, the classical form of democracy, despite the attempts of the Athenians to establish democratic governments in some of the cities of her fifth century empire, never established a stable interpolis community of citizens (de Ste Croix 1972: 34–49). The difference in eligibility becomes most clear when we consider that the exclusion of women, slaves and foreigners indicates that Athens was neither a cosmopolitan nor a liberal democracy.

More differences appear when we look at the mechanics of democracy, and in particular those through which popular power was put into practice. Athenian citizens were powerful because they were able to speak, debate, and vote on matters of great political significance. In modern democratic theory since Burke and Mill, the answer to the question of how popular power is to be effectuated has lain in the manipulation of systems of delegation or representation (Blaug and Schwarzmantel 2001: 92–5, 150–6). Theoretical and practical experiments with direct forms of democracy have, however, been undertaken in the modern world. Some of these make room for popular initiative: the practice of offering citizens the right to place issues to the vote has been tried in the state of California (Dunn 2005: 177); a nearly extinct form of direct democracy which has endured in a few rural cantons of Switzerland since the thirteenth century is that of annual popular assemblies (*Landesgemeinde*) which offer every citizen the right to speak and vote (Hansen 2005a: 14, 60 n3, 62 n14). Other experiments in direct democracy have included the use of small randomized panels of citizens in British Columbia, and Marcus Schmidt's theory of popular digitally enabled decision-making (Hansen 2005a: 53–7). Despite the reported success of the experiment in British Columbia, it is unclear how direct democracy, given its reliance on participation and initiative, might be affected by the problems of apathy, disengagement, and self-interest. A more widespread form of direct democracy is the referendum, but the usual form of the procedure means that the choices put in front of citizens are determined by politicians (Butler and Ranney 1994): the absence of initiative means that the procedure is less direct than it at first seems.

Athenian democracy looks very different to modern democracy given the absence of a comprehensive constitution, separation of powers, or supreme court. A further important difference between ancient and modern democratic institutions concerns the selection of magistrates. In some modern democracies (such as the United States), the head of state is elected by popular ballot, a process which bestows political legitimacy on the leader. In the United Kingdom, a hereditary sovereign appoints a prime minister from the elected members of parliament; in effect this is usually the leader of the political party which holds the majority of elected representatives in the House of Commons; this means that the prime minister is elected by only a small number of constituents. Lesser offices are selected by committees or elected officials, while many key public officials and administrators (in the UK, the Civil Service) are unelected. But in Athens most public officials and administrators were selected by lottery (Headlam 1933; Dow 2004; C. Taylor 2007a). While the use of lot may have had its origins in religious procedures, its use was explained on the basis of the idea that the election of magistrates was an aristocratic means of selection (Arist. *Pol.* 1300b4–5; cf. Isoc. *Areop.* 23). The effect of lot was twofold: it made the issue of selection of magistrates, a highly momentous but often controversial occasion in modern democracies, a relatively insignificant process (Headlam 1933: 25–6); it reinforced political equality, as it gave all citizens an equal chance to hold office regardless of their profession. Voting, therefore, is much more central to the modern practice of democracy; nevertheless, a small number of ancient Athenian officers were selected by popular election (Ps-Xen. *Ath. Pol.* 1.3; Arist. *Ath. Pol.* 61.1; C. Taylor 2007a), including the ten generals. These two methods of selection were central to the Athenian democracy's support of coexisting modes of elite and mass participation.

What Is the Use of Studying Ancient Democracy?

It has emerged in this essay that while both ancient and modern democracies place a premium on the idea of equality, modern interpretations of that value go beyond the Athenian stress on political equality. In terms of political activity, the Athenians were more successful at securing significant popular contributions to the infrastructure of their community. Such differences, and in particular the fundamentally different scale of modern democracies, has led some modern thinkers to deem the Athenian example insignificant for modern democracy (Dahl 1989: 23; Bryce 1921: 1.207). But such differences do not mean that ancient democracy has little to offer a world in which ostensibly (but often superficially) democratic political practices, foremost among them that of election, have become close to representing a universal ideal. The study of ancient democracy offers three potential contributions: in terms of its ideals and aspirations, its institutions and practices, and its historical experiences and epistemological value.

The overlap of ancient and modern democratic values like liberty and equality has led certain recent analysts to suggest that the study of ancient Athenian democracy may remind modern democratic communities of the desirability of democratic ideals (Woodruff 2005), even if the Athenians themselves were far from ever making those ideals practicable (Sagan 1991: 64). One of the most significant contributions of the history of ancient Athenian democracy is to illustrate how difficult it is to sustain political practices which live up to the standard of democratic values; the history of Athens in the hellenistic period (323–146 BC), periodically dominated by the kingship of Alexander the Great's successors, illustrates how easily democratic ideology and institutions may degenerate into little more than hollow sloganeering (see Habicht 1997).

The institutions and practices of ancient Athenian democracy have generally been thought of as less relevant to the modern practice of democracy than have its ideals and values. Before the revival of Athenian democracy in nineteenth century liberal thought by George Grote and J. S. Mill, there had been a long antidemocratic tradition, with origins in ancient critiques of democracy (Roberts 1994): thus, when the founders of the American constitution talked about Athenian democracy, it was usually as an example of political practices best avoided (Madison, Hamilton, and Jay 1987: 248, 372–3). The most scathing recent attack on Athenian democracy has come in the work of L. J. Samons, who suggests that the practices of both ancient

Athenian and modern American democracy are damaging to public virtue (Samons 2004). But it is possible that the Athenian experience of democracy may offer something of interest even for those who do not share its ideals. At the most basic level, studying ancient democracy (and ancient political systems in general) serves as a reminder of the different agendas of ancient and modern democracy: modern democracies must strive toward forms of cosmopolitanism that ancient Greek political systems were unable to internalize (Balot 2006: 302). In some ways, difference is a key factor in making ancient democracy good to think with: indeed, in the aftermath of the collapse of Soviet and Soviet-inspired communism, some North American scholars suggested that ancient democracy might replace Marxism as the central political and theoretical interlocutor of western democracy (Euben, Wallach, and Ober 1994b: 9).

But the example of ancient Athenian democracy may be held up as a worthwhile example of a political system which achieved a high level of participation. Moses Finley, for instance, thought that the Athenian example might inspire a new form of popular participation at a time of widespread disengagement from the political process (1985a: 37, 108). Mogens Hansen's interest in Athenian democracy has recently focused on the systems of sortition and rotation: he has suggested that recent experiments in direct democracy are "based on institutions and principles borrowed from ancient Athens" (2005a: 56; cf. Hansen 2002a): accordingly, the study of Athenian history is one way of assessing the merits of wide participation and direct democracy. Direct democracy demands a broad political education of its participants: such an education may, as it was in ancient Athens, be based upon direct engagement with political realities. However, direct democratic institutions will give rise to rational and beneficial decisions only if the groups or individuals are well informed of both local issues (as the ancient Athenians were) but also global issues (upon which matters the ancients were less well informed). Moreover, the relevance of the Athenian example to the prospect of direct democracy in the modern world becomes less simple when we consider that if there is a future in this form of democracy, it will be heavily reliant on the development and availability of appropriate digital technology (see Barney 2000; Gibson, Römmele, and Ward 2004).

The value of individual engagement with political realities is stressed by those thinkers who take a more philosophical approach to the question of how the practices of Athenian democracy are relevant to the modern world. The political theorist Hannah Arendt suggested that ancient democracy gave men a means of public self-expression, and thereby fulfilled their capacity for action and freedom (1958: 41–3). Arendt's work has much in common with that of recent formulations of the notion of deliberative democracy (a theory which places emphasis on political debate and speech-making as factors in shaping democratic activity) which employ the history of Athenian democracy as an instructive case study (Fontana 2004; Saxonhouse 2004; Urbinati 2002: 54–122; generally see Blaug and Schwarzmantel 2001: 492–521). A related development has led some North American scholars to emphasize the educative role of Athenian democracy: the political and judicial experiences of democratic life helped Athenian citizens develop a political understanding of the world around them (Euben 1993: 479; Wallach 1994). Coinciding with the view of J. S. Mill (Urbinati 2002; Blaug and Schwarzmantel 2001: 59–67), Josiah Ober has suggested that Athenian democracy offered a form of civic education: democracy, he suggests, enabled the ancient polis to become an "effective network of people, of knowledge, of trust" (Ober 2005b: 42). One formulation of his thesis suggested that Athens offers a model to for-profit businesses in the modern world: just as Athens made its citizens free and equal members of an organization, so businesses should make their employees free and equal members in the hope they will feel more personally invested in a company (Manville and Ober 2003). Applying the same principle to a global concern, it might be suggested that while the history of the Athenian democracy cannot offer technical solutions to the problems of environmental degradation and human-induced climate change, understanding the ways in which the Athenians attempted to pool ideas, knowledge, and concerns might suggest ways of focusing local and global action on concerted solutions. Organizations which encourage participation necessarily broaden the pool from which they can draw and develop good ideas.

As noted in the second section above, in democratic Athens, debates about the qualities of democracy often gave rise to the clearest expressions of democratic virtues; I have also stressed the co-existence of parallel discourses on the value of participation and expertise in Athenian democracy. The history of Greek democratic ideas, therefore, suggests the importance of criticism and contention to the vitality of the idea of democracy. But such debates may be more productive if they recognize the plurality of interpretations of democracy. While the democracy that this essay has focused upon was the Athenian form, it should be noted that, as Aristotle recognized, different communities were suited to different kinds of democracy (Arist. *Pol.* 1289b 27–35, 1317a 12–29). In the ancient Greek world, forms of politics practiced at both polis and federal level were highly contingent on cultural and geopolitical factors. The modern world would do well to remember this: as Bhikhu Parekh has observed, if the west intends to secure and propagate its own interpretation of democracy, it must be ready to negotiate with culturally oriented critics (Blaug and Schwarzmantel 2001: 419).

Finally, the fact that a sophisticated set of ideas about and institutions of popular government emerged in ancient Greece should serve to remind us that democracy is not the exclusive property of the post-Enlightenment western cultural tradition. Ancient Athens was not the only nonwestern expression of democratic values, as the examples of the Cossacks of the sixteenth century AD, or the Ochollo people in Ethiopia show (Detienne 2007: 101–25). As Amartya Sen has argued, democracy is a universal not a "western" value (Blaug and Schwarzmantel 2001: 420–3). The example of Greek democracy might help the modern west realize that the interpretation of what constitutes democracy is not its exclusive privilege.

FURTHER READING

Robinson 2004 (a collection of ancient sources and modern essays) is a good introduction to ancient and modern debates on the relationship between political theory and reality. The best surveys of the fits and nonfits between ancient and modern democracy and of the modern reactions to ancient democracy are Rhodes 2003a and Hansen 2005a; Cartledge 1999 and Euben 1993 are concise; Saxonhouse 1996 is also relevant. Finley 1985a is an important work which attempts to "develop a dialectical discourse between the ancient and modern conceptions of democracy" (1985a: x). Ober and Hedrick 1996 and Euben, Wallach, and Ober 1994a are collections of essays which address the question of the extent to which ancient democracy might serve as a palliative for modern democracy.

CHAPTER 10

"Rights," Individuals, and Communities in Ancient Greece

Paul Cartledge and Matt Edge

"Rights-talk" is all the rage in contemporary political theory; and "taking rights seriously" is a major preoccupation in political practice too (cf. Dworkin 1987). It is therefore a striking discontinuity between the political world of the ancient Greeks and our own that they, so far as we know, had no conception of individual, subjective rights (Rahe 1992: 19, 31; Ostwald 1996; Ober 2005a). It is the contention of this chapter, however, that this long recognized and long accepted, yet problematic, claim is of relatively little interest and, in fact, obscures a number of important things in the political history of ancient Greece (meaning for present purposes classical Athens in particular, on which we concentrate for lack of relevant evidence for other poleis and *ethnē*, though we regret this inevitable Athenocentrism; cf. Brock and Hodkinson 2000; Hansen and Nielsen 2004).

It is of relatively little interest, because the contemporary, western notion of rights, highly contentious as it is,[1] is a product of a much later development that has its origins in medieval or later medieval scholasticism (Tuck 1979; Brett 1997, 2003) and employs a conceptual language simply not known in the ancient Greek world (e.g. Cartledge 2000: 18). It is problematic because, to contemporary minds, any government or form of social organization that does not give a catalog of basic rights to its citizens is generally thought to be despotic or, at best, misguided, such has become the hegemonic force of rights-talk in contemporary language. That the Athenians did not endorse a concept of "rights" immediately casts them in a certain negative light, and likewise questions the (direct, participatory) democracy that was their form of sociopolitical organization. It obscures, finally, because the simple statement that the Athenians did not recognize a concept of rights is often the end of the story. Yet there is – as we hope to show in this chapter – much more to the story than that. What the Athenians do have to say on this matter ought in itself to be of interest to contemporary political philosophy.

We have in mind here a prominent theme in the historical philosophy of Quentin Skinner (2002a: 6): "One of the uses of the past arises from the fact that we are prone

A Companion to Greek and Roman Political Thought, First Edition. Edited by Ryan K. Balot.
© 2013 Blackwell Publishing Ltd. Published 2013 by Blackwell Publishing Ltd.

to fall under the spell of our own intellectual heritage. As we analyze and reflect on our normative concepts, it is easy to become bewitched into believing that the ways of thinking about them bequeathed to us by the mainstream of our intellectual traditions must be *the* ways of thinking about them." In other words, our language of rights represents just one way, historically speaking, in which the liberty of the individual has been protected by the society in which he or she lived. Simply because the Athenians did not have a conception of rights does not logically entail that they did not understand the need for, and did not seek to secure, individual liberty. As Skinner himself has argued in relation to his work on Machiavelli (2002b: 126), "we are prone to think that there can be no theory of individual liberty in the absence of a theory of rights. But as I try to show … one value of investigating the pre-modern history of political philosophy is to show that there need be no necessary connection between the two."

The purpose of a right, or of rights in general, is to guarantee the individual protection from the invasion of his or her freedom (of speech, of association, of thought, and so on) and of his or her property, and to protect him or her from forms of bodily harm and abuse (torture, violence, slavery, abduction, arbitrary arrest and imprisonment, and so forth). In short, rights protect individual liberty, safety, dignity, and well-being. In these terms, they are commonly grouped in the analysis of political societies and institutions alongside such notions as the rule of law and the separation of powers (e.g., Rawls 1999: 38, 206–13; cf. Brett 2003: 97). This is, essentially, the thinking behind Isaiah Berlin's celebrated analysis of liberty (Berlin 2002a; cf. I. Harris 2002 for a full analysis of the literature that Berlin's celebrated lecture has inspired). His "negative liberty" is precisely a clearly defined area within which the individual is free to move without coercion or interference from others, provided he or she treats others likewise (and does not seek to coerce and interfere with them); and the existence of this space is guaranteed by a catalog of rights and the rule of law (Berlin 2002a: 169–78). It is also for alleged ignorance of this idea (Berlin 2002b: 34) that Athens and, indeed, ancient Greece as a whole, have long been condemned, possibly beginning with Hobbes (Hobbes 1996: 142–4) but most famously in Benjamin Constant's lecture/essay of 1819, "The Liberty of the Ancients Compared with That of the Moderns" (Constant 1988). Did the Athenians, then, fail to understand the negative concept of liberty and seek instead to violate individual freedom? What was, in the terms of this chapter, the relationship of the individual to the democratic community?

In actual fact, contrary to what is often suggested, Athenian democrats did recognize a clearly defined concept of negative individual freedom, and it is this we shall focus on briefly in the first part of this chapter. This conception of liberty resembles that adopted by the later neoclassical tradition, both by such well-known authors as Machiavelli, James Harrington, Joseph Priestley, and Richard Price, and by a host of less famous writers and pamphleteers, as it has been excavated by among others Skinner (1984, 1986, 1998, 2001, 2002c, 2002d, 2003) and Philip Pettit (Pettit 1993, 1997).[2] Both of these theories – the Athenian and the neoclassical – claim that, in order to be free, you need to be living as the citizen of a self-governing community freed from dependence upon the will of a tyrant or monarch, though they diverge quite sharply on what is required for the constitution and makeup of that community. The neoclassical theorists are satisfied so long as one is living under representative or mixed governments, both of which can uphold the common good and secure equality under the law. But they repudiate participatory democracy, often viewing it as a dangerous form of government arguably posing no less of a threat to individual liberty than a tyrant or monarch (see, for example, Pettit 1997: 12, 81, Skinner 1992: 59; 1998: 31–2).[5]

The Athenian theory, however, suggests you can be truly free only if you are living as the equal citizen of a participatory, Athenian-style democracy, and not allowing anyone to make laws on your behalf and, thereby, dictate the content of your life. If you lived under a tyranny, or an oligarchy, or were ruled by another polis (or *ethnos*), this immediately placed you in a condition of slavery (*douleia*), since, like legally defined slaves, you were under the direct control of others. To avoid such a condition of "slavery" you had to live in a *dēmokratia*.[4] This theory is not anywhere given an extended, coherent theoretical exposition, but may be pieced together from various kinds of sources, including drama.

Thus, Euripides' King Theseus in the *Supplices* (444–55) gives a good indication of what thinking Athenian democrats worried about. Tyrants, Theseus says, kill the young who threaten their position, rape girls, and take money at their whim because they have the power to, the law and the tyrant's will being one and the same. This was also a familiar complaint in the fourth century. As Demosthenes (17.3–4) put it, "the victims of tyranny may be executed without trial, as well as outraged in the persons of their wives and children." In his speech against Leptines (20.16–17), Demosthenes contrasts democracy with tyranny and oligarchy, claiming that "whereas with those [constitutions] the fear of what is to come is greater than the present grace, with you a man could keep what he won without fear of loss."

Athenian writers were, then, not concerned solely with the power that oligarchic or tyrannical "masters" (*despotai*) could theoretically wield, but also with the very presence of these powerful individuals within the polis, a presence which had an immediately detrimental effect on your individual liberty. The effect of tyrannical rule on its citizens was a notable theme of some other fifth-century tragedies, appearing also in Euripides' *Bacchae*, in Sophocles' *Antigone* and, in perhaps its most interesting deployment, Sophocles' *Electra* (Edge 2006: 74–7). Jocasta, in Euripides' *Phoenician Women* (391–3), points out that it is indeed a slave's lot not to enjoy openness of free speech (*parrhēsia*) and that one has to endure the stupidity of one's rulers.

This atmosphere of fear under "slavery" thus restricted both what one did and also what one said, according to the writers we are discussing. The author of the Demosthenic funeral oration states that "although juntas [*dunasteiai*] dominated by a few create fear in their citizens, they fail to awaken the sense of shame …; democracies, however, possess many other just and good features, to which right-minded men should hold fast, and in particular it is impossible to deter openness of free speech [*parrhēsia*]" (60.25–6). Demosthenes himself says elsewhere, in his speech against Androtion (22.32), that "in oligarchies, even if there are men living more shamefully than Androtion, one is not able to speak badly of one's rulers."

Democracy, therefore, was considered to offer respite from these evils of "slavery." As Demosthenes succinctly put it (24.5), "I suppose no man living will attribute the prosperity of the polis, the popular government and our freedom to anything other than the laws?" He stresses elsewhere (21.188) that "equality [*to ison*] follows to you from the law." This was very different from living under tyrants and oligarchs.

> Whereas those in oligarchies both undo the things which have been transacted and are sovereign to give orders concerning things of the future according to their whim, our laws, on the other hand, declare what must needs be concerning the future, having been settled by persuading people that they will be beneficial to those who live under them. (Dem. 24.76)

Hyperides (fr. 15 D) expressed a similar idea in relation to tyranny, claiming that "living in a democratic state where justice is established by the laws is different from passing into the power of one tyrant where the caprice of an individual is supreme. We have either to put our trust in laws and so remember freedom or else to be surrendered to the power of one man and brood daily over slavery." Or, as the same writer put it elsewhere:

> if men are to be happy, the voice of law, not the threat, must be sovereign; if men are to be free, they must not be fearful of [groundless] blame but of [fair] trial, nor must the safety of our citizens depend on those who slander them and truckle to their leaders but on the force of the laws alone. (Hyp. 6. *Epit.* 25)

In short, what is being stressed is that democracy, to borrow Berlin's terminology, is a "negative," protective, idea which guards the liberty of its citizens from the over-mighty power and will of tyrants and oligarchs who are able to invade the freedom of their own citizens at their whim.

Freedom from the arbitrary wills of tyrants and oligarchs had a further benefit. The fact that you were not a "slave," and therefore not under the direct control of others, meant that you were under your own will and, as a result, able to live your own life as you saw fit. This was the aspect stressed by the Thucydidean Nicias when he reminded the Athenians at Syracuse that their fatherland was "the most free" city and possessed "the unhindered potential for all to live the lifestyle [*diaita*] they wished" (Thuc. 7.69.2). Demosthenes (19.69) repeated the boast in the fourth century when he said that Athens was "the most free of cities." But the best known illustration of the theme is provided by the funeral oration credited to Pericles in Thucydides. Here Pericles is made to assert:

> No one, so long as he has it in him to be of service to the state, is kept in political obscurity because of poverty. We live freely both concerning the public realm and as regards the [lack of] suspicion towards others of their daily pursuits. We do not get exercised by our next-door neighbor if he enjoys himself in his own way, nor do we give him the kind of black looks which, though they inflict no real harm, still can be found offensive. But though free and tolerant in our private lives, in public affairs we observe the law. (Thuc. 2.37.1–3)

Demosthenes also drew the distinction between private and public life which had been further developed in the fourth century. The laws of public life, he says (24.193), which guide the conduct of politicians and the polis in general, are strict and are laid down vehemently, "whereas those laws concerning private life are laid down mildly and philanthropically on behalf of the masses." This aspect of democratic liberty aroused consternation among ancient opponents of democracy, who construed "living as you will" as a form of anarchy. Thus Plato, discussing the "democratic man" in the *Republic* (557b), has Socrates ask: "are they not all free, and is the city not full of freedom and freedom of speech and has not every man authority to do as he likes?" Aristotle in the *Politics* (1310a31–4) similarly castigates the freedom of democracy as living as one wishes and adds that Euripides called it "living for the fancy of the moment."

We have a number of useful indications of what the consequences of "enslavement" to an oligarchic constitution might have meant. Lysias (12.5) reports that when the Thirty came to power in 404 they declared that the Athenians must be "converted" to "excellence" and "justice." The oligarchic author of the *Athenian Constitution* preserved among the works of Xenophon (sometimes referred to as the "Old Oligarch") provides a blatantly partisan indication of the purpose and direction of oligarchic attacks on democratic freedom. The author explains that the "better sort" are always hostile to democracy and says that this is because "among the best men there is less intemperance and injustice, but a great deal of strictness regarding serviceable matters, whereas among the people, there is much ignorance and disorder and badness" (Ps-Xen. *Ath. Pol.* 1.5). He expressly states that he wants the people to fall into *douleia* through what he calls "good governance" (*eunomia*), meaning oligarchy (Ps-Xen. *Ath. Pol.* 1.6–9).

> If you seek good governance, you will first see the laws being put into place by the most clever themselves. Next, the better sort will punish the worse sort, and the better sort will determine the policy for the city and not allow madmen to sit on the council nor to speak nor to form assemblies. So then from these excellent things the people would quickly sink into slavery. (Ps-Xen. *Ath. Pol.* 1.9)

Note that the author is referring here to freedoms we count among our basic rights (the right to assemble and the right to speak freely); the type of freedom is in principle no different from ours, except that in a direct democracy every Athenian citizen had the liberty to speak and propose within a wider political realm. Plato (*Resp.* 562d) adds that, if the officials in democracies are not "very mild" and do not "supply much freedom," they are accused of being oligarchs. Democratic writers put the same point positively: "if you care to enquire why a man would sooner live under a democracy than an oligarchy, you would discover that the most common reason is that everything is more mild in a democracy" (Dem. 22.51).

What the "Old Oligarch" is getting at expresses well the essential claim of the democratic concept of liberty we have been discussing. It also brings out the essential difference in its use in the later neoclassical tradition and in contemporary liberal political thought (Edge 2006: 94–106, and forthcoming). For what the author is advocating is the end of democratic conditions in which all are able to serve in the government and speak "according to equality" (Ps-Xen. *Ath. Pol.* 1.6). But he concedes that "the people do not want to be slaves themselves through good governance but to be free and to rule" (Ps-Xen. *Ath. Pol.* 1. 8). In other words, by ending political equality (equality of voting, of free speech, of freedom to assemble in the *ekklēsia* and serve on the council and so on), the people will fall into slavery thanks to the stricter rule of the few.

It was precisely this link between liberty and equality which was fundamental to the democratic concept of freedom we are attempting to excavate. Athenian writers (and those who follow them in discussing this democratic concept of freedom, such as Aristotle and Cicero: Edge 2006: 90–4) often seem to be confused or inconsistent: at one moment, they mention liberty and at the next equality (cf. Dem. 21.188 and 24.5, both quoted above). But actually this is far from being inconsistent. The fundamental insight of this Athenian democratic concept of freedom is that the moment you surrender political equality, the moment you stop living in a democracy, you immediately lose your individual freedom and are straightforwardly "enslaved."

This idea again stretches back to the fifth century, where it appears prominently in Euripides' *Supplices*. Theseus says that he has made the people free by establishing equality of voting (*isopsēphia*) for all, thereby negating the situation of tyranny where the monarch's will is law (Eur. *Supp.* 352–3). "The polis," he says, "is not ruled by one man but is free. Sovereignty belongs to the people, who take turns to govern in annual succession. Wealth receives no special recognition from us; the poor man has an equal voice [*ison echōn*]" (*Supp.* 404–8). He goes on to make a number of the complaints against tyranny that we have discussed, namely that there are no common laws and the power of the laws rests in one man's hand. This, he says, is no longer equal (*Supp.* 429–32). Written laws, on the other hand, provide equal justice for all (*Supp.* 433–4). "Freedom is this," Theseus points out. Those who wish to set a proposal before the people can do so, those who do not wish to simply stay quiet. "Where," he concludes, "could a city enjoy greater equality than this?" (*Supp.* 438–41). Theseus is far from being confused. Freedom is secured by the establishment of political equality (equality of voting, *isēgoria*, or equality of freedom of public political speech, and equality under the laws).

This is also a firmly negative concept. The idea is not to give political freedom to all so that they may interfere with, and dictate the contents of, the lives of others, but to prevent others from doing that to you. If all are equal through the natural political makeup of a democracy, none is in a position to enforce his will upon you, rendering you straightforwardly a "slave." In short, you did not have a "master" or *despotēs*. As Demosthenes puts it in comparative terms, "whenever a certain man is elected to the senate, or Gerousia, as they [the Spartans] call it, he is a master [*despotēs*] of all the rest. For there the prize of excellence is to become sovereign over the constitution with one's peers, whilst with us the people is sovereign" (20.107). Plato borrowed this notion for his mock funeral oration of the democratic city (*Menex.* 238d; cf. *Resp.* 463a, 562d, 563e). The moment you surrendered political equality was the moment liberty was lost, since this placed you under the control of others. Demosthenes declared in the *Fourth Philippic* of 351:

Those in the cities have divided into two factions. One desires neither to rule by force nor to enslave others but instead to govern with freedom and laws according to equality, whereas the other lusts after power to rule their fellow citizens, and to be subjected by some other [i.e. Philip II of Macedon], whom they believe to be able to accomplish these ends for them. These partisans of Philip, who lust after tyrannies and juntas, have everywhere prevailed. (10.4)

Demosthenes gave another good illustration of this thesis in his speech *On the Liberty of the Rhodians*, also of 351. Wars, he says, are fought against democracies for a number of reasons (private quarrels, border disputes, rivalries, and so on), but they are fought against oligarchies "on behalf of none of these things, but on behalf of your constitution and freedom" (15.18). Only democrats, he explained, were free men, and he made it clear exactly why this was so.

I should not hesitate to say that I think it a greater advantage that all the Greeks should be your enemies under democracy than your friends under oligarchy. For with free men I do not think you would have any difficulty in making peace whenever you wished, but with oligarchs I do not believe that even friendly relations could be permanent, for the few can never be well disposed to the many, nor those who covet power to those who have chosen a life of equality of free speech. (Dem. 15.18)

"I recommend you," he went on, "to consider those who destroy free constitutions and change them into oligarchies as the common enemies of all those who set their hearts upon freedom" (Dem. 15.20).

The Lysianic funeral speech (Lys. 2), written at the end of the fifth century, gives another clear indication of how a loss of political equality meant slavery and loss of freedom. Painting a typically rose-tinted picture of Athens' history (a *topos* of funeral orations), Lysias claims that the Athenians were the first to drive out narrow juntas and to establish democracies in their place, "believing the freedom of all to be the greatest concord" (Lys. 2.18). He later gives a similar gloss to the Athenian empire, claiming that the Athenians' ancestors had "delivered their allies from civil war [*stasis*], determining not to enslave the many to the few, but compelling equality for everyone" (Lys. 2.55–6). In a forensic speech delivered on his own behalf, Lysias praises the loyalist democratic grouping for winning a victory over the Thirty Tyrants and "freeing" the men of the City (*astu*) – the oligarchic faction – from the Thirty (Lys. 12.97; cf. Lys. 12. 73, 78). He had earlier claimed that, if the faction of the *astu* had won this conflict, they would have "enslaved" themselves to the Thirty, but because the democratic grouping won, all are equal with the victors (Lys. 12.92–3).

The essence of the democratic concept of freedom we have been examining, and, indeed, the essence of the democracy which housed it, was firmly negative in Berlin's sense. Democracy, in other words, is not conceived as a form of majoritarian rule which can justifiably coerce the minority and interfere with the lives of its citizens at will. It is seen as precisely the opposite of this: it prevents such interference and control in the first place. As Aeschines nicely puts it, "in a democracy the private individual is a king because of the law and the vote, but when he hands these over to another man, he has by his own act put himself under an illegitimate form of government" (3.233). The Greek of this last clause translates literally as "he has dissolved himself into a *dynasteia*"; this neatly reflects the concerns of the concept of freedom we have discussed, a *dynasteia* being an extreme form of oligarchy.

One of the benefits of the exploration of the past and its ideas is to help us challenge some of those deeply rooted, perhaps even hegemonic, beliefs which are so encoded in everyday language that they assume the status of truths. To that end, we would like briefly to consider how the Athenians sought to protect this individual liberty. For one such "truth" is the idea that participatory, Athenian-style democracy is necessarily a despotism. This is argued on the grounds that it cannot possibly embrace the doctrine of the separation of powers (since the people control all branches of government and public administration) and is therefore naturally inimical to the rule of law. This view was popularized first by Immanuel Kant (1996, AK: 8: 350–3, 322–5), who claimed that democracy was necessarily a despotism. He then contrasted this with republican (representative) forms of rule. More recently it has been revived within the discipline of ancient history in Raphael Sealey's *The Athenian Republic: Democracy or the Rule of Law?* Note the disjunctive "or." Sealey indeed concluded that, "if a slogan is needed, Athens was a republic not a democracy" (1987: 146).

Similarly, Josiah Ober has claimed that "there is indeed a philosophical and constitutional contradiction between sovereign laws and the sovereign popular will" (1989: 300). He further observed:

> Raphael Sealey concluded a seminal article on the Athenian concept of law by stating that "the Athenians achieved something far more valuable and even more fundamental than democracy. They achieved the rule of law." I imagine that the Athenians could have understood the opposition. And if required to choose between the two ideals, I think they unhesitatingly would have chosen democracy. (Ober 1989: 304)

As we hope has already been made clear, actually the Athenians felt that it was democracy and democracy alone which could guarantee the "rule of law," since it alone did not place the laws in the hands of others. There was no real "philosophical and constitutional contradiction" between the two; far from it. This is a case, rather, of imposing our own normative beliefs and confusions on the Athenians.

The Athenians did not speak the language of rights or the separation of powers. But this is not to say that they were unaware of these issues or of the threat that power posed to individuals and their freedom. How then did the Athenians seek to ensure that their notion of individual liberty was honored? Perhaps it was because of the harsh lessons learnt at the end of the fifth century, or perhaps it is simply a function of the chance survival of the evidence, but there is apparent for the first time in the fourth century a clear concern with the protection of individuals and their freedoms against the democracy and the democratic community.

First, no decree (*psēphisma*) of the Assembly was to override a law (*nomos*), a measure which had the aim and effect of significantly curtailing the powers of the Assembly (see, for example, Andoc. 1.87; Aeschin. 1.177–8; Dem. 23. 87, 218; 24.30; Hyp. 3. *Athen.* 22). Second, no law was to be applied which was not written down (Andoc. 1. 85); and, third, the democracy "forbids the introduction of any law that does not affect all citizens alike, enacted well and democratically. For just as equality follows from the rest of the constitution to everyone, in this way everyone is worthy of enjoying an equal share in these things" (Dem. 24.59; cf. Dem. 23.86; 24.59; 46.12). No wonder Demosthenes (21.188) could fairly claim that equality followed to all Athenians from the laws.

Fourth, and possibly the most interesting development of all, the Assembly itself was forbidden from legislating. Significantly, Demosthenes calls this limitation on the powers of the fourth-century Assembly "democratic" and philanthropic. This is contrasted with oligarchy, which is "savage" and "violent." This is so because, first, it is up to the people themselves to initiate the process of legislation and decide whether there is to be a new law, and, second, the people themselves are forbidden from legislating and allowed only to appoint the terms on which the legislative committee (the *nomothetai* or "lawgivers," drawn from the annually empanelled album of 6,000 jurors) shall sit. Not that the people themselves were excluded from this process entirely by any means. "In the intervening time," Demosthenes (24.20–6) continues, "they instructed persons wishing to introduce laws to exhibit them in front of the Heroes, so that anyone who wishes may inspect them, and, if he discovers anything prejudicial to you, may inform you and have time to speak against the law." Any citizen throughout the year could also propose changing an existing law, so long as he provided the *nomothetai* with an alternative. As a collectivity, the people in assembly were forbidden from legislating, but any individual who wished (known in Athens as *ho boulomenos*) could play a part in the lawmaking process if he discovered laws which were prejudicial to his interests or those of the Athenian people as a whole.

This ties in neatly with another vital aspect of Athenian legal procedure, the actions against unconstitutional decrees (*graphē paranomōn*) and against unconstitutional laws (*graphē nomōn mē epitēdeion theinai*), which again could be brought by any Athenian who wished. These devices have not generally received the attention they deserve (but see Hansen 1974; cf. Hansen 1999, esp. 205–12), and they have a special relevance to the question at hand. These *graphai* (public writs), first attested in 415 BC (Hansen 1999: 22), were a very intelligent means of offering individual volunteer citizens the opportunity to defend their rights and freedoms without having to rely on anyone else. Simply put, if any citizen proposed a new decree in the Assembly, or a new law to the *nomothetai*, it was open to any other citizen to indict the proposer as the author of an unconstitutional decree (against which the *graphē paranomōn* was used) or law (*graphē nomōn mē epitēdeion theinai*) and force him to defend his proposal before a jury-court. Plaintiffs could then cite laws such as the ones discussed above (no law to apply to any Athenian unless it applied to all, no decree to override a law) to demonstrate that a given law or decree was a threat to the lives and liberties of Athenians. The Athenians did not, then, have to rely on parliamentarians or representatives to defend their lives and freedoms, but had the tools to do the job themselves, at least in theory. "What," demanded Demosthenes (24.87; cf. e.g. Ar. *Plut.* 908–18), "is the only just and secure guardian of the laws?" His response? "You, the masses."

To concentrate on theory as we have done (in line with this volume's major concern) is of course to paint rather a rosy picture of the system, and no doubt the Athenian system suffered abuses both in its own terms and in ours. Nor are we ignorant of the differences between "the rule of law" in its ancient as opposed to modern applications. Some citizens (such as adulterers caught in the act) could be executed in hot blood without trial (Hansen 1976), and Athenian law certainly suffers in any modern comparison so far as issues of precise legal definition are concerned (the Athenian law against *hybris*, for example, Aeschin. 1.9–17, Dem. 21.47, does not define *hybris*, *contra* Arist. *Rhet*. 1.13.10; 2.2.6). The same goes, as Socrates found out to his great cost, for *asebeia*, impiety. But when evaluating it, it is crucial to apply appropriate standards and not introduce anachronistic concepts.

Freedom is fundamentally a concept of degree, which is why approaches such as Benjamin Constant's should be avoided. His contention that in the ancient world individual freedom was sacrificed to the freedom of the whole (1988: 311–12) not only fails to do justice to the complexities raised by the issue of individual liberty. It misses the point entirely that the Athenians, or, more correctly, some democratic Athenians, firmly believed that they could hope to be free as individuals only when living as citizens of a particular community, a democracy. The two were vitally interlinked.

What a society considers crucial to its interests differs necessarily and often greatly from one society to the next. The degree of space a society allows its inhabitants for free movement will depend very much on its complex matrix of social, moral and religious beliefs, as well as on the general ideas, notions and prejudices it endorses through language. Freedom will evolve (in terms of both restriction and growth) depending on how quickly societal truths and dogmas are challenged, shed, or, indeed, allowed to develop. Equally, of course, the degree of individual freedom available to the members of any given society will itself differ, especially in relation to the wealth each possesses, which gives them different access to opportunities and choices. This, in turn, gives further weight to our claim that we must not blindly assume that a capitalist, representative, liberal democracy gives its inhabitants "liberty." Rather it gives them (or, perhaps more correctly, some of them) a particular degree (of a particular conception) of liberty. Shedding this preconception itself allows further development of free, individual, thought in relation to the concept of liberty itself!

So, for instance, democratic Athens is thought to be defective in any comparison with a modern "liberal democracy" as regards its wholesale endorsement of slavery, its subjection of women, its exclusion of these groups from the political sphere, and its lack of an understanding of modern law. Equally, of course, many would urge the execution of Socrates as a counterexample, together with the execution of the Arginusai generals, to what we have written here. At no point – providing the complexities of these two events are given due attention[5] – would we wish to deny that they do represent, as we have already indicated, violations of the theory in practice.[6] Regrettably, however, modern liberal democracies also provide a number of discrepancies in practice from the "equal rights" theoretically bestowed not only upon their citizens, but also all within their borders, and cannot, therefore, be immune from the same criticism. The recent British antiterror laws, which have directly resulted in a number of flagrant violations of human rights (cf. Skinner 2003: 25), and the appalling conditions of destitution and isolation endured by asylum-seekers in the same country (not to mention the homeless and other radically disadvantaged groups), are but two such discrepancies. Equally, from an Athenian democratic point of view, the modern world suffers by comparison to the ancients' freedom of political activity, freedom of movement, lack of a popular stigma toward homosexuality (male homosexuality, at least), and the absence of what we would today term the "state" with its accompanying bureaucratic and administrative apparatus which enables the government to keep a more thorough watch on its citizens.[7] This is a very brief survey, and our inadequate list is merely to illustrate the point of cultural difference (for a fuller discussion, see Wallace, this volume, chapter 11).

A study focusing on this practical side of individual freedom in Athens (how and where the Assembly, and other bodies, *did*, in practice, interfere in the lives of Athenians and, indeed, how and where it did not) would, we think, be useful and would provide a far more comprehensive list of similarities and differences between the freedoms enjoyed by modern individuals and their Athenian counterparts. But the practice of individual liberty has not been our concern in this paper, so we will conclude with our central issue, theory. The Athenians did not speak the language of individual, subjective, rights, but they did possess a concept of individual freedom and sought to defend that freedom, however imperfectly to modern eyes. Solely because they confronted similar problems to us, we should not make them speak our conceptual language if they do not use it themselves. Were we to do so, we might obscure potentially interesting differences from our view. The same goes for other, modern societies. Rights talk is just one way of looking at the question of the individual's relationship to society, and, by imposing a language of rights on those societies and peoples which did not – and do not – speak in this way, we lose the natural diversity of the history of political thought. This diversity ought also to provide us with the means of measuring our own normative world and seeing whether perhaps there are other ways of speaking than the language we currently employ.

The Athenians did not understand the concept of rights, but they did understand the concept of individual liberty, and, perhaps, by looking at the way they spoke about it, we might be led to wonder whether we, ourselves, have actually got it – and, indeed, our approach to it – right. It seems to us that we do have something to learn from the Athenian insight that the moment one surrenders political equality and the (equal) political freedoms that go with it (*isēgoria, isopsēphia, isonomia* and so on, in Athenian terms), one immediately surrenders one's individual liberty by placing oneself under the control of others. To be sure, rights are one particularly ingenious way of getting this power back from governments (though in a different way), but we are prone to assume somewhat blindly that the concept of freedom currently in general use is the correct one (cf. Skinner 1998: 116–20; 2002a), or that it expresses some neutral truth about our world, so it is well worth our reflecting on this Athenian insight.

In fact, because this concept of liberty does not have anything like the hegemonic authority of rights talk (and does not possess anything like a genuine tradition in western political thought), it might even have some use beyond our own societies in solving some of the problems that "rights" have brought with them.[8] Equally, the point works the other way around. Our own political language would greatly benefit from a far greater interaction with "alien" traditions, whether Islamic, African, Indian, or Chinese, than it enjoys currently. For instance, rather than the present obsession with spreading western, capitalist, representative democracy throughout the globe and standing bemused, our mouths agape, when other peoples and cultures feel resentment toward it, we might do well to listen to what those peoples and cultures have themselves been saying.

For classicists, a very different conception of "democracy" readily exists in classical Athens that may be fruitfully compared with its modern equivalent. But there exist other conceptions too. We have in mind here, for instance, Kwasi Wiredu's exhortation to philosophers and, indeed, rulers to pay more attention to what he refers to as the traditional African politics of consensus (see Wiredu 1996: part IV; 2001). He sees this embodied in the famous phrase – borrowed by the former president of Tanzania, Julius Nyerere, for example – "the Elders sit under big trees, and talk until they agree" (Nyerere 1975: 478). And he believes this notion of nonparty, consensual government (premised, he correctly points out, on difference of opinion and free thought) to be much richer than the impoverished western idea of representative, party-based and majoritarian democracy.

Western governments do, indeed, have much to gain from shedding the assumption that they have "got it right" in the ways they talk about human beings, their well-being, liberty, safety, and dignity. Such an open-minded approach to our normative concepts, whether it be "democracy," "rights," "liberty," or "justice," and a willingness to listen to the languages of other cultures on a genuinely free and open and level playing-field, would represent genuine cosmopolitanism from a cosmopolitan point of view. Such an approach to politics, and to political theory, we believe, promises a great deal and ought to open our minds to new ways of thinking and speaking about how we might wish our world to be reconstructed and what we can realistically expect from the process of construction. As Donald Davidson wrote, "there are no definite limits to how far dialogue can or will take us" (2001: 219).

Indeed, to conclude, there are very many ways of speaking about, and seeking protection for, human dignity and human liberty, and it would do a great deal for human dignity and human liberty if we paid more attention to this vast cosmopolitan storehouse of meanings (and approaches). To that end, we hope to have added this one, long-forgotten, Athenian conception to the spectrum of potential choices.

FURTHER READING

For a full discussion of negative liberty as nondependence in Athens, and of the difference between this conception and the ways in which individual liberty is generally construed in the modern world, see Edge 2006 and forthcoming. On "rights" in ancient Greece, see Rhodes 1979 as a useful introduction. There are a number of important articles in Ober and Hedrick

1996, particularly the papers by Wallace and Ostwald. Ober 2005a is another important, and controversial, paper looking into the notion of rights in classical Athens, taking a very different perspective from the one we have adopted here and including an interesting and timely discussion on the rights of noncitizens in Athens. Another controversial and engaging work, F. Miller 1995, argues for the presence of subjective rights in Aristotle and has initiated a lively debate on the subject. We have, in this essay, focused primarily on rights in relation to ancient communities (or, more correctly, a particular ancient community) rather than philosophy, so it has not been our purpose to comment on Miller and the literature he has generated. This is not to dismiss the importance of Miller – far from it. Instead, as the last pages hope to illustrate, we aim to provide a slightly different way of conceptualizing individual liberty, as well as looking at the problem of (what we moderns call) "rights" from a different perspective by considering a neglected stream of (Athenian) thought. A good place to start with the responses to Miller's stimulating contribution to the subject of rights is Schofield 1999.

The literature surrounding contemporary questions and issues of rights is unsurprisingly vast, and there are many contested aspects. Waldron 1993, written by one of the most important thinkers on rights in contemporary political philosophy, is a good starting point. The essays in Waldron 1984 are a useful way into a number of issues relating to rights and moral philosophy, especially the important contributions by Hart, Mackie, Dworkin, and Vlastos. Dworkin 1987 is a very influential – and readable – defense by a heavyweight political and legal thinker of the theory and practice of rights. See also the literature cited in note 1 below for an introduction to (some of the) further debates on the problem of rights. Hohfeld 2001, dating from 1919, remains influential despite its age and can still frequently be found cited in much of the contemporary literature on rights.

NOTES

1   In a number of ways. What "rights" do we actually possess, and do these always give rise to legally enforceable duties on the part of other individuals or the state? For instance, in an important book, Thomas Pogge demands that the international community (especially the fortunate inhabitants of the wealthier countries) have a positive obligation to realize in practice Article 25.1 of the Universal Declaration of Human Rights ("everyone has the right to a standard of living adequate for the health and well-being of himself and of his family, including food, clothing, housing and medical care"), but it is clear that a world which allows some 18 million people to die each year from poverty-related causes (cf. Pogge 2002: 2) is woefully failing to fulfill the obligations and duties of this "right" (not, of course, in this case a legally enforceable claim – ought it not to become so?). See Pogge 2002. Second, there is an important debate over whether human rights are supported and endorsed by all nations, races, and cultures, for instance over "human rights and Asian values." See, for example, Donnelly 1999; Ignatieff 2001: 53–98; Sen 1999: 227–48. The approach of Othman 1999 promises a great deal to the solution of this question. Third, of course, "rights talk" is far from being the only approach to moral philosophy, and the role of rights within other schools of moral philosophy (utilitarianism and a number of its variants in particular) remains hotly contested. See especially Dworkin 1984; J. Mackie 1984. Cf. Sen 1982. Indeed, in the material political world, utilitarian-style arguments can often be used to circumvent and override basic rights. For instance, the British government justifies its Draconian antiterror legislation on the grounds that it is "beneficial to the public

interest" (or some similar phrase) to ignore certain rights in some cases. Nor, of course, must we be misled into thinking that rights are the only means of preserving human freedom and dignity, but we shall return to this.

2 For a much fuller discussion of the neoclassical (or "Republican") tradition and its relationship(s) to antiquity, see the interesting discussion by Nadon, this volume, chapter 33.

3 This divergence between the two is dealt with in greater detail in Edge 2006: 94–106 and forthcoming. Despite this difference, it is important to state that the two conceptions of liberty do share common ground since both refute absolutely the claim of liberal writers (from Hobbes, through David Hume to Constant and, later, Berlin himself) that the form of government you live under is of no intrinsic importance to your individual liberty. What seems to happen is that, via Cicero's *De republica*, the radical democratic conception of liberty is replaced by a less radical, republican version, where the self-governing and free community is no longer a participatory democracy but a representative, or mixed, republic. Indeed, to Cicero's eyes, and to many who followed him in part or in full, an Athenian-style democracy is no less of a tyrant, and, therefore, no less of a threat to individual liberty, than the archetypal absolute monarch.

4 Examples: Aesch. *Pers.* 241; Eur. *Heracl.* 61–2, 113, 197–8, 243–6, 286–7, Eur. *Supp.* 476–7; Lys. 2.14; Thuc. 1.141.1. Similarly, Athenian writers often speak of the threat of "enslavement" at the hands of the Persians (e.g., Dem. 14.31–2, 15.15; Lys. 2.21, 26, 33, 35, 41–2, 44, 46–7, 55, 57, 59–60) and Macedon (e.g., Dem. 1.5, 23; 2.8; 3.20; 8.46, 49, 60, 62; 9.22, 36, 59, 66, 70–1; 10.25; 18.66, etc.; Din. 1.19; Hyp. 6. *Epit.* 10–11, 19, 24, 34). Equally, Athenians linked their "freedom" to the expulsion of the tyrants in 510 (e.g., Dem. 17.3–4; Lyc. 1.61; Lys. 31.26, 31–2; Thuc. 8.68.4) and spoke of their "slavery" at the hands of the Thirty Tyrants in 404/03 and their "liberation" from dependence on that brutal regime (e.g., Andoc. 2.27; Lys. 12.39, 67, 73, 78, 92–4, 97; 13.17; 14.34; 18.6, 24, 27; 26.19–20).

5 Although both cases should not be considered examples of the infamous "tyranny of the majority" *simpliciter*, they do, at the very least, represent failings in the Athenian legal and democratic system because such abuses of individual liberty *could* happen. In Socrates' case that he could be put on trial for impiety and found guilty (regardless of the number of votes for acquittal). In the generals' case that all six could be condemned by a single vote, regardless of the machinations of Theramenes and his oligarchic followers.

6 We should also point out that similar violations will not readily be seen in the later fourth century, and it must be acknowledged that the Athenians could, just as we can, learn from their mistakes and, in fact, seem to have made a pretty good job of doing so, especially in relation to the apparently more stringent legal protections for individuals put in place at the beginning of the fourth century (discussed above).

7 On this point, see the interesting debate between Mogens Hansen and Moshe Berent on whether we can legitimately speak of an ancient "state." Berent prefers the term "stateless political community." See Berent 2000a, 2000b, 2004; Hansen 2002b.

8 We mean by this that, because it represents a different (and, arguably, far more radical) way of speaking about liberty than that currently on offer as the norm in western liberal democracies, other cultures, from the perspective of the (free and equal) cosmopolitan conceptual dialogue outlined in the following passage, might be more open to it. In the Athenian conception of liberty we have been discussing, the individual, as Aeschines neatly put it, is king and the guard of his own area of liberty and free movement (now, belatedly, modern writers can add "her" to this equation). This represents a very different approach from the "liberty" we are told we enjoy under representative governments, where power to

make laws, and dictate the area of free movement for individuals, is in the hands of others, the very thing the Athenian concept we have been discussing is wary of. An entire political philosophy could, indeed, usefully be built on this notion of the sovereign individual (and we should also point out that we are certainly not claiming that the Athenians ever did so), having due regard for a fundamental question of political philosophy – what is the degree of liberty I can expect to enjoy, assuming an equal amount for my fellows in political society? The Athenian democratic concept of liberty places each of us as individuals, you and me together, at the center of this question, as the ones who decide what liberty we are to enjoy when living (in Rawls's terms) and cooperating in human society over time. Of course, it is worth pointing out, to return to history, that it is precisely these terms that the Athenians, and the ancient Greeks and Romans as a whole, with the possible exception of a few enlightened souls, were ignorant of. The language of equal rights and universal human equality, the fundamental basis of modern political philosophies, is a regrettably late development in human moral evolution and is arguably still a very long way from being realized in practice.

CHAPTER 11

Personal Freedom in Greek Democracies, Republican Rome, and Modern Liberal States

Robert W. Wallace

Although Greek democracies and Republican Rome each promoted freedom – *eleutheria, libertas* – as a cardinal value, they differed profoundly in tolerating personal freedoms, just as they differ from modern liberal states. While many components of modern liberalism are historically contingent, core personal values include the freedoms of speech, thought, and religious belief, equality especially of rights and opportunities, and the decriminalization of private conduct such as drug use and various sexual practices by consenting adults. By these criteria (and notwithstanding the absence of "rights": see Cartledge and Edge, this volume, chapter 10), Athens and (so far as we can determine) other Greek democracies stand as far more tolerant than any modern liberal democracy. First attested in Sophocles' *Ajax* (1071–84), probably in the 440s, Athens' democratic ideal was "to live as you like." Beyond constitutional type, key mentalities best known from Athenian democratic sources reflect broader Greek trends, including egalitarianism, communitarianism, and tolerance. In the hundreds of archaic Greek laws collected by van Effenterre and Ruzé (1994–5) from every kind of polity, none regulates personal conduct. A central issue for modern liberalism, Greek religion was regulated almost only in connection with public cult, rather than belief (see Osborne, this volume, chapter 8). Except for the fourth century elite reaction against democracy most visible in Plato, legally regulating another person's private life was not an idea that occurred to the Greeks.[1] As for social pressure, even public insults in Athens' comic theater and courtrooms, however delicious or titillating, apparently did little actual damage. So for example, Aristophanes' main target Kleon continued to dominate Athenian politics until his death in battle in 422. In Thucydides' Funeral Oration Pericles remarks, "in our day-to-day lives, we are not angry with our neighbor if he does something according to pleasure, nor do we give him those black looks which, though they do no real harm, still are painful. In our private lives we live together in a tolerant way" (2.37).

A Companion to Greek and Roman Political Thought, First Edition. Edited by Ryan K. Balot.
© 2013 Blackwell Publishing Ltd. Published 2013 by Blackwell Publishing Ltd.

In republican Rome, by contrast again, *libertas* even excluded personal freedom, which could be considered *licentia*, license. If *libertas* became a cardinal value partly because of *eleutheria*'s importance for Greece, it mostly bore a different sense. *Libertas* designated the quality of a free citizen rather than a slave, thus implying all that was required of a Roman. Rome's core values included order, hierarchy, discipline, and obedience. For citizens' personal lives, these qualities were symbolized by that state's highest public official, the *censor*, exercising a *regimen morum*: general control over morals and conduct. Recent attempts to posit for Rome personal freedom in the Greek sense – "living as you like" – have fallen on stony ground.

In Greek democracies, *eleutheria* embraced what Isaiah Berlin (1958) called both positive and negative freedoms: to participate equally in government, and to live one's personal life without interference. In Aristotle's summation,

> a basic principle of the democratic form of government is freedom ... for every democracy has freedom as its aim. Ruling and being ruled in turn is one element of freedom ... Another is to live as you like. For this, they say, is a function of being free, since living not as you like is the function of a slave. (*Pol.* 1317a40–b17)

In Athens, "living as you like" was a reality in both ideology and practice. In addition to Thucydides' Funeral Oration, as Cartledge and Edge note (chapter 10), the general Nicias calls Athens "the freest country," praising "the unregimented powers – *exousiai* – for all in daily life," to encourage his soldiers (Thuc. 7.69.2). An ardent democrat, the native Syracusan speechwriter Lysias said that in a democracy "people can live as they like" (26.5). Anticipating the libertarian J. S. Mill, the northern Greek democratic philosopher Democritus wrote: "the laws should not prevent each person from living according to his own powers" – *exousiai* – "provided one person does not hurt another" (DK 68 B 245).

Beyond ideology, few will dispute what so outraged fourth century conservatives, that day by day Athens was remarkably tolerant in personal matters. Private citizens were free to visit prostitutes, get drunk, or engage in homosexual relations, although public standards of morality condemned these practices (Davidson 2001). During the war with Sparta, a conspicuous number of upper-class Athenians (with hangers-on like Socrates) felt free to dress and behave like Spartans, and openly praised the enemy (see, e.g., Dunbar 1995: 636). For years the Cynic philosopher Diogenes – "he preferred freedom to everything": Diog. Laert. 6.71 – lived naked in the Agora, doing everything including masturbating and defecating in public. And yet, his biographer reports, "the Athenians loved him" (Diog. Laert. 6. 46, 58, 69; 6.41).

Exploiting democratic principles of free speech, courtroom litigants could say almost anything. In 323, Dinarchos calls Demosthenes – a senior statesman, now over 60 – "this beast" (Din. 1.10), "this hireling" (1.28), "open to bribes," "a thief and a traitor" (1.41, cf. 77), this "juggler" (1.92), "this person to be spit upon! this Scythian! – really I cannot contain myself" (1.15). Coarse, libelous, even impious language was typical of the comic stage. As Horace remarked, "Eupolis, Cratinus and

Aristophanes poets, and the other good men to whom Old Comedy belongs, if there was anyone worth describing as a rogue and thief, as an adulterer or cut-throat or as scandalous in any other way, they set their mark upon him with great freedom" (*Satires* 1.4.1–4). As Moses Finley observed, Aristophanes and other playwrights repeatedly criticized Athens' war against Sparta. Yet year after year, their plays were performed for the demos at public expense. "The phenomenon has no parallel known to me" (Finley 1973: 83–4). Aristophanes even treats the gods with mocking irreverence. In *Frogs*, parodying the sacred formula "*ekkechutai* [it's poured], call the god," Dionysos tells his slave Xanthias "*ekkechoda* [I've shit myself], call the god." Xanthias replies, "You're ridiculous, get up before someone sees you" (479–80).

As drama relentlessly questioned social norms (Goldhill 1987; Gibert, this volume, chapter 28), tragedies, too, presented unconventional, subversive, and impious notions about religion. Euripides' *Bellerophon* included the lines, "Does any man say there are gods in heaven? No, there are none" (*TGF* fr. 286). *Iphigeneia at Aulis* 1034–5 asks "if there are gods ... , but if there are not ..." In *Trojan Women* 884–90, the sympathetic, later devastatingly intellectual Hecabe prays to Zeus, "Conveyance of the earth and you who have a base on earth, whoever you are, most difficult to know, whether you are the necessity of nature or the mind of mortals." Slow-witted Menelaus replies, "What's this? What strange new prayers do you make to the gods?" his verb *kainizein* prefiguring the charge against Socrates. Whatever Euripides' religious views, it is easy to understand how Aristophanes might say, "he has persuaded men that the gods do not exist" (Ar. *Thesm.* 450–1). The city welcomed all sorts of new thinkers, some saying outrageous things against the social and religious bases of society.

Even the city's most brilliant politicians, including Pericles and Alcibiades, lived unconventional private lives, yet the demos returned them to office as best skilled in politics and war. Like other contemporary intellectuals Pericles was probably an atheist (in Thucydides he never mentions the gods). For years he lived unmarried with the foreigner Aspasia, producing two illegitimate sons. Alcibiades flagrantly violated every virtue of restraint, moderation, and self-control. Xenophon, who knew him and was sympathetic, quotes his detractors that he was "most intemperate" (*akratestatos*), "most outrageous" (*hubristotatos*), and "most violent" (*Mem.* 1.2.12). Describing him as self-interested and deceitful, Thucydides – also a sympathetic eyewitness – wrote that the demos feared "the magnitude of his violations of laws and conventions in matters concerning his body in his daily life, and of the thinking of what he did in everything he was involved in" (6.15, cf. 5.43, 5.45, 6.12). At the *Symposium* party, Plato – another sympathetic eyewitness – shows Alcibiades shouting drunk in the courtyard, then staggering to the house helped by a flute girl, and standing in the doorway "with a mass of ribbons and an enormous wreath of ivy and violets sprouting on his head" (*Symp.* 212d). Nonetheless, the people elected him general in 420 as soon as he was eligible, and then in 419, 418, 417, 416, and 415. He was driven out only by his aristocratic competitors, despite immense popular support.

In some contexts, the Athenians extended personal freedoms to women, and sometimes even to slaves. Plato complains "how much equality and freedom there is among women toward men and among men toward women" in democracies (*Resp.* 563b). In Aristophanes' *Frogs* Aeschylus rebukes Euripides because so many women and slaves speak in his plays. "But," Euripides protests," that's democratic what I was doing" (948–52). If social ideals stipulated that citizen women remain inside the home, Aristotle (*Pol.* 1300a4–9) notes that in democracies many poor citizen women went outside to work, some in the fields, others selling food or other simple products such as garlands. Some worked as midwives, innkeepers, bakers, laundresses, or wet nurses (Herfst 1922). Even in inflammatory areas such as adultery, women's realities could be complex (D. Cohen 1991: 129–32). If the law sanctioned severe punishments, extant evidence also reveals "silence, extortion, or complicity" (1991: 133). Isaeus 3 records a dispute over the estate of one Pyrrhus: had he been properly married to Phile's mother? Evidence from Pyrrhus' uncles supported Phile's claim (29–34), but one court had already rejected it, and the speaker's assertion that Phile's mother was a *hetaira* (courtesan) was supported by allegations of quarrels, noisy parties, and other wild behavior (13–14). The mother's status may always have been unclear. However, for many years she had been well taken care of by Pyrrhus' family, despite any bad behavior. She apparently felt free to engage in nonconformist behavior, even though it affected the major civic issues of marriage, citizenship, and inheritance.

As for slaves, "even in private homes," Xenophon complains, "those who had rather more than the usual number of slaves, and some who had only a few, were nevertheless, though nominally masters, quite unable to assert their authority over even those few" (*Cyr.* 1.1). Aristotle regards as "characteristic of popular government" the "lack of rule over slaves ... and tolerating everyone living as he wants" (*Pol.* 1319b 27–31). Plato's indignation produced the provocative inversion that Athens' slaves were free (*Resp.* 563b).

Athenian texts document an ongoing debate over the merits of allowing people to live, speak, and think as they liked. Elite conservatives unhappy with democracy deplored personal freedoms as "licentious" (*akolastoi*), perverting "living as one likes" into "doing what one wants," a tyrant's vice which even democrats condemned. Athens' premier enemy of freedom and democracy, Plato complains that the democratic city "is full of freedom and free speech and everyone in it is allowed to do what he likes ...., each man can plan his life as he pleases." Citizens, foreigners, slaves, women, even the animals are "full of freedom," horses and donkeys "walk freely and arrogantly, bumping into everyone who meets them in the street if they do not step aside" (*Resp.* 557b). In his antidemocratic pamphlet "The Athenian Polity," the so-called Old Oligarch laments, "among the best people there is minimal licentiousness and injustice ..., but among the demos there is a maximum of ignorance, disorder, and wickedness" (Ps-Xen. *Ath. Pol.* 1. 5, 10). The antidemocratic Thucydides took wicked pleasure in having Athens' democratic leader Cleon criticize the incompetence of the people's Assembly, praising "ignorance with self-control [*sōphrosunē*]" – Spartan qualities – over the demos's "cleverness with licentiousness" (3.37). With delicious pleasure he has Alcibiades – another democratic leader – tell the Spartans that democracy is licentious and "an acknowledged folly" (6.89). When his Nicias commends to his soldiers Athens' "*anepitaktoi* [unregimented] powers for all," the irony of *anepitaktoi* – scarcely a military virtue – reveals this writer's devilishly clever bias. So too, in the Funeral Oration Thucydides has Pericles pervert the democratic ideal of "living as you like" into "doing something according to pleasure." Echoing that perversion, Thucydides shortly afterwards says the Athenians acted "according to pleasure" during (what he claims was) a period of moral collapse following the plague (2.53.1), and as they were later turned to pleasures by Athens' demagogues (2.65.10).[2] One remembers Plato's allusion to the democratic judiciary as a doctor being prosecuted by a pastry cook before a jury of children (*Grg.* 521e–522a).

In modern liberal democracies, issues of social tolerance and control remain important topics of discussion and public policy. Legal philosophers continue to dispute the value of legislating personal morality. An iconic western democracy, Athens has sometimes played a role in these controversies. Yet for Athens itself, current debate has centered not on the merits of liberal tolerance, but on whether Athens was tolerant – how far each Athenian was free to live, speak, and think as he wished. The Athenians' own debate makes clear that both democrats and conservatives thought the Athenians were free, but conservatives disliked this. As we have seen, much evidence documents the Athenians' extraordinary tolerance. Modern scholars question these freedoms because, despite ideologies and tolerant practices, the Athenians sometimes violated individuals' freedoms in ways modern liberals find disturbing. Despite free speech, Assembly speakers were often shouted down or even dragged off the speaker's platform. According to Xenophon, while attempting to become Athens' leader although not yet 20, Plato's brother Glaucon was more than once dragged from the speaker's platform "an object of ridicule" (*Mem.* 3.6). Plato's Socrates remarks that if a non-expert tries to advise the Assembly on technical matters, "however handsome or wealthy or nobly born he may be, it makes no difference. They reject him noisily and with contempt, until he is shouted down and desists, or is dragged off or ejected by the police on the orders of the presiding authority" (Pl. *Prt.* 319c).

In some areas Athens did not grant its citizens freedom. Pericles himself sponsored a law against marrying a foreigner. A citizen who discovered his wife in adultery was obliged by law to divorce her. In the fifth century a citizen could not bequeath his property as he wished: laws stipulated a fixed group of inheritors. In ca. 443 the Athenians ostracized Damon, a music theorist and Pericles' adviser; between 440 and 437 they apparently curtailed the comic poets' freedom to criticize; in 399 they executed Socrates (Wallace 1994, 2005). Despite widespread religious freedom, the main legal charge against Socrates was "refusing to recognize the gods whom the city recognizes, but introducing other new spiritual beings." In *The Ancient City*, Fustel de Coulanges listed many kinds of state interference in private life (1882: 293–8), including compulsory military service to the age of 60; a law against idleness; and a law permitting no one to remain neutral in political conflicts. In addition, the "state system of justice ... could strike when one was not guilty, and simply for its own interest." The demos could ostracize a fellow citizen for ten years simply because they thought him undesirable.

No one disputes that Athens' adult male citizens enjoyed a number of positive freedoms, in particular "to share in" many functions of citizenship and government (Rhodes, this volume, chapter 4; cf. Ostwald 1996). How far they possessed other positive freedoms, such as addressing the Assembly, has been judged more ambiguous – in the Assembly, because they could be shouted down. As for negative freedoms – the freedom from oppression in daily life, the right to be left alone, to think, say, or "live as one wished" – most modern critics claim that because these freedoms could at any moment be taken or else legislated away, they cannot be considered freedoms. Finley observed,

> what was wholly lacking was a conception of precisely those inalienable rights which have been the foundation of the modern libertarian doctrine: freedom of speech, of religion and so on ... The Athenian state ... could make inroads into freedom of speech and thought, and did so when it chose ... Provided the procedures adopted were themselves lawful, there were no limits to the powers of the *polis*, other than self-imposed (and therefore changeable) limits, outside the sphere in which deep-rooted and ancient taboos remained powerful. (1976: 21–2)

Among many examples, Finley noted that "a Greek had his freedom severely restricted ... in the field of marriage and family law. The state determined the legitimacy of a marriage ... by specifying the categories of men and women who could, or could not, marry each other." Josiah Ober remarked, "The Athenians never developed the principle of inalienable 'negative rights' (freedom from governmental interference in private affairs) of the individual or of minorities vis-à-vis the state – a central tenet of modern liberalism" (1989: 15), despite their ideology of citizens' freedoms. Berlin wrote,

> I have found no convincing evidence of any clear formulation of [the notion of individual freedom] in the ancient world. Some of my critics ... cite the ... celebrated paean to liberty in the Funeral Oration of Pericles, as well as the speech of Nicias before the final battle with the Syracusans, as evidence that the Greeks, at any rate, had a clear conception of individual liberty. I must confess that I do not find this conclusive ... The issue of individual freedom, of the frontiers beyond which public authority ... should not normally be allowed to step, had not clearly emerged at this stage; the central value attached to it may, perhaps, ... be the late product of a capitalist civilization, an element in a network of values that includes such notions as personal rights, civil liberties, the sanctity of the individual personality, the importance of privacy, personal relations, and the like. (1958: xl–xli)

Fustel concluded,

> At Athens ... a man's life was guaranteed by nothing so soon as the interest of the state was at stake ... It is a singular error... to believe that in the ancient cities men enjoyed liberty. They had not even the idea of it. ... To have political rights, to vote, to name magistrates, – this was called liberty; but man was not the less enslaved to the state. The ancients, especially the Greeks, always exaggerated the importance, and above all, the rights of society. (1882)

Modern historians question Athens' freedoms because the demos had the untrammeled power to interfere in virtually any aspect of people's lives, by regulations, interventions, and sometimes arbitrary punishments.

How are we to reconcile the Athenians' violations of individuals' freedoms with their own deeply felt ideologies and practice of tolerance? Under what circumstances might freedoms be constrained, and did any underlying principles inform community interventions?

Two fundamental historical and conceptual differences between ancient Greek communities and modern liberal states suggest complementary approaches to Athens' infringements of freedom. First, in contemporary liberal states, freedoms are guaranteed by laws and rights. In the United States, the Declaration of Independence, the Constitution, and the Bill of Rights extend to all citizens various rights including free speech, religious choice, public assembly, firearms, and a fair and speedy trial. In this context, "right" is a rigid, absolute term, implying a clear principle, and inalienable except under specified circumstances. The Declaration of Independence guarantees the right to life, liberty, and the pursuit of happiness, qualified only by the state's right to execute or imprison those judged to be criminals after the due process of law. All citizens have the right to free speech, especially in the "high value" areas of social, political, and artistic expression. This right is qualified only when the courts have determined that the unrestrained exercise of free speech is detrimental to the common good, as in libel, sedition, perjury, or "falsely shouting fire in a crowded theater." Restrictions apply especially in "low value" areas, including deceptive commercial speech, common obscenity and pornography if conflicting with community values, and what the Supreme Court has called "fighting words."

Finley, Ober, and other critics view Athens' abuses of personal freedom from the modern perspective of rights. Finley notes, "What was wholly lacking was a conception of . . . inalienable rights" (see above). They are correct: an Athenian's freedoms were not guaranteed by a concept of rights. "Right" in this sense was unknown to the Greeks, they had no word for it.[3] None of Socrates' defenders argue that prosecuting him for his religious beliefs violated even Athens' ideology of free speech.

Yet how far does freedom depend on rights? In fact, rights prove to be poor promoters of freedom, in comparison with Athens' alternatives. In Athens, even without rights, many laws protected important "negative" freedoms against personal interference, for example by making it illegal for the government or any private person to kill, imprison, enslave, or beat anyone (including noncitizens) except under specified circumstances.

It has been objected that, although ancient writers (Thuc. 2.37.3, Hdt. 3.83.3) said that people were free to live as they liked provided they obeyed the law, this conception offers individuals little protection, because laws can target any aspect of private life (D. Cohen 1995: 192, cf. 54). However, Athens simply had no laws that regulated private life. Its legislation before 350 displays a single, unwavering orientation toward private conduct. If a person did not materially harm others, violate another citizen's household, or infringe on community obligations, it was the democracy's principle and practice not to regulate personal conduct. Before 350 no laws had the primary purpose of preventing "self-degradation" or self-inflicted harm, for example by prostitution or drug use by private citizens. Catalogs of Athens' public and private offenses, and the many legal cases in the orators and elsewhere, indicate that most Attic laws regulated interpersonal crimes or disputes concerning matters like theft and inheritance, or else relations with the polis – for example, citizenship, military service, and taxation. Their general statute outlawing impiety was used almost exclusively against violations of public cult. The Athenians regulated marriage and adultery because the citizen community was obsessed about the purity of citizen blood. They did not care what a man did, including having children with a foreigner. Those children, however, could not be citizens. The statute against idleness targeted heads of household who neglected household property, to the detriment of heirs. Athens had no laws of a paternalistic or educatory type. The Athenians were conscious of this principle and most of them were proud of it. Laws regarding private individuals should be "gentle and humane," Demosthenes states (24.193). Aeschines notes, "the law does not investigate private citizens" (1.195). This "gap" guaranteed that personal freedom was free of legal regulation. As I have mentioned, no archaic polis, regardless of political type, appears to have regulated the private conduct of individuals. Sparta was no exception, even if the ever present danger of helot revolts necessitated the militarization of society, transferring much of private life – such as the need to produce children (future soldiers) – into the public sphere.

Finally, positive personal freedoms at Athens were actively promoted by various democratic principles, mentalities, and ideologies, including "living as you like," "free and candid speech" (*parrhēsia*), and "equal speech" (*isēgoria*). As we have seen, the Greeks called these not rights but "powers," *exousiai*. By contrast, rights can protect freedoms but mostly do not promote them. US citizens have the right to vote and to speak freely. However, these rights are typically invoked only when threatened, not to encourage their use. At Athens, principles, ideologies, and mentalities contributed to a feeling of civic duty, encouraging citizens to use the freedoms that society extended to them. In addition, American states can restrict personal freedoms in any area not expressly protected by the Constitution, Bill of Rights, or Declaration of Independence. The US Equal Employment Opportunities (EEO) Laws (Title VII of the US Civil Rights Act of 1964) prohibit discrimination based on race, color, religion, sex, national origin, disabilities, or being over 40(!); some (but only some) states and municipalities also include sexual orientation in this list. Discrimination based on other factors, such as dress codes or physical attractiveness, is common. Until recently, Texas outlawed sodomy, but not for heterosexual couples. Such inconsistencies, and the need for further supralegal guarantees, are reflected in the US controversy over the Equal Rights Amendment to the Constitution. The premise of that amendment is that laws stipulating equal treatment for women offer only uneven and uncertain protections. In *Anarchical Fallacies* and elsewhere, Jeremy Bentham argued that rights present a fundamental paradox: they purport to be absolute but are arbitrary. Different societies value different qualities and at different times. An advocate of laws to regulate the relations between community and individuals, Bentham called the rights of man "nonsense on stilts," the revolutionaries' *Déclaration des droits de l'homme* "a metaphysical work – the *ne plus ultra* of metaphysics."

As a further defect in rights, in the US, at least until recently, the citizen privileges of African Americans – and during World War II, citizens of Japanese descent – were routinely flouted despite the paper guarantee of rights.

For these reasons, Athens' laws, principles, mentalities, and ideologies were stronger forces for freedom than rights. Finley may object that in Athens "there were no theoretical limits to the power of the state," but as Hansen points out (1991: 80), theory is not so important as practice. Britain has no theoretical limits to state intrusion into people's private lives, but in practice usually respects most freedoms. No supralegal texts prevented the Athenians from legislating private morality, but before 350 they did not. US rights constitute theoretical limits to the state's power, in all the ambiguity of that qualification. Most Athenians lived much freer and more actively free lives than citizens of modern liberal states, and felt little anxiety that their freedoms were at risk.

A second difference between ancient democracies and modern liberal states supplies an alternative perspective on Athens' occasional restrictions of freedom. Modern liberalism is informed by the notion of the primacy of the individual over the state, and the paramount importance of protecting individual liberties against state interference. This orientation is in part the product of the continuous struggle against religious oppression since the Roman Empire. It is also the product of the struggle against so-called "heavy states," where regimes or faceless bureaucrats dominate an alienated populace by what Max Weber called a monopoly of legitimate violence: censorship, taxation, and the police. In the seventeenth century, liberalism itself emerged out of debates over the extent to which any state might restrict citizens' freedoms. For the founding fathers of modern liberalism such as Baruch Spinoza and John Locke, freedom meant, among other things, shielding a realm of private life from interference by government. Although the US Constitution permits states to set aside individuals' rights when "the public safety may require it" (Article I, section 9), the legal system of the United States is so far oriented toward protecting individuals that even known criminals (even if noncitizens) are set free if representatives of the state have inadvertently committed some minor procedural mistake. The American Civil Liberties Union opposes indiscriminate security screening of passengers at airports, and police sobriety checkpoints against drunk drivers. In a famous statement (*Omstread v. United States*, 1928), Justice Louis Brandeis of the Supreme Court wrote, "Experience should teach us to be most on guard to protect liberty when the Government's purposes are beneficent. Men born to freedom are naturally alert to repel invasions of their liberty by evil-minded rulers. The greatest dangers to liberty lurk in insidious encounters by men of zeal, well-meaning but without understanding." Although patriotism in the US is not a discredited ideal, many Americans feel entitled to oppose their government for reasons of conscience, through civil disobedience. A significant number refuse to pay taxes for military purposes. A significant number refused induction during the Vietnam War. Mohammad Ali remarked, "I got no quarrel with them Viet Cong." In *What I Believe*, published in 1939, E. M. Forster observed, "if I had to choose between betraying my country and betraying my friend, I hope I should have the guts to betray my country." Chauvinism, jingoism – Samuel Johnson defined patriotism as "the last refuge of a scoundrel" (J. Boswell, *Life of Johnson*, entry for April 7, 1775).

Antistate sentiment has shaped modern attitudes toward Athens, not least by inducing sympathy for rebellious individuals like Socrates or subordinated groups such as women and slaves. The sensitivity of modern citizens to any infringement of liberty as first steps on the "slippery slope" to tyranny has sensitized us to any infringement of freedom in Athens, not least because of the continued significance of Athens' democracy in political discourse. From the perspective of history since the Roman Empire, these attitudes are understandable and these reactions are valid.

The views of most Athenians were different. While questions of loyalty to family or political comrades could sometimes be discussed, it was a basic ideology and also common practice that the community took precedence over any individual. Democrats supported freedom, but virtually everyone held that the substantive, material interests of the city came before the freedom of any individual. No text, conservative or progressive, displays any ambiguity about this value. Ostensibly progressive, Thucydides' Pericles remarks: "When the whole polis is on the right course it is a better thing for each separate individual than when private interests are satisfied but the polis as a whole is going downhill" (2.60.2). More cautious and traditional than Pericles, Nicias claims that a person who cares for his own safety and property is still a "good citizen," because in his own interests he "would be most anxious that the city's affairs prosper too" (Thuc. 6.9.2, see also 6.12.2). Thucydides himself remarks that after Pericles' death the city suffered because politicians acted "in accordance with their personal ambition and personal gain" (2.65.7).

In Aristophanes' *Frogs*, Euripides says "I hate the kind of citizen who'll prove to be / Slow to assist his country, swift to harm her greatly / For his own good astute, but useless for the City's" (1427–9). According to the conservative Xenophon (*Hell.* 1.7.21), Euryptolemos called it "disgraceful" to put the interests of his relatives over the interests of "the whole polis." The democrat Lysias, the oligarch Andocides, the contemporary speech Ps-Andocides 4 all proclaim the priority of the community over individual concerns. Demosthenes states to the demos, "I have never received anything from you and I have spent on you all but a fraction of my fortune" (21.189). Individuals constantly boast how much more they pay in taxes than required. As Dover notes (1974: 175–6), no modern person would do this – we boast of avoiding taxes. In court, defendants typically plead how much they have served the community. In Lysias a speaker asks the dikasts (lay judges) "to give whatever verdict you choose as to which of the [litigants] behaves better toward your city" (fr. 7). Virtually every Greek understood and accepted this limitation on personal freedom. The ethical message of the first Greek text lies in the price all pay when Achilles put his own anger at being slighted ahead of his community's welfare. In early sixth century Athens, Solon proclaimed to fellow citizens, "obey the public authorities, right or wrong" (fr. 30 West), and compelled them to take sides in civil strife. Democritus wrote: "One should think it of greater importance than anything else that the affairs of the polis are conducted well ... For a polis which is conducted well is the best means to success. Everything depends on this, and if this is preserved everything is preserved and if this is destroyed everything is destroyed" (B 252). Classical Greece had no "heavy states" oppressing an alienated populace. The anachronistic connotations of the word "state" argue that for classical Greece we should avoid it, in favor of polis or community, acting together in common self-interest.

An Athenian's freedoms were almost entirely unrestrained provided he posed no substantive, material threat to others or the polis. Apparent exceptions to this principle, regarding for example marriage or adultery, are few, and reflect modern rather than ancient perspectives, differently demarcating private and public. Athenians active in government were asked five questions about personal conduct never asked of private citizens – had they beaten their parents, not supported them, not performed military service, not thrown their shield away, and not prostituted themselves (e.g., Aeschin. 1.28–32). To safeguard the community, military service was obligatory, although only by wealthier citizens. Thucydides' Pericles boasts how mild military service was (2.39), and many sources attest military indiscipline (Pritchett 1974: 232–45). Antidemocratic or impious philosophers went unharmed, except on rare occasions when their political entanglements were judged to threaten the city. Confronted with material danger, the demos sometimes intervened, sometimes abruptly and with insufficient deliberation. Yet even those who appear unfairly treated did not challenge the prior interests of the community in which everyone shared. Even Plato's Socrates endorsed the greater claim of the demos, at the cost of his own life. In *Crito* 51a–c the "Laws" say to Socrates,

> your fatherland is more to be honored than your mother, father, and other ancestors … You must persuade your fatherland or do what it commands, and endure in silence what it orders you to endure, whether you are beaten or bound, whether you are led into war to be wounded or killed … for there justice lies.

Speech, thought, and conduct posing no material threat to others remained unregulated. In guarding their common interests, the Athenians were much more tolerant of nonconformity than any modern state.

Alien to the Greeks in not publicly tolerating personal deviance from strict social norms, Roman society was closely regulated by moral codes, effected through social disapproval and legal sanction. Most famously, Rome's highest magistrates, the censors, exercised the authority even to disfranchise citizens for immoral or disrespectful conduct. Every census saw expulsions from the senate, as for example Cornelius Rufinus was expelled in 275 for owning ten pounds of silver goblets; other moral crimes included harshness or indulgence toward children. The Lex Orchia (187 BC) limited the number of guests at private parties; the consumption of dormice and other delicacies was outlawed at banquets; "living respectably," *honeste vivere* (Ulpian, *Dig.* 1.1.10.1) was a legal duty: all in defense of *mores* ("a term of notable imprecision": Astin 1989: 19) and the *mos maiorum* – "the customs of the ancestors." Although Brunt (1988b: 304) rightly mentions some resistance to some of these restrictions, Rome's oligarchy mostly tolerated them, partly in an attempt to remain cohesive against the temptations resulting from empire (Baltrusch 1989), partly as a product of basic social mentalities. The moral regulation of Rome's upper class stands in contrast with the Athenians, who after 350 regulated some aspects of the lives of women and the young, but almost never constrained their own freedoms. And if Roman moral codes were mostly enforced against the upper classes (Astin 1988: 17–19) – the morals of the lower orders weren't worth worrying about – Roman society was "always hierarchical" (Brunt 1988b: 288) and many constraints applied to all: sons obeyed fathers ("complete subjection": 1988b: 285); citizens spent 20 years on active military service; *disciplina* responded to *imperium*. In an iconic episode, in 340 the consul T. Manlius Torquatus had his son decapitated for breaking ranks to attack the Latins. As for women, during the republican period men had the legal right to kiss any female relative, in an effort to detect wine drinking at home when men were absent.

Libertas designated the quality of a free citizen (Mommsen in fact identified *libertas* with *civitas* (1887–8: iii 1), as did Cicero, *Balb.* 9.24), simultaneously embracing the hard-won civic protections of free citizens and the constraints imposed by law, by moral virtues, and by civic and family rights and duties. *Libertas* meant freedom from both *regnum* and servitude (Schulz 1936: 140–1). It was often contrasted with tyranny and monarchy (Syme 1939, ch. 11). "From the individual's point of view *libertas* was primarily a guarantee of equality under the law ... and an assurance that the rules of judicial procedure would be known, published and impartially applied ... the certainty that the magistrates' coercive power was not unlimited" (Nicolet 1980: 320). All citizens possessed many protections against upper class abuse. In particular, all had the legal right to a trial and judicial appeal, and not to be tortured. The Roman principle that each citizen was *liber* also led to what has been called "extreme individualism in the domain of private law" (Schulz 1936: 146 and ff.). The state did not regulate marriage or most aspects of married life (e.g., not requiring a husband to support his wife); an owner's power was to be "as unrestricted as possible" (1936: 153); rules of succession maintained to the fullest extent the freedom of the individual. So, too, as Brunt notes (1988b: 300), philosophy, religion, and political thought went largely unregulated. At the same time, however, these freedoms were constrained within the boundaries of Roman values and institutions, such as the patron–client relationship ("no doubt social pressures restricted the individual far more than the state did": Brunt 1988b: 307) and virtues, including *fides* and *pietas* (Wirszubski 1950: 7–8). *Pudicitia* ("a sense of public shame") was often paired with *libertas* (Cic. *Mil.* 77, *Part. or.* 86.4–5; Liv. 3.52.4; Sen. *Ben.* 1.11.4). In the early second century Ennius (fr. 308–11 = Warmington 1935 (Loeb) I 332) grounded *libertas* in *virtus*. "It is proper for a man to live a life inspired by true *virtus* / to stand steadfast and blameless against the enemy / The man who bears his heart both pure and staunch – that is *libertas*. / All else is servile, lies lurking in dim darkness." Later in that century Scipio Africanus Minor proclaimed, "from integrity springs worthiness, from worthiness public recognition, from public recognition civil and military power, from civil and military power *libertas*."[4] *Libertas* here cannot be translated "liberty" or "freedom," but "civic standing." As Livy wrote (23.12.9): "the arrogant man has forgotten another man's *libertas*; the coward has forgotten his own."

Especially in the late republic, *libertas* became a political slogan (Syme 1939: ch. 11). The masses invoked *libertas* against the dominant oligarchy of patricians and senate; *populares* interpreted *libertas* to mean rule by the popular assemblies; Brutus and Cassius invoked *leibertas* on their coins and in their letters to Antony (Cic. *Fam.* 329, 336 = XI. 2, 3); *nobiles* considered it the freedom to exercise their *dignitas* in ruling, even to the extent of dominating others. Clodius called Cicero *tyrannus* and *ereptor libertatis* (Cic. *Sest.* 109) for executing Roman citizens (the Catilinarians) without a trial; after Cicero was driven into exile, Clodius damaged his house and erected a shrine to Libertas (Cic. *Dom.* 131, *Leg.* 2.42). Cicero in turn called this shrine a Templum Licentiae and symbol of the slavery to which Clodius had subjected Rome (*Dom.* 110). He alleges that its statue of Libertas was the image of a prostitute at – [nb] Greek – Tanagra, and once graced a tomb plundered by Clodius's brother (*Dom.* 111).

Finally, *libertas* did not mean that "everyone could do as he pleased" (Schulz 1936: 158). " 'Freedom,' to the Romans, never meant the capacity to do or leave undone what one pleased, to live at one's own sweet will" (1936: 140, contrasting the Greeks). Conduct was guided by "*pietas, fides, humanitas,* in short *officium* ["duty"] as enforced by public opinion" (1936: 159). Nicolet's chapter "Libertas" (1980: 317–42) is subtitled "the citizen and the authorities": it ignores personal freedom. For the Romans, the idea of living as you like was anathema: *libertas* was in fact the opposite of *licentia* (Liv. 34.1.14). The most important exploration of how far any Roman could "live as he liked" (Brunt 1988b) in fact reveals how limited our Roman evidence for that conception is. Although what passed for Roman political theory was heavily influenced by the Greeks (compare for example Cicero's claim (*Leg.* 3.5) that a citizen's duty is "to rule and be ruled in turn" with Aristotle), the attempts in recent years especially by Brunt and Fergus Millar (esp. Millar 1998) to find similarities between the Roman Republic and Greek democracy have yielded only mixed success (see among others J. North 1990; W. Harris 1990), including on personal freedom. The Stoics conceived of *libertas* as living as one wished, *potestas vivendi ut velis,* but as guided by moral principles (Brunt 1988b: 311), that is, by a normative conception of what people truly wished. With uncertain evidence, Brunt (1988b) claims that Ennius's grounding *libertas* in virtue must also be a Greek ideal, "as a more natural usage." Even Millar (1998: 46–7) rejected Brunt's attempt to argue that the Roman people exercised various forms of free speech (1988b: 314–17). Along with Rome's "democracy" (cf. Tatum, this volume, chapter 14), its links with the personal freedoms of the Greeks must be doubted.

FURTHER READING

On Greek freedom generally, see Raaflaub 2004b; on personal freedom, see my essays Wallace 1994, 1995, 2004, 2005, and later my book in preparation; compare now Liddel 2007. On republican Rome, works by E. Badian are recommended for political history and by P. Brunt for social history (if not on personal freedom).

NOTES

1 See Raaflaub and Wallace in Raaflaub, Ober, and Wallace 2007: 22–48, and (e.g.) Vernant 1989: 213–14, 220–3. On the partial reaction against tolerance in post-350 Athens, partly reflecting the influence of fourth century conservative intellectuals, see Wallace 1995.

2 On Thucydides, see Wallace forthcoming a. Although Cartledge and Edge (chapter 10) claim that "democracy … is not conceived as a form of majoritarian rule which can justifiably coerce the minority and interfere with the lives of its citizens at will," in fact

some antidemocrats viewed it that way, and therefore for example opposed democracy's laws (Wallace 2007a). Also, the democracy did interfere with citizens' lives, as we shall see.

3   See Cartledge and Edge, chapter 10. Ober (2005a: 96) says the Athenians possessed "quasi rights, ... performative and contingent, ... to be enjoyed by those who deserved them." In that venerable formulation, are "quasi rights" like "quasi pregnant"?

4   "ex innocentia nascitur dignitas, ex dignitate honor, ex honore imperium, ex imperio libertas": Malcovati, *ORF*^{2} no. 32, p. 134.

CHAPTER 12

The Mixed Constitution in Greek Thought

David E. Hahm

The mixed constitution was one of antiquity's most productive contributions to western political thought. The application of the conception of mixture to describe characteristics of the constitution of a state originated in Athens in the wake of the violent political upheavals of the late fifth century. Athens was a city that early in her history had learned the value of compromise as a way to deal with the tensions that inevitably developed between the leisured landowning families and the ordinary citizens who had to work for a living. The Greeks always valued civic harmony. They named it *homonoia* ("thinking alike") and thought of it as an absolute consensus on public issues, with full cooperation in pursuit of the city's goals. A difference of opinion among the citizens of a Greek city-state constituted a breach of *homonoia* and raised the possibility of a rupture in the civic body (*stasis*) and an inability to function with the full force of its resources (Cartledge 2000: 17–20).

Despite their recognition of the dangers of disunity the Greeks rarely achieved the civic harmony they desired because most Greeks had difficulty compromising and settling for less than full satisfaction of their personal, familial, or class aspirations. In Athens the compromises of Solon, Cleisthenes, Ephialtes, and Pericles, and the resulting progressive democratization for a time spared it the debilitating civil strife that marked other Greek city-states. As a result Athens in the fifth century found herself in a position of power, prosperity, and influence in the Aegean. These compromises preserved Athens from civic strife for a time, but in 411 BC the radical democracy fell to an oligarchic coup. This was overthrown shortly afterwards and followed by a constitution that Thucydides describes as "mixed":

> Indeed, during the first period [of the rule of the 5,000] the Athenians were better governed than ever before, at least during my time; for there was a moderate blending (*metria ... xungkrasis*) of the few and the many. It was this [their good government]

A Companion to Greek and Roman Political Thought, First Edition. Edited by Ryan K. Balot.
© 2013 Blackwell Publishing Ltd. Published 2013 by Blackwell Publishing Ltd.

that first brought the city out of the evil circumstances into which it had fallen. (Thuc. 8.97.2; cf. Gomme, Andrewes, and Dover 1945–81: 5: 330–40)

This was the first time in extant literature that the concept of mixture was used to characterize a form of government.

Thucydides had personally experienced three Athenian governments: the classical fifth century democracy, the oligarchic government of the 400 brought in by the coup of 411 BC, and the government of the 5,000, introduced when the oligarchs were deposed by Athenian hoplites who were as opposed to narrow oligarchy as they were to "radical" democracy. He deemed the government of the 5,000 the best and explained its superiority by appealing to the notion of a constitutional mixture in the form of a "moderate blending of the few and the many." Thucydides apparently identified the nature of this blending as a compromise regarding the constituency of the ruling elite. Earlier he had pointed out that the 400 considered even 5,000 citizens sharing in the government to be tantamount to a democracy (8.92.11); yet the 5,000 wealthiest Athenians would hardly have constituted a democracy in Athens with approximately 50,000 adult male citizens (Gomme, Andrewes, and Dover 1945–81: 5: 323–30). Thucydides construed the constitution of the 5,000 as assigning the ultimate authority to a segment of the population defined by wealth and property (cf. 8.65.3), but possessing an intermediate degree of that wealth. It was a mixture of the few and the many in the sense that the ruling body comprised both the few wealthiest citizens and the wealthier of the many remaining citizens, viz. an economic middle class. With its center of authority securely anchored in the upper middle class, the ruling body of citizens was unable to be dominated either by a handful of the very wealthiest landowners or by the poor masses.

When Thucydides concluded that a blend of the few and the many had produced a compromise government better than either democracy or oligarchy, he was drawing on a form of political thinking that had evolved over several centuries and that was prevalent among Greek intellectuals of the time (Meier 1990b). There is a hint in Pindar (*Pyth.* 2.86–8) that as early as the 470s BC Greek thinkers were classifying governments as species of three simple types of rule: rule by one (monarchy), rule by a few (oligarchy), and rule by many (democracy). Herodotus placed a debate on the relative merits of these three types in the mouths of three Persian nobles after the suppression of the revolt of the Magi in 520 BC (Hdt. 3.80–3). Though the debate is hardly historical, Herodotus' composition of it proves that by the second half of the fifth century the Greeks not only classified constitutions into three primary types on the basis of the proportion of citizens participating in rule (one, some, or all), but also assessed the relative merits of each type and recognized two different modes of rule, rational rule for the common good and intemperate exploitative rule. Moreover, they had begun reflecting on the processes by which seemingly decent, well-qualified and well-intentioned men became impulsive self-aggrandizing rulers. In this project, as Herodotus indicates, history and current events provided the raw material for reflective theoretical analysis and theoretical analysis provided guidance for future practice.

Thucydides worked in this fifth century tradition when, in his reflection on Athenian government during the Peloponnesian War, he applied the concept of blending to understand and evaluate the changes that the Athenian constitution underwent. For Thucydides the tripartite division of constitutions into monarchy, oligarchy, and democracy seems to have been inadequate to explain the development of the Athenian constitution, in which the boundary between those who were among the ruling elite and those who were not shifted, first moving down to embrace all citizens regardless of social or economic class, then up to comprise only 400, and finally down again (partially) to embrace 5,000. Thucydides' solution transcended the simple trichotomy of one–few–many by construing the government of the 5,000 as a proportioned or moderate blend or mixture of the few rich oligarchs with the multitude of democratic poor. It was a minority of the population, situated closer to the wealthy upper class than to the poorest of the Athenians; but in principle it represented an intermediate economic group holding the balance of power in the state.

From Thucydides' time on it was constitutional mixing that served to express the principle of compromise in Greek political thinking and that was used to think through the options for compromise in the political realm. The different theories that followed explored what an acceptable compromise looked like, how one could realistically expect opposing parties to accept it, and how one could integrate conflicting political goals and practices to achieve constructive and mutually beneficial outcomes, that is, an approximation of the absolute unanimity (*homonoia*) that was the Holy Grail of Greek constitutional theory.

Plato

In the fourth century the concept of mixing or blending was exploited by Athenian statesmen, orators, historians, and philosophers, both to describe governments and to promote political policies and agendas (Blythe 1992: 14–24). It was the philosophers Plato and Aristotle, however, who applied the concept to constitutional theory in a rigorous way and developed its theoretical foundations.

Plato lived through the tumultuous times at the end of the fifth century, when democratic Athens was defeated by the nondemocratic Dorian states allied with Sparta, was terrorized by an oppressive homegrown oligarchy (the "Thirty Tyrants"), and then reacted by restoring its democracy and executing Plato's mentor Socrates. Disgusted by the violent upheavals of his native city and disillusioned with both democracy and oligarchy, Plato yearned for civic harmony and rationality and sought it in his own imagination in a city-state ruled by philosophers.

Plato described such a state in his *Republic*, along with utopian social and educational institutions and practices to bring it about and keep it functioning. The best possible ruler in this imaginary state or in any actual state, he concluded, was a self-disciplined, virtuous and wise king with extensive philosophical training (*Resp.* 2–7); but he also recognized that even such a philosopher-king could degenerate into a tyrant. He later observed that a utopian city such as this could not be realized among ordinary people; it could exist only "among gods and sons of gods" (*Leg.* 5.739d).

In the *Laws*, his last work, Plato proposed a social and institutional structure that, though admittedly not the best, stood a better chance of being established in the real world (*Leg.* 5.739a–e). In *Laws* 3–4, before elaborating on its specific structure and laws, he expounded a theoretical basis for it. Just as he held that the goal of human life is not merely to live, but to live well, that is to live a life of virtue, so he was convinced that the goal for a city-state was not merely to survive, but to be well governed and to function virtuously and successfully (701e; cf. 693e, 698a, 702a). For both stability and a life of virtue and happiness Plato appealed to constitutional mixing. His experiments here with the use of the concept of mixture to define and justify the best forms of government laid the foundation for much subsequent constitutional theorizing and ensured that the so-called mixed constitution would take center stage in debates regarding the best constitution down to modern times.

Plato's discussion in the *Laws* took the form of a dialog between an unnamed Athenian and two travelers whom he had just met, a Spartan and a Cretan. The Athenian proposed a model constitution for the Cretan, who had been appointed to a small group charged with framing a constitution for a new colony (702b–d). By way of prolog the Athenian elicited theoretical foundations for his proposed constitution from the histories of Athens and of Athens' major fifth century adversaries, Persia and the Dorian Greeks (cf. *Leg.* 683a–684a). First, in a review of the history of the Dorian cities of Argos, Messene, and Sparta he attempted to uncover the causes of and remedies for civic strife (*stasis*), paying special attention to what he regarded as the principal cause of rebellion, the degeneration of kings or rulers into tyrants (*Leg.* 683c–692c). Then in a review of the histories of Persia and Athens he identified the basis for the defining characteristics of good government, namely, freedom, civic unity, and rationality (*Leg.* 693d–701e). For the goals of both constitutional stability and civic happiness a mixed constitution was in his judgment essential; but the nature of the mixing, the constituents of the mixture, and the nature of the resulting moderation were entirely different. His critique of these constitutions provided principles for his own model constitution, expounded in books 4–12.

For Plato mixing was a device by which a legislator or founder of a city-state could affect the behavior of its rulers and citizens to ensure stability, unity, rational governance, virtue, and happiness. To assist the would-be legislator in discovering the foundational principles for the first goal, civic stability, he compared the Dorian cities of Argos and Messene with Sparta. In Messene and Argos the kings over time acquired wealth and distinction, began to pursue all the desires of their hearts in defiance of the guidance of reason, and fell victim to the highest form of folly or ignorance, namely, disharmony (*diaphonia*) between rational judgment and feelings of pleasure and pain (683d–689e; cf. 696c). In their constant pursuit of more and more (*pleonektein*) the kings trampled on the established laws and customs and brought discord and ultimately ruin to their cities (690a–691a).

The history of the third Dorian city, Sparta, showed the way for a city to avoid this fate. Under the guidance of divine providence Sparta had developed a mixed constitution that recognized due measure (*to metrion*) and assigned to each ruler his due degree of authority. For if a ruler is given too much authority, the Athenian noted, his soul will go to hubristic excess (*exubrizonta*) and "beget injustice, the offspring of *hubris*" (691c, cf. 713c). The Athenian observed that if a young man who accedes to absolute rule without limitations or accountability is predisposed by nature to degenerate into a tyrant (691c, cf. 875a–d), the best remedy is to construct a constitution that neutralizes the effects of the three conditions that predispose him to decline: youth, absolute authority, and absence of accountability. Plato read the history of Sparta as the sequential development of institutions to compensate for each of the three conditions (691d–692a; Morrow 1960: 38–41, 54–8).

First, some providential god gave Sparta two kings instead of the usual single king, thereby preventing either from having absolute authority. Then a divinely inspired lawgiver "blended [*mignusi*] the sane and sober power of age with the self-willed strength of noble birth" by giving a body of 28 elders (*gerousia*) an equal vote with the kings. From a constitutional point of view this provision blended the few (the elders) with the one (viz. the two kings) by giving each an equal degree of power (*dunamin*); but since the few in this case were the older members of the community, the effect was to compensate for the second factor promoting degeneration, namely, youth. Finally, a third lawgiver "put a bridle, as it were," on the power of the kings and elders through the agency of the ephors. The ephors approximated the power of a lottery system and added a democratic element by making the kings and the *gerousia* answerable to officials elected by and from the people. By this three-stage process the Spartan kingship became "mixed with [*symmiktos*] what it needed and acquired measure [*metron*]." It was thereby itself saved and became a salvation to others (691d–692a).

On Plato's interpretation the Spartan constitution was the first mixed constitution in the history of the world. Its mixture consisted in requiring three different organs of government (the kings, a small group of elite elder citizens, and representatives of the citizen body as a whole) to cooperate in order for the city to function fully. If they did not, any one could serve as a check on the actions of the others. The effect was to moderate the decisions and actions of the kings and other leaders. It also satisfied aspirations for a role in government on the part of the senior leaders of the principal families and the people as a whole. In effect, the Spartans arrived at a compromise on who should rule the city and in whose interests. By doing so its mixed constitution reduced the incentive for the oligarchic and democratic elements to rebel against the monarchy and ensured the stability of the constitution.

Simply removing the causes of civil strife, however, was, in Plato's view, not enough to produce a well-governed city. For good governance a city also needed three additional qualities: freedom, friendliness, and intelligence (*eleuthereia, philia, phronēsis, Leg.* 693b–d, 701d). For this interrelated set of conditions the Athenian appealed to a mixture of constitutions for a second time, but this time to a different kind of constitutional mixing:

> There are two mother-constitutions, as it were, from which one might rightly say the others have been born. One is rightly named monarchy and the other democracy. Of the one the Persians have the extreme form; of the other we [Athenians] do. Nearly

all the other constitutions, as I said, are variations of [literally, "embroidered with" (*diapepoikilmenai*)] these two [viz. strands of constitutional form]. So it is imperative for a constitution to partake of both of these if it is going to have freedom and friendship along with intelligence. That, in fact, is the point of our argument, when we said that a city that does not partake of these can never be rightly governed [*politeuthēnai … kalōs*]. (693d–e)

To explain how this mixture of monarchy and democracy produced freedom, friendship, and intelligence, Plato identified the two constituents, taking care to distinguish them from the monarchic and democratic elements that characterized the Spartan mixed constitution previously discussed (Stalley 1983: 77–9; Laks 2000: 278–85; Schofield 2006: 77–84). He used the despotism of Persia at its worst and the libertarianism of Athens at its most extreme as examples of pure unmixed monarchy and democracy (693e; cf. 3.694a–d; 6.756e–757a). By calling these components "the free" and "the monarchic" or "the despotic" (693e, 697c; cf. 701e) he indicated that the components of this mixture were the qualitative characteristics of the political relationships that prevailed under these constitutions. Moreover, he emphasized the qualitative nature of the components by observing that virtually all the other constitutions were "embroidered" or "threaded through" with them, implying that all constitutions were permeated by these two strands of constitutional character and each of them was defined in its own way by the degree to which the despotic and the free were mixed into its particular constitutional structure.

In this way Plato indicated that he was attempting to isolate two characteristics underlying all constitutions, generative principles ("mother-constitutions"), as he called them, from which constitutions ultimately derive their essential nature. He wanted to make clear that the mixture of monarchy and democracy now under discussion did not refer to a combination of competing segments of society or interest groups in a single governmental structure or to a combination of sociopolitical institutions and practices used by these competing groups (small council, large assembly, election, lottery, etc.). It referred instead to the type of authority exercised by the rulers and the attitude of rulers and subjects toward each other and toward the city as a whole regardless of its institutional structure. It was this psychological and motivational aspect of civic constitutions that was the key to the quality of governance in any state and to its ultimate success or failure in achieving its end as a well-ordered city-state.

Plato illustrated his conception in separate accounts of the histories of Persia and Athens and of their oscillation between what he classified as extreme unmixed forms of either one (the despotic or the free) and moderate mixtures of the two (694a–701d). Both Persia and Athens over the course of their history shifted from a moderate blend of the despotic and the free to an extreme form of one or the other. When the Persian kings, Cyrus and Darius, treated their subjects more like equals than like slaves and gave them a degree of freedom and equality, even tolerating free speech, their soldiers became friendly to their commanders and eager to undertake risks for them, while those who were wise (*phronimos*) among them began to contribute advice to the common pool of intelligence in the kingdom. The admixture of freedom in a monarchic regime led to friendship and unity (*koinōnia*), military strength, and an increase in intelligence available to the leadership (694a–b, 695c–d).

Similarly when Athens at the time of the Persian Wars lived under the "old constitution," which was "a measured degree of rule by others" in the form of magistrates with different degrees of authority, its government embodied respect (*aidōs*) like a queen (*despotis*), so that the people willingly lived as slaves (*douleuontes*) to the prevailing laws (698a–c; cf. 700a). The Athenian interpreted this constitution as a mixture of monarchy and democracy in the sense that free people voluntarily submitted to their rulers, to the law and to respect for the law. Under these conditions the Athenians developed a friendship among themselves that bonded them together for a successful defense against the Persians. Moreover, since law (*nomos*) is the ordering (*dianomē*) brought about by mind (*nous*), which is an immortal, divine element in the human race (cf. also Pl. *Plt.* 300c), the Athenians' submission to the law (700a) and to their hierarchically ordered rulers produced a state governed by some degree of intelligence. The moderate blending of democratic freedom with monarchic authority thus resulted in freedom, friendship, and intelligent leadership, the marks of good government and the grounds for Athenian strength and military supremacy. What Plato is talking about in this mixture of monarchy and democracy in both Persia and Athens is a compromise in which the ruler (whether the king or the people) voluntarily surrenders a degree of autonomy to the other part of the state to gain the benefit of the intelligence in the other and the harmony that is proportional to the degree of equality among the parts of the state.

This compromise and voluntary cooperation can be achieved only at the price of appropriate upbringing from youth on. Since such cooperation is predicated on the foundational psychological assumption that the best life for an individual or city is one in which the feelings of pleasure and pain follow the judgment of reason, the city must provide a psychological and intellectual upbringing to develop that condition. The histories of both Persia and Athens showed the importance of upbringing and the devastating results of ignorance and following the lead of pleasure and pain. Plato later summarizes the difference between good and bad government: Any ruler whose soul strives after pleasures and desires is headed for disaster (714a). The only hope for any state is for its leaders to order themselves in obedience to the immortal element within all human beings, namely the mind (*nous*), submitting to the order that is expressed in the law (713e–714a).

In the *Laws* Plato has attempted to extend the concept of constitutional mixing to account for the qualitative differences that he recognized in his classification of constitutions in the *Statesman*. There he had subdivided the three basic types of constitution (rule by one, few, or many) into two subtypes, the law-bound, in which the rulers rule in accord with law, and the lawless (Pl. *Plt.* 300e–303b). Now in the *Laws* he explains this subjection to law as a result of the mixing of the despotic with the free, in that it arises from a free and voluntary submission to the absolute rule of rational law.

In his constitutional theory Plato has refined the basic concepts circulating since the fifth century and has given them a new theoretical formulation. The commonplace fifth century insight that any type of simple constitution can be abused to oppress and exploit the powerless he refined by defining the difference between benevolent and autocratic versions of each type. Genuine or correct constitutions he defined as law-abiding (*kata nomous*), with rulers that follow reason and rule on behalf of the city as a whole and with citizens that submit voluntarily to their rulers. Imitation constitutions, which he deemed unworthy of the name "constitution" and more accurately designated "factionalities" (*stasiōtereiai*), are lawless, with rulers following their desires, oppressing their subjects for their own benefit, and demanding obedience from their subjects by force (*Leg.* 715b, 832c; cf. Pl. *Plt.* 303c). Plato also explored the psychology that underlay the transformation of a ruler into an autocrat and the consequent hostility and rebellion of his subjects; and he stipulated particular civic arrangements and political structures that would prevent or retard degeneration and promote benevolent regimes. It was in this regard that he made two novel attempts to apply the concept of mixture to constitutional theory.

First of all, he introduced a new conception of constitutional mixture, namely, functional complementarity of different organs of government. In the case of Sparta, these were the kings, the *gerousia*, and the ephors. With no single group having exclusive control, the constitution embodied a compromise that gave three organs, reflecting three different political agendas and points of view, the power to support or block each other. In this way Plato could view the mixed constitution as a way to deploy the psychological factors underlying political decision-making to moderate the actions of the rulers and to prevent their degeneration into oppressive governments. This innovative conception of constitutional mixture had profound historical significance. It brought all three types of simple constitutions into play in a single mixed constitution instead of only two (democracy and oligarchy), as Thucydides' analysis had done. More importantly, Plato here introduced for the first time in history the concept of curbs and checks among organs of government, a concept that was adopted by Polybius and that became a model for government from the Middle Ages to Montesquieu and the American constitution (Morrow 1960: 39–40).

Plato's second innovation was an attempt to introduce the concept of mixture into his analysis of constitutional forms to explain the qualitative difference between benevolent and autocratic constitutions. He used the concept of mixture to describe a political state that mediates between the civic conditions of freedom or equality on the one hand, and servitude or hierarchy on the other, and thereby optimizes harmony, esprit de corps, rational action, virtue, and happiness among its citizens. Plato argued that balancing individual freedom and submission to the authority of rational leadership would bring the benefits both of rational leadership and of the knowledge, talent, and strength residing in the rest of the population. This bold attempt to explain the difference between benevolent and autocratic regimes in terms of mixture never caught on. Plato's successors, including Aristotle and Polybius, continued to explore both the difference between benevolent and oppressive regimes and the individual and social psychology that accompanied them, but without formal appeal to mixing constitutional characteristics.

Aristotle

Aristotle, Plato's student and associate for 20 years, followed his teacher in theorizing constitutional developments that he observed among the Greek city-states. Though he was not an Athenian or even a citizen of any surviving Greek state (his own native city, Stagira, having been destroyed by the Macedonians) he remained a lifelong admirer of the Greek city-states and sought in his *Politics* to develop a general theory applicable to all Greek city-states.

Aristotle defined the nature of the constitution (*politeia*) in conjunction with the related concepts of city-state (*polis*) and citizen (*politēs*) (*Pol.* 3.1–9). Like Plato he regarded the goal of the city-state and its citizens as more than physical survival. Human beings are "political animals," animals who come together into city-states to achieve their common good, which in its fullest realization consists in the good life for all its citizens (*Pol.* 1.1–2; 3.6, 9; 7.1–3, 13).

Aristotle acknowledged that Greek city-states organized themselves in various ways. He defined a constitution as "the organization of the offices and in particular of the office that is sovereign over all [the others]," such as the people (*dēmos*) in democracies and the few (*oligoi*) in oligarchies (3.6.1278b8–13). The few who are sovereign in an oligarchy, he observed, are those with property, whereas the people who are sovereign in a democracy are the poor, the mass of those who have nothing except their freedom (3.8.1279b17–19). Thus Aristotle constructed his constitutional theory around the authority or power exercised by citizens who were differentiated according to economic class (cf. *Pol.* 4.4; Yack 1993: 209–39). Aristotle formally classified constitutions following the traditional tripartite division into rule by one, by a few, or by many. He then subdivided each of them by modes of rule: (a) right rule in the interests of the city as a whole (the common good); or (b) deviant rule in the interests only of the ruler(s). Aristotle thus recognized six primary constitutions: three correct constitutions, kingship, aristocracy, and the constitution that goes by the name of "polity" (*politeia*, lit. "constitution"), and three deviant constitutions, tyranny, oligarchy, and democracy (*Pol.* 3.7).

One of Aristotle's major projects in the *Politics* was to define and evaluate these constitutions and to explain the changes from one to another, above all the changes between oligarchy and democracy. This was the most common change in Greek cities and one that occurred even in Athens (*Pol.* 3.9–6.8). His explanations were designed to discover ways to promote stability and improved governance for a city as a whole. His prescription for alleviating civic conflict (*stasis*) and for stabilizing the typically deviant Greek constitutions was for rulers to govern with a view to the common good, that is, to establish a right form of constitution. This, he contended, would not only improve stability, but also enable the city and its citizens to achieve success or happiness (*eudaimonia*), the proper end of the city-state. Of the six constitutions, Aristotle regarded polity as the best option for a typical Greek city, most of which were either oligarchies, organized around and for the pursuit of wealth, or democracies, organized around and for the pursuit of liberty (*Pol.* 4.8–9). His advocacy of polity derived from his confidence in its stability. This confidence, in turn, was predicated on polity's status as a mixed constitution. In the final analysis, Aristotle, like Plato, regarded a mixed constitution as the best practical choice for Greek city-states.

Aristotle, however, had a different conception from Plato of what constituted a mixed constitution. This became apparent in his critique of Plato's proposal in the *Laws* for the second-best constitution (*Pol.* 2.6). Aristotle found much to criticize in it, including Plato's conception of the role of constitutional mixture. In viewing Plato's proposal through the lens of his own classificatory scheme, Aristotle determined that it was a "mean" (*mesē*) constitution: "It is neither democracy nor oligarchy, but midway (*mesē*) between them, the constitution called 'polity' " (2.6.1265b26–9). Regardless of how Plato construed the constitution of the *Laws*, Aristotle understood it as equivalent to the constitution to which he had given the name "polity" and as such, a mixture (*mixis*) of oligarchy and democracy (cf. *Pol.* 4.8–9).

By construing Plato's proposed constitution as a polity Aristotle could see its value in gaining acceptance among Greek cities; but he could not accept Plato's ranking it as the second-best constitution, surpassed only by a monarchy governed by a philosopher-king, such as the one Plato advocated in the *Republic*. He attacked Plato's ranking by arguing that there are other constitutions superior to it, such as the Spartan constitution, which many regarded as the best of all because it was mixed from all three basic types. Plato, he pointed out, constructed his allegedly second-best constitution from only two constitutions, and the two worst ones at that, that is, democracy and tyranny (2.6.1265b29–1266a5). Aristotle did not deny that the constitution of the *Laws* was mixed or that a mixed constitution was superior to an unmixed. His point was that Plato's mixed constitution contained an inferior mixture. He added that it also suffered from inconsistency in misidentifying the components that constitute the mixture. The constitution proposed in the *Laws* was actually a combination of oligarchy and democracy, like his own constitution called "polity." There were no monarchical elements to be found in it, only democratic and oligarchic elements (2.6.1266a5–22).

Aristotle's treatment of Plato shows that he was not interested in attempting to understand Plato on his own terms or in acknowledging any debts to Plato, but only in refuting Platonic claims that on their surface appeared inconsistent with his own theory. His biased reading reveals his essential difference from Plato. Aristotle's use of political control mechanisms and practices to define simple constitutions and to diagnose the constituents of the mixed constitutions proposed by others indicates that Aristotle conceived of constitutional mixture as a sharing of governing authority by the various economic subdivisions of the citizen body.

His analysis of the Spartan constitution in *Politics* 2.9 shows how he thinks this sharing produces constitutional stability. In Aristotle's analysis the consequence of the Spartan division of governing functions among three governing bodies, the kings, the elders, and the democratically elected ephors, was that each of the social classes from which these rulers came, viz. two royal dynasties, the elder citizens, and the people as a whole, had a significant stake in governing and hence in the survival of the constitution. The principle he drew from this was: "For a constitution to be secure and stable it is necessary that all the parts desire it to exist and to remain the same as it is" (2.9.1270b21–2). He agreed with Plato in crediting the psychological effects of shared governance for the stability of the Spartan constitution; but he did not agree in identifying the causal mechanism behind the stability as the moderation and restraint that results from a fear of being thwarted by another governing agent. Instead, he appealed to the fact that each party had a stake in the government and therefore had an interest in preserving the government that gave it that stake. Thus, though Plato and Aristotle both construed the Spartan constitution as a mixed constitution in which three components shared the rule, Aristotle saw the mixture as a way to involve more segments of the population and increase support for the constitution; he made no use of Plato's conception of curbs or checks among the organs of government.

In his own theory Aristotle took the same approach, but explicitly grounded in his comprehensive theoretical framework. Throughout his exposition in *Politics* 3–6 Aristotle used division of governing authority by the constituent economic classes, specifically the rich and the poor, as the defining mark of a mixed constitution. He defined "polity," the constitution that he rated as the most viable for actual Greek cities, as a "mixture [*mixis*] of oligarchy and democracy." There was, he assumed, a continuum of proportions in mixtures of oligarchy and democracy. When a constitution leaned toward democracy, it was commonly called "polity"; when it leaned toward oligarchy, it was called "aristocracy" (4.8.1293b31–8). He was keen to stipulate the two relevant populations that constituted the mixture and to identify the ways of mixing structures and practices to implement an equitable sharing of authority because he believed shared governance to be the key to constitutional stability: "A well-mixed constitution remains stable through itself ... because no part of the city would even wish to have a different constitution" (4.9.1294b36–40; cf. 4.12.1297a6–7). It was the voluntary acceptance of the constitution by both parties that guaranteed its stability. When Aristotle went on to spell out in detail the different types of combination and mixing (*synthesis kai mixis*) that constituted a polity, he invariably cited practices of political control as evidence of mixture. He defined a well-mixed constitution as one that combines the respective practices so completely that it may legitimately be described either as a democracy or as an oligarchy, as in the case of Sparta (4.9).

In *Politics* 5 he explored the threats to constitutional stability and the causes of constitutional change. Following in the Platonic tradition he focused on the psychological state of the two principal social classes, the wealthy nobles and the poor masses. He underscored the importance of feelings of exploitation or inadequate respect by the dominant class as the primary motivation for faction and revolution. The best way to assuage these feelings of hostility, Aristotle argued, was to treat the nondominant class justly and to compromise on traditionally hierarchical practices by assigning all members of the city enough honor and political authority so that they would accept the constitution and work for its preservation (5.8–9; cf. 4.8.1296b14–16). In effect, to maintain an oligarchy or democracy he recommended a compromise. That was tantamount to transforming the constitution into a mixed constitution, that is, into a polity with justice for rich and poor alike and governing authority divided fairly between the two classes (Yack 1993: 231–9).

A sharing of power by rich and poor in a polity may not always be enough to ensure stability. The growth of one of the parts or the cumulative effect of slight changes may upset the balance and lead to dissatisfaction and civil strife (5.4; 5.8). For this Aristotle saw a solution in reimagining the constitution as a combination of three, rather than the typical two, economic classes, rich and poor. Wealth is by definition a continuous scale, in which there are not only some very wealthy and some very poor, but people in between, whom Aristotle called the "middle people" (*hoi mesoi*). Every state, he claimed, consists of three, not two parts. Even polity, a mixture of wealthy oligarchs and poor democrats, has citizens that fall between them in degree of wealth, however few they may be. A state in which this middle part is large in comparison to the very rich and the very poor, Aristotle argued, will be well run and the most harmonious and stable constitution of all. It would be best, he claimed, if the middle part were the largest of the three classes; but even if it is not, as long as it is more numerous than either of the extremes, it can outweigh one extreme by siding with the other and prevent either from becoming dominant and going to excess. Thus a large middle will ensure that a majority of the citizen body are satisfied and will support the preservation of the constitution. Aristotle called this a "middle constitution" (*mesē politeia*). Whether he regarded it as a form of polity or as a distinct type, he hailed it as the best constitution possible in the real world (4.11–12; cf. 5.1.1302a14; Johnson 1990: 143–54). Aristotle admitted that a middle constitution with a significant number of middle people never existed or only rarely; but because of its superior stability he advised both oligarchies and democracies to include the middle class as beneficiaries of their constitutions.

Aristotle consistently recommended a mixed constitution, construed as a coalition of socioeconomic classes through an equitable distribution of governing authority, as the most stable constitution and did so because it satisfied the natural desire of every citizen for a share in governing the city. The few wealthy citizens and large numbers of ordinary citizens each had assigned roles to play, commensurate with the ability of each to contribute to the good of the whole. Those equally qualified for governing would take turns in office, so none would be excluded. Policy decisions would be made on the basis of free public debate, in which Aristotle confidently predicted the right view and the virtuous action would generally prevail (cf. 3.11).

Like Plato Aristotle saw shared governance as the key to stability because of its psychological effect on the citizens, but his understanding of the psychological mechanism behind it was different. Plato saw parts of the state, like parts of the Platonic soul, in potential conflict. The mixed constitution, he believed, mitigated the conflict by using one organ of government to impose restraints on another, so that, ideally at least, the embodiment of reason might lead the whole. Aristotle, in contrast, saw the parts of the state as interconnected and operating (ideally) in harmonious conjunction for the common good (F. Miller 2000: 330–4). It was a concept that was going to have a long and fruitful life in later European political thought (Blythe 1992).

When Aristotle moved beyond constitutional stability to the virtue, well-being, and happiness (*eudaimonia*) of the state and its citizens, he made no use of the concept of mixture per se as a defining feature of a correct constitution. In contrast to Plato, Aristotle viewed the difference between right and defective constitutions not as a matter of degree (excess or deficiency of some quality), but as a difference in kind. They are two different species of rule, originating in the household: viz. in the rule of the master over slaves (despotic) looking out primarily for the good of the master, and in the rule of the male/father over the free and equal female/mother, where the ruler looks out for the good of the whole family. The latter type of rule he calls "political," corresponding, as it does, in a city to shared or reciprocal rule, in which free and equal citizens take turns ruling each other and looking out for the good of the city as a whole (F. Miller 2000: 325–34). In other words, Aristotle formally distinguished benevolent from autocratic government by its ends, whether the common good or the good of the rulers. Nevertheless, mixture was not irrelevant to the best constitution available to the typical state. Since the common good comprised the good of both rich and poor citizens, polity, which as a mixture of oligarchy and democracy gave a share of rule to both rich and poor, met the criterion of a constitution in which rule is for the common good. Thus by means of the single mechanism of mixing democracy and oligarchy Aristotle achieved both stability and right rule for the city. There was no need for Plato's two different kinds of mixing of constitutions.

He did, however, leave the door open for Plato's psychological explanation of moral degeneration to play a role alongside mixture in the best constitution. In his explanation of why the rare middle constitution with a majority of middle people is the best, he appealed to the psychological phenomenon that Plato had used to explain the stability of the Spartan mixed constitution, the tendency of wealth and power to turn rulers into despots (*Leg.* 3.687b–691a, 694c–695b). The superfluity of goods with which the few wealthy citizens are endowed leads to an inability and unwillingness to be ruled, Aristotle claimed. In a city with many poor and powerless, who do not know how to rule, the affluent inevitably establish despotic rule, with a high incidence of criminal injustice on the part of both rulers and ruled. A large body of citizens with a moderate degree of wealth, however, will be obedient to reason, willing both to rule and to be ruled in turn and to enter into political associations as friends and equals. They will constitute a virtuous well-run city, free of factions and divisions (4.11.1295a4–1296b21). Aristotle thus ascribed to the middle constitution essentially the same qualities (intelligence, freedom, and friendship) that Plato had ascribed to the constitutions of Athens and Persia at the times when they successfully blended the two mother-constitutions, the monarchic (despotic) and the democratic (free) (*Leg.* 694a–701d).

Polybius

Plato and Aristotle each left a school of followers who pursued their particular lines of thought and approach to philosophy. Dicaearchus among the Peripatetics and some of the Stoics in the third century BC wrote on the mixed constitution, but not enough survives to determine their precise contribution to the history of the idea (Blythe 1992: 24–5). The next chapter known to us was written in the second century BC by the historian Polybius (von Fritz 1975; Walbank 1972, esp. 135–50; Hahm 1995; 2000: 464–76).

By this time the political landscape in Greece had changed. After Alexander's conquest of the Near East the Greek city-states found themselves in a world dominated by regional federations, like the Achaean and Aetolian leagues, and by the king of Macedonia, one of the powerful regional kings of the eastern Mediterranean. Late in the third century BC the Romans, having expanded their power over the western Mediterranean, began encroaching on Greece and during Polybius' lifetime brought Greece under their control. It was the Roman conquest of Greece that prompted Polybius to write his history, crediting Rome's mixed constitution for her success in bringing "virtually the entire world" under her rule (1.1.5; 6.2.3; cf. 3.1.4).

Polybius was a citizen of Megalopolis, a member of the Achaean League in the Peloponnesus. The cities of the league, though dominated by a narrow group of old wealthy families, regarded themselves as democratic (2.41–2; 4.1.5). By this they meant they had a high degree of local autonomy and were not controlled by an agent of the Macedonian monarchy. Polybius went further and regarded the league as a whole as a democracy, with the same democratic institutions as its constituent cities (2.37.7–11; 2.38.5–9). In fact, he thought it fair to call the Peloponnesus a single city in every respect but one, namely, in not being surrounded by a single wall (2.37.11; 4.1.7). The sharp classical distinction between oligarchy and democracy had receded into the background by this time, and the operative distinction now was between democratic self-rule and monarchic rule by an agent of one of the powerful regional kings.

Polybius made productive use of the political theories circulating in his day to account for Rome's success in taking control of the Mediterranean world. He constructed his theory around the standard six constitutions: the three generic types differentiated by proportion of rulers (one, few, or many), with each subdivided into an improved and an unimproved or deviant type (6.3.5–6.4.6). He defined the improved constitutions as ones based on consent of the governed, consent that is earned by a ruler's intelligent and virtuous governance. The deviant constitutions in Polybius' thinking are characterized by government based on force and fear or in the case of democracy on bribery and corruption (6.4.2; 6.6.10–12; 6.8.4–5; 6.9.5–7). In this he differed from Plato and Aristotle, who defined right constitutions respectively as those based on law and those aiming at the common good. He also differed from them in taking the defective or unimproved constitutions as the natural ones, from which the good constitutions were constructed by human intervention. Plato and Aristotle, with their teleological perspective, prioritized the best forms and regarded the worst as constitutions that had degenerated.

For each generic type of constitution Polybius postulated a natural historical development from its generic type to an improved version, typically followed by a decline to its deviant form. He illustrated this in the case of monarchy by a progression from the generic form of monarchy, ruled by the strongest, to an improved version, kingship, in which the people recognize the intelligence and fairness of their ruler and submit voluntarily (6.5.4–6.7.5). This improved version inevitably declines to its defective version when a ruler achieves the rule by right of birth. Feeling secure in his position, he begins to oppress and exploit his subjects, eventually triggering revolt. While the process of decline and its explanation are recognizable as preoccupations of Plato, the process leading to what Polybius called the improved or corrected version is new, though, just as in the case of Plato and Aristotle, explained in terms of the psychology of the participants. Polybius offered psychological explanations for the improvement and degeneration of each of the three generic types and for the change of one generic type into another.

In explaining these changes in sequence, Polybius portrayed a series of ostensibly successive constitutions: monarchy, kingship, tyranny, aristocracy, oligarchy, democracy, and tyranny, the last of which sets the stage for the reemergence of the first, monarchy (Polyb. 6.4.7–10; 6.5.4–6.9.10). The purpose of laying out the series of changes, he claimed, was to allow statesmen to make predictions. He called his account a "generalized conception" (*koinē epinoia*) or a "generic pattern" (*katholikē emphasis*, 6.5.2–3), by which he seems to have meant a universal description covering all or most cases of constitutional change (Hahm 1995: 8–37, esp. 8 n5, 12–13) and concluded that "one who has an overall view of how each naturally develops may be able to see when and how and where the growth, flowering [*akmē*], change for the worse [*metabolē*] and end will occur again" (6.4.12). Though Polybius did not claim that one can predict the timing of constitutional change, he does seem confident that one can predict which type will follow which. In the end, he summed up the process as a whole as "the cycle [*anakuklōsis*] of constitutions, nature's pattern of administration [*physeōs oikonomia*] according to which the constitutional structure develops and changes and returns again to its original state" (6.9.10).

Polybius has often been interpreted as postulating a rigid cycle of constitutional changes. Yet as a historian he could not have failed to notice that the sequence of changes as a whole cannot be perfectly mapped onto the historical evidence (von Fritz 1975:74–5); only a few of the changes can be found in the history of some city-state (Trompf 1979: 107–9, cf. 69–75). A closer examination of the changes, however, shows that Polybius explained all of these changes in terms of human psychology. The changes are thus as natural and predictable as human behavior. He generalized Plato's "law" of the degeneration of kings into tyrants when they are born into their position by stipulating the necessary conditions for each of the constitutional changes. These conditions take the form of natural laws of social and political change (Hahm 1995: 15–37). Some of these laws or explanations of change stipulate sufficient conditions and make the change absolutely predictable, such as the deterioration of good governments into vicious forms as soon as the rulers begin holding office by hereditary succession. It was these and only these that Polybius compared to a segment of the biological cycle of birth, growth, maturity, decline, and death. The rest, including a change in the proportion of rulers, involve contingent factors and are not absolutely predictable. They are nevertheless understandable by anyone who has grasped the principles and natural laws of social psychology that Polybius had enumerated. They are thus useful for statesmen in deliberating on their city's political policies.

In his review of constitutional change Polybius laid heavy stress on the inevitable degeneration of improved simple constitutions, because it was this degeneration that threatened constitutional stability and national strength. If Polybius wished to account for Rome's stability and strength, he had to account for Rome's ability to avoid degeneration and to act in full civic harmony for a common goal. Since degeneration results from a ruling power's unqualified security, Polybius, following

Plato, contended that the only way to prevent it was to limit the ruling power's security. He was aware that it was difficult to maintain such limitation in a simple constitution indefinitely. So he, like Plato, concluded the best constitution had to be a mixed constitution, because it created conditions that preclude unqualified security for rulers (6.3.7–8, 6.10.1 11).

Polybius distinguished two kinds of mixed constitutions: (1) those created deliberately by a lawgiver following an intentional plan, like Sparta; and (2) those that evolved naturally over a period of time, like Carthage and Rome. The Spartan constitution (*politeia*) was created, Polybius claimed, when the Spartan lawgiver Lycurgus

> brought together all the virtues and distinctive features of the best [simple] governments [*politeumata*], so that none might grow beyond its proper point and change into its corresponding evil, but rather, with the force of each being counteracted by [that of] another, none would tilt [the scale] and outweigh the other for any length of time, but the government would over time be balanced in equilibrium and would last indefinitely in accord with the principle of counteracting forces. (6.10.6–7)

Polybius adopted Plato's idea of the organs of government curbing each other, but he understood the dynamics differently. Plato had imagined the organs of government per se as having the capability of thwarting the actions of another organ. He seemed to suppose the individuals who constituted the organs of government possess an awareness of the limited scope of their authority as well as of their need for cooperation, or at least need for the consent of another government agency. This he had assumed caused them to restrain their impulses to act solely in their own self-interest and to practice moderation in ruling. He imagined the rulers involved interacting directly with each other in the execution of their governmental functions and individually choosing self-restraint to avoid being thwarted by others.

Polybius, in contrast, imagined the interaction occurring between what he called "governments" (*politeumata*). Polybius' mixed constitution (*politeia*) did not combine merely three organs of government or three governing bodies (kings, elders, and ephors), but three "governments" (*politeumata*, 6.10.6). This had the effect of combining the virtues (*aretai*) and distinctive properties (*idiotētas*) of the best governments. He identified the best simple constitutions as kingship, aristocracy, and democracy (6.3.5–6.4.5), that is, the three improved varieties of constitution. What made their combination superior to any single one of them was its stability. The constituents of Polybius' mixed constitution were political structures (*politeumata*) that embodied the essential characteristics of each of the three improved simple constitutions (6.10.8–11). When he identified these as kingship (*basileia*) or kings (*basileis*), the people (*dēmos*) and the elders (*gerontes*), he made it clear that he was talking about the relationship of a body of rulers to the city and the political institutions that mediate that relationship. Each component was a demographic element of the city-state in its capacity to participate in the government of that city-state through its particular political institutions, the dual kingship, the aristocratic body of elders, and presumably the ephors (though he did not here explicitly identify the organ of government that mediates the democratic element). Each might be called a "government" (*politeuma*) and the combination of them a mixed "constitution" (*politeia*).

As separate governments, each would follow the course of development of a simple constitution and could be expected to degenerate if its rulers held their positions securely for life (6.45.5); but combined in the mixed constitution, they did not degenerate because the three governments counteracted (*antispōmenēs*) each other by tending in opposite directions, as do the pans of a balance scale. The mechanism of the counteracting forces was psychological. The kingship was restrained from arrogance by fear of the people in their governing capacity (presumably through the ephors). The people were restrained from treating the kings with contempt because of fear of the elders, who adjudicated between the kings and the people on the basis of justice (6.10.8–10).

It is worth noting that Plato had also concentrated on the way in which the Spartan constitution prevented the degeneration of the kingship. He viewed the relationship among the three organs of government as a way to restrict the scope of the royal authority by splitting it between two kings, giving the elders the power of veto, and by authorizing the ephors to rein in both kings and elders if they together went too far. He had likened the function of the ephors to a bridle or curb. Polybius changed the metaphor to one of a balance scale where the tendency of one pan to decline was counteracted by the weight of the other pan. The king and the people, he contended, naturally pulled in opposite directions and counteracted decline in each other as long as neither grew too strong. The third government in the mixture, the elders, for its part, having been selected on the basis of virtue, brought justice to the civic interaction. The elders swung from one side to the other to maintain a just balance and parity of authority between them. In substituting the analogy of a balance scale for the bridle he was, in effect, following Aristotle, who used the balance scale in his middle constitution as an analogy for the way that the shifting support of the middle people kept the extremely wealthy and extremely poor from going to immoderate excess (Arist. *Pol.* 4.11.1295b34–9). In Polybius' view this arrangement produced the most enduring government known to him (6.10.11).

The Spartan mixed constitution could potentially have lasted forever; but having been constructed by an individual, it was also susceptible to being deconstructed by an individual. So it was in the third century BC, when Cleomenes abolished the mixed constitution and changed Sparta into a hellenistic autocracy, a tyranny on Polybius' classification (2.47.3; 4.8.14). The Spartan constitution, the best and most stable the world had seen up to the third century BC, was nevertheless deficient in equipping the Spartans for conquering and ruling others (6.50). The Roman constitution surpassed it in just this respect.

The Roman constitution was a mixed constitution that evolved naturally. It arose by "many struggles and actions, in which the Romans repeatedly chose the better course, on the basis of a new understanding acquired in disasters" (6.10.14). Its constituent parts were comparable to those of the Spartan constitution: two consuls, embodying the monarchic form; the senate, embodying the aristocratic form; and the people. The political mechanism by which they interacted with one another, however, was different. Unlike the Spartan constitution in which the kings and the people prevented excessive growth in each other by opposition, with the elders switching from one side to the other to maintain the equilibrium, the Roman constitution prevented any part from carrying out its function without the cooperation of both the other parts. For example, the consul was responsible for leading the army and conducting warfare; but it was the senate that appropriated the money and that reappointed the consul as proconsul to continue conducting the war. The people, moreover, had to ratify or annul the consul's action and arrangements (6.12, 15). The consuls could not carry out their functions without the cooperation of the other two parts (6.13–14, 16–17).

As in Polybius' analysis of the dynamic of simple constitutions, the operative factor in the cooperative functioning of the Roman mixed constitution was fear. An extreme threat compelled all to come to agreement and act in unity to meet the need of the hour, so that this particular form of government possessed irresistible power and achieved its every decision. It was also self-correcting, for when Rome became secure and prosperous and one of the governmental parts grew out of proportion and gained too much power, as governments tend to do, the others opposed it. This not only prevented the execution of self-interested actions, but the fear of intervention prevented even their proposal (6.18). Unlike the Spartan mixed constitution, the Roman constitution not only prevented degeneration, but also bonded the entire state together, directed all its force at its chosen objectives, and thereby enabled it to take control of an extensive empire.

When one looks more carefully at the construction of this union, one can see that just as in the case of the Spartan constitution, it comprised not merely three organs of government, but three governments, each consisting of a segment of the population along with its governing institutions. So, for example, the people as a governing body act through the election process, the popular courts, the council of the plebs and the tribunes with their vetoes (6.14–16). But the most revealing evidence for the relationship of the parts of the state to each other came in Polybius' account of the decline of natural mixed constitutions (6.57.6–9). Polybius found a basis for his prognostication of the future of Rome in the history of the Carthaginian constitution, which was also a mixed constitution, but one that had already begun to decline by the time of the Second Punic War (6.51; cf. 6.52–6).

In his prognostication of the future of Rome Polybius articulated two additional laws of sociopolitical change, stipulating the conditions that would determine the decline of the mixed constitution (Hahm 1995: 41–5; 2000: 475–6). These differ from the laws that govern changes in simple constitutions precisely in the fact that they specify the change that will take place in two of the governments in the mixture, namely the government of the few (the aristocratic) and the government of the many, that is, the people. The outcome would depend on the interaction between them. As Polybius stipulated, prosperity affected the few and the many in different ways. It turned the aristocratic few to oligarchic greed and competitive display of wealth at the same time that it turned the democratic many to excessive love of political office, a characteristic of mob rule (ochlocracy). The greedy few alienated the people, making them ripe for revolt whenever they found a leader. At the same time, the people, now a deviant democracy, had many would-be leaders craving office, with leaders and people lacking the shared moral values of an improved constitution. When these masses revolted against the leadership of the now oligarchic few and refused to obey them, they de facto dissolved the mixed constitution. Since they themselves had already degenerated from democracy, their rule reconstituted the state as an ochlocracy or mob rule.

Most of Polybius' political theory sounds as it if were being summarized from current thinking in the circles in which he moved, the elite families of Megalopolis and the leaders of the Achaean League; but there can be little doubt that his application to Rome and the Roman constitution was his own work. It showed most clearly how the mixture of a mixed constitution was assumed to work. It integrated three governmental structures so that they could cooperate with or oppose each other, while still remaining independent and subject to the natural laws of sociopolitical evolution and change.

The Mixed Constitution in Retrospect and Prospect

Polybius' theory was the last of the Greek constitutional theories known to us. The Greek theories show how constitutional mixing became an analytical tool to identify the most effective compromises for preventing civic strife and ensuring the survival of a city-state. Each one was developed consciously on the basis of empirical evidence from actual governments that displayed superior stability or civic excellence. As time went on, the scope of the examples was extended. Thucydides looked only at three Athenian constitutions and explained the best as a mixture. Plato, having witnessed Athens' defeat, expanded his range of comparative examples to include Athens' rivals, the Persians and the Dorian Greeks, as well as Athens' governments in the more distant past. Aristotle made an effort to include all Greek cities over their entire histories, as well as Carthage. Two centuries later Polybius added Rome to his repertory of effective constitutions that could most aptly be analyzed as mixed constitutions.

From Plato onward, the standard basis for judging the effectiveness and quality of a model of political compromise was its conformity to normal human psychology. For service in the real world, and not only in an imaginary utopia, this was essential. Though all the models recognized the tendency of security, luxury, and power to corrupt rulers and the complementary tendency of their exploited subjects to feel hostile to the point of rebellion, there was no agreement on what kind of compromise would promote self-control and moderation in rulers. Three strategies for implementing compromise and reconciling opposed factions appear in the four mixed constitutions that are known to us:

1 Privileging the economic mean among citizens, as Thucydides noted in the Athenian constitution of the 5,000 or as Aristotle advocated in respect to his "middle" constitution.

2 Splitting the authority and honors of rule fairly among the contenders, as Aristotle proposed for his "polity."
3 Balancing or linking opposing organs of government or regimes so they cannot succeed without cooperating with the opposition, as Plato found in the Spartan constitution and Polybius found in both Sparta and Rome.

The choice of strategy depended on the agents entering into the compromise. Determining the relevant agents was crucial, for unless the source of the conflict was correctly identified, the opposing components could not be reconciled. For Thucydides and Aristotle it was the socioeconomic classes of the city, for Plato the various organs of government, the individuals and bodies assigned to make decisions in the city-state. For Polybius it was the regimes operating in and through the state, the sociopolitical segments of the population that constitute sources of authority in the citizen body and the individuals or groups who mediate that authority in the governing process.

These diverse attempts to theorize mixed constitutions were not ivory tower exercises, but serious attempts to bring rationality, the lessons of history, and the results of contemporary social science to bear on the most urgent political problems of ancient times: how to achieve civic cohesion and benevolent governance for the common good. There is no evidence that any of them were successful in furthering these goals in their own states. In fact, the concept of compromise through a "mixed constitution" was eventually forgotten. It had not been a central independent concept in Plato or Aristotle, but developed incidentally in their quest for the best constitution. When its strategic importance was recognized, it was by practical statesmen, Polybius in Greece and later Cicero in Rome; but the books in which they defended the idea were eventually lost. The relevant portion of Polybius' *History* survived only in a Byzantine collection of excerpts of the work. Cicero's account in *De republica* was completely lost and not rediscovered again until the nineteenth century.

But the principles of the Greek mixed constitution were not lost; they found a warm reception in medieval and early modern Europe and stimulated reflection on contemporary politics and history and profoundly shaped medieval and early modern political thought. With the translation of his *Politics* into Latin in the thirteenth century, Aristotle's theorizations came to serve as a basis for medieval political theory and for analyzing governance in England, France, and the Italian republics (Blythe 1992). In the fifteenth century the Latin translator of Plato's *Laws* tendentiously claimed that the Venetians had derived their mixed constitution from Plato (Gilbert 1968: 468–70). When the Byzantine excerpts of book VI of Polybius' *History* were finally translated in the sixteenth century, his formulation came to supplant the medieval Aristotelian formulation in Florence and England (Blythe 1992: 265–307). In England Polybius' conception of a mixed constitution, combining monarchic, aristocratic, and democratic elements, not only shaped the development of the British government, but was also transplanted to the British colonies in the western hemisphere, where it became the model for the American constitution. Through these modern embodiments of constitutional compromise, the ancient Greek principle of the mixed constitution continues to challenge the political agendas of nations around the globe.

David E. Hahm

FURTHER READING

The most comprehensive discussions are Aalders 1968 and Nippel 1980, both in German. Briefer surveys in English may be found in von Fritz 1975; Blythe 1992: 12–35; and Lintott 1997: 70–87; 1999a: 214–32, all with bibliography. For the origins of constitutional thinking in general see Meier 1990b. The individual theories of Plato, Aristotle, and Polybius are surveyed with references and extensive bibliography in C. Rowe and Schofield 2000; see also Balot 2006. Plato's theory is also discussed by Morrow 1960; Stalley 1983, esp. chs 7 and 11; and Schofield 2006. For additional discussions of Aristotle's theory see also Johnson 1990; Yack 1993; and Lintott 2000. Polybius' theory is discussed by von Fritz 1975; Walbank 1972; Trompf 1979; and Hahm 1995.

CHAPTER 13

Republican Virtues

Malcolm Schofield

In his recent monograph *Paideia Romana*, Ingo Gildenhard contrasts two lists of virtues presented by Cicero in his philosophical writings, one at the beginning of *De republica*, the other at the beginning of *Tusculan Disputations*. The argument of the passages in which they are embedded, Gildenhard suggests, is "virtually identical," and, he says, "rests on Cicero's programmatic belief in the superiority of [Roman] practice over [Greek] theory in the realm of politics and ethics" (Gildenhard 2007: 119). Specifically:

> Just as *Rep.* 1.2 insists that those generations who founded human communities antici-pated every meritorious insight reached by philosophers, so *Tusc.* 1.2 maintains that the ancestors organized the sociopolitical aspects of human existence better than any other people, without the benefits of (philosophical) theory and learning.

But though the contexts are in Gildenhard's view so similar, the lists are very different. As well as the creation of law, *De republica* mentions *pietas* (devotion), *religio* (religious observance), *iustitia* (justice), *fides* (trustworthiness), *aequitas* (fairness), *pudor* (modesty), *continentia* (self-control), *fuga turpitudinis adpetentia laudis et honestatis* (aversion to vice and disgrace, appetite for honour and goodness), *fortitudo* (courage).[1] And as Jonathan Powell points out in a forthcoming paper, the fourth of the canonical cardinal virtues, *sapientia* (wisdom), is ascribed in the immediate sequel (*Rep.* 1.3) to those who rule cities by *consilium* (judgment embodied in advice) and *auctoritas* (authority). By contrast, in the *Tusculans* Cicero offers us what Gildenhard describes as a "peculiar selection of ancestral excellences" (2007: 110): *gravitas* (seriousness), *constantia* (steadfastness), *magnitudo animi* (greatness of spirit),[2] *probitas* (integrity), *fides* (trustworthiness). Only *fides*, Gildenhard observes, appears twice.

Why the difference? Gildenhard points above all to radically different extratextual political contexts. *De republica* was composed and published in the late 50s BC, when Rome was still a republic in which those who actively participated in politics

A Companion to Greek and Roman Political Thought, First Edition. Edited by Ryan K. Balot.
© 2013 Blackwell Publishing Ltd. Published 2013 by Blackwell Publishing Ltd.

could expect that they might at some point play a role in government of the commonwealth. The dialogue takes as its subject matter the ideal form for the constitution of a commonwealth and the ideal statesman to guide its fortunes. The *Tusculan Disputations* were composed in 45 BC under the tyranny of Julius Caesar, when there was no longer scope for someone like Cicero to contribute meaningfully to public life or for constitutional theory to flourish. Instead of a focus on communal values, the *Tusculans* are accordingly much more preoccupied "with developing an anthropology and philosophy of self-sufficiency, which find their archetypal articulation in *gravitas* and *constantia*"[3] – in uneasy and unstable tension with a continuing "insistence on service for the community as the supreme realization of our human potential" (Gildenhard 2007: 129). The outcome is a "philosophical redefinition of Roman *virtutes* under tyranny" (2007: 130), which turns them from classic attributes of republican commitment into something as well attuned to the private as to the public sphere, and to coping with the "agony" of political exclusion.

There is much to stimulate and reward in Gildenhard's treatment of this material. But this programmatic contrast between *De republica* and *Tusculan Disputations* doesn't work. In particular, the grounds for seeing the *Tusculans* as engaged in a revisionary project vanish on closer examination. The *Tusculans'* list of virtues figures in a larger textual context (on which to be sure Gildenhard has already been commenting). The greater wisdom (*sapientia*) of the Romans is what Cicero begins with. It is illustrated first by the superiority of their *mores*, the conventions governing life, and family arrangements, then by the superior laws and practices by which public affairs are regulated. In war they have excelled in *virtus* (here prowess or courage), but still more through better training (*disciplina*). The emphasis here is throughout on social acculturation.[4] But Cicero goes on to talk of something else: the Romans' *natural* advantages. It was superior natural endowment which enabled their ancestors to attain *gravitas, constantia, magnitudo animi, probitas*, and *fides* – and indeed (something to which Gildenhard does not draw attention in his contrast with *De republica*) outstanding *virtus* (here to be understood generically as moral excellence) of every kind.

So the opening page of the *Tusculans* in fact covers much the same ground as *De republica* in its treatment of virtue. The *Tusculans* too are concerned with law, social life, and the public sphere (including war, rather more prominently and specifically than *De republica*, which speaks simply of "courage in hardship and danger"), and with the wisdom required to create and sustain them. The main differences are two. The *De republica* passage stresses throughout the role of training, *mores*, law in producing the virtues, whereas the *Tusculans* emphasize the way natural endowment underpins their development, without underplaying law and acculturation. This difference is connected with another. Although *De republica* couches its account of the virtues in terms that are designed to carry multiple Roman resonances (in particular, launching it with reference to *pietas, religio*, and *ius aut gentium aut hoc ipsum civile quod dicitur* [law, whether the law of nations or "civil" law] is clearly designed to play these up for all they are worth), the account is a general one. Cicero is claiming that virtues are the product of civilization, not philosophy. Contrary to what Gildenhard claims, the argument of the *Tusculans* is importantly different.

Cicero is now looking for an explicit explanation of what makes the Romans different. The grave, loyal, reliable character natural to the Romans (as evidenced by their ancestors) is an equally important part of the story. In other words, the focus on nature is also a point – unparalleled in the *De republica* passage – specifically and explicitly about what it is to be Roman.[5]

These two differences are sufficient to explain the divergences in the membership of the two lists of virtues observed by Gildenhard: differences in the intellectual projects Cicero undertakes in the two passages, not in the political circumstances of their composition. Our quarry in this chapter is republican virtue. So we shall be looking more closely at some of the qualities Cicero highlights in the *Tusculans* as ancestral Roman virtues. It is not that those listed at the beginning of *De republica* weren't conceived as Roman: simply that in the *Tusculans* we are being offered Cicero's preferred selection when he attempts an explicit account of why Romans are Romans. It will turn out that Cicero's conceptualization and rhetorical exploitation of these particular virtues remain remarkably stable over a long period, spanning the years of senatorial government and Caesar's dictatorship and its immediate aftermath. What leads him to talk about them at any juncture is indeed a function of the changing political climate (sometimes the microclimate), but they retain the same identity as Roman virtues throughout.

There are of course many other possible routes into the topic of republican virtue than a study of a few key passages from one author, albeit the author of the late republic whose work survives in massively greater quantity than any other; an author who clearly had a huge personal investment in the subject; and the only author from whom we have theorized discussions of the issues – though for Cicero theory cannot be the otherworldly speculation of a Plato, whose account of justice is "totally at odds with normal life and civic customs" (*De or.* 1.224; a virtually identical comment on Plato's ideal city: *Rep.* 2.21).[6] One alternative might be to work from a comprehensive lexical database of literature of the period and look systematically at significant collocations and distributions. Another might be to offer a comprehensive historical account of Roman politics of the late republic, in which virtue vocabulary and its manipulation could be situated and evaluated as ingredients in the dynamics of the political culture as a whole.[7] This study attempts to achieve some of the benefits of these alternative approaches while capitalizing on the particularity of the texts and episodes it comments upon – and in the course of that other voices than Cicero's will get a hearing. Talk about virtues is inevitably harnessed to some particular intellectual or political agenda: this is not a study of republican virtue *sub specie aeternitatis*.

Gravitas and *Constantia*

There is one further important dimension in which the *Tusculans'* treatment of its topic differs from *De republica*'s. It is here that Gildenhard's analysis yields particular dividends. What he argues is that by the time Cicero wrote the *Tusculans*, he had come to think that the Stoic virtues of Cato, who committed suicide at Utica in North

Africa when the forces of the republic were finally defeated, rather than live under Caesar's rule and accept his *clementia* (clemency), epitomized what it was to be truly Roman.[8] Gildenhard (2007: 121) quotes Lily Ross Taylor, writing in 1949: "Cato's unconquered soul speedily became identical with the republic and liberty" (L. Taylor 1949: 170). And he cites a telling passage from a letter Cicero wrote to Atticus in the early summer of 46 BC in which he comments on the difficulty he was having in writing his (now lost) eulogy *Laus Catonis* (*Att.* 12.4.2, trans. Gildenhard 2007):

> But with the *Cato* it is like trying to square a circle. I don't manage to write anything that your dinner-companions could read with pleasure or at least without losing their temper. Even if I were to leave aside his votes in the senate, his whole attitude towards politics and his public counsels, and simply wish to praise his seriousness and steadfastness, this alone would still be hateful to their ears.

The two words *gravitas* and *constantia* are alone enough to annoy the Caesarians. They epitomize refusal to compromise republican values and collude with what anti-Caesarians conceived as tyranny.[9] And, of course, they are the first two virtues on the *Tusculans* list. Cicero is not there excluding other kinds of virtue from consideration: as we have seen, he speaks of outstanding virtue "in each *genus.*" But *gravitas* and *constantia* are given pride of place.

Important though Cato was in this connection, the prominence of these two virtues is nothing very novel in Cicero's writing. His forensic speeches from the very outset are littered with references to them in his frequent plaudits of his contemporaries. The two are often paired. The early speech (quite how early is disputed) on behalf of the actor Q. Roscius says of one C. Cluvius (*Q Rosc.* 7): "quem hominem? levem? immo gravissimum. mobilem? immo constantissimum" ("What sort of a person is he? Lightweight? No one more serious. Fickle? No one more steadfast"). Among the praises Cicero heaps on his provincial client in the peroration to *Pro Cluentio,* composed and delivered in 66 BC, ancestral Roman virtues are emphasized: "nobilitatem illam inter suos locumque a maioribus traditum sic tuetur, ut maiorum gravitatem, constantiam, gratiam, liberalitatem adsequatur" ("his regard for the distinction of his family and the ancestral position he has inherited from them is such that it is ancestral seriousness and steadfastness, kindness and generosity that he practices" (*Clu.* 197)). In more politically charged speeches of 56 BC, not long after his return from political exile, we find virtually identical tributes to M. Bibulus, consul in 59 BC, when he resisted Caesar's legislative proposals ("adest praesens vir singulari virtute, constantia, gravitate praeditus": "here today is a man of exceptional courage, steadfastness, seriousness" (*Dom.* 39)), and to Pompey, the warlord on whom Cicero was always pinning his hopes for the rescue of the Republic ("hunc ... incredibili quadam atque inaudita gravitate, virtute, constantia praeditum": "this man of a seriousness, courage, steadfastness hitherto unheard of and indeed beyond belief" (*Balb.* 13)).[10]

So if the Caesarians interpreted attribution of *gravitas* and *constantia* as code for commitment to republican values and the republican cause, they had every reason to do so. And that is how Cicero must have intended these words to be read at the beginning of the *Tusculans*. It does not follow that everywhere he twins the terms they carry the same connotation. In his philosophical writings Cicero can introduce the pairing in contexts not explicitly Roman or public. Even Epicureans can be "faithful in friendship and steadfast and serious in their whole conduct of life" (*Fin.* 2.81: perhaps Cicero is thinking of his own close friend Atticus). When Democritus said: "I came to Athens, and nobody recognized me," he showed himself "a person of constancy and seriousness – for glorying in the fact that glory had not come his way" (*Tusc.* 5.104). Perhaps he thereby showed himself an honorary Roman?

In other contexts *gravitas* and *constantia* are not so much moral as intellectual virtues. There is a particularly clear example in the next dialogue Cicero composed after the *Tusculans*. In the preface to *De natura deorum*, Cicero finds it necessary to explain and defend his Academic sceptic position in philosophy with particular care, no doubt in part because of a need not to be perceived as undermining religion. The defence is couched in decidedly Stoic terms (cf. *Academica priora* 53):

> What is more open to criticism than the rashness involved in giving assent where the matter is an uncertain one? What can there be that is rasher or more unworthy of the *gravitas* and *constantia* of the wise person (*sapientis*) than to hold a false opinion or to maintain without any hesitation something that is not perceived or known on the basis of sufficient explanation? (*Nat. D.* 1.1)

In other words, in epistemology only the Academic is a true Stoic. Arcesilaus agrees with Zeno on what the *gravitas* of the sage requires (*Academica priora* 66), but it is the Academic, not the Stoic, who passes the test.

Cicero's fullest exploration of *constantia* as a moral virtue comes in the last of his philosophical writings, *De officiis*. The account of the virtues he presents in book 1 of *De officiis*, following the Stoic Panaetius, makes constancy or consistency a hallmark of the fourth virtue, the *decorum*, the "just right" character of behaviour (1.14).[11] As he sums it up at one point (1.125): "There is nothing which is so 'just right' as maintaining constancy (*constantia*) in all one undertakes and in the conceiving of all one's purposes." The Stoic Cato was its great exemplar (1.112): "Nature had endowed him with unbelievable *gravitas*, and he had himself reinforced it with unswerving constancy (*constantia*) and always stuck to the purposes he had conceived and undertaken: so rather than having to look upon the countenance of the tyrant death was the imperative." *Constantia* here remains thoroughly Roman and republican. But it is now accorded a fully theorized treatment. There is clearly an intimate connection with the Stoic conception of the goal of life: living consistently, or as Cicero has Cato put it in the exposition of Stoic ethics in book 3 of *De finibus*: "choice constant [*constans*] and in agreement with nature" (*Fin.* 3.20). He then sums it up in the word he offers as his translation of the Greek *homologia*, *convenientia*, "conformity" or "consistency."

Gravitas, by contrast, is never subjected to similar philosophical analysis. Indeed in the *De officiis* passage just quoted Cicero goes so far as to portray Cato's *gravitas* as a natural endowment, scarcely a philosophical virtue at all. Nor in general does the word appear to function as the Latin equivalent of any canonical Greek virtue.

In Cicero it seems often to be associated with the moral and intellectual impressiveness – the weight and seriousness – of philosophy itself. If we count white teeth, attractive eyes, a pleasant coloring as good things, then what is there – Cicero asks, adopting a Stoic perspective – in the seriousness (*gravitas*) of a philosopher[12] that is more serious (*gravius*) or elevated than the opinion of the crowd or the rabble of the foolish (*Tusc.* 5.46)? Epicurus speaks of living honourably, wisely, with justice. Nothing could be more serious (*gravius*), more worthy of philosophy, did he not make pleasure their focus (*Tusc.* 5.26). Of course, Epicurus often represents pleasure as simply the absence of pain. So by his own criterion, what this "austere and serious philosopher" specifies elsewhere as the good (the pleasures of ears and palate) isn't anything we're in need of, and shouldn't be pursued (*Fin.* 2.29). In passages like these, it is tempting to construe the polarities in play in terms of an opposition between Epicureanism and Stoicism. But Cicero is elsewhere at pains to give the *gravitas* of the philosopher a more venerable pedigree. In book 3 of the *Tusculans*, for example, he contrasts "these pleasure-seeking philosophers" with "those serious philosophers of old" (*Tusc.* 3.40). And in *De legibus* Plato is described as the "most serious [*gravissimus*] of all philosophers" (*Leg.* 2.14).

Magnitudo Animi

Cato and his *gravitas* first figure in Cicero's writings in a notable forensic speech of 63 BC, the year of his consulship. Cato had joined in the prosecution of L. Licinius Murena, successful candidate for the consulship the following year, on a charge of bribing the electorate. Cicero's speech for the defense begins with a rebuttal of Cato's attack on him for taking on the case. His line is that in doing so he is no less conscientious than the conscientious Stoic Cato himself – "gravissimo atque integrissimo viro" "a man of the utmost seriousness and integrity" (*Mur.* 3). Later in the speech Cicero turns to Cato again, and in a memorable passage ridicules his lack of judgment. The critique turns on a contrast between the wholly admirable qualities which spring from Cato's own nature, and the less appealing and unnatural characteristics which he had acquired through embracing the Stoic system of philosophy. In that system "all sins are equal, every slip-up is a wicked crime" (*Mur.* 61); and Cicero has a field day inventing examples illustrating the principle, designed to convince the judges of the inhumanity and absurd lack of proportion Stoicism instills in its adherents. This contrasts sharply with what Cato is in himself: "nature herself has moulded you into nobility [*honestas*], seriousness [*gravitas*], temperance, greatness of spirit [*magnitudo animi*], justice – in short a person of towering stature" (*Mur.* 60).

In an important article of 1935 Ulrich Knoche wrote as follows about this passage:

> I can't think it an accident that Cicero here ascribes to Cato three of the Stoic cardinal virtues – sōphrosunē, megalopsuchia, dikaiosunē [temperance, greatness of spirit, justice] – in fact the three main virtues of the *vita activa* [the life of action] identified by the Middle Stoa. ... No more can it be an accident that Cicero ... acknowledges that his

disinterested conduct has turned Cato into a *magnus et excelsus homo* ["a person of towering stature"]: this too is a Stoic value predicate. (1935: 56)[13]

Knoche (1935: 56) found it no less significant that in surviving Latin literature this is the first appearance of the expression *magnitudo animi*. It was not in reality, he argued, a traditional Roman virtue (we may note in his support that in this list *honestas* and *gravitas* are the terms striking the traditional note), but a value imported into Roman discourse from Stoicism: specifically the version of Stoicism associated with the name of Panaetius (mid-second century BC), who seems to have understood it as the disposition to rise above merely human contingencies. These were not the terms in which Romans had been accustomed to thinking of *fortitudo*, the traditional virtue with which Cicero will in due course most closely associate *magnitudo animi* – physical and mental toughness and robustness are the usual keynotes.

Cicero tries to have it both ways with Stoicism, and not only in *Pro Murena*. He admires its logical consistency and the high moral demands it makes on us, but is constantly irritated by its embrace of exaggerated positions that in the end innovate more in *verba* than in *res*.[14] By the subtle allusions to Cato's Stoicism diagnosed by Knoche Cicero enhances the compliment. At the same time he signals to the *cognoscenti* that his own grip on Stoic vocabulary and ideology is as good as Cato's.[15] Is he actually innovating: himself putting the Greek *megalopsuchia* into Latin for the first time? Knoche (1935: 57) thought it more likely that it was Cato who was responsible. I agree.

A piece of evidence cited elsewhere by Knoche (1935: 46) looks particularly indicative. In the preface to a much later work by Cicero (probably early 46 BC), his own elegant exposition of the Stoic paradoxes, we can infer that *magnitudo animi* was an expression Cato was indeed in the habit of using. Cicero refers to the eloquence of which Cato is capable in public performance when he talks of *magnitudo animi*, self-control, death, virtue, the gods, love of country (*Paradoxa Stoicorum* 3). It's striking that *magnitudo animi* comes first on the list: surely because it was almost a Catonian trademark. Something else that supports the hypothesis is the single occurrence of the expression in Sallust's account of the Catilinarian conspiracy (ca. 41–40 BC). His character sketch comparing Cato and Caesar portrays them as evenly matched in age, family, and a range of personal characteristics. They were equal, too, he says, in *magnitudo animi*: as if to acknowledge the expression's established association with Cato, but at the same time to contradict any assumption that the virtue was his exclusive preserve (Sall. *Cat.* 54.1).

So it was in highly particular circumstances that *magnitudo animi* entered Cicero's vocabulary. But he evidently took to the expression. It recurs at intervals in his writings at interesting junctures, in letters and speeches usually as a key republican virtue. The very next year (62 BC), for example, he applied it to himself in connection with his suppression of the Catilinarian conspiracy, in both a speech (*Sull.* 14) and a letter to Pompey (*Fam.* 5.7.3), and again in a letter to Atticus of March 60 (*Att.* 1.19.6), whom he had by then also credited with the virtue in a letter of December 61 (*Att.* 1.17.5): a sure index of the grip the idea was exercising on his moral imagination. Then we hear no more of *magnitudo animi* until he returns from political exile in 57 BC, and in the following year delivers the speech in defense of Publius Sestius, who as tribune had taken a leading part in promoting Cicero's recall, which constitutes his classic manifesto for senatorial government, and the unique capacity of the *optimates* (the "best people," the nobility) to protect the liberty of the populace at large (the *plebs*) and to guide the elected magistrates by their wise counsel (*consilium*) (cf. Cic. *Sest.* 137).

Cicero talks a great deal about *magnitudo animi* in *Pro Sestio*.[16] The virtue is inevitably ascribed again to Cato (Cicero speaks of his *gravitas, integritas, magnitudo animi*, and *virtus*, and then of his "exceptional" *magnitudo animi* and "amazing" *virtus*: 60, 62). It is also exemplified by other named individuals: L. Ninnius, another tribune who had supported Cicero's recall, a man of amazing *fides, magnitudo animi*, and *constantia* (26); and T. Annius Milo, yet another supportive tribune, endowed with extraordinary and hitherto unknown *magnitudo animi, gravitas*, and *fides* (85) – Cicero will have to defend Milo in the courts four years later, charged with the murder of the Caesarian populist politician Publius Clodius, and will reiterate his praise of Milo's *magnitudo animi* (*Mil.* 1, 61, 69). But in fact the defense of Rome against internal subversion by the entire company of good men and true has been due to their *auctoritas, fides, constantia*, and *magnitudo animi* (*Sest.* 139). Rome herself is the very birthplace of *gravitas* and *magnitudo animi* (141).

The expression recurs in Cicero's letters and speeches of 56 (e.g. *Fam.* 1.7.3, *Att.* 4.6.1, *Prov. cons.* 27). Needless to say it is never defined there, no more than are the other virtues he clusters with it. Nonetheless it may be indicative that in his dialogue *De oratore*, written the following year, *magnitudo animi* and *sapientia* (wisdom)[17] are distinguished from social virtues such as *clementia, iustitia, benignitas, fides*, and *fortitudo* (2.143). The latter are reckoned beneficial to humanity, and prompt a warm reaction in us when people talk of them. The former, by contrast, are not conceived as related primarily to *mores*, but as conditions of the mind. "Greatness and strength of spirit" is then explained as the mindset in which "all human affairs are thought of as of slight concern and worth nothing" – in line with the Stoic definition. We admire these qualities, but the admiration is less tinged with warmth. Is that true of the *magnitudo animi* so much on Cicero's lips in *Pro Sestio*? Very probably so, where the austere and severe Cato was concerned. And throughout the speech Cicero wishes to impress upon his hearers and readers the awesome, almost superhuman qualities of the defenders of the Republic to whom he ascribes *magnitudo animi*. Their *fides* may endear them to us, but the vocabulary is for the most part chosen to evoke respect for something exceptional – something, of course, which should inspire the audience to set prejudices and petty interests aside. In the simplest terms, *magnitudo animi* is the virtue of a *magnus vir*, whatever it is that makes such a man great.

When in retirement from politics Cicero turned ten years later to writing philosophy and rhetorical theory, it was only to be expected that in passages which list and categorize the virtues, *magnitudo animi* should receive frequent mentions. In the last of his philosophical writings, *De officiis* (44 BC), it decisively displaces *fortitudo* (courage) in the canonical quartet. But from as early as *De republica* (54–51 BC) a tendency to reinterpret *fortitudo* in terms of *magnitudo animi* is apparent. There for example we find Cicero explaining *fortitudo* as the virtue in which *magnitudo animi* is present, further specified as "huge contempt for death and pain" (*Rep.* 5.9 (= 5.7 Powell)). In expounding Stoicism in *De finibus* (45 BC) he has Cato state that it is "the elevated and distinguished man with greatness of spirit [*vir altus et excellens magno animo*] that is truly brave, who thinks all things human beneath him" (*Fin.* 3.29). Similarly in the *Tusculans* that same year he writes of *fortitudo* and "what goes with it": *magnitudo animi, gravitas, patientia* (endurance), contempt for things human *Tusc.* 2.32). In *Partitiones oratoriae* (perhaps 46 BC), where a formal classification of the virtues is presented, *magnitudo animi* now embraces *fortitudo*, *patientia*, and *liberalitas* (*Part. or.* 77). These reconfigurations of the virtues clearly reflect developments in hellenistic Stoicism we can detect (for example) in Greek sources containing definitions, alternative to more orthodox formulations, of virtues such as *karteria* (endurance) and *enkrateia* (self-control), in effect making them species of *megalopsuchia* (cf. Sext. Emp. *Math.* 9. 153, 161).

Zeno of Citium, largely followed by other early Stoics, had simply taken over the canonical quartet of virtues that we find, for instance, in Plato's *Republic* (Plut. *De Stoic. rep.* 1034C, *De Virt. mor.* 441A), and defined each of the others Socratically in terms of wisdom (*phronēsis*; Chrysippus subsequently substituted knowledge (*epistēmē*) for wisdom). But there was no very obvious or decisive rationale for his selection of just this set of four, with choice (for *sōphrosunē*), endurance (for courage) and distribution (for justice) as their respective responsibilities. The major alternative scheme which survives is very probably due to Panaetius, the mid-second century BC Stoic who had a close association with the younger Scipio Africanus, hero of Cicero's *De republica*. He rethought the quartet of cardinal virtues in terms of different fundamental human impulses. We have rational impulses to pursue truth, to associate with others and care for them, to rise above dependence on anybody or anything, and to exhibit order and consistency and balance in all we think and say and do. The person in whom these impulses are perfected has attained the principal virtues: wisdom (*sapientia* and *prudentia*), justice (*iustitia*) and beneficence (*beneficentia*), greatness of spirit (*magnitudo animi*) – and a fourth which is harder to sum up in just one or two words, since it manifests itself variously as respect (*verecundia*), restraint and self-control (*temperantia* and *modestia*), and measure and order in behavior (*ordo et modus*). Cicero brings *constantia* under this heading. To epitomize the fourth virtue he adopted Panaetius's expression *to prepon*, and Latinized it as *decorum*: what is and seems "just right."[18] We are in fact very largely dependent on Cicero in *De officiis* for our knowledge of the entire theory; the account given above summarizes the main points of *Off.* 1.11–17 (cf. also 1. 20, 93).

There can be no surprise to find Cicero happy to present *magnitudo animi* as the third of the four virtues, given all the various contexts in which we have seen him wax eloquent on its importance in sustaining the defence of the *res publica*. More unexpected is the note he strikes at the very outset of his detailed discussion in *Off.* 1.61–92. He starts with an acknowledgment of how nothing seems more brilliant (*splendissimum*) than deeds performed with "great and elevated spirit, and contempt for things human," above all those which bring military glory (1.61). But he issues an immediate warning: *elatio et magnitudo animi* (elevation and greatness of spirit) driven not by concern for the common good, but by willfulness and an excessive desire for preeminence (or even sole preeminence) is not a virtue at all. Without justice it can't be anything honorable (*honestum*). It isn't bravery but audacity. Deeds not glory are the test of "true and wise *magnitudo animi*." Nobody can be regarded as a great man if his "greatness" depends on the folly of an ignorant mob (1.62–5).

As the commentators note, this nuanced and indeed critical treatment of *magnitudo animi*, unprecedented in Cicero's writings, is clearly prompted by reflection on Roman politics, and above all – with its reference to ambition for "sole preeminence" – on the career of the recently assassinated Julius Caesar. Indeed an earlier passage (1.26) had singled him out as a case of the lust for "honor, empire, power and glory found in the greatest spirits [*maximis animis*] and most brilliant talents." It may be that we catch here a sign, confirmed by Sallust's verdict that Cato and Caesar were equal in *magnitudo animi* (*Cat.* 54.1), that ownership of the expression was contested, and that the senatorial party hadn't managed to secure exclusive rights in it. At *Off.* 1.26 Cicero seems to concede that Caesar *was* a big man: he did have a sort of *magnitudo animi*. Though the words must have stuck in his throat when two years earlier in the *Pro Marcello* (*Marcell.* 19) he had felt he had to include in his praise of the dictator mention of the brilliance of *true* glory (*splendor in laude vera*) and the impressiveness conferred on a person by *magnitudo animi et consili* – except that he managed to invest his syntax with a certain ambiguity: is he actually ascribing these qualities to Caesar, or is he reminding his audience and readership of what it *would* be like to be truly virtuous?

A. A. Long rightly reads *De officiis*'s assault on perverted *magnitudo animi*, and more generally its sustained critique in both books 1 and 2 of "false glory," as an attempt to promote a "reformist ideology," a "reform of the Roman honour code" which would "turn glory into a co-operative value, grounded in justice" (Long 1995: 230, 224, 233). In attacking particularly the assumption that war is the preeminent sphere for the display of *virtus*, Cicero is indeed picking an argument with the entire Roman aristocratic tradition. He himself endeavors to claim that it is his own standpoint that is truly traditional, by representing his agenda as restoration rather than reform. From the time of the suppression of the Catilinarian conspiracy onward, he and those public figures whose *magnitudo animi* he had praised had in his eyes practiced true virtue and earned true praise. Devotion to the *res publica* and to Roman tradition (*instituta maiorum*) had been what motivated them. Their example proved that there was nothing intrinsically wrong with the Roman honor code. But what he perceived as the devastation produced during his lifetime by political ambition now prompted Cicero to analysis of the temptations to which great powers and achievements are subject, and to extended examination of a quality such as *magnitudo animi*. In short, *De officiis* accepts the need to develop an *argument* for and about the values Cicero had been trumpeting for decades, not just to reiterate them, as in the letters and forensic speeches. In the process – as Long argues – something new in Roman discourse is forged: above all, a fully articulated distinction between meretricious and genuine glory.

In exploring *magnitudo animi* at length, Cicero is able to develop other themes that carry contemporary Roman resonances. He returns as often to the superior claims of the public over the private life (*Off.* 1.69–73), and insists that statesmanship and government are more important spheres for the exercise of virtue than is war, with Roman as well as Greek examples (1.74–80). P. Scipio Nasica did no less service to the *res publica* by eliminating Tiberius Gracchus than the younger Scipio Africanus in destroying Numantia (1.76), and even when wars have to be fought their initiation and subsequent conduct requires statesmanship – witness Marcus Cato's role with regard to the Third Punic War (1.79). Inevitably he cites once more his own achievement in the year of his consulship in saving the *res publica* from subversion or destruction: an achievement like that requires greater energy and devotion even than military prowess (1.77–8). *Ratio* (reason) in settling disputes when guided by calculation of *utilitas* is more desirable than courage in fighting over the issue (1.80). Keeping one's head as a statesman is a form of courage and constancy that requires both "a great and exalted spirit and one reliant on wisdom [*prudentia*] and counsel [*consilium*]" (1.81). And government has a greater scope and affects more lives than any other undertaking (1.92). Bellicose and addicted to violent masculinity though the Romans were, it is hard to doubt that war weariness and horror of civil strife would have commended Cicero's thesis to many of his readers – who will have perhaps recalled how much store was set on the gentler virtues of *lenitas* and *misericordia* by Caesar himself.[19]

The public utility of *magnitudo animi* and its inseparability from justice are brought out in the analysis of the structure of the virtue. Although in this section of the book Cicero never adverts to the idea of the unity and interdependence of the virtues (as he will in discussing the *decorum* at 1.94–8), its importance for understanding *magnitudo animi* is made clear enough (1.66–8). At the core of *magnitudo animi* are two things: knowledge that only the honorable and what is "just right" (*decorum*) are good, and the freedom from the passions that goes with that. In other words, the virtue is grounded in *sapientia* and *moderatio*. When someone of such a disposition experiences that impulse to excel in difficult and dangerous circumstances which is special to *magnitudo animi*, its supreme expression – given that humans are designed for community – will be in the conduct of great enterprises that will sustain the *res publica* or exhibit *beneficentia* and *liberalitas*: the province of justice (see especially 1. 86, 92).[20]

The *De officiis* accordingly presents both Cicero's theorization of the *magnitudo animi* which had stirred him to eloquence at crucial junctures during the previous two decades, representing it unequivocally as a cardinal virtue (it isn't here the culminating member of a list), and a new justification of political activity in the service of the *res publica* as the highest expression of human excellence. *Magnitudo animi* has made a remarkable journey from its first appearance in his writings back in the *Pro Murena* (63 BC) to its now dominant role in his articulation of Roman republican ideology. Its absorption into Roman political discourse – due of course to Cato and no doubt others as well as Cicero – is one of those cases where philosophy has made its mark on the wider vocabulary of a language.

As *De officiis* was being completed, Cicero returned to the public stage, above all in the series of speeches (the "Philippics") he launched against Mark Antony, now standard-bearer of the Caesarian cause, from September 44 well into the following year. Once more he hymns the virtues exemplified by those he sees as champions of the *res publica*. C. Vibius Pansa, consul in 43, is portrayed as a man of *magnitudo animi*, *gravitas*, and *sapientia* (*Phil.* 7.7); Cassius the tyrannicide – in words which seem to echo *De officiis* 1.81 – is equal in *magnitudo animi* and in wisdom (*consili*) (11.28). Everybody knows the *consilium*, *ingenium*, *humanitas*, *innocentia*, and *magnitudo animi* displayed by Cicero's friend Trebonius in liberating the country (from Caesar's tyranny) (11.9). Most grandiloquent of all is the roll call of virtues exemplified in their liberation of the Roman people by the three commanders Pansa, Hirtius, and Octavian, as Cicero describes them on the last page of the last of the *Philippics*: *imperium*, *consilium*, *gravitas*, *constantia*, *magnitudo animi* – and (a surprise – we were thinking *magnitudo animi* was as so often to be the crowning item) *felicitas*: good luck (14.37).[21]

Epilogue

When in the *Tusculan Disputations* Cicero had listed *gravitas*, *constantia*, *magnitudo animi* first among the Roman ancestral virtues, Gildenhard saw this as in reality a redefinition – of what it was to be Roman under tyranny. *Gravitas* and *constantia* articulated a philosophy of self-sufficiency (Gildenhard 2007: 125), *magnitudo animi* "an *ethos* of lofty indifference"[22] to life under Caesar: in short, a retreat into the private sphere which nonetheless signaled its active republican inheritance. The evidence amassed in this chapter demonstrates on the contrary that over two decades (or more, in the case of *gravitas* and *constantia*) Cicero consistently represented these attributes as the qualities typically exhibited by great political actors in their defense of the common good against attempts to subvert it. *Magnitudo animi* entered his vocabulary only when he was forced to think about Cato and what gave him his particular strength and authority as a public figure. But once it did, he was glad to appropriate it and associate it with others of the ancestral virtues he liked to celebrate in those devoted in their public life to the cause of the *res publica*: *fides*, *integritas*, *auctoritas*, for example, as well as *gravitas* and *constantia*. And when he turned to writing philosophy in 46–44 BC, he found it natural to employ *gravitas* and *constantia* in Stoicizing vein to characterize philosophy itself and philosophical consistency. The scope and moral foundations of *magnitudo animi*, always understood in Stoic terms, were to be thoroughly explored in *De officiis*.

In 45 BC Cicero delivered a speech before Julius Caesar on behalf of Deiotarus, whom Pompey had made king of Galatia, and who was now charged with plotting to assassinate the dictator. He praises Deiotarus's *magnitudo animi*, *gravitas*, and *constantia*, after rehearsing all the many motions passed in the senate in gratitude for his services rendered to Roman generals campaigning in the east. With gross rhetorical exaggeration (which he must have known would be perfectly apparent to Caesar) Cicero claims that all the philosophers make these virtues the only true good, sufficient for the life of happiness – but Deiotarus, he adds at once, attributes all his tranquillity and peace of mind to Caesar's *clementia* (*Deiot.* 37–8).[23] The message is clear. The philosophers would go so far as to make such a person a Stoic sage in his moral perfection. But Deiotarus knows that he owes a quiet old age to Caesar. His devotion to the *res publica* deserves no less. His virtues mark Deiotarus as a great public servant, an honorary Roman.

The associations of the vocabulary are just the same as they were under the Republic. By exploiting them, Cicero within a few short sentences achieves the ingenious feat of coded reiteration of republican ideals, as forcefully expressed as ever, coupled with calculated flattery of the dictator made all the more effective by a mediating play on philosophical ideas that would have been common ground between the two of them. In Cicero republican virtues, as this chapter will have made plain, always live within argument, forensic or philosophical as the case may be.

FURTHER READING

A still useful and readable general account of the whole topic is Earl 1967. There are many serviceable political histories of Rome in the late republic: one that retains its value is Beard and Crawford 1985 (2nd edn 2000). Atkins 2000 offers an accessible overview on Cicero. A good recent book that examines Cicero's writings as contributions to the political and cultural arguments of his times is Steel 2005. Gildenhard 2007 makes the *Tusculan Disputations* the focus of a stimulating examination of Cicero's philosophical writings from a similar viewpoint. For *De officiis* use the excellent English edition of Griffin and Atkins 1991. The virtues in *De republica* are discussed in Powell forthcoming. On Cato see Griffin 1986, on Sallust Earl 1961. A valuable resource is the sequence of surveys of the semantic behavior of a whole gamut of virtue words constituted by Lind 1979, 1989, 1992. There is an ambitious study of Roman political vocabulary in the republican period by Hellegouarc'h 1972. Benferhat 2005 contains much of interest on the vocabulary of mercy in late republican and Caesarian Rome. Examples of treatments of particular virtues and virtue words are Heinze 1925 (*auctoritas*), Knoche 1935 (*magnitudo animi*), Balsdon 1960 (*auctoritas, dignitas*), Wagenvoort 1980 (*pietas*), Atkins 1990 (*iustitia*), M. Griffin 2003 (*clementia*), and the major study by Kaster 2005a (*verecundia, pudor, integritas*). On *gloria* see Long 1995. A wide-ranging and provocative study of Roman conceptions of virtue, exploiting a range of modern perspectives, is Barton 2001. Noreña's chapter 17 in this volume is a concise introduction to the virtues expected of the emperor in the period of the early and high empire.

NOTES

My thanks to Ryan Balot for the invitation to contribute to this volume, and for some challenging editorial comments which have helped to improve the chapter.

1   For the most part I reproduce the English equivalents proposed by Gildenhard. Throughout the chapter I shall usually present a single English equivalent for any Greek or Latin term introduced. These translations are intended to suggest to the reader only the roughest of mappings: modern English moral vocabulary differs from Latin and ancient Greek systematically in its semantic range and sociopolitical density. Each Latin virtue word deserves extended discussion not possible within the compass of this chapter.

2   Gildenhard says "magnanimity of spirit." But as we shall see from Cicero's use of the
    expression, it seems rather to connote for him a loftiness of perspective, an ability to rise
    above the contingencies of human life.

3   Gildenhard 2007: 125. Gildenhard puts particular weight on an interesting passage at
    Tusc. 5.12–13, where – he suggests – these attributes are "identified as 'inalienable'
    qualities of the *vir bonus*, quite regardless of his fortune" (2007: 125 n114). This is to
    misread the argument. Cicero's opponent is resisting the Stoic thesis that virtue is
    sufficient for happiness, regardless of whether a person has any of the other things in life
    generally regarded as good to have. He produces the standard example of torture: you can
    live rightly, honourably, praiseworthily – and for that reason live well. What does he mean
    by "well"? Steadfastly (*constanter*), seriously (*graviter*), wisely (*sapienter*), courageously
    (*fortiter*) – as we shall see below, this is code for "like a good republican." All that is
    subjected to the thumbscrews too: the thumbscrews are not the happy life one is after (i.e.
    that a good republican is hoping for). Cicero's reply effectively challenges his interlocutor
    to show that a person with these virtues *will* be deprived of happiness in the torture
    chamber. It doesn't redefine or imply redefinition of those virtues.

4   So Gildenhard is wrong to state: "While Cicero evokes the state of the ancestors, he does
    so without foregrounding the set of social values that made it work" (2007: 130).

5   Much of Cicero's agenda in the rest of *De republica* of course takes an explicitly Roman
    focus, notably in the representation of the Roman republican "mixed" constitution as
    ideal in book 2. But in the preface to book 1 (1.1–12) his arguments are quite general, even
    where their Roman applications are obvious enough and sometimes explicitly articulated.

6   I shall be referring to Sallust's discussion of the contrasting virtues of Caesar and Cato in
    chapter 54 of his *Catilina* below (p. 205): reflective and pointed, if not theorized.

7   See the suggestions for further reading.

8   On Cato's Stoicism and his suicide see M. Griffin 1986.

9   Tyranny is how Cicero habitually thinks of Caesar's rule, on occasion even to the point of
    using the Greek expression *turannos*, whether neat, as privately in correspondence with
    Atticus in March 49 (*Att.* 9.13.4), or in transliteration, as publicly in 44 after Caesar's
    assassination (*Off.* 3.19). But others spoke of Caesar differently. Sallust, for example,
    speaks not of the concentration of power in the hands of one man (Cic. *Div.* 2.6), but
    says of him that he sought for himself *imperium, exercitum, bellum novom* so that his *virtus*
    could shine forth (not that Cicero would have disagreed with that: cf. e.g. *Off.* 1.26) –
    reflecting Caesar's own claim that in crossing the Rubicon what he was defending above all
    was his own *dignitas* (*B Civ.* 1.9.2; cf. Cic. *Att.* 7.11.1). Caesarians would speak of his
    lenitas and *clementia* in victory (*B Afr.* 86, 92), although Caesar himself – writing again in
    March 49 – preferred words like *misericordia* and *liberalitas* (Cic. *Att.* 9.7C; echoed in
    Sallust's talk of his *beneficia* and *munificentia*, his *mansuetudo* and *misericordia*: Sall. *Cat.*
    54.2), no doubt because they sounded less monarchical than *clementia*. In this connection
    the brilliant discussion of "political catchwords" in Syme 1939: ch. 11 is still well worth
    consulting; on the political subtleties of the vocabulary of mercy at Rome during the civil
    war and its aftermath see Griffin 2003, Benferhat 2005: chs 4 and 5.

10 On Cicero's economy with the truth in the story he liked to tell of the circumstances of his
    exile, see Robert Kaster's analysis in this volume, chapter 20.

11 See further Schofield forthcoming.

12 A phrase repeated e.g. at *Fin.* 2.100.

13 For the Stoic credentials of *magnus et excelsus homo* he cited the account of Stoic ethics in
    Stobaeus: "The virtuous person is big and powerful and tall and strong" (*Ecl.* 2.99.12–14;

these seemingly physical attributes are then all explained in terms of moral psychology in the sequel: 2.99.14–19).

14 See e.g. Schofield 2002a.

15 He pretends at this point in the speech that his audience are all of them *cognoscenti* (*Mur.* 61 *ad init.*).

16 For more on *Pro Sestio* see Robert Kaster's discussion in chapter 20.

17 These virtues are coupled as qualities Cicero salutes (along with *gravitas*) in the proconsular P. Lentulus, in a letter to him of February 56 (*Fam.* 1.5a.4); and he accords them to his friend Trebonius, in a letter to him of June 45 (*Fam.* 6.11.2), in connection with his *dignitas*. At *Fin.* 3.25 (also 45), in Cicero's exposition of Stoic ethics, *magnitudo animi* is actually identified along with *iustitia* as a form of *sapientia*, characterized by judging that everything that can happen to a human being is beneath notice.

18 On the fourth virtue see Schofield forthcoming.

19 See the references at note 9 above.

20 How would such behaviour exemplify "contempt for things human" (1. 13, 67, 72)? Cicero's discussion (1.72–3) suggests that great spirits are free from worry about what will happen to them or about what resources they have in life. In other words, they despise not human life itself, but the preoccupations which usually dominate people's minds. Unlike other men, they "appreciate the frailty of things human and the variability of fortune," as Panaetius is quoted as saying, and are unimpressed by them (1.90).

21 On *felicitas* – and Caesar's luck in particular – see Murphy 1985–6.

22 Gildenhard 2007: 122 n100 (here using a phrase in Dyck 1998: 228, of which he says: "it is hard to find a more appropriate characterization of Cato's attitude to life under Caesar").

23 On *clementia* see M. Griffin 2003.

CHAPTER 14

Roman Democracy?

W. Jeffrey Tatum

The Roman constitution, never comprehensively codified, resided in the Romans' accumulation of customary practices, traditional regulations, and public legislation. The result was a system of government that remained complicated and untidy (see Hammer, this volume, chapter 2). Polybius, in the earliest analysis of the Roman constitution known to us, concentrated his attention on what he perceived to be the three principal elements of Rome's government – the magistrates, the senate, and the people – all of which combined, in their mutual competition, to yield what he deemed to be a mixed constitution (Polyb. 6.11–18). Greek political theory recognized three fundamental kinds of constitution: government by one, by a few, and by the many, the manifestations of which could be either attractive (in which case one had to do with monarchy, aristocracy, or democracy) or the opposite (thus furnishing tyranny, oligarchy, or ochlocracy). More complicated states were viewed as conglomerations of these basic bits, resulting, for instance, in Aristotle's complicated discussions of constitutional compounds that required careful scrutiny before one could determine whether they were, in the end, more like a democracy or more like an aristocracy (Arist. *Pol.* 2.1266a26–8; 4.1294b13–16, 34–6; cf. Rowe 2000b: 384–7).

A mixed constitution was one that successfully joined the virtues of monarchical, aristocratic, and popular government in order to create a stable and just state. This view was already ancient when Polybius brought it to bear on Rome (Walbank 2002: 281), where it found the consuls exercising a limited version of regal power, the senate, composed of Rome's wealthiest men, supervising Roman finances, the management of Italy and the conduct of Roman foreign policy, and, in the power of the popular assemblies to dispense honor and punishment, to accept or to reject laws and to decide questions of war and peace, Rome's democratic dimension. Roman stability, in Polybius' assessment, was owing to the checks each element put on the superiority of any other: a consul at war, for example, because he required the cooperation of the senate and the people if he hoped to secure victory and glory, could not be indifferent to their wishes. This was not to say that the balance was in every way even: Polybius

A Companion to Greek and Roman Political Thought, First Edition. Edited by Ryan K. Balot.
© 2013 Blackwell Publishing Ltd. Published 2013 by Blackwell Publishing Ltd.

observes that the superiority of the Roman to the Carthaginian constitution (another mixed constitution) at the time of the Hannibalic War was an effect of the latter's greater inclination toward democracy than to aristocracy (Polyb. 6.51; see Hahm, this volume, chapter 12).

Polybius was aware that his account of the Roman constitution was incomplete and reductive (Polyb. 11.3–8). It did not occur to him, however, to inquire whether Greek political theory furnished the best means for understanding the complications of Roman government. One might without unfairness attribute his conclusions to the simple coincidence that (i) in Polybius' opinion, Rome enjoyed a superlative constitution, and (ii) as every Greek intellectual was aware, a superlative constitution must be a mixed constitution. Consequently it was merely left to Polybius to discover in the actualities of Roman government what he knew had to be there in the first place: monarchical, aristocratic, and democratic institutions (Seager forthcoming). This train of thought might, for instance, help to explain his failure to observe that Roman consuls were all of them senators before their elevation to high office and all of them senators once more at the completion of their magistracy, a reality that tended to narrow the gap between those two elements of the constitution in contrast to the distance between the many who constituted the people and the few who inhabited the senate and the magistracies (Hölkeskamp 2004: 266–7; cf. the approaches outlined by Hahm, chapter 12). Nor, as we shall see, is the democratic quality of the popular assemblies entirely incontestable or unqualified. It has in fact been objected that Greek categories are entirely useless and even misleading concepts for understanding Roman society, the dynamics of which must be understood on their own terms (Meier 1980: 45–63; Flaig 1995: 88–9; Hölkeskamp 2004: 259–60).

But Polybius' approach to the Roman constitution was not limited to its formal institutions: he extended himself to an ample discussion of the Roman army and of various and, in Polybius' view, important aspects of Roman society, such as their approach to religion – in sum, the customs and way of life (*ēthē kai nomima*) exhibited by Roman culture (Polyb. 6. 19–56). Furthermore, Polybius was well aware of the significance of extrainstitutional factors in explaining the relationships among the elements he discerned in the Roman constitution. The senate's hold over the people, to take the most obvious example, he explains entirely in terms of the latter's economic and social dependence on the former (Polyb. 6.17). And it cannot pass unnoticed that Polybius' analysis of the Roman constitution, in its essential outline, proved quite acceptable to Cicero (Cic. *Rep.* 1–2, notwithstanding his important adjustments and very different perspective). The inevitable limitations of Polybius' account of the Roman constitution ought not to be ignored. At the same time, its value, not least because it was obvious enough to Cicero, who embraced the appositeness of the concept of a mixed constitution (*Rep.* 1.69), must not go unappreciated (see Hahm, chapter 12).

The evidence of Polybius has proved an important stimulus in recent discussions of the Roman Republic that wish to stress the importance of the role of the people in political life. It has long been acknowledged that, along with the authority of the senate (*senatus auctoritas*), the sovereignty of the Roman people remained a fundamental principle of Roman government. *Res publica*, insists Cicero, means *res populi*

(*Rep.* 1.39), nor is the orator too shy to declaim that "it is fitting that all powers, all commands, all commissions are granted by the Roman people" (*Leg. agr.* 2.17). But it has long been an academic reflex to derogate the importance of popular sovereignty, the prevailing assumption being that the senatorial class, or certainly the noble elite of that class, possessed the means – wealth, prestige, influence, patronage – effectually to eliminate the independence of the common people, who, distracted by their daily struggles, were obliged to lend their support to the political designs of their superiors. "The Senate," as Ronald Syme put it, "being a permanent body, arrogated to itself power, and after conceding sovranty to the assembly of the People was able to frustrate its exercise. The two consuls remained the head of the government, but policy was largely directed by ex-consuls. These men ruled, as did the Senate, not in virtue of written law, but through *auctoritas*" (Syme 1939: 10).

Here we see a manifestation of the "iron law of oligarchy" that simplifies all governments to this common distillation (Rhodes 2003a: 44–5; cf. Syme 1939: 7 – "in all ages, whatever the form and name of government, be it monarchy, republic, or democracy, an oligarchy lurks behind the façade"; cf. Hammer, chapter 2). But this approach ignores too many obvious realities of Roman society. In fact, only popular assemblies could create legislation, commonly referred to as *iussa populi*, the people's commands (the senate possessed no *legal* authority not granted it by popular legislation), a state of affairs that rendered the popular assemblies far from impotent, at least in theory. Furthermore, because the senatorial aristocracy was a political aristocracy, that is, because the realization and consequently the demonstration of one's standing depended not simply on inherited splendor but above all else on election to public office (Hopkins and Burton 1983: 44–5; Hölkeskamp 2004: 268–9), the assemblies played a major role in regulating the composition of the governing elite. Election to the quaestorship or tribunate was the regular route to membership in the senate. And, with only a very few and remarkable exceptions, election to the praetorship or consulship was necessary for military command, triumph, and *gloria*. Elevation to the consulship, the signal aristocratic honor during the Republic, ennobled one's family forever and, for the aspiring *nobilis*, confirmed the reputation of his ancestry as well as the reality of his individual superiority. In the end, then, aristocratic greatness relied on its recognition by and within the *res publica* and (what amounts to the same thing in practical terms) on its ratification in the voting assemblies of the Roman people. As Polybius recognized, in Rome honor was dispensed by the popular assemblies.

These assemblies, it will be clear, matter very much to any attempt to assess the democratic qualities of the Roman constitution. Consequently a brief and somewhat technical description of their operations will be necessary here (see Rhodes, this volume, chapter 4). Out of this complexity will emerge an awareness of the limitations, in theory and in practice alike, imposed on the voice especially of vulnerable sections of the populace – despite an authentic and in certain particulars even robust respect for the realities of popular sovereignty in Roman government.

The people exercised its powers only when it was articulated into one of the city's voting assemblies (Lintott 1999a: 40–60). No public assembly was legal unless summoned by a magistrate. Magistrates summoned unorganized crowds in order to address them on any matter of public importance, such as the recitation of edicts or, more commonly, the delivery of political speeches in favor of or in opposition to an item slated to come before a voting assembly: an assembly of this type was called a *contio*, at which no restrictions were placed on attendance and at which no formal decisions were put to the audience, although whatever throng gathered was free to express itself in cheers and jeers. Voting assemblies, on the other hand, were far more restrictive. They were permitted only on certain days in the Roman calendar, and whereas legislative or judicial assemblies might be called throughout the year, elections were held only once in a year, usually during the summer. Instead of a promiscuous crowd, popular participation was limited to Roman citizens (free and freed men of at least 17 years), organized into well-defined political units. Only in these configurations did the sovereign Roman people emerge with the capacity to act officially.

Three voting assemblies defined the Roman people: the tribal assembly, the assembly of the *plebs* and the centuriate assembly. The first two of these can here be treated together, inasmuch as the differences between them were relatively minor. In each, the fundamental voting unit was the *tribe*, an affiliation determined, at least originally, by the voting districts into which citizens were distributed: from 241 BC there was a total of 35 tribes. Of these there were four urban tribes, into which all freed slaves were deposited in order to minimize their influence in the assemblies, a restriction that, despite the efforts of reformers, was never overcome. The remaining so-called rural tribes were, at least when it came to legislative assemblies, regularly populated by city dwellers of rural origins and citizens from rural territories lying very near the city (matters will have been different during elections, when prosperous types from throughout Italy often traveled to the city). It is certainly the case that the urban *plebs* appear to have dominated most legislative assemblies (Lintott 1999a: 204). The method of voting in both assemblies was the same: the population was sorted into tribes. The number of voters in a particular tribe at any election was irrelevant: each tribe cast a single vote, which was determined by a simple majority of the individual votes of its participating membership. A simple majority of 18 votes sufficed to secure election or passage of a bill into law. At elections, winners were announced whenever they received the necessary 18 votes (and so the order of counting ballots and announcing results was important for individual candidates during elections). These assemblies, especially the assembly of the *plebs*, were Rome's principal legislative bodies, and here we find practical if qualified evidence that speaks in favor of a democratic element in Roman government.

Matters become very different when we turn to the centuriate assembly. Though it too carried legislation, though rarely in the late republic, this was the body that elected praetors and consuls, the chief magistracies. In this assembly, the whole of the voting public was articulated into 193 units denominated as *centuries*. Citizens were assigned to individual centuries on the basis of their wealth and age, with the result that the membership of different centuries varied greatly in terms of their number: the centuries of the rich had relatively few members, those of the poor, especially the very poor, were teeming. Each century possessed a single vote – however numerous its members – and all elections in the centuriate assembly were decided on the basis of a simple majority of 97 votes. Centuries voted in a specific order (generally speaking, the rich voted first and thereafter groups of centuries voted in descending order of wealth). Results were announced at specific points during the voting. Whenever a candidate for office secured 97 votes, his election was announced. It was rarely necessary for everyone who was present at an election to cast ballots. This was because the wealthy, who constituted the smallest portion of Roman voters, were distributed among 88 centuries (nearly half the possible votes in the assembly and only nine votes shy of the simple majority needed to elect a magistrate or carry an issue), whereas the poorest citizens were crammed into far fewer centuries.

According to Dionysius, the *proletarii* (Rome's poorest citizens) constituted more than half the citizen population (*Ant. Rom.* 4.18.2; 7.59.6), although this no doubt reflects nothing more than his impression of the urban situation. Whatever the scale of the *proletarii*, however, by the time of the late republic the wealthy classes certainly represented a very small part of the overall population: Cicero, again reacting to his perceptions from electoral assemblies, tells us that one century of the lower classes (in which group he counts all but the rich) included more citizens than almost the entirety of the membership in the wealthy centuries (Cic. *Rep.* 2.40). This was by design. As Cicero proudly describes the system, it was organized "in such a way that the greatest number of votes lies in the power, not of the multitude, but of the rich" (*Rep.* 2.39), or, as Livy puts it, "levels were designed so that no one appeared to be excluded from an election and yet all of the clout resided with the leading men" (Liv. 1.43.10). In practice, the lowest classes were rarely asked for their votes (Liv. 1.43.11; Dion. *Ant. Rom.* 4.20.5).

Now the constitutional clout of these assemblies, whatever their restrictions in terms of individual equality, is obvious. In addition, one must not overlook another aspect of popular influence in the Roman constitution: the office of tribune of the *plebs*, which originated in early republican conflicts between patricians and plebeians and subsisted, in principle, as a safeguard of the rights and privileges of the Roman people, the *telum libertatis* (Sall. *Hist.* 3.34.12 McGushin). Each year ten tribunes were elected by the assembly of the *plebs*, and it was by way of that assembly, under the presidency of tribunes, that the bulk of middle and late republican legislation was passed, including a considerable body of legislation described as *popularis* (i.e. legislation gratifying to the people). Tribunes possessed the power to rescue citizens from any magisterial excess (*auxilium*), and Polybius adduces the tribunate as an aspect of the democratic element in Rome on account of its power to veto decrees of the senate: "if a single one of the tribunes interposes his veto, the senate is unable to pass a decree about any matter, nor can it even sit – and it is necessary to observe that tribunes are always obliged to act in accordance with the views of the people and attend to its wishes" (Polyb. 6.4–5). Tribunes could also exercise their veto at legislative assemblies, if a proposed measure was deemed harmful to the interests of the people.

In a series of important publications, Fergus Millar has defended the accuracy of Polybius' representation of the Roman constitution and has vigorously emphasized the significant role played by the people in Roman politics (articles collected in Millar 2002b: 85–182; cf. also Millar 1998). In different degrees, this claim has proved persuasive. The recurring practices of republican Rome – descending to the Forum, speechifying from the Rostra, campaigning for office for oneself or on behalf of another – all supply evidence of the need on the part of Rome's political leadership to cultivate the people, or at least some component of the people, in pursuing their legislative or electoral ends: after all, only the people could elect a magistrate or carry a law. An appreciation along these lines of the practical importance of the people complements nicely the opinion that in republican Rome popular rights (*iura*) and privileges (*commoda*), manifestations of popular freedom (*libertas populi*), constituted traditional and legitimate concerns of Rome's governing class, a condition that helps to explain why it was possible for a Roman politician to play the part of a *popularis* without descending (in the judgment of his peers) into demagoguery (Meier 1980:116–28; Brunt 1988a: 57–61; Tatum 1999: 7–11). The relationship between the prestige of the senate and the sovereignty of the people remained dynamic.

Now it has long been recognized that the people mattered on account of their sheer numbers, not least in a state that relied on civic restraint and obedience instead of a state police force as the essential means for sustaining public order (Nippel 1995). But the natural deference and economic vulnerabilities of the masses made it possible for the senatorial order and especially for the noble elite within the senate to minimize the role of the Roman people in politics by inhibiting the development of collective identities among the poor and by cultivating extensive and often hereditary individual ties, such as the patron–client relationship (MacMullen 1974: 123–7; cf. Hammer, chapter 2). The social disparity between rich and poor was not lost on the Romans: Sallust's Licinius Macer, for example, in urging the people to assert themselves in claiming their rights (in this instance, the restoration of the powers of the tribunate that had been removed by the dictator Sulla), scolds them for selling themselves cheap: "you reckon you have the fullness of liberty because your backs are not whipped and you can go where you please, all of this the gift of your rich masters" (Sall. *Hist.* 3.32.26 McGushin).

These social circumstances, it has been argued in the past, eliminated the reality of popular sovereignty, it being assumed that the men at the top, once they determined how best to preserve their own interests, simply deployed their assets (their own privileged votes in the centuriate assembly as well as the votes of their dependents) in order to select the candidate of their choice (e.g., Gelzer 1912; Münzer 1920; Syme 1939; Scullard 1973; cf. Brunt 1988a: 382–502 for criticism). But this approach is too mechanical to explain adequately the complicated realities of Roman politics, in which sound specimens of the nobility fail, sometimes to complete newcomers to the ranks of the senate (derisively dubbed *novi homines*: new men). Take the election of the new man Gaius Marius to the consulship of 107 BC – in the teeth of noble opposition. Marius, it must be said, was by no means unacceptable to the wealthy – there were many rich equestrians who supported him – but, according to Sallust, his election was secured when tribunes of the *plebs*, in frequent *contiones*, roused Rome's artisans and farmers to attend Marius in his canvass (Sall. *Iug.* 65.4–5; 73.3–7). The importance of individual appeals to the masses for their support and for their attendance during a political campaign is registered elsewhere in republican literature

(Cic. *Mur.* 44–5, 70–1; *Planc.* 21; Q. Cic. *Comm. Pet.* 35–8). The masses must have mattered.

But to whom and why? An obvious answer is that they mattered for aspirants to the senatorial order, whose honor ultimately depended on popular election. Elections in Rome are consistently represented as competitive, at every level, and it is evident from their results that, in campaigns for the quaestorship or tribunate, new men, who can hardly have commanded expansive networks of inherited dependents, were very likely to succeed (Hopkins and Burton 1983): the senate was by no means a hereditary body. On the other hand, the nobility dominated the consulship throughout the middle and late republic: it was rare for a new man to reach the top (Badian 1990). The Roman people, one must conclude, were conservative and inclined to reward inherited splendor – although not invariably: the examples of Marius and Cicero have already been adduced. And so campaigns remained essential even for the nobility – because what each candidate cared most about, naturally enough, was his own success and not the collective accomplishment of his class, which could never compensate for the pain of his rejection by the people (*dolor repulsae*). And the point must be made that individual nobles frequently lost in Roman elections, both to other nobles and (at levels beneath the consulship) to new men. The noble M. Iuventius Laterensis was defeated by the new man Cn. Plancius in the aedilician elections for 55. Q. Lutatius Catulus, the consul of 102, was defeated in the consular elections for 106, 105 (by a new man) and 104 (again by a new man). The reasons for failure are not always clear to us. Still, one example illustrates the importance of popular ingratiation. A certain P. Scipio Nasica, in campaigning for the aedileship, in shaking hands with a farmer, responded to the roughness of the man's hands by inquiring whether it was his habit to walk on his hands. This insulting witticism was soon current and the public became convinced that Scipio despised the poverty of Roman farmers. He was defeated. The lesson of this episode, according to Valerius Maximus, by whom it is related (Val. Max. 7.5.2, from a section devoted to electoral defeats), is that public offices (*honores*) do not simply lie open to the nobility, a condition that increases their prestige (*auctoritas*).

Hence the intense and often ruthless competitiveness of Roman elections. This was true even in elections conducted by the plutocratic centuriate assembly. It has recently been demonstrated that in some elections (and especially in the praetorian elections), competition was strong enough and the pool of viable candidates was deep enough that the lower classes were called on to vote, which means that, in Roman elections, the actual participation of the lower classes – as *voters* – could sometimes matter (Yakobson 1999). It is sufficient that this was only sometimes the case, because that fact alone compelled candidates to seek the (potential) votes of the masses. It is beside the point that the number of actual voters each year may regularly have been quite small, even, perhaps especially, among the lower classes (Mouritsen 2001: 32–7); because there could be no knowing in advance who would actually attend the assembly in any particular year – it was very likely the case that in different years different voters turned out (Tatum 1999: 29–30) – a diligent candidate had to solicit as many voters among all classes as he possibly could. Although the nobility dominated high office in Rome, the competition, because it was individual, entailed the energetic solicitation of the public: the electioneering advice recorded in Q. Cicero's *Commentariolum petitionis* emphasizes repeatedly the necessity of energetic deportment in securing the support of Romans at every social level. At *Comm. Pet.* 53 he describes the ideal candidate for the consulship as the man who the senate believes will be the guardian of its authority, the *equites* and prosperous classes believe will be a supporter of peace and tranquility, and the multitudes believe will not be hostile to their entitlements.

Let us turn now to legislative assemblies. There was almost no limit to the people's power to legislate (it was restrained only by the forces of tradition or religious scruple: cf. Cic. *Leg. agr.* 2.18). Although measures could be proposed only by a competent magistrate, a not unimportant limitation to the people's capacities, it nonetheless lay exclusively within the power of the assemblies to accept the proposed measure – in toto – or to reject it outright. Legislative assemblies entailed no deliberation. But debates and harangues, by magistrates and leading citizens, over the merits and faults inherent in any promulgated bill were regular – and apparently crucial – antecedents to legislative assemblies. It is in this context that the *contio* becomes a central intersection between the governing class and the population: hopeful legislators explicated and justified their propositions, while their opponents endeavored to persuade the public to reject them (Morstein-Marx 2004). It is owing to this critical dimension of the legislative process that eloquence constituted an essential virtue of the aristocracy (Liv. 30.1.5; Plin. *NH* 7.139.3; cf. Cic. *Off.* 2.31–8) and an element of the prestige by means of which a sound consul could deflate the ambitions of irresponsible and dangerous demagogues (Cic. *Mur.* 24). Not every *contio*, it is clear, was an honest attempt to influence popular sentiment: many were carefully orchestrated demonstrations (Mouritsen 2001: 38–62). Still, there could be little point in staging such pageants if it were not believed that there was something to be gained in creating the impression that a legislative proposal either was or was not popular with the crowd. Put differently, even demonstrations represented a vehicle of persuasion, by stimulating the elite's sensible concern for popular dissatisfaction and the Roman public's natural inclination toward conformity.

Two examples will illustrate the varying strains of legislative practice. Shortly after the conclusion of the Hannibalic War, the senate concluded that war with Philip V of Macedon, who in the senate's view had become intolerably aggressive in the east, was unavoidable. In this period, declarations of war remained within the power of the centuriate assembly. But the prospect of further warfare was far from attractive in the aftermath of recent exhaustions, and the people, including the wealthy classes, were stirred to resist the proposal by the exertions of a tribune of the *plebs*. When the question of the war came before the assembly, it was rejected, to the consternation of the senatorial majority. Nevertheless, the senate lacked the competence to set aside the people's decision. Instead it was decided that the consuls should put the matter before the assembly a second time. A *contio* was held at which further and forceful arguments for the necessity for war were ventilated, this time persuasively, and the people acquiesced. There was apparently no further tribunician resistance. A rather different situation occurred during Cicero's consulship, when a tribune promulgated a measure for distributing public land to impoverished citizens, a form of social legislation that had been passed by the assemblies in the past, though invariably with controversy. In this instance, the bill would be brought before the assembly of the *plebs*, which could be predicted to support the measure. In a series of speeches delivered at *contiones*, none of which speaks very highly for the level of political debate in the presence of the people, Cicero attacked this measure as disadvantageous to the masses, convincingly enough that it never became law (indeed, another tribune threatened to veto the measure). Naturally a complex variety of incentives (and disincentives) will have attached themselves to every legislative proposal. Nonetheless, the centrality of popular persuasion remains conspicuous.

Only a few instances are known in which a legislative measure was rejected by a vote of the assemblies (Flaig 1995: 80 assembles the evidence). This is probably an accident of our historical record. A single episode will make this clear: C. Papirius Carbo, when tribune of the *plebs* (probably in 130), put forward a measure that would allow tribunes to extend their tenure by reelection. We know from more than one source that the bill was opposed by Scipio Aemilianus. We also know that the proposal failed. But only one source informs us that the measure was actually voted down in the assemblies, Cicero's essay on friendship (Cic. *Amic.* 96). This is serendipity, and illustrative of the precarious nature of our evidence. Still, it is very likely the case that, rather than endure the humiliation of summoning a legislative assembly only to suffer rejection by the voters, magistrates took pains to observe the public's responses at *contiones*. A measure that was clearly unpopular could only be pressed if it had the nearly universal backing of the senatorial order (in which case it might be hoped that the collective prestige of that body might ultimately prevail, as occurred in the matter of war with Philip). But it was always necessary for magistrates to take their case, by whatever means at their disposal, to the public: in matters of legislation, the people were without question sovereign. By way of the assemblies, then, both elective and legislative, the Roman people exercised genuine political power: as Cicero puts it, in a speech delivered to the public, "your influence resides in your votes" (*Leg. agr.* 2.102).

That there were democratic elements in the Roman constitution seems undeniable. But do they suffice to make it a fair claim that Rome was a democracy? From a purely formal perspective, in Fergus Millar's view, the Roman Republic was a democracy. Furthermore, owing to the assemblies' exclusive hold on legislative power, Rome was in many respects also functionally democratic, "a direct democracy" (Millar 1998: 208–26; cf. Yakobson 1999). Similarly, on the basis of the powers of the assemblies and the role of the tribunes as guardians of the people's interests, Lintott insists that Rome was "some kind of democracy" (Lintott 1999a: 199–208). These claims cannot be adjudicated easily, and the problem is not simply a matter of semantics. Neither Millar nor Lintott is suggesting that Rome resembled democratic Athens, in which every (male) citizen was invested with political equality and enjoyed the freedom to express his views to the popular Assembly that governed the city (see Rhodes, chapter 4). Instead, each is making a claim about the theoretical and (more importantly) the practical power of the people in Roman society, thereby rejecting any approach to the Roman Republic that locates the totality of political power in the senatorial class and reduces the theoretical sovereignty of the people to "a screen and a sham" (Syme 1939: 15).

In like manner, modern students of government make their own determinations, often controversial, about the democratic qualities of ancient and modern regimes: despite its invention of *demokratia*, to introduce a common example, the institution of slavery and the exclusion of women from full citizen rights render classical Athens less than entirely democratic to twenty-first century sensibilities, and there is no shortage of contemporary debate about the quality of democracy in any number of modern states, including those that insist on exporting their own version of it. Popular power and individual rights become the real subject of inquiry, and the degree of their fulfillment becomes an important measure of the suitability of any state's designation as a democracy (e.g. Dahl 1971).

Modern students of democracy, then, tend to go beyond mere formalism (see Hammer, chapter 2). After all, the simple existence of democratic institutions, such as elections, do not in practice suffice to establish a democratic regime: there exist, for instance, numerous authoritarian states whose elections display genuine competition among candidates, but, owing to deficiencies in electoral inclusiveness or fair practices, resist characterization as democratic (L. Diamond 2002). Democratic institutions must not merely exist but they must function under conditions that sustain and even enhance the state's responsiveness to the wishes and to the rights of its citizens. In most modern discussions, these conditions include (but are hardly limited to) political equality for all citizens, universal suffrage, an unrestricted access to balloting, pluralism, and accountability on the part of the government (Dahl 1971: 1–16; L. Diamond and Morlino 2005). It is obvious that these conditions, which introduce to the assessment of democracy a set of values that in itself can entail complications in definition and evaluation, reveal what is at stake in any discussion of Roman democracy. The Roman constitution, it must be observed, did not endorse political equality for all its citizens, nor the right to vote; many citizens, a majority by the late republic, when the whole of Italy became Roman, were always unable to make their way to the city to cast their ballots; and apart from the penalties that could be imposed in the courts for violations of the law, there was very little in the way of accountability in Roman government. But the question is not whether republican Rome, either in theory or in practice, attained to contemporary standards of democracy (whatever they turn out to be), but rather, how, within the actualities of Roman society and the regular conduct of Roman political institutions, the people mattered to the actions of the governing class and to the decisions taken by the state.

The observations of Polybius and Cicero are relevant here. Polybius maintains that Rome was not an oligarchy, a common misapprehension he attributes to the many Greek states whose dealings with Rome were limited to its magistrates and to the senate (Polyb. 6.13.8–9). Cicero shared Polybius' opinion that Rome could not properly be regarded as an oligarchy (Cic. *Rep.* 1.43). Nor could Rome be deemed a democracy: Polybius, who, as a citizen of democratic Achaea, was familiar with the genuine article, never describes Rome as such, and in fact it is essential to his explication of the mixed quality of the Roman constitution that it not be simplified to the status of either an oligarchy or a democracy. For Cicero, equity (*aequitas*) was the essential element in a mixed constitution (*Rep.* 1.53), but this was wanting in a democracy, the requirement of which for equality (*aequabilitas*) was anything but equitable because it made no allowance for the varying degrees of prestige existing among the citizenry (*Rep.* 1.43). Although *res publica* entailed *res populi*, a point which Cicero conceded, there was no republic at all when everything fell into the power of the *multitudo* (Cic. *Rep.* 3.45). Rome, in Cicero's opinion, was not a democracy, nor even markedly democratic.

This was not an entirely uncontested assessment, as Cicero himself makes plain. In his dialogue *Laws*, Cicero represents his brother, Quintus, reporting only to reject the common opinion that the power of the people is so great as to be irresistible (Cic. *Leg.* 3.34). That view was no straw man, and it is an interesting complication to Quintus' position that, although he minimizes the extent of the people's power, he is also hostile to the office of tribune of the *plebs*, which, he fears, by abusing its powers, can unleash the dangerous realities of popular sovereignty (Cic. *Leg.* 3.19–26). Cicero disagrees with his brother in the matter of the tribunate, an institution which, he argues, allows humble citizens to imagine that they are the equals of the leading men in the state (*Leg.* 3.24): Quintus – and Atticus, the third participant in the dialogue – remain unconvinced. They do, however, share Cicero's opinion that, under ordinary circumstances, by which, it is meant, in the absence of a demagogic senator, the Roman people are entirely deferential to their superiors (*Leg.* 3.24). The people, Cicero maintains, rely on the expertise and the prestige of the best men, and it is this reliance that sustains the Republic (*Leg.* 2.30), a claim that acknowledges the potential power of the assemblies even as it makes the point that the Republic would be disrupted by its genuine actualization. Indeed, the masses, content simply with the right to cast ballots, allow themselves to be guided by the prestige (*auctoritas*) and the influence of the best men – to the extent that, when voting, they strive to ratify the judgments of the senatorial elite (*Leg.* 3.39). It had been possible, Cicero observes, to organize the Roman constitution in such a way that the public possessed authentic and not merely nominal freedom: instead, the people were granted liberty in such a manner that they were induced by many excellent customs to defer to the prestige of the senatorial order (*Leg.* 3.25).

This was perhaps not merely wishful thinking on the part of a conservative like Cicero. The principal interlocutor of Cicero's *On the Republic*, Scipio Aemilianus, offers justifications of democracy (*Rep.* 1.47–50) and aristocracy (*Rep.* 1.51–3) in advance of his explication of Rome's mixed constitution, which constitutes the bulk of the work. Scipio's democratic discourse includes a swipe at states whose citizens are only nominally free ("in quibus verbo sunt liberi omnes"), by which he means:

> States in which the people cast ballots, elect generals and magistrates, are canvassed by candidates for office, have legislative proposals put before them in assemblies, but in fact they simply ratify what they would have to ratify, even if they were unwilling to do so, while others seek from them things which they themselves do not possess – for the people have no share in power, in public deliberations, or in the juries that preside over the courts, all of which are granted on the basis of birth or wealth. (*Rep.* 1.47)

This assessment of the role of the people in "certain states," suspiciously similar to Cicero's representations of Rome in his *Laws*, Scipio immediately contrasts with authentic democracies like Rhodes or Athens. In doing so this text indicates that the Romans were well aware that mere formalism was less important for the realization of democracy than prevailing social conditions.

The formal and circumstantial limitations to the people's participation in government have been noted: the magistracies and the senate remained the reserves of the rich, and they were not in practice significantly accountable to the public, the centuriate assembly was plutocratic in design; it was a physical impossibility for a majority of voters to participate in the assemblies; there were no opportunities for popular deliberation or for popular initiatives, an impediment that cannot be ignored even if politicians seeking favor occasionally responded to public discontents. But the most serious obstacle to the democratization of Roman politics was the sheer narrowness of the people's aspirations. It is obvious that the exploitation of the poor is facilitated when the masses are inclined to accept their circumstances as fixed and natural (L. Diamond and Morlino 2005: xxvii–xxviii). In the matter of rights (*iura*) and entitlements (*commoda*), the Roman people can hardly be described as ambitious. In his public oratory, Cicero can claim that nothing is more popular with the masses than security, stability, and the absence of interference by others (*Leg. agr.* 2.102: *pax, tranquillitas, otium*; cf. *Leg. agr.* 2.9; 3.4). In a catalog of popular entitlements, Cicero lists influence (at elections), freedom, the right to vote, prestige, the enjoyment of the city, the delights of the forum, the games, and religious festivals (*Leg. agr.* 2.71). This list, already thin in practical advantages, cannot be greatly expanded. The urban population, for instance, relished their neighborhood associations (*collegia*): we know this because, when the senate deprived some of the people of this opportunity, a tribune achieved popularity by restoring and expanding this simple privilege (Tatum 1999: 117–19). And the most important entitlement of the late republic, unmentioned by Cicero, was the state's (relatively modest) grain subsidy (Tatum 1999: 119–25). The disproportionate gratitude inspired by this policy, and the public's anxiety to preserve it, are captured in the acid remarks to the people that Sallust attributes to the tribune Licinius Macer: "through this measure, they have appraised the value of the freedom of all of you at five bushels per man, an allowance not much greater that the rations of a prison" (Sall. *Hist.* 3.34.19 McGushin). Of course, the people may have desired a good deal more than their betters believed – but if so they were apparently unable to communicate any of it to the senatorial order or to posterity.

The relationship between the senate and the people should not be viewed simply in terms of their relative clout. The theoretical sovereignty of the people, hallowed by tradition, and their practical role in sorting successful from unsuccessful candidates at elections and mere bills from actual laws in legislative assemblies, made them the unavoidable object of a range of solicitations on the part of the senatorial order. At elections, for example, it was obligatory that a candidate canvass the public energetically, always resorting to techniques of ingratiation that were anathema to aristocratic sensibilities (e.g. Cic. *De or.* 1.112 ; cf. Tatum 2007). And while it is true that, during political campaigns, the lower orders were solicited owing to the possible usefulness of their votes, it is unmistakably clear that popularity among the masses was also an asset in winning the endorsement of prosperous voters. Attendance by great crowds was important to electoral success, not least because it conferred high repute (*opinio*) and prestige (*dignitas*) on any candidate so attended (Cic. *Mur.* 44–5, 70–1; *Planc.* 21; Q. Cic. *Comm. Pet.* 35–8). Inasmuch as public order and sustained government depended to an extraordinary degree on the respect that the city's magistrates commanded, a massive following signified popular favor and lent to the candidate who attracted it an aura of soundness: this was a man whom the people could count on (thus the popular inference) and this was a man whose capacity for commanding deference among the masses could be relied on to sustain stability (thus the elite inference). After all, the elite could not sensibly support a candidate who was incompetent in his dealings with the multitude: a consul must possess the *dignitas* requisite to foil irresponsible tribunes and to overawe popular agitations.

Deference to authority preserved public order and sheltered the advantages of the senate. It was certainly useful to that class that its customary superiority was perpetuated in the experience of Roman elections, an almost constant pageant that enacted the responsibilities and industry – and excellence – of the candidates as well as the legitimate expectations and the right to recognition – and the inferiority – of the masses. This was especially the case in elections conducted in the centuriate assembly, which exploited the participation of the poor in such a way that their actions tended to reaffirm their subordination. Year after year they helped to select their leaders (and they did in fact select their leaders) from among their superiors, showing their support for their betters through mass gestures: assembling in the atrium of a great man's house, descending with him to the forum, following him about during the day, cheering his words in *contiones*, and, *possibly*, casting one of many votes in a teeming century – all in the expectation of preserving their present condition (on the regular activities of canvassing, see Tatum 1999: 22–30; Yakobson 1999). In legislative assemblies the people enjoyed a greater opportunity to assert their political power, but only within the circumstances created by divisions within the senatorial order and never on their own initiative or in their own terms. In sum, then, the political importance of the people, although significant, was clearly constrained. If, then, we must include the Romans' political system within the set of all democracies, we may prefer the denomination "delegative democracy," in which system there is electoral competitiveness as well as civil and political freedom, all of which obtained in the Roman Republic, but very little in the way of responsiveness to the preferences of the public on the part of elected magistrates, whose authority suffers few practical limitations (O'Donnell 1994).

The sovereignty of the Roman people was entirely real, but it was, in practice, restricted by the social conditions and the aristocratic traditions of the Republic. The people always mattered, however, in theory and in the actual performance of government, and popularity remained a critical asset for ambitious politicians. The complex and constantly dynamic interconnectedness of the various constituencies of the Roman people with the highly competitive membership of the senatorial class was an exceedingly unsimple affair that resists categorization. Polybius was clearly correct to discern what everyone would concede are democratic elements in republican Rome, and Roman historians have often erred in ignoring the significance of his observations. Whether or not the democratic dimension of Roman society is its most conspicuous feature, however, introduces an altogether different claim, and it would be a mistake to overreact to the tendency of past scholarship to neglect the importance of popular sovereignty in the Roman constitution. It was no accident that the collapse of the Roman Republic was set in motion when Caesar, who as proconsul was for a decade rendered unaccountable and impervious to senatorial interference by legislation carried in the popular assemblies, induced the tribunes of the *plebs* to exercise their powers, in the teeth of senatorial hostility, in defense of his personal prestige, an aristocratic contest in which the wishes of the people counted for little or nothing.

FURTHER READING

An excellent introduction to the Roman constitution, in practical and theoretical terms, is Lintott 1999a, with ample bibliography. The essays in Brunt 1988a reveal the difficulties that ensue from attempting to understand Roman politics in excessively mechanical and top-down terms. The most robust statement for the case of democratic Rome is Millar 1998, which remains provocative in every sense of the word. Yakobson 1999 applies Millar's views to elections in the centuriate assembly, with intelligent if not uncontroversial results. In L. Taylor 1949, Wiseman 1971, and Tatum 1999 one can find sensible and readable accounts of the details of Roman canvassing: none embraces a democratic characterization of Rome yet each stresses the importance of broad popular support for political success. Mouritsen 2001 argues that, in spite of the rhetoric of Roman politics, the rich and the poor were essentially ships passing in the night, and he reminds readers of the consistently tendentious nature of public discourse about "the Roman people." A different line is taken by Morstein-Marx 2004, who, by demonstrating how crucial the *contio* remained in Roman politics, underscores the importance of the people without ignoring the restrictions imposed on them by Roman custom and by constitutional realities.

PART III

The Virtues and Vices of One-Man Rule

CHAPTER 15

The Uses and Abuses of Tyranny

Sara Forsdyke

Despite the virtual disappearance of tyranny in the major Greek city-states (*poleis*) by the end of the sixth century, representations of single rulers remained prominent in the literature of fifth and fourth century Greece. The reason for the continued presence of one man rule in the Greek imagination is that it was "good to think with" in the sense that it was a powerful, yet ambiguous, cultural symbol that could be appropriated by poets, political thinkers, and popular traditions alike to represent their ideals, desires, and anxieties about political life. This essay will examine the dynamic interaction between competing traditions about tyranny in particular ideological and historical contexts from the archaic period to the late fourth century.

Historical Background: One-Man Rule in Ancient Greece

Single rulers of various types were an important feature of early Greece. In the middle and late Bronze Age, powerful monarchs ruled over extensive territories, enriching themselves through a palace-centered economy of collection and redistribution. Though these kingdoms were successively destroyed or collapsed and finally disappeared ca. 1200 BCE, their material remains survived and served as a stimulus for "memories" and practices that evoked the great era of kingship for later generations of Greeks. In addition to the cults established at remains of Bronze Age structures, oral poetry and prose traditions – surviving for us in the form of the Homeric epics, Greek tragedy, and works of such authors as Herodotus and Thucydides – recalled the kings of Bronze Age Greece. In these works, we hear of mythic kings such as Agamemnon, Nestor, and King Minos of Crete. As we shall see, the representation of these kings in later literature reveals more about conceptions of one-man rule in later times than the realities of Bronze Age monarchies. Nevertheless, the continued

A Companion to Greek and Roman Political Thought, First Edition. Edited by Ryan K. Balot.
© 2013 Blackwell Publishing Ltd. Published 2013 by Blackwell Publishing Ltd.

interest in Bronze Age kingship in later texts attests to the power of the concept of a single absolute ruler in collective thinking about modes of political organization.

After the collapse of the Bronze Age kingdoms, the new leaders who emerged were not so much hereditary kings as what anthropologists call "big men" or "chiefs." Unlike their Bronze Age predecessors, these *basileis* ("kings") not only had to continually justify their position through displays of military and deliberative prowess, but were constrained by the relatively small gap between themselves, a group of fellow elites, and the wider community. By the mid-seventh century, a power-sharing agreement between the elites at the top of the political hierarchy had evolved. As the earliest written laws attest, it was at this time that formal public offices and rules regulating regular rotation of power emerged in ancient Greece. Only a small number of wealthy men were eligible for public office. Nevertheless, the appearance of formal institutions marks the emergence of a civic order that was to become the hallmark of the ancient Greek city-states. It was against this background that the earliest "tyrants" of Greece first arose.

The non-Greek word *tyrannos* was adopted into the Greek language from the Near East probably in the seventh century. The term designated a single all-powerful ruler, and was sometimes used interchangeably with Greek words for single rulers, e.g., *mounarchos, basileis*. Tyrants usually numbered themselves among the small group of elites who were eligible for public office, but, through force or persuasion, they established preeminent power for themselves (G. Anderson 2005). Often archaic tyrants performed valuable services for their communities; they built temples, improved roads and harbors, and enhanced the civic festivals that served as a focus for collective identity and cohesion. Furthermore, by relying more directly on the support of the wider community than on their fellow elites, archaic tyrants set the stage for more active involvement of the masses in politics. In Athens, this latter development culminated in the emergence of the first democracy in 508/7 BCE (Forsdyke 2005a: 101–43; cf. Lavelle 2005). In this way, the archaic tyrants, paradoxically, were the cause of their own decline.

Despite the decline of tyranny and the emergence of democracy in Greece at the end of the sixth century BCE, many city-states remained oligarchic throughout the classical period. Besides the idiosyncratic Sparta (see below), major Greek city-states, such as Corinth, Megara, and Thebes, rejected both tyranny and democracy in favor of moderate oligarchy. Tyranny, moreover, did not disappear altogether. In Sicyon, for example, one Euphron ruled briefly as tyrant between 368 and 366 (Xen. *Hell.* 7.1.44–6 and 7.3 with S. Lewis 2004), and in Corinth, the cavalry commander Timophanes made himself tyrant even more briefly in 365 (Plut. *Tim.* 4–5; Diod. Sic. 16.65.3–9 with Riess 2006). In addition, one-man rule of various types remained prominent on the margins of mainland Greece (Jason of Pherae, the kings of Thessaly and Macedonia), in Sicily (Gelon, Hieron, Dionysios I and II of Syracuse) and in the Near East (the Achaemenids of Persia). In the fourth century, the Macedonian kings extended their power to include mainland Greece, thereby effectively ending the era of self-governing Greek city-states. Henceforth, large territorial kingdoms governed by monarchs of Macedonian descent were the dominant form of rule in the Greek world.

The Ideological Construction of Tyranny in the Archaic Period

While the Homeric epics are clearly concerned with the problem of political authority, their composition probably predates the introduction of the word *tyrannos* into the Greek language (Janko 1982a; contra: Nagy 1996). Nevertheless, these epics present a wide array of single rulers (*anakes* or *basileis*) and illustrate both ideological justifications of early Greek kingship and the tensions that arose from this form of rule. As many have noted, the Homeric epics seem to present the dominant ideology of the ruling elites, but hint at the competing discourses of other groups (I. Morris 1986). The epics therefore provide a window on competing claims about the best form of rule in eighth and early seventh century Greece.

The clearest expression of the justification of one-man rule in the Homeric epics is put in the mouth of a Trojan leader, Sarpedon, though the claims he makes are representative of arguments made by Greek leaders in the poems.

> Glaucus, why are we two honored most of all in Lycia with seats of honor, cuts of meat and full cups? And all look upon us as gods, and we possess a great estate, rich in orchards and wheat-bearing land, on the banks of the river Xanthus. It is necessary that we now make our stand in the front and take up our share of raging battle so that some strong-armed Lycian might say "Not without fame do our kings rule Lycia and eat fat sheep and drink choice sweet wine. For indeed their strength is superior, since they fight among the first men of Lycia." (Hom. *Il.* 12.310–21)

In other words, the kings of early Greece abided by a social contract of sorts, whereby the kings provided leadership, particularly in war, and were rewarded in turn with various honors and privileges by the community (chiefly political power and material wealth). Indeed, it is precisely Agamemnon's failure to live up to his side of the social contract that sets off the plot of the *Iliad*. In the quarrel between Achilles and Agamemnon over the correct distribution of honor, we see the tensions that could arise when there was an imbalance between services rendered and rewards demanded by the rulers in early Greece. Achilles complains bitterly about Agamemnon's cowardice and greed:

> You wine-sack, with the eyes of a dog and heart of fawn,
> Not once have you undertaken to arm for war with the people
> Or go out on an ambush with the best of the Achaeans.
> For you know that you would die. Indeed, it is much easier
> to take away the gifts of anyone who speaks against you.
> People-devouring king, since you rule non-entities.
> If not, you would now have committed your last outrage. (*Il.* 1.225–32)

Since Achilles' complaints about Agamemnon are echoed shortly afterwards by a character on the lower rungs of the social hierarchy – an ordinary soldier named Thersites – the poem hints that these criticisms of one-man rule could arise not only from elite rivals of the king, but also from the wider community. Nevertheless, the poem quickly masks this brief glimpse of tensions over elite rule by representing the Greek army as unmoved by Thersites' expression of outrage. Indeed, the soldiers laugh heartily when Odysseus heaps verbal abuse on Thersites and beats him over the head. Achilles' complaints are taken more seriously, however, and serve not so much to question the propriety of one-man rule as to emphasize to rapacious elites that they must provide services to the community and distribute rewards fairly if they expect their supremacy to endure. The *Odyssey* echoes this conception of politics through the representation of Odysseus as ideal king who treats his people benevolently in contrast to the suitors whose greed and indolence place great strains on the community.

The Homeric epics, therefore, establish the ideological foundations of elite rule and articulate some tensions regarding elite claims to power. These tensions are echoed in non-epic archaic poetry. The lyric and elegiac poetry of Alcaeus, Theognis, and Solon, in particular, expresses the difference between good and bad forms of rule in terms of the contrast between rulers who protect and serve the community and those who destroy it in their relentless quest for power and wealth. These poets, however, were writing during the late seventh and sixth centuries when elite power was being institutionalized through the creation of formal public offices and written laws. As we have seen, these early formal institutions sought not only to reinforce elite claims, but more importantly to place restraints on the ability of individual elites to seize absolute power (Osborne 1996: 186–97). The poetry of this era can be viewed as the ideological equivalent of the institutionalization and formal regulation of power through written laws. By representing the consequences of unrestrained pursuit of power and wealth, these poets sought to buttress the formal institutions of the state through discursive means. It was at this time that the word *tyrannos* appeared in Greek poetic traditions as the favored term for the unprincipled quest of absolute power. Tyranny stood as the antithesis of the good governance (*eunomia*) of self-restrained elites serving in the formal public institutions of the state (magistracies, council). The fact that this poetry was performed by and for elites explains why its ideological constructions took this particular form.

For example, the poetry preserved under the name of Theognis of Megara gives a dire illustration of the consequences of lack of restraint among the elite for the civic order.

> Cyrnus, this city is pregnant, and I fear that it will give birth to a man who will be a corrector of our misbehavior.
> The citizens are still prudent, but the leaders are inclined to fall into wickedness.
> Good men have never destroyed the city, Cyrnus,
> But whenever it pleases evil men to commit outrages
> They destroy the people and give justice to unjust men
> For the sake of private gain and power.
> Don't expect that city to remain peaceful for long
> Not even if now it is at peace,
> When these things are dear to evil men – gain that comes with public misfortune.

From this, comes civil discord, internecine strife
And monarchs. Let these things never please this city. (39–52)

The poet suggests that if elite leaders do not restrain their greed for wealth and power, they will destroy the people, generate civil conflict, and a single-ruler will emerge to punish their outrages. In effect, Theognis warns the elite to behave justly and responsibly toward the rest of the community; if not, an absolute ruler (*mounarchos*) will overturn the civic order. Theognis' elitist perspective is unabashedly evident: although single rulers may correct abuses by the elite against the community, they are a threat to the (elite-dominated) institutions of the state and therefore must be avoided.

The Athenian lawgiver Solon paints a similar picture of the consequences of misrule by the elite, warning that civil conflict and single rulers (*mounarchoi*) will result (Solon frr. 4, 9 West). Since Solon was appointed as mediator to resolve conflict in Athens ca. 594, however, his poetry functioned not simply as a didactic tool guiding elite behavior in the abstract, but more immediately to place his reforms in relation to past discourses on good and bad forms of rule. Consequently, he explains his moderate position – providing basic protections of life and property to the ordinary citizens, while preserving the wealth and power of the elite – by echoing the ideology of elite rule that was articulated in the Homeric epics. Essential to this ideology, as we have seen, is the idea that good leadership entails protecting the community, not destroying it through the selfish pursuit of wealth and power. Unlike in Homeric poetry, however, where good rulers could be monarchs, for Solon and other sixth century poets, all the evils of irresponsible rule were encapsulated in the concept of a particular form of absolute rule, namely, tyranny. "If I spared my country, and I did not adopt a tyranny and unrestrained violence, thereby staining and destroying my reputation, I am not ashamed. For in this way I believe I will win over all men" (Solon fr. 32 West). Drawing on a rhetorical strategy that goes back to the seventh century Parian poet Archilochus, moreover, Solon invokes the natural human desire for wealth and power through the imaginary figure of an elite aspirant to tyrannical power.[1] "But if I had so wished and had ruled, taking unlimited wealth and ruling as tyrant over Athens even one day, I would later have been flayed like a wine-skin and my family would have been destroyed" (Solon fr. 33 West). Whereas Archilochus rejected tyrannical wealth in favor of a generalized moral goal of moderation (Archil. fr. 19 West), Solon suggests more pragmatically that the "unlimited wealth" of tyrants is short-lived and usually results in retribution from the community.

Solon's attempt to deter elites from tyrannical ambitions by invoking a frightening image of potential retribution, however, was unsuccessful. Following Solon's reforms, rival elites fought for exclusive power until one among them – Peisistratus – established a lengthy period of absolute rule for himself and his sons. Poetic injunctions similarly failed to restrain elites in other city-states, as the appearance of tyrannies in Corinth, Megara, Mytilene, Samos, Sicyon, and Argos, among other places, attest. Sometimes we hear from the losers in this struggle for dominance. In Mytilene, the poet Alcaeus laments the rise of his fellow elite, Pittacus, who became sole-ruler of

Mytilene for ten years in the late seventh century. Alcaeus addresses Pittacus abusively calling him pot-bellied and base-born (frr. 129, 348 Lobel-Page). Later sources, drawing on Alcaeus' own poems, claim that Pittacus was an elected leader and remember him as a wise lawgiver. Alceaus, however, grounds his abuse in terms of the familiar dichotomy between a single-ruler who "devours his people" and a group of elite leaders who protect the people and rule through the established institutions of the state (frr. 129, 130 Lobel-Page).

In sum, against the historical background of various forms of one-man and oligarchic rule in archaic Greece, we see discourses about good forms of rule develop from a simple contrast between good and bad forms of one-man rule to the conception of all forms of one-man rule as pernicious. This discourse developed solely within elite circles in the archaic period. With the rise of democracy in the late sixth century, however, the negative image of the absolute ruler was appropriated and embellished in polis-wide traditions as the inverse of democracy. In this way, as in many others, democratic ideology appropriated preexisting elite discourses and adapted them to its own ends (Ober 1989; Forsdyke 1999).

Fifth Century Uses of the Concept of Tyranny

It is useful to break down the classical period into two subperiods since, as we shall see, historical events at the end of the fifth and beginning of the fourth centuries ruptured certain ideological structures. In the first period, from the establishment of democracy in Athens in 508/7 BCE to the end of the fifth century, democracy proved to be an effective and stable form of rule. Athens, in particular, grew in prominence during this period. Athens began as a relatively insignificant state and became the leader of an empire whose power was rivaled only by Sparta and its alliance of Peloponnesian states. As a result, Athenian democrats created the dominant ideological structures of the time. As we shall see, the concept of tyranny played a central role in democratic discourse, and was also a key term in the critical responses of elites.

The prominence of tyranny in democratic discourse is surprising since tyrants had largely disappeared from the mainland Greek world. The main alternative to democracy in classical Greece was oligarchy. Three factors explain the continued importance of tyranny in the ideology of democrats and oligarchs. Foremost among these is the legacy of elite discourses of the archaic period. As we saw, tyranny was represented as the opposite of good government (i.e. the sharing of political power among elites serving in formal public offices). This conceptual scheme continued to be useful to oligarchs, who still needed to buttress their rule ideologically against the threat of a charismatic leader who might become all-powerful by winning the support of the masses. Even more important however, was the utility and adaptability of the good-government versus tyranny scheme for democratic purposes. For example, democrats expanded the meaning of good government (*eunomia*) to include the orderly sharing and rotation of power among all citizens, not just among the elite. The terms *isonomia* (equality before the law), *isēgoria* (equal right to speak publicly), and *isokratia* (equal power) that – along with *eunomia* – had probably served as watch-words for institutionalized elite rule in the archaic period, were now recast by democrats to embody the principle of political equality for all citizens (cf. *Carmina convivialia* 893, 896 (Page) and Raaflaub 2004b). Tyranny stood as the antithesis of these values, and indeed it was often through the (sometimes graphic) representation of the negative features of one-man rule that the positive features of democracy were articulated (Dewald 2003; Raaflaub 2003b; Forsdyke 2001; Pelling 2002; cf. Wohl 2002; Kallet 2003).

The utility of the image of tyranny to democrats and oligarchs alike demonstrates a second factor behind the continued prominence of tyranny in Greek political thought. Tyranny, like all effective political symbols, was a condensed, multivocal and ambiguous term that could serve as a vivid negative example against which the positive features of both oligarchic and democracy could be articulated. Tyranny, in other words, was something that both oligarchs and democrats could agree upon, though for different reasons.

As I noted at the beginning of this essay, historical tyrants played a key role in developing the civic unity and strength of the polis. Nevertheless, elites had always presented tyranny as a threat to the wider community and not just to their own claims to power. Democrats in turn adopted and further embellished the image of the tyrant as destructive to his people. A favorite image was the portrait of the tyrant confiscating property and exiling and killing citizens indiscriminately in order to preserve his own power. In one such rendition, the tyrant Periander of Corinth consults his fellow tyrant Thrasybulus of Miletus on how best to secure his power. Instead of responding directly, Thrasybulus takes Periander's messenger out into a field and begins to chop off the ears of grain that stick out above the rest (Hdt. 5.92). Periander understands Thrasybulus to be advising him to kill anyone who sticks out, and therefore undertakes to banish and kill the Corinthian citizenry indiscriminately. Indeed, the rule of Periander and his father the tyrant Cypselus was remembered in democratic traditions according to a stereotypical triad of abuses: "[Cypselus] banished many Corinthians, and he confiscated the property of many others. But he murdered many more by far" (Hdt. 5.92e.2, cf. 5.92h.1 with Forsdyke 1999).[2]

The idea of one-man rule as destructive to the lives and livelihood of its people is represented perhaps most graphically in Greek literature through the portrait of the Persian kings (Dewald 2003; Forsdyke 2001). Indeed, after the Greek victories over the Persians in 490 and 480/79, the Persian kings served as the exemplars par excellence of the evils of one-man rule. The conflict against Persian monarchies was therefore a third, and perhaps most important, factor determining the prominence of one-man rule in Greek political thought. In Aeschylus' *Persians* and in Herodotus' *Histories* the dramatic representation of the conflict between Greeks and Persians is cast as a confrontation of moral and most particularly, political values. The hoards of barbarian troops are driven into battle with a whip like slaves; they fight only because they fear punishment; and they die in droves. By contrast, the courageous and orderly regiments of Greeks fight heroically to preserve their freedom and they win a decisive victory despite their inferior numbers. While this ideological structure was flexible enough to be applicable to all Greeks who fought against the Persians (both democratic and oligarchic), it was also explicitly applied by the Athenians to reinforce the values of democracy (Forsdyke 2001, 2002, 2006).[3] The Athenians believed that democratic government produced a spirited and strong citizen body whereas single-rulers made their subjects submissive and weak (Aesch. *Pers.* 188–96; Hdt. 5.91.1–2). Herodotus seems to reflect this aspect of official Athenian polis ideology when he writes (of an earlier victory against Athens' neighbors):

> It is clear that democracy [*isēgoria*] is an excellent thing, not just in one aspect but in every way. For the Athenians, when ruled by tyrants, were no better than any of their neighbors in war, but when they had gotten rid of the tyrants, they became first by far. This shows, therefore, that when they were held down, they were cowardly, on the grounds that they were working for a master, but when they had been liberated, each man was eager to work for himself. (5.78)

One of the most striking examples of the focus on one-man rule as the antithesis of democracy in fifth century Greek thought is the celebration in democratic ideology of a pair of elite lovers for their attempt to kill the tyrant Hippias in 514 BCE (Boedeker and Raaflaub 1998; Monoson 2000: 21–50; Ober 2003; Neer 2002: 168–81; Osborne 2006). These men were honored as founders of democracy, despite the fact that their act did not end the tyranny and was motivated by their anger over the unwanted amorous attentions of the younger brother of the tyrant. In a striking case of "willing collective amnesia" the Athenians erected statues of these men in the central public space (*agora*) and granted rewards to their descendants even through-out the fourth century.[4] The importance of the tyrannicides in Athenian democratic discourse is one further example of the ways that the democracy used tyranny as a bogeyman against whom the Athenians were continually summoned to rise up in defense of their political system(Ober 2003). Another aspect of this same phenom-enon was the promulgation and publication of laws declaring the tyrannicide exempt from prosecution (Arist. *Ath. Pol.* 16.10; *SEG* 12.87 with Ober 2003).

Although Athenian sources focus more frequently on the evils of tyranny as a way of signaling indirectly the strengths of democracy, occasionally we get explicit con-trast of the defining features of each regime (Raaflaub 1989a). For example, in Euripides' *Suppliants*, a messenger arriving at Athens from Thebes asks to speak to the tyrant of the land and is told, "You began your speech incorrectly by seeking a tyrant here, for our city is not ruled by one man, but is a free city. The people rule through the annual rotation of public offices and they do not give a greater share to wealth, but even a poor man has an equal share" (Eur. *Supp.* 403–8).[5] In a particu-larly unique passage in Herodotus' *Histories*, a relatively systematic discussion of the strengths and weaknesses of each type of regime is provided. While this "constitu-tional debate" is set in Persia, it clearly derives from Greek political thought (Pelling 2002). In accord with the patterns we have noted already, moreover, the main emphasis is on the contrast between tyranny and democracy (oligarchy gets less attention). Even more strikingly, the speech in favor of democracy focuses on the evils of tyranny and has relatively little to say about the positive features of democracy. After expanding at length on the tyrant's power "to do whatever he likes" (*poieein ta bouletai*) without being held to account (*aneuthunos*), the advocate of democracy says: "First, the rule of the masses has the most beautiful name of all – political equality [*isonomia*] – and second it does none of the things that the monarch [*mounarchos*] does. Political offices are determined by lot, officials are held to account, and all public affairs are decided collectively" (3.80.6).[6]

So far I have focused on the use of tyranny to articulate democratic values. Oligarchs, however, found tyranny a powerful concept for *criticizing* democracy. For oligarchs, the lack of accountability and unrestrained violence toward citizens that was conventionally associated with autocratic rule were the defining flaws of late fifth century democratic rule. The equation between tyranny and democracy in elite discourse took two forms.[7] First, Athens' increasing control over other Greek states over the course of the fifth century meant that it exercised power in ways that could be interpreted as tyrannical (Connor 1977; Raaflaub 1979). Not only did the Athenians exact tribute from other Greeks in ways that resembled the Persian king's control of his Asiatic subjects, but they responded forcefully and sometimes brutally to any threats to their power. As Pericles, a leading politician of this period, is made to say in Thucydides' *History*: "You already hold your power like a tyranny: it was unjust to take it in the first place, but it is dangerous to let it go" (2.63.2).[8] An anonymous critic of the democracy, known as the Old Oligarch, expands on the equation between tyranny and the Athenian empire by applying the conventional triad of abuses associated with tyranny (see Hdt. 5.92e.2 above) to Athenian democracy's behavior as imperial power: "[In order to preserve their power], the Athenians disenfranchise the good men [in subject Greek cities], and exile them and kill them; by contrast, they empower base men" (1.14).[9]

The second way in which critics equated democracy with tyranny was to suggest that the democracy treated elite citizens in ways that resembled the tyrant's mistreatment of his subjects (Kallet 2003; Raaflaub 2003b; Ober 2003; Forsdyke 2005a: 267–77). This critique was based on three factors – the financial "exploitation" of elites through the liturgy system, the scapegoating of elite leadership for decisions made collectively, and ostracism. Since many public activities (e.g., festivals, naval warfare) were organized and financed by the wealthiest citizens, elites effectively subsidized the poor and consequently felt unduly burdened (Christ 2006: 143–204). As the disgruntled Old Oligarch put it: "The people think it right that they earn money by singing, running, dancing, and sailing in the ships, so that they themselves have money and the rich become poorer" (1.13). This same writer touches on an even more keenly felt criticism when he adds: "And in the courts, the people concern themselves less with justice, than what is advantageous for them" (1.13). The idea that the people do what is in the best interest of preserving the democracy, rather than what is just, is the animating idea behind this short treatise, and recalls the traditional image of the tyrant who is willing to do whatever it takes to secure his power (Hdt. 5.92z.2).

Perhaps the most powerful representation of the democracy as tyrannical is Thucydides' account of the downfall of Alcibiades. Thucydides reports that, despite Alcibiades' brilliant leadership of the war against the Spartans, the Athenians grew alarmed by his flamboyant private lifestyle, and suspected him of tyrannical ambitions

(6.15). Fearful for their democracy after a series of bizarre incidents involving elite social groups, the Athenians recalled Alcibiades from his command of the newly launched campaign in Sicily in order that he stand trial in Athens (6.53). Thucydides represents the Athenians as cracking down harshly on those whom it suspected (on the flimsiest of evidence) of plotting against the democracy (6.53–61). Both in its language and themes – not to mention his digression in the same passage on the Peisistratid tyranny – Thucydides evokes the traditional image of the tyrant in his portrait of the democracy's behavior towards one of its "best" citizens (Forsdyke 2005a: 267–70). Just as Thrasybulus advised his fellow tyrant to cut down anyone who stood out (Hdt. 5.92 above; cf. Plato *Resp.* 567c5–7), so the Athenian democracy got rid of its "best" citizens in order to preserve its own power.

Xenophon paints a similar portrait of the Athenian people as unrelentingly harsh and willing to subvert justice in order to selfishly pursue their own interests. In his account of the trial of the generals who commanded the Athenian fleet at Arginusae in 406, Xenophon depicts the Athenian assembly as outraged when a speaker suggested that they follow the laws and grant the generals individual trials: "The masses shouted out that it was monstrous if someone prevented the people from doing whatever they wanted." In its use of the catch-phrase "to do whatever one wants," Xenophon recalls the traditional portrait of the tyrant who can do whatever he wants without being held to account (Hdt 3.80.3, see above). Plato echoes Xenophon's application of tyrannical lack of restraint to democracy in his more systematic critique in the *Republic* (557b5; Forsdyke 2005b; Saxonhouse, this volume, chapter 23; and below).

The institution of ostracism was perhaps the most potent symbol of the tyrannical tendencies of the democracy according to elite critics. This institution allowed the Athenians to expel a single individual once a year by collective vote. Although the Athenians used this power moderately and limited the term of exile to ten years, elites (who were the primary victims of the procedure) considered ostracism the crowning injustice of democratic rule. Aristotle reflects elite views when he equates ostracism with the traditional image of the tyrant removing his political opponents. After retelling the story of Thrasybulus and Periander, Aristotle observes "ostracism has the same effect: to cut down the outstanding men, and to exile them" (*Pol.* 1284a36–8 with Forsdyke 1999 and 2005a: 274–7).

So far we have seen how elites criticized democracy by drawing on traditional portraits of the evils of one-man rule. But critics of democracy did not simply attack the prevailing political system. Rather, they argued for alternative political systems that sometimes entailed one man rule. We can catch a glimpse of these positive constructions of single rulers in the arguments made by the advocate for monarchy in Herodotus' constitutional debate: "Nothing would appear to be better than [the rule] of the best man. For by using intelligence of such a sort, he would govern the masses blamelessly, and he would guard plans against the enemy best" (3.82.2). Thucydides develops this theory of good monarchy further in his portrait of Pericles. In Thucydides' judgment, Pericles had the moral authority to guide the masses into making the right decisions. As a consequence, Pericles became more of an absolute ruler than merely a leader in a democracy: "Because he was powerful both in his reputation and in his intelligence, and, because he was manifestly incorruptible, he restrained the masses without compulsion. He was not led by the masses, but rather he himself was the leader ... And what was in name a democracy, became in fact the rule of the foremost man" (2.65). Thucydides drew a strong connection between the moral qualities of Pericles and his ability to check what he perceived to be the unethical tendencies and thoughtless impulses of the masses, namely their propensity to swell up with overweening arrogance in good times and to fall into despondency and cowardice in bad times.

The monarchist solution, then, avoided the pitfalls of tyranny by suggesting that single leaders must meet the highest ethical standards, since it is only then that they can avoid becoming tyrants on the one hand, or pandering to the basest desires of the people and becoming demagogues on the other hand.[10] The dangers of the latter scenario were illustrated for Thucydides and other critics by the fate of Athens following Pericles' death. According to Thucydides, rival politicians looking to their narrow self-interest, fed the base desires of the people and ruined the city (2.65; Ar. *Knights*). On the other hand, the short-lived oligarchies of the late fifth century (411/10 and particularly 404/3) showed that restricting power to the "better" classes did not guarantee ethical and effective rule. Indeed, the oligarchs of 404/3 became known as the Thirty Tyrants because of the brutal nature of their regime. Their example invalidated any simple equation between wealth, social standing, and good government. One solution to this impasse, as we shall see, was to focus on the moral education of the rulers.

Tyranny in the Fourth Century

In the fourth century, critics of democracy were compelled to develop new models of oligarchic and monarchic rule that avoided the celebrated abuses of the tyrant who could "do whatever he likes." They did this mainly by imagining a new type of ruler who – in order to ensure that he ruled in the interests of the people – had undergone intensive training in the political virtues of intelligence, wisdom, and self-restraint. The life of single rulers was no longer to be imagined as "like the gods" insofar as they had unlimited wealth and power. Rather they were to be disciplined and self-denying, so that not only did they avoid becoming corrupted by power, but their virtue would be the guiding principle of the entire state. As Isocrates put it to the Cyprian monarch Nicocles, "Do not think it right that others live in an orderly fashion, while kings may live licentiously. Rather, let your self-control stand as an example to the rest, knowing that the ethos of the whole city-state is derived from the rulers" (2.31).

Fourth century advocates of monarchy used various means to articulate this new conception of political leadership. Some composed admiring portraits of monarchs based on a blend of actual and wished-for virtues. So Xenophon wrote a biography praising King Agesilaus of Sparta, and a longer fictional account of the virtues of King Cyrus of Persia. Others sought to exhort existing monarchs to virtuous behavior through treatises and dialogues – and occasionally direct tutorials – on good leader-ship. Plato tried unsuccessfully to educate the tyrants of Syracuse and Isocrates addressed several treatises to the kings of Cyprus. In one treatise, for example, Isocrates undertook to teach the young Cypriot king Nicocles "how he might manage his polis and his kingdom best" (*To Nicocles* 2.2). In contrast to the trad-itional portrait of the tyrant who is advised to "remove" anyone who attempts to rival him (cf. Hdt. 5.92 above), Isocrates advises Nicocles to cultivate his virtue, intelli-gence and wisdom (*To Nicocles* 2.8, 11–14). For Isocrates, the benefits of the virtuous rule of a single ruler are greater security for the monarch and milder government for the people (2.8). These benefits accrue because wise rule entails ruling in the interests of the masses, ensuring both that the best men are honored, and that the rest suffer no injustices (2.15). In these latter aspects, Isocrates' ideal monarchy somewhat resembles the moderate democracy that he associated with Solon (*Panath.* 138). Indeed, Isocrates places more emphasis on the character of the rulers than on the type of regime as a determinant of good government. If the ruler(s) in a democracy, oligarchy, or monarchy rule in the common interest, then they will govern well; if they rule in the their own interests or through greed, then they will rule badly (*Panath.* 132–3).

In *To Nicocles*, Isocrates argued that it is actually in the interest of the ruler to govern in the interest of the masses, since in this way he will be admired and his regime will endure. Xenophon developed another tack in his curious dialogue *Hiero*. In this imaginary dialogue between the tyrant Hiero of Syracuse and the poet Simonides, Xenophon represents tyranny as undesirable insofar as the tyrant lives in constant fear of his life, cannot enjoy the goods at hand, and cannot trust that anyone truly honors or loves him. After Hiero's long exegesis of the miseries of the tyrannical life, Simonides provides a much shorter recipe for ruling and winning the affection of his subjects. By delegating the less pleasant tasks of governing – like overseeing punishments – to his subordinates, and by focusing his own energies on public works and the distribution of honors to citizens, the tyrant can become both a strong ruler and well liked.

In the *Republic*, Plato takes a much more radical step in making the life of his ideal rulers different from conventional conceptions of leadership by denying them any private property or family life. Like Xenophon and Isocrates, Plato focuses on the moral education of the rulers, but he formalizes the means to this education and explains how it can be effectively reproduced over time. Plato draws a sharp contrast between the politicians of his own day, and the rulers of his ideal state, "Beautiful-city" (*Callipolis*). Current politicians are mere rhetoricians who have no real knowl-edge, but rather cultivate the ability to persuade the masses by pandering to its base desires. Contrary to the popular perception that such individuals enjoy power similar to a tyrant, and therefore are to be envied, Plato suggests that the power to do whatever one likes (including wrongdoing) does not make one happy (*Grg.* 466c–475e). On the contrary, the happiness of both individuals and the state depends on their moral goodness. Moral goodness in the state can only be achieved, moreover, by making philosophers rulers, since only philosophic men (and women!) have been trained from youth in knowledge of The Good. This is not the place to describe the metaphysical basis of Plato's conception of The Good, but suffice it to say that Plato reimagines political leadership in the form a single (*Statesman*) or small number (*Republic*) of philosophical individuals who constantly keep in mind the underlying moral order of the universe and mold both their own souls and the larger community according to this principle (*Republic*).[11]

In his final work, *Laws*, Plato modifies his idealism by acknowledging that even such rulers might fall prey to the corruption that results from absolute power (cf. Bobonich 2002; Laks 2000; Hitz, this volume, chapter 24). In place of the ideal monarch or aristocracy of his earlier works, therefore, Plato advocates a mixed constitution similar to that of the Spartans and Romans (Polyb. 6.10; Fink 1962; von Fritz 1975). In this solution, checks are placed on power by balancing different bodies of the state against one another. Sparta not only had two kings (cf. the two Roman consuls) but power was distributed between these, the Gerousia (cf. the Roman senate) and the assembly of the Spartans (cf. Roman popular assemblies). In addition, the Ephors oversaw the kings and were empowered to depose them if they failed to rule according to the laws. It was this solution of checks and balances that most attracted early modern political thinkers such as Machiavelli, and, more significantly, the American Founding Fathers (cf. Pocock 1975; Sellers 1994; Roberts 1994; and below).

In line with the focus on the moral education of leaders, fourth century political theorists developed a more complex typology of states than had previously existed. Fifth century theorists had conceptualized the options for constitutions as threefold: rule of one man (monarchy, kingship, tyranny); rule of a few men (aristocracy, oligarchy), and rule of the masses (*isonomia, isokratia, isēgoria*, democracy). In the fourth century, this tripartite scheme was further subdivided in a systematic way according to the character of the regime, among other criteria. The rule of one man was subdivided into kingship, if the ruler governs in the interest of his subjects, or tyranny, if the ruler governs in his own interest. The regimes were correspondingly divided into "correct" and "deviant" forms, with kingship, aristocracy, and constitutional government falling into the former category, while tyranny, oligarchy, and democracy fell into the latter. "Tyranny is one-man rule in the interest of the monarch, and oligarchy is [rule of the few] in the interest of the wealthy, and democracy is [rule of the many] in the interest of the poor. None of these [deviant] forms rules in the common interest" (Arist. *Pol.* 1279b7–10).

It was in the context of Plato's earlier typology of regimes in the *Republic* that Plato developed the most searing portrait of what he viewed as the most defective form of rule, namely tyranny. While Herodotus depicted the tyrant as transgressor of norms without accountability (3.80), Plato focuses on the soul of the tyrant. Plato identifies four types of deviant regimes and identifies them with the souls of four types of individuals. The unifying feature of these deviant regimes and individuals is that all are ruled by desire, not reason (Schofield 2006). The timocratic man desires honor and focuses his efforts on this to the exclusion of all else (*Resp.* 547). The oligarchic man sets his sights on wealth and neglects education and virtue (550–4). The democratic man strives after freedom and consequently abandons all distinction between good and bad desires: "He doesn't deprive any desire of its rights and treats them all equally" (561b5). From the democratic man emerges the tyrannical man who is completely consumed by uncontrollable desires: "Lust, the tyrant within, takes over the soul completely" as "many terrible desires grow and take root day and night" (573d). With this move, Plato is able to equate absolute freedom to do what one likes with absolute slavery to one's desires. Thus paradoxically, the tyrant who is free to do what he likes is the most enslaved of all (577). In this way, Plato, like Xenophon in the *Hiero*, argues that the tyrant is the most miserable of all human characters since he is "driven mad by desires and lusts" and lives as if imprisoned in the jail of his own desires (578–9). Thus, contrary to popular wisdom, Plato argues, the tyrant is the least happy of all individuals (cf. *Grg.* 490–9). By contrast, the king, who is ruled by knowledge and reason, is the most happy (587b8). With this, Plato returns full circle to one of the main themes of the *Republic*, namely that the just man is happier than the unjust (588a7).

In his late dialogue, the *Statesman*, Plato dismisses the classification of constitutions according to standard criteria, and suggests that only those rulers who are educated in the science of rulership (whether they be one, two or more men) are correct and true forms of constitution (*Plt.* 291c–293e). Similarly, Aristotle was willing to entertain the idea that the rule of a single individual, if he were of preeminent virtue and political skill, might be the best form of government (*Pol.* 1284a4–b35). It is even possible that Aristotle viewed Alexander of Macedon as a potential candidate for the position of king over all Greece (Ober 1998: 342–7). Isocrates had earlier exhorted Alexander's father Philip to take up the position of panhellenic leader. For Isocrates, however, Philip's qualifications were not so much his virtue and political skill, as his military leadership. By directing Greek energies toward external foes, Isocrates believed, Philip might resolve the conflicts that were currently consuming the Greek city-states.

So far I have focused on the ways that critics of popular rule responded to the new circumstances of the fourth century by adapting and reformulating earlier conceptions of one-man rule. For these critics, the education in political virtue of a new breed of leaders was the key to avoiding the well-known flaws of oligarchic and monarchic rule. This response must be read against the background of a dominant democratic ideology in which tyranny and oligarchy symbolized all the ethical and political flaws which democracy sought to avoid. In a speech before the popular courts in 346/5, for example, Aeschines grouped tyranny and oligarchy together as the antithesis of democracy: "Among all men it is agreed that there are three types of constitution: tyranny, oligarchy and democracy. Tyrannies and oligarchies are managed according to the characters of those in power, while democratic cities are governed by the laws" (1.4). Similarly, when Demosthenes wished to represent Philip II of Macedon as a grave threat to Greece, he described him as a tyrant before the democratic assembly of the Athenians: "What do you seek? Freedom. But do you not see that Philip's titles are incompatible with this [freedom]? For every king and tyrant is the enemy of freedom and the law" (6.24–5).[12] As we have seen, fourth century critics of democracy sidestepped this critique by distinguishing monarchy from tyranny, and aristocracy from oligarchy. Moreover, these critics, like fifth century critics of democracy, waged ideological warfare against democracy by suggesting that tyranny and democracy shared the same flaws, namely lawlessness and the license to live as one likes. For example, Plato turned the democratic concept of freedom on its head by associating democratic freedom with the tyrant's freedom to live as he likes, unconstrained by the law (*Resp.* 557b–564a).

It is fascinating to see how both sides of the political spectrum used the same concept – tyranny – as the ideological and theoretical counterpoint to radically different forms of government. The appropriation of the concept of tyranny for opposing political agendas illustrates once again the ideological flexibility and conceptual utility of the figure of the tyrant. This statement is true not only for the historical periods covered in this essay, but also for later western political thought. For example, a recent US Supreme Court decision made use of the concept of tyranny in striking down special tribunals for terror suspects. In support of the majority opinion in the case, Justice John Paul Stevens drew on a seminal quote from James Madison on the nature of tyranny: "The accumulation of all powers, legislative, executive and judiciary, in the same hands, whether of one, a few or many, and whether hereditary, self-appointed or elective, may justly be pronounced the very definition of tyranny" (*Federalist* #47). This quotation shows not only that the concept of tyranny is easily adapted to radically different circumstances, but more importantly, that it has lost none of its potency, despite the intervening thousands of years of historical change.

FURTHER READING

For an excellent up-to-date overview of the political development of Greece from the Late Bronze to the Archaic Period see Hall 2007. For a superb recent discussion of historical tyranny in Archaic Greece, see G. Anderson 2005 (with earlier bibliography cited). On the Peisistratid tyranny in Athens, see Lavelle 2005 and Forsdyke 2005a: 101–33. For fifth and fourth century tyranny and tyrannies outside mainland Greece, including the Black Sea, Sicily, and even Rome, see Brock and Hodkinson 2000 and Lewis 2006. On oligarchy, see Ostwald 2000. On the Macedonian kings, see Lewis et al. 1994.

On kingship in Homer, see Raaflaub 1997 and Osborne 2004. On Solon and the relation between his poetry and politics in Athens, see Blok and Lardinois 2006. For the ideological construction of tyranny in the classical period, see the essays in Morgan 2003 and S. Lewis 2006. For a fascinating argument for the ambiguity of the concept of tyranny even among democratic Athenians, see Wohl 2002. For the representation of oriental kings and Greek tyrants in Herodotus and Greek tragedy, see Dewald 2003; Seaford 2003; Pelling 2002; Forsdyke 2001.

For fourth century political thought, see Ober 1998, chs 4–6 and Rowe and Schofield 2000, chs 6–19. An excellent recent overview of Plato's political thought can be found in Schofield 2006. On Plato's *Laws*, see Bobonich 2002; Laks 2000. On the reception of Greek political thought and ideologies in the modern era see Roberts 1994 and Osborne 2006. Scholars continue to debate the importance of ancient Greek political thought and experience to contemporary democracy; see, for example, Rhodes 2003a and Ober 2005c.

NOTES

1 The natural human desire for the goods that follow the acquisition of tyrannical power is conceptualized in both Archilochus and Herodotus in erotic terms ("love of tyranny" or "being a lover of tyranny"): Archil. fr. 19 West; Hdt. 1.96.2; 5.32; 3.53.4; cf. Wohl 2002: 220.

2 See also Cartledge and Edge in this volume (chapter 10) for the representation of tyrannical abuses (including sexual transgressions against the wives and daughters of citizens).

3 The panhellenic version of this ideology was often cast in terms of the poverty, strength, and freedom of the Greeks versus the wealth of Persia with its weak and servile subjects. See for example, Hdt. 7.101–4; Hippoc. *Aer.* 23. For a democratic version of the wealth/poverty contrast see Democritus, DK fr. 251.

4 The phrase "willing collective amnesia" is adapted from Saxonhouse 2006. I emphasize willing, because the demos was fully aware but, under certain circumstances, chose not to recall that the Spartans overthrew the tyranny at the behest of the family of the Alcmeonidae and their allies (cf. Thuc. 6.53; Ar. *Lys.* 1150–5; Hdt. 6.123; R. Thomas 1989: 238–82).

5 This passage echoes a similar one in Aeschylus' *Persians* (241–2) and has the same dramatic purpose as the conversation between Xerxes and Demaratus in Herodotus 7.102–4. See also Aesch. *Pers.* 213, 591–7 where tyranny serves as a foil for democratic accountability and free speech. See Forsdyke 2001 for discussion.

6 For the connection between democracy and protection of individual liberty, see Cartledge and Edge in this volume (chapter 10); for tyrannical abuses, see Saxonhouse (chapter 23).

7 For the equation between democracy and tyranny in ancient and early modern criticisms of democracy, see also the essays in this volume by Cartledge and Edge (chapter 10) and Saxonhouse (chapter 23).

8 In Thuc. 3.37, Cleon states this point even more starkly, and, we may assume that this equation was a topos of political oratory, particularly of the realist brand, in late fifth century Athens. We should of course never equate Thucydidean speeches with historical speeches. Nevertheless, as many scholars have shown, the ideas articulated in Thucydides' speeches may fairly represent some themes in late fifth century critical discourse (cf. Ober 1998: 52–121).

9 See further Saxonhouse (chapter 23) on Plato's critique of the Athenian empire as a tyranny.

10 For further discussion of the relation between the character of leaders and good governance in ancient Greek and Roman political thought, see the essays in this volume by Stadter (chapter 29) and Noreña (chapter 17).

11 For further discussion of Plato's conception of political virtue, see the essays in this volume by Saxonhouse (chapter 23) and Hitz (chapter 24).

12 See Cartledge and Edge (chapter 10) for further discussion of the connection between democracy, freedom, and rule of law in Athenian democratic theory.

CHAPTER 16

Hellenistic Monarchy in Theory and Practice

Arthur M. Eckstein

The political culture of the classical Greek city-state, or polis, whether it was an aristocratic republic or a democracy, was ideologically opposed to monarchy. The Greeks of the fifth century BC knew absolute rulers mostly from what they saw on the tragic stage, and the depiction there was negative: men such as Creon in *Antigone*, whose absolute power led to overweening arrogance.[1] And aside from Sparta with its double constitutional monarchy, what the Greeks saw of kingship in the real world was characteristic of half-barbarian places such as Macedon or Thrace – and of course the Persian empire, the realm of the Great King. The power of the Shah-an-Shah was, naturally, respected. But thinkers of the classical period were contemptuous of his subjects, seeing them as no better than slaves who endured a despotism that Greeks would find intolerable. They thought it natural that free men such as themselves, despite being hugely outnumbered, had beaten such creatures at Marathon in 490 and during the great Persian invasion of Greece in 480–479.[2] The absolutism of the Great King was in fact a Greek fantasy, for the Shah often confronted a powerful aristocracy and his conduct was hedged about with custom. Nevertheless, this was the ideology.[3]

King Philip II of Macedon and his son Alexander the Great, and then the Successors of Alexander, forced the Greeks into a new political world in which monarchy replaced the city-state as the dominant Greek political institution. This was a profound political and intellectual revolution. Philip gave monarchy a new prestige based on its political effectiveness, for he gained control over all of European Greece, an achievement that had been beyond the capabilities of any city-state. And his son Alexander went on to conquer Persia and much of the known world. After Alexander's death in 323, his gigantic empire fell apart; but the size and power of the separate monarchical regimes forged by his generals were enormous compared to poleis. The Greeks of the city-states, with their tradition of freedom for the citizen and their fierce desire for polis autonomy, were forced to deal now with the brutal

A Companion to Greek and Roman Political Thought, First Edition. Edited by Ryan K. Balot.
© 2013 Blackwell Publishing Ltd. Published 2013 by Blackwell Publishing Ltd.

concentration of great military-political power in huge political units overseen by kings. This power could rarely be escaped; it had to be (somehow) accommodated. Intellectuals responded to this revolutionary political situation by idealizing the monarch and hoping to put his enormous power to work for the benefit of Hellas. Whether the monarchs who came to dominate the hellenistic world after 340 BC actually lived up to that ideal is a separate question.

Can Scholars Speak of "Hellenistic Monarchy" as a Political Category?

The new world created by Philip, Alexander, and the Successors stretched from Ionia and Egypt to Afghanistan, and it was highly varied in culture. And in the chaos after 323 it was not only Macedonian generals who founded large royal regimes: so did powerful indigenous dynasts among the Bithynians, the Pontians, the Parthians, and eventually the Jews. Among the indigenous kings, customs and internal balances of political power created monarchies differing from the absolutist ideal propagated by Alexander. Thus the Parthian king, whose realm eventually included Iran and Mesopotamia, confronted a powerful aristocracy that imposed significant constraints on his rule (Wiesehöfer 1996). The Hasmonean kings after 140 BC were themselves constrained by a powerful Jewish priesthood that demanded royal adherence to the precepts of God and the Torah; nothing like this existed among the Greeks (Rajak 1996). Moreover, the great Greek monarchies differed among themselves. The Ptolemies' kingdom, based in Egypt, was quite homogeneous ethnically, had one great capital at Alexandria, and there the king could usually be found; but the Seleucids constantly traveled around their far-flung and ethnically diverse dominion, and they had two capitals, at Antioch in Syria and at Seleucia-on-the-Tigris.[4] The Attalids of Pergamum had wealth and ambition but their geographical scope was limited to western Asia Minor. The Antigonids, though militarily powerful via their hold on the old Macedonian homeland, led a far less extravagant lifestyle than the Ptolemies or the Seleucids, because of Macedonian custom and comparative lack of wealth. One can understand why some scholars conclude that "no singular formula existed for a Hellenistic king" (Bilde et al. 1996b: 11).

Nevertheless, F. W. Walbank is closer to the mark when he argues that the various monarchies did come to resemble each other significantly. This makes it possible to discuss "hellenistic monarchy" as a specific political category.[5]

First, all these monarchies originated as usurper-states.[6] Macedonian royal legitimacy ceased with the murder of Alexander's 12-year-old son in 311, and the end of the Argead line. This allowed various Macedonian warlords to proclaim themselves kings in their own right. Antigonus the One-Eyed and his son Demetrius, ruling western Asia, began the process (306), and they were soon followed by Ptolemy's proclamation of kingship, Seleucus' proclamation in Mesopotamia, and the proclamations of several others. A great victory won against the Celts allowed Antigonus Gonatas, the grandson of Antigonus the One-Eyed, to proclaim himself king over a disordered

Macedon in 277.[7] Similarly, a victory over the Celts in 241 led Attalus, the local warlord of Pergamum, to declare that he, too, was a king; and the continued victories of his descendants kept them in that status.[8] The indigenous monarchies were themselves usurpatory in nature. Victory over Macedonian forces in 297 led the Thracian warlord Zipoetes to declare himself king in Bithynia (northwest Asia Minor). In the same period the Persian aristocrat Mithridates of Cius became a king by seizing Pontus (north-central Asia Minor).[9] This ruthless principle of usurpation, with successful violence as justification for rule, is put straightforwardly in the *Suda*, a text of Byzantine provenance but based on an early-hellenistic precursor: "Kingship [*basileia*] does not derive either from royal descent or from formal legitimacy, but rather from the ability to command armies and to govern effectively. We see this with the Successors of Alexander."

Usurpers themselves, it was natural that kings were often threatened by usurpers. The main threat came from talented men from minor branches of the royal family, and any sign of weakness at the center could bring it forth. The Seleucids were especially bedeviled by this, and internal divisions after 150 would destroy the dynasty entirely. But it was a problem faced by many royal families, including the Hasmoneans. The Greek historian Polybius, writing about 150, praises the Attalids of Pergamum for an unusual tradition of mutual loyalty (18.41.9–10).[10]

Again, because the fundamental justification for rule was personal military success, there was a similarity in the official depiction of the monarch. All the kings of the hellenistic period, of realms large and small, Greek or indigenous, were portrayed in military attire. The official symbol of monarchy was the Macedonian diadem, a white or purple-and-white headband with two long loose ends behind. Even the descendants of non-Greek kings appear on their coinage wearing this quintessential hellenistic symbol of royalty.[11] But military regalia was the official royal attire of all these men: we have no statues of hellenistic kings dressed as civilians.[12]

Similarly, the extent of the royal realm was based on successful military violence. Powerful armed forces were central to these regimes not merely because they existed in a brutal anarchy of states characterized by the absence of international law (that was true of the hellenistic republics and democracies as well),[13] but also because, in the absence of inherited legitimacy, sheer conquest was the greatest justification for large territorial power. Hence kings tended to describe their territory by the term *doriktētos chōra*, "spear-won land." This was a brutally direct claim, prominent in the generation of the Successors.[14] And though monarchs of later generations could also make claims to territory on the basis of inheritance, or marriage dowry, conquest remained the strongest claim to the land. Thus Antiochus III, whose wars re-established Seleucid power from Afghanistan all the way to the Hellespont, claimed northwest Asia Minor and Thrace as spear-won land in 196 because of his own victories in the region as well as those of Seleucus I a century before (see Polyb. 18.51.3–6). His son Antiochus IV said as he prepared to invade Egypt in 170 that he "regarded possession through warfare as the surest claim and the best" (Polyb. 28.1.6).[15]

To sum up: hellenistic monarchy, whether large or small, whether Greek or indigenous, was above all a uniquely military and personal monarchy, with an origin in usurpation, a military character of great intensity, and an explicit justification in successful violence both for the rule of the dynasty and the extent of its possessions.

Of course, because of Alexander the Great's legitimacy as a member of the traditional royal family of Macedon, his military achievements, and his eventual reputation as a superhuman figure, any link with Alexander himself could also be a powerful legitimating principle. None of the men who created the Successor kingdoms had a kinship tie with him. Nevertheless, a claimed link to Alexander was a common feature among hellenistic monarchies. Ptolemy I seized Alexander's corpse in 321 and built a gigantic tomb for it in the Ptolemaic capital of Alexandria; Alexander's portrait appeared on Ptolemaic coinage; Ptolemy wrote a famous memoir of his campaigns with Alexander; and Alexander eventually became a central figure in the religious cult of the dynasty, and thus a putative ancestor.[16] Seleucus claimed to have had a dream in which Alexander promised him monarchy (Diod. Sic. 19.90.3–4); his descendants issued coinage with Alexander's image; and eventually they falsely claimed a blood tie.[17] The Antigonids were probably the first falsely to claim the kinship, so that their rule over Macedon could be seen as a continuation of the rule of the Argeads.[18] Even indigenous monarchs relied on Alexander to prop up their legitimacy: the Thraco-Iranian Mithridates VI of Pontus proclaimed himself the New Alexander, while the Syrian Antiochus I of Commagene declared himself his descendant.[19]

Beyond their common origins as usurper-states and their common ways of seeking legitimacy, the hellenistic kingdoms also employed similar institutions of royal governance. The first was the court, the royal headquarters. Its surroundings were often luxurious – though Antigonid Macedon was restrained in this respect, whereas the Ptolemies were extravagant. In general, the court's absolutist atmosphere and detailed protocol was an adaptation from Achaemenid Persia. Situated in a palace complex which was often magnificent, here was to be found an elaborate system for caring for the personal needs of the king (doctors, eunuchs, slaves, concubines). But no king could rule a kingdom by himself, and so here at court was also situated the central governing bureaucracy. This included not only the military chiefs, but the men responsible for handling the flood of correspondence and petitions that was always coming in to the king (Walbank 1984: 68).

Within every court, a crucial institution was the Friends (*philoi*) of the king. These were men of talent whom the monarch appointed to important military or administrative positions. The title of Friend was employed by all the monarchical regimes. The Friends often came from the king's territorial realm, but equally often not from within his territorial realm at all.[20] Monarchs customarily convened councils of these Friends to give advice on serious matters. They constituted a corps of professional administrators and military men, and – for the sake of the efficacy of his regime – one of the central tasks of a king was to keep them satisfied.[21]

One way to keep the Friends satisfied was to invite them to royal banquets. The royal feast and drinking party (the *basilikon symposion*) was typical of all hellenistic courts. These banquets were often given for hundreds of people, and they symbolized, in a world where simply getting enough to eat was a problem for many, the power and benevolence of the monarch (Tondriau 1948). The banquets of Antigonus II were famous for their philosophical conversation; and one source depicts Ptolemy II discoursing over a several days' feast on issues of political philoso-phy with 70 Jewish elders.[22] We need not believe that things were always so staid, for Antiochus IV had a fine time indeed at the huge feast he organized at Antioch in 166.[23] Nor, once again, was the *basilikon symposion* limited to the Greco-Macedonian courts; Mithridates VI of Pontus, surrounded by Greek philosophers and poets, turned banquets into seminars.[24] The symposium allowed the king to appear on a more amiable and open level with his high-ranking lieutenants and Friends than was usual under court etiquette, and thus helped solidify the personal ties that were crucial to running the regime (O. Murray 1996).

As already noted, the king and his court were to be found in the capital city. The capital was often a brand new foundation artificially designed to be the seat of government, and huge funds were lavished on it for palaces and administrative buildings. Alexandria of the Ptolemies and Antioch of the Seleucids were the most famous, but Seleucia-on-the-Tigris must have been a sight to see, and Pergamum of the Attalids, on its great mountain, was a tremendously impressive place. Again, the Greeks were not alone in this: in the 260s King Nicomedes I, son of the Thracian warlord Zipoetes who had seized Bithynia, founded a great new Greek-style capital city on the coast of the Propontis; a typical hellenistic monarch, he named it after himself – Nicomedia. Half a millennium later it was still suitable as an imperial residence for the Roman emperor Diocletian (Hannestad 1996: 75).

These capital cities came with wonderful public amenities. Alexandria was famous for its two huge libraries, its temples, the museum, and the medical school; and Seleucid Antioch and Attalid Pergamum were not far behind. In all three cities the great libraries were presided over by well-paid intellectuals.[25] Thus the king displayed himself both as an exemplar and a patron of Greek culture – and his enormous wealth was proclaimed. For just as a weak king was a contradiction in terms in this world, so was a poor one (Austin 1986: 459). Hence an important and enjoyable political event in any capital city was the great royal procession, such as that of Ptolemy II in 279/278 in Alexandria, with its dozens of floats and 80,000 troops.[26]

Hellenistic monarchies, whether large or small, Greco-Macedonian or indigenous, always spent a huge amount of attention and money on their armed forces.[27] This was not only because of the military nature of hellenistic monarchy and its direct foun-dation on force (see above), but also because of the harsh nature of the interstate environment (see below). Armies were often huge: the citizen field-army of Athens in 431 had numbered about 13,000 infantry and 1,000 cavalry, but the Ptolemaic army at Raphia in 217 numbered about 75,000 men and it confronted a Seleucid army numbering 68,000; the Seleucid army at Magnesia in 189 numbered some 60,000 infantry and 12,000 cavalry.[28] As for the navies of the kings, they were sometimes comparable in numbers of ships to the famous fifth century Athenian fleet, but the warships were themselves larger, with the quinquireme having replaced the trireme (Lévêque 1968: 273–4).

In all these usurper-states, it was natural also that the new royal houses sought legitimacy through claims to special protection from the divine (Lévêque 1968: 85). Sometimes the royal family and its individual members were merely declared to be under a divinity's special protection. Thus the Attalids claimed a special relationship with Athena-Bringer-of-Victory, and each year organized a spectacular parade of thanksgiving for her at Pergamum; the Seleucids claimed the special protection of Apollo of Miletus, who (they said) had prophesied that the original general Seleucus would become a king.[29] Indigenous dynasties followed suit: the Mithridatic kings in Pontus claimed the special protection of Zeus Stratios.[30]

A stage beyond this was the direct assimilation of kings to divinities. The Ptolemies identified themselves with Dionysus. Coins of Antigonus II of Macedon have on the obverse the head of the god Pan – bearing the features of Antigonus himself (Walbank 1984: 86). Some regimes also encouraged placing a great statue of the monarch in a temple shared with a divinity, so that the king became "a temple-sharing god" (*synnaos theos*). Thus Attalus III of Pergamum during his own lifetime shared a temple with the god Asclepius. Indigenous monarchs again followed suit: in the 80s BC the Persian dynast Ariarathes V, king of Cappadocia in east-central Asia Minor, was sharing a temple with Zeus the Savior.[31]

The next step was the king as a god in his own right. When Alexander demanded that he receive worship in 324 and 323, it was a turning point; Greek states granted him divine honors (cult statues, a sanctuary, a priest, animal sacrifices, incense, an annual festival) – for who could resist his mighty power?[32] The Successors, seeking ways to legitimate their regimes, happily accepted the cult images, sanctuaries, altars, priests, and festivals offered in their honor by their allegedly grateful subjects. Most often, this was indeed in celebration (or expectation) of acts of royal benevolence. Antigonus the One-Eyed and his son Demetrius allowed themselves to receive divine honors at Scepsis in Asia Minor as early as 311 (*OGIS* 6) and then famously at Athens in 307, where, following their liberation of the city from their rival dynast Cassander, they were worshiped as Savior-Gods. Other monarchs soon imitated them: thus there were cults throughout the northern Aegean in the 280s to King Lysimachus the overlord of Thrace, when Lysimachus' power was at its height; and after Seleucus I defeated him, then Seleucus, too, was worshipped as a god in the region.[33] Indigenous rulers again followed the Greeks; Antiochus I of Commagene (northwest Syria) established a cult for himself in the mid-first century BC (Dörner 1967).

One should not imagine that most Greeks thought of monarchs as gods in the same sense as Zeus or Apollo, and intellectuals sometimes protested the worship ceremonies.[34] But as with monarchy itself, the ultimate rationale for giving kings divine honors was their benevolent efficacy in the real world. The famous Athenian hymn to Demetrius the Besieger ca. 290 makes the main point: Demetrius has accomplished good things for Athens and will accomplish still more, whereas "other gods are either far away or have not ears, or do not exist, or heed us not at all."[35] Eventually the entire royal dynasty could itself be worshiped as divine, precisely for this reason – legitimacy indeed![36]

The most important aspects of the monarchies that came to dominate the eastern Mediterranean after Alexander were thus widely shared, common both to Greco-Macedonian and indigenous royal regimes, common to realms large and less so. All these regimes possessed a common problematic origin (usurpation), similar organization, political structure, and capital cities, a shared focus on militarism, regime display, and religious justification. It is for these reasons that we can speak of

"Hellenistic Monarchy" as a specific political category of monarchy – a category subject to its own historical analysis.

The Theory of Monarchy in the Hellenistic Age

Greek intellectuals evolved an elaborate theory of monarchy to justify this new world of absolutist states. But given the background of deep Greek political distrust of absolutism, this theory also sought to tame royal power through an image of the ideal king – the fierce and effective but benevolent man who imposes order and provides benefits to his subjects, receiving in return a loyalty that was a reasonable response to his services for them.

After the disasters of the Peloponnesian War some Greek intellectuals were already thinking about monarchy as a good form of government. We see this in Isocrates's essays on King Euagoras of Cyprus and his successor Nicocles (ca. 375), in Xenophon's biography of Agesilaus of Sparta (ca. 370), and in his fictional account of Cyrus the founder of the Persian empire (the *Cyropaedia*). These works laid out the virtues of a model king: he was just, generous, and feared the gods; he was incorruptible, and self-controlled in food, wine, and sex; he was courageous in battle and patriotic.[37] Plato, of course, went further; in the *Statesman*, he proposed monarchy as the best of all forms of government. Aristotle was more skeptical of monarchy, but still believed that a man with truly superior virtue could rightfully assume kingship over a city, ruling for the common good.[38]

These ideas had little impact at the time beyond a small cadre of intellectuals. But when, after Philip and Alexander and the Successors, the question became not which form of government was theoretically good, but how to provide a philosophical accommodation with the real monarchies that had emerged, the answers were already available. Our sources on the hellenistic treatises on kingship are fragmentary and often late, but they allow us to see that the ideas set out in the first half of the fourth century were now deployed both to educate monarchs on how to use their absolute power in a philosophically acceptable (i.e. benevolent) way, and to educate the population on why monarchical rule was acceptable.[39] We also possess a great amount of surviving propaganda from the royal governments themselves, in the form of coinage, inscriptions on stone, and papyrus documents in the case of Egypt. These official statements enable us to see how the governments wished to view themselves and to be viewed by their populations. In sum: we can see fairly well how the good monarchy was supposed to work.

The king was, of course supposed to have martial virtues. He was not only to be a strategist but personally brave in battle – as we see in official inscriptions praising courageous royal behavior and in the passages in Polybius praising royal courage in battle and condemning royal cowardice.[40] Because enemies included the tribal peoples ("barbarians") who from ca. 280 BC constantly threatened the settled city-life of the Mediterranean coast from the north, there emerged the ideal of the monarch as defender of Greek civilization. It finds its finest artistic expression in

Eumenes II's great Pergamene Altar of Zeus (ca. 170 BC), with its dramatic reliefs of the battles of the gods against the giants – symbolizing the Attalid kings as the protectors of the Asia Minor coastal cities against the terrible assaults of the Galatian Celts who had settled in upland Anatolia.[41] The Antigonids fulfilled a similar role, protecting Macedon and Greece against the Thracians and Celts.[42] Still, war was not waged against barbarians alone, as we see in the Canopis Decree of 238 BC, which praises Ptolemy III for having "maintained the country at peace by fighting in its defence against many nations and their rulers" (*OGIS* 96, lines 12–13, trans. Austin 1981: 336) – none of them, in this case, barbarians (Walbank 1984: 82).

The ideal king also had to be wealthy: it was part of his power to do good (Austin 1986: 457). Royal wealth derived primarily from taxes, though sometimes from war booty. In the ideal, it was to benefit the king's friends and subjects, to relieve the needy, and to fund the armed forces necessary to defend the realm (see Stob. *Ecl.* 4.7.62). No doubt the vast royal wealth and power displayed in the gigantic processions of Ptolemy II in Alexandria in 279/278 and Antiochus IV at Antioch in 166, or in the vast palaces and public buildings of Alexandria, Antioch, Pergamum or Nicomedia, also served to impress the kings' subjects and hence led back once again to regime stability. Ideally, wealth also constituted a specific moral challenge: for the king as a superior man had to overcome the great temptations of sloth, luxury, and sensuality which wealth offered (Aristaeus, *Letter to Philocrates* 207).

Another central virtue of kings set forth by the theoreticians was the provision of justice and benevolent administration. The king made the laws for all; and though some thinkers argued that he did not have to obey the laws himself (as Anaxarchus allegedly told Alexander after Alexander murdered a friend in a drunken rage), the thrust of the treatises on kingship was otherwise – that the good king should voluntarily submit to the laws he made. Here was another area where the philosophers could depict monarchy as the most honorable of challenges toward moral behavior on the part of a man of superior quality.[43] Similarly, magnanimity and generosity (*megalopsuchē, philanthrōpia*) are the most common royal virtues in intellectual treatises and on official inscriptions.[44] And a major theoretical text asserts that a king must above all show self-control (*enkrateia*) toward his subjects, and indeed that to show such self-control was to gain "the greatest empire of all" – empire over oneself (Aristaeus, *Letter to Philocrates* 207 and 221). The result of a king showing such affection for his subjects was – supposedly – that they would in turn be affectionate and loyal toward him.[45]

This understanding of how to mitigate absolutist control is also shown in the official view of relations between kings and the "free and autonomous" cities both within and beyond their realms. Most Greek poleis were now democratic in form, so that the contrast with monarchy was stark; and at any one time there were dozens of cities in Greece and the Aegean free from direct monarchical domination (though only Rhodes and the Aetolian League could claim such a history continuously).[46] Relations between kings and cities outside their power were polite (unless they were about to go to war). And in keeping with the ideals, kings liked to appear as great benefactors of cities: hence both the Attalids and Seleucids financed spectacular public buildings in free Athens after 229 BC.[47] Even with subordinated poleis in his realm, there developed a rhetoric of highly polite communication, stressing the king's benevolence and special favor on the one side, and corresponding good will and loyalty on the other. The king often granted formal freedom and autonomy, and aided these poleis economically and militarily. This is of course not the entire story (see below), but the rhetoric of benevolence and loyalty did act as a factor to mitigate the brutal imbalance of power.[48]

In sum, the hellenistic ideal of monarchy required a king "to throw his weight on the side of good," employing his immense power to the benefit of all (Walbank 1984: 83). In this conception, monarchy became – as Antigonus II is supposed to have said – a "glorious servitude," with the king taking constant care for the common interest.[49] But in laying out the virtues necessary both for royal personal goodness and to justify monarchy to a people with a history of freedom, the theoreticians were not naive – for writings on royal virtue acknowledged the terrible temptations of unlimited hedonism, irresponsibility, and cruelty inherent in absolute power. To overcome those enormous temptations required a man of the highest moral stature (Walbank 1984: 83). How many men, in reality, achieved this goal?

Hellenistic Kingship in Practice

We must begin with a few hard facts. First, all the monarchies were machines for extracting wealth from the population (mostly the peasants, but including artisans and merchants in the cities), and employing this wealth for the government: that is, for the king, the army, the bureaucracy. The wealth was extracted via taxation.[50] It was this extracted wealth which, in turn, allowed the king to control the realm – funding the army that imposed order, funding the bureaucracy that both imposed order and extracted those taxes. Since in the vast dominions of the Ptolemies and the Seleucids, as well as in Greek kingdoms as far away as Bactria (Afghanistan), the king, the army, and the bureaucracy were made up overwhelmingly of Macedonians and Greeks, this meant that in the east monarchy acted as the agent of a Greco-Macedonian aristocracy which led a relatively good life based on the extraction of indigenous wealth – a "colonial" situation.[51] This conformed to the view that the kings and their supporters based their privileged position on "spear-won land" – that is, successful military violence.[52]

There was certainly some upward mobility for hellenized indigenous people.[53] But in Ptolemaic Egypt, the weakening at the top after 207 was enough to call forth a massive indigenous rebellion against Greek rule which lasted for over 20 years; and the Seleucids had little enthusiastic support from their own indigenous population.[54] In parts of Asia Minor, and in Iran with the rise of the Arsacid Parthian empire (its territory won at the expense of the Seleucids), there grew up indigenous monarchies on the hellenistic model. But these regimes, too, were machines for extracting wealth in the form of taxes from the peasantry – this time to support indigenous masters. And even the indigenous kings in Asia Minor were aided by a large corps of privileged Greco-Macedonian experts.

This is a grim picture, somewhat mitigated by the fact that the kings managed to impose a good deal of internal order: the Seleucids suppressed bandits; the Ptolemies ran an elaborate system of courts which dealt fairly efficiently with property disputes. And if the monarchies had also managed to provide international peace in exchange for the wealth they extracted to support the structures of absolutist government, this would have mitigated the situation far more. But here the monarchies failed (see below).

Second, whatever the theory, the monarchies were at heart absolutist states in which the king did what he wished. Naturally, no monarch wished to be perceived as an ogre, and some men did try to live up to the ideals espoused both by intellectuals and by their own government propaganda.[55] But when the monarch wished to depart from those ideals, there was nothing to stop him – and plenty of men did so. Thus, while philosophers mandated self-control for kings in regard to both alcohol and sex, the Antigonid king Demetrius the Besieger appropriated the Parthenon itself for the use of his personal harem (ca. 290 BC), and the lead float in the great procession of Ptolemy II in Alexandria in 271/270 was a penis 150 feet long with a 20-foot star coming out of its tip. Ptolemy IV ca. 225 BC was a notorious drunk, as was the Seleucid king Demetrius I (ca. 150), and even efficient men such as Philip V and Antiochus III behaved badly when they had been drinking.[56] The ideal of dynastic unity was upheld by intellectuals, but in the real world the sons of Antiochus II fought a large-scale war for their father's throne in the 240s, causing widespread damage in Asia; Philip V murdered his own son Demetrius in 180 on suspicion of plotting against him; the polygamous-incestuous marriage of Ptolemy VIII with his sister and his niece (both named Cleopatra) ended badly in 130 with civil war in Alexandria.[57] And when Philip V launched surprise attacks on his own allies, or raped citizen women at Argos, or betrayed his promises to cities that surrendered to him on terms (selling their free Greek populations into slavery instead, in order to get money to finance his wars), many were outraged but no one could stop him.[58] Monarchs might be worshipped as divine because of the power of their beneficence, but Plutarch's judgment was that the adoption of the royal title "stimulated men's pride and raised their ambitions, and made them arrogant in their style of living and obnoxious in their dealings with others" (*Demetr.* 18). Polybius' judgment was similar: while kings frequently began their reigns with impulses toward treating people democratically, and a few kings did live up to the ideals of rulership, most kings eventually treated everyone not as allies and friends but as slaves (15.24.4).[59]

Third, and most important, is that the kings were almost always at war with each other.

The Greco-Macedonian state system that arose in the late fourth century was the result of Alexander's enormous conquests, followed by the terrible struggle for power among his marshals after 323. The system was a heavily militarized anarchy. There were a few informal norms of interstate conduct – such as maintaining good faith in sworn treaties – and they helped somewhat to ameliorate the prevailing harsh conditions; but these informal norms were not always obeyed, and there were no mechanisms for enforcing them. There were also numerous attempts at mediation and arbitration of disputes between the less powerful states – a considerable Greek effort toward resolving interstate problems peacefully. Yet no state of the first rank ever submitted itself to the process. This is true not only of the great monarchies, but also of the most powerful of the hellenistic city-states, such as Rhodes.[60] For the great states, conflicts of interest were decided by might alone. Polybius is explicit that the primary cause of war in his world was the absence of enforceable international law (5.67.11–5.68.2).

This bleak picture has not always been the predominant view of the hellenistic state system.[61] But the picture of hellenistic international relations held by many current students of the period is now more grim than previous scholarly opinion. Political scientists, led by Kenneth Waltz, have in general emphasized the negative impact of such anarchic and militarized state systems upon the behavior of all states within these systems, and conditions in the hellenistic world confirms the political scientists' grimmest conclusions.[62] Every state within the hellenistic world had to depend upon its own self-help in order to survive amid the disorder, which meant that every state had to be heavily militarized: "states must meet the demands of the political eco-system or court annihilation" (Sterling 1974: 336). The logic of self-help led to the maximizing of power: a state could be secure only by increasing its power and influence, thus gaining more control over its harsh surrounding environment. But since every hellenistic state was under this same pressure, and responded in the same harsh way, competition was unrestrained, and tensions persistently led to crises over real or perceived conflicts of interest.[63] The primitive nature of ancient diplomacy during such crises – where diplomatic interactions consisted mostly of threats – was not conducive to their peaceful resolution, since ancient concepts of honor, and the necessity to maintain prestige, required resistance to threats.[64]

These factors almost led to warfare among hellenistic states, and because the units in conflict were large and the resources available to the most powerful states great, the damage done was often enormous.[65] The devastation in the Greek world caused by the constant wars of the great monarchies becomes clearer the more inscriptions are discovered.[66] The ravaging of city territory and the destruction of rural property was a common occurrence, while the great dynasties even employed pirates to attack enemy commercial shipping and raid coastal areas.[67]

It is notorious in ancient studies that the Roman Republic went to war almost every year; but this does not set the Romans apart from other hellenistic states.[68] Rather, it was a typical response to the anarchy, as is shown by the fact that the great hellenistic kings went to war every year too. Men such as Seleucus II, Antiochus III, or Philip V spent *every* year of their reigns leading their troops into battle. For Antiochus, that meant 36 straight years in the field; for Philip V it was 42 straight years. Many kings were famous generals – and all of them tried to be. As we saw above, this was partly because successful violence was the fundamental justification for all these royal regimes; but it was also a necessity in a harsh interstate world. Monarchs took titles indicating their ferocity: "the Eagle," "the Hawk," "the Invincible Victor," "the Glorious Victor"; and hellenistic rulers were praised in official inscriptions for being "avid for battle."[69] In sum, successful warfare was a necessity for hellenistic kings.[70]

This is why we have no statues of hellenistic kings in civilian attire. But, strikingly, we *do* have statues of kings posing in what is called "heroic masculine nudity," showing off their muscles, and other things.[71] Such men naturally boasted of their predatory masculinity. Philip V symbolized his insatiable sexual appetite on his coinage, by means of his famous helmet with goat's horns; Ptolemy II ordered that float with the 150-foot penis.[72] Images of sheer physical strength were also central: Lysimachus claimed to have fought a lion with his bare hands (and he had the scars to show it); Seleucus I, like Lysimachus a man of exceptional size, boasted of having subdued with his bare hands a raging bull in front of Alexander.[73] And while kings decided foreign relations and grand strategy, they also led their forces into battle in person – as Alexander had done. Thus of the first 14 kings of the Seleucid dynasty, 12 died in battle or on campaign. As late as 146, Ptolemy VI died at the head of a cavalry charge while attempting to conquer Syria.[74] King Hiero II of Syracuse (ca. 250 BC) could boast of having killed many men in single combat (Justin 23.4.12); so could Pyrrhus, king of Epirus in 297–272.[75] Attalus I of Pergamum often fought at the head of his forces (both on land and sea) – and was several times almost killed; Philip V and Antiochus III were famous warriors in the battle-line. This was the definitional essence of kingship.

The bellicosity and constant warfare characteristic of monarchies also held for second-tier states such as the Achaean League or the Aetolian League, and even for small hellenistic city-states, which pursued their own local military rivalries and mini-imperialisms. This was all part of – and a response to – the prevailing anarchy.[76] But Lévêque calculates that in the 163 years between Alexander's death in 323 BC and 160 BC, the eastern Mediterranean was without war involving one or more of the three great monarchies in only four years. This prevalence of war is to be explained, Lévêque argues, primarily because war was the natural way in which the natural antagonisms among these great hellenistic states was regulated. Yes, there was an amount of interstate diplomacy, and the creation of alliances (including via marriage among the dynasties). But at its heart, in hellenistic interstate relations "la guerre est le recours essential"; and – in a phrase reminiscent of Kenneth Waltz's general hypothesis regarding the life of states under anarchic international systems – "la guerre est … le recours *normal*."[77]

In such a world, even the largest states were at great risk if they showed any weakness. Polybius provides us with an example of the ruthless nature of hellenistic politics and the kings who dominated it in his discussion of what occurred when Ptolemy IV died prematurely in 204, leaving the throne at Alexandria to a son who was only six years old:

> When Ptolemy [IV] died, leaving an infant son whom it was the natural duty of Philip [V] and Antiochus [III] as kings to maintain in possession of his realm, they hastened instead to divide the child's kingdom between themselves, plotting to destroy the orphan. Nor did they, as tyrants do, even attempt to provide themselves with some flimsy pretext for the shameful deed. Who can look at their treaty [of alliance to destroy young Ptolemy V] and not see the image of all impiety towards the gods, all savagery towards men, and the unbounded greed of these two kings?[78]

Doubts have been cast, wrongly, in my opinion, about the historicity of this pact between Philip and Antiochus to destroy the Ptolemaic realm;[79] but the point is that Polybius, writing for an audience of Greek statesmen, expected his readers to believe that such utterly ruthless conduct was possible – indeed, usual – among the great monarchies (Austin 1986: 458).

The same realities of power determined royal relations with the Greek cities. True, the kings were often anxious to gain for themselves the public support of "free" poleis, and they did it via benevolence: exemption from taxes; the granting of local autonomy; the funding of public buildings and public education; the providing of economic subsidies or military protection in times of need. Relations were usually conducted in a rhetoric of effusive politeness on both sides, and we have seen above how such polite rhetoric might even work a bit to mitigate the impact of the real imbalance of power. Moreover, kings – beset on all sides by threats – might well need the military-political support of cities: Smyrna could even describe itself as a benefactor of King Seleucus II, because of its help to him during wars in the 240s (*OGIS* 229).[80] And local goodwill was in general important to procure the efficient running of an empire under premodern conditions, because the projection of coercive military power overland was difficult and expensive. Thus the balance of power was not totally on the side of the kings (Shipley 2000: 74).

But the people of the city of Abydus on the Hellespont preferred in 200 BC to commit mass suicide rather than be under the control of a monarch – and they win Polybius' approbation (16.30–4).[81] One should not speak of any "parity" between the cities and the king; the power imbalance was too large.[82] Indeed, monarchical "violence" was implicit in the very scale of the gifts which kings could give (autonomy, exemption from taxes): these gifts were assertions of royal superiority, while to the ancients the accepting of such large benefactions constituted in itself a definite (even shameful) sign of inequality. When in the 180s King Eumenes II of Pergamum politely offered to subsidize the functioning of the council of the Achaean League, he was harshly refused, because the Achaeans, a proudly independent and indeed quite powerful state, did not wish to be, or be seen to be, so beholden to a king (Polyb. 22.8). But many cities were.

Thus the enormous military power concentrated at the royal center, and the enormous wealth available for distribution, remained the heart of the situation forced upon the cities by the rise of the kings. They could adapt to it, and manipulate the ideology of ideal kingship to their own advantage and to moderate the impact of royal hegemony. But it was the imbalance of power – not the politeness of the language on honorific inscriptions – that determined the real relations between the cities and the kings. A final example: the great city-state of Rhodes had withstood the attack of Demetrius the Besieger in 304 BC, but a century later was unable to deal with the threatening might of Philip V and Antiochus the Great – and so the Rhodians were forced to join with several other states in calling upon Rome to intervene and save them. This action opened up another chapter in the story of imperial power in the Mediterranean.[83]

Conclusion

After Philip II, the father of Alexander, defeated the Greeks at Chaeronea in 338 BC, he established the League of Corinth. The League was intended as an instrument of Macedonian control over the poleis, but also as a forum for settling disputes among them, a way of enforcing a *koinē eirēnē*, a Common Peace; in exchange for submission to Philip's domination and the loss of their beloved freedom of action, the city-states would for the first time in their history gain peace among themselves.[84] And if Alexander had lived, his gigantic Greco-Macedonian empire, stretching by 323 from Greece to the Indus, would have been a harsh despotism, but it would at least have provided relative peace to the peoples of this enormous region.

The above discussion of the realities of hellenistic monarchy suggests that the dynastic realms that emerged after Alexander's premature death mostly lived up to the despotic potential of the projects of Philip and Alexander, but failed the potential which those projects held for bringing peace to an anarchic world. No doubt many kings were hard-working rulers (one thinks of Seleucus I, Attalus I, Hiero II, Philip V, Antiochus III); they were generally able to impose a modicum of internal order within their large realms; and royal despotism was somewhat ameliorated by an ideology that stressed justice and self-restraint – or occasionally by some hard facts of power (as with Seleucus II's relations with the city of Smyrna). But at heart the kings were all warlords. Their power was based on usurpation through military violence, their legitimacy was unstable, their territory was "spear-won land," their public appearance was militaristic, their main task was military campaigning. Alexander's vast empire had fallen apart into large, rivalrous, and often mutually hostile kingdoms. This division of power among the three great dynasties allowed political space for lesser powers to have some freedom of maneuver, and even for smaller Greek city-states, for example, those on the western coast of Asia Minor, to negotiate an ameliorated political status with their overlords. But the royal rivalries also led to destructive wars. If either Philip or Alexander had lived long enough, the Greeks might have traded freedom and anarchy for peace under despotism; but instead, they faced despotic power while anarchy and war continued.

The greatest of the dynasties never stopped dreaming of the reunification of the imperial space that had once belonged to Alexander. At the end of the third century, Philip V and Antiochus III banded together to destroy the realm of the Ptolemies, which was in the hands of a child (see above). If these ruthless and ambitious rulers had succeeded, then the history of the Mediterranean would have been dramatically different: the Greek state system might have evolved from a tripolar balance of power (Antigonids, Seleucids, Ptolemies) into a bipolar structure dominated by two great monarchical states of enormous strength, or perhaps (after another round of massive war), either the Antigonid or the Seleucid dynasty would have emerged as sole hegemon over the Greek world. But as it was, the action of the desperate second-tier states in calling in the Republic of Rome when confronted by the tremendous power and aggression of Philip and Antiochus eventually led to Roman domination of the entire East. By 188 BC, after a surprising sequence of events, the Romans had defeated both Philip and Antiochus.[85] From that point onward the Romans were increasingly able to impose peace (the *pax Romana*) upon the previous anarchy that had always characterized the eastern Mediterranean – and eventually they would impose an emperor as well.[86]

FURTHER READING

The best general introduction to hellenistic monarchy, both the political theory behind kingship and in its practice, is Walbank 1984. Also excellent is the chapter on "Kings and Cities" in Shipley 2000, which employs different information in discussing daily practicalities. On the warlike nature of hellenistic kingship, the basic study in English is Austin 1986. A fascinating discussion of the interplay of masculinity and military violence in hellenistic monarchy is Roy 1998. On the savage character of the hellenistic interstate anarchy in general, see chapter 4 in Eckstein 2006. On the militarizing impact of the anarchy even among weaker states, Ma 2000 is a fascinating essay. For an image of the king that is less bellicose and more benevolent (and even shows the monarch as occasionally an intellectual), see Oswyn Murray's fine essay on hellenistic royal feasts (O. Murray 1996). For the often striking portraiture of these monarchs, and an impression of what these men (and women) looked like (or rather, what they wanted to look like), see the rich collection of images in Smith 1988.

NOTES

1   See Walbank 1984: 62; cf. Bilde et al. 1996b: 9–10.
2   On Greek belief in Persian absolute despotism, see, e.g., Hdt. 3.31.5 and Arist., *Pol.* 1285a. The ideological framework given for the defeat of the Persians in 490 and 480–479: see e.g. Waters 1971: 75–85; Raaflaub 2007: 58–89.
3   On what is now thought about Persian political realities, see Billows 1995: 68–9.
4   Our Greece-focused sources tend to put too much emphasis on Antioch; Seleucia was actually larger: see Invernizzi 1989–90.
5   Walbank 1984: 65. Besides Walbank 1984, there are good discussions in Billows 1995: chs 2 and 3; Shipley 2000: ch. 3.
6   Rightly emphasized by Austin 1986.
7   On "the Year of the Kings" (306/305), see Muller 1973 and Gruen 1985. On the Antigonids' strangely peripatetic career before they eventually seized Macedon permanently in 277, see Billows 1995.
8   For the rise of the Attalids, see McShane 1964: ch. 2.
9   Zipoetes appears to have presented himself as a continuation of earlier Achaemenid rule: see Hannestad 1996: 72 and n36 (with references to earlier scholarship). The rise to power of the Mithridatic family: see McGing 1986: 13–16. The family later falsely claimed descent both from Cyrus the founder of the Achaemenid Persian empire and from Alexander the Great (!): see Hind 1994.
10 Similarly, we have an inscription praising Apollonis, the wife of Attalus I, for her ability to maintain harmonious relations not only with all her royal children but even with her daughters-in-law (*OGIS* 308).

11 See Fleischer 1996, figs 3 and 4. Another example of this indigenous adaptation of the Macedonian diadem is King Tarcondimotus I of Cilicia: Fleischer 1996, fig. 21.

12 See the comments of Roy 1998: 114.

13 On the absence of international law in Mediterranean antiquity and its negative consequences for the behavior of every state, see now Eckstein 2006, and below.

14 See Diod. Sic. 18.39.5; 18.43.1 ("Ptolemy gained kingship over Egypt through his spear"); 19.85.3; 19.105.5; 20.76.7; cf. 53.3; 21.1.5. This material probably derives from the contemporary observer Hieronymus of Cardia. For discussion, see esp. Billows 1995: 25–6.

15 See Walbank 1984: 66; Billows 1995: 26 and n5.

16 Good summary in Billows 1995: 37–8. For Alexander as eventually central to the religious cult rendered to the Ptolemaic family, see, e.g., Strabo 17.1.8, with Fraser 1972: 225–6 and Stewart 1993: ch. 8.

17 Seleucid coinage with Alexander's portrait: see Hadley 1974; H. Smith 1988: 60; Morkholm 1991: 78. The false claim to a blood tie: see Billows 1995: 41 and n46.

18 For the claim, see Polyb. 5.10.10, with Walbank 1993: 1721–2; the claim of kinship with Alexander provoked cynical remarks from their competitors: Walbank 1993: 1722.

19 Mithridates as the New Alexander: see McGing 1986: 44–6, 101–2, 141–2. The claim of Antiochus I of Commagene, made on his impressive "Ancestor Monument" at Nimrud Dagh, came through his maternal link to the Seleucids and their false claim: see Dörner 1967.

20 Example of Friends drawn from within the kingdom: see the family of Lysias, important Seleucid generals and administrators, in bar-Kochva 1976: 88. "International" professionals: the Aetolian general Scopas, who commanded the army of Ptolemy V (Polyb. 18.53.).

21 On the Friends, see Habicht 1958; on the potentially subversive political power of these men, see Austin 1986. They were almost always Greeks and Macedonians, not indigenous people.

22 On Antigonus II's philosophical feasts, see Billows 1995; on Ptolemy II and the Jewish elders, see O. Murray 1996: 22.

23 Antiochus IV: Polyb. 30.25–6; Diod. Sic. 30.16. We also hear mention in Antigonid Macedon of naked dancing girls – at breakfast (Athen. 13.607b; cf. 4.162b).

24 On Mithridates' hellenized court, see McGing 1986: 92–3.

25 For convenient discussion, see E. Turner 1984: 170–2.

26 On the procession of Ptolemy II, see Athenaeus 196a–203b, with Rice 1983. In Macedon every spring the capital at Pella witnessed the spectacular procession and then war game of the Antigonid army: see Livy 40.6.1 and Curtius 10.9.12 with Walbank 1979: 233–4. At Pergamum every year there occurred the royal procession and festival in honor of Athena-Bringer-of-Victory: E. Hansen 1971: 448–50.

27 For recent discussion, see Beston 2000.

28 Lévêque 1968: 270–1. Including reserves and garrison troops, the total size of the Ptolemaic army in the 250s may have approached 240,000 (so App. *Proemium* 10; cf. Lévêque 1968: 270). By contrast, the fifth century Athenian field army of 13,000 infantry was backed by 16,000 reserves, for a grand total of about 30,000 men: see Thuc. 2.13.6. Similar figures can be found in Diod. Sic. (12.40.4–5): 12,000 infantry in the Athenian field army, backed by 17,000 reserves.

29 On the cult of Athena Nicephorus at Pergamum, see E. Hansen 1971: 280–2 and 448–50. The Attalid family also claimed the protection of Dionysus: E. Hansen 1971: 451–3.

It helped Seleucus I that he had an anchor-shaped birthmark on his thigh – the symbol of Apollo of Miletus: see Justin 15.4.2.

30 Since this dynasty was Iranian in origin, probably Zeus Stratios was originally some form of the Persian Ahura-Mazda: see McGing 1986: 10 and n37.

31 Attalus: see Nock 1972: 1:219; Ariarathes: Nock 1972: 1: 346 n8. On this family's seizure of Cappadocia and subsequent claim to royalty (probably based on victories won against the Seleucids), see Billows 1995: 106–7.

32 General official acceptance of Alexander's claims, despite some famous protests: see Walbank 1984: 90–1. Classic example: Arr. *Anab.* 7.32.1 (the Greek envoys to Alexander in spring 323).

33 Lysimachus was worshipped at Priene and on Samothrace, Seleucus at Ilium (apparently for liberation *from* Lysimachus), Erythrae, Colophon, and Magnesia-on-the-Meander: see Bickermann 1938: 243–6; Walbank 1984: 92.

34 See Shipley 2000: 157, with evidence.

35 On the circumstances surrounding the Hymn to Demetrius, see conveniently Habicht 1997: 92–3. Similarly, the Ionian League decreed divine honors for King Antiochus I in expectation of specific favors (*OGIS* 222). Athen. 6.253e condemns the servility of the Athenians – the former victors of Marathon – toward Antigonus and Demetrius.

36 On "royal holy families," see Billows 1995: 42. The Ptolemies: Fraser 1972: 225–6. The Seleucids: see Welles 1934: nos 36 and 37 (with Robert 1967: 281–96), and *OGIS* 245.

37 On all this, see Walbank 1984: 75–6.

38 See Arist. *Pol.* 1284a and 1287a–1288a, with Billows 1995: 58 and n5.

39 There were numerous treatises on kingship written in the hellenistic period, some by prominent intellectuals (e.g., Zeno the founder of Stoicism, and Demetrius of Phalerum); but little directly survives. We are dependent upon later (sometimes much later) summaries of what such thinkers wrote: see Walbank 1984: 76–8. In addition, there were letters of advice written for the kings, the most important surviving one being the *Letter to Philocrates* by Aristaeus: on which see O. Murray 1967.

40 See Eckstein 1995: 35–7 and 45–6, and Beston 2000. Official propaganda: *OGIS* 219 (Antiochus I) and 332 (Attalus I). If there was no war at the moment, the king could be praised for his courage in hunting (Polyb. 22.3.5–9: Ptolemy V).

41 On the strategic role of Attalid Pergamum in the struggle of the coastal cities to survive against the Celts of the Anatolian Plateau, see McShane 1964: 52–4, 60–1, and 158–9.

42 On the role of Macedon as "the shield of Greece" against attack from the barbarian north, see Polyb. 9.35.3, 18.37.9 and 31.29.3–5 with Walbank 1967: 598; 1979: 512–13.

43 On the relationship of kingship to law, see Walbank 1984: 76–7.

44 See, e.g., Aristaeus, *Letter to Philocrates*, esp. 291–2; Theophrastus, *On Kingship* (*P Oxy* 1611, lines 42–6); *OGIS* 229, lines 6–7 (Seleucus II); *OGIS* 332 (Attalus III); all with Walbank 1984: 83.

45 See Xen. *Oec.* 21.12; or Welles 1934: no. 35, line 12 (Amynander, king of Athamania in northwest Greece, ca. 200 BC).

46 Cf. Shipley 2000: 106.

47 Good discussion in Shipley 2000: 87–8.

48 See Ma 2002; cf. Shipley 2000: 74.

49 Ael. *VH* 2.20; cf. Volkmann 1967.

50 The greatest taxers were the Ptolemies, who imposed 1,600 different kinds of taxes upon the population of Egypt. See E. Turner 1984: 144–53.

51 See the astringent comments of Billows 1995: 20–3, 56.

52 See Billows 1995: 45–55 (on the ideology behind the Boscoreale paintings).

53 For examples from Ptolemaic Egypt, see N. Lewis 1986: ch. 7.

54 See Green 1990: 187–9. Though the Ptolemies did much to try to placate the Egyptian priestly class, it was only in the reign of Cleopatra VII ca. 45 BC that we find a Ptolemaic ruler who could even speak Egyptian.

55 A point emphasized by Billows 1995: 65, 74–5.

56 Demetrius and the Parthenon: Plut. *Dem.* 29; Ptolemy II's penis float: Athen. 196a–203b. Ptolemy IV's drunkenness: Polyb. 5.34.10; Demetrius I: Polyb. 31.13; 33.19. Antiochus III and Philip V: Polyb. 20.8; 25.3.7.

57 On the War of the Brothers, see Ma 2002: 45–6; on Philip V's murder of his son, see Derow 1989: 295. Ptolemy VIII and the two Cleopatras: see Diod. Sic. 34/35.14 and 20; Justin 38.8.12–9.1 and 39.1–2, with Gruen 1984: 713, 715.

58 See Polyb. 3.19.10–11 and 7.12–14, cf. Plut. *Arat.* 49–50 (Messene); Polyb. 10.26, cf. Plut. *Mor.* 760a (Argos); Polyb. 15.22.3–4 (Cius); Polyb. 15.24.1–2 (Thasos), with Eckstein 1995: 88–90.

59 Still fundamental on Polybius' attitude toward kingship is Welwei 1963.

60 On interstate arbitration, see Ager 1996. But on the harsh attitude of the most powerful states, see Badian 1983: 402; Shipley 2000: 80.

61 See the optimistic reconstructions of a self-restrained hellenistic state system and balance of power offered by Droysen 1878: 182; Tarn 1913: 1; Braunert 1964: esp. 80–1;Welles 1965: 220–1; Veyne 1975: 823, 837–8; Klose 1982: 80–8; Will 1982: 61; and Bederman 2001: 43 and n63.

62 Waltz 1979 is the classic study of international-system anarchy and its impact; see now also Mearsheimer 2001.

63 On the negative impact of international anarchy upon states – militarization, dependence upon self-help, power maximization, the constant friction and unrestrained clashes of interest – see Waltz 1979 and Mearsheimer 2001; and now for the ancient world Eckstein 2006.

64 See the shocked comments of modern political scientists on the primitive and counter-productive nature of ancient crisis diplomacy: Lebow 1991; Kauppi 1991. On honor culture and resistance to threats: see B. Strauss 1986: 31–6. Examples from the hellenistic period: the refusal of Byzantium to bow to Rhodian threats, the result being war: Polyb. 4.47–8; the failure of peace talks between Ptolemy IV and Antiochus III in winter 218/217 BC, the result being war: Polyb. 5.67–8; the refusal of Philip V to bow to Roman threats in 200, the result being war: Polyb. 16.34.

65 The breakthrough article here is Lévêque 1968; cf. Austin 1986, followed now by Eckstein 2006: ch. 4.

66 See, from the 240s, the examples of Smyrna: *OGIS* 220, lines 3–5; and Telmessus: *OGIS* 55, line 10. From the end of the century, see Cius (Polyb. 15.21), and Thasos (15.24.6).

67 See the grim picture in Préaux 1978: 425–32. On the damage caused to the smaller states from the continuous wars among the great Greek powers in the third century, see Ager 2003: 49. Pervasive use of pirates: see conveniently Garlan 1978 (with sources).

68 Despite the implication of W. Harris 1979: chs 1–3, 5.

69 *OGIS* 219 (from Troy in the 270s, praising Antiochus I); cf. also Plut. *Pyrrh.* 13.1.

70 See e.g. Plut. *Demetr.* 44.3 (explicit on the devastating impact of perceived weakness).

71 Roy 1998: 114. Note also that official depictions never showed kings as older than early middle age even when they were quite old: Roy 1998: 133–4; cf. Shipley 2000: 69.

72 The goat-horn coinage of Philip V: see e.g. Perseus Coin Catalogue (online), Museum of Fine Arts, Boston, coin acquired 1984, no. 44. Ptolemy II's float: see again Athen. 196a–203b, with Rice 1983.

73 Lysimachus: Plut. *Demetr.* 22.3 and *Pausanius* 1.9.5 ; Seleucus: App. *Syr.* 57.

74 Seleucid statistics: Bickermann 1938: 13, cf. Walbank 1984: 63. Militaristic images on coinage, militaristic titles of kings, and the "theology of victory": Lévêque 1968: 276–9. Ptolemy VI: Polyb. 28.21 and 39.7.1, with Eckstein 1995: 30.

75 Plut. *Pyrrh.* 7.5 (with spears, then swords, against the opposing commander), 28.4, 34.1–2; for an early Roman view of Pyrrhus' personal ferocity: Enn. *Ann.* 183–6.

76 On the constant warfare engaged in by the Achaean League, still valuable is Walbank 1933; for Aetolia, see Scholten 1999; on the warlike behavior of small city-states in this period, see the brilliant article by Ma 2000.

77 That is, war was the essential tool in hellenistic interstate relations, and the normal recourse when there was a severe clash of interest. Lévêque 1968: 279. For Waltz's general rule, see Waltz 1959: 160; 1979: 102; 1988: 620–1. Note the parallel conclusion of de Romilly 1968: 207 on the earlier classical period.

78 Polyb. 15.20.2–4, on which see now Eckstein 2005.

79 See esp. Errington 1971, 1986.

80 Cf. Shipley 2000: 78.

81 Discussion: see Eckstein 1995: 50–4.

82 On the theme of monarchical control, see the classic study of Orth 1977. The emphasis on "parity" in Ma's own otherwise excellent study of Antiochus III and the cities is now modified by Ma himself in the second edition: Ma 2002: 383–4.

83 The Rhodians in 201/200 BC were joined by Pergamum, Athens, and Ptolemaic Egypt in desperately calling for help from Rome in the face of the overwhelming threat from the Antigonids and Seleucids. For discussion, see now Eckstein 2008: chs 4–6.

84 In political science terms, a situation of anarchy and nondifferentiated polities (all warlike) would have exited into a situation of empire in which most states would not be warlike, though the hegemonic state (Macedon) would still be. See Wilkinson 1999 for the scenario.

85 Useful discussion of the complex confrontations and massive wars of 200–188 BC: Errington 1989.

86 On the surprisingly early emergence of the *pax Romana* under the Republic, see Cornell 1993.

CHAPTER 17

The Ethics of Autocracy in the Roman World

Carlos F. Noreña

Political Thought in the Roman Empire

Most political thought during the Roman Empire was expressed either in direct appeals to or judgments of individual Roman emperors, or in abstract theoretical treatises that aimed for, and nearly achieved, total detachment from contemporary society. There was very little in the way of sustained, critical engagement with the nature of the political order upon which the Roman imperial state was based, very little reflection upon its normative claims or informed discussion of possible alternatives. That is hardly surprising. After the accession of the emperor Tiberius in AD 14, the monarchy, as an institution, was a fact, beyond deliberation, and for many years before this the permanence of the empire could simply be taken for granted. Indeed, ancient readers of Vergil's *Aeneid* could be forgiven for accepting Jupiter's prophecy about the Romans' infinite empire (1.278–9) and for concluding, like Francis Fukuyama some 2,000 years later, that history had come to an end.

The most conspicuous symbol of Rome's imperial might was the figure of the emperor. Sitting alone at the apex of a steep political and social hierarchy that encompassed over 50 million subjects, the Roman emperor wielded power of unprecedented scope. In attempting to come to grips with this dominant figure on the political and conceptual landscape, writers of the imperial period could not escape the conclusion that the emperor's power was, in principle, absolute. The Roman jurists (who ought to have known) were explicit on this point. "The emperor is freed from the laws," as Ulpian proclaims (*Dig.* 1.3.31), an open declaration of autocracy that rather undermines the logic, dubious in any case, that the emperor's opinion had "the force of law" because his *imperium* (legal authority) had been voted to him by a law of the *populus Romanus* (*Dig.* 1.4.1 *praefatio*; cf. Gai. *Inst.* 1.2.5). Seneca is more elegant but no less to the point, opening his *De clementia* with a striking tableau of Nero's awesome power, as the emperor himself might imagine it:

A Companion to Greek and Roman Political Thought, First Edition. Edited by Ryan K. Balot.
© 2013 Blackwell Publishing Ltd. Published 2013 by Blackwell Publishing Ltd.

I am the arbiter of life and death for the nations [*gentes*]; it rests with my power what each man's lot and state shall be; by my lips Fortune proclaims what gift she would bestow on each human being; from my utterance peoples and cities gather reasons for rejoicing; without my favor and grace no part of the wide world can prosper; all those many thousands of swords which my peace restrains will be drawn at my nod; what nations shall be utterly destroyed, which banished, which shall receive the gift of liberty, which have it taken from them, what kings shall become slaves and whose heads shall be crowned with honor, what cities shall fall and which shall rise – this it is mine to decree. (1.1.2; trans. Basore 1928)

Even Pliny, who strives in his *Panegyricus* to represent Trajan as a civilian ruler respectful of the senate and, above all, subject to the laws (65.1), cannot avoid acknowledging that the emperor's power was total, "equal to that of the immortal gods" (4.4). And in all these writers and their contemporaries we can discern an unspoken but nevertheless pervasive assumption that this state of affairs was permanent. This or that emperor may come or go, but the monarchy was here to stay. For a venerable Greco-Roman intellectual tradition of political thought that was rooted in formal analysis of different constitutions and their attendant advantages and disadvantages for everything from the management of the state to the cultivation of the soul, this was something of a conceptual prison.

Conditions in the Roman empire, then, were not exactly propitious for major advances in the field of political theory. The contrast with the dynamic and labile world of Greek city-states in the archaic and classical periods is quite pronounced in this respect (see Forsdyke, this volume, chapter 15). In a world in which the cycle of constitutional change had apparently ceased to operate, traditional analysis of different constitutional forms held little appeal. And in an apparently stable political system in which the emperor's power was notionally absolute, formal analysis of that system would have been otiose. One potentially attractive subject, by contrast, was the emperor himself, and in particular his personal character. Because there were no legal constraints on his behavior, the emperor's own character stood in theory as the sole determinant of his actions. The nature of the emperor's personality was therefore a vital political question. And this was not lost on contemporaries. Following his vignette of Nero's power, for example, Seneca turns immediately to the individual qualities that should hold this terrifying power in check, observing that a "good" emperor will not be motivated by anger, youthful passion, rashness, or stubbornness (*Clem.* 1.1.3). Many other writers, too, explored the nexus between the emperor's character, his actions, and the quality of political and social life in the empire (mainly, it must be said, from the perspective of the educated elite). Even in more theoretical works on ideal rulership in which the emperor was not the ostensible subject, praise of monarchy as a form of government generally gave way to celebration of the ideal ruler's character. As a result, most political discourse in the Roman Empire was really an ethical discourse on the personal character of monarchs.

In developing this discourse, writers of the imperial period were able to draw on a longstanding biographical and philosophical tradition, going back to Isocrates, Xenophon, and Plato in the fourth century BC, in which rulers were judged primarily in moral terms (see in this volume Forsdyke, chapter 15, and Stadter, chapter 29). Even in other genres, such as historiography, the personal character of the main actors was always a central concern (cf. Stadter, chapter 29). But the range and precision of the terminology now employed to render such judgments represented something new and distinctive. Whereas classical Greek political theorists tended to work with small constellations of virtues – the most famous being the Platonic canon of justice (*dikaiosunē*), wisdom (*sophia* or *phronēsis*), temperance (*sōphrosynē*), and bravery (*andreia*) – writers under the Roman Empire, both Roman and Greek, often presented their readers with elaborate panoramas of virtues and vices. This allowed for quite nuanced treatments of a ruler's personal character and its impact on state and society.

The political thought of the Roman Empire may be characterized, therefore, by the near total convergence of political and ethical language, on the one hand, and by the development of a highly articulated vocabulary of virtue and vice for the judgment of emperors and other rulers, on the other. The overwhelming power of the Roman emperor was the inescapable fact on the ground that structured this body of thought and dictated the sharp focus on the politics of one-man rule. And though this power militated against bold innovation in the field of political theory as a whole, it did nevertheless encourage incisive thinking on the relationship between power and virtue, which, over time, produced a robust "ethics of autocracy" that helped to shape political discourse in the Roman Empire and the normative framework in which emperors operated.

Romans on Monarchy: From Theory to Reality

When Roman political theory was inaugurated by Cicero in the late 50s BC, the advent of monarchy at Rome, in the idiosyncratic form of Augustus' "restoration of the republic" in 28–27 BC (*Res Gestae* 34.1), was still a generation away. This makes the political thought of this period critically important for our understanding of Roman theories of monarchy, because this thought was not yet conditioned by the presence of an actual monarch. But this valuable analytical window was shortlived. In fact, within a relatively brief period from the late 50s down to the early years of Augustus' reign, we can trace an evolution in Roman approaches to monarchy, from the theoretical to the practical (see also Stadter, chapter 29). Before turning to the writings of the imperial age, then, it will be useful to consider this formative period in Roman thinking on monarchy, with special attention to three key texts: Cicero's *De republica*, composed between 54 and 51 BC; his *Pro Marcello*, based on a short speech delivered to the senate in 46 BC; and the first book of Livy's *Ab urbe condita*, completed between 27 and 25 BC.

The *De republica*, a philosophical dialogue in the Platonic mold, examined the relationship between the ideal commonwealth (*res publica*) and the ideal citizen (Zetzel 1995: 1–34). The first book centers on a discussion of the best commonwealth. When asked to declare which commonwealth is best, Scipio Aemilianus, the main character of the dialogue, chooses monarchy (*Rep.* 1.54–5). This choice has been the subject of much discussion, but it must be set in the context of Scipio's overall argument. Scipio had already made it clear to his interlocutors that a mixed commonwealth was best (1.45), a view repeated at the end of book 1 and then underlined by the assertion that Rome's mixed commonwealth is in fact the best of all (1.69–71; cf. Lintott 1997). In addition, in an important passage that precedes discussion of the different types of commonwealth, Scipio subordinates these individual types to their shared purpose, which is both to provide long-lasting *consilium* ("deliberation") (1.41) and "to defend that bond which first bound men together in the association of a commonwealth" (1.42), a bond explained earlier as "consensus on the law" and "shared advantage" (1.39). For Scipio, then, monarchy is inferior to a mixed commonwealth and only "tolerable" (1.42) insofar as it preserves the implicit contract upon which organized society is based.

Scipio's choice of monarchy is nevertheless significant, because it is ranked ahead of both aristocracy and democracy as the unmixed commonwealth best suited to preserving this contract. There are two main arguments in favor of monarchy in book 1. The first is that it is analogous to other types of legitimate unitary authority, including the sole rule of Jupiter over the other gods (1.56); the supremacy of reasoned judgment (*consilium*) over anger, greed, ambition, and lust in men's minds (1.60); and the authority of the *paterfamilias* over the rest of the household (1.61). The second is that individual leadership is more effective than communal leadership in times of emergency (1.62–3). Underpinning both arguments is the notion that a monarch's legitimate authority depends on his administration of justice, without which monarchy degenerates into tyranny (1.65–8). Cicero then fleshes out these views on monarchy in book 2, in which he offers, still through the voice of Scipio, a historical overview of Rome's regal period. Here we learn that the prerequisite for a legitimate monarch is not pedigree, as the Spartans mistakenly believed, but rather individual character, especially *virtus* ("manliness, courage; virtue") and *sapientia* ("wisdom") (2.24). And though the people lack *libertas* ("freedom") under a monarchy, that form of rule is nevertheless superior to aristocracy and democracy as long as the monarch can maintain security, equality, and peace through his power, justice, and wisdom (2.43). Without these qualities, and especially without justice, the monarch becomes a tyrant (2.48). The figure most beneficial to the community is therefore the opposite of a tyrant, which the reader might reasonably expect to be a monarch. But through a type of dialectical reasoning, Cicero arrives at something rather different:

> Let there be opposed to this man [the tyrant] another, who is good and wise and knowledgeable about the interests and the reputation of the state, almost a tutor and manager of the commonwealth [*quasi tutor et procurator rei publicae*]; that, in fact, is the name for whoever is the guide and helmsman of the state [*rector et gubernator civitatis*]. Make sure you recognize this man; he is the one who can protect the state by his wisdom [*consilium*] and efforts. (2.51; trans. Zetzel 1995)

The metaphorical language of the passage (signaled by *quasi*) makes simple identification with a conventional monarch untenable. In addition, it should be noted that Cicero elsewhere employs the terms *rector* and *gubernator* to identify the ideal republican statesman in contexts in which monarchy is out of the question (*De or.*

1.211; *Sest.* 98). It is also unlikely that Cicero was inviting a political strongman, such as Pompey, to take control of the state, or that he was calling for the rise of a charismatic *Führer*, as some Nazi propagandists of the 1930s claimed (Zetzel 1995: 27–9). Given the emphasis in book 1 on the superiority of the mixed constitution, and in light of Cicero's own republican convictions, it is best to see this passage as a description of a traditional republican statesman (Powell 1994). After all, Cicero himself described the dialogue as an inquiry into the nature of the "best citizen" (*optimus civis: Q Fr.* 3.5.1). The *De republica* was not an argument for establishing monarchy at Rome.

With the *Pro Marcello* we come to a transformed political landscape and to a new stage in Cicero's thinking on one-man rule. Frankly accepting that Caesar, on the cusp of total victory in the civil wars of 49–45 BC, was in a position to dominate the Roman world, Cicero attempts to channel this power in the interests of the community as a whole. He first praises Caesar for having pardoned his enemy M. Claudius Marcellus, and then invites him to undertake no less a task than the restoration of the entire commonwealth (esp. 27–9). Cicero bases his rhetorical strategy in part on a celebration of Caesar's virtues, especially *clementia* ("mercy") and *sapientia* (1, 9, 18–19), and in part on an extended appeal to Caesar's desire for immortal glory, which will come not from his past military victories, shared, as they were, with Fortune and with the rank-and-file soldiers, but rather through his future restoration of the commonwealth, which Caesar alone can accomplish (7, 11, 28–9). It is a complex mix of praise, focused not on achievements but on character, and prescription (S. Braund 1998). For Cicero, then, the question was no longer what form the commonwealth should take – indeed, Caesar himself is closely identified with the commonwealth in several passages (21, 22, 25, 32) – but how the new form represented by Caesar's dictatorship should operate. The generic requirements of the *Pro Marcello* and above all the political exigencies of the times explain this shift in perspective from that of the *De republica*.

We find a new perspective on monarchy in the first book of Livy's *Ab urbe condita* (Ogilvie 1965: 30–232; Miles 1995: esp. 137–78). Written between 27 and 25 BC, just after Octavian's assumption of the title Augustus and the so-called "first settlement" of his anomalous position in the state, book 1 treats Rome's foundation and regal period, conventionally dated from 753 to 509 BC, from the perspective of one watching the reemergence of monarchy before his own eyes. In describing the investiture of Rome's kings, Livy is always careful to specify the legitimate basis of their authority, which ultimately rested on the consent of the people (1.7.1–3, 17–18; 22.1, 32.1, 35.6, 46.1). Only when Tarquinius Superbus acceded to the throne through a violent usurpation did "just and legitimate" kingship at Rome come to an end (1.47–8). Whether or not these details are accurate is beside the point. What is significant is Livy's sensitivity to the question of the "constitutional" procedures by which Rome's kings were (or were not) made legitimate, so typical of an age in which unrepublican powers were routinely defined in traditional, legal terms.

Even more important is Livy's attitude to the relationship between constitutional form and popular *libertas*. In several passages in book 1 Livy alludes to the absence of *libertas* under the kings (1.17, 46, 48), despite the fact that legitimate accession to the throne depended upon the people's will. Evidently the prerogative to choose a monarch did not constitute freedom, in Livy's opinion. The opening lines of book 2 make this abundantly clear (2.1): "I will now write the history of a free Roman people and their annual magistrates, when the commands of the laws were stronger than those of men" ("imperiaque legum potentiora quam hominum"). Here Livy echoes Cicero's views in the *De republica* on the incompatibility of monarchy and *libertas* (1.43.1, 47, 50.3, 55.2; 2.43.5); there is also a parallel with Cicero's claim in the *De officiis* that when justice can no longer be secured from a single ruler, men turn to the protection of the laws (2.41–2; cf. Ferrary 1995). For Livy, then, *libertas* (freedom) was the right of "the people" (i.e. the citizen body) to choose annually elected officials whose authority was subject to the laws which the people themselves had promulgated. But Livy makes the additional point that the Roman people would not have been ready for *libertas* before the reign of Tarquinius Superbus, developing an evolutionary schema in which the monarchy is presented as necessary, at an early stage of development, both to preserve concord and to teach Romans to love their families and their land (2.1.4–6). Once the people had reached maturity in these things, monarchy was no longer necessary or desirable, and true freedom could begin with the annual election of consuls (2.1.7). In Livy's eclectic treatment of monarchy, then, we find an emphasis on "constitutional" authority; an evolutionary model of society in which the monarchy plays a vital role in bringing about the republic by establishing the necessary conditions and attitudes in which republicanism could flourish (a point that Machiavelli would later highlight in his *Discourses on Livy*, 1.9, 1.11, 1.19 etc.); and the courageous suggestion that there can be no *libertas* under a monarchy, even one that is "just and legitimate."

In these three texts we have three sets of ideas on monarchy. Elements of the *Pro Marcello* and Livy book 1, both written under autocrats, stand as precursors to several characteristic features of political thought under the empire. The refrain of Caesar's personal virtues in the *Pro Marcello* and the subtle blending of praise and prescription throughout the speech together provide the basic formula for later imperial pan- egyric. Livy's projection onto the past of judgments about individual rulers and about monarchy as an institution prefigures much imperial historiography and biography, both of which, through their focus on the past, and especially on past emperors, can offer only oblique commentary on contemporary politics. And the valuation of individual *libertas* as an aristocratic ideal in opposition to autocracy becomes a major theme of political discourse in the early empire (Wirszubski 1950: esp. 124– 71; Roller 2001: 213–87; cf. Brunt 1988b for the republican background). It is no accident that of these three texts, it is Cicero's *De republica*, written before the advent of monarchy, that does not have much formal influence on later political thought, which is mostly devoid of typological analyses of different constitutions. In one important respect, however, the *De republica*, as well as its companion piece from the late 50s, the *De legibus*, contains the roots of a simple idea that will flourish under the empire, and that is the fundamental distinction between individual monarchs and the institution of monarchy as such. As Cicero puts it in the *De legibus*, "the monarchic form of constitution, which was once approved, was repudiated afterwards, not because of the faults of monarchy, but because of the faults of the monarch" (3.15; cf. *Rep.* 2.43). A useful thought – for even though Cicero's aristocratic heirs under the empire could not overthrow the Principate, they could still judge, and indeed repudiate, individual emperors.

The Kaleidoscope of Royal Virtues and Vices

From the late republic and early Augustan period we turn now to the imperial period. We move from diachronic to synchronic analysis, and to works that range from a focus on the Roman emperor to those that address rulership more generally, written in both Latin and Greek. This approach can be justified in part by the timeless questions that these texts address, and in part by the broad coherence of this body of thought (the complexities of individual authors and texts naturally deserve systematic analysis, too, but that is beyond the scope of this chapter). This coherence results largely from the prominence accorded to personal character in these texts and to their shared conceptual framework for the judgment of rulers. As a result of this basic orientation, the political discourse of the imperial period has something of a kaleidoscopic quality, as virtues and vices are endlessly rearranged in different configurations in order to evaluate specific emperors or imagined rulers. As we shall see, this ethical program not only defined the profile of the ideal monarch, but also transcended the universe of ideas by producing a real-world model of monarchic behavior that Roman emperors ignored at their peril.

The texts under consideration range from concentration on one or a few human qualities to discussion of dozens of virtues and vices. At one end of the spectrum is Seneca's *De clementia*, completed in AD 55–6, near the beginning of Nero's reign, and devoted to the exposition of a single imperial virtue, mercy (Adam 1970; M. Griffin 1976: esp. 129–71; Barden Dowling 2005: esp. 169–218; Braund forthcoming). *Clementia*, according to Seneca, is "the moderation of the soul when taking vengeance or the gentleness of the stronger towards the weaker in meting out punishments" (2.3.1). Though *clementia* is, of all the virtues, the one most appropriate to man (1.3.2; cf. 1.25.1 on the cruelty of wild beasts), it is especially important for an emperor in particular (1.3.3), because it is the principal quality that restrains his absolute power and distinguishes him from a tyrant (1.11–13). Seneca emphasizes that *clementia* is not to be confused with pity (*misericordia*), which is not a virtue (2.4.4), and that its opposite is not strictness (*severitas*), but rather cruelty (2.4.1). Indeed, he had already offered a sketch of imperial cruelty in his *Apocolocyntosis*, a wicked mockery of Claudius' deification which sharply criticized the emperor's perversion of justice; the short text culminates in Claudius' own trial in Hades in which the dead emperor is charged with the murder of 35 senators, 221 *equites*, and "countless others" (*Apoc.* 14).

At the other end of the spectrum from Seneca's meditation on a single imperial virtue is Pliny's *Panegyricus*, a speech of thanks to the emperor Trajan, delivered on the occasion of Pliny's election to the consulship in AD 100 and later circulated as a written text (Durry 1938; Fedeli 1989; Bartsch 1994: 148–87; Braund 1998: 58–68;

Gowing 2005: 120–30). In this text Pliny bombards the reader with a dizzying cascade of more than 30 imperial virtues. The theme is established right from the outset. Pliny first lauds the emperor for his sense of duty (*pietas*), restraint, clemency, humane character, moderation, and good nature (2.6–7), and then offers a serial contrast between imperial virtues and vices:

> For there is no risk that when I speak about his humane character, he [Trajan] will think that he is being censured for arrogance, or that I am referring to licentiousness instead of temperance, savagery instead of mercy [*clementia*], greed instead of generosity [*liberalitas*], malice instead of kindness, wantonness instead of self-control, sloth instead of toil, fear instead of courage. (Plin. *Pan.* 3.4)

And all of this is just an introduction to the extended discourse on human qualities that follows, which includes both standard imperial virtues, such as *iustitia* ("justice," e.g. 33.2), *indulgentia* (e.g. 21.4), and *fides* ("good faith," 67.1), and less common ones, such as *simplicitas* ("candor," 4.6), *hilaritas* ("cheerfulness," 4.6), and *comitas* ("friendliness," 71.6). Like the *Pro Marcello*, the speech combines praise with prescription, and like its predecessor it dwells less on concrete achievements than on personal character. This rhetorical strategy allows Pliny not only to draw an effective contrast between the "good" Trajan and the "bad" Domitian – for the latter's imperial achievements were not negligible, and Trajan's reign had just begun – but also to guide the emperor's future actions in positive ways, especially toward the beneficent paternalism implied by *indulgentia* (Cotton 1984); toward the courteous treatment of senators that befits a *civilis princeps* endowed with *modestia* and *moderatio* ("humility" and "self-control," 3.2) (Wallace-Hadrill 1982); and toward the virtuous behavior that would justify the honorific title "Optimus" (88.4–10).

Between these two ends of the spectrum lie the bulk of texts that address rulership in one way or another, in which a handful of virtues and vices play a more or less substantial role. And it is in these texts, taken as a whole, that a profile of the ideal-typical monarch or tyrant can be discerned, defined above all by the human qualities that were thought to shape monarchic or tyrannical action. Not all human qualities, however, were equally significant for rulers. In the kaleidoscope of royal virtues and vices, to return to the metaphor employed above, certain qualities tend to stand out again and again.

The most important royal virtue was justice (*dikaiosunē, iustitia*). This conception goes all the way back to ancient Near Eastern belief systems (cf. Raaflaub 2000: 52–7 and Raaflaub, this volume, chapter 3), of course, and had long since been canonized in Plato's *Republic*, but the theme remains prominent under the Roman Empire, especially in Greek authors. In the "kingship orations" of Dio Chrysostom (Dio. *Or.* 1–4; cf. Desideri 1978; Moles 1990), for example, composed in the early second century and probably addressed to Trajan, justice is repeatedly invoked as a defining quality for a king (e.g., 1.45, 2.26, 2.54, 3.7, 3.32, 4.24). As he asks, "for whom is a sense of justice more important than for the one who is above the laws" (3.10)? In this Dio is followed by Aelius Aristides, whose encomium of an unnamed emperor (*Eis Basilea*), probably Antoninus Pius (C. Jones 1972; cf. Swift 1966 for a third century date), also identifies justice as a distinctive royal virtue (Aristid. *Or.* 35.8, 15, 17).

Justice is also prominent in the Stoic writers of the imperial period. According to Epictetus, it was specifically his dispensation of justice that made Heracles, a frequent model for monarchs (e.g. Dio *Or.* 1.83), a true king (3.26.31–2). The ideal is also stitched into the very fabric of Marcus Aurelius' *Meditations* (e.g., 3.6.1, 5.12.2, 6.47.6, 50.1; 7.54, 7.63.1, 8.39, 10.11.2, 11.1.5, 12.1.2–4, 12.15), written by a private individual for his own edification, to be sure, but inevitably reflecting the preoccupations of a Roman emperor (Brunt 1974; Hadot 1998). And for one who knew the meaning of the royal office better than anyone, justice was deemed to be the virtue "upon which all others depend" (11.10.4). It is no surprise, then, that this virtue is also prominent in the imperial panegyrics of the late third and fourth centuries AD (e.g., *Pan. Lat.* 3.21.4, 4.1.5, 6.6.1, 7.3.4, 11.19.2; cf. Seager 1984; Nixon and Rodgers 1994). Indeed, Menander Rhetor, in his brief manual on how to praise a king (Russell and Wilson 1981), encourages discussion of a number of virtues under the heading of justice, which usefully distinguishes the king from the tyrant (375). Emphasis on royal justice reaches an apogee of sorts in the "pseudo-Pythagorean" kingship treatises (*Peri Basileas*) of Ecphantus, Sthenidas, and Diotogenes, written perhaps in the second or third century AD (Delatte 1942; Centrone 1990: 13–44; for the texts, Thesleff 1965). It is Diotogenes who goes furthest, opening his essay with an esoteric amalgamation of justice, law, and the king himself:

> The king ought to be the one who is most just [*dikaiotatos*], and the one who is most just is the one who is most lawful [*nomimōtatos*]. For without justice no one can be king, and without the law there can be no justice. Justice exists through the law, and the law, of course, is the cause of justice. And the king is either the living law [*nomos empsychos*] or the lawful ruler; for these reasons, therefore, the king is most just and most lawful. (71.18–23; all citations of pseudo-Pythagorean texts by page and line number in Thesleff 1965)

Though the language of this passage is rather abstract, and the logic less than airtight, it is a sentiment with which Cicero, for whom *iustitia* was "the queen of all the virtues" (*Off.* 3.28), would have agreed.

The repeated citation of justice as a royal virtue reflects the deeper concern to define the correct relationship between a monarch and the law, a critically important issue in classical Greek and Hellenistic political thought as well (see in this volume, Forsdyke, chapter 15, and Eckstein, chapter 16). For Cicero and Livy, writing before the full flowering of monarchy after Augustus, one-man rule and the rule of law were simply incompatible (see above). Later authors, who were forced to confront autocracy, openly admitted that emperors were freed from the laws, but developed the ideal that the "good" emperor should nevertheless submit to them. Hence the centrality and enduring appeal of justice, which more than any other virtue ensured the monarch's voluntary submission to the same laws that bound his subjects.

Following justice in importance comes a set of four royal virtues, all of which have slightly different inflections in Greek and Latin authors: courage (*andreia, virtus, fortitudo*), temperance (*sōphrosynē, enkrateia, moderatio, temperantia, continentia*), reverence for the gods (*eusebeia, hosiotēs, pietas*), and benevolence (*philanthrōpia, liberalitas, indulgentia, humanitas*). Courage is equally prominent in Greek (e.g., Dio *Or.* 2.26, 2.54, 3.7, 3.32, 3.58, 4.24; Aristid. *Or.* 35.29, 38; M. Aur. *Med.* 3.6.1, 3.11.3, 5.12.2, 11.18.21; Men. Rhet. 372–3) and Latin authors (e.g., Plin. *Pan.* 3.4; Suet. *Aug.* 21.3; *Pan. Lat.* 2.40.3, 3.5.4, 4.1–5, 7.3.4, 11.19.2). For most Greek authors of the imperial period, courage is a generic royal quality that does not require comment. Of the passages cited above, for example, only Menander associates it with actions in war (372–3). In the Latin moral lexicon *virtus*, like *andreia*, could be an ethical quality – sometimes closer, in fact, to *aretē* than to *andreia* (McDonnell 2006) – but as an imperial virtue it normally referred to the courage on the battlefield that guaranteed imperial victory. Typical is the anonymous panegyric to Constantine from 313 (*Pan. Lat.* 12), in which the speaker declares, "every type of war, weapon, and enemy yields to you alone, as well as the monuments of courage preserved in writing from the memory of every age" (24.3).

Temperance was a more elastic virtue, denoting a range of behaviors that pointed to moderation and self-control – especially desirable in autocrats unencumbered by external restraints – with particular reference to bodily pleasures and to the emotions (e.g., Plin. *Pan.* 2.7–8, 3.2; Aristid. *Or.* 35.27–9; Diotog. 72.25–9; Men. Rhet. 376; cf. Dio *Or.* 3.7, 3.32, 3.58, 3.85; M. Aur. *Med.* 3.6.1, 5.12.2, 7.63.1; *Pan. Lat.* 3.5.4, 4.1.5, 7.3.4, 11.19.2). It was an imperial virtue more often remarked in the breach than in the observance. In Suetonius' imperial biographies, in particular, composed in the mid-second century AD, the vices of personal excess, such as extravagance (*luxuria*) and lust (*libido*), are standard markers of "bad" emperors (e.g., *Calig.* 56.1; *Nero* 26.1, 29.1; *Vit.* 13.1, 17.2; *Dom.* 22.1; cf. Wallace-Hadrill 1983: esp. 142–75).

Reverence for the gods is a consistent theme in the Greek authors (e.g., Dio *Or.* 1.15; Aristid. *Or.* 35.8, 15; cf. Epict. 3.26.32 on Heracles), but it is elevated to the status of a major virtue, almost on a par with justice, in the Latin authors. For the Romans, in fact, *pietas* was a core ideal, one that expressed the fulfillment of obligations to anyone or anything, including but not limited to the gods, to whom or to which they were owed. As a result, a Roman emperor was expected to display *pietas* not only toward the gods (cf. *Pan. Lat.* 11.6.1), but toward other objects as well, especially his subjects (Plin. *Pan.* 2.3–6; *Pan. Lat.* 7.5.1), his parents (natural: Tac. *Ann.* 14.3.3; Amm. Marc. 15.8.14; adoptive: Plin. *Pan.* 10.3; Pliny, *Ep.* 10.1), and the state (Amm. Marc. 15.8.14).

Finally, benevolence. Greek authors tended to treat *philanthrōpia*, like *andreia*, as a crucial but nevertheless generic royal virtue (Dio *Or.* 1.17, 20; 2.26, 4.24; Aristid. *Or.* 35.8; Philo, *Mos.* 2.9; Men. Rhet. 374). As the pseudo-Pythagorean writer Archytas put it, "The true ruler must not only possess the knowledge and power of ruling well, but must also be a lover of man [*philanthrōpos*]; for it would be absurd for a shepherd to hate his flock" (36.1–5). For Latin authors, by contrast, this sort of benevolence was best understood through its concrete manifestations, the most prominent of which were acts of personal generosity, especially in the material realm. This virtue was expressed by the concept of *liberalitas* (Kloft 1970; for *liberalitas* as a "humane" virtue, see Sen. *Ep.* 66.13, 115.3). *Liberalitas* is the dominant Trajanic virtue in Pliny's *Panegyricus* (3.4, 25.3, 25.5, 27.3, 28.4, 33.2, 34.3, 38.2, 38.4, 43.4, 51.5, 86.5), a regular marker of "good" emperors in Suetonius (*Aug.* 41.1; *Vesp.* 17; cf. *Nero* 10.1; *Dom.* 9.1), and a theme that still finds resonance in the late antique panegyrics (esp. *Pan. Lat.* 9, a request for the rebuilding of the rhetorical schools at Augustodunum).

In addition to these five virtues, many other royal qualities were routinely cited in discussions of rulers, from canonical virtues such as wisdom (Dio *Or.* 3.7, 3.58; M. Aur. *Med.* 5.9.5, 18.3; Ecph. 84.6; Men. Rhet. 373, 375) to novel ones such as gentleness (Dio *Or.* 2.26; Aristid. *Or.* 35.10; Sthenidas 188.2–4) and sense of humor (Suet. *Vesp.* 22). But it was these five virtues in particular that gave shape and structure to all the rest. The monarch of the imperial period, then, was above all a paradigm of justice, but also endowed with courage, especially in war, reverence for the gods (together with the related sense of duty in other relationships), mastery over his desires and passions, and love of his subjects, as expressed most clearly in his material benefactions to them. It is a profile that combines elements of Platonic philosophy, hellenistic kingship theory (see Eckstein, this volume, chapter 16), Roman aristocratic ethics – though it should be noted that some of the virtues "coded" by Cicero as republican, especially *constantia* ("steadfastness") and *gravitas* ("seriousness") (see Schofield, this volume, chapter 13), were not especially prominent in imperial discourse – and Roman imperial ideology, and, with due allowance made for differences of language and genre, it is one that defines both the ideal ruler described in abstract treatises on kingship and the "good" emperor constructed by Roman aristocrats. And it was not empty rhetoric. Because this profile of the ideal monarch was relatively stable and repeatedly evoked, it presented Roman emperors, addressed in these texts (whether directly or indirectly) by the same social elite to which they themselves belonged, with a rather formidable set of expectations for their public and private behavior.

Anxieties and Strategies

One of the defining characteristics of political thought under the Roman Empire was the unremitting concern to define what, precisely, an emperor or monarch was. There were two principal approaches to this problem. The first was to set up simple, binary oppositions between the ideal-typical king and tyrant, and the second was to conceptualize the nature of royal power by means of analogy with other types of authority. The king/tyrant dichotomy was a staple of this tradition. He who rules on behalf of his subjects is a king, according to Dio Chrysostom, while he who rules on behalf of himself is a tyrant (Dio. *Or.* 3.38–41). The king promulgates just legislation, the tyrant unjust (Men. Rhet. 375). Kings are only cruel out of necessity and reason, while tyrants are cruel for their own pleasure (Sen. *Clem.* 1.11.4). Kings have many friends, tyrants have no friends (Dio *Or.* 3.86–116). The list could be substantially extended from Dio's writings alone (cf. *Or.* 1.67 ff., 2.67–8, 3.45–8, 4.45). Analogies are even more common. The emperor/monarch is to his subjects as the mind is to the body (Sen. *Clem.* 1.3.5); a father to his children (Sen. *Clem.* 1.16.2; Ecph. 82.3–6); a teacher to his pupils (Sen. *Clem.* 1.16.2); a commander to his soldiers (Sen. *Clem.* 1.16.2; Dio *Or.* 3.66–7); a "king" (i.e. queen) bee to the rest of the swarm (Sen. *Clem.* 1.19.1–3; Dio *Or.* 3.50); a shepherd to his flock (Dio *Or.* 1.13, 3.50, 4.45; Aristid. *Or.* 35.22; Ecph. 82.3–6; Arch. 36.1–5). Closely related to analogies of this sort are those passages in which imperial or monarchic authority is modeled on that of other symbols of power, such as the bull, which uses its awesome strength only on behalf of the herd as a whole (Dio *Or.* 2.67–8); the sun, which never complains about its toils (Dio *Or.* 3.82–3); and especially Zeus, the ruler of the heavens (Dio *Or.* 1.39–41, 3.50; Diotog. 75.8–9). And for those seeking to define not monarchy but tyranny by means of analogy, the master/slave relationship offered an irresistible model (Roller 2001: 213–87).

That the very essence of emperorship, kingship, monarchy, and tyranny was so regularly defined in these ways points to some underlying anxieties about the nature of autocratic rule. One explanation for such anxieties is the possibility that these definitions could be contested, resulting in an ongoing struggle over the most appropriate principles by which rulers should be judged. But there does not seem to have been too much disagreement about what it was that made a "good" or a "bad" emperor, a king or a tyrant. Another possibility is that there was a troubling epistemological uncertainty about the essence of autocracy in the Roman world. If so, these incessant definitions and articulations could be seen as attempts to pin down an elusive quarry. And the stakes of such definitions were high indeed, because the emperor or monarch was not only a model *of* authority, he was also a model *for* his subjects. In the words of the Tiberian historian Velleius Paterculus, "The emperor who is best [*optimus*] instructs his citizens to do right by doing it, and even though the emperor is greatest in power, he is even greater through his example" (2.126.5). So too Pliny: "We do not need power [over us] so much as an example. Indeed, fear is an unreliable teacher of what is right. Men learn better from examples" (*Pan.* 45.6). The emperor or ruler as model was in fact a standard conceit (cf. Sen. *Clem.* 2.2.1 ff.; Philo, *Mos.* 1.160–1; Cass. Dio 52.34.1; Ecph. 80.22–4). Menander even advises his pupils to connect marital bliss and the production of legitimate children to the behavior of the emperor: "Because of the emperor, marriages are chaste, fathers have legitimate offspring, spectacles, festivals, and competitions are conducted with proper splendor and due moderation. People choose a style of life like that which they observe in the emperor" (Men. Rhet. 376; trans. Russell and Wilson 1981). Understanding the essence of imperial or monarchic authority was crucial, then, because it was this authority, in the eyes of contemporaries, that set the basic parameters within which the rest of society operated.

The function of the ruler as a paradigm for his subjects increased the already very high premium placed on the ruler's personal character. From this concern arose the further anxiety that the royal office corrupted the character of the individual who occupied it. To counter this suspicion, supporters of imperial rule often asserted that the emperor's character had not been degraded by autocratic power. Aristides, for example, insists that the emperor being celebrated in his encomium did not change after acceding to the throne (*Or.* 35.9, 26; cf. Plin. *Pan.* 44.2). This is the context for Marcus Aurelius' resolution not to let himself become too "Caesarized" or "dipped in the royal purple" (M. Aur. *Med.* 6.30.1–2). And it gives real force to Tacitus' observation that Vespasian was the only person whose character actually improved upon becoming emperor (*Hist.* 1.50.4). One way for observers to assess the character of the monarch *qua* monarch was through examination of his capacity for friendship – for how could one with a debased character have true friends? The theme of royal friendship is especially pronounced in Dio's third oration on kingship (*Or.* 3.86–116, with Konstan 1997b), but it also finds expression in Pliny (*Pan.* 85), Marcus Aurelius (*Med.* 1.16.10, 6.30.13 on Antoninus Pius' friendships), and the late antique panegyrics (*Pan. Lat.* 3.18.4, 21.2 ff.; 2.16.1 ff.).

But the deepest political anxiety of the imperial period was simply that the emperor might be a bad person who would rule poorly and to the detriment of his subjects. Because the emperor was not formally constrained by laws or institutions, there was good reason for this concern. As a result, a major strand of political thought under the Roman Empire was the development of various strategies for persuading the emperor to rule well. Most arguments were instrumentalist in nature, designed to convince the emperor that ruling well was in his own interests. Both Seneca and Dio Chrysostom claim that a ruler should rule in a virtuous manner because this is the best way to guarantee eternal fame and glory (*Clem.* 1.10.2, 1.17.3, 1.18.3, 1.20.3; Dio. *Or.* 1.33, 3.83); vicious rule, by contrast, ensures eternal execration (Plin. *Pan.* 53.5). For a world in which posthumous reputation was highly valued, these arguments could carry real weight. A related argument pertained to the ruler's lot after death. Good rulers enjoy a blessed afterlife (Dio *Or.* 2.75–8; Cass. Dio 52.36.1), while bad ones suffer eternal punishment (Sen. *Apoc.* 14–15). Among the more prosaic arguments for virtuous rule is Cassius Dio's claim, embedded in Maecenas' speech on behalf of monarchy, that citizens are more willing to pay their taxes under a moderate emperor (52.29.2). Sometimes we find the proposition that subjects love good rulers (Dio *Or.* 1.20, 3.112), but this, too, is normally given an instrumentalist spin, since it is precisely the love of their subjects that conduces to the security of the ruler himself (Sen. *Clem.* 1.8.6, 1.10.2, 1.13, 1.19.6–8; Dio *Or.* 3.83; Cass. Dio 52.39.2). As Seneca asks: "Mercy, then, makes rulers not only more honored, but safer, and is at the same time the glory of sovereign power and its surest protection. For why is it that kings have grown old and have handed on their thrones to children and grandchildren, while a tyrant's sway is accursed and short?" (*Clem.* 1.11.4; trans. Basore 1928). Rulers who rule well are also happy, as various authors declare (Sen. *Clem.* 1.13.2, 1.26.5; Dio *Or.* 1.45; Cass. Dio 52.39.2), and enjoy good health and pleasant memories as well (Dio *Or.* 3.60–1, 83). In all these cases it is implied that tyrants experience the opposite of these things. At least one author, Seneca, could base his claim for virtuous imperial rule on the intrinsic good of the virtues themselves – an appropriate stance for a Stoic philosopher. "No reward is fitting for the virtues," he writes, "apart from the very virtues themselves" (*Clem.* 1.1.1). Appeals to monarchic self-interest, however, were the norm. But what difference, if any, did such appeals – or the larger discourse on royal power and virtue of which they were a part – really make?

Conclusion

Writers under the Roman Empire were confronted with the stark reality of autocratic power. Though official censorship was never systematic or prolonged, the very fact of autocracy was by itself enough to put a damper on the free exchange of ideas. But the writers of the imperial period nevertheless managed to produce a valuable political philosophy to go with the times. Indeed, the texts considered in this chapter may be seen as so many contributions to a shared project to articulate an ethics for autocracy. The effectiveness of this ethical program for influencing political action in the Roman Empire, and in particular for helping to guide the behavior of emperors, is impossible to measure. But there are several reasons for thinking that its effect was considerable. First, there existed a broad consensus, drawing on centuries of philosophical speculation, on what constituted an ideal monarch. No emperor who deviated from this norm could appeal to a competing ideology. Second, the omnipresence of virtues and vices in the political discourse of the Roman Empire gave rise to an emphatically ethical vocabulary of political action, which in turn created a coherent and durable framework for the normative behavior of emperors. Emperors could not help but be influenced by this discourse and its attendant ideology (for a classic statement of how public language shapes political action, see Q. Skinner 1974). Not only did they rule in full awareness of what was expected of them, but as aristocrats themselves, they had been raised to share the same ideology of virtuous rule as the educated elite who were its main exponents. And if that were not enough, the fates of canonically "bad" emperors like Nero, Domitian, Commodus, and Elagabalus, who openly abandoned the principles of this ethical system and died violent deaths as a result, offered a salutary reminder of the risks of tyranny. The effort to equip imperial autocracy with an ethics of its own was not in vain.

FURTHER READING

For a short, general introduction to Roman political thought, see Connolly 2007a. Potter 2006, written by a team of experts, provides an excellent, up-to-date overview of the period considered in this chapter, and is equipped with a massive bibliography; those seeking more detailed treatments of the history of the Roman Empire should consult volumes 10–14 of the revised *Cambridge Ancient History*. The approach of this chapter has been mainly thematic. For a different approach to the political thought of the imperial period, arranged mainly by author and by text, see C. Rowe and Schofield 2000. The rhetorical dimensions of Roman political thought, with a focus on the Republic, are examined in Connolly 2007b. Two outstanding studies of political thought in the early imperial period are M. Griffin 1976 and Roller 2001 (but note that "politics" is a much broader category for Roller than it is for Griffin); Braund's major commentary on Seneca's *De clementia*, forthcoming, will add a third. For the later imperial period, Russell and Wilson 1981 and Nixon and Rodgers 1994 offer useful introductions. The Greek authors treated in this chapter can be elusive for students, but there are now several incisive ways into this body of thought, including Swain 1996 and Whitmarsh 2006.

PART IV

The Passions of Ancient Politics

CHAPTER 18

Political Animals: Pathetic Animals

Giulia Sissa

The social sciences are rediscovering the emotions. We can see a renewed awareness of
their significance in philosophy, anthropology, the cognitive sciences, and political
theory. For the reader of classical texts this does not come as a surprise. Ancient
historians, orators, and philosophers enrolled the passions among the most compelling motives for action – be it the heroic acting out of an outraged tyrannicide
(Aristotle), or the imperial decision to wage a war, in retaliation for an old offense
(Herodotus), or the deliberation of a collective body about a preemptive strike, out of
fear of a threatening neighbor (Thucydides).

   The language of politics, descriptive as well as normative, accommodates a vocabulary and syntax of the passions. By a passion, or an emotion, I mean a feeling of
pleasure or pain, which occurs in a particular situation: a state of mind, in response to
a state or the world (Arist. *Eth. Nic.* 2.5.2). A passion, or an emotion, is made of two
components: it is a thought, accompanied by a bodily alteration – one that, today, we
would locate in the brain, but one that Homer, Aristotle or the Stoics would map
onto the diaphragm, the heart, the *thumos*, or the blood. It is this physical change
that is felt as either pleasure, or pain.

   Passions are reasons. As Bernard Williams (1993) and Christopher Gill (1996) have
forcefully pointed out, already Homer has his characters enact their most intense
feelings in words. Feeling is thinking, often aloud. This occurs not only when *erōs* is
involved, but when power, authority, and recognition are at stake. In the *Iliad*,
Achilles' anger is made of honor hurt, the thought that Agamemnon's ingratitude
is quite unfair, and the firm intention to undermine the king's effort to take Troy. All
this grief comes across in streams of tears and waves of music, but also in articulate
complaints and thorough explanations. Later, all kinds of political leaders, from
Herodotus' Xerxes to Thucydides' Alcibiades, from Aeschines to Lysias, will perform
as effective speakers, able to exploit the interface of arguments and affects. Their
phrases, proofs, and examples act in the skillful tuning of what an audience must feel.

A Companion to Greek and Roman Political Thought, First Edition. Edited by Ryan K. Balot.
© 2013 Blackwell Publishing Ltd. Published 2013 by Blackwell Publishing Ltd.

Finally, in his profound understanding of hellenic culture, Aristotle will offer a theory of that interface.

The experience of social relations – especially those relations which, being asymmetrical, entail a dialectic of submission and command, acknowledgment of a superiority and reward for service – this experience is felt as either gratifying or humiliating, either exhilarating or mortifying. Egalitarian democracy too, as we shall see, by redistributing power, reconfigures its emotional experience. Politics is the place where social relations find a normative (more or less stable) order; where their trial of strength culminates in a particular form of (more or less stable) government. Politics is the place where the pleasures and pains derived from recognition, authority, and power find their ultimate expression.

There is a great variety of political orders in the Greek world. Tyrannies, monarchies, oligarchies, democracies, and mixed constitutions. Different governments are compatible with different manners of political agency; they establish different sets of rights, they impose or tolerate the cultivation of different habits and characters, different virtues and emotions. Through the teaching of civility, self-control and sport, different cities mold different bodies. Each configuration of power shapes the person, singular or plural, in charge, on the one hand, and creates expectations on the receiving side, for the subjects or the citizens, on the other. This fashioning produces qualities which, as we shall see, are moral as much as they are emotional. Classical political thought shows a pervasive understanding that forms of authority and forms of affectivity are coherent. The political animal, we should say, is a pathetic animal.

From Herodotus to Polybius, the variety of political orders is always seen in motion. History is political history: one which can be captured only in progress, in the biography of individuals as well as the vicissitudes of a polis or an empire. These storylines involve the translation of emotional fields into emotional sequences. The pathetic animal, we should add, is a narrative animal.

Passion and Power

In each form of government, emotions make up a dynamic system, one that we can call a "pathetic apparatus." By "apparatus" I mean a pragmatic notion: in a society, there are normative values that bridge words and deeds, rules and practices, models and speech-acts, status and agency. All these values solidify into rights, habits, and bodies, as I mentioned, but can be met with either compliance or resistance. It is in this ramified and dynamic manner that power acts within a society. Each particular apparatus of rights, habits, and bodies creates the conditions for a particular set of emotions. The pathetic apparatus of tyranny, for instance, includes greed, envy, and arrogance on the one hand; terror and subservience on the other. The pathetic apparatus of democracy requires different feelings and character traits: a self-governing multitude is, above all, courageous, proud, competitive, and potentially envious. States remain stable or, on the contrary, collapse when their pathetic apparatus loses its balance: when they reach a breakage point, such as the last straw in tyrannical humiliation, or a popular rule that verges on unmanageable conflict. This is, at least, the vision of historical change shared by political theorists such as Herodotus and Thucydides, Plato and Aristotle, but also by political agents such as democratic public speakers.

The most obvious characterization of a passionate rule is that of a tyrant. In his Persian dialogue on the forms of government, Herodotus has a relative of the Great King, Otanes, the son of Hystaspes, claim that monarchy is not pleasant, *hedus*, nor good, *agathos* (Hdt. 3.80–3). It is bad and it makes its subjects suffer. This occurs because of the *hubris* and the *phthonos* that inevitably affect any king. Offensiveness and envy are the reasons why a certain exercise of power – unlimited, exclusive, and unchecked – is unworthy: that level of supremacy can set the best of all men astray from what is proper; it corrupts his character, and fatally stokes those foul emotions. The flaws of monarchy, therefore, are the vices the monarch acquires once in that position, and these vices consist of strong feelings: his envious inability to bear the excellence of young men; his predatory sexual appetite that makes him rape women, thus dishonoring their families; his indiscriminate temper toward flatterers and friends alike; and his immeasurable arrogance. A tyrant is insolent, erratic, insatiable, and volatile. This is why, the Persian grandee claims, it would be best to place power in the hands of the many.

Does this mean that a democracy would be based on reasonable, dispassionate deliberation? A democracy, Otanes argues, would grant publicity, transparency, and responsibility. Magistrates would take turns in office and give account of their doing. Justice would be the same for all. There would be no place, as a consequence, for the intense concentration of wealth, means, and command that induces a king to want more. But what Otanes fails to mention is a form of excellence that lies at the core of any praise of the people empowered: military valor. In 521 BCE, long before Cleisthenes' reforms in Attica, conventionally considered the birthday of democracy, a Persian grandee was its very first inventor. He missed, however, one crucial point: he failed to acknowledge that individual motivation for freedom which, together with equality before the law, makes the substance of a popular rule. For Herodotus himself, at least when he speaks on his own behalf, it is the process of democratization that was responsible for Athens' prosperity and warlike strength. One of the features of this government was its improbable success in the noblest of all virtues, which is also an emotional performance: fearlessness on the battlefield.

Two years after Salamis, 50 years before Herodotus' *Histories*, Aeschylus' *Persians* set the stage for Athens's self-representation. Redistributed and shared in an egalitarian plural, power political and military would prove far superior to an authoritarian administration and a hyperhierarchical chain of command. The emotional resource of manliness and fearlessness was the secret of the unexpected victory at Salamis, as the character of Xerxes himself is obliged to explain back in Susa, to his devastated courtiers. "The people from Ionia do not flee from the spear," claims the Chorus. And Xerxes: "They are manly! I have seen a disaster I never expected" (Aesch. *Pers.* 1025–6). As his mother, Atossa, has to learn with great surprise, the Athenians could be called neither the slaves, nor the subjects, of any human being (Aesch. *Pers.* 242).

After the Persian Wars, we shall see in a moment, political rhetoric would never cease to reiterate that signature fantasy, especially in the template of funeral panegyrics.

Democratic warriors, be they hoplites or marines or even sailors, were no less intrepid than Heracles, Achilles, or Ajax, the Homeric icon whom Cleisthenes himself chose as an eponymous hero for one of his new tribes.

The Pathetic Apparatus of Monarchy

When concentrated in the hands of one man, power generates insolence, greed, erotic frenzy, and injustice. We can see this with the Great Kings of Persia, when even a relatively measured and flexible sovereign such as Xerxes ends up lusting after his brother's wife, then seduces this woman's daughter, and finally kills his own brother. We can see it in the biographies of Greek tyrants, inclined to eliminate any possible competitor, and to rape young women, as Theseus, a most improbable democratic king, claims in Euripides' *Suppliants*.

> How then could a city remain stable, where one cuts short all enterprise and mows down the young like meadow-flowers in spring-time? What good is it to acquire wealth and livelihood for children, merely to add to the tyrant's substance by one's toil? Why train up daughters virtuously in our homes to gratify a tyrant's whim, whenever he wishes, and cause tears to those who rear them? (Eur. *Supp.* 447–54, trans. Coleridge 1938)

We can see it in monumental figures of authority – stubborn, unbending and despotic – such as Creon in Sophocles' plays.

And, finally, we can understand the logic of this subversive vision of monarchy, once again, in Aristotle's definition of injustice. Injustice is a wrongdoing that contravenes the law. If we examine the subjective conditions of its accomplishment, we can see that it is carried out deliberately, thus by a morally flawed person, because that person deems it possible, *dunaton*. The ability to act against the law, with the certainty of being able to get away with it, is the reason why an intrinsically unjust person commits a particular act of injustice (Arist. *Rhet.* 1.12.1). People usually select the kind of behaviors that correspond to their vicious dispositions, Aristotle claims, but the actual decision to do the deed requires the assessment that the deed can be done, and can be done by us.

Political power, especially tyranny, makes a lot possible with a great deal of advantage and almost no risk of retribution (Arist. *Rhet.* 1.12.9–10): it creates the perfect incentive to injustice. Power entails authority, wealth, honor, a high idea of oneself, and the expectation of having always more than everyone else. Individuals who are ambitious, honored, and fortunate in all sort of ways tend to want everything, and become envious of those who possess any of the goods they feel entitled to (Arist. *Rhet.* 2.10). This is why *phthonos* is the emotion of the small-minded, but also of the successful. For analogous reasons, individuals who are wealthy (and young) are prone to wrongdoing (Arist. *Rhet.* 1.12.2), and offensive arrogance, *hubris*. "They think that, in acting badly, they make themselves superior" (Arist. *Rhet.* 2.2.6). *Hubris* is the imposition onto others of one's sense of superiority; more precisely it is the creation of that superiority, through the very act of offending and dishonoring, therefore diminishing, the other person. The paramount example of *hubris* is Agamemnon, when he deprived Achilles of his prize.

The response to *hubris* is anger, *orgē*. And this emotion too is the consequence and the expression of a high self-esteem. Eminently irascible will be the same kind of man who must be hubristic: "the man in position of ruling towards the one who is ruled, and the man who believes he is worthy to rule, in regards to the one who is worthy of being ruled" (Arist. *Rhet.* 2.2.7). With analytical precision, Aristotle corroborates the portrait Otanes had sketched in the Persian debate.

The Pathetic Apparatus of Democracy

Ancient democratic theory, in its various voices, had to respond to the challenge of the plural. In the aristocratic tradition, the many were the obverse of the one, their multiplicity being profoundly associated with vulgarity, lack of education, and therefore the unreasonable. Think of Pindar, Theognis, Parmenides, Plato or the Old Oligarch. But the actual government of the many requires a cognitive reassessment of the multitude. A minimal wisdom of crowds must be admitted if we are to appreciate the ability of the people to govern themselves. Furthermore, a minimal morality has to be attributed to the masses if we are to acknowledge their political fitness. The zero degree of excellence is patriotism, with its corollary virtues that are nothing but good emotions, such as emulation, *zēlos*, anger, *orgē*, and *erōs* for the city.

Funeral Orations, again, offer a template of democratic manliness in its emotional nuances. To take the most paradigmatic sample of that form of rhetoric: in Pericles' speech in honor of the dead during the first year of the Peloponnesian War (431 BCE), as reconstructed by Thucydides, we can follow the speaker's words at work on the emotions of the audience. While extolling the dead on the battlefield, Pericles becomes aware that praise might be triggering envy in the listeners. He then instructs them to convert that potential *phthonos*, a base emotion, into a cognate, and yet noble feeling: emulation, *zēlos*. *Phthonos*, Aristotle will argue, is our displeasure at another person's prosperity, when that person is like us, thus we feel deprived of something we should possess, not them. It is a negative, passive, and destructive emotion, focused on what others have, but, in our opinion, should cease having. *Zēlos*, on the contrary, is our desire to get for ourselves something another person already has: in this case we act, strive, and compete in order to acquire that same thing. In the situation created by an encomium, *phthonos* would be for the audience to feel bitter at the hyperbolic celebration of the dead soldiers; *zēlos* would mean, for the same spectators, to grow excited by those men's example, and to wish to rise to the challenge.[1] The next generation, Pericles argues, should endeavor to become even more outstanding than those heroes. The Athenians should love their city, even become enamored of Athens, with an unbound *erōs* (Thuc. 2.43.1).

Aristotle will call *paraskeuazein* a strategy of preparation, modification, or orchestration of the emotions of the audience, in order for the speaker to make them feel and think what he wishes. This skill is as important as the choice of topics and the montage of enthymemes, as demonstrated by the second book of the *Rhetoric*, with its know-how to excite, appease, or transform the emotions. Now, this strategy appears to be deliberately executed in the existing speeches of Athenian orators. Pericles was a perfect example for Aristotle (who actually mentions the Funeral Oration). Lysias would be too.

A rhetoric of just wars, intended to protect and spread freedom, flourishes after the *stasis* that culminates with the coup of the Thirty and ends with the victory of the *demos*, in 403 BCE, a success that the People handled with remarkable elegance, as Aristotle observes, by making the decision to reconcile the population and "not to remember the evil," *me mnēsikakein*. The ordinary citizens fighting at the Piraeus were the true heroes, rising against the tyrants and their friends. Lysias commends them as the worthy men, the *andres agathoi* ready to take risk (*kindunos*), acquire fame (*doxa*), and accomplish worthy deeds, *agatha*.[2] They face the culprits of terrible things: the slanderers, the greedy, the unjust few who put innocent people to death without trial, confiscated the property of resident aliens only to raise funds, and fundamentally betrayed the city, making it smaller and weaker. These commoners were both excellent and the victims of injustice (Lys. 12.57). Their excellence took shape as a string of emotions, from shame to fearless audacity, but culminates with anger, the most active passion of all, that which drives us to take up arms:

> Compelled by no law, but induced by their nature; imitating in fresh encounters the ancient valor of their ancestors; ready to purchase with their own lives a common share in the city for the rest; choosing death with freedom rather than life with slavery; no less ashamed of their disasters than angered against the enemy; preferring to die in their own land rather than live to dwell in that of others; and having as allies their oaths and covenants, and as enemies their open foes of aforetime and their own fellow citizens. Nevertheless, having felt no fear of the multitude of their opponents, and having exposed their own persons to the peril, they set up a trophy over their enemies, and now find witnesses to their valor. (Lys. 2.61–65, trans. Lamb 1930)

Lysias' speeches addressed, after 403 BCE, to the Athenians, as the victorious party, now in control of the city, offer a perfect example of the rhetorical manipulation of *orgē*, in the context of the democratic heroization of the people. The worthy men who resisted at the Piraeus were no less ashamed at what had happened to them than furious (*orgizomenoi*) against their enemies (Lys. 2.62). These men, Lysias argued, were still in a position to get angry. And anger is the emotion they were supposed to feel and they ought to feel. Along with other feelings and beliefs – such as revulsion for slavery, love of freedom, sacrifice of their lives for the sake of the common good, and fearless courage in taking risks – the rage, *orgē*, of the men at the Piraeus was an expression of their nature, their *phusis* (Lys. 2.61), in other words of their natural excellence. This innate nobility was the cause of their uprising, in anger, against the humiliations inflicted on the city by the oligarchs. And *orgē* is the passion Lysias insisted in awakening and keeping alive, by recalling those events, in a number of speeches delivered in the years immediately afterwards. Lysias will keep remembering and reminding his audience of the events of 403, by stoking the most aristocratic of all passions.

Consider the following passages:

I fully understand you, gentlemen of the jury, when hearing such statements and remembering the events, you get angry [*orgizesthai*] in the same way against all those who remained in the city. (Lys. 25.1)

I consider, gentlemen, that you would not be justified in hating those who have suffered nothing under the oligarchy, when you can indulge your wrath [*orgizesthai*] against those who have done your people mischief. (Lys. 25.18)

You feel anger [*orgizesthe*] against everyone who entered your houses in search either of yourselves or of some member of your household. (Lys. 12.30, trans. Lamb 1930)

"One absolutely must get angry [*sphodra chre orgizesthai*]," Lysias claims, when a man such as Pheidon, trusted to reconcile the city, ends up betraying it (Lys. 12.58). Sometimes one has to get angry, *dei orgizesthai*, as Aristotle would also later acknowledge.

Now, the excellence of these men is presented to the audience as the remake of the *aretē* of the men at Marathon. They all defy danger, take daunting risks and, in so doing, become worthy men.[3] They all excite the competitive and admiring emulation – the *zēlos* – of mankind.[4] The same democratic drive was there at the outset. In the most remote past, the Athenians "were the first and the only people to drive out the *dunasteias* of their states and to establish a democracy, believing the liberty of all to be the strongest bond of agreement" (Lys. 2.18).[5]

The Athenians began their democratic life with a revolution. That foundational war – a *stasis* – was the condition of possibility for the establishment of the power of the people, a hard-won success. And that was the very first expression of their intolerance of slavery, and their wish to give freedom a political reality, in a collective act of angry valor.

Whereas democratic rhetoric praises the demos and its *aretē*, poets and political theorists, I mentioned, resist recognizing the intelligence and the virtues of the many. Aristotle was the first to argue that a group has more chances of reasoning well than one of its members. He claimed, firstly, that the wisdom of numerous individuals amounts to a cumulative, higher insight; secondly, that a multitude is less prone to persuasion than one person (cf. esp. *Pol.* 3.11). All this is at a far cry from Herodotus' comments, when he recounts how, under the pressure of Aristagoras of Miletus, the Athenian Assembly voted to invade Lydia: a thoughtless, and yet momentous, decision that set in motion the Persian Wars. It is easier to sway 30,000 people than one king, Herodotus added (5.97) – and it was not meant as a compliment. This is also at odds with Thucydides' repeated allusions to the haste and fickleness inherent in collective deliberation. And this inverts Plato's philosophical characterization of democracy in *Republic* 8. Democracy, Socrates argues, is the reign of multiple opinions, casual political activity, contradictory decisions, changes of mind, and mere conflicts of

interest. A demos is but a capricious, moody, and instable beast, to be coaxed with
skillful words (Pl., *Resp.* 8.557a–562a). Demos personified, as Aristophanes shows in
his *Knights* (424 BCE), is an old man, exceedingly irascible, half-deaf, demented and
gullible, now at the mercy of his cunning slave – a master of flattery (40–68).

Aristotle, the most insightful anthropologist of hellenic culture, was the first elitist
philosopher to offer a coherent theory of common sense as the ground of collective
deliberation. Consistently, he also offered a theory of emotions as reasons: reasons
accompanied by intense feelings of pleasure or pain, reasons that are predictable,
often hasty, stubborn and not necessarily good, but reasons that can be prepared,
modified, and orchestrated through words and arguments. His cognitive reassessment of the passions is consistent with his serious treatment of rhetoric, an indispensable component of political life, especially in a democracy. Aristotle's complex
views on the role of *pathos* in human agency culminate in his notion of spiritedness,
thumos, as the source of anger and courage, as the cause of collective valor. Manliness,
Aristotle, thought, was the only form of excellence available to a great number of
men: "Although it is possible for one man or a few to excel in virtue, when the
number is larger it becomes difficult for them to possess perfect excellence in respect
of every form of virtue, but they can best excel in military valor, for this is found with
numbers" (Arist. *Pol.* 3.1279a–b, trans. Rackham 1944).

Although critical vis-à-vis *dēmokratia*, a regime too intent on liberty, Aristotle
designed an ideal city-state that was a *politeia*, a "city of the citizens," where a club
of highly educated and completely virtuous citizens/soldiers would govern themselves, taking turns in office. This aristocratic democracy was for him the perfect polis,
and such a thought would have been impossible without a novel response to the
challenge of the plural.

Political Animals, Moral Animals, Pathetic Animals

In order to measure the consistency of Aristotle's theory of political agency, we need
to place the emotions within the framework of Aristotelian ethics.

Virtue is the faculty (*hexis*) of producing and preserving good things. Good things,
that is, which are valuable in themselves but also beneficial to others (Arist. *Rhet.*
1.9.5–7; cf. *Eth. Nic.* 2.6.1–10). These faculties are justice, courage, self-control,
magnificence, magnanimity, liberality, and gentleness; practical and speculative wisdom. They are not innate, but the result of education, training, and habituation. They
make up our character (Arist. *Eth. Nic.* 2.1.1–6). Now, these acquired qualities enable
us, or dispose us, to actions as well as passions. "Moral virtue is concerned with
emotions and actions, in which there is excess, deficiency and the mean" (Arist. *Eth.
Nic.* 2.6.10; cf. 2.6.12). They generate our acts as well as our feelings, by setting us to
do certain things and feel in a certain way (Arist. *Eth. Nic.* 2.5.1–2). Between the two
(vicious) extremes of irascibility and slavish indifference to any offense lies the
virtuous ability of the even-tempered, and yet dignified, person to get angry when
she must respond to an undeserved slight. Between the excesses of daring and fear lies
the noble valor of the warrior.

Like emotions, virtues are related to pleasure and pain: they allow us to act well in those matters (Arist. *Eth. Nic.* 2.3.6; cf. 2.3.10). Reciprocally, emotions can be classified following a moral criterion: they are worthy either of a good person or of a despicable one. "Emulation is virtuous and characteristic of virtuous men, whereas envy is base and characteristic of base men" (Arist. *Rhet.* 2.11.1). Shame is the *pathos* through which we respond to our own vice, from cowardice to sexual incontinence, to meanness (Arist. *Rhet.* 2.6). Because a virtue is but the correct mean as opposed to vices that are intense passions, the constant intertwining of virtues and emotions regulate our life (Arist. *Eth. Nic.* 2.6.10–12).

Pathe or *pathemata* make the texture of a person's morality. This intrinsic connection is possible because, first of all, for Aristotle, passions are reasons: only, as briefly mentioned, they are reasons accompanied by pleasure or pain (Arist. *Eth. Nic.* 2.5.2). I have been slighted, I did not deserve it; I feel aggrieved; I wish to retaliate. This sequence of thoughts, excruciatingly felt, is what we call "anger." I can restrain my anger in an effort to think differently. I can govern my passions because they are not alien to reason. Secondly, happiness is the enjoyment of excellence, in all its forms (Arist. *Rhet.* 1.5.3). I only feel well if I am good. Therefore, my emotional state is the result of my ethical condition. And, reciprocally, my excellence is made of virtues, those dispositions which make me do the right things, and feel the right emotions. Thirdly, emotions are causes of agency, and of voluntary acts. Therefore they contribute to the decency or the wrongdoing of a moral agent.

Now virtues are all interactive. Excellence is composed of faculties, we said, which are intrinsically good, but also beneficial to others: a virtue is a *dunamis euergetikē*. Virtues always regulate our dealings with other people. Think of justice, courage, liberality, moderation, or gentleness. The very exercise of these dispositions implies the existence of others, involves others, and engages us with others. This is what it means to be political animals. We are political animals not superficially, because we resemble the bees in our spontaneous inclination to live together, but more profoundly because our personal quality, our excellence, is made of excellent social manners. In order to fulfill our potential to live well, therefore to attain a full-fledged *aretē*, we must live in a community; ideally in a political order that allows and fosters a complete flourishing. The political animal, therefore, is a moral animal.

The emotions too imply the interaction with others. Think of courage, gentleness, love and hatred, fear, hope, anger, shame, envy, emulation, indignation. It would be impossible to define them without including, in their definition, a relation to others. Aristotle classifies the emotions on the basis of three binary oppositions: pleasure versus pain; what is deserved versus what is undeserved; I versus other people. Facing another person's pleasure (be it happiness, well-being, or success), I can either rejoice (friendship) or feel sorry, and this because that pleasure is not well deserved (indignation), or because I fail to have that pleasure (envy), or because I strive to have it (emulation). Facing another person's suffering, I either feel sorry and afraid that the same horror might happen to me (pity), if it is undeserved; or I rejoice if the pain looks well deserved to me. This dilemma presupposes my ethical quality. If I am a mean person, prone to envy, I will enjoy other people's diminishment, as much as

I would resent their prosperity. If I am a decent human being, I will be inclined to pity, indignation, and emulation. The moral animal is a pathetic animal.

This is a script for the performance of politics, between the Pnyx and the courts of law. How an individual responds with his pleasure and pain to the pleasure and pain of others – their pleasure and pain consisting in their welfare or their misery: this is a *pathos*. And a *pathos* is a social manner: a pleasure or a pain that I feel in the comparative, competitive game of communal life. The list of the emotions in *Rhetoric* composes a web of intersubjective adjustments which hinge on what one thinks about oneself. Expectations, self-representations, self-descriptions are the cause of our responses to others. Whereas the inconsistency of others' views of us with our image of ourselves causes pain, recognition gives pleasure.

Pleasure and pain are, for Aristotle, the object of political theory. Political theory studies the end of human life, its highest good: happiness. Happiness cannot be reduced to pleasure, but it entails a sense of pleasure. Happiness requires excellence. Now, excellence exists through the virtues. And virtues are dispositions to feel the right emotions. Happiness, therefore, being made of virtues, is also made of emotions: those which are beautifully pleasurable.

The political animal who finds his accomplishment – that is his happiness – within a polis is a *polites*, thus a virtuous/emotional living.

A political environment, a given *politeia* is what shapes the characters, thus the virtues and the emotions of the people. Lawgivers, Aristotle claims, make citizens good by training them to acquire proper habits: those forms of excellence which will result in the right acts and the right emotions. And within a society governed by certain principles, human beings learn, through practice and habituation, to behave and to feel.

Consider the following:

> It is by taking part in transactions [*sunallagmata*] with fellow-men that some of us become just and others unjust; by acting in dangerous situations and forming a habit of fear or of confidence we become courageous or cowardly. And the same occurs also as far as desire [*epithumia*] and anger [*orgē*] are concerned. Some people become moderate and gentle, others profligate and irascible, by actually comporting themselves in one way or the other in relation to those passions. (Arist. *Eth. Nic.* 2.1.5–7)

> We display justice, courage and other virtues in our intercourse with our fellows [*pros allēlous prattomen en sullagmasin*], when we respect what is due to each in contracts and services and in our various actions, *and in our emotions also* [*en te tois pathesi*]. (Arist. *Eth. Nic.* 10.8.1–2, trans. Rackham 1944, slightly modified)

This is exactly what Pericles or Lysias endeavored to accomplish in their speeches. The pathetic and moral animal is a political animal.

FURTHER READING

On the Persian dialogue on the forms of government, see Waters 1972; Gammie 1986; and Thompson 1996, who examines previous scholarship, such as Benardete 1969, 1981;

Brannan 1963; Lasserre 1976; Lateiner 1984, 1989; Myers 1991. On the emotions, democracy, and rhetoric, see Ober 1989; Roisman 2003; Yunis 1996; Wohl 2002; Thalmann 2005. On courage, manliness and democracy, recent discussions can be found in Saxonhouse 1980; Balot 2001a, 2001b, 2004; Sluiter and Rosen 2004; Salkever 1991; and Forsdyke 2001. On the most problematic corollary of courage, anger, see D. Allen 2000; Braund and Most 2004; W. Harris 2002. On the complexities of democracy in Euripides, excellent discussions can be found in Mills 1997 and Mendelsohn 2002.

NOTES

1   Thuc. 2.45.1 (avoidance of *phthonos*); Thuc. 2.43.4 (imperative to feel *zēlos*).

2   See Lysias 25.28: "And you should consider that, in the Peiraeus party, those who are in highest repute, who have run the greatest risk, and who have rendered you the most services, had often before exhorted your people to abide by their oaths and covenants, since they held this to be the bulwark of democracy: for they felt that it would give the party of the town immunity from the consequences of the past, and the party of the Peiraeus an assurance of the most lasting permanence of the constitution." Cf. Lys. 2.61–5.

3   The men at the Peiraeus: "You came, despite many adversities, to the Peiraeus. Beset by many great perils, you proved yourselves men of true valor, and liberated one party while restoring the other to their native land" (Lys. 12.97, trans. Lamb 1930). The men at Marathon: "They proved their worth as men, neither sparing their limbs nor cherishing their lives when valor called, and had more reverence for their city's laws than fear of their perils in face of the enemy; and so in their own land they set up on behalf of Greece a trophy of victory over the barbarians, who had invaded others' territory for money" (Lys. 2.25, trans. Lamb 1930).

4   The men at Marathon: "No wonder, then, that these deeds performed long ago should be as though they were new, and that even to this day the valor of that band should be envied by all mankind" (Lys. 2.26, trans. Lamb 1930). The men at the Peiraeus: "Thus the struggles at the Peiraeus have earned for those men the envy of all mankind" (Lys. 2.66, trans. Lamb 1930).

5   Thucydides opposes *dunasteia* (in Thessaly) and *isonomia* in Athens (4.78). He characterizes it as a regime near to tyranny: "Our city" – claims a Theban orator – "at that juncture had neither an oligarchical constitution in which all the nobles enjoyed equal rights nor a democracy, but that which is most opposed to law and good government and nearest a tyranny – the rule of a very small group [*dunasteia*]" (3.62). Aristotle defines *dunasteia* in opposition to *politeia* and democracy (Arist. *Pol.* 1272b, 1292b, 1302b). He sees it as the most elitist form of oligarchy, close to monarchy: "And if they carry matters further by becoming fewer and holding larger properties, there comes about the third advance in oligarchy, which consists in their keeping the offices in their own hands, but under a law enacting that they are to be hereditary. And when finally they attain very great pre-eminence by their wealth and their multitude of friends, a dynasty of this nature is near to monarchy, and men become supreme instead of the law; and this is the fourth kind of oligarchy, the counterpart of the last kind of democracy" (*Pol.* 1293a, trans. Rackham 1944).

CHAPTER 19

Anger, Eros, and Other Political Passions in Ancient Greek Thought

Paul W. Ludwig

Passions bridge the gap between what modern liberals think of as the private and the public spheres. In ancient political philosophy, passions such as anger and love were not private indulgences but public servants in the project of binding political regimes together. The ancients saw passions as changes which the soul "passively" undergoes, as opposed to the soul's activities, such as thinking. Thinking plays a role in politics, but passion arguably plays a greater role. Philosophers, lawgivers, and statesmen therefore attempted to discover the best passions for citizens to have. Perhaps the single most perplexing aspect of ancient political psychology is the centrality of anger in Plato and its continuing relevance for Aristotle. "Spiritedness" – the middle bond between reason and desire in the tripartite soul of Plato's *Republic* – connotes a quickness to anger, and its many forms can be traced back to anger. Why base political life on this apparently antisocial passion? If anger tends to force out or replace gentler passions, then Plato's conceding the central place in the soul to spiritedness might be strategic rather than strictly normative. Plato may accommodate anger, making the best of what he considers the bad hand dealt by human psychology. But the *Republic*'s assurances that the spirited part of the soul normally listens to reason are undercut by the dialogue itself, as we shall see. How would Plato's strategy differ from simply caving in to humanity's most destructive impulse and letting it rule? If we approach the political use of anger by first examining the alternatives, we may gain perspective on the question. To misappropriate Churchill's dictum on democracy: anger may be the worst political passion, except for all those other political passions that have been tried from time to time.

Honor, Shame, and Awe

The background of traditional passions against which classical thought made its innovations is partly on display in the Funeral Oration by the great Athenian statesman

A Companion to Greek and Roman Political Thought, First Edition. Edited by Ryan K. Balot.
© 2013 Blackwell Publishing Ltd. Published 2013 by Blackwell Publishing Ltd.

Pericles, as retold by Thucydides. The Funeral Oration is a sophisticated, enlightened Greek perspective on political passion, intended to inspire citizens who were not yet themselves (or not in every case) sophisticated or enlightened. The needs of the occasion required that Pericles look back to the past and give at least lip service to the opinions enshrined there. Thucydides' Pericles selects some traditional passions to motivate his fellow citizens; other passions are conspicuous by their absence.

The wish to be honored and remembered motivates citizens to sacrifice their lives for their community (Thuc. 2.41.5, 2.43.2–3). This passion for honor to which Pericles appeals is as old as Homer's poetry: the heroes of the *Iliad* fought to gain glory or fame (*kleos*). But desire for individual fame is questionable as a political passion because fame can also be won at the expense of the community. Achilles harmed his fellow Greeks when he withdrew from the Trojan War, winning the greatest fame by returning to the battlefield – thus showing how the whole war depended on his personal prowess. Pericles is careful to make his appeal not simply to fame but to communally bestowed honor (*timē*). Honors were often quite concrete perquisites actually conferred by the community,[1] as opposed to the vague but powerful rumors or reputation of fame. In contrast to fame, such honors were firmly under civic control. It was thus useful for a political community to encourage a passion for honors: the love of honor.[2] As Pericles says, "The love of honor [*to philotimon*] alone never grows old, and the better enjoyment ... is not material gain as some say, but receiving honor" (Thuc. 2.44.4). But the socially engineered incentive of honor remains in tension with the passion for fame, which transcends the community.[3]

Pericles makes far less use of honor's traditional flip side – shame (*aiskhunē*). Archaic Spartan civic poetry vouches for the fact that the stick of shame had often been used in tandem with the carrot of honor. One group of lines by Tyrtaeus begins "It is beautiful to die in the front ranks" but then goes on to paint a picture of the horrific shame – civic exile – that awaits a man who fails to risk his life (West 1993). In oligarchic Sparta, citizens were not so much attracted into doing their duty by the prospect of honors and higher office as they were shamed into it and motivated by the fear of dishonor and disgrace if they failed.[4] Or so Pericles wishes to claim, to provide a contrast for his Athenians. We catch only glimpses of shame in Pericles' speech: the same citizens who sought and won eternal remembrance by building Athens into a great imperial power simultaneously displayed a keen sense of shame (*aiskhunomenoi*, 2.43.1); but this shame is only a concomitant of honor – the participle is in fact often translated "sense of honor."[5] Love of honor entails avoidance or abhorrence of disgrace. Pericles mentions some innovations in Athenian shame: poverty does not make them ashamed, but failure to work their way out of it does; and Athenians have a sliding scale of respect for laws, culminating in unwritten laws that everyone agrees it is shameful to break (2.37.3; 2.40.1). But in contrast to Sparta, Pericles considerably downplays shame as a tool of social control. Pericles would prefer to attract Athenians into citizen virtue, unlike the Spartans who, he says, are forced to be virtuous (2.39).[6]

Although Pericles' dichotomy between free Athenians and forced Spartans is self-serving, the dark side of the Spartan psychology of shame is evident from the way Sparta deliberately shamed their serf population in order to edify the elite. Citizen youth were encouraged to humiliate and terrorize the Helots as a part of their educational rites of passage. They also shared in the Helots' shame by living for a time in a liminal state between slave and free – a period which seared into the boys' consciousness the benefits of being in the citizen group and the horrors of falling below that status. Shaming outsiders thus helped to educate insiders.[7]

However, there was also a different, more positive side to shame in Homer and in archaic thought. Awe or respect (*aidōs*) was the passion aroused in Greeks when they sensed the mystery that enwraps entities of great worth: a god, a sacred precinct, a parent, a maiden, or anything else that ought to remain inviolate. Self-respect or self-reverence is also a common meaning of *aidōs*.[8] The relation of awe to shame (i.e. of *aidōs* to *aiskhunē*) is complex, and at times the Greek words are used nearly synonymously. But one salient difference may be simplified into a formula: the violation of awe is an occasion for shame. The violator feels shame at having transgressed against the awesome, while the violated feels shame at having his or her curtain of awe rent asunder and thus being exposed or laid bare. Respect or awe helps keep citizens' behavior within bounds of propriety.[9]

Even more than shame, awe is downplayed by Pericles. The word does not occur in his oration. He says Athenians obey the law out of reverent fear (*deos*, 2.37.3), but in context the passage is about how the unusual degree of Athenian freedom does not lead to public lawlessness. Pericles' ideal citizen cannot be strongly reverent or awestruck without relinquishing the daring spirit of achievement with which Pericles wishes to imbue him. Awe felt toward the ancestral was crucial for the preservation and transmission of the received laws and constitution, as Pericles recognizes; yet he begins his oration by pointedly neglecting to follow the custom of praising the lawgiver who instituted the funeral speech (2.35.1).[10] Instead, he criticizes that law. He continues by scanting the customary praise of the forefathers: the citizens' distant progenitors achieved mere political freedom. By contrast, the generation just past performed the much greater achievement of acquiring empire (2.36.1–2). At the apex stands the current generation.

As we shall see, Pericles does not want citizens so in awe of Athens that they cannot love her with that dynamic love which generates new achievements. Pericles does not want unquestioning, unthinking reverence for Athens but rather a love sensible of merits and flaws: a love that compares Athens to other cities and finds her superior in actual fact. Such a critical, merit-based love is in many ways opposed to feeling awe. Instead of respecting Athens like a parent, the citizens should fall in love with her. Hence Pericles' primary exhortation will be that Athenians should open themselves to a new political passion: erotic love.

Eros

This first experimental political passion in our account can be said to inaugurate the preoccupation with the passions among classical political theorists. We cannot know for certain the extent to which eros (in Greek, *erōs*) made its way out of political rhetoric and theory into the realm of political practice; we do know that Thucydides was intensely interested in it, and that he had a stake in making his account credible to his audience. Non-erotic love had long provided solutions to Pericles' problem of attracting citizens into civic duty rather than forcing them. Patriotic love, like the passions discussed above, formed part of the archaic legacy which classical thought inherited and revised. In addition, homoerotic attraction between pairs of comrades was believed to have political relevance.[11] But as we shall see, the lens of the Funeral Oration will transform these traditional loves dramatically.

Pericles exhorts Athenian citizens to become erotic lovers (*erastai*) of Athens.[12] Not only is a new, unusual object (the city) supposed to arouse eros, but citizens are also required to play the social role of lover in relation to the city, imitating the gallantry which homoerotic lovers were thought to show toward their beloveds. Rivalry with other suitors is a key aspect of this social role. Pericles' citizens are to serve Athens chivalrously, sacrifice for her, perhaps die on her behalf, and, in this game of courtship, compete for her favors to show who is most worthy. People in love, then as now, were routinely seen to neglect their own interests for the sake of the beloved. Examples from homoerotic courtship included camping out on the beloved's doorstep, disregarding one's business affairs, going without food, all in the service of eros. Eros makes people willingly enter bonds that would otherwise look like slavery. In seeking to motivate free, democratic citizens toward civic sacrifice and duty, Pericles here discovers a passion that is at once perfectly free and perfectly committed.

Pericles' reconception of the city into an erotic object flies in the face of a more traditional conception, in which the city – or at least the land – was the object of a very different kind of love. Myths and metaphors in which the native land was one's mother (e.g. Aesch. *Sept.* 17), together with the common paternal or ancestral designation of the "fatherland" (*patris, patroia gē*) bespeak an attitude more properly called filial love. In place of the love a child owes to a parent, Pericles substitutes the more energetic passion of the lover. Such eros is dangerous because it overrides the awe or reverence (*aidōs*) traditionally felt for the motherland or fatherland.[13] A sacred object cannot be embraced without losing its sacredness. Pericles does not seem to anticipate that one suitor might actually *win* the competition for Athens, giving him rights of possession over the city – the way a beloved gives a lover erotic rights.

Fear of such a takeover eventually undermines Athens' most erotic moment, in Thucydides' narrative. Thucydides shows Pericles' audience fulfilling his expectations of citizenship-as-courtship, but only after his death and in a manner he did not intend. The intense erotic rivalry to serve Athens best comes to a head in the citizens' peacock behavior during the preparations for their disastrous expedition to conquer Sicily (6.30–2). Eros was the passion at the heart of this imperial overstretch, according to Thucydides (6.24.3; cf. 6.13.1).

But the Athenians lose their nerve in the face of all that erotic citizenship entails, Thucydides implies. The erotic longing to win Sicily is largely the work of Pericles' young, flamboyant, and tyrannically ambitious nephew Alcibiades, who nevertheless manages the public's affairs ably (6.15.4). He is put in joint command of the expedition to Sicily. Alcibiades' rivals for the hand of Athens (6.28.2, 6.29.3) move the Assembly to recall him, leaving lesser talents in charge of the fleet. His rivals cannot bear the possibility that Athens might wish to be tyrannized by Alcibiades if he should prove successful in the monumental enterprise. Eros used as a political passion unexpectedly entails a benign tyranny under the greatest citizen. The Athenians could have had this, Thucydides implies, and with it possibly victory in the Peloponnesian War, but only at the cost of their democracy. In wanting Athens so much that they feel eros for her, Alcibiades and his rivals are prepared to harm her interests (6.92.2–4). The upshot of Thucydides' explorations is that eros is an indispensable model for describing certain aspects of imperialism, of regime transformation, and of political psychology, but erotic courtship is no normative model for citizenship, nor is a political psychology based on erotic passion the most desirable psychology for citizens.

Anger and the Idea of Spiritedness

What can restrain the erotic desire that leads to imperial overstretch? Problems with too much or too little restraint have plagued each of the passions discussed so far. The passion for fame is not easy to keep control of – it can outgrow the community's system of honors. The social tool of shame can be savage and illiberal in its administration, while awe is incompatible with political dynamism. Perhaps each of these passions – and many others besides – deserve a place in an adequate political psychology; but none deserves the central place. Plato will institute a surprise in the *Republic*, making spiritedness (proneness to anger) the center of the soul, and making anger the common factor linking several political passions, including some of those already discussed.

Anger erupts when individuals believe they are suffering an injustice (*Resp.* 4. 440c–d). Here we see the rudiments of a mechanism by which anger could serve the public good. Anger acts as a deterrent to injustice. Yet what prevents anger from taking justice into its own hands, starting a series of reprisals or a feud worse than the initial injustice? Anger or spirit (*thumos*) makes an alliance "with apparent justice" – not necessarily with true justice – and hangs on like a dog (4.440c–d). Such *thumos*, according to the *Republic*, is altogether unconquerable and indomitable (2.375b). These savage or animalistic descriptions give the reader pause. Does Plato make spiritedness (*to thumoeides*, 440e–441a) the linchpin of the soul because it is good, or because anger is too strong to be overcome by gentler passions? Aristotle will make a similar move when analyzing courage. Wounded animals, according to Aristotle, often attack because they are carried by their mere basic anger (*thumos*) against the ones who wounded them. But this is not courage, even though they are risking their lives. Courage requires more than just anger, it requires reason and choice. Nevertheless, courageous people are "spirited" (*thumoeideis*), implying that anger does indeed contribute something to courage, or at least that courage is like anger (*Eth. Nic.* 3.8.1116b23–1117a9). The animal passion or instinct supports the virtue. Everything then hinges on the degree to which reason can be added to spiritedness, that is, the degree to which spiritedness can listen to reason (*Resp.* 4.441e).

Reason can sometimes turn anger inward against other parts of the soul; anger can be given a constructive job, the position of internal policeman. Just as men good at violence can be integrated into a polity by making them soldiers and police, so anger's role in the soul can be to defend and purify. Anger represses bad desires the way the *Republic*'s guardians will repress criminals and repel enemies. Socrates tells an anecdote about a man named Leontius who, passing by a sordid spectacle of corpses left by the public executioner, gets angry at himself for wanting to stare (*Resp.* 4.439e–440c). The ugly desire to view gore is at odds with Leontius' self-idea. He thought he was better than that, superior to such vulgar behavior. He accordingly gets angry at his own eyes and at his own baser self. Such anger can be used to combat the desires, to prevent other passions (like eros) from getting the upper hand.

What is political about *thumos*? High-strung people, individuals who are prickly or nettlesome, quick to take umbrage or to sense an injustice, seem to have anger near the surface even when they are not currently angry. They must be defending something, or else why would they get angry at seeing it slighted? They seem to defend their sense of self-worth, their sense of self. They become indignant when someone fails to recognize them, or does not recognize their worth. Just as defensiveness is a precondition for survival in the case of Aristotle's wounded animals, so human defensiveness is a precondition of being taken seriously, of asserting oneself, whether politically or otherwise.

The added suffix -*eidos* or "form" raises the possibility that *thumos* may appear in various different forms or guises.[14] What seem to be separate passions may actually be diverse manifestations of *thumos*. "Thumoeid" would then be a description that shows the angry origin of a whole range of passions – passions "in the form of anger," or irascible passions. If so, then we would expect Plato's revolutionary new political psychology to be able to incorporate some of the traditional passions canvassed above rather than merely replacing them. This turns out to be the case. Plato shows the interrelatedness of several passions while placing them on a new, common basis – *thumos*. The desire for honor is a good example: the spirited part of the soul will later be said to be the "honor-loving" part of the soul (*Resp.* 9.581a–b). That the wish to be honored is one of the "thumoeid" passions follows immediately from *thumos*'s defensiveness about self-worth. If Leontius in the anecdote had not been a proud man, he would not have minded permitting himself a little self-indulgence. Proud people get angry at their own moral slip-ups. Although the extreme of pride can be imagined as being totally self-contained – too proud to care what other people think – Socrates treats spiritedness like a dog that responds to (at least some) other people: its own family or those to whom it has become accustomed (*Resp.* 2.375e). Spiritedness can apparently be influenced by what other people think, as a dog responds to its master's approval or disapproval. Similarly, the most spirited members of the city will respond to the approval and disapproval of their fellows if, as Socrates hopes, the whole city or entire class of guardians can become one giant family (e.g. *Resp.* 5.463c–465b). Civic rewards and punishments – such as honors and shame – become incentives and curbs that keep spiritedness on the straight and narrow (e.g. 468c–e). Seeking honors is a way of feeding one's sense of self-worth, which in turn is defended and asserted via anger. Eventually,

Socrates will base an entire regime on honor (timocracy), a regime in which spiritedness reigns supreme (*Resp.* 8.547b–553a).

Shame is a second "thumoeid" passion that follows directly from this account of spiritedness. Spirit, like a noble dog, is vulnerable to the disapproval of its "family." However, Plato's Socrates, like Pericles, conspicuously scants shame as a tool of social control, at least in one crucial regard. Flying in the face of traditional wisdom about the social utility of shame, Socrates goes out of his way to make his citizens sexually shameless, for instance, forcing women and men to exercise naked together (5.452a–e). His eschewal of (at least one form of) shame appears motivated by both political and philosophical concerns. First, he rends the curtain of shame (or perhaps awe) that surrounds marriage and family life: the family is abolished in order that the city may be unified as one great family. Second, the eros of the guardians is increasingly turned toward philosophic pursuits. As with Pericles' erotic citizens (who must see Athens' merits as they really are in order to fall in love with her), the philosophic class in the *Republic* must penetrate through the curtains of awe to the heart of mysteries without being held back by shame. Yet the guardians, being nettlesome types, will probably have the thumoeid passion of shame in abundance just as they have in abundance the wish for honor. So the philosophic part of their education is somewhat at odds with the *thumos* that fits them to be guardians.

Does spiritedness represent an advance for political psychology? The answer partly depends on the political question, "Who will guard the guardians?" Socrates says that spirit accepts punishment if it thinks it right (*Resp.* 4.440c), and this rings true. A remarkable fact of human psychology is that a part of us wishes to submit the rest of us to justice. But what is to guarantee that spirit agrees with reason about which punishments are just? One can easily imagine the justly condemned prisoner using his spiritedness to fight back hard against the jailor or executioner. Socrates' claim that spiritedness never allies with desire against reason (440b) seems manifestly wishful thinking.[15] It is true that spirit never wants a pleasure for its own sake, the way desire does. But spirit often does want pleasures as perquisites of status, aggrandizing the self – as the wish for "relishes" bears out (2.372c). According to Socrates' young interlocutor Glaucon, a simple city without luxuries or relishes is a "city of pigs"; its denizens deserve better unless they are to be wretched. As a result of this wish, Socrates' city becomes "bloated" with lavish extravagances and must begin practicing for war in order to support its tastes (2.372d–373e). The whole need for a Guardian-class arises – at least dramatically – from this "thumoeid" wish for pleasures. Thus spirit does ally with desire (against reason) when it thinks the self or its city deserves nothing but the best.[16] Moreover, the anger that issues from frustrated desire is so obvious as not to require further evidence, whether the desire be a rational one or not. Spiritedness appears from these examples to be a useful passion but also a two-edged sword.[17]

Spiritedness has one further resource that enhances its excellence as a political passion: its connection to a form of love. Admitting that spiritedness is capable of destroying its own (*tous oikeious*) fellow citizens along with the enemy (2.375b–c), Socrates hopes to direct this savagery *only* toward outsiders, as watchdogs growl at and attack strangers. He recognizes that spiritedness, like a dog, is protective. It will fight to protect the familiar against the alien (2.376b). Like a dog, spirit "owns" its owner in both senses of possessing and recognizing the persons to whom it belongs. The dog discerns not what is true and good but what is its own. While spirit's master can in theory be reason (4.440d), in practice the master is whatever is most familiar. Spiritedness is capable of recognizing a face that is dear to it (*philēn*; 2.376b). This holding-dear is far and away the most surprising aspect of angry passion — its connection to its ostensible opposite: affection.

Affection and Civic Friendship

Spiritedness is the "heart" of political psychology in part because it is a source of civic friendship and other forms of affection. Previously, spiritedness was shown to be the seat of the political passions honor and shame. But now Aristotle goes much further, asserting that spiritedness is the faculty of soul through which most of us experience affectionate, non-erotic love (*Pol.* 7.7.1327b38–1328a17). *Philia*, a very different passion from eros, denotes affection for the near and dear, family members and friends.[18] But on what grounds does Aristotle base his claim that *thumos* creates affection?

Aristotle asks us to consult our experience when we feel slighted. Our anger is kindled more when relatives and friends (*philoi*) slight us than when strangers do. The greater anger felt toward relatives and friends must be connected, at the source, to the greater love felt toward them (*Pol.* 7.7.1327b38–1328a17). But if affection and anger are two sides of the same, underlying coin of spiritedness, what does that imply about affection? We earlier said that spiritedness was responsible for the sense of self, and that anger was aroused when the self-idea was endangered. Affection for others would then appear to be an enlargement or extension of one's sense of self. The self is enlarged so as to infuse itself into other people and things. Affection on this account would be a possessive love because the self would come to regard those people and things as its own (or itself as their own). Affection would always go together with the possessiveness and protectiveness of a watchdog.

Such a "low" view of affection makes more sense of Plato's doglike guardians (whom the *Politics* 7.7 passage criticizes) than it does of the rational friendships Aristotle discusses in the *Ethics*. Unlike the *Politics*, the *Ethics* does not claim that spiritedness is the source of affection. Friendships ethically considered are based on three lovable things: pleasure, utility, and virtue (e.g. *Eth. Nic.* 8.2.1155b16–20). Civic friendship – love for a fellow citizen *qua* citizen – would seem ordinarily to be a species of utility friendship. By contrast, *thumos* most often means mere anger in the *Ethics*, and it can be argued that Aristotle does not accept the tripartite division of the soul for truly ethical and philosophical people, whose choices and whose very being should be a harmonious blend – or even identification – of reason with desire (e.g. 6.2.1139b5–6; cf. Sachs 2002). Spiritedness would thus be a feature of the merely political soul. In short, it is by no means clear how to reconcile the very different accounts of friendship found in the *Politics* and the *Ethics*.

One way of reducing the gap between the two accounts is to examine how far the apple of friendship falls from the tree of the self in the *Ethics*. The self looms very large in all three types of friendship. The true friend or loved one (*philos*) is a second self, literally an *alter ego* (*Eth. Nic.* 8.12.1161b29, 9.4.1166a32, 9.9.1170b7). Of the three bases of friendship, use and pleasure are explicitly self-seeking (8.3.1156a11–19). But virtuous people, too, are selfish for Aristotle, albeit in a different way. They love others who are a lot like them: the highest friendships are loves between sames or similars (8.4. 1156b20–4). Such friends do not *need* each other's virtues and are far more likely to *share* the same virtue. By contrast, user and used are opposites because what one lacks the other fulfills (8.8.1159b12–24). Virtuous friends admire in the other what they admire in themselves (it takes one to know one). The happiest man wants to contemplate his *own* good actions, but since actions are easier to contemplate in others, he enjoys contemplating his friend's actions, which are equivalent to his own (9.9.1169b33–1170a5). This ethical friendship is a love of one's own kind[19] and, as such, is an extended form of self-love. The virtuous man is the ultimate self-lover, according to Aristotle (9.8.1168b25–1169a15).

The fact that the most exalted friendships of the *Ethics* remain self-centered – even without reference to spiritedness – may provide a further clue to the problems of ordinary "thumoeid" affection in *Politics* 7. Unaware of the selfish roots of love, such political friends are surprised and hurt by betrayals, and their love quickly turns to anger and hatred.[20] Such friends probably fall into the common errors discussed in the *Ethics*: believing that good people should act "for the sake of a friend" and neglect their own (*Eth. Nic.* 9.8.1168a28–1168b1), they are disappointed when these expectations are not fulfilled. Such a low view of affection lacks the altruism of much modern thought, but it makes sense of such phenomena as possessiveness, love which turns to hate, love which "smothers" the loved one, as well as the way identity often gets bound up with people and things other than the self. The political friendships are mostly based on spiritedness for Aristotle.

But while taking over Plato's *thumos*, Aristotle rejects Plato's innovation or thought-experiment of making the city into one great household. Instead of stretching family relations to include fellow citizens, Aristotle appeals to the more traditional *philia* he observed within and among small (especially familial) groups inside the city (e.g. *Pol.* 2.3.1261b16–2.4.1262b25; cf. *Eth. Nic.* 8.10–12). *Philia* was indeed a traditional political passion. To take one of the most important instances: military arrangements sometimes relied on family *philia* to motivate unit cohesion. Hoplite armies were traditionally organized by tribe and thus were partially family affairs. Three generations of men from the same family might all be stationed near enough to see one another during battle. Rather than fighting for an abstract cause, they fought for each other: they wanted to protect their comrades who were also friends and loved ones (*philoi*). Clearly, the traditional arrangement assumes that men do not love their fellow citizens *qua* citizens as much as they love their own family and friends. The traditional wisdom made civic use of friendships that were private rather than civic. In the *Theognidea*, for example, *philia* is essentially a private alliance (or even pact) between two aristocratic families (cf. Figuera and Nagy 1985).

One may be forgiven for wondering if the historical progression of thought from Thucydides to Plato to Aristotle has not merely been a long road back to the obvious. The obvious superiority of *philia* over eros – its stability as opposed to eros' volatility, *philia*'s connections to honor and pride and its source in the indomitable *thumos* – seems to render further experimentation pointless.

But can one be friends with every member in a whole polis (let alone a modern nation-state)? Aristotle practically admits that the really strong ties that bind will always obtain within and among nepotistic, factional groups inside the polity. The specter of nepotism is ever present, for example, in the *philia* between aristocrats in the *Theognidea*. Such powerful families no doubt believe that, together, they constitute the true polis of peers, but their dominance means subservience for everyone else. Plato's thought-experiment of abolishing real families serves to highlight this problem with families, as Aristotle also shows (*Pol.* 2.2–2.4). The *Republic* assumed that all guardians could be made to share "one belief" about their own (*oikeion*; 5.464d). But in the absence of communism, "one's own" will include much that other citizens do not share. Thus *philia* is good for cities, but any *philia* wide enough to encompass the whole citizen body will probably be shallow. We have learned that affection is self-centered, that the objects of affection form a target pattern with the self at the bull's-eye: the inner circle is loved most, the middle ring less, the outer perimeter is not much loved at all.

In defense of civic friendship, it might be argued that people can become friends to the extent that they share something in common (*Eth. Nic.* 8.9.1159b29–30). And the polity does aim at no mere partial advantage, as Aristotle says (*Eth. Nic.* 8.9.1160a14–30). In theory, then, this most common of advantages ought to bind citizens together in the strongest friendships. In practice, however, partial advantages closer to home and strong parochial bonds draw citizens away from care of the public good. Nothing guarantees that civic friendship will be adequate to its aim. And that is only internally. Little or nothing of later antiquity's preoccupation with cosmopolitanism and friendship across national boundaries is visible in classical theory. Foreign enemies may even be needed to remind citizens that they are supposed to have a bond with their fellow citizens as citizens – people for whom otherwise they would feel nothing. Fear and hate of outsiders creates solidarity among insiders. The problem with civic friendship remains its selfish, angry roots. Only because the alternatives are so problematic did this *thumos*-inspired passion emerge as the front-runner. Thus the upshot or normative recommendation of ancient theory is civic friendship. But when today's political theorists apply ancient ideals of civic friendship to modern problems without taking cognizance of the problems out of which the recommendation emerged, the results can be confusing.

Civic Friendship and Modern Liberalism

How best to apply the ancient theory of civic friendship to politics today? Modern liberal thought privatized the passions, relegating them to the private sphere.

Friendship, too, is now supposed to be private: whom we choose to associate with is our own business and properly off-limits to state control or even recognition. This privatization has been the source of inestimable benefits.

Yet modern liberalism has been overly ambitious about the extent to which passions can be kept private. Marriage is a good example: people continue to desire that the state recognize their ostensibly private love relationships. The state, in its turn, has an interest in stable marriages because they help to socialize the next generation of citizens at low cost. Furthermore, the passions which liberal marriage keeps in the private sphere have increasingly been subject to criticism: everyone is now familiar with arguments that power politics informs private associations and relationships, particularly those with a history of inequality. The politics of sex, the politics of the family, now even the politics of friendship (e.g. Derrida 1997): "the personal is political" has become a truism and an implicit challenge to liberalism's distinction between public and private. Both the desire for marriage and the critique of marriage show how the passions have a way of breaking out of their private sphere, a way of seeking to make public issues of themselves.

The most useful application of ancient theory is not to bandwagon with recent critiques of liberalism but to supplement and bolster liberalism's attempts to negotiate these difficulties, in part by providing richer descriptions of what the passions are. The passions figure prominently in two schools of thought that have challenged liberalism in recent years: postmodernism and communitarianism. Among their other criticisms, these schools of thought have argued that liberal epistemology has scanted the passions. According to postmodernists, the dispassionate, objective reason on which liberalism is founded is rare or impossible; instead, preconditions of our living together (such as power and language) constitute us as thinking subjects and decisively shape our thoughts. Similarly for communitarians, the loves which liberalism leaves to personal choice in fact constitute us as who we are. Liberal selves which freely choose where to live, whom to associate with, do not really exist. Instead, people are always already passionately embedded in communities and families.

Ancient theory about civic friendship can help to inoculate liberalism against these challenges. Ancient theory shows us a political science that acknowledges these passions and their distorting influence on reason without giving up on rationality. Liberalism need only concede to postmodern and communitarian critiques that liberal rationality is fallible, not that it is bankrupt. It is the forever unfinished character of the epistemological foundations of liberalism that most invites attack. The modern expectation that political theory should establish firm foundations and then build upon them creates a scandal when the foundations turn out to be just as much subject to inquiry as the superstructures built on them. But it is a scandal of our own creating. In ancient philosophy, by contrast, foundational questions are the least solvable of problems, those most open to further inquiry. Ancient rationalism provides a model in which inquiry into the foundations continues simultaneously with inquiry into the political superstructures. A fallibilist liberalism informed by ancient theory can point out the excessive normative aspirations cherished by communitarian and postmodern critics, who would replace sober liberal practices with attempts, respectively, to create tighter communities and to widen civic friendship to include all humanity. Friendship's rootedness in the self places grave limitations on these hopes; it is unlikely that a community can ever approach the love that private families enjoy. Much less is it likely that all humankind can enjoy anything like the civic friendship that parochial communities sometimes achieve. Extending the bonds of friendship to include more and more "Others" cannot go on indefinitely.

Ancient theory of the passions can also help to deter liberalism from some of its own excesses. Many liberals have been at the forefront of attempts to extend democratic fairness into the new areas known as identity and recognition. On the one hand, classical scholars must welcome the richer description of politics inherent in these attempts. Pride in identity and the desire for recognition are clearly manifestations of spiritedness. For example, Gutmann (2003: 14–15) cites the example of black Americans who could pass for white and receive all the social perquisites of whiteness but choose instead to remain true to a group identity. Such cases show clearly that politics is about more than self-interest; liberal theory has too often reduced politics to the pursuit of private interests such as security and comfort. Yet Plato and Aristotle could add context to a second example of Gutmann's: a deaf-mute student who would refuse an ear implant on the grounds that it would change his deaf identity (Gutmann 2003: 117). Here we see how individuals identify with their own (the *oikeion*) regardless of the goodness of their own (see above). No necessary connection exists between spiritedness and the group it has trained itself to love. The value that spiritedness confers sometimes contains all the perversity of anger. Such arbitrariness poses problems for liberal theories of recognition. In a recent formulation, recognition politics consists of creating the "hospitable conditions of identity formation" and fighting against factors that lock an individual into his or her current identity or current idea about what the said identity is (Patten 2004). Such a fostering of identities would have to rely on a fostering of angers, according to ancient theory. Therefore liberalism's earlier resolve to ignore group identities and let individuals assert their identities under their own power seems more prudent than liberal recognition politics, at least from the standpoint of ancient theory about the passions.

FURTHER READING

For the interrelated passions connected with honor, shame, and awe, Riezler 1943 and E. Straus 1966 give invaluable theoretical treatments from the perspectives of social psychology and phenomenology, respectively. Campbell 1982 provides notes on the archaic Spartan poet Tyrtaeus; the (mostly) preclassical *Theognidea* is another excellent source of archaic attitudes, this time from Megara, a city neighboring Athens. For translations of both Tyrtaeus and the *Theognidea*, see West 1993. The volume edited by Figueira and Nagy (1985) contains discussions of friendship, love, and other emotions in the *Theognidea*. For a general treatment of archaic and classical emotions, see Konstan 2006. Padel 1992 provides a wealth of material on pre-Platonic *thumos*. On Platonic *thumos* and on eros in classical Greek political theory, see Ludwig 2002. For a very full discussion of friendship in Plato's *Lysis* and Aristotle's *Nicomachean Ethics*, see L. Pangle 2003. On classical friendship generally, see Konstan 1997a. For recent applications of Aristotelian civic friendship to modern liberal democracy, see D. Allen

2004 and Frank 2005. For postmodernism and friendship see Derrida 1997. For communitarianism and friendship, see Sandel 1982. On the politics of recognition, see C. Taylor 1994; Markell 2003; and Patten 2004. Walzer 2004 criticizes – from within liberalism – liberal assumptions of passionless politics and free association.

NOTES

1 Seats, meats, full cups, and lands are some of the concrete honors which Homeric heroes receive in contradistinction to their overarching goal: fame (Hom. *Il.* 12.310–28). See Redfield 1994.
2 In the *Iliad* it is a malfeasance in *timē* – i.e. a misadministration in the public conferral of honors, concretely expressed in the spear-won slave women Chryseis and Briseis – which instigates Achilles' anger and sets the stage for his winning the greatest fame by withdrawing from the war. Properly managed *timai* might have kept Achilles' thirst for fame at the beck and call of his society.
3 Pericles uses the Homeric term for fame, *kleos*, only negatively and only in a tiny section of the Funeral Oration devoted to womanly excellence (Thuc. 2.45.2).
4 What distinguishes Athenians is their freedom from that suspicious surveillance (Thuc. 2.37.2) over one another that characterizes Spartans. The critical "gaze" of shame (see Williams 1993) is relatively absent: Pericles even claims that Athenians refrain from harmless grimaces at their neighbors' living as they please.
5 The disposition to feel shame (as opposed to being "shameless") is sometimes denoted by *aidōs* (see below), while shame that actually occurs is usually *aiskhunē*. See Cairns 1993. Shameful reproach is the only thing the glorious dead ever "fled" (Thuc. 2.42.4).
6 Even Spartan courage is mere ignorance of the pleasures they are giving up, Pericles implies (2.40.3). On the epistemological component of Athenian courage, see Balot 2001b.
7 On Spartan "contempt" for the Helots generally, see Ducat 1990.
8 See e.g. Hom. *Il.* 22.104–7; cf. 6.441–3.
9 Ordinary citizens' courage relies in part on awe (in its sense of self-respect), according to Aristotle (*Eth. Nic.* 3.7, 1116a16–30). *Aidōs* falls short of being a virtue for Aristotle (in part because it is only a passion), and he makes little distinction between *aidōs* and *aiskhunē* (4.9, 1128b10–35; cf. 2.7, 1108a32–1108b1). See especially Straus 1966; Riezler 1943.
10 He agrees to speak, he implies, in bare obedience to the law and to the opinion of the men of old times (2.35.3).
11 Xen., *Lac.* 2.12–14, *Symp.* 8.32–5, *Hell.* 4.8.39; Ephorus in Strabo 10.4.21; Pl. *Leg.* 636a–d, *Symp.* 178d–179a, 182a–d; Thuc. 1.20, 6.53–9; cf. 2.43; Cartledge 1981; Figuera and Nagy 1985; Ludwig 2002.
12 Or of her power (*dunamis*, 2.43.1). See Ludwig 2002 for a further discussion of the ideas in this section.
13 Compare Plut. *Caes.* 32.6: the night before Caesar crosses the Rubicon to attack Rome, he was said to have dreamt of committing incest with his mother.
14 See Benardete 1989: 55.
15 Ferrari 2007: 187 points out that it is only because Glaucon is noble that he never noticed his (or anyone's) *thumos* allying with desire against reason. Socrates' language immediately relativizes the assertion: the *nobler* a man, the *less* he rebels against just punishment.

16 Glaucon is characterized as possessing the victory-loving aspect of the timocratic man (8.548d–e). See Ludwig 2007 for a discussion.

17 Aristotle, too, admits (at *Eth. Nic.* 7.6, 1149a25–b4) that *thumos* listens to reason very poorly, and has the advantage over desire only insofar as desire does not listen to reason at all.

18 Technically, *philēsis* is the passion (*pathos*) while *philia* is a settled disposition (*hexis*) to love by deliberate choice, a love that is reciprocated, for Aristotle (*Eth. Nic.* 8.5, 1157b29–32; cf. 8.2, 1155b27–34 with *Rhet.* 2.4, 1381a1–2; I am indebted to David Konstan for pointing out to me the latter passage).

19 In a comparable way, Plato's *Lysis* arrives at *aporia* by first assuming that people love utility rather than whatever happens to be their own (*oikeion*; *Lys.* 209c–210d; cf. 214d–221c). Socrates and his interlocutors then find that they are forced to reconsider the possibility that the *oikeion* is the basis of love (221d–222d).

20 Aristotle salts his account with poetic quotations: "Harsh are the wars of brothers" and "Those who loved excessively will hate excessively too" (*Pol.* 7.7.1328a15–17).

CHAPTER 20

Some Passionate Performances in Late Republican Rome

Robert A. Kaster

No one who has witnessed the opening years of the twenty first century needs to be told that emotion is inseparable from political thought and political action. So many today – individuals, parties, sects, whole nations – "are full of passionate intensity," and so thoroughly do their passions govern their deeds that we could fancy Yeats's drafting "The Second Coming," in January 1919, as an act of prophecy, not a retrospective meditation on the Easter Rising and the First World War. But of course no decade in no century has ever wanted for the like, including the decades and centuries of Rome's Republic; nor is the enactment of political passion ever, quite, just a symptom of "mere anarchy ... loosed upon the world." Political passions serve multiple purposes – expressive, effective, and normative – in making ideology manifest and urgent. In this chapter we will survey a few of these purposes in the time of Cicero, the better to see how such passions illuminate the values that sustained the republican community and inspired people to gestures mimicking stable unanimity amidst the tumult of competing factions.[1]

We can organize the survey around a story that Cicero never tired of telling about himself, though it meant revisiting, again and again, a time of disfiguring disgrace. The story appears as the main structural element in no fewer than four extant speeches, delivered before quite diverse audiences, and significant elements of it reappear in several other orations and in the correspondence.[2] The story goes like this:

> Late in 63 BCE Cicero, as consul, uncovered the plot of Catiline and his confederates to overthrow Rome's civil regime. Acting with the senate's authoritative support, he oversaw the execution of five chief conspirators at Rome, including a praetor of the Roman people; not long after, Catiline was defeated in a pitched battle in Tuscany. The Republic was rescued, and – though some malicious types grumbled that citizens had been executed without trial and the people's judgment, contrary to Roman law and tradition – there was general agreement that Cicero was the Republic's "unique savior."[3]

A Companion to Greek and Roman Political Thought, First Edition. Edited by Ryan K. Balot.
© 2013 Blackwell Publishing Ltd. Published 2013 by Blackwell Publishing Ltd.

But as the next few years passed there came to prominence an enemy of Cicero, and of all right-thinking patriots, the patrician Publius Clodius Pulcher, a dissolute and violent brigand, a plague on the community. After engineering a transfer from his patrician family to a plebian family in 59, so that he could become a tribune of the plebs, he gained that office for the following year and opened his term with a barrage of legislation that overturned several of the Republic's key institutions. Clodius then turned his attention to Cicero, promulgating a law, "on the life [*caput*] of a citizen," intended to punish with exile – retroactively as well as prospectively – anyone who put a Roman citizen to death without trial. This move was greeted by a great public outcry, massive and passionate demonstrations, and demands from both the senate and the people that the consuls take action to protect Cicero and thwart Clodius. But Clodius had already purchased the consuls' connivance with a promise of rich provincial assignments, and Cicero was left defenseless. After first contemplating armed resistance or even suicide, he resolved that self-sacrifice would be the most patriotic course: he would withdraw and thereby spare his fellow citizens the bloodshed that resistance would bring.

So Cicero went out from Rome on the day Clodius' law was passed [March 18(?), 58], leaving behind his wife, children, and all he held dear. Very quickly Clodius promulgated a second law, declaring that Cicero had been exiled: once this law was passed, his property would be confiscated, his civic status and family rights would be lost, and he could be executed on sight if found within 400 miles of Italy. So Cicero fled to the Greek mainland, staying first at Thessalonica in Macedonia and then at Dyrrachium on the Adriatic Coast, and for almost 18 months tracked from afar the efforts of patriots to gain his recall.

These efforts began barely a month after he left Italy and gradually gained momentum through the balance of 58: Pompey the Great, whose impulse to help had been "slowed" during Cicero's crisis,[4] began to work on his behalf, and the elections for the magistrates of 57 both brought in a cadre of tribunes loyal to the good cause and gave the consulship to a man who would be Cicero's champion, Publius Cornelius Lentulus. When in December the new tribunes entered office they immediately promulgated legislation for Cicero's recall; the senate soon expressed strong support for such legislation at its meeting on the first day of the new year; and an assembly was convened to vote on the tribune's law on 23 January. But before that vote could be held the assembly was violently disrupted by Clodius' thugs: "the Tiber was filled then with the bodies of citizens, the sewers stuffed, the blood had to be cleared from the forum with sponges" (*Sest.* 77).

With this mayhem the public life of Rome was brought to a standstill, through February and beyond, partly under the oppressive influence of Clodius' lawless gangs, partly as an expression of outraged protest and sympathy on the part of Cicero's allies in the senate. But by late spring, the consul Lentulus was able to mobilize the forces of good order and set in motion the events leading to Cicero's recall. In late May or early June the senate met in the temple of Honos and Virtus built by Marius, Cicero's fellow native of Arpinum, whose generalship had saved Rome from German hordes just as Cicero's statesmanship had saved Rome from Catiline. There the senate passed a decree directing all provincial governors to ensure Cicero's safety and directing the consuls to send letters to the towns of Italy calling on "all who wished the commonwealth's safety" to gather in Cicero's support: the language intentionally echoed the formula used to declare a state of emergency and effectively identified the commonwealth's well-being with Cicero's own. During the *ludi Apollinares* in July those crowds did gather, in vast numbers, to show their favor, while the senate, following Pompey's lead, met to pass further supportive decrees. The law restoring Cicero's civic status was promulgated, and on August 4, as the centuriate assembly was convened for the vote, Cicero set sail from Dyrrachium and touched Italian soil again at Brundisium the next day. A stately, triumphant procession the length of the Appian Way brought him to Rome on September 4, and to a joyous reception signaling that Cicero and the commonwealth had been restored at one and the same time.

Such, at any rate, was the story that Cicero told; and as a story, it derives much of its shape and point from omissions, distortions, and – it must be said – downright falsehoods. To mention only a few of these falsifying touches here: though Cicero repeatedly says that Clodius' legislation overturned the use of auspices and destroyed the censorship, it is plain that these assertions are false, and tolerably clear that Clodius' measures aimed only at normalizing procedures (in the case of the auspices) and strengthening due process (in the case of the censorship); though Cicero repeatedly says the suppression of the Catilinarians was attacked as illegal only by *inimici et invidi* – personal enemies and those who were envious or spiteful – one did not have to belong to either category to think that such summary executions rode roughshod over several basic principles of republicanism; though Cicero repeatedly blames the consuls of 58 for their corrupt connivance at Clodius' attack, he also claims to have had the support of almost all the other tribunes, any one of whom could have vetoed the bills Clodius aimed at Cicero – if the bills had been even nearly as unpopular as Cicero represents them as being; though Cicero repeatedly speaks of his departure from Rome as a willing act of patriotic self-sacrifice, his correspondence from exile shows that it was a move he came bitterly to regret; and though Cicero repeatedly stresses the support he received from Pompey in the run-up to his restoration, he cloaks in silence or euphemism the fact that Pompey had flagrantly betrayed him in the weeks and months before his exile, when the great man refused an appeal from Cicero's son-in-law, equivocated with a delegation of Cicero's senatorial supporters, and literally turned his back on Cicero himself, not even bidding him to rise when he had thrown himself at Pompey's feet in supplication.[5]

But for our purposes here the various ways in which Cicero was economical with the truth in fashioning his story are less important than the story itself, which turns the drama of Cicero's exile and return into a late republican morality play.[6] The play is obviously organized around a central conflict between personal interests and communal interests, between individual willfulness and the subordination of one's will to the common good: it reaches its crisis in the triumph of the few over the many that sends Cicero out of Rome, and it finds its resolution in the triumph of the many over the few that brings him home. Of course, the *dramatis personae* are drawn to suit the plot.[7] The role of the ego that knows no bounds – the individual who willfully pursues his own advantages while ignoring the just claims of others and of the community – is played to the hilt by Clodius: he is, to use Cicero's favorite term, the *latro* – "brigand" – who is prepared to use violence, in defiance of the community's laws, for merely personal ends. To play off the brigand we have the men who embody the proper use of power and authority, and those who should do so but fail. The latter are the consuls of 58, Lucius Calpurnius Piso and Aulus Gabinius, who personify the perversion of public office: a hypocritical hedonist and a debauched wastrel (respectively), they take the power delegated to them by the people, and – instead of using it for the common good under the guidance of the senate's authority – they prostitute it to Clodius' ends, not just turning a blind eye but actually shielding him in his assault on Cicero and the commonwealth; fouler still, they abuse their trust for self-interested reasons, to gain provincial assignments that will allow them to divert funds rightly owed to the treasury and apply them to their own insatiable appetites.[8] Fortunately, these men are balanced by two figures of consular righteousness, Cicero himself and Lentulus, his champion in 57. It was Cicero's own use of consular power, exercised as the minister of the senate in suppressing the threat to the civil community, that set the drama in motion; and it was Lentulus' use of consular power, orchestrating the senate's authority and the people's will, that in the end produced the consensus of all patriots, the outpouring of the *populus Romanus universus* that called Cicero back and received him when he returned.

Within the story the actions of Cicero and Lentulus together illustrate the patriot's obligations and his reward. The good man must not hesitate to risk his *caput* ("head" = "life") for the *res publica*, whether it entails the literal sacrifice of his *caput*, his life – say, in defense of Rome at war – or the sacrifice of his metaphorical *caput*, his life as a citizen. It was exactly the latter that Cicero chose to give up when (as he claims) he chose to leave Rome rather than subject his fellow citizens to the mayhem that resistance would have brought: he thereby destroyed his civic self for the sake of the common good. When the good man has satisfied his obligation to the *res publica* in this way, the only thing he should expect and accept in return is glory: the good opinion of other patriots that, when spread abroad and preserved in memory, will cause his peers to judge him excellent and posterity to remember him respectfully, "forever."[9] And as Cicero liked to note, few if any Romans before him had been gifted with glory like his own. We have already seen, and we are about to see in greater detail, how his drama was punctuated by episodes in which his fellow citizens responded to and commented on the action in the manner of a tragic chorus, making their sentiments plain through speech and stylized gestures alike: among those sentiments was exactly the proposition that Cicero's civic well-being was inseparable from, in fact identical with, the well-being of the civil community as a whole.

So we come to the passionate performances of my title. As a point of entry, consider the set of vivid tableaux that Cicero describes in one telling of the story, at just the moment when Clodius has promulgated the first of his laws aimed at Cicero and the crisis has begun to build:[10]

> At this the senate grew concerned; you, gentlemen of the equestrian order, were aroused; all Italy together was thrown into a tumult. In short, all citizens of every sort and rank thought that in this matter, *where the public interest was critically at stake*, aid should be sought from the consuls and their high office. ... Daily they were called upon, by the laments of all patriots and especially the senate's entreaties, to look after *my interests*, to do something, finally, to refer the matter to the senate. [The consuls] took the offensive, not just refusing these requests but even laughing in the face of all the most substantial

men of the senatorial order. Hereupon, when a crowd of unbelievable size had gathered on the Capitol from every part of the city and all of Italy, a unanimous decision was taken to put on mourning dress and to *defend me* in every way possible, as a matter of individual initiative, seeing that [the consuls] had failed *the public interest*. At the same time, the senate met in the temple of Concord – the very precinct that called to mind the memory of my consulship[11] – and there the entire senatorial order, in tears, made its appeal to the ... consul [Gabinius]. ... Oh, the arrogance with which that slimy blot spurned the prayers of that most substantial body and the tears of our most distinguished citizens! ... You came to the senate – I mean you, gentlemen of the equestrian order, and all patriots with you – dressed in mourning, and *for the sake of my life as a citizen* [*caput*] you prostrated yourselves at the feet of that utterly filthy pimp; and when your entreaties had been spurned ... Lucius Ninnius [a tribune loyal to Cicero] ... brought the issue before the senate as *a matter touching the public interest*, and a packed meeting of the senate voted to assume mourning dress for the sake of my well-being.

We can start with the adoption of mourning dress. In making this gesture, the "crowd of unbelievable size" (20,000 strong, Cicero elsewhere says: *Red. pop.* 8) was doing something at once very familiar and completely novel. The familiarity derived from the various occasions – other than those of actually mourning the death of someone close – when an individual or a group adopted mourning, to represent the suspension of life's normal concerns under the impact of overwhelming psychic pain. It had become customary, for example, for a defendant in a "capital" trial, where his "life as a citizen" (*caput*) was at stake, to "change garments" (*vestem mutare*) – putting on a dark-dyed toga, or simply one that was unclean – and to go about in an unkempt state – unwashed, unshaven, and with hair untrimmed – to signal that he faced an unjust calamity and so deserved the pity of others, especially the judges, and his family and friends would join him in a show of solidarity.[12] Cicero remarks (*Red. sen.* 31) that there was a time within living memory when senators, at least, did not normally assume mourning when on trial, but by the mid-first century it appears to have been expected: one defendant's refusal to don mourning was reportedly interpreted as a sign of arrogance and contributed to his conviction.[13] It is easy to find other circumstances, too, when an individual used the gesture to arouse pity for a person presumed to be suffering unjustly and to stir indignation against the person or persons responsible for the suffering: one or another aggrieved suppliant came in mourning from Sicily to protest the depredations of the corrupt governor Verres; in the field against Catiline early in 62, the praetor Metellus Celer put on mourning when his brother, Metellus Nepos, was suspended from his tribunate in the aftermath of rioting he was held to have instigated; as governor of Asia, Quintus Cicero did the same when his brother was driven into exile, and so did the son of Cicero's champion, Cornelius Lentulus, when a law unfavorable to his father was proposed in 56.[14]

In most such instances the purely "private" element of mourning – the sharp personal grief felt for an intimate – is obviously blended, at least implicitly, with a "political" element, as the gesture is aimed at a lamentable state of affairs caused by official action in the public sphere; and the political element is dominant when the gesture is performed by a group working in concert. Consider, for example, some responses to the actions of tribunes: in 133 the landholders opposed to Tiberius Gracchus donned mourning to protest his agrarian legislation; in early 62 the members of the senate did the same to express their dismay at the rioting caused by the clashing tribunes Cato and Metellus Nepos, then again in 56 to protest another tribune's vetoes; and in 55, the consuls Pompey and Crassus, together with their senatorial partisans, "changed their garments" in response to some tribunes' opposition on various fronts.[15] In all such cases the point the demonstrators wish to make is not that they feel aggrieved because their personal interests are at stake – a position that would be either absurd or dishonorable in the circumstances described – but that their grief is honorably public-spirited: the calamity that provoked it should be understood to touch the entire *res publica*, and their common dress shows that they share the sentiments that *all* decent people should share. Such was the point, more clearly still, when the population at large assumed mourning in 63, as war with Catiline threatened, or when the senate and people together did so late in 50, on the eve of civil war.[16] *And* such was plainly the point of the Senate and people's demonstration in 58, when (according to in Cicero's account) they wished to show that "the public interest (*res publica*) was critically at stake," while the consuls "had failed the public interest (*res publica*)."

But that is just where the demonstration passed from the familiar to the novel. As Cicero puts it (*Sest.* 27):

> What a day that was, judges, mournful for the senate and all patriots, a source of woe to the commonwealth, a grievous one for me in the sorrow it brought my household – but for the memory that posterity will have of me, glorious! For what greater distinction could anyone find in all history than this, that all patriots, on their own and in concert, and the entire senate, as a matter of public policy, took on the dress of mourning for one of their fellow citizens?

What greater distinction, indeed? The senate, as a matter of "public policy" (*publico consilio*), and the people, in a display of passionate consensus apparently embracing all but the villainous consuls, had together acted out their belief that a threat against the civic status of a single man was tantamount to a threat against them all, against the public interest – the commonwealth, *res publica* – as a whole. As Cicero was to claim – truthfully, so far as we know – that equation had never before been made (*Planc.* 87), and in that respect it was a unique honor comparable to having a period of thanksgiving declared in his name as a civil magistrate (not a victorious general) for saving Rome from the Catilinarians (*Cat.* 3.15, 4.5, 20). The unprecedented character of the honor, combined with the extravagant claim it implied, would have been sufficient grounds for the consuls to do what they did next: issue an edict bidding the senators to resume normal dress, an act for which Cicero never forgave them.[17]

Related to the demonstrative use of mourning dress, but of wider application, is another gesture that appears in Cicero's account already quoted: "You came to the senate – I mean you, gentlemen of the equestrian order, and all patriots with you – dressed in mourning, and for the sake of my life as a citizen [*caput*] you prostrated yourselves at the feet of that utterly filthy pimp [the consul Gabinius]" (*Sest.* 26, cf.

Red. sen. 12). Cicero's account of his drama recurs often to the same image, of people groveling in supplication on his behalf: a tribune, on the verge of vetoing a measure favorable to Cicero, found his own father-in-law at his feet; Cicero's daughter and her husband abased themselves before the husband's distant relative, the consul Piso; Cicero's brother, Quintus, "in a gesture of unbelievable devotion and unprecedented affection, groveled in utter disarray at the feet of our worst enemies."[18]

I imagine that most readers of this essay, like its author, have never seen anyone actually behave this way in everyday life, and that distance might tempt us to suppose that in such cases Cicero is speaking metaphorically; but that would surely be mistaken. In fact, the practice appears to have been so common as to have had a highly formalized, quasi-scripted character: it is difficult to imagine how else we should visualize the account of a defendant and his supporters supplicating a panel of judges who were about to render their verdict in court – an effort so carefully choreographed as to ensure that six of the group clasped the knees of the judges on the left while five clasped the knees of the judges on the right; or the account of Clodius – in a tight spot earlier in his career – throwing himself at the feet of every single senator in turn at a meeting attended by over 400 members, a process that – even granting no more than a rather feverish five seconds per senator – would have taken over half an hour.[19] Like the assumption of mourning, the act aims to stir pity in the person entreated, and thereby gain a request, when that person is able to relieve your wretchedness; when the person entreated is also held responsible for your wretchedness – as very commonly – the gesture also typically aims to arouse onlookers' pity and their indignation against the offender, to shame him into action. In all cases it is understood to be a voluntary act of self-humiliation. Actually to kick someone who thus abased himself before you was a mark of monstrous arrogance (Val. Max. 8.1 (absol.).3); to spurn the suppliant arrogantly, as Gabinius is represented as doing in Cicero's account, hardly better.

But a different, more public, and perhaps more interesting form of supplication plays an important role in Cicero's story, nearer the joyful climax than the mournful beginning. Early in July 57, when the bill that gained Cicero's recall was about to be presented to the people, the consul Lentulus convened an assembly (*contio*) at which he invited all the foremost men of the community (*principes civitatis*) to speak in support of the measure.[20] The first of these to speak was Pompey, whose remarks were summarized in the speech of thanks that Cicero delivered before the people not quite two months later (*Red. pop.* 16):

> First he instructed you [the *populus*] that the commonwealth had been saved by my policies, he yoked my cause together with that of the general well-being [i.e., he restated the premise of the earliest demonstrations on Cicero's behalf, above], and he urged you to defend the senate's authority, the civil regime, and the fortunes of a citizen who had earned your gratitude. Then, in rounding off the argument he asserted that you were being petitioned by the senate, by the equestrian order, and by all Italy; and in conclusion he not only petitioned you for my well-being but even implored you.

Though Cicero describes the speech's first part less tactfully in the contemporary speech of thanks to the senate (*Red. sen.* 26: "he commended my cause to those of practical intelligence [viz., the senate] and gave a thorough lesson to the ignorant [viz., the *populus*]"), the final contrast between petitioning (*rogare*) and imploring (*obsecrare*) is described in similar terms in all of Cicero's frequent references to the speech:

> [he] not only exhorted but even implored [*obsecrari*] the Roman people on my behalf as though on behalf of a brother or parent. (*Red. sen.* 29, similarly 31 "he implored the Roman people as a suppliant")

> in assemblies of the people he presented himself not only as a defender of my well-being but even as a suppliant on my behalf [*supplex pro me*]. (*Pis.* 80)

> he roused … the Roman people … not only with his *auctoritas* but also with his entreaties [*preces*] (*Har. resp.* 46)

> [Lentulus] then introduced Pompey, who not only put his moral weight behind my well-being but <presented> himself as a suppliant of the Roman people. (*Sest.* 107 "se non solum auctorem … sed etiam supplicem … <praebuit>")

The latter two passages especially, which contrast putting the moral weight of one's *auctoritas* behind a request and acting as a suppliant (*supplex*), suggest why Cicero so stresses this point. In a request based on *auctoritas* the petitioner occupies a superior position in the other party's eyes, and he expects to gain his aim just because the other party is disposed to grant it; in supplication, the hierarchical positions are reversed, as the petitioner presents himself as the dependent party. Since any *contio* was, as a matter of ideology, an assembly of the people as a whole, Pompey was acting out his dependence on the people as whole, making plain in visually unmistakable terms where sovereignty lay. For one of Pompey's vastly preeminent social standing (*dignitas*) to present himself thus was an extraordinary, self-humbling gesture, of the sort made only for a very close connection (cf. *Red. sen.* 29: "as though for a brother or parent"): it both implied great emotional involvement in the request and placed on the persons being supplicated a pressure made more intense by the sudden, vertiginous reversal of authority.

The arousal of pity – the painful awareness that an innocent has been wronged, coupled with the desire to make the wrong right – pervades the performances of mourning and supplication that we have surveyed; but yet another performance, more striking still, is prominently associated with the public rousing of pity in Cicero's story. A more formally staged performance, at least at its start, it took place a month or so before the supplication of Pompey just described, as the movement to restore Cicero gathered steam. In late May or early June the consul Lentulus convened a meeting of the senate in the temple of Honos and Virtus and there saw to the passage of several decrees. These included the decree directing the consuls to send letters to the towns of Italy calling on "all who wished the commonwealth's safety" to gather in Cicero's support: this was the summons that effectively equated Cicero's well-being with the commonwealth's as a matter of public policy, and it resulted in the crowds that received Pompey's supplication in early July. But Lentulus did not just leave matters to the senate: he simultaneously gave a set of extraordinary theatrical games – games outside the official cycle of festivals – at which he saw to it that a veteran actor's virtuoso performance of a carefully chosen script created in the crowd a heady blend of pity, grief, and shame.[21]

Here are the words in which Cicero, giving a virtuoso performance of his own, evokes the scene he was not present to see (*Sest.* 120–2):

[Weren't] the true and uncorrupted judgment of the people as a whole and the most deep-seated feelings of our civil community [made plain] when – as soon as word of the senate's decree passed in the temple of Virtus was relayed to the theater, at the games where a vast crowd was gathered – [the actor Aesopus] pled my case before the Roman people, with tears of fresh joy mixed with grief and longing for me, and with much weightier words than I could have done myself? He gave expression to [the poet Accius'] talent not only through his craft but also through his grief: for when he forcefully delivered the lines on

> the one who, with mind resolved, aided the commonwealth,
> set it upright, and stood with the Achaeans,

he was saying that *I* stood with all of *you*, he was pointing at all the categories of the citizenry! Everyone called for a reprise –

> when the going was uncertain
> he scarce balked to put his life at risk, unsparing of his fortunes.

What a clamor greeted that performance! ... Applause rained down for the poet's words, the actor's intensity, and the thought that I was going to return:

> greatest friend amidst the greatest war –

then in the spirit of friendship he added, and people approved, perhaps from some yearning they felt:

> endowed with greatest talent.

And what a groan arose from the Roman people when soon ... he delivered this phrase:

> Oh father –

I, I in my absence should be mourned as a father, he thought – I whom Quintus Catulus and many others in the senate had called "father of the fatherland." What copious tears he shed in lamenting my fall in flames and ruin – the father expelled, his home set afire and razed to the ground, the fatherland beset – and what an effect he achieved: first gesturing toward my early good fortune, then whirling round to say,

> All this I saw in flames!

He roused to weeping even those hostile to my person and envious of my success! By the immortal gods! What a performance then followed! ...

   Oh ungrateful Argives, thankless Greeks, unmindful of the favor done you!

... The following line that the poet wrote ... the actor ... delivered with reference to
me, when he pointed to all the categories of the citizenry and indicted the senate, the
equestrian order, the Roman people as a body:

   You leave him in exile, you left him to be driven out, and now he's driven out
   you put up with it!

How they all joined then in a demonstration, how the Roman people as a body made
plain its feelings ... – well, I for my part only heard the report, those who were present
can more readily judge.

The script was presumably chosen by the man who gave the games, Cicero's supporter Lentulus, and it was a shrewd choice: the *Eurysaces*, in which the title character – the son of Ajax and grandson of Telamon – laments the expulsion of his
grandfather from his *patria*. It was child's play for the actor to make the lines
pointedly refer to Cicero's plight, and in fact Roman audiences were accustomed to
that sort of topical adaptation: two years earlier, when an actor delivered a line from a
tragedy – "To our misery are you great" – in a way that was taken to refer to Pompey
the Great, the audience called on him to repeat the line over and over, and Clodius,
more recently, had been treated to a similar discomfiture.[22] But the actor Aesopus'
skill in working upon the audience's feelings called upon still more sophisticated
techniques. Having delivered the first half of a line from Accius' script – "greatest
friend amidst the greatest war" ("summum amicum summo in bello") – he then
improvised a second half with particular bearing on Cicero – "endowed with greatest
talent" ("summo ingenio praeditum") – to produce a full trochaic line. Another
improvisation was still more venturesome, in the manner of a jazz musician quoting a
snatch of melody from one song while playing on the chord structure of another: for
the words "Oh father ... All this I saw in flames" are not from Accius' play at all but
are inserted from Ennius' *Andromacha*, evoking the fall of Troy and applying it to the
destruction of Cicero's grand house on the Palatine, after he left for exile. And
Aesopus augmented the impact of this improvisation with a theatrical stroke that
capitalized on the placement of the temporary stage in the center of the city: for when
Cicero says that the actor "gestur[ed] toward [Cicero's] early good fortune," he
means that he pointed to the north rim of the Palatine, where Cicero's house had
stood, then whirled back to the audience to exclaim, "All this I saw in flames!" There
was, Cicero assures us, not a dry eye in the house.
   Thus "the Roman people as a body" – *populus Romanus universus* – made its
feelings known, as it had at every significant stage of the drama. The beginning,
middle, and end of Cicero's story are all strongly marked by moments of passionate,
highly formalized behavior that sweep up – and are meant to sweep up – "all the
categories of the citizens" and cause them to think and feel the same thing: the
episodes serve as forms of punctuation in the narrative flow at the same time as they
help to move the action along to its resolution. And though we are exceptionally well
informed about this story, thanks to Cicero's repeated retellings, there is no reason to

think that the story is atypical in either the amount or the kinds of passionate behavior it represents. Much of Roman public life comprised the sorts of exuberant street theater that we have surveyed, and other sorts too; and much of that street theater must have been as carefully mobilized and staged as the episodes we have seen in Cicero's tale, none of which was simply a spontaneous upwelling of popular response, for all that Cicero seeks to represent them as such. They are all more or less calculated attempts to shape popular opinion by kindling popular emotion, or by appearing to do so in ways that could be represented as the authentic voice of an aroused populace.

This shaping was done for plainly practical, instrumental ends, to influence magistrates or to whip up support for a piece of legislation. Yet it would surely be a mistake to assume that it was done simply for such purposes, with an aim as narrow as influencing a given vote: after all, the law that restored Cicero to Rome was voted in the centuriate assembly, which was so organized that the wealthy exercised disproportionate power and any given issue was typically decided before the great majority of potential voters – "the Roman people as a body" – had had a chance to vote. I suggest that so much effort and passion were also spent for a reason both less focused and more fundamental: so that the public men who lived out their lives "in the sight of the Roman people" (*in conspectu populi*) could claim to be figures of consensus, men with whom all patriots stood and whom only "brigands" opposed, who were devoted only to the common good and who therefore rightly enjoyed the only sort of prestige consistent with republicanism's communitarian ideology. Being such a man was, in the minds of the political class, as important as, and inseparable from, being the sort of man who commanded the material realities of wealth, kinship, and power. Cicero's repeated retellings of his story before various audiences – before the senate and before the people, before the college of priests and before a panel of judges, before (in fact) "all the categories of the citizens" – were clearly motivated by various forms of self-interest: reclaiming his house, discharging obligations to friends, taking vengeance on enemies, justifying his life to date. But we should resist any impulse to reduce the story to those ends, or to suppose that Cicero did not value it for any other reason. However self-interested and utilitarian those repeated retellings undoubtedly were, they also evoked something that was, to Cicero and his audiences, desirable in itself, by momentarily creating, and inscribing in the hearers' minds, the cohesive, consensual community of the republican ideal.

FURTHER READING

For an excellent overview of the period from the consulship of Cicero to the aftermath of his return from exile see Wiseman 1994a, 1994b; for accounts with a biographical focus on Cicero, see Gelzer 1969: 97–152, Rawson 1975: 89–121, and Mitchell 1991: 63–168, and on his exile see G. Kelly 2006 (ch. 4.4); the best treatment of Clodius is Tatum 1999. On the adoption of mourning and the use of supplication as instruments of "popular justice," see esp. Lintott 1999: 16–20; on these and other means used to arouse righteous indignation (*invidia*) against abusive individuals, see Kaster 2005a: 96–9; and on the "ritualized" nature of public life in the late republic, see Flaig 2003. The political role of "the crowd in Rome in the late republic" and its management in formal assemblies (*contiones*) and elsewhere have been much debated in the last two decades, and will continue to be debated: see esp. Vanderbroeck 1987; Hölkeskamp 1995: 25 ff.; Pina Polo 1996; Laser 1997: 138–82; Millar 1998; Mouritsen 2001; Morstein-Marx 2004. On demonstrations at the games and shows, see Nicolet 1980: 363–73, Edwards 1993: 110–19, Leach 2000 (treating the games discussed above), Stärk 2000; on the "theatricality" of Roman political culture more generally, see esp. Bartsch 1994.

NOTES

1   For a discussion of the political passions, from a normative point of view, in the thought of (especially) Thucydides, Plato, and Aristotle, see Ludwig, this volume, chapter 19.

2   The same story is told, with minor variations in detail, in *Red. sen.* and *Red. pop.* (both Sept. 57), *Dom.* (Oct. 57), and *Sest.* (Mar. 56); elements appear in all the "post return" speeches broadly so called, most importantly *Pis.* (late summer 55), and in the important political *apologia* addressed to Cornelius Lentulus, Cicero's main supporter in 57 in *Fam.* 1.9 (esp. 13–14: late 54). On the genesis of the story, and its often misleading character, see Kaster 2006: 1–14, with further refs.

3   That he "alone" was responsible for saving the Republic is among the notes Cicero strikes most insistently, both in his own voice (e.g., *Fam.* 5.2.6–7, *Prov. cons.* 23, *Pis.* 6, 21, cf. *Sull.* 33–4, *Rep.* 1.7) and esp. in reporting the view of others (e.g., *Att.* 1.19.7, similarly *Att.* 2.1.6; *Red. sen.* 29, *Red. pop.* 5, 16–17, *Dom.* 73, 122, 132, *Sest.* 129, *Har. resp.* 58, *Prov. cons.* 43, 45, *Pis.* 23, 34, *Mil.* 39, 73).

4   The euphemism appears at *Sest.* 67; cf. below at note 5.

5   On Clodius' legislation regarding the auspices see Kaster 2006: 194–6, with further refs.; on the censorship, Tatum 1999: 133–5. On the legal status of the Catilinarians' execution see Ungern-Sternberg 1970: 86 ff., esp. 123–9; Drummond 1995: esp. 95 ff.; Berry 1996: 178. For Cicero's regret at his decision to leave Rome see esp. Cic. *Q Fr.* 1.4.4, *Fam.* 14.3.1–3. For Pompey's equivocations and evasions in the period leading to Cicero's departure see Cic. *Pis.* 77, *Q Fr.* 1.4.4, *Att.* 10.4 3 (written in April 49 but referring to the events of 58); Plut. *Cic.* 31.2; Cass. Dio 38.17.3; cf. Cic. *Q Fr.* 2.37.3.

6   For Cicero's own conception of the story as a literary drama, see *Fam.* 5.12.4–6; he treated the story of his exile and return in a lost epic poem in three books, *On His Times*, on which see S. Harrison 1990.

7   With the discussion of Cicero's character drawing here, cf. Stadter's discussion, in chapter 29 of this volume, of the ancient historians' views on the role of character in politics.

8   For Cicero's attacks on Gabinius see esp. *Red. sen.* 10–13, *Red. pop.* 11, *Sest.* 18, 20, 71, 93, *Prov. cons.* passim; for his attacks on Piso, beyond *Prov. cons.* and *Pis.*, see esp. *Red. sen.* 13–17, *Red. pop.* 10, *Dom.* 62, *Sest.* 19, 21–4, 71, 94.

9   On "glory" in Cicero's thought, see Sullivan 1941; Knoche 1967; Haury 1974; Lind 1979: 16–19, 57–8; J.-F. Thomas 1994; and esp. Long 1995.

10   *Sest.* 25–6 (emphasis added) (spoken in a trial before a panel of judges comprising both senators and equestrians, hence the address to "gentlemen of the equestrian order"). For the demonstration and the consuls' response see also Cic. *Red. sen.* 12, 31, *Red. pop.* 8, *Dom.* 26, 99, *Pis.* 17–18; Plut. *Cic.* 30.4, 31.1, *comp. Dem. et Cic.* 4.1; App. *B Civ.* 2.15; Cass. Dio 38.14.7.

11 Cicero had presided over critical meetings held there on Dec. 3–5, 63 to determine the Catilinarians' fate: *Cat.* 3.21; Sall. *Cat.* 46.5, 49.4; Plut. *Cic.* 19.1.

12 See, e.g., *Clu.* 18, 192, *Mur.* 86, *Sest.* 1, *Cael.* 4, *Planc.* 21, 29, *Scaur.* 49, *Lig.* 32–3; Plut. *Cic.* 9.2, 19.2, 30.4, 35. Implied in all such gestures is an understanding of emotion that grants a great deal to cognition: Roman "pity," for example, does not just respond instinctively and irrationally to the spectacle of suffering but depends on the judgment that the sufferer does not deserve to suffer. On the importance of cognition in the ancient understanding of emotion, from Aristotle on, see esp. Konstan 2006; on the Romans, Kaster 2005a, 2005b.

13 Plut. *Cic.* 35.4, on the trial of Milo in 52.

14 Sicilian suppliants: Cic. *Verr.* 2.2.62, 2.3.6, 2.4.41, 2.5.128. Metellus Celer: Cic. *Fam.* 5.1.2. Quintus Cicero: Cic. *Att.* 3.10.2. Young Lentulus: *Sest.* 144.

15 See, respectively, Plut. *Ti. Gracch.* 10.6–7; Cass. Dio 37.43.3; Cass. Dio 39.28.1–4, 39.30.3–4 (= Livy *Periochae* 105); Cass. Dio 39.39.2.

16 See, respectively, Cass. Dio 37.33.3; Plut. *Pomp.* 59.1, *Caes.* 30.3.

17 Cicero often decries this "enormity": see *Red. sen.* 12, *Red. pop.* 13, *Dom.* 55, *Sest.* 32–3, *Pis.* 18, *Planc.* 87; cf. Plut. *Cic.* 31.1; Cass. Dio 38.16.3; the distinction between private and public behavior drawn at *Red. sen.* 12 ("[Gabinius] issued an edict that, while saying nothing to keep you from groaning over your own woes in private, bade you not lament the fatherland's misfortunes in public") perhaps is a distorted echo of the edict's wording, cf. Bailey 1991: 11 n34. In none of his accounts of these demonstrations does Cicero mention that they took their cue from Cicero himself, who assumed mourning when Clodius' bill was promulgated, a move he later regretted (*Att.* 3.15.5).

18 Respectively, *Sest.* 74 (cf. *Att.* 4.2.4); *Red. sen.* 17, cf. *Sest.* 54; *Sest.* 145.

19 Defendant and supporters: Asc. 28.16 ff. Cl., on the trial of Marcus Aemilius Scaurus, at which Cicero spoke (but did not join in the supplication). Clodius: Cic. *Att.* 1.14.5 (Feb. 61), at the height of the Bona Dea scandal; similarly *Q Fr.* 2.6.2, an account of the senator Fulvius Flaccus. Cf. also Cic. *Quinct.* 96–7, *Phil.* 2.45, *Att.* 8.9.1, 10.4.3, *Lig.* 13 with *Fam.* 6.14.2; Plut. *Pomp.* 3.3

20 On the assembly, *Red. sen.* 26, *Red. pop.* 16, *Sest.* 108, *Pis.* 34, and below; on the chronology and the relation of the assembly to the bill's promulgation, Kaster 2006: 401 n26.

21 On the date of the games and their place outside the regular festal calendar see Kaster 2006: 400 n25.

22 For these episodes, see Cic. *Att.* 2.19.3 and *Sest.* 118, respectively; for demonstrations at games and gladiatorial shows more generally, see *Sest.* 124, *Pis.* 65, *Att.* 1.16.11, 2.21.1, 4.15.6, 14.2.1, *Q Fr.* 2.15.2, 3, 3.1.14, *Fam.* 8.2.1 (Caelius); Plut. *Cic.* 13.

PART V

The Athens of Socrates, Plato, and Aristotle

CHAPTER 21

The Trial and Death of Socrates

Debra Nails

Athens, birthplace of democracy, executed the philosopher Socrates in the year 399
BCE for the crime of impiety (*asebeia*), that is, irreverence toward the gods of the
polis, which his accusers – Meletus, Anytus, and Lycon – had said was a corrupting
influence on the young men who kept company with Socrates and imitated his
behavior. But the city had been hearing complaints and jokes about Socrates for
some 30 years by then. A popular comedian had in 414 added the term "to Socra-
tize" (*sōkratein*) to the Athenian vocabulary, describing the conduct of long-haired
youths who refused to bathe and carried sticks, affecting Spartan ways (Aristophanes,
Birds, 1280–3). What was different in 399 was a wave of religious fundamentalism
that brought with it a steep rise in the number of impiety cases in Athenian courts.
Socrates, maintaining in his defense that he was not an atheist and that he had never
willingly corrupted the young or indeed knowingly harmed anyone, was found guilty
and went willingly to his execution against the exhortations and the plans of his
companions, preferring death to the alternatives of desisting from philosophy or
leaving his beloved polis to engage in philosophy elsewhere. Plato narrates the
indictment, trial, and execution of Socrates in a series of five dialogues, the *Theaetetus*,
Euthyphro, *Apology*, *Crito*, and *Phaedo*, set in the spring and summer of that year.

 This singular event has been examined and reexamined ever since. There are other
accounts,[1] but it is Plato's that has become philosophy's founding myth and that has
immortalized Socrates in the popular imagination as a man of profound moral
strength and intelligence – though also as a uniquely peculiar and inscrutable individual. When brought to trial, Socrates was 70 years old, married, the father of three
sons ranging in age from 1 to 17, and poor; his net worth, including his house, was 5
minae (Xen. *Oec.* 2.3.4–5), the equivalent of what a sophist might charge for a single
course (Pl. *Ap.* 20b9), and less than a skilled laborer could earn in a year and a half.
He perished without publishing but having inspired his young companion Plato
(424/3–347 BCE) and other men known as Socratics to compose dialogues and
memoirs in which Socrates was featured. There were enough of these that Aristotle

A Companion to Greek and Roman Political Thought, First Edition. Edited by Ryan K. Balot.
© 2013 Blackwell Publishing Ltd. Published 2013 by Blackwell Publishing Ltd.

was later to refer to such Socratic works as a literary genre (*Poetics* 1447b11). What was it about democratic Athens in 399, its politics, religion, culture, laws, or courts – or about Socrates, or his accusers, or their charges – that might help explain what has appeared to so many as a great miscarriage of justice? In laying out some of the issues raised by Socrates' trial and death, I will follow the five dialogues mentioned above in relation to the legal thread through the events: summons, preliminary hearing, pretrial examination, evidentiary and penalty phases of the trial, imprisonment, and execution (A. Harrison 1968–71: vol. 2; MacDowell 1978).

Anyone who reads the five dialogues, amidst the telling of Socrates' final story, encounters indestructible philosophy – argumentation concerning being, knowing, and philosophical method.[2] So provocative and engaging are the extended philosophical passages in the *Theaetetus* and *Phaedo* that anyone inquiring into Socrates' trial and execution must make a conscious effort not to be distracted by brilliant arguments, not to be seduced away from the narrative line of Socrates' last days. That this should be so is Plato's ultimate defense of the philosopher, his highest tribute to Socrates and to the very idea of what it is to live the life of a philosopher: one's circumstances, no matter how dire, are never more than a backdrop for the conduct of philosophy.

Meletus' Summons and the Political Background

Several things had already happened when Socrates, the summons in his hand, greeted Theodorus in the spring of 399 (*Tht.* 143d1–2), and it is best to set them out in order.

Meletus of Pithus was Socrates' chief accuser. He was the son of a poet also named Meletus, but was himself "young and unknown" (*Euthphr.* 2b8).[3] To charge Socrates, a fellow citizen, Meletus was obliged to summon him to appear at a preliminary hearing before the relevant magistrate, namely, the king-archon (*archōn basileus*), who had jurisdiction over both homicide and impiety. This Meletus did by composing a speech or document that stated the complaint and demanded that the defendant, Socrates, appear on a specified day. It was not necessary to put the summons in writing, or for the king-archon to agree in advance about the date of appearance, but at least four days had to be granted between the notification and the hearing.

Athenian public prosecutors, selected by lot and paid a drachma per day, had only narrow functions, so, when Meletus made his accusation, he became both plaintiff and prosecutor in Socrates' case. The summons had to be served on Socrates personally and preferably in public: active participation in Athens' extensive religious life was a civic obligation; thus to prosecute impiety was to act in the public interest. Any citizen could serve and, though it was not obligatory, could add his name to Meletus' document, if Meletus put his complaint in writing (as *Ap.* 19b3–c1 implies he did). If a defendant could not be located, it may have been permissible to announce the summons in front of his house (as allowed some decades later); but the sanctity of Socrates' house could not be violated for that purpose. One or two witnesses accompanied Meletus in his search for Socrates, men who would later swear that the summons had been properly delivered. These may have been the two men who would be Meletus' advocates (*synēgoroi*) in the trial, Anytus of Euonymon and Lycon of Thoricus, men of very different dispositions.[4]

Anytus was rich, having inherited a tanning factory from his self-made and admirable father (Pl. *Meno* 90a). Plato emphasizes his hatred of sophists at *Meno* 90b, 91c, and 92e. He was elected general by his tribe, and in 409 tried but failed because of storms to retake Pylos from the Spartans. Prosecuted for this failure, he escaped punishment by devising a new method of bribery for use with large juries that was later given the name *dekazein* and made a capital crime. In 404, he supported the government of the Thirty, but it soon banished him, whereupon he became a general for the exiled democrats (though his protection of an informer to the Thirty cast doubts on his loyalties). When the democracy was restored in 403, he became one of its leaders. Anytus served as a character witness in another of the impiety trials of 399, that of Andocides. Xenophon calls Anytus' son a drunkard (Xen. *Apology* 31.1–4).

Lycon is known to us through an extended and sympathetic portrayal by Xenophon (in *Symposium*) who depicts him as the doting father of a devoted son, Autolycus, a victorious pancratist in 422 who was later executed by the Thirty. Lycon was a man of Socrates' generation who had become a democratic leader after the fall of the oligarchy of 411. In comedies, his foreign wife and his son are accused along with him of living extravagantly and beyond their means; he is accused with his son of drunkenness; but he alone is accused of treachery, betraying Naupactus to the Spartans in 405.

It is sometimes said that political animosity lay behind the impiety charges against Socrates, both because some of the men he was rumored to have corrupted were political leaders; and because, it has been claimed, he could not *legally* be charged with the political crime of subverting democracy (Stone 1988; cf. Burnyeat 1988). Although the labels "democracy" and "oligarchy" are ubiquitous, politics in Athens in the late fifth century resists reduction to a simple clash between broad-franchise democrats and narrow-franchise oligarchs for several reasons: many central figures changed sides, sometimes repeatedly; the oligarchies themselves varied in number (the 400, the 5,000, the 30); clan and family interests as well as individual loyalties often cut across affiliation. During the long Peloponnesian War, from 431, Athens remained a democracy except for a brief period in 411. After a decisive Spartan victory in 404, however, the Assembly (*ekklēsia*) elected 30 men, three per tribe, to return the city to her predemocratic ancestral constitution. The Thirty quickly consolidated their power and wealth through executions and confiscations, driving supporters of the democracy into exile. After about eight months of tyranny, in 403, the exiles retook the city in a bloody civil war, later driving the leaders of the Thirty and their supporters to Eleusis. An amnesty was negotiated with Spartan help that separated the two sides and made it illegal from 402 to bring charges against anyone on either side for crimes committed during the rule of the Thirty. Suspecting that the former oligarchs were hiring mercenaries, the democrats raided Eleusis in the early spring of 401 and killed all who were left. In the courts, from 400, the amnesty was observed for criminal charges, but residual hostility continued, and it was common to attack one's opponent for remaining in the city instead of joining the democrats in exile, as had Socrates' childhood friend Chaerephon (*Ap.* 20e8–21a2). Socrates did remain in the city, but he opposed the Thirty – as his record shows – and there is no evidence that there was an underlying political motive in Socrates' case.

Upon receipt of the summons, to resume the narrative, Socrates enjoyed a citizen's right not to appear at the preliminary hearing, though Meletus' suit would then proceed uncontested to the pretrial examination stage. Even if charged with a murder, short of parricide, a citizen also had the right to voluntary exile from Athens, as the personified laws remind Socrates (*Crito* 52c3–6). Socrates exercised neither of those rights. Rather, he set out to enter a plea before the king-archon and stopped at a gymnasium on his way.

The *Theaetetus*: Trial and Death in Prospect

The *Theaetetus*, replete with references to Socrates' impending trial and execution,[5] opens the five-dialogue exploration of what it is to lead the examined life of a philosopher. Philosophy begins in wonder (*Tht.* 155d3) with the study of mathematical patterns, and, in Socrates' case, ends – if it ends – with his death as presented in the *Phaedo*. Although the *Theaetetus* stands first in Plato's narrative, it is rarely read in that context because of its overwhelming philosophical importance in distinguishing perceptions and true beliefs from *knowledge*.[6] Yet the Athenians' failure to make precisely these distinctions is crucial to what happened in 399. Why the polis executed Socrates comes starkly into focus four times in the dialogue, showing that – however well intentioned – *the Athenians mistook their friend for their enemy and killed him.*

The first is a famous passage (*Tht.* 148e–151d) in which Socrates likens himself to his mother, Phaenarete, for both are midwives, she of bodies, he of minds. As she is beyond child-bearing age, he is beyond wisdom-bearing age. As she runs the risk of being confused with unjust and unscientific procurers when she practices her art, he runs the risk of being confused with sophists when he practices his (cf. 164c–d). Through Socrates' maieutic art, others "have themselves discovered many admirable things in themselves, and given birth to them" (150d6–8).[7] He admits he is considered strange and has a reputation for questioning others and making them suffer birth pains without proffering his own views; some men want to bite him when he disabuses them of the silliness they believe. As he draws the midwifery comparison, Socrates presages what he will later say in court: that his mission is compelled by the god; that he has a personal *daimonion* or spiritual monitor,[8] which here sometimes forbids his association with youths who return to him after choosing bad company; and that no god can wish evil to man – the denial of which serves as an example of "silliness." The gods acknowledged by the polis were those of the poets, gods who often wished, and even caused, evil; but Socrates acknowledged no such gods. Plato makes it easy to imagine Socrates playing into the hands of his accusers, for Socrates volunteers examples of youths whose corruption he could not prevent and says Homer's gods Oceanus and Tethys are really flux and motion (152e7–8, cf. 180d), that Homer's golden chain is the sun (153c9–d1).

A second perspective arises out of the discussion of Protagorean relativism. If knowledge is perception, then every juryman is "no worse in point of wisdom than anyone whatever, man or even god" (162c2–5; cf. majority opinion, 171a). Protagoras, impersonated by Socrates, says: "about matters that concern the state, too – things which are admirable or dishonorable, just or unjust, in conformity with religion or not – it will hold that whatever sort of thing any state thinks to be, and lays down as, lawful for itself actually is, in strict truth, lawful for it" (*Tht.* 172a1–b5; cf. 167c–d, 177c–d, *Prt.* 320d–328d); from which it follows that if Athens thinks it is just, then it *is* just for the city that it execute Socrates. But it is another matter entirely, Socrates objects, when one considers justice not judicially but legislatively, that is, considers what laws *ought* to be enacted in the interest of the polis – for a polis can judge its own good incorrectly. "Whatever word it [the state] applies to it [the good], that's surely what a state aims at when it legislates, and it lays down all its laws, to the best of its ability and judgment, as being most useful for itself" (*Tht.* 177e4–6; cf. 179a), says Socrates. However, one state's decision may approximate the truth, actual justice, less well than another's, and the counselor-gadfly of one polis may be wiser than that of another (cf. 177d). The implication is that Socrates' execution could be legalistically just yet unjust in itself, unjust by nature, thereby raising two further issues pursued in the *Apology* and in the *Crito*: whether a citizen must obey an unjust law, and whether punishment is justifiable. If a polis unwillingly does wrong, it deserves instruction, not punishment – as Socrates replies to his Athenian jury (*Ap.* 26a).

The third is the central section, well known as the philosophical digression (*Tht.* 172c–177c) comparing the practical man and the philosopher, corresponding to "two patterns set up in that which is."[9] The description of the philosopher shows why the polis would condemn him. In Athens, philosophers are completely misunderstood; they "look ridiculous when they go into the law courts" (172c4–6), and worse. The philosopher's inexperience in court is mistaken for stupidity, his inability to discredit others personally is ridiculed, his genuine amusement is taken for silliness; he thinks of rulers as livestock keepers, fails to value property, wealth, or noble ancestry; he is arrogant, ignorant, and incompetent (174c–175b). If such a man should violate the law as well, wouldn't it be right to kill him? Two further opinions Socrates expresses about the philosopher of the digression will feature in the undoing of Socrates himself: he studies natural science (173e–174a), and his gods are not those of the city (176b–c). For such a godlike man, "the fact is that it's only his body that's in the state, here on a visit" (173e2–5); he "ought to try to escape from here to there as quickly" as he can (176a8–b1).

Fourth and finally, while discussing whether knowledge is true judgment, Socrates asks Theaetetus whether a jury has knowledge when it has been persuaded to a true judgment by an orator or a skilled litigant (201a–c) – reflecting exactly Socrates' situation with his own jury. By the strict letter of the law, Socrates is guilty of not believing in the vengeful Olympian gods of the Athenians and the poets, and thus his jury is persuaded to a true judgment by the orator Lycon and the skilled litigant Anytus, if not by the feckless Meletus. But the result is legalistic justice, not justice itself; it reflects a correct judgment, but not knowledge. As the digression puts it, the point is "to give up asking 'What injustice am I doing to you, or you to me?' in favor of the investigation of justice and injustice themselves" (*Tht.* 175c1–2).

The *Euthyphro* and Piety

The *Euthyphro*, on the nature of piety, takes place just before Socrates enters his plea before the king-archon. The diviner-priest, Euthyphro, a man in his mid-forties who will prove inept at grasping piety when Socrates questions him, nevertheless predicts impending events well, fearing that Meletus will harm "the very heart of the city by attempting to wrong" Socrates (*Euthphr.* 3a7–8), and inferring that Socrates' spiritual monitor signals religious innovation "easily misrepresented to the crowd" (3b5–9). Socrates replies by zeroing in on the crux: the Athenians would not mind his spiritual monitor or his opinions if he were not imitated by the young (3c7–d2; cf. 2c–d); the reason he is a defendant, he says, is that he does not accept the poets' stories about the gods' wrongdoing, "and it is likely to be the reason why I shall be told I do wrong" (6a8–9). Socrates leaves no doubt that the quarreling gods Athenians accept are not the ones he believes in: what he formulates as questions at 6b–c, he states unambiguously elsewhere: "we can state the truth like this. A god is by no means and in no way unjust, but as just as it's possible to be" (*Tht.* 176b8–c1). For Socrates, the gods agree perfectly in their goodness, justice, wisdom, etc., and could not come into conflict – something Euthyphro cannot accept.

But Socrates' insistence that what the Athenians are most concerned about is how the youths are affected introduces the topic of education that plays a role in the background. Athenian males of the propertied classes sought higher education in their late teens. Since success in democratic public life was enhanced by the ability to influence the citizenry in the Assembly and courts, many studied with rhetoricians to learn the latest techniques of effective public speaking. In the latter fifth century, however, new intellectual influences from abroad began making headway in Athens among the young: sophists and natural scientists. The former could outdo the ordinary rhetoricians by teaching new ideas about what constitutes a good life or a good state, and some of them taught logic-chopping and hair-splitting as well, to make "the worse into the stronger cause" (*Ap.* 19b5–c1), encouraging the young to get ahead without regard for justice or even custom. Natural scientists too seemed a threat to social order, giving naturalistic explanations for natural phenomena, and were lampooned repeatedly in comedy. Over the years, as Athens suffered war, plague, loss of empire, and defeat, its citizenry became increasingly alarmed that the new learning was somehow to blame, and anti-intellectualism grew.

The Preliminary Hearing

Although the rough content of the summons is given by the conversation in the *Euthyphro*, how Socrates would later that day answer the charge at his preliminary hearing probably led to greater precision in the formulation of the charge itself. The preliminary hearing designated the official receipt of the case (*dikē*) by the king-archon who, in office for one year, would later preside at the pretrial examination and the trial. Meletus stated or handed over his complaint, and Socrates answered by entering his plea. The king-archon was authorized to refuse Meletus' case on technical procedural grounds, to redirect it to an arbitrator, or to accept it. If Socrates took substantive exception, challenged the admissibility of the charge in relation to existing law, he had the right at this preliminary stage to file a countersuit (*paragraphē*) that would have been heard first – but he did not. In the case of an oral or improperly written complaint, the king-archon rendered the charge in appropriate legal language, marking the official acceptance of the case, now an indictment in the modern sense. It was then published on whitened tablets in the agora and a date was set for the pretrial examination (*anakrisis*); from this point, word would have spread that old Socrates, that big-mouth, hair-splitting, long-time target of the comic poets, had been charged with impiety.

The indictment that we have – via Diogenes Laertius (2.40.3–7), who took it from Favorinus (second century CE), who said he saw it in the public archive, the Metroön – is so formulated that, taking both the *Euthyphro* passage and this one into account, a secondary literature has grown up over exactly how many separate charges Socrates faced: "This indictment [*graphē*] is brought on oath by Meletus, son of Meletus, of Pithus, against Socrates, son of Sophroniscus, of Alopece: Socrates is guilty of not believing in the gods the city believes in, and of introducing other divinities [*daimonia*]; and he is guilty of corrupting the young. The penalty assessed is death." Athenian law forbade impiety, and that is the single law Socrates is charged with breaking – in two ways (not believing ..., introducing ...), with one result: corruption of the young.

Narrowly and legalistically, the prosecution faced some obstacles: base individuals who could testify to Socrates' direct influence would be suspect as witnesses; the upright citizens who would have been convincing witnesses, Socrates' actual companions, would testify only to his piety and propriety (*Ap.* 33d–34b). But the prosecution had the advantage that the charge of impiety was not limited to the period 403–399, for it was not a political crime; Meletus, Anytus, and Lycon had only to persuade the jury that Socrates had at some time in his long life been impious and, since some of Socrates' associates, whom he might be alleged to have corrupted, were already dead – Critias, Charmides, Alcibiades, and others associated with the particularly notorious sacrileges of 415 – the prosecution could cast aspersions without blatantly violating the law against hearsay evidence.[10] It is probably unwise to be too narrow or legalistic, however, for juries could be swayed by innuendo and fallacious argument, swept along by powerful orations. Besides, the king-archon's acceptance of the case is prima facie evidence that there was a case to be made.

The Pretrial Examination

The court fees normally assessed of a plaintiff at this point, to be reimbursed by the defendant if found guilty, were waived in Meletus' suit because impiety prosecutions were "in the public interest." Yet his action would not have been without risk: to discourage frivolous suits, Athenian law imposed a heavy fine on plaintiffs who failed to obtain at least one-fifth of the jury's votes, as Socrates points out (*Ap.* 36a7–b2). Unlike closely timed jury trials, pretrial examinations were occasions for questions to and by the litigants, including questions of one another, to make more precise the legal issues of a case so a verdict of guilt or acquittal would be more straightforward. It was no time for speeches. This procedure had become essential because of the susceptibility of juries to bribery and misrepresentation by speakers who deliberately and often skillfully interpreted laws to their own advantage. Originally intended to be a microcosm of the citizen body as a whole, juries were now manned by volunteers – the old, disabled, and poor – who needed the meager pay of three obols, half the drachma that an able-bodied man could earn for a day's work (cf. Aristophanes, *Wasps* 291–311). In 399, Athenian men age 30 or over were eligible to volunteer for jury service at the beginning of the archon year, in midsummer. Six thousand were impaneled, probably by lotteries for 600 from each tribe, to be deployed repeatedly in different configurations to the various civil and criminal courts throughout the year. When Socrates' trial took place at the approach of midsummer, the jurors were experienced if not jaded.

Also, unlike trials, the pretrial examinations could be adjourned and reconvened repeatedly – when, for example, one of the principal parties needed to collect information. If a litigant wished to delay proceedings for weeks or months, this was a rich opportunity. Magistrates could also use the pretrial examination to compel a litigant to reveal information. We do not know what went on at Socrates' pretrial examination, though his complaints at *Theaetetus* 172e acknowledge some constraints.

The Trial and Socrates' Defense: The *Apology*

Plato takes up the story again in the month of Thargelion (May–June), a month or two after Meletus' initial summons, when Socrates' trial occurred. Onlookers gathered along with the 500 or 501 jurors (*Ap.* 25a)[11] for a trial that probably lasted most of the day, each side timed by the water clock. Plato does not provide Meletus' prosecutorial speech or those of Anytus and Lycon; or the names of witnesses called, if any (*Ap.* 34a3–4 implies Meletus called none). *Apology* – the Greek "*apologia*" means "defense" – is not edited as are the court speeches of orators. For example, there are no indications in the Greek text after 35d8 and 38b9 that the two votes were taken; and there are no breaks after 21a8 or 34b5 for witnesses, although Socrates may in fact have called Chaerecrates or the seven named men. Also missing are speeches by Socrates' supporters; it is improbable that he had none, even if Plato does not name them.

It is sometimes said that Socrates was the first person in the west to be convicted for his beliefs – for a thought-crime or crime of conscience; and not believing in the gods of the Athenians is exactly that. In classical Athens, however, religion was a matter of public participation under law, regulated by a calendar of festivals in honor of a variety of deities, with new ones introduced from time to time. The polis used its revenues to maintain temples and shrines, and to finance festivals; it mandated consultation with Apollo's oracle at Delphi at times of important decisions or crises; generals conferred with seers before deploying troops; and the lottery system for selecting public officials left decisions to the gods. Prescribed dogma or articles of faith, however, were unknown, so compliance was measured by behavior; and it is very unlikely, based on extant Socratic works, that there would have been *behavior* to offer in evidence of Socrates' beliefs, such as neglecting sacrifices or prayers, for Socrates continues his religious observance through his dying day. Moreover, unlike the case of the acquitted Anaxagoras a generation earlier (cf. *Ap.* 26d6–e2), there were no writings to present as evidence of unorthodox beliefs.

Socrates divides the accusations against him into old and new, addressed in that order. He had a reputation fueled by several comic poets from about 429 that conflated him with both natural scientists and sophists, often emphasizing his egregious effect on the young:[12] he "busies himself studying things in the sky and below the earth" (*Ap.* 19b5). The single case Socrates mentions explicitly in *Apology* is Aristophanes' *Clouds* (produced in 423, revised in 418). As clear as it is with hindsight that the *character* Socrates who introduces new gods, denies the old ones, and corrupts the young in the play is a composite of several different sophists, natural scientists, and philosophers (Dover 1968), the jury made no subtle distinctions. Besides, Aristophanes had made fresh attacks in *Birds* (in 414) and *Frogs* (in 405), both times emphasizing that the city's young men imitated Socrates. In the latter, the Socrates imitators are accused of attacking the poets. Socrates says himself that the young men question and thereby anger their elders (*Ap.* 23c2–d2). Though Socrates denies outright that he is a natural scientist, his familiarity with their investigations and his own naturalistic explanations make it no surprise that the jury could not tell the difference (e.g., *Tht.* 152e, 153c–d, 173e–174a; *Phd.* 96a–100a). Those who had witnessed Socrates in philosophical conversation (*Ap.* 19d1–7), his respondents becoming angry or confused, were not likely to have appreciated fine distinctions between philosophical inquiry and sophistry. Socrates' excuse for his strange behavior – the god makes me do it (20e–23b) – appears from the crowd's reaction only to have exacerbated their misunderstanding.

Turning to the new charges, Socrates easily defeats Meletus in argument, demonstrating in turn that Meletus (1) has not thought deeply about the improvement and corruption of the young, (2) should have sought to instruct Socrates privately before hauling him into court, (3) confuses Socrates' views with those of Anaxagoras, and (4) holds incompatible theses: Socrates is an atheist; and Socrates introduces new divinities. Yet the very exhibition of Socratic questioning, coupled with Socrates' belittling of Meletus (26e6–27a7) may have boomeranged. The jury, riled again, may have found Socrates' tactics indistinguishable from those of sophists: they saw, but they did not understand. Socrates' relentless honesty, easily mistaken for arrogance, casts doubt on his every claim: he will do no wrong, even to avoid death; he is like Achilles; he has risked death in battle; he does not fear death; he will never cease to do philosophy, to examine himself and others, even for the promise of acquittal; he is god's greatest gift to the city; his accusers cannot harm him, and the jurors will harm themselves if they kill him.

A defendant is wise to refute what he can, and Socrates does address some of the evidence against him directly. (5) He admits he has had, since childhood, the spiritual monitor that Meletus ridicules, but he defends it. He attributes to it his inability to "yield to any man contrary to what is right, for fear of death, even if I should die at once for not yielding" (32a6–7), and offers two instances of his defiant behavior in proof of it: presiding (as *prytanis*) over the Council (*boulē*) in 406, he opposed the Assembly's unlawful denial of separate trials to six generals who were tried and executed as a group. As a citizen under the lawfully elected but corrupt government of the Thirty, he refused the order to seize a fellow citizen, a general allied with the democrats in exile.[13] In both cases Socrates cites, crediting his spiritual monitor, the Athenians had later come around to Socrates' view. (6) He denies being anyone's teacher, receiving a fee for conversing, teaching or promising to teach, and is thus unwilling to answer for the conduct of others (33a–b). (7) The Athenian god Apollo ("the god"), he says, ordered him to question wise guys – which the youths of Athens enjoy (33c); and he says oracle-like that he believes in the gods "as none of my accusers do" (35d7). (8) Socrates three times takes up the charge that he corrupts the young, twice in the same hypothetical way: "Either I do not corrupt the young or, if I do, it is unwillingly." If unwillingly, he says he should be instructed because "if I learn better, I shall cease to do what I am doing unwillingly" (25e6–26a4). Later: "if by saying this I corrupt the young, this advice must be harmful, but if anyone says that I give different advice, he is talking nonsense" (30b5–7). He also argues that many of his former and current young companions are present with their guardians, but that none of them have testified to his corrupting influence (33d–34b). Anytus had warned the jury that Socrates should perhaps not have been brought to trial but, since he was, must be executed or else the sons of the Athenians will "practice the teachings of Socrates and all be thoroughly corrupted" (29c3–5). Can this 70-year-old who insists he will continue to philosophize possibly yield to instruction? Socrates claims his advice is that the soul is more important than the body or wealth (30a–b), but there has also been testimony that he teaches the young to despise the gods of the city and to question their elders disrespectfully. Even Socrates could not blame the jury for finding him guilty, for it is mistaken about what is truly in the interest of the city (cf. *Tht.* 177d–e). So the gadfly is swatted. The verdict is guilty, and the trial passes into the penalty phase.

Socrates blames one of Athens' laws: "If it were the law with us, as it is elsewhere, that a trial for life should not last one but many days, you would be convinced, but now it is not easy to dispel great slanders in a short time" (*Ap.* 37a7–b2). This isolated complaint in the *Apology* is supported by the running criticism of the court in the *Theaetetus* noted earlier, for example, "is what's true to be determined by the length or shortness of a period of time?" (158d11–12; cf. *Grg.* 455a). And it stands opposed to the remark of the personified laws that Socrates was "wronged not by us, the laws, but by men" (*Cri.* 54c1).

Socrates goes on to describe himself as the city's benefactor; to maintain that he mistreats no one and thus deserves a reward, not punishment; to insist that he cannot and must not stop philosophizing, for "the unexamined life is not worth living" (*Ap.* 38a5–6) – confirmation to some that incorrigible Socrates opposes the will of the city. In a last-minute capitulation to his friends, he offers to allow them to pay a fine of 30 minae, six times his net worth. He is sentenced to death and reflects that it may be a blessing: either a dreamless sleep, or an opportunity to converse in the underworld.

Socrates' trial was no evil conspiracy against an innocent, but something more profound and at the same time more tragic – a catastrophic mistake, a misunderstanding that could not be reconciled in the time allowed by the law.

The *Crito* and Socrates' Refusal to Escape

The day before Socrates' trial begun, the Athenians launched a ship to Delos, dedicated to Apollo and commemorating Theseus' legendary victory over the Minotaur (*Phd.* 58a–b). During this annual event, Athenian law demanded exceptional purity, so no executions were allowed. Although the duration of the voyage varied with conditions, Xenophon says it took 31 days in 399 (*Mem.* 4.8.2); if correct, Socrates lived 30 days beyond his trial, into the month of Skirophorion (June–July 399). A day or two before the end, Socrates' childhood friend Crito – sleepless, distraught, depressed – visits Socrates in the prison, armed with arguments for why Socrates should escape before it is too late. Socrates replies that he "listens to nothing ... but the argument that on reflection seems best" (*Cri.* 46b4–6), whereupon a reflective conversation begins.

Socrates' argument that he must not escape is a continuation of his refrain from the *Apology* (28b, 29b, 32a, 32b, 37a, 37b) that he never willingly does wrong (*Cri.* 49b–d). The principle is absolute. Wrongdoing, mistreating people, and injustice are the same, "in every way harmful and shameful to the wrongdoer" (49b5), never to be inflicted, not even in return for wrongdoing suffered (cf. *Tht.* 173a8), not even under threat of death (cf. *Ap.* 32a), not even for one's family (*Cri.* 54b3–4). Clearly Socrates cannot be morally consistent and inflict harm on Athens in return for harm endured, as Crito would prefer (50c1–3). Note, however, that although one should keep one's agreements (49e6–8) – one's social contract as it were – one cannot always keep all one's agreements at the same time. Socrates is right not to equate injustice with lawbreaking. We have already seen that (a) cities legislate their good to the best of their ability, but can be mistaken about what is in their interest, consequently establishing unjust laws; (b) Athens' law against impiety, insofar as it required acceptance of the quarreling, wrongdoing gods of the poets, was an unjust law; (c) orders from lawful governments to commit wrongdoing are not binding because they are unjust; and (d) Athens' one-day limit on all trials was an unjust law. Socrates had already found it necessary to violate the law of (b) when it conflicted with both his spiritual monitor and reason, and to disobey an order of type (c) when following it would have harmed someone else. Nevertheless, Socrates says he would be mistreating Athens to escape and must therefore remain in prison (49e9–50a3). To understand why that is so, we should take into account the argument of the *Theaetetus* and the *Apology* that (e) the correct response to unwilling wrongdoing is not punishment but wise counsel, instruction – the positive corollary to the negative principle of do-no-harm. When the laws tell Socrates to persuade or obey them (*Cri.* 51b9–c1), they give a nod to this principle. Like keeping agreements, however, persuasion is not always possible and is thus subordinate to do-no-harm.

One might say Socrates should have attempted to persuade the Thirty, and perhaps he did, but that situation differed importantly: undermining a corrupt government by refusing to harm a good man was unlawful, but it was not unjust. In the present case, having already said that death may be a blessing, Socrates cannot point to a harm that would outweigh the harm he would be inflicting on the city if he now exiled himself unlawfully when he could earlier have left lawfully (52c3–6). In this case, the laws are right to say that if Socrates destroys them, he will manifestly confirm the jury's judgment that he is a corrupter of the young (53b7–c3).

The impiety law Socrates violated is interesting in a different way. Whereas one can destroy laws by undermining them, one cannot *persuade* laws; one must rather persuade men. And that presents an insurmountable obstacle: in 410, a commission was established to inscribe all the laws, the Athenian Constitution, in stone on the walls of the king-archon's court. Just as the task was completed in 404, a series of calamities – Athens' defeat by Sparta, the establishment of the Thirty, then bitter civil war – persuaded the citizens that, however useful it was to have the newly inscribed laws readily available, those laws themselves had failed to prevent disastrous decisions over a generation of war in which the empire had been lost. When the democracy was restored in 403, a board of legislators (*nomothetai*) was instituted to write additional laws, assisted by the Council. A new legal era was proclaimed from the year 403/2, Ionic lettering replaced Attic for inscriptions, and a public archive was established so laws written on papyrus could be consulted and cited. From that year, only laws inscribed from 410 to 404, or from 403 at the behest of the new legislators, were valid; an official religious calendar was adopted and inscribed; and decrees of the Assembly and Council could no longer override laws (such as had enabled the six generals to be tried as a group over Socrates' objections).

However useful the reforms were, the board was not a public institution seeking advice or holding hearings. Furthermore, it was a crime for anyone else even to propose a law or decree in conflict with the inscribed laws. Still, Socrates did what he could: he never shrank from discussing whether the gods were capable of evil and conflict. It is anachronistic to use the phrase "academic freedom" of the era before Plato had established the Academy, but what is denoted by the phrase owes its authority to Socrates' steadfast principle of following nothing but the argument that on reflection seemed best to him.

The Execution of Socrates in the *Phaedo*

Plato sets the final conversation and execution of Socrates in a metaphysically specu-lative, Pythagorean dialogue where intricately intertwined arguments, mythology, and Socratic biography have roles to play. The *Phaedo* is Plato's most dualistic dialogue, exploring the soul's troubled relationship with the body; and it is the only dialogue in which Plato's absence is explicitly remarked (59b10). What in the *Theaetetus* is Socrates' down-to-earth maieutic method, is in the *Phaedo* the soul's recollection of transcendent Forms. What in the *Theaetetus* is the philosopher's escape from the earthly mix of good and bad, is in *Phaedo* the soul's escape from the body.

Phaedo is, by custom, the dialogue most concerned with what it is to be a philosopher and to lead the life of philosophy – though in more rarefied air than when the rough Socrates practices his questioning techniques on anyone willing to be engaged by him. It is perhaps closer to the truth to say that the dialogue is about dying in philosophy, for the recurring image is of the soul's purification and final flight from the imprisoning body that distracts it with pleasures and pains, needs and desires, throughout life. Phaedo tells the Pythagorean community at Phlius that – while Socrates' companions felt "an unaccustomed mixture of pleasure and pain at the same time ... sometimes laughing, then weeping"[14] – the philosopher himself, on his last day of life, "appeared happy both in manner and words as he died nobly and without fear" (58e3–4), a proem sustained in the conversations about the soul that follow.

Without ever claiming certainty, and sometimes flatly denying he has it, Socrates wants to put his argument before his "judges," his friends: one who has spent a lifetime doing philosophy should face death cheerfully. He says, "other people do not realize that the one aim of those who practice philosophy in the proper manner is to practice for dying and death" (64a4–6) – which raises a laugh and Simmias' joke that people think "true philosophers are nearly dead" (64b4–6; cf. 65d, 80e). But the seriousness of the day's talk is plain when Simmias and Cebes have delivered themselves of arguments against the immortality of the soul, depressing everyone. Socrates rallies: "If you take my advice, you will give but little thought to Socrates but much more to the truth. If you think that what I say is true, agree with me; if not, oppose it with every argument and take care that in my eagerness I do not deceive myself and you and, like a bee, leave my sting in you when I go" (*Phd.* 91b8–c5). Philosophical argument resumes. Near the end, Socrates breaks into a long story of the afterlife that "no sensible man would insist" were true, but where "Those who have purified themselves sufficiently by philosophy live in the future altogether without a body" (114c2–6).

In sharp contrast, realism dominates the opening and closing scenes in the prison. In the morning, Socrates visits with Xanthippe and their baby, and rubs his ankle where the bonds have been removed, speaking of pleasure and pain; the Eleven, prison officials chosen by lot, are already gone (59e–60b). Now, sometime in the afternoon and with the philosophical conversation ended, attention focuses again on the body. Socrates has no interest in whether his corpse is burned or buried, he says, but he wants to take a bath to save the women of his household from having to wash the corpse; then he meets with his family before rejoining his companions. The servant of the Eleven, a public slave, bids Socrates farewell by calling him "the noblest, the gentlest, and the best" (116c5–6), but cannot forbear weeping. The poisoner describes the physical effects of the poison, the *Conium maculatum* variety of hemlock (Bloch 2001). Socrates cheerfully takes the cup, "without a tremor or any change of feature or color" (117b3–5), and drinks. The emotions that have been threatening Socrates' companions now erupt violently – and are immediately checked by Socrates' shaming, "keep quiet and control yourselves" (117e2). The poison begins to work, and the poisoner follows its numbing progress from the feet to the belly – touching, testing, pressing Socrates' body. Socrates makes a last request of Crito. Presently, his body gives a jerk, after which his eyes are fixed. Crito closes them. Phaedo, the former slave, echoes the servant of the Eleven, ending the dialogue with an epithet for Socrates, "the best, ... the wisest and the most upright" (118a16–17).

FURTHER READING

Background. Cooper 1997b is important not only for its widely used translations, but for Cooper's sober and wide-ranging introduction. Nails 2002 is a reference for information about the persons in the dialogues, their historical context, and evidence for dramatic dates. Harrison 1968, 1971 remains unsurpassed for the details of the issues that arise in connection with the trial and execution of Socrates. MacDowell 1978 is essential for understanding the major changes in Athenian legal procedures at the end of the fifth and beginning of the fourth century. Mackenzie 1981 is an authoritative, comprehensive source on punishment, thus important for the views Socrates alludes to in *Theaetetus* and articulates in *Apology.* Camp 1992 includes line drawings and photographs of places and artifacts relevant to Socrates' last days; and Bloch 2001 identifies *Conium maculatum* as the specific hemlock poison that produces the exact symptoms described by Plato. Nails 1995, in a study of Socratic and Platonic method, examines a variety of conflicting claims about Plato's philosophical development. Thesleff 1967 is a handbook of Platonic composition technique, dialogue structure, and comparative classification of styles.

Interpretations. Clay 2000, brilliant and idiosyncratic, develops the explicit allusions in the texts insightfully. Blondell 2002 provides a deeply moving treatment of the dramatic elements of the *Theaetetus* and especially of its digression (ch. 5). McPherran 1996 seeks the religion of the historical Socrates through an extensive survey of Greek religious practices, close readings of Socratic texts, especially the *Euthyphro*, and dialogue with Vlastos 1989 (an influential paper taking the position that Socrates rationalized Athenian religion). Vlastos 1983 argues that Socrates preferred democracy to other forms of government but faulted men who misused democratic institutions for unjust ends. Weiss 1998 argues persuasively that the personified laws of the *Crito* do not speak for Socrates, who follows the argument that seems best to him. Euben 1997 is an engaging essay on Socrates' role as educator within the democracy, drawing compelling parallels to contemporary culture–war debates.

Controversies raised by Socrates trial. Dover 1968 describes the intellectual milieu in Athens in the late 420s, arguing that the Socrates of Aristophanes' *Clouds*, whom the jury confused with the historical Socrates, was a composite of foreign and local intellectuals. Woozley 1979 argues that disobedience to law would be permissible for Socrates only if the illegal action were itself intended to persuade. Kraut 1984 goes further, examining Socrates' attitude toward democracy and arguing that living an examined life would require Socrates, if he disobeyed a law, to persuade a court that he had been right to disobey. But other authors have disagreed. R. Allen 1984 argues that Socrates' foremost commitment was not to laws, but to a "single, self-consistent standard of justice, fixed in the nature of things" against which any set of laws must be measured. Burnyeat 1988 finds Socrates guilty of not believing in the gods in which the city believes, amidst a masterful review of Stone 1988; the great journalist Stone had cited political reasons for Socrates' conviction, paying tribute to Athenian democracy by telling "Athens' side of the Socrates story." Brickhouse and Smith 1989 is a watershed work on the arguments, historicity, and context of Plato's *Apology*, downplaying the role of politics in a miscarriage of justice that resulted in Socrates' conviction. Similarly, Reeve 1989 argues that the Socrates of the *Apology*, having defended himself convincingly against the indictment, was unjustly convicted. According to Brickhouse and Smith 1994, however, Socrates always obeys the law, which it is always just to do; thus obeying an unjust law would not bring blame to Socrates but to the legislators and the law itself.

NOTES

1 Xenophon is often cited, though he was not in Athens at the time: see discussions in Stone (1988), Brickhouse and Smith (1989: §§1–2), and McPherran (1996 passim); later accounts, mostly fragmentary, tell how Socrates was viewed in later centuries (see Brickhouse and Smith 2002).

2 Cf. allusions at, e.g., Pl. *Sph.* 216a–d, and *Plt.* 299b–300e, set dramatically when the indicted Socrates was at liberty pending trial.

3 *Euthphr.*, *Ap.*, *Cri.*, and *Phd.*, trans. G. M. A. Grube, revised by John Cooper, in Cooper 2002.

4 Anytus appears in the works of 11 different contemporaneous authors, Lycon in six (Nails 2002: 37–8, 188–9).

5 Litigation is a topic (172a–173b, 173c–d, 174c, 178e, 201a–c); but there are additional allusions to legal proceedings: (a) the ad hoc adoption of legalistic language (145c, 170d, 171d, 175d, 176d–e, 179b–c); (b) reminders about the time required by philosophy and limited by litigation (154e, 158d, 172c–e, 187d, 201a–b; cf. *Ap.* 24a, 37b). Moreover, there are thematic ties to *Phd.* (*Tht.* 144e–145a, 145c–d, 154c, 173e–174a, 176a–b, 205c).

6 By discussing *Tht.* in dramatic order, I make no claims about when it was written, though I reject the so-called developmental hypothesis that Plato's views evolved in some linear way: Plato tendered positions tentatively, leaving them open for revision, and returned to them repeatedly to address material for various purposes (Nails 1995: 219–31).

7 *Tht.* trans. McDowell 1973.

8 See Pl. *Resp.* 496c4 (cf. 509c1), *Phdr.* 42b9, *Euthd.* 72e4, *Euthphr.* 3b5, *Ap.* 31d1, 40a4, 41d6, and *Tht.* 151a4.

9 Thesleff (1967: 57–61) surveys three types of central section, arguing that Plato, like Pindar et al., occasionally sets a visionary speech at the center of a dialogue, e.g. the divided line passage in *Resp.* Blondell's (2002: 289–303) account of the digression notes the special role of the central section and cites more recent bibliography. The passage here shows, by the way, why Socrates would fit more comfortably in the primitive communal society of *Resp.* 2 (369b–372d) than in even a purged Athens, though it is the latter that he loves (*Tht.* 143d).

10 Critias was a leader of the Thirty; Charmides was a member of the Piraeus Ten in the same period. The mutilation of herms and profanation of the mysteries is treated in Nails (2002: 17–20s.vv.); contemporaneous ancient sources are Thuc. 6.27–9, 6.53, 6.60–1; Andoc. 1.11–1.70; inscriptions on stelae from the Eleusinium in Athens (*IG* I 421–30); and

Xen. *Hell.* 1.4.13–21. Plutarch (*Alc.* 18–22) and Diodorus Siculus (13.2.2–4, 13.5.1–4, 13.69.2–3) may have used contemporaneous sources, no longer extant, in their much later accounts.

11 The round number 500 continues to appear in contemporaneous accounts long after we know 501 were employed to avoid ties.

12 See Nails (2002: 266–7) for Ar., *Clouds*; *Birds* 1280–3, 1553; *Frogs* 1491–9, et al.; and for fragments of Callias' *Pedētae*, Teleclides, Amipsias' *Connus*, and Eupolis.

13 A more complete account appears in Nails (2002: 79–82), citing Xen. *Hell.* 1.7.8–35; Diod. Sic., *Library of History* 13.98–103; and contemporary sources; cf. pseudo-Aristotle, *Athenian Polity* 34.1. The election and rule of the Thirty, with numerous ancient and contemporary sources, is at Nails (2002: 111–13). Leon of Salamis has an entry at Nails (2002: 185–6) with reference to Thuc. 5 and 8, passim; Xen. *Hell.* 1 and 2, passim, esp. 2.3.39–41; Andoc. 1.94; Lys. 10, 13.44; Pl., Letter 7.324e–325a, and *Ap.* 32c–d; and contemporary sources.

14 *Phd.* 59a4–9. Considerable information about these companions is known. Of some 23 persons, only two are attested in the liturgical class, five or fewer are Athenian men under 30. There are three slaves and a (foreign) former slave, the illegitimate son of a rich man, two to three women, three children, and six foreigners, one of whom seems to have been wealthy (Nails 2002: xxxix). The prison cell, which could not have held them all at once, has been unearthed (Camp 1992: 113–16).

CHAPTER 22

The Politics of Plato's Socrates

Rachana Kamtekar

Examining in this way what would be the virtue of a good leader, he [Socrates] stripped away all the other qualities but left this remaining: to make whomever one leads happy.
Xenophon, Memorabilia 3.2.4

Modern readers of Plato find it easier to admire Socrates as an exemplary citizen in relation to his polis than as a political philosopher. As a citizen, Socrates refused to obey the orders of a violent and unscrupulous regime to arrest a fellow citizen for execution (*Ap.* 32c–e); he was the sole member of the Council to oppose the illegal mass trial of the generals who had failed to rescue the survivors of the battle of Arginusae (*Ap.* 32b–c); he openly criticized his city's government, and was willing to die for his principles – do no injustice (*Ap.* 32c–e; *Cri.* 49a–b); obey the god's command to philosophize even if the cost of doing so is death at the hands of your city (*Ap.* 29d, 38a); abide by the decision your city makes concerning you even if it is unfavorable to you (*Cri.* 50a–53a).[1] On the other hand, the reasoning Socrates provides for abiding by the city's decision – that not doing so would constitute an attempt to destroy the law; that since the laws are like a citizen's parents, it is not permissible to retaliate against them; that by remaining in the city and not expressing dissatisfaction with its laws the citizen agrees to obey those laws – fails to recognize reasonable limits on what a city may require of its citizens. And the leitmotif of Socrates' political thought – the criticism of democracy as rule by the ignorant (Pl. *Cri.* 44d; *Prt.* 319b–d; *Grg.* 454e–455a, 459a–461c) in the pursuit of desire gratification (*Grg.* 502e–503d, 521e–522a) resulting in the corruption of the citizens (*Grg.* 515d–517c) – seems to be based on an implausibly low estimate of most people's capacity for political judgment and an implausibly high estimate of the specialized knowledge required for politics. Finally, there is no avoiding Karl Popper's criticism that Plato mistook the fundamental question of politics to be "who shall rule the

A Companion to Greek and Roman Political Thought, First Edition. Edited by Ryan K. Balot.
© 2013 Blackwell Publishing Ltd. Published 2013 by Blackwell Publishing Ltd.

state?" and ignored the far more important question of how to design institutions so
as to check the abuses of political power,[2] a matter which greatly occupied Athenian
democratic practice and thought.

In these circumstances, it is tempting to distinguish the exemplary individual
Socrates from the theorist Plato. Popper himself excuses the historical Socrates
(who survives in Plato's *Apology* and *Crito*) for neglecting the issue of checks on
political power on the grounds that because of his "emphasis upon the human side of
the political problem, he could not take much interest in institutional reform."[3]
According to Popper, Socrates was engaged with the Athenian democracy critically
but constructively, attempting to reform its (usually oligarchic-leaning) political elites
by forcing them to think critically. By contrast, Popper argues, Plato betrayed the
legacy of Socrates by having him speak on behalf of an antidemocratic constitution in
the *Republic* (1962: 189–97).[4] More recently, Terry Penner has argued that Socrates'
intellectualist moral psychology commits him to the view that only the nonpolitical
activity of engaging with one's fellow citizens in philosophical dialogue can benefit
them.[5] Socrates' response to politics is, on this view, to "change the subject" – that is,
to try to reform the characters of the politically ambitious young men with whom he
interacted. And this project of moral reform through critical conversation must soften
Socrates' attitude toward democracy. As Richard Kraut puts it, Socrates "thinks that
the many will always rule badly, and he would prefer a society of moral experts [in this
regard he is as authoritarian as Plato]. But he sees little hope for anything better than
democracy, and he values the intellectual freedom provided by this political system."[6]

Approaching Socrates' politics as politics in some extraordinary sense, consisting
of critical and oppositional activity focused on individual intellectual transformation, has the advantage of reconciling Socrates' claim that he does not participate
in politics (*Ap.* 31d) with his claim that he alone of all the Athenians undertakes
the true political expertise and engages in political affairs (*Grg.* 521d): there is a
sense, a special Socratic sense, in which Socrates' moral engagement with individuals is political; yet this is not politics in the ordinary sense at all.[7] But while there
is something to this conception of Socrates, if criticism and the attempted moral
transformation of individuals were the whole of Socrates' contribution to politics,
it would be hard to see why courses in political theory or the history of political
philosophy should, as they commonly do, begin with the Socrates of the "early
dialogues." Surely the more plausible beginning would be Plato's *Republic*,
which both describes an ideal constitution, including the details of an educational
system for moral cultivation, and systematically criticizes other actual and ideal
constitution-types.

Leo Strauss wrote that Socrates was "the founder of political philosophy."[8] The
present chapter attempts to show in what sense this is true – and it will be for rather
different reasons than Strauss thought (see the section below). In brief, the argument
is that Plato's Socrates[9] transforms the traditional "who should rule?" question by
yoking its consideration to the idea that ruling is a profession; Socrates thereby
introduces a nonpartisan basis from which to discuss that question. In the next
section of the chapter, I sketch the ancestry of the "who should rule?" question in
Socrates' predecessors and identify two justifications they offer for the privilege of

ruling. Then, I argue that Socrates' contribution to this debate develops out of his internal criticism of a quite separate discourse, that of the advertisements, made by contemporary sophists and orators, for a new professional education in politics. These figures professionalize political rule in the sense that they describe it as an activity in which success can be achieved by mastery of the skills that may be acquired by studying with them. Socrates accepts their characterization of political rule as a profession, and uses this characterization to insist that success in this profession consists in improving the citizens – rather than in any personal advantage of the ruler. Thus (although the teachers of the political profession are not eager to admit it) the professionalization of political rule has implications for the constitutional debate because it entails a certain account of what correct rule is, and what its goal is. Socrates' criticism of the professional discourse results in a novel and nonpartisan basis for answering the question "who should rule?" but it does so by replacing a prevalent conception of political rule as a privilege, the claim to which demands justification, with a conception of political rule as a profession, in which the claim to expertise demands a show of credentials. Referring the debate about who should rule to a discussion of what skills the job of ruling requires not only inaugurates nonpartisan evaluation of political regimes, it also invalidates some considerations previously given in support of certain partisan answers. I discuss these results of Socrates' reconceptualization of the question "who should rule?" in the final section.

The Constitutional Debate

In Plato's *Laws*, the Athenian lists seven bases on which people may claim to be worthy to rule others: that they are their ancestors, that they are of higher birth, that they are older, that they are masters and the others slaves, that they are stronger, that they are wise and the others ignorant, and finally, that having been chosen by lot, they are favored by the gods and fortune (690ac). Readers of Plato will associate the sixth claim, of the wise to rule the ignorant, with Socrates. But just how does Socrates argue that the wise should rule the ignorant? To understand Socrates' contribution to the debate about who should rule, we need first to get a sense of the shape of the debate before Socrates. (The first evidence that Socrates is concerned with the question "who should rule?" may be in the *Crito*, where the Laws remind Socrates he has always praised Crete and Sparta for being well governed (53a), but this may have been praise for the conformity of behavior in Crete and Sparta to Cretan and Spartan law, rather than for the laws themselves.)

Herodotus puts in the mouths of sixth century Persian nobles who have lately seized power a debate about which form of government – democracy (the rule of many), oligarchy (the rule of a few), or tyranny (the rule of one man) – they should choose (the discussion is a little anachronistic because it refers to fifth century Athenian institutions like the selection of officials by lot and public examinations for officials). The argument for the superiority of democracy to tyranny is that there are no checks on a tyrant, the result of which is that the tyrant becomes arrogant and commits many atrocities; by contrast, democracy's institutions allow no one that kind of power; instead, in a democracy, all citizens are equal before the law. The argument for the superiority of oligarchy adds to the criticisms of tyranny criticisms of democracy: democracy puts in power ignorant men who are even more arrogant than a tyrant; oligarchy, on the other hand, puts the best men (present company included) in power, and the best men will produce the best policies. The argument for the superiority of tyranny adds to the criticisms of democracy criticisms of oligarchy: oligarchy leads to feuding and bloodshed; further, conflicts within oligarchies and democracies lead to tyranny anyway; finally, if the tyrant is the best, then nothing is better than his government (*Histories* 3.80–2). Herodotus may have taken these arguments from a sophistic source, perhaps Protagoras, who is said to have written a *Peri Politeias* (Diogenes Laertius, *Lives of Eminent Philosophers* 9.55) and whose *Antilogikai* is said by Aristoxenus to have been the source of Plato's *Republic* (3.38). (The Herodotus passage's exhaustive rehearsal of all arguments on all sides supports the attribution to Protagoras' *Antilogikai*.)

Common to debates about who should rule is the view that ruling is a privilege the possession of which has to be justified; those who would rule have to show themselves to deserve the privilege of ruling – either in exchange for something they provide or because they are simply worthy of ruling. The giving of justifications for ruling may even precede any debate about or contestation of any leader's claim to rule. For instance, Homer's Sarpedon gives a general justification of elite privilege when he explains that aristocrats have the privileges that they do (and common people don't) because they fight where the battle is fiercest (*Il.* 12.310–21). The suggestion is that the courage of the aristocrats is both intrinsically good and valuable to the community.

Two kinds of considerations in support of the different forms of government inform the debate as to who should rule. One consideration is the *protection of the citizens* – so just as democracy promises protection from the whims of one who would place himself above the law, the tyrant too is described as a guardian of the people, whose rule preserves them from the violence of faction and feud. A second consideration is that *the ruling individual or group be "the best."* This consideration might be expressed in terms of divine right, as in Homer, by Zeus' gift of the scepter to the king (*Il.* 2.100, cf. 7.412, 9.96). Even though these two considerations – providing protection and being superior – usually go together in actual arguments, as long as the content of the superiority is not simply superiority in providing protection, they are quite separate considerations.

The pseudo-Xenophon *Constitution of the Athenians* is one text that distinguishes superiority in protecting the citizens from some other kind of superiority. The author disapproves of the Athenian constitution because the Athenians prefer the well-being of the inferior at the expense of the superior (*chrēstoi*) (1.1). But he also suggests that it is just for the (inferior) common people to have more than the nobility, on the grounds that it is the common people – that is, the navy rather than the hoplites – who defend Athens (1.2). So his point of view seems to be that it would be best if the intrinsically superior on the one hand had more, and on the other hand, did more by way of protecting Athens. However, since they don't protect Athens, justice doesn't demand that they have more; rather, it demands that those who actually protect Athens have more. Still, despite their failure to protect Athens, the "superior" surpass the common people by their many intrinsic merits: they have the least injustice, the most self-restraint and concern for good things (1.5). The Athenians (i.e. common Athenians), for their part, can tell who's superior and who's inferior, but they prefer the inferior because the inferior are more useful to them (2.19).

The most remarkable instance of the view that intrinsic superiority entitles one to rule is of course Callicles' speech in Plato's *Gorgias*, which characterizes as "nature's justice" the rule by the superior (482e–484c). Although Callicles does not explicitly oppose the condition in which the stronger and more capable have a greater share to the condition in which the common good is achieved (he opposes it instead to the condition in which all have a "fair share"), his examples of the superiors who by nature's justice have a greater share are conquerors, raiders, and lions. And the reason the lion is king of the animals is not that he protects them.

Callicles' is obviously an extreme position, but it is evidence that a party's intrinsic superiority could be taken as by itself a reason for that party to rule. This may be the sentiment in, for example, Democritus' pronouncements that it is by nature fitting for the superior to rule (DK B267), that it is hard to be ruled by an inferior (49), and that it is proper to yield to a law or a ruler or someone wiser (47). Alongside this belief in a reason for the superior to rule, Democritus remarks that poverty under democracy is preferable to prosperity under a dictator to the same extent as freedom is preferable to slavery (251); perhaps the thought is that democracy at least limits the extent of an inferior's power over one. That Democritus is no Calliclean is shown by his advice that his audience not try to acquire power for themselves contrary to the common good (252).

The other consideration in favor of a kind of rule – that it protects the people – is more widely used, and there is usually more to be said about just how a ruler/rule of that kind can or will protect the people. So, for example, in Thucydides' account of the debate at Syracuse (*History of the Peloponnesian War* 6.39), the oligarchs contend that the wealthy are best able to rule because they are the least tempted to take the city's money for themselves, and the democrats counter that the "demos" whose interests are served by democracy includes all the citizens, and that all citizens in a democracy have a fair share – by contrast with the oligarchy, in which the dangers, but not the profits, are shared.

I have documented the use of and emphasized the distinctness of these two considerations in favor of someone's or some group's rule in order to bring out Socrates' distinctive contribution to the debate. By contrast, Leo Strauss argues that the question "who should rule?" arises naturally out of the politically engaged stance of the classical political philosopher, and the answer "the best should rule" arises equally naturally and prephilosophically, and needing the philosopher only to spell out its implications and defend it against objections by "bad or perplexed men."[10] But this account assumes that "rule by the best" is not a controversial ideal. Yet the interpretation of "best" is seen to be a matter of contention in Thucydides' Syracusan debate. And the democrats in Herodotus' constitutional debate do not even try to claim on behalf of democracy that the demos are the best.

In the constitutional debate, the alternatives for rule – by the many (the poor), the few (the rich or historically rich), or one man – are idealizations of actual constitutions. It is not as if Socrates can argue in favor of rule by the wise by pointing to or idealizing some existing constitution in which the wise rule. Yet to make a case for rule by the wise, it would seem necessary to address the claims to rule of the wealthy, the nobly born, the military, and so on. In the *Republic*, when Plato does describe and argue for the superiority of a constitution in which the wise rule, he helps himself to the conception of a ruler who is motivated to rule because his ruling is necessary rather than because ruling is something fine or good (347cd, 520e–521a) and whose rule is justified by his qualifications. There has been a quiet revolution between the idea of rule as privilege, claim to which requires justification, and this idea of rule as a job the performance of which calls for certain qualifications. The question "who should rule?" has come to depend on the question "what does the job of ruling demand?" In the next section, I argue that Socrates takes the conception of ruling as a job requiring certain skills from contemporary sophists, but that he argues that determining what the requisite skill is depends on the answer to the question "what is the goal of ruling?"

Professionalizing Political Rule

In all likelihood Socrates takes over the idea that political rule is a job requiring certain skills from some of his older contemporaries. Plato includes among these Protagoras, who claimed to teach "sound deliberation [*euboulia*], both in domestic matters – how best to manage one's household, and in public affairs – how to realize one's maximum potential for success in political debate and action" (*Prt.* 319a),[11] and Gorgias, who claimed to teach rhetoric, "the ability to persuade by speeches judges in a law court, councilors in a council meeting, and assemblymen in an assembly or in any other political gathering that might take place" (*Grg.* 452e) which produces "freedom for humankind itself and ... the source of rule over others in one's own city" (452d). Both Protagoras and Gorgias characterize politics as a field in which one can excel when one has achieved the mastery over the skills (deliberation, rhetoric) that they teach.

Before we delve into Socrates' engagement with the sophists and orators, a word about what they were doing in Athens. The demand for sophists and orators seems to have arisen with two changes in Athenian circumstances in the fifth century which made traditional elites' claim to political power and prior political skills obsolete: democracy and empire. If the vote of the demos was required for a politician's plan to carry, it was no longer enough to be a great general; the politician had to be able to speak persuasively to the assembled demos, and since he did not have a common culture and education with them, he had to learn what appealed to them in particular. In addition, Athens' new status as an imperial power complicated its affairs and this, combined with the requirement that any issue be decided by the Assembly in a single day, created a demand for politicians who could devote themselves to mastering

Athenian political affairs. Plato's contemporary Isocrates expresses one kind of response to the complexity of Athens' affairs when he denies the possibility of scientific knowledge (*epistēmē*) of "what we should do or what we should say" and instead upholds the importance to the politician of "insight" (*phronēsis*) and the ability "by his powers of conjecture [*tais doxais*] to arrive generally at the best course" (Isoc. *Antid.* ca. 271).[12] But however desirable mastery of political affairs or good judgment may have been in a politician, the democratic system made the ability to speak persuasively not just a desideratum but a necessity.[13]

In this context, "professionalizing" political rule amounts to claiming that there is a body of knowledge, sufficiently wide in scope and precise in formulation, upon the learning of which the would-be political leader should expect success. Describing a new discipline as a *technē* (profession, craft, art) or *epistēmē* (science) is a way of claiming for it a status possessed by better-established practices like medicine. That status derives in part from the professional's ability to bring about a valued result (such as health) on the basis of some understanding of the factors involved (rather than by luck). (I have chosen the term "profession" to translate *technē* rather than the more usual "craft" or "art" for several reasons. First, in English, "craft" sounds as if it refers to something one does with one's hands and "art" to something in the fine arts, perhaps as opposed to the sciences, whereas *technē* has none of these connotations; like the *technai* about which there are disputes, such as medicine and politics, a profession is thought to have an important intellectual component. Second, in contemporary English "professional" has normative connotations that seem to resonate with those of *technē*: people speak today of professional standards and professional (or unprofessional) behavior.)[14]

I mean this to be a minimalist account of what is entailed by calling the subject one practices or teaches a *technē*, and I want a minimalist account because it seems to me that more substantial accounts reflect controversial innovations by Socrates (and other fifth century intellectuals) to which we will want to pay special attention. So, for example, Aristotle characterizes a *technē* as involving knowledge of universals, by contrast with experience (*empeiria*) or knowledge of particulars; as involving knowledge of causes; and as teachable (*Metaphysics* 1.1). But these may be peculiarly Socratic emphases (on the contrast with experience, and on knowledge of universals and causes, see e.g. *Grg.* 464c–465a; on teachability, *Prt.* 319b–e, 361a–c). Aristotle's characterization is quite different from that of the late fifth century Hippocratic *On Ancient Medicine*, according to which medicine's claim to be a science rests on its answering a need, having a starting point and longstanding method for discovery, and being explicable to laypersons (2). While this text also insists on medicine's having a precise and complete understanding of causes and their effects on the body (20), it insists that these are found out by experience, which allows distinctive causes to be investigated by the method of difference – by contrast with causal and explanatory principles that derive from a more general physical investigation. Again, Socrates' insistent demand that any claimant to a *technē* specify its product (*ergon*) (Plato *Grg.* 447d–454b; *Prt.* 318a–319a; *Euthd.* 288e–292d; *Cleit.* 409b–d) builds on what must have been a widespread expectation that a professional could name or point to the beneficial product he had on offer, but it goes beyond that expectation in demanding that the professional give an account of this product. After all, a doctor might be expected to tell his patient the symptoms of his disease and of his cure, but it is not reasonable to expect him to give a nonexpert an explanation of how the disease produces the symptoms, or how the treatment effects the cure, or of what health is, particularly in any given case. (However, Socrates is himself subjected to this higher standard of giving an account of the product of a craft when Thrasymachus demands that he say what the just (which Socrates has been treating as the product of the *technē* of justice, *Resp.* 332d ff.) is without saying that it is the advantageous or beneficial and so on (*Resp.* 336c–d; cf. *Cleit.* 409c–d).)

In his conversations with the sophists and orators, Socrates accepts the formal claim that expert knowledge in politics brings about good political results. His questions focus on the content of the expert knowledge they profess (What is it about? What is the evidence that they really have it?), on their conception of good political results (Are these really good? If not, what are the good results to be brought about by political rule?), and on the relationship between the two (Does their expertise really have the results they claim it does? Or what sort of expert knowledge would it take to bring about these results, or genuinely good results?). So, for example, in the *Gorgias*, Socrates counters Gorgias' claim that rhetoric is an expertise which produces the good political result of enhanced social and political power for the orator-politician (452d–e) by pointing out that however rhetoric achieves its effects, it is not through any knowledge of the matters of justice and injustice about which it makes speeches (459a–e, 461b), and that even if it enables the orator-politician to visit evil upon anyone he wishes, it does not enable him to bring about any good for himself or anyone else (466b–468e). So rhetoric fails to be political expertise on two counts: it lacks knowledge of central political matters (the just and unjust), and it fails to bring about any genuine good.

The sophists and orators contemporary with Socrates cannot have welcomed his agreement with their claim that expert knowledge in politics brings about good political results. For Socrates not only agrees with them that expert knowledge brings about successful political rule, but also adds that only those with expert knowledge are qualified to (thus should, or may) rule. Sophists and orators like Gorgias, Protagoras, and Thrasymachus, noncitizens in Athens, would have shied away from being seen as telling the Athenians how they should run their city; they claimed only to be helping aspirants to political power within the existing constitution, thereby allowing their professional training to be equally attractive to partisans of democracy and oligarchy. Socrates, on the other hand, was centrally in the business of evaluating ways of living, both individual and communal. Further, while the need to attract students led sophists and orators to allow the conception of successful political rule to depend on the would-be student's conception of success or advantage, Socrates' insistence on a substantive account of the (goods) produced by successful political rule brought into the limelight the difficulties of making recommendations without any views on what is noninstrumentally good.

In *Republic* 1, Plato points out both the common ground and the differences between Socrates and a contemporary sophist, Thrasymachus. It is Thrasymachus who introduces the idea of a professional expertise of ruling which enables its possessor, insofar as he is a professional, to rule unerringly (340c–341b). Socrates accepts the idea that there is a profession of ruling; he disagrees with Thrasymachus, however, about the goal of this profession. According to Thrasymachus, the professional ruler rules to his own advantage. But the introduction of the idea of a professional ruler opens up other dimensions of the profession of ruling. Socrates argues, by analogy with the other professions, that a profession's goal is always the improvement of that over which it has power. He seems to be reasoning: if [as you Thrasymachus maintain] ruling is a profession, then [you must concede that] its product is like that of other professions, and the product of any other profession is the improvement of that over which it has jurisdiction. For example, the doctor in the precise sense is so called because he treats the sick, the healing of the sick being the advantage which the profession of medicine is directed toward (341c–d, 342c). He generalizes, "No kind of knowledge seeks or orders what is advantageous to itself . . . but what is advantageous to the weaker, which is subject to it" (342c–d; trans. Grube, rev. Reeve in Cooper 1997b). If political rule is rule over citizens, then its goal must be their betterment, not the ruler's. In the *Gorgias*, Socrates announces that he himself is a practitioner of the political profession (521d), perhaps the only one. If improving citizens is the goal of the political professional, then, since Socrates' protreptic and elenctic activities have that goal, he can reasonably count himself a political professional.

In this argument, Socrates claims that the professions "by nature" aim at the betterment of whatever they have jurisdiction over; for example, medicine was discovered to remedy the deficiencies of the human body (341d–e). This seems a deliberate departure from the common line of thought that the professions were discovered for the benefit of mankind: Protagoras' myth gives us many other examples of the deficiencies to remedy which Prometheus and Zeus gave humans the various professions (*Prt.* 321c–322d). The common line is, although initially more plausible, perhaps more vulnerable to misuse than Socrates'. If we specify the goal of a profession by the benefits it gives us humans – saying with Thrasymachus that the goal of shepherding is surely not the welfare of the sheep but rather the production of the meat and wool the sheep provide for the shepherd's benefit (343b) – then it is open to someone to specify the goal of another profession by the benefits it gives some one subgroup of humans, perhaps even by exploiting another subgroup. (Thrasymachus' choice of an example is particularly striking, given the standard characterization of the ruler as a shepherd (e.g. Hom. *Il.* 2.243; Xen. *Mem.* 3.2.1; Arist. *Eth. Nic.* 8.11, 1161a12–15; criticized at Pl. *Plt.* 267c ff.).) Safer, then, to look for an internal connection between a profession and its goal. And to specify the internal connection when we also have to determine the goal, it makes sense to turn to the other professions as models, on the assumption that the professions resemble each other. Resemblance between the professions seems to be the basis of Socrates' argument that injustice isn't an expertise and the unjust person isn't clever or good because the unjust try to outdo each other whereas experts only try to outdo nonexperts, not other experts (349a–350c).

Socrates' conception of the relationship between a profession and its goal is stronger than might be thought. Socrates does not claim that in no circumstance can it ever benefit the practitioner of a profession to practice his profession (a view which, as long as he wants to treat justice as a profession, would deliver him right into the hands of Thrasymachus, who claims that justice is another's good (343c)). He only claims that benefiting its practitioner is not the goal of any profession. Benefit to the practitioner might be an incidental result of the profession; it might be the result of practicing the profession, perhaps in a given social context – doctors might get monetary payment, recognition, or gratitude for practicing medicine, but the goal of medicine remains healing. Similarly, rulers may get wages, honors, or they may only avoid the "penalty" of having worse people than themselves ruling (347a–d), but it will not do to confuse the job of ruling with any of these socially mediated consequences. But that is just what people who think of ruling as a privilege, like Thrasymachus, do.

Socrates' answer to the question "what is the goal of the job of ruling?" converges with one answer to the question "who should rule?": the goal of the job of ruling is the benefit of the ruled; that individual or group should rule who is best qualified to benefit the ruled.[15] We saw above that advocates of democracy, oligarchy, and tyranny all claim to benefit the ruled – so Socrates is hardly being controversial by claiming that political rule aims at the benefit of the ruled. Rather, he is showing that the sophists, who would prefer to remain silent on the "who should rule?" question, are committed by the very notion of a profession of ruling to the answer "he who best fulfills the goal of ruling" – for any profession has action-guiding norms which are structured by the profession's goal(s).

Socrates' use of the notion of a profession deprives Thrasymachus of the respectability associated with being a professional practitioner or teacher – insofar as Thrasymachus himself pursues the injustice he praises (343c–344c). If one's motive for engaging in a profession conflicts with the goal of that profession, one's claim to be a professional of that sort is invalidated. Not everyone will care about this loss, and this marks the limits of the normative force of the notion of a profession. Anyone who can swallow the loss of prestige that goes with having to take a position that says, "I don't care about being a professional, I just want my own advantage," will need a deeper response than Socrates gives to Thrasymachus. (On this point, it is worth noting that while Thrasymachus is unmoved by Socrates' argument that someone who uses his power to benefit himself rather than those he rules is, contrary to Thrasymachus, no expert ruler, he sweats and blushes when Socrates argues that the unjust person is neither clever nor good.) It is perhaps in recognition of this need for a deeper argument that from *Republic* 2 on, Plato takes on the more fundamental question of why it is better to be just rather than unjust.

Consequences for Political Thought

One consequence of defining ruling as a profession aimed at benefiting citizens and using this definition to answer the question "who should rule?" is that it provides a position from which to criticize existing regimes without becoming an ally of any of the parties vying for power – in the particular case of Socrates' criticism of the Athenian democracy, of the oligarchs. So although Socrates' criticism of democracy as rule by a foolish mob resembles the criticism of the oligarchs, because Socrates ties the content of the wisdom that could qualify someone to rule so closely to the job of ruling, and because he defines the job of ruling in terms of its goal of improving the citizens, he cannot but be a critic of oligarchy, tyranny, and the like, as well. Rulers in existing oligarchies and tyrannies are no less ignorant, and so no less incapable of improving the citizens, than the demos.

For Plato, himself disillusioned with the injustice of successive political regimes in Athens (*Seventh Letter* 324b–326b), it would have been important to find a kind of political criticism that did not play into partisan hands. Plato certainly portrays Socrates as a nonpartisan individual: the *Apology* carefully balances Socrates' opposition to democratic injustice against his refusal to participate in oligarchic injustice (32b–c and 32c–e). Further, among Socrates' associates are Critias, one of the Thirty Tyrants who terrorized Athens after coming to power in 404, and his cousin Charmides, appointed by the Thirty to govern the Piraeus; but Socrates' longtime friend Chaerephon, who was told by the Delphic oracle of Socrates' wisdom, and who was lampooned by Aristophanes for "Socratizing," was an ardent enough democrat to go into exile in 404. While we might find it unsettling that Socrates should have associated with both kinds of people, perhaps he found partisan political affiliations none too deep given the example of his beloved Alcibiades, who, after having been an Athenian general, defected to Sparta, then worked for the Persians, but was subsequently forgiven and welcomed back by democratic Athens.[16]

It may be objected that the position from which to criticize existing regimes provided by the sophistic professionalization of ruling is redundant because the very considerations raised in favor of one kind of rule or another – that the rule secures some common good, or that it puts in power the intrinsically superior who deserve to rule – can themselves be given nonpartisan readings. But possibility is not history, and we do not see nonpartisan evaluations of forms of rule prior to Socrates. The *Theaetetus* opposes speech in the service of personal and political interests to speech that seeks the truth about justice and injustice (173a–e, 175c–d). It is of course contentious to treat these as mutually exclusive kinds of speech – after all, interested speeches from different perspectives could conceivably further an inquiry into the truth – but the distinction between partisan and nonpartisan political speech is useful. Prior to Socrates, debates about who should rule are partisan: although the parties offer arguments which can in principle be detached from the partisan point of view advancing them – oligarchic or democratic or monarchic – in practice they are never so detached, and there are no instances of a neutral investigation of the question from some agreed-upon starting point. Perhaps it is the hope of a debate in which each party gives the strongest arguments in favor of its view and against the alternatives that the winner will not only seem best to all concerned but will also be best, objectively. But even in this case, the process leading to agreement involves the parties *qua* partisans of some or other arrangement, rather than *qua* investigators who begin with objective or even just shared principles. Further, we should not underestimate the conceptual breakthrough required to go from dealing with political issues only in partisan argument and dealing with them disinterestedly. Alongside the attitudinal difference between partisan and disinterested, significant conceptual resources have been developed in the tradition of political philosophy since Socrates (the idea of aggregation, the impartial spectator, the technique of universalization). My claim here is that the idea of political rule as a profession is the conceptual resource that Socrates uses to engage in nonpartisan evaluation.

A second consequence of Socrates' professionalizing political rule is the invalidation of one of the considerations given in support of answers to the "who should rule?" question; namely, that the superior, just in virtue of being superior, deserve to rule. In the *Gorgias*, Callicles says that nature's justice demands that the superior rule over and have more than the inferior (which they may accomplish by force) (488b). Although Callicles identifies the superior, the better and the stronger, he does not believe that these qualities are constituted by having power, as the many do in Athens (488d–489b); rather, his idea is that some people are intrinsically superior and for that reason deserve to rule and have more; at Socrates' suggestion, he identifies the superior with the more intelligent (489c–e).

Callicles' invocation of nature shows him to be committed to an ideal of justice different from Socrates', and so Socrates needs to show him what is wrong with that ideal of justice. The obvious way for Socrates to do this would be to question Callicles: Why does superior wisdom justify having more? Or, alternatively, what is the connection between ruling and having more?

However, instead of raising these challenges, Socrates seems to grant Callicles the point that superior wisdom (about some F) justifies having more (of F) – but, Socrates adds, this must be in order to facilitate proper use (of F). So, Socrates asks Callicles (490c–e), if you think that the more intelligent should have more, then should the doctor, the one who is more intelligent about food and drink, have more food and drink than the others, or should he be given the job of distributing food and drink to everyone including himself, on the basis of their strength or weakness (which determines how much food they need)?

At first sight, it seems as if Socrates is just not hearing the normative claim in Callicles' words, that the superior or more intelligent deserve to rule over and have more than the others. Socrates speaks as if the only thing that follows from greater intelligence is entitlement to manage whatever the intelligence is about.

In his commentary, Irwin writes,

> Here and in 490e Socrates does not seem to distinguish "have more," *pleon echein*, and "take more" or "outdo," *pleonektein*; cf. 483c. But "getting the advantage," *pleonektein*, 491a, seems to be the result of getting a larger quantity, *pleon echein*. Perhaps Socrates argues: superior wisdom gives no claim to have more, *pleon echein*, and therefore, contrary to Callicles, it gives no claim to advantage, *pleonektein*.[17]

However, if we assume that Socrates (unlike Callicles) does distinguish having more (i.e. having the charge of more) and taking more (i.e. more than one's share, for oneself), then we can take Socrates at his word: superior wisdom justifies having more of what one is wise about (because one can use it properly); it does not, however, justify taking more of it for oneself (*ou pleonektēteon*, 490c4). The idea that wisdom justifies possession because it enables correct use is very close to the idea that most things ordinarily thought to be good are only good if accompanied by wisdom, because only wisdom reliably enables the correct use required for such things to benefit us (*Euthd.* 280c–282b).

Socrates challenges Callicles' claim that intrinsic superiority entitles anyone to taking more of anything for himself not by defending some other ground for privilege than intrinsic superiority, but instead by embracing the idea that intellectual superiority of some kind is relevant to ruling, and treating it as the basis for assigning responsibilities, just as the doctor's knowledge of the body dictates that he perform the task of assigning food and drink to bodies in accordance with what they need.

I do not think this recasting of Callicles' idea is partisan. It does not favor any of the traditional political regimes or parties. And it raises the excellent question what on earth intrinsic superiority has to do with ruling unless it is superiority at ruling. This question is a pressing question for Callicles in a way that it is not for Thrasymachus, for Callicles believes that it is nature's justice – that is, really just – for the superior to rule and take more, whereas Thrasymachus makes no claim about what is just by nature, contenting himself with an exposé of existing societies' conceptions of justice as a front for norms that in reality benefit the rulers, and a critique of adherence to these norms as contrary to subjects' self-interest. Conceiving of ruling as a profession rather than a privilege leaves a number of questions unanswered. Even if only the professionally qualified can do the job of ruling (i.e. really do the job, so that its goal is achieved), are professional qualifications sufficient to entitle someone to rule? (In the *Lysis*, Socrates suggests the answer is yes, 209d.) And if rule by the professionally qualified alone counts as political rule, what else must be in place to require the professionally qualified to rule? Finally, if ruling is not a privilege or prize, how is a ruler to be compensated? Plato takes up these questions in the main books of the *Republic*, where detaching jobs from the privileges that usually go along with them frees him to imagine a distribution of social goods which – instead of only compensating citizens for their contribution – enables people to do their jobs and to enjoy whatever goods they can.[18]

I'd like to return, finally, to the Popperian complaint that Plato's Socrates misguidedly focuses on the question of sovereignty or "who shall rule the state?" to the neglect of the question of how to design political institutions to check the abuses of political power. I hope to have shown why his thought has the focus it does. It is not that he (or Plato) subscribed to a theory of unchecked sovereignty, nor that he (or Plato) was obsessed with (re)establishing hierarchies. Rather, it is that his far more intellectually radical project of transforming the conception of ruling from privilege to profession, and spelling out the normative implications of ruling being a profession, provides a new basis for answering the question of sovereignty.

FURTHER READING

This chapter focuses on the distinctive and original contributions to political thought made by Plato's Socrates; for further reading on these the reader may pursue the references in the notes.

But we also have extensive portrayal of Socrates' political ideas in Xenophon, and more contentiously, Aristophanes, and for their and other perspectives, see Brickhouse and Smith 2002. On the role played by religion and partisan politics in the trial and execution of Socrates see Burnyeat 1998 and Irwin 2005. On the question of how (or whether) to distinguish Socrates' political views from Plato's, see Kraut 1984, and, for a different approach, Schofield 2006.

NOTES

For comments on this paper, I'm very grateful to Steve Gardiner and to the audience of the (2005) Arizona Ancient Philosophy Colloquium on The Socratic Legacy.

1　But see Vlastos 1994b for a criticism of Socrates as a political actor.
2　Popper 1962: 120–1. Note that in the *Laws*, Plato does address the issue of checks on political power.
3　Popper 1962: 191.
4　Cf. Grote 1875: III.240.
5　Penner 2000.
6　Kraut 1984: 244. By contrast, Kraut argues, Plato found this same freedom horrifying (1984: 277).
7　An exception is E. Brown (2000b), who attributes to Socrates cosmopolitan rather than local (polis-wide) commitments. However, in Brown's own expression, the cosmopolitan commitments are part of Socrates' "extraordinary" politics of investigating along with anyone, citizen or foreigner (*Ap.* 23b). My focus here is on Socrates' ordinary, i.e. polis-restricted, politics.
8　Strauss 1989a: 76.
9　I focus on Plato's Socrates in works from the *Apology* through *Republic* 1 not out of a firm conviction that their Socrates represents Socrates' own teachings rather than Plato's views, but because I find in them a significant development in political thought that risks being overshadowed by the constructive project beginning with *Republic* 2.
10　Strauss 1989a: 68–9.
11　*Protagoras* translated by S. Lombardo and K. Bell. This, and all translations of Plato, are from Cooper 1997b.
12　Isocrates translations Norlin 1929.
13　Ober 1989; Connor 1971.
14　For discussion of Socrates' use of the notion of *technē* see Irwin 1977.
15　Cf. Parry 1996: 22–3, who says that if Socrates had the notion of legitimacy, he would have said that the legitimate ruler cannot just improve rulers but must improve the ruled.
16　For more on Socrates' associates, see Nails 2002.
17　Irwin 1979 *ad loc.*
18　I discuss the *Republic*'s principles for distributing social burdens and benefits in Kamtekar 2001.

CHAPTER 23

Freedom, Tyranny, and the Political Man: Plato's *Republic* and *Gorgias*, a Study in Contrasts

Arlene W. Saxonhouse

In Plato's *Republic*, Socrates creates a regime in speech that attempts to incorporate justice into its orderly structure, where philosophers rule, guardians guard, and workers work. It is a regime that rejects the principal institutional practices and ideologies of Athenian democracy, such as equality of participation by its citizens, offices assigned by lot, the sharing of rule and being ruled, and the practice of free speech. Athenian democracy, with its openness to free expression and its refusal to allow itself to be hierarchically structured among its citizens, would be – in the context of the *Republic* – not only unjust, but lead to the brink of tyranny. The caricature of democracy in book 8 of the *Republic* identifies the underlying principles of democracy as freedom and free speech,[1] but it does so to show how democracy, in its failure to identify the ruler and to attend to distinctions of worth among individuals and among speeches, leads to the greatest injustices of tyranny.

In contrast, Plato's dialogue *Gorgias* finds Socrates not constructing in speech the just regime, but extolling the practice of free speech among the Athenians and engaging in conversation with one whom he describes as a lover of the demos about the political life of Athenian democracy. In the *Gorgias* Socrates debates with the Sophist Gorgias, his student Polus, and Gorgias' Athenian host Callicles about the meaning of freedom, power, and the purposes of speech. This direct engagement in the *Gorgias* about the nature of political participation rather than the construction of an imagined political regime leads to Socrates' proclamation that he himself is among a few – if not the only – Athenian who truly practices the art of politics. His concern for Athens' citizens, that they become the "best," not that they experience the most enjoyment, makes him the *politikos* or political man. Such an assertion puts Socrates into competition not only with the Sophists, who offer their students

A Companion to Greek and Roman Political Thought, First Edition. Edited by Ryan K. Balot.
© 2013 Blackwell Publishing Ltd. Published 2013 by Blackwell Publishing Ltd.

power in the city, and with Callicles, who portrays himself as one who understands how to function in the political regime, but also with the great democratic leaders of Athens such as Cimon, Themistocles, and Pericles. I argue below that Socrates' discourse, especially about the nature of freedom and power that underlies his claim to be the true political actor in democratic Athens, and his transformation of the language of power and freedom serve as a stronger guard against tyranny than does the "prayed for" hierarchical justice of the philosopher-kings in the Callipolis of the *Republic.*

Callipolis: The Anti-Athens

Challenged by Glaucon and Adeimantus in the *Republic* to help them understand the nature of justice and why they should want to be just, Socrates proposes founding a city in which they will find justice coming into being. He begins his task as founder by proposing the city by nature: a regime in which each member does that task for which he (or she) is best suited. The house-builder builds houses; he does not craft shoes. And the farmer farms; he does not weave cloth. This is the "true" city, Socrates tells Glaucon, who has just complained that such a city without any luxuries is fit for pigs (372e). Since Glaucon wants more than acorn tea and rude houses, Socrates persists and takes his audience through the founding of the fevered city of luxuries and then the city where those luxuries are purged, in part through the transformation of the poetry that is to be told to the young warriors of the city. "We'll persuade nurses and mothers to tell the approved tales to their children and to shape their souls with tales more than their bodies with hands" (377c).[2] And while the warriors are so molded by the revised and censored poetry, there emerges another group, the guardians, who are filtered out from the warriors to be the rulers of the entire city. Socrates offers the city his myth of the metals whereby the workers are forged in the earth with iron, the warriors or auxiliaries with silver and the rulers with gold. The myth affirms a hierarchy among the inhabitants of Callipolis according to the nature of their souls. By the middle of book 4 of the *Republic* Socrates announces to Adeimantus that his city has been founded (427c): the poetry has been reformed, the warriors will protect the city from its enemies, internal and external, and the warriors and guardians shall live in common, sharing goods and wives and children. Now it is time to find justice. "In the next place," Socrates says to Adeimantus, "get yourself an adequate light somewhere; and look yourself – and call in your brother and Polemarchus and the others – whether we can somehow see where the justice might be and where the injustice" (427d).

Justice is not so easy to find in this city. First they discover wisdom: it is "good counsel [*euboulē*]" (428b); then courage, "preserving of the opinion by law through education about what – and what sort of thing – is terrible" (429c); next, moderation, "an accord of worse and better, according to nature, as to which must rule in the city and in each one" (432a). And finally there is the virtue that is left over (432b, 433b), rolling around at their feet (432d), and we learn: "justice is the minding of one's own business and not being a busybody" (433a). As we see in the construction of the just regime that emerges from the fevered and then the purged regime, and just as in the original city according to nature, the city of pigs according to Glaucon, justice is each person performing that task for which he or she is best suited. To slide from one job to another job is a violation now of the principle of justice.

On this understanding of justice, the regime of democratic Athens is most unjust; it is built on the principle of sharing in rule and everyone performing a multitude of tasks within the city. The system of offices distributed according to a lottery assures that individual citizens will not do only those tasks for which they are best suited. They will do all sorts of tasks – from serving as the tax collector to supervising weights and measures, from serving as road commissioners to carrying out executions. Only the ten generals, the supervisors of the water supply, the treasurers of the military funds and a limited number of other offices were elected.[3] Further, the citizen who may have been the farmer and executioner one year is also sitting in the Assembly 40 times a year voting on the policies of the city. In the language of the Athenians, the citizen was a "busybody," the *polupragmōn*, one who did many tasks and as a result exemplified exactly the opposite of what Socrates defines as justice in the *Republic*.[4] Democratic Athens is the antithesis to the just city of Callipolis, where everyone had one task and no more,[5] where there could not even be theater because in the very act of participating in the theatrical production one would play more than one role (394c–398c).

In a curious touch, in book 8 we find Socrates exploring the fundamental principles of a series of other regimes besides Callipolis, namely, timocracy, oligarchy, democracy, and tyranny. There he offers a powerful description of what he calls a "democracy," a regime with some similarities to – but also major differences from – the democracy in which Socrates and the Callicles of the *Gorgias* lived. This democracy is also the antithesis of Callipolis in its rejection of hierarchy and the fundamental principle of one man (woman)/one job. Indeed, the central characteristic of this regime is its refusal to identify any particular form for any being; boundaries between forms are permeable. We hear Socrates talk of animals who do not step aside for citizens (563c), of the freedom in the relations between women with men (563b), of fathers who habituate themselves to be like their children and fear their sons (562e), of teachers who fawn before their students and students who make light of their teachers (563a). And when we turn our attention to the democratic individual we find him marked by a refusal to attend to any particular job; instead "he lives along day by day, gratifying the desire that occurs to him, at one time drinking and listening to the flute, at another downing water and reducing: now practicing gymnastics, and again idling and neglecting everything; and sometimes spending his time as though he were occupied with philosophy" (561cd). So difficult is it in this regime to make any distinction between individuals or jobs that even executions are not carried out and we find the condemned stalking the land like a hero (558a). This floating between forms or definition captures what Socrates says is the primary characteristic of this regime. It is a regime defined most of all by freedom and license and the freedom of speech (557b). No poetry need be censored to purge citizens of extraneous desires. The city indeed welcomes the speech of all.

This is a regime marked by freedom, but not by power. It is a gentle democracy,[6] but what follows is not gentle, though it imagines itself as free. It emerges from the inability to identify hierarchies, to distinguish necessary from unnecessary. It is the tyrannical regime with the tyrant at its helm that arises when "the leader of a people … tak[es] over a particularly obedient mob, does not hold back from shedding the blood of his tribe but unjustly brings charges against a man … and … murders him, and doing away with a man's life, tastes of kindred blood with unholy tongue and mouth, and banishes, and kills" (565e). Later, Socrates adds to this picture of the tyrant: "He will stick at no terrible murder, or food, or deed. Rather, love lives like a tyrant within him in all anarchy and lawlessness: and being a monarch, will lead the man whom it controls, as though he were a city, to every kind of daring that will produce wherewithal for it and the noisy crowd around it" (575a). The daring tyrant will attempt to subdue all those around him, to make them serve his lusts and imagined necessities. The tyrant Socrates imagines here matches the tyrant who will be extolled by Polus in the *Gorgias*, but it also captures fifth century Athens ruling over her empire, enslaving the Greeks.[7] This is the Athens Socrates is eager to reform through his own political art in the *Gorgias*.

As presented in the *Republic*, then, democracy leads directly into the savagery of the tyrannical regime. To escape the injustices and violence of that tyranny, Socrates had founded Callipolis, though in doing so he had destroyed all freedom – from the simplest laughter, which may lead to a change in form (388e), to the censorship of poetry and the silencing of the one who sings songs not approved by the city, to the banning of performing multiple tasks in the process of self-rule. It is a regime in which a man like Socrates, who proudly proclaims himself to be a busybody (*polupragmonō*, Pl. *Ap.* 31c), could not live and where he could not go around caring for the souls of the multiple members of the community. In the tightly organized Callipolis, Socrates' attention to the particularity of the individual would violate the principles of the regime founded on conformity. Callipolis protects itself against tyranny through the creation of just the closed society with which Karl Popper, writing his *The Open Society and Its Enemies* (1962) in the wake of mid-twentieth century fascism, found so much fault.[8] In the democratic city of Athens that appears in the *Gorgias* there is a place for the philosopher Socrates, who offers an alternative defense against tyranny. Here Socrates speaks to individuals privately, in the homes of citizens, in the agora, revising their understanding of power and freedom rather than creating the uniformity of a stultifying and sterile Callipolis. The Socrates of the *Gorgias* delights in multiplicity and variety; he does not excise diversity from his city. The philosopher-king yields in the *Gorgias* to the democratic philosopher who engages with and does not stand above the other members of the regime.

Freedom and Power in the *Gorgias*

In the *Republic* Socrates has eager followers who, after book 2, seldom ask him hard questions. Even Thrasymachus, who expresses the frustration of many of Socrates' interlocutors (Socrates just doesn't see the obvious, that people want to serve their own interests), ends up in book 6 welcomed by Socrates as having become a friend, "though," Socrates adds "we weren't even enemies before" (498d). Socrates may be engaging in selective memory here. Book 1 had seen a sputtering Thrasymachus spewing forth numerous snide comments (345b, 352b, 354a). The story of Socrates' engagement with his interlocutors in the *Gorgias* is not quite the same. In this dialogue Socrates starts out on friendly terms with Callicles, a character who imagines himself an expert on political life. Callicles eagerly invites Socrates to his home and offers him advice on how to survive and succeed in politics. By the end of the dialogue Callicles can barely endure Socrates' presence and continues to talk with Socrates only under considerable pressure from the other guests. Callicles, who begins his conversation with Socrates with long and grand speeches, ends by granting Socrates at most monosyllabic responses, that is, when Socrates does not have to answer for him.

The *Republic* takes place in the port city of the Piraeus, away from the city of Athens, and Socrates is forcibly brought to Cephalus' house, where he pursues the meaning of justice. In the *Gorgias* Socrates himself specifically searches out Gorgias to "learn from him what the power [*dunamis*] of the man's art is" (447c).[9] The *Gorgias* has Socrates immersed in the life of the city, eager to understand power and freedom and setting himself in conflict not only with the aspiring politician Callicles, but also with the great heroes of the democracy.

The discussion with Gorgias and Polus in the first half of the *Gorgias* sets up the question about freedom and power and politics that will coalesce in the extended interchanges with Callicles. Space prevents detailing the elaborate arguments, but certain points need highlighting in order to understand the discussion with Callicles. Near the beginning, Gorgias responds to Socrates' queries about the nature of the art of rhetoric by defining rhetoric as the greatest good for human beings (452d). He explains that it is the cause (*aition*) of freedom (*eleutheria*).[10] At first, Gorgias ignores the double-edged quality of freedom, but it soon becomes clear that for Gorgias freedom refers not to the individual unburdened by the control of others, but rather entails rule over others – whether we are referring to life within the city or to one city ruling over another, as the Athenians do with their empire. Gorgias explains that the freedom enjoyed by one skilled in the art of rhetoric comes from knowing how to enslave others, to make of them, as he says explicitly, a slave (*doulon*). Socrates had wanted to learn the "power" of the man's art; Gorgias tells him: "With this power [*dunamis*], you will be able to make the doctor into a slave [*doulon*], the trainer into a slave [*doulon*]" (542e). Gorgias imagines that this power will be used for benign purposes, to persuade the sick man to listen to medical advice, or an assembly of Athenians to listen to the advice of a Pericles or Themistocles, that the slave, whoever that may be, will benefit from the "freedom" of the enslaver. Without rhetoric the doctor's art would lie useless, unable to heal the suffering patient, and the advice of a Pericles would not transform Athens into the glorious city she had become.

Polus, elaborating on the soft definition of rhetoric offered by Gorgias, is not so blindly benign in his vision of the power of rhetoric. He describes one who acquires the art of speaking persuasively as the most powerful in the cities ("*megiston dunantai en tais polesin,*" 466b), but unlike Gorgias, he does not talk about enslaving the artisan to do good deeds. The man he envies as the exemplar of power and freedom, the man after whom he wishes to model himself, is Archelaus, the tyrant of Macedonia. Archelaus, once the mere son of a slave to the king, managed to become free and powerful, a master rather than a servant. He killed his uncle and his cousin, he threw the young son of the former ruler into a well, all in order to acquire power. Now, with the power of a tyrant he has the freedom to do as he wishes, the freedom Polus craves and imagines would be available to him should he learn the art of rhetoric from Gorgias.[11] Archelaus may have committed many crimes in order to acquire this freedom, killed many and deceived others, but now that he is free and not a slave to another, Polus assumes, Archelaus must be happy. Having exchanged slavery for freedom, how could he not be? Archelaus' freedom enables him to do whatever he wishes; he can take away his subjects' property, he can kill them, he can send them into exile, all without the fear of punishment.[12]

The young Polus, perhaps less ready to invite his relatives to dinner and then slit their throats or throw young boys down wells, nevertheless dreams of the power he might have over others, turning them with the art of rhetoric into slaves who serve his – not their – interests. He refuses to believe, at least at first, that Socrates does not also crave this power: "As if indeed you, Socrates, would not welcome the possibility of your doing what seemed good to you in the city, rather than not, and would not feel envy when you see someone killing whomever it seemed good to him or confiscating possessions or putting him in fetters" (468e). Incredulous, he says to Socrates: "You would not welcome ruling as tyrant? ... The possibility of doing in the city whatever seems good to oneself, killing and expelling and doing all things in accord with one's opinion" (469c).

In the subsequent interchange between Polus and Socrates, Socrates shames Polus into admitting that Archelaus' actions are unjust, but what concerns us here is that both Polus' and Gorgias' definition of freedom is limited by the city walls. Both Polus and Gorgias talk of the power rhetoric gives within the city, the mastery they will acquire over fellow citizens; they do not deal with the mastery over other cities such as the Athenians have acquired with their empire.[13] Both Polus and Gorgias, restrained by the context of the city, are likewise inhibited by the language of the city, where terms such as shame and justice control speech and actions and thus make the two subject to Socrates' own art of rhetorical manipulation. Callicles, who is willing to look beyond the city to nature and the relations between cities, initially suffers no such constraints. Polus may envy the power and freedom of Archelaus, but he cannot call the actions that come from that freedom "good." They are, he admits, "shameful." So too had been Gorgias' experience: he refused to take responsibility when the rhetoric he taught and the freedom it offered might be used unjustly – not to heal the patient, but to harm him.

For Callicles, freedom and power are not modified by the conventional language of justice and shame. He looks outside the city and disregards traditional values, looking to a nature independent of the customs of the city. He speaks of a natural justice that entails inequality and taking what is not one's own by those who are stronger. This is the justice practiced by the Athenians when they acquired their empire, claiming the support of the gods for their actions. "[N]either our pretensions nor our conduct [is] in any way contrary to what men believe of the gods, or practice among themselves," the Athenians tell Melians, according to Thucydides. "Of the gods we believe, and of men we know, that by a necessary law of their nature they rule where they can ... we found it existing before us, and shall leave it to exist for ever after us ... as far as the gods are concerned, we have no fear and no reason to fear that we shall be at a disadvantage" (5.105).[14] Callicles affirms that the manly man (*andros*) (and by implication the manly city) does not suffer injustice; such suffering belongs to the slave, "for whom it is superior to die than to live" (483b). Callicles assigns laws and feelings of shame to those who are too weak to commit what some might call injustices, to cities that are too weak to acquire power over others.[15] Nature, Callicles tells Socrates, supports the desire to have more, and the strong to acquire what they can – but they can do so only insofar as they do not let themselves be bound by conventions that tell them that it is "shameful" or "unjust" to act in this way. For evidence Callicles points to the kings of Persia, to the animal kingdom, to the poems of Pindar, to the actions of the god Heracles.

At the beginning of this panegyric for a justice according to nature, Callicles accuses Socrates of being a "demagogue" – manipulating his audience (in this case the young Polus) through the powerful emotion of shame to contradict himself and admit (much to Polus' shock) that the art of rhetoric should be used – if at all – to ensure that friends and oneself are punished for any injustice they commit and to help enemies escape punishment. Only by playing the demagogue and bringing his interlocutors to conclusions that serve his own interests could Socrates get Polus to accept such an absurdity. Callicles' accusation is part of his retort to Socrates' suggestion of a similarity between himself and Callicles, in which he implies that Callicles is the demagogue. They both, Socrates had claimed, have two lovers, or "boyfriends" (*paidika*). Callicles loves the Athenian demos as well as the young man Demos, son of Pyrilampes (481d); Socrates has as his "boyfriends" Alcibiades and philosophy. Socrates develops the analogy: while Callicles adjusts his speech to the wishes of the Athenian demos and his beloved Demos, so too does Socrates adjust his speech – but in his case only to one of his boyfriends, namely philosophy, who, Socrates tells us, is much less variable than the son of Cleinias. Callicles does not respond to the issue of being a "lover" of the people, but by calling Callicles a "lover," Socrates makes ambiguous Callicles' power. Is not the lover a slave of the beloved?[16] Is the lover of the demos a slave of the people? This is not how Callicles, so eager for freedom and power, wants to think of himself. Socrates, in contrast, would not deny his subjection to philosophy, though he clearly does not allow himself to be Alcibiades' slave (Pl. *Symp.* 216e–219e). Callicles, in his own speech, however, does not accept Socrates' portrait of himself as a slave of the people; he is a leader, not a lover of the people.

In the second half of Callicles' speech, after he has extolled the natural justice of the strong, who take what they want, the tone of his speech changes and in avuncular fashion Callicles advises Socrates on how to function within the city, how to protect himself from those who will find him an easy target for their animus. Portraying himself as a leader knowledgeable about both politics and the demos, he advises

Socrates to develop political skills by abandoning his beloved philosophy. Should Socrates continue to love philosophy, he will have no power in the city (i.e. he will not be free). Weak, Socrates will be enslaved by those who are strong. Callicles couches his warning in a series of oppositions: philosophy versus the engaged politician, youth versus maturity, effeminacy versus manliness, slavery versus freedom. Socrates' attachment to philosophy calls to mind, Callicles claims, a boy who, whether in a private or political affair ("tina idian ē politikēn praxin," 484d), never grows up and ends up looking "exceedingly laughable" (*katagelastoi*, 484e), just as, he continues, political men (*politikoi*) are exceedingly laughable (*katagelastoi* again) when they spend too much time practicing philosophy. For a youth, Callicles explains, philosophy may be the mark of a "free man" (*eleutherion*), but for an adult it is a sign of being somewhat "slavish" (*douloprepes*, 485b). Callicles continues:

> it falls to this [slavish] man, even if he is of an altogether good nature, to become unmanly [*anandrōi*] through fleeing the central area of the city and agora, in which the poet says men "become highly distinguished," and through sinking down into living the rest of his life whispering with three of four lads in a corner, never to give voice to anything free [*eleutheron*] or great or sufficient. (485de)

According to Callicles, then, the philosopher remains the slave "never giving voice to anything free or sufficient," while the one who navigates successfully the political world (as he pretends to do) is the free man. Claiming that he speaks from friendship,[17] Callicles warns Socrates: "You are careless, Socrates, of the things that you ought to take care of ... you would not contribute a speech correctly to the councils of justice, nor cry out something probable or persuasive, nor advise any new proposal on another's behalf" (486a). "Predicting" exactly what will happen at Socrates' trial, Callicles cautions Socrates:

> If someone seized you ... and carried you off to prison, claiming that you were doing an injustice when you were not, you know that you would not have anything of use to do for yourself, but you would be dizzy and gaping ... without anything to say; and when you stood up in the law court, happening to face a very lowly and vicious accuser, you would die, if he wished to demand the death penalty for you. (486ab)

While Callicles exhorts cities to enslave others when they can, for a Socrates so uninterested in power over others, he appears to advise simply self preservation.

Unlike most (indeed, all) other characters who inhabit Plato's dialogues, Callicles has no presence in the ancient literature outside this particular dialogue. Though Callicles may offer himself as the savvy political man able to advise a naive Socrates, and though Socrates describes him as one "beginning to do the city's business" (515a), this peculiar absence may suggest that Callicles would not garner for himself the reputation that attended, for example, a Pericles, Themistocles, or Cimon. Given his speech extolling the freedom of the powerful, we can assume that he longs for the fame of a Pericles – just as he longs for the power that Polus imagines the tyrant has. Socrates as the political actor he claims to be later in the dialogue must purge Callicles of this longing. Socrates' political action is to divert Callicles from his tyrannical conception of the freedom of political power, an understanding of politics held as well by Polus and Gorgias. Callicles is the potential tyrant emerging from democracy that the *Republic* had warned its readers about. Socrates as the self-proclaimed political man of this dialogue disarms Callicles with his discourse and subversive questioning. He thus saves Athens, we can imagine, from the potential tyrant Callicles. Polus was a somewhat comical character. Callicles with his language of a natural justice that supports the strong is a powerful threat whom Socrates with his own political skill learned from his "boyfriend" philosophy disarms. Insofar as we never hear of Callicles again in the ancient literature, in this case Socrates may have been successful.[18]

Disarming the Tyrant

In the subsequent interchange, Socrates disarms Callicles by showing Callicles how he had misconstrued the nature of the political man when he imagined him as one who has power over others and who is free because he has that power. Callicles in his efforts to be the political man sought influence for himself in the city and empire for his city, but such influence and empire is neither power nor freedom as Socrates comes to redefine these political terms. The challenge addressed to Callicles, and the claim that Socrates makes when he defines himself as the only political man in Athens, depend crucially on the transformation of the meaning of freedom and power, not on the complex transformation of regime he tries with the founding of Callipolis. Again, space prohibits detailing the steps that lead to the disarming of Callicles, but let me briefly indicate how Socrates exercises his transformative powers, ones that may have been powerful enough to force Callicles to withdraw from his own pursuit of political power with the potential to enslave others. These interchanges enmesh Socrates in the discourse of democratic Athens; they do not enable him – as in the *Republic* – to escape it.

By remarking on Callicles' love for the demos, Socrates had made Callicles appear the democrat, but in the questions that follow Socrates undermines that portrait. Callicles had passionately extolled the power of the strong to do what they want, to enslave the weak, to be free. Socrates responds by wondering who exactly "the strong" may be. Who are these strong and (he adds, with no objection from Callicles) "the better" (*ton beltiō*) men who rule over lesser men and who ought to have more than the paltry ones (488b)? Socrates wonders whether we can say that the many are not stronger than the one. Democrat that Socrates claimed Callicles to be in his "love for the demos," Callicles concurs with Socrates on this point, only to become angered when Socrates follows through with the suggestion that then the belief held by the "strong many" that the just is having equal shares and that doing injustice is shameful is clearly according to nature. Now the antidemocrat in Callicles surfaces and the contradictions he harbors in his soul become apparent. "[D]o you think I am saying that, if a rabble of slaves and human beings of all sorts, worth nothing except perhaps for the exertion of bodily might, was collected together, and if these people asserted some things, these things are lawful?" (489c).

Socrates pushes Callicles so far that Callicles almost appears to defend the philosopher-kings of the *Republic* by arguing that the "just by nature is this, for one who is superior [*beltiō*] and more intelligent [*phronimōteron*] both to rule and to have more than the lowlier ones" (490a), and that such men are those "who are intelligent [*phronimous*] in regard to the affairs of the city and courageous [manly, *andreious*]." These are the ones, Callicles says, for whom "it is fitting" that they rule the cities (491c). Socrates in the *Republic* had imagined the philosophers as rulers with intelligence, knowing how the people may be well governed; in this conversation with Callicles he defends democracy. Callicles does not hesitate to express his frustration with a Socrates who "always talk[s] without stopping about cobblers, cooks, and doctors, as if our speech were about these people!" (491a). Instead, Callicles wants to talk about those who are "not only intelligent but also courageous, being sufficient to accomplish that which they intend and not flinching through some softness of soul" (491b).[19] So much for Callicles the democrat; so much for Callicles the lover of the demos.

Having gotten Callicles to express his clear disdain for the many, Socrates then focuses on this superior individual who rules in the city. Does he, Socrates asks, rule over himself? Baffled by this question, Callicles asks: "What do you mean, ruling himself?" – to which Socrates, again taking the side of the many and their beliefs, responds: "Just what the many mean: being moderate and in control of oneself, ruling the pleasures and desires" (491de). Callicles, who had understood power as the freedom to exercise rule over others and therefore as a means to satisfy all one's cravings, is stunned. The man who rules over himself is a fool and allows himself to become a slave. Those who are courageous and intelligent satisfy their desires. They can because they have acquired power in the city either "as sons of kings or themselves by nature sufficient to supply for themselves some rule or tyranny or dynasty [like Archelaus, we might note]" (492b). And for those in power there is the satisfaction of desires. As Callicles concludes one of several speeches that express amazement at Socrates' claims, he affirms: "luxury, intemperance, and freedom [*eleutheria*], when they have support – this is virtue and happiness" (492c).[20]

Socrates thus moves Callicles from the problem of the definition of who is "strong," since the democratic answer disturbs Callicles, to the question of what human good does one seek to attain with the power that one has when one is strong. Callicles, focusing on pleasure, imagines that the strong satisfy their desires in much the same way that Polus first imagines Archelaus the tyrant doing whatever he wants, and as Athens the empire does, as Pericles says, when it draws "the produce of the world into our harbor" (Thuc. 2.38). Callicles, like Polus, imagines that the tyrant, whether individual or city, must be happy. But Socrates, as with Polus, will not let Callicles rest satisfied with his strong, superior men satisfying their desires through rule over others. Though Callicles may consider those who control their desires and therefore need nothing as no more than stones or corpses (492e, 494a), Socrates tries to persuade Callicles that the soul of the man of immoderate desires, strong or otherwise, is like a leaky jar, never filled, always searching for more, or still more crudely he is like the man who scratches an itch. The life Callicles (and Polus) imagine for themselves is no better, Socrates proposes, than that of a "catamite." As Nichols (1998: 87 n109) explains, a catamite is the man or boy who is the "passive object" in sexual relations.

This is hardly the vision Callicles embraces as he loftily praises the ones who are "not only intelligent but also courageous, being sufficient to accomplish what they intend and not flinching through softness of soul" (491b). The frustration Callicles feels as the conversation proceeds is palpable. Callicles wants to talk of great men, leaders, those who hold empires under their sway, and all Socrates does is talk of the cobblers and cooks and the desire to drink when one is thirsty or eat when one is hungry, "small and narrow things," as Callicles calls them (497c). It is Socrates who expresses throughout the conversation his concern not with the great, but with the average man, the one whom Callicles is so eager to subdue and exploit. Socrates is eager to make those cobblers and cooks "better" and insists that Callicles take him seriously about these everyday men:

> For you see that our speeches are about this – and what would a human being [*anthrō-pos*] who had even a little intelligence [not a great deal, not the men of intelligence about whom Callicles had been so eager to speak] be more serious about than this? That is, in what way one must live, whether the life to which you urge me on, doing these things of a man [*tou andros*], speaking among the people and practicing rhetoric and acting in politics in this way in which you now act in politics; or this life in philosophy. (500c)

So angered and resistant does Callicles become as his arguments melt before Socratic questioning that Socrates is left to carry on the dialogue himself. Callicles no longer tries to defend his understanding of freedom and power; he is thrown into silence as the dialogue turns to the good of the soul, virtue, and the dependence of the pleasurable on the good. Socrates concludes, with Callicles' grudging consent, that happiness comes from moderation and escape from the intemperance that leads one to seek domination over others. The potential tyrant has been tamed and perhaps finds it impossible after his encounter with Socrates to play the part of the courageous man of intelligence, ruling over the paltry and taking what he wants from them. If this is simply the life of the catamite, Callicles would want no part of it.

Socrates has undermined the meaning of power as Callicles understood it. He has shown that political power leads to the life not of the manliest of men satisfying their desires for empire, but to the life of the lowliest of the low. Along with power he has undermined meaning of freedom as enslaving others. Instead, freedom is ruling over oneself. Rhetoric, if used as Polus and Gorgias initially envision it, leads to power and freedom, in other words tyranny. No, says Socrates, it leads to one's own slavery, not to domination over others. A man always seeking more is a slave to his passions. A polity like that of the Athenians expressing so much pride in the empire that Pericles helped them acquire only increases the slavery of its citizens. They become, because of Pericles, "corrupted ... lazy, cowardly, babbling, and money lovers" (515e). Athens as a tyrant city has transformed its citizens into men enslaved by their passions and the desire to rule, "more savage than they were when [Pericles] took them over ... [and] ... if more savage, then more unjust and worse" (516c). Rulers in a democracy who provide confections for their citizens as Pericles, Themistocles, and Cimon did, Socrates suggests, become themselves the subjects of wild and unruly citizens. In Pericles' case, "they voted a condemnation of him for theft, and came close to sentencing him to death, clearly on the grounds that he was base" (516a). Callicles had urged Socrates to abandon philosophy and become a political man making speeches. He did not recognize how that would make Socrates a slave of the people, turning him into a pastry chef before a tribunal of children (e.g. 521e), just like Pericles and the other politicians in Athens.

No, thank you, says Socrates. In private or in the agora, leading the philosophic life, he rules over himself and endeavors to educate others to rule themselves rather than seek to rule over others. Rule over the self is freedom; rule over others is slavery. The "power" of Gorgias' art, while it may lead to the enslaving of others, does not lead to freedom for oneself. The only man in Athens who practices the true political art is the one who frees the Athenians from being tyrants over others and thus slaves to their desires. That is where Pericles and other democratic heroes had led them. In Thucydides, Pericles had told the Athenians: "For what you hold is, to speak somewhat plainly, a tyranny; to take it perhaps was unjust, but to let it go is unsafe" (2.63), recognizing, as does Socrates, that the possession of a tyranny constrains rather than frees the city that cannot stop fighting lest they become the slaves of their enemies. What Pericles had described as "perhaps unjust," Socrates says has made the city "swollen and festering with sores underneath." Those who made Athens the tyrant of Greece "have filled up the city with harbors, dockyards, walls, tribute, and such drivel" (518e–519a).

The true political actor frees the city from such "drivel." Freedom, Socrates teaches, is not tyranny. To the degree that he acts in the city, Socrates the busybody butting into everyone's affairs has the potential to protect citizens from becoming themselves enslaved by a false understanding of the meaning of freedom. Thus the many might learn to protect themselves through freedom properly understood from the most dangerous of potential tyrants, themselves. At least in this dialogue, Socrates – not Pericles or Themistocles or Cimon – is the hero of the democracy preserving the freedom of its citizens from tyranny.

Conclusion

We cannot take what Plato writes in any of his dialogues as the definitive statement of his "political theory." Plato's dialogues are exploratory, not didactic. He investigates the possibility of justice in the city in the construction of Callipolis, but finds there a sterile world where the "busybody" Socrates would have no home. As founder, he stands outside and builds a city of dreams far from the center of Athens. In the *Gorgias* Socrates proclaims himself to be a political actor within the context of the democratic regime and does not absent himself from it. He recognizes that following Callicles' advice to engage in democratic politics on Callicles' terms might lead to his execution for being like the doctor in a contest with the pastry chef before a jury of children (521e), but he also points to democracy's strengths in contrast to Callipolis. A democracy would allow Socrates to wander, talking to those like Polus and Callicles who long for tyranny and befuddling them by pointing to the ambiguity of the language of freedom as the power over others. The survival of Callipolis ultimately relies on a magical number to determine the proper mating among its guardians; the survival of Athens would come from the human engagement of a busybody to free her citizens from false understandings of power.

FURTHER READING

The secondary literature on the *Republic* is vast; that on the *Gorgias* not nearly as vast, but substantial nevertheless. The following indicate only a limited number of works that approach the dialogues with interpretive tools similar to that used in this chapter. There are many other ways of reading the dialogues that are not captured either in the chapter or the suggested readings. Leo Strauss's *The City and Man* (1964) and Allan Bloom's interpretive essay appended to his translation of the *Republic* (Bloom 1968) present readings of the *Republic* that draw on the dramatic elements of the dialogue and do not accept Callipolis as the obvious expression of Plato's vision of an ideal regime. They both find systemic problems in the construction of that regime.

The classic work on the *Gorgias* is E. R. Dodds's edition of the dialogue (Dodds 1959); it includes important contextual, historical, and interpretive material. James H. Nichols (1998) adds an insightful introductory essay to his translation of the *Gorgias*. A recent study of the dialogue suggesting Socrates' recognition of the power of rhetoric to assist philosophy is Stauffer 2006. J. Peter Euben includes an important chapter on the *Gorgias* in Euben 1997. For a more general study of Socrates as a political actor, see Villa 2001.

NOTES

1 See Wallace, this volume, chapter 11.
2 I use the translation of the *Republic* by Bloom 1968 throughout.
3 M. Hansen 1991: 233–4 suggests that there were "just over 100 magistrates chosen not by lot but by election." In the fifth century it was primarily the military officers that were elected; in the fourth century, with establishment of new financial posts, those officers were also elected.
4 For a full discussion of the status of the busybody in Athens see Adkins 1976.
5 See 397e where Socrates describes Callipolis thus: "It's only in such a city that we'll find a shoemaker a shoemaker, and not a pilot along with his shoemaking, and the farmer a farmer a farmer, and not a judge along with his farming, and the skilled warrior a warrior, and not a moneymaker along with his warmaking, and so on with them all." In one of the many tensions that mark the construction of Callipolis we can note that the philosopher-king violates the very principle of justice that founds Callipolis, for he both philosophizes and rules. It is this contradiction that raises for some such as myself, Saxonhouse 1986, and others (L. Strauss 1964: ch. 1; Bloom 1968) questions about how seriously we are to take Socrates proposals about Callipolis as the "ideal" city.

6 See Saxonhouse 1996: ch. 4.

7 See e.g. the Corinthians' exhortation to the Spartans in Thucydides 1.69. Also Forsdyke in this volume, chapter 15.

8 It is important here to keep in mind the differences between totalitarianism (the modern regime whose origins Popper finds in Plato and Hegel) and the tyranny that Socrates portrays in book 9 of the *Republic*, the orderliness and precision of the former and chaos and arbitrariness of the latter. See further, Arendt 1973.

9 I use the translation of the *Gorgias* by Nichols 1998 throughout.

10 On the emergence of the political meaning of *eleutheria* (freedom) see Raaflaub 2004b.

11 There is an irony here: Raaflaub argues that *eleutheria* emerges as the opposite of tyranny, but in his discussion of the history of the fifth century he also emphasizes it as the "interdependence of freedom and power" both within the city and as rule over other cities in the fifth century (2004b: 120 and esp. chs 4 and 5). Plato in this dialogue and in the *Republic* expands on this connection.

12 See in this volume, Wallace, chapter 11, and Forsdyke, chapter 15.

13 Nor, we might note, does Socrates address his own participation in the acquisition of this empire through his participation in Athens' battles such as those at Potideia and Delium (though we might also note that in both these battles Athens suffered defeats).

14 I use the translation of Thucydides by Crawley 1982 throughout.

15 This is the language the Melians use when they try to respond to the Athenians who affirm the right of the strong: "We are just men fighting against unjust" (Thuc. 5.104).

16 See e.g. *Symp.* 183a; 183c; 219e.

17 I suggest that it may also be from fear of Socrates' potential power; Socrates, recognizing the fallibility of the *nomoi* and capable of shaking himself free from the opinions of the many, has the potential to be the superman (Saxonhouse 1983).

18 We need to recall that Socrates was not always successful in taming the tyrant. Consider the histories of Alcibiades, Charmides, and Critias, all companions of Socrates who exercised their tyrannical aspirations, the latter two as members of the nefarious Thirty Tyrants put into power by the Spartans after the defeat of Athens in the Peloponnesian War.

19 This is the language the Corinthians use of the Athenians at the Congress at Sparta when describing the Athenians who have enslaved much of Greece, in Thucydides' rendition (1.70).

20 See also in this volume, Forsdyke, chapter 15, and Wallace, chapter 11.

CHAPTER 24

Plato on the Sovereignty of Law

Zena Hitz

The Rule of Law and Platonic Ideals

By far the most prominent political ideal expressed in the Platonic dialogues is the ultimate authority of political knowledge. From the *Charmides* and *Euthydemus* to the *Gorgias* and *Republic*, the dominant idea is that political power ought be exercised only by those who know the good. Just as doctors, navigators, and generals, in virtue of their expertise, are granted authority over certain practices aimed at certain goods, so, Socrates speculates again and again, there must be experts capable of attaining the political good who ought to hold political power.

The notion of political knowledge, while nearly ubiquitous in the dialogues, is persistently unclear. Its existence is a premise of the construction of the just city in Plato's central political work, the *Republic*, and lies at the root of his most famous political doctrine, the rule of philosopher-kings. All the same, the nature of this knowledge is never fully explained or fleshed out in any of the dialogues that appeal to it. Its appearance in the *Gorgias* and *Euthydemus* is only brief and suggestive. The knowledge of the good possessed by the philosopher-kings of the *Republic* is gestured at through metaphors and earmarked as something that needs further explanation (*Resp.* 506c–e). A similar architectonic political knowledge is the source of considerable paradox in the *Charmides*. (On the philosopher-king, see Saxonhouse, this volume, chapter 23; for Aristotle on political knowledge, see Depew, this volume, chapter 26).

While a full analysis of the ideal of knowledgeable rule is outside the scope of this chapter, a sketch of an explanation of the vagueness and paradox surrounding it seems warranted. One could doubt the sincerity of the endorsement of the rule of knowledge in the dialogues; or suspect that Plato himself believed political knowledge not to be attainable by human beings (see, for example, L. Strauss 1964). However, an alternative is available, namely that while the rule of knowledge is meant to be minimally attainable, its primary function as an ideal is not practical: it is not meant, at least not primarily, as a plan of political action. The lack of clarity and detail given to political

A Companion to Greek and Roman Political Thought, First Edition. Edited by Ryan K. Balot.
© 2013 Blackwell Publishing Ltd. Published 2013 by Blackwell Publishing Ltd.

knowledge in the dialogues suggests rather that its philosophical use is hypothetical: it functions as a standard by which other constitutions or current conditions might be evaluated, rather than as a practical political program. So, for example, it serves as a hypothetical model to illustrate what is wrong with current conditions, as for example in the *Gorgias*, when the rule of knowledge is contrasted with the democratic use of political power for whatever the people happen to want (see Saxonhouse, chapter 23). Likewise, in the *Republic* it is held out as the only condition under which humans can live free from the evils of greed, injustice, and tyranny – but it is clear that neither Socrates nor his interlocutors think that such a condition is ever likely to hold (*Resp.* 544a; cf. 445c, 545a). What one actually knows when one has political knowledge, and how, practically speaking, it might help one rule, is never fully discussed; and given its hypothetical function in the relevant contexts, it does not need to be.

Versions of the ideal of the rule of knowledge also surface in Plato's last writings on politics, the *Statesman* and the *Laws*. The *Statesman* seeks to provide a formal definition of political knowledge (*politikē*) and to distinguish it clearly from its subsidiary rivals, the arts of rhetoric, judging, and generalship; and, more importantly, to distinguish the true statesman (*politikos*) from conventional politicians or "experts in conflict" (*stasiastikoi*). It does provide a richer picture of political knowledge than that seen elsewhere: the true statesman will know the right time to use the subsidiary forms of expertise, and will "weave" them together in his efforts to produce virtue in the city (Pl. *Plt.* 305e ff.).

Likewise, the *Laws* claims that under the best circumstances someone with knowledge would rule (*Leg.* 875d), and, while praising the rule of law, also finds a role for philosophic wisdom within its model regime in the form of the Nocturnal Council (951d–952d, 961a–968c). While the actual administrative role of the Council is somewhat unclear in the text, it is clear that its members have the general role of securing and "saving" the laws. Their knowledge is said to consist in knowledge of the way virtue is one thing while at the same time divided into its components, courage, moderation, justice, and wisdom (961d–965e). They are also said to know about the plurality and unity of the beautiful and the good (966a–c), as well as certain doctrines about god, the immortality of the soul, and related issues in mathematics and music (966e–968a).

While a detailed account of political knowledge across dialogues would require a great deal more discussion, it remains clear that the rule of political knowledge is consistently held out as ideal, and that this knowledge is said to rely crucially on knowledge of virtue or human excellence. Thus so far it may seem that these two dialogues, by a broad consensus thought to have been written late in Plato's life (see Cooper 1997a), present a political philosophy broadly consistent with that of the *Republic* and other non-late dialogues. However, the *Statesman* and the *Laws* also quite clearly undertake a different project than the earlier dialogues, namely, to give concrete and detailed advice about practical politics. This among other differences has led many scholars to believe that they represent a significant change in Plato's thinking about politics (Bobonich 2002; Klosko 1986). Alternatively, one could argue that the differences can be explained by the use of the political ideal of knowledge for distinct purposes across Plato's life (Kahn 1995); or that Plato does not have a political theory, as such, at all (Saxonhouse, chapter 23).

How is the focus of the *Laws* and *Statesman* more pragmatic? While both dialogues clearly endorse the ideal of the rule of knowledge, both suggest that this ideal is not attainable, or at any rate, not usually. Both dialogues describe a time in the mythic past, the age of Cronus, when gods governed humans, suggesting that political success is limited when mere human beings are in charge (*Leg.* 713e, *Plt.* 275c). What is most striking about these two dialogues in contrast with the rest is that they also outline a second-best alternative, a way that mortals can approximate the lost divine regime: the rule of law.

"The rule of law," like "freedom" or "democracy," functions as a slogan in our contemporary political life and in contemporary political theory, as it has in a variety of political cultures from ancient Athens to republican Rome and their many imitators. As is suggested in the account of rhetoric in the *Gorgias*, slogans do not get their power because of their clear and distinct denotation of real values, but because they satisfy some audience: they are used to gain a certain effect. We should expect, then, that the various rhetorical uses of "the rule of law" have rendered its meaning less than clear. This lack of clarity, in turn, makes it difficult to follow a philosophical or theoretical inquiry into the notion of the kind Plato pursues. For the purposes of this essay I assume that "the rule of law" describes a cluster of ideas surrounding the legal or constitutional restriction of political power to prevent its misuse. For example, a political community may achieve the rule of law by operating under fixed rules governing the appointment of officials and their duties, and by having legal remedies for the abuse of power. Sovereignty in such a community is treated as belonging to offices or to the laws themselves rather than to particular persons, and accordingly there are limits on the extent to which officials can exercise their private judgment. As a means to ensure the law is followed, the rule of law requires publicity: that the laws be clearly stated, easily available, and publicly known.

In the latter part of the *Statesman* (*Plt.* 297d–303d), regimes are praised as desirable (with qualifications) when the rulers – kings, oligarchs, or democratic assemblies – rule "according to the laws." These regimes are contrasted with their degenerate counterparts, democracies, oligarchies, and monarchies, whose rulers act "contrary to law." These phrases by themselves are highly ambiguous. (Because the Greek word for law, *nomos*, refers both to written positive law and the informal customs that govern and define a community, Greek discussions of law are often ambiguous.) However, it is clear in the *Statesman* that the lawful regimes are regimes in which written law holds ultimate authority. All types of regime – knowledgeable, lawful, and lawless – have laws. In the best regime ruled by knowledge, the laws are modified or suspended by the statesman-king when appropriate – the laws are subject to change in the light of the ruler's knowledge (300c). The lawless regimes, on the other hand, are not those where law doesn't exist, but where law is overrun by rulers seeking private profit or personal favors (300a). In lawful regimes, by contrast, strict obedience to the written laws and ancestral customs is enjoined (298d–e, 301a). In both lawless regimes and under the rule of knowledge it is the ruler that is sovereign – he changes or disobeys the laws, for good or ill (300d). In the lawful regimes, since the laws effectively restrict the actions of the rulers, it is clear that they, not the rulers, hold the ultimate authority.

The account of the rule of law in the *Statesman* does not, unfortunately, go much beyond this in describing how exactly the rulers will be restricted by law. Ultimately, then, the dialogue does not give a clear idea of what a law-governed regime would look like. By contrast the *Laws* begins from a discussion of the origin and nature of law, and its central project is the sketch of the laws for a new colony, Magnesia, to be founded on Crete. The laws of Magnesia as well as the role they play in its constitution are described exhaustively in the dialogue.

The construction of laws and a regime from scratch already distinguish the law-governed regime in the *Laws* from the parallel regime in the *Statesman*: in the latter, it is suggested, one makes a regime lawful simply by sticking to such laws as happen to be on the books.[1] All the same, there are significant parallels between the rule of law as we have sketched it in the *Statesman* and the rule of law in the *Laws*. As in the *Statesman*, the laws if not fixed are quite difficult to change (*Leg.* 772b–d, 957a–b; see Bobonich 2002: 395–408 for a different interpretation), and strict obedience to the laws is emphasized (as I discuss below, along with the idea of "slavery to the law"). While it is clear that all of the citizens of Magnesia are called to be "slaves to the law," strict obedience is most emphatically enjoined for the magistrates or officers of the regime.

Correspondingly we find two types of law or legal organization in the *Laws*: on the one hand, "constitutional" laws, setting up magistracies or offices, and giving rules on how they are to be filled; and on the other, the actual laws the magistrates are meant to enforce, which govern the behavior of citizens through their birth, education, pastimes, marriage, and death (Laks 2000: 263–7). It is the former sort of laws that the chief interlocutor, the Athenian, may have in mind when he proclaims that "where the law is master over the rulers, and the rulers slaves to the law, then the city will have security and all the good things that the gods give cities" (*Leg.* 715d3–6). Strict rules are set down in Magnesia as to how offices are to be filled. Among those rules is the scrutiny of magistrates before they take office, and audit afterward: every magistrate is subject to review both by other magistrates and by the citizens, creating a broad system of reciprocal audit. In this way, every magistrate or official exercises power under the constraint of law (Morrow 1960: esp. 215–28 and ch. 11). Because the laws are difficult to change, it is difficult for them to be manipulated in order to support some particular person's hold on power. Lastly, the laws of the regime are publicly available and widely known; the *Laws* itself is required reading for all schoolchildren (*Leg.* 811c–812a).

The ideal of legal controls over magistrates to prevent the abuse of power had precedents in the constitutions of both ancient Athens and Sparta, both of which, along with Crete, serve as explicit models for the regime of the *Laws*. Sparta's ephors audited its kings, and its divided or "mixed" regime is praised in the *Laws* (*Leg.* 691d–692a; Morrow 1960: 54–8 and ch. 10); the procedures in Athens for scrutiny and audit of magistrates, and its judiciary are models for the parallel systems in Magnesia (Morrow 1960: 544–61). Likewise, the publicity and clarity of the law was a significant goal of the Athenians in the wake of the oligarchic revolutions of 411 and 404 BC: legislative commissions with authority to collect and write down the laws were put under way, in order to prevent the manipulation and abuse of the law that took place under those brief regimes (Andoc. 1.81–9; Aeschin. 3.38; Dem. 20.91–4).

The use of law as a response to revolution and civic conflict or *stasis* is not only clear in Athenian practice in the late fifth and early fourth century, but it is also significant in nonphilosophical political writing in Athens prior to and contemporary with Plato. We find in this writing that the rule of law is contrasted both with the rule of force or violence – as in Xenophon's fictional dialogue between Pericles and Alcibiades (Xen. *Mem.* 1.2.40–6) – and with the rule of men, their private interests and private judgment. For instance, in Theseus' well-known speech in Euripides' *Suppliants*, he contrasts a tyranny, where the law is the private possession of one man, to democratic Athens, where the law is "common" or "belongs to the community," and claims that where the laws are written down, rich and poor alike have equal access to justice (Eur. *Supp.* 429–36; D. Allen 2000: 89–91). A natural empirical connection between the rule of private persons, the rule of those persons in their private interest, and civic conflict means that the rule of law is often ambiguous between what prevents force and violence and what prevents private rule. The sixth century Athenian lawgiver Solon writes of *eunomia* or lawfulness as what produces order and justice in cities, as what puts an end to both "crooked judgments" and civic conflict (Solon fr. 4, West). So also the fifth century sophist known as Anonymus Iamblichi writes of obedience to the law as contrasting with seeking one's own advantage, and he likewise praises *eunomia* or lawfulness as key to the prevention of civic conflict (see bibliographic note). Set against these more mainstream views is the challenge of Thrasymachus in *Republic* 1 that law in fact serves as a mask for the ruler's interest, and so promotes civic conflict rather than preventing it.

And so for the Athenians the rule of law seems to be appealed to in the service of distinct, if often overlapping goals: to protect the weak or the poor; to restrain oligarchic revolutionaries and tyrants; and to prevent self-seeking or overreaching behavior in officials. All of these goals fall under the general heading of the prevention of *stasis* or civic conflict, and to this extent, as I will discuss in more detail below, the law and the rule of law serve a similar function in Plato's *Statesman* and *Laws*. The extent to which the Athenians meant to set up a regime of laws sovereign even over the people, as is key in Plato's model regimes, or whether they meant simply to restrain the powers of oligarchs and possible revolutionaries and so to secure the power of the demos or the majority, is fiercely debated by scholars today (law is sovereign: Ostwald 1986: 497–524; skeptics: Ober 1989: 299–304; D. Allen 2000: ch. 8). By contrast, it is clear and explicit that Plato means to restrict the power of the majority as well as individuals, and so to aim at a good that is common to all regardless of class or faction.

Liberalism, Perfectionism, and the Rule of Law

So Plato's praise of law in the *Statesman* and the *Laws* resonates with our own notion of the rule of law in its emphasis on the ultimate authority of law, the importance of constraining official power, and on publicity and clarity. Nor would it have sounded strange at first hearing to an audience of ancient Athenians. But perhaps it ought to have; and perhaps it ought to us. For one thing, the rule of law in both dialogues is said to be second best to the rule of political experts, and furthermore to "imitate" expert rule. One plausible way to understand this is to see the two forms of rule as aimed at the same goal, the production of human excellence (virtue) and human well-being (happiness). Plato, like Aristotle, is what we would call in the terms of contemporary political theory a *perfectionist*, one who believes that the central goal of government is to promote good characters and well-being among its citizens (see Depew, chapter 26). This explains his overriding concern with education and training from birth in the virtues of moderation, justice, wisdom, and courage, as seen in the *Republic*, *Statesman*, and *Laws* alike. The goal of human excellence is shared both by the knowledge-governed regimes described in the *Republic* and *Statesman*, and the law-governed regime of the *Laws*, and it is reasonable to think that this overarching end is at least one key way in which law-governed regimes imitate knowledgeable ones.

How, exactly, does the rule of law promote virtue? One puzzle here is what role the sovereignty of law over magistrates plays in instilling virtue or preventing vice. But it is even reasonable to ask how the laws governing the lives of citizens promote virtue. This question may seem trivial: after all, the laws for citizens prescribe certain beneficial or virtuous behaviors, like marriage or honorable ways of hunting, and forbid the various forms of vice and injustice such as theft, assault, and murder. As Aristotle points out, even ordinary criminal laws aim at virtue (Arist. *Eth. Nic.* 5.1). The difficulty that arises is that real virtue requires choosing the right things for the right reasons, choosing the good because it is recognized and desired as good – while a law, for Plato as for us, is *coercive*: it threatens punishment against those who transgress it. What role can coercive law play, then, in the promotion or inculcation of virtue?

This question, it should be recognized, is broad, deep, and universal. Today's right-wing perfectionist does not want laws governing sexual morality or euthanasia to be obeyed merely out of fear of punishment or force of habit. Rather, he or she wants citizens to grasp the relevant value – the sanctity of life or the primary value of the family. Likewise it is hard to see how a left-wing perfectionist can attain a more compassionate or socially just society only by coercing the rich to contribute to the support of the poor. Beyond any partisan perfectionism, I do not think that any of us want to live in a community where the injunctions of the criminal code, laws against rape, murder, or theft, are obeyed merely out of fear of punishment or force of habit. We want rather that our neighbors not want to do these things, and that they not want to do so for the right reasons.

Laws governing educational systems, as we find in *Republic* 2–3 and *Laws* 7, are a straightforward application of perfectionist ideals. Likewise, it is not as puzzling or surprising that restrictive criminal codes might play some role in a perfectionist scheme, as a last resort, for instance, or a concession to the intractably vicious. And so Socrates concedes a role for coercive law even within the highly optimistic and ambitious just state of the *Republic*, when he argues that the manual worker, if he cannot be ruled by his own reason, ought to be ruled by reason from the outside via law (*Resp.* 590d). Here the coercion of the law is seen as a last resort, so that those who are not ruled by their own reason may still benefit from its guidance. (If one takes into account the laws restricting the Guardians, for instance the ban on private property, the question about coercion and virtue arises in the *Republic* as well.) There is the further mysterious claim, repeated throughout the dialogues, that punishment itself is curative and in some way improves the moral condition of the lawbreaker (Stalley 2007: 74–5 has a summary with references; see also Stalley 1995a).

But in the perfectionist law-state described in the *Laws*, the laws are central, not peripheral, to the ordering of the state, and the promotion of virtue is the explicit overarching end of the laws and of obedience to them. The interlocutors of the *Laws* seem to recognize the dangers of coerced obedience, and accordingly they suggest that explanatory "preludes" be attached to the laws, so that the laws seek persuasion in the first order, and threaten punishment only as a last resort. We will look at whether and how the preludes dispel worries about the relation between law-enforced virtue and real virtue in the next section. The difficulty will be even more pressing for the *Statesman*, as it advocates not the making of new virtue-promoting laws but simply strict obedience to whatever laws happen to be in place. Assuming that the innovations of the *Laws* have a chance to solve the difficulty, how will following *ordinary* laws, of the kind found in regimes claimed to be degenerate or vicious, be of any use in the improvement of the characters of the citizens? And if they are not useful for promoting virtue, in what sense does Plato think they have any value at all?

In what follows I will look first at how laws instill virtue under more ideal circumstances in the *Laws*. Then I will turn to the ordinary laws endorsed in the *Statesman*, and speculate about what use obedience is meant to be in that context. I will conclude with some general remarks about law and virtue for Plato.

The Rule of Law and the Rule of Reason

As in the *Statesman*, the *Laws* describes a mythical lost era – "the time of Cronus" – when superior beings (*daimōnes*) ruled men as shepherds rule sheep. Since weak and fallible mortals were not in charge, the city achieved "peace, modesty, good laws, justice in full measure, and so made the tribes of men free from *stasis* or civic conflict and happy." The rule of mortals, unfortunately, can never fully achieve the ends of political community. The only hope, says the Athenian, is that

> We ought by every means to imitate the life in the age of Cronus, as tradition paints it, and order both our homes and our cities in obedience to the immortal element within us, giving to reason's ordering the name of "law." But if an individual man or an oligarchy or a democracy, possessed of a soul that strives after pleasures and appetites and seeks to fill itself with these things … if such a one shall rule over a city or an individual by trampling on the laws, then there is, as I said just now, no means of salvation. (*Leg.* 713e)[2]

The passage encapsulates the main principles of political theory in the *Laws*. A good political community is one with determinate goals, virtue, and happiness; and the chief means to those goals (given current less-than-ideal conditions) is the law or laws. The rule of law is said to be akin to the rule of reason, "the immortal element within us."

The passage also makes clear what political problem the law is meant to solve – *stasis* or civic conflict – and explains that such problems result from the rule of men rather than laws, and the rule of appetite and pleasure rather than reason.

How, then, do laws prevent *stasis*? They do so on several levels. Specific laws, for instance the laws on the distribution of property, will be designed to eliminate causes for conflict, such as extreme wealth or poverty (*Leg.* 744d, cf. 729a1 and 757a). More generally, the sovereignty of law itself over any ruler, group, or faction means that the laws can benefit the whole city. When law is not sovereign, the Athenian argues, but rather the ruler or rulers are, those rulers will seek their own benefit at the expense of others. Such states, named as oligarchies, democracies, and tyrannies, are not true constitutions (*politeiai*) but are rather "conflict-tutions" (*stasiōteiai*) (715b–d). Further, because the laws of Magnesia do not aim at the good of a particular faction, but rather at the whole city or citizenry, they are not threatened by the development of virtue throughout the whole political community. The city aimed at the common good, virtue and happiness, is also said to be "free"; it consists of "voluntary rule over willing subjects," as opposed to the rule of a faction, which is said to be "voluntary rule over unwilling subjects accompanied by force of a sort" (832c).

A "conflict-tution" may have criteria for holding office, such as wealth (as in oligarchies), or "strength, size, or birth"; by contrast, Magnesia's criterion for office is obedience to the law: with the most obedient citizen qualifying for the highest magistracies, and so on proportionately down the hierarchy (715b). Magistrates ought to recognize the law as "master" – they ought, indeed, in the Athenian's peculiar phrase, to be "slaves to the laws" (715b–d). Nor is this true only of magistrates: "every man" ought to serve the laws first, since one cannot be a good master without being a good servant (762e).

While the phrase "slaves to the laws" might suggest forceful rule or at the least robotic citizens carrying out orders in blind obedience, a closer look indicates otherwise. The language of slavery here is meant to explain the relationship between reason as embodied in the laws and one's appetites and desires; the human excellence sought by the laws is constituted by the authority of reason in the soul. At the beginning of the general prelude to the laws in book 5, the Athenian describes the relationship between the soul and the body as a master and a slave:

> Of all a man's own belongings, the most divine is his soul, since it is most his own [*oikeiotaton*]. A man's own belongings are invariably twofold: the stronger and better are master [*despozonta*], the weaker and worse are slavish [*doula*]; wherefore of one's own belongings one must honor those that are master above those that are slaves [*douleuōn-tōn*]. (*Leg.* 726e1–6)

One ought to be a slave to the laws as one is a slave to reason – which is to say that reason ought to rule over one's appetites and desires as a natural superior over a natural inferior, as a shepherd over his sheep. The appetites have nothing to offer as a standard for the guidance of one's life, although properly directed they can of course drive one to live the life reason demands. The exclusion of the appetites as such as standards for how we ought to act is suggested in the definition of injustice as the domination or tyranny of the soul by anger, fear, pleasure, pain, envy, and desire (*Leg.* 864a), as well as in the age of Cronus passage quoted above. (For Aristotle on the rule of reason, see Depew, chapter 26).

The citizens are thus "slaves" to the laws in that they treat them, as expressions of divine reason, as having absolute authority over appetites, desires, and emotions. Reason's authority is necessary for one to attain one's good and to achieve human excellence or virtue. Furthermore, since in the passage above about the slavery of the body to the soul, the soul is said to be "most one's own," and since at least in some sense no one does wrong or is vicious willingly (*Leg.* 860de, 861d), there is a way in which following reason involves doing what we really want.

The promotion of virtue and the prevention of *stasis* or civic conflict so turn out to involve the same central condition: the rule of reason in the souls of magistrates and citizens. Just as the law must be sovereign over the will of any individual magistrate or potential ruler, preventing self-serving or faction-serving behavior, so must it be sovereign over the impulses, appetites, and desires of the individual citizen. In other words, *stasis* is a manifestation of vice; it results from self-seeking or greedy behavior in magistrates or citizens. It is prevented by the promotion of virtue – the rule of reason – which in Magnesia is attained chiefly by obedience to the law. And obedience to the law is meant, in the end, to promote virtue and the rule of reason not just by coercion, but by the education required by laws as well as the persuasive prefaces attached to them.

However, the identification of law as an expression of reason deepens the question that I raised earlier. If law is reason, and as such is truly "one's own" and commands one's true good, what one in fact really wants, to what extent are laws simply correct moral rules that allow for the self-fulfillment and well-being of a rational creature, and to what extent are they coercive injunctions? What accounts for maintaining the coercive function of law, if law is so truly in accord with one's nature and if it correctly produces one's good?

The answer must be that the effectiveness of laws as reason must depend on the rational capacities of the citizens. If then, the laws fail to be utterly persuasive on their own terms, it must be, in the view of Plato in the *Laws*, because of a failure in rationality in the person persuaded. And this in turn would seem to indicate a failure to achieve the central goal of the laws, virtue. To explore this question in detail, and to see clearly whether and how it is problematic for Plato, we will have to look at Plato's chief innovation in lawmaking: the preludes.

The Preludes

So far in my discussion of the *Laws* I have left the means by which the laws promote virtue vague and unspecified, apart from suggesting that "slavery to reason" and the subjugation of the appetites are somehow involved. And this has left the most pressing question open: what kind of obedience to the law is attained in Magnesia, and how does that obedience relate to being virtuous?

One way of sharpening the question is to look at what sort of obedience might *not* be virtuous. Here is the kind of obedience that I originally questioned in this respect: that the citizens obey the laws without really wanting to. In other words:

(i)   The citizens follow the rules out of coercion, rather than desiring what the law demands as something good.

The identification of law with reason, however, and the emphasis throughout the *Laws* on the effects of education and law on the desires and emotions suggest that a distinct kind of worrisome obedience may be in play, that the citizens may obey the law without understanding it. In other words:

(ii) The citizens are habituated by the shaping of their desires and pleasures to obey the law, rather than understanding why what the law commands is good.

Virtue, for Plato, as is clear from the passages I have already cited, involves life under the authority of reason. This seems fine for those with sufficient rational capacity to understand exactly why they live as they do. But will the citizens of Magnesia have this capacity? This question turns out to be crucial for the overall success of the regime of the *Laws* on its own terms. How exactly will the citizens avoid nonvirtuous obedience?

The interlocutors of the *Laws* address this question through Plato's major innovation in legal theory. The laws will have attached to them "preludes" or prefaces that explain the reasoning behind the law (718b–724b). If the prelude is successful, the coercive part of the law, the part threatening punishment, will be unnecessary. It seems to be assumed, however, that the coercive part must always remain in place regardless. For example, the interlocutors set a law for Magnesia that one must marry before age 35, on penalty of yearly fines. This prescription, threatening punishment if not followed, is prefaced by an explanation of the role that marriage plays in the best life – namely, by securing immortality through procreation (721b–e).

The analogy that the Athenian uses to explain the preludes is a comparison between "slave doctors" and "free doctors." Slave doctors are slaves and have slaves for patients. A slave doctor gives no account of their patient's condition or their treatment, but "like a tyrant" prescribes what he judges best and rushes off without further explanation. The free doctor, a free man who treats free men, investigates the condition of his patient, and tries so far as is possible to give explanations and "to teach [*didaskei*]" the patient, so that he does not begin treatment until he has persuaded the patient and obtained his consent (720b8–e2). In a later passage referring back to this one, the Athenian describes the free doctor as "nearly philosophizing" when he talks with his patient, as "practically educating" him as if he were being trained to become a doctor (857c2–e5).

The doctor analogy strongly suggests that the preludes to the laws are to persuade the citizens by appeal to their reason, so that their own reason is brought into accord with the reason embodied in the law. To some extent, the preludes we find in the *Laws* bear out this goal. The prelude to the laws against impiety in *Laws* 10, for example, is a series of fairly sophisticated theological arguments apparently designed to convince the citizens that the theological theses ordained by the state (that gods exist, are good and cannot be bought off) are actually correct (888a–907c). Likewise, we find philosophical discussions – meant for the citizens to understand – of the distinction between voluntary and involuntary, as well as the nature of justice and injustice (861d–864c). It is also clear enough, given the nature of virtue and the goal of the law to promote it, that rational understanding ought to be sought where possible.

It is less clear, however, how much rational persuasion is actually sought and achieved by the preludes we find in the *Laws*. Our first sign that something is amiss is that the chief interlocutors, Cleinias and Megillus, get lost in the midst of the sophisticated theological arguments of book 10 (892 dff.). If the interlocutors cannot follow the argument and so be rationally persuaded, why should we think that many or most of the citizens will? There is furthermore an often noticed gap between the preludes as described in the doctor passages and the actual preludes the interlocutors attach to the laws. In addition to (a) the philosophical preludes I have mentioned, we also find (b) sermon-like exhortations, explaining the role of obedience to the law in the good life. The prelude to the law that one must marry before age 35 is an instance of this; it gives a hortatory description of the role procreation has in a good life, and explains that it achieves a certain kind of immortality (721b–e). The "general prelude" to the whole law code, found in book 5, is an even better example: here we find the passages cited above about the relation between the law and reason and the importance of reason and obedience to it in the best life. And further, there are preludes consisting of (c) simple rhetorical flourishes, praising or condemning the behavior in question, as for instance the prelude to the law restricting hunting exclusively to hunting quadrupeds (823e–824b), as well as the preludes to the laws about temple-robbing (854b–c), beatings (879c–880a), and fraud (916d–917b). Lastly, we find (d) preludes threatening punishment after death, as in the laws against injustice (870e, 872e). (The laws themselves threaten bodily punishment, exile, or fines.)

How should we understand the gap between the preludes as they are described in the doctor analogy and the preludes that the interlocutors actually attach to the laws? One possibility is that the doctor analogy describes a certain ideal of the role of law in producing virtue, an ideal that often must be compromised in light of the actual rational capacities citizens have (Laks 2000). Another possibility is to argue that virtue in the *Laws* has a lower bar than we find in other dialogues, and consists of a fairly low-level rational grasp of good (Bobonich 2002). This fits well with much of the language in the *Laws* that suggests that virtue can be attained with a true belief about what is good (and a sincere desire for it), as opposed to full-fledged knowledge or understanding (*Leg.* 653b–c, 654b–d, 659d–e). A citizen persuaded by the prelude to the law concerning marriage, for example, would have a correct belief that he ought to get married, along with some understanding of why he ought to do it: because procreation helps him attain immortality. The prelude thus may not require excellence in reasoning to the highest degree, but it will involve some low-level rational grasp of the relevant good.

One might worry that the conception of virtue that the preludes help achieve on this latter view, consisting as it does of a fairly unsophisticated grasp of the good, is a weak or limpid conception of virtue. After all, virtue involves the rule of reason, and

Zena Hitz

reason seems to involve real understanding and not simply the unreflective behavior one might expect from someone with a correct belief about how to live and a sincere desire to live that way, even if in some cases they have a crude justification for that belief. Crude and roughly correct justifications are awfully easy to find: for instance, a person who gets married because he has an idea this would make him happy may well have a low-level grasp of the good of marriage; similarly, a soldier who fights because he judges his native political order to be a good thing. But such a grasp of the good seems not to demonstrate much in the way of human excellence, much less excellence in reasoning. So while the view does successfully provide an account of how a citizen of Magnesia may have *some* grasp of the good, and so is not simply an obedient robot, the virtue indicated looks substandard or at least very ordinary. The inadequacy of this type of virtue to grasp and secure the overall aim of the city is made explicit late in the *Laws*, when the Nocturnal Council is said to provide the expert knowledge and surpassing virtue needed (962b; 964b; cf. 632c). Those with merely common virtue (*dēmosia aretē*) are thus not capable of ruling the entire city (968a). Virtue thus seems to have two levels in the *Laws*, the ordinary subexpert level, and the level attained by members of the Nocturnal Council.

There is a further difficulty, however, for those who think that the preludes in principle give the rational understanding needed for authentic virtue, and that is that there is a certain lack of connection between the general exhortations of the preludes to the good life and the enormous detail and specificity demanded by the laws themselves. The *Laws* as a whole contains far more in the way of regulative detail than it contains explanation or justification of those regulations. This means that the citizens may obey the laws willingly, understanding the importance of law and of reason generally, but they will not understand the specific rules they are commanded to follow. The prelude about marriage (that reproduction provides a share in immortality and so a key human good) may well convince the citizens that they ought marry. But how will it convince them that they ought to marry before age 35? And likewise with many of the detailed laws about inheritance, buying and selling, hunting and fishing, and so on found in the dialogue. The "general prelude" to the law code found in book 5 is particularly worrisome on this point. It may convince the citizens that they ought to honor the soul and follow reason in the form of laws, but how does it explain to them that reason demands the particular laws that follow? These features of the preludes raise the disturbing specter that the preludes encourage citizens to obedience generally, without giving much of an explanation of why they ought to obey in these particular and very specific ways.

That the preludes simply soften up citizens into an obedient frame of mind is supported both by the fact that the preludes are meant as preparations for the law itself, and by the dual function of law as both persuasive and compulsive. The preludes are not sufficient on their own, or self-standing without their coercive counterparts, on this view, because they are not capable of justifying the specific types of obedience that the laws command, but only obedience generally. Hence the worry: that the persuasion provided by the preludes is a persuasion to obey whatever laws the lawgivers hand down, and not persuasion that these laws in particular provide the goods promised.

Both worries about the preludes can be generalized in the following way. If the preludes do not produce rational understanding, or if they do so only at a crude level, to obey laws for the sake of the ideal of a certain kind of rational life may yet mean to obey laws that one does not oneself understand. Life under the authority of reason, then, might mean life in obedience to someone else's reason, as is suggested in the final parts of the *Republic* (590a–e). Indeed, even the seemingly optimistic analogy of the lawgiver to a doctor that we saw in the discussion of the preludes could suggest that the citizens of Magnesia are not themselves the source of the rational understanding that guides their lives, any more than the free patient could heal himself on his own.

If it is correct that the grasp of the good sought for the citizens of the *Laws* is very general, so that obedience is judged to be good even without detailed understanding of what sort of obedience is best, this might help to explain why, in the *Statesman*, obedience to ordinary laws is also praised. The *Statesman*'s praise of obedience to the law even in cities with ordinary laws has puzzled commentators (see C. Rowe 1995, 2000a). After all, given the suspect sources of these laws, in ordinary common sense and the commonplace wisdom of the village elder (*Plt.* 300b1–5) why should these regimes be praised? What good – from the perspective of Platonic perfectionism – could obedience to ordinary laws obtain?

There are clear parallels between the *Statesman*'s praise of obedience to laws as such and the inculcation of general obedience, as sought by the general prelude of *Laws* 5, in Magnesia. In both cases, one constrains one's appetites in accordance with public, general rules that aim at least roughly at some good. (A key difference will be that in the *Statesman*, this good is factional – hence the leaders even of lawful regimes are called "experts in faction [*stasiastikoi*]" – whereas in the *Laws*, a common good is sought.) This opens the possibility that obedience is praised in the two dialogues for similar reasons: that deliberate orderliness, even if partly coerced or encouraged by coercion – even in the absence of the sophisticated grasp of the good that the *Republic*'s philosopher-kings and the *Statesman*'s expert ruler have – constitutes a desirable, if second-rate, form of human excellence for Plato.

Law and Order

Law, for Plato, is an expression of reason. Reason is the "immortal element" within us and has its ultimate source in divine reason, *nous* or understanding, which orders everything into its best condition (*Leg.* 713e; 903a–905b). Law is associated with order and harmony throughout the dialogues (e.g. *Grg.* 503e–504d; *Phlb.* 26b), but in the *Laws* the connections between divine reason and the forms of human order are perhaps clearest (Morrow 1960: 560–1; Bobonich 2002: 93–7; Laks 2000: 260–1, 275–8).

There is no question that, in Plato's *Laws* and related dialogues, reason is the source of real order, and accordingly, beings capable of reason (human souls, divine intellects) are higher and more authoritative than the passive recipients of order (bodies and materials) (Bobonich 2002: 97). The difficulty that becomes clear from our discussion so far is that there is some evidence that certain forms of order can be achieved by passive obedience rather than active understanding; and while a passive, orderly soul is not the ideal result of the rule of knowledge, it may well be all that the regime outlined in the *Laws* can obtain for a great many of its citizens.

It thus seems plausible that even an externally enforced order, or an order attained without full or proper grasp of its goodness, is a weak form of human excellence for Plato. This would explain why the preludes aim at the rule of reason in citizens even while providing not much more than a very general and low-level grasp of the good. The scale of human excellence, on this view, would then correspond to a scale of orderliness: from the least orderly, whose behavior is coerced; to the "common" virtue of the average citizen of Magnesia, consisting of sincere desires and correct, loosely justified, beliefs; to the most orderly and most virtuous person, whose own reason fully grasps the good in his life and who actively shapes the world accordingly. Unity and order within the soul are still the highest human achievement – and each citizen does live in accordance with reason to the best of his ability – but conformity with an external unity or an external order may yet provide a similar, if weaker, form of human good.

We began by noticing close connections between the rule of law as an ideal of contemporary liberalism, as a way of restraining the use and abuse of political power, and the rule of law as described in both the *Statesman* and the *Laws*. These connections are undeniable, as is the influence of the legal structures of the *Laws* on liberal political ideals, via Aristotle and Roman writers. What I have suggested is that a closer look at the rule of law in Plato indicates deep and unbridgeable differences: the law for Plato remains an explicit second-best alternative to political expertise; the rule of law, like the rule of political expertise, is ultimately and irreducibly perfectionist in its aims; and, to the extent that the rule of law does indeed consist of an externally imposed order, it is baldly inconsistent with contemporary liberal ideals of autonomy and the rights of the individual.

FURTHER READING

Laks 2000 gives an excellent and relatively brief general overview of the philosophical issues in the *Laws*, and C. Rowe 2000a does likewise for the *Statesman* in the same volume. For more in-depth general reading on the *Laws*, Morrow 1960 gives the seminal account of the Magnesian regime's constitutional and legal structures and their historical parallels, while Bobonich 2002 provides an invaluable survey of the major philosophical issues, along with many provocative arguments. For a valuable recent discussion of the role of knowledge in Plato's political philosophy, see Schofield 2006: ch. 4. There is strong historical evidence that the *Laws* was unfinished at Plato's death, and so was written last, and strong linguistic and stylistic reasons to think that the *Statesman* (along with the *Sophist, Philebus, Timaeus, Critias*) was written at around the same time. For a judicious and sensible discussion of the chronology of the dialogues, see Cooper 1997a. For developmental accounts of Plato's political thought, see Bobonich 2002 and Klosko 1986; for an alternative, see Kahn 1995. On the rule of law and its many contemporary interpretations, see Shklar 1987 and Raz 1977. For a very interesting account of the relation between the rule of law for the Athenians on the one hand and for Plato and Aristotle on the other, see Cohen 1995. On the rule of law in ancient Athens, see Ober 1989: 299–304 and D. Allen 2000: ch. 8 for arguments that the Athenians did not distinguish between the sovereignty of the democratic Assembly and the sovereignty of law; for counterarguments, see Ostwald 1986: 497–524 and M. Hansen 1987. For discussion of the Athenian movement to codify and clarify the laws in the late fifth and early fourth century, see M. Hansen 1999: 162–79 and Ostwald 1986: 405–11, 414–20, and 511–23. On the importance of *stasis* or civic conflict to Greek political thought, especially Plato, see Balot 2001a. For an extensive and powerful argument that the preludes seek rational persuasion and that the citizens of Magnesia are capable of rationally grasping the laws, see Bobonich 2002, esp. 93–119. For an argument that the preludes in fact chiefly involve nonrational forms of persuasion, see Stalley 1994. For the view that they seek rational persuasion as a utopian ideal, but end up seeking nonrational persuasion as a concession to real conditions, see Laks 2000, 1991. Plato's account of the function of punishment is surveyed in Mackenzie 1981 and an account of the view in the *Laws* in particular is found in Stalley 1995a and Saunders 1991. I believe that the goal of the lawful regimes of the *Statesman* like that of the *Laws* is virtue, but this point is disputed by Christopher Rowe, who argues that these regimes aim only at minimal stability and order (C. Rowe 1995: 14–18; 2000a: 244–51). For strong disagreement with the point of view of the essay's conclusion, see Bobonich 2002 and D. Cohen 1993, both of whom argue that the political philosophy of the *Laws* is broadly compatible with contemporary liberalism.

NOTES

I am very grateful to Julia Annas, whose manuscript "Virtue and Law in Plato" first got me thinking about these questions, and from which I have learned a great deal. Thanks also to the audience at the 2006 Princeton Classical Philosophy Colloquium, where I presented comments on Annas's paper, and to Ryan Balot, who commented on an earlier draft of this essay.

1 So it seems from the fact that the lawful regimes come in different kinds, monarchies, oligarchies, and democracies; and from the Eleatic Visitor's description of the laws having their origins in experience and the agreement of some wise advisors with the people (*Plt.* 300b). However, the Visitor also describes lawful regimes as using the written documents belonging to the knowledgeable regime (297d), and calls the laws of the lawful regimes "imitations" of the truth handed down as far as possible from those "who know" (300c). It is not clear from the text whether the Visitor means (a) that the lawful regimes will literally use the statesman's laws; (b) that the village elders who suggest the laws approved by the majority have statesman-like knowledge; or (c) that in some way, ordinary laws aim imperfectly at correct ones, because in a mysterious way traces of truth are available to nonexperts.

2 All translations in this essay are based on Bury 1967–8 with modifications.

CHAPTER 25

"Naturalism" in Aristotle's Political Philosophy

Timothy Chappell

Five Senses in Which We Should Not Call Aristotle a Naturalist

In classical Greek, the nearest equivalent to the English "naturalist" is *phusikos*, literally "a man concerned with *phusis*, nature." The match is not close. To write a treatise "about nature," *peri tēs phuseōs*, was not to write a book on what we would call physics – though indeed Aristotle's own work, the *Physics*, introduced a shift in the sense of the Greek *ta phusika* (literally "natural things") toward the sense of our word "physics." Rather it was to write a book on *whatever has grown or come to be* (the root verb is *phuesthai*, with this range of meanings): a book on everything, or a book on nature (Latin *natura*, cognate with *nascere* "to be born").

A classical Greek philosopher who, like Aristotle, is a self-declared *phusikos* is not a philosophical naturalist in either of our two commonest senses of the word. When philosophers today talk of naturalism, they usually mean either a general view opposed to supernaturalism, or a specifically ethical view opposed to nonnaturalism, or both (see Pettit 1992). As opposed to supernaturalism, naturalism is the view that a complete understanding of reality need not posit the existence of God, gods, angels, or the like. As opposed to nonnaturalism, naturalism is the view that a complete understanding of moral reality need not posit the existence of special moral properties. The Greek *phusikos* is no closer to these technical senses of "naturalist" than to the colloquial sense in which a naturalist is a bird-watcher.

Aristotle would have rejected the anti-supernaturalist form of naturalism. The existence of a God – indeed of more than 40 gods – is (literally) a first principle of his philosophy (*Metaphysics* 12.8; cf. *Physics* 8). As for the anti-nonnaturalist form of naturalism – and it is telling that this awkward locution is the easiest name for the position – Aristotle's response, I suspect, would be that he does not know what the modern naturalist and nonnaturalist mean by "special moral properties." The modern

A Companion to Greek and Roman Political Thought, First Edition. Edited by Ryan K. Balot.
© 2013 Blackwell Publishing Ltd. Published 2013 by Blackwell Publishing Ltd.

ethicists' idea of the "specially moral" is heavily dependent for its sense on G. E. Moore's famous doctrine of the "naturalistic fallacy" in his *Principia Ethica*. But it seems unlikely that Aristotle would even have understood Moore's distinction between "good," an indefinable "non-natural property," and every other property, which is "natural." Nor is it necessarily discreditable for Aristotle not to comprehend this: as MacIntyre 1984 and Anscombe 1958 have pointed out, there may well not be anything comprehensible in Moore's doctrine.

A similar problem confronts a third way of distinguishing ethical naturalists from nonnaturalists, which appeals to the alleged "uncodifiability" of the moral (see McDowell 1979, 1981, 1987). On this story the naturalist thinks that moral properties have a nonmoral "shape," such as some suppose could be given by, for example, equating "the right thing to do" with "the act that maximizes utility." The nonnaturalist, by contrast, denies that moral properties have any nonmoral "shape." They may supervene on nonmoral properties, but the ways they do so are (as they appear from a nonmoral perspective) too chaotic to have a shape.

Like the first and the second, this third way of telling naturalists from nonnaturalists presupposes that we have a plausible way of demarcating "the natural" from "the nonnatural." If (as I would argue) we have no such demarcation, it does not even make sense. But even if it did make sense, and could be applied to the ancient Greeks, in any case it does not do what we might have wanted it to do, namely sort Aristotle from Plato. Both authors say things that can be heard (and often are) as endorsements of uncodifiability: with Aristotle's famous remarks about only seeking the measure of precision appropriate to the subject matter (*Eth. Nic.* 1094b12–14), compare Plato's famous question (*Resp.* 331c) whether you should keep your promise to return a knife to a madman – the expected answer is No, which supports the view that morality is uncodifiable. On the other side, both philosophers also say things that can be heard as rejections of uncodifiability. Socrates' insistence in the *Phaedo* that every token of the action-type suicide is a wrong action is as unconditional as Aristotle's insistence at *Eth. Nic.* 1107a9 that there are action-types that do not admit of a mean.

The uncodifiability hypothesis presupposes distinctions and doctrines that were unknown to Aristotle. As Williams 1985 and Anscombe 1958 have pointed out, these modern distinctions are not obviously improvements on any related distinctions that Aristotle did know about. For instance Aristotle's practical/theoretical contrast (see e.g. *Eth. Nic.* 1103a6) is quite different from, and a good deal clearer than, the modern moral/nonmoral contrast.

It begins to look as if Aristotle can be called a naturalist only in the bird-watching sense. (In that sense Aristotle most certainly was a naturalist, perhaps the first great one in western history.) But perhaps there is some other, looser sense in which Aristotle can reasonably be called a naturalist. Here is a fourth suggestion: Aristotle counts as a naturalist because he rejects Platonism. If "rejecting Platonism" means rejecting "the separation of the Forms," then certainly Aristotle makes this move (*Eth. Nic.* 1.6) – but that alone does not qualify him as a naturalist: Parmenides too rejects the separation of the Forms. Or if "rejecting Platonism" meant rejecting top-down explanatory principles whose reality goes beyond the spatiotemporal, this move would qualify Aristotle as a naturalist. But Aristotle does not make it. He is just as committed as Plato is to top-down transcendent explanatory principles: simply to different ones.

There remains a fifth proposal: that any philosopher will count as a naturalist if he makes some sort of appeal to nature central to his method, or makes it his ambition to explain this or that part of nature "in terms of the rest of nature." This last phrase I quote from Bernard Williams: "The question for naturalism is always: can we explain, by some appropriate and relevant criteria of explanation, the phenomenon in question in terms of the *rest* of nature?" (Williams 2002: 23).

In this meaning of the word Aristotle clearly is a naturalist. The only difficulty is that it is hard to think of a philosopher who is not. Plato, for instance, is certainly a naturalist in this sense, as the *Timaeus* makes abundantly clear. Apparently Parmenides at one end of the history of western philosophy, and G. E. Moore at the other, are naturalists too in this sense – though it is usual to classify Parmenides (arguably) and Moore (unarguably) as paradigm *non*naturalists. So this fifth proposal fails too. Compared to other philosophers, and in particular to his teacher Plato, Aristotle is not different, or more naturalistic, in having the ambition to explain things – the optimal shape for human society, for instance – "in terms of the rest of nature"; *pace* Williams (apparently), that ambition is universal among philosophers.

Still, this last proposal does bring us to a point where there is a real contrast between Aristotle and those, such as Plato, who are less naturalistically inclined. This is a matter of the weighting of the evidence, of our sense of what counts as a conclusive argument. *This* contrast between naturalism and antinaturalism is real, and applicable to Aristotle. It is the first of three real contrasts that I shall say more about in the next section.

Three Senses in Which We Should Call Aristotle a Naturalist

Plato, in the *Republic*, had no difficulty seeing that many of his political proposals – his elevation of the role of women, for example, or his abolition of the family among the Guardian class – were proposals that most people in Plato's own milieu would find profoundly counterintuitive. Similarly, Plato knew that some of his central philosophical methods – not only the appeal to the Form of the Good at the heart of the argument of the *Republic*, but the whole idea of Socratic interrogation – would not be accepted by most of his contemporaries. Plato's insistence (at the level of doctrine) on abolishing the family life of his Guardians, and (at the level of method) on corralling his interlocutors into a particular mode of argument and response, both naturally meet with the simple objection: "But that's not how things are in real life." One real contrast between Plato and Aristotle comes out in their reactions to this objection – the Real Life Objection as we may call it. Crudely, the contrast is that Plato does not take it seriously, and Aristotle does.

It *is* crude to say that Plato "does not take seriously" this objection, because he is certainly not simply dismissive of it. The Real Life Objection exerts a constant philosophical pressure upon Plato's thought. There are well-known signs in his later political writings, especially the *Laws*, that he is less resistant to that pressure than he was at earlier points in his career, most obviously in the *Republic* (cf. Hitz, this volume, chapter 24). Even in the famously rationalistic *Republic*, Plato does not assign the Real Life Objection a nil deliberative weight without thinking about it carefully; still, *after* careful thought, nil pretty well is the deliberative weight that he awards to it. The *Republic*'s argument against the Real Life Objection   not a completely explicit one, but see the Myth of the Cave in *Republic* 7 for some of the key moves – is strikingly reminiscent of Marx and Engels' theory of "false consciousness." The basic point is that our society, being corrupt, has corrupted us, so that what *we* count as "real life" is not a critical conception that can be used to address what is wrong with our society, but just another symptom of its sickness.

In this sense the *Republic*'s pessimistic political philosophy exactly parallels its pessimistic epistemology. Given the reprobate condition of humanity, naive commonsense intuitions about what is knowable by perception are no more trustworthy or authoritative than naive commonsense intuitions about what political or human reality is, or what it demands, or where the boundary is to be set between the genuine needs of an actually good city, and what a "pampered" or "febrile" city (*truphōsan polin, phlegmainousan polin*: *Resp.* 372e4, 372e9) merely imagines it needs.

Aristotle rejects Plato's apriorism in political philosophy just as surely as he rejects it in epistemology, and for parallel reasons. In the theory of knowledge Aristotle will write that "what appears to all men, that we say *is*; for the person who takes away this trust [*pistin*] will have no chance at all of replacing it with anything else *more* trustworthy [*pistoteron*]" (*Eth. Nic.* 1173a1–2). Aristotle opposes apriorism about knowledge with the sturdy obstinacy of common sense, and with more than a hint of a Moorean antiskeptical strategy. Like Moore 1959, Aristotle asks how any argument to undermine our most basic certainties could deserve a higher level of credence from us than those basic certainties themselves.[1] Similarly in politics, Aristotle's focus, in his critique of Plato's *Republic* and *Laws* in *Politics* book 2, is squarely on the practical consequences of attempting to implement their programs. For him, the key question is *what will happen* if we try to realize these political ideals "in real life." And he shows no interest in the likely Platonic retort "What kind of 'real life' would that be, then?"; or in the charge of false consciousness that lies behind the retort.

This, then, is the first sense in which it is right to describe Aristotle as a naturalist about politics. A second sense connects Aristotle's political naturalism directly to his ethical naturalism. Aristotle, as is well known, sees humans as one kind of animal among others, and tells us that the business of ethics is to clarify the nature of human well-being, *eudaimonia*, and identify what sort of life and what sort of character traits we need to have if we are to be *eudaimones*. Since this is the business of ethics, and since politics and ethics are, for Aristotle, contiguous and continuous studies – the *Nicomachean Ethics* famously ends with the words "Let us begin," that is, "begin to study politics" – it follows that Aristotle's ethical naturalism will carry straight over into a political naturalism.

With what specific results, though? No one is going to dispute that Aristotle is a political naturalist in that he believes that human nature has to be recognized as a determinant of what is possible and what is ideal in political theory. No one will dispute this, because the belief is a truism: as we have seen, even Plato at his most rationalist accepts it. The interesting question is how *exactly* our conception of (human) nature can act as a determinant of our detailed political outlook.

In the remainder of this chapter I shall look closely at two answers to this question. The first of these answers yields a third sense in which the term "political naturalism" is appropriate for Aristotle's approach to political questions; I discuss it in the next two sections. The other answer brings us to Nussbaum's capability approach, which I discuss in the final section.

Aristotle's Doctrine That the Polis Is Natural

In the third sense, Aristotle is a naturalist about politics because he holds that the state is natural:

> The community [*koinōnia*] formed of numerous villages is the complete city-state [*teleios polis*]. This has achieved the limit [*peras*] of pretty well entire self-sufficiency [*autarkeia*]: though it came about merely for the sake of survival, once in existence, it is for the sake of the good life. For this reason [*dio*] every polis is by nature [*phusei*], if at least the first communities also are. For the polis is itself the natural aim (*telos*) of those communities, and nature *is* what it naturally aims at [*hē de phusis telos esti*]; for what a thing is when its coming-to-be is fully completed, we say that that is its nature, whether it is a man, a horse, or a house. (*Pol.* 1252b28–36)

In Aristotle's philosophy the claim that something is *phusei* ("by nature," "natural") can stand in more than one opposition. The development of an organism, or any similar process, can be natural as opposed to spontaneous (*automatōi*) or subject to mutilation (*pērōsis*) (*Part. an.* 656a7–12, 686b2–5; *Gen. an.* 767b5). Events can happen naturally; they can also happen by luck (*tuchēi*) or accidentally (*kata sumbebēkos*), or again spontaneously (*Metaphysics* 5.30). A different distinction is between events happening naturally and being made to happen, either by skill (*technēi*) applied in "production" (*poiēsis*) or by deliberate choice (*proairesei*) applied in "action" (*praxis*) (*Pol.* 1254a7; *Metaphysics* 1069b). Further, an agent's possession of a character trait can be a result of nature, or of habituation (*ethismos*) (*Eth. Nic.* 2.1). Another and more traditional opposition is taken up by Aristotle when he agrees that human behavior and belief can be natural as opposed to conventional (*nomōi*) (see e.g. *Pol.* 1253a31). Finally, Aristotle contrasts what is natural (*kata physin*) with what is *un*natural (*para physin*) (see e.g. *Pol.* 3.6; compare Pl., *Leg.* 890a2–9, and *Grg.* 483c for a sophistical argument that the polis is unnatural). Which of these oppositions does Aristotle have in mind when he says that the polis is natural?

He cannot mean all of them. Aristotle cannot mean, for instance, that the polis is natural in the way a flower is natural – that it comes about by biological process rather than by human skill and ingenuity. Nor can he mean that the polis is more like an innate character trait than one acquired by habituation, such as a virtue: Aristotle clearly thinks of a good constitution as the equivalent in a city of virtue in an individual, which makes the development of the polis more the work of "second nature" than of nature itself (*Eth. Nic.* 1103a24–5). On the other hand, Aristotle surely does mean that the polis is not *un*natural; and that it is not (*pace* Callicles) merely conventional; and also that it is not spontaneous.

No doubt; but for an adequate understanding of his claim that the polis is natural, we need to see that claim as moving beyond all these senses of the natural/unnatural opposition. When the claim is first made (at *Pol.* 1252b28–36), Aristotle presents it as the terminus of a line of reasoning about self-sufficiency – a line of reasoning that is more than a little reminiscent of the one Plato uses to establish the "city of pigs" in *Republic* 2: "The polis comes into being … because of the fact that each of us is not self-sufficient, but lacks many things; no other principle [*archē*] establishes the polis" (*Resp.* 369b5–7). So, first, male and female individuals seek each other out because without each other they "could not even exist" (*mē dunamenous einai*, 1252a27). (Interestingly, Aristotle explicitly says that this seeking-out happens not by conscious purpose, *ek proaireseōs*, but because "the urge to leave behind another individual like oneself" is *phusikon*, "part of nature" – "instinctive," as we might also translate it (1252a29).) Then "the natural master and the natural slave" (*archon de kai arch-omenon phusei*, 1252a31) likewise seek each other out – "for the sake of security," *dia tēn sōtērian* (1253a31). Evidently Aristotle thinks that the natural master and the natural slave too could not even exist without each other, the master because he could not do all his own work, the slave because he needs the master's protection and direction. Once these two partnerships are in place we have the household, *oikia*, a form of natural partnership that suffices "for everyday needs," *eis pasan hēmeran* (1252b13). Then, Aristotle goes on, "the first partnership that is established on account of needs that are not everyday [*chrēseōs heneken mē ephēmerou*] is the village [*kōmē*]" (1252b17). This brings us up to the stage that the argument has reached in the passage quoted above: it is by the combination of these villages (possibly Aristotle has in mind the relation of its demes to the city of Athens[2]) that we finally get the city-state itself, *pasēs echousa peras tēs autarkeias.*

This is only the sketch of an argument. Aristotle wants to motivate each step of the development from individuals to polis by appealing to a need that is not yet met. But he does not tell us what the need is that gets us from household to village, or from village to polis, beyond saying that the former need is "not everyday," and that the polis is unlike families or villages in being "for the sake of the good life, not merely of life." As for the two mutual needs that he does tell us about – of the two sexes, and of the master and slave – his account of these is decidedly unconvincing. A man does not seek out a woman (or vice versa) merely for the sake of survival, or because without her *he* will not exist. A "natural master" who will die unless he finds a slave hardly seems worthy of the name. And Aristotle's suggestion (1252a35) that the natural slave's interests are identical with the natural master's seems a transparent piece of ideology.

However, we must not allow these superficial faults to distract us from the argument's deeper faults. The thought behind the argument is that political association is natural just where it meets some sort of need (*anangkē*) that is unmet by any smaller unit of political association. Hence, the largest natural unit of political association is the one that meets *every* human need, and when we reach this we have reached the natural terminus of the process of political development: so the polis is natural because it is self-sufficient. The argument's key notions of need and self-sufficiency both need to be scrutinized. In the next section I consider them in turn.

Need and Self-Sufficiency

Aristotle's deployment of the notion of need seems a good deal less critical than Plato's in the *Republic*. Aristotle, to put it bluntly, just offers us assertions about what is natural – and not especially convincing assertions. It would be nice to be able to say that these assertions were at least well rooted in Aristotle's philosophical biology. But as my close look at *Politics* 1252b28–36 has already suggested, honesty compels us to regard them as little more than bolt-on additions to his serious science.

Plato, by contrast, does not offer us mere assertions about need; instead, he offers us an explanation of why such assertions cannot establish much even about, say, the kind of family structures that are genuinely needed in the good state. A passage we have already touched on, *Republic* 369b–372e, demonstrates this by working out, more as a step in the dialectic than as anything like Plato's own considered view, a simple outline account of the good city the development of which is explicitly driven by the (commonsense) notion of need: "What will make the city, apparently, is our neediness" (*hē hēmetera chreia, Resp.* 369e8). This "city of pigs" is contrasted at length with the *truphōsa polis* (372e4–373e6), the city which goes beyond "the limit set by our needs" (373e1) and is therefore exposed to the greatest evils that can come to states, including war (373e3–7). How then are we to locate the true limit set by our real needs?

Plato pointedly does not answer this question. He moves on, instead, to discuss the nature of the good soldier (374a–d), and then the nature of the good ruler and his education – the discussion that takes us into the heart of the *Republic*'s concerns. The point of this significant silence is that, at this stage of Plato's inquiry, there is no way to fix the boundary between our true and our merely apparent needs – any more than a good response to the Real Life Objection could begin by just asserting a demarcation between what is and what is not really "Real Life." At 373e it may seem to Socrates and Glaucon and Adeimantus that the development of the luxurious city out of the city of pigs is as inevitable and indeed as "natural" as any other development. Plato is, of course, convinced that it is neither inevitable nor natural. But he does not think that he can prove that simply by stipulating a content and scope for the notion of need. To show it, he thinks, requires a journey to a viewpoint on philosophy that will change the way we look at *everything*: namely, the journey to the Form of the Good that the central books of the *Republic* take us on. There can, for Plato, be no ideologically innocent account of need, any more than there can of "Real Life." To a Platonist, Aristotle's attempt to help himself to one must seem at best naive.

Aristotle's use of the notion of self-sufficiency is equally exposed to objections. The guiding idea of the argument is that a natural limit to political development has been reached when we arrive at the point where human living becomes self-sufficient. Now for something to be a self-sufficient unit in Aristotle's sense is for it to be able to provide, by itself, for all its own *needs*. So clearly the objections to Aristotle's notion of need that I have just raised are also objections to his notion of self-sufficiency. But that is not the only or even the main difficulty about Aristotle's notion of self-sufficiency. That notion is hopelessly unclear anyway – and unclear in both directions, so to speak.

In the one direction (toward smaller units than the polis), Aristotle is famous for saying that the life of contemplation is self-sufficient: *"hē te legomenē autarkeia peri tēn theōrētikēn malist' an eiē"* (*Eth. Nic.* 1177a27–8). So it is his own view that the individual human can be self-sufficient. Aristotle's adherence to this view is not restricted to the *Nicomachean Ethics*: the *Eth. Nic.*'s package of views about the contemplative life is briefly reaffirmed at *Politics* 1325b17–22. So either Aristotle should have accepted that the truly self-sufficient unit was not the city-state but the (enlightened) individual; or he should have further explained his notion of self-sufficiency in order to show how it fitted the polis better than the individual.

We could respond that there is a distinction between personal and political self-sufficiency: the ideal of self-sufficiency that is achieved by the contemplative individual is one sort of *autarkeia*, the ideal that is achieved by the *teleia polis* is another. But this suggestion merely prompts the question "Why just these?" If there can be two Aristotelian ideals or notions of self-sufficiency, why not three (perhaps counting as the third the self-sufficiency of a world trade-system – more about that in a minute)? Why not four, or five, or as many as you like?

Going in the other direction (toward larger units than the polis), international trade was hardly an unknown phenomenon in Aristotle's day, and not all of it was trade in unnecessary luxury items. Thus every polis in Aristotle's famous collection of constitutions will have been a polis that was not, economically, a self-sufficient community. So either Aristotle should have accepted that the truly self-sufficient unit in politics was not the city-state but the international trading community of city-states and other states (including Egypt, Persia, Carthage, China? And the states that traded with them?); or else he should have further explained his notion of self-sufficiency in order to show how it uniquely fitted the polis.

Perhaps Aristotle means that the polis is the terminus of a natural process of development because it is the smallest self-sufficient political unit – rather as, in the metaphysics of the *Categories*, individual substance is the least abstract and most concrete thing to which predicates can be applied (*Categories* 2a34–6). This suggestion, like the parallel suggestion in metaphysics, merely prompts the question "Why stop there?" We have been given no argument that the natural process of development is completed when we reach the smallest viable self-sufficient state. Why couldn't someone retort that the natural process of association goes on beyond the level of the polis, and that these smallest possible states are themselves merely raw material for an ever wider union – such as, to give one obvious example, Alexander's empire? (There is a well-known irony in the idea of a "resident alien" philosophy professor, sitting in Athens writing out an eight-book defense of the Greek city-state as exemplified by Athens, just as his most famous pupil Alexander was busying himself with the final and permanent destruction of the Greek city-state in general, and the Athenian city-state in particular.)

Aristotle says something about this second objection at 1280a25–b10. The difference between an economic relationship and a political relationship, he suggests there, is that an economic relationship is only for the sake of life, whereas a political relationship is for the sake of the good life. The suggestion is, presumably, that the city-state "is self-sufficient in respect of virtue": the polis is uniquely the context in which we have all the resources that we need to achieve full virtue (perhaps, of the active rather than the contemplative kind), and where we have those resources in a way in which they are not available at any lower level of political organization.

We only need to develop this suggestion to see how unpromising it is, whether we apply it to Aristotle's society or to our own; though it is surprising how much rose-tinted idealization of the Greek polis we will have to see past in order to get the point. As any reader of Thucydides' *Histories* will quickly gather, the idea that politics is not the practice of virtue but merely the art of the possible is as much a classical Greek idea as a modern one. As any reader of Sophocles' *Antigone* will see, Aristotle's idea that the state is there for the good life, the family only there for the sake of survival, can quite easily be stood on its head – even in a classical Athenian context. What *Antigone* shows us with stark clarity (and it is not the only classical Greek drama to do so: compare, for instance, the *Oresteia*, or Sophocles' *Philoctetes*) is that the state and its imperatives can easily become the most important *obstacle* to an agent's practice of virtue; and that the Athenians of Sophocles' time knew this perfectly well.

The idea that engagement in the public life of the state is necessarily more an exercise of virtue than life at more local levels of association, such as family life, therefore deserves little credit either from us or Aristotle, who was in no worse a position to be critical of it than we are. The idea that life at more global levels of association than the polis is necessarily less of an exercise of virtue does not deserve much credit either, as any supporter of the United Nations or the European Community might point out. But this too is not just a modern point, it is a point that Aristotle was in a position to see. Presumably the exchange of philosophical ideas is a form of association for the sake of the good life if anything is. But the Athenians' practical cosmopolitanism about philosophical exchange was proverbial – as St Luke reports (*Acts* 17.21), and as Plato repeatedly illustrates. Athenians like Socrates would talk philosophy with anybody, and learned as much from foreigners like Protagoras and the "Eleatic Stranger" as from fellow citizens of the Athenian polis like Glaucon, Adeimantus, Phaedo, or Theaetetus. Plato, then, gives us a picture of ethical interaction and mutual instruction that is at least panhellenic in its scope. The idea that there can be fruitful ethical debate with an even wider scope is presented repeatedly by the Athenian playwrights. Euripides' *Troiades* (415 BC), for instance, is a sustained meditation on the wrong done by the Greeks to the Trojans, with a studied contemporary reference to the Athenian city-state's rape of the city-state of Melos (416 BC). The meditation is presented, moreover, by characters who are both barbarians and women, and so presumably have a double dose of Aristotelian natural inferiority.

I suspect that Aristotle is only led in the first place to talk of self-sufficiency as an ideal in ethics[3] and political theory because of the strong analogy with his talk of independence as a criterion of substance in metaphysics (see e.g. *Metaphysics* 1029a28). The analogy does little real work in political theory unless we take seriously an organic conception of the state. Plato takes that conception seriously, with familiarly sinister consequences for any conception of individual freedom worthy of the name. Aristotle, to his credit, usually does not. Of course he does sometimes gesture in the direction of the organic conception; as for instance in the opening lines of the *Politics*, where we are supposed to derive the priority of the polis over the individual from a hierarchy of *telē* of a familiar sort (1252a1–7); and again a little later, where Aristotle tells us that the individual is related to the state as part (*meros*) to whole, and that the state is "prior in nature" (*phusei proteron*) to the individual (1253a27). If it is to be taken as more than mere metaphor, such talk is bound to conflict with the deeper substantial individualism of Aristotle's metaphysics.

The fallout of that conflict includes, apparently, the series of philosophical problems that I have reviewed in this section. Aristotle should not have sought, and did not need to seek, to make self-sufficiency the mark of the naturalness of the city-state. Indeed, in order to defend the polis in a way that is true to his own most important commitments, Aristotle did not even need to be a naturalist about the polis in the sense that this section has explored – the sense of taking the polis to be the natural endpoint of a process of development toward complete self-sufficiency. The conclusion about the naturalness of the polis that is (from Aristotle's own point of view) really worth having is, I suggest, not a point about self-sufficiency at all. It is only the thesis (which Aristotle of course accepts) that living in poleis contributes in a distinctive and nonreplaceable way to individuals' *eudaimonia*. But this thesis could be true without the much stronger thesis about natural self-sufficiency that Aristotle tries to argue for. Suppose it is agreed that no particular form of human association is any more *natural* than any other is. Even then, we can intelligibly discuss the question which sorts of friendships or associations best contribute to *eudaimonia*. After all, in just the same way we can intelligibly discuss the question which board-games we find most worthwhile. This is possible even though we all agree that the only relevant natural fact is that it is human nature to devise and play *some* sort of games; that no board-game is any more natural than any other; and indeed that all board-games are paradigms of conventionality. Even, to take Aristotle's own favorite example, chess (1253a8).

This conclusion brings us back to the second way of spelling out the details of an Aristotelian political naturalism that I identified at the end of the second section: namely, by working up an account of the human good such as that offered by Martha Nussbaum under the name of "the capability approach." I look at this line of thought in the next section.

The Capability Approach

Nussbaum's capability approach explicitly aims at producing a defensibly universalistic ethics. She seeks this by starting with *human* universals: aspects of human life which all humans in all societies share in, areas of experience and choice in which all humans must have some conception or other of what well-being is, and how it can be achieved.

> We begin from the general intuitive idea of a creature who is both capable and needy ... the question we are asking is: What are the features of our common humanity, features that lead us to recognise certain others, however distant their location and their forms of life, as humans and, on the other hand, to decide that certain other beings who resemble us superficially could not possibly be human? The question directs us to cross boundaries ... (Nussbaum 1990a: 219)[4]

When we cross these boundaries and look around, what we find ourselves working toward is "a kind of story about what seems to be part of any life that we count as a human life" (Nussbaum 1990a: 219). This story generates a list of aspects of human potential for well-being, "functionings" as Nussbaum sometimes calls them:

> The list we get if we reflect this way is open-ended ... like most Aristotelian lists, our working list is meant not as a systematic philosophical theory, but as a summary of what we think so far, and as an intuitive approximation, whose intent is not to legislate, but to draw attention to certain areas of special importance. And the list is not only intuitive, but also heterogeneous; for it contains both limits against which we press and powers through which we aspire. (1990a: 219)

These aspects of potential for well-being are the eponymous capabilities. Nussbaum's own list runs: (1) Mortality; (2) The human body; (3) Capacity for pleasure and pain; (4) Cognitive capability: perceiving, imagining, thinking; (5) Early infant development; (6) Practical reason; (7) Affiliation with other human beings; (8) Relatedness to other species and to nature; (9) Humor and play; (10) Separateness (1990: 219–24).

This list gives the capability approach a theory of the good: a "list theory," as such theories are often called. Indeed it is worth comparing Nussbaum's list with some other list theories of the good, in particular with those offered by the neo-Thomist "new natural law theorists" such as John Finnis, who offers a list of seven goods: life (cf. Nussbaum's 1, 2, 10), knowledge (cf. her 3), play (9), beauty (8), friendship (7), practical reasonableness (6), and religion (1).

On the basis of this list of the human capabilities, the capability approach then offers a foundational normative claim. And here I pause to query the vague connective "on the basis of": *how* does the list of capabilities generate the normative claim? There are many routes that might get us from a theory of the good to the theory of the right. Contrast consequentialist and deontological routes, for instance, and bear in mind that this is only one of many contrasts that might be drawn. There is much work still to be done by capability theorists in deciding between these alternatives.

The foundational normative claim of the capability approach is egalitarian in two distinct ways. The capability approach posits it as the good that ethical and political choice should work toward the (a) equal support and realization of citizens' capacities, which in themselves are thought of as (b) broadly equal capacities – in general, citizens do not differ *enormously* in what they are able or unable to do or achieve or experience.

> The task of Aristotelian politics is to make sure that no citizen is lacking in sustenance. With respect to each of the functionings ... citizens are to receive the institutional, material and educational support that is required if they are to become capable of functioning in that sphere according to their own practical reason – and functioning not just minimally, but well ... Politics examines the situations of the citizens, asking ... what the requirements of the individual for good functioning are, in the various areas. Both the design of institutions and the distribution of resources by institutions is done with a view to their capabilities ... [Politics'] aim is ... to design a comprehensive support scheme for the functionings of all citizens over a complete life. (Nussbaum 1990a: 228)

This, in quick outline, is the capability approach. What are we to make of it? The quick reply is that it is an extremely plausible application of neo-Aristotelianism to political philosophy. However, there are reasons to doubt that the Aristotelianism is more than neo-.

It is clear that the capability approach deals well, or can deal well, with the most obvious objections that it raises. For example, the approach is not really vulnerable at all to Bernard Williams's objection to all forms of Aristotelian and neo-Aristotelian naturalism, that they depend on an antiquated teleological biology:

> In Aristotle's teleological universe, every human being ... has a kind of inner nisus toward a life of at least civic virtue, and Aristotle does not say enough about how this is frustrated by poor upbringing, to make it clear exactly how, after that upbringing, it is still in this man's real interest to be other than he is. If Aristotle, with his strong assumptions about the nisus of each natural kind of thing toward its perfection, cannot deliver this result, there is not much reason to think that we can. Evolutionary biology, which gives us our best understanding of the facts that Aristotle represented in terms of a metaphysical teleology, cannot do better in trying to show that an ethical life is one of well-being for each person [because] evolutionary biology is not at all directly concerned with the well-being of the individual, but with fitness. (Williams 1985: 44)

Williams assumes here that evolutionary biology and "metaphysical teleology" are two understandings *of the very same facts*. This seems mistaken. The facts about human life that Nussbaum appeals to in spelling out her list of functionings or capabilities are facts about human ethology *as it is now*. They are not facts about how that ethology developed in the past, as evolutionary facts are. Moreover, there need be nothing particularly "metaphysical" about the kind of teleology needed by the capability approach. For sure, the approach needs the claim that we do have various sorts of "inner nisus," such as the nisus to avoid our own deaths, or the nisus to deploy practical reason in planning our own lives. That is a claim against which Bernard Williams has another important argument, his famous argument against external reasons: he only gestures toward this argument in the quotation above, though on reflection it may well seem that it is really Williams's anti-external-reasons argument that is, subterraneously, driving his thinking here. To assess that argument would be another paper.[5] The point for now is that it does not seem very ambitiously metaphysical to say that we have more than one inner nisus. Nor does that claim conflict with the facts about evolution: it could be an evolutionary fact that we have evolved these inner nisus.

This is one place where we should distinguish Aristotle from neo-Aristotelians. Williams may have a good point against the historical Aristotle's own ethics and politics; he may be right that *Aristotle* is committed to, and bases his normative views on, a defunct metaphysical and teleological science. (Though even with the historical Aristotle, that seems an overly uncharitable reading, given the possibility of separating ethology from scientific theories about how that ethology came into being.) Williams is surely wrong to say that *any neo-Aristotelian* has to share that commitment to implausible antique science – and certainly Nussbaum seems able to avoid any such commitment. (For Nussbaum's own rather different arguments against Williams's objection, see her 1995.)

A different objection asks why it should be assumed that all basic human capabilities are essentially benign. If we can say that there are human capabilities for practical reason and humor, why can't we also say that there are human capabilities for spite, murder, adultery, war, treachery, embezzlement? If there are no such malign capabilities, we need to know why not, given the striking prevalence of these sorts of activity in human life. Or if there *are* malign capabilities, we need to decide how to respond to this fact. Perhaps it means that the capabilities approach cannot be applied at all – we need to try some other approach. Or perhaps it means that the capabilities approach can be applied, but yields immoralism rather than a conventionally moral outlook. The point is not that the capability approach cannot deal with this sort of objection. It is that it is a virtue of the capability approach to raise this problem so clearly, since the problem is central for any biologically based ethics.

A third sort of objection to the capabilities approach will begin in suspicion of the sheer scope and ambition of the kind of state that Nussbaum envisages: "[Politics'] aim is ... to design a *comprehensive* support scheme for the functionings of *all* citizens over a *complete* life" (1990a: 228); "The job of government ... does not stop until we have removed *all* impediments that stand between [the] citizen and fully human functioning" (1990a: 215).

It sounds like the capability approach has a worrying tendency toward statism and centralism. But here we come back to the problem I noticed above, about how to get from a theory of the good to a theory of the right. The objection to sweeping claims like these is not that the capability approach inevitably yields a worryingly strong form of statism. It is that there seems to be no inevitability at all about the emergence of these strongly statist views alongside the theory of the good with which the capability approach begins. The capability approach cannot be a complete political philosophy without clear answers to crucial questions of liberty and rights: about the balance between state and individual, about what sorts of state intervention and confiscation are permissible and why, and indeed about what justifies the very existence of the state in the first place. Again, I am not suggesting that these questions cannot be answered by adherents of the capability approach – though I am suggesting that they have not been answered yet.[6]

A different kind of question about the capability approach, to which I briefly turn in closing, is not whether it is plausible, but whether Nussbaum is right to claim that it is genuinely Aristotelian. To answer that, let us take the components of the capability approach one by one.

First, I said above, the capability approach aims to offer us a *universalistic* approach to ethics and politics, by identifying aspects of human life which all humans in all societies share in, and in which all humans must have some conception or other of what well-being is, and how it can be achieved. In its concern to identify these functionings, the theory is certainly very like Aristotle's own, though Nussbaum identifies them more clearly and systematically than Aristotle does.

However, the reasons why Aristotle and Nussbaum wish to identify a set of capabilities and found a normative theory on them seem to be different. Nussbaum 1988 takes her own universalism to be an ambition that Aristotle shares: she sees him as someone who engages in a cosmopolitan critique of all known ethical and political outlooks. But it is surely clear that Aristotle does not share Nussbaum's ambition. Unlike some other Greeks – Herodotus, for instance – he is simply not interested in being able to engage in normative debate in a cosmopolitan way. Aristotle certainly wants to vindicate his own ethical and political views as the absolute truth, but the vindication is for his own and his friends' and peers' sake, not for the sake of just any interlocutor at all. If the barbarians disagree with him, Aristotle does not wish to argue with them. He simply doesn't care. They are barbarians.

This mention of barbarians brings us to the most striking difference of all between the neo-Aristotelian capability approach and anything that is actually in Aristotle himself – the difference that makes the capability approach acceptable to modern liberal individualists like me, while Aristotle's own political naturalism is not. As I noted above, the central normative claim of the capability approach is doubly egalitarian: we are to work toward the (a) equal support and realization of citizens' capabilities, which are thought of as (b) broadly equal capabilities. The problem with taking these egalitarian claims as not only neo-Aristotelian, but also historically Aristotelian, is not that Aristotle does not make similar sounding claims. As Nussbaum goes to great lengths to demonstrate, he certainly does. The problem is that Aristotle's egalitarian claims only *sound* similar. The trick is in the word "citizens," *politai*.

Nussbaum tells us that, for the Aristotelian, "the task of political arrangement is both *broad* and deep. *Broad*, in that it is concerned with the good living not of an elite few, but of each and every member of the polity. It aims to bring every member across a threshold into conditions … in which a good human life may be chosen and lived" (Nussbaum 1990a: 209). On the face of it this seems the plainest of exegetical sailing. After all, doesn't Aristotle similarly say this, in a passage that Nussbaum has just quoted? "It is evident that the best *politeia* is that arrangement according to which anyone whatsoever [*hostisoun*] might do best and live a flourishing life."[7]

But here we come to it. "Anyone whatsoever": A slave? A barbarian? A woman? Of course not. Here and everywhere in the *Politics* that he uses this sort of general language, Aristotle means "anyone whatsoever *who is naturally qualified to be a citizen in the first place*," and takes this to be such an obvious qualification on his remarks that he does not bother to state it. (Any more than we might state the real, but to us easily invisible, limits on a claim true in our society such as "Everyone can vote.")[8]

Here a great gulf opens up between Aristotle's "anyone whatsoever" and Nussbaum's supposedly parallel "each and every member of the polity." She and Aristotle disagree fundamentally: not about what is owed to a citizen, but about who is entitled to be a citizen in the first place. Nussbaum contrasts a defensible concern for the well-being of every citizen with an indefensible concern only for the well-being of what she calls "an elite few." But, in her terms, the citizenry that Aristotle has in mind *is* "an elite few."

Remember the sheer number of slaves that, in Aristotle's time, were working in Athenian society. (For more on slaves, cf. Depew, this volume, chapter 26.) Pretty well every Athenian citizen, even the poorest, had at least one domestic slave; in the true style of a Hegelian master and slave dialectic, poor citizens saw the possession of a slave as a mark of their own freedom. The rich would certainly not stop at a single domestic slave (rich households might include 50). There were many other categories of slaves besides domestic ones. Most, perhaps all, Athenian businesses presupposed the existence of slavery: large-scale businesses owned slaves who worked in factories and mines and docks and galleys; smaller-scale businesses like farms involved something like serfdom. The city of Athens deployed 1,200 "public slaves" (*dēmosioi*) as its police force (these are the Scythians often mentioned in Aristophanes); other public slaves worked as clerks in the Athenian treasury and the Assembly, as executioners and torturers, at producing coins in the Athenian mint, as temple attendants like Ion in Euripides, and so on.

Familiar though they may be, these facts cannot be emphasized enough if we want, for the purposes of political philosophy, a clear view of exactly what kind of society it is that Aristotle was admiring and advocating, in his admiration and advocacy of the Athenian style of city-state. For instance, the facts about slavery at Athens should help us to get a proper perspective on Aristotle's well-known doctrine (see e.g. *Pol.* 1278a22) that certain forms of work, and in particular manual labor, are inconsistent with the dignity of citizenship. Against the background of the socioeconomic facts about slavery at Athens, this is not an admirably high-minded proto-Marxian plea for "the construction of fully human and sociable forms of labor for all citizens" (Nussbaum 1990a: 231). Rather it is the fiercely conservative doctrine that slaves should be kept in their place, so that the citizens can be kept in theirs.

More widely, the sheer number of slaves as opposed to citizens that were found at Athens should help us to see the crucial ambiguity of that tricky phrase "all citizens." Restricted in the way that Aristotle means to restrict it, and in the way that it was in fact restricted at Athens in his time, "all citizens" does not mean the universal-suffrage group of all mentally competent adults that liberals like myself and Nussbaum readily assume must be meant. The Aristotelian citizenry are nothing like the citizenry of a modern liberal democracy. They may indeed be equal among themselves, but then so are the members of a gentlemen's club; what is more to the point is the number of *non*equals who are excluded from their sort of equality. Given the racial distinctions that there usually were between Athenian freemen and their slaves, who were usually brought from the Middle East or central Asia as victims of war, terror, or professional slave-hunting (*Pol.* 1256b24), the closest equivalent to the Athenian citizenry in the modern world is the white elite of South African apartheid. And, remember, Aristotle in the *Politics* is busy arguing for this sort of polity: he goes to as much effort to show that slavery is natural as he does to show that the polis is natural, and indeed his arguments for the two theses are connected.

The uncomfortable conclusion of this train of thought is that Aristotle uses the resources of something like a capability approach to argue for a racist and suprema-cist segregationism. That fact should give us a little pause before we claim, as we might in a brash moment, that the neo-Aristotelian in political theory derives pretty well directly from the historically Aristotelian. It might also prevent us from being completely confident that an Aristotelian, or neo-Aristotelian, capability approach leads inevitably to a plausible and attractive liberal political theory like Nussbaum's. It would be nice if it did, of course; but the fact is that Aristotle manages to take the approach to an embarrassingly different conclusion.

It is interesting to try to think out the reasons why this difference is possible. One of the reasons, at least, is obvious: in between Aristotle's resolute chauvinism and Nussbaum's resolute universalism, there came the radical cosmopolitanism and egali-tarianism of Pauline Christianity.

FURTHER READING

The standard edition of Aristotle's *Politics* is W. Ross 1957. Good translations include Barker's (see Stalley 1995b) and Jowett's, revised by Jonathan Barnes (in Barnes 1984). Valuable secondary reading includes Keyt and Miller 1991; Kraut 2002; F. Miller 1995; Mulgan 1977; Salkever 1990; Simpson 1998; and Yack 1993. The best online resource is F. Miller 2002.

NOTES

Thanks to Ryan Balot and Sarah Broadie for helpful comments; neither is, of course, respon-sible for my mistakes.

1 Cf. Denyer 1991, last chapter ("Aristotelian Optimism"), and Hedrick in this volume, chapter 27.
2 Unless the demes were not ancient entities but artefacts of Cleisthenes' reforms, a question on which ancient historians do not agree: see Ostwald 1986: 175–81.
3 Self-sufficiency as an ethical ideal faces other objections, too. What is so great about needing no one else? Why shouldn't it be a sign that I *lack* well-being that I am never vulnerable or dependent? Perhaps we should celebrate human interdependence, not see it as a flaw to be

remedied: cf. MacIntyre 2001. In any case Aristotle's emphasis on self-sufficiency is not entirely easy to reconcile with another emphasis that he frequently makes much of – namely his emphasis on friendship.

4 Nussbaum's question has a curious implication: that a group of creatures with human chromosomes and genetic lineage might *not* be human, and that a group of creatures with no such chromosomes or lineage might *be* human. This distances her use of "human" from the scientist's sense of the word. It makes "human" in her mouth, like "person" in many contemporary philosophers' mouths, an "evaluative concept," as she agrees at Nussbaum 1995: 126 n17; indeed she tends to treat "person" and "human" as synonyms. I share Williams 2006b's reservations about any such use of "human": even in its ethical deployment it is much better kept a straightforwardly biological term.

5 Williams 1981; for further discussion see Chappell 2006.

6 They are not answered, for instance, by Wolff and de-Shalit's impressive book (2007), which takes their version of the capability approach as its theory of the good, and adds their version of egalitarianism as its theory of the right; but, explicitly, not so much by arguing for egalitarianism over nonegalitarianism, as by seeking a consensus *among* egalitarians: Wolff and de-Shalit 2007: 3.

7 Nussbaum's own translation; the reference is to *Pol.* 1324a24.

8 For an examination of a similar invisibility in Socrates' ethical and political thought, see my paper "Why Wasn't Socrates a Cosmopolitan?" which is available on my webpage at www. open.ac.uk/Arts/philos/why_wasnt_Socrates_cosmopolitan.pdf.

CHAPTER 26

The Ethics of Aristotle's *Politics*

David J. Depew

Politics and Ethics

> The most authoritative and architectonic science seems to be political science. For it prescribes which of the sciences are to be used in the polis, who is to learn them, and to what extent. (*Eth. Nic.* 1.1.1094a26–b2)

At the beginning of *Nicomachean Ethics* we find Aristotle searching for the master science in the sphere of human activity by constructing hierarchies in which bridle-making, for example, is instrumentally related, and hence subordinated to, horsemanship, horsemanship to military expertise (*stratēgikē*), and military expertise, finally, to political science (*politikē epistēmē*) (*Eth. Nic.* 1.1.1094a9–26). Other chains converge on political science as well. Moderns – the authors of the American constitution, for example – might admit the primacy of politics in this sense. As founders of a state, and hence practitioners of *politikē*, the framers could not help making it their business to weigh in on economic, legal, social, and educational matters. They said, for example, that religious instruction would not be given by officers of the state or supported by it. We might imagine, however, that their warrants for such judgments were ethical, not political. By their time ethics had been distinguished from politics. So the framers envisioned a state whose citizens were empowered to pursue their own happiness, an ethical concept, by means of justly framed and fairly applied laws. For these lawmakers politics was to be informed and constrained by ethics. But Aristotle, too, declares happiness (*eudaimonia*) to be the "highest of all goods in the sphere of action" (*Eth. Nic.* 1.4.1095a16–18). So shouldn't ethics have been the master science for him as well? Perhaps. Still, the fact is that for Aristotle the buck really does stop at politics (*Eth. Nic.* 1.4.1095a16). His ethics is entirely political.

Why is that? It is not because Aristotle treated individuals as mere cogs in the wheel of the state, as fascists did. He regarded any notion of a happy state not founded on the happiness of its individual citizens as incoherent (*Pol.* 2.5.1264b17–21). But

A Companion to Greek and Roman Political Thought, First Edition. Edited by Ryan K. Balot.
© 2013 Blackwell Publishing Ltd. Published 2013 by Blackwell Publishing Ltd.

neither does Aristotle's commitment to the autonomy of each citizen entail a political theory that enjoins merely minimal norms of public conduct in order to ensure that maximal room is left for private persons to identify and realize their own conceptions of happiness. With one wrinkle, his ethical theory identifies, analyzes, and commends a single objectively adequate, if complex, conception of happiness. With the exception of a relatively few theoretical adepts – that is the wrinkle, to which I will return at the end (see also Brown, this volume, chapter 31) – his conception identifies "only those activities [as] part of the human good which are activities of good citizens in the good polis" (Garver 2006: 128; *Pol.* 3.18. 1288a40–b2). If ethics is neither subordinate to politics nor superior to it it is because for Aristotle ethics simply *is* political science in its most normative and least circumstance-burdened aspect.

What aspect of political science is that? Aristotle is keenly aware that the polis-oriented activities that are constitutive of individual happiness depend on the acquisition of certain habits and values. So he insists that socialization (*ethismos*) and education (*paideia*) should be the primary concerns of lawmakers (*Pol.* 7.14.1333a35–b10; *Eth. Nic.* 5.2.1130b22–6). Ethics is the aspect of politics that commends to leaders the set of moral virtues to which citizens *qua* citizens should be habituated and the norms of justice they should embrace in their dealings with one another. It also specifies the forms of affection (*philia*) they should cultivate and the kinds of leisure activities (*diagōgē en tē scholē*), including branches of art and learning, in which they should engage. These four topics – virtue, justice, friendship, and leisure, in this order – structure the table of contents of *Nicomachean Ethics*. In sum, Aristotle's answers to questions about happiness double as first principles of normative politics because they identify the virtues, activities, and values that are required if citizens of Greek poleis, or something very much like them, are to flourish.

Aristotle nowhere relativizes these norms. On the contrary, his ethnocentric contempt for barbarians – with notable exceptions, he simply means foreigners – embodies the notion that there can be no better, or indeed other, form of social and political organization than the Greek polis as a matrix for fully developing and expressing human capacities. Does this mean that his ethics is useless for anyone not living in a Greek city-state? Does it mean that people who embrace Aristotle's ethics must do what they can to bring back the city-state? Or that those who even today claim to find his ethical texts helpful in public as well as private matters, but who live in entirely different sociopolitical worlds, must have misinterpreted him? There are no easy answers to these questions. Nonetheless, in musing about them we would do well to acknowledge that the reception history of these texts usually betrays more about the cultural assumptions of Aristotle's fans at this or that time than about Aristotle himself, even if the most creative of these time-bound appropriations do manage to find partial support in genuinely Aristotelian claims.

Aristotle's medieval interpreters, for example, whether they were Islamic, Jewish, or Christian, could see at a glance that he liked kingship, in large part because he thought it afforded more scope for matching the claims of individuals to their social and moral worth than the ham-handed uniformity of even the best laws, which Aristotle regarded as standing in for virtues that most people do not fully acquire (*Eth. Nic.* 5.10.1137612–32; Hedrick, this volume, chapter 27). In economic exchange, qualification for office, punishment for crimes, and constitution making, proportional equality *is* Aristotle's idea of justice (*Eth. Nic* V.3.1131a29–b31). He thought kings could best render justice so conceived because their flexibility in addressing particular circumstances rested on their own (or, suspiciously, their family's, *Pol.* 3.17.1288a16) incommensurably greater virtue, wealth, and freedom of action when compared to other citizens (*Pol.* 3.13.1284a3–10; 15.1288a10–12; 17.1288a26–9). Medievals made Aristotle safe for dynastic kingship by following this line of thought, and anti-republican defenders of the ancien regime followed suit.

Freedom-loving liberals,[1] whether they stress free markets or free personal behavior, including the right not to participate in political life, are offended by such a doctrine, as well as by other unpalatable features of *Politics*, such as its defense of slavery and its denial of citizenship to women. If they read Aristotle's *Ethics* sympathetically, as commending to reflective persons everywhere a philosophically justified way of defining and achieving personal happiness, they will try to find ways to pry the *Ethics* loose from the *Politics*. They might in this event try to make something of the slippage Aristotle himself acknowledges between the good citizen of this or that state, whose conduct conforms to its laws, and the good man as such, whose actions flow from virtuous dispositions and desires tutored by rationality (*Pol.* 3.4.1276b29–1277a4; *Eth. Nic.* 5.1.1130b25–30). If they are honest enough to recognize that, even if not all of Aristotle's good citizens are good men, his good men must also be good citizens, they may still try to make him safe for liberal democracy by limiting the explicitly political application of his moral theory to behaving justly toward others (Striker 2006; see *Eth. Nic.* 5.1.1129b31–5; 2.1130b20–2). If, following this line of thought, they acknowledge that Aristotle's conception of justice as proportional equality seems to stress treating unequal cases unequally more than, like our own, treating equal cases equally (*Pol.* 3.9.1280a9–15), they may try to find ways to show that under scrutiny this theory of justice is closer to our own than we might initially have imagined (F. Miller 1995).

In recent decades, attempts to find either a monarchical authoritarian or a proto-liberal in Aristotle have given way to efforts to find in his stress on virtue a communitarian political theorist. Virtue ethicists use Aristotle's conviction that morality depends on habituation to shared norms of behavior as a stick with which to beat merely proceduralist conceptions of morality and justice, whether utilitarian or Kantian (MacIntyre 1984, 1999). People whose virtuous habits are acquired by the inculcation and subsequent internalization of strong social norms, they argue, are most likely to find and do what morality demands in particular, often complex, circumstances (Hedrick, chapter 27). While not every virtue theorist is a communitarian, those that are argue that ineffectively thin, rule-governed criteria for moral judgment are closely tied to liberal political institutions and that in practice these institutions produce people whose habits, values, and behavior regularly fall short of what common life requires, thereby threatening the very possibility of a good society (Bellah et al. 1985). All communitarians thus agree with Aristotle that orientation toward active participation in some kind of community life is required to turn out good people. That still leaves open what kind of community is required (see F. Miller 1995: 361–6). But most communitarians think that there can be no substitute for orientation to active citizenship in a political community for forming a moral identity and being able to make prudent judgments in particular cases. In effect, they agree with Aristotle that the good person must be a good citizen. Of those who take this view, some have attempted to refigure liberalism itself in order to accommodate this requirement (Sandel 1996; Walzer 1983; Barber 1984). Others have distanced themselves from liberalism in favor of corporativist political theories (Etzioni 1993).

Politically oriented communitarian virtue theorists are fond of citing Aristotle's warrant for forging a tight connection between morality and citizenship. That warrant, in the words of the would-be historian of philosophy and Aristotle scholar Karl Marx, is that "man is in the most literal sense of the word a *zōon politikon* [political animal], not merely a gregarious [herd] animal, but an animal that can individuate itself only in the midst of society" (Marx 1973: 84; see also 496). Nonetheless, communitarians and virtue theorists generally tend to draw back from the anthropological grounds on which Aristotle himself bases this claim. That, it has been said, is because we moderns no longer share Aristotle's biological teleology, and hence his theory of human nature (MacIntyre 1984: 52–3). There is some worry, too, that whenever a biological "is" is used to enjoin an ethical or political "ought" there almost always lurks an assumption of the biologically grounded superiority of some persons over others. Aristotle's example does nothing to assuage this worry. Accordingly, interpreters of Aristotle's practical philosophy must consider whether or to what degree the anthropology that undergirds his ethical theory imposes insuperable barriers to our appropriation of that theory. To do so we must first recount his anthropology as accurately as we can.

The Ethical Implications of Aristotle's Anthropology

A human being is by nature [*phusei*] a political animal [*politikon zōon*] … Actually, the human being [*anthrōpos*] is more political than any sort of bee and every herd animal. For … alone among the animals the human being has articulate speech [*logos*]. (*Pol.* 1.2. 1253a2–9)

For Aristotle, *anthrōpos* is not the only political animal, even though human beings do express this concept paradigmatically, and so define what appears less clear and developed in other cases. In the spirit of this semantics of exemplarity, which is closely related to Plato's theory of forms, Aristotle recognizes in his biological treatises social insects and cranes, in addition to humans, as political animals because they communicate with one another and, by doing so, divide roles in pursuit of a common work (*koinon ergon*) (*Hist. An.* 1.1.488a8; 8.589a3; *Pol.* 1.2.1253a7–9; see Cooper 1990; Kullmann 1991; Depew 1995). Aristotle also notes that the specifically human way of being a political animal relies on our inclination to "couple up" (*sunduazetai*) into permanent male–female pairs (*Eth. Eud.* 7.10.1242a25). (Some nonpolitical and a few other political animals, such as cranes, also do this.) These bonds are very important. Permanent coupling creates natural ties not only between parent and child, but also links that extend across generations through kinship. Households are thus parts of villages, and villages either of tribes, clans, and nations or, in a less common but superior trajectory of social development, of poleis (*Pol.* 1.2.1252b16–30).

What diffuses these bonds and drives them into highly role-differentiated social structures is the uniquely human capacity for articulate speech (*logos*). All political animals have a way of communicating with one another in order to cooperate. But political animals other than human have only touch or sound to serve as a communication medium, whereas humans also have language. They can thus communicate with one another not merely "what is painful and pleasant ... but what is useful and useless ... just and unjust ... good and bad" (*Pol.* 1.2.1253a11–15). This capacity, Aristotle infers, makes human beings "more political than any bee or herd animal" (*Pol.* 1.2.1253a8–9), presumably because speech, by its intentionality, multiplies the number, intensity, and nature of our mutual engagements far beyond those of other political animals (Cooper 1990). In sum, we are the only species that lives in a niche constituted by the webs of discourse in and through which we interact with one another and the environment. Aristotle views human nature through the eyes of a natural historian (Chappell, this volume, chapter 25). But from this perspective he asserts that the distinctively human way of being biological is to be cultural.

In this respect, the solitary (*monadikos*) animal is the polar opposite of the political. (Between these extremes lie scattered (*sporadikos*) and herd (*agelaios*) animals (*Hist. An.* 1.1.488a2–4; Depew 1995).) Being naturally political in their cultural, discursive way, humans risk forfeiting the sources of their selfhood when they are made, or even worse make themselves, into solitaries.[2] As Marx recognized, the solitary never becomes an individual at all in the sense of a well-realized instance of his natural kind. Rather, he degenerates into a self-absorbed monster, more wild beast than man, whose natural passions are warped into love of violence for its own sake and whose intelligence, rather than serving as a medium of cooperation, is turned into a frighteningly powerful instrument of bestial desires. Armed to the teeth by his cunning, the solitary man "is the most unholy and most savage of animals, and the worst with regard to sex and food" (*Pol.* 1.2.1253a35–7, trans. Lord 1984). His desires are bottomless, like those of the tyrant whose inner life is laid bare in Plato's *Gorgias* and the final books of *Republic*. If anything, Aristotle is more realistic than Plato in stressing not the frustrations of forever chasing after new pleasures, but the real delight that the greedy man takes in being unconstrained by the claims of others and the very notion of "enough" (*Eth. Nic.* 5.1130b4; Balot 2001a: 25–33; Nagle 2006: 297). We should fear this "clanless, lawless, heartless" condition (*Pol.* 1.2.1253a4–5, quoting Hom. *Il.* 9.63–4). Moreover, we should pity good people like Philoctetes or Hecuba who through no fault of their own are stripped of the communities that sustain, as well as generate, their identities. Driven to the edges of civilization, their very selves can be unmade (Nussbaum 1986: 378–421).

Admittedly, discursively mediated social bonds come in all shades. But Aristotle's cultural anthropology is no more relativist than his political theory. He rank orders cultures by the quality of their discursive life. (That is why Aristotle buys into the astounding Greek prejudice that underlies the word "barbarian," those who go "ba-ba-ba" rather than having fully articulate speech.) The scale on which he measures cultures is the degree to which, in the course of communicative interaction, objects accessible *only* to speech and thought, and so expressive of the distinctive potentialities of mind (*dianoia*), become the focus of shared life rather than serving merely as more powerful tools for the satisfaction of needs and desires that are shared with other animals (*Eth. Nic.* 1.7.1097b22–1098a19; *de An.* 2.3.414a29–32). In the ideal case, discursive speech becomes a conceptual medium in which aspects of the *kosmos* that are not open to nonrational animals, but have intrinsic value, are constituted as objects of desire, discussion, and contemplative apprehension (on "the open," see Agamben 2004). This can happen only on the basis of polis life, even when it transcends it, because the discursive activity that makes such revelations possible grows only in the soil of the polis. "Community [*koinonia*] [in perception of the useful just, and good]," Aristotle says, "is what constitutes a household and a polis" (*Pol.* 1.2.1253a18).

The intimate tie between ethics and polis life follows from these supposed anthropological facts. Unless human beings are socialized from childhood in good habits, moral underdevelopment ensues and moral disaster looms (*Eth. Nic.* 1.4.1095b4–9; Burnyeat 1980; McDowell 1996; Hedrick, chapter 27). When, on the other hand, good socialization is succeeded by the practice of deliberative reason-giving – a practice reliably and pervasively available only in and through polis life – the young will become virtuous in proportion as they internalize the noble (*kalos*) values that for Aristotle, no less than Plato, integrate the self. This requires learning to distinguish in everyday practice between internal and external goods and, relatedly, between instrumentally and intrinsically valuable uses of rationality. Because the quality of their discursive interaction is poor, Aristotle infers, such distinctions do not operate in barbarian cultures. They are also at risk in poleis whose "deviant" constitutions substitute the apparent good of particular persons (tyrannies) or classes (oligarchies and democracies) for the common (*koinon*) good of the political community (*koinonia*). Aristotle thinks that internalizing what is intrinsically noble into the core of the self will in turn protect citizens when for one reason or another access to the modest supply of external goods such as health, wealth, and beauty necessary for stable happiness comes under strain (*Eth. Nic.* 1.10.1100b23–33). The cultivation of virtuous activity and leisured activities for their own sake makes the polis more, not less, secure because Aristotle believes that the external goods necessary for its well-being are normally consequences, not direct aims, of its devotion to the pursuit of intrinsic goods through its encouragement of virtuous acts done for their own sake (*Pol.* 7.1.1323a39–b6). This upbeat claim is licensed not only by the view that good values make the self a harmonious whole that is resilient in the face of difficulties, but also by Aristotle's confidence in the protective and prophylactic webs of polis life. By contrast, he takes barbarian conurbations – pleasure-loving Babylon, for example – to be constantly vulnerable to conquest because their denizens have no public spirit (*Pol.* 3.3.1276a29–30; Garver 1994).

None of this will occur, however, unless highly intrusive, well-conceived public educational norms and practices (*paideia*) are put in place. That is why Aristotle thinks, as I noted above, that the most important aspect of constitutional law and the standard by which founding lawmakers should be judged is provision for a common education (*Pol.* 7.14.1333a35–b10; *Eth. Nic.* 5.2.1130b22–6). Neglecting education, misconstruing it as the Spartan legislator did with his one-sided stress on military virtues to the neglect of the proper uses of leisure (*Pol.* 2.9.1271b1–7; 7.14.1333b15–23; 8.3.1337b30–3), or just leaving it up to individual heads of households, as Athenian democrats do – all these are recipes for trouble.

We should at this point be clear about Aristotle's ethical theory. He is a moral perfectionist. To be sure, he believes that most citizens of most poleis can be educated by good customs and laws only to the extent of acquiring what he calls "citizen's virtue," which enables them to resist passions that they actually feel (*Pol.* 3.3.1276b33–5). A desire to run away from battle, for example, can be countered by shame (*Eth. Nic.* 3.8.1116a18–b3). But a distinctive aspect of Aristotle's moral philosophy is that citizenly self-control (*enkrateia*) is a poor measure of fully developed human capacities. His version of virtue theory has it that good men, and therefore the very best citizens living in the very best states, can be so fully drawn to what is good and noble that they will enjoy, with no hint of repression, being temperate about food and sex; will be pleased, being friends, to treat fellow citizens justly and generously; and will even be able to take pleasure in courageous acts in battle (on temperance, see Young 1988; friendship, Cooper 1975, 1990; courage, Garver 1994).

This doctrine of perfection will seem less odd if we remind ourselves once more that Aristotle's ethics is political. We ourselves are often pleased to find pretty much the same suite of admirable character traits and, not coincidentally, practically wise decisions that he commends in people like, say, Nelson Mandela. But we have also been inescapably influenced by the rise since late antiquity of the notion that good character traits are to be measured by altruistic acts that extend beyond the circle of one's own (in Christian ethics, for example (Hedrick, chapter 27)). This has led, on one hand, to ethical ideals that are more strenuous than Aristotle's and, on the other, to lower expectations about what is actually possible, given our nature. For his part, Aristotle would simply disagree with Kant, and with the Christian anthropology he inscribed into the notion of practical rationality, that "nothing better can be made out of the crooked wood of humanity" than mere resistance to our pathologies. By the same token, Aristotle would think that Kant's notion that a set of devils or Hobbesian natural solitaries can form a state provided only that they know how to reason validly is doubly incoherent. It misconstrues the state as an alliance or contract between persons whose core identities are antecedent to the relationships into which they enter, as in social contractarian thought experiments. It also misconstrues reason as simply a calculating tool for getting whatever our untutored passions want. For this reason, Aristotle would also disagree with utilitarians like John Stuart Mill, who, even though they are as eudaimonistic as he, believe that moral reasoning reduces, by an unrestricted practice of socially negotiated trade-offs, to the best way of securing for everyone (and not, as Aristotle would have it, in proportion to merit as measured by contribution to the common good of the political community) the external goods whose enjoyment utilitarians take to constitute happiness. (This is the moral theory embedded in our own political practices.) As long as even a hint remains that one's thoughts and actions are instrumentally aimed at securing external goods and satisfying untutored passions instead of being oriented toward intrinsic goods that are accessible to mind, Aristotle will discern cracks between one's actual desires and one's grasp of, attraction to, and choice of what is inherently noble.

As long as such cracks exist the self will not be whole and its happiness will be either inaccessible, imperfect, or at risk.

The same considerations that reveal Aristotle to be neither a deontologist nor a utilitarian also show that neither is he what, in our frame of reference, *we* call an ethical naturalist (for a contrary view, see Chappell, chapter 25). If anything, he is a moral intuitionist. He believes that the intrinsically good, right, and noble are intentional objects of virtuous dispositions (*Eth. Eud.* 2.11.1227b13–1228a3). Even so, Aristotle's denial that moral intuitions are innate to all will surely lead most commentators to reject this characterization; embedding ethics within politics as deeply as he does, he cannot help but affirm that moral insight is comparatively rare and so deeply contingent on good institutions and practices that it depends on "moral luck." At the same time, the dependence of morality on training to acquire good values does serve to show why Aristotle's ethical-political perfectionism is more alive to and repulsed by the evils of which men are capable than any Calvinist, Hobbesian, or Machiavellian. Aristotle's anthropological stress on humans as naturally community-forming animals (*koinōnika zōa*; *Eth. Eud.* 7.10.1242a22–7) leads him to the perception that "the wickedness of human beings is insatiable" when the bonds of community are shattered, perverted, abrogated, or never formed (*Pol.* 2.7.1267b1, trans. Lord 1984).

Does this mean that for Aristotle human nature is "basically" bad? Certainly not. We have seen that unlike modern social contractarians Aristotle does not think of human nature as consisting in a fixed set of passions (*pathēmata*), desires (*epithumiai*), and impulses (*hormai*) that are preformed before our engagements in social life. Nor does he imagine that we maximize and manage these fixed passions by using an equally innate, if incurably self-regarding and content-neutral, calculative rationality. For Aristotle "the nature of each thing, such as a human being, a horse, or a house, is reached only when its process of coming-to-be is finished" (*Pol.* 1.2. 1252b30–1253a2). Given this teleological view, naked passion and purely calculative rationality are not the beginning points from which persons or states are formed. On the contrary, they are evidence of failure to actualize the distinctive potentialities of naturally discursively political animals. Reason itself is developed and oriented toward its proper ends by communicative interaction. To define our species without reference to the ends that its highest capacities can reach if properly cultivated by discourse, then, is not only to privilege passions over reason – the distinctive faculty that marks us off from all other animals – but to treat what for Aristotle are species specific potentialities as dissipated into bad habits from the very outset. Unfortunately, he seems to think this defect is both widespread and for the most part irreversible.[3]

A precisely opposed anthropology has been vividly set forth by Thomas Hobbes. That is because Hobbes, who was no mean Aristotle scholar, is simply Aristotle turned upside down. Because he rejected Aristotle's teleological semantics, as well as his teleological conception of nature, Hobbes took human beings to be natural solitaries in Aristotle's sense. He also thought that their naturally solitary lives were as "poor, nasty, brutish, and short" as Aristotle assumed. Hobbes therefore found it easy to imagine that these solitaries would use whatever calculative rationality they could muster to enter contractually into civil society, which in consequence he clearly saw must exist not by nature, *pace* Aristotle, but by constitutional art (Hobbes, *Leviathan*, "Introduction"; Keyt 1991a; F. Miller 1995). Would Aristotle recognize Hobbes's civil society or any contractually grounded state, including our own, as a political community? Probably not (*Pol.* 3.9.1280a33–40, b29–32), although he might recognize that our political institutions are actually or at least potentially less contractual, and more oriented toward the good life, than our own theories allow us to see. To appreciate this skepticism we must examine the political institutions that Aristotle thinks his own ethical norms call for and rule out.

The Politics of Aristotle's Ethics

The polis is the sort of community [*koinōnia*] that arises from [the integration of] a number of villages into a completed [*teleia*] community. [It is completed] because it reaches, as it were, a level of full sufficiency [*autarkeia*]. Coming into being for the sake of life itself [*zēn*], it exists for the sake of living well [*eu zēn*]. It is evident, then, that the polis is among things that exist by nature [*phusei*]. (*Pol.* 1.2.1252b27–1253a3)

If Aristotle's ethics are political, what sorts of political institutions do they countenance? We may begin an inquiry into this subject by noting that Aristotle's anthropology does indeed contain the claim that Hobbes rejects, that the polis – not this or that polis, but the polis as a form of human social life – exists by nature because it comes to be by a natural, not an artificial, process of development. Plants and animals, except for those that are spontaneously generated, come into being naturally and exist by nature as well. Since each is a substance, it has been tempting to interpret the natural status that Aristotle ascribes to the polis as conferring on it substantial existence in its own right. This is, however, as incorrect as regarding the polis as a product of constitutional *technē*. If poleis were substances, Aristotle would have to give up his conviction that human beings become individuated within them and that the measure of good poleis is the happiness of the individuals who live in them.[4] Fascists both see this and embrace the inference. Ontologically considered, however, the polis falls under the category of relationship, not substance. It is a certain kind of community (*koinōnia*): a reliably reconstructed, transgenerational pattern of relationships among naturally political human animals that obtains when their characteristically discursive form of communicative interaction reaches its final state of development, its *telos*.

It happens this way. As permanently coupling, socially embedded, discursively communicating animals, human beings are "always already" painfully, universally, and naturally oriented toward social interaction as a way of acquiring mates, offspring, land, food, population, military security, luxury goods, and rest from labor. Getting, and more importantly reliably reproducing, these means of material self-sufficiency (*autarkeia*) can be ensured only to the extent that the master–slave, woman–man, and parent–child relationships come to be distinguished within the household by the assignment of special roles, and appropriate degrees of virtue, to each; and when, not coincidentally, the male heads of these households (*oikonomikoi*) appear in public as citizens (*politai*) who deliberate about the common good with other citizens. Role differentiation of this sort is necessary because if heads of households were simply masters of slaves (*despotai*) they would treat their wives, too, as slaves and not as partners in deliberation, and could never appear in public as freely deliberating citizens. Indeed, only when the household comes to be distinguished from the public deliberative sphere by acquiring full internal role differentiation – Aristotle's version of Plato's one-person-one-job criterion (*Pol.* 1.2.1252b1–3) – does it actually become functionally or teleologically defined *as* a household and as a proper, constitutive part of the polis (*Pol.* 1.2.1253a19–21). Aristotle thinks that precisely these differentiations, and consequently the key distinction between "a large household and a small polis" (*Pol.* 1.1.1252a12–13), do not emerge among barbarians, who "take the social position [*taxis*] of the woman and the slave to be the same" (*Pol.* 1.2.1252b4–9).

The polis, then, consists of a number of "polis-households" – not too many or too few to sustain a rationally deliberative, leisured way of life – linked by a variety of permanent, multigenerational bonds (*Pol.* 3.1.1275b17–20; 7.4.1326b3–5; Nagle 2006). The capstone of these bonds is shared commitment to the common good as secured by public deliberation among citizens under the assumption that leisured self-sufficiency is the *telos* of their association. In seeing this we may see more clearly why Aristotle takes economic self-sufficiency to be a good effect, rather than the properly final end, of polis life. The reason is that only in a space of citizenly deliberation, where means and ends are reflexively discussed, can it be recognized that economic security is a means to an end, and that when enough security has reliably been attained the community is in a position to make the very point of its association the maintenance of a leisured sphere in which citizens and the free members of their households spend whatever time is not required by work (*Pol.* 1.8.1256b29–39). The notion that wealth is limited by the ends to which it is put is what protects a society from overreaching and undermining itself.

Some of this leisure time is to be spent in the discursively constituted self-governance that makes greater security, and so enhanced leisure, possible. But citizens can also be expected to treat the shared enjoyment of shared ties and festivals and other ways of "passing time together in a leisured way [*diagōgē en tē scholē*]" as more end-like (*Pol.* 7.15.1334a32–4). Activities that cultivate and express rationality are so end-like, in fact, that for Aristotle they provide the appropriate measure of whatever external goods are required for a fully realized human life (*Eth. Eud.* 8.3.1249b17–21; Cooper 1975: 136–9), thereby canceling what Hobbes called "the restless desire of power after power that ceases only in death" (Leviathan I.11) that characterizes naturally solitary humans, as well as the presumption of scarcity that continues to shadow all human communities except the polis. This reversal of values is what Aristotle means by the shift from "mere life" (*zēn*) to "good life" (*eu zēn*) in the passage quoted at the outset of this section. The shift leads away from a conception of scarce leisure as rest before renewed labor (*anapausis*; *Pol.* 8.3.1337b36–38a2) toward abundant leisure conceived as civic, religious, artistic, and, in a wide sense of the word, philosophical engagement (*Pol.* 7.15.1334a32–4; Depew 1991). Along the way, the very meaning of the term self-sufficiency (*autarkeia*) changes. From referring to freedom from the dependent, hence slavish, labor (*ponos*) necessary to maintain "mere life" it comes to mean engagement in activities that citizens autonomously, and hence unslavishly, pursue for their own highly pleasurable sake (Cole 1988–9; Brown, this volume, chapter 31).[5]

We are now in a position to observe Aristotle's natural teleology at work in his political theory. The fact that the discursive life of the polis equips it with an end beyond which it will not overreach – the pursuit of leisure in its highest forms – as well as with developed deliberative abilities to attain and preserve that end in particular situations is what makes the polis a natural existence. For the nature of something, we recall, is the point in the unfolding of a natural process that cannot be improved by further change. The polis is the terminal point of social development because leisure activities in civic friendship are themselves so ineluctably end-like (Cooper 1990). Only in the polis, Aristotle thinks, can religious festivals, artistic performances, practices of reflective criticism, and all forms of systematic inquiry appear to all as "the very best [*aristen*] way of passing time" (*Pol.* 7.3.1338a23–31, quoting Hom. *Od.* 9.5–6).

This account of the genesis of the polis as moving naturally from mere life to good life also provides Aristotle with an efficient cause of the step-by-step social complexification that reaches its *telos* in the polis. It is, of course, true that Aristotle's maxim that "nature does nothing in vain" entails that the polis arises because it is necessary for the actualization of human potential (F. Miller 1995: 40–1). But in order to avoid the circular rabbit-out-of-a-hat reasoning that was among the reasons why Hobbes and other early moderns abandoned final causes and natural teleology, Aristotle must adduce a concrete efficient cause for the development of the polis. The efficient cause is not simply the fear of not having enough, which is intensified in animals who deal with their environment by way of forethought, imagination, and anticipation of their own death, but also the positive impulse that naturally political animals have to maximize shared leisure-time activities.

There is, as usual, both a controversial background and a normative implication in Aristotle's analysis. His genealogical account of the polis differs from Plato's in *Republic* by declining to take the division of labor in an exchange economy as the locus that leads by self-purification toward the emergence of the proper parts of the polis. Instead, Aristotle locates the genesis of the polis in the movement from subsistence households through households linked by kinship into villages that "generate more than is required for daily needs" to fully self-sufficient polis-households (*Pol.* 1.2.1252b10–1253a1). He strongly implies that, while Plato's heart is in the right place, the story he tells stresses the quest for security more than the positive reinforcement of pleasurable social leisure activities. Even when transcended, Plato's economism is shadowed by need and want. Accordingly, Aristotle complains that when Plato puts a stop to the imperialist expansion of mere life in his genealogy of the polis in *Republic* he does so by constraining the self-actualizing, enjoyable activities of the citizens by making temperance (*sōphrosunē*), rather than the liberality (*eleutheria*) with which citizens freely share their possessions with one another, the most prominent characterological presupposition of justice (*Pol.* 2.6.1265a29–37). Moreover, Plato makes justice rather than friendship (*philia*) the bond of men in states.

Aristotle, on the other hand, believes that proportional equality (in claims to office, shares of the common wealth, and redress for crimes) can be as sensitive to the differential merits of claimants in particular cases as the concept of justice requires because (in contrast to Plato's tendency to multiply laws unnecessarily) justice is ringed about by friendship within and between households. "Friendship," Aristotle writes, "is the conscious choice [*prohairesis*] of sharing life together [*suzēn*] for its own sake" (*Pol.* 3.9.1280b39–40). The fact that Aristotle's discussion of justice in *Ethics* is followed by an extended treatment of the many dimensions of friendship, which in turn gives way to reflections on the best ways of using the leisure that economic security confers on citizens (entertainment? political engagement? philo sophical inquiry?) shows, if any further proof be asked, just how intimately connected ethics and politics are for him. It also suggests that for Aristotle political morality cannot be restricted to the practice of justice toward one's fellow citizens, no matter how justice is parsed.

Is this account meant to be historical? Whatever the answer, it should be acknowledged that Aristotle is less interested in anthropological facts than in analyzing, differentiating, and integrating the proper parts (in this case the constitutive relationships) of the polis in order to use its natural developmental *telos* as a normative model. His model is, in this respect, as analytical as that of his early modern social contractarian opponents. Still, Aristotle takes it for granted that there are real places, times, and peoples in which the transition from mere life to good life seldom, if ever, occurs and others in which it is more probable. It never occurs, for example, in climates that are too extreme for agriculture, which alone seems to produce the surplus necessary for polis life – a true observation to this day. It occurs especially frequently, he thinks, though not exclusively, in Greece. Whenever and wherever it does occur, however, we must distinguish between the polis as a type of social and cultural integration and this or that actual, historical polis. Athens, Thebes, Carthage, Sparta, or other individual political communities typically come into being when a founding legislator, whose name is usually preserved in collective memory, imposes constitutional form on the proximate matter of the natural polis (*Pol.* 8.4.1325b40–1326b5). This, plus any subsequent constitutional revolutions, individuates *a* polis.

To be sure, in Aristotle's own sketch of a best polis in *Pol.* 7–8 constitutional form sits so lightly on, and emerges so "naturally" from, highly wrought social matter that it is probably better not to see the result as an individuated polis at all, but as deploying the literary genre of ideal states to further draw out the normative implications of Aristotle's genealogy of the polis in *Pol.* 1 and his critique of Plato and other reformers in *Pol.* 2. As we might expect, the citizens of Aristotle's ideal state spend a good deal of time in civic celebration, musical performances, and other forms of leisure (*Pol.* 7.14.1333a31–b3). There is, however, no founding legislator and the laws are customary. Citizens simply take turns ruling and being ruled, the young deferring to their elders until the generational cycle, rather than some explicit constitutional procedure, brings them their turn (*Pol.* 7.9.1329a6–16). The presumption is that a more fully spelled-out constitution is not needed because in this

fantasy Aristotle is imagining that the three prima facie just claims on which citizenship rest – free birth, wealth, and virtue (*Pol.* 3.13.1283a30–40; *Eth. Nic.*
5.3.1131a25–8; see Keyt 1991b; F. Miller 1995) – happen to coincide ("as if in
answer to a prayer:" *Pol.* 4.1.1288b23; 7.4.1325b37) in each and every citizen and
household. Yet this is precisely what fails to occur in the open space that looms up
between the natural development of the polis and the achievement of its end in
particular, real social circumstances. Practical wisdom affects real history when a
lawmaker imposes constitutional form, and often class compromise, on proximate
social matter in which the freeborn and the wealthy happen not to be as virtuous as
Aristotle's good men.[6] Those who bring virtue, wealth, and free birth to the table all
deserve something. But they hardly ever deserve the same thing (*Pol.* 3.9.1280a9–15;
Eth. Nic. 5.3.1131a10–30). Aristotle is keenly aware that in circumstances as contingent as these failure to impose a good constitution, or perversion of one, is common.

Enter history, if somewhat typologically. Although Aristotle purports to base his
generalizations on data provided by the narrative histories of over 150 poleis (of
which only the *Constitution of Athens* has been found), he thinks there are two ways
of imposing constitutional form on social matter: those that accord with nature (*kata
phusin*) because they conserve, reach, or restore the shared leisured life of the natural
polis, and those that are contrary to nature (*kata phusin*). The latter have about them
an "element of mastery" because they dedifferentiate the social matter of the polis.
They turn it aside (*parekbasein*) from its articulated natural *telos*, in which the master–
slave relation is fully contained within the household and disappears from the public
sphere.[7] "Regimes that look only to the advantage of the rulers," Aristotle writes,
"are deviations [*parekbaseis*] from correct [*orthōn*] regimes. For they involve mastery.
But a *polis* is a community of free persons" (*Pol.* 3.6.1279a17–22, trans. Lord 1984,
punctuation amended; see 7.1.1323b41–1324a23; 1325a27–9; 2.1324b3–5;
14.1333a3–6 for more links between slavery, constitutional deviation, and failure to
prize leisured freedom).

On each side of the normative divide between correct and deviant constitutions lie
three possible generic constitutional forms, allowing Aristotle to re-derive Plato's
sixfold taxonomy of constitutions in *Statesman* from his own theory (*Pol.*
4.2.1289b5–10). When a single person is disproportionately more virtuous (and
economically secure) than other citizens kingship accords with nature and justice
(*Eth. Nic.* 8.10.1160b4–7; *Pol* 3.17.1288a16).[8] Tyranny, the polar opposite of
kingship and the extreme of all departures from what accords with nature (*Pol.*
4.2.1289b1–2), exists when a single person without virtue establishes unjust mastery
over other citizens and denies their rightful claims to participation in self-governance
(*Pol.* 3.8.1279b16–17; *Eth. Nic.* 8.10.1160b1–4). An aristocracy obtains when virtue
is more evenly divided between a number of citizens and families who rule in accord
with the common good (*Pol.* 3.7.1279a34–7). Elite rule degenerates into oligarchy,
however, when it is the wealth, not the virtue, of the elite that imposes its norms,
values, and interests on both the people and the virtuous (*Pol.* 3.8.1279b17–18; see
2.11.1273a35–b7). When both the virtuous and the wealthy are constrained by the
poor, who in almost all cases comprise a majority of the freeborn, one or another sort
of democracy exists (*Pol.* 3.8.1279b17–20). Although some are less bad than others,

Aristotle says that all democracies work against nature because they exercise mastery over the virtuous and the wealthy, who do not deserve to be collectively subordinated to the many. This condition can be alleviated if collective action or a wise legislator moves existing states toward what Aristotle calls a constitutional regime or polity (*politeia*), which empowers a moderately wealthy middle class judiciously to allocate different offices and other social goods to oligarchical and democratic elements (*Pol.* 4.6.1293a33–4).

History enters with a vengeance into Aristotle's political theory with his recognition that by his own time the claims of virtue, wealth, and free birth have separated so far that almost all contemporary states take themselves to be either oligarchies or democracies, the wealthy sanctimoniously pretending to be virtuous, aristocratic, and genteel, the people thinking of themselves as the collectively infallible guardians of their polis's spirit (*Pol.* 4.11.1296a21–7). This situation seems to have occurred because of the massive increase of wealth and military power since what Aristotle calls "the olden days" (*ta archeia*, *Pol.* 3.4.1277b2–3, for example). Money and might have combined to enlarge the franchise to meet military needs (*Pol.* 4.13.1297b16–28). This requires paying poor people to abstain from the labor of their bodies and the work of their hands enough to think of themselves as leisured citizens, who promptly dissipate that leisure into mere entertainment (*bios apolaustikos*). Just what, if anything, Aristotle proposes to do about the prevalence of deviant states is not entirely clear. He sometimes recommends constitutional regimes or polities, a proposal that has had wide historical influence (*Pol.* 3.13.1284b19–20). But he also seems to intimate that monarchy (of a certain benevolently absolute type) is in a better position to turn a polis toward the highest uses of leisured self-sufficiency (*Pol.* 4.2.1289a40–b1).

Ethical Sticking Points in Aristotle's Political Theory

A slave by nature is a possession ... a human being that is a physically separable organ of action of another human being ... (*Pol.* 1.4.1254a16–17)

A slave has no deliberative part [of the soul] [*bouleutikon*] at all. A woman has it, but not authoritatively [*akuron*]. A [free] child has it too, but incompletely. (*Pol.* 1.13.1260a11–13)

Aristotle's constitutional taxonomy has had more influence on the subsequent history of political theory than his appeal to nature in grounding it. Especially in the long history of republican theorizing about constitutional states and class compromises, this influence has led to interpretations of the distinction between correct and deviant constitutions as holding between schemes that are and are not governed by law or, alternatively, between those that aim at or subvert the common good. The former view is unsupported by the text. With Plato's Thrasymachus in *Republic* 1, Aristotle recognizes not only that tyrannies, oligarchies, and democracies have laws too, but that enough justice, if not friendship, is embodied in those laws to require citizens to obey them. The criterion of common good is more supportable – Thomas Aquinas, for example, made much of it – but it has seldom been spelled out in ways that stress Aristotle's substantive conception of the common good as a shared life of leisure pursuits. In this chapter, I have used this substantive conception to draw contrasts between Aristotle *ad litteram* and appropriations of his thought. In one way, the result should feel liberating. When it comes to human beings, as I noted earlier, much of what Aristotle means by nature we call culture. It is in this space that ethical norms appear. In this space, too, arises much that we ourselves can regard as ideal. Still, in the matter of individuating human political animals, Aristotle's implicit conception of culture is "thicker" than even the thickest of contemporary culture concepts (on "thick culture," see Geertz 1973). As a result, his assumptions about the fundamental and irremediable inegalitarianism of cultural life reveal real ethical sticking points in his political theory. One can get around these difficulties. But, having done so, it is no longer clear that what remains will be Aristotle's theory.

Consider slavery. The history of Aristotle scholarship and Aristotelian philosophizing is haunted by his doctrine that some people are slaves by nature (*Pol.* 1.4.1254a12–17). This single greatest impediment to the appropriation of his ethics and politics has made desperation the mother of interpretive invention. He didn't really mean it, some say; it is a thinly disguised critique (Ambler 1987). He did mean it, but unreflectively; it was simply a cultural given (Williams 1993). He meant it all right, but only in ways that we too could accept, or at least excuse; his natural slaves are mentally damaged persons who can and should be put to work doing simple tasks (Nussbaum 1995; Schofield 1990). Unfortunately, Aristotle's theory of natural slavery is more deeply embedded in his political theory than any of these interpretations suggest. To be sure, chattel slavery, in which slaves are acquired in a commercial market into which the commodities they produce are fed back, is not justified by that theory. But household slavery is indispensable to it. The leisure-oriented value system that informs and supports political deliberation, choice, and action (*praxis*) depends on freeing not only heads of households, but their wives and children from bodily labor and its orientation toward "mere life," the inherent brutishness of which cannot mentally, emotionally, behaviorally, and even physiognomically (natural slaves are supposed to look like slaves, *Pol.* 1.5.1254b27–32) be transcended. Worse is Aristotle's smug conviction that cultures whose social structures are in his opinion unable to generate and sustain the role differentiations required for political life provide a steady supply of justly enslavable individuals. In particular, he thinks that Asians are fit to be enslaved (by war, not by commerce, *Pol.* 1.8.1256b24–6) – not because they lack intelligence of a calculative, planning sort, but because the social structures that generate them also propagate the deficiency in spirit (*thumos*) on which self-respect, devotion to fellow citizens, ethical norms, and so political life proper depends (*Pol.* 1.2.1252b4–9; *Pol.* 7.7.1327b23–33; Garver 1994).[9] It does not follow, of course, that such persons ought to be enslaved unless Aristotle thinks that since someone is always enslaving such people it might as well be Greeks, who can put them to good use in the construction of a leisured society. Unfortunately, he probably does think this (*Pol.* 3.1285a18–22).

Marx, among others, tried to find a way out by taking on board Aristotle's musings about Homer's fantasy that "each of the [inanimate] instruments might perform its work on command or by anticipation, as they assert those of Daedalus did, or the tripods of Hephaesthus … so that shuttles would weave themselves and picks play the lyre." In this event, "master craftsmen would no longer have need of subordinates or masters of slaves" (*Pol.* 1.4.1253b34–1254a1, trans. Lord 1984; see Hom. *Il.* 18.376). But Aristotle rejects this technological fix. He thinks that a householder or his wife who constantly uses labor-saving devices would be engaging too directly in tasks whose inherent instrumentalism would render them as vulgar as factory hands (about whose virtues Marx had a decidedly higher opinion). This is why he thinks of domestic slaves as extended organs of the master's physiology, not as instruments of production (*Pol.* 1.4.1254a1–8); why he thinks they must come under the control of moral, not technical, training (*Pol.* 1.13.1259b37–1260a8); and why he is contemptuous of "how-to-run-your-slave" advice (*Pol.* 1.7.1255b20–7). It is also why he wants the political system to constrain market activity, with its inherently vulgar values, and criticizes Plato for implicitly conceding the citizenly status of the artisans in *Republic* (*Pol.* 2.5.1264a25–6). In his own ideal state, production and exchange will be consigned entirely to foreigners who live in a port some distance from the polis and who interact with its slave-owning farmer-citizens only in carefully monitored sites (*Pol.* 7.6.1327a37–9). A lesson again and again taught by Aristotle's political philosophy is that its core values are threatened by commercializing and technologizing political life. Every move in this direction threatens his distinction between mere and good life, reducing politics to a function of civil society and construing shared leisure as mere entertainment.

A second ethical stumbling block is Aristotle's argument that even the freest of free women cannot be citizens. To be sure, Aristotle regrets that noble women, such as Helen or Hecuba, are sometimes enslaved (*Pol.* 1.6.1255a23–8). Free women administer the property that their husbands acquire (*Pol.* 3.4.1277b24–5) and play a crucial role in educating their sons to be citizens and their daughters to be wives of citizens, and so themselves must be virtuous and oriented toward good values. "Women are half of the free population and from their children come those who share in the constitution" (*Pol.* 1.13.1260b18–20). Why, then, should they not be citizens themselves? Aristotle's stated reason is that the deliberative judgments of free women are less authoritative than those of their husbands because their reason cannot transform their emotional structure quite as far (*Pol.* 1.13.1260a12–13). We see ideology at work whenever Aristotle's cultural analysis, which is natural in his teleological sense, gives way to reductionistic biological speculations about efficient causes, as in Aristotle's physiognomy of slaves, which even he does not quite believe (*Pol.* 1.5.1254b25–33). In the case of women's lack of authority, this tendency shows itself in his effort to trace the postulated limitation to women's embryological development, which fails to reproduce the paternal form and so constitutes a deviation from it (*Gen. an.* 2.3.737a28; see Mayhew 2004 for an attempted defense of Aristotle against the charge of ideological distortion). Should we conclude that this biologism is a grounded inference from his political-ethical theory, Aristotle's own misapplication of it, or an unreflective reflection of his times? All three, I think.

A third cluster of ethical difficulties arises from Aristotle's assertion that the citizenly life of engagement in the affairs of state and household (*bios politikos*) can be transcended by a relatively few people who are able to lead an even more leisure-oriented theoretical way of life (*bios theōrētikos*). Aristotle himself is among those who lead such a life, which includes raising to consciousness the nature and norms of political life. There has been considerable debate about whether this way of life is so superior that it transcends the bonds of polis life, rendering the intellectual as solitary as a god and as indifferent to social duties (*Eth. Nic.* 10.7.1177a11–1178a8). There is undeniably a tension between the *bios theōrētikos* and the *bios politikos* (Brown, this volume, chapter 31; Kraut 1989: 199). But it can be exaggerated. Aristotle says that, while there is a philosophy of human affairs (*ta anthropina philosophia*, *Eth. Nic.* 10.9.1181b15) and a political science (*epistēmē*), they would not be worth thinking about (humans not being the best things in the universe) if we were not inescapably interested, as human beings ourselves, in what we should do (*Eth. Nic.* 1.1.1095a5–6; 6.7.1141a20–30). It follows that social and political life would be theorized falsely by anyone who did not share in the virtuous norms that reveal its nature to thought. No one who fails to acknowledge and largely act in accordance with these norms could even grasp them. Uncovering the intelligibility of the political world, moreover, is a valuable enterprise; it not only presupposes the moral virtues, but justifies the leisure-oriented values of correct poleis (*Pol.* 7.3.1325b16–21). It follows that good states must do more than merely tolerate philosophers. They should hold them up as exemplars of their own fundamental commitments (Depew 1991; Broadie 1991: 383–98). This, combined with an urge to distance himself from philosophical quietism, is why Aristotle says that the theoretical life is itself a life of action (*praxis*) (*Pol.* 7.3.1325b14–32; see in this volume, Brown, chapter 31; Chappell, chapter 25). Nor was this an entirely idle thought. Under the influence of the Lyceum, the Macedonian rulers of Alexandria predicated the legitimacy of their rule on making the cultivation of artistic and scientific uses of leisure the very point of civilized life. The downside of this program, however, was the establishment of an imperial *raj* over native peoples, often justified by Aristotle's contempt for slavish barbarians (Nagle 2006: 315).

Aristotle's political science is also practical because it takes itself to be able to provide guidance to rulers. The general tenor of this advice is to urge rulers to move from bad to good constitutions, in part by illuminating them about the greater, more differentiated range of possibilities than the simple oligarchy–democracy duality in which fourth century political discourse was mired (*Pol.* 4.1.1289a6–11). A difficulty is that Aristotle is willing to give advice not only to well motivated statesmen who would try to move deviant states to the nearest accessible correct form (*Pol.* 3.13.1284b19–20), but also to those who wish to preserve deviant forms, even tyrannies (*Pol.* 5.11.1313a33–1315b10, sounding very much like Machiavelli). One might blunt this objection by pointing to Aristotle's recognition that social stability is itself a good (*Pol.* 6.5.1319b33–40). This seems right, but only if stability is not seen, as it sometimes is, as a separate, second-best good. Even badly governed poleis are still poleis, that is, communities whose way of life is superior to those of gregarious, scattered, and especially solitary animals. Aristotle is keenly aware that, although virtue armed and well equipped preserves the polis (*Pol.* 1.6.1255a12–16), the uncoupling of wealth and might from virtue in what he clearly regards as modern times threatens to turn the Greek world toward the viciousness of armed solitaries. Under these conditions stability might not seem to him all that different from political improvement (*Pol.* 4.1.1288b28–30).

Attempts to discount Aristotle's views about slavery, sexism, and imperialism are fruitless. Even when his efforts to ground these practices in embryological consider- ations are recognized as ideological, they still remain too close to the very point of his political theory to simply ignore. But that does not mean that Aristotle's political ethics is crude realism. On the contrary, his aim is to foster institutions and practices in which the highest capacities of human beings can be developed. We, too, share that aspiration. The problem, as Hegel, that great reader of Aristotle, saw is that his philosophy epitomizes the proposition that "only some are free." The modern separ- ation of ethics from politics, and the concomitant insistence that the former must be the measure of the latter, was and remains an ongoing effort to insist that "all are free." We should never think that that demand has been fully met. Reading Aristotle can help us reflect critically on how embedded in our own institutions, practices, and anthropological assumptions our formally universal ethical norms actually are. It can also help us to see, as he did, that the point of ethics is to foster good politics.

FURTHER READING

Those working through the text of *Politics* have at their disposal three comprehensive com- mentaries: Newman 1887–1902; Schütrumpf 1991–2005, which is recent and is especially good on the vast number of Aristotle's intertextual references to Plato's dialogues; and Simpson 1998, which consists of syllogistic reconstructions of the arguments of each chapter written in the spirit, and sometimes under the tutelage, of Thomas Aquinas (who himself wrote an incomplete commentary on *Politics* in the high Middle Ages that has now appeared in English (Regan 2007)). Another commentary that may be usefully consulted is Susemihl and Hicks 1984. Barker 1946 sometimes shows up on reading lists. It is not entirely trustworthy either as a translation or a commentary.

The student will find various volumes of the compact Clarendon (Oxford) translations and commentaries helpful. Although Saunders's frequent confessions of incomprehension are distracting, Saunders 1995 summarizes the definitional and theoretical problems of the first two books of *Politics*. In reading these arguments it becomes clear that one cannot understand Aristotle's view about the polis unless one understands his account of the household (*oikos*). Brendan Nagle has written an informative book on the subject (see Nagle 2006). Nagle argues for a tighter fit between Aristotle's political theory and Greek political reality than has been customary. The Clarendon series also offers David Keyt and Richard Robinson's translation of and commentary on *Politics* 3–4 (Keyt and Robinson 1995) and Keyt's translation and commentary on *Politics* 5–6 (Keyt 1999). Keyt 1999 deals with the principles of justice and political realism. The same topics are at the heart of F. Miller 1995. In his Clarendon translation and commentary on *Politics* 7–8 (1997), Richard Kraut deals intensively with the tension between the active and philosophical lives, as he does in Kraut 2002. See also Natali 2001.

Scholarly articles on the most interesting and persistent problems in Aristotle's *Politics* can be found in Keyt and Miller 1991 and in Patzig 1990.

Treatments of Aristotle's ethical treatises are numerous. Those most helpful in the present context take seriously the relation between ethics and politics. Among these are Cooper 1975; Broadie 1991; and Garver 2006.

NOTES

Unless otherwise noted, translations are my own. Many of these are adapted from Lord 1984. In my view this is the best English translation currently available. Where I adopt Lord's rendering *in toto* I cite him.

1   I am using the term liberal in its foundational nineteenth century sense. It refers to a politics built on equal access to the laws, universal voting rights, laissez-faire economics, and freedom to behave as one wants in private. Twentieth century conservatives and liberals are both liberal in this sense, even though their stresses differ.

2   It is sometimes said that humans who exceed political life by engaging in the theoretical life proper to gods are solitary animals as well. For reasons against this, see Depew 1995: 176–7.

3   For Aristotle a species-specific capacity (*dunamis*), once taken up by an individual's ontogeny (first nature) and habituation (second nature), is no longer available for any further actualization. Its potentiality has become the capacity to continue to be its substantial self, as it were. See Kosman 1984; 1987: 366. Thus barbarians, having come to be the individual human beings they are by internalizing the dispositions, behaviors, and ways of life of their cultures have no remaining capacity for polis life either as heads of households or citizens. Accordingly, from the fact that "political animal" refers paradigmatically to capacities for life in a polis household and active engagement in political life it by no means follows that every real human being has an accessible capacity for such a life. Inside most human beings there does not lurk a frustrated citizen just dying to get out – any more than there exists the rational economic man that for the last three centuries has been Europe's replacement for this mythical being.

4   The technical reason is that complete substances cannot be parts of complete substances.

5   Chappell, this volume, chapter 25, uses the "material needs" sense of *autarkeia* to gloss Aristotle's "natural" as "based on needs, desires, and urges." Through this lens, he sees Aristotle as less subtle, if more empirical, than Plato. This analysis does not recognize that Aristotle follows Plato in tracing the genesis of the polis to a point where the satisfaction of material needs dialectically reverses itself, although, in contrast to Plato, he takes the family rather than the exchange economy as the locus of differentiation and self-limitation. Chappell's approach finds self-sufficiency (*autarkeia*) in the philosopher's rejection of bodily needs, but not in the nonslavish freedom from needs possessed by political communities that consciously limit the pursuit of mere life to what is needed for leading the good life.

6   The addition of constitutional art to the social polis poses difficult questions for the natural status of individual poleis. See Keyt 1991a and F. Miller 1995 for statements of the problem and possible solutions.

7   That Hannah Arendt (1958) makes much of these differentiations is not odd; Aristotle was her source. But she exaggerates the difference between the citizenly sphere and the household, conceiving the former as permeated by friendship (*philia*) and the latter by violence (*bia*). The issue turns on the status of household slavery, which Arendt believes undermines

the very possibility of friendship in the household. It is difficult to find in Aristotle a claim anything like this. The issue was first posed by Hegel.

8 Aristotle argues that the definition of a citizen (*politēs*) is best realized in a democracy (*Pol.* 3.1.1275b4–5). That is not because he favors democracy, but because even kingship of an absolute sort logically depends on judgments of relative merit that are conceptually available only on the assumption of citizenly deliberation. Just as the concept of citizen emerges from the concept of householder (*oikonomikos*), so the concept of ruler (*archontos*) emerges from that of citizen (*politēs*) (*Pol.* 3.4.1277a20–3). Aristotle makes Plato's inadequate differentiation of these differences a guiding theme of his entire political theory (*Pol.* 1.1.1252a7–17).

9 The assumption that all normal humans are born with a more or less equal and equally accessible capacity for rational deliberation and can flourish as soon as they are placed in an appropriate environment has generated the notion that human rationality is simply the generic calculative capacity we call IQ. This assumption dominates the literature on Aristotle's natural slaves. Garver (1994) has shown that Aristotle's natural slaves are not especially deficient in calculative intelligence; their incapacity for deliberation and choice derives from affective weaknesses that are endemic according to Aristotle in many societies.

PART VI

Constructing Political Narrative

CHAPTER 27

Imitating Virtue and Avoiding Vice: Ethical Functions of Biography, History, and Philosophy

Charles W. Hedrick, Jr

In his speech honoring the memory of the Cypriot king Euagoras, probably written around 370 BC, Isocrates claimed to be the first to praise a man's virtue (*aretē*) in prose (cf. Momigliano 1971: ch. 3; Halliwell 1990). Traditionally, he says, such encomia had been the monopoly of poets, who, with their fantastic embellishments and seductive rhythms, enjoyed an advantage. Orators, by contrast, were restricted to common speech and relevant facts (Isoc. *Euagoras* 8–11). Isocrates' predecessors, such as Gorgias, had praised famous figures of the legendary past, but none had dared speak about the great of the contemporary age, for fear of envy (5–6, 8). The great may be honored with fine monuments and portraits, but such representations are only rudimentary and superficial: character may be reflected in physical appearance (e.g. 23), but verbal portrayals of deeds (*praxeis*) and intentions (*dianoiai*) are far more useful, and by their nature can be disseminated easily, wherever men can speak (73–4). Furthermore, while "no one can make his bodily nature resemble sculpture or paintings, it is easy to imitate the characters [*tropoi*] of others and their intentions [*dianoiai*], as represented in language" (75). His composition will inspire auditors, and particularly the youth, to imitation (5–6, 75, 80). By tricking out his account of the life of Euagoras with rhetoric, Isocrates can transport the souls (*psuchagōgein*) of his audience, just as the poets do, and incite them to emulation of virtue (10, 73, 76–7, 80).

As a rule, modern professional historians have despised biography as the foppish, degenerate love-child of prim history, a narcissistic clothes-horse for rhetorical frippery. Isocrates claims, however, that biography is written for the most serious of reasons, to provide instruction in virtue, and that rhetorical flourishes are essential to the project: affective speech excites the sentiments of readers, and emotional engagement, admiration or contempt, motivates readers to imitate virtue and despise vice. The ancient Greeks and Romans believed that ethical instruction had to be

A Companion to Greek and Roman Political Thought, First Edition. Edited by Ryan K. Balot.
© 2013 Blackwell Publishing Ltd. Published 2013 by Blackwell Publishing Ltd.

communicated in evocative, inspiring language, specifically the morally charged idiom of praise and blame.

Isocrates' speech stands at the beginning of the Greco-Roman biographical tradition; his ideas would have a decisive impact on the future course not only of biography, but of history as well. As he says, poets had long sung the praises of great men. Historians too had shown an interest in the people who populated their stories, but this interest was incidental. Isocrates made the narrative of the individual's life and the elucidation of his virtues the cynosure of the story. His essay was doubtless stimulated by the writings of the Socratics, and in turn stimulated them. The first preserved Greek biography, Xenophon's account of the life of the Spartan king Agesilaus, was written around 360 and transparently relies on Isocrates' encomium of Euagoras.

Isocrates' emphasis on virtue (*aretē*) as a quality of character is novel and complicit with the emergence of the genre of biography. The idea of virtue was traditional; in the earlier authors, however, it was understood to refer above all to virtue in warfare, valor. This virtue is competitive, and was evaluated in the way we might judge the excellence of an athlete: by its effectiveness. The word *aretē* connoted at all times in Greek the notion of function, but by the third quarter of the fifth century, under the influence of the sophistic movement, the semantic range of the word had expanded to include also virtues that we can characterize as social, or cooperative, such as justice and self-control. Such virtues are not to be understood in terms of objective effectiveness, but, as Isocrates suggests, in relation to subjective disposition and intent: character. Here we see the beginnings of another of the central ideas of ancient ethical narratives: deeds are exemplary and can consequently expose the connection between the concrete and the abstract, the specific and the general, the apparent and the hidden: external action and internal moral quality.

In the *Euagoras* Isocrates distinguishes three kinds of compositions that communicate virtue: poetry, pictures, and speeches of praise. Of these, only the encomium has the potential to reveal the inward character. It is remarkable that he does not include philosophical writing in the list.[1] Since the 420s sophists had been exploring the nature of *aretē*; and after the execution of Socrates in 399, episodes in the life of the philosopher had been recounted by a number of writers (Danzig 2003: 285). Platonic dialogues often revisited the nature of virtue. By putting such ideas in the mouth of Socrates and situating discussions in contentious, vivid encounters, Plato presented Socrates as himself an exemplary character, an avatar of virtue. Xenophon too concluded his *Memorabilia* with an account of Socrates' teaching and example in virtue (4.8.11).

It may also seem surprising that Isocrates ignores the contributions of earlier history-writing to the celebration of virtue. Biography, though evidently regarded as distinct from history from its beginnings, nevertheless shared similar concerns, and from the fourth century on its preoccupation with the virtues of the individual came to be foregrounded in histories as well. Even so, historians before the time of Isocrates and Xenophon, such as Herodotus and Thucydides, while interested in virtue, did not engage so much in the kind of character study that preoccupies Isocrates. They tended to think of virtue in terms of its traditional, competitive aspect, and so did not understand it in terms of internal character, but in relation to the realization of power.

Aristotle's *Nicomachean Ethics* marks a watershed in the history of Greek conceptions of virtue: it sums up a tradition and, through the abiding influence of the Peripatetic school, determines an agenda for the future; its influence will be felt to the end of antiquity and beyond. Aristotle, unlike Plato, was concerned in his philosophy to rationalize commonly held social views; as a consequence his ethical philosophy is manifestly linked to contemporary ethical practices. He also usefully poses the question of the practical utility of writing about virtue at all, and so suggests a framework for considering the relative value of the discursive arguments of philosophers and narrative descriptions of historians and biographers. For the ancients, historians, biographers and philosophers all wrote to educate: the most important reason to read about virtue is to become virtuous oneself (cf. Burnyeat 1980). Narrative proceeds by example; philosophy by argument; narrative incites, philosophy reasons. Which offers more effective instruction?

In this essay, with Aristotle as my guide, I consider the ancient association of ethical instruction with evocative prose narrative, especially biography and history, and the relationship of such exemplary narratives to the discursive arguments of philosophy. In the argument I will give more attention to the positive idea of virtue than to vice; nevertheless, the two are of a piece, two sides of the same coin. Narratives of praise indicate virtues to be imitated as blame does vices to be avoided; the two serve the same function, as Livy later famously suggested in the proem to his history (10) (Stadter, this volume, chapter 29). I begin with an account of the idea of virtue in ancient Greece, outlining the history of its development in early authors and philosophers down to Aristotle. I then discuss the role of virtue in the fifth century BC historians, Herodotus and Thucydides, and the changes that come to history-writing with the fourth century and the rise of biography. Finally I turn to the question of the relationship between exemplary narrative and philosophical discourse and the potential of each to instruct, giving special attention to Aristotle's treatment of the problem in the *Nicomachean Ethics*.

Greek Virtue

The contemporary western tendency to think of morality in terms of abstract rules or laws of behavior owes its beginnings to Christian doctrine. Many subsequent philosophical theories, even the avowedly irreligious, were erected on religious bedrock, that is, on the presumption that morality was to be explained in terms of some general rule or law. Some 50 years ago in an epochal article G. E. M. Anscombe argued that the most influential statements of modern western ethical philosophy, including Kant's deontological ethics with their "categorical imperative" and the utilitarian pleasure principle developed by Hume and J. S. Mill, relied, willy-nilly, on defunct religious belief. The idea of law presumes a lawgiver. Absent God, there can be no foundation for moral law. As an alternative to the "philosophy of moral law,"

Anscombe urged a return to the classical Greek philosophy (Anscombe 1958). In contrast with religious, legalistic notions about ethics, classical thought about ethics began from virtue, *aretē*. The great exposition of classical "virtue ethics" is found in Aristotle's *Nicomachean Ethics* (Depew, this volume, chapter 26). Aristotle took the position that ethics are to be understood in terms of individual dispositions. So, for example, where modern-day protesters invoke justice as if it were an entitlement, Aristotle understands the word as a personal commitment to giving people what they deserve. So he begins his discussion of justice in book 5 of the *Nicomachean Ethics* by defining justice as a disposition (*hexis*): "we see that all men mean by justice that disposition that makes them perform just actions, which makes them act justly and wish what is just" (*Eth. Nic.* 5.1). Laws are impersonal, virtues are characterological; laws are absolute and systematic, virtues are circumstantial and pragmatic. Since Anscombe's time these arguments have been developed in a movement known as "Virtue (or sometimes Aretaic) Ethics."

The Greek word for virtue, *aretē*, derives from a root (the *ar-* part of the word) that connotes the idea of "the fitting." Thus virtue was generally understood in terms of functional excellence. The word was used by the Greeks as broadly as we might use the word "excellence."[2] Thus, for example, the virtue of a racehorse might be to run swiftly; the virtues of a hammer might include efficiency in driving or drawing nails. This popular idea of function underpinned the arguments developed by Greek philosophers (cf. Dover 1974: 1–5, 66–73).

Homer celebrated the virtues of the warrior, including courage, or even simple efficiency in killing. Of course, other, more social virtues, such as justice, *dikaiosunē*, and self-control, *sophrosunē*, are known from the time of Homer on, but they are not as a rule conceived in relationship to the competitive virtues, nor are they as highly valued. The history of Greek ethical thought to the fourth century can be understood in terms of a developing opposition and ultimate reconciliation of the brutal excellence of *aretē* with the social virtues (Adkins 1960: 3–7). The beginnings of this development can be traced as early as the philosophy of the archaic period: so, while Democritus continues to equate virtue and courage in his book "On *Aretē*, or Courage [*Andragathia*]" (Diog. Laert. 9.46), Heraclitus (fr. 112) can remark that "the greatest of the virtues is self-control [*sophrosunē*]" (Kahn 1985). The relationship of the competitive and cooperative ideas of virtue became a philosophical problem under the influence of the sophistic movement in the second half of the fifth century BC. The particular issues debated can be followed in the series of concepts to which it was opposed. So, for example, when virtue was coupled with pleasure (*hedonē*) it connoted asceticism; when with fortune (*tuchē*), industriousness. The most important of these dichotomies was the contrast between virtue and artifice (*technē*). This dichotomy recapitulated many of the traditional social issues surrounding virtue. Virtue, for example, had long been conceived as an aristocratic quality, while *technē* was the realm of the lower-class artisan; virtue was inherited, *technē* acquired. On the other hand, the sophists claimed to be able to teach virtue, and if virtue was an innate quality, it could not be taught (Guthrie 1971: 250–60). The social elite claimed a monopoly on natural virtue. Protagoras responded by merging virtue and artifice: in Plato's dialogue he refers both to the *aretai* and *technai* of craftsmen (*Prt.* 322 b and d).[3] People, like animals, inherited the capacity for certain activities; these native capacities however can be developed with training. Protagoras' position becomes dogma in the Greco-Roman world. By the time of Horace it is a truism: "As eagles give birth to eagles, so the strong and good give birth to the strong and good; teaching however advances inbred power" (*Odes* 4.4.33).

The association of *aretē* with competitive aristocratic excellence was too strong to be easily overthrown. The assimilation of the competitive and cooperative virtues, of *aretē* and *dikaiosunē*, begins with a modification in the connotation of their opposites, the shameful (*aischra*) and base (*kaka*). In the latter part of the fifth century BC these are increasingly equated with injustice (*adika*). This complex of vice is then opposed to both competitive *aretē* and cooperative *dikaiosunē* – a contrast that strengthened the sophist tendency to distinguish between natural and conventional virtue (Adkins 1960: ch. 9).

Plato was preoccupied with the question of virtue (cf. above all the *Meno* and *Protagoras*). He especially insisted that the virtues could not be considered piecemeal, in terms of particular personal manifestations, but that the problem had to be the general definition of virtue (this is a manifestation of the notorious "Platonic Theory of Ideas").[4] To the extent that we can recognize certain characters as just, for example, there must be some general idea of "the just," and the problem for those who love justice is to know this abstraction. The Platonic "idea" is not the same as a religious notion of a divinely ordained law, it is an abstraction implied by its particular manifestations. Christian justice, by contrast, is an imposed and received law, a law not of our making, and perhaps even inscrutable to us, as the ways of god are ultimately inaccessible to man.[5]

At the same time Plato self-consciously turned the discussions surrounding *aretē* away from the competitive abilities that had been emphasized in the Homeric accounts of warfare (see Pl. *Leg.* 666e and 922a). Such functional excellence continued to be recognized as virtue, and routinely served as a point of departure for discussion of the cooperative virtues. With Plato, however, the central problem of virtue becomes a recognizable question of ethics in the modern, popular sense: What is the virtue of a human being, generally understood? And what does this virtue have in common with the functional *aretē* of a knife? Here he was opposing the sophistic tendency to understand virtue as something circumstantial, defined according to context. The Socratic solution to this question devolved unsurprisingly to the question of knowledge: if only we can know what virtue is we shall be virtuous; no one with such knowledge can be unvirtuous, because vice is a falling off from excellence, and is thus self-destructive. And who would knowingly harm themselves?

Aristotle inherited these ideas about virtue from Plato and others. Nevertheless, though Plato had been his teacher and friend, he did not hesitate to disagree with him, rejecting also his "theory of ideas" and the related argument that virtue was tied to knowledge: "Plato is a friend, but truth is a greater friend." (*Eth. Nic.* 1.4).[6] Experience proved that people could behave unvirtuously though they knew what was just and good (*Eth. Nic.* 7.1–2); Plato himself had allowed Socrates to admit the point (*Prt.* 352d–e). For Aristotle, virtue is not realized through knowledge, but through practice. In fact, Aristotle argues, there can be no philosophy of ethics:

virtuous behavior arises from imitation, discipline, and habit not from philosophical proofs. The philosopher can at most aspire to clarify the thoughts of those who are already virtuous. As a consequence, he denied Plato's notion that virtue could be understood in the absolute at all; he agreed with the sophists, that virtue had to be understood circumstantially. As he says in the *Politics* (1260a25), "Those who speak in general terms, saying that virtue 'is the well being of the soul' or 'right action' or the like, are wrong. To enumerate the virtues, as Gorgias did is much nearer the mark than to make this kind of definition." Virtuous people do not act in consultation with some airy-fairy "idea" or for that matter inflexible moral law; rather they act as circumstances permit, in conformity to their disposition. This conception of virtue implies a novel approach to the idea of the individual, a focus on internal character rather than external action.

For Aristotle, ethics elucidates our actions. As the name (from "ethos") suggests, ethics are a disposition, or habit, or even character, and this character finds its particular manifestations in particular virtues or vices. Since the Greeks understood virtue as functional excellence, the relation between its actual and ideal end (*telos*) provides the standard of evaluation: people are to be accounted virtuous to the extent that they achieve their end. Of course individuals conceived for example as economic actors may have different ends: a doctor's, for example, is to heal, as a cobbler's is to make shoes. When we contemplate humankind in its humanity, however, what is its end? Various "ends" may be prioritized. Money, for example, may be the immediate end of many human undertakings, but it is of no use in and of itself, but only for what it can buy; it must therefore be considered subordinate to other ends. Conceived at the most general level, Aristotle argues that the specific natural quality that discriminates people from animals is their ability to think: he consequently argues that the "natural" virtue of people is intellectual excellence.[7] Against this he allows for the "moral" virtues – justice, courage, temperance and so on – which are to be judged against the ultimate aspiration of human life: happiness, or fulfillment (*eudaimonia*).

For Aristotle, it is not that proper exercise of the virtues *leads* to the acquisition of happiness; because virtue is a disposition, its practice properly *is* fulfillment or happiness, as the possession of health *is* well-being. In such cases (happiness, health) the end is subsumed in the practice itself. Thus, in contrast to modern law-based theories of morality, the Aristotelian virtue ethics focus on character rather than accomplishment, on being good, rather than on doing good. For this reason it makes sense to say, as Aristotle does (*Eth. Nic.* 2.4), that a good action is not to be understood by appeal to some external standard of morality. What makes an action good is that it is done by a person of virtuous character, because it is good only insofar as it is a fulfillment of human nature; the goodness of the action is merely the character expressing itself externally. This way of understanding, though alien to modern popular understanding of morality, allows for almost infinite refinement in the assessment of the moral quality of action. It has always been a problem for legalistically minded moral philosophers that proper moral action requires situational thinking; a rule-based approach to moral action, mindlessly and brutally applied, quickly leads to ethical absurdity. The point is assumed by the common qualification that in ethics intention matters. The disinterested act of helping an elderly lady across the street may be ethically admirable, even if it results in the pedestrians being killed by a truck. The same act, committed with the selfish intent of gaining her confidence in order to defraud her of her pension, is morally despicable, even if the plot fails and is never found out. In such cases, what matters is not the act or even its consequences, but the disposition of the actor: what makes an act virtuous is not that it conforms to a certain type or rule, but that the agent is in a certain state of mind when the act is accomplished: he must act with knowledge, choose the act deliberately and for its own sake, and the act must spring from a permanent disposition (*Eth. Nic.* 2.4.3) (Williams 2006a).

Virtue and Exemplary Narrative

According to Aristotle, virtue is a "condition of the soul," of which there are three kinds: emotion, capacity, and disposition. We neither praise nor blame people for their emotions or for their capacities; consequently virtues (and vices) must be dispositions (*hexeis*) (*Eth. Nic.* 2.5.5). The association of virtue here with praise and blame is important and seldom emphasized.[8] It is not that people should be virtuous in order to earn praise or blame, though as Aristotle points out elsewhere praise is a sweet reward for virtue. People are virtuous because of their dispositions, which make it possible for them to accomplish noble deeds. It is rather that praise and blame are the criteria by which we can identify virtues among the "conditions of the soul." It is only through praise and blame that virtue can be either described or appreciated; this is the language of virtue. Praise, Aristotle says, is about the relation of its object to an absolute standard. Just so Greek virtue, *aretē*, is about the striving for what is good, and for this reason it is deserving of praise. By contrast, it seems absurd to praise what is absolute; we do not praise the gods, because this would imply that they are judged against a human standard. Instead we honor them (*Eth. Nic.* 1.12.1–4). Praise, like virtue, is inherently relative; it does not reflect being, but longing. In this respect the nature of praise recapitulates that of virtue. By this criterion Isocrates' encomium is not just appropriate, but necessary as a vehicle for any practical discussion of virtue.

As virtue is a quality of character, it cannot be directly apprehended; it is manifested only indirectly, in behavior: as Aristotle remarks, for those who would know the nature of virtue, "it is necessary to use visible evidence for what is invisible" (*Eth. Nic.* 2.2.6) (Halliwell 1990: 51–2). In narratives of virtue, then, deeds described must be understood as examples. "Exemplarity" is the chief form of "argument" in narrative accounts of virtue. We might define an example as a generalized particular: that is, it is a specific, understood as standing in place of something abstract or absolute (cf. Lyons 1990; Gelley 1995). The nature of the example recapitulates the Aristotelian definition of praise: by praising a thing, we relate it to an absolute standard; that is to say, we treat it as exemplary.

Traditionally two distinct kinds of examples have been recognized. The first is the kind of example used in argument: a particularity that is regarded as illustrative of a general rule or law. The second is the moral example: a particular person or thing that is regarded as worthy of imitation. The two, though distinct, are related, even reducible. It is precisely the general aspect of the example that makes it imitable, and it is the desire to imitate that leads to the recognition of the general aspect. What makes the individual worthy of imitation is the perception that his quality or qualities partake of something larger – moral standards – in which the imitator may potentially share. A moral deed is an action perceived as exemplary; what makes a deed exemplary is the perception that it is worthy of emulation or contempt; emulation, the desire to assimilate oneself to what is admirable or avoid what is despicable, provides the minimum basis for generation of a community of moral agents (Alderman 1982).

The effectiveness of exemplarity is ultimately based on identification, or more precisely, the longing for identification. So for the past to have an exemplary ethical force, present and past must be regarded as forming a continuum. A senior colleague can serve as an example for me to the extent that we share common circumstances; if our situations become incomparable then his example becomes irrelevant. So, if I were to say that my older colleagues are the "children of another generation," I would not be saying that their behavior is bad (or good), but dismissing them altogether as ethical beings: their example has become morally irrelevant (Koselleck 1985; Hedrick 2006: 48–51).

In the Greco-Roman tradition, at least from the fourth century BC on, history was regarded as a form of ethical teaching (*askēsis*). This attitude should be understood as underpinning traditional historical narratives even where it is not explicitly avowed. Historians fostered a nuanced sense of their culture's standards of right and wrong not by expounding philosophical rules but by presenting examples, from which readers abstracted the nature of virtue and vice. It can be difficult for moderns to understand the ethical dimension of ancient historiography, because it presumes an ethically absolute vision of the past (Hedrick 2005). Ethics were decisively displaced from historiography and from modern understanding generally with the rise and spread of German historicism in the course of the nineteenth century. Historicist method is a form of systems analysis: actions must be interpreted contextually, in accordance with the historical unities of time and space, rather than in light of some absolute standard of knowledge or morals. Thought itself is understood to be historically conditioned. From the historicist perspective, ethical commitments impede understanding. Historians may allow themselves to be personally outraged by the material they study, but the task at hand for historians is not to praise or condemn, but to understand (Hedrick 2006: 1–26).

Some of the presumptions of exemplarity, ideas about the unity of past and present and of the prestige of tradition, are implicit in all Greek narratives about the past, although the exhortation to emulation, so important in the Greek traditions of biography and history-writing after the end of the fifth century, is scarcely to be found earlier. Already in the *Iliad* and the *Odyssey* we find the notion that the men of the past were stronger, more warlike, and better. The idea through which the attitude toward tradition is articulated is *kleos* (renown). The Homeric influence is palpable in the opening lines of the first preserved Greek history, the investigation (*historiē*) of Herodotus. Herodotus claims that he writes for three reasons: so that the deeds of men should not be evanescent; so that the great and marvelous accomplishments alleged by Greeks and Barbarians should not lose their renown (*kleos*); and to explain why Greeks and Barbarians fought one another (cf. Nagy 1990b: 221–7; Hedrick 1993: 24–6). Some of the ideas of exemplarity are also to be discerned, I believe, in Thucydides' claim (1.22) that his history will be useful to those wanting to know clearly things that have happened, and which will, in accordance with human nature, occur again in comparable and very similar form (cf. e.g. Lisle 1977). Both Herodotus and Thucydides presume the constancy of human nature and the comparability of past and present. Neither, however, says that he writes to furnish ethical examples for imitation.

Elements of Aristotle's argument about the nature of virtue and happiness are to be found in Herodotus, most notably the emphasis on happiness as the fulfillment of the human condition. The point is made most famously in the anecdote about Solon and Croesus (1.30–1) – a story that Aristotle cites in the *Nicomachean Ethics*, attributing it to Solon (1.10–11). The Lydian tyrant supposedly displayed his wealth to the Athenian sage, and then asked him who he thought was the happiest of men. Solon surprised him by choosing others, among them an Athenian named Tellus, whose name puns on the idea of "the end." Croesus, offended, asked if his own prosperity was so contemptible. Solon answered that he would call no man happy before the end; that only in death do we know happiness – a point that Croesus is made to realize years later when he falls from prosperity and faces death on a pyre. Aristotle finds it odd to attribute happiness to the dead, but nevertheless mentions the story in support of his own discussion of the ultimate goals of human aspiration (Pritzl 1983).

This episode epitomizes a central theme of Herodotus' history: fortune is fleeting and happiness seldom abides long in one place. Happiness (*eudaimoniē*) is produced through chance rather than human striving and virtue.[9] The point is made at other places in the history: for example the tyrant Polycrates is said to suffer a comparable reversal of fortune. At the beginning of the history, Herodotus speaks of the mutability of states: those once small have become large and those once great have become small; because he knows that human happiness never abides long in the same place, he will make mention of both alike (1.5.4) (cf. recently T. Harrison 2005: 31–63).

In his discussions of happiness Herodotus says nothing of virtue; chance is the important variable. By contrast, for Aristotle, virtue and happiness are intertwined; the cultivation of virtue does not just produce happiness, rather the state of virtue is the state of happiness. Because of the identification of the two the virtuous man is more (but not absolutely) invulnerable to the buffetings of fortune (*Eth. Nic.* 1.10.14). The difference in conceptions is in part due to Herodotus' understanding of virtue, which is Homeric. Virtue here is still a competitive virtue rather than a cooperative one, and is consequently not a matter of habitual personal self-cultivation, but of competitive advantage.

Herodotus most famously uses the concept of *aretē* in this competitive sense in the anachronistic "constitutional debate" (Winton 2000: 101–11). After the death of Persian King Cambyses' double, the "false Smerdis," three claimants to the throne meet to discuss the future of the Persian state. Each urges a different form of government: monarchy, oligarchy, and democracy (3.80–2). In the last of the speeches, which is given to the future king Darius, the downfall of oligarchy is attributed to the virtue of the oligarchs themselves (3.82.3). In an oligarchy, he explains, many, desiring to be preeminent in counsel, cultivate virtue, which in turn exacerbates enmities. Virtue is excellence, and its pursuit leads to competition for power and influence, which is ultimately destabilizing to the political order.

Virtue is not central to Thucydides' notions about the value of reading and writing of history, though it does play an important part in his considerations of power and community (M. Palmer 1989). Such discussions occur notably in the speeches, where he is free to consider and contrast the various ideas current in his day. The association of *aretē* with the "cooperative" virtues is not completely absent from these discussions, though it is comparatively rare (cf. Bétant 1969 s.v.). The most notable elaboration of the "cooperative" ideal of virtue in Thucydides is to be found in the appeal of the Mytilenian oligarchs to the Spartans for help and protection against the Athenians, whose league they had deserted (3.10):

> Concerning justice [*dikaiosunē*] and virtue [*aretē*] we shall first make our speech, especially as we are asking for an alliance, because we know that solid friendship [*philia*] between individuals or community [*koinōnia*] between cities does not come into being, unless they behave toward each other with apparent virtue [*dokousē aretē*] and in other respects be of similar character [*homoiotropoi*].

Here (apparent!) virtue is the basis of cooperation, not of competitiveness.

More often, the word *aretē* in Thucydides refers to competitive excellence, especially the excellence of the fighting man. This virtue plays an important part in Thucydides' notions about politics. The Periclean funeral oration, a speech that is largely concerned with the values of community and warfare, contains a number of occurrences of the word in this sense (Loraux 1986: 106–7). One of the most interesting, complex, and compressed passages is to be found at 2.43. The section begins with praise of Athenian ancestors, who have produced the great state that the Athenians have inherited. Those who listen now should fix their eyes on the power (*dunamis*) of the state daily, become lovers of it, and recognize that it was by daring and knowledge of what was necessary that their ancestors obtained this power. They did not hesitate to deprive the state of their virtue (*aretē*) by sacrificing their lives (2.43.1). Present Athenians should imitate (*zēlōsantes*) them, and judging that happiness (or fulfillment – *to eudaimon*) is freedom (*to eleutheron*) and freedom bravery (*to eupsuchon*), they should not shirk the dangers of war (2.43.4). In this passage we see the notion that virtue is presented to be imitated; that (military) virtue produces power; and that through bravery comes freedom and through freedom fulfillment. Fulfillment, or happiness, as we have seen, was conventionally regarded as the end of human striving, and will be considered by Aristotle as produced through virtue. Thucydides' interest in the relationship between virtue and power is characteristic of certain thinkers of the sophistic movement, such as Callicles (as portrayed in Plato's *Gorgias*) or Thrasymachus (as portrayed in Plato's *Republic*).

While Herodotus and Thucydides use *aretē* almost exclusively in its traditional competitive sense, the broadening use of its antonyms, such as *aischros* and *kakos*, is remarkable. Both historians use words deriving from these stems to describe both competitive ineffectiveness and moral deficiency. The stakes involved in this widening of the sense of the shameful is summarily and perfectly expressed in the Melian dialogue, where Thucydides has the Athenians urge the Melians not to act from fear of incurring the charge of (moral) shame, when they are embroiled in actual dangers; to fall prey to these dangers, that is to fail in the competitive world of warfare, would itself be far more shameful (5.111.3) (cf. Adkins 1960: 178, 193 n17).

Certainly Thucydides thinks carefully about the nature of virtue and its political functions. Nevertheless, the engendering of moral excellence is not central to his conception of the purpose and function of the writing of history itself. For that we need to wait for the beginnings of Greek biography.[10] The first surviving biographies date to the beginning of the fourth century and were produced, under the palpable influence of Socratic philosophy, by Xenophon. Interest in the lives of great men can be traced earlier than the beginning of the fourth century, both in history and rhetoric, especially in encomiastic speeches. I have already briefly noticed the biographical digressions to be found in Herodotus and Thucydides and Isocrates' encomium of *Euagoras*, a speech that had a notable impact on the earliest preserved Greek biography, Xenophon's *Agesilaus*. At the same time, biographical interests continue to be found in the writings of certain fourth century historians, the notable example being a biographical digression about the life of Alcibiades found among the fragmentary remains of Theopompos' *Philippica* (*FGrH* 115) (Momigliano 1971: 62–3; Connor 1968; Shrimpton 1991). But Xenophon's biographies, especially the *Agesilaus* and *Education of Cyrus*, had such an enormous impact on subsequent writing that they arguably obscured the earlier tradition of biographical writing to the point where we know little about it.

Xenophon is well known for his continuation of Thucydides' unfinished history, the *Hellenica*. Arguably his most innovative and influential works, however, were his biographical essays: the *Agesilaus*, the various accounts of the life of Socrates, including an *Apology* and the *Memorabilia*, and the enormously popular and influential *Education of Cyrus* (*Cyropaedia*) (cf. Momigliano 1971: 49–57; Stadter, this volume, chapter 29). In these the notion of virtue is divorced from the struggle for power and associated with individual character. The cultivation of morality now becomes essential to the purpose of the work: the *Education of Cyrus* is not just about the education of the prince; it is intended to be an education to the reader. Here it will be enough to consider the *Agesilaus*.

The *Agesilaus* provides an account of the life and virtues of the Spartan king, a man of whom Xenophon had long personal experience. After a brief introduction, in which Xenophon complains of the difficulty of writing an account of Agesilaus' life that is worthy of his virtue (*aretē*) and reputation (*doxē*), Xenophon gives a brief account of the life and deeds of his hero (*Ages.* 1–2). This section shows the influence of Isocrates. Throughout the passage Xenophon also quotes verbatim from his earlier political history, the *Hellenica*. Next Xenophon turns to an account of Agesilaus' virtues, a section that will take up the major part of the essay (3–9): "now I shall try to show the virtue [*aretē*] in his spirit [*psuchē*], through which he accomplished these things and loved all that is good and put aside all that is shameful." He treats these in the following order: piety, justice, self-control, courage, and wisdom. The order is conventional: we find the same list in Xenophon's enumeration of the virtues of Socrates at the end of the *Memorabilia*; in his catalog of the virtues of Cyrus

(*Cyr.* 8.1.23–33); and in Agathon's speech in Plato's *Symposium*. Socrates afterward remarks that Agathon's speech reminds him of Gorgias (192c), and on this basis most believe that this ordering of virtues goes back to that sophist. Also, as I noted above, Aristotle claims that it is better to enumerate virtues, as Gorgias did, rather than attempt a general definition of the term (*Pol.* 1260a25). There follows a formal conclusion (*Ages.* 10) in which Xenophon urges his readers to imitate the virtue of Agesilaus: "The virtue [*aretē*] of Agesilaus seems to me to provide a fine example [*paradeigma*] for those who wish to cultivate [*askein*] morality [*andragathia*]." People do not become reprobates by imitating [*mimoumenos*] the just. The essay concludes (11) with a summary list of Agesilaus' virtues, so that they can be more easily remembered (*eumnēmonesteros*).

Xenophon's quotations from the *Hellenica* in the *Agesilaus* demonstrate the similar natures and subject matters of history and biography. On the other hand, given this common ground, we must ask why Xenophon does not show a comparable interest in the personal virtues in his political history. The answer must be that he considered this subject inappropriate to history: for him, biography and history are distinct, and the distinction is marked precisely by the question of character, which provides biography both with its distinctive character and even its justification for being. History is not the place for ethical portraits; we read and write biography to learn about virtue. As we have seen the point holds true for earlier historians as well. Thucydides cares about virtue insofar as it provides the basis for the production of power or community, not to illustrate the exemplary characters of great men.

The rise of biography and the interest in virtue as excellence of character should be seen as complicit. Both of them reflect a growing interest in the late fifth and early fourth century in character, personality – the inside of the person, so to speak. It is against this backdrop that we must understand the virtue ethics expounded by Aristotle in the *Nicomachean Ethics*. Xenophon does not so much apply philosophical thought to biography as Aristotle theorizes biographical practice.

Instruction in Virtue

From the beginning, the implication of virtue and politics was obvious to the ancient Greeks: in authors from Homer to Thucydides, virtue was understood competitively and its end was power. With the merging of the competitive and social virtues and the emergence of the ideal of virtue as an internal, characterological excellence at the time of sophists, the connection between virtue and politics changes. As we have seen Thucydides recognizes that social solidarity and trust are only possible if there is the appearance of virtue. Likewise, for the Greek philosophers from Plato on, cultivation of the proper ethical attitudes was a political problem. Plato frequently pointed out that the lawgiver's mandate was not so much to govern as to make people better. Xenophon makes a comparable point about Agesilaus toward the end of his biography: Agesilaus did not so much pride himself on ruling over others as for ruling himself; he did not aspire to lead his people against the enemy, but to lead them to virtue (10.2).

Aristotle took up the point in his *Nicomachean Ethics*, which was avowedly written as a prologue to his *Politics* (*Eth. Nic.* 10.9.8–23) (Adkins 1984: 29–49). While he is concerned in this work to describe how individuals become good, "to secure the good of one person only is better than nothing, to secure the good of a nation or a state is a nobler and more divine achievement. Therefore our investigation is in some sense the study of politics" (*Eth. Nic.* 1.2.4–8). Or again, "lawgivers make citizens good by training them in the habits of right action – this is the aim of legislation, and if it fails to do this it is a failure; this is what distinguishes a good form of constitution from a bad one" (*Eth. Nic.* 2.1.5).

The central problem in discussions of virtue henceforth will be education. The problem remains as much alive today as it was in ancient Greece. Few modern parents would admit that they are indifferent to the ethical instruction of their children. The question of who should be allowed to contribute to this education and how it should be accomplished, however, is a contentious issue. Certainly most would agree that ethical instruction is a matter for the family or for religious groups. Many believe that in addition schools should play a part in molding the characters of students; programs of ethical instruction, however, are chiefly to be found in religious and private schools. The modern state has generally shied away from becoming involved in moral pedagogy. The administrators and instructors of modern public schools and universities are accustomed to define education in terms of a content imparted, rather than of a disposition formed, as though it would be better to tell students what justice is, instead of instilling in them a love of justice. From the perspective of the secular state, ethical instruction has come to be generally regarded as the proper province of the family or church, not of the state. The idea that state-sponsored schools should presume to "condition" children to embrace a particular ethical or aesthetic sensibility not only offends the old Enlightenment strictures about the separation of church and state, but conjures up the more recent specter of totalitarianism. Up until the eighteenth century, by contrast, it was widely accepted that the chief function of education was character formation. Public political disengagement from the project must in my view be understood in relation to various related trends since the nineteenth century, notably the secular solution to the problem of multiculturalism and the plethora of value systems that come with it, problems which emerged with the rise of vast, heterogeneous nations, and the emergence of relativizing historicism as the dominant intellectual movement in the academy.

The question now, as then, is how to instill virtue. If virtue is an internal quality, manifest only through actions, how is it to be inculcated in the young? Obviously we can compel action; but how do we instill not just the forms of morality, but the love of virtue? The ancient historians taught by example. For most philosophers, from Plato on, virtue comes from knowledge. For Aristotle the problem is more complex (Depew, this volume, chapter 26). In the *Nicomachean Ethics* the question of the relative educational value of historical narratives and philosophical speculations is posed.

Granted that social groups and institutions can exercise an ethical influence on people, whether they aspire to do so or not, what is the ethical function of writing? Would it be unreasonable of me to aspire to improve readers through this essay? Does an essay have the potential to make people better? And how frequently do authors write for that reason? I wonder, for instance, how many contemporary academic ethical philosophers write in order to improve the ethics of their readers?[11] For Plato, at least, the writing of ethical philosophy should ideally have an improving function, because, he argued, there was a link between understanding and moral behavior: people who behave badly do so out of ignorance; for those who know, it is impossible to behave other than rightly. Thus a writing that promotes understanding also promotes virtue. The argument doubtless remains an inspiration for many philosophers.

By contrast, in the *Nicomachean Ethics* Aristotle argued that philosophy never made anyone virtuous. Windy speculation is a refuge for loafers and imposters – diddlers who are complacent enough to imagine that cloistered meditation and polite academic disputations can somehow substitute for the bloody school of action. As though the empty wagers of the lecture hall recreate the stakes and consequences entailed in a conscientious life! People do not become virtuous by discoursing windily about temperance and justice, or by listening to others cavil. As Aristotle tells us in the second book of the *Nicomachean Ethics*, we become virtuous through practice, not speculation: "by doing just acts one becomes just; by doing temperate acts one becomes temperate" (*Eth. Nic.* 2.4; cf. 10.9.1–7).

He makes this point paradoxically in the context of a general, philosophical discussion of virtue, and wakeful readers must wonder what he imagines he is doing by writing. If philosophy cannot teach virtue, if the Platonic equivalence of knowledge and moral excellence does not hold, what is the point of reading or writing about ethics? Aristotle's explanation is not well developed. Part of the answer is doubtless to be sought in his unexpressed assumption of the ancient ideal of philosophy as a vocation, not simply a quest for knowledge; in this regard, philosophers themselves are not just teachers, but moral exemplars. First, he insists that his purposes in writing the *Nicomachean Ethics* are chiefly practical, not theoretical: he is less concerned to provide a rigorous definition of virtue than to make his readers better (*Eth. Nic.* 2.2). He does not write for those who lack virtue: for a person inadequately prepared, it would be as unimproving to read his discussion of the virtues as it would be for a criminal to memorize laws (*Eth. Nic.* 1.3). Virtues, he says, are habits (*Eth. Nic.* 2.4 and 2.1–6 passim), and we acquire them in the same way we might learn to ride a bicycle: not through theoretical discussion and abstract diagrams and prescriptions, but by wobbling over the pavement, falling, skinning our knees, and getting back in the saddle (*Eth. Nic.* 2.2–3). People are not born virtuous; they learn to be virtuous through discipline, including even the cruel school of the belt-strap (*Eth. Nic.* 10.9.10). We learn ethical excellence in the same way we might learn to play the guitar or build a house: through imitation and repetition (*Eth. Nic.* 2.1, 10.9). Virtue then begins with the conditioned disposition of the organism rather than the deliberate choice and reflection of the conscious mind; it is an attitude so ingrained as to be reflexive, like the manual dexterity of a virtuoso pianist or the efficient and economical motions of an expert sculler. It is acquired through practice, and a person with this "practical wisdom" is virtuous (the idea of "practical knowledge" is developed at length in *Eth. Nic.* book 6). It is for such people that Aristotle writes, in the expectation that general and critical consideration of virtuous dispositions and actions will be useful for the virtuous – who are, in any event, the only ones in a position to profit from such reflection (*Eth. Nic.* 1.3).

The idea that ethical knowledge is initially communicated in the same way that bears are taught to dance in carnival sideshows will offend the sensibilities of most philosophers. It is not, I think, that anyone doubts that it is practically possible through such conditioning to mold the tastes and dispositions of people, whether this means their appetite for certain foods or their contempt and admiration for certain qualities; rather we believe that to be virtuous, actions must be voluntary, consciously considered. Aristotle agrees. Reflex may be a necessary foundation, but it is insufficient for the realization of virtue. No action is ethical in itself; a deed only becomes good or bad when viewed from the perspective of the state of mind of its perpetrator: "Though actions are entitled just and temperate when they are such acts as just and temperate men would do, the agent is just and temperate not when he does these acts merely, but when he does them in the way that a just and temperate man would do them" (*Eth. Nic.* 2.4.6). For an action to be virtuous the agent must act with knowledge, choose the act deliberately and for its own sake, and the act must spring from a permanent disposition (*Eth. Nic.* 2.4.3) (Williams 2006a).

How then do people make the transition from enforced routine to deliberate performance, from Pavlovian salivation to self-aware pursuit of virtue? Aristotle does not develop an argument, though he intimates that the answer must lie in the association of the affections with ethical ideals. One must learn from one's earliest age to love what is good, and hate the shameful (*Eth. Nic.* 10.9.8; cf. 1.4, 1.7, 2.1); it is essential to be trained from childhood to like and dislike the proper things (*Eth. Nic.* 2.3). Love and hatred are enlisted in support of ethics, are even the essence of ethics, especially through their association with our earliest and most elementary role models: our parents. As children love and fear their mothers and fathers they also take them as examples and model their behavior after them. Aristotle makes this point briefly in his account of the authority of the lawgiver:

> Paternal exhortations and family habits have authority in the household, just as legal enactments and national customs have authority in the state, and more so on account of the ties of relationship and the benefits conferred that unite the head of the household to its other members: he can count on their natural affection and obedience at the outset. (*Eth. Nic.* 10.9.14)

The point might have been made by Freud – in fact, it was made by Freud: there is a link between the affection with which we regard exemplary individuals and the cultivation of a self-governing ethical sensibility; so conscience (the superego) is fostered by love and fear for the father, as the affection of patient for analyst (transference) can be exploited in treatment (cf. e.g. Wollheim 1990: 166–70, 223–33). It is for this reason among others, as I argued above, that the praise and blame are the proper languages for the representation of virtues and vices: the logic of morality is exemplary.

Philosophical writing, then, can only be a kind of supplemental instruction, useful for those who come to it with a firm practical grounding in virtues. Aristotle's discussion of the formation of habits in virtue suggests that other narrative forms of writing may play a more effective role in the production of ethical individuals. One of the most important ways in which we learn in our early years, he suggests, is through imitation. Our love and admiration for certain examples motivates us. The first examples of virtuous behavior are the parents. It is our recognition of something transcendent in the behavior of these exemplars, something in which we can potentially share, that provides us with the common ground: let us call these transcendent qualities ethics. As Aristotle remarks, since virtue is a quality of character it cannot be directly perceived. We can know it only as it is instantiated in exemplary actions. The mutual dependence of character and action is recognized by Aristotle throughout the *Nicomachean Ethics* (see esp. 1.8 and 2.1). Character is prior to and determinative of actions, yet it is the nature of the virtuous disposition to act virtuously; a person who does not act cannot be virtuous: as at the Olympics, the prize does not go to the strongest, but to the strongest competitor.

There is a fundamental difference between philosophical argument and exemplary illustration, despite the fact that the one often includes the other. The opposition can be seen in philosophical discomfort with examples, which are often seen as extraneous to the rigors of argument, digressions that are as often weaknesses as clarifications. At its most basic the argument boils down to a formal dichotomy: metonymy versus metaphor. Philosophical argument is systematic, discursive, whereas exemplary description is descriptive, narrative.

Aristotle's remarks suggest that narrative, in its formal similarity to the lived experience of exemplarity, has a more basic part to play in the moral formation of people's characters than does philosophy. The ethical effectiveness of narrative was widely acknowledged by the ancients, and continued to be assumed by philosophers as late as Rousseau.[12] The qualities of heroes and villains, the very logic of the story, including the resolution of conflict and the sense of an ending, convey and instruct people in profound questions of cultural standards of good and evil, and just or unjust resolution. And even if these lessons are not as nuanced or self-reflective as philosophers might like, the moral paradigms of stories are generally accessible, far more so than abstract philosophical arguments. Jesus' parables and Grimm's fairy tales remain far more accessible than Kant's categorical imperative has ever been, even to philosophers.[13] The most banal Hollywood action film teaches moral lessons about good and evil, courage and self-sacrifice: the morality plays of Clint Eastwood and Arnold Schwarzenegger assuredly have a greater impact on the ethical lives of contemporary Americans than academic philosophy for the simple reason that their lessons are easy to understand and apply. We all have learned ethical lessons, but very few of us have learned them from philosophers. While we may reasonably be interested in philosophical reflection about ethics, if we wish to understand how people became ethical in ancient Greece or how we become ethical now we can more profitably consult Herodotus than Aristotle. Aristotle seems to have agreed with this point.

Conclusion

Aristotelian ideas about virtue and education dominate both Greek and Roman narratives of the past, whether biography or history, to the end of antiquity.[14] Aristotle's successors, the Peripatetics, famously collected anecdotes illustrating virtues and vices and wrote biography, illustrations of Aristotle's arguments (Momigliano 1971: 66–100). The impact of Aristotelian ethical writing about virtues can subsequently be detected in the attention given by Greek and Roman historians and biographers to character (Stadter, this volume, chapter 29). Roman students of Greek philosophy absorbed his teaching. Cicero, who provided the Romans with a developed Latin philosophical vocabulary with which to deal with Greek ideas, elaborated the Greek philosophy of virtues, notably in the *De republica*, the *Tusculan Disputations* and the *De legibus* (Schofield, this volume, chapter 13).[15] Here he emphasizes Aristotle's crucial demurral from Plato, that virtues consist not in knowledge, but in action: "It is not enough to possess virtue as though it were some skill, unless you use it. For a skill, even when not used, can nevertheless be retained by knowledge of it alone; *virtus* depends entirely on its use" (*Rep.* 1.2).

"In Christ there is no east or west, in him no south or north / but one great fellowship of love, throughout the whole wide earth." The hymn verse (1908) recalls the universalizing claims of the Christian faith: "There is neither Jew nor Greek, there is neither bond nor free, there is neither male nor female: for you are all one in Christ Jesus" (Galations 3.28; cf. Colossians 3.11). God's law applies to all, and provides a common ethical measure across cultures.

As faith in Christianity has waned, so has western assurance about the possibility of an ethics that applies across cultural boundaries. For humanists it is equally a matter of faith that every culture has its own ethics; all values are relative. "Oh, East is East and West is West and never the twain shall meet / till Earth and Sky stand presently at God's great judgment seat," as Kipling famously declared in the opening stanza of his "Ballad of East and West."

Christian belief and humanist doubts both presume a morality authorized by law and lawgiver. Greek discussions of virtue by contrast are framed with a view to human nature: for Aristotle, human virtue should be evaluated with reference to the extent that it leads to the realization of the natural potential of the person (Depew, this volume, chapter 26). Some will not like the notion that humans have a nature at all; others will agree that humans have a nature but will not wish to allow that it can be distinguished from that of animals. Even if we were to subscribe to the arguments of Aristotle's "Virtue Ethics" there is no reason that we should be limited by Greek writings in our contemplation of what it means to be human and what the ends of human life should be; but given this conception of virtue, to the extent that we recognize others as sharing in our own humanity, we must all share in the same virtues. Consequently the Greeks believed they could as easily learn moral lessons from Persians such as Cyrus as from Agesilaus. The second couplet of Kipling's stanza is not so well known as the first: "But there is neither East nor West, Border nor Breed nor Birth / when two strong men stand face to face, though they come from the ends of the earth."[16]

Philosophical essays are appropriate to the contemplation of moral regulations. The virtuous, however, do not bend the knee to rules and consistency; they are governed in any circumstance only by their dispositions, their love of virtue. So, as Aristotle says, what makes an action virtuous is only the character of the person performing it.

Caprice is an embarrassment to philosophy. The unsystematic and contextual behavior of the virtuous finds its suitable and morally exemplary expression in descriptive narratives of praise and blame, of biography and history.

FURTHER READING

The nineteenth century scholarship on ancient biography remains essential to an appreciation of the form: see above all Leo 1901. The classic modern essay is Momigliano 1971; for a more recent and succinct account see e.g. Cox 1983: ch. 1.

Aristotle's *Nicomachean Ethics* is generally acknowledged as the seminal work on "virtue ethics." In the vast bibliography on this work, the standard point of entry is Hardie 1980; beginners can usefully consult next Rorty 1980. There are a number of recent student's introductions: see e.g. Hughes 2001. Lines 2002 provides a useful survey of the *Nachleben* of the *Ethics* from antiquity through the early modern period. The most important general discussion of the more general Greek idea of virtue is Adkins 1960; cf. his succinct statement in Adkins 1989. Two of the most important recent contributions to the revival of the "virtue ethics" movement are MacIntyre 1984 and R. Taylor 1985. Among the many introductions to the discussion, R. Taylor 2002 provides a vigorously written statement of the issues for the general reader.

NOTES

1   He does refer to earlier "philosophers," who have not dared explore the virtues of their great contemporaries (at e.g. 8), but by this he means orators. For the famous Isocratean identification of rhetoric with philosophy see recently Ober 2004: 26–7, with earlier bibliography cited at notes 8–9.
2   The most important general discussion of the Greek idea of virtue is Adkins 1960; cf. his succinct statement in Adkins 1989.
3   On the *aretē–technē* dichotomy, Adkins 1973. For the *aretē–technē* distinction as applied to military virtue see recently Lendon 2005: 109–14.
4   On Plato's concept of virtue see e.g. Adkins 1989. It should be emphasized that the so-called "theory of ideas" at least has since the time of Aristotle generally been conceded to be a Platonic, not a Socratic, idea.
5   The classic example is the biblical story of Job; cf. too the discussion of God's injustice in Romans 9.14 ff. For the fallibility of human justice, Augustine *De civ. D.* 19.6.
6   "Amicus Platon, sed magis amica veritas." The Latin proverb translates and adapts a line from this section of the *Nicomachean Ethics*.
7   The distinction between human and animal has been fundamental to philosophical thought since at least the time of the Greeks; recent blurring of the distinction will consequently require rethinking of many fundamental ideas, including ethical ideas.
8   For an interesting, though slightly different discussion of this connection, see Halliwell 1990: 45, 50.
9   Tellos dies at a moment of supreme happiness: his children and grandchildren are alive; he has died performing a glorious deed. In the context of the story, however, it is not that he has achieved his happiness through virtue. Solon is making the point that before death,

fortune can strip a person of everything, regardless of deserts, and that it is only with the stability of death that one has the potential to achieve happiness. So Croesus, despite his wealth, will not end happily, but will succumb to fortune.

10 Of course, on occasion, as when dealing with Nicias (7.86) or Antiphon (8.68), he refers to their virtue: cf. Adkins 1975.

11 This was the traditional function of philosophy, before it became an academic discipline: see Hadot 1995, and more briefly, Hadot 1990.

12 For treatment of the point by ancient philosophers see e.g. Pl., *Resp.* 2–3; Arist., *Pol.* 8. The question is central to Rousseau's writing: see e.g. his *Discourse on the Arts and Sciences*, or his book on education, *Émile*; cf. Froese 2001. Psychologists have also begun to make this claim: see Walker 2002. The relationship between narrative forms and human experience of time is the subject of Ricoeur 1984–90.

13 Cf. Dover 1974: 2–3 n3: "I cannot recall experiencing a temptation to use the word 'duty' in its Kantian sense (except, of course, when talking about Kant) and, at least in the course of the last five or six years, I do not think I have heard the word so used. Unless I am seriously deceiving myself, I and most of the people I know well find the Greeks of the Classical period easier to understand than the Kantians."

14 For example, Plutarch appeals to Aristotelian (or at least Peripatetic) ideas in espousing the importance of good examples in biography: see the beginning of his *Life of Timoleon*; for the usefulness of bad examples, the beginning of his *Life of Demetrius*. The general influence of Aristotle on Plutarch, writing in the mid-second century AD, is patent. The clearest example is his *De virtute,* which relies in detail directly or indirectly on the *Nicomachean Ethics:* see e.g. Babut 1969. Of the general bibliography on Aristotle's influence in antiquity, see e.g. Sandbach 1985; for an account of his influence on ancient historiography, von Fritz 1958.

15 The Romans rendered *aretē* as *virtus*, a traditional word with religious and military connotations. Its use to translate *aretē* goes back in my view to at least the third century and the Scipionic epitaphs – and is perhaps to be found even earlier, in the Twelve Tables. Generally on *virtus* in the Roman tradition, see Earl 1967 and McDonnell 2006. See further Cic., *Rep.* 1.1.5–1.2.1 (with the commentary provided by Zetzel 1995) and 5.9.

16 In this poem, Kipling alludes to the universality of the "competitive," martial virtues, that is the point of the reference to "*strong* men." This idea is developed in Alderman 1982; cf. particularly the example of Richard Burton's experience in Dahome, discussed there at 140–2.

CHAPTER 28

Greek Drama and Political Thought

John Gibert

Drama can contribute greatly to the understanding of political thought as defined in this volume, and several qualities of fifth century Athenian tragedies and comedies increase their value for this purpose. They often go out of their way to politicize their content, they offer political thought in forms (e.g., representational, narrative) not abundantly supplied by other sources for the period (narrative history, discussed in chapter 27, being an obvious exception), and they delight in argumentative rhetoric. Above all, created at a time and place of unmatched importance in the history of ancient democracy, Greek play-texts are the record of a communication involving individual artists, a large number of performers, and a mass audience within a notably politicized setting.

Scholarship has much to offer on the subject. It is a commonplace that few critics nowadays conceive of "aesthetic" or "literary" objects that can be isolated from the "political," or that better attain some well-defined purpose of their own the less political they are. Indeed the student sampling work on Greek drama from the last 30 or 40 years will find few sustained readings that are not political in some sense. The flip side of this is that "political" might mean just about anything. Not only does a (legitimate) recourse to etymology (*ta politika* meaning "everything to do with life in a polis") encourage a broad view of the subject, but the idea that *excluding* anything from the political is a political gesture has gained wide currency. If the richness of the material is one attraction of the subject, the opportunity to think about such basic definitional issues is another (see also Hammer, this volume, chapter 2).

Tragedy and comedy appear to have very different political preoccupations and are usually discussed separately. With one exception (Aeschylus' *Persians*, produced in 472), surviving Greek tragedies dramatize stories set in a mythic past. Their main characters are heroic or divine, and few are Athenian. The resulting distance from the world of the audience plays no small part in making the stories suitable vehicles for certain kinds of political thought, but it also requires theorizing these "filters." The nine fifth century comedies of Aristophanes, in contrast, engage contemporary issues

A Companion to Greek and Roman Political Thought, First Edition. Edited by Ryan K. Balot.

more or less directly, and their characters are recognizable social types, many of them Athenian. Even allowing ample room for comic distortion, it is clear that we are dealing with a very different relation to reality.

Citizens and Others, Institutional Setting

Tragedy's heroic and monarchical protagonists can be studied as historical, ethical, or religious problems with political dimensions. Thus, in a widely cited essay, Jean-Pierre Vernant takes a very long historical view, defining a tragic "moment" that pits heroic individuals against the values of the polis (Vernant 1988). Richard Seaford's complex and challenging book *Reciprocity and Ritual* in some ways develops this idea, with an emphasis on religious discourse and a reminder that the values embodied in heroic tradition are older than archaic epic, which also attained the form in which we know it against the background of emerging poleis (Seaford 1994; cf. Seaford 2000). The tragic discourse of tyranny is interpreted variously. For example, some start by observing that disapproval of tyranny unites all elements of Athenian society, while others (not incompatibly) argue that the tyrant focuses anxieties fifth century Athenians felt about the individual autonomy they increasingly enjoyed (Raaflaub and Seaford, respectively, in Morgan 2003; see also in this volume, Forsdyke, chapter 15, and Liddel, chapter 9).

Another approach is to consider how the citizen (*politēs*) is defined by what he is not. It is widely believed that Greeks were especially prone to antithetical thinking. The question is which "others" are most instructive, and in the study of drama, candidates include slaves, non-Greek foreigners, and non-Athenian Greeks (E. Hall 1989, 1997; Zeitlin 1990; Vidal-Naquet 1997). The fact that tragic principals are usually (mythic) Thebans, Argives, and so on encourages us to think about how tragedy achieves its effects for Athenians through these categories. Broadly speaking, two opposing tendencies appear to be at work: while others, by being excluded, can define and stabilize the Athenian's identity, they also invite him to look beyond difference, think and feel inclusively, and expand the boundaries of his self. In assuming a masculine subject, I am doing what many believe tragedy itself does. For good reasons, the feminine is often seen as the other par excellence and crucial to Greek drama, in the interpretation of which it has received much sophisticated attention (e.g., Zeitlin 1996; Wohl 1998; Foley 2001; see also Sissa, this volume, chapter 7).

No attempt can be made to summarize work on "alterity" here, but a few points may be helpful.[1] First, many insist that more is at stake in drama's engagement with the other than language and thought (fundamental though these are). Stage figures possess something of the roundedness of real life, and in representing them, Greek actors (who were always male) literally "played the other." The tragic chorus typically represents a marginal and/or powerless group (women, slaves, old men). That the men who played them were citizen amateurs and can be seen as modeling audience response implies that engagement with the other was meant to be intimate and intense for the spectators as well. In other words, alterity may be a privileged source of drama's power (and thus its value as political thought), though the precise effect is hard to pin down. Second, the relative strength of what I am calling inclusive and exclusive tendencies is always a matter of interpretation. In practice, the inclusive (expansive, destabilizing) potential tends to be given most play in discussions of emotional effect, and to depend heavily on the representation of women and non-Athenian Greeks. More narrowly political readings tend to stress the exclusive (defining, stabilizing) tendency, asserting the need of Athenians, according to the circumstances, to see themselves as, on the one hand, not "barbarians," not slaves, not Thebans, etc., and on the other, not divided further by class or partisan political tendency. In such readings, exclusion of women may also play a constitutive role, as (most would say) in Aeschylus' *Eumenides*. Such assessments are always contestable: there are usually worthy arguments on both sides, and no reason to assume that the balance of forces is simple or constant. Third, although a focus on Athenian male citizens as the implied or majority audience makes sense for some purposes, it should not be forgotten that they had company (see below). Aside from bringing the effects on these other spectators themselves into the conversation, this leads to the question whether diversity in the audience complicates the response of Athenian citizens.

An obviously important aspect of the citizen's self-definition in fifth century Athens is that he lives in a democracy, but how much this matters to drama is disputed. In the case of comedy, we are again dealing with a relatively overt relationship, reflected in the well-known story that Plato responded to the Syracusan tyrant Dionysius' request for information about Athens' *politeia* by sending him the works of Aristophanes (anonymous *Life of Aristophanes* 42–5). In the case of tragedy, whose fictional settings are nondemocratic, we must be alert first of all to such anachronistic allusions to democracy as may occur (Raaflaub 1989a), and then to more general evidence of democratic mentality. In both genres, a great many topics invite consideration under the heading "drama and democracy," for example deliberation and decision-making, ways of resolving or containing conflict, the dynamics of leadership, and attitudes toward outsiders. Some of these will concern us later, but now is the time to say a little more about drama's institutional setting, which has become a cornerstone of the argument that its contributions to political thought must be seen in the light of democracy.

All our plays were originally performed at Athenian festivals of the god Dionysus organized and paid for, in part, by the state (details in Pickard-Cambridge 1988; Csapo and Slater 1994). The performances were organized as a competition, and some of the responsibilities borne by officials had to do with maintaining a level playing field. Thus the state and its officials chose the poets who would compete, recruited and paid actors, appointed wealthy citizens as *choregoi* to train and equip the choruses, and awarded prize money. Meanwhile, (male) citizens were involved in various ways. At the City Dionysia, large numbers of them actually performed. Ten, chosen by lot (one per tribe) from a list approved by the Council, were empaneled as judges. After the festival, a special session of the Assembly examined the conduct of the officials who had run it and any incidents that had arisen.

Citizens were also involved, of course, as audience members, and seating may have reflected political and social divisions of the populace. Estimates of how many spectators the fifth century Theater of Dionysus held vary widely; it now looks as if earlier estimates as high as 17,000 will have to be brought down, perhaps to 7,000 or even lower (Revermann 2006: 168 n117). It is also uncertain how many of the audience were not Athenian citizens (Carter 2004: 10–13), whether the citizens in attendance were representative in socioeconomic terms (Sommerstein 1997; Bowie 1998: 58–60), and whether women attended at all (opposing views in Henderson 1991 and Goldhill 1994; cf. Goldhill 1997. 62–6). At some point, a fund was created to subsidize citizens' purchase of tickets, but the date is disputed, as are the political implications for the periods before and after the practice began. There is good reason, then, to be cautious before asserting that the festival audience mirrored the democratic Assembly or law courts.[2]

In an influential article, Simon Goldhill explores the significance of four aspects of "pre-play ceremonial" (libation by elected generals, recognition of benefactors, display of tribute from the empire, award of armor to war orphans) (Goldhill 1987; cf. Connor 1989). Jasper Griffin objects that Goldhill's emphasis on these framing events leads him to exaggerate the role of politics in the audience's experience of the plays themselves (J. Griffin 1998). Goldhill counters that his case depends on the institutional setting as a whole, not just the preliminaries (Goldhill 2000a: 37–8). P. J. Rhodes and David Carter have recently reexamined the evidence and found some of it wanting (Rhodes 2003b; Carter 2004; cf. Henderson 2007). Rhodes argues, to my mind convincingly, that the salient aspect of drama's institutional setting is that it is a polis, not that it is a democracy, and Carter makes a strong case that the ideology on display at the festival is best seen in the light of Athenian imperialism (cf. Rosenbloom 1995, 2006; Kurke 1998; Kennedy 2006; D. Carter 2007).

Drama and Ideology

Of course, Goldhill and others also address ideology in the texts. An at least superficially gratifying picture of Athens and Athenians can hardly be denied (Zeitlin 1990; Mills 1997); some equate this with civic or democratic ideology and argue that tragedy basically affirms it. Others work with subtler notions of ideology (a notoriously tricky concept) and find in tragedy's many kinds of complexity – ethical, emotional, and intellectual as well as political – support for other conclusions about its ideological import, for example that it is didactic, admonitory, interrogative, or subversive.[3] Of course the relation may vary with different authors and plays and for different members of the audience. And, we may add, for different audiences. While attention to the plays' premieres remains indispensable, scholars increasingly recognize the importance of drama's early spread beyond Athens. Whatever meanings the plays had when received by democrats, reperformance in other settings was not only possible, but quite successful, and at times the poets may have anticipated it when composing.[4]

An aspect of self-definition in which there were obvious differences among Athenian citizens is social or economic class, and this suggests the possibility of *competing* ideologies in drama. For many, containing or neutralizing its competitors is, so to speak, all in a day's work for democratic ideology – which is not to deny that close attention reveals contradictions, occlusions, mystifications, and so on. For others (e.g. Rose 1992, 1995; Griffith 1995), tragedy offers more or less consistent validation for elite ideology (even if that is not all it does). The disagreement leads still others (e.g. J. Griffin 1999a) to wonder whether there are sufficient grounds for either view; for whatever reason, tragic critics do often avoid the subject. Interpreters of comedy, on the other hand, almost always explore its political thought in terms of identities at least as specific as "mass" and "elite" (Henderson 1990, 1993; Konstan 1995; with his emphasis, more typical of tragic studies, on what *unites* citizens, McGlew 2002 is something of an exception). A brief look at the ideological import of Aristophanes' early comedies will lay some groundwork for the discussions that follow.

In two of Aristophanes' plays from the years 425–421, a comic hero devises a fantastic scheme to get relief from some oppressive aspect of contemporary reality; in his way stand "the powers that be." After attaining his goal, he is approached by others who want to share his good fortune, but he doesn't let them. He humiliates and routs these "impostors" and secures his hold on prosperity (defined in comic terms as food, wine, and sex). The other three plays from this period offer variations in place of the hero but a similar opposition between the ordinary citizen (whose fictional name often marks him as a kind of Everyman) and the prominent or powerful (including real contemporaries singled out by name). The latter are "elite" in that they can be portrayed as getting more than their share of good things, the former "demotic" in that they (and the group they represent) are being cheated of theirs.

Concerning the political implications of this scenario, three main positions have emerged.[5] According to the first, the comic poet is fundamentally an opportunist, who does not mock if he thinks it will hurt his chances of winning the prize (Heath 1987a, 1997). The second sees Aristophanes as playing to the demos, offering it a vision of itself as blocked from gratifying its every desire only by the malfeasance of its leaders. He gets away with mocking the demos for its stupidity because it is after all not to blame; the people can wise up, throw the bums out, and set the city back on course (Henderson 1990, 1993). According to a third view, the lists of those Aristophanes satirizes and spares (as well as the few he praises) reveal systematic bias in favor of the traditional elite (Sommerstein 1996a).

These views leave room for varying conclusions about comedy's political effect. Some degree of opportunism – perhaps even a high degree – is consistent with a desire to affect decisions outside the theater. Heath denies Aristophanes that desire because he *also* thinks the audience regarded comedy as irrelevant to practical politics. On the other hand, playing to the demos could be merely opportunistic, if the demos played an important part in awarding the prize and that was all Aristophanes wanted. Henderson takes comedy's political effect seriously because he *also* thinks the Athenian understanding of politics was broad enough to encompass comedy as a forum that mattered, and that Aristophanic comedy empowers its audience by reminding it that, all appearances to the contrary, it is sovereign. Finally, if Aristophanes systematically favors the traditional elite, that does not have to be the result (only) of his own beliefs. Sommerstein's findings in fact lead him to suggest that the comic audience belonged to a higher socioeconomic status, on average, than assemblymen or jurors; Aristophanes may still play to his audience's prejudices, but comedy as an institution appears in a new and less democratic light (Sommerstein 1997). More convincing is Henderson's harmonization of Sommerstein's findings with his own. Aristocratic bias was well established in political and cultural discourse, and spectators did not have to be aristocrats themselves to tolerate it. It remains significant that the comic poets did not "offer illegal advice, question the right of the demos to full sovereignty, or suggest any changes in the rules of democracy" (Henderson 1998: 271). Occupying the political center, comedy tends toward inclusive rather than divisive or partisan effects.

As we shall see, critics have favored a similar conclusion about Aeschylus (and tragedy in general). Before turning to his *Eumenides* and the other plays to be studied briefly in the rest of this chapter, I note that the selection is not meant to be representative. The tragedies (*Eumenides* and Euripides' *Ion*) are unusual both in their overt relationship to Athens and, perhaps not coincidentally, their lack of the catastrophic outcomes that are so common in, and eventually come to define, the genre. The comedies (*Birds* and *Lysistrata*) vary and extend the ideological model just sketched; other unusual features have led to interpretation in modes more typical of tragedy than comedy. As a group, then, the plays bring out some common themes in the political thought of Greek drama's two main genres. At the same time, they indicate the wide range of political issues on which drama has something interesting to say. While many of these can only be mentioned in passing here, I have tried to be generous with references and suggestions for further reading. As for the Athenocentricity of the examples, I suggest that it makes for homogeneity of only a fairly unimportant kind. My interest is in how drama's political thought, which constantly puts Athenian identities themselves to the test, is broad enough to engage non-Athenians, including modern readers, in reflection that is of much more than antiquarian interest.

Eumenides

Aeschylus' *Oresteia* trilogy (458 BCE) dramatizes the return of the Greek commander Agamemnon from Troy and his murder in Argos by his wife Clytemnestra and her lover Aegisthus (*Agamemnon*); the murder of these two by Agamemnon's and Clytemnestra's son Orestes, acting on the god Apollo's instructions (*Choephoroe*); and the Furies' punishment of Orestes for this crime and his trial and acquittal in Athens (*Eumenides*). The most obvious narrative challenge the trilogy sets for itself is what to do about a potentially endless cycle of revenge killing. Because Clytemnestra and Aegisthus usurp Argive royal power, there is also a problem of royal succession, and because Apollo commands matricide, which it is the age-old duty of the Furies (the chorus of the third play) to avenge, there is a crisis of cosmic order. These all come to a head in the trial, which is made relevant to fifth century Athens in ways that are both unusual for tragedy and clearly important. Some of the issues that demand attention are political in a rather narrow sense, but their interpretation inevitably involves broader contexts. Indeed, by virtue of their number, variety, and increasing sophistication, political readings of the *Oresteia*, and of *Eumenides* in particular, have acquired paradigmatic status in the study of Greek drama and require somewhat more detailed treatment here.

We may summarize the features that would most strongly encourage an Athenian audience in 458 to think of its own historical experience as follows:[6] (1) Athens is promised a beneficial alliance with Argos; (2) high hopes are expressed for Athenian success in war, which is contemplated almost cheerfully (a most unusual attitude); (3) repeated warnings of the dangers of civil strife are given; and (4) Orestes' trial becomes the mythical explanation (*aition*) of the Athenian Areopagus Council. All of these can be linked with issues that were or recently had been of intense partisan interest. Just three years earlier the Athenians had abruptly abandoned all pretence of cooperation with Sparta and made an alliance with Sparta's old rival Argos. Almost immediately, they embarked on a series of military adventures which by 458 included open conflict with Sparta (the "first Peloponnesian War"). With the change in foreign policy came the adoption of domestic reforms urged by Ephialtes, including a reduction in the duties and influence of the Areopagus Council, which, consisting of former archons (an office for which members of only the two highest property classes had been eligible), was associated with aristocratic tendencies. Soon after the reforms were enacted, Ephialtes was killed, assassinated (his supporters assumed) by his political opponents. Civil war may have seemed a real possibility.

Debate once centered on Aeschylus' personal opinion of these changes and/or others the Athenians might yet make. Contemporary scholars, among whom the most common view is that the plays do suggest support of what the democrats had done so far, have not altogether abandoned this question (references in Goldhill 2000b: 77; Kennedy 2006: 39), but they usually go on to consider other political effects experienced by Aeschylus' audience. One view is broadly allegorical and straightforwardly didactic: the Furies represent the old (traditional aristocratic government), trial by jury the new (democracy), and the audience is warned not to let the new run roughshod over the old (Meier 1993: 102–16, Boedeker and Raaflaub 2005: 116–18).

Similarly, the effect of the contemporary allusions themselves is often taken to be promotion of solidarity among Athenian citizens. At least three routes (which may be combined) have been taken to this conclusion. First, observation of textual indeterminacy. For example, Alan Sommerstein writes that "Nowhere in *Eumenides* is there an avowedly partisan utterance relating to domestic Athenian politics." Where specific issues are broached at this level, artful ambiguities ensure that each audience member can hear what he wants to hear, and the play as a whole insists on "the vital importance of avoiding anything that might lead to civil conflict" (Sommerstein 1989: 31–2). Second, appeal to historical context. Thus Malcolm Heath argues that what had been highly contentious partisan issues in 462/1 were no longer so three years later: "Aeschylus is taking both the reforms and the new political consensus for granted, and is doing for it what came so naturally to the Greeks; he is using myth to furnish an aetiological charter for the political *status quo*. The significance of this is obviously pan-Athenian, not partisan" (Heath 1987b: 69). Third, appeal to other aspects of the play, especially its means of achieving closure. The many who take this route emphasize, for example, that the solution to revenge killing is found in Athens, the Furies are incorporated into the city's religious order as Reverend Goddesses inspiring respect and moderation, and the trilogy ends in a procession like that of the Panathenaic festival, in which the elements of the population are harmoniously ordered.

The combination of warnings against civil strife and avoidance of unambiguously partisan views on domestic matters makes for a strong case that the text promotes solidarity. It should be remembered, though, that some degree of indeterminacy is a feature of all texts, and viewers and readers cannot avoid choices (and thus disagreements) about whether and how to respond. For example, disagreement as to *who* is warned (aristocrats, democrats, or everyone) has arisen because the text does not spell it out. About the cheerful acceptance of war implied by *Eumenides*, Sommerstein argues that it makes no sense except as support for the new Athenian foreign policy. Aeschylus does not avoid clarity on *this* issue, he believes, because "Athens is embattled on many fronts … and the proponents of war feel entitled (as always in such circumstances) to the support of every loyal citizen" (Sommerstein 1989: 31–2). In other words, Sommerstein determines both that the unusual attitude (less jarring in its fictional context than, say, mention of the Areopagus Council) must have been received in the light of current events, and that it was compatible with promoting solidarity. These moves are reasonable, but in place of the second, one could argue that soft-pedaling domestic issues while exploiting war fervor was precisely the most effective partisan strategy for a "radical democrat" in 458. Obviously, Heath's appeal to history is also contestable: if he is wrong about consensus, *Eumenides* is not so obviously pan-Athenian. Where evidence is so slight, his dismissal of Thucydides 1.107.4, which mentions a conspiracy to overthrow the democracy in 458 or 457, is tendentious, and Christopher Pelling rightly emphasizes the danger of circularity in the whole argument (2000: 173).

Appeals to closural devices are another way of imposing determinacy. Evidence can be found to support open readings, too, but recent critics who tackle this issue prefer to avoid simple alternatives and see *Eumenides* not as promoting some one effect, but as reflecting or constituting political discourse or ideology, negotiating between competing ideologies, or the like. Both Griffith and Goldhill, for example, present the relationship of tragedy and ideology as anything but simple. They agree that tragic conflict is not always resolved, but sometimes suppressed, contained, or displaced. They also agree that tragedy offers different subject positions to its audience, and that some measure of validation is available to many, if not all, positions. For Griffith, "the actual or implied outcome of the whole process is a mutual assurance of the continuation in authority of a class of aristocratic leaders, vulnerable, occasionally flawed, but in the last resort infinitely precious and indispensable" (1995: 110). For Goldhill, on the other hand, the privileged discourse is democratic. The disagreement mirrors the one we saw earlier concerning the ideological import of Aristophanic comedy. Like Sommerstein in the case of Aristophanes, Griffith highlights aristocratic bias; like Henderson, Goldhill insists on the affirmation of the relatively new democratic framework. Since Athens in the fifth century did in fact see the persistence of aristocratic ideology and privilege alongside democratic ideology and institutions, the choice is largely one of emphasis. We may speak of a tension, rather than a contradiction or incoherence, because the effect of drama on most spectators was probably to promote thought and feeling rather than political action.

Outside the theater, of course, citizens did act directly. Choice might be easy or hard, but it was unavoidable; also, its motives might remain hidden. Because *Eumenides* so conspicuously politicizes its subject matter (Goldhill 2000b: 79), those spectators who were also citizens doubtless thought of the Athenian jurors' vote on Orestes' case at least partly in terms of political action. For reasons that remain inaccessible, the vote is split, and the jurors thus become a figure for the impossibility of simple meaning.[7] Goldhill (2000a: 55) suggestively connects this impossibility, in turn, with the inscription of political language in a "narrative web" that includes "the discourse of divinity, action, causation, power, memory, ritual that so dominate the narrative of the trilogy." Once again, a banalization is possible: as the original Areopagus Council, the jurymen are open to partisan reading as aristocrats. But the ways in which they are underdetermined seem equally or more important. Anonymous, idealized, silent, and the only Athenian men present (including in the closing procession), they are a fit projection of Athenian unity. Like the trilogy's political thought, however, this unity is irreducibly diverse.

Birds

In Aristophanes' *Birds*, produced in 414, two Athenians leave Athens in search of a *topos apragmōn*, a place free of trouble (line 44). They believe Tereus, who was a man but has been changed into a bird, can help them find it. While talking with him, one of the Athenians, Peisetaerus, conceives the plan of founding a city in the air. Called Cloudcuckooland, it will prosper by threatening the Olympian gods with a blockade and demanding that humans make their sacrifices from now on to the birds, who (he says) were the original rulers of the universe. The plan succeeds, and the play ends with Peisetaerus supremely triumphant; Zeus' promise to give up power is symbolically fulfilled by the arrival of a young woman called Basileia ("sovereignty"), whom Peisetaerus marries.

Birds reprises elements of the comedies discussed earlier, but a major difference is that there is no topic of immediate relevance to Athenian politics. As a result, it has been called "escapist," but while the atmospheric setting and mythical resonances of the plot make this understandable, Athenian content is pervasive, and Jeffrey Henderson insists that "Neither in the play nor in any external source is there the slightest suggestion that in spring 414 the Athenians generally were in an escapist mood; on the contrary, Thucydides portrays their mood as buoyant to the point of hubris (6.24–31)" (Henderson 1997: 136). Indeed, some detect more than a hint of hubris in the play itself: Peisetaerus' arrogant contempt for the gods and eventual displacement of Zeus convey a warning, and his triumph must be seen in an ironic light (Hubbard 1997; Romer 1997). Others doubt that Aristophanes would make such a warning central to the meaning of his play and suspect that the move to "irony" (the idea that the play really means the opposite of what it appears to mean), unusual in the interpretation of Aristophanes, is driven by a preconceived notion of what it *ought* to mean.

But if the move to irony is desperate, the way the play distances and generalizes its political content – a technique rare in surviving comedy but typical of tragedy – does call for an unusual mode of interpretation. Henderson, for example, continues, "The utopian fantasy of *Birds* was indeed generated by contemporary realities, but it is too large, distant, and autonomous to be limited by them"; the way the play comments on reality "is bound to be ambiguous and complex, and its mode suggestive or 'interrogative' rather than allegorical or didactic" (Henderson 1997: 136). The critic's task is "not to find one 'correct' meaning but rather to determine a range of meanings whose coexistence is topically significant" (1997: 137). Henderson fulfills this task in part by putting forward an intriguing new idea about Peisetaerus. Briefly, while Peisetaerus shares many traits with other Aristophanic hero(in)es, he differs from them in (1) being so full of contradictions that he represents no one social type; (2) possessing some elite traits (e.g., ambition, rhetorical and intellectual sophistication, contempt for religion) at which Aristophanes elsewhere takes satirical aim; and (3) undergoing a transformation from *apragmon* to ruler of the universe. The historical background Henderson assumes is that, under the democracy, some "well-to-do and cultivated Athenians" had "decided not to be ambitious for public distinction" until, in 415, a number of them (notably Alcibiades) stepped forward with a bold plan for Athenian expansion, of which they were to be the (natural) leaders. (On *apragmones*, "quietists," see also Brown, this volume, chapter 31.)

Henderson suggests that Peisetaerus may have evoked this brand of elite identity, though not, perhaps, for every spectator. After all, his talents are useful for the protagonist of any comedy to have, and his name ("persuader of comrades") can betoken the fundamentally democratic value of free and open debate. That "elite" is included among the hero's *possible* identities, however, is taken by Henderson to hint at Aristophanes' satisfaction that some members of that class had (re)entered politics, and/or his hope that still more would. In the event, Alcibiades' self-assertion provoked a backlash, and was soon followed by the divisive affairs of the Herms and the Mysteries. According to Henderson, *Birds* both contains hints of Aristophanes' disappointment at these developments and offers a fantasy in which the "true" elite assume their natural role without causing such a rift.

Crucially, a relationship to civic ideology like that with which Aristophanes had been successful earlier in his career (see above) remains available, and the new articulation of political identities differs only subtly from the old. The earlier distribution of satirical targets already offered evidence of bias (and in general, Aristophanes' appeals to the good old days are "conservative"), but unlike *Birds*, the plays from the 420s contain few if any positive hints that the "true" elite could actually lead. A hopeful and inclusive new vision of leadership is possibly to be seen in a few further details. First, Peisetaerus at least nominally acts on behalf of a community. (Critics disagree as to whether his roasting of allegedly rebellious birds at 1583–5 is a passing joke or unmasks his apparently sympathetic concern for the birds as a sham; see further Sommerstein 2005: 79–84.) And while his treatment of impostors is in most respects typical, the scene with the Father Beater suggests how internal unity may be achieved. The young man is given a panoply (like a war orphan) and urged to enlist in the army and find an acceptable outlet for his aggression (1360–9). It is also at least arguable that the treatment of hated types who profited from the empire (Inspector, Decree Seller, and Informer) represented a somewhat conciliatory gesture toward Ionian and other "allies" in the audience, at a time when Athens was no doubt keen to avoid conflict in the Aegean. In this case, the notion of "internal" unity expanded to include non-Athenians.

Ion

Euripides' *Ion* dramatizes the reunion of Creusa, last living child of the mythical Athenian king Erechtheus, and Ion, the son she bore after being raped by the god Apollo. My summary of an intricate background and plot must be limited to a few points of political significance. Erechtheus and Creusa are descended from Erichthonius, said by a popular Athenian myth to have been born from the earth. This is one meaning of the word "autochthonous"; literally true of Erichthonius, it applies by extension to his descendants by ordinary sexual reproduction, and in some sense to the community as a whole by association with its rulers. Myth also told that the Athenians had not, like other Greeks, come to their territory from elsewhere, but had always inhabited Attica; all Athenians could claim to be "autochthonous" in this second sense, even though they knew very well that many of them, or their forebears, had more or less recently immigrated, and indeed other myths praised Athens for opening itself to them. (On autochthony, see, e.g., Loraux 1993; Zacharia 2003: 56–65.)

Few stories were told of Ion; his one indispensable function is as eponym of the Ionian Greeks. Athens claimed to be the base from which colonial expansion into the lands inhabited by Ionians occurred, and in the fifth century, this became a charter myth for Athenian domination of the region. What most Greeks believed about Ion's place in hellenic genealogy is reflected in the Hesiodic *Catalogue of Women* (fr. 1a.20–4 MW), where he is the son of the Erechtheid Creusa and Xuthus, son of Hellen; his brothers are Dorus and Aeolus, eponyms of Dorians and Aeolians. Euripides alters this: in *Ion*, Athena tells Creusa she will bear Xuthus sons, Dorus and Achaeus (1589–94). While using the new or little known story of Apollo's paternity to associate Athenians and Ionians with divinity and each other, then, Euripides brazenly demotes Dorians and Achaeans to lesser descendants of the Athenian royal house. (On Ionianism and genealogy, see Parker 1987; J. Hall 1997; Zacharia 2003: 48–55.)

Myths of Athenian autochthony became popular after the Persian Wars and remained so throughout the fifth century; their uses included "propaganda" throughout the Peloponnesian War. Likewise, Euripides' revision of Hellenic genealogy, taken at face value, would be welcome to Athenians at any time during that war. No external source gives a date for *Ion*, but metrical criteria point to the second half of the 410s, a period about which we know so much that assigning *Ion* to a particular year could have enormous implications for nuanced political interpretation. And one still has to gauge the tone of the play, an unusually difficult task that cannot detain us here. Most scholars see the effect of both autochthony and Ionianism on Athenian viewers as affirmative and cohesive, but a few take the opposite view or, more subtly, argue that the play invites searching questions about the supposed purity of the citizen body (Walsh 1978; Saxonhouse 1986). Also, in light of what we have said about *Birds*, it is worth mentioning that Ionianism seems to presuppose an audience in which the presence of Ionians matters.

While they have a fifth century history, autochthony and Ionianism work by making claims about the mythic past in which the play is set. At one point, however, the issue of Ion's participation in practical politics is framed anachronistically in ways that strongly suggest fifth century realities. Halfway through, when he believes wrongly that he is the son of Xuthus and an unknown but probably non-Athenian woman, Ion explains that he would rather stay in Delphi than go to Athens because, among other reasons, (1) he is the bastard son of a foreigner rather than an autochthon (589–92); (2) if he tries to lead, he will be hated by the mass of unprivileged citizens, laughed at by elite quietists, and opposed by rival leaders (593–606); and (3) he will not enjoy *parrhesia*, the privilege of frank speech, unless his mother turns out to be Athenian (670–5). Ion is "in fact" the son of an Olympian god and an Athenian princess. Projected in one way onto fifth century reality, this looks like as elite an identity as it is possible to have. But here and elsewhere (especially 1539–45, which raise issues of legitimacy and inheritance) the text dwells on practical and legal obstacles he will face, not only on the mistaken assumption underlying the passage just summarized, but also on the basis of his true identity, the revelation of which might have been expected to remove them. All of the following identities bear on Ion's case, at some point and/or at some level: temple slave; bastard son of a non-Athenian man who may or may not have been naturalized as a citizen; adopted son of that man and an Athenian woman; bastard son of an Athenian woman and a god. One of these (the third) might just entitle him to citizen rights under Athenian law, but even that one is a far cry from the ideal of legitimate offspring of two Athenian parents envisaged by the Periclean Citizenship Law enacted in 451 (for details and bearing on *Ion*, see Ogden 1996: 59–77, 155–6). One effect of this jumble of identities could be that the discourse of political participation is in some subtle way broadened. The significance of this is not its bearing on any policy issue actually before the Athenians at the time – though at dates close to *Ion* Athens found itself rethinking such matters amid oligarchic revolution and military collapse. It is rather that Ion, in many respects an ideal Athenian, is no Athenian at all according to the usual, exclusionary definition.[8]

Lysistrata

The title figure of Aristophanes' *Lysistrata* (produced in 411) masterminds a two-part plan to force the Athenians and Spartans to make peace. The wives of Greece refuse to have sex with their husbands, and older women seize the Acropolis and deny Athenian men access to the treasure used to finance the war. The first action is carried out by individual women, whose struggle to maintain their resolve and torment of their husbands make for several bawdy scenes; the second is the work of a half-chorus, fecklessly opposed by a half-chorus of old men. Representatives of Athenian male authority appear and negotiate with Lysistrata, who leads (while standing somewhat aloof from) both prongs of the attack. Eventually, the men capitulate. The half-choruses reconcile and unite, and Lysistrata brings a woman called "Reconciliation" before the Athenian and Spartan representatives, who come to terms by dividing the sexual "territory" represented by her body.

An obvious question to ask about the play's political significance is whether Aristophanes wants to be understood as seriously favoring a negotiated end to the war. The actual terms the Athenians might have obtained at the time would have involved much more sacrifice than the play even remotely suggests; as in other plays, real obstacles are conveniently elided (Henderson 1987: xix–xx). A way of attributing serious purpose to the play nonetheless is to say that it reminds those in authority that the people are tired of war and won't put up with it forever. Further dimensions of political thought follow from two important innovations. First, as in the 420s plays, a dominant character engineers a solution to a pressing contemporary issue, but for the first time, that character is female. Second, delaying the success of the heroine's plan produces a tension more typical of tragedy than old comedy (Henderson 1987: xxviii–xxxiii).

Within the comic fantasy of "women on top," the women speak and act in ways that are both laughable and serious (Pelling 2000: 209–18). Much potentially serious content is offered by Lysistrata herself, who is allowed several more or less overt claims to authority. She has an apparently longstanding interest in public affairs, which she hears about from men at home or even, surprisingly, in the streets (lines 507–24). She points out that women contribute sons to the community – an obvious point, but one whose seriousness is underscored by the pained reaction it gets from the Athenian magistrate ("Proboulos") at 589–90. At 1124–7, she proclaims her own intelligence and says she has been educated by listening to her father and other elders; the adaptation of a tragic heroine's words here constitutes another implicit claim to authority. As for her arguments themselves, when she describes managing the city's affairs in terms of women's traditional role in managing the household, inventive humor may or may not overshadow a fundamentally sound idea; many modern readers find the extended metaphor of working wool and weaving a cloak for the city plausible and even moving (567–86, lines which seem to have influenced Plato at *Plt.* 308d–11c). When she lectures the Athenian and Spartan representatives, her broad and nostalgic program unseriously elides real difficulties but is probably not without emotional appeal (1129–61). If so, it is lost on the men, who ignore her and lust for Reconciliation; for the audience, it may be the same, or humor may provide the cushion enabling her to be taken seriously. Mention should also be made of the possibility that Lysistrata ("Army-Disbander") reminded the original audience of Lysimache ("Battle-Disbander"), Priestess of Athena Polias at the time. Lysimache is in fact mentioned at 554; association of the heroine with a real woman (who may even have had known views on public matters such as the war) in a genre that avoids even naming respectable women would be a remarkably bold step. It is disputed whether Aristophanes took it (Henderson 1987: xxxviii–xl; Revermann 2006: 236–43), but a more general association of Lysistrata with Athena herself constitutes yet another claim to authority. Fewer such claims are evident in the case of the half-chorus of women, but their remark that they owe good advice to the city because they have participated in important religious rituals is noteworthy (638–48), as is their repetition of Lysistrata's point that contributing sons gives them a stake in the community (649–51).

Crucially, Lysistrata acts on behalf of the whole community; the contrast with the selfish heroes of earlier plays (with the very partial exception of Peisetaerus, as discussed above) could hardly be sharper. Delayed success means that there is no parade of "impostors" denied a share of blessings; on the contrary, Lysistrata makes sure the men and women of Greece all get what they want. She is so self-effacing that there is no trace of her in the text after 1188, though the idea that she presides, Athena-like, over the final scene is attractive (Henderson 1987: 215). Even more significant is the form her success takes: not fulfillment of individual sexual fantasy, but restoration of domestic happiness for everyone, perfectly symbolized by couple dancing (1273–end).

Conclusion

To say that the uniquely inclusive celebration at the end of *Lysistrata* somehow widens public discourse is not to deny that the heroine's self-effacement and assimilation to Athena's sexless image represent a triumph for the feminine that is at best highly qualified. And as in *Ion*, a reminder that the play's political thought has nothing to do with any contemplated extension of political rights in the usual sense is in order. *Eumenides* can be heard with an emphasis on what unites Athenians or what divides them; if *Birds* varies the ideological model with which Aristophanes rose to success, it does so without becoming unfamiliar or threatening. Drama is not a call to direct political action, and its effect on some spectators may even be to stifle it (Griffith 2005: 348–50). But although there is no simple, progressive story to be told about fifth century Greek drama, we do not have to believe that all its audiences ever wanted was to see their prejudices confirmed, and there is every reason for modern readers, interested as we are in more expansive notions of participatory citizenship than Greek drama seems at first to offer, to look for the seeds of such notions wherever we can, and then to consider which if any bore fruit, why or why not, and when and for whom. When we do, we find a wide range of issues articulated with a subtlety and intelligence that make them very much worth studying today.

FURTHER READING

Several recent handbooks cover Greek tragedy (or tragedy generally) in all its aspects and provide plentiful bibliography: Easterling 1997; Bushnell 2005; J. Gregory 2005. For both tragedy and comedy, see Storey and Allan 2005. On Greek drama's festival setting, the classic work is Pickard-Cambridge 1988; Csapo and Slater 1994 translate and interpret most of the sources and give greater attention to theatrical production outside Athens and later than the fifth century BCE. See also the work on reception studies cited in note 4. Book-length treatments of literature (or tragedy), history, and political thought include Rose 1992; Meier 1993; Pelling 2000; and D. Carter 2007. On comedy and political thought, see Heath 1987a; Konstan 1995; and McGlew 2002. Menander, poet of Athenian "New Comedy," has had to be left out of account here; see Konstan 1995; Major 1997; and Lape 2004. Much of the most important work on drama and political thought is in collections of essays or conference proceedings: Euben 1986; Winkler and Zeitlin 1990; Sommerstein et al. 1993; Goff 1995; Dobrov 1997; Pelling 1997; Boedeker and Raaflaub 1998; J. Davidson et al. 2006; Cairns and Liapis 2006.

NOTES

I am grateful to the editor and to Peter Hunt for perceptive and helpful comments on this chapter.

1 See also Gellrich 1995; Pelling 1997: 228–31 and esp. Cartledge 2002a.
2 Regarding women, my own guess is that they attended. Although their marginal status may have been reflected in low numbers or segregated seating, their presence nevertheless had the potential to affect the gender dynamics of dramatic performance radically. The degree to which this potential was realized will have varied according to the subject matter and treatment of the plays and the dispositions of individual spectators, but it must be taken seriously.
3 On tragedy and ideology see, e.g., Gregory 1991; Meier 1993; Croally 1994, 2005; Foley 1995; Pelling 1997: 224–35; 2000: 177–84; work cited in the next paragraph in the text, and below on *Eumenides*. On ideology in general, see Rhodes, this volume, chapter 4. The idea that tragedy is didactic, emphasized in different ways by Gregory, Meier, and Croally (cf. Boedeker and Raaflaub 2005: 109–11), is ancient, but modern critics do not limit themselves to the simple (and often interested) "lessons" discerned by ancient authors, nor should they.
4 Easterling 1994; Taplin 1999. A major current of contemporary work on Greek drama, reception studies, considers the plays as they have been reperformed, translated, adapted, and used intertextually from the fifth century BCE to the present. The increasing quantity and sophistication of reception studies, in which political thought is a favored topic, are stimulating new ways of thinking about original performance. See Easterling 1997: chs 9–12; Hardwick 2003; Rehm 2003; and especially work written and inspired by Oliver Taplin, Edith Hall, Fiona Macintosh, and others associated with the Archive of Performances of Greek and Roman Drama, whose website (www.apgrd.ox.ac.uk) may be consulted for references and further information.
5 Tempted perhaps by certain features of the genre (in particular the *parabasis*, a traditional form in which the chorus typically sheds its fictive identity and purports to speak directly to the audience on behalf of the poet), some comic critics write about the poet's personal views and intentions rather more confidently than tragic ones typically do. There are reasons to resist the temptation (Hubbard 1991), but it matters even more that discussion also include

the role of context and recipients in shaping meaning. As to comedy's political effects, Aristophanes' legal trouble with Cleon and the sporadically attested efforts to control comic satire by legislation also enter the discussion (e.g. Sommerstein 1996a: 331–3; 2004; Henderson 1998).

6 I follow Sommerstein 1989: 25–32, expanded at 1996b: 392–402. For a similar survey of approaches to the *Oresteia*, see Carter 2007: 21–63. For historical discussion of Ephialtes' reforms, see Rhodes 1992: 67–77.

7 The long-running debate over how many votes are cast is ably summarized by Sommerstein 1989: 221–6; Seaford 1995 and Goldhill 2000a: 51–6 consider its implications for open versus closed reading.

8 Ober 2005c approaches what I regard as related issues from several angles. For example, he is interested in whether the homogeneity of the Athenian citizenry has been exaggerated, and in the implications of the Athenians' often lax enforcement of the supposedly strict boundary between citizens and others, particularly the question whether this liberality (a term he uses with all due caution) followed a logic inherent, if apparently unrecognized, in Athenian democracy itself. The exclusivity of Athenian compared to Roman notions of citizenship is stressed by Champion, this volume, chapter 6 (esp. on *Ion*, pp. 91–92).

CHAPTER 29

Character in Politics

Philip A. Stadter

He held power because of his stature, his judgment, and his obvious disinterest in money.
                                                                                    Thucydides

I pray for good emperors, but I put up with whomever I get.

                                                                                    Tacitus

In classical thought, the character of political leaders, good or bad, had a direct effect
on events at least as important as other impersonal factors such as the inherent
irrationality of human nature, the relation of financial strength to military prepared-
ness, and the eccentricities of fortune. To take one famous example, Thucydides
attributed Pericles' success as a politician to his character as well as his intellectual
abilities. His foresight was important, but was only effective when combined with his
integrity regarding money, his devotion to Athens, and his willingness to speak
frankly to his fellow citizens. In contrast, Thucydides presented later politicians as
ambitious, greedy, and undisciplined. Their weaknesses created discord in the city and
led to Athens' defeat by Sparta. Character counted.

In everyday life, persons recognize and evaluate character through words and
actions, but frequently disagree on the implications and interpretations of the same
person's character. In interpreting the character of historical persons, readers must
rely on the historian, who chooses salient features and offers an interpretation.
Different historians will focus on different features, and draw different conclusions.
Readers then must make their own judgment given the evidence presented. Speaking
of character is an act of interpretation.

This essay will begin by considering how three fourth century BC authors, Xenophon,
Plato, and Aristotle, laid the theoretical basis for speaking of character in politics. The
second part will look at how Polybius and Livy related Rome's extraordinary success
to individual character. Finally, the establishment of the Roman Principate provoked
new understandings of the effect of character on politics. Examples from Tacitus,
Pliny the Younger, and Plutarch will illustrate the new and searching appraisal of the

A Companion to Greek and Roman Political Thought, First Edition. Edited by Ryan K. Balot.
© 2013 Blackwell Publishing Ltd. Published 2013 by Blackwell Publishing Ltd.

character of the good leader and the good subject, and the defects in statesmen and emperors which brought turmoil, defeat, civil war, and tyranny.

Fourth Century: Theory and Practice

In the first half of the fourth century BC thinkers came to realize that more was needed of a political leader than the traditional qualities of good birth and intelligence, or even the new rhetorical training advocated by the sophists. Even the rigid Spartan civic structure and educational program was no longer able to produce successful leaders. Xenophon, Isocrates, Plato, and Aristotle attempted to define the virtues necessary for political leadership; Plato also attempted to describe new programs of education and of civic life and structures or constitutions which could inform citizens with these virtues (see in this volume, Hedrick, chapter 27, and Forsdyke, chapter 15).

Xenophon, a young Athenian gentleman and contemporary of Plato's, lived through the defeat of Athens in 404. He was particularly conscious of the effect of character in politics in the narrative of his *Greek History* (*Hellenica*) and in other semihistorical works. In the *Anabasis*, he offered sketches of many leaders, including the admirable Persian prince who had hired the army, but had lost his life in a rash cavalry charge, and three Greek commanders killed by the Persians: Clearchus, the Spartan "war-lover," a stern and often violent martinet, who was nevertheless valued by his men in the moment of battle; Proxenus, Xenophon's personal friend, "who thought all men were as good as he was" and so could not control his troops; and Meno, who considered duplicity and treachery as the best route to success. Meno, after betraying his fellow generals, was tortured and killed by the Persians (*Anab.* 2.6). Xenophon's own character as commander emerges in contrast to these: responsible, firm, quick to learn and to innovate, and devoted to his troops but not soft on them. Throughout, Xenophon consciously distinguishes different character traits by behavioral patterns and appropriate adjectives, and relates these traits to actions and consequences.

The formation of the character of a good leader by proper training and self-fashioning is the grand theme of Xenophon's *Cyropaedia*, a fictional biography of Cyrus the Great of Persia. The good ruler must keep focused on one goal, deserving and winning the support of others. To do this he must self-consciously keep his own desires under careful control and instead think constantly of the needs of his allies and subjects and win them with generosity, while keeping a cool eye on the realities of power. The *Cyropaedia* is meant to inspire the reader to shape his own life in similar fashion; it was often cited by Cicero and other Roman authors.

Xenophon also exalts the virtue of a real leader whom he had known, King Agesilaus of Sparta, in an encomium, *Agesilaus*, which lists the king's virtues and gives examples of each in action, drawn from the history, while tacitly passing over his weaknesses. Isocrates' *Euagoras* similarly presents the virtues of a recently deceased king of Cyprus as a model for the king's son and for all political figures. In both works, the subject's virtues are seen as the product of conscious choice, which others might imitate.

Plato and Aristotle attempted to formulate a more theoretical understanding of the interaction of different elements within the self and the individual's role within a society, building on Greek traditions going back to Homer. Within the self, reason ideally should set goals according to universal values and moderate and direct the dynamics of the self's irrational tendencies and passions in the pursuit of these goals. Aristotle argued that virtues are dispositions which permit us to choose to act according to reason so as to attain our proper (good and noble) goal. Good character is learned, though innate qualities will affect the individual outcome. The principal sphere of action of the virtuous man is in society and his virtues are the same as the virtues of a ruler or leader. Practical reason is prized, not simply because it is useful, but because reason is the highest human capacity and is intrinsically noble, since it helps us to see what is the true good, independent of an individual's preexisting preferences or tendencies.

Unlike Enlightenment thinkers, classical writers attributed a person's character much more to moral training than to preformed desires inherent from birth. Proper training depended on the community's encouragement of right behavior through laws, customs, and the structures of civic government, as well as teachers and individual self-improvement. For this reason Plato and other philosophers gave special emphasis to the description of the ideal community, one suited to produce good character.

Ancient historians attributed different character traits to different peoples, based on their different customs and civic constitutions. Polybius is noteworthy for devoting the whole of book 6 to the special qualities of the Romans, discussing the army, honors for military success, and the role of religion. He discusses the particular excellence of the Roman constitution at length, comparing it to those of other states – Thebes, Athens, Crete (which he considers steeped in treachery), Carthage, and Sparta. Livy touches on the qualities of peoples encountered by the Romans, noting for example the Greeks' preference for talk over action and the Numidians' sexual appetite (8.22.8, 29.23.4, 30.12.18). In his *Germania*, Tacitus admires the freedom and rough simplicity of the German tribes, contrasting it to the subservience and decadence of contemporary imperial Rome. Pliny speaks of the responsibility of ruling Greeks, who "gave us justice and laws," and where "civilization, literature, and agriculture are thought to have originated" (Pliny, *Ep.* 8.24). However, apart from Polybius, such evaluations are usually hardly more than stereotypes and have relatively little influence on the historians' analysis of political action or of individual character.

Ancient views of the person focus on his or her role as a moral agent. Although individuals may be constrained by poverty or by a weak and factious state, or buffeted by external circumstances, it was considered a fallen state, not the norm, for them to be passive objects of internal impulses or upbringing. Thus descriptive adjectives describing character tend to be evaluative, either directly or implicitly. Different thinkers gave different emphases, but generally speaking, the good man, and the ideal leader of a state, is one who through his training has learned to channel his irrational urges and desires toward rationally chosen and noble goals, that is, to exercise virtue.

Historians of the Roman Republic

These concepts of character and moral agency form the basis of presentation of individuals by the historians of the hellenistic and Roman periods. Nevertheless, each historian's interpretation of character and its effects reflects his own background and political context. The rise first of the hellenistic monarchies and then of the Roman Republic meant that the underlying civic structure changed considerably from that of the city-states of fourth century Greece, and with it the virtues most important in a given society. In particular, the communal government of the Roman republican oligarchy required a respect for others and a limitation of one's own ambitions, but was not well fitted to control great men who rose to power in times of crisis, especially in the last years of the Republic. Nevertheless, historians continued to focus on the presence or absence of virtues in political leaders, as we see in the histories of Polybius and Livy.

Polybius (ca. 200–ca. 118 BC) was trained in the Greek aristocratic tradition of honor, duty, and glory. Taken to Rome after the defeat of Macedonia in 168 BC, he conceived the idea of a grand history of Rome's rapid conquest of the Mediterranean world. Many factors contributed to Rome's success, including her unusually stable constitution, highly organized army, and customs which promoted courage and moral character. Polybius finds the Roman constitution much superior to those of Sparta and Carthage in exactly this respect, and moreover, in that it was well adapted to acquiring and holding an empire (Polyb. 6.43–58). Not the least factor in its greatness was the character of its leaders and that of its opponents. Although only fragments survive of much of his history, many of these derive from a Byzantine collection of excerpts on virtue and vice, and thus are especially illuminating in this regard. Three features distinguish his treatment of character.

First, Polybius recognized the difficulty of establishing a person's character. Analyzing Hannibal's behavior, he comments on the difficulty of pinning down a person's underlying qualities, because the pressure and complexity of circumstances and the persuasion of friends can strongly influence action (9.22–6). Obviously Hannibal was outstandingly capable, managing not only the campaign in Italy, but those in Spain and Sicily. But was he extraordinarily cruel and greedy for money, as many said? Polybius questioned the accusation, and cited several examples of persons who had acted harshly under one set of circumstances, and nobly under others. In particular, he thought Hannibal's harsh treatment of his Italian allies after the Roman capture of Capua in 211 BC forced on him by circumstance, not a feature of his character. Men, he noted, can act contrary to their basic direction. Similar passages discuss the Greek leader Aratus (4.8) and other rulers (9.23).

Second, even when the city offered a conducive environment, a proper education was essential to the formation of character. He praised the Greek hero Philopoemen's early training, which taught him courage, endurance, and a moderate style of life (10.22). He himself became a mentor for the young Scipio Aemilianus and writes at some length, full of pride and pleasure, of the young man's moderation (*sophrosunē*) regarding sex and other diversions, his liberality and lack of avarice regarding money, and the physical courage he learned while hunting (31.25–30). Polybius conceived his own work as both a moral and a political education for his readers.

Third, as Eckstein says, "Polybius viewed human character as complex and malleable, but fundamentally weak" (1995: 239). Of the many persons among the Romans, their allies, and their opponents whose character he sketches, very few show great virtues. The Second Punic War produced the greatest number: men like Hamilcar Barca, Hannibal, and Scipio Africanus; later, Greece could boast of Philopoemen. The victories of Scipio Africanus had changed the whole Mediterranean world; the others were worthy opponents of Rome. Taking advantage of the fact that Philopoemen, Hannibal, and Scipio all died in the same year, he reviews their characters (23.12–14). Philopoemen had an active political career for 40 years, and had spoken frankly at all times, but never aroused envy. Hannibal was a born leader, for although he led a motley army of many nationalities and barbarian tribes, he never was conspired against or deserted by those who served under him. Scipio won unprecedented popularity with the people and respect from the Roman senate. But many men were dominated by passion or vice and so accomplished little. A great general, like Hannibal before Cannae, considers the character of his opponent, Polybius observes, and lists possible weaknesses: idleness, drunkenness, sexual pleasure, cowardice, rashness, foolish ambition, and vanity (3.81.3–9). Polybius' pessimism seems to grow as his work progresses. Even at Rome luxury and self-interest come to overwhelm virtue. Cato the Censor and Aemilius Paullus showed some of the old virtue (31.25.5a, 31.22), but such figures were rare. Among the young men, Scipio Aemilianus' moderation was exceptional.

Polybius, initially impressed by the outstanding success of the Romans, sadly reflected that most men, too weak to develop the moral strength and inner discipline to restrain their less noble impulses, could never become suitable leaders.

Livy and Sallust wrote during the last days of the Roman Republic, when its collapse was complete and the new structure of monarchy was emerging. Both saw the decay of moral character in the state's leaders as a major cause of the crisis. Sallust wrote of the arrogance, greed, and lust for power of the aristocracy at Rome. Livy (59–17 BC) took a longer view, choosing to trace the history of Rome from its foundation, in the hope that his readers would find models to imitate. He proudly asserts, "No country has ever been greater or more upright than ours or richer in fine examples; none has been free for so many generations from the vices of avarice and luxury" (*Preface* 11). For Livy, as for Polybius, early Rome was a city in which virtue could flourish. The sturdy simplicity of the farmer-warrior could shape a courageous, honest, and straightforward leader. As the centuries wore on, Rome's virtue declined, until the Republic finally collapsed. In the first ten books, treating the earliest history of Rome and its expansion in Italy, Livy retells on the basis of flimsy traditions exemplary stories of good and bad behavior. These include the tales of Lucretia, Horatius at the bridge, and Camillus, the victor over Veii, who patiently endured an unjust exile, then returned to save Rome from the Gauls and rebuild the city. The books treating the Hannibalic War and Rome's expansion eastward (20–45) draw upon Polybius' history, but reconceive the period from a Roman and mid-first century perspective. The later books, which chronicled the struggles for domination by the great generals and dynasts, Marius, Sulla, Pompey, Caesar, and Augustus, are lost. Not surprisingly, given the tumult of his age, Livy constantly favors moderation and concord in individuals and in the state as a whole.

In contrast to Polybius, Livy prefers an indirect presentation of character to direct authorial statements. He much prefers to use speeches by the person in question (which according to convention he himself composed), in combination with opinions expressed or reactions shown by contemporaries. He will rewrite a direct judgment by Polybius as an opinion, speech or letter by another party. From time to time he will offer a few sentences at the death of important persons. These obituaries are not simple eulogies, but compressed evaluations of the impact of the person's character and career on the city.

On a few occasions, Livy will offer a full character sketch. One of the most impressive introduces his reader to Hannibal (21.4). Livy's portrait rhetorically combines standard features of a great general and an implacable enemy, without attempting a particularized analysis of character. As a leader, Hannibal is vigorous, able both to command and obey, a risk-taker and skilled tactician, tireless and tough in mind and body, and an unequaled warrior on foot or horseback. As an enemy, he is cruel, treacherous, and without regard for truth, honor, the gods, oaths, or anything sacred. This characterization states the challenge that Rome faced from the implacable hatred of a brilliant general and creates the background against which Roman virtues will be demonstrated.

The great figure in our extant books is Scipio Africanus, the victor over Hannibal. Livy praises his generalship, but gives little attention to the finer details of tactics or strategy, preferring to emphasize his moral qualities. In war, his courage, dynamism, hard work, courage, and commanding presence make him an ideal military leader. But he also shows self-control, clemency, and amiability in interacting with Romans and with enemies. His extraordinary pursuit of glory did provoke envy, however, and he was attacked by Cato and others. In the unseemly trials to which he and his brother were subjected at the end of his life, he stands out as a unique individual, the savior of Rome, imperious and self-confident in his extraordinary service to the state and the blessings of the gods. Even a personal enemy, Sempronius Gracchus, delivers a speech recognizing Rome's debt to him (38.50.4–53, cf. 38.55.10–13). Nevertheless, Livy notes that Scipio excelled more in war than in peace; he could not endure the pettiness of political life after the greatness of his achievements.

The outstanding hero presages the great dynasts of the late republic, hungry for glory and power, and unwilling to respect the customs of oligarchy. Scipio may have reminded Livy of Pompey the Great, who hoped that his many victories would give him an honored and secure place in political life, without the need constantly to defend and strengthen his position. The fragment preserving Livy's opinion on Cicero, immediately after his murder on the orders of Mark Antony (frr. 60–1 Weissenborn from book 120 = Sen. *Suas.* 6.17, 22), speaks to the violence of those years:

> he bore none of his misfortunes like a man, except his death, which, if one judges rightly, might seem less unsuitable, since he suffered nothing worse from his victorious enemy

than, if had been fortunate, he would have done to his defeated opponent. Nevertheless,
if one should weigh his vices against his virtues, he was a great and memorable man, who
would need a Cicero to speak his praises properly.

Livy compresses into a few words his disgust at the viciousness of civil war and his
admiration for Cicero's eloquence and service to Rome. Both Antony and Cicero
exceeded any usual civic norms: their violence and extremism are both symptoms and
causes of the destruction of the Republic.

Historians of the Roman Empire

The foundation of the monarchy by Augustus changed the dynamics of power. New
questions presented themselves. What kind of character did the autocrat have, and
what would be desirable? What was the character of a subject? (see Noreña, this
volume, chapter 17). Under Tiberius, the senate still preserved some importance. In
succeeding reigns, however, the palace, with the imperial women and freedmen close
to the emperor, overshadowed the senate. At all periods, the character of the emperor
dominated all. Great strains pulled those citizens who wished to stand out in the
society but dared not challenge the emperor. Monarchy offered the possibility of civic
peace and order after the murderous factional battles of the first century BC. But it
also changed the way in which both monarch and subject could learn and practice
virtue. Succession to power by birth or the army, the rise of freedmen administrators
and confidants, and the threat which a strong leader presented to the monarchy were
some of the factors constraining the development and practice of a leadership based
on virtue. Three authors must suffice to give a sense of the issues raised: Tacitus, Pliny
the Younger, and Plutarch.

Tacitus (ca. AD 56–ca. 120), writing a century later than Livy, found it hard to find
examples of moral greatness or nobility under the emperors who followed Augustus.
The play of character, politics, and power in Tacitus' works is too complex to give
more than two small samples. The first looks at the characterizations of Tiberius and
his potential successor Germanicus; the second at that of Agricola, governor of
Britain under Domitian.

"The inborn arrogance of the Claudian family and signs of a harsh disposition kept
breaking out, though he tried to suppress them" (Tac. *Ann.* 1.4): thus, we are told,
gossip about Tiberius ran even while Augustus was alive. Tacitus' final notice, looking
back over 23 years of rule, ends with these words: "As long as he supported or feared
Sejanus [his chief agent for many years before his abrupt execution], the cruelty of
Tiberius was hated, but his lusts were kept secret. Afterwards he followed only his
own nature and erupted in crimes and vice, throwing aside fear and shame" (6.51). In
between these two passages, using a variety of techniques – reported speeches,
innuendo, suggestion, comments by observers, and direct statements – Tacitus
makes us understand Tiberius' duplicity, arrogance, and cruelty. Most difficult to
penetrate was his secretiveness. In a speech to the senate after the funeral for

Augustus, Tiberius spoke of the difficulty of ruling the empire, and asked for help. Tacitus comments, "whatever Tiberius said, even when he did not aim at conceal-ment, was – by habit or nature – always hesitant, always cryptic." In this case, he adds, "his words became more and more equivocal and obscure" (1.11). The senators could not trust what he said, and thus began a game in which neither they nor the emperor spoke directly. For the senators, there was fear of a misstep: some word which would result in disgrace, exile, or death; for Tiberius, some real or imagined threat to his position. From the first, the regime proceeded in an atmosphere of tension and oppression.

The gloom is made darker by the contrasting figure of Germanicus, whom Tacitus presents as the opposite of his uncle and adoptive father: friendly, mild, dignified, restrained in his pleasures, a warrior known especially for his clemency (*Ann.* 2.72–3). He is first introduced leading the troops in Germany, where he is much loved for his openness and rapport with the troops. In fact, too much so: at the news of Augustus' death, the troops rise against their commanders, and demand that Germanicus accept their acclamation as emperor. Suddenly, Germanicus seems well out of his depth, floundering in the sea of the soldiers' emotions, hardly a resolute leader of men. He remains loyal to Tiberius, but can restore order only with much bloodshed (*Ann.* 1.31–45). Soon after he was assigned to the east, where he had some significant diplomatic successes but also made a naive visit to Egypt which threatened imperial prerogative. Shortly thereafter he fell sick and died, perhaps, Tacitus intimates, poisoned at Tiberius' orders (2.53–61, 69–72).

At this point Tacitus reports the praise Germanicus received at his funeral, with-holding his own comments. They compared him favorably with Alexander, claiming that he was more kind to his friends, more restrained in his pleasures, and more merciful. He was Alexander's equal as a commander, but less rash (2.73). The virtues ascribed to Germanicus contrast sharply with Tiberius' arrogance, sensuality, and cruelty, yet the comparison with Alexander seems ridiculously exaggerated, besides revealing Germanicus' very limited success as a field commander. Tacitus seems bitterly ironic with respect to the characters of both Tiberius and Germanicus. The latter is no Alexander, but his naive goodwill contrasts with the suspicious and constricted climate of Tiberian Rome.

Those who compared Germanicus to Alexander offered a vision of a simpler world, where daring men did great deeds and the rhetoric of glory and virtue responded to the needs of leader and populace. Tacitus' characters live a more complex history, where devious plans are shaped in the recesses of the imperial palace, and success depends more on astuteness, deception, and suspicion than simplicity and goodwill.

Neither man appears from their words and actions to justify these portraits. Tacitus overlays his own interpretation on the events, but his narrative allows us also to construct alternative histories and ascribe different characteristics to Tiberius. The continuing fascination with this period of Roman history derives in no small part from the ways in which Tacitus challenges us to envision the emperor's character. The reader, like Tiberius' contemporaries, is left to read ambiguous signs, never sure whether he has penetrated the enigma. Tantalizingly, at the end of the Tiberian segment of his narrative, Tacitus points us in two different directions. Was Tiberius' character perhaps "transformed and deranged by absolute power," as one man asserted, or had it always been vicious, but kept hidden, and was revealed fully only "after all fear and shame were removed," as Tacitus' own words affirm (*Ann.* 6.48, 51)?

The unveiling of Tiberius' hidden character functions as a metaphor for the monarchy, which only reveals its true nature over time. The unlimited and unaccountable power of the emperor renders every ruler a tyrant. For a time, like Tiberius, he may live under powerful influences which inhibit his behavior, but soon the true nature of the ruler will emerge. Different rulers may favor different vices, but at heart they are the same. It is the monarchy itself which "follows its own inner nature." In autocracy, the function of the good citizen is to limit and direct the power of the *princeps*, if he dares to do so.

Tacitus portrays just such a good citizen in his biography of his father-in-law, Agricola, a senator, consul, and governor of Britain. Success was dangerous, especially under the emperor Domitian, in whom suspicion of rivals gradually grew to paranoia. Agricola early learned to temper his ambition with moderation, and pursued a military career away from Rome with diligence and spirit. In reporting his victories to Domitian, he carefully avoided boastfulness, but even so, Tacitus says, Domitian was fearful of a rival (*Agr.* 39). On his return to Rome, he tried to be as inconspicuous as possible, and with difficulty avoided the dangerous honor of being appointed to a higher position (40, 41). Tacitus praises his behavior:

> The emperor ... was softened by the moderation and prudence of Agricola, who neither by a perverse obstinacy nor an idle parade of freedom challenged fame or provoked his fate. ... There may be great men even under bad emperors, and obedience and submission, when joined to activity and vigor, may attain a glory which most men reach only by a perilous career, utterly useless to the state, and closed by an ostentatious death. (*Agr.* 42, trans. Church and Brodribb 1942)

The courage of the Stoic senators Thrasea Paetus and Helvidius Priscus, who opposed Nero and Domitian and were executed, should be admired, but their confrontational style not imitated. The description of Agricola might fit Tacitus himself, who also made his career under Domitian, and all those senators who tried to live with honor under difficult emperors, avoiding dangerous and futile opposition.

One of these was Tacitus' friend Pliny (ca. AD 61–ca. 112). His nine books of letters to his friends, including Tacitus, also address the proper role of a senator under an autocracy. They describe meetings of the senate, defense and prosecution of senatorial governors, and leisure activities, and refer often to the difficulties of political life under Domitian. Taken as a group, they imply that senators can contribute positively to the welfare of the state, even in difficult times. The tenth book of letters presents Pliny's correspondence with Trajan when he was governor of Bithynia, which in its own way portrays the character of both the emperor and Pliny. Trajan appears a just, thoughtful, and caring ruler, friendly to Pliny, flexible but firm with the provincials. Pliny is loyal, respectful, just, and diligent. A much fuller and even more idealized image of the emperor's character appears in the *Panegyric* he addressed to the emperor. In part descriptive, in part hortatory, Pliny lays out the qualities of an ideal emperor. Naturally, he builds on the ancient tradition treating the virtuous monarch, as does his contemporary Dio Chrysostom in his orations *On Kingship*. However, Pliny's characterization reflects in a special way the heritage of the first century. His emphasis is on social virtues, not military or administrative ones. In particular, he praises Trajan's *humanitas*, the basic recognition that the emperor shares a common humanity with the senators and other citizens. This knowledge appears in the emperor's moderation, mildness, and temperance. Trajan, Pliny asserts, is at ease with others, and is good-humored, cheerful, easy to meet with – in a word, friendly. To the senators, the simple actions of entering Rome on foot, or being gracious at audiences and dinners, separate the just ruler from the tyrant. For Pliny, Trajan might possess no less autocratic power than Tiberius or Domitian, but the way his character was perceived changed the political scene and won the support of the upper class of the empire.

Pliny certainly painted an idealized portrait, but his perception of Trajan's greater virtue in comparison with earlier rulers seems to describe what modern historians can recognize as a real change in the behavior of Trajan and the immediately succeeding emperors. This change, coupled with a new attitude among the senators, contributed to decades of good government in the first half of the second century AD, free from civil war and much of the suspicion and fear which had preceded.

The philosopher and biographer Plutarch (ca. AD 46–ca. 120), a Greek contemporary of Tacitus and Pliny, could not write of imperial politics from direct experience as had they, both Roman senators. However, by combining the psychological insights of Plato and Aristotle with the political record found in earlier historians, he composed biographies of remarkable moral penetration.

Plutarch's great work is his *Parallel Lives*, an extensive review and rethinking of the characters of the great men of Greece and Rome, as seen in their political and military activity. Shining his searchlight on every sort of political leader in both peoples, he creates a kind of encyclopedia of character in politics. In comparing leaders, Plutarch was quite conscious of the different character of different states, noting that a politician would behave quite differently in Athens than in Sparta, or Carthage, and that Lycurgus was able to make reforms in Sparta which were impossible in Athens (*Political Precepts* 799b–e; *Sol.* 16, 22). He believed that there was something uniquely civilizing about Greek culture, whose presence or lack in a Roman significantly influenced his character toward restraint or savagery. He criticizes Coriolanus or Marius for their focus on military valor without the civilizing qualities he associates with Greek philosophy. Yet he also noted that many of his Greek heroes lacked the "Greek" qualities of moderation and self-control, and a Roman like Numa could be more "Greek" than the Greeks. Character was influenced but not determined by cultural context. The *Lives* encourage thoughtful consideration of how personal character relates to historical achievement and especially to the creation of peace and concord through good government. Although they describe many fine moments and actions, they do not usually display paragons of virtue. In each life, the statesmen show strengths and weaknesses, virtues and flaws.

The depiction of character (*ēthos*) is Plutarch's principal aim; his techniques vary with the subject and the sources. For Alexander, "it is often the small incident or saying or joke which reveals the soul, rather than battles with thousands of dead" (*Alex.* 1.2); for Pompey, Plutarch needs room "for the greatest deeds and experiences, which show best his character" (*Pomp.* 8.7). Character can be learned from events, but often anecdotes, individually or in clusters, give better insights into individual traits. Opinions ascribed to "the better (or more sensible, or wiser) people" indicate value judgments of particular actions. His most powerful tool is comparison, which operates at many levels, internal and external to the life. The *Parallel Lives* set two lives side by side in one unit, thus revealing the individual expressions of basically similar characters and their different impacts on their cities. Aristides "the Just" died poor; Cato the Elder was just too, but left his family rich. Contrasts within a life also cast light on the hero, as the rational arguments of Cineas and the stern moral code of Fabricius rebuke Pyrrhus of Epirus' ambitions of conquest (*Pyrrh.* 14, 20).

The fundamental issue for Plutarch as for Plato was the degree to which the individual hero had learned to channel the drive of his passions into a rational and productive course. An education which could develop moderation and self-control was essential, whether it be through Greek philosophy, Spartan discipline, or the Roman moral code. Alcibiades, despite his tutoring by Socrates, never had learned to seek true values rather than the favor of his lovers and the applause of the populace. Coriolanus learned courage, but could not regulate either his ambition or his scorn of the people, and preferred violence to compromise. Nicias could not conquer his fear of the Athenian people or of the gods; Crassus driven by ambition, rashly invaded Parthia. The case of the Gracchi brothers is exemplary: they were driven by a passion for praise to ultimately destructive political action, despite their noble intentions. Plutarch recognized the arrogant self-serving of the senatorial opposition. But the brothers went beyond the limits of acceptable action, enflamed by the admiration and encouragement of the irrational populace. Even for those with moral training, the results were mixed, but those who positively rejected its influence destroyed themselves and the state. Ambition was a common trait of many of Plutarch's heroes, but could easily lead to disaster, for the individual and the state. Worst of all was the competition which led to factional fighting and civil war. Marius and Sulla are two of Plutarch's most vicious examples, combining insatiable ambition with unprecedented savagery.

The most intractable problems for the Greek cities of Plutarch's days as for the Roman Empire of which he was a subject were created by the ambitions, self-interest, competitiveness, and greed of the ruling class. His analysis of character in the *Lives* was meant to heighten his reader's awareness of the effect of character upon their lives and their societies. The examples of two extraordinary statesmen, Pericles and Caesar, may speak for his whole project.

Pericles' chief qualities, as we have seen, are identified by Thucydides as foresight, integrity, and eloquence. That portrait reflects the historian's admiration for his penetrating judgment and independence from the hasty, poorly informed, and unstable opinions of the mass of Athenians. With these traits, Pericles fostered a dynamic, independent Athens that dared face Sparta down over its role in Greece. Thucydides' portrait also points to the intellectual and moral errors which he believes weakened Athens and led to her defeat and establishes a standard against which to judge the political performance of later Athenian leaders who would appear in his history, notably Cleon, Nicias, and Alcibiades.

Plutarch accepts the virtues of honesty, foresight, and eloquence as basic parameters, but redraws Pericles' character to emphasize his self-possessed temperament (*praotēs*) and loftiness of mind (*megalophrosunē*). The former trait, learned especially from the philosopher Anaxagoras, limits his competitiveness in political rivalry, so that he can reconcile himself with Cimon, his political opponent (*Per.* 10.7). Guided by rational strategy, he dissuades the angry Athenians from engaging the Spartans in an uneven battle. His loftiness of spirit permits him to imagine a grand peace project for Greece (17) and to oppose yielding to the Spartans (31). Plutarch refuses to consider Pericles' building program on the Acropolis simple demagoguery, but finds it justified by its eternally fresh beauty (13). The reasons for initiating the wars with Samos and Sparta did raise special problems. How could wars between Greek states be justified? Did Pericles yield to the importuning of his mistress Aspasia, or were these rational decisions to defend Athenian interests? After exploring the opposing views, Plutarch aligns himself implicitly with the latter position. He concludes the life with his own evaluation: the Athenians had never seen a leader "more moderate in his gravity and more venerable in self-possession" (39).

This life expresses Plutarch's opinion on some necessary qualities for a leader in his own day: an even temperament guided by philosophical principles, limiting one's own ambitions to maintain concord in the city, an ability to rule wisely without succumbing to the temptations of luxury and violence, and military prowess exercised against foreign opponents, never against one's countrymen.

Plutarch's *Life of Caesar* portrays a markedly different kind of man, one dedicated to his own honor, who makes being first in his state his single-minded goal. Unlike other lives, it offers very little direct moral commentary, even on points, like Caesar's early lavish spending to win popularity, which he would normally condemn. Caesar's relentless pursuit of honor reminds the reader of other protagonists who suffer from excess ambition, like Marius and Sulla. Yet Caesar was neither a Marius nor a Sulla, though he had elements of both. Like Marius, Caesar was a great general who used popular support to challenge the senatorial aristocracy; like Sulla, he was able to dominate his enemies and become dictator. However, he was immensely more able as a politician than the former, and much milder as a victor than the latter.

Unlike many of Plutarch's statesmen, including his rival Pompey, Caesar was able to function equally well as a general in the field and as a politician in Rome. (Contrast Plutarch's comments on Pompey's confusion at *Pomp.* 23, and Clodius' mockery of him at *Pomp.* 46, 48–9.) Completely focused on his goal, he surprised his contemporaries by his determination and flexibility. For instance, when Cato opposed the triumph which Caesar wished in 60 BC, he immediately abandoned that to pursue the consulship, which would advance his status more surely. Again, he took advantage of the quarrel of the two most prominent men then in Rome, Crassus and Pompey, to broker a deal which would satisfy them both, but to use their strength to further his own ambitions. Caesar was a risk-taker, bold, willing to throw all his resources into politics as into war. While in Gaul, he never forgot the political situation in Rome, and employed the loot of his wars to win support there. Pompey, so dynamic as a general, never engaged himself so fully in domestic politics, expecting rather to live on his prestige. Even when events came to a crisis, and Pompey was chosen sole consul, Plutarch reports, he found time to marry a young wife and spend time with her (*Pomp.* 55). Caesar never paused, never rested, and like a good general, never allowed himself to be trapped. He preferred compromise to confrontation, but accepted confrontation if necessary. As his term in Gaul neared an end, he suggested various compromises which would allow both Pompey and himself to keep their armies, or to resume civil status. Pompey and the senate refused to accept an agreement: Caesar threw the die, crossed the Rubicon, swept into Rome with his army, and Pompey and the senate fled.

Character determined two momentous events that followed. First, when Caesar took Rome, there was no bloodbath. Caesar welcomed those who would accept his preeminence. Second, when the armies of Caesar and Pompey met in Greece, Pompey, although an outstanding general with superior forces, could not manage the arrogant and contentious senators in his army. His better judgment overwhelmed by their carping, he allowed Caesar to take the initiative, and was defeated at Pharsalia. His weak reluctance to insist with his friends on what he knew was tactically essential had undercut his military talent. Caesar's restraint of a natural feeling for revenge, however, continued even after he had won the war: he pardoned those who fought for Pompey, and gave high positions at Rome to many, including his future assassin, Brutus.

Caesar finally achieved his ambition: he became the undisputed first man in Rome, was chosen dictator, and showered with honors. Dynamically, he initiated projects of every sort to improve Rome, from the calendar, to buildings, to new colonies. Plutarch writes that he held the position of a tyrant, but acted "beyond reproach" (*Caes.* 57). But the other side of honor is envy, and the senators who had opposed him on his rise, and had been pardoned by his clemency, were now even more eager to bring him down. Within a year of his final victory over the Pompeians, he was murdered.

Other men, with other characters, had played their own roles. Cato lived according to stern Stoic principles, and attempted to cut back the power of both Pompey and Caesar. His intransigence weakened Pompey but unwittingly strengthened Caesar; finally, he made it impossible for Caesar to surrender his army without fearing for his life. Mark Antony's dissolute life harmed Caesar's government, and would later lead to his own defeat by the future Augustus. Brutus, admired for his integrity, convinced himself that he was acting for Rome and liberty in removing a tyrant, but opened the way to more wars and more killing, and finally a permanent monarchy.

Unusually, Plutarch reserves moral comment throughout the life, preferring to observe. Scholars think that a final comparison between Alexander and Caesar has been lost, which might have expressed praise or condemnation. Perhaps Caesar was just too great, or too similar to Trajan, to allow comment. But the final chapter does pose a question: was it all worth it? "The rule and power Caesar had finally attained, after a lifelong and enormously dangerous pursuit, brought him nothing except the name and the glory so much resented by his fellow citizens," he writes (*Caes.* 69).

And yet, Plutarch adds, a divinity avenged him after his death. The monarchy was fated to come and Caesar's life was a major step in bringing that to pass. For Plutarch, living under the rule of emperors, in a world where honor was the highest prize, Caesar's confidence in his superiority and unremitting quest for preeminence is extraordinary, but carries a terrible warning. Honor, prestige, glory – even the senate's grant of divine honors – may still be hollow.

The various ideal schemes of Xenophon, Plato, and Aristotle envisioned leaders who had formed their character through training and self-discipline, in a state whose constitution and customs could promote this process. Reason would channel the unruly passions in noble directions. Moderation, judgment, self-possession, integrity, and justice would be the basis of political leadership. These theories had been prompted by the collapse of leadership during and after the Peloponnesian War, and encouraged an educational program which might train good leaders. Unsurprisingly, perhaps, given the intractability of human nature, the succeeding centuries gave birth to few such ideal leaders. The historians chronicle occasional outstanding men, who were able to lead their cities to victory in war and prosperity in peace. More often, the tale tells of men of outstanding talent whose flawed characters lead to civic turmoil, unnecessary wars, defeat abroad and oppression at home. In either case, they use the philosophical framework established in the fourth century to observe the action of character, adapting their analysis to the new circumstances created by the rise of Rome, the collapse of the Republic, and the foundation of the monarchy.

Polybius celebrated a hero like Scipio, but as his history went forward, he saw the world as increasingly dominated by irrational politicians or an erratic Fortune. Livy was proud of the many examples that Rome could offer of noble action, and of the late date of its moral decline, but could find little solace in his own day, when he recognized that even someone as cultivated as Cicero was liable to be as savage as his enemy Mark Antony, who had impaled the orator's hands and head in the Roman forum.

Politics depended on character, but what place could good character have when a society went mad, each man's distorted character contributing to the maelstrom of emotions, reprisals, ambitions, and violence? Plutarch writes of Sulla (*Comparison of Lycurgus and Sulla* 1),

> it was not surprising that Sulla held power when men like Glaucias and Saturninus drove a Metellus from the city, when sons of consuls were murdered in the assemblies, ... and fire and sword wrote the laws and put down opponents. I don't blame anyone for managing to seize power in such circumstances, but I don't consider being first in a city in such condition as an indication of being best.

The Principate set one man in power at Rome, but that did not mean he was the best in character. On the contrary, for Tacitus, one-man rule fostered duplicity, betrayal, and surrender to the worst urges. It was extremely difficult to win honor or build a career under such conditions. With Trajan, there were new hopes, expressed eloquently by Pliny. Plutarch was cautious. He clearly desired to encourage statesmen to fashion their character in the most virtuous way possible, and thus preserve the state in harmony and prosperity. But the reality of history all too often demonstrated that even great men were seriously flawed.

How then does character affect politics? Historians living in good times may be optimistic, believing that one or another great leader can steer the state with integrity, justice, and humility. Those happy times unfortunately are rare. Good character, Aristotle said, needs the support of the whole community to develop. The writers discussed here, from Polybius to Plutarch, wished to strengthen the process of character development by educating their community, and through their study of past leaders to train, warn, and inspire statesmen.

FURTHER READING

Modern philosophers have shown a great deal of interest in ancient ethics, character, and virtue theory. Gill 2004 gives a survey of modern responses to classical ethical thinking. On ancient ethics in general and Aristotle in particular, see Annas 1993; Pakaluk 2005; and Kraut 2006. Burnyeat 1980 treats Aristotle's thinking on moral education. For various perspectives on the issues of ancient characterization, see Pelling 1990; on the distinction of character and personality, Gill 1990. The recent revival of Xenophon studies has improved his reputation: for contrasting arguments on the treatment of character in the *Cyropaedia* see e.g. Tatum 1989; Due 1990. For Polybius on character, moral thinking, and politics, see Eckstein 1995: 237–71, esp. ch. 8, "Optimism and Pessimism"; for Livy, Walsh 1963: 82–109 (ch. 4, "Roman Morality Historically Characterised") is still valuable. The character of Tiberius is intimately bound to the understanding of his years under Augustus, his reign, and the problem of succession, for which, among many authors on the subject, Levick 1999 offers a good introduction. For Tacitus, the fundamental study is Syme 1958. Martin 1981 gives a good basic introduction. The discussion in Pelling 1993 addresses the issue of inconsistency in Tacitus' treatment of Germanicus. Plutarch presents his theory of moral virtue, which is heavily influenced by Aristotle, in his work *On Moral Virtue*, and discusses adult character formation in a number of essays, such as *On Anger*. The Platonic roots of his theory of the soul, and its relation to the program of the *Parallel Lives*, are ably discussed in Duff 1999.

PART VII

Antipolitics

CHAPTER 30

Cosmopolitan Traditions

David Konstan

If we may trust Diogenes Laertius, the third century AD historian of philosophy (*Lives of the Philosophers* 6.63), then the earliest attested occurrence of the Greek word "cosmopolite" (*kosmopolitēs*) can be dated to the fourth century BC (there is no ancient Greek equivalent for "cosmopolitan," which is made up of a Latin ending attached to a Greek root). Diogenes Laertius ascribes it to the Cynic thinker Diogenes, who is said to have died in 323 (the same year as Alexander the Great). The word is found in one of a series of anecdotes revealing Diogenes' wit and flair for spontaneous repartee: "When he was asked where he was from, he replied: 'I am a cosmopolite,' " that is, a citizen (*politēs*) of the cosmos. But aphorisms of this sort were often invented later and then credited to Diogenes, so the attribution is insecure – the more so since the next occurrence of the term (nine times) is in the writings of Philo of Alexandria (ca. 20 BC–ca. AD 50). Nevertheless, John Moles (1996: 107–9) has argued that the sentiment is consistent with what we know of Diogenes' views, and in particular with another saying of his quoted by Diogenes Laertius (6.72): "He used to make fun of noble birth and reputation and all such things, calling them "cosmetics [*prokosmēmata*] of vice," and affirming that "the only right polity [*politeia*] was that which resides in *kosmos*." The problem is determining the sense of *kosmos* here; the Greek word could mean "good order" or "behavior" (this is the source of our word "cosmetic"), and the pun in Diogenes' pronouncement suggests that he may have meant that the only correct form of government lies in one's own comportment (the absence of the definite article before *kosmos* also points to this interpretation). We shall have occasion to return to the precise sense of *kosmo-* in the compound *kosmopolitēs*.

Just what Diogenes might have meant, had he used the term (or something like it), is disputed. On one interpretation, he intended merely to indicate that there was no particular city or polis with which he identified or to which he professed allegiance. This is what Moles calls the "purely negative" view (1996: 107), and it is, as Moles observes, the prevailing one in modern scholarship. In itself, it is radical enough.

A Companion to Greek and Roman Political Thought, First Edition. Edited by Ryan K. Balot.
© 2013 Blackwell Publishing Ltd. Published 2013 by Blackwell Publishing Ltd.

The polis was the dominant form of social organization in the Greek-speaking world (or at least it was thought of as such), and in refusing to acknowledge any city as his own Diogenes would have been perceived as rejecting society per se (he in fact came from Sinope, a port city on the Black Sea, far from Athens where he spent his adult life). Such a critical attitude toward the polis was maintained, it appears, by the Cyrenaic philosopher Aristippus, an earlier contemporary of Diogenes, as reported by Xenophon (*Mem.* 1.1.11–13); in order to avoid either ruling others or being ruled by them, Aristippus chose a third path, which he called "freedom," and to achieve this, he declared, "I do not lock myself into any polity, but I am everywhere a stranger [*xenos*]."[1]

But perhaps there was a more positive content to Diogenes' assertion. It could mean, for example, that he was equally at home in all the cities of the world. Alcibiades, for instance, is said to have been highly adaptable to different customs. As Plutarch reports (*Alc.* 23.5, trans. Dryden 1947), "At Sparta, he was devoted to athletic exercises, was frugal and reserved; in Ionia, luxurious, gay, and indolent; in Thrace, always drinking; in Thessaly, ever on horseback; and when he lived with Tisaphernes the Persian satrap, he exceeded the Persians themselves in magnificence and pomp." There is a model for this kind of versatility, perhaps, in the Odysseus of the *Odyssey*, who "saw the cities of many men and knew their minds" (1.3). Although such flexibility may be merely strategic, it may also rest on a more profound belief in the relativism of human customs, with the implicit suggestion that all are equally valid. Herodotus, for example, affirms (3.38) that one ought never to ridicule the practices of others, since everyone, if asked to choose the finest laws of all that exist, after examining them all would vote for his own. In proof of this, Herodotus records a scene staged by Darius, in which he horrified some Greeks by asking them at what price they would eat their dead, and equally shocked members of an Indian tribe called Callatians, who traditionally consumed their dead, by asking at what price they would consent to burn them, as the Greeks did – making sure that the Greeks understood their response by providing an interpreter (contrast Plutarch *De Alex. fort.* 328c, where a philosophically minded Alexander persuades the Scythians to bury rather than eat their dead). The very idea of reviewing all the customs or *nomoi* in the world suggests that they are in some sense on a par, and that preference for one's own is a matter of tradition and habit, not natural superiority (though this does not prevent Herodotus from approving some customs over others).

This is not the kind of adaptability, however, that Diogenes will have expounded, since he was given rather to despising than to respecting traditions, whether his own or those of others, in favor of practices that he considered natural and therefore in principle universally valid (cf. Diog. Laert. 6.71). Thus he deliberately comported himself in such a way as to shock rather than assimilate to prevailing norms. To take one of the most outrageous instances, he is said to have masturbated in the agora and to have exclaimed: "If only it were possible to rub one's stomach and so not feel hunger" (Diog. Laert. 6.46). That human beings are alike in their underlying nature, despite the ostensible differences between one people and another, was an idea already familiar to earlier generations. Thus Antiphon the Sophist announced (fr. 44b, col. 2.10–15 DK = *P Oxy* 11.1364): "By nature we are all similarly constituted in all respects, both barbarians and Greeks." Again, in Plato's *Protagoras* (337c6–d3), the sophist Hippias states: "Gentlemen here present, I believe that you are all kin and relations and fellow citizens – by nature, not by convention [*nomos*]: for things that are similar to one another are by nature kindred, but convention, which is a tyrant over human beings, forces many things to go against nature." So conceived, the appeal to nature as opposed to law or custom (*phusis* versus *nomos*) is essentially ecumenical in scope.

Now, one way to be a world citizen is to acquire statutory citizenship in a large variety of polities. To take an example from a much later period, at the height of the Roman empire (ca. AD 200) a renowned athlete from Alexandria, who was undefeated in pankration contests throughout Greece and elsewhere, set up an inscription at Rome in which he proclaimed: "I am Markos Aurelios Asklepiades, also called Hermodorus, senior temple warden of the great god Sarapis, chief priest of the Universal Athletic Guild. ... I am a citizen of Alexandria, Hermopolis, and Puteoli; a member of the City Council of Naples, Elis, and Athens; and also a citizen and member of the Council of many other cities" (*IG* 14.1102 = *Inscriptiones Graecae Urbis Romanae* 240, lines 4–10; trans. König 2005: 1; see also Rhodes, this volume, chapter 4). Alexandria, Athens, Naples: like his name, the man is transnational. Whether Markos Aurelios Asklepiades, aka Hermodorus, felt any difficulty in assuming his offices in such varied communities is unknown; Roman rule, while it respected local differences, at the same time tended to result in a certain homogeneity (we shall return to this point below). Diogenes, however, did not claim to be a citizen of many cities, but rather of the cosmos as a whole. It is as though the world at large were a single city – and he a citizen of it.

The idea that the world is one's country is not without precedent in early Greek thought. To cite but a few examples, a character in a lost play of Euripides declares: "The whole earth [*khthōn*] is a noble man's fatherland [*patris*]" (*TrGF* 1047.2; cf. *TrGF* 777, 902). The passage is preserved by Musonius Rufus, the first century AD Stoicizing writer, in his essay on why exile is not an evil (*Discourse* 9), where he ascribes the view also to Socrates: "isn't the cosmos the common fatherland [*patris*] of all human beings, as Socrates believed?" Indeed, the formula was common enough for Lysias (31.6) to give it a negative twist, and condemn those who were by nature – that is, by birth (*phusei*) – citizens of Athens, but "were of the opinion that the whole earth was their fatherland, wherever they had business," and therefore were ready to put their private interests ahead of loyalty to the state (for more passages and references to modern bibliography, see Moles 1996: 109 n18). The use of the term *patris* or fatherland, rather than polis or *city*, may be significant here, since it does not carry with it the sense of a regular polity with its own laws and criteria for citizenship. In this, it perhaps has something of the vagueness of the term cosmos in the expression "cosmopolite."

But Diogenes may have had a more ambitious concept in mind. John Moles affirms that "Cynic cosmopolitanism implies a positive attitude toward the natural world" (1996: 112), an attitude that "may extend to the heavenly bodies" and include even the gods. Such an expansive conception of the sage's place in the universe is more often associated with the Stoics. It is not entirely clear whether the early Stoics actually employed the word *kosmopolitēs* (although three of the nine mentions of the term in Philo, our earliest source for it, are cited among the fragments of Chrysippus in von Arnim's *Stoicorum Veterum Fragmenta* (*SVF*)), but for them a citizen of the cosmos – a term that by the late fourth century signified the whole natural order – would have been someone who lived in accord with universal, that is, divine reason. Such a sage would be a fellow citizen not only of all other human beings, but of the gods themselves, and would participate in the same social compact or constitution (*politeia*). Expressions of this view are to be found in Cicero and, a century and a half later, in Dio Chrysostom, who elevate the notion to a philosophical and quasi-religious sense of communion with the natural world. In his *Republic* (1.19 = fr. 338 *SVF*), for example, Cicero affirms that "the gods have given this world [*mundus* = *kosmos*] to us as a home and a fatherland [*patria*], in common with themselves"; and in *On the Laws* (1.7.23 = fr. 339 *SVF*) he says that since human beings and gods have reason, and hence law and justice (*ius*), "they must be considered members of the same city [*civitas*]," and that "this whole universe is a city common to gods and human beings" (cf. *Fin.* 3.62 = fr. 340 *SVF*; Dio Chrysostom *Or.* 36.23 = fr. 334 *SVF*; *Or.* 1.42 = fr. 335 *SVF*). And Philo asserts (*On the Creation of the Universe* 143 = fr. 337 *SVF*) that, "since every well-ordered polis has a constitution [*politeia*], it is necessary that a citizen of the cosmos [*kosmopolitēs*] abide by the constitution which the whole cosmos does as well" (cf. also *On the Creation of the Universe* 3 = fr. 336 *SVF*). Still in the Stoicizing tradition, Musonius Rufus (*Discourse* 9) affirms that an *epieikēs* or decent person "believes that he is a citizen of the city [*polis*] of Zeus, which is composed of humans and gods," and Epictetus (*Diss.* 1.9.1) declares: "If what the philosophers say about the kinship of god and humans is true, humans can but acknowledge the dictum of Socrates: 'When someone asks whence you come, never say you are an Athenian or a Corinthian, but rather that you are a Cosmian [*Kosmios*]'" (the adjective *kosmios* ordinarily means "well-ordered" or "well-behaved").

There is, however, a catch to the Stoic (and possibly Cynic) association of reason with cosmic citizenship. For while all human beings, or at least the great majority, are endowed with the capacity to become fully rational creatures, and hence virtuous, only a very few succeed in realizing this potential, namely those who become sages. It is they who are cosmopolites, living in harmony with natural reason and the gods. Diogenes did not say, "We are all citizens of the world," but rather, "I am a citizen of the world." Cosmopolitanism on this view is an elite status, and takes the form of membership in the international community of the wise and good – one that includes the gods among its citizens. Thus Seneca writes (*De otio* 8.4):

> We embrace two republics in our soul, one great and truly public, in which gods and men are contained, in which we do not have regard for this corner or that but measure the limits of our polity by the sun, the other to which the condition of our birth has assigned us. This latter will be that of the Athenians or Carthaginians or some other city which belongs not to all human beings but only to some.

This seems an affirmation of a universal, if ideal, state, but Seneca at once adds: "Some devote their energies to both republics at the same time, the greater and the lesser, some only to the lesser, some only to the greater" (cf. Saint Paul's Letter to the Ephesians 2.19: "You are, then, no longer strangers and resident aliens, but you are fellow citizens [*sumpolitai*] of the saints and members of God's household"; centuries later, this ideal would inspire Saint Augustine's vision of a City of God). In Lucian's dialogue *Hermotimus*, Lucinus, a stand-in for Lucian himself, challenges Hermotimus' blind faith in the Stoic sect. Pressed to offer his own definition of virtue (*aretē*), Lucinus defines it as a city inhabited by happy, wise, just, and temperate citizens (22). In such a polis, he goes on to say,

> all are immigrants [*epēludes*] and foreigners [*xenoi*], and no one is a native [*authigenēs*], but many barbarians and slaves are citizens of it and also ugly and short and poor people, and in general anyone who wants to participate in the city . . . ; for someone to become a citizen, intelligence and a desire for what is noble and hard work suffice. . . . Superior and inferior and noble and commoner and slave and free neither exist nor are spoken of in this city. (24)

In this utopian community, there is no discrimination on the basis of origins, and the only criterion for citizenship is virtue. But it is none the less exclusive for that.

If we try now to sum up the versions of cosmopolitanism that we have identified so far, we may begin by recognizing at the most general level two forms: a negative, that is, the rejection of allegiance to any polis, which we may associate with the Cyrenaic philosopher Aristippus; and a positive, which presupposes some kind of commitment to society beyond the confines of the city-state. This latter may, in turn, be subdivided into two further classes. On the one hand, there is the relativistic view, according to which norms and customs are understood to differ radically from one community to another, with no basis on which to privilege one's own. One may simply respect the differences, or else, like Alcibiades, exhibit a protean or, in Plutarch's phrase, chameleon-like adaptability to the kaleidoscopic variety of folkways in the world at the cost of any local identification. On the other hand, there is what we may call the abstract or reductive view, which we may identify with the figure of Diogenes. Here, the basis of cosmopolitanism is the conviction that, at bottom, all human beings are alike, whatever their local practices. Crucial to this view, in ancient thought, is a division between custom or convention (*nomos*) on the one side, and nature (*phusis*) on the other. One need not take the extreme position that human beings are no more than "bare forked creatures" (in King Lear's phrase), and that all cultural refinements or distinctions are mere cosmetics. Diogenes himself, despite his contempt for material superfluities and conventional codes of behavior, seems to have held that virtue (in some sense of the term) is a fundamental attribute of mankind, and the ground of its unity. The problem in identifying virtue with behavior according to nature, however, is that it restricts membership in the cosmic community to the good and wise (including, at the metaphysical extreme, the gods themselves), thereby converting the ideal of the commonality of mankind into an imaginary polity of sages. Indeed, Diogenes Laertius (6.105) ascribes to the Cynics the view that "the wise man is a friend to one who is like him."

What the several types of cosmopolitanism catalogued above have in common, however, is that they are all what we may call personal or subjective in nature: that is, they all depend on individual belief in the community of mankind (or of the wise, at all events), whether relativistically or on the basis of some conception of shared human nature, but they do not presuppose the actual political unity of all people under a single civic government. There was a model for such an ecumenical regime in the Persian empire, which incorporated a wide variety of peoples under its rule. Indeed, Herodotus (7.8) ascribes to Xerxes the ambition to conquer Europe and thereby convert all the lands under the sun into a single land (*khōra*). To Herodotus, this was an overweening aspiration, since Europe was a distinct continent and was not meant to be united with Asia (Xerxes' bridging of the Hellespont, which divides the two land masses, was a sign that he was violating natural geographical boundaries). In fact, an incipient sense of panhellenic identity worked against the ideal of universal government, marking off the Greeks as a separate and, most often, superior people. Herodotus records (8.144.2–3) how, after the battle at Salamis (480 BC), the Persians sent envoys to Athens to propose a separate treaty, in the hope of detaching the Athenians from the common cause. As Herodotus tells it, the Athenian spokesmen reminded the other Greeks of their own obligation to avenge the burning of the temples and statues of the gods in Athens, and then continued:

> But there is also the fact that the Greek people [*to Hellēnikon*] are of the same blood and the same tongue, that we have in common the edifices of our gods and our sacrifices, and that our traditional ways are all alike, and it would not be well that the Athenians should be traitors to all this. Know then, if you did not already know it, that so long as one Athenian survives, we shall never make a pact with Xerxes.

Kinship, language, religious practices, and common customs define what it is to be a Hellene, and set the Greeks off from other peoples.

The Persian invasion undoubtedly provided a huge impetus to the ideological contrast between Greeks and "barbarians," and Edith Hall (1989) has argued forcefully that Athenian tragedy was among the major vehicles for sharpening and propagating this opposition. It is true that the Homeric *Iliad* narrates a war between peoples who are collectively identified as "Achaeans," "Danaans," or "Argives" (in Homer, "Hellene" refers to a specific ethnic group in Thessaly; cf. *Il.* 2.684), on the one side, and Troy and its allies on the other, and in later times this conflict would be interpreted as one between Greeks and barbarians (e.g. Isoc. 4.158–9). We may note, however, that "Achaeans" and "Danaans" occur only in the plural in Homer: no individual is a "Danaan" or "Achaean," as opposed to being a Myrmidon like Achilles or an Ithacan like Odysseus ("Argive" in the singular signifies a person from Argos rather than a Greek as such). Local affiliation defines identity. The Greeks do share a common language, whereas the Trojan allies speak a variety of tongues (*Il.* 2.802–6, 2.867, 4.433–8; cf. *Od.* 19.172–7; whether the Trojans themselves speak Greek is unclear), and Shawn Ross (2005: 314) concludes from this that the *Iliad* reflects "a nascent Panhellenic identity based on linguistic unity," but one that was still "lacking systematic opposition with a non-Hellenic Other" (it is interesting that Plato (*Plt.* 262c–e) denies that the barbarians constitute a single *genos* opposed to the Greeks precisely on the basis of the multiplicity of their languages). Perhaps it is worth remarking that the royal household of Troy is distinguished from all others by the practice of polygamy. And yet, all the peoples in the *Iliad* worship the same gods, who show no special preference for Achaeans over non-Achaeans. So too, Greeks and non-Greeks have common genealogies and bonds of friendship, and the final scene of mutual compassion between the Trojan king Priam and the Greek warrior Achilles stands as one of the finest expressions in all literature of common feeling across ethnic lines. If it is not too fanciful a thought, I suspect that the reference, when Achilles is pursuing Hector and is on the point of slaying him, to twin springs of the Scamander river, one steaming hot, the other ice cold even in winter (*Il.* 22.147–52), hints at the underlying identity of these mortally opposed enemies.

The possibility of an ecumenical state first presented itself with the conquests of Alexander the Great, who briefly brought under a single command Greece and what had been the Persian empire, together with lands still further east. Plutarch, in a rhetorical showpiece called *On the Fortune of Alexander*, attributes to Alexander the conscious intention of forming a world polity (329a–329c, trans. Babbitt 1936):

> the much-admired *Republic* of Zeno, the founder of the Stoic sect, may be summed up in this one main principle: that all the inhabitants of this world of ours should not live differentiated by their respective rules of justice into separate cities and communities, but that we should consider all men to be of one community and one polity, and that we should have a common life and an order common to us all, even as a herd that feeds together and shares the pasturage of a common field. This Zeno wrote, giving shape to a dream or, as it were, shadowy picture of a well-ordered and philosophic common-wealth; but it was Alexander who gave effect to the idea. For Alexander did not follow Aristotle's advice to treat the Greeks as if he were their leader, and other peoples as if he were their master ... But, as he believed that he came as a heaven-sent governor to all, and as a mediator for the whole world ..., he brought together into one body all men everywhere, uniting and mixing in one great loving-cup, as it were, men's lives, their characters, their marriages, their very habits of life. He bade them all consider as their fatherland the whole inhabited earth, as their stronghold and protection his camp, as akin to them all good men, and as foreigners only the wicked.

Plutarch (329d–330a) treats Alexander's decision to adopt Persian garb, and to promote the intermarriage of Greeks and foreigners, as part of a grand plan to unite all peoples in kinship. And he explains (330c–d):

> For he did not overrun Asia like a robber nor was he minded to tear and rend it, as if it were booty and plunder bestowed by unexpected good fortune, after the manner in which Hannibal later descended upon Italy. ... But Alexander desired to render all upon earth subject to one law of reason and one form of government and to reveal all men as one people, and to this purpose he made himself conform. But if the deity that sent down Alexander's soul into this world of ours had not recalled him quickly, one law would govern all mankind, and they all would look toward one rule of justice as though toward a common source of light. But as it is, that part of the world which has not looked upon Alexander has remained without sunlight.

Plutarch's vision of a single, homogeneous world under Alexander's leadership seems to treat local customs as impediments to international harmony, or at best as superficial phenomena that a wise ruler like Alexander will either ignore or attempt to blend into a uniform mixture. At the same time, Plutarch regards Alexander's as a civilizing mission, which will replace barbarous traditions with practices based on reason. We have already seen that Plutarch, unlike Herodotus, assumes that interring rather than eating the dead is by nature rational and right, and in the same passage he presents a series of changes inaugurated by Alexander that are seen as improving the uncouth habits of barbarians:

> But if you examine the results of Alexander's instruction, you will see that he educated the Hyrcanians to respect the marriage bond, and taught the Arachosians to till the soil, and persuaded the Sogdians to support their parents, not to kill them, and the Persians to revere their mothers and not to take them in wedlock. O wondrous power of Philosophic Instruction, that brought the Indians to worship Greek gods. ... [T]he children of the Persians, of the Susianians, and of the Gedrosians learned to chant the tragedies of Sophocles and Euripides. ... [T]hrough Alexander Bactria and the Caucasus learned to revere the gods of the Greeks. ... Alexander established more than seventy cities among savage tribes, and sowed all Asia with Grecian magistracies, and thus overcame its uncivilized and brutish manner of living.

There is thus a tension in Plutarch's account of Alexander's cosmopolitanism, and it corresponds in a rough way to the difference between the relativist version of cosmopolitanism, which we associated with Alcibiades, in which the conventions or *nomoi* that govern the behavior of different peoples are regarded as equally valid, and the appeal to nature as providing the common denominator among all human beings – the view of the Stoics and perhaps of Diogenes – where the universal polity is based upon reason that is inherent in the cosmos itself. To be sure, both Diogenes and the early Stoics, such as Zeno and Chrysippus, are said to have approved both cannibalism and incest, and neither were high on marriage as such. But the idea that the wise were in a favorable position to identify the rules by which a universal polity should be governed lent itself to the privileging of the traditions of the conqueror, above all in the case of Greeks who perceived themselves as superior to all other peoples in philosophy.[2]

It is possible that Plutarch drew inspiration for his idealizing portrait of Alexander's cosmopolitan ambitions from historians in the retinue of Alexander himself,[3] although among surviving sources (Diod. Sic. 77.4–5, Curtius 6.6.4, Justin 12.3.8, Arrian 4.7.4), Plutarch is unique in his unqualified support for Alexander's program of cultural integration (cf. Ramelli 2001: 182).[4] Given the loss of virtually all hellenistic prose, however, it is difficult to determine just how Alexander was represented, and because his world empire dissolved into separate and often mutually antagonistic states immediately after his death, its practical implications were stillborn. Plutarch himself wrote in the late first and early second century AD, when Rome ruled over most of the territories conquered by Alexander, and the whole of Western Europe and North Africa to boot, and it is surely with Rome in mind that he holds up Alexander as a model or a mirror.[5] The Romans developed, along with their empire, the view that they were particularly destined to rule: as Anchises, the father of Aeneas, instructs his son in Virgil's *Aeneid* (6.851–3): "You, Roman, remember to govern peoples by your authority [*imperium*] (these will be your arts), to impose the habit of peace, to spare the conquered and battle down the arrogant."

The privilege of naked power, together with a carefully cultivated taste for military glory, were sufficient motive and justification for extending Roman rule (for the Romans' enthusiasm for war during the Republic, see Harris 1979: 9–53). Nevertheless, the Romans entertained an image of themselves as especially humane, and at least from the first century BC onward they might excuse or rationalize their empire as being in the service of a cosmopolitan ideal. Three interrelated political circumstances contributed to this ecumenical attitude. First, the pragmatic pressures of governing a vast empire demanded a certain uniformity of practices. As Andrew Wallace-Hadrill (1997) has argued, in the sphere of law the role of amateur patrons who defended their clients and friends gave way to learned jurisconsults whose efforts would one day result in the systematization of the Roman judicial code. So too, the calendar, which had previously been managed by the priests or *pontifices*, was rationalized under Augustus with the help of professional mathematicians. Even language was affected, as grammarians began to dictate how to speak and write correctly. Common to all these transformations, according to Wallace-Hadrill, is the replacement of local knowledges, which are traditional and specific to particular communities, by a universal knowledge or *scientia*. Fixing the date of a religious celebration – or the celebration of the emperor's birthday – across a far-flung empire demanded an astronomically calibrated and accurate year, as opposed to the random intercalations that had served the needs of a small city. Latin had to be standardized just because Latium was not the ancestral home of most of the people who spoke it. Law grew in complexity *pari passu* with the Roman state. The great merit of Augustus was to perceive that the new order must be constructed on the basis of *ratio* or reason, not *consuetudo* or custom (Wallace-Hadrill 1997: 22).

The second factor in promoting Roman cosmopolitanism, which gained momentum after the Social Wars of 92–89 BC, was the extension of Roman citizenship to an ever larger segment of the people under Roman rule, a development which culminated in the famous decree of Caracalla, in 212 AD, by which virtually all free men in the Roman Empire were granted the franchise (see Rhodes, this volume, chapter 4). Finally, there is the circumstance that the Roman Empire tended to draw its governing class from local urban elites throughout its territories; this stratified system, which Ernest Gellner (1997) has argued is characteristic of premodern imperial societies, promoted the global integration of the higher, more educated orders of ancient society, and hence a sense of common identity; at the same time, it permitted the retention of local practices among those of lower status.

Affirmations of Rome as the *communis patria* or common fatherland of all nations are legion. In the first century AD, the poet Valerius Flaccus composed an epic poem on the voyage of the Argo. In the course of encouraging Medea to follow Jason back to Greece, Venus (here disguised as Circe) advises: "You must understand that this world and the gods are common to all living creatures; call that your country [*patria*] – from where the day begins to where it ends" (*Argonautica*, 7.227–9). No difference is recognized between Greek and barbarian lands, and while Rome is not mentioned (the action is set well before the foundation of that city), the spirit is that of Roman universalism, and quite unlike that of Apollonius of Rhodes' Greek *Argonautica* (third century BC). Aelius Aristides (second century AD), in his *Encomium of Rome* (207), intones: "you [Romans] govern the entire world as though it were a single city." The emperor Marcus Aurelius, in his *Meditations* (3.11.2), sees each human being as "a citizen of the highest city, of which the other cities are like households." Because reason is in common, so too is law, and hence we are all "fellow citizens [*politai*] and participate in a kind of civic entity [*politeuma*]; and if this is so, then the cosmos is a city [*polis*], as it were" (4.4.1). The language is general, but the supreme city is implicitly Rome. As Marcus says (6.44.2): "My city and country, insofar as I am Antoninus, is Rome, but insofar as I am a human being, it is the cosmos" (on Marcus' vision of a universal state, see Stanton 1968).

An oration of Themistius (34.25), who wrote popular paraphrases of Aristotle's treatises and tutored the sons of both Valens and Theodosius I, as well as serving as senator (in Constantinople) from 355 on, provides a particularly clear statement of Roman universalism. After comparing Theodosius favorably with Agamemnon in the *Iliad*, who notoriously urged that not a single Trojan should be allowed to live, not even the unborn child in its mother's womb (*Il.* 6.55–60), Themistius expands upon the gentleness of the Romans, who do not hate their enemies but "deem them worthy of being spared, as human beings." He goes on to explain that "he who proceeds to the utmost against arrogant barbarians makes himself king of the Romans alone, but he who conquers and yet spares knows himself to be king of all human beings, and one might justly call this man truly humane [*philanthrōpos*]." Playing on the root sense of *philanthrōpos* as "lover of mankind," Themistius affirms that Cyrus was a lover of Persians (*philopersēs*), not of humanity, Alexander a lover of Macedonians, Agesilaus of Greeks, Augustus himself a lover of Romans; but a true lover of mankind and a king in the unqualified sense (*haplōs*) is he who inquires simply whether a person who begs for clemency is a human being, irrespective of nationality. This is clearly a top-down version of a universal empire, predicated on a ruling power that acknowledges diversity among its subjects but treats all as equally entitled to imperial benevolence (we may note that Themistius, unlike his contemporary Libanius, for example, was in favor of the integration of barbarians into the empire, a policy that was followed by Theodosius).[6]

Under the Roman Empire, the political project of a universal state, as opposed to a subjective ideal of an international community of the wise, inevitably took the form of an imperial system. Such regimes, whatever their ideological pretensions to equality, normally arose as a result of conquest and coercion; hence the odor of bad faith that modern readers, at least, detect in the more extravagant encomia of Roman ecumenicism. Modern European cosmopolitan ideals have been more varied, in accord with the emergence of independent political states across the continent.[7] True, the term "cosmopolitan" today has mostly a nonpolitical connotation; the first two definitions provided by the online Merriam-Webster dictionary are "having worldwide rather than limited or provincial scope or bearing" and "having wide international sophistication: worldly." This personal sense of worldliness has its roots in eighteenth century conceptions of universal man; as Pauline Kleingeld and Eric Brown (2002) observe, cosmopolitanism commonly indicated "an attitude of open-mindedness and impartiality," characteristic of a person "who led an urbane life-style, or who was fond of traveling, cherished a network of international contacts, or felt at home everywhere." They cite Fougeret de Montbron's *Le Cosmopolite* (1753), in which he declares: "All the countries are the same to me" (p. 130).

Two eighteenth century figures, however, are prominently associated with more political proposals. In his influential tract, *Perpetual Peace* (1795), Immanuel Kant recommended a universal association in which states would maintain their sovereignty, including military independence, but would agree voluntarily to certain principles governing external relations. This is essentially the structure of a league (Kant's model inspired the formation of the League of Nations), and it has a certain analogue in the local defensive associations, such as the Aetolian League, in classical antiquity. I do not know of an ancient proposal for a universal government on this basis. (A league might be transformed into an empire if one of its members was far superior in power to the rest, as in the case of the Delian League, which began as a federation of independent city-states but ended up subservient to the compulsory hegemony of Athens.)

Anacharsis Cloots (Jean-Baptiste du Val-de-Grâce, baron de Cloots, 1755–94), in turn, "advocated the abolition of all existing states and the establishment of a single world state under which all human individuals would be directly subsumed" (Kleingeld and Brown 2002), and where sovereignty resides with the people, that is, with the entire human race (cf. *La république universelle ou adresse aux tyrannicides*, 1792; *Bases constitutionelles de la république du genre humain*, 1793). This model too, which rests on Enlightenment doctrines of the popular will, has no parallel in the classical world, save insofar as the Roman empire might be represented as governing in the interests of all its subjects. But Roman sovereignty was always located in the emperor, even when, in the third century and later, political authority was to some degree decentralized and distributed across two or more capitals.

We have seen that, just as in the case of subjective cosmopolitanism, so too in the imperial ideology of ancient Rome there was an abiding tension between an implicit recognition of local differences (one thinks of the millet system of the Ottoman Empire as a paradigm of this kind of tolerance for indigenous traditions) and a tendency to ground claims to universal hegemony in theories of the natural kinship or homogeneity of mankind – always on the basis of Greco-Roman interpretations of what counted as rational and in accord with nature. Any conception of human solidarity that transcended the repressive authority of the state and rested on the free cooperation of human beings was necessarily visionary in character. I conclude this chapter on cosmopolitanism with a passage from Philo of Alexandria, to whom we owe, as we have seen, the earliest citations of the term *kosmopolitēs*. In his treatise, *On Virtues* (119–20), Philo writes:

> The most holy prophet [that is, Moses] desired to establish this above all in all his laws: concord, fellowship, like-mindedness, and the mixture of characters, from which households and cities and peoples and countries and the whole race of mankind [*to sumpan anthrōpōn genos*] might advance to the highest happiness. But up to the present these are but prayers; yet they will be, as I believe, the most true facts, if God grants fruitfulness to our virtues like yearly harvests.[8]

FURTHER READING

An early book that is readable and still useful is Baldry 1965. Brown 2006 covers the early philosophical views, especially those of the Stoics and Cynics. For the Cynics in particular, one may consult Moles 1996. A more technical but readable account of Plutarch's special contribution, in relation to the conquests of Alexander the Great, is Whitmarsh 2002. A very useful survey of the idea from antiquity to modern times may be found in Kleingeld and Brown 2002. Appiah 2006 discusses issues involved in cosmopolitan ideals today in a thoughtful and illuminating way; one may also consult Fine 2007. Several articles on cosmopolitanism are in Daedalus 137 (2008), including Long 2008 on ancient conceptions. For the texts of the hellenistic philosophers, the best collection is Long and Sedley 1987.

NOTES

1   On the cosmopolitanism of the Cynics and Cyrenaics, see Brown, this volume, chapter 31.
2   On the political ideals of the early Stoics, and in particular Zeno's *Republic*, see Alesse 1998; Boys-Stones 1998; and Schofield 1991, 2002b.
3   Onesicritus, who had Cynic connections, is a possible source, but his account of the life of Indian sages is perhaps better characterized as utopian rather than cosmopolitan; see T. Brown 1949: 43–77.
4   See Ramelli 2001: 180 n6 for bibliography on Alexander's attitude toward Persian integration; for a skeptical view, see Baldry 1965: 113–27. As Ramelli notes (2001: 183–4), Plutarch is polemicizing against Aristotle. Strabo (1.4.9) reports Eratosthenes' view that Alexander did well not to treat Greeks as friends and barbarians as enemies, but to distinguish rather on the basis of virtue and vice.
5   For parallels, not all of them equally cogent, between Plutarch's account of Alexander's vision and the universal Christian mission, see Georgi 1991: 28–34.
6   Cf. Cameron 1991: 131–3.
7   For recent contributions to the theory of cosmopolitanism, see Pogge 1992; Kymlicka and Straehle 1999; Scheffler 1999; Lu 2000; Nussbaum 2000; Waldron 2000; Gamwell 2003; Pojman 2005; and Nielsen 2005.
8   On *philanthrōpia* in Philo, cf. Berthelot 2003: 265–8. Philo's mention of laws, cities, and countries distinguishes his vision from more general anticipations of universal harmony, as in Isaiah 2.4, Virgil's fourth *Eclogue*, and the conclusion of the *Liber legum regionum*, deriving from the school of Bardesanes (Bar Daysan; second century AD); for the last, see Ramelli 1999: 349 (Syriac text and English translation in Cureton 1855).

CHAPTER 31

False Idles: The Politics of the "Quiet Life"

Eric Brown

The Ideology Opposed to Withdrawal

In Thucydides' *History*, Pericles gives the funeral oration for the first of the Athenian war dead, and he calls the living to arms by praising their way of life. In Athens, he says, "In the same men there is concern both for their own affairs and at the same time for those of their fellow citizens, and those who are busy with their work know enough about public affairs, for we alone think that the man who takes no part in public affairs is not unbusied [*apragmōn*] but useless [*achreios*]" (Thuc. 2.40.2). The Athenians, says Pericles, participate in politics, and they scorn the man who avoids the business (*ta pragmata*) of the polis. Other Greeks might say, interchangeably, that such a man is "unbusied" (*apragmōn*) or that he "minds his own business" (*to ta hautou prattein*). But Pericles insists that Athenians do not accept these labels. They rebuke him.[1]

Despite Pericles' rhetoric, this attitude was common throughout the Greek world. (Indeed, the Athenian citizenry, with its democratic freedoms, was among the least rigorously committed to political engagement. That is why Pericles has to try to inspire greater commitment.) Moreover, there was good reason for the widespread hostility to quiet withdrawal from politics. Throughout the Greek world, the security of the polis depended upon its citizens. Anyone who withdrew from politics to live a quiet life was a "free rider," reaping benefits of the city without contributing his fair share of effort (cf. Plut. *Adv. Col.* 1127a). Worse, his inattention made him useless when trouble came to the polis. During war, especially, the city needed the help of every citizen.

Not that the opposition to the quiet life was limited to wartime. In Plato's *Republic*, Socrates imagines a "good father who lives in a polis that is not well governed, who avoids honors, political office, lawsuits, and all such 'busybodiness' [*philopragmosunēn*], and who is willing to be disadvantaged to avoid business [*pragmata*]" (549c1–5). Socrates also imagines what this man's wife will say about him:

A Companion to Greek and Roman Political Thought, First Edition. Edited by Ryan K. Balot.
© 2013 Blackwell Publishing Ltd. Published 2013 by Blackwell Publishing Ltd.

She complains that her husband is not one of the rulers and that this disadvantages her among the other women, and then she sees that he is not very serious about money, that he does not fight or squabble in private courts or public assembly, but that he bears all such things easily, and when she perceives that he is always absorbed in his own thoughts, not much regarding or disregarding her – as a result of all these things, she complains and says that he is unmanly and too easygoing. (549c7–d7)

The nagging wife is not alone. The man's son hears similar things from the household slaves (549e2–3), and "when he goes out, he hears and sees other things of this sort: men who mind their own business [*tous ta huutōn prattontas*] in the city are called fools and of little account, while those who do not are honored and praised" (550a1–5).

Call this the dominant ideology. It attaches honor to the busy, political life and dishonor to the unbusied, quiet life. It contrasts the manly vigor of public action with the feminine weakness of private withdrawal. Politics, on this conception of value, is a necessary outlet for human excellence.[2]

The dominant ideology waxed and waned but persisted throughout antiquity. It is commonly believed that polis-centered life collapsed in the wake of Alexander the Great's conquests, but the dominant ideology continued to exert force throughout the hellenistic period under the successor kingdoms. Nor was it limited to Greece. Rather, it underlay Cicero's appeals for political action in the prologue to *On Republic* and in the first book of *On Duties*. And it remained a force at the end: Augustine wrote *City of God* to defend the Christians from the charge that their withdrawal from public affairs left Rome vulnerable to the barbarians.

But the dominant ideology did not go unopposed. In this chapter, I show how defenders of the quiet life challenged the view that ordinary political engagement should be central to the lives of citizens. To find these challenges, I concentrate chiefly on philosophical writings.[3] Greek and Roman philosophers engaged in a longstanding dispute about whether it was best to live as an active citizen or as a detached philosopher, and this debate offers a rich source of reasons to resist the dominant ideology. I focus on three distinct challenges, with the aim of taking the measure of their significance for ancient political thought.

Three Defenses of Withdrawal

Although I will focus on philosophical writing, I begin with Euripides' *Antiope* because this play raises all three challenges and reminds us of the intellectual connections between authors that modern academe too often keeps apart. Only fragments of *Antiope* survive, but they record an interesting disagreement between two brothers. Zethus accuses Amphion of betraying his "noble nature [*gennaian phusin*]" by taking on a "womanish shape" and refusing to "offer vigorous counsel" (fr. 185 *TGF*). He charges, "Any man well-equipped for life who neglects the affairs of his house and runs after the pleasures of music and dance will be useless (*argos*) to his house and the city and a nobody to his friends. One's nature [*phusis*] is ruined when one gives way to sweet pleasure" (fr. 187 *TGF*). Zethus also singles out for scorn the pleasures of intellectual inquiry, and he beseeches Amphion to reject "these refined subtleties" and "idle babbling" that threaten his house and weaken his city (frr. 188 and 219 *TGF*).

But Amphion can offer three distinct replies. First, he can defend his quiet pursuit of pleasure. This involves two distinct moves. Amphion first has to defend the pursuit of pleasure in general. He argues that uncertainties governing other pursuits make it a reasonable option (cf. Horace, *Odes* 1.11): "Such is the life of struggling mortals: not always fortunate or unfortunate; sometimes successful and sometimes not. Since we are faced with uncertain blessedness, why should we not live as pleasantly as we can and avoid pain?" (fr. 196 *TGF*). Amphion's second move is to insist that the best route to pleasure leads not through politics but through quiet withdrawal. He says, "He who busies himself in many things [*prassei polla*] that he might avoid is a fool, when he might live pleasantly as an unbusied man [*apragmona*]" (fr. 193 *TGF*). The two steps of this argument are related. In a life of public engagement, one struggles against rivals to secure honor, prosperity, and security for oneself and one's friends. But the goals of such competition are subject to fortune. Amphion argues that it is more sensible to pursue a goal that one can achieve reliably and that one can achieve one's goal reliably if one pursues pleasure in a quiet life.

Amphion can also defend the life of quiet withdrawal by defending more particularly the intellectual inquiries that Zethus scorns. Another fragment that might belong to *Antiope* suggests how he could do this. This complicated fragment contrasts the life spent studying nature with sordid business: "Blessed is he who gives his attention to research, desiring neither the misery of his fellow citizens nor unjust actions, but contemplating the ageless order of immortal nature – how it is constituted, and whence, and why. Concern for shameful deeds never sits near such things" (fr. 910 *TGF*).[4] Again, Amphion draws attention to the competition that political life involves. Such competition involves wishing ill to one's rivals and temptations to do wrong to promote one's own projects. So even when things work out fortunately, politics is a disagreeable way of procuring what one wants. Quiet study, by contrast, is entirely free of such nastiness. It is not a disagreeable way of procuring what one wants; it *is* something that one wants. Quiet study simply makes one blessed because it is, if not valuable for its own sake, at least intrinsically pleasant. (If it is intrinsically pleasant, it brings about pleasure all by itself, and pleasure, according to Amphion, is valuable for its own sake.)

Third, and perhaps most surprisingly, Amphion can argue that his detached life makes him a more effective citizen. Again, his argument has more than one part. His general claim is that wise advice takes precedence over manly vigor: "With a man's sound advice a city and a house thrive, and there is, in addition, great strength for war. For one bit of wise counsel conquers many hands, and ignorance is the greatest evil with the mob" (fr. 200 *TGF*). Then Amphion suggests that he will be a more effective source of wise advice: "I hope I shall have a sense of proportion [*aidōs*] and say something wise, and so make no disturbance which harms the city" (fr. 202 *TGF*). It is not difficult to imagine that Amphion rests this hope on his quiet way of life. As we have seen, he expects that busily engaged citizens will show "concern for shameful deeds." So that kind of life *threatens* a "sense of proportion." Presumably, then, if Amphion thinks that he will have a "sense of proportion" and so be able to give wise advice, it is because his quiet life enables him to protect his balanced sense of right and wrong. So understood, Amphion connects the quiet life and wise citizenship.

It is perhaps surprising to see someone hold that one can mind one's own business *and* engage in politics. But if being unbusied (*apragmosunē*) is generally opposed to being nasty and meddlesome (*polupragmosunē*), and if there is no word for the condition of engaging in others' business without nasty meddling, then one might want to characterize the middle ground as a way of being unbusied or minding one's own business. That appears to be how Amphion sees himself. He does not entirely abandon politics, but nonetheless withdraws from the hustle and bustle of political competition in favor of research and pleasure. All told, then, he prefers the (relatively) quiet life for pleasure, intellectual inquiry, *and* wiser politics.[5]

It is not clear how Amphion would fit these aims together and balance his pursuit of pleasure, research, and the good of the city, nor is it clear how much political action or what kind of political action he would allow himself as one who minds his own business. Perhaps his position would display more obvious coherence if we had the rest of Euripides' play. Perhaps not: he is a character in a drama and not a theorist striving for consistency.

In any case, later philosophers who were eager to justify withdrawal from ordinary politics typically separated these aims. They independently prioritized just one of the three aims to argue that it would be better to live a quiet than a political life. The significance of their arguments lies not just in their ramifications for ancient ethical theory and its account of how a person should live. The philosophers who argue for withdrawal also challenge the dominant ideology about politics in different ways, and they all suggest an alternative conception of politics.

To offer a first approximation of how they do this, I need to tease out some of the dominant ideology's implicit commitments. The ideology explicitly holds that human excellence requires political action. If the ideology assumes, with Aristotle and many Greeks, that human excellence is the fulfillment of human nature, then it is committed to the idea that human beings are naturally political animals (see also Depew, this volume, chapter 26). But two other commitments offer a more relevant explanation of the dominant ideology. First, according to the dominant ideology, the good of a human's life is (at least primarily) not private and exclusive to him but shared or common; it is (at least primarily) located not in some state of himself but in activities that necessarily involve others. Second, the dominant ideology identifies these activities that necessarily involve others and (at least partly) constitute the good of a human life as the traditional activities of the active citizen. These two commitments explain why the dominant ideology holds that excellence and achieving the good so obviously require political engagement.

The three philosophical defenses of withdrawal challenge different features of the ideology and suggest different alternatives. The first, developed by Plato and Aristotle on behalf of philosophical contemplation, accepts both of the dominant ideology's implicit commitments but argues that some exceptional human beings do better by trying to transcend human nature and ordinary political activity. Like Amphion, they favor quiet study. Perhaps unlike Amphion, they think that only an exceptional few should favor quiet study, and they favor quiet study for its own sake, as the best activity a human can perform, and not for the sake of pleasure, although it is extremely pleasant. To the extent that Plato and Aristotle, and especially some heirs of their argument, suggest a community of like-minded people who avoid traditional political activity, they also introduce an alternative vision of a political community, and one that does not require face-to-face interaction.

The second defense of withdrawal, developed by Epicurus on behalf of pleasure, rejects the dominant ideology's first implicit commitment by arguing that the good for human beings is private – each person's good is his own pleasure and not a shared activity – and concludes that humans best realize their good outside traditional political activity. By turning their backs on the hazards of competition and embracing pleasure, including a defense of some intellectual inquiry, the Epicureans follow Amphion closely, although their concomitant embrace of a separatist community of Epicureans might well differ from his, which is uncertain.

The third defense of withdrawal, developed by Socrates and some of his followers on behalf of reforming politics, accepts that the human good lies in shared activity but rejects the second implicit commitment of the dominant ideology by radically transforming the picture of what that activity should be. On this approach, politics should not be the traditional competitive endeavor but a quiet, shared education in what is good. Perhaps this develops Amphion's proposal to offer wise counsel from a quiet life. At the least, Socrates and his followers develop Amphion's curious combination of withdrawal and engagement, and they offer various ways of developing this combination as a new kind of politics.

Withdrawal to Transcend Politics

Plato and Aristotle do not reject the dominant ideology, but their attraction to the ideal of minding one's own business leads them to plead for exceptions. They are in a difficult spot, wanting to motivate the ideal of minding one's own business without rejecting the dominant ideology. At first glance, it might seem that Plato succeeds in doing this by transforming what it means to mind one's own business. But in the end, the transformation is not enough. Plato is still drawn to the ideal of minding one's own business as traditionally understood, as the quiet life. He and Aristotle both argue that an elite few can live the best possible human life by withdrawing from politics, and their case for this introduces tension into their ethics and puts pressure on the dominant ideology.

Plato transforms the idea of minding one's own business in the *Republic* when he makes "minding one's own business" essential to justice, the paradigmatic excellence of the political life.[6] He maintains that the just person is one in whose soul each part minds its own business (*Resp.* 441d–e, 443c–d), and a just city is one in which each class of citizens minds its own business (*Resp.* 434c). This is a transformation because "minding one's own business" now has little to do with avoiding the business of the polis. Indeed, on Plato's scheme, the ruling class of the ideal city "minds its own business" (that is, it does its own job) by *ruling the city*! So it would appear that this transformation allows Plato to stand by the dominant ideology's rejection of withdrawal while co-opting the quiet life's ideal of "minding one's own business."

But his support for the dominant ideology is uneasy, for two reasons. First, Plato's transformed ideal of "minding one's own business" is highly restrictive. In his view, the just soul is ruled by its rational part (*Resp.* 441e), which must have knowledge (441e with 442c), and knowledge requires grasping the Forms, the nonsensible properties that explain the way things seem (*Resp.* 476a–479e with books 6 and 7). But only philosophers grasp the Forms (*Resp.* 476a–479e), and so only philosophers are, strictly speaking, just. On Plato's view, too, the just city is ruled by its rational part, which must have knowledge. So the just city must be ruled by philosophers (*Resp.* 473c–e). According to these standards, very few people and even fewer cities are just.

What is more, Plato holds that those who *are* just and who perfectly manifest the transformed ideal of "minding their own business" – that is, the philosophers – also want to mind their own business in the traditional sense of withdrawing from politics.[7] According to the *Republic*, a philosopher who has grasped the knowable reality that underlies and explains the world of perceptual experience wants nothing so much as to continue to contemplate this reality, and so she disdains politics. That is why, in the *Republic*, the founders of the ideal city have to compel the philosophers to rule (see E. Brown 2000a, 2004). These philosophers will "mind their own business" in the transformed sense and engage in politics only if they are compelled to, and those who willingly engage in politics must, according to Plato, fail to "mind their own business" in the transformed sense. So it would seem that the transformation of "minding one's own business" fails to save Plato's attachment to the dominant ideology.

In fact, Plato expounds upon the gulf between the best, philosophical life and political activity in several dialogues. When the *Republic* addresses how philosophers should live in ordinary cities, it is clear that they should and will justifiably indulge their love for wisdom, far from politics (520a–b; cf. 496c–497a and 592a). In the *Phaedo*, Socrates insists that philosophers are completely different from anyone else, including regular citizens, for the philosophers are lovers of wisdom while everyone else is a lover of body (68b–c). And in his digression in the *Theaetetus*, he asserts that these utterly different interests involve incompatible skills: philosophers are ignorant and incapable in law courts and political proceedings (173c–d) while politicians are ignorant and incapable when it comes to philosophical discussions of justice (175b–d). In these works, Plato urges withdrawing from politics to live the best life a human being can live, the life of contemplative philosophy.

Plato's ideal of the quiet life of contemplation is not exactly Amphion's. Amphion defends intellectual activity in part because it brings him maximal pleasure and in part because it will enable him to give political advice. Plato's contemplators are not interested in giving political advice, and while they believe that contemplation is the most pleasant activity, pleasure is not their reason for contemplating. They are attracted to contemplative activity for its own sake, on account of their love of wisdom.

The contemplative ideal might be Plato's invention. Plato himself and the later tradition attribute the contemplative ideal to some Presocratic philosophers, but it is not clear if the attribution is correct.[8] It is clear, however, that Aristotle retains the contemplative ideal. This is clearest in the *Nicomachean Ethics* (but see also *Pol.* 7.2–3 and *Eth. Eud.* 1.4–5). In book 1, chapter 5, Aristotle distinguishes four sorts of lives that people lead, and he dismisses two of them, the money-making life and the "apolaustic" life devoted to bodily pleasure. But he postpones the comparison of the political and philosophical lives. When he returns to the subject, in book 10, chapters 7 and 8, he argues that it is better to act always for the sake of philosophical contemplation than to act always for the central activities of the political life.

Plato and Aristotle do not give all the same reasons for living a contemplative life, but they agree on two important claims. First, contemplative activity is intrinsically superior to political activity. That is why Plato's philosophers prefer it, and why Aristotle favors the philosophical over the political life. Second, the philosophical life involves transcending human nature to become as much like god as possible (Pl., *Resp.* 613a–b, *Tht.* 176b, *Tim.* 90a–d, and Arist. *Eth. Nic.* 1177b31–4; cf. Depew, this volume, chapter 26).

These claims, in fact, introduce a tension into the ethics of Plato and Aristotle. On the one hand, both want to say that the best human life perfects human nature (see esp. Arist. *Eth. Nic.* 1098a7–18). But on the other hand, they acknowledge that philosophical contemplation involves acting like a god and not a human. This tension left room for disagreement. If contemplation is more than human and the best life is truly human, then perhaps the best life is political, after all. Aristotle's pupils Dicaearchus and Theophrastus disagreed about whether the philosophical life is really better than the political life (see Cic. *Att.* 2.16.3).

The tension lurks because Plato and Aristotle agree that the contemplative ideal is *exceptional.* In their view, at best a few people have the ability to transcend human nature and contemplate like the gods. In other words, Plato and Aristotle want to leave the dominant ideology largely intact: for most human beings, in their view, it is best to engage in politics (see also Depew, chapter 26). But their passion for the contemplative ideal calls the ideology into question, nonetheless, in three ways.

First, Plato and Aristotle threaten the dominant ideology's conception of certain fundamental values to explain why the contemplative life is best. According to the dominant ideology, excellence expresses itself in action, and action is political (see, e.g., Pl., *Meno* 71e and Xen. *Mem.* 4.2.11). But this makes it impossible to say that a contemplative philosopher who minds his own business has excellence. So Plato and Aristotle have to reject the ideology's conception of excellence and activity. Plato does it one way: when he says that the contemplative philosopher is unwilling to engage in politics, he says that she is unwilling to *act* (*Resp.* 517c), and so he rejects the connection between excellence and activity. Aristotle does it another: when he says that the contemplative philosopher is unwilling to engage in politics, he insists, nevertheless, that he is *acting* (*Pol.* 1325b14–32), and so he rejects the connection between activity and politics.

Sometimes, too, the contemplative ideal makes problems for the dominant ideology not by overturning its values but by making explicit tensions that were already there. So, for example, according to the dominant ideology, the best humans and poleis display self-sufficiency, but it is not entirely fixed whether self-sufficiency requires independence or is compatible with extensive alliances. Aristotle exploits this. He builds up the picture of self-sufficiency as interdependency to accommodate the political life that is the best most could hope for, and he argues that for the few, contemplation realizes the self-sufficiency of independence, which surpasses what befits human beings as political animals (*Eth. Nic.* 1097b6–16 and 1177a27–b1 with E. Brown forthcoming a).

Finally, the contemplative ideal hints at alternative politics. Consider, for example, the Academy or Lyceum as a community of people who mind their own business and share a contemplative life. Such a community offers a concrete example of a community apart from the dominant ideology's polis. Nor does the threat of an alternative community depend upon face-to-face interactions. Plato and Aristotle wrote works to exhort others to take up the philosophical life, and these writings might be viewed as tools for building dispersed philosophical communities. At least, that is the way the Roman Stoic Seneca saw the early Stoics' philosophical work when he was justifying his retirement from politics (*Dial.* 8.6.4). In two ways, then, those who live as contemplative philosophers, minding their own business, can see themselves as citizens of a community outside the bounds of the traditional polis.

Plato and Aristotle do not pursue these implications of the contemplative ideal, probably because they do not want to threaten the dominant ideology. And in fact, their contemplative ideal poses no immediate threat to politics unless it becomes widely available. But Christianity, in a way, made the contemplative ideal widely available and fostered a community, not always face-to-face, that stood as an alternative to traditional politics. That is why Augustine's *City of God* must toil to defend the Christians. It also helps to explain why philosophers who embrace the dominant ideology rejected that contemplative ideal: they recognized the threat posed by that ideal to traditional political work. The great third century Stoic Chrysippus, for example, rejected the life of leisure both for those who openly avow their pursuit of pleasure (Epicureans) and for those who pursue pleasure cryptically (Academics and Peripatetics) (Plut. *De Stoic. rep.* 1033cd). He and his Stoic followers – Seneca's *On Leisure* notwithstanding – agreed that "the sage will participate in politics, if nothing prevents him" (Diog. Laert. 7.121).

So, when Cicero, who wholeheartedly embraces the dominant ideology, tries to defend his beloved Plato, he gives no support to the contemplative ideal. Rather, he claims that Plato taught Dion of Syracuse to be a better citizen (*Off.* 1.155). Cicero, in other words, defends Plato the man against Plato the theorist. It is not hard to imagine that Plato, Aristotle, and their immediate followers would have done the same. After all, they respected the dominant ideology despite the special exceptions, and in both schools, there were in fact several philosophers who advised politicians. So perhaps, in practice, and despite the contemplative ideal, Plato and Aristotle would have defended the quiet life by citing Amphion's third reason, that it facilitates wiser political advice.

Still, by proposing a way of life greater than politics, Plato and Aristotle call into question the dominant ideology, and their evaluative demotion of the political life had long-term consequences.

Withdrawal to Reject Politics

Epicurus also demotes the value of political activity. He believes that politics has merely instrumental value, because he thinks that everything besides pleasure has value if and only if it brings about pleasure. This private conception of the good – each person should pursue his or her *own* pleasure – departs radically from the dominant ideology's conception of the good. But Epicurus' understanding of pleasure is unusual, and although he generally favors the quiet life, he also lays the groundwork for a countercultural conception of politics.

Epicurus understands pleasure to be not sensual satisfaction but the absence of mental disturbance and physical pain. Thus he proposes that success in life requires cultivating bulwarks against disturbance and pain and avoiding circumstances that are likely to give rise to disturbance and pain. These two strategies might be thought to pull in two different directions. After all, the better one is equipped to shrug off what would pain most people, the less one needs avoidance, and the more one avoids pains, the less practice one has absorbing troublesome circumstances without trouble. But generally speaking, Epicurus prefers the odds of avoidance, and so he counsels against the political life (*Sent. Vat.* 58 and *RS* 14; cf. Diog. Laert. 10.119 and Plut. *Adv. Col.* 1126e–1127c).

Of course, this is general advice, and it admits of exceptions. If *no one* takes charge and political instability threatens, then the calculation might change. Epicurus' pupil Colotes explains, "Those who arranged laws and customs and established kings and rulers in cities brought much security and tranquility to life and banished turmoil. If anyone takes these things away, we shall live the life of beasts, and one man who chances upon another will practically devour him" (Plut. *Adv. Col.* 1124d). This would be worse than a life engaged in politics. So, as Seneca reports, "Epicurus says that the sage will not engage in politics *unless* something intervenes" (*Dial.* 8.3.2). This no doubt explains why some Epicureans, such as Cassius, did engage during the Roman civil war in the first century BCE (see Momigliano 1941).

It is worth noting, too, that one might accept the general framework of Epicurean ethics and nevertheless infer that one should engage in politics. One need only recalculate how politics and withdrawal would promote one's private good. There is some reason to believe that Epicurus' atomist predecessor Democritus favored this alternative calculation. According to later reconstructions, Democritus held that one should act always for the sake of one's "good-spiritedness" (*euthumia*), and he identified "good-spiritedness" as something distinct from pleasure but reliably tracked by "enjoyment" (*terpsis*) (Diog. Laert. 9.45; Clem. Al. *Strom.* II 130; cf. fr. 189 DK). This makes his account of ethics a close cousin to Epicurus': both locate the good in a private state of the individual. But unlike Epicurus, Democritus roundly encourages politics, at least according to our surviving fragments (Plut. *Adv. Col.* 1126a and 1100c (= fr. 157 DK) and fr. 252 DK).

The difference between Democritus' support for the dominant ideology and Epicurus' rejection of it seems to turn on a disagreement over the effects of one's reputation. The fragments of Democritus include this: "If a man neglects the affairs of the people, he becomes ill spoken of, even if he does not steal or do anything wrong. Later, for the man who is negligent or does wrong, there is a risk of being ill spoken of and of suffering something. To err is inevitable, but it is not easy for human beings to forgive" (fr. 253 DK). Democritus does not encourage pursuit of the greatest honors (Plut. *De tranq. anim.* 465c = fr. 3 DK), but he *does* say that minding one's own business will bring trouble. That is, given the dominant ideology, one does not want the reputation of minding one's own business. Epicureans surely faced the dominant ideology's complaint that they were "free riding" (see Plut. *Adv. Col.* 1127a). But Epicurus nonetheless advises his followers to "live unnoticed" (fr. 551 Usener). He seems to believe that those who engage in politics are mistaken about how best to obtain security. They think that political power and honor will give them freedom from fear (*RS 7*). But in fact, Epicurus maintains, it is riskier to seek security among such people than it is to try to avoid notice. The Epicureans simply calculate the risks differently than Democritus, for they, unlike him, consistently conclude that it would be better to avoid politics (see also Roskam 2007).

But Epicureanism is not entirely apolitical, and the Epicureans who mind their own business do not entirely leave politics behind. They do not withdraw to live as separate individuals, each minding his own business. Rather, they cultivate friendship with other Epicureans as the greatest security against pain and disturbance (*RS 27* and 28, *Sent. Vat.* 34). In fact, the Epicureans lived together in Epicurus' "Garden" (see Clay 1983). They established a community of like-minded people who helped each other by providing security so that each could best pursue pleasure (*RS 40*). The ideals of this community departed sharply from those of the polis from which the Epicureans withdraw: theirs was a countercultural community (see E. Brown forthcoming b; cf. Eur. *Hipp.* 1013–1020).

The Epicureans do not draw attention to the fact that their Garden counts as countercultural *politics*. This should not be surprising; they aim to "live unnoticed." But the founder of Stoicism, Zeno of Citium, seems to have proposed a similarly countercultural community of friends, and he *did* draw attention to this in a work called *Republic* (*Politeia*). In this work, Zeno proposes an ideal political arrangement that embarrasses Plato's *Republic* by its impracticality. The ideal, Zeno suggests, would obtain were every adult human to be a Stoic sage. Any power-sharing arrangement among nonsages is doomed to faction: political peace requires like-mindedness (*homonoia*) which requires genuine wisdom. So on Zeno's radically deinstitutionalized picture of ideal politics, a community of sages can be counted on to be friends and to educate the young to be virtuous adults. They will need no law courts or temples. Nor will they need a military, so long as the world is filled with cities each of which is filled exclusively with sages, sharing the same, Stoic way of life.

It is hard to see how such an ideal could have any practical import, since the Stoic sage is "rarer than the Phoenix." But Zeno insisted on the relevance of his *Republic* right from its start (Phld. *De Stoicis* 12.2–8), where he also impugned the standard Greek education (Diog. Laert. 7.32). This suggests that he imagines that people might reject the standard education and seek to build a community with like-minded individuals who are committed to a Stoic education. If that is the import of Zeno's *Republic*, and it is not easy to be sure about this, then it resembles the lesson of Epicurus' Garden, with the challenge to traditional political theorizing made explicit (see E. Brown forthcoming c: ch. 6). Although Zeno and Epicurus start from very different assumptions about human beings and their good, Zeno's proposal highlights the political implications of Epicurus' particular way of minding his own business.

Withdrawal to Transform Politics

The third defense of withdrawing from politics accepts wholeheartedly the dominant ideology's claim that the good for a human being is activity that must be shared with other human beings, but it rejects the thought that this activity can be found in ordinary politics. Its sponsor is Socrates, at least as he appears in Plato's Socratic dialogues.[9]

Socrates uses paradox to characterize his attitude toward the political life: "It might perhaps seem strange that I go around giving advice and minding others' business privately but do not dare to go into your assembly and advise the city publicly" (Pl. *Ap.* 31c4–7). This is paradoxical because Socrates considers himself both a busybody (*polupragmōn*) and yet outside traditional politics. But he fully explains the paradox.

On the one hand, Socrates explains his rejection of traditional politics. He acknowledges that he gave Athens conventional political service on each of the three or four occasions when his city called upon him: he fought in battles at Potidaea, Amphipolis, and Delium (Pl. *Ap.* 28de; cf. *La.* 181b); he was at least once – but not more than twice (Arist. *Ath. Pol.* 62.3) – a member of the Council of Five Hundred (Pl. *Ap.* 32b1); and when the Thirty summoned Socrates to carry out an order, he answered the call, though he refused to carry out the order (*Ap.* 32c4–d7). But the divine voice has told him to keep away from engaging in politics (*Ap.* 31d2–5), and Socrates believes that it is entirely right to do so (*Ap.* 31d5–6). He explains,

> For know well, men of Athens, that if I had long ago tried to engage in political affairs, I would have long ago perished and would have benefited neither you nor myself. Do not be angry with me when I speak the truth, for no one at all will survive if he genuinely opposes either you or any other assembly and prevents many injustices and illegalities from occurring in the city. Rather, anyone who really fights on behalf of the just, if he is going to survive for even a short time, must live privately, and not publicly. (*Ap.* 31d6–32a3)

In order to benefit himself and the Athenians, Socrates believes that he had to withdraw from the traditional political life. So Socrates lived a philosophical life that "minds its own business" (cf. Pl. *Grg.* 526c).

Yet, on the other hand, Socrates did not live a life of quiet contemplation (cf. Pl. *Ap.* 36b), and he did not withdraw from the business of helping the general public, for he believed that his examinations provide the greatest benefit to Athens that anyone could provide (*Ap.* 36c). This explains why he also characterizes himself as a "busybody" (*Ap.* 31c, quoted above), and it explains why he insists, in Plato's *Gorgias*, that he is the only Athenian of his time even to *try* to engage in true politics, which is to say, he is the only one who tries to improve others' lives instead of trying merely to make them *feel* better (*Grg.* 521d).

Socrates, then, is a special case, and his argument for withdrawing from ordinary politics depends upon rethinking what politics should be. He rejects thoroughly the values of contemporary Athenians, their love of honor and wealth (*Ap.* 36b and *passim*), and he argues instead that no one should engage in the affairs of the city before straightening out the affairs of his own soul (cf. Pl. *Symp.* 216a). Socrates in a way inherits a traditional aristocratic rejection of democratic politics. But instead of offering reactionary proposals, he radically rethinks what politics should be. He opposes not just the values of the Athenian democrats but also those of their oligarchic rivals. That is why Callicles is right to draw on Zethus' critique of Amphion when he wants to cast Socrates as someone who neglects traditional political values and activities (Pl. *Grg.* 485e–486d).

How special Plato's Socrates is can be seen by looking at Isocrates, who offers a rival conception of how to transform politics through a life that minds its own business. Isocrates is Plato's chief rival for students who wish to study what both call "philosophy." But whereas Plato's students learn to study and contemplate the nature of the world, and to reshape their lives in accordance with what they discover, Isocrates promises a more narrow revision of traditional rhetorical training, revamped to suit more aristocratic aims than those served by other fourth century orators. Accordingly, he stays closer to the traditional aristocratic ideal of "minding one's own business." He attacks earlier and rival rhetoricians for teaching "busybodiness" (*polupragmosunē*) (*C. soph.* 20 and *Antid.* 48, 230, 237). He cultivates instead being unbusied (*apragmosunē*) (*Antid.* 4, 151, 227), and he defends himself against the charge of having taught busybodies (*polupragmosunē*) (*Antid.* 98). Isocrates uses his writings to try to change Greek politics, but his aims are far less radical than Socrates'. He yearns for a return to past glory that attracted Greek allies to Athens' leadership and kept the barbarians at bay (see e.g. *Aerop.* 79–81).

So Socrates' life was unusual, both because it simultaneously minded its own business and meddled and because it thoroughly critiqued traditional political values. But it is not easy to see what the concrete political implications of Socratic politics are. How would a polis be arranged if all the citizens successfully examined themselves and each other? Socrates, like some other prominent political theorists – Marx leaps to mind – is clearer about what is wrong with the status quo than he is about how things would be if they were set right.

Perhaps because he was so unusual and perhaps because his vision of an alternative future was indeterminate, Socrates attracted a wide range of followers. In a way, Plato's and Aristotle's thoughts about how a city ought to be governed respond to Socrates' call for reform, as they insist that rulers should be the most virtuous people, but Aristotle, especially, shows how the Socratic conception of virtue can be tamed to accommodate traditional Athenian values. Other so-called "Socratic" followers stay closer to the radical challenge that Socrates presents to business as usual, although they differ widely in their interpretation of how to reform politics and realize the aim of benefiting others.

The Cyrenaics and Cynics both go further than Socrates in removing themselves from traditional politics. Like Socrates, they avoided the Assembly and the courts and thereby rejected the traditional political life. But Socrates, despite his philanthropic (Pl. *Eu.* 3d) desire to examine and benefit "anyone, whether fellow citizen or foreigner, whom I think is wise" (Pl. *Ap.* 32b, cf. 30a), stayed in Athens. He need not have thought that he was obligated to benefit the Athenians especially. He might simply have thought that Athens, with its free speech, best suited his controversial way of life (Pl. *Grg.* 461e; cf. *Ap.* 37c–e and *Meno* 80b). Nonetheless, he did not renounce his ties to Athens. The Cyrenaics and Cynics, by contrast, noisily rebuked local attachments. Aristippus the Elder, who is in some sense the founder of the Cyrenaic sect, says, "I do not shut myself up in a political community but am a stranger everywhere" (Xen *Mem.* 2.1.13; cf. Plut. *an virt. doc. possit* 2, 439e). The later Cyrenaic Theodorus names the cosmos his father-city (*patris*) (Diog. Laert. 2.99). And, most noisily of all, Diogenes the Cynic declares himself a "citizen of the world" (Diog. Laert. 6.63) and embraces his existence "citiless, homeless, deprived of a fatherland" (6.38). These cosmopolitan Socratics spread sharply contrasting visions of the good human life, but both Cyrenaics and Cynics were clearly inspired by Socrates' conception of politics outside the traditional bounds.[10]

The Stoics, whose founder apparently studied with the Cynic Crates and in the Academy (Diog. Laert. 7.2), offer a more nuanced response to Socrates' example. On the one hand, they partly rehabilitate traditional political engagement and the dominant ideology. At least by the time of Chrysippus, Stoics believe that one should engage in politics if the circumstances permit (Diog. Laert. 7.121), and Chrysippus even allows that a Stoic might speak in public as though wealth and health were good even though Stoicism holds that only virtue is, strictly speaking, good (Plut. *De Stoic. rep.* 1034b; cf. 1048a). There seems to have been no fixed political program in the Stoa, as different circumstances would call for different regimes and laws to achieve the aims of politics, which are to restrain vice and promote virtue. But the Stoics attempt to join Socrates' uncompromising views about value with traditional political action.

On the other hand, the Stoics also insist, with Socrates and against the dominant ideology, that a good human life does not *require* traditional political engagement. It requires, instead, agreeing with nature, and this demands sensitivity to the particular circumstances in which one finds oneself. So one person might do best by engaging in politics, and another as a private farmer, and a third as a philosophical teacher. Here the Stoics resemble the other philosophers in seeking to divorce the notions of excellent activity and traditional politics, but like Socrates – and unlike the advocates of contemplative activity or pleasant withdrawal – the Stoics do this by transforming the notion of politics and by yoking *all* excellent activity to the inherently political project of seeking a common good with other human beings. For them, even the private life of philosophical teaching is the life of a political animal, and its excellent activity aims at a common good with other humans just as surely as the traditional political life does (see E. Brown forthcoming c: ch. 7). So the Stoics remain true to the Socratic revolution in rethinking the aims and means of politics even though they encourage traditional forms of political action to realize this revolution.

With time, the contrast between the Cynic and the Stoic responses to Socrates became more pronounced. Especially once Stoicism settled in Rome, Stoic ideas drifted further from their radical roots, and they were frequently joined to conventional Roman ideals. But interestingly, philosophers in the Roman world who often espouse Stoic–Roman ideals that are opposed to the radical proposals of Socrates and the early Socratics continue to make a special exception for Socrates and his immediate followers. So, for example, Cicero declares, "No one should be led into this error, that if Socrates or Aristippus did or said something contrary to custom or political practice, this same thing should be permitted to him. For those men acquired such freedom by their great and divine goods. But the whole theory or approach of the Cynics must be rejected" (*Off.* 1.148). Seneca goes one step further, and finds room to praise Diogenes the Cynic. He says, "In benefits, I am necessarily defeated by Socrates, necessarily defeated by Diogenes, who marched naked through the middle of the Macedonians' treasures, treading upon the wealth of a king" (*Ben.* 5.4.3). These accommodations suggest that the Socratic challenges to the dominant ideology are allowable only as exceptional provocations to virtue. Broader allegiance to the Socratic program, such as one finds in the vogue for Cynicism in first and second century (CE) Rome, would have to be tamer (see Billerbeck 1996).

Contesting the Political

Philosophers in antiquity sought to justify the quiet life against the dominant ideology's insistence that excellence requires engaging in the affairs of the polis in the Assembly and the courts. It is not hard to find in these arguments an appearance of rationalization or self-justification. But I have tried to show why it would be a mistake to dismiss these arguments or set them apart from "Greek and Roman political thought." By these arguments, the philosophers raise, sometimes merely implicitly and sometimes explicitly, deep and important questions about politics. Some of them merely challenge the values and virtues of the political agents around them. More searchingly, some of them go one step further, and offer a model of political activity that is not confined by the geography and institutions of the polis. When we are asking about what politics is, who does or should engage in politics, and how they should do so, these challenges matter.

FURTHER READING

The best study of Greek withdrawal from politics is L. Carter 1986, which covers the last third of the fifth century as the background to Plato's defense of the contemplative life. There is no adequate survey in English of the longstanding philosophical dispute between the philosophical and political lives. Perhaps the best work remains Jaeger 1948. In French, there is Joly 1956, which should be read warily. Also relevant are André 1966; Demont 1990; and Grilli 1953. For more specialized inquiries, see the notes and citations.

NOTES

Ryan Balot proposed this chapter, offered many helpful suggestions for developing the chapter, and improved it with his critique of a penultimate draft. I am very grateful to him for all of this and for much else.

1   There are other senses of "minding one's own business" that I leave aside in this chapter. Consider how Pericles attacks those who "mind their own business" in his final speech in Thucydides' history (2.63.2–3). Here those who "mind their own business" are attempting to persuade their fellow Athenians to surrender their empire (see also 2.64.1 for the attempt to persuade and 2.61.4 for the opposition to empire). So they are not *entirely* minding their own business. Perhaps, then, "minding one's own business" is a relative term, always understood by contrast to some state of "busybody-ness" or "meddlesomeness" (*polu-pragmosunē*). (Compare the discussions of Amphion and Socrates below.) Often, the terms do work this way, and with wide variability: what is considered meddlesome varies because different people in different circumstances are expected to take different degrees of interest in the affairs of another (see Adkins 1976). For the most part, I set this aside, to concentrate on "minding one's own business" where it indicates withdrawal from politics. On the other hand, and perhaps more likely, Pericles might identify the anti-imperialists as "minding their own business" not because they are less meddlesome but because they want *Athens* to "mind its own business" and surrender its empire. (Thucydides has the Corcyraean envoys say that Corcyra was formerly committed to minding its own business (*apragmosunē*) (1.32.5). Compare Arist. *Pol.* 7.2–3.) It is doubtful that the anti-imperialists themselves would embrace this label, since it smears them with political inexperience and inattention, but "minding one's own business" and "meddlesomeness" were often slogans in debates over Athenian foreign policy (see Ehrenberg 1947 and Kleve 1964). I set this usage aside, as well. For the identity of the anti-imperialists Pericles targets, see W. Nestle 1926; Wade-Gery 1932; and Dienelt 1953. And with Pericles' attack, compare how Alcibiades characterizes Nicias' opposition to the Sicilian expedition as "minding one's own business" (*apragmosunē*) (Thuc. 6.18.6).

2   For the dominant ideology's transformation of Homeric values, see Adkins 1960. Wallace (this volume, chapter 11) excellently situates this ideology. Rahe 1984 reflects expansively on it.

3   L. Carter 1986 discusses the historical quietists in fifth century Athens by inferring their existence from largely literary evidence. Although he does not name many names, he identifies three distinct groups: the nobles who withdrew from the democratic regime they could not support (e.g. some of the youths in Socrates' circle); the peasant farmers of Attica who had neither the time nor the money to go to the Assembly or the courts in Athens (e.g. various characters in Euripides' and Aristophanes' plays); and rich quietists, some of whom could not engage because they were metics, who feared prosecution and entanglement (e.g. some of Lysias' defendants).

4   The source for this fragment does not name the play. Nothing much turns on whether it comes from *Antiope*. For my purposes, it is enough that Zethus' charges establish that Amphion was engaged in intellectual inquiries of some sort. That sets up the need for Amphion to defend such inquiries. If this fragment does not record his defense, it at least expresses a related idea, and thus introduces one of the three motivations for withdrawal that I want to explore.

5   North says that "minding one's own business," "the watchword of the aristocrats" in the fifth century, was later "absorbed into the Attic ideal of citizenship" (1966: 137). This seems to me to go too far. There remains in the fourth century BCE (and beyond) an element of detachment in "minding one's own business," and there remained people who insisted on "minding their own business" by staying out of politics altogether. Notice that in the *Oration on the Scrutiny of Evandrus* that North immediately cites, Lysias warns that Evandrus will *contrast* his life minding his own business with most Athenians' (26.4).

6 In the *Charmides* (161b–163d), Socrates is less optimistic about "minding one's own business" as a characterization of virtue (in this case, moderation or temperance).

7 In the *Statesman* (305e–309b), the Eleatic Stranger explains that people who are keen to mind their own business are those with the quiet nature that is associated with moderation or temperance, as opposed to those with the lively nature associated with courage and the warring life. But one should not suppose that the philosophers of the *Republic* have quiet natures. Rather, they manifest a blend of both natures, just the sort of blend that the Stranger wants the statesman to bring about in the citizens. But notice the similarity between the Stranger's complaint about the quiet natures (at 307e) and the wife's complaint about the father who minds his own business in *Republic* 8 (549c–d, quoted above).

8 Jaeger 1948: 429, for example, doubts it. The strongest contender would seem to be Anaxagoras. See DK 59A29–30. If Euripides studied with him (Diog. Laert. 2.10), Anaxagoras' leanings toward a contemplative life might also help to explain Euripides' *Amphion* (or whoever speaks fr. 910 *TGF*).

9 Xenophon's Socrates is at least sometimes a very different character, who endorses the dominant ideology and encourages political engagement. See esp. *Mem.* 3.7.

10 For an excellent survey of cosmopolitan ideas from Greek antiquity, see Konstan, this volume, chapter 30.

CHAPTER 32

Citizenship and Signs: Rethinking Augustine on the Two Cities

Todd Breyfogle

In Canto 13 of Dante's *Purgatorio*, the poet arrives at the cornice where the sin of envy is purged.[1] "Does any Italian soul dwell among you?" he asks, hoping to find wisdom and solace among fellow countrymen. A shade replies with gentle admonition:

> O frate mio, ciascuna è cittadina
> d'una vera città; ma tu vuo' dire
> che vivesse in Italia peregrina (lines 94–6)

> (O my brother, everyone is a citizen of a true city.
> What you meant to say was
> "who [here] lived in Italy as a pilgrim.")

The Dante of the poem has wrongly seen his ties to the earthly city, and the brotherly shade of the pool of envy renders in image and rhyme the complicated Augustinian contrast between earthly citizenship and pilgrim status: *cittadina è peregrina*. The shade reaffirms the value – indeed, the inescapable requirement – of citizenship while suggesting a temporal mode of being which is in but not of the world, which does not participate in the envious ground which gives rise to the earthly city.

As the Dante of the poem departs this level of purgatory, the voice of another, more ominous brother cries out "as a bolt lanced sudden from a downward-rushing cloud." "Whosoever finds me will slay me ..." Dante shrinks beside his Roman guide as Virgil continues: "There was the galling bit, which should keep man within his boundary ... Heaven calls and, round about you wheeling, courts your gaze with everlasting beauties. Yet your eye turns with fond doting still up on the earth. Therefore he smites you who discerneth all."[2]

A Companion to Greek and Roman Political Thought, First Edition. Edited by Ryan K. Balot.
© 2013 Blackwell Publishing Ltd. Published 2013 by Blackwell Publishing Ltd.

Thematically, verbally, theologically, these central passages of the *Purgatorio* – and thus hence of the whole *Commedia* – reflect Augustine's treatment of the story of Cain and Abel in *De civ. D.* 15.5–8: the corrosive effect of *invidia*, citizenship in the earthly and heavenly cities respectively, the personifications of *amor sui* and *amor Dei*, the preference of one's own to the inexhaustible store of divine goods. Yet the symbolic significance of Cain and Abel is not as straightforward as it seems at first glance. For Augustine, as for Dante, Cain is a compact and complicated sign which characterizes the full range of human social possibilities manifest respectively in *societas*, *civitas*, and *ecclesia*.

De civ. D. 15.1–8, and especially 15.2, has long been seen as the central passage for assessing Augustine's linguistic and conceptual terminology concerning the nature and relation of the two cities. The possibility that the *civitas Dei* is a Platonic exemplar of which the *civitas terrena* is only an image has been decisively disproven.[3] But the difficulty remains as to how to talk about the two eschatological cities with respect to actual historical institutions: Rome, Israel, and Church. Rome is a historical city founded on the misplaced worship of Romulus – for Augustine, the name of the city epitomizes the idolatrous character of the love that forms it (*De civ. D.* 22.6).[4] Jerusalem (coterminous with Israel for Augustine) also is a historical city which serves as a special symbol or prophetic image of the *civitas Dei*, a shadowy reminder that the *civitas Dei* is eschatological, not fully present in time (*De civ. D.* 15.2). *Ecclesia* is that society of those who love and serve God, the *civitas Dei* on pilgrimage in this world prophetically suggested by Jerusalem in her captivity and indicated obliquely by way of negative example by the historical manifestations of the *civitas terrena* (*De civ. D.* 15.2).[5]

The root of this confusion is the failure properly to determine things from loves, institutions from allegiances. Rome, Jerusalem, and the Church are historical things, institutions; *civitas terrena* and *civitas Dei* are eschatological societies formed by individual loves, allegiances – citizenship. Insofar as the historical institutions are reflections of their formative loves, they are also signs of those loves, their opposites, and what they shall become. Augustine speaks of the *civitas* and the *ecclesia* as actual historical *societates*. All members of a *societas* are citizens of one or the other of the eschatological *civitates*, but not all human relations are civic relations, that is, relations defined by citizenship in an actual, historical polity. Cain is born a member of the eschatological *civitas terrena*, but founds an actual, historical *civitas*. Abel is born a member of the eschatological *civitas Dei* and does not found a *civitas*, but is a pilgrim (*De civ. D.* 15.1). Augustine's bewildering play of terms underscores the complex tension between eschatological citizenship and historical citizenship, disclosing an interpenetration whose contours shift beneath the weight of mixed motives of love and the creative possibilities of human invention.[6] The several kinds of *civitates* and *ecclesia* are all *societates*. While all members of a *societas* are eschatological citizens, not all social relations are civic relations in the historical sense. All human beings are members of either one or the other eschatological *civitates*; regardless of their historical citizenship, they live out their lives either as earthly citizens possessing temporal goods or as pilgrims seeking an eternal home. To summarize, then, here is Augustine's conceptual framework:

societas – fellowship or association, human or divine
civitas^c = *in ordo causarum* – the *societas* of just and loving command and obedience in the mind of God (Christ)[7]
  in eternity
    civitas Dei – eschatological heavenly city (spiritual citizenship); the redemption of *civitas^c* (Abel; Seth = resurrection 15.18)
    civitas terrena – eschatological earthly city (spiritual citizenship); the eschatological fulfillment of *civitas^t* (Cain)
  in time
    ecclesia – that historical *societas* of citizens of the *civitas Dei* who, while possessing citizenship in a *civitas^t*, live in sin but under grace as pilgrims whose primary love or allegiance is to God; the positive (hopeful) deformation of *civitas^c* (spiritual pilgrimage)
      Jerusalem/Israel – a specific *civitas^t* which, in bondage, signifies *ecclesia* (Abel)
    civitas^t = *in ordo temporum* – the *societas* of command and obedience under the condition of sin; the negative (damned) deformation of *civitas^c* (material citizenship)
      Rome/Babylon – a specific *civitas^t* which, in domination, signifies by negative example the *civitas Dei* on earth[8] (Cain)

The theological–political conflict, then, is between those who are material citizens (Cain) and spiritual pilgrims (Abel) with respect to the goods of this world.

The bifurcation of *civitas^c* into the two eschatological cities is precipitated by Adam and Eve in their sinful refusal of obedience to God. Husband and wife, each with duties of care with respect to each other, reject divine sociability and are cast into a world of pain, toil, and natural mortality. The natural sociability for which human beings were created became bifurcated in time with sin – the *civitas* which would have obtained became two *civitates*, each imperfect, each aiming toward different eschatological resolutions. The story of Cain and Abel signifies the refusal of human sociability, the rejection of natural fraternity in favor of a world of unnatural mortality. Brothers in a condition of sin, one under damnation the other under grace, signify the twofold temporal deformation of *civitas^c* into *civitas^t* and *ecclesia*. Over and against the regime theories of classical antiquity, Augustine reduces the animating spirits of human sociability to two – the two cities formed by the two loves.

These two loves nonetheless yield three units of analysis: *societas*, *civitas*, and *ecclesia*. *Civitas* Augustine understands to be the perceptible continuity of loves shared by a people, whether understood in historical or eschatological terms. *Societas* refers to that web of interpersonal relations, however weak, formed in the daily conduct of the business of living, reaching from passing familiarity to formal contract. *Ecclesia* represents a specific set of relations shaped by participation in common ritual and eschatological hope. Of the three, *societas* opens most widely to encompass a wide variety of human associations; *civitas* concerns the relations of citizen; *ecclesia* expresses the mutual relations of Christians. While each of these institutional conceptualizations of human bonds is discrete, Augustine also comes to see them as integral to a more general conception of order, though whether these units of theoretical analysis are different in kind or related as genus and species remains to be determined.

Societas

Societas refers to the plurality of associations or fellowship among persons, whether human or divine, including trading partnerships, friendship, marriage, household and neighborly relations (including communities of interest), political associations, the community of mankind, both demonic and angelic community, and the communion of the divine persons.[9] Human beings are created for sociability, having a similarity of species nature because they are derived from one man and bound together also by affinities of individual natures to one another (*b. conjug.* 1.1; *De civ. D.* 12.22, 14.1). To be a being endowed with *intellectus* and *voluntas* is to be a being drawn to others in common knowledge and common interest. This sociability is perfected in heaven where all share "the full enjoyment of the beauty of reason" and where wills no longer conflict because they rest in that true peace, "the will willing nothing unbecoming and yet retaining its freedom" (*De civ. D.* 22.30). The beatific vision is social (*De civ. D.* 22.29); the peace of the heavenly city is "the most ordered and harmonious society in the enjoyment of God and of one another in God" (*De civ. D.* 19.13).[10]

The primary natural bond of society is the relationship between husband and wife, extending to include children and the broader household.[11] Procreation is, indeed, "a duty to society [*officium societatis*]" (*b. conjug.* 1.1, 9.9; *Gn. litt.* 9.7.12, 9.9.14). God created Eve for Adam's company, "a precious gift" to serve as a recognition and reminder that the solitary man is not self-sufficient (*Gn. litt.* 9.12.21). The manner of Eve's creation from Adam's side is an indication of her equality with Adam under God; she is not created from his foot to be trampled or from his head to lord over him, but from his side to be embraced in fellowship (*De civ. D.* 22.17).

Sin is intrinsically a disruption of *societas*; the perverse self love separates us from the *societas* for which we were created (*Gn. litt.* 11.14.19, 11.31.41). In delighting in his own power, the devil "separated himself from the society of angels" (*Gn. litt.* 11.14.18). Yet even the divisive impulses of sin thrust us inexorably into *societas*, if only to misdirected ends. The band of thieves to which Alexander's empire is likened is formed by a pact of *societas* (*De civ. D.* 4.4 *pacto societatis astringitur*) and the embittered gather themselves into a *societas* to taste the bitter water of their sins

(*Conf.* 13.17–18). In stealing the pears, Augustine longs for the approval of the society of his peers (*Conf.* 2.4.9ff.). Adam himself sins, Augustine says, not from concupiscence but out of concern (*benevolentia*) in his "attachment and affection" for Eve (*Gn. litt.* 11.42.59). Adam's sinful attachment is a lesser good, though it is a *societas* which shapes in Adam "the deformity of confusion, not the humility of confession" (*Gn. litt.* 11.35.47: "Habet confusionis deformitatem, et non habet confessionis humilitatem").

That the punishment of pride is confusion is the story also of the Tower of Babel, which caused different *societates* to become "divided according to different languages" (*Gn. litt.* 9.12.20). The cause of divided *societates* is pride, but in the punishment God has planted the seeds of the remedy – for there is a beauty in the sharing of ideas and we long to communicate (to commune sociably) with those who do not speak our language (*trin.* 10.1.2). Babel is the occasion of our having to learn humility so that we may delight more fully in sociability (as anyone who has tried to learn a language knows). Naturally, intellectually, and in disposition or "affectus", human beings are created for sociability according to their common origin, their rational desires, and feelings of affection – the familiarity of the company of good people and good things (*De civ. D.* 15.4). Our very nature resists the drive to solitary power and redirects the deformations of confusion to the pursuit of a common good, however weak or misconstrued.

It is in the midst of these reflections on the sociability for which we were created that Augustine seems first to have conceived his motif of the two cities developed in *Gn. litt.* 11. Avarice is the root of all evil (Augustine is commenting on 1 Timothy 6.10) insofar as it is a function of

> the attitude by which a person desires more than what is due by reason of his excellence, and a certain love of one's own interest, his private interest, to which the Latin word *privatus* was wisely given, a term which obviously expresses loss rather than gain. For every privation [*privatio*] diminishes. Where pride, then, seeks to excel, there it is cast down into want and destitution, turning from the pursuit of the common good to one's own individual good out of a destructive self-love. (*Gn. litt.* 11.15.19)[12]

The inordinate attachment of the heart to one's own to the exclusion and indeed domination of others distracts us from the true *societas* for which we were created.[13] Opposed to the "disease" of perverse self-love which separates us from society is "charity, who *seeks not her own* [1 Cor. 13:5], that is, does not rejoice in her own [*privata*] excellence" (*Gn. litt.* 11.15.19). Having established the rupture in *societas* in the substitution of the private for the common good, Augustine launches into his formative conception of the two cities (*Gn. litt.* 11.15.20).

Distinct from our predominant modern usage, Augustine's description of *societas* as expressed in the two *civitates* is not a political abstraction but always the discrete, concrete relations among persons – between father and son, among neighbors, between imperial official and citizen, and among trading partners.[14] Augustine's letters are infused with a pathos for those who hold civic or ecclesiastical office, making clear that formal bureaucratic relationships are informed by an understanding of personhood. An official may represent the ruling power, but insofar as he is

Christian, for example, his dealings should be Christian.[15] Put another way, Augustine has no conception of a corporate person (such as exists in systems of common law) usurping the humane responsibilities of moral persons.[16] A *societas* is the sum total of those innumerable single and repeated engagements between people, engagements as diverse as trade, neighborliness, familial relations, and civic friendship – the love of neighbor, where one's neighbor is construed most broadly. Like the command to love God, which assists us in our ignorance, the command to love our neighbor binds us to the natural but corrupted impulse to sociability.

Love of country is a Christian duty because one's fellow citizens are also one's neighbors and the historical city is the context in which they live well or poorly. Even Rome can be ordinately loved, for by God's permission Rome brought the whole world into "a single society of common goods and law" (*De civ. D.* 18.22: "unam societatem rei publicae legumque"). *Societas* opens more widely than *civitas* and *ecclesia*, and in principle ought to extend to the whole human race.[17] Often Augustine will speak of *societas* as synonymous with *civitas* (*De civ. D.* 15.1, 15.20 *civitas societasque*), even as the definition of the city itself: "a multitude of men linked together by some bond of association [*societatis vinculo*]" (*De civ. D.* 15.8; also 19.17). The term is used with equal facility in reference to the *civitas terrena* (*De civ. D.* 15.8, 15.22) and the heavenly city (*De civ. D.* 15.18, 15.22, 16.10), of the community of demons as well as that of angels (*De civ. D.* 18.18, 20.15). All cities are *societates*, but not every *societas* is political. Yet the natural rational and affective impulse to *societas* resolves itself into the formation of both material and spiritual *civitates*.

Civil harmony or disharmony are by-products, as it were, of the network of varied concrete relationships of sociability. The degree to which temporal law is brought to bear on a people is properly proportional to the character of their sociability (*lib. arb.* 1.5), for temporal law concerns itself with the "compromise between human wills in respect of the provisions relevant to the mortal nature of man."[18] The society of spiritual pilgrims will have less need of temporal law than those whose citizenship is defined by material things. The degrees of earthly peace and just rule are goods which are both derivative from and responses to people pursuing essentially "private" – that is, not explicitly political – relationships.[19]

The household, for example, is

> the beginning, or rather a small component part of the city, and every beginning is directed to some end of its own kind, and every component part contributes to the completeness of the whole of which it forms a part. The implication is quite apparent, that domestic peace contributes to the peace of the city – that is, the ordered harmony of those who live together in a house ... contributes to the ordered harmony concerning authority and obedience obtaining among the citizens.[20]

Private sociability need not be incompatible with the common good. The private love (*caritas privata*) of the household, for example, also supports the *ecclesia* and is in no way incompatible with the "public love in the house of God" ["*publica in domo Dei caritas*"].[21] Both the civic and ecclesiastical orders reflect the character of the souls and relationships which comprise them – the character of the individual loves.

When Augustine comes, in *De civ. D.* 19, to reformulate Cicero–Scipio's definition of a republic, he stresses the character of the people's social bond. Under the initial definition advanced at *De civ. D.* 2.22, a people is defined by its agreement as to *ius* (what is right) and common *utilitas* (what is useful), criteria impossible to meet under the condition of sin (*De civ. D.* 19.23). Augustine's difficulty is both theoretical and empirical – "Without a people [*populus*] there can be no republic" (*De civ. D.* 19.23), yet we need a tool of conceptual analysis and see around us plausible if temporally contingent examples of "a people." But, Augustine continues,

> if we discard this definition of a people, and, assuming another, say that a people is an assemblage of reasonable beings bound together by a common agreement as to the objects of their love, then, in order to discover the character of any people, we have only to observe what they love … and it will be a superior people in proportion as it is bound together by higher interests, inferior in proportion as it is bound together by lower. (*De civ. D.* 19.24)[22]

This new definition allows Augustine to detach earthly politically constituted society from a definition of justice which only the *civitas* could attain. It also provides a unit of theoretical analysis which accords with both the eschatological character of the two cities and the empirical reality of functioning historical *societates*. Finally, the definition extends the conception of earthly social relationships beyond that of material citizenship to encompass the whole texture of human relations, not simply the formal legal relations of citizens and noncitizens. One's neighbor is not simply a political creature with some degree of legal standing, but a human being with whom one shares both a species nature and affinities with other individual natures.

These new horizons complement rather than replace the original definition of a people – Augustine refines but does not abandon Cicero–Scipio's definition – which presupposes a common understanding of *ius*, what is mine and thine, and the derived *leges* (laws) which regulate disputes about *ius*.[23] Likewise, the new definition reaffirms the customary relationships of any established society, together with the individual habits and collective traditions which regulate daily life. Even bad loves form some degree of social peace, and the Christian must value that peace as far as it extends, not for its own sake but for the sake of his neighbor. It is, then, with a joint view of peace and the common good that the *paterfamilias* frames his domestic rule "in accordance with the law of the city, so that the household may be in harmony with the civic order" (*De civ. D.* 19.16). This injunction need not be read – as is often the case – as a complacent acceptance of the status quo. In the condition of sin, the Christian father must assess how far what passes for peace is in fact conducive to the common good – where a people aims at a higher peace, he orders his domestic precepts accordingly; where the governing laws and customs of a people are not conducive to peace, his precepts aim to teach the higher good. Coming in *De civ. D.* 19 chapter 16, the injunction to take account of prevailing law recognizes the tension which obtains under the condition of sin but in the hope of grace. How far one is to resist unjust laws is a matter of prudence subject to the same criteria as the just war: defense of neighbor, proportionality, and the likelihood of success.[24] The task, and not infrequently the tragedy, of Christian love in Augustine's eyes is the difficulty of shaping and being shaped by the historical city while on pilgrimage in this world.

Although it takes account of the overall character of a people's sociability, Augustine's robust vision of the common good proceeds, as it were, from the bottom up, beginning with the individual soul whose improvement will naturally though perhaps imperceptibly contribute to the common good.[25] At the same time, common goods are the context in which human beings come to recognize that they are neither intellectually nor socially self-sufficient. Just as our intellectual restlessness prompts us to learn again how to love God, our desire for human companionship throws us together into a multiplicity of *societates* in which we learn to love our neighbor.

That "river" or "torrent" of the human race bears two streams: "in the original evil, there are two things: sin and punishment; in the original good there are also two: propagation and conformation" (*De civ. D.* 22.24: "In originali malo duo sunt, peccatum atque supplicium; in originali bono alia duo, propagatio et conformatio"). The former arose "from our audacity", while the latter are bestowed by God, who never inhibited "the fecundity originally bestowed ... in the condemned stock." While sin implicated us in mortality, it did not compromise that "marvelous seminal power" ["illam vim mirabilem seminum"] by which all things – natural and of human design – are propagated in the course of time. If the mixture of good and evil is the torrent of a river, two blessings flow "as from a fountain": the natural propagation of beings and ideas begun by God and from which he rested on the seventh day, and the conformation of human beings in time to God's ongoing creative work of voluntary providence. In this long and lyrical passage (*De civ. D.* 22.24), which rivals Sophocles' "Ode on Man," Augustine celebrates not only biological regeneration but the "countless astonishing arts" of "human genius," from agriculture and medicine to the theater to music and philosophy – all of these the work not of single individuals but of persons in *societas*. Even in sin, man's voluntary sociability in conformation with God's propagation adorns the universe with loveliness.

Civitas

Civitas in Augustine's thinking takes two forms, the *civitas* according to the *ordo causarum*, and the *civitas* according to the *ordo temporum*. In the *ordo temporum*, *civitas* is bifurcated into two *civitates*, the *civitas Dei* and the *civitas terrena*, both eschatological cities of spiritual citizenship which, though distinct, are inseparable in the course of time. As a deformation of *civitas*, the *civitas terrena* is an animating spirit which indicates the *civitas Dei* against which it rebels. Had there been no sin, there would have been one *civitas* – both historical and eschatological – the unity of the historical *civitas* and the historical *ecclesia* as they emerge under the condition of sin in the course of time. The eschatological *civitas terrena* is not coterminous with the historical *civitas*, though empirically the historical *civitas* would seem to be formed by citizens of the *civitas terrena*, those whose loves are of self to the exclusion of God. And in its double valence, the historical *civitas* points to its animating loves in the *civitas terrena*, and to its opposite, by negative example, the animating love of the *civitas Dei*. Nonetheless, whatever its corruption, the historical *civitas* is one of those marvelous goods of human invention, a remarkably varied creative experiment in the exercise of human intellect and will.

The present discussion of *civitas*, then, will be restricted to the historical *civitas*, of which Rome (and sometimes Babylon) will serve as the shorthand and the example. Augustine is intimately familiar with the contours and many details of Roman history, and of republican and imperial apologetics, as well as the civic and religious myth-ology which supported those apologetics. Yet his primary concern in *De civ. D.* is not what Rome does, but what Rome *means* as an expression of the will to self-love which forms the eschatological *civitas terrena*. Augustine treats the history of Rome as the expression, in time, of those divided, selfish loves which form the eschatological *civitas terrena*. It is the *mystical* not material meaning of the historical *civitas* which, for Augustine, animates human and salvation history.

"This race we have distributed in two parts, the one consisting of those who live according to man, the other of those who live according to God. And these we also mystically [*mystice*] call the two cities, or the two communities of men" (*De civ. D.* 15.1). One's membership in one city or the other is predetermined. Cain, we are told, is both born a member of the *civitas terrena* (ontologically) and its founder (histor-ically); Abel was "predestined by grace" to be a citizen of the *civitas Dei*. All history is thus conceived in terms of a specifically Christian structure, that is to say, a structure that is linear and teleological. Indeed, Augustine takes great pains to refute the notion that the world is eternal and that history is cyclical (*De civ. D.* book 12). History begins with creation and ends with judgment (*De civ. D.* book 20) and the imposition of eternal punishment (*De civ. D.* book 21) and reward (*De civ. D.* book 22). The structure of *De civ. D.* as a whole illustrates Augustine's understanding of history and Rome's place in it.

De civitate Dei contains 22 books and divides broadly into deconstructive and constructive parts, books 1–10 and 11–22 respectively, though Augustine weaves criticism and constructive positions throughout. In books 1–10, Augustine argues that the old Roman gods should not be believed in either for the sake of temporal security (1–5) or for reward in the life to come (6–10). Thus, when Augustine comes to discuss explicitly the history of the two cities, he has already conducted an extensive philosophical engagement with every major school of classical philosophy and the intellectual foundations of Roman religion.

In the second part of the work, books 11–22, Augustine addresses the two cities directly. "I will," he writes, "endeavor to treat of the origin, and progress, and deserved destinies of the two cities … which, as we said, are in this present world commingled, and as it were, entangled together" (11.1). In accordance with this plan, books 11–22 contain a history of the two cities, tracing creation, the Fall and its implications (11–14), the Christian remedy for the ills of the present (15–18), and the Christian hope of the world to come (19–22). More specifically, the division of this second part pertains to the history of the two cities in the past (11–14), the present (15–18), and the future (19–22). Augustine's primary treatment of the history of Rome in the second part of *De civ. D.* comes in book 15. Why this is significant will become apparent upon a closer examination of Augustine's treatment of the two topics.

The origins of the two cities are treated in books 11–14. Here, we learn of creation and the initial foundation of the cities in the pride of angelic disobedience (11), the origin of evil (12), the imposition of death as a punishment for Adam's sin (13), and the consequences of sin (14). The very distant past, for Augustine, thus consists in what we might call a mythical or philosophical past, one that is real and potent but which is not considered to have taken place in time – or at least one that is not accessible as *historical* truth, as he makes clear also in *Gn. litt.*

The present, then, comes to include the whole human past, from the earliest record of the Hebrew scriptures to Augustine's own day. And, whereas the philosophical treatment of the two eschatological cities (in books 11–14) was clear, the historical treatment of the two eschatological cities (in books 15–18) must reckon with their complicated intertwining, the historical record rendering each city "more conspicuous" (16.12) at one time than at another. Thus the middle section of *De civ. D.* part 2 treats the history of the earthly city from Adam to the flood (book 15), the history of both cities from Noah to Abraham (book 16.1–11) and of the heavenly city alone from Abraham to the Kings of Israel (book 16.12–43), the heavenly city again from the Kings to David, Samuel and Christ (book 17), and finally both cities again from Abraham to the end of the world (book 18).

We would expect Augustine to treat Roman history in the course of book 18, as part of the history of the earthly city after Abraham. Yet we find virtually nothing of Rome in that book. Indeed, if we are to find Augustine's substantive treatment of Roman history, we must look elsewhere. Specifically, we find Roman history treated most straightforwardly as an example of the expression of the loves of the citizens of the *civitas terrena* (book 15) and en passant as part of Augustine's attack on Roman religion (books 1–5).

Augustine has, he notes at the beginning of book 15, already treated of the beginning of the world, the soul, and the human race itself. That is, he has established – deconstructively in books 1–10, and constructively in 11–14 – the metaphysical foundations of human history. In book 15, by contrast, he treats the expression of the loves of the citizens of the two eschatological *civitates* in their emergence as historical events.

The two cities make their historical emergence in the story of Cain and Abel. Cain, we are told, was born a member of the mystical *civitas terrena*. "Accordingly [*itaque*]," Augustine writes, 'it is recorded of Cain that he built a city, but Abel, being a sojourner built none" (*De civ. D.* 15.1). The building of that city is held, *tout court*, to be the product of one who acts from self-will. Cain's city is thus an expression of the mystical *civitas terrena*, a deformation of the sociability (*civitas^c*) for which we were created. The historical city is not a creation, strictly speaking – it does not have a nature, but is an expression of nature. God did not create it, but man cannot create ex nihilo. Sociability is part of that marvelous fecundity that overflows under the aspect of propagation; the historical city (and *ecclesia* also) is that innovative, experimental, voluntary work of human beings to order their sociability under the aspect of conformation.

Augustine interrupts his account of Cain in book 15 by an affirmation of the historical city (and by a fascinating allegorical interpretation of Abraham's two sons (chs 2–3) whose intricacies must be neglected here). As a human invention, the historical city is not everlasting, though "has its good in this world, and rejoices in it with such joy as such things can afford" (*De civ. D.* 15.4).[26] Formed as it is by divisive loves, it is frequently divided against itself by dissension and war. It enjoys its victories with price, for "its victory is life-destroying" in that its rule quickly turns to domination (*De civ. D.* 15.4). And in addressing the mortal cares of our temporal condition, it is anxious that its success is like "glass in its fragile splendor [*ut vitrea laetitia comparetur fragiliter splendida*]" (*De civ. D.* 4.3).

Nonetheless, "it cannot rightly be said that the things which this city desires are not good, insofar as it is in itself the best of all humanly generated goods. For it desires earthly peace for the sake of enjoying earthly goods, and it makes war in order to attain this peace" (*De civ. D.* 15.4: "Non autem recte dicitur ea bona non esse, quae concupiscit haec civitas, quando est et ipsa in suo humano genere melior. Concupiscit enim terrenam quamdam pro rebus infimis pacem; ad eam namque desiderat pervenire bellando"). The peace enjoyed by the historical city is the sine qua non of enjoying the natural and inventive fecundity of creation, for the peace of the historical city is that for which people are willing to die. In some sense, *civitas* is a shorthand for all of those good things which are "ours for a time," for the *civitas* is that which preserves these things, insofar as they can be preserved: "the body, freedom (not true freedom, which is reserved for those who abide by eternal law), family, acquaintances" (*lib. arb.* 1.15.107–11).[27] The *civitas* and its degree of peace in accordance with virtue "are good things, and without doubt the gifts of God" (*De civ. D.* 15.4).[28] Nonetheless, an inordinate attachment to these goods to the neglect of the love of God will undermine the peace upon which the enjoyment of those goods depends. The natural and inventive fecundity of creation is rendered virtuous only insofar as human beings conform themselves to divine love.

Despite this affirmation of the blessings of the *civitas*, its actual history is one of deformation rather than conformation. "Thus," he begins chapter 5, "the founder of the earthly city was a fratricide." Cain's murder of Abel is archetypal, and so it comes as no surprise, says Augustine, that the crime should be repeated at the founding of Rome: "For of that city also, as one of their poets has mentioned, 'the first walls were stained with a brother's blood,' or, as Roman history records, Remus was slain by his brother Romulus" (15.5).

The foundation of Rome and the foundation of Cain's city are identical in Augustine's eyes, with one exception. Whereas Cain and Abel were animated by different desires (earthly and heavenly respectively), Romulus and Remus strove for the glory of unchallenged earthly rule. Cain's murder of Abel stemmed from the pure envy the evil have of the good – Abel did not desire to rule in the city which his brother had built. Romulus and Remus, on the other hand, are doubly violent because the goods they desired were mutually incompatible: "both desired to have the glory of founding the Roman republic, but both could not have as much glory as if one only claimed it." Here, the conflict is within the earthly city and is motivated by lust for rule or lust for glory, that is, by pride (cf. *De civ. D.* 12.8 and 14.13). Augustine sums up the difference in this way: "The quarrel, then, between Romulus and Remus shows how the earthly city is divided against itself; that which fell out between Cain and Abel illustrated the hatred that subsists between the two cities, that of God and that of men." The founding of Rome is the reenactment of the historical foundation of the division between the earthly and heavenly cities, yet the Roman founding is more base, for it arises out of the struggle for purely worldly gain. No citizen of the *civitas Dei* is present at the founding of Rome.

Consistent with the deformation of its founding, the history of Rome is a history not of rule (which regulates goods in common) but of imperial subjugation (which appropriates goods unto itself). Augustine writes with reference to Rome's founding: "In order, therefore, that the whole glory might be enjoyed by one, his consort was removed; and by this crime the empire was made larger indeed" (*De civ. D.* 15.5). It is no surprise, then, that when we turn to book 18, where Augustine's treatment of Roman history ought properly to occur, we read that two kingdoms (*regna*),

> settled and kept distinct from each other both in time and place, have grown far more famous than the rest, first that of the Assyrians, then that of the Romans. First came one then came the other. The former arose in the east, and, immediately on its close, the latter in the west. I may speak of other kingdoms and other kings as appendages of these. (*De civ. D.* 18.2)[29]

Just as Cain and Abel are archetypes *mystice*, Rome and Assyria are paradigmatic of the historical *civitas* in which "the strongest oppress the others, because all follow after their own interests and lusts" (*De civ. D.* 18.2). Those who accept imperial subjugation do so in concert with the "voice of nature," which prefers the good of life, even in captivity, to the evil of death. Of the world's many kingdoms, Assyria and Rome stand out for the intensity of their "earthly interest or lust." The history of the earthly city, then, is the history of the passing of the torch of empire from Cain, to the Assyrians, to the Romans, in succession. The passing is true, for Augustine, both chronologically – Rome appears as Assyria fades from power – and typologically. "Babylon, like a first Rome, ran its course along with the city of God. ... Rome herself is like a second Babylon" (*De civ. D.* 18.2). To the identification of Rome with Cain's fratricide and Assyrian imperialism is added the confused folly of Babel/ Babylon (cf. *De civ. D.* 16.4–5). Human history is the history of the deformation of our original *societas* in the confusion of tongues and of incommensurable temporal loves, the history of the divisions internal to the *civitas terrena* in its historical expression (*De civ. D.* 18.2). Both Rome and its eschatological archetype are cities divided against themselves and so cannot stand.

This division of course is born out in the actual events of Roman history which Augustine discusses in *De civ. D.* books 1–5, the history of qualified virtue and vice in the deformations of the impulse to *societas*. Even in the impiety of not worshiping the true God, Romans exhibited the genuine goods of sociability: "industry at home, just government without, a mind free in deliberation, addicted neither to crime nor to lust" (*De civ. D.* 5.12). The presence of only a few great men outstanding in their virtue, such as Regulus (*De civ. D.* 1.15, 24) and Cato (*De civ. D.* 1.23) may mitigate the corrosive temptations of decadence and dominion. The love of glory, itself an impulse to sociability, may suppress the desire to dominate and support the love of liberty (*De civ. D.* 5.12–13, 18). In these empirically rare moments, the historical *civitas* intimates, however weakly, the natural capacity for human sociability.

These moments are, nonetheless, mere respites in the civil war of man's attempt to restore under his own power the created sociability which he lost. For the linchpin of that sociability was obedience to divine command, and where there is no true piety there can be no felicity (*De civ. D.* 4.3, 4.23). Rome mistook greatness for true happiness. Augustine details the "unscrupulous ambition" of "a nation corrupted by avarice and luxury" and made weak by prosperity (*De civ. D.* 1.31). The destruction of Carthage bears witness to the "unmitigated intensity" of Rome's *libido dominandi* over the worn and weary (*De civ. D.* 1.30). In a passage poignantly reminiscent of Tacitus, Augustine writes: "Peace vied with war in cruelty, and surpassed it: for while war overthrew armed hosts, peace slew the defenceless" (*De civ. D.* 3.28).

The whole of the history of the earthly city reduces, for Augustine, to the mystery of Cain's fratricide of the defenseless, unsuspecting Abel, to that inexplicable spiritual darkness of the human heart bent on willing the destruction of the good. Further, the mythological-metaphysical themes of books 11 to 14 find their culmination in the Cain and Abel story which dominates book 15, which stands as the pivot linking biblical mythological and historical time. Having dealt with exemplary events in Roman history in *De civ. D.* books 1–5, Augustine's interest in Rome at this stage of his work is solely typological, a means by which to view the contest for command under the condition of sin.

The *ecclesia* is not a combatant in this temporal civil war; history, viewed *mystice*, is not an epochal, Manichean battle of saints and sinners.[30] In showing Rome *mystice* for what it is, Augustine has inverted the frame in which to see the entry of *ecclesia* into the limelight of the stage of human history. The effect is twofold. First, *ecclesia* is not part of Rome's story; Rome is part of *ecclesia*'s story. Second, *ecclesia* contests Rome not on Rome's terms – those of domination – but on its own, eschatological terms, the witness of peace and service. The *ecclesia* is not complacent, but properly resists the temptation to do battle with the deformed *civitas* on that city's own terms and with its own tools. *Ecclesia* seeks not to match domination with domination, but takes the form of the suffering servant whose strength is made perfect in weakness. The pilgrim *ecclesia*'s quiet witness is to true peace, the attentive *societas* which yields the fecund conformation of love, the root harmonic basso continuo which the tumultuous drive for power and glory can never overcome.

Ecclesia

Ecclesia is that *societas in ordo temporum* comprising the citizens of the eschatological *civitas Dei* who are pilgrims under grace but in the condition of sin. While *ecclesia* strives to live out the natural loving relations of command and obedience, it is not and properly does not strive to be a historical *civitas*.[31] *Ecclesia*, like Abel, is conditioned by sin, but insofar as it is formed by the love of God, the character of its aspirations to sociability is set apart from those who seek unity by domination.

   Having traced the history of the earthly city backwards in time, as it were, to find its origins in the mysteries of the human heart laid bare in the story of Cain and Abel, Augustine also traces forward the temporal expressions of the two eschatological *civitates* from that moment of violence. In *De civ. D.* 18, the history of Rome becomes woven into the narrative of scripture, not vice versa. *Ecclesia* is not a haphazard bandage introduced in response to human sinfulness; it is the anchor of history around which political life inevitably, inexorably, and turbulently revolves. As the expression in time of the citizens of the *civitas Dei*, *ecclesia* is the primary unit of social meaning, that which measures all things. Abel is the firstborn; the city of Cain strives in vain to usurp Abel's glory. The challenge of *ecclesia* is not to be seduced by Babylon, to remain true to what it already is eschatologically, not to create a parallel idolatry in response to threats of usurpation.

   Ecclesia and *civitas*, as the bifurcated deformations of *civitas* in *ordo temporum*, nonetheless can only be understood in relation to one another. The typology of the two eschatological *civitates* is embedded in the complex literary trope of the story of Cain and Abel. A careful reading of Augustine's spinning out this trope in *De civ. D.* 15 addresses three misconceptions: the natures of the two eschatological *civitates* and their relationship in time.

   First, the trope of Cain and Abel confirms analysis by other means that the historical *civitas* is not the imperfect reflection of a Platonic ideal type. Whether explicitly grounded in Platonic participation or not, this essentially Eusebian–Constantinian view of the heavenly kingdom on earth cannot be sustained.[32] Second, the story of Cain and Abel undermines the opposite position, that *ecclesia* is the perfect and holy assembly of the saints, as the Donatists might have it, and on which later claims to sovereign temporal ecclesiastical power will be based. This ecclesiological optimism is matched by a Pelagian, theological overestimation of the capacities of human beings to perfect their individual and collective intellects and wills.[33] Third, Augustine's reading of Cain and Abel cannot sustain the positing of a secular realm of liberal neutrality between the *civitas terrena* and *ecclesia*. There is no space of political neutrality in Augustine's critique of temporal power understood as the spiritual contest for command.[34]

   The story of Cain and Abel reveals a historical and eschatological tension which cannot be resolved in time and which to some extent resists even logical analysis, and Augustine's reading is designed to forestall oversimplifications of this tension, whether on the part of the historical *civitas* or the *ecclesia*. Augustine's treatment is designed to reinforce not alleviate the discomfort of the confrontation with the complexity of the mystery of the human hatred of God, self, and others and the metaxy of existence. Augustine strives then for a spiritual rather than logical precision in his exegesis of the biblical narrative of Cain and Abel in which the ambiguities of the *ecclesia*'s historical existence begin to be disclosed.

   In Augustine's exegesis, Cain functions simultaneously as a datum in linear history and as a highly complex organizing symbol for the spiritual dynamic which animates that history. Cain is both a thing and a sign, a *res* and a *signum* (to use the terms of *De doctrina christiana*) something both "sensed or understood" and "something sensed which shows the mind something else beyond this sense" (*De doctrina christiana* 2.2.1). At its best (or worst), the sign of Cain does not just point beyond itself, but comes to function as a conjunctive sign, a *signum* which instantiates meaning immediately, a sign of such resonance and force that the mind traverses the distance between sign and signified in an instant. In Augustine's hands, Cain both is *not* and *is*, in some important way, Nimrod, Romulus, and (potentially) *us*.

But just as a string struck, or plucked, or bowed requires a sounding board if it is to be heard, a sign is only as effective as the background against which it resonates. What then, to continue the musical metaphor, are the sympathetic strings which vibrate when Augustine plays Cain's tune? Simply, how do the many layers of the sign of Cain work?

Augustine has already established the primary frame: "Two cities have been formed by two loves: the earthly by the love of self, even to the contempt of God; the heavenly by the love of God, even to the contempt of self" (14.28). Cain and Abel are signs of the two cities and the two loves that animate them. The simplicity of this formulation is deceptive. For underlying the apparently straightforward identification is a cluster of images which play off one another as light between two facing mirrors, projecting figures which become images of themselves and, sometimes, images reversed and inverted.

In the beginning of book 15, Augustine sets up a series of pairings or dichotomies which he sustains throughout his wandering exposition of Cain and Abel – an exposition which is centered in 15.5–8, but really extends from 14.28 (the two cities), through the end of 15, to his discussion of the tower of Babel in 16.4. These pairings may be summarized as follows.

Cain is first born, Abel second. Cain signifies the natural man (in St Paul's usage), Abel the spiritual man (the true natural man, in the order of creation). Invoking 1 Corinthians 15.46, Augustine lines up Cain and Abel with the Old and New Adam, the earthly and heavenly, sin and redemption. Cain, the citizen of the world, built a city. Abel, a sojourner (*peregrinus*) on earth built none but had an eternal city and served an eternal *Princeps*. These opposed human types or dispositions are also sequences in time. "Born of Adam evil and carnal" we become spiritual only later through rebirth in Christ. Wickedness is prior in the order of time, goodness in the order of value, just as the potter's first vessel (here Augustine invokes Romans 9.21) is dishonored and the second honored. Augustine does not cite the gospels here, but clearly we are to understand that the last shall be first and the first shall be last.[35]

The pairings of 15.2 shift from the ontological structure of sin and grace to the historical-biblical mechanism of redemption. Cain and Abel represent two kinds of law: the old law and new law, the law of bondage and the law of freedom, the old and new covenant, the realm of flesh and the realm of promise, Sinai and the New Jerusalem, Ishmael and Isaac, iniquity and justice.[36] Underlying these oppositions is, of course, the separation of Jews and Christians – specifically law and church – a division Augustine sets up explicitly in 15.7 and which, as he tells us there, he has already developed more fully in *Contra Faustum*.[37] In that work, Augustine writes that Cain is "cursed from the earth,"[38] a tiller of soil which does not yield fruit. The earth which swallowed Abel's blood is the Church, says Augustine, clearly evoking Eucharistic imagery, which does not yield to the Jews in their impiety. Cain is "the carnal mind that tills the ground, but does not obtain its strength."[39] Without the light that penetrates the rent veil at the crucifixion, the old law does not bear fruit. The sterility of the earth is not Cain's punishment, Augustine argues in *Contra Adimantum*, but the spiritual sterility of law without grace.[40] The sterility of Cain's city mirrors the sterility of his soil; the seed not watered by God's grace will not grow.

Augustine emphasizes this spiritual interpretation in chapters 3 and 4 of *De civ. D.* 15. Nature is good and given by God – Cain is the son of Adam, God's child. But in the absence of grace – Cain has hid himself from God's face – nature is barren. Cain's earthly city has its goods, but true joy and *concordia* are not among them. Like Cain's sacrifice, earthly goods are not first fruits but secondary. Citizen Cain is divided against himself – he is born free, but binds himself to vice and the *libido dominandi*. As a *signum*, Cain is made to bear the mystery of creation, of salvation history, and of the *saeculum* all at once. Cain is the negative principle but he is also good as far as he goes. His more imperfect nature implies the possibility of grace bringing nature to its proper end.

By the time Augustine begins his full treatment of the Cain and Abel story in 15.5, then, he has already established Cain as an ontological and eschatological sign, that much more powerful when deployed for a secular-historical purpose. Augustine's polemical purpose in 15.5–8 is to expose envy – *invidia* – as the fundament of the earthly city in history. In so doing, he departs from Ambrose, who identified Cain and Abel with Babylon and Jerusalem and held that Cain's sin was submission to sensual pleasure.[41] Augustine also departs (knowingly or unknowingly) from Philo for whom the identification of Cain and Abel with Athens and Jerusalem indicted classical philosophy divorced from piety.[42] For Augustine, Cain is the archetype (Augustine uses the Greek *archetypoi*) of envy: Cain is *sui generis imago*, an image unto himself and so intrinsically incomprehensible. The first crime resounds through the history of the earthly city as the voice of blood shed in the violence of foundings. Rome's fratricidal founding is no different, save "that Romulus and Remus were both citizens of the earthly city" (15.5). "The quarrel, then," Augustine writes, "between Romulus and Remus shows how the earthly city is divided against itself; that which fell out between Cain and Abel illustrated the hatred [*inimicitia*] that subsists between the two cities, that of God and that of man" (15.5).

Thus there is only a partial parallel between Cain and Abel and Romulus and Remus. The brothers at Rome's founding contested for a glory only one of them could enjoy. The economy of earthly enjoyment is, in modern parlance, a zero-sum game. By contrast, heavenly goods are not zero-sum; God's favor cannot be exhausted. Unlike glory, goodness is increased and diminished as it is shared and not shared. Further, Abel did not want to rule, he did not contest with Cain for any earthly goods. Cain himself signifies the earthly city's division against itself, he is both Romulus and Remus, and something more, for he signifies the division of the earthly from the heavenly city defined by the mysterious but palpable "diabolical, envious hatred with which the evil regard the good" (15.5).

Augustine is cautious to avoid setting up a Manichean dualism and further qualifies the Cain–Abel dichotomy. Abel cannot stand for the eternal heavenly city because, as a man, he fell short of perfection.[43] Insofar as he too is divided in himself, he is a qualified sign of the heavenly city. Abel signifies the Church which still awaits perfection. In human time, Augustine emphasizes, the spiritual and the carnal contend (by *concupiscentia*) against one another, both within individuals (even Abel) and between the wicked and the good. So long as there is imperfection there will be strife. The divisions internal to Cain and Abel mirror each other – one strives against the good, the other strives against evil.

Augustine further qualifies this apparently intractable, dualistic opposition. In chapter 6, he again turns the tables on his reader. The earthly strife of the intermixed cities is not a call to vanquish the opponent but an occasion for incremental transformation, a striving for mutual healing and forgiveness as Christ becomes present, "little by little, and piece by piece" in his members, that is, in the *ecclesia* which is his body (*De civ. D.* 20.5). Upon the troubled waters of primordial fratricide, the Holy Spirit moves to calm and heal. Augustine shifts from martial language to medicinal language. God the judge is also God the teacher and healer.

Cain's sacrifice was unacceptable to God, and at last we have reached the beginning of the story, for Augustine has been giving us the story backwards. He has been reading the sign of Cain from the outside in, from the mysteries of eschatology and history to the mystery which lies in the human heart.

> And the Lord said unto Cain: Why are you angry, and why is your countenance fallen? If you offer rightly but do not rightly divide [*recte autem non dividas*], have you not sinned? Be still, for to you shall be its turning and you shall rule over it [*Quiesce: ad te enim conversio eius, et tu dominaberis illius*]. (*De civ. D.* 15.7)

Augustine will not allegorize on this occasion: God speaks directly to Cain, just as he spoke to Adam and Eve in the garden.[44]

This passage from Genesis is notoriously difficult to interpret and Augustine himself admits that it is at best unclear. What is clear to Augustine, however, is that God speaks directly to Cain in admonition but with an eye to providing Cain with the opportunity to repent. But of what educative value, Augustine asks, was God's speech? Neither God's admonition about the failed sacrifice nor God's (oblique) warning to master the impulse to murder has any effect on Cain. Instead, as Augustine notes elsewhere, Cain "seeks to refer wickedness to another" in blaming Abel for the imperfection of his own sacrifice and in his disingenuous protestation "am I my brother's keeper?" The denial of sin, the pretended ignorance, is worse than the sin itself (14.14).[45] In opposition to the love of neighbor which is referred to God, the hatred of neighbor is referred to neighbor in self-deceptive self-love. The sin of further pride compounds the rift in the soul already divided against itself and refuses the medicine of repentance.

But what is Cain's original sin? "In which of these particulars," of Cain's sacrifice his sin lies, Augustine notes, "it is difficult to determine." The failure of Cain's sacrifice did not make him wicked (Augustine cites 1 John 3.12) but his wickedness rendered the sacrifice unacceptable. Cain simply does not rightly distinguish yet God does make a distinction. The visible sign of sacrifice discloses no error but God nonetheless discerned some sign. There are for God no ambiguous or misleading signs, for God's knowledge is not dependent upon the mediation of signs.

Augustine makes a handful of speculations as to the inappropriateness of Cain's sacrifice – Cain kept himself to himself, he offered sacrifice to God not in a spirit of worship but for divine aid, he did not seek healing but an extension and satisfaction of his passions, he acted out of a love of rule rather than a love of doing good,[46] he sought to use God for earthly enjoyment rather than to use the world that he might enjoy God. Elsewhere, Augustine suggests that Cain lacked *caritas*,[47] that he was not content, and that, like the Jews, he failed to distinguish (*divisio*) rightly the time and his need for a physician. In contrast to Abel's "harmless service of grace," Cain preferred "earthly observances."[48] Cain remains bewitched by the visible image. He is a sign who cannot see.

More precisely, Cain obscures his own sight by the restless misdirection of his will. He is convinced he is not responsible for his sin. In Augustine's interpretation, God's obscure command ("ad te enim conversio eius, et tu dominaberis eius") is an injunction to rule over sin. This mastery is qualified. Reason should rule over sin and soul rule flesh as the husband rules his wife. "And therefore, says the apostle:[49] 'He that loves his wife loves himself; for no man ever yet hated his own flesh.' This flesh, then, is to be healed because it belongs to ourselves: is not to be abandoned to destruction as if it were alien to our nature" (15.7). The mastery to which Cain is enjoined is not that of owner over slave but a healing of what belongs to him, an integration of what is good, a love of self rightly understood.

Augustine concludes chapter 7 with a reminder that Cain bound himself to restless strife in refusing to make amends. God charges Cain to be still (*quiesce*) – and though the verse is not cited the biblical ear hears "and know that I am God" – recalling the peace of man's created nature. Just as the Jews refused to repent of their stubbornness and killed Christ, the Good Shepherd, Cain slew Abel, the shepherd of sheep. Yet, even to this stubbornness God responds in mercy. The death penalty is suspended[50] and the mark upon Cain places a heavy punishment on any who seek to initiate judgment or vengeance.[51]

Augustine does not make much of the mark of Cain in his treatment in *De civ. D.* 15, but refers the reader explicitly (at the end of 15.7) to his treatment of the matter in *Contra Faustum*. In that work, Augustine emphasizes Cain's earthly exile. Just as the scattered Jews mourn the loss of their kingdom, Cain worries more about being shunned or killed by earthly inhabitants than about being hidden from God's face (*c. Faustum* 12). But Cain and the Jews are protected by God, preserved not as objects of abuse or destruction but as a new sign, a reminder that Christians too, apart from grace, deserve punishment for remaining more attached to the earthly than to the heavenly city. This sign has historical instantiation – alone of all those conquered by Rome, the Jews maintain their observance of the Jewish law (of which Cain himself is a sign). Cain and the Jews are scattered and inhabit a "land of commotion, of carnal restlessness"; like heretics, "they are not content" and are "strangers to the Sabbath of the heart" (*c. Faustum* 13). In contrast to the Garden of Eden, in time the earthly city we will always have with us, Augustine cautions his readers, lest we forget that heavenly city in which our rest truly lies.

One further text outside *De civ. D.* deserves mention at this point. In his *Enarrationes in Psalmos*, 61, Augustine takes up the image of the sojourning city. Cain built a city where there was no city. Jerusalem by contrast (and here Augustine relies upon Joshua 18.28 for his historical data) was built upon a preexisting city: "This having been captured, overcame, made subject, there was built a new city, as though the old were thrown down; and it was called Jerusalem, vision of peace, City of God." The good city, correspondingly, is built up by changing evil men to good, while the city of Cain does not throw down the old self, and builds upon nothing at all. Cain's barren land is contrasted with the transformation of existing material, the healing balm of the New Jerusalem.

If chapters 1–4 cast light forward upon Cain's treatment in 5–8, chapters 15–23 cast light backwards, illuminating the earlier narrative even further. The biblical account of the lineages of Cain and Abel add additional layers to Cain as a sign. Cain begets Enoch and a line that ends in Lamech with another murder. Seth is born as a replacement of Abel – a new Abel, Abel born again by adoption as it were – and begets a line that ends with Noah. Abel's sacrificial death – a *mirabile sacramentum* (15.17) – ushers new life in Seth who, Augustine tells us, is a sign of regeneration, an emblem of chosenness before the covenant with Noah or the institution of circumcision (15.16). Abel's death becomes an invisible sacrament forever evoked by the visibly bloodstained hands of the line of Cain.

The descendants of Cain and Abel allow Augustine to enrich further Cain and Abel as symbols in themselves. Cain means "possession" (*possessio*) because either Adam or Eve said that, in Cain, they had acquired a man through God ("Adquisivi hominem per Deum"). If Adam and Eve possess Cain *per Deum*, Cain sees himself in terms of self-possession, he belongs to himself and not to God. Enoch, Cain's son, means "dedication" (*dedicatio*) for he (and the city named for him) is dedicated to earthly ends. Cain and his line have usurped what is properly possessed by and dedicated to God.

By contrast, Seth (whose name means *resurrectio*), names his son Enos, which means *homo*. As distinct from *Adam*, the Hebrew name applied to both male and female, Augustine continues, Enos/*homo* stands for the child of resurrection. The son of resurrection lives in *hope*, a topic reinforced by the fact that in naming Enos, Seth is recorded as having "hoped to call on the name of the Lord God." For his part, Abel means "grief" (*luctus*) which in death gives way to resurrection, just as Christ's death is followed by eternal life. The chronological and theological supplanting of Abel by Seth is supernatural – Seth is the third brother, not Abel's natural son. Unlike the natural line of Cain, Abel's genealogy is defined not by natural relations but by grace. So it is (15.17) that while women are named in Cain's lineage, there is no marriage mentioned among Seth's offspring, for there is no need for the natural generation of offspring in the resurrection. Abel's lineage is not the work of human beings, but the ongoing divine action of generation under voluntary providence in conformation to God's love.

The hope which informs the peregrination of the heavenly city on earth begets faith. More specifically, faith in death and resurrection – in the sign of Abel – is begotten by the city of God in this world. The line of Abel hopes and calls upon (*invocare*) God. Enos, says Augustine, prefigures a man, or rather a human *societas* which lives according to hope. Cain hopes in man and human artifice (his sons, Augustine notes, are tent-dwellers, musicians, and metal workers); Abel hopes in God. *Ecclesia*, then, is that *societas* which recognizes that its organs are not in men but in God.

Augustine makes interesting use of the numerological significance of the respective generations. In the line of Seth, seven generations from Adam, is another Enoch or "dedication," signifying the Sabbath rest. Not including Adam, this Enoch belongs to the sixth generation and so also signifies the creation of man as the consummation of God's work. Genesis 5.24 records that God takes Enoch away, prefiguring Christians' deferred dedication as well as Christ's own translation. The line of Seth from Adam to Noah is recorded as 12 generations, a number of fulfillment. The progeny of Adam in the line of Cain is completed by 11 generations, where 11, the number of transgression, signifies sin and the violation of the law. This line ends with Lamech and so Cain's line begins and ends with a murderer who refers things to himself and not to God. The sons of Cain (including Romulus), Augustine reminds his reader, "call their lands after their own names" (15.21).[52]

Both Cain's city and *ecclesia* participate in a common iniquity in this world, though their inescapable mixedness contains possibilities of limited concord. The offspring of Cain and Abel/Seth intermarry, further extending social bonds rather than preserving a pure lineage. Still, Augustine does not want us to forget that the divergent lineages which populate and animate the intermixed earthly city derive from a single set of parents. The children of Hagar by right may be claimed for adoption by Sarah. While Cain represents the everlasting history of the envious hatred of the good, the battle with Abel takes place within the temporal framework of a common nature born of a single source with two conflicting wills, with the potential destination of spiritual adoption.[53] Cain persists as a sign – he does not die; scripture does not record his death – and has been marked by God as a neighbor in the earthly city who is to be loved and not harmed; the descendants of Abel do not pursue and vanquish those of Cain. The mark of Cain signifies to all that justice is preserved not in vengeance but in mercy.

In his collected works, Augustine shifts his emphasis in interpreting the Cain and Abel story depending upon his polemic purpose. Against the Manicheans, he argues that material nature is not bad; Against the Pelagians, he maintains that Abel is not perfect. Against the Donatists, he stresses that schism requires healing. Against the pagans, he recalls the violence of the historical *civitas*. Against the Jews, he invokes a reminder of God's providential purpose.[54] All of these uses have echoes in *De civ. D.* and of course they are not mutually contradictory. On the contrary, they constantly supply undertones which enrich the sign's many layers.

This is not, of course, a startling conclusion, for this is how signs work. Writing of Abel, Augustine remarks "all such sacrifices are significant, being symbols of certain things by which we ought to be roused to search or know or recollect the things which they symbolize."[55] The sign of Cain and how it works has roused us to search and know and recollect that the story of Cain and Abel – and the motif of the two eschatological cities of which they are citizens – are more complicated than we often recall. Cain's footfalls echo for Augustine and his reader. Cain is both a type of the earthly city's division against itself and a type of the separation of the *civitas terrena* and the *civitas Dei*. The conflict between the spirit and the flesh (as well as the temporal intermixedness of the two cities) is represented both between Cain and Abel and *within* each of them.

Cain is a sign that sets us on our feet, only to destabilize us when we think we have caught our balance. Cain is the natural man who kills his better nature, the man whose name is possession but who is himself possessed, the man who masters Abel and in so doing is a slave to the *libido dominandi*, the man who does not rightly divide because he has refused the healing offered to his divided self, the wanderer in the fields who is exiled to the permanent restlessness of the earthly city. Like Dante's Virgil, Cain points the pilgrim to a promised land that Cain himself can never enter.

"We have here [no] continuing city." These words of the writer of *Hebrews* – even in Augustine's day there was uncertainty about the attribution to Paul – are double-edged in Augustine's intellectual world. The ambiguities of *civitas* and *ecclesia* understood properly, that is, understood mystically (*mystice*), reinforce our pilgrim status, the fundamental instability of earthly life. The question Augustine poses is not whether one will be an earthly pilgrim, but what sort of pilgrim one will be. Cain's pilgrimage is never-ending and a journey without respite or resting place. The *civitas terrena* is a necessary good in the postlapsarian world, but it cannot be for Augustine (as would seem to be true for Aristotle) sufficient. Conscious of their self-deception or not, the sons of Cain move from distraction to distraction by distraction.

Yet the sons of Abel are always and everywhere already implicated in original sin. Abel's pilgrimage is cut short, but it is still a pilgrimage. *Ecclesia* is a place of rest, but not a resting place, the balm of grace for the sores of distraction, a place of convalescence, but not of perfection. The Church is the mystical body of Christ; it is a sign which can be too easily mistaken for a thing. The Church is not a legal fiction but a divine reality (*Ep.* 185.4). *Ecclesia*, like *civitas*, is no less equally susceptible to idolatry and complacency (too great an attachment and too little, respectively). The Church, no less than the city, must be understood *mystice*.

For Augustine *ecclesia* must keep three elements in tension and in view simultaneously – God's eternal truth, the teaching and disciplinary authority of those occupying church office, and catholicity – what it taught and practiced everywhere and always. We could reformulate these as divine reason, submission to grace and sacramental authority, and habits and dispositions. Or again: understanding, assent (intellect, will) and practice. The Church, consistent with Augustine's philosophical anthropology, works backwards – beginning with practice one moves to assent and, perhaps, to understanding.

If the minimal criterion for a *civitas* is that it keeps peace, what is the end of *ecclesia*? *Ecclesia* is a *societas* bound together as the body of Christ by a love of God and participation in a sacramental life inherited from scripture and tradition (*De civ. D.* 22.17). The *ecclesia*'s spirit of sociability has as its model the Mediator who is both in the form of God and in the form of a servant (*Gn. litt.* 5.19.37). The Church is, therefore a living body constituted as it were, both horizontally and vertically – what is believed and practiced everywhere and always. Put simply, the Church for Augustine is Catholic.

Much of Augustine's conception of *ecclesia* is defined in terms of what the Church is *not*. Augustine's theological and ecclesiological contestations with the Donatists and Pelagians are also political in that both sects represented, for Augustine, an impatience with the Christian's pilgrim status and with the mystical character of the Church. In other words, Augustine saw both the Donatists and the Pelagians as substituting a visible sacrifice for an invisible one. Donatism demanded a visible sign of a purity which could neither be materially achieved nor visibly manifest. Pelagianism likewise claimed an achievement which overcame the ambiguity of sin. Both substituted the idolatry of a completed journey for the ambiguity of Abel's status as a sojourner.

The Church, properly understood, then, is no less subject to *ignorantia* and *infirmitas* than the historical *civitas*. It is a *societas* which remains self-conscious of its own tincture of original sin while availing itself – responding to divine command – of the sacramental balm. The promise of *ecclesia* is that healing is both already and not yet, like God's work, already completed and yet begun anew. Even those souls purified for the vision, those who live justly, are exiled as pilgrims in the world, walking by faith not by vision but gathered by the Church into "the bosom of her charity" – to Jerusalem, "the vision of peace," a sign of "our eternal mother in heaven" (*Gn. litt.* 12.28.56). The relation between Christ and Church is prefigured in the manner of Eve's creation. Adam's sleep signifies Christ's death, and from his sleep "the woman" is "built up," just as Paul speaks of the edification of the body of Christ (*De civ. D.* 22.17; cf. *Gn. litt.* 9.18.33–5 and 9.15.6). Ecclesiastical authority, properly under- stood, is the extension of love of neighbor to all, and the *disciplina* of the wisdom and humility of the cross. The true unity of *societas* represented *mystice* by the Church is this: "we should be made one in the one just one." This passage from *De trinitate* (4.2.11) encapsulates the central insights of both *Gn. Litt.* and *De civ. D.* Christ

> wants his disciples to be one in him, because they cannot be one in themselves, split as they are from each other by clashing wills and desires, and the uncleanness of their sins; so they are cleansed by the mediator that they may be one in him, not only by virtue of the same nature whereby all of them from the ranks of mortal men are made equal to the angels, but even more by virtue of one and the same whole and harmonious will reaching out in concert to the same ultimate happiness, and fused somehow into one spirit in the furnace of charity. This is what he means when he says *That they may be as we are one* [John 17.22] – that just as Father and Son are one not only by equality of substance but also by identity of will, so these men, for whom the Son is mediator with God, might be one not only by being of the same nature, but also by being bound in the fellowship [*societas*] of the same love. (*trin.* 4.2.12)[56]

A common nature, a common fellowship, a common love – such are in the fabric of the divine and so in the fabric of all creation. In the order of time, for Augustine, the fabric is ruptured by the divisive loves which separate us from God, from neighbor and from ourselves. For the divine being, there is only one citizenship. Human beings, however, are inexorably implicated in a complex of dual citizenships: earthly and heavenly, temporal and eternal, civil and ecclesial, citizenships of parallel structure yet not reducible one to another. Each citizenship is a sign reminding the earthly citizen of his eternal destiny and enjoining the heavenly citizen of his obligations to the world.

The structure of dual citizenship supplies the theoretical and practical backbone of the Gelasian doctrine of the two swords which animated medieval political thought and practice and whose breakdown ushered in the contractarian theories of early modern political thought. And in the *Commedia*, Dante anticipates in Christianity's division against itself the unitary citizenship of his fellow Florentine Machiavelli and, later, Hobbes. Yet modern attempts to resolve the political-religious problems do not eliminate the fundamental aspects of the human condition. In Augustine we find these perennial tensions – good and evil, the divine and the human, the symbols that inform the character of our regard for one another in politically constituted society. The terms of our pilgrim status may have changed, but the fundamental, irresolvable tensions still remain as we await the theoretical analysis of a new, if very different, St Augustine.

FURTHER READING

The literature on Augustine's political thought is vast, complex, and full of disagreement. Markus 1988, Deane 1963, and Cranz 1972a, 1972b remain fundamental, with the critiques offered by O'Donovan 1987 and Burnell 1992, all with bibliography. P. Brown 2000 and 1972 offer important biographical and historical context, as do O'Donnell 2005, O'Daly 1999, Ruokanen 1993, and Van Oort 1991. Recent works, again with bibliography, explore important aspects of Augustine's moral-philosophical anthropology (Burnell 2005), political theology (Dodaro 2004; O'Donovan 2002), ethics (O'Donovan 1980; Wetzel 1992; Arendt 1996; Burnaby 1991) and his relation to liberalism (E. Gregory 2008; Milbank 1991; Fortin 1972, 1996; von Heyking 2001; Elshtain 1995; Bathory 1981). Also valuable are the collections by Doody, Hughes, and Paffenroth 2005 and Vessey et al. 1999.

NOTES

1   I am grateful for the comments of audiences at the North American Patristics Conference at Loyola University, Chicago (2000) and at the University of Saskatchewan (2003), where some of these ideas were presented and developed, and for countless conversations on the subject with Professor Peter Burnell, who has generously shared of his wisdom even as I have distinguished my position from his own. In citing passages from Augustine in English translation, I have used, sometimes in adapted form, the following translations: Benjamin and Hackstaff 1964; Bettenson 2003; Chadwick 1991; Dods 2000; Dyson 1998; Hill 1998; Robertson 1958; and J. Taylor 1982. In translating *De civ. D.* in particular, I have often revised Dods's translation to reflect more accurately Augustine's Latin meaning, consulting additionally the translations of Bettenson and Dyson.
2   13.135ff. (Dante 1931).
3   See Cranz 1972a, 1972b; Deane 1963; Markus 1988; Milbank 1991; Ruokanen 1993; and Van Oort 1991.
4   Romulus, Augustine writes (*De civ. D.* 22.6), was loved as a god, in "false dignity," and so named Rome after himself; by contrast, Augustine continues, to love Christ is to name the city Jerusalem, city of peace.

5   See also Cranz 1972b: n22. For a more recent treatment of the two cities, see C. Harrison 2000: 194–222.

6   An argument could be made that Augustine's ambiguities on this subject are intentional – a) to safeguard against too close an identification of historical human institutions with either eschatological city, and b) as a pedagogical device to develop the nuanced analysis necessary to sort through the theological-political-historical problem. If Augustine's ambiguities are indeed intentional, one might argue that he was too clever by half, but then he could not possibly have foreseen the ways in which the concerns of subsequent thinkers have obscured the key Augustinian insights.

7   Had this *civitas* existed in time without the corruption of sin, its members would have understood themselves to be pilgrims en route, through the wisdom learned in a life of virtue, to the *civitas Dei*. More generally, see Wetzel 1992.

8   *De civ. D.* 15.8. *Civitas* has no ontological status and so, both historically and eschatologically, indicates only the privation of the *societates* for which we were created and redeemed.

9   *b. conjug.* 1.1, *De civ. D.* 12.22, 18.18, 20.15, *Conf.* 4.4.7, *Gn. litt.* 5.19.37, *lib. arb.* 1.15.107–11, *trin.* 3.1.6, *Gn. litt.* 11.14.18, *trin.* 4.2.11. See also Deane 1963: 78–80; Elshtain 1995: 34–42. I have covered some of this same ground in Breyfogle 2005, revising here some important elements of that earlier essay.

10 "pax caelestis civitatis ordinatissima et concordissima societas fruendi Deo et invicem in Deo" (*De civ. D.* 19.13, also 19.17)

11 For the background of marriage and household according to classical Roman law, see Schulz 1951: 103–41 (on marriage), and 142–61 (on parents and children).

12 "si avaritiam generalem intellegamus, qua quisque appetit aliquid amplius quam oportet, propter excellentiam suam, et quemdam propriae rei amorem: cui sapienter nomen latina lingua indidit, cum appellavit privatum, quod potius a detrimento quam ab incremento dictum elucet. Omnis enim privatio minuit. Unde itaque vult eminere superbia inde in angustias egestatemque contruditur, cum ex communi ad proprium damnoso sui amore redigitur."

13 Augustine treats *privatus* and *proprius* as synonymous (see J. Taylor 1982: 2: 290 n41).

14 In classical Latin, and especially in Cicero, *societas* encompasses "fellowship" and partnership, especially in trading relationships; e.g., Cicero *Leg.* 1.10.28, *Off.* 3.6.32, and Quint. 3.11. On contracts and corporations, see Schulz 1951: 465–7 (contracts) and 86–102 (corporations). Also Rist 1994: 203–55 on individuals, social institutions, and political life.

15 Augustine's treatment of pagan and Christian emperors in *De civ. D.* 5.24–5 makes this clear.

16 See Schulz 1951 for the legal concept of corporation (86–102), and of *societas* as not constituting a corporation or legal person (549–54, esp. 550); see further Fortin, Gunn, and Kries 1994 and Fortin 1996.

17 In *De civ. D.* 15, Augustine frequently uses the phrase *societatis hominum, societas humana*, or a comparable formulation. See also *De civ. D.* 18.2.

18 *De civ. D.* 19.17

19 In the *Apology*, Plato's Socrates says that he has lived a private life, but it is clear that this private life has profound political consequences; cf. Balot 2008.

20 *De civ. D.* 19.16.

21 *Ep.* 243.4.

22 "Si autem populus non isto, sed alio definiatur modo, velut si dicatur: 'Populus est coetus multitudinis rationalis rerum quas diligit concordi communione sociatus,' profecto, ut videatur qualis quisque populus sit, illa sunt intuenda, quae diligit. Quaecumque tamen diligat, si coetus est multitudinis non pecorum, sed rationalium creaturarum et eorum quae diligit concordi communione sociatus est, non absurde populus nuncupatur; tanto utique melior, quanto in melioribus, tantoque deterior, quanto est in deterioribus concors." *De civ. D.* 19.24; cf. *De civ. D.* 2.21. Also *De civ. D.* 1.15, where the *civitas* is solely a "harmonious collection of individuals [*concors hominum multitudo*]."

23 See O'Donovan 1987. Also, August. *lib. arb.* 1.7: "For a nation consists of men, united under one law which, as I have said, is temporal [Nam ex hominibus una lege sociatis populus constat, que lex, ut dictum est, temporalis est]." For the understanding of *gens* in classical Roman law, see Schulz 1936: 109–39.

24 For a more extensive, political assessment of this topic, see Burnell 1992, 1993; Langan 1991.

25 Not unlike, perhaps surprisingly, Adam Smith's discussion of the "invisible hand." See also Weithman 1992.

26 At *De civ. D.* 22.6, Augustine observes that in Cicero the political regime strives for immortality; the death of the political regime is unnatural.

27 "Deinde parentes, fratres, coniux, liberi, propinqui, affines, familiares, et quicumque nobis aliqua necessitudine adiuncti sunt. Ipsa denique civitas, quae parentis loco haberi solet; honores etiam et laus, et ea quae dicitur gloria popularis." Benjamin and Hackstaff 1964 neglect the sentence division and, eliding the *denique*, pass over the fact that *ipsa civitas* encapsulates all that has gone before and makes possible the *honores* and *laus*. Augustine here does not commit himself to the notion that the *civitas* is held to have the place of a parent, but the weight of the supposition does not suggest that the *civitas* is to its citizens what a *paterfamilias* is to his household; rather, the *civitas* is simply the place where one is raised, as if by a parent.

28 While Augustine notes that the proper enjoyment of earthly prosperity must not be overvalued, it remains, nonetheless, a good (*De civ. D.* 1.8; *Serm.* 50.5); cf. *De civ. D.* 22.24; *De civ. D.* 19.13; *Serm.* 311.11 (see Burnaby 1991: 114ff.). Also *De sermone domini in monte* 2.8ff

29 This is the only substantive reference to Rome in all of book 18, which charts the present history of the expression of the *civitas terrena*.

30 Nor should the earthly and heavenly cities be understood anachronistically as the equivalents of state and church, a distinction which begins with Gelasius I and reached its fullness in the later Middle Ages. For a comparison of Augustine and Orosius, see Frend 1989: 1–38. Strictly speaking, the medieval period distinguishes between spiritual and civil power; to speak of church and state is to deploy terminology which emerges as a description of the phenomenon of the modern nation-state. See further Tierney 1964.

31 In *De civ. D.* in book 22, Augustine uses *ecclesia* to indicate either a physical building or as the mystical body of Christ, but never as a temporal bureaucracy. Clearly, he understood the *auctoritas* of the temporal bureaucracy, but its standing comes not from itself but from its part in the mystical body of Christ.

32 See Cranz 1972a, 1972b; Markus 1988. Also C. Harrison 2000: 117–57.

33 The presentation by Cranz 1972b nonetheless affirms Israel as the sole example of an historical *civitas* which in fact instantiates the *civitas Dei* in time, leaving open attempts to create "God's New Israel" – a kind of Pelagian drive to political perfection.

34 Essentially the position of Markus 1988, well critiqued by O'Donovan 1987 and Burnell 1992. See also Ruokanen 1993; Van Oort 1991.

35 See *En. Ps.* 77.9 for use of this scripture in reference to Cain.

36 This last distinction is implied in 15.2 but made explicitly at *En. Ps.* 48.2.11.

37 See *c. Faustum*, 9ff.

38 *c. Faustum*, 11.

39 *c. Faustum*, 12. See further Bonner 1994.

40 *Contra Adimantum*, 4.

41 See Ambrose, *Cain and Abel*.

42 See Philo, *De Sacrificiis Abelis et Cain*, 2ff., and elsewhere. See also Quinones 1991.

43 See *nat. et gr.*, 44–5.

44 Cf. *trin.* 2.

45 See also *c. Faustum*, 10.

46 See also *Ep.* 102.17.

47 *In epistulam Johannis ad Parthos tractatus*, 5.

48 *c. Faustum*, 9

49 Eph. 5.28–9.

50 Cf. *Contra litteras Petiliani*, 2.86.191.

51 On the mark of Cain, and the difficulty of interpreting the Genesis passage, see Delaney 1996.

52 Quoting Ps 52.8; see also *De haeresibus ad Quodvultdeum*, 18, where Augustine says that the Cainites take the name for Cain (*caiani*).

53 On one nature, two wills, see *Contra Julianum opus imperfectum* 2.181.

54 Despite Ambrose's moralizing and homiletic example, Augustine employs Cain and Abel only twice in his sermons. Augustine's use of Cain and Abel in the *Enarrationes in Psalmos*, however, is more extensive.

55 *Ep.* 102.17.

56 "vult esse suos unum, sed in ipso quia in se ipsis non possent dissociati ab invicem per diversas voluntates et cupiditates et immunditiam peccatorum; unde mundantur per Mediatorem ut sint in illo unum; non tantum per eamdem naturam qua omnes ex hominibus mortalibus aequales Angelis fiunt, sed etiam per eamdem in eamdem beatitudinem conspirantem concordissimam voluntatem in unum spiritum quodam modo caritatis igne conflatam. Ad hoc enim valet quod ait: Ut sint unum sicut et nos unum sumus, ut quemadmodum Pater et Filius, non tantum aequalitate substantiae, sed etiam voluntate unum sunt, ita et hi inter quos et Deum Mediator est Filius, non tantum per id quod eiusdem naturae sunt, sed etiam per eamdem dilectionis societatem unum sint."

PART VIII

Receptions

CHAPTER 33

Republicanism: Ancient, Medieval, and Beyond

Christopher Nadon

Republicanism rests at bottom on man's claim to be capable of ruling himself. What has come to be known today as "classical republicanism" rests on the claim that it is through political participation in a republican regime that man comes to perfect his nature. Classical republicanism was not known to the classics (cf. Depew, this volume, chapter 26). It is, like the Renaissance or the Middle Ages, a term of art or taxonomy used by contemporary intellectual historians and political theorists to give or bring out a retrospective shape or meaning to the past that might not have been apparent to its actual inhabitants. It owes its current sense largely to the work of J. G. A. Pocock and his book *The Machiavellian Moment: Florentine Political Thought and the Atlantic Republican Tradition* (1975). Pocock built his paradigm on a foundation begun by the Renaissance historian Hans Baron in *The Crisis of the Early Italian Renaissance: Civic Humanism and Republican Liberty in an Age of Classicism and Tyranny* (1955). According to Baron, fifteenth-century Florentine humanists developed "a new ideology" over the course of their city's protracted military struggles against a tyrannically ruled and imperialistic Milan, an ideology that was republican in character and potentially even democratic. Pocock traced this "civic humanist" embrace of republican liberty over and against monarchic oppression from its exemplar Machiavelli back to its classical origins in Polybius and Aristotle, and in addition showed the profound influence of this tradition on later republicans such as James Harrington, Henry St John Bolingbroke, Cato, Thomas Jefferson, and others in America. His great innovation was to do so by discovering that the common thread that tied these thinkers together is not simply a shared understanding of and commitment to republicanism, but a common language or vocabulary for justifying that commitment. Thus, for Pocock, terms like "material," "form," "*isonomia*," "virtue," "*zōon politikon*," "*res publica*," "corruption," and "the common good" become markers for republican thinking.

Pocock's avowed intention was to challenge and replace overly Whiggish interpretations of the history of political thought that understood it as a progressive march

A Companion to Greek and Roman Political Thought, First Edition. Edited by Ryan K. Balot.
© 2013 Blackwell Publishing Ltd. Published 2013 by Blackwell Publishing Ltd.

toward greater and more secure individual rights and liberties. Certainly the most outstanding result of his approach was to displace Locke as the philosophic spirit presiding over the American Revolution and early Republic (Pocock 1975: 423, 436, 507, 527). The possibility held out by Pocock of formulating a non-Marxist and non-utopian critique of liberal capitalism grounded in a sober reassessment of forgotten historical possibilities, rather than a desperate vision of the future, contributed in no small measure to the appeal of his version of republicanism. Pocock's framework was taken up and over time significantly modified most notably by Quentin Skinner along with other Cambridge School historians, embraced by communitarians, and became the basis for a nuanced contemporary theory of freedom in the work of Philip Pettit.

Under Pocock's influence liberalism and republicanism have frequently come to be viewed as antithetical ideologies. If liberalism puts the stress on negative liberty and the protection of individual rights, republicanism privileges positive liberty or at least political participation and duty in some form or another. For Pocock, then, the fundamental political conflict is the conflict between the individual's particular good and the universal or common good of the community, and the difficulty of making sure the latter prevails (1975: 74). According to him, republicans since Aristotle have done this by considering devotion to the universal good as "itself a good of a higher order than the particular goods which the citizen as social animal might enjoy." This view allows political participation to become the means by which citizens achieve perfection. Within the republican tradition thus understood, Machiavelli's distinct contribution was to extend the transformative power of political participation to the soldier's virtue of risking his life for his community, that is, to the virtue of accepting "in a totally non-cynical way, the adage that one should love one's own country more than one's soul" (1975: 68, 74–5). "The republic is the common good; the citizen directing all his actions toward that good, may be said to dedicate his life to the republic; the patriot warrior dedicates his death, and the two are alike in perfecting human nature by sacrificing particular goods to a universal end" (1975: 201). Under the proper conditions, the energies generated by this experience of citizenship and the politicization of virtue could transform a city's way of life forever (1975: 76, 165, 167, 211, 386; cf. Depew, chapter 26).

Again, Pocock's vision of participation in a republican regime as the means to perfect human nature was not known to the classics. But the classical world did in fact know something like the phenomenon Pocock describes as the politicization of virtue and agreed it could take place only within a framework of relatively widespread political participation. The development was of political not philosophic origin. Sparta, of course, ultimately came to be considered the incarnation of the spirit of republicanism for later Greek, Roman, and European thinkers (Rawson 1969). Yet in the pages of Herodotus, the first thinker to give a systematic analysis of the virtues and vices of different regimes, Athens emerges as the city that most clearly demonstrated the dynamic potential of widespread political participation and the politicization of virtue to which it subsequently gave rise. Indeed, Herodotus portrays Spartan politics both before and after the heroics at Thermopylae as dominated by the intrusion of the private or familial and dynastic interests of the various Spartan kings into both domestic and foreign affairs. Athens stagnated as a third-rate power under the tyranny of the Peisistratids. But it very quickly increased in activity and power after their expulsion and in the wake of Cleisthenes' civic reforms. Herodotus explains why:

> This makes clear that equal political participation [*isēgoria*] is in every respect important. If under the tyrants the Athenians were no better at war than any of those around them, when freed from them they were far and away the first. This makes clear that when held down they willingly slacked off as working for a master. Once free, however, each one eagerly strived on his own behalf. (Hdt. 5.78, trans. Grene 1987)

This is not yet Pocock's ideal of the republican preference for the universal or common good over particular or private interest. Yes, the city grows in power. But the reason for it is that each Athenian works, and works hard, on his own behalf. Yet over time the Athenians do move in a "republican" direction as they come to see their own good as primarily political and identify it more and more with the city's power. Herodotus documents this process with two anecdotes. During the time of their relative weakness, the Athenians had a dispute with their neighbors, the Aeginetans, over the possession of certain votive images. The Athenians suffered a terrible defeat in the conflict, from which only one man returned. When he told what had happened, the Athenian women surrounded him and stabbed him to death with the brooches used to fasten their robes, each one demanding, "And where is my husband?" This violent act seemed to the men to be worse than the defeat itself. So they punished the women by compelling them to change their dress from the traditional Dorian robe to the Ionian tunic, a garment that requires no such pin (Hdt. 5.85–8).

The parallel story from the post-tyrannical, democratic regime based on *isēgoria* dates from the time of the Persians' second occupation of Athens. The Persian general sent a messenger to the Athenian council to offer terms of peace that would allow the Athenians to return to their homes. One counselor, Lycidas, said he thought that as the situation was dire, the proposal should at least be brought before the people. For this suggestion he was surrounded and stoned to death by the other counselors and those of the people outside who somehow got word of his proposal. When the Athenian women learned what had happened they marched on their own initiative to Lycidas' house and stoned his wife and children to death. Herodotus records no shocked reaction from the men on this occasion (Hdt. 9.4–5).

If tyranny blurs the difference between men and women in the direction of the feminine, the effects of *isēgoria* almost completely efface the natural distinction in the opposite direction. Thus the familial and domestic motives of love of one's own and grief at personal loss, which earlier proved stronger than the shame of political defeat, come to be replaced by an enthusiasm so public-spirited that it overwhelms the boundary between public and private.[1] From here it is only a short step to Pericles' exhortation to the Athenians to become "lovers" (*erastas*) of a city whose greatness outweighs any private benefit to its citizens, and to the imperial longings to which such a disposition necessarily gives rise (Thuc. 2.43, 2.65, 6.24). Yet the fact that each citizen remains eagerly striving for his own benefit, especially when added to the difficulty of attributing an end or purpose to the city which is then denied to the individuals within it (Thuc. 2.63; Arist. *Pol.* 1324a5–13), means that the politicization of virtue can pose a genuine threat to the stability of the political order. The Greek cities that allowed for political participation had to devote considerable resources to developing a civic education and political institutions that would dampen the risk of *stasis* or civil war without altogether extinguishing their citizens' public-spiritedness (Rahe 1992).

For Aristotle, man is a being possessed of speech or reason, capable of distinguishing by his own lights the just and advantageous. He can therefore attain his full natural potential or perfection only within the city (*polis*). Someone either incapable of participating in political life or in no way in need of it stands beneath or beyond the city as a beast or a god (Arist. *Pol.* 1253a1–28). These premises are certainly compatible with and even support man's wish to rule himself. Yet the further claim in book I of the *Politics* that "every city exists by nature," apparently without regard to its particular form or constitution (*politeia*), would seem to be a poor foundation on which to rest an argument specifically for republican government (1252a30, trans. Lord 1984). This claim does, however, establish a standard or framework for evaluating various forms of government and makes of politics a legitimate subject of philosophic inquiry: results difficult to obtain when beginning from either the then traditional conception of the city as essentially sacred or the sophistic deprecation of it as a purely conventional artifact. And it also in some way anticipates or facilitates Aristotle's ultimate preference for the mixed or balanced constitution. For by declaring every city to exist by nature, he deprives any particular form of government of the advantage of having a natural or prepolitical precedence that might allow it an undisputed superiority over the others. Thus Aristotle never says of the good forms of government (kingship, aristocracy, and polity) that they are according to nature, although he is willing to say that the three bad forms (tyranny, oligarchy, and democracy) are "against nature" (1287b38–9; cf. Hahm, this volume, chapter 12). Indeed, these pure or simple forms of government seem not to exist (e.g., 1292a16–18, 1293b22–36, 1295a1–3). All actual cities are in fact made up to some extent or another of the haves and have-nots, the rich and the poor, oligarchs and democrats (1279b38–40). In order for men to vindicate the claim to be capable of self-rule, they must find some way to reconcile the potentially fatal conflicts between these groups without recourse to external powers (1294b35–9). Again, Aristotle's preferred solution is the mixed constitution or regime (this volume, Hahm, chapter 12, Depew, chapter 26).

On the level of political institutions, the mixed regime requires ruling to be divided into different functions: deliberating, judging, and the offices that put those deliberations and judgments into effect (Arist. *Pol.* 1297b37–1298a3). These functions and offices can be constituted on either oligarchic or democratic principles (choice or lot), divided, and then distributed to different parts of the city. A proper distribution allows the two principal parts of the city to trust one another and act in common because they have the institutionalized capacity to distrust one another through supervision, auditing, or a veto. For example, in more oligarchic regimes it is advisable to allow the multitude a veto over measures passed by the few, but not to pass their own; and, in more democratic regimes, to predispose a greater number of the notables to take part in deliberations while discouraging the poor (1298a33–1298b40). Such institutions make it more difficult to say of any one particular regime whether it is a democracy or an oligarchy, and therefore make it less likely for the different parts to wish for some other political order (1294b35–9). But they also make it impossible for the reasonable part of the city, wherever it happens to reside, simply to determine the outcome of deliberations (cf. Hitz, this volume, chapter 24). If man's ability to reason about the just and unjust is what makes him capable of self-rule, the mixed regime favored by Aristotle would seem to stand in the way of or compromise reason's ability to rule directly. But perhaps compromise is reasonable.

Men may be capable of reasoning about justice but that does not necessarily mean they always reason well about justice. Political life especially provides an occasion for bad judgment since it always requires us to deliberate about matters that touch us. And "most people are bad judges concerning their own things" (Arist. *Pol.* 1280a14–15, trans. Lord 1984). Men commonly have a partial view of justice because they remain partial to themselves even when they are parts within a whole and should take the larger view. The body politic does not possess the same integrity as does the human body. *Esprit de corps* is a quality of mind rather than body; yet man is both. Democrats therefore tend to have a democratic view of justice and posit a democratic purpose for the city, oligarchs an oligarchic view and oligarchic purpose. Neither is altogether right or altogether wrong. "All fasten on a certain sort of justice but go only up to a certain point and do not speak of the whole of justice in its authoritative sense" (1280a9–11, trans. Lord 1984). Because neither side sees the consequences of favoring its partial conceptions, Aristotle tries to show them where the arguments they do advance must end.

Democrats, who view the city as existing primarily for the sake of goods all can enjoy, such as freedom and security, believe it just to make the goods of the wealthy available to all through redistribution. Oligarchs, who view the city as existing primarily for the sake of wealth, believe it just to exclude the poor from rule altogether. Both inclinations in fact destroy the city (Arist. *Pol.* 1280b19–30, 1281a15–20, 1281b17–20, 1281b25–35). Moreover, when thought through or pushed to their logical conclusion, the arguments they advance to support their claims in fact undermine their own positions and end up justifying monarchic rule. To say wealth should rule could justify the rule of the less well off who nonetheless collectively possess more than the rich, or rather the rule of the one wealthiest. The same holds true with the claims based on free birth or ancestry. And especially if virtue is taken to be the end of the city, the unlimited rule of the most virtuous is best. Thus, according to Aristotle, in the presence of superior virtue it remains only "for everybody to obey such a one gladly" (Arist. *Pol.* 1284b33–4).[2] Cicero, who in the fiercely antimonarchic tradition of Rome goes so far as to elaborate a doctrine of tyrannicide (e.g. Cic. *Off.* 3.19), defends the mixed regime on the basis of its equitable balance and stability (Cic. *Rep.* 1.45). Yet when judging by the standard of virtue, even he acknowledges the superiority of monarchic rule (1.34; cf. Hahm, chapter 12). However unlikely the presence of such an outstanding individual may be, there is nothing unjust or unlikely in his rule. But in his absence the mixed regime remains the preferred practical solution. However, the theoretical superiority of monarchy means that the mixed regime is to be understood as comprising not just a mix and balance of different parts or social classes in the city, but also a mixture and balance of the different ends and partial or incomplete conceptions of justice that these parts advance.

The copresence of these different aims and opinions ideally acts to moderate partisan passions through mutual understanding, or, absent that, at least to make fellow citizens more respectful out of mutual fear (Arist. *Pol.* 1295b4–34). The mixed regime necessarily falls short of perfection (Polyb. 6.57; cf. Hahm, chapter 12). Moreover, active participation in it or any other regime is not, for Aristotle, necessary for human perfection since philosophic contemplation is the peak of human activity (Arist. *Eth. Nic.* 1177a12–14, 1178a5–9, 1178b1–11, 28–32). Yet reflection on the nature of political life, the typical claims to justice it engenders, and the manner in which they can be transcended remains an essential part of philosophic education and self-knowledge. And the way of life embodied in the independent ancient city-states permitted the tensions inherent in claims to self-rule to be seen with particular clarity. Thus, quite apart from serving as a genuinely practical guide for actual statesmen and rulers, the *Politics* also provides a kind of historical record making the fundamental premises of republican political life accessible to those living in other times and places where their direct experience might no longer be possible or likely (cf. Depew, chapter 26).

As Machiavelli notes in the *Discourses*, the superlative virtue or strength of the Roman Republic led to its becoming the Roman Empire. This empire in turn destroyed "all republics and civil ways of life," ultimately dissolved itself, and left behind a legacy that made it difficult for cities to restore a civil way of life "except in a very few places of that empire" (Machiavelli, *Discourses* 2.2.2, trans. Mansfield and Tarcov 1996). In the eleventh century one of those places was northern Italy, where some cities enjoying de facto independence from the Holy Roman Empire began to put in place communal forms of government. At first they sought to justify their position through recourse to various interpretations of the Roman Law (Q. Skinner 1978: 1: 27–65). Yet the recovery and diffusion of Aristotelian political thought, largely through the medium of Moerbeke's translation of the *Politics* and Thomas Aquinas' commentaries, quickly shifted the grounds of political debate to a more philosophic and universal level.

Aquinas might seem to be an unusual and unexpected source for republicans. He was initially, and continues today, to be interpreted as a proponent of monarchic and even absolute rule. After all, for Aristotle, nature could rarely be counted on to produce the kind of superlative virtue that justifies monarchy. But in the Christian context, belief in God's providential intervention to perfect nature through grace would seem to make this condition more likely. And whereas Aristotle suggests that men originally projected their experience of a primitive form of monarchy onto Zeus' rule over the other gods, Aquinas seems to move in the opposite direction and begins with Christian metaphysics as the basis for the superiority of monarchic rule.[3] Yet Aquinas is also concerned to temper monarchy to prevent its decline into tyranny and to temper the Christian tendency to follow the analogy of God's rule in the direction of political absolutism in its various forms, thus his special emphasis on natural law (cf. Depew, chapter 26). And, at the institutional level, he offers several practical arguments in favor of the mixed regime. More importantly, however, he supplies it with a basis that can perhaps withstand or hold its own against the claims of grace. He manages this by interpreting the form of government God first established for the Jews through Moses as a mixed constitution, and declares it best on the authority of Scripture (*Summa Theologiae*, 1.2.105.1).

Whatever Aquinas' motive for injecting this theological element into his justification of the Aristotelian mixed regime, the need for him to have done so indicates a problem. The claim to rule based on the grace of God cannot be dialectically disputed, transcended, and thus moderated as were the more natural or typical claims of oligarchs and democrats. It can only be met with another equally transcendent claim. Yet such claims tend either to cancel one another out or to overawe and upset the balance between the worldly elements of the city, thus making stability and peace less likely. If, as Pocock writes, republicanism appealed to the "*esprits forts*" and "toughly and secularly civic minds" of those in fifteenth century northern Italy who sought to carve out a place for liberty between the overarching claims of emperors and popes (1975: 80, 113), its appropriation in the thought and career of the Thomist and Dominican friar Savonarola provided a striking example of the inability of the traditional mixed regime to moderate the new extremes.

Savonarola adapts the Aristotelian mixed regime to the context of late fifteenth century Florence in good Thomistic fashion. After quoting Aquinas' *Summa* for support, he declares monarchy to be the best form of government: "And because the government of God, which is concentrated in one, namely, in Him alone, is most perfect, so, when government is similarly concentrated in one leader who is good, then it can be called a good and perfect government" (Savonarola 2006: 171). Yet the particularly clever, intelligent, and subtle spirits of the Florentines make them unfit to be ruled by a king, even a good one (2006: 182, 196). So Savonarola proposed that Florence be governed instead by a mixed regime like that so successful in Venice, although, again, in deference to local circumstances, one less aristocratic and more popular than the model. More originally, he suggested that Florence put Christ in the place of the monarch, not metaphorically, but in a special way with himself as his prophet, and that it devote the city's political life to the attainment of eternal life and felicity (2006: 230, 166–7). Both Savonarola's own position and the end toward which he directs the Florentine republic are difficult to balance and fit ill within the confines of the traditional mixed regime.[4] Nontraditional, too, were the principal means by which the republic was to be governed. Alluding to the almost pagan views of Cosimo de' Medici, he tells the Florentines, "You say that cities and the state are not governed with paternosters nor with prayers. You are greatly deceived, and in the end you will find yourselves deceived" (2006: 167–8). The poet and eyewitness Benedetto Varchi described the continued influence and effect that Savonarola had in the midst of the Florentine republic's final crisis some 30 years after the Frate's execution for heresy in 1498:

> Because of the words and sermons of Fra Girolamo, which they called prophecies, the more their enemies pressed Florence, the more greatly they rejoiced, holding firmly to

the belief that when the city had been reduced to such a point that she had no remedy left and could not be defended by any human power in any way, then, at last, and not before then, angels would be sent from heaven to the walls of the city to liberate her with their swords. Not only common and uneducated men believed this, but also noble and cultured ones. (quoted and translated in Weinstein 1970: 372 n170)

Machiavelli rejected the mixed regime of Venice favored by Savonarola (and with it that of ancient Sparta) in part because it could not adapt to the kind of expansion made necessary in his view by the constant flux of human affairs, but also because it proved itself susceptible of being redirected toward the attempt to expiate imagined sins at the expense of increasing real ones, and all to the neglect of addressing the genuine political necessities it had originally been designed to accommodate and balance (Machiavelli, *Discourses* 1.6.4, 1.11.5, 1.45.2, 3.30.1; *Prince*, 12.2, 15). He took instead the Roman Republic as his model. But in choosing a classical model, Machiavelli gave a decidedly nonclassical interpretation of its constitution. Whereas the ancients understood the city to be made up of oligarchs and democrats, divided by their opinions as to what constitutes a just claim to rule yet brought together in a way that allows each to contribute its own distinctive virtues, Machiavelli separates nobles and plebs into two diverse humors characterized either by the desire to oppress or to be free from oppression (*Discourses* 1.4.1; cf. Polyb. 6.10; Mansfield 1979: 37, 43). With the conflict stated in such terms, it is hardly surprising that Machiavelli eschews the Aristotelian role of umpire and declares for the people, not least but not only because their end "is more decent [*onesto*] than that of the great" (*Prince* 9.2, trans. Mansfield 1985).

Aristotle could perhaps be thought to share something of this view when he maintains that "the aggrandizements of the wealthy are more ruinous to the regime than those of the people," and that "the poor are willing to remain tranquil even when they have no share in offices so long as no one acts arrogantly to them nor deprives them of any of their property" (Arist. *Pol.* 1297a10–13, 1297b5–8, trans. Lord 1984). But Aristotle refuses to reduce the end of politics simply to freedom from oppression. Despite acknowledging the questionable origins of the wealth that makes gentlemanly leisure possible, he defends the resulting freedom from material necessity on the grounds that it makes possible the practice of the virtues that contribute to human happiness or perfection, a good of a different kind and higher than security (1280a39–b8, 1293b37–1294a2). Machiavelli, on the other hand, explains what appeared at first to be a moral difference between the humors of the people and the great in a manner that tends to dissolve the moral character of the distinction. The people are more trustworthy simply because they are not able to oppress (Machiavelli, *Discourses* 1.5.2). What unites both plebs and patricians is a common desire to feed themselves, that is, to acquire, a desire Machiavelli is keen to baptize as altogether natural without specifying any limit or end toward which it might be directed (*Discourses* 1.5.2, 1.16.5, 1.46, 3.8.1, 1.6.4; *Prince* 3.12). His rejection of the traditional Aristotelian classification of regimes, which was based on their ends and forms, in favor of a scheme that looks more to their origins, reflects the greater importance Machiavelli places on acquisition or founding (*Prince* 1, 6). Far from then maintaining that virtue consists in "placing the common good above the pursuit of any individual or factional ends" (Q. Skinner in Bock, Skinner, and Viroli 1993: 304), or that such devotion serves to perfect human nature (Pocock 1975: 201), Machiavelli does not hesitate to draw the necessary conclusion that follows from his premises. Political virtue consists in the ability to acquire and maintain a state and it can therefore vary according to circumstances as much as do the characters and deeds of Moses, Agathocles, and Severus (*Prince* 6, 8, 19; *Discourses* 1.9.3, 2.13.1, 3.6.19, 3.30.1). As shocking as it may be to find these characters associated with each another, it is even more so to discover the difficulty of elucidating any solid distinction between them on Machiavelli's grounds.

Montesquieu's *Spirit of the Laws* would seem to be a more likely source for the kind of republicanism advocated by Pocock and Skinner. In the "Author's Foreword" to the 1757 edition, Montesquieu apparently seeks to clarify what he means by virtue in the first four books of that work, and that he intends to keep separate what earlier forms of republicanism confounded: religion and politics. "It is not a moral virtue or a Christian virtue; it is a political virtue, and this is the spring that makes republican government move" (Montesquieu 1989: xli). In the body of the work he tells us that a good man must love the state less for his own sake than for itself and that political virtue consists in the love of the fatherland, something which requires both "a continuous preference for the public interest over one's own" and "the continuous sacrifice to the state of oneself and one's aversions," to say nothing of enduring poverty (1989: 26, 35–6, 69, 98). He even suggests that the modern spirit of commerce is the antithesis and corruption of republican virtue (1989: 22–3, 36–8, 40). Here, in the pages of the *Spirit of the Laws*, is the citizen of "the classical republicans," complete with classical credentials (1989: 35).

Yet Montesquieu fails to speak of this virtue as perfecting man's nature, as a good "classical republican" apparently should. This is puzzling, as is the fact that after claiming to distinguish between political virtue and moral or religious virtue in the Foreword, he directs the reader to book 3, chapter 5. There he claims, "I speak here of political virtue, which is a moral virtue in the sense that it points toward the common good." But if political virtue is admittedly a moral virtue, Montesquieu still maintains that it has nothing to do with "that virtue which relates to revealed truths." He again directs the reader to a specific chapter: "This will be seen in Book V, chapter ii" (Montesquieu 1989: 25 n9). That chapter does spell out that virtue in a republic is simply love of the republic, and shows how it is instilled through repression. "The less we can satisfy our particular passions, the more we give ourselves over to passions for the general order." Yet the example he uses to illustrate his point undermines the distinction he had promised to respect between religious and political virtue.

> Why do monks so love their order? Their love comes from the same thing that makes it intolerable to them. Their rule deprives them of everything upon which ordinary passions rest; what remains, therefore, is the passion for the very rule that afflicts them. The more austere it is, that is, the more it curtails their inclinations, the more force it gives to those that remain. (1989: 43)[5]

Rather than distinguishing between political, moral, and religious virtue, Montesquieu in fact amalgamates them to the disadvantage of each. He brings out the element of repression common to them all in a manner that makes it appear senseless or particularly cruel (cf. 1989: 318; Manent 1998: 12–31). Thus Montesquieu deflates the education in magnanimity and self-control that was the pride of republican politics in antiquity. He claims that because the Greeks held commerce and the banausic arts in contempt they had to institute gymnastics to keep the citizens from being idle. But as these exercises made them harsh and savage, they had then to soften them with music or the practice of homosexuality. Far from aiming at man's natural perfection, in Montesquieu's analysis, classical education is simply a hardening followed by a softening made necessary by a mistaken prejudice against commerce (1989: 39–41; cf. 337–41). In addition, it requires citizens to police themselves to an extraordinary degree, something which ultimately renders their individual security quite precarious (e.g., 1989: 38–9, 77–80, 81–2, 189–93).

Like Machiavelli, Montesquieu rejects both classical and Christian virtue and sides with the people in the sense of taking their ends, security and liberty, as the proper ends of politics. "Men being made to preserve, feed, and clothe themselves, and to do all the things done in society, religion should not give them an overly contemplative life" (Montesquieu 1989: 466; cf. 39–41). Indeed, he defines political liberty as "that tranquility of mind that comes from the opinion each one has of his security (1989: 157). But whereas Machiavelli thought this end best attained by means of encouraging princely ambition, Montesquieu thought liberty could be better secured through institutions that restrict and temper the more violent modes of acquisition employed by Machiavellians (e.g. 1989: 389–90). He takes as his model England, which can be considered as "a nation where the republic hides under the form of monarchy." But unlike the ancient republics, England does not have virtue as its spring (1989: 70, 22); and unlike the modern Italian republics, it separates the powers of legislation, execution, and judging and distributes them to different bodies in a manner that makes it much less likely that one citizen will fear another. Rather, it "has political liberty for its direct purpose." England is still in some sense a mixed society with its nobles and people divided by different passions and interests (1989: 157–8, 156, 163). The government, however, is mixed, not so much because it blends the different virtues of the one, few, and many, but because it assigns to each a separate power and balances them accordingly. In fact, nobles and people are both assigned the legislative power which they exercise by means of representatives. The real balancing takes place between the executive and legislative, with parties forming around them and each individual shifting his allegiance back and forth between them in a manner that maintains their equilibrium, a fluidity made impossible when political institutions are constructed wholly on the basis of social classes thought to possess specific virtues (1989: 325–6; cf. Cartledge and Edge, this volume, chapter 10).

Echoing the views of republicans like Thomas Paine with their arguments for simple forms of government, the Abbé Turgot criticized the early American republics for a thoughtless adherence to traditional English forms in their various state constitutions. He thought a balance of powers no longer necessary in societies without strict social classes, that is, "in republics founded upon the equality of all citizens." He feared such institutions would contribute to the establishment of different orders of men, something which, in turn, could become "a source of divisions and disputes." John Adams defended the attachment of most of the States to the kind of balance and separation of powers embodied in Montesquieu's description of the mixed regime because he considered it to be based "in nature and reason," not mere habit or prejudice (Adams 1971: 1.4 5). But if Adams thought "we shall have reason to exult if we make our comparison with England and the English constitution," he was also convinced of the inevitable emergence in America of an aristocracy that would require an independent institution so as to keep it in equilibrium with the first magistrate and people (1971: 95–6, xxii).[6] It was left to the authors of the *Federalist Papers* to disentangle the doctrine of the separation of powers from the mixed regime and to show its continued importance for a republic that rests simply on the will of the people rather than on an accommodation between nobles and plebs.

For Pocock, however, *Federalist #10* forms the *locus classicus* of what he takes to be the antirepublican or "liberal" legitimization of "particular interest," and the abandonment of "virtue in the classical sense" (1975: 522). No one could deny that the protection of individual rights, especially of property rights, is a central concern of the *Federalists* ("Publius" 1961: 46). Yet Publius concludes *Federalist #10* with this proud boast: "In the extent and proper structure of the Union, therefore, we behold a republican remedy for the diseases most incident to republican government. And according to the degree of pleasure and pride we feel in being republicans ought to be our zeal in cherishing the spirit and supporting the character of federalists" (1961: 52). What Publius understands by republican government is "popular government" where all powers are derived "directly or indirectly from the great body of the people" (1961: 45, 209). The republicanism of the *Federalist Papers* therefore demands an "unmixed" republic (1961: 69). The self-rule it envisages is not the direct participation of different elements of society checking each other, but rather governing in the absence of a controlling authority either independent or above an altogether democratic society. While not demanding selfless devotion to the common good, and thus the complete denial of private interest, republican government does, in Publius's view, presuppose the existence of noble human qualities "in a higher degree than any other form." Among these qualities, an honorable determination to vindicate or prove "the capacity of mankind for self-government" is prominent. Genuine self-rule also requires institutions to be formed by "reflection and choice," not "accident and force" (1961: 314, 208, 1). Government must be an affair altogether of human making, and proudly so.

As we have seen, one problem with the mixed regime as embodied by the English constitution is that it requires the existence of different orders of men who are lacking in America. More important, and at a more general or universal level, even the English constitution seems to be in the process of unmixing itself over time. Thomas Jefferson observed this phenomenon as early as his *Rights of British America* and gave a diagnosis of its cause that shows he understood the change as anything but a corruption: the kings in England have somehow become "conscious of the impropriety of opposing their single opinion to the united wisdom of two houses of parliament," to say nothing of the long term implications of the Act of Settlement (Jefferson 1975: 14). And according to the Federalists, once the House of Commons came to be understood as the element most representative of the people, and hence conferring upon the whole the legitimacy that derives from consent rather than contributing some particular virtue or ability, it tended to enjoy a "continual triumph" and overawe the other branches of government ("Publius" 1961: 327). In America, without king and lords, the problem diagnosed as "the impetuous vortex" of the legislative body becomes even more acute since the very closeness of the people to their representatives serves to undermine the rights their representative bodies are intended to protect. Publius's doctrine of the separation of powers, understood as a system of checks and balances within the government, is primarily directed against the legislative branch and the people's inclination to place too much trust in it (1961: 277).

Thus the political philosophy of the Federalists calls upon citizens to make a liberal calculation of their self-interest, but a self-interest properly understood to encompass the desire to vindicate the cause of republican government. All popular forms of government have hitherto proved incapable of stability because they lacked the proper institutional structures. In light of this sobering reflection, the American people must collectively decide to exclude themselves from any further collective participation in their government, and this for the collective good of not just themselves but all mankind ("Publius" 1961: 1). Under modern conditions, particularly when religious diversity would seem to exclude the possibility of giving all citizens the same passions and opinions (1961: 46), republicanism requires liberal institutions. But no less so do liberal institutions require a republican pride or spirit if both their founding and continued preservation are to remain matters of "reflection and choice," not "accident and force." Modern republicanism and liberalism can exist in symbiosis, not simply opposition. Quentin Skinner very nicely demonstrates this point when he sums up the contemporary lesson to be derived from the study of classical republicanism. It teaches us that "unless we place our duties before our rights, we must expect to find our rights themselves undermined" (Q. Skinner 1991: 205; cf. this volume, Cartledge and Edge, chapter 10; Hitz, chapter 24). Of course, if we put our duties first for the sake of securing our rights, it is our rights that we in fact place first and value most. What Skinner's statement lacks in terms of logical consistency, it more than makes up for in political good sense, not least in recognizing the potential compatibility between our liberal rights and republican duties, properly understood.

FURTHER READING

The contemporary study of the history of republican institutions and political theory was given much of its impetus by Pocock 1975. Pocock himself was inspired by Baron 1955, 1968 and Arendt 1958 to give great weight to the role of citizen participation in this tradition. Q. Skinner 1978, 1990 followed Pocock's lead in focusing attention on the conceptual vocabulary of republicanism, but did so in such a manner as to depart from or qualify Pocock's focus on the Aristotelian roots of republicanism. In Skinner's account, Roman and late medieval theorists and lawyers predominate, with freedom being understood primarily as the freedom from arbitrary oppression rather than the positive freedom to participate in the common enterprise of rule. The common thread linking the enterprise of these scholars is a lament at the depoliticization of modern life, in which the economic interests of corporate bodies often supplant the deliberations of an engaged citizenry, and an effort to recover a historical alternative to counterbalance contemporary liberalism and its excessive concern with security, property, and the protection of other individual and economic rights. Pettit 1997 and Viroli 2002 elaborate applications of this standpoint to contemporary debates and issues.

In part as a reaction to the widespread influence of Pocock's approach, and in part as a deepening or reconsideration of his insights, an alternative account of the republican tradition has emerged. Mansfield (1979, 1989, 1996), Rahe (1992), and M. Zuckert (1998) have been its chief exponents, arguing that Machiavelli is best understood to have broken with rather than revived Aristotelian republicanism, and that his distinctively modern version is compatible with or even contributes to the rise of liberal politics. Hankins 2000 offers critiques of the "classical republicanism" thesis from this and other perspectives. Yet even these "revisionist" accounts share something with that of the "classical republicans" as they too call into question the triumphalism of overly Whiggish or progressive interpretations of our political history, a point given special emphasis by Manent 1998.

NOTES

1   I am indebted to Clifford Orwin for the connection of these two stories to Herodotus' understanding of *isēgoria* (Clifford Orwin, "Herodotus on Athenian Democracy," a public lecture delivered at Boston College in December 2004).

2   "Such is the dazzling paradox showing monarchy at the base of all politics" (Mansfield 1989: 39). See also Newell 1987: 176.

3   e.g. "Every natural governance is governance by one. . . . Even among the bees there is one king and in the whole universe there is one God, maker and director of all things" (Aquinas, *De Regimine Principum*, 1.2; cf. *Summa Theologiae*, 1.103.3, 1–2.90.3). See Blythe 1992: 41, 46–7.

4   Compare Savonarola's understanding of his role in the republic with the place Aristotle reserves for priests in his best regime (Arist. *Pol.* 1322b18–20, 1328b11, 1329a27, 1331b5, 1284b30–1).

5   Montesquieu's earlier pairing of Lycurgus to William Penn (1989: 37) anticipates the comparison to which he draws special attention here.

6   "Wherever we have seen a territory somewhat larger [than San Marino], arts and sciences more cultivated, commerce flourishing, or even agriculture improved to any great degree, an aristocracy has risen up in a course of time, consisting in a few rich and honorable families, who have united with each other against both the people and the first magistrate" (Adams 1971: 94).

CHAPTER 34

Twentieth Century Revivals of Ancient Political Thought: Hannah Arendt and Leo Strauss

Catherine H. Zuckert

In the wake of World War II, two influential political theorists warned their contemporaries that they were in danger of losing not merely their liberty, but their very humanity, if they did not recover certain aspects of ancient political thought. The innovative as well as influential character of their respective attempts to revive antiquity in the midst of late modernity is indicated by the fact that Hannah Arendt has often been taken to be one of the leading theorists of the "New Left" whereas Leo Strauss has recently been publicly associated with the development and thought of the "New Right."

Arendt and Strauss were both Jewish émigrés who fled the horrors of Nazi Germany. As students of philosophy in early twentieth century Germany, both Arendt and Strauss had not only witnessed the weakness and eventual fall of the Weimar Republic; they had also sympathetically learned and absorbed Friedrich Nietzsche's radical critique of modern philosophy and politics. Both feared that modern thought and politics would produce the moral and physical degeneration of Nietzsche's "last man" ("Zarathustra's Prologue," 5: see Nietzsche 1968b: 128–31), that is, human beings who have no higher goal or yearning, but seek only to live and die with minimal pain. But neither thought such degeneration would necessarily occur, because neither thought, like Hegel and Marx, that there was a necessary direction or end to human history. Both sought to deflect, if not entirely to avoid, the threatened moral and political corruption by reviving an ancient understanding of politics that had been forgotten, if not entirely obliterated.

The similarities in their backgrounds – educational, personal, and political – as well in the overall structure of their philosophical-political projects make the differences between Arendt and Strauss stand out (cf. Beiner 1990; Villa 2001: 246–98).

A Companion to Greek and Roman Political Thought, First Edition. Edited by Ryan K. Balot.
© 2013 Blackwell Publishing Ltd. Published 2013 by Blackwell Publishing Ltd.

Although both Arendt and Strauss thought that modern totalitarian regimes threatened to eradicate human freedom, they had quite different understandings of the distinctive characteristics of these regimes. Whereas Arendt argued that the totalitarian regimes constituted an entirely new form of government, arising out of mass society and based on terror and ideology, Strauss insisted that the character of these regimes would not be understood by anyone who did not see that they represented a more dangerous form of the ancient phenomenon of tyranny. (Arendt 1973; Strauss 1991: 22–4. On the ancient understanding of tyranny, see Forsdyke, this volume, chapter 15.)

Thinking that the threat to the preservation of humanity arose from the abolition of distinctions among individual human beings in mass society along with the power of modern technology to re-form everything, Arendt sought to revive the ancient understanding and practice of politics as an activity undertaken for its own sake, not as a means of securing our lives, liberty, and estates. The ancient Greek understanding of the polis as the place where individuals distinguished themselves by engaging in contests in speech had first been subordinated to the rule of reason in the philosophy of Plato. Only with the rise of Christianity, however, had the *vita contemplativa* become generally more valued than the *vita activa*. Machiavelli was the last political theorist to assert the value of politics, with its striving for individual glory, against the contemplative model embraced by the Christians. When later modern theorists and practitioners turned back from the contemplation of eternal truths to the world, they made political activity subservient to the requirements of self-preservation and thus lost all sense of its human importance and fragility.

Observing that the most immediate threat to the preservation of human liberty in the twentieth century arose from a lack of conviction on the part of liberal democrats in the value or truth of their own principles and hence a reluctance to fight and die in defense of them (Strauss 1953: 3, 6; 1964: 3), Strauss sought to revive a version of Platonic political philosophy that would provide his contemporaries with an understanding of "right" grounded in nature, as opposed to mere opinion, agreement or "convention." The version of Platonic political philosophy Strauss sought to revive was, however, very different from the two-world model of the opposition between truth and appearance that Arendt thought had first led to the depreciation of the importance of politics. The explicitly untraditional reading Strauss gave of Plato emphasized the tension between politics and philosophy. Rather than indifference to or contempt for political activity, Strauss argued, Plato's presentation of Socrates emphasized the need for philosophers to take account of the political context and potentially damaging effects of their investigations. Although Strauss reaffirmed the Platonic and Aristotelian judgment that the contemplative life was, in the end, superior to a life devoted to practical politics, he also argued that Plato and Aristotle saw the need to maintain a distinction between theory and practice that had been lost in modern philosophy. Like Arendt, Strauss thus tried not only to reintroduce that distinction but also to remind his contemporaries of the dignity and importance of politics.

Arendt's Advocacy of Political "Action"

Arendt begins her most general and comprehensive account of *The Human Condition* by reminding her readers of the distinction Aristotle draws at the beginning of his *Politics* between "activity" (political and philosophical), which is undertaken for its own sake, and "production," which is undertaken primarily by slaves in order to provide the necessities of life (1958: 22–78). In the ancient polis, "production" belonged to the "private" sphere of the household or *oikos*. Obviously the source of the name of the modern science of "economics," the *oikos* was the association devoted to accumulation of the goods and provision of services necessary to sustain life. Only those free from the need to provide such necessities were able to enter and engage in public life, and only those who engaged in public debates were considered to be truly or fully human. Like everything associated merely with bodily preservation, "private" life was thought to be properly hidden.

Modern people no longer have a sense, much less an understanding of the character and importance of "public" or distinctly political life, because public and private concerns have gradually been merged into the "social." After Rousseau, the private sphere came to be associated particularly with "intimacy" and affection, and the provision of necessary goods and services or "economics" became the chief concern of "public" business.

Regarded merely as needy or even infinitely desirous animals, Arendt saw, human beings do not differ much from one another. The elevation of economic concerns to the top of the public agenda has thus been one of the major factors which have produced modern "mass" society and the condition for the emergence of totalitarian regimes.

Human beings distinguish themselves from each other as well as from other animals by means of their speech, not the labor or work by means of which they satisfy their needs and transform the world in which they find themselves. But Arendt did not simply endorse the Aristotelian definition of the human being as *zōon politikon* or *echon logon*, that is, a political or rational animal, who actualizes its natural potential only by participating in public deliberations about what is good and bad, just and unjust, useful or useless. She objected to Aristotle's definition of the human species as a kind of being, a "what" rather than a "who." She thought that human beings differ from all other animals inasmuch as each human being differs from all others from birth. Each has his or her own experience and perspective on the world. These differences become manifest only in speech, however, and human beings develop their ability to speak only in relation to others. We test the accuracy of our own perceptions and conclusions about ourselves as well as about other things in the world by comparing them with the opinions of others who see the same things from a slightly different perspective. Arendt did not think, therefore, that we should follow Aristotle and talk about human "nature." On the contrary, she emphasized, human life is thoroughly conditioned, and the conditions – like the polis or the various languages human beings speak – are products of human artifice.[1]

Human beings develop and display their distinctive traits – both as individuals and as a species – only by engaging in what Arendt calls political "action," that is, by articulating and exchanging individual views in public. But people do not necessarily or always establish and maintain the kinds of "public spaces" which make such action possible, even though the requirements for establishing the public space are relatively simple. A group of people need simply mark off the boundaries of a certain territory and establish a set of rules or laws that allow exchanges of opinions. The ancient Greeks established poleis when they acquired enough leisure to reflect on the evanescence of human life. The individuals who had persuaded others to follow them and their opinions wanted their preeminence and deeds to be remembered. Only a community that reproduced itself and so lasted beyond the lifetime of a single generation could promise such individuals that they could achieve immortal glory by living on in the memories of those who came later.

Arendt admits that actual historical examples of the kind of "action," that is, public speech, she calls "political" are rare. It occurred in Greek poleis, at the founding of the American Republic, and the beginning of the French Revolution, in the first soviets and at the outbreak of the Hungarian revolution.

There are three reasons, she suggests, why "politics" properly understood occurs so infrequently and tends to degenerate rather quickly into more utilitarian forms of action. First, the distinctive character of political "action" or activity is rarely, and even then incompletely, understood. Even the ancient Greeks and Romans were confused, as shown by the words they used to describe it. Unlike modern languages, Arendt observed, Greek and Latin have two words that both mean "to act." The Greek verbs *archein* ("to begin," "to lead," finally "to rule") and *prattein* ("to pass through," "to achieve," "to finish") correspond to the two Latin verbs *agere* ("to set into motion," "to lead") and *gerere* (whose original meaning is "to bear"). The ancients seem to have thought that each action was divided into two parts, the beginning, made by a single person, and the achievement, in which many could join. Over time, however, "the word[s] that originally designated only the second part of action, its achievement ... became the accepted word[s] for action in general, whereas the words designating the beginning of action ... came to mean chiefly 'to rule' and 'to lead' " (1958: 189).

The second reason the distinctive character of political action is easily misunderstood and, consequently, lost is that people want to see concrete results. Because each and every human being is different, the results of their interactions are essentially unpredictable. And because human beings are individually weak, they want to achieve security along with the order that makes exchanges of opinions possible. "Thus the role of the beginner and leader, who was a *primus inter pares* (in the case of Homer, a king among kings), changed into that of a ruler," who had the prerogative of giving commands to subjects who were obliged to obey them.

Third, political action becomes identified with rule based on force, because everyone cannot take part in public debate, certainly not all of the time. Most people have been excluded from taking part in the decisions that determine much of the course of their lives by being forced to provide goods and services for those with the power to make the laws.

It is not clear what the content of the "political action" or speech Arendt praises actually was or is. "What is it that they talked about together in that endless palaver in the agora?" quipped Hanna Pitkin (1981). In fact, readers of ancient Greek texts know that they talked primarily about questions Arendt explicitly excludes: Who should rule? How goods should be acquired and distributed, or what is just? Should the city go to war or remain at peace? Arendt excludes such topics, because they involve the realm of necessity, that is, the provision and distribution of goods needed to preserve human life and for the use of force. Debates about such topics did not constitute true displays of human freedom and individuality embodied in what she called "political action."

Although Arendt differs from Aristotle both about the natural basis and the content of "political" debate, she could nevertheless have obtained a good deal of support for what she says is distinctively "political" from the *Politics*. In the first place, Aristotle observes (1255b20, 1259b1–5, 1277b7–10), political relations exist among equals. Since everyone cannot rule at once, fellow citizens rule and are ruled in turn. Second, Aristotle points out (1277b25–9), it is necessary to hold public office and make public decisions in order to demonstrate one's own practical wisdom or *phronēsis*. Third, Aristotle emphasizes (1254b3–5), political rule occurs by means of *logos* (speech or reason). It does not rest on superior force like the power of a despot or master over his slaves. (See Depew, this volume, chapter 26.)

Arendt probably chose not to cite Aristotle in her description of political "action" because he continues to speak in terms of "rule." He does not emphasize the importance of individuals showing who they are by articulating their opinions in front of others to see whether they can persuade others. He suggests, moreover, that some people or parts of a political community will always rule others.[2]

Arendt's understanding of political "action" is more egalitarian than Aristotle's. She does not recognize the existence of natural differences between slaves and masters or between men and women, nor does she suggest that political participation should be restricted on the basis of such differences. (See Depew, chapter 26.) She has nevertheless been criticized for her "elitist conception of great action as being incomplete unless it is accompanied by great speech." Like Nietzsche, Sheldon Wolin observes (2004: 455–6), Arendt thought that the value and meaning of human life was determined by its highest examples. Following Nietzsche, Arendt was, like Strauss, concerned above all to see that the conditions under which truly great individuals could emerge and flourish were not forgotten or destroyed.

It would be a mistake, however, to conclude that Arendt or her thought were fundamentally "fascist," because of the Nietzschean roots. On the contrary, it was her "Nietzschean" concern about the importance of recognizing and preserving the individual differences that emerged in the contests (*agōnes*) characteristic of the Greek polis that distinguished her political thought from that of her mentor, Martin Heidegger. As Dana Villa has shown in his masterful study *Arendt and Heidegger* (1996: 171–240), Arendt took her understanding of distinctively human existence as an "open space" in which "truth" appears to those who exist "with others" in a shared "world" from her one-time teacher. By explicitly politicizing Heidegger's analysis of human existence in *Being and Time*, however, Arendt changed it significantly. Heidegger had emphasized the difference between a shared but "inauthentic" understanding of things, which gradually loses its basis in genuine insight and becomes ever more flat as it is repeated without thought in empty, everyday chatter, and the "authentic" insight individuals acquire into the fundamental uncertainty and non-necessity of their own existence if they reflect on the basis of the underlying anxiety they feel. Such individuals have the option only of intentionally resolving to persist in the way of life of the people at the time and place in which they happen to have been born as a matter of their own choice rather than as the result of extrinsic accident. They do not have the power to change the fundamental character of their community or its dominant opinions. By emphasizing the differences among individuals that emerge in political debates, Arendt not merely brought the description of a distinctively human existence closer to its origin in Aristotle's *Politics* and so made it more accurate. She also and more fundamentally emphasized the divisions within every people or polity and thus gave a more concrete account of the source of the "strife" Heidegger argued was responsible for creating the "open" space and the freedom that comes with it (Heidegger 1959). For Arendt public speech was capable not merely of disclosing the truth, which revealed the distinctive character of each and every individual; it was capable of creating a new public, more generally shared understanding of the world.

Arendt followed Heidegger in arguing that Plato changed his readers' understanding of "truth" and the highest form of human existence, so that the original experience of both was gradually forgotten. But where Heidegger emphasized the change from an understanding of truth as disclosure (*a-letheia*) to correctness (in the correspondence of being to idea), Arendt emphasized the change in the understanding of the relation between politics and philosophy. She attributed the change not to Plato's reworking of the original understanding of "*eidos*" as shape or appearance, but to his reaction to a specific event – the trial and condemnation of Socrates. (Cf. Arendt 1990: 81; Heidegger 1962.)

In a lecture she delivered at the University of Notre Dame in 1954, but which was not published until 1990, Arendt suggested that it was Socrates' failure not only to persuade his fellow Athenians that philosophy was beneficial to the city but also to convince his philosophical friends that political action was important that led Plato to turn away from the sphere of opinion and seek a more reliable eternal truth upon which to base both politics and philosophy. "Platonic truth, even when *doxa* is not mentioned, is always understood as the very opposite of opinion" (1990: 81). But Socrates' famous claim in the *Apology* that the Delphic oracle had declared him to be the wisest human being, because he knew only that he did not know, meant not only that he had only opinions but also that he knew it.[3] Socrates explicitly eschewed rhetorical speeches intended to persuade a multitude in order to engage in a dialectical conversation or dialogue with one other individual, because he saw that such rhetorical speeches were not true acts of persuasion. They represented attempts to force one's own opinions on others by enacting them in law. "To Socrates, as to his fellow citizens, *doxa* was the formulation in speech of what *dokei moi*, that is, of what appears to me." For Socrates and his fellow Athenians "opinion" thus had the character of Heidegger's original "truth," although Arendt insisted, contra

Heidegger, this opinion or truth is different for each and every individual. This "truth" could, moreover, only become manifest in public. "The word *doxa* means not only opinion but also splendor and fame. As such, it is related to the political realm, which is the public sphere in which everybody can appear and show who he himself is." Although Socrates refused to speak in the public Assembly, unless required to do so by law, he did not retire into the private life of his own household (*oikos*). On the contrary, Socrates "moved in the marketplace, in the very midst of these *doxai*. … What Plato later called *dialegesthai*, Socrates himself called … the art of midwifery: he wanted to help others give birth to what they themselves thought …, to find the truth in their *doxa*" (Arendt 1990: 81).[4]

Socrates thus showed himself to be an individual who did not fit the previous understanding of a wise man (*sophos*) any more than he fit Plato's later conception of a philosopher-king. Unlike previous wise men, Socrates did not neglect human affairs in order to study cosmic or eternal truths. Recognizing he did not possess knowledge, he went to the marketplace to test his own opinions in comparison with others. Socrates' method rested on "a twofold conviction: every man has his own *doxa*, his own opening to the world," so that he can "not know beforehand" how things appear to others. "Just as nobody can know beforehand the other's *doxa*, so nobody can know by himself and without further effort the inherent truth of his own opinion."

Socrates wanted to bring out the truth that everyone potentially possesses. Using his own metaphor of midwifery, we might say: "Socrates wanted to make the city more truthful by delivering each of the citizens of their truths. The method of doing this is *dialegesthai*, … but this dialectic brings forth truth *not* by destroying *doxa* or opinion, but on the contrary reveals *doxa* in its own truthfulness." The role of the philosopher, as represented by Socrates, "is not to rule the city but to be its 'gadfly,' not to tell philosophical truths but to make citizens more truthful" (1990: 81).

Unfortunately, Socrates' fellow Athenians could not tell the difference between Socrates and his predecessors. Nor did they understand the way in which the kind of philosophy he practiced was politically useful. So they convicted him, and Plato concluded that persuasion was not a sufficient basis for politics or philosophy.

As a result, Plato and his successors lost two of Socrates' essential insights. One arose from the Delphic command to know thyself, which led the philosopher to examine both his own opinions and those of others. The second was that "it is better to be in disagreement with the whole world than, being one, to be in disagreement with myself." This experience of "being one" and yet able to talk to oneself, as if one were two, is the basis not only of our ability to contradict ourselves but also of our fear of doing so. Someone who is not of one mind and thus vacillates or even opposes herself is not reliable. This experience of talking to oneself, as if one were two, is also the basis of friendship; and, as Aristotle saw, friendship rather than justice is the basis of political community. Only "because I am already two-in-one, at least when I try to think, can I experience a friend, to use Aristotle's definition, as an 'other self.' " A "friend understands how … the common world appears to the other." And "this kind of understanding – seeing the world (as we rather tritely say today) from the other fellow's point of view – is the political kind of insight *par excellence*" (1990: 83–4).

Plato distorted Socrates' insight into the essential plurality of human existence, which begins and is expressed in the dialogue we have with ourselves in attempting to understand who we are, by recasting the internal division we experience as a conflict between soul and body and insisting that the soul must rule. "To the philosopher, politics ... became the field in which the elementary necessities of human life are taken care of" (Arendt 1990: 101–2). Practical political activity thus came to be seen as far inferior to the contemplative life, and in modern times both practice and theory were devoted to providing the goods human beings need to survive. The western philosophical tradition came to an end when Marx declared that labor was the source of all value and that technology would relieve human beings of the need to labor. Human life no longer had any distinctive purpose or meaning.

"To find a new political philosophy from which could come a new science of politics," Arendt thought, it would be necessary to regain the Socratic insight.

> Solitude, or the thinking dialogue of the two-in-one, is an integral part of being and living together with others, and in this solitude the philosopher, too, cannot help but form opinions ... His distinction from his fellow citizens is not that he possesses any special truth from which the multitude is excluded, but that he remains always ready to endure the *pathos* of wonder and thereby avoids the dogmatism of mere opinion holders. (1990: 103, 101)

Leo Strauss's Revival of Platonic Political Philosophy

Strauss shared Arendt's Nietzsche-inspired concern about the perpetuation of human greatness, as well as her very anti-Nietzschean desire to revive a Socratic understanding of political philosophy. In a letter he wrote to Karl Loewith in 1935 Strauss admitted that "Nietzsche so dominated and bewitched me between my 22nd and 30th years that I literally believed everything that I understood of him." Loewith had shown Strauss that the aspects of Nietzsche that had attracted him were only part of Nietzsche's work and that "with Nietzsche something 'is not right.' " But Strauss did not think that Loewith had taken "those intentions of Nietzsche which point beyond Nietzsche's teaching" seriously enough. "It is not sufficient simply to stop where Nietzsche is no longer right; rather one must ask whether or not Nietzsche himself became untrue to his intention to repeat antiquity, and did so as a result of his confinement within modern presuppositions" (1988: 183–4).

Strauss later praised his friend Jacob Klein for being "the first to understand the possibility which Heidegger had opened without intending it: the possibility of a genuine return ... to the philosophy of Aristotle and of Plato" (1978: 1). But Strauss did not approach ancient politics and philosophy on the basis of a fundamentally Heideggerian framework the way Arendt had. On the contrary, Strauss thought that he had obtained a fresh, more original reading of ancient political philosophy by taking an untraditional path back to it. That path led through medieval Jewish and Islamic political philosophy, which differed in notable respects from the Augustinian appropriation of Plato and the Thomist appropriation of Aristotle that remained dominant not only in the early modern philosophical reactions against Christian scholastic theology but also in the contemporary critiques of Plato put forward by Heidegger and Arendt.

In his early book *Philosophy and Law* (1995) Strauss argued that the Jewish medieval philosopher Moses Maimonides and his Islamic teacher, Farabi, began with an essentially Aristotelian understanding of the cosmos and reinterpreted Islamic and Jewish law in light of that understanding in order to establish and preserve the conditions, especially the moral beliefs, necessary to maintain political order. But Strauss later came to see that Maimonides' teacher Farabi had followed Plato, not Aristotle, in thinking that philosophy consisted in the search for wisdom, not in contemplation of the eternal beings. Farabi, moreover, followed a Plato very different from Plato as normally understood in the western tradition. That Plato argues that suprasensible, disembodied "forms" or "ideas" are the true beings, of which the things we experience are mere reflections or imitations. He teaches that there is an immortal soul which exists separately from the body. And he advocates the rule of philosophers. This is the Plato Heidegger and Arendt thought had distorted and so covered over the original way in which the truth of Being or about individuals in political debate was disclosed.

In Farabi's tripartite work *The Aims of the Philosophy of Plato and Aristotle*, Strauss observed, the Islamic philosopher argued that happiness is the aim of human life, according to both ancient philosophers. Since man's perfection and thus his happiness consist in philosophy, and since, as the fate of Socrates makes clear, philosophy arouses political opposition, Plato taught that it was necessary to seek a city different from the cities that existed in his time: the city in speech of the *Republic* where the philosophers rule. At least that was what Farabi seemed to say at the beginning of his treatise on Plato. Reading further, Strauss observed, Farabi provided a number of grounds on which to challenge the textbook version of Plato's *Republic*. Having initially claimed that Plato thought philosophy needed to be supplemented by a royal art in order for human beings to attain happiness, Farabi then stated that Plato "teaches that philosophy does not need to be supplemented by something else in order to produce happiness." Farabi's second statement thus contradicted what he had said at first. Having first suggested that the happiness of the philosophers, as well as of their fellow citizens, depended upon the establishment of the perfect city, that is, the city of the philosopher-kings, "toward the end of the treatise, Farabi ma[de] it absolutely clear that there can be, not only philosophers, but completely perfect human beings … in imperfect cities." Philosophers do not need to rule in order to achieve their end. Philosophers can live and even thrive as members of imperfect regimes.

Nor did Farabi think that, according to Plato, the happiness of the philosopher depends upon his contemplating eternally existing, unchanging beings. Although he purportedly summarized the *Phaedrus, Phaedo,* and *Republic,* Strauss pointed out, Farabi did not mention the immortality of the soul or the unchanging Platonic ideas. Yet Farabi had claimed to present "the philosophy of Plato, its parts, and the grades of dignity of its parts, from its beginning to its end." How could Farabi leave out topics so prominent in the dialogues he was interpreting, topics that were apparently so central to Platonic philosophy? Strauss concluded that when Farabi omitted a topic, this meant that he thought it was unimportant or merely an exoteric (surface) doctrine. To avoid being persecuted for impiety like Socrates, Farabi saw that Plato and philosophers in general had to claim not only that they could help their fellow citizens live better, but also that the philosophers themselves believed in eternal beings and in an afterlife. Writing in his own name in the preface to *The Aims*, Farabi thus distinguished "the happiness of this world" from "the ultimate happiness in the other life." But in the central chapter of *The Aims* on Plato, he silently dropped this distinction. And "in his commentary on the *Nicomachean Ethics* [in part 3] he declare[d] that there is only the happiness of this life and that all divergent statements are based on 'ravings and old women's tales.' "

Farabi could express such impious views without fear of persecution, Strauss suggested, because as a commentator, Farabi was not explicitly presenting his own views. Strauss nonetheless thought he could discern Farabi's own views and his deeper understanding of Plato's views through his subtle way of presenting Platonic philosophy. Even as a commentator, Farabi was not simply summarizing what Plato wrote. Plato had explicitly argued for the immortality of the soul and hence some kind of afterlife in the *Phaedrus*, *Phaedo*, and *Republic*. Farabi was thus almost "compelled [by the Platonic texts] to embrace a tolerably orthodox doctrine concerning the life after death." By choosing to attribute another opinion to the philosopher he most highly revered, "Farabi avail[ed] himself then of the specific immunity of a commentator, or of the historian, in order to speak his own mind" (Strauss 1945: 359–83).[5]

Strauss thought that he had learned from Farabi's *Plato* that the goodness of a philosophic way of life does not depend upon the possibility of human beings' attaining complete theoretical knowledge. It was possible, therefore, to revive Platonic political philosophy without insisting on or even affirming the truth of Aristotelian cosmology in the face of modern physics. The model of the philosophic life is Socrates, not Aristotle. In Plato's *Apology* Socrates tells his Athenian jurors that the Delphic oracle declared him to be the wisest, because he at least knows that he does not know. (Knowing that one does not know is, of course, not knowing nothing; one has to know, among other things, what it is to know.) Socrates recognized that his fellow citizens might find his story about the oracle ironic. All he claimed to know on the basis of his own experience was that the "unexamined life is not worth living, but to make speeches every day about virtue and the other things about which you hear me conversing is the greatest good for a human being" (*Ap.* 38a). Whether or not Socrates ever attained the knowledge he sought, Plato's presentation of his life represented the contention that philosophy is a way of life, is *the* form of human life that is by nature best. If that claim could be made good, it would constitute a decisive response to Nietzsche and modern nihilism, without requiring questionable metaphysics or cosmology.

Although Socrates is famous for having maintained that virtue is knowledge, in the *Republic* (485b–487a) he suggests that human beings who merely seek wisdom possess all four of the cardinal virtues as a result of their overwhelming desire for truth. It is not necessary, in other words, to possess knowledge so much as passionately to seek it. Desiring truth above all else, Socrates argues, people with philosophical natures are not tempted to be immoderate or unjust by taking more than their share or seizing the goods of others. Recognizing that all sensible things must pass away, they are not afraid in the face of death. The philosopher's over-whelming desire for truth frees him from the desires for wealth, power, and status or recognition that lead most other human beings to be immoral. Philosophers do not need to possess the knowledge, for example, of the Idea of the Good, Socrates suggests they would need to rule in order to be virtuous themselves. (See Hitz, this volume, chapter 24.)

As Socrates' own life and death demonstrated so dramatically, however, philo-sophers came into conflict with political authorities as a result of the questions they posed in their quest for knowledge. Strauss nevertheless thought that Socrates had been correct, as Cicero put it, to bring "philosophy down from the heavens" (Strauss 1953: 121). Philosophers seek knowledge of the whole. The philosopher himself, or more broadly humanity, is not merely a part of the whole, however; the philosopher is a particularly central or significant part, because human beings are the only parts of the whole that raise the question about the whole. The first commandment of the philosophic life thus becomes, "know thyself." Humanity exists first and foremost within social and political orders. To understand themselves, philosophers thus have to understand the social and political life of human beings, and how the life or questioning of the philosopher relates to this universal and in a sense defining feature of human existence.

Unlike Arendt, however, Strauss did not think that the trial and death of Socrates led Plato to conclude that philosophers needed to rule. In his essay "On Plato's *Republic*" Strauss (1964: 122–8) recognized that Socrates maintains that evils in cities will not cease until philosophers become kings or kings become philosophers. But, Strauss also pointed out, in the *Republic* Socrates emphasizes that philosophers do not want to rule; they would be the only just rulers precisely because they are the only people who cannot attain or hope to attain what they want by means of rule. Philosophers can justly be compelled to rule, moreover, only by a city that provides them with the education that enables them to become philosophers. It is unlikely that they will be compelled to rule in any existing city, because most people outside the just city will continue to believe that philosophers are at best useless. But, Strauss recognized, philosophers are just human beings, and there is such a thing as self-compulsion. "It should not be necessary, but it is necessary to add that compulsion does not cease to be compulsion if it is self-compulsion." Will a philosopher in a less than perfectly just regime feel obliged to rule? The implicit answer is, no. The fact that philosophers do not feel duty-bound to rule does not mean, however, that philosophers will not attempt to benefit their fellow citizens, for example, by advising the government. Free from the competitive desires for wealth and honor that make human beings hostile to one another, philosophers are able to act on the natural affection all human beings feel for others, especially for members of their own families and community.

Strauss (1964: 50–7) emphasized the importance of taking the literary form of the dialogues seriously if we wish to understand Plato's writing. Like a playwright, Plato does not speak to his readers directly. "The decisive fact is that Plato … points away from himself to Socrates. If we wish to understand Plato, we must take … seriously … his deference to Socrates. Plato points not only to Socrates' speeches but to his whole life, to his fate as well" (1983: 168).

Socrates never went into the public Assembly or sought to rule. Had he done so, he states in both the *Republic* (496a–e) and his *Apology* (31c–32a), he would not have survived. Like a good citizen, he had risked his life by serving in the Athenian army at Potidaea, Delium, and Amphipolis. He had also served, when required by law to do so, as part of the jury for the trial of the Arginusae generals. But he had angered his fellow citizens by insisting that they ought to obey their own laws and not try the ten generals together. Socrates recognized both that the Athenians did not understand the kind of service he provided for the city as a philosopher, and that the young people who imitated his questioning would irritate the elders. But Socrates nevertheless persisted. In his *Apology* (29c–d) he went so far as to say that the only law he would disobey would be a law that forbade him from philosophizing in his accustomed manner.

In *On Tyranny* Strauss explains that like Socrates,

> the philosopher must go to the marketplace in order to fish there for potential philosophers. His attempts to convert young men to the philosophic life will necessarily be regarded by the city as an attempt to corrupt the young. The philosopher is therefore forced to defend the cause of philosophy. He must therefore act upon the city or upon the ruler.

But that does not mean "the philosopher must desire to determine or codetermine the politics of the city or of the rulers." On the contrary, "there is no necessary connection between the philosopher's indispensable philosophic politics and the efforts which he might or might not make to contribute toward the establishment of the best regime. For philosophy and philosophic education are possible in all kinds of more or less imperfect regimes" (1991: 205).

The fact that philosophers like Socrates did not seek to rule did not mean that they were not politically engaged and active. Like Arendt, Strauss insisted that "political activity" and rule are not synonymous. But where Arendt argued that Socrates' examinations of the opinions of his contemporaries were an expression and extension of the distinctively human capacity for "political action" in general, Strauss insisted that Socrates was engaged in a certain kind of philosophical education.

> If justice is taken in the larger sense according to which it consists in giving to each what is good for his soul, one must distinguish between the cases in which such giving is intrinsically attractive to the giver (these will be the cases of the potential philosophers) and those in which it is merely a duty or compulsory.

If philosophers' overwhelming desire to acquire knowledge were taken into account, it would be clear that no philosophers would choose to spend their time attending to public business and hence, of necessity, give up the leisure necessary to pursue wisdom, their own greatest love. But that does not mean that they would not attempt to help their fellow citizens. "There is no reason why the philosopher should not engage in political activity out of that kind of love of one's own which is patriotism" (Strauss 1964: 128). That is what Socrates did when he went to his fellow citizens in private to reproach them for seeking wealth, honor, and safety rather than truth, prudence, and the good of their souls or when he willingly served the city in war. (See Saxonhouse, this volume, chapter 23.)

Although he understood the peak of human existence differently, Strauss agreed with Arendt in thinking that modern conditions threatened to make the achievement of this peak impossible. The combination of the universal principles characteristic of modern politics with the power of modern technology created the specter of the complete suppression and destruction of philosophy as an open-minded quest for truth by rulers claiming to act on the basis of the "true philosophy," that is, ruling ideology. When governments persecuted dissenters and critics in the past, Strauss observed, philosophers had simply gone underground or left the country. But if a government now acquired universal power and insisted that everyone under it subscribe to its "truth," there would be nowhere to flee. (Strauss 1991: 211). It was essential for the preservation of both human liberty and human dignity, therefore, to preserve a number of different nations with different regimes.

Like Arendt, Strauss thus emphasized the limitations of modern political philosophy and tried to revive an Aristotelian appreciation not only of the difference between theory and practice, but also of the autonomy and dignity of politics. By limiting politics to the preservation of life, liberty, and estate, Strauss argued, modern political philosophers had transformed government into a public means of achieving private, individual ends. The line they attempted to draw between "public" and "private" was not tenable, however. As Aristotle pointed out, the economy, social institutions, and character of individuals living in communities are decisively shaped by the government or "regime."

Modern political philosophy also downplayed, if it did not altogether deny the importance of individual leaders. As James Madison observed in *Federalist #10*, "enlightened statesmen will not always be at the helm." Modern philosophers thought that it would be better, therefore, to rely on institutions than on individuals. Recognizing that laws and institutions did not always have the intended effects, they found it necessary to look at the underlying, often unacknowledged, if not unconscious drives that impel human beings to act as they do. Political acts were thus reduced to reflections or results of subpolitical economic, social or psychological needs. (Cf. Strauss 1968: 203–23; Arendt 1958: 22–78.) In fact, Strauss suggested, it was impossible to explain either the rise of "totalitarian" regimes or the successful resistance by the western democracies in World War II without reference to individual leaders. "The weakness of the Weimar Republic made certain its speedy destruction," he observed, but that weakness "did not make certain the victory of National Socialism":

> The victory of National Socialism became necessary in Germany for the same reason the victory of Communism had become necessary in Russia: the man who had by far the

strongest will or single-mindedness, the greatest ruthlessness, daring, and power over his following, and the best judgment about the strength of the various forces in the immediately relevant political field was the leader of the revolution. (Strauss 1997: 1)

The defense of the liberal democracies had likewise depended upon the practical wisdom of Winston Churchill. One of the ways a philosopher could most help his people, Strauss urged, was to educate other potential political leaders.

In returning to the ancients, Strauss thus attempted to revive not only a Socratic understanding of philosophy, but also an Aristotelian understanding of political science. Whereas modern political philosophers like Hobbes (and the contemporary behavioral social scientists who have followed him) recognized only one kind of science and thus attempted to reform the study of politics so that it would be more like modern physics, Aristotle argued that there were two kinds of science, theoretical and practical or political. And Strauss saw, this "distinction between theoretical and practical sciences implies that human action has principles of its own which are known independently of theoretical science (physics and metaphysics)" (1968: 205–6).

In his *Politics* (1324a13–1325b30), Aristotle concludes that the choice between the life of theory and the life of practice is the most difficult, because the most important, choice a human being can make. By agreeing that their contemporaries needed to be reminded of both the character and importance of a distinctively human form of existence, but disagreeing about whether the highest form is essentially practical or philosophical, Arendt and Strauss revived a sense of the importance and dignity of both for their modern readers. In evident contrast to both Nietzsche and Heidegger, Arendt and Strauss reminded people who still contemn mere "politicians" of the way in which "politics" not merely pervades, but fundamentally determines the character of our common lives. By celebrating Socrates, both Arendt and Strauss showed the way not merely ancient political philosophy, in general, but the deeds and speeches of a historical individual, in particular, continue to inspire modern readers in the twenty-first century.

FURTHER READING

Students wishing to learn more about the way in which Arendt and Strauss attempted to revive ancient political thought should, of course, begin by reading their works. In the case of Arendt, a student should begin with *The Human Condition* (1958) along with her two essays on Socrates published in *Social Research* (Arendt 1984, 1990). Strauss's writings on ancient political philosophy are much more extensive. Students should begin with his essays on "What Is Political Philosophy?" "Classical Political Philosophy," "Classic Natural Right" in Strauss 1989a and 1953. *The City and Man* (1964) contains his most comprehensive statement on ancient political philosophy. Strauss wrote not only on "Farabi's 'Plato' " but also "On the *Minos*" and liberal education in Strauss 1968 as well as essays on ancient political philosophy, reprinted in Strauss 1989b and Strauss 1983. He wrote a book-length study of *Socrates and Aristophanes* (1966) and three books on Xenophon: *On Tyranny* (1991), *Xenophon's Socratic Discourse* (1970), and *Xenophon's Socrates* (1973). Hinchman and Hinchman 1994 provides a useful introduction to the debates among the commentators on Arendt's thought. Discussions of Strauss's "return to the ancients" can be found in S. Smith 2006; Zuckert and Zuckert 2006; and Pangle 2006. Other comparative studies include Kielmansegg, Mewes, and Glaser-Schmit 1995; Beiner 1990; and Villa, "Hannah Arendt and Leo Strauss," in Villa 2001.

NOTES

1 Arendt initially wanted to entitle her major work the *Vita Activa*, to emphasize what she wanted to recover and its traditional opposition to the *vita contemplativa*, but her publisher objected.

2 On the inaccuracy of Arendt's description of the ancient polis and her "flat-footed" readings of Plato, see J. Peter Euben, "Arendt's Hellenism," in Villa 2000: 151–2.

3 Strictly speaking, Socrates says that he does not know "the greatest things." To know that one does not know, one has to know what knowledge is. At *Apology* 29b Socrates states that disobeying a superior is evil, and at 37b he refuses to propose what he knows to be an evil as a penalty, as opposed to death, which he does not know to be good or bad.

4 One problem with Arendt's account of Socrates in this lecture is that, in the only dialogue in which he explicitly characterizes his activity as the "art of midwifery," Socrates shows the young geometer Theaetetus that he does not even know what knowledge is, i.e. that his previous opinions were ungrounded or empty "wind-eggs," not truths. In "Thinking and Moral Considerations" she observed that "nobody among Socrates' interlocutors ... ever brought forth a thought that was no windegg" (1984: 23).

5 Drury (1988) accuses Strauss of using the same tactic.

References

For ancient authors, texts, and editions of fragmentary source material occurring in the chapters, see also the Abbreviations at the front of the volume.

Aalders, G. J. D. 1968. *Die Theorie der gemischten Verfassung im Altertum.* Amsterdam: Hakkert.

Adam, T. 1970. *Clementia Principis.* Stuttgart: E. Klett.

Adams, C. D. (trans.) 1919. *Aeschines.* Cambridge, MA: Harvard University Press.

Adams, F. (trans.) 1849. *The Genuine Works of Hippocrates.* London: Sydenham Society.

Adams, J. 1971. *A Defence of the Constitutions of Government of the United States of America.* 3 vols. New York: Da Capo Press.

Adkins, A. W. H. 1960. *Merit and Responsibility: A Study in Greek Values.* Oxford: Oxford University Press.

Adkins, A. W. H. 1973. "*Aretē, Technē*, Democracy and Sophists: *Protagoras* 316b–328d." *Journal of Hellenic Studies* 93: 3–12.

Adkins, A. W. H. 1975. "The *Aretē* of Nicias: Thucydides 7.86." *Greek, Roman and Byzantine Studies* 16: 379–92.

Adkins, A. W. H. 1976. "*Polupragmosunē* and 'Minding One's Own Business': A Study in Greek Social and Political Values." *Classical Philology* 71: 301–27.

Adkins, A. W. H. 1984. "Classical Greek Political Thought II: The Connection between Aristotle's *Ethics* and *Politics*." *Political Theory* 12: 29–49.

Adkins, A. W. H. 1989. "Plato." In R. J. Cavalier, J. Gouinlock, and J. P. Sterba (eds), *Ethics in the History of Western Philosophy.* Basingstoke: Macmillan.

Agamben, G. 2004. *The Open: Man and Animal.* Stanford: Stanford University Press.

Ager, S. L. 1996. *Interstate Arbitrations in the Greek World, 337–90 BC.* Berkeley: University of California Press.

Ager, S. L. 2003. "An Uneasy Balance: From the Death of Seleukos to the Battle of Raphia." In A. Erskine (ed.), *A Companion to the Hellenistic World*, 35–50. Oxford: Blackwell.

Alcock, Susan, Gates, Jennifer, and Rempel, Jane 2003. "Reading the Landscape: Survey Archaeology and the Hellenistic *Oikoumene*." In A. Erskine (ed.), *A Companion to the Hellenistic World*, 354–72. Oxford: Blackwell.

A Companion to Greek and Roman Political Thought, First Edition. Edited by Ryan K. Balot.
© 2013 Blackwell Publishing Ltd. Published 2013 by Blackwell Publishing Ltd.

Alden, Maureen 2000. *Homer beside Himself: Para-Narratives in the Iliad*. Oxford: Oxford University Press.

Alderman, H. 1982. "By Virtue of a Virtue." *Review of Metaphysics* 36: 127–53.

Alesse, F. 1998. "La repubblica di Zenone di Cizio e la letteratura socratica." *Studi Italiani di Filologia Classica* 16: 17–38.

Allam, S. 1987. "Aspects of Law in Ancient Egypt." *Bulletin of the Center of Papyrological Studies* (Cairo) 4: 9–31.

Allen, D. S. 2000. *The World of Prometheus: The Politics of Punishment in Democratic Athens*. Princeton: Princeton University Press.

Allen, D. S. 2004. *Talking to Strangers: Anxieties of Citizenship since Brown v. Board of Education*. Chicago: University of Chicago Press.

Allen, R. E. 1984. *The Dialogues of Plato*, vol. 1: *Euthyphro, Apology, Crito, Meno, Gorgias, Menexenus*. New Haven, CT: Yale University Press.

Alty, J. 1982. "Dorians and Ionians." *Journal of Hellenic Studies* 102: 1–14.

Ambler, W. 1987. "Aristotle on Nature and Politics: The Case of Slavery." *Political Theory* 15: 390–410.

Anastasiadis, V. 1999. "Political Parties in Athenian Democracy: A Modernising *Topos*." *Arethusa* 32: 313–35.

Anderson, B. 1991. *Imagined Communities: Reflections on the Origin and Spread of Nationalism*. New York: Verso.

Anderson, Elizabeth 2006. "The Epistemology of Democracy." *Episteme: Journal of Social Epistemology* 3: 8–22.

Anderson, G. 2003. *The Athenian Experiment: Building an Imagined Political Community in Ancient Attica, 508–490 BC*. Ann Arbor: University of Michigan Press.

Anderson, G. 2005. "Before Turannoi Were Tyrants: Rethinking a Chapter of Early Greek History." *Classical Antiquity* 24.2: 173–222.

Ando, Clifford 2000. *Imperial Ideology and Provincial Loyalty in the Roman Empire*. Berkeley: University of California Press.

André, J.-M. 1966. *L'otium dans la vie morale et intellectuelle romaine des origins à l'époque Augustéenne*. Paris: Presses Universitaires de France.

Andrewes, A. 1938. "Eunomia." *Classical Quarterly* 32: 89–102.

Andrewes, A. 1982. "The Growth of the Athenian State." In J. Boardman and N. G. L. Hammond (eds), *The Cambridge Ancient History*, vol. 3: 360–91. 2nd edn. Cambridge: Cambridge University Press.

Annas, J. 1993. *The Morality of Happiness*. Oxford: Oxford University Press.

Anscombe, G. E. M. 1958. "Modern Moral Philosophy." *Philosophy* 33: 1–19.

Apfell, H. 1957. "Die Verfassungsdebatte bei Herodot (3.80–82)." Diss., Erlangen. (Repr. New York: Arno Press, 1979.)

Appiah, K. A. 2006. *Cosmopolitanism: Ethics in a World of Strangers*. New York: W. W. Norton.

Arendt, H. 1958. *The Human Condition*. Chicago: University of Chicago Press.

Arendt, H. 1973. *The Origins of Totalitarianism* [1951]. New York: Harcourt, Brace.

Arendt, H. 1984. "Thinking and Moral Considerations: A Lecture." *Social Research* 51.1 (Spring): 7–37. (Originally in *Social Research* 38.3 (1971): 417–46.)

Arendt, H. 1990. "Philosophy and Politics." *Social Research* 57.1: 73–103.

Arendt, H. 1996. *Love and Saint Augustine*. Chicago: University of Chicago Press.

Assmann, J. 1990. *Ma'at: Gerechtigkeit und Unsterblichkeit im Alten Ägypten*. Munich: Beck.

Assmann, J. 1993. "Politisierung durch Polarisierung. Zur impliziten Axiomatik altägyptischer Politik." In Raaflaub and Müller-Luckner 1993: 13–28.

Astin, A. 1988. "*Regimen Morum.*" *Journal of Roman Studies* 78: 14–34.

Atkins, E. M. 1990. "*Domina et Regina Virtutum*: Justice and *Societas* in *De officiis.*" *Phronesis* 35: 258–89.

Atkins, E. M. 2000. "Cicero." In C. Rowe and Schofield 2000: 477–516.

Austin, M. M. 1981. *The Hellenistic World from Alexander to the Roman Conquest: A Selection of Ancient Sources in Translation*. 1st edn. Cambridge: Cambridge University Press.

Austin, M. M. 1986. "Hellenistic Kings, War, and the Economy." *Classical Quarterly* 36: 450–66.

Austin, M. M. 2006. *The Hellenistic World from Alexander to the Roman Conquest: A Selection of Ancient Sources in Translation*. 2nd edn. Cambridge: Cambridge University Press.

Babbitt, Frank Cole (ed. and trans.) 1936. *Plutarch. Moralia*, vol. 4. Cambridge, MA: Harvard University Press.

Babut, D. (ed.) 1969. *Plutarque. De la vertu ethique*. Paris: Belles Lettres.

Badian, E. 1958. *Foreign Clientelae (264–70 BC)*. Oxford: Clarendon Press.

Badian, E. 1968. *Roman Imperialism in the Late Republic*. Oxford: Blackwell.

Badian, E. 1983. "Hegemony and Independence: Prolegomena to a Study of Rome and the Hellenistic States in the Second Century BC." In *Actes du VIIe Congrès de la FEIC*, 397–414. Budapest.

Badian, E. 1990. "The Consuls, 179–49 BC." *Chiron* 20: 371–413.

Badian, E. 1996. "*Tribuni Plebis* and *Res Publica*." In J. Linderski (ed.), *Imperium sine Fine: T. Robert S. Broughton and the Roman Republic*, 187–213. Stuttgart: Franz Steiner.

Balakrishnan, G. (ed.) 2003. *Debating Empire*. London: Verso.

Baldry, H. C. 1965. *The Unity of Mankind in Greek Thought*. Cambridge: Cambridge University Press.

Balot, R. 2001a. *Greed and Injustice in Classical Athens*. Princeton: Princeton University Press.

Balot, R. 2001b. "Pericles' Anatomy of Democratic Courage." *American Journal of Philology* 122.4: 505–25.

Balot, R. 2004. "The Dark Side of Democratic Courage." *Social Research* 71.1: 73–106.

Balot, R. 2006. *Greek Political Thought*. Oxford: Blackwell.

Balot, R. 2008. "Socratic Courage and Athenian Democracy." *Ancient Philosophy* 28.2: 49–69.

Balsdon, J. P. V. D. 1960. "*Auctoritas, Dignitas, Otium.*" *Classical Quarterly* 10: 43–50.

Balsdon, J. P. V. D. 1979. *Romans and Aliens*. Chapel Hill: University of North Carolina Press.

Baltrusch, E. 1989. *Regimen morum: Die Reglementierung des Privatlebens der Senatoren und Ritter in der römischen Republik und frühen Kaiserzeit*. Munich: Beck.

Barber, B. 1984. *Strong Democracy: Participatory Politics for a New Age*. Berkeley: University of California Press.

Barden Dowling, M. 2005. *Clemency and Cruelty in the Roman World*. Ann Arbor: University of Michigan Press.

Barker, E. 1918. *Greek Political Theory: Plato and his Predecessors*. 2nd edn. London: Methuen.

Barker, E. 1946. *The Politics of Aristotle*. Oxford: Oxford University Press.

Bar-Kochva, B. 1976. *The Seleucid Army: Organization and Tactics in the Great Campaigns*. Cambridge: Cambridge University Press.

Barnes, J. (ed.) 1984. *The Complete Works of Aristotle: The Revised Oxford Translation*. 2 vols. Princeton: Princeton University Press.

Barney, D. 2000. *Prometheus Wired: The Hope for Democracy in the Age of Network Technology*. Vancouver: UBC Press.

Barnish, S. J. B. 1994. "Late Roman Prosopography Reassessed." *Journal of Roman Studies* 84: 171–7.

Baron, H. 1955. *The Crisis of the Early Italian Renaissance: Civic Humanism and Republican Liberty in an Age of Classicism and Tyranny.* Princeton: Princeton University Press.

Baron, H. 1968. *From Petrarch to Leonardo Bruni: Studies in Humanistic and Political Literature.* Chicago: University of Chicago Press.

Barta, H. 2006. "Solons *Eunomia* und das Konzept der ägyptischen *Ma'at* – Ein Vergleich. Zu Volker Fadingers Übernahme-These." In Robert Rollinger and Brigitte Truschnegg (eds), *Altertum und Mittelmeerraum: Die antike Welt diesseits und jenseits der Levante. Festschrift für Peter W. Haider,* 409–43. Stuttgart: Steiner.

Barton, C. A. 2001. *Roman Honor: The Fire in the Bones.* Berkeley: University of California Press.

Bartsch, S. 1994. *Actors in the Audience: Theatricality and Doublespeak from Nero to Hadrian.* Cambridge, MA: Harvard University Press.

Basore, John W. (ed. and trans.) 1928. *Seneca. Moral Essays,* vol. 1: *De Providentia. De Constantia. De Ira. De Clementia.* Loeb Classical Library. Cambridge, MA: Harvard University Press.

Bathory, P. 1981. *Political Theory as Public Confession: The Social and Political Thought of St Augustine of Hippo.* New Brunswick, NJ: Transaction.

Bauman, Richard. 1992. *Women and Politics in Ancient Rome.* London: Routledge.

Beard, M. 1990. "Priesthood in the Roman Republic." In Beard and North 1990: 19–48.

Beard, M. and Crawford, M. 1985. *Rome in the Late Republic.* London: Duckworth. (2nd edn 2000.)

Beard, M. and North, J. 1990. *Pagan Priests: Religion and Power in the Ancient World.* London: Duckworth.

Beard, M., North, J., and Price, S. R. F. 1998. *Religions of Rome.* 2 vols. Cambridge: Cambridge University Press.

Bederman, E. 2001. *International Law in Antiquity.* Cambridge: Cambridge University Press.

Beiner, R. 1990. "Hannah Arendt and Leo Strauss: The Uncommenced Dialogue." *Political Theory* 18.2: 238–54.

Beiner, R. 1992. *What's the Matter with Liberalism?* Berkeley: University of California Press.

Beiner, R. (ed.) 1995. *Theorizing Citizenship.* Albany: State University of New York Press.

Bellah, R. N., Madsen, R., Sullivan, W., Swidler, A., and Tipton, S. 1985. *Habits of the Heart: Individualism and Commitment in American Life.* Berkeley: University of California Press.

Benardete, S. 1969. *Herodotean Inquiries.* The Hague: Martinus Nijhoff.

Benardete, S. 1989. *Socrates' Second Sailing.* Chicago: University of Chicago Press.

Benferhat, Y. 2005. *Cives Epicurei: Les épicuriens et l'idée de monarchie à Rome et en Italie de Sylla à Octave.* Brussels: Latomus.

Benjamin, Andrew (ed.) 1988. *Post-structuralist Classics.* London: Routledge.

Benjamin A. S. and Hackstaff L. H. (trans.) 1964. *Augustine: On Free Choice of Will.* Indianapolis: Bobbs-Merrill.

Berent, Moshe 1996. "Hobbes and the 'Greek Tongues.' " *History of Political Thought* 17: 36–59.

Berent, M. 2000a. "Sovereignty: Ancient and Modern." *Polis* 17: 2–34.

Berent, M. 2000b. "Anthropology and the Classics: War, Violence and the Stateless Polis." *Classical Quarterly* 50: 257–89.

Berent, M. 2004. "In Search of the Greek State: A Rejoinder to M. H. Hansen." *Polis* 21:107–46.

Berkowitz, P. 2000. *Virtue and the Making of Modern Liberalism.* Princeton: Princeton University Press.

Berlin, I. 1958. *Four Essays on Liberty.* Oxford: Oxford University Press.

Berlin, I. 2002a. "Two Concepts of Liberty" [1958]. In H. Hardy (ed.), *Liberty*, 166–217. Oxford: Oxford University Press.

Berlin, I. 2002b. "Introduction" [1969]. In H. Hardy (ed.), *Liberty*, 3–54. Oxford: Oxford University Press.

Berlinerblau, J. 1999. *Heresy in the University: The Black Athena Controversy and the Responsibilities of American Intellectuals*. New Brunswick, NJ: Rutgers University Press.

Bernal, M. 1987–2006. *Black Athena: The Afroasiatic Roots of Classical Civilization*. 3 vols. New Brunswick, NJ: Rutgers University Press.

Bernal, M. 1993. "Phoenician Politics and Egyptian Justice in Ancient Greece." In Raaflaub and Müller-Luckner 1993: 241–61.

Bernal, M. 2001. *Black Athena Writes Back: Martin Bernal Responds to His Critics*, ed. D. C. Moore. Durham, NC: Duke University Press.

Berns, W. 2001. *Making Patriots*. Chicago: University of Chicago Press.

Berry, D. H. 1996. *Cicero. Pro P. Sulla Oratio*. Cambridge Classical Texts and Commentaries 30. Cambridge: Cambridge University Press.

Berthelot, K. 2003. *Philanthrôpia Judaica: le débat autour de la "misanthropie" des lois juives dans l'antiquité*. Leiden: Brill = Supplements to the *Journal for the Study of Judaism* 76.

Beston, P. 2000. "Hellenistic Military leadership." In van Wees 2000: 315–35.

Bétant, É. A. 1969. *Lexicon Thucydideum* [1843–7]. 2 vols. Hildesheim: Olms.

Bettenson, H. 1972. *Concerning the City of God against the pagans; a new translation*. Harmondsworth: Penguin.

Bickermann, E. J. 1938. *Institutions des Séleucides*. Paris: Librarie Orientaliste Paul Geuthner.

Bickermann, E. J. 1952. "Origines Gentium." *Classical Philology*, 47: 65–81.

Bilde, P., Engberg-Pedersen, T., Hannestad, L., and Zahle, J. 1996a. *Aspects of Hellenistic Kingship*. Aarhus: Aarhus University Press.

Bilde, P., Engberg-Pedersen, T. Hannestad, L., and Zahle, J. 1996b. "Introduction." In Bilde et al. 1996a: 9–14.

Billerbeck, M. 1996. "The Ideal Cynic from Epictetus to Julian." In R. Bracht Branham and M.-O. Goulet-Cazé (eds), *The Cynics: The Cynic Movement in Antiquity and Its Legacy*, 205–21. Berkeley: University of California Press.

Billows, R. 1995. *Kings and Colonists: Aspects of Macedonian Imperialism*. Leiden: Brill.

Billows, R. 2003. "Cities." In A. Erskine. (ed.), *A Companion to the Hellenistic World*, 196–215. Oxford: Blackwell.

Bintliff, John 1982. "Settlement Patterns, Land Tenure and Social Structure: A Diachronic Model." In C. Renfrew and S. Shennan (eds), *Ranking, Resource, and Exchange: Aspects of the Archaeology of Early European Society*, 106–11. Cambridge: Cambridge University Press.

Blaug, R. and Schwarzmantel, J. (eds) 2001. *Democracy: A Reader*. Edinburgh: Edinburgh University Press.

Bleicken, J. 1990. *Zwischen Republik und Prinzipat: Zum Charakter des zweiten Triumvirats*. Göttingen: Vandenhoeck and Ruprecht.

Bleicken, J. 1994. *Die athenische Demokratie*. 2nd edn. Zurich: Ferdinand Schöningh.

Bloch, E. 2001. "Hemlock Poisoning and the Death of Socrates: Did Plato Tell the Truth?" *Journal of the International Plato Society* (Jan.), at http://gramata.univ-paris1.fr/Plato/article9.html.

Blok, J. M. and Lardinois, A. (eds) 2006. *Solon of Athens: New Historical and Philological Approaches*. Leiden: Brill.

Blondell, R. 2002. *The Play of Character in Plato's Dialogues*. Cambridge: Cambridge University Press.

Bloom, Allan 1968. *The Republic of Plato*. New York: Basic Books.

Blythe, J. M. 1992. *Ideal Government and the Mixed Constitution in the Middle Ages*. Princeton: Princeton University Press.

Bobonich, C. 2002. *Plato's Utopia Recast: His Later Ethics and Politics*. Oxford: Clarendon Press.

Bock, G., Skinner, Q., and Viroli, M. (eds) 1993. *Machiavelli and Republicanism*. Cambridge: Cambridge University Press.

Boedeker, D. and Raaflaub, K. A. (eds) 1998. *Democracy, Empire and the Arts in Fifth-Century Athens*. Cambridge, MA: Harvard University Press.

Boedeker, D. and Raaflaub, K. A. 2005. "Tragedy and City." In Bushnell 2005: 109–27.

Boegehold, A. L. 1994. "Perikles' Citizenship Law of 451/0 BC." In Boegehold and Scafuro 1994: 57–66.

Boegehold, A. L. and Scafuro, A. C. (eds) 1994. *Athenian Identity and Civic Ideology*. Baltimore: Johns Hopkins University Press.

Bonner, Gerald 1994. "Augustine's Understanding of the Church as a Eucharistic Community." In F. LeMoine and C. Kleinhenz (eds), *Saint Augustine the Bishop: A Book of Essays*, 39–64. New York: Garland.

Bottéro, Jean 1992. "The 'Code' of Hammurabi." In J. Bottéro, *Mesopotamia: Writing, Reasoning, and the Gods*, trans. Z. Bahrani and M. van de Mieroop, 156–84. Chicago: University of Chicago Press.

Bourdieu, P. 1970. "The Berber House or the World Reversed." *Social Science Information* 9: 151–70.

Bourdieu, P. 1977. *Outline of a Theory of Practice*, trans. R. Nice. Cambridge: Cambridge University Press.

Bourdieu, P. 1990. *The Logic of Practice*, trans. R. Nice. Stanford: Stanford University Press.

Bourdieu, P. 1991a. "Political Representation: Elements for a Theory of the Political Field." In J. Thompson (ed.), *Language and Symbolic Power*, trans. G. Raymond and M. Adamson, 171–202. Cambridge, MA: Harvard University Press.

Bourdieu, P. 1991b. "Social Space and the Genesis of 'Classes.' " In J. Thompson (ed.), *Language and Symbolic Power*, trans. G. Raymond and M. Adamson, 229–51. Cambridge, MA: Harvard University Press.

Bowie, E. 1998. "Le portrait de Socrate dans les *Nuées* d'Aristophane." In Trédé et al. 1998: 53–66.

Boyle, A. J. 2003. *Ovid and the Monuments: A Poet's Rome*. Bendigo: Aureal.

Boys-Stones, G. 1998. "Eros in Government: Zeno and the Virtuous City." *Classical Quarterly* 48: 168–74.

Bracht Branham, R. (ed.) 2002. *Bakhtin and the Classics*. Evanston, IL: Northwestern University Press.

Brannan, P. 1963. "Herodotus and History: The Constitutional Debate Preceding Darius' Accession." *Tradition* 19: 427–38.

Braund, D. and Gill, C. (eds) 2003. *Myth, History and Culture in Republican Rome: Studies in Honour of T. P. Wiseman*. Exeter: University of Exeter Press.

Braund, S. M. 1998. "Praise and Protreptic in Early Imperial Panegyric: Cicero, Seneca, Pliny." In M. Whitby (ed.), *The Propaganda of Power: The Role of Panegyric in Late Antiquity*, 53–76. Leiden: Brill.

Braund, S. M. forthcoming. *Seneca. De Clementia*. Oxford: Oxford University Press.

Braund, S. M. and Most, G. (eds) 2004. *Ancient Anger: Perspectives from Homer to Galen*. Cambridge: Cambridge University Press.

Braunert, H. 1964. "Hegemoniale Bestrebungen der hellenistische Grossmächte in Politik und Wirtschaft." *Historia* 13: 80–104.

Bremmer J. (ed.) 1987. *Interpretations of Greek Mythology.* London: Croom Helm.

Bremmer, J. 1994. *Greek Religion: Greece and Rome.* New Surveys in the Classics 24. 2nd edn. Oxford: Oxford University Press.

Bremmer, J. 1999. *Greek Religion: Greece and Rome.* Repr. with addenda. Oxford: Oxford University Press

Bremmer, J. and Horsfall, N. M. 1987. *Roman Myth and Mythography.* London: Institute of Classical Studies.

Brennan, G. and Pettit, P. 2004. *The Economy of Esteem: An Essay on Civil and Political Society.* New York: Oxford University Press.

Brett, A. 1997. *Liberty, Right and Nature: Individual Rights in Later Scholastic Thought.* Cambridge: Cambridge University Press.

Brett, A. 2003. "The Development of the Idea of Citizens' Rights." In Q. Skinner and B. Strath (eds), *States and Citizens: History, Theory, Prospects*, 97–112. Cambridge: Cambridge University Press.

Breuer, Stefan 1985. "Stromuferkultur und Küstenkultur Geographische und ökologische Faktoren in Max Webers 'ökonomischer Theorie der antiken Staatenwelt.' " In W. Schluchter (ed.), *Max Webers Sicht des antiken Christentums: Interpretation und Kritik*, 111–50. Frankfurt am Main: Suhrkamp.

Breyfogle, Todd 2005. "Toward a Contemporary Augustinian Understanding of Politics." In Doody, Hughes, and Paffenroth 2005: 217–36.

Briant, P. 2002. *From Cyrus to Alexander: A History of the Persian Empire*, trans. P. T. Daniels. Winona Lake, IN: Eisenbrauns.

Brickhouse, T. C. and Smith, N. D. 1989. *Socrates on Trial.* Princeton: Princeton University Press.

Brickhouse, T. C. and Smith, N. D. 1994. *Plato's Socrates.* New York: Oxford University Press.

Brickhouse, T. C. and Smith, N. D. (eds) 2002. *The Trial and Execution of Socrates: Sources and Controversies.* Oxford: Oxford University Press.

Broadie, S. 1991. *Ethics with Aristotle.* Oxford: Oxford University Press.

Brock, R. 1991. "The Emergence of Democratic Ideology." *Historia* 40: 160–9.

Brock, R. and Hodkinson, S. (eds) 2000. *Alternatives to Athens: Varieties of Political Organisation and Community in Ancient Greece.* Oxford: Oxford University Press. (Corrected repr. 2002.)

Broughton, T. Robert 1972. "Senate and Senators of the Roman Republic: The Prosopographical Approach." In H. Temporini (ed.), *Aufstieg und Niedergang der römischen Welt*, 1.1, 250–65. Berlin: Walter de Gruyter.

Brown, E. 2000a. "Justice and Compulsion for Plato's Philosopher-Rulers." *Ancient Philosophy* 20: 1–17.

Brown, E. 2000b. "Socrates the Cosmopolitan." *Stanford Agora: An Online Journal of Legal Perspectives* 1: 74–87. At http://agora.stanford.edu/agora/libArticles/brown/brown.pdf.

Brown, E. 2004. "Minding the Gap in Plato's *Republic*." *Philosophical Studies* 117: 275–302.

Brown, E. 2006. "Hellenistic Cosmopolitanism." In M. L. Gill and P. Pellegrin (eds), *A Companion to Ancient Philosophy*, 549–58. Oxford: Blackwell.

Brown, E. forthcoming a. "Aristotle on the Choice of Lives: Two Concepts of Self-Sufficiency." In P. Destrée (ed.), *Quel choix de vie? Études sur les rapports entre theôria et praxis chez Aristote.* Louvain: Peeters.

Brown, E. forthcoming b. "Politics and Society." In J. Warren (ed.), *The Cambridge Companion to Epicureanism*. Cambridge: Cambridge University Press.

Brown, E. forthcoming c. *Stoic Cosmopolitanism*. Cambridge: Cambridge University Press.

Brown, Peter 1972. "Political Society." In Markus 1972: 311–35.

Brown, Peter 2000. *Augustine of Hippo: A Biography* [1967]. Rev. edn. Berkeley: University of California Press.

Brown, T. S. 1949. *Onesicratus: A Study in Hellenistic Historiography*. Berkeley: University of California Press.

Brunt, P. A. 1966. "Athenian Settlements Abroad in the Fifth Century BC." In E. Badian (ed.), *Ancient Society and Institutions*, 71–92. Oxford: Oxford University Press.

Brunt, P. A. 1971. *Social Conflicts in the Roman Republic*. London: Chatto and Windus.

Brunt, P. A. 1974. "Marcus Aurelius in his *Meditations*." *Journal of Roman Studies* 64: 1–20.

Brunt, P. A. 1988a. *The Fall of the Roman Republic and Related Essays*. Oxford: Clarendon Press.

Brunt, P. A. 1988b. "*Libertas* in the Republic." In Brunt 1988a: 281–350.

Brunt, P. A. 1993. "Athenian Settlements Abroad in the Fifth Century BC." In P. A. Brunt (ed.), *Studies in Greek History and Thought*, 112–36. Oxford: Oxford University Press. (Rev. from original publication in 1966.)

Brunt, P. A. 2004. "*Laus Imperii*." In Champion 2004b: 163–85.

Bryce, J. 1921. *Modern Democracies*. 2 vols. London: Macmillan.

Bultrighini, U. (ed.) 2005. *Democrazia e antidemocrazia nel mondo Greco. Atti del convegno internazionale di studi, Chieti 9–11 aprile 2003*. Alessandria: Edizioni dell'Orso.

Burckhardt, Leonhard, Seybold, Klaus, and von Ungern-Sternberg, Jürgen (eds) 2007. *Gesetzgebung in antiken Gesellschaften (Israel, Griechenland, Rom)*. Berlin: De Gruyter.

Burke, Edmund 1992. "The Economy of Athens in the Classical Era: Some Adjustments to the Primitivist Model." *TAPA* 122: 199–226.

Burkert, W. 1979. *Structure and History in Greek Mythology and Ritual*. Berkeley: University of California Press.

Burkert, W. 1992. *The Orientalizing Revolution: Near Eastern Influence on Greek Culture in the Early Archaic Age*. Cambridge, MA: Harvard University Press.

Burkert. W. 2004. *Babylon – Memphis – Persepolis: Eastern Contexts of Greek Culture*. Cambridge, MA: Harvard University Press.

Burnaby, John 1991. *Amor Dei: A Study of the Religion of St Augustine*. The Hulsean Lectures for 1938. Norwich, Norfolk: Canterbury Press.

Burnell, Peter 1992. "The Status of Politics in St Augustine's *City of God*." *History of Political Thought* 13.1: 13–29.

Burnell, Peter 1993. "The Problem of Service to Unjust Regimes in Augustine's *City of God*." *Journal of the History of Ideas* 54.2: 177–88.

Burnell, Peter 2005. *The Augustinian Person*. Washington, DC: Catholic University of America Press.

Burnyeat, M. F. 1980. "Aristotle on Learning to be Good." In A. O. Rorty (ed.), *Essays on Aristotle's Ethics*, 69–92. Berkeley: University of California Press.

Burnyeat, M. F. 1987. "Cracking the Socrates Case." *New York Review of Books*, Mar. 31.

Burnyeat, M. F. 1997. "The Impiety of Socrates." *Ancient Philosophy* 17: 1–12.

Burton, A. 1972. *Diodorus Siculus Book I: A Commentary*. Leiden: Brill.

Bury, R. G. (trans.) 1967–8. *Plato. Laws*. Cambridge, MA: Harvard University Press.

Bury, R. G. (trans.). 2005. *Plato. Timaeus, Critias, Cleitophon, Menexenus, Epistles*. Loeb Classical Library. Cambridge, MA: Harvard University Press.

Bushnell, R. (ed.) 2005. *A Companion to Tragedy*. Oxford: Blackwell.

Butler, D. and Ranney, A. 1994. *Referendums around the World: The Growing Use of Direct Democracy.* Basingstoke: Macmillan.

Cairns, D. 1993. *AIDOS: The Psychology and Ethics of Honour and Shame in Ancient Greek Literature.* Oxford: Clarendon.

Cairns, D. and Liapis, V. (eds) 2006. *Dionysalexandros: Essays on Aeschylus and His Fellow Tragedians in Honour of Alexander F. Garvie.* Swansea: Classical Press of Wales.

Calame, Claude 2005. *Masks of Authority: Fiction and Pragmatics in Ancient Greek Poetics*, trans. Peter Burk. Ithaca, NY: Cornell University Press.

Camassa, Giorgio 1994. "Verschriftung und Veränderung der Gesetze." In Gehrke 1994: 97–111.

Cameron, A. 1991. *Christianity and the Rhetoric of Empire: The Development of Christian Discourse.* Berkeley: University of California Press.

Camp, J. M. 1992. *The Athenian Agora: Excavations in the Heart of Classical Athens.* Corrected edn. London: Thames and Hudson.

Campbell, D. A. 1982. *Greek Lyric Poetry.* Bristol: Bristol Classical Press.

Carandini, Andrea 1988. *Schiavi in Italia: Gli strumenti pensanti dei Romani fra tarda Repubblica e medio Impero.* Rome: La Nuova Italia Scientifica.

Carney, T. F. 1973. "Prosopography: Payoffs and Pitfalls." *Phoenix* 27: 156–79.

Carter, D. M. 2004. "Was Attic Tragedy Democratic?" *Polis* 21: 1–25.

Carter, D. M. 2007. *The Politics of Greek Tragedy.* Exeter: Bristol Phoenix Press.

Carter, L. B. 1986. *The Quiet Athenian.* Oxford: Clarendon Press.

Cartledge, P. A. 1975. "Toward the Spartan Revolution." *Arethusa* 8: 59–84.

Cartledge, P. A. 1981. "The Politics of Spartan Pederasty." In *Proceedings of the Cambridge Philological Society* 207: 17–36.

Cartledge, P. A. 1999. "Democratic Politics Ancient and Modern: From Cleisthenes to Mary Robinson." *Hermathena* 166: 5–29.

Cartledge, P. A. 2000. "The Historical Context." In C. Rowe and Schofield 2000: 11–22.

Cartledge, P. A. 2001. *Spartan Reflections.* London: Duckworth.

Cartledge, P. A. 2002a. *The Greeks: A Portrait of Self and Others.* 2nd edn. Oxford: Oxford University Press.

Cartledge, P. A. 2002b. *Sparta and Lakonia: A Regional History 1300–362* BC. 2nd edn. London: Routledge.

Centrone, B. 1990. *Pseudopythagorica ethica. I trattati morali di Archita, Metopo, Teage, Eurifamo. Introduzione, edizione, traduzione e commento.* Naples: Bibliopolis.

Chadwick, Henry (trans.) 1991. *Confessions / Saint Augustine.* Oxford: Oxford University Press.

Champion, C. B. 1997. "Review of *Contra Arma Verbis: Der Redner vor dem Volk in der später römischen Republik* by F. Pina Polo." *Bryn Mawr Classical Review*, 97.3.6, online journal. At http://ccat.sas.upenn.edu/bmcr/.

Champion, C. B. 2004a. *Cultural Politics in Polybius's Histories.* Berkeley: University of California Press.

Champion, C. B. (ed.) 2004b. *Roman Imperialism: Readings and Sources.* Oxford: Blackwell.

Champion, C. B. and Eckstein, A. M. 2004. "Introduction: The Study of Roman Imperialism." In Champion 2004b: 1–10.

Chaniotis, A. 2005. *War in the Hellenistic World: A Social and Cultural History.* Oxford: Blackwell.

Chaplin, Jane 2000. *Livy's Exemplary History.* Oxford: Oxford University Press.

Chappell, T. 2006. "Bernard Williams." In *The Stanford Encyclopedia of Philosophy.* At http://plato.stanford.edu/contents.html.

Charpin, D. 2005. "Le statut des 'codes de lois' des souverains babyloniens." In P. Sineux (ed.), *Le législateur et la loi dans l'Antiquité. Hommage à Françoise Ruzé*, 93–107. Caen: Presses Universitaires.

Chilcote, R. H. (ed.) 2000. *Imperialism: Theoretical Directions*. Amherst, NY: Humanity Books.

Christ, M. R. 2006. *The Bad Citizen in Classical Athens*. Cambridge: Cambridge University Press.

Church, A. J. and Brodribb, W. J. (trans.) 1942. *Tacitus. The Complete Works*, ed. M. Hadas. New York: Modern Library, 1942.

Clay, D. 1983. "Individual and Community in the First Generation of the Epicurean School." In *Syzetesis: Studi sull'epicureismo greco e romano offerti a Marcello Gigante*, vol. 1: 255–79. Naples: Bibliopolis.

Clay, D. 2000. *Platonic Questions: Dialogues with the Silent Philosopher*. University Park: Pennsylvania State University Press.

Cohen, D. 1989. "Seclusion, Separation, and the Status of Women in Classical Athens." *Greece and Rome* 36: 3–15.

Cohen, D. 1991. *Law, Sexuality, and Society: The Enforcement of Morals in Classical Athens*. Cambridge: Cambridge University Press.

Cohen, D. 1993. "Law, Autonomy and Political Community in Plato's *Laws*." *Classical Philology* 88: 301–18.

Cohen, D. 1995. *Law, Violence and Community in Classical Athens*. Cambridge: Cambridge University Press.

Cohen, E. E. 1992. *Athenian Economy and Society: A Banking Perspective*. Princeton: Princeton University Press.

Cohen, E. E. 2000. " 'Whoring Under Contract': The Legal Context of Prostitution in Fourth-Century Athens." In V. Hunter and J. Edmondson (eds), *Law and Social Status in Classical Athens*, 113–47. Oxford: Oxford University Press.

Cohler, Anne 1989. *Montesquieu. The Spirit of the Laws*. Cambridge: Cambridge University Press.

Cole, E. 1988–9. "*Autarkeia* in Aristotle." *University of Dayton Review* 19: 35–42.

Coleridge, E. P. (trans.) 1938. *Euripides. The Suppliants*. In W. J. Oates and E. O'Neill, Jr (eds), *The Complete Greek Drama*. New York: Random House.

Collins, S. 2006. *Aristotle and the Rediscovery of Citizenship*. Cambridge: Cambridge University Press.

Connolly, J. 2007a. "Political thought." In A. Barchiesi and W. Scheidel (eds), *The Oxford Handbook of Roman Studies*. Oxford: Oxford University Press.

Connolly, J. 2007b. *The State of Speech: Rhetoric and Political Thought in Ancient Rome*. Princeton: Princeton University Press.

Connor, W. R. 1968. *Theopompus and Fifth-Century Athens*. Cambridge, MA: Harvard University Press.

Connor, W. R. 1971. *The New Politicians of Fifth-Century Athens*. Princeton: Princeton University Press.

Connor, W. R. 1977. "Tyrannis Polis." In J. H. D'Arms and J. W. Eadie (eds), *Ancient and Modern: Essays in Honor of Gerald F. Else*, 95–109. Ann Arbor: University of Michigan.

Connor, W. R. 1987. "Tribes, Festivals and Processions: Civic Ceremonial and Political Manipulation in Archaic Greece." *Journal of Hellenic Studies* 107: 40–50.

Connor, W. R. 1989. "City Dionysia and Athenian Democracy." *Classica et Mediaevalia* 40: 7–32.

Connor, W. R. 1996. "Festivals and Athenian Democracy." In M. Sakellariou (ed.), *Colloque International Démocratie Athénienne et Culture*, 79–89. Athens: Academy of Athens.

Consolo Langher, S. 2005. "Democrazia e antidemocrazia a Siracusa: isotes e ges anadasmos nelle lotte sociali del IV secolo." In Bultrighini 2005: 235–50.

Constant, B. 1988. "The Liberty of the Ancients Compared with That of the Moderns" [1819]. In B. Fontana (ed.), *Constant: Political Writings*, 309–28. Cambridge: Cambridge University Press.

Cooper, J. 1975. *Reason and Human Good in Aristotle*. Cambridge, MA: Harvard University Press.

Cooper, J. 1990. "Political Animals and Civic Friendship." In Patzig 1990: 220–41.

Cooper, J. M. 1997a. "Introduction." In Cooper 1997b: vii–xxvi.

Cooper, J. M. (ed.) 1997b. *Plato: Complete Works*. Associate ed. D. S. Hutchinson. Indianapolis: Hackett.

Cooper, J. M. (reviser) 2002. *Plato. Five Dialogues: Euthyphro, Apology, Crito, Meno, Phaedo*, trans. G. M. A. Grube. 2nd edn, rev. J. M. Cooper. Indianapolis: Hackett.

Corbier, Mireille 1995. "Male Power and Legitimacy through Women: The *Domus Augustus* under the Julio-Claudians." In R. Hawley and B. Levick (eds), *Women in Antiquity*, 178–93. London: Routledge.

Cornell, T. J. 1993. "The End of Roman Imperial Expansion." In J. Rich and G. Shipley (eds), *War and Society in the Roman World*, 139–70. London: Routledge.

Cornell, T. J. 1995. *The Beginnings of Rome: Italy and Rome from the Bronze Age to the Punic Wars (c. 1000–264 BC)*. London: Routledge.

Cotton, H. 1984. "The Concept of *Indulgentia* under Trajan." *Chiron* 14: 245–66.

Cox, Cheryl Anne 1998. *Household Interests: Property, Marriage Strategies, and Family Dynamics in Ancient Athens*. Princeton: Princeton University Press.

Cox, P. 1983. *Biography in Late Antiquity: A Quest for the Holy Man*. Berkeley: University of California Press.

Cranz, F. E. 1972a. "The Development of Augustine's Ideas on Society before the Donatist Controversy." In Markus 1972: 336–403.

Cranz, F. E. 1972b. "*De Civitate Dei*, XV, 2, and Augustine's Idea of the Christian Society." In Markus 1972: 404–21.

Crawford, M. H. (ed.) 1996. *Roman Statutes*. 2 vols. London: Institute of Classical Studies.

Crawley, Richard (trans.) 1982. *Thucydides. History of the Peloponnesian War*. Revised; introd. T. E. Wick. New York: Modern Library/Random House.

Crifò, G. 1972. "Le legge delle XII tavole. Osservazioni e problemi." In Hildegard Temporini (ed.), *Aufstieg und Niedergang der römischen Welt* I.2, 115–33. Berlin: De Gruyter.

Croally, N. T. 1994. *Euripidean Polemic: The Trojan Women and the Function of Tragedy*. Cambridge: Cambridge University Press.

Croally, N. T. 2005. "Tragedy's Teaching." In J. Gregory 2005: 55–70.

Crook, John 1967. *Law and Life of Rome*. Ithaca, NY: Cornell University Press.

Csapo, E. and Slater, W. J. 1994. *The Context of Ancient Drama*. Ann Arbor: University of Michigan Press.

Cureton, W. (ed. and trans.) 1855. *Spicilegium Syriacum: Containing Remains of Bardesan, Meliton, Ambrose and Mara Bar Serapion*. London: F. and J. Rivington.

Dagger, R. 1997. *Civic Virtues: Rights, Citizenship, and Republican Liberalism*. New York: Oxford University Press.

Dahl, R. A. 1971. *Polyarchy: Participation and Opposition*. New Haven: Yale University Press.

Dahl, R. A. 1989. *Democracy and Its Critics*. New Haven: Yale University Press.

Dahl, R. A. and Tufte, E. R. 1973. *Size and Democracy*. Stanford: Stanford University Press.

Dalby, A. 1992. "Greeks Abroad: Social Organisation and Food among the Ten Thousand." *Journal of Hellenic Studies* 92: 16–30.

Dante Alighieri 1931. *The Divine Comedy*, trans. H. F. Cary. New York: E. P. Dutton.

Danzig, G. 2003. "Apologizing for Socrates: Plato and Xenophon on Socrates' Behavior in Court." *Transactions of the American Philological Association* 133: 281–321.

Davidson, D. 2001. "Three Varieties of Knowledge" [1991]. In D. Davidson, *Subjective, Intersubjective, Objective*, 205–20. Oxford: Oxford University Press.

Davidson, James 1997. *Courtesans and Fishcakes: The Consuming Passions of Classical Athens*. New York: St Martin's Press.

Davidson, J. 2001. "Dover, Foucault and Greek Homosexuality: Penetration and the Truth of Sex." *Past and Present* 170: 3–51. (Repr. in Osborne 2004a: 78–118.)

Davidson, J. et al. (eds) 2006. *Greek Drama III: Essays in Honour of Kevin Lee*. London: Institute of Classical Studies.

Davies, J. K. 1971. *Athenian Propertied Families, 600–300 BC*. Oxford: Clarendon Press.

Davies, J. K. 2004. "Athenian Citizenship: The Descent Group and the Alternatives." In Rhodes 2004: 18–39 (edited version). (Originally in *Classical Journal* 73 (1977–8): 105–21.)

Deane, H. A. 1963. *The Political and Social Ideas of St Augustine*. New York: Columbia University Press.

De Blois, Lukas, Erdkamp, Paul, Hekster, Olivier, de Kleijn, Gerda, and Mols, Stephan (eds) 2003. *The Representation and Perception of Roman Imperial Power*. Amsterdam: J. C. Gieben.

Deininger, Jürgen 1985. "Die politischen Strukturen des mittelmeerisch-verderorientalischen Altertums in Max Webers Sicht." In W. Schluchter (ed.), *Max Webers Sicht des antiken Christentums. Interpretation und Kritik*, 72–110. Frankfurt am Main: Suhrkamp.

Deininger, Jürgen 1989. "Die antike Stadt als Typus bei Max Weber." In W. Dahlheim, W. Schuller, and J. von Ungern-Sternberg (eds), *Festschrift Robert Werner zu seinem 65. Geburtstag dargebracht von Freunden, Kollegen und Schülern*, 269–89. Konstanz: Universitätsverlag Konstanz.

De Jong, Irene J. F. and Sullivan, J. P. (eds) 1994. *Modern Critical Theory and Classical Literature*. Leiden: Brill.

De Laix, Roger Alain 1973. *Probouleusis at Athens: A Study of Political Decision-Making*. Berkeley: University of California Press.

Delaney, D. K. 1996. "The Sevenfold Vengeance of Cain." Diss., University of Virginia.

Delatte, L. 1942. *Les Traités de la Royauté d'Ecphante, Diotogène et Sthenidas*. Paris: E. Droz.

Demont, P. 1990. *La Cité grecque archaïque et classique et l'idéal de tranquillité*. Paris: Belles Lettres.

Dench, E. 1995. *From Barbarians to New Men: Greek, Roman and Modern Perceptions of Peoples from the Central Apennines*. Oxford: Oxford University Press.

Dench, E. 2005. *Romulus' Asylum: Roman Identities from the Age of Alexander to the Age of Hadrian*. New York: Oxford University Press.

Denyer, N. 1991. *Language, Thought and Falsehood in Ancient Greek Philosophy*. London: Routledge.

Depew, D. 1991. "Politics, Music, and Contemplation in Aristotle's Ideal State." In Keyt and Miller 1991: 346–80.

Depew, D. 1995. "Humans and Other Political Animals." *Phronesis* 40: 156–81.

de Romilly, J. 1968. "Guerre et paix entre cités." In Vernant 1968: 207–20.

Derow, P. S. 1989. "Rome, the Fall of Macedon, and the Sack of Corinth." In *The Cambridge Ancient History*, vol. 8: 290–323. 2nd edn. Cambridge: Cambridge University Press.

Derrida, J. 1997. *The Politics of Friendship*, trans. G. Collins. London: Verso.

De Ste Croix, G. E. M. 1972. *The Origins of the Peloponnesian War.* London: Duckworth.

De Ste Croix, G. E. M. 1981. *The Class Struggle in the Ancient Greek World.* London: Duckworth.

De Ste Croix, G. E. M. 2004. *Athenian Democratic Origins and Other Essays*, ed. D. Harvey and R. Parker. Oxford: Oxford University Press.

De Sélincourt, Aubrey and Marincola, John (trans.) 1996. *Herodotus. The Histories.* New edn. Harmondsworth: Penguin.

Desideri, P. 1978. *Dione de Prusa. Un'intellettuale greco nell'impero romano.* Messina: G. D'Anna.

De Souza, P. 1999. *Piracy in the Graeco-Roman World.* Cambridge: Cambridge University Press.

Detel, Wolfgang 2005. *Foucault and Classical Antiquity: Power, Ethics and Knowledge*, trans. D. Wigg-Wolf. Cambridge: Cambridge University Press.

Detienne, Marcel 1977. *The Gardens of Adonis: Spices in Greek Mythology*, trans. J. Lloyd. Baltimore: Johns Hopkins University Press.

Detienne, M. 2007. *The Greeks and Us: A Comparative Anthropology of Ancient Greece*, trans. J. Lloyd. Cambridge: Polity.

Dewald. C. 2003. "Form and Content: The Question of Tyranny in Herodotus." In Morgan 2003: 25–58.

Diamond, L. 2002. "Thinking about Hybrid Regimes." *Journal of Democracy* 13: 21–35.

Diamond, L. and Morlino, L. (eds) 2005. *Assessing the Quality of Democracy.* Baltimore: Johns Hopkins University Press.

Diamond, M. 1977. "Ethics and Politics: The American Way." In Robert H. Horwitz (ed.), *The Moral Foundations of the American Republic*, 39–72. Charlottesville: University of Virginia Press.

Dickinson, Oliver. 1994. *The Aegean Bronze Age.* Cambridge: Cambridge University Press.

Dienelt, K. 1953. "*Apragmosyne.*" *Wiener Studien* 66: 94–104.

Dignas, B. C. 2002. *Economy of the Sacred in Hellenistic and Roman Asia Minor.* Oxford: Oxford University Press.

Diller, Hans 1956. "Der vorphilosophische Gebrauch von *kosmos* und *kosmein.*" In *Festschrift Bruno Snell zum 60. Geburtstag … überreicht*, 47–60. Munich: Beck. (Repr. in Diller, *Kleine Schriften zur antiken Literatur*, ed. H.-J. Newiger and H. Seyffert, 73–87. Munich: Beck, 1971.)

Dillery, John 1998. "Hecataeus of Abdera: Hyperboreans, Egypt, and the *Interpretatio Graeca.*" *Historia* 47: 255–75.

Dobrov, G. W. (ed.) 1997. *The City as Comedy: Society and Representation in Athenian Drama.* Chapel Hill: University of North Carolina Press.

Dodaro, Robert 2004. *Christ and the Just Society in the Thought of Augustine.* Cambridge: Cambridge University Press.

Dodds, E. R. 1959. *Plato. Gorgias.* Oxford: Clarendon Press. (Repr. 1979.)

Dods, Marcus (trans.) 2000. *The City of God / Augustine.* New York: Random House.

Donlan, Walter 1989. "The Pre-state Community in Greece," *Symbolae Osloenses* 64: 5–29.

Donlan, Walter 1993. "Duelling with Gifts in the *Iliad*: As the Audience Saw It." *Colby Quarterly* 29: 155–72.

Donlan, Walter 1997. "The Relations of Power in the Pre-state and Early State Polities." In L. Mitchell and P. J. Rhodes (eds), *The Development of the Polis in Archaic Greece*, 39–48. London: Routledge.

Donnelly, J. 1999. "Human Rights and Asian Values: A Defense of 'Western' Universalism." In J. R. Bauer and D. A. Bell (eds), *The East Asian Challenge to Human Rights*, 60–87. Cambridge: Cambridge University Press.

Doody, John, Hughes, Kevin L., and Paffenroth, Kim (eds) 2005. *Augustine and Politics.* Lanham, MD.: Lexington Books.

Dörner, F. K. 1967. "Zur Rekonstruktion der Ahnengalerie des Königs Antiochos I. von Kommagene." *IM* 17: 195–210.

Dougherty, Carol 1993. *The Poetics of Colonization: From City to Text in Ancient Greece.* New York: Oxford University Press.

Dougherty, C. and Kurke, L. (eds) 1993. *Cultural Poetics in Archaic Greece: Cult, Performance, Politics.* Cambridge: Cambridge University Press.

Dougherty, Carol and Kurke, Leslie 1998. "Introduction." In C. Dougherty and L. Kurke (eds), *Cultural Poetics in Archaic Greece: Cult, Performance, Politics,* 1–12. Repr. edn. Oxford: Oxford University Press.

Douglass, R. B., Mara, G. M., and Richardson, H. S. (eds) 1990. *Liberalism and the Good.* New York: Routledge.

Dover, K. J. 1968. *Aristophanes: Clouds.* Oxford: Clarendon Press.

Dover, K. J. 1974. *Greek Popular Morality in the Time of Plato and Aristotle.* Oxford: Blackwell.

Dow, S. 2004. "Aristotle, the Kleroteria, and the Courts." In Rhodes 2004: 62–94.

Doyle, M. W. 1986. *Empires.* Ithaca, NY: Cornell University Press.

Driver, G. R. and Miles, J. C. (eds) 1952. *The Babylonian Laws,* with translation and commentary. Vol. 1. Oxford: Clarendon Press.

Driver, G. R. and Miles, J. C. (eds) 1955. *The Babylonian Laws,* with translation and commentary. Vol. 2. Oxford: Clarendon Press.

Droysen, J. G. 1878. *Geschichte des Hellenismus,* vol. 3: *Geschichte der Epigonen.* 2nd edn. Gotha.

Drummond, A. 1995. *Law, Politics and Power: Sallust and the Execution of the Catilinarian Conspirators.* Hermes Einzelschriften 93. Stuttgart: F. Steiner.

Drury, S. 1988. *The Political Ideas of Leo Strauss.* New York: St Martin's Press.

Dryden, J. (trans.) 1947. *Plutarch. The Lives of the Noble Grecians and Romans,* trans. revised A. H. Clough. New York: Modern Library.

Ducat, J. 1990. *Les Hilotes.* Athens: École Française d'Athènes.

Due, B. 1990. *The Cyropaedia: A Study of Xenophon's Aims and Methods.* Aarhus: Aarhus University Press.

Duff, T. 1999. *Plutarch's Lives. Exploring Virtue and Vice.* Oxford: Oxford University Press.

Dunbar, N. 1995. *Aristophanes. Birds.* Oxford: Oxford University Press.

Dunn, J. 2005. *Setting the People Free: The Story of Democracy.* London: Atlantic.

Durry, M. 1938. *Panegyrique de Trajan.* Paris: Belles Lettres.

Dworkin, R. 1984. "Rights as Trumps." In J. Waldron (ed.), *Theories of Rights,* 153–67. Oxford: Oxford University Press.

Dworkin, R. 1987. *Taking Rights Seriously.* New edn. London: Duckworth.

Dyck, A. R. 1998. "Narrative Obfuscation, Philosophical *Topoi,* and Tragic Patterning in Cicero's *Pro Milone.*" *Harvard Studies in Classical Philology* 98: 219–41.

Dyson, R. W. (trans.) 1998. *Augustine: The City of God against the Pagans.* Cambridge: Cambridge University Press.

Earl, D. C. 1961. *The Political Thought of Sallust.* Cambridge: Cambridge University Press.

Earl, D. C. 1967. *The Moral and Political Tradition of Rome.* London: Thames and Hudson.

Easterling, P. E. 1994. "Euripides outside Athens: A Speculative Note." *Illinois Classical Studies* 19: 73–80.

Easterling, P. E. (ed.) 1997. *The Cambridge Companion to Greek Tragedy.* Cambridge: Cambridge University Press.

Eck, Werner 1984. "Senatorial Self-Representation: Developments in the Augustan Period." In F. Millar and E. Segal (eds), *Caesar Augustus: Seven Aspects,* 129–67. Oxford: Clarendon Press.

Eckstein, A. M. 1995. *Moral Vision in the Histories of Polybius.* Berkeley: University of California Press.

Eckstein, A. M. 2005. "The Pact between the Kings, Polybius 15 20 6, and Polybius' View of the Outbreak of the Second Macedonian War." *Classical Philology* 100: 228–42.

Eckstein, A. M. 2006. *Mediterranean Anarchy, Interstate War, and the Rise of Rome.* Berkeley: University of California Press.

Eckstein, A. M. 2008. *Rome Enters the Greek East: From Anarchy to Hierarchy in the Hellenistic Mediterranean, 230–170 BC.* Oxford: Blackwell.

Eder, Walter 1986. "The Political Significance of the Codification of Law in Archaic Societies: An Unconventional Hypothesis." In K. A. Raaflaub (ed.), *Social Struggles in Archaic Rome: New Perspectives on the Conflict of the Orders,* 262–300. Berkeley: University of California Press.

Eder, Walter 1991. "Who Rules? Power and Participation in Athens and Rome." In Molho, Raaflaub, and Emlen 1991: 169–96.

Eder, Walter 1992. "Polis und Politai: Die Auflösung des Adelsstaates und die Entwicklung des Polisbürgers." In W.-D. Heilmeyer and I. Wehgartner (eds), *Euphronios und seine Zeit,* 24–38. Berlin: Staatliche Museen.

Edge, M. 2006. "The Road to Modern Liberty: Freedom and Democracy Athenian and Modern." Ph.D. thesis., University of Cambridge.

Edge, M. forthcoming. "Athens and the Spectrum of Liberty."

Edwards, Catharine 1993. *The Politics of Immorality in Ancient Rome.* Cambridge: Cambridge University Press.

Edwards, Catharine 1997. "Self-Scrutiny and Self-Transformation in Seneca's Letters." *Greece and Rome* 44: 23–38.

Ehrenberg, V. 1947. "Polypragmosyne: A Study in Greek Politics." *Journal of Hellenic Studies* 67: 46–67.

Ehrenberg, V. 1950. "Origins of Democracy." *Historia* 1: 515–48.

Ehrenberg, V. 1965. "Eunomia." In K. F. Stroheker and A. J. Graham (eds), *Polis und Imperium,* 139–58. Zurich and Stuttgart: Artemis.

Ehrenberg, V. 1967. *From Solon to Socrates: Greek History and Civilization during the 6th and 5th centuries BC.* London: Methuen.

Eliot, T. S. 1968. *Four Quartets.* San Diego: Harcourt.

Elshtain, Jean Bethke 1995. *Augustine and the Limits of Politics.* Notre Dame, IN: University of Notre Dame Press.

Elster, J. 1979. *Ulysses and the Sirens: Studies in Rationality and Irrationality.* Cambridge: Cambridge University Press.

Elster, J. (ed.). 1986. *Rational Choice.* Oxford: Blackwell.

Elster, J. 1999. *Alchemies of the Mind: Rationality and the Emotions.* Cambridge: Cambridge University Press.

Elster, J. 2000. *Ulysses Unbound: Studies in Rationality, Precommitment, and Constraints.* Cambridge: Cambridge University Press.

Elster, Jon 2007. *Explaining Social Behavior: More Nuts and Bolts for the Social Sciences.* Cambridge: Cambridge University Press.

Errington, R. M. 1971. "The Alleged Syro-Macedonian Pact and the Origins of the Second Macedonian War." *Athenaeum* 49: 336–54.

Errington, R. M. 1986. "Antiochos III. Zeuxis und Euromus." *Epigraphica Anatolica* 17: 1–8.

Errington, R. M. 1989. "Rome against Philip and Antiochus." In A. E. Astin et al. (eds), *The Cambridge Ancient History*, vol. 8: 244–89. Cambridge: Cambridge University Press.

Erskine, A. 1990. *The Hellenistic Stoa: Political Thought and Action*. Ithaca, NY: Cornell University Press.

Erskine, A. 2001. *Troy between Greece and Rome: Local Tradition and Imperial Power*. Oxford: Oxford University Press.

Erxleben, E. 1975. "Die Kleruchien auf Euboia und Lesbos und die Methoden der attischen Herrschaft." *Klio* 57: 83–100.

Etzioni, A. 1993. *The Spirit of Community*. New York: Touchstone Books/Simon and Schuster.

Euben, J. P. (ed.) 1986. *Greek Tragedy and Political Theory*. Berkeley: University of California Press.

Euben, J. P. 1990. *The Tragedy of Political Theory: The Road Not Taken*. Princeton: Princeton University Press.

Euben, J. P. 1993. "Democracy Ancient and Modern." *Political Science and Politics* 26.3: 478–81.

Euben, J. P. 1997. *Corrupting Youth: Political Education, Democratic Culture, and Political Theory*. Princeton: Princeton University Press.

Euben, J. P. 2003. *Platonic Noise*. Princeton: Princeton University Press.

Euben, J., Wallach, J., and Ober, J. (eds) 1994a. *Athenian Political Thought and the Reconstruction of American Democracy*. Ithaca, NY: Cornell University Press.

Euben, J., Wallach, J., and Ober, J. 1994b. "Introduction." In Euben, Wallach, and Ober 1994a: 1–21.

Evans, J. A. S., 1981. "Notes on the Debate of the Persian Grandees in Herodotus 3.80–82." *Quaderni Urbinati di Cultura Classica* 36: 79–84.

Fadinger, V. 1996. "Solons Eunomia-Lehre und die Gerechtigkeitsidee der altorientalischen Schöpfungsherrschaft." In H. J. Gehrke and A. Möller (eds), *Vergangenheit und Lebenswelt. Soziale Kommunikation, Traditionsbildung und historisches Bewusstsein*, 179–218. Tübingen: Narr.

Farenga, V. 2006. *Citizen and Self in Ancient Greece: Individuals Performing Justice and the Law*. Cambridge: Cambridge University Press.

Fedeli, P. 1989. "Il 'Panegyrico' di Plinio nella critica moderna." In *Aufstieg und Niedergang der römischen Welt* (*ANRW*) 2.33.1: 387–514.

Feeney, D. C. 1991. *The Gods in Epic*. Oxford: Clarendon Press.

Feeney, D. C. 1998. *Literature and Religion at Rome: Cultures, Contexts, and Beliefs*. Cambridge: Cambridge University Press.

Fehr, B. 1984. *Die Tyrannentöter, oder Kann man der Demokratie ein Denkmal setzen?* Frankfurt: Kunststück.

Feldherr, Andrew 1998. *Spectacle and Society in Livy's History*. Berkeley: University of California Press.

Felson-Rubin, Nancy (ed.) 1983. *Semiotics and Classical Studies*. Special Issue of *Arethusa* 16 (Spring and Fall).

Ferguson, N. 2004. *Colossus: The Price of America's Empire*. New York: Penguin.

Ferrari, G. R. F. 2007. "The Three Part Soul." In G. R. F. Ferrari (ed.), *The Cambridge Companion to Plato's Republic*, 165–201. Cambridge: Cambridge University Press.

Ferrary, J.-L. 1995. "The Statesman and the Law in the Political Philosophy of Cicero." In A. Laks and M. Schofield (eds), *Justice and Generosity: Studies in Hellenistic Social and Political Philosophy*, 75–83. Cambridge: Cambridge University Press.

Figueira, T. J. and Nagy, G. (eds) 1985. *Theognis of Megara: Poetry and the Polis.* Baltimore: Johns Hopkins University Press.

Fine, R. 2007. *Cosmopolitanism.* London: Routledge.

Fink, Z. 1962. *The Classical Republicans* [1945]. Evanston, IL: Northwestern University Press.

Finley, M. I. 1973. *The Ancient Economy.* London: Chatto and Windus.

Finley, M. I. 1974. "Athenian Demagogues." In Finley, *Studies in Ancient Society,* 1–25. London: Routledge and Kegan Paul.

Finley, M. I. 1976. "The Freedom of the Citizen in the Greek World." *Talanta* 7: 1–23. (Repr. in. Finley 1982b: 77–94.)

Finley, M. I. 1977. *The World of Odysseus.* 2nd edn. London: Chatto and Windus.

Finley, M. I. 1978. "Empire in the Greco-Roman World." *Greece and Rome,* n.s. 25: 1–15.

Finley, M. I. 1981. *Early Greece: The Bronze and Archaic Ages.* London: Chatto and Windus.

Finley, M. I. 1982a. *Authority and Legitimacy in the Classical City-State.* København: Munksgaard.

Finley, M. I. 1982b. *Economy and Society in Ancient Greece,* ed. B. Shaw and R. Saller. New York: Viking.

Finley, M. I. 1983. *Politics in the Ancient World.* Cambridge: Cambridge University Press.

Finley, M. I. 1985a. *Democracy Ancient and Modern* [1973]. 2nd edn. New Brunswick, NJ: Rutgers University Press.

Finley, M. I. 1985b. "Max Weber and the Greek City-State." In Finley, *Ancient History: Evidence and Models.* London: Chatto and Windus, 88–103.

Flaig, E. 1995. "Entscheidung und Konsens. Zu den Feldern der politischen Kommunikation zwischen Aristokratie und Plebs." In M. Jehne (ed.), *Demokratie in Rom? Die Rolle des Volkes in der Politik der römischen Republik,* 77–127. Stuttgart: Franz Steiner.

Flaig, E. 2003. *Ritualisierte Politik: Zeichen, Gesten und Herrschaft im Alten Rom.* Göttingen: Vandenhoeck and Ruprecht.

Fleischer, R. 1996. "Hellenistic Royal Iconography on Coins." In Bilde et al. 1996a: 28–40.

Fleming, D. 2004. *Democracy's Ancient Ancestors: Mari and Collective Governance.* Cambridge: Cambridge University Press.

Foley, H. 1995. "Tragedy and Democratic Ideology: The Case of Sophocles' *Antigone.*" In Goff 1995: 131–50.

Foley, H. 2001. *Female Acts in Greek Tragedy.* Princeton: Princeton University Press.

Fontana, B. 2004. "Rhetoric and the Roots of Democratic Politics." In Fontana, Nederman, and Remer 2004: 27–56.

Fontana, Benedetto, Nederman, Gary, and Remer, Gary (eds) 2004. *Talking Democracy: Historical Perspectives on Rhetoric and Democracy.* University Park: Pennsylvania State University Press.

Fornara, C. W. 1983. *Archaic Times to the End of the Peloponnesian War.* Translated Documents of Greece and Rome 1. 2nd edn. Cambridge: Cambridge University Press.

Forsdyke, S. 1999. "From Aristocratic to Democratic Ideology and Back Again: The Thrasybulus Anecdote in Herodotus' *Histories* and Aristotle's *Politics.*" *Classical Philology* 94: 361–72.

Forsdyke, S. 2001. "Athenian Democratic Ideology and Herodotus' Histories." *American Journal of Philology* 122: 329–58.

Forsydke, S. 2002. "Greek History, c.525–480 BC." In E. Bakker et al. (eds), *Brill's Companion to Herodotus,* 521–49. Leiden: Brill.

Forsdyke, S. 2005a. *Exile, Ostracism and Democracy: The Politics of Expulsion in Ancient Greece.* Princeton: Princeton University Press.

Forsdyke, S. 2005b. "Revelry and Riot in Archaic Megara: Democratic Disorder or Ritual Reversal?" *Journal of Hellenic Studies* 125: 73–92.

Forsdyke, S. 2006. "Herodotus, Political History and Political Thought." In C. Dewald and J. Marincola (eds), *The Cambridge Companion to Herodotus*, 224–41. Cambridge: Cambridge University Press.

Fortin, Ernest 1972. *Political Idealism and Christianity in the Thought of St Augustine*. Villanova, PA: Augustinian Historical Society.

Fortin, Ernest 1996. *The Birth of Philosophic Christianity: Studies in Early Christian and Medieval Thought*, ed. J. Brian Benestad. Lanham, MD: Rowman and Littlefield.

Fortin, Ernest, Gunn, Roland, and Kries, Douglas (eds) 1994. *Political Writings / Augustine*, trans. M. W. Tkacz and D. Kries. Indianapolis: Hackett.

Foster, B. O. (trans.) 2002. *Livy: History of Rome, Books 1–2*. Loeb Classical Library. Cambridge, MA: Harvard University Press.

Foucault, Michel 1977. "Nietzsche, Genealogy, History." In Foucault, *Language, Counter-Memory, Practice*, ed. D. Bouchard, 139–64. Ithaca, NY: Cornell University Press.

Foucault, Michel 1988. "An Aesthetics of Existence." In L. Kritzman (ed.), *Politics, Philosophy, Culture*, 47–53. New York: Routledge.

Foucault, Michel 1990a. *The History of Sexuality*, vol. 2: *The Use of Pleasure*, trans. R. Hurley. New York: Vintage.

Foucault, Michel. 1990b. *The History of Sexuality*, vol. 3: *The Care of the Self*, trans. R. Hurley. New York: Vintage.

Foucault, Michel 1997. "The Ethics of the Concern for Self as a Practice of Freedom." In P. Rabinow (ed.), *Ethics: Subjectivity and Truth*, vol. 1: 281–301. New York: Free Press.

Foucault, Michel 2005. *The Hermeneutics of the Subject: Lectures at the Collège de France 1981–1982*, ed. F. Gros, trans. G. Burchell. New York: Palgrave.

Fowler, Don 2000. *Roman Constructions: Readings in Postmodern Latin*. New York: Oxford University Press.

Foxhall, Lin 1989. "Household, Gender and Property in Classical Athens." *Classical Quarterly* 39: 22–44.

Foxhall, Lin 1998. "Pandora Unbound: A Feminist Critique of Foucault's *History of Sexuality*." In D. Larmour, P. Miller, and C. Platter (eds), *Rethinking Sexuality: Foucault and Classical Antiquity*, 122–37. Princeton: Princeton University Press.

Frank, J. 2005. *A Democracy of Distinction: Aristotle and the Work of Politics*. Chicago: University of Chicago Press.

Fraschetti, Augusto (ed.) 2001. *Roman Women*, trans. Linda Lappin. Chicago: University of Chicago Press.

Fraser, P. 1972. *Ptolemaic Alexandria*, vol. 1. Oxford: Oxford University Press.

Freeland, C. A. 1998. *Feminist Interpretations of Aristotle*. University Park, PA: Penn State University Press.

Frend, W. H. C. 1989. "Augustine and Orosius: On the End of the Ancient World." The 1989 Saint Augustine Lecture. *Augustinian Studies* 20: 1–38.

Frier, B. W. 1999. *Libri Annales Pontificorum Maximorum: The Origins of the Annalistic Tradition*. Ann Arbor: University of Michigan Press.

Froese, Katrin 2001. *Rousseau and Nietzsche: Toward an Aesthetic Morality*. Lanham, MD: Rowman and Littlefield.

Fustel de Coulanges, N. D. 1882. *The Ancient City*, trans. W. Small. 4th edn. Boston: Lee and Shepard.

Gaddis, J. L. 2004. *Surprise, Security, and the American Experience*. Cambridge, MA: Harvard University Press.

Gagarin, M. 1974. "*Dike* in Archaic Greek Thought." *Classical Philology* 69: 186–97.

Gagarin, M. 1981. *Drakon and Early Athenian Homicide Law*. New Haven, CT: Yale University Press.

Gagarin, M. 1986. *Early Greek Law*. Berkeley: University of California Press.

Gagarin, M. 2008. *Writing Greek Law*. Cambridge: Cambridge University Press.

Gagarin, M. and Woodruff, P. 1995. *Early Greek Political Thought from Homer to the Sophists*. Cambridge: Cambridge University Press.

Galinsky, G. K. 1969. *Aeneas, Sicily, and Rome*. Princeton: Princeton University Press.

Galinsky, Karl. 1996. *Augustan Culture: An Interpretive Introduction*. Princeton: Princeton University Press.

Gammie, J. 1986. "Herodotus on Kings and Tyrants: Objective Historiography or Conventional Portraiture?" *Journal of Near Eastern Studies* 45.3: 171–95.

Gamwell, F. I. 2003. "The Moral Ground of Cosmopolitan Democracy." *Journal of Religion* 83: 562–84.

Gardner, R. (trans.) 2005. *Cicero. Orations* (*Pro Caelio, De Provinciis Consularibus, Pro Balbo*). Loeb Classical Library. Cambridge, MA: Harvard University Press.

Garlan, Y. 1978. "Signification historique de la piratie grecque." *Dialogues d'Histoire Ancienne* 4: 1–16.

Garnsey, P. D. A. and Whittaker, C. R. (eds) 1978. *Imperialism in the Ancient World*. Cambridge: Cambridge University Press.

Garnsey, Peter, Hopkins, Keith, and Whittaker, C. R. (eds) 1983. *Trade in the Ancient Economy*. Berkeley: University of California Press.

Garver, E. 1994. "Aristotle's Natural Slaves: Incomplete *Praxeis* and Incomplete Human Beings." *Journal of the History of Philosophy* 32: 173–95.

Garver, E. 2006. *Confronting Aristotle's Ethics*. Chicago: University of Chicago Press.

Gay, R. 1988. "Courage and *Thumos*." *Philosophy* 63.244: 255–65.

Geertz. C. 1973. *The Interpretation of Cultures*. New York: Basic Books.

Gehrke, H.-J. (ed.) 1994. *Rechtskodifizierung und soziale Normen im interkulturellen Vergleich*. Tübingen: Narr.

Gehrke, H.-J. 2000. "Verschriftung und Verschriftlichung sozialer Normen im archaischen und klassischen Griechenland." In Lévy 2000: 141–59.

Gelley, A. (ed.) 1995. *Unruly Examples: On the Rhetoric of Exemplarity*. Stanford: Stanford University Press.

Gellner, E. 1997. *Nationalism*. New York: New York University Press.

Gellrich, M. 1995. "Interpreting Greek Tragedy: History, Theory, and the New Philology." In Goff 1995: 38–58.

Gelzer, M. 1912. *Die Nobilität der römischen Republik*. Leipzig: B. G. Teubner. (Trans. R. Seager as *The Roman Nobility*. Blackwell: Oxford, 1969.)

Gelzer, M. 1969. *Cicero: Ein biographischer Versuch*. Wiesbaden: F. Steiner.

Georgi, Dieter 1991. "Reflections of a New Testament Scholar on Plutarch's Tractates De Alexandri Magni fortuna aut virtute." In B. A. Pearson et al. (eds), *The Future of Early Christianity: Essays in Honor of Helmut Koester*, 20–34. Minneapolis: Fortress Press.

Gibson, R., Römmele, A., and Ward, S. 2004. *Electronic Democracy: Mobilisation, Organisation, and Participation via New ICTs*. London: Routledge.

Gilbert, F. 1968. "The Venetian Constitution in Florentine Political Thought." In N. Rubenstein (ed.), *Florentine Studies: Politics and Society in Renaissance Florence*, 463–500. London: Faber.

Gildenhard, I. 2007. *Paideia Romana: Cicero's* Tusculan Disputations. Cambridge: Cambridge University Press.

Gill, C. 1990. "The Character–Personality Distinction." In Pelling 1990: 1–31.

Gill, C. 1996. *Personality in Greek Epic, Tragedy, and Philosophy: The Self in Dialogue*. Oxford: Clarendon Press.

Gill, C. 2004. "The Impact of Greek Philosophy on Contemporary Ethical Philosophy." In L. Rossetti (ed.), *Greek Philosophy in the New Millennium: Papers in Honour of Thomas M. Robinson*. Sankt Augustin: Academia, 209–26. (A shorter version appeared as "Introduction" in C. Gill (ed.), *Virtues, Norms, and Objectivity: Issues in Ancient and Modern Ethics*, 1–7. Oxford: Clarendon Press, 2005.)

Gleason, Maud 1995. *Making Men: Sophists and Self-Presentation in Ancient Rome.* Princeton: Princeton University Press.

Godelier, Maurice 1977. *Perspectives in Marxist Anthropology*, trans. R. Brain. Cambridge: Cambridge University Press.

Godley, A. D. (trans.) 1920. *Herodotus. The Histories*. Loeb Classical Library. Cambridge, MA: Harvard University Press.

Goff, B. (ed.) 1995. *History, Tragedy, Theory: Dialogues on Athenian Drama*. Austin: University of Texas Press.

Goldhill, S. 1987. "The Great Dionysia and Civic Ideology." *Journal of Hellenic Studies* 107: 58–76. (Repr. in Winkler and Zeitlin 1990: 97–129.)

Goldhill, S. 1994. "Representing Democracy: Women at the Great Dionysia." In Osborne and Hornblower 1994: 347–69.

Goldhill, S. 1997. "The Audience of Athenian Tragedy." In Easterling 1997: 54–68.

Goldhill, S. 1999. "Programme Notes." In Goldhill and Osborne 1999: 1–29.

Goldhill, S. 2000a. "Civic Ideology and the Problem of Difference: The Politics of Aeschylean Tragedy, Once Again." *Journal of Hellenic Studies* 120: 34–56.

Goldhill, S. 2000b. "Greek Drama and Political Theory." In C. Rowe and Schofield 2000: 60–88.

Goldhill, S. and Osborne, R. (eds) 1999. *Performance Culture and Athenian Democracy.* Cambridge: Cambridge University Press.

Goldman, Alvin I. 1999. *Knowledge in a Social World*. Oxford: Clarendon Press.

Gomme, A. W., Andrewes, A., and Dover, K. J. (eds) 1945–81. *A Historical Commentary on Thucydides*. 5 vols. Oxford: Clarendon Press.

Gordon, R. L. 1990a. "The Veil of Power: Emperors, Sacrificers and Benefactors." In Beard and North 1990: 201–31.

Gordon, R. L. 1990b. "Religion in the Roman Empire: The Civic Compromise and Its Limits." In Beard and North 1990: 235–55.

Gould, John 1980. "Law, Custom and Myth: Aspects of the Social Position of Women in Classical Athens." *Journal of Hellenic Studies* 100: 38–59.

Gowing, A. 2005. *Empire and Memory: The Representation of the Roman Republic in Imperial Culture*. Cambridge: Cambridge University Press.

Gradel, I. 2002. *Emperor Worship and Roman Religion*. Oxford: Oxford University Press.

Green, P. 1990. *From Alexander to Actium: The Historical Evolution of the Hellenistic Age*. Berkeley: University of California Press.

Greengus, S. 1995. "Legal and Social Institutions of Ancient Mesopotamia." In J. Sasson (ed.), *Civilizations of the Ancient Near East*, vol. 1: 469–84. New York: Scribner.

Gregory, Eric 2008. *Politics and the Order of Love: An Augustinian Ethic of Democratic Citizenship*. Chicago: University of Chicago Press.

Gregory, J. 1991. *Euripides and the Instruction of the Athenians*. Ann Arbor: University of Michigan Press.

Gregory, J. (ed.) 2005. *A Companion to Greek Tragedy*. Oxford: Blackwell.

Grene, D. (trans.) 1987. *Herodotus. Histories*. Chicago: University of Chicago Press.

Griffin, J. 1977. "The Epic Cycle and the Uniqueness of Homer." *Journal of Hellenic Studies* 97: 39–53.

Griffin, J. 1980. *Homer on Life and Death*. Oxford: Clarendon Press.

Griffin, J. 1998. "The Social Function of Attic Tragedy." *Classical Quarterly* 48: 39–61.

Griffin, J. 1999a. "Sophocles and the Democratic City." In Griffin 1999b: 73–94.

Griffin, J. (ed.) 1999b. *Sophocles Revisited: Essays Presented to Sir Hugh Lloyd-Jones*. Oxford: Oxford University Press.

Griffin, M. T. 1976. *Seneca: A Philosopher in Politics*. Oxford: Clarendon Press.

Griffin, M. T. 1986. "Philosophy, Cato, and Roman Suicide." *Greece and Rome* 33: 64–75, 192–202.

Griffin, M. T. 2003. "Clementia after Caesar: From Politics to Philosophy." In F. Cairns and E. Fantham (eds), *Caesar against Liberty? Perspectives on His Autocracy*, 157–82. Papers of the Langford Latin Seminar 11. Cambridge: Francis Cairns.

Griffin. M. T. and Atkins, E. M. (eds) 1991. *Cicero: On Duties*. Cambridge: Cambridge University Press.

Griffith, M. 1995. "Brilliant Dynasts: Power and Politics in the *Oresteia*." *Classical Antiquity* 14: 62–129.

Griffith, M. 2005. "Authority Figures." In Gregory 2005: 333–51.

Grilli, A. 1953. *Il Problema della Vita Contempletiva nel Mondo Greco-Romano*. Milan: Fratelli Bocca Editori.

Grossmann, G. 1950. *Politische Schlagwörter aus der Zeit des Peloponnesischen Krieges*. (Diss. University of Basel 1945.) Zurich: Leemann AG.

Grote, G. 1875. *Plato and the Other Companions of Sokrates*. London: John Murray.

Grote, G. 1906. *A History of Greece*. 12 vols. London: Dent.

Gruen, E. S. 1974. *The Last Generation of the Roman Republic*. Berkeley: University of California Press.

Gruen, E. S. 1984. *The Hellenistic World and the Coming of Rome*. Berkeley: University of California Press.

Gruen, E. S. 1985. "The Coronation of the Diadochoi." In J. Eadie and J. Ober (eds), *The Craft of the Ancient Historian: Essays in Honor of Chester G. Starr*, 253–71. Lanham, MD: University Press of America.

Gruen, E. S. 1991. "The Exercise of Power in the Roman Republic." In Molho, Raaflaub, and Emlen 1991: 251–67.

Gruen, E. S. 1992. *Culture and National Identity in Republican Rome*. Berkeley: University of California Press.

Gruen, E. S. 1996. "The Roman Oligarchy: Image and Perception." In J. Linderski (ed.), *Imperium Sine Fine: T. Robert S. Broughton and the Roman Republic*, 216–34. Stuttgart: Franz Steiner.

Gummere, Richard (trans.) 1996. *Seneca. Epistles*. Cambridge, MA: Harvard University Press.

Gunderson, Erik 1998. "Discovering the Body in Roman Oratory." In M. Wyke (ed.), *Parchments of Gender: Deciphering the Bodies of Antiquity*, 169–89. Oxford: Clarendon Press.

Gunderson, Erik 2000. *Staging Masculinity: The Rhetoric of Performance in the Roman World*. Ann Arbor: University of Michigan Press.

Guthrie, W. K. C. 1971. *The Sophists*. Cambridge: Cambridge University Press.

Gutmann, A. 2003. *Identity in Democracy.* Princeton: Princeton University Press.

Habicht, C. 1958. "Die herrschende Gesellschaft in den hellenistischen Monarchien." *Vierteljahrsschrift fur Sozial- und Wirtschaftsgeschichte* 45: 1–16.

Habicht, C. 1997. *Athens from Alexander to Antony,* trans. D. Schneider. Cambridge, MA: Harvard University Press.

Habinek, Thomas 1998. *The Politics of Latin Literature: Writing, Identity, and Empire in Ancient Rome.* Princeton: Princeton University Press.

Hadley, R. A. 1974. "Dynastic Propaganda of Seleucus I and Lysimachus." *Journal of Hellenic Studies* 94: 50–65.

Hadot, P. 1990. "Forms of Life and Forms of Discourse in Ancient Philosophy." *Critical Inquiry* 16: 483–505.

Hadot, P. 1992. "Reflections on the Notion of 'The Cultivation of the Self.' " In F. Ewald (ed.), *Michel Foucault, Philosopher,* trans. T. Armstrong, 225–31. New York: Routledge.

Hadot. P. 1995. *Philosophy as a Way of Life: Spiritual Exercises from Socrates to Foucault.* Oxford: Oxford University Press.

Hadot, P. 1998. *The Inner Citadel: The Meditations of Marcus Aurelius.* Cambridge, MA: Harvard University Press.

Hahm, D. E. 1995. "Polybius' Applied Political Theory." In A. Laks and M. Schofield (eds), *Justice and Generosity: Studies in Hellenistic Social and Political Philosophy,* 7–47. Proceedings of the Sixth Symposium Hellenisticum. Cambridge: Cambridge University Press.

Hahm, D. E. 2000. "Kings and Constitutions: Hellenistic Theories." In C. Rowe and Schofield 2000: 457–76.

Hahn, István 1975. "Der Klassenkampf der *plebs urbana* in den letzten Jahrzehnten der römischen Republik." In J. Herrmann and I. Sellnow (eds), *Die Rolle der Volksmassen in der Geschichte der vorkapitalistischen Gesellschaftsformation,* 121–46. Berlin: Akademie.

Hall, E. 1989. *Inventing the Barbarian: Greek Self-Definition through Tragedy.* Oxford: Clarendon Press.

Hall, E. 1997. "The Sociology of Athenian Tragedy." In Easterling 1997: 93–126.

Hall, J. M. 1997. *Ethnic Identity in Greek Antiquity.* Cambridge: Cambridge University Press.

Hall. J. M. 2001. *Hellenicity: Between Ethnicity and Culture.* Chicago: University of Chicago Press.

Hall, J. M. 2007. *A History of the Archaic Greek World, ca. 1200–479* BCE. Oxford: Blackwell.

Hallett, Judith 1984. *Fathers and Daughters in Roman Society: Women and the Elite Family.* Princeton: Princeton University Press.

Hallett, Judith and Skinner, Marilyn (eds) 1997. *Roman Sexualities.* Princeton: Princeton University Press.

Halliwell, S. 1990. "Traditional Greek Concepts of Character." In Pelling 1990: 32–59.

Halperin, David 1990. *One Hundred Years of Homosexuality and Other Essays on Greek Love.* London: Routledge.

Halperin, David 1995. *Saint Foucault: Towards a Gay Hagiography.* New York: Oxford University Press.

Halperin, David, Winkler, John, and Zeitlin, Froma (eds) 1990. *Before Sexuality: The Construction of Erotic Experience in the Ancient Greek World.* Princeton: Princeton University Press.

Hamel, D. 2003. *Trying Neaira: The True Story of a Courtesan's Scandalous Life in Ancient Greece.* New Haven, CT: Yale University Press.

Hamilton, C. D. and Krentz, P. (eds) 1997. *Polis and Polemos: Essays on Politics, War, and History in Ancient Greece in Honor of Donald Kagan.* Claremont: Regina.

Hammer, Dean 2002. *The Iliad as Politics: The Performance of Political Thought*. Norman: University of Oklahoma Press.

Hammer, Dean 2004. "Ideology, the Symposium, and Archaic Greek Politics." *American Journal of Philology* 125: 479–512.

Hammer, Dean 2005. "Plebiscitary Politics in Archaic Greece." *Historia* 54: 107–31.

Hammer, Dean 2006. "Bourdieu, Ideology, and the Ancient World." *American Journal of Semiotics* 22.

Hammer, Dean 2008. *Roman Political Thought and the Modern Theoretical Imagination*. Norman: University of Oklahoma Press.

Hampe, Roland 1955. "Eukleia und Eunomia." *Mitteilungen des Deutschen Archäologischen Instituts, Römische Abteilung* 62: 107–23.

Hanfmann, G. M. A. 1951. *The Season Sarcophagus in Dumbarton Oaks*. Cambridge, MA: Harvard University Press.

Hankins, James 2000. *Renaissance Civic Humanism: Reappraisals and Reflections*. Cambridge: Cambridge University Press.

Hannestad, L. 1996. " 'This Contributes in No Small Way to One's Reputation': The Bithynian Kings and Greek Culture." In Bilde et al. 1996a: 67–96.

Hansen, E. V. 1971. *The Attalids of Pergamum*. 2nd edn. Ithaca, NY: Cornell University Press.

Hansen, M. H. 1974. *The Sovereignty of the People's Court in Athens in the Fourth Century BC and the Public Action against Unconstitutional Proposals*. Odense, Denmark: Odense University Press.

Hansen, M. H. 1976. *Apagoge, Endeixis and Ephegesis against Kakourgoi, Atimoi and Pheugontes*. Odense, Denmark: Odense University Press.

Hansen, M. H. 1986. *Demography and Democracy: The Number of Athenian Citizens in the Fourth Century BC*. Herning, Denmark: Systime.

Hansen, M. H. 1987. *The Athenian Assembly in the Age of Demosthenes*. Oxford: Blackwell.

Hansen, M. H. 1988. *Three Studies in Athenian Demography*. Copenhagen: Royal Danish Academy.

Hansen, M. H. 1989a. "On the Importance of Institutions in an Analysis of Athenian Democracy." In Hansen, *The Athenian Ecclesia II: A Collection of Articles 1983–89*, 263–9. Copenhagen: Museum Tusculanum Press.

Hansen, M. H. 1989b. "Review Article: Athenian Democracy: Institutions and Ideology." *Classical Philology* 84: 137–48.

Hansen, M. H. 1991. *The Athenian Democracy in the Age of Demosthenes*. Oxford: Blackwell.

Hansen, M. H. 1993. "The Polis as a Citizen State." In Hansen, *The Ancient Greek City-State*, 7–29. Copenhagen: Royal Danish Academy of Sciences and Letters.

Hansen, M. H. 1996. "The Ancient Athenian and the Modern Liberal Views of Liberty as a Democratic Ideal." In Ober and Hedrick 1996: 91–104.

Hansen, M. H. 1999. *The Athenian Democracy in the Age of Demosthenes*. 2nd edn. London: Duckworth/Bristol Classical Press.

Hansen, M. H. 2002a. "Direct Democracy, Ancient and Modern." In P. McKechnie (ed.), *Thinking like a Lawyer: Essays on Legal History and General History for John Crook on His Eightieth Birthday*, 135–49. Leiden: Brill.

Hansen, M. H. 2002b. "Was the Polis a State or a Stateless Society?" In T. H. Nielsen (ed.), *Even More Studies in the Ancient Greek Polis*, 17–47. Papers from the Copenhagen Polis Centre 6; Historia Einzelschriften 162. Stuttgart: F. Steiner.

Hansen, M. H. 2004. "The Concept of the Consumption City Applied to the Greek Polis." In T. H. Nielsen (ed.), *Once Again: Studies in the Ancient Greek Polis*, 9–47. Papers from the Copenhagen Polis Centre 7; Historia Einzelschriften 180. Stuttgart: Steiner.

Hansen, M. H. 2005a. *The Tradition of Ancient Greek Democracy and Its Importance for Modern Democracy.* Historisk-Filosofiske Meddelelser 93. Copenhagen: Royal Danish Academy.

Hansen, M. H. (ed.) 2005b. *The Imaginary Polis.* Copenhagen: Royal Danish Academy of Sciences and Letters.

Hansen, M. H. 2006a. *Polis: An Introduction to the Ancient Greek City-State.* Oxford: Oxford University Press.

Hansen, M. H. 2006b. *Studies in the Population of Aigina, Athens and Eretria.* Copenhagen: Royal Danish Academy.

Hansen, M. H. and Nielsen, T. H. (eds) 2004. *An Inventory of Archaic and Classical Poleis: An Investigation Conducted by the Copenhagen Polis Centre for the Danish National Research Foundation.* Oxford: Oxford University Press.

Hanson, V. D. 1989. *The Western Way of War: Infantry Battle in Classical Greece.* Berkeley: University of California Press.

Hanson, V. D. 1996. "Hoplites into Democrats: The Changing Ideology of Athenian Infantry." In Ober and Hedrick 1996: 289–312.

Hardie, W. F. R. 1980. *Aristotle's Ethical Theory.* 2nd edn. Oxford: Oxford University Press.

Hardin, G. 1968. "The Tragedy of the Commons." *Science* 162: 1243–8.

Hardin, R. 1982. *Collective Action.* Baltimore: Johns Hopkins University Press.

Hardin, R. 2002. "Street Level Epistemology and Democratic Participation." *Journal of Political Philosophy* 10: 212–29.

Hardt, M. and Negri, A. 2000. *Empire.* Cambridge, MA: Harvard University Press.

Hardt, M. and Negri, A. 2004. *Multitude: War and Democracy in the Age of Empire.* New York: Penguin.

Hardwick, L. 2003. *Reception Studies: Greece and Rome.* New Surveys in the Classics 3. Oxford: Oxford University Press.

Harris, E. 1992. "Pericles' Praise of Athenian Democracy, Thucydides, 2.37.1." *Harvard Studies in Classical Philology* 94: 157–67.

Harris, E. 2005. "Was All Criticism of Athenian Democracy Anti-democratic?" In Bultrighini 2005: 11–24.

Harris, I. 2002. "Berlin and His Critics." In I. Berlin, *Liberty*, ed. H. Hardy, 349–64. Oxford: Oxford University Press.

Harris, W. V. 1979. *War and Imperialism in Republican Rome, 327–70 BC.* Oxford: Oxford University Press. (Repr. 2000.)

Harris, W. V. 1989. *Ancient Literacy.* Cambridge, MA: Harvard University Press.

Harris, W. V. 1990. "On Defining the Political Culture of the Roman Republic: Some Comments on Rosenstein, Williamson, and North." *Classical Philology* 85: 288–94.

Harris, W. V. 2002. *Restraining Rage: The Ideology of Anger Control in Classical Antiquity.* Cambridge, MA: Harvard University Press.

Harrison, A. R. W. 1968–71. *The Law of Athens.* Vol. 1: *The Family and Property.* Vol. 2: *Procedure.* Oxford: Oxford University Press. (Reissued with a foreword by Douglas M. MacDowell, Indianapolis: Hackett, 1998.)

Harrison, Carol 2000. *Augustine: Christian Truth and Fractured Humanity.* Oxford: Oxford University Press.

Harrison, S. J. 1990. "Cicero's *De temporibus suis*: The Evidence Reconsidered." *Hermes* 118: 455–63.

Harrison, S. J. (ed.) 2001. *Texts, Ideas, and the Classics: Scholarship, Theory, and Classical Literature.* Oxford: Oxford University Press.

Harrison, Thomas 2005. *Divinity and History: The Religion of Herodotus*. Oxford: Clarendon Press.

Harvey, D. 2003. *The New Imperialism*. New York: Oxford University Press.

Hatscher, Christoph 2000. *Charisma und Res Publica: Max Webers Herrschaftssoziologie und die Römische Republik*. Stuttgart: Franz Steiner.

Haubold, Johannes 2002. "Greek Epic: A Near Eastern Genre?" *Proceedings of the Cambridge Philological Society* 48: 1–19,

Haury, A. 1974. "Cicéron et la gloire. Une pédagogie de la vertu." In *Mélanges de philosophie, de littérature et d'histoire ancienne offerts à Pierre Boyancé*, 401–17. Paris: École Française de Rome.

Havelock, Eric A. 1978. *The Greek Concept of Justice: From Its Shadow in Homer to Its Substance in Plato*. Cambridge, MA: Harvard University Press.

Haynes, Holly 2003. *The History of Make-Believe: Tacitus on Imperial Rome*. Berkeley: University of California Press.

Headlam, J. 1933. *Election by Lot at Athens*. Cambridge: Cambridge University Press.

Heath, M. 1987a. *Political Comedy in Aristophanes*. Göttingen: Vandenhoek and Ruprecht.

Heath, M. 1987b. *The Poetics of Greek Tragedy*. Stanford: Stanford University Press.

Heath, M. 1997. "Aristophanes and the Discourse of Politics." In Dobrov 1997: 230–49.

Hedrick, Charles W., Jr 1993. "The Meaning of Material Culture: Herodotus, Thucydides and Their Sources." In R. Rosen and J. Farrell (eds), *Nomodeiktes: Greek Studies in Honor of Martin Ostwald*, 17–38. Ann Arbor: University of Michigan Press:

Hedrick, Charles W., Jr 2005. "The Ethics of World History." *Journal of World History* 16: 33–49.

Hedrick, Charles W., Jr 2006. *Ancient History: Monuments and Documents*. Oxford: Blackwell.

Heidegger, M. 1959. *An Introduction to Metaphysics*, trans. R. Manheim. New Haven, CT: Yale University Press.

Heidegger, M. 1962. "Plato's Doctrine of the Truth," trans. John Barlow. In W. Barrett and H. D. Aiken (eds), *Philosophy in the Twentieth Century*. New York: Random House.

Heidegger, M. 1996. *Being and Time*, trans. J. Stambaugh. Albany: State University of New York Press.

Heinze, R. 1925. "*Auctoritas*." *Hermes* 60: 348–66.

Helck, Wolfgang 1986. *Politische Gegensätze im alten Ägypten: ein Versuch*. Hildesheim: Gerstenberg.

Hellegouarc'h, J. 1972. *Le Vocabulaire latin des relations et des partis politiques sous la République*. Paris: Belles Lettres.

Henderson, J. 1987. *Aristophanes: Lysistrata*. Oxford: Oxford University Press.

Henderson, J. 1990. "The *Demos* and Comic Competition." In Winkler and Zeitlin 1990: 271–313.

Henderson, J. 1991. "Women and the Athenian Dramatic Festivals." *TAPA* 121: 133–47.

Henderson, J. 1993. "Comic Hero versus Political Élite." In Sommerstein et al. 1993: 307–19.

Henderson, J. 1997. "Mass versus Elite and the Comic Heroism of Peisetairos." In Dobrov 1997: 135–48.

Henderson, J. 1998. "Attic Old Comedy, Frank Speech, and Democracy." In Boedeker and Raaflaub 1998: 255–73.

Henderson, J. 2007. "Drama and Democracy." In Samons 2007: 179–95.

Henry, M. 2007. *Neaera: Writing a Prostitute's Life*. London: Routledge.

Herfst, P. 1922. "Le travail de la femme dans la Grèce ancienne." Diss., Utrecht.

Herman, G. 2006. *Morality and Behaviour in Democratic Athens: A Social History*. Cambridge: Cambridge University Press.

Hignett, Charles 1952. *A History of the Athenian Constitution to the End of the Fifth Century BC*. Oxford: Clarendon Press.

Hill, Edmund (trans.) 1998. *The Trinity / Augustine*. New York: New City Press.

Hinchman, L. P. and Hinchman, S. K. (eds) 1994. *Hannah Arendt: Critical Essays*. Albany: State University of New York Press.

Hind, J. G. F. 1994. "Mithridates." In J. A. Crook, A. Lintott, and E. Rawson (eds), *The Cambridge Ancient History*, vol. 9: 129–64. 2nd edn. Cambridge: Cambridge University Press.

Hindess, Barry and Hirst, Paul 1975. *Pre-capitalist Modes of Production*. London: Routledge.

Hirzel, R. 1907. *Themis, Dike und Verwandtes. Ein Beitrag zur Geschichte der Rechtsidee bei den Griechen*. Leipzig: S. Hirzel. (Repr. Hildesheim: Olms, 1966.)

Hobbes, T. 1996. *Leviathan: Or the Matter, Forme and Power of a Commonwealth Ecclesiasticall and Civill* [1651], ed. J. C. A. Gaskin. Oxford: Oxford University Press.

Hodkinson, S. 2000. *Property and Wealth in Classical Sparta*. London: Duckworth/Classical Press of Wales.

Hoffman, Gail 1997. *Imports and Immigrants: Near Eastern Contacts with Iron Age Crete*. Ann Arbor: University of Michigan Press.

Hohfeld, W. L. 2001. *Fundamental Legal Conceptions as Applied in Judicial Reasoning* [1919], ed. D. Campbell and P. Thomas. Aldershot: Ashgate.

Hölbl, G. 2001. *A History of the Ptolemaic Empire*. London: Routledge.

Hölkeskamp, Karl-Joachim 1992a. "Arbitrators, Lawgivers and the 'Codification of Law' in Archaic Greece: Problems and Perspectives." *Metis* 7: 49–81.

Hölkeskamp, Karl-Joachim 1992b. "Written Law in Archaic Greece." *Proceedings of the Cambridge Philological Society*, n.s. 38: 87–117.

Hölkeskamp, Karl-Joachim 1994. "Tempel, Agora und Alphabet. Die Entstehungsbedingungen von Gesetzgebung in der archaischen Polis." In Gehrke 1994: 135–64.

Hölkeskamp, Karl-Joachim 1995. "*Oratoris Maxima Scaena*: Reden vor dem Volk in der politischen Kultur der Republik." In M. Jehne (ed.), *Demokratie in Rom? Die Rolle des Volkes in der Politik der römischen Republik*, 11–49. Historia Einzelschriften 96. Stuttgart: F. Steiner.

Hölkeskamp, Karl-Joachim 1999. *Schiedsrichter, Gesetzgeber und Gesetzgebung im archaischen Griechenland*. Stuttgart: Steiner.

Hölkeskamp, Karl-Joachim 2002. "*Ptolis* and *Agore*: Homer and the Archaeology of the City-State." In F. Montanari (ed.), *Omero tremila anni dopo*, 297–342. Roma: Edizioni di Storia e Letteratura.

Hölkeskamp, Karl-Joachim 2004. *Senatus Populusque Romanus. Die politische Kultur der Republik – Dimensionen und Deutungen*. Stuttgart: Franz Steiner.

Holmes, S. 1979. "Aristippus in and out of Athens." *American Political Science Review* 73: 113–28.

Hölscher, Tonio 2000. "Augustus und die Macht der Archäologie." In A. Giovannini (ed.), *La révolution romaine après Ronald Syme. Bilans et perspectives*, 237–73. Geneva: Fondation Hardt.

Hopkins, K and Burton, G. 1983. "Political Succession in the Late Republic (249–50 BC)." In K. Hopkins, *Death and Renewal*, 31–119. Sociological Studies in Roman History 2. Cambridge: Cambridge University Press.

Hornblower, S. 2004. " 'This was Decided' (*edoxe tauta*): The Army as Polis in Xenophon's *Anabasis* – and Elsewhere." In R. Lane Fox (ed.), *The Long March: Xenophon and the Ten Thousand*, 243–63. New Haven, CT: Yale University Press.

Hornung, E. 1971. "Politische Planung und Realität im alten Ägypten." *Saeculum* 22: 48–58.

Howarth, R. S. 2006. *The Origin of Roman Citizenship*. Lewiston, NY: Mellen.

Hubbard, T. K. 1991. *The Mask of Comedy: Aristophanes and the Intertextual Parabasis*. Ithaca, NY: Cornell University Press.

Hubbard, T. K. 1997. "Utopianism and the Sophistic City in Aristophanes." In Dobrov 1997: 23–50.

Hughes, G. J. 2001. *Routledge Philosophy Guidebook to Aristotle on Ethics*. London: Routledge.

Hume, David 1978. *A Treatise of Human Nature* [1733], ed. L. A. Selby-Bigge and P. H. Nidditch. Oxford: Clarendon Press.

Humphreys, S. C. 1991. "A Historical Approach to Drakon's Law on Homicide." In Michael Gagarin (ed.), *Symposion 1990: Papers on Greek and Hellenistic Legal History*, 17–45. Cologne: Böhlau.

Humphreys, S. C. 1993. "Diffusion, Comparison, Criticism." In Raaflaub and Müller-Luckner 1993: 1–11.

Humphreys, S. C. 2004. *The Strangeness of Gods: Historical Perspectives on the Interpretation of Athenian Religion*. Oxford: Oxford University Press.

Huntington, S. P. 1996. *The Clash of Civilizations and the Remaking of the World Order*. New York: Simon and Schuster.

Huntington, S. P. 2004. *Who Are We? The Challenges to America's National Identity*. New York: Simon and Schuster.

Hursthouse, R. 1999. *On Virtue Ethics*. Oxford: Oxford University Press.

Ignatieff, M. 2001. *Human Rights as Politics and Idolatry*. Princeton: Princeton University Press.

Invernizzi, A. 1989–90. "Séleucie du Tigre, métropole grecque d'Asie." *Revue Archéologique* 23: 180–5.

Irani, K. D. and Silver, M. (eds) 1995. *Social Justice in the Ancient World*. Westport, CT: Greenwood Press.

Irwin, T. 1977. *Plato's Moral Theory*. Oxford: Clarendon Press.

Irwin, T. 1979. *Plato: Gorgias*. Oxford: Clarendon Press.

Irwin, T. 2005. "Was Socrates against Democracy?" In R. Kamtekar (ed.), *Plato's Apology, Crito and Euthyphro*, 127–49. Lanham, MD: Rowman and Littlefield.

Jacobsen, T. 1946. "Mesopotamia." In H. Frankfort et al.(eds), *The Intellectual Adventure of Ancient Man: An Essay on Speculative Thought in the Ancient Near East*, 123–219. Chicago: University of Chicago Press.

Jaeger, Mary 1997. *Livy's Written Rome*. Ann Arbor: University of Michigan Press.

Jaeger, W. 1948. "On the Origin and Cycle of the Philosophic Ideal of Life." In Jaeger, *Aristotle: Fundamentals of the History of His Development*, trans. R. Robinson, 426–61. 2nd edn. Oxford: Oxford University Press. (Originally "Über Ursprung und Kreislauf des philosophischen Lebensideals" in *Sitzungsberichte der preussischen Akademie der Wissenschaften*, Philosophische-historische Klasse, 1928.)

Janko, R. 1982a. *Homer, Hesiod and the Hymns: Diachronic Development in Epic Diction*. Cambridge: Cambridge University Press.

Janko, R. 1992. *The Iliad: A Commentary*, vol. 4: *Books 13–16*. Cambridge: Cambridge University Press.

Janko, R. 1992. *The Iliad: A Commentary*, vol. 5: *Books 17–20*. Cambridge: Cambridge University Press.

Jefferson, Thomas 1975. *The Portable Thomas Jefferson*. Harmondsworth: Penguin.

Jehne, Martin (ed.) 1995. *Demokratie in Rom? Die Rolle des Volkes in der Politik der römischen Republik*. Stuttgart: Franz Steiner.

Johnson, C. N. 1990. *Aristotle's Theory of the State*. London: Macmillan.

Johnston, David 1999. *Roman Law in Context*. Cambridge: Cambridge University Press.

Joly, R. 1956. "Le thème philosophique des genres de vie dans l'antiquité classique." *Mémoires de l'Académie Royale de Belgique* 51.3: 7–201.

Jones, A. H. M. 1957. *Athenian Democracy.* Oxford: Blackwell. (Repr. 1960.)

Jones, A. H. M. 1960. "How Did the Athenian Democracy Work?" In *Athenian Democracy*, 99–133. Oxford: Basil Blackwell.

Jones, A. H. M. 1964. *The Later Roman Empire 284–602: A Social, Economic, and Administrative History.* 2 vols. Norman: University of Oklahoma Press.

Jones, C. P. 1972. "Aelius Aristides, *Eis Basilea.*" *Journal of Roman Studies* 62: 134–52.

Jones, C. P. 1999. *Kinship Diplomacy in the Ancient World.* Cambridge, MA: Harvard University Press.

Jonnes, L. and Ricl, M. 1997. "A New Royal Inscription from Phrygia Parorcios: Eumenes II Grants Tyraion the Status of a Polis." *Epigraphica Anatolica* 29: 1–30.

Just, R. 1989. *Women in Athenian Law and Life.* London: Routledge.

Kahn, Charles H. 1985. "Democritus and the Origins of Moral Psychology." *American Journal of Philology* 106: 1–31.

Kahn, Charles H. 1995. "The Place of the *Statesman* in Plato's Later Work." In C. J. Rowe (ed.), *Reading the Statesman*, 49–60. Proceedings of the III Symposium Platonicum. Sankt Augustin: Academia.

Kaiser, Brooks A. 2007. "The Athenian Trierarchy: Mechanism Design for the Private Provision of Public Goods." *Journal of Economic History* 67: 445–80.

Kallet, L. 2001. *Money and the Corrosion of Power in Thucydides: The Sicilian Expedition and Its Aftermath.* Berkeley: University of California Press.

Kallet, L. 2003. "Demos Tyrannos: Wealth, Power and Economic Patronage." In Morgan 2003: 117–53.

Kamtekar, R. 2001. "Social Justice and Happiness in the Republic: Plato's Two Principles." *History of Political Thought* 22.2: 189–220.

Kant, I. 1996. "Toward Perpetual Peace: A Philosophical Sketch" [1795]. In Kant, *Practical Philosophy*, ed. M. J. Gregor, 311–51. Cambridge: Cambridge University Press.

Karavites, P. 1992. *Promise-Giving and Treaty-Making: Homer and the Near East.* Leiden: Brill.

Kaster, R. A. 2005a. *Emotion, Restraint, and Community in Ancient Rome.* Oxford: Oxford University Press.

Kaster, R. A. 2005b. "The Passions." In S. J. Harrison (ed.), *A Companion to Latin Literature*, 319–30. Oxford: Blackwell.

Kaster, R. A. 2006. *Cicero: Speech on Behalf of Publius Sestius.* Clarendon Ancient History series. Oxford: Oxford University Press.

Kateb, George 1992. *The Inner Ocean: Individualism and Democratic Culture.* Ithaca, NY: Cornell University Press.

Katz, Marilyn 1999. "Women and Democracy in Ancient Greece." In T. Falkner, N. Felson, and D. Konstan (eds), *Contextualizing Classics: Ideology, Performance, Dialogue*, 41–68. Lanham, MD: Rowman and Littlefield.

Katznelson, I. 1997. "Structure and Configuration in Comparative Politics." In M. Lichbach and A. Zuckerman (eds), *Comparative Politics: Rationality, Culture, and Structure*, 81–112. Cambridge: Cambridge University Press.

Kauppi, M. V. 1991. "Contemporary International Relations Theory and the Peloponnesian War." In Lebow and Strauss 1991: 101–124.

Kelly, Christopher 2004. *Ruling the Later Roman Empire.* Cambridge, MA: Harvard University Press.

Kelly, Gordon 2006. *A History of Exile in the Roman Republic*. Cambridge: Cambridge University Press.

Kennedy, R. F. 2006. "Justice, Geography and Empire in Aeschylus' *Eumenides*." *Classical Antiquity* 25: 35–72.

Kerferd, G. 1981. *The Sophistic Movement*. Cambridge: Cambridge University Press.

Kerschensteiner, J. 1962. *Kosmos: Quellenkritische Untersuchungen zu den Vorsokratikern*. Munich: Beck.

Keyt, D. 1991a. "Three Basic Theorems in Aristotle's Politics." In Keyt and Miller 1991: 118–41.

Keyt, D. 1991b. "Aristotle's Theory of Distributive Justice." In Keyt and Miller 1991: 238–78.

Keyt, D. 1999. *Aristotle. Politics. Books V and* VI. Oxford: Clarendon Press.

Keyt, D. and Miller, F. (eds) 1991. *A Companion to Aristotle's Politics*. Oxford: Blackwell.

Keyt, D. and Robinson, R. 1995. *Aristotle. Politics. Books III–IV*. Oxford: Clarendon Press.

Kielmansegg, P., Mewes, H. and Glaser-Schmit, E. 1995. *Hannah Arendt and Leo Strauss*. Cambridge: Cambridge University Press.

Kienast, B. 1994. "Die Altorientalischen Codices zwischen Mündlichkeit und Schriftlichkeit." In Gehrke 1994: 13–26.

Kienast, Dietmar 1999. *Augustus: Prinzeps und Monarch*, 3rd edn. Darmstadt: Wissenschaftliche Buchgesellschaft.

King, B. L. 1997. "Wisdom and Happiness in Herodotus' Histories." PhD diss., Department of Classics, Princeton University.

King, H. 1998. *Hippocrates' Woman: Reading the Female Body in Ancient Greece*. London: Routledge.

Kirk, G. S. 1970. *Myth: Its Meaning and Function in Ancient and Other Cultures*. Berkeley: University of California Press.

Kirk, G. S. 1988. "The Development of Ideas, 750–500 BC." In J. Boardman et al. (eds), *The Cambridge Ancient History*, vol. 4: 389–413. 2nd edn. Cambridge: Cambridge University Press.

Kirk, G. S. 1990. *The Iliad: A Commentary*, vol. 2: *Books 5–8*. Cambridge: Cambridge University Press.

Kitchen, K. A. 1995. *The Third Intermediate Period in Egypt (1106–650 BC)*. 2nd edn. Warminster: Aris and Phillips.

Kleingeld, Pauline and Brown, Eric 2002. "Cosmopolitanism." In E. N. Zalta (ed.), *The Stanford Encyclopedia of Philosophy*. At http://plato.stanford.edu/archives/fall2002/entries/cosmopolitanism/.

Kleve, K. 1964. "*Apragmosyne* and *Polypragmosune*: Two Slogans in Athenian Politics." *Symbolae Osloenses* 39: 83–8.

Kloesel, H. 1935. "Libertas." Diss., Breslau.

Kloft, H. 1970. *Liberalitas Principis*. Cologne: Böhlau.

Klose, E. 1972. *Die völkerrechtliche Ordnung der hellenistichen Staatenwelt in der Zeit von 289–168 v. Chr*. Munich: C. H. Beck.

Klosko, George 1986. The *Development of Plato's Political Theory*. London: Methuen.

Knoche, U. 1935. *Magnitudo Animi: Untersuchungen zur Entstehung und Entwicklung eines römischen Wertgedankens*. *Philologus*, Supplementband XXVII, Heft 3. Leipzig: Dieterich.

Knoche, U. 1967. "Die römische Ruhmesgedanke." In H. Opperman (ed.), *Römische Wertbegriffe* (Wege der Forschung 34), 420–45. Darmstadt: Wissenschaftliche Buchgesellschaft.

Koebner, R., and Schmidt, H. D. 1964. *Imperialism: The Story and Significance of a Political Word, 1840–1960*. Cambridge: Cambridge University Press.

Koerner, R. 1993. *Inschriftliche Gesetzestexte der frühen griechischen Polis*, ed. K. Halloff. Cologne: Böhlau.

Köhne, Eckart, Ewigleben, Cornelia, and Jackson, Ralph (eds) 2000. *Gladiators and Caesars: The Power of Spectacle in Ancient Rome*. Berkeley: University of California Press.

Kolb, Frank 1977. "Die Bau-, Religions- und Kulturpolitik der Peisistratiden." *Jahrbuch des Deutschen Archäologischen Instituts* 92: 99–138.

König, Jason 2005. *Athletics and Literature in the Roman Empire*. Cambridge: Cambridge University Press.

Konstan, D. 1983. *Roman Comedy*. Ithaca, NY: Cornell University Press.

Konstan, D. 1994. *Sexual Symmetry: Love in the Ancient Novel and Related Genres*. Princeton: Princeton University Press.

Konstan, D. 1995. *Greek Comedy and Ideology*. New York: Oxford University Press.

Konstan, D. 1997a. *Friendship in the Classical World*. Key Themes in Ancient History series. Cambridge: Cambridge University Press.

Konstan, D. 1997b. "Friendship and Monarchy: Dio of Prusa's Third Oration on Kingship." *Symbolae Osloenses* 72: 124–43.

Konstan, D. 2006. *The Emotions of the Ancient Greeks: Studies in Aristotle and Classical Literature*. Toronto: University of Toronto Press.

Koselleck, R. 1985. "Historia Magistra Vitae: The Dissolution of the Topos into the Perspective of a Modernized Historical Process." In Koselleck, *Futures Past: On the Semantics of Historical Time*, 21–38. Cambridge, MA: Harvard University Press.

Kosman, A. 1984. "Substance, Being and *Energeia*." *Oxford Studies in Ancient Philosophy* 2: 121–49.

Kosman, A. 1987. "Animals and Other Beings in Aristotle." In A. Gotthelf and J. Lennox (eds), *Philosophical Issues in Aristotle's Biology*, 360–91. Cambridge: Cambridge University Press.

Kovacs, D. (ed. and trans.) 1999. *Euripides: Trojan Women, Iphigenia among the Taurians, Ion*. Loeb Classical Library. Cambridge, MA: Harvard University Press.

Koziak, B. 2000. *Retrieving Political Emotions. Thumos, Aristotle, and Gender*. University Park: Pennsylvania State University Press.

Kraus, Christina 1994. " 'No Second Troy': Topoi and Refoundation in Livy, Book V." *Transactions of the American Philological Association* 124: 267–89.

Kraus, Christina and Woodman, A. J. 1997. *Latin Historians*. Oxford: Oxford University Press.

Kraut, R. 1984. *Socrates and the State*. Princeton: Princeton University Press.

Kraut, R. 1989. *Aristotle and the Human Good*. Princeton: Princeton University Press.

Kraut, R. 1997. *Aristotle. Politics. Books VII–VIII*. Oxford: Clarendon Press.

Kraut, R. 2002. *Aristotle: Political Philosophy*. Oxford: Oxford University Press.

Kraut, R. (ed.) 2006. *The Blackwell Guide to Aristotle's Nicomachean Ethics*. Oxford: Blackwell.

Kraut, R. and Skultety, S. (eds) 2005. *Aristotle's Politics: Critical Essays*. Lanham, MD: Rowman and Littlefield.

Kreutz, N. 2004. "Fremdartige Kostbarkeiten oder sakraler Müll? Überlegungen zum Stellenwert orientalischer Erzeugnisse in Olympia und zum Selbstverständnis der Griechen im 7. Jh. v. Chr." In M. Novák, F. Prayon, and A.-M. Wittke (eds), *Die Aussenwirkung des späthethitischen Kulturraumes*, 107–20. Münster: Ugarit-Verlag.

Kuhrt, A. 1995. *The Ancient Near East, ca. 3000–330 BC*. 2 vols. London: Routledge.

Kuhrt, A. 2001. "The Achaemenid Persian Empire (c.550–330 BCE): Continuities, Adaptations, Transformations." In S. E. Alcock, T. D'Altroy, K. D. Morrison, and C. M. Sinopoli (eds), *Empires: Perspectives from Archaeology and History*, 93–123. Cambridge: Cambridge University Press.

Kullmann, W. 1991. "Man as a Political Animal." In Keyt and Miller 1991: 94–117. (Originally "Der Mensch als Politisches Lebeswesen bei Aristoteles." *Hermes* 108 (1980): 419–43.)

Kunkel, Wolfgang and Wittman, Roland 1995. *Staatsordnung und Staatspraxis der römischen Republik*. Munich: C. H. Beck.

Kurke, L. 1991. *The Traffic in Praise: Pindar and the Poetics of Social Economy*. Ithaca, NY: Cornell University Press.

Kurke, L. 1998. "The Cultural Impact of (on) Democracy: Decentering Tragedy." In Morris and Raaflaub 1998: 155–69.

Kurke, L. 1999. *Coins, Bodies, Games, and Gold: The Politics of Meaning in Archaic Greece*. Princeton: Princeton University Press.

Kymlicka, W. and Straehle, C. 1999. "Cosmopolitanism, Nation-States, and Minority Nationalism: A Critical Review of Recent Literature." *European Journal of Philosophy* 7: 65–88.

Laks, A. 1991. "L'utopie législative de Platon." *Revue Philosophique* 4: 417–28.

Laks, A. 2000. "The *Laws*." In C. Rowe and Schofield 2000: 258–92.

Lamb, W. R. M. (trans.) 1930. *Lysias*. Loeb Classical Library. Cambridge, MA.: Harvard University Press. (Repr. 1988.)

Lamberton, R. 1988. *Hesiod*. New Haven, CT: Yale University Press.

Landman, T. 2000. *Issues and Methods in Comparative Politics: An Introduction*. London: Routledge.

Landsberger, Benno 1939. "Die babylonischen Termini für Gesetz und Recht." In J. Friedrich, J. G. Lautner, and J. Miles (eds), *Symbolae ad Iura Orientis Antiqui Pertinentes Paulo Koschaker Dedicatae*, 219–34. Leiden: Brill.

Langan, John, S.J. 1991. "The Elements of St Augustine's Just War Theory." In W. S. Babcock (ed.), *The Ethics of St. Augustine*, 169–89. Atlanta, GA: Scholars Press.

Lape, S. 2004. *Reproducing Athens: Menander's Comedy, Democratic Culture, and the Hellenistic City*. Princeton: Princeton University Press.

Laqueur, T. 1990. *Making Sex: Body and Gender from the Greeks to Freud*. Cambridge, MA: Harvard University Press.

Larmour, David, Miller, Paul, and Platter, Charles (eds) 1998. *Rethinking Sexuality: Foucault and Classical Antiquity*. Princeton: Princeton University Press.

Larsen, J. A. O. 1948. "Cleisthenes and the Development of the Theory of Democracy at Athens." In M. Konvitz and A. Murphy (eds), *Essays in Political Theory: Presented to George H. Sabine*, 1–16. Ithaca, NY: Cornell University Press.

Larsen, Mogens T. (ed.) 1979. *Power and Propaganda: A Symposium on Ancient Empires*. Copenhagen: Akademisk Forlag.

Laser, G. 1997. *Populo et scaenae serviendum est: Die Bedeutung der städtischen Masse in der späten römischen Republik*. Bochumer Altertumswissenschaftliches Colloquium 29. Trier: Wissenschaftlicher Verlag Trier.

Lasserre F. 1976. "Hérodote et Protagoras: le débat sur les constitutions." *Museum Helveticum* 33: 65–84.

Lateiner, D. 1984. "Herodotean Historiographical Patterning: The Constitutional Debate." *Quaderni di Storia* 20: 257–84.

Lateiner, D. 1989. *The Historical Method of Herodotus*. Toronto: University of Toronto Press.

Latte, Kurt 1946. "Der Rechtsgedanke im archaischen Griechentum." *Antike and Abendland* 2: 63–76. (Repr. in Latte, *Kleine Schriften zu Religion, Recht, Literatur und Sprache der Griechen und Römer*, 233–51. Munich: Beck.)

Lavelle, B. 2005. *Fame, Money and Power: The Rise of Peisistratos and "Democratic" Tyranny at Athens*. Ann Arbor: University of Michigan Press.

Leach, E. W. 2000. "The *Spectacula* of Cicero's *Pro Sestio*: Patronage, Production, and Performance." In S. K. Dickison and J. P. Hallett (eds), *Rome and Her Monuments: Essays on the City and Literature of Rome in Honor of Katherine A. Geffcken*, 369–97. Wauconda, IL: Bolchazy and Carducci.

Leach, Eleanor 2003. "*Otium* as *Luxuria*: Economy of Status in the Younger Pliny's Letters." *Arethusa* 36: 147–65.

Lebow, R. N. 1991. "Thucydides, Power Transition Theory, and the Causes of War." In Lebow and Strauss 1991: 125–65.

Lebow, R. N. and Strauss, B. S. (eds) 1991. *Hegemonic Rivalry: From Thucydides to the Nuclear Age*. Boulder, CO: Westview.

Lefkowitz, Mary 1996. *Not Out of Africa: How Afrocentrism Became an Excuse to Teach Myth as History*. New York: Basic Books.

Lefkowitz, Mary and Rogers, Guy M. (eds) 1996. *Black Athena Revisited*. Chapel Hill: University of North Carolina Press.

Leigh, Matthew 1997. *Lucan: Spectacle and Engagement*. Oxford: Clarendon Press.

Lekas, Padelis 1988. *Marx on Classical Antiquity: Problems of Historical Methodology*. New York: St Martin's Press.

Lendon, J. E. 1997. *Empire of Honour: The Art of Government in the Roman World*. Oxford: Clarendon Press.

Lendon, J. E. 2005. *Soldiers and Ghosts: A History of Battle in Classical Antiquity*. New Haven, CT: Yale University Press.

Leo, F. 1901. *Die griechische-römische Biographie nach ihrer litterarischen Form*. Leipzig: Teubner.

Lévêque, P. 1968. "La guerre a l'époque hellénistique." In Vernant 1968: 261–87.

Levick, B. 1999. *Tiberius the Politician*. 2nd edn. London: Routledge.

Lévy, E. (ed.) 2000. *La Codification des lois dans l'antiquité*. Strasbourg: Centre de Recherches sur le Proche-Orient et la Grèce Antiques.

Lévy, E. 2005. "Isonomia." In Bultrighini 2005: 119–37.

Lewis, D. M. et al. (eds) 1992. *The Cambridge Ancient History*, vol. 5: *The Fifth Century* BC. 2nd edn. Cambridge: Cambridge University Press.

Lewis, D. M., Boardman, J., Hornblower, S., and Ostwald, M. (eds) 1994. *The Cambridge Ancient History*, vol. 6: *The Fourth Century* BC. Cambridge: Cambridge University Press.

Lewis, N. 1986. *Greeks in Ptolemaic Egypt: Case Studies in the Social History of the Hellenistic World*. Oxford: Clarendon Press.

Lewis, S. 2004. " 'Kai saphos tyrannos en': Xenophon's account of Euphron of Sicyon." *Journal of Hellenic Studies* 124: 65–74.

Lewis, S. (ed.) 2006. *Ancient Tyranny*. Edinburgh: Edinburgh University Press.

L'Homme-Wéry, L. M. 1999. "Eleusis and Solon's *Seisachtheia*." *Greek, Roman, and Byzantine Studies* 40: 109–33.

Lichbach, M. 1997. "Social Theory and Comparative Politics." In M. Lichbach and A. Zuckerman (eds), *Comparative Politics: Rationality, Culture, and Structure*, 239–76. Cambridge: Cambridge University Press.

Licht, Robert A. 1978. "Reflections on Martin Diamond's 'Ethics and Politics: The American Way.' " *Publius: The Journal of Federalism* 8.3: 183–211.

Liddel, P. 2007. *Civic Obligation and Individual Liberty in Ancient Athens*. Oxford: Oxford University Press.

Lincoln, B. 2007. *Religion, Empire, and Torture: The Case of Achaemenian Persia, with a Postscript on Abu Ghraib*. Chicago: University of Chicago Press.

Lind, L. R. 1979. "The Tradition of Roman Moral Conservatism." In C. Deroux (ed.), *Studies in Latin Literature and Roman History* I, 7–58. Brussels: Collection Latomus 164.

Lind, L. R. 1986. "The Idea of the Republic and the Foundations of Roman Political Liberty," in C. Deroux (ed.), *Studies in Latin Literature and Roman History* IV, 44–108. Brussels: Collection Latomus 196.

Lind, L. R. 1989. "The Idea of the Republic and the Foundations of Roman Morality I." In C. Deroux (ed.), *Studies in Latin Literature and Roman History* V, Brussels. Collection Latomus 206.

Lind, L. R. 1992. "The Idea of the Republic and the Foundations of Roman Morality II." In C. Deroux (ed.), *Studies in Latin Literature and Roman History* VI, 5–40. Brussels: Collection Latomus 217.

Lines, David A. 2002. *Aristotle's Ethics in the Italian Renaissance (ca. 1300–1650): The Universities and the Problem of Moral Education.* Education and Society in the Middle Ages and Renaissance 13. Leiden: Brill.

Lintott, A. W. 1981. "What Was the 'Imperium Romanum'?" *Greece and Rome,* n.s. 28: 53–67.

Lintott, A. W. 1993. *Imperium Romanum: Politics and Administration.* London: Routledge.

Lintott, A. W. 1997. "The Theory of the Mixed Constitution at Rome." In J. Barnes and M. Griffin (eds), *Philosophia Togata II: Plato and Aristotle in Rome,* 70–85. Oxford: Oxford University Press.

Lintott, A. W. 1999a. *The Constitution of the Roman Republic.* Oxford: Clarendon Press.

Lintott, A. W. 1999b. *Violence in Republican Rome.* 2nd edn. Oxford: Oxford University Press.

Lintott, A. 2000. "Aristotle and the Mixed Constitution." In Brock and Hodkinson 2000.

Lisle, Robert 1977. "Thucydides 1.22.4." *Classical Journal* 72: 342–7.

Lloyd, A. B. 1975–88. *Herodotus, Book II,* I: *Introduction* (repr. 1994); II: *Commentary.* Leiden: Brill.

Loewenstein, Karl 1973. *The Governance of Rome.* The Hague: Martinus Nijhoff.

Long, A. A. 1995. "Cicero's Politics in *De officiis.*" In A. Laks and M. Schofield (eds), *Justice and Generosity: Studies in Hellenistic Social and Political Philosophy,* 213–40. Cambridge: Cambridge University Press.

Long, A. A. and Sedley, D. (eds) 1987. *The Hellenistic Philosophers.* Cambridge: Cambridge University Press.

Long, Tony 2008. "The Concept of the Cosmopolitan in Greek and Roman Thought." *Daedalus* 137: 50–8.

Loraux, N. 1986. *The Invention of Athens: The Funeral Oration in the Classical City,* trans. A. Sheridan. Cambridge, MA: Harvard University Press.

Loraux, N. 1993. *The Children of Athena: Athenian Ideas about Citizenship and the Division between the Sexes,* trans. C. Levine. Princeton: Princeton University Press. (French original 1984.)

Loraux. N. 2000. *Born of the Earth: Myth and Politics in Athens,* trans. S. Stewart. Ithaca, NY: Cornell University Press.

Lord, C. (trans.) 1984. *The Politics of Aristotle.* Chicago: University of Chicago Press.

Love, John 1991. *Antiquity and Capitalism: Max Weber and the Sociological Foundations of Roman Civilization.* London: Routledge.

Low, Polly 2007. *Interstate Relations in Classical Greece: Morality and Power.* Cambridge: Cambridge University Press.

Lowry, S. Todd 1979. "Recent Literature on Ancient Greek Economic Thought." *Journal of Economic Literature* 17: 65–86.

Lu, Catherine. 2000. "The One and Many Faces of Cosmopolitanism." *Journal of Political Philosophy* 8: 244–67.

Ludwig, P. W. 2002. *Eros and Polis: Desire and Community in Greek Political Theory.* Cambridge: Cambridge University Press.

Ludwig, P. W. 2007. "Eros in the *Republic.*" In G. R. F. Ferrari (ed.), *The Cambridge Companion to Plato's Republic*, 202–31. Cambridge: Cambridge University Press.

Luraghi, Nino, and Alcock, Susan (eds) 2003. *Helots and Their Masters in Laconia and Messenia: Histories, Ideologies, Structures.* Washington, DC: Center for Hellenic Studies.

Lutz, M. 1998. *Socrates' Education to Virtue: Learning the Love of the Noble.* Albany: State University of New York Press.

Lyons, John D. 1990. *Exemplum: The Rhetoric of Example in Early Modern France and Italy.* Princeton: Princeton University Press.

Ma, J. T. 2000. "Fighting Poleis in the Hellenistic World." In Van Wees 2000: 337–76.

Ma, J. T. 2002. *Antiochus III and the Cities of Western Asia Minor.* 2nd edn. Oxford: Oxford University Press.

MacDowell, D. M. 1978. *The Law in Classical Athens.* Ithaca, NY: Cornell University Press.

Machinist, P. 1993. "Assyrians on Assyria in the First Millennium BC." In Raaflaub and Müller-Luckner 1993: 77–104.

MacIntyre, A. 1984. *After Virtue: A Study in Moral Theory.* Notre Dame, IN: University of Notre Dame Press.

MacIntyre, A. 1988. *Whose Justice? Which Rationality?* London: Duckworth.

MacIntyre, A. 2001. *Dependent Rational Animals.* LaSalle, IL: Open Court.

MacKendrick, Paul 1969. *The Athenian Aristocracy, 399 to 31 BC.* Cambridge, MA: Harvard University Press.

Mackenzie, M. M. 1981. *Plato on Punishment.* Berkeley: University of California Press.

Mackie, G. 2003. *Democracy Defended.* Cambridge: Cambridge University Press.

Mackie, J. L. 1984. "Can There Be a Right-Based Moral Theory?" In J. Waldron (ed.), *Theories of Rights*, 168–81. Oxford: Oxford University Press.

MacMullen, R. 1974. *Roman Social Relations, 50 BC to AD 284.* New Haven, CT: Yale University Press.

MacMullen, R. 1988. *Corruption and the Decline of Rome.* New Haven, CT: Yale University Press.

MacMullen, R. 2000. *Romanization in the Time of Augustus.* New Haven, CT: Yale University Press.

Madison, J., Hamilton, A., and Jay, J. 1987. *The Federalist Papers*, ed. I. Kramnick. London: Penguin.

Major, W. 1997. "Menander in a Macedonian World." *Greek Roman and Byzantine Studies* 38: 41–74.

Malkin, I. 1987. *Religion and Colonization in Ancient Greece.* Leiden: Brill.

Malkin, I. 1998. *The Returns of Odysseus: Colonization and Ethnicity.* Berkeley: University of California Press.

Mandelbaum, M. 2005. *The Case for Goliath: How America Acts as the World's Government in the 21st Century.* New York: Public Affairs Books.

Manent, Pierre 1998. *The City of Man.* Princeton: Princeton University Press.

Mansfield, Harvey C., Jr 1979. *New Modes and Orders: A Study of the Discourses on Livy.* Ithaca, NY: Cornell University Press.

Mansfield, Harvey C., Jr (trans.) 1985. *Niccolò Machiavelli. The Prince.* Chicago: University of Chicago Press.

Mansfield, Harvey C., Jr 1989. *Taming the Prince: The Ambivalence of Modern Executive Power.* Baltimore: Johns Hopkins University Press.

Mansfield, Harvey C., Jr 1996. *Machiavelli's Virtue.* Chicago: University of Chicago Press.

Mansfield, Harvey C., Jr and Tarcov, Nathan (trans.) 1996. *Machiavelli. Discourses.* Chicago: University of Chicago Press.

Mansfield, H. 2006. *Manliness.* London and New Haven: Yale University Press.

Manville, P. B. 1990. *The Origins of Citizenship in Ancient Athens.* Princeton: Princeton University Press.

Manville, P. B. 1994. "Toward a New Paradigm of Athenian Citizenship." In Boegehold and Scafuro 1994: 21–33.

Manville, B. 1997. "Pericles and the 'both/and' Vision for Democratic Athens." In C. D. Hamilton and P. Krentz (eds), *Polis and Polemos: Essays on Politics, War, and History in Ancient Greece, in Honor of Donald Kagan*, 73–84. Claremont, CA: Regina.

Manville, B. and Ober, J. 2003. *A Company of Citizens: What the World's First Democracy Teaches Leaders about Creating Great Organizations.* Boston: Harvard Business School Press.

Marchand, Suzanne, and Grafton, Anthony 1997. "Martin Bernal and His Critics." *Arion* 5.2: 1–35.

Markell, P. 2003. *Bound by Recognition.* Princeton: Princeton University Press.

Markle, M. 1985. "Jury Pay and Assembly Pay at Athens." In P. Cartledge and F. Harvey (eds), *Crux: Essays in Greek History Presented to G. E. M. de Ste Croix on His Seventy-Fifth Birthday*, 265–97. London: Duckworth.

Markus, R. A. (ed.) 1972. *Augustine: A Collection of Critical Essays.* Garden City, NY: Doubleday.

Markus, R. A. 1988. *Saeculum: History and Society in the Theology of St Augustine.* New York: Cambridge University Press.

Martin, Jochen 1994. "Der Verlust der Stadt." In C. Meier (ed.), *Die Okzidentale Stadt nach Max Weber: Zum Problem der Zugehörigkeit in Antike und Mittelalter*, 95–114. Munich: R. Oldenbourg.

Martin, R. H. 1981. *Tacitus.* Berkeley: University of California Press.

Martin, R. P. 1993. "The Seven Sages as Performers of Wisdom." In Dougherty and Kurke 1993: 108–28.

Marx, K. 1973. *Grundrisse: Introduction to the Critique of Political Economy.* New York: Vintage.

Marx, Karl 1975. Letter from Marx to Arnold Ruge, May 1843. In *Early Writings*, trans. R. Livingstone and G. Benton, 200–6. New York: Vintage.

Matthes, Melissa 2000. *The Rape of Lucretia and the Founding of Republics.* University Park: Pennsylvania State University Press.

Mayhew, R. 2004. *The Female in Aristotle's Biology: Reason or Rationalization.* Chicago: University of Chicago Press.

McCarthy, George 2003. *Classical Horizons: The Origins of Sociology in Ancient Greece.* Albany: State University of New York Press.

McDonnell, Miles 2006. *Roman Manliness: Virtus and the Roman Republic.* Cambridge: Cambridge University Press.

McDowell, J. (trans.) 1973. *Plato. Theaetetus.* Oxford: Clarendon Press.

McDowell, J. 1979. "Virtue and Reason." *Monist* 62: 331–50.

McDowell, J. 1981. "Non-cognitivism and Rule-Following." In S. Holtzman and C. Leich (eds), *Wittgenstein: To Follow A Rule*, 141–62. London: Routledge and Kegan Paul.

McDowell, J. 1987. "Projection and Truth in Ethics." Lindley Lecture, University of Kansas.

McDowell, J. 1996. "Deliberation and Moral Development in Aristotle's *Ethics*." In S. Engstrom and J. Whiting (eds), *Kant and the Stoics*, 19–35. Cambridge: Cambridge University Press.

McGing, B. C. 1986. *The Foreign Policy of Mithridates VI Eupator, King of Pontus.* Leiden: Brill.

McGlew, James 1993. *Tyranny and Political Culture in Ancient Greece*. Ithaca, NY: Cornell University Press.

McGlew, J. 2002. *Citizens on Stage: Comedy and Political Culture in the Athenian Democracy.* Ann Arbor: University of Michigan Press.

McGushin, Patrick (ed. and trans.) 1994. *Sallust. The Histories*, vol. 2: *Books III–V*. Oxford: Oxford University Press.

McKeown, Niall 1999. "Some Thoughts on Marxism and Ancient Greek History." *Helios* 26: 103–28.

McManus, Barbara (ed.) 1997. *Classics and Feminism: Gendering the Classics*. New York: Twayne.

McPherran, M. L. 1996. *The Religion of Socrates*. University Park: Pennsylvania State University Press.

McShane, R. B. 1964. *The Foreign Policy of the Attalids of Pergamum*. Urbana: University of Illinois Press.

Mead, W. R. 2004. *Power, Terror, Peace, and War: America's Grand Strategy in a World at Risk*. New York: Knopf.

Mearsheimer, J. J. 2001. *The Tragedy of Great Power Politics*. New York: W. W. Norton.

Meier, C. 1980. *Res Publica Amissa: Eine Studie zu Verfassung und Geschichte der späten römischen Republik*. Frankfurt: Suhrkamp.

Meier, C. 1988. "Max Weber und die Antike." In C. Gneuss and J. Kocka (eds), *Max Weber: Ein Symposion*, 11–24. Munich: Deutscher Taschenbuch.

Meier, C. 1990a. "C. Caesar Divi filius and the Formation of the Alternative in Rome." In K. A. Raaflaub and M. Toher (eds), *Between Republic and Empire: Interpretations of Augustus and His Principate*, 54–70. Berkeley: University of California Press.

Meier, C. 1990b. *The Greek Discovery of Politics*, trans. D. McLintock. Cambridge, MA: Harvard University Press.

Meier, C. 1993. *The Political Art of Greek Tragedy*, trans. A. Webber. Baltimore: Johns Hopkins University Press. (German original 1988.)

Meier, Christian 1994a. "Bemerkungen zum Problem der 'Verbrüderung' in Athen und Rom." In Meier 1994b: 18–33.

Meier, Christian (ed.) 1994b. *Die okzidentale Stadt nach Max Weber: Zum Problem der Zugehörigkeit in Antike und Mittelalter*. Munich: R. Oldenbourg.

Meiggs, R. 1972. *The Athenian Empire*. Oxford: Clarendon Press.

Meikle, S. 1995. *Aristotle's Economic Thought*. Oxford: Clarendon Press.

Mendelsohn, D. 2002. *Gender and the City in Euripides' Political Plays*. Princeton: Princeton University Press.

Metzler, Dieter 1980. "Eunomia und Aphrodite. Zur Ikonologie einer attischen Vasengruppe." *Hephaistos* 2: 73–88.

Mewes, Horst 1976. "On the Concept of Politics in the Early Work of Karl Marx." *Social Research* 43: 276–94.

Michell, H. 1952. *Sparta*. Cambridge: Cambridge University Press.

Milbank, John 1991. *Theology and Social Theory: Beyond Secular Reason*. Oxford: Blackwell. (Repr. 2006.)

Miles, G. B. 1995. *Livy: Reconstructing Early Rome*. Ithaca, NY: Cornell University Press.

Mill, J. S. 1991. "On Liberty" [1859]. In Mill, *On Liberty and Other Essays*, ed. J. Gray, 5–128. Oxford: Oxford University Press.

Millar, F. 1977. *The Emperor in the Roman World (31 BC–AD 337)*. London: Duckworth.

Millar, F. 1984. "The Political Character of the Classical Roman Republic, 200–151 BC." *Journal of Roman Studies* 74: 1–19.

Millar, F. 1986. "Politics, Persuasion, and the People before the Social War (150–90 BC)." *Journal of Roman Studies* 76: 1–11.

Millar, F. 1989. "Political Power in Mid-Republican Rome: Curia or Comitium?" *Journal of Roman Studies* 79: 138–50.

Millar, F. 1998. *The Crowd in Rome in the Late Republic*. Ann Arbor: University of Michigan Press.

Millar, F. 2002a. *The Roman Republic in Political Thought*. Hanover: University Press of New England for Brandeis University Press.

Millar, F. 2002b. *Rome, the Greek World, and the East*, vol. 1: *The Roman Republic and the Augustan Revolution*. Chapel Hill: University of North Carolina Press.

Miller, D. 1999. *On Nationality* [1995]. Oxford: Oxford University Press.

Miller, F. 1995. *Nature, Justice, and Rights in Aristotle's* Politics. Oxford: Clarendon Press.

Miller, F. 2000. "Naturalism." In C. Rowe and Schofield 2000: 321–43.

Miller, F. 2002. "Aristotle's Political Theory." In E. N. Zalta (ed.), *The Stanford Encyclopedia of Philosophy*. At http://plato.stanford.edu/archives/fall2002/entries/aristotle-politics/.

Miller, M. C. 1997. *Athens and Persia in the Fifth Century* BC: *A Study in Cultural Receptivity*. Cambridge: Cambridge University Press.

Miller, Paul 1998. "Catullan Consciousness, the 'Care of the Self,' and the Force of the Negative in History." In Larmour, Miller, and Platter 1998: 171–203.

Miller, Walter (trans.) 1914. *Xenophon: Cyropaedia*, vol. 5. Loeb Classical Library. Cambridge, MA: Harvard University Press.

Millett, P. 1998. "The Rhetoric of Reciprocity in Classical Athens." In C. Gill, N. Postlethwaite, and R. Seaford (eds), *Reciprocity in Ancient Greece*, 227–53. Oxford: Oxford University Press.

Mills, S. 1997. *Theseus, Tragedy and the Athenian Empire*. Oxford: Oxford University Press.

Mitchell, T. N. 1991. *Cicero: The Senior Statesman*. New Haven, CT: Yale University Press.

Moles, J. 1990. "The Kingship Orations of Dio Chrysostom." *Papers of the Leeds International Latin Seminar* 6: 297–375.

Moles, J. L. 1996. "Cynic Cosmopolitanism." In R. Bracht Branham and M.-O. Goulet-Cazé (eds), *The Cynics: The Cynic Movement in Antiquity and Its Legacy*, 105–20. Berkeley: University of California Press.

Molho, Anthony, Raaflaub, Kurt, and Emlen, Julia (eds) 1991. *City States in Classical Antiquity and Medieval Italy*. Ann Arbor: University of Michigan Press.

Momigliano, A. D. 1940. "Review of R. Syme, *The Roman Revolution*." *Journal of Roman Studies* 30: 75–80.

Momigliano, A. D. 1941. "Review of B. Farrington, *Science and Politics in the Ancient World*." *Journal of Roman Studies* 31: 149–57.

Momigliano, A. D. 1951. "Review of Wirszubski, *Libertas as a Political Idea at Rome during the Late Republic and Early Principate*." *Journal of Roman Studies* 41: 146–53.

Momigliano, A. D. 1971. *The Development of Greek Biography*. Cambridge, MA: Harvard University Press.

Momigliano, A. D. 1987. *Essays in Ancient and Modern Historiography*. Middletown, CT: Wesleyan University Press.

Mommsen, Th. 1887–8. *Römisches Staatsrecht*. 3 vols. 3rd edn. Leipzig: Hirzel.

Monoson, S. S. 2000. *Plato's Democratic Entanglements: Athenian Politics and the Practice of Philosophy*. Princeton: Princeton University Press.

Montesquieu, C.-L. de Secondat 1989. *The Spirit of the Laws*, trans. A. Cohler. Cambridge: Cambridge University Press.

Moore, G. E. 1903. *Principia Ethica*. Cambridge: Cambridge University Press. (Rev. edn with "Preface to the Second Edition" and other papers, ed. T. Baldwin, Cambridge: Cambridge University Press, 2002.)

Moore, G. E. 1959. "Proof of an External World." In *Philosophical Papers*, 127–50. London: Allen and Unwin.

Morenz, S. 1960. *Ägyptische Religion*. Stuttgart: Kohlhammer.

Morenz, S. 1973. *Egyptian Religion*, trans. A. E. Keep. London: Methuen.

Morgan, K. A. (ed.) 2003. *Popular Tyranny: Sovereignty and Its Discontents in Ancient Greece*. Austin: University of Texas Press.

Morkholm, O. 1991. *Early Hellenistic Coinage from the Accession of Alexander to the Peace of Apamea (336–188 BC)*. Cambridge: Cambridge University Press.

Morley, N. (ed.) 1999. *Marx and Antiquity*. *Helios*, special issue, 26.2.

Morley, N. 2004. *Theories, Models and Concepts in Ancient History*. London: Routledge.

Morris, I. 1986. "The Use and Abuse of Homer." *Classical Antiquity* 5: 81–138. (Repr. in D. Cairns (ed.), *Oxford Readings in Homer's Iliad*, 57–91. Oxford: Oxford University Press, 2001.)

Morris, I. 1994. "Review Article: The Athenian Economy Twenty Years after *The Ancient Economy*." *Classical Philology* 89: 351–66.

Morris, I. 1996 "The Strong Principle of Equality and the Archaic Origins of Greek Democracy." In Ober and Hedrick 1996: 19–48.

Morris, I. 1999. "Archaeology and Gender Ideologies in Early Archaic Greece." *Transactions of the American Philological Association* 129: 305–17.

Morris, I. 2000. *Archaeology as Cultural History: Words and Things in Iron Age Greece*. Oxford: Blackwell.

Morris, I. 2005. "The Athenian Empire (478–404 BC)." Princeton/Stanford Working Papers in Classics. At www.princeton.edu/~pswpc/pdfs/morris/120508.pdf/.

Morris, I. and Raaflaub, K. A. (eds) 1998. *Democracy 2500? Questions and Challenges*. Dubuque, IA: Kendall/Hunt.

Morris, S. P. 1992. *Daidalos and the Origins of Greek Art*. Princeton: Princeton University Press.

Morrow, G. R. 1960. *Plato's Cretan City: A Historical Interpretation of the* Laws. Princeton: Princeton University Press.

Morschauser, S. N. 1995. "The Ideological Basis for Social Justice/Responsibility in Ancient Egypt." In Irani and Silver 1995: 101–13.

Morstein-Marx [Kallett Marx], R. 1995. *Hegemony to Empire: The Development of the Roman Imperium in the East from 148 to 62 BC*. Berkeley: University of California Press.

Morstein-Marx, R. 2004. *Mass Oratory and Political Power in the Late Roman Republic*. Cambridge: Cambridge University Press.

Morwood, J. 2007. *Euripides: Suppliant Women*. Oxford: Aris and Phillips.

Mouritsen, H. 2001. *Plebs and Politics in the Late Roman Republic*. Cambridge: Cambridge University Press.

Mueller, Dennis C. 2003. *Public Choice III*. Cambridge: Cambridge University Press.

Mühl, Max 1933. *Untersuchungen zur altorientalischen und althellenischen Gesetzgebung*. Klio Supp. 29. Leipzig: Dieterich.

Mulgan, R. 1977. *Aristotle's Political Theory*. Oxford: Oxford University Press.

Mülke, Christoph 2002. *Solons politische Elegien und Iamben (Fr. 1–13; 32–37 West). Einleitung, Text, Übersetzung, Kommentar*. Leipzig: Sauer.

Muller, O. 1973. *Antigonos Monophthalmos und das "Jahr der Könige."* Bonn: Rudolf Habelt.

Münzer, F. 1920. *Römische Adelspartien und Adelsfamilien.* Stuttgart: Carl Ernst Poeschel. (Trans. T. Ridley as *Roman Aristocratic Parties and Families.* Baltimore: Johns Hopkins University Press, 1999.)

Murphy, P. R. 1985–6. "Caesar's Continuators and Caesar's *felicitas.*" *Classical World* 79: 307–17.

Murray, A. T. (trans.) 2001. *Demosthenes: Orations L–LIX.* Loeb Classical Library. Cambridge, MA: Harvard University Press.

Murray, O. 1967. "Aristeas and Ptolemaic Kingship." *Journal of Theological Studies* 18: 337–71.

Murray, O. 1993. *Early Greece.* 2nd edn. Cambridge, MA: Harvard University Press.

Murray, O. 1996. "Hellenistic Royal Symposia." In Bilde et al. 1996a: 15–27.

Murray, O. and Price, S. (eds) 1990. *The Greek City: From Homer to Alexander.* Oxford: Clarendon Press.

Myers, R. 1991. "La démocratie chez Hérodote. Une étude du débat sur les régimes." *Canadian Journal of Political Science/Revue Canadienne de Science Politique* 24.3: 541–55.

Nagle, B. 2006. *The Household as the Foundation of Aristotle's Polis.* Cambridge: Cambridge University Press.

Nagy, G. 1990a. *Greek Mythology and Poetics.* Ithaca, NY: Cornell University Press.

Nagy, G. 1990b. *Pindar's Homer: The Lyric Possession of an Epic Past.* Baltimore: Johns Hopkins University Press.

Nagy, G. 1996. *Homeric Questions.* Austin: University of Texas Press.

Nails, Debra 1995. *Agora, Academy, and the Conduct of Philosophy.* Dordrecht: Kluwer.

Nails, Debra 2002. *The People of Plato: A Prosopography of Plato and Other Socratics.* Indianapolis: Hackett.

Natali, C. 2001. *The Wisdom of Aristotle.* Albany: State University of New York Press.

Neer, R. T. 2002. *Style and Politics in Athenian Vase-Painting: The Craft of Democracy, ca. 530–460 BCE.* Cambridge: Cambridge University Press.

Nehamas, A. 1998. *The Art of Living: Socratic Reflections from Plato to Foucault.* Berkeley: University of California Press.

Nestle, D. 1972. "Freiheit." *Reallexikon für Antike und Christentum* 8: 269–306. Stuttgart: Hiersemann.

Nestle, W. 1926. "*Apragmosunē* (zu Thukydides II 63.)." *Philology* 81: 129–40.

Neustadt, Richard and May, Ernest 1986. *Thinking in Time: The Uses of History for Decision-Makers.* New York: Free Press.

Newell, W. R. 1987. "Superlative Virtue: The Problem of Monarchy in Aristotle's *Politics.*" *Western Political Quarterly* 40.1: 159–78.

Newman, W. L. 1887–1902. *The Politics of Aristotle.* 4 vols. Oxford: Clarendon Press.

Nichols, James H. 1998. *Plato's Gorgias.* Ithaca, NY: Cornell University Press.

Nichols, M. 1992. *Citizens and Statesmen: A Study of Aristotle's Politics.* Lanham, MD: Rowman and Littlefield.

Nicolet, C. 1980. *The World of the Citizen in Republican Rome.* Ithaca, NY: Cornell University Press.

Nicolet, C. 1990. *Space, Geography, and Politics in the Early Roman Empire.* Ann Arbor: University of Michigan Press.

Nielsen, K. 2005. "Cosmopolitanism." *South African Journal of Philosophy* 24: 273–88.

Nietzsche, F. 1967. *On the Genealogy of Morals* [1887], trans. W. Kaufmann and R. J. Hollingdale. In Nietzsche, *On the Genealogy of Morals and Ecce Homo.* New York: Vintage.

Nietzsche, F. 1968a. *The Birth of Tragedy,* trans. W. Kaufman. New York: Modern Library.

Nietzsche, F. 1968b. *The Portable Nietzsche,* trans. W. Kaufman. New York: Viking.

Nippel, W. 1980. *Mischverfassungstheorie und Verfassungsrealität in Antike und Frühere Neuzeit.* Geschichte und Gesellschaft 21. Stuttgart: Klett-Cotta.

Nippel, W. 1994. "Max Weber zwischen Althistorie und Universal-geschichte: Synoikismos und Verbrüderung." In Meier 1994b: 35–57.

Nippel, W. 1995. *Public Order in Ancient Rome.* Cambridge: Cambridge University Press.

Nixon, C. E. V. and Rodgers, B. S. 1994. *In Praise of Later Roman Emperors: The Panegyrici Latini.* Berkeley: University of California Press.

Nock, A. D. 1933. *Conversion: The Old and the New in Religion from Alexander the Great to Augustine of Hippo.* Oxford: Clarendon Press.

Nock, A. D. 1972. *Essays on Religion and the Ancient World*, ed. Z. Stewart. 2 vols. Oxford: Clarendon Press.

Norlin, G. (trans.) 1929. *Isocrates*, vol. 2. Loeb Classical Library. Cambridge, MA: Harvard University Press.

North, H. 1966. *Sophrosyne: Self-Knowledge and Self-Restraint in Greek Literature.* Ithaca, NY: Cornell University Press.

North, J. 1990. "Democratic Politics in Republican Rome." *Past and Present* 126: 3–21. (Repr. in R. Osborne 2004a: 140–58.)

Nozick, R. 1974. *Anarchy, State and Utopia.* New York: Basic Books.

Nussbaum, M. C. 1986. *The Fragility of Goodness.* Cambridge: Cambridge University Press.

Nussbaum, M. C. 1988. "Non-relative Virtues: An Aristotelian Approach." In P. A. French, T. E. Uehling, Jr, and H. K. Wettstein (eds), *Ethical Theory: Character and Virtue*, 32–53. Midwest Studies in Philosophy 13. Notre Dame, IN: University of Notre Dame Press.

Nussbaum, M. C. 1990a. "Aristotelian Social Democracy". In B. Douglass, G. Mara, and H. Richardson (eds), *Liberalism and the Good*, 203–52. London: Routledge. (Repr. in Tessitore 2002: 47–104.)

Nussbaum, M. C. 1990b. *Love's Knowledge: Essays on Philosophy and Literature.* Oxford: Oxford University Press.

Nussbaum, M. C. 1994. *The Therapy of Desire: Theory and Practice in Hellenistic Ethics.* Princeton: Princeton University Press.

Nussbaum, M. C. 1995. "Aristotle on Human Nature and the Foundations of Ethics." In J. E. J. Altham and R. Harrison (eds), *World, Mind, and Ethics*, 86–131. Cambridge: Cambridge University Press.

Nussbaum, M. C. 2000. "Duties of Justice, Duties of Material Aid: Cicero's Problematic Legacy." *Journal of Political Philosophy* 8: 176–206.

Nussbaum, M. C. 2001. *Upheavals of Thought: The Intelligence of Emotions.* Cambridge: Cambridge University Press.

Nussbaum, M. C. and Cohen, J. (eds) 2002. *For Love of Country?* [1996]. Boston: Beacon Press.

Nussbaum, Martha and Sihvola, Juha (eds) 2002. *The Sleep of Reason: Erotic Experience and Sexual Ethics in Ancient Greece and Rome.* Chicago: University of Chicago Press.

Nyerere, J. K. 1975. "Democracy and the Party System" [1963]. In M. Mutiso and S. W. Rohio (eds), *Readings in African Political Thought*, 478–81. London: Heinemann.

Ober, J. 1989. *Mass and Elite in Democratic Athens: Rhetoric, Ideology and the Power of the People.* Princeton: Princeton University Press.

Ober, J. 1993. "The Athenian Revolution of 508/7 BCE: Violence, Authority, and the Origins of Democracy." In Dougherty and Kurke 1993: 215–32.

Ober, J. 1996. *The Athenian Revolution: Essays on Ancient Greek Democracy and Political Theory.* Princeton: Princeton University Press.

Ober, J. 1998. *Political Dissent in Democratic Athens: Intellectual Critics of Popular Rule.* Princeton: Princeton University Press.

Ober, J. 2000. "Political Conflicts, Political Debates, and Political Thought." In R. Osborne (ed.), *The Shorter Oxford History of Europe I: Classical Greece*, 111–38. Oxford: Oxford University Press.

Ober, J. 2003. "Tyrant-Killing as Therapeutic Stasis: A Political Debate in Images and Texts." In Morgan 2003: 215–50.

Ober, J. 2004. "I, Socrates ... The Performative Audacity of Isocrates' *Antidosis.*" In T. Poulakos and D. Depew (eds), *Isocrates and Civic Education*, 21–43. Austin: University of Texas Press.

Ober, J. 2005a. "Aristotle's Natural Democracy." In Kraut and Skultety 2005: 223–43.

Ober, J. 2005b. "Quasi-Rights: Participatory Citizenship and Negative Liberties". In Ober 2005c: 92–127. (Originally published in *Social Philosophy and Policy* 12 (2000): 27–61.)

Ober, J. 2005c. *Athenian Legacies: Essays on the Politics of Going on Together.* Princeton: Princeton University Press.

Ober, J. 2006. "Thucydides and the Invention of Political Science." In A. Rengakos and A. Tsakmakis (eds), *Brill's Companion to Thucydides*, 131–59. Leiden: Brill.

Ober, J. 2007. "Natural Capacities and Democracy as a Good-in-Itself." *Philosophical Studies* 132: 59–73.

Ober, J. 2008. *Democracy and Knowledge: Learning and Innovation in Classical Athens.* Princeton: Princeton University Press.

Ober, J. and Hedrick, C. (eds) 1996. *Dēmokratia: A Conversation on Democracies, Ancient and Modern.* Princeton: Princeton University Press.

O'Daly, Gerard 1999. *Augustine's* City of God*: A Reader's Guide.* Oxford: Clarendon Press.

O'Donnell, G. 1994. "Delegative Democracy." *Journal of Democracy* 5: 55–69.

O'Donnell, James J. 2005. *Augustine, Sinner and Saint: A New Biography.* London: Profile.

O'Donovan, O. M. T. 1980. *The Problem of Self-Love in Saint Augustine.* New Haven, CT: Yale University Press.

O'Donovan, O. M. T. 1987. "Augustine's City of God XIX and Western Political Thought." *Dionysius* 11: 89–110.

O'Donovan, O. M. T. 2002. *Common Objects of Love: Moral Reflection and the Shaping of Community.* Grand Rapids, MI: Eerdmans.

Offner, A. 1995. "Going to War in 1914: A Matter of Honor?" *Politics and Society* 23: 213–41.

Ogden, D. 1996. *Greek Bastardy in the Classical and the Hellenistic Periods.* Oxford: Oxford University Press.

Ogilvie, R. M. 1965. *A Commentary on Livy. Books 1–5.* Oxford: Clarendon Press.

Ogle, W. (trans.) 1882. *Aristotle. On the Parts of Animals.* London: Kegan Paul, Trench.

Oldfield, A. 1990. *Citizenship and Community: Civic Republicanism and the Modern World.* London: Routledge.

O'Leary, Timothy 2002. *Foucault: The Art of Ethics.* London: Continuum.

Olson, Mancur 1965. *The Logic of Collective Action: Public Goods and the Theory of Groups.* Cambridge, MA: Harvard University Press.

O'Neill, Eugene, Jr (ed. and trans.) 1938. *Aristophanes. Ecclesiazusae.* In vol. 2 of *The Complete Greek Drama.* New York: Random House.

O'Neill, J. 1995. *The Origins and Development of Ancient Greek Democracy.* Lanham, MD: University Press of America.

Orth, W. 1977. *Königlicher Machtanspruch und städtische Freiheit.* Munich: C. H. Beck.

Osborne, M. J. 1981–3. *Naturalization in Athens.* Verhandelingen van de Koninklijke Academie voor Wetenschappen 98, 101, 109. Brussels: Koninklijke Academie.

Osborne, R. 1985a. *Demos: The Discovery of Classical Attika.* Cambridge: Cambridge University Press.

Osborne, R. 1985b. "Law in Action in Classical Athens." *Journal of Hellenic Studies* 105: 40–58.

Osborne, R. 1996. *Greece in the Making, 1200–479 BC.* London: Routledge.

Osborne, R. (ed.) 2004a. *Studies in Ancient Greek and Roman Society.* Cambridge: Cambridge University Press.

Osborne, R. 2004b. "Homer's Society." In R. Fowler (ed.), *The Cambridge Companion to Homer*, 206–19. Cambridge: Cambridge University Press.

Osborne, R. 2006. "When Was the Athenian Democratic Revolution?" In S. Goldhill and R. Osborne (eds), *Rethinking Revolutions through Ancient Greece*, 10–28. Cambridge: Cambridge University Press.

Osborne, R. (ed.) 2007. *Debating the Athenian Cultural Revolution: Art, Literature, Philosophy, and Politics 430–380 BC.* Cambridge: Cambridge University Press.

Osborne, R. and S. Hornblower (eds) 1994. *Ritual, Finance, Politics: Athenian Democratic Accounts Presented to David Lewis.* Oxford: Oxford University Press.

Ostwald, M. 1969. *Nomos and the Beginnings of the Athenian Democracy.* Oxford: Clarendon Press.

Ostwald, M. 1986. *From Popular Sovereignty to the Sovereignty of Law.* Berkeley: University of California Press.

Ostwald, M. 1995. "Freedom and the Greeks." In R. W. Davis (ed.), *The Origins of Modern Freedom in the West*, 35–63. Stanford: Stanford University Press.

Ostwald, M. 1996. "Shares and Rights: Citizenship Greek Style and American Style." In Ober and Hedrick 1996: 49–61.

Ostwald, M. 2000. *Oligarchia: The Development of a Constitutional Form in Ancient Greece.* Stuttgart: Franz Steiner.

Ostwald, M. 2005. "The Sophists and Athenian Politics." In Bultrighini 2005: 35–51.

Othman, N. 1999. "Grounding Human Rights Arguments in Non-Western Culture: *Shari'a* and the Citizenship Rights of Women in a Modern Islamic State." In J. R. Bauer and D. A. Bell (eds), *The East Asian Challenge to Human Rights*, 169–92. Cambridge: Cambridge University Press.

Owen, E. R. J. and Sutcliffe, R. (eds) 1972. *Studies in the Theory of Imperialism.* London: Longman.

Padel, R. 1992. *In and Out of the Mind: Greek Images of the Tragic Self.* Princeton: Princeton University Press.

Pakaluk, M. 2005. *Aristotle's Nicomachean Ethics. An Introduction.* Cambridge: Cambridge University Press.

Palmer, M. 1989. "Machiavellian virtù and Thucydidean aretē: Traditional Virtue and Political Wisdom in Thucydides." *Review of Politics* 51.3: 365–85.

Palmer, R. 1997. *Rome and Carthage at Peace.* Stuttgart: Steiner.

Pangle, L. S. 2003. *Aristotle and the Philosophy of Friendship.* Cambridge: Cambridge University Press.

Pangle, T. 1988. *The Spirit of Modern Republicanism: The Moral Vision of the American Founders and the Philosophy of Locke.* Chicago: University of Chicago Press.

Pangle, T. 1992. *The Ennobling of Democracy: The Challenge of the Postmodern Age.* Baltimore: Johns Hopkins University Press.

Pangle, T. 1998. "The Retrieval of Civic Virtue: A Critical Appreciation of Sandel's *Democracy's Discontent*." In A. L. Allen and M. C. Regan, Jr (eds), *Debating Democracy's Discontent: Essays on American Politics, Law, and Public Philosophy*, 17–31. Oxford: Oxford University Press.

Pangle, T. 2006. *Leo Strauss: An Introduction to His Thought and Intellectual Legacy.* Baltimore: Johns Hopkins University Press.

Parker, R. 1987. "Myths of Early Athens." In Bremmer 1987: 187–214.

Parker, R. 1996. *Athenian Religion: A History.* Oxford: Clarendon Press.

Parker, R. 2005. *Polytheism and Society at Athens.* Oxford: Oxford University Press.

Parry, R. 1996. *Plato's Craft of Justice.* Albany: State University of New York Press.

Passavant, P. and Dean, J. (eds) 2004. *Empire's New Clothes: Reading Hardt and Negri.* London: Routledge Press.

Paterson, Jeremy 1985. "Politics in the Late Republic." In T. P. Wiseman (ed.), *Roman Political Life: 40 BC–AD 69*, 21–43. Exeter: University of Exeter Press.

Patten, A. 2004. "Review of Markell, *Bound by Recognition*." *Perspectives on Politics* 2.4: 826–8.

Patterson, C. 1981. *Pericles' Citizenship Law of 451/0.* New York: Arno Press.

Patterson, C. 1994. "The Case against Neaira and the Public Ideology of the Athenian Family." In Boegehold and Scafuro 1994: 199–216.

Patterson, O. 1991. *Freedom, I: Freedom in the Making of Western Culture.* New York: Basic Books.

Patterson, O. 2003. "Reflections on Helotic Slavery and Freedom." In Luraghi and Alcock 2003: 289–309.

Patzig, G. (ed.) 1990. *Aristoteles' Politik.* Göttingen: Vanderhoeck and Ruprecht.

Pelling, C. (ed.) 1990. *Characterization and Individuality in Greek Literature.* Oxford: Clarendon Press.

Pelling, C. 1993. "Tacitus and Germanicus." In T. J. Luce and A. J. Woodman (eds), *Tacitus and the Tacitean Tradition*, 59–85. Princeton: Princeton University Press.

Pelling, C. (ed.) 1997. *Greek Tragedy and the Historian.* Oxford: Oxford University Press.

Pelling, C. 2000. *Literary Texts and the Greek Historian.* London: Routledge.

Pelling, C. 2002. "Speech and Action: Herodotus' Debate on the Constitutions." *Proceedings of the Cambridge Philological Society* 48: 123–58.

Penner, T. 2000. "Socrates." In C. Rowe and Schofield 2000: 164–89.

Peradotto, John 1997. "Modern Theoretical Approaches to Homer." In I. Morris and B. Powell (eds), *A New Companion to Homer*, 380–95. Leiden: Brill.

Perlman, Shalon 1963. "The Politicians in the Athenian Democracy of the Fourth Century BC." *Athanaeum* 41: 327–55.

Pettit, P. 1992. "The Nature of Naturalism." *Proceedings of the Aristotelian Society* (supp. vol.) 66: 245–66.

Pettit, P. 1993. "Negative Liberty, Liberal and Republican." *European Journal of Philosophy* 1: 15–38.

Pettit, P. 1997. *Republicanism: A Theory of Freedom and Government.* Oxford: Oxford University Press.

Pickard-Cambridge, A. 1988. *The Dramatic Festivals of Athens.* 2nd edn. Rev. with supplement by J. Gould and D. M. Lewis. Oxford: Oxford University Press.

Pina Polo, F. 1996. *Contra Arma Verbis: Der Redner vor dem Volk in der späten römischen Republik.* Heidelberger Althistorische Beiträge und Epigraphische Studien 22. Stuttgart: F. Steiner.

Pitkin, H. 1981. "Justice: On Relating Public and Private." *Political Theory* 9: 327–52.

Platt, A. (trans.) 1910. *Aristotle. De generatione animalium.* Oxford: Clarendon Press.

Pocock, J. G. A. 1975. *The Machiavellian Moment: Florentine Political Thought and the Atlantic Republican Tradition*. Princeton: Princeton University Press.

Pocock, J. G. A. 1985. *Virtue, Commerce, and History: Essays on Political Thought and History, Chiefly in the Eighteenth Century*. Cambridge: Cambridge University Press.

Pogge, T. 1992. "Cosmopolitanism and Sovereignty." *Ethics* 103: 48–75.

Pogge, T. 2002. *World Poverty and Human Rights*. Cambridge: Polity.

Pojman, Louis P. 2005. "Kant's *Perpetual Peace* and Cosmopolitanism." *Journal of Social Philosophy* 36: 62–71.

Pollitt, J. J. 1972. *Art and Experience in Classical Greece*. Cambridge: Cambridge University Press.

Popper, K. 1962. *The Open Society and Its Enemies*, vol. 1: *The Spell of Plato*. Princeton: Princeton University Press.

Porter, James 2005. "Foucault's Ascetic Ancients." *Phoenix* 59: 121–32.

Potter, David 1996. "Performance, Power and Justice in the High Empire." In Slater 1996: 129–59.

Potter, D. S. (ed.) 2006. *A Companion to the Roman Empire*. Oxford: Blackwell.

Pounder, R. 1984. "The Origin of *theoi* as Inscription-Heading." In K. J. Rigsby (ed.), *Studies Presented to Sterling Dow on His Eightieth Birthday*, 243–50. Durham, NC: Duke University Press.

Powell, J. G. F. 1994. "The *rector rei publicae* of Cicero's *De Re Publica*." *Scripta Classica Israelica* 13: 19–29.

Powell, J. G. F. forthcoming. "Cicero's *De Republica* and the Virtues of the Statesman." In W. Nicgorski (ed.), *Cicero's Practical Philosophy*. Notre Dame, IN: University of Notre Dame Press.

Préaux, C. 1978. *Le Monde hellénistique. La Grèce et l'Orient (323–146 av. J.-C.)*. 2 vols. Paris: Presses Universitaires de France.

Price, S. R. F. 1984. *Rituals and Power: The Roman Imperial Cult in Asia Minor*. Cambridge: Cambridge University Press.

Price, S. R. F. 1999. *Religions of the Ancient Greeks*. Cambridge: Cambridge University Press.

Pritchard, D. 2007. "How Do Democracy and War Affect Each Other? The Case Study of Ancient Athens." *Polis* 24.2: 328–52.

Pritchett, W. K. 1974. *The Greek State at War*. Part II. Berkeley: University of California Press.

Pritzl, K. 1983. "Aristotle and Happiness after Death." *Classical Philology* 78: 101–11.

"Publius" 1961. *The Federalist Papers*, ed. C. Rossiter. New York: New American Library.

Quinones, Ricardo J. 1991. *The Changes of Cain: Violence and the Lost Brother in Cain and Abel Literature*. Princeton: Princeton University Press.

Quirke, Stephen 1994. "Translating *Ma'at*." *Journal of Egyptian Archaeology* 80: 219–31.

Raaflaub, K. A. 1979. "Polis Tyrannos. Zur Entstehung einer politischen Metapher." In G. Bowersock et al. (eds), *Arktouros*, 237–52. Berlin: De Gruyter.

Raaflaub, K. A. 1984. "Freiheit in Athen und Rom. Ein Beispiel divergierender politischer Begriffsentwicklung in der Antike." *Historische Zeitschrift* 238: 529–67.

Raaflaub, K. A. 1986a. "The Conflict of the Orders in Archaic Rome: A Comprehensive and Comparative Approach." In Raaflaub (ed.), *Social Struggles in Archaic Rome: New Perspectives on the Conflict of the Orders*, 1–46. Berkeley: University of California Press.

Raaflaub, K. A. 1986b. "From Protection and Defense to Offense and Participation: Stages in the Conflict of the Orders." In Raaflaub (ed.), *Social Struggles in Archaic Rome: New Perspectives on the Conflict of the Orders*, 198–243. Berkeley: University of California Press.

Raaflaub, K. A. 1989a. "Contemporary Perceptions of Democracy in Fifth-Century Athens." *Classica et Mediaevalia* 40: 33–70.

Raaflaub, K. A. 1989b. "Homer and the Beginning of Political Thought in Greece." *Proceedings of the Boston Area Colloquium Series in Ancient Philosophy* 4: 1–25.

Raaflaub, K. A. 1993a. "Homer to Solon: The Rise of the Polis: The Written Sources." In M. H. Hansen (ed.), *The Ancient Greek City-State*, 41–105. Copenhagen: Munksgaard.

Raaflaub, K. A. 1993b. "Politics and Society in Fifth-Century Rome." In M. A. Levi (ed.), *Bilancio Critico su Roma arcaica fra monarchia e repubblica, in memoria di Ferdinando Castagnoli*, 129–57. Rome: Accademia Nazionale dei Lincei.

Raaflaub, K. A. 1996a. "Born to Be Wolves? Origins of Roman Imperialism." In R. W. Wallace and E. M. Harris (eds), *Transitions to Empire: Essays in Greco-Roman History, 360–146 BC, in Honor of E. Badian*, 273–314. Norman: University of Oklahoma Press.

Raaflaub, K. A. 1996b. "Equalities and Inequalities in Athenian Democracy." In Ober and Hedrick 1996: 139–74.

Raaflaub, K. A. 1996c. "Solone, la nuova Atene e l'emergere della politica." In Salvatore Settis (ed.), *I Greci* II.1: 1035–81. Turin: Einaudi.

Raaflaub, K. A. 1997a. "Homeric Society." In I. Morris and B. Powell (eds), *A New Companion to Homer*, 624–49. Leiden: Brill.

Raaflaub, K. A. 1997b. "Power in the Hands of the People: Foundations of Athenian Democracy." In I. Morris and K. A. Raaflaub (eds), *Democracy 2500? Questions and Challenges*, 31–66. Dubuque, IA: Kendall/Hunt.

Raaflaub, K. A. 1997c. "Soldiers, Citizens and the Evolution of the Early Greek Polis." In L. G. Mitchell and P. J. Rhodes (eds), *The Development of the Polis in Archaic Greece*, 49–59. New York: Routledge.

Raaflaub, K. A. 2000. "Poets, Lawgivers, and the Beginnings of Political Reflection in Archaic Greece." In C. Rowe and Schofield 2000: 23–59.

Raaflaub, K. A. 2001. "Political Thought, Civic Responsibility, and the Greek Polis." In Johann P. Arnason and Peter Murphy (eds), *Agon, Logos, Polis: The Greek Achievement and Its Aftermath*, 72–117. Stuttgart: Steiner.

Raaflaub, K. A. 2003a. "Freedom for the Messenians? A Note on the Impact of Slavery and Helotage on the Greek Concept of Freedom." In Luraghi and Alcock 2003: 169–90.

Raaflaub, K. A. 2003b. "Stick and Glue: The Function of Tyranny in Fifth-Century Athenian Democracy." In Morgan 2003: 59–93.

Raaflaub, K. A. 2004a. "Archaic Greek Aristocrats as Carriers of Cultural Interaction." In Rollinger and Ulf 2004a: 197–217.

Raaflaub, K. A. 2004b. *The Discovery of Freedom in Ancient Greece*. 1st English edn, rev. and updated. Chicago: University of Chicago Press.

Raaflaub, K. A. 2004c. "Zwischen Ost und West: Phönizische Einflüsse auf die griechische Polisbildung?" In Rollinger and Ulf 2004b: 271–90.

Raaflaub, K. A. 2005. "Polis, 'the Political,' and Political Thought: New Departures in Ancient Greece, c.800–500 BCE." In J. Arnason, S. N. Eisenstadt, and B. Wittrock (eds), *Axial Civilizations and World History*, 253–83. Leiden: Brill.

Raaflaub, K. A. 2006. "Athenian and Spartan *eunomia*, or What to Do with Solon's Timocracy?" In Blok and Lardinois 2006: 390–428.

Raaflaub, K. A. 2008. "Zeus und Prometheus. Zur griechischen Interpretation vorderasiatischer Mythen." In M. Bernett, W. Nippel, and A. Winterling (eds), *Autorencolloquium am Zentrum für Interdisciplinäre Forschung der Universität Bielefeld*, 33–60. Stuttgart: Steiner.

Raaflaub, K. A. forthcoming a. "Charaxos the Merchant, Rhodopis the Courtesan, Pittakos the Tyrant, and Greek-Nongreek Interaction in the Archaic Age." In A. Pierris (ed.), *Symposium Lesbium: Poetry, Wisdom, and Politics in Archaic Lesbos: Alcaeus, Sappho, Pittacus*.

Raaflaub, K. A. forthcoming b. "Das frühe politische Denken der Griechen im interkulturellen Zusammenhang des Mittelmeerraumes." In H. Matthäus (ed.), *Die Ursprünge Europas und der Orient. Kulturelle Beziehungen von der Späten Bronzezeit bis zur Frühen Eisenzeit.*

Raaflaub, K. A. 2009a. "Intellectual Achievements in Archaic Greece." Forthcoming in Raaflaub and van Wees, 2009.

Raaflaub, K. A. 2009b. "Learning from the Enemy? Athenian Imperial Policies and Persian 'Instruments of Empire.' " Forthcoming in J. Ma, N. Papazarkadas, and R. Parker (eds), *Interpreting the Athenian Empire: New Essays.* London: Duckworth.

Raaflaub, K. A., and Müller-Luckner, E. (eds) 1993. *Anfänge politischen Denkens in der Antike. Die nahöstlichen Kulturen und die Griechen.* Munich: Oldenbourg.

Raaflaub, K. A. and van Wees, H. (eds) 2009. *A Companion to Archaic Greece.* Oxford: Blackwell.

Raaflaub, K. A. and Wallace, R. W. 2007. " 'People's Power' and Egalitarian Trends in Archaic Greece." In Raaflaub, Ober, and Wallace 2007: 22–48.

Raaflaub, K. A., Ober, J., and Wallace, R. W. 2007. *Origins of Democracy in Ancient Greece.* With chapters by Paul Cartledge and Cynthia Farrar. Berkeley: University of California Press.

Rabinowitz, Nancy Sorkin and Auanger, Lisa (eds). 2002. *Among Women: From the Homosocial to the Homoerotic in the Ancient World.* Austin: University of Texas Press.

Rabinowitz, Nancy and Richlin, Amy (eds.) 1993. *Feminist Theory and the Classics.* New York: Routledge.

Rackham, H. (trans.) 1944. *Aristotle*, vol. 21. Cambridge, MA: Harvard University Press.

Rahe, Paul A. 1984. "The Primacy of Politics in Classical Greece." *American Historical Review* 89.2: 265–93.

Rahe, Paul A. 1992. *Republics Ancient and Modern: Classical Republicanism and the American Revolution.* Chapel Hill: University of North Carolina Press.

Rajak, T. 1996. "Hasmonean Kingship and the Invention of Tradition." In Bilde et al. 1996a: 99–115.

Ramelli, I. 1999. "Linee generali per una presentazione e per un commento del Liber legum regionum con traduzione italiana del testo siriaco e dei frammenti greci." *Rendiconti del Istituto Lombardo, Classi di Lettere e Scienze Morali e Storiche* 133.1: 311–55.

Ramelli, I. 2001. "Il problema dell'integrazione culturale in Plutarco." *Rivista Storica Italiana* 113: 179–94.

Rawls, J. 1971. *A Theory of Justice.* Cambridge, MA: Belknap.

Rawls, J. 1999. *The Law of Peoples.* Cambridge, MA: Harvard University Press.

Rawls, J. 2001. *Justice as Fairness: A Restatement.* Cambridge, MA.: Harvard University Press.

Rawson, E. 1969. *The Spartan Tradition in European Thought.* Oxford: Clarendon Press.

Rawson, E. 1975. *Cicero: A Portrait.* Ithaca, NY: Cornell University Press.

Raz, J. 1977. "The Rule of Law and Its Virtue." *Law Quarterly Review* 93: 195–202. (Repr. in *The Authority of Law: Essays on Law and Morality.* Oxford: Clarendon Press, 1979.)

Redfield, J. M. 1994. *Nature and Culture in the Iliad: The Tragedy of Hector.* 2nd edn. Durham, NC: Duke University Press.

Reeve, C. D. C. 1988. *Philosopher-Kings: The Argument of Plato's* Republic. Princeton: Princeton University Press.

Reeve, C. D. C. 1989. *Socrates in the "Apology": An Essay on Plato's Apology of Socrates.* Indianapolis: Hackett.

Regan, Richard J. (trans.) 2007. *Aquinas: A Commentary on Aristotle's Politics.* Indianapolis: Hackett.

Rehm, R. 2003. *Radical Theatre: Greek Tragedy and the Modern World.* London: Duckworth.

Renger, J. 1994. "Noch einmal: Was war der 'Kodex' Hammurapi – ein erlassenes Gesetz oder ein Rechtsbuch?" In Gehrke 1994: 27–59.

Revermann, M. 2006. *Comic Business: Theatricality, Dramatic Technique, and Performance Contexts of Aristophanic Comedy.* Oxford: Oxford University Press.

Rhodes, P. J. 1972. *The Athenian Boulē.* Oxford: Oxford University Press.

Rhodes, P. J. 1979. "A Graeco-Roman Perspective." In F. E. Dowrick (ed.), *Human Rights: Problems, Perspectives and Texts*, 62–73. Westmead, UK: Saxon House

Rhodes, P. J. 1981a. *A Commentary on the Aristotelian Athenaion Politeia.* Oxford: Oxford University Press.

Rhodes, P. J. 1981b. "The Selection of Ephors at Sparta." *Historia* 30: 498–502.

Rhodes, P. J. 1984a. "A Graeco-Roman Perspective." In F. E. Dowrick (ed.), *Human Rights: Problems, Perspectives and Texts*, 62–77. Aldershot: Gower.

Rhodes, P. J. 1984b. *Aristotle: The Athenian Constitution.* Harmondsworth: Penguin.

Rhodes, P. J. 1988. *Thucydides, History, II.* Warminster: Aris and Phillips.

Rhodes, P. J. 1992. "The Athenian Revolution." In D. Lewis et al. 1992: 62–95.

Rhodes, P. J. 2000. "Who Ran Democratic Athens?" In P. Flentsed-Jensen et al. (eds), *Polis and Politics*, 465–77. Copenhagen: Museum Tusculanum Press.

Rhodes, P. J. 2003a. *Ancient Democracy and Modern Ideology.* London: Duckworth.

Rhodes, P. J. 2003b. "Nothing to Do with Democracy: Athenian Drama and the Polis." *Journal of Hellenic Studies* 123: 104–19.

Rhodes, P. J. 2003c. "Sessions of *nomothetai* in Fourth-Century Athens." *Classical Quarterly* 53: 124–9.

Rhodes, P. J. (ed.) 2004. *Athenian Democracy.* Edinburgh: Edinburgh University Press.

Rhodes, P. J. with Lewis, D. 1997. *The Decrees of the Greek States.* Oxford: Oxford University Press.

Rhodes, P. J. and Osborne, R. 2003. *Greek Historical Inscriptions 404–323 BC.* Oxford: Oxford University Press.

Rice, E. E. 1983. *The Grand Procession of Ptolemy Philadelphus.* Oxford: Oxford University Press.

Rich, J. and Shipley, G. (eds) 1993. *War and Society in the Roman World.* London: Routledge.

Richardson, J. S. 1991. "*Imperium Romanum*: Empire and the Language of Power." *Journal of Roman Studies* 81: 1–9.

Richlin, Amy 1991. "Zeus and Metis: Foucault, Feminism, Classics." *Helios* 18: 160–80.

Richlin, Amy 1992. *The Garden of Priapus: Sexuality and Aggression in Roman Humor.* Rev. edn. New York: Oxford University Press.

Richlin, Amy 1998. "Foucault's *History of Sexuality*: A Useful Theory for Women?" In Larmour, Miller, and Platter 1998: 138–70.

Ricoeur, P. 1984–90. *Time and Narrative.* 3 vols. Chicago: University of Chicago Press.

Riess, W. 2006. "How Tyrants and Dynasts Die: The Semantics of Political Assassination in Fourth Century Greece." In G. Urso (ed.), *Terror et Pavor. Violenza, intimidazione, clandestinità nel mondo antico. Atti del convegno internazionale, Cividale del Friuli, 22–24 settembre 2005*, 65–88. Pisa: Edizioni ETS.

Riezler, K. 1943. "The Social Psychology of Shame." *American Journal of Sociology* 48.4: 457–65.

Rist, John M. 1994. *Augustine: Ancient Thought Baptized.* Cambridge: Cambridge University Press.

Robert, L. 1967. "Encore une inscription grecque de l'Iran." *Comptes Rendus de l'Académie des Inscriptions et Belles-Lettres (CRAI)* 1967: 281–97.

Roberts, J. T. 1994. *Athens on Trial: The Antidemocratic Tradition in Western Thought.* Princeton: Princeton University Press.

Roberts, J. T. 1996. "Athenian Equality: A Constant Surrounded by Flux." In Ober and Hedrick 1996: 187–202.

Robertson, D. W., Jr (trans.) 1958. *On Christian Doctrine / Augustine*. New York: Liberal Arts Press.

Robinson, E. 1997. *The First Democracies: Early Popular Government outside Athens*. Historia Einzelschriften 107. Stuttgart: Steiner.

Robinson, E. 2004. *Ancient Greek Democracy: Readings and Sources*. Oxford: Blackwell.

Roisman, J. 2003. "The Rhetoric of Courage in the Athenian Orators." In R. Rosen and I. Sluiter (eds), *Andreia: Studies in Manliness and Courage in Classical Antiquity*, 127–43. *Mnemosyne* supp. vol. 238. Leiden: Brill.

Rolfe, J. C. (trans.) 2005. *Sallust*. Loeb Classical Library. Cambridge, MA: Harvard University Press.

Roller, M. B. 2001. *Constructing Autocracy: Emperors and Aristocrats in Julio-Claudian Rome*. Princeton: Princeton University Press.

Röllig, W. 1993. "Aktion oder Reaktion? Politisches Handeln assyrischer Könige." In Raaflaub and Müller-Luckner 1993: 105–13.

Rollinger, R. 2004a. "Das fünfte internationale 'Melammu'-Meeting in Innsbruck. Überlegungen zu Kulturkontakt und Kulturaustausch in der Alten Welt." In Rollinger and Ulf 2004a: 20–30.

Rollinger, R. 2004b. "Die Verschriftlichung von Normen: Einflüsse und Elemente orientalischer Kulturtechnik in den homerischen Epen, dargestellt am Beispiel des Vertragswesens." In Rollinger and Ulf 2004b: 369–425.

Rollinger, R. 2006. " 'Griechen' und 'Perser' im 5. und 4. Jahrhundert v. Chr. im Blickwinkel orientalischer Quellen, *oder* Das Mittelmeer als Brücke zwischen Ost und West." In B. Burtscher-Bechter et al. (eds), *Grenzen und Entgrenzungen. Historische und kulturwissenschaftliche Überlegungen am Beispiel des Mittelmeerraumes*, 125–53. Würzburg: Königshausen und Neumann.

Rollinger, R. and Ulf, C. (eds) 2004a. *Commerce and Monetary Systems in the Ancient World: Means of Transmission and Cultural Interaction*. Stuttgart: Steiner.

Rollinger, R. and Ulf, C. (eds) 2004b. *Griechische Archaik: interne Entwicklungen – externe Impulse*. Berlin: Akademie.

Romer, F. 1997. "Good Intentions and the *hodos hē es korakas*." In Dobrov 1997: 51–74.

Rorty, A. O. (ed.) 1980. *Essays on Aristotle's Ethics*. Berkeley: University of California Press.

Rose, Peter 1992. *Sons of the Gods, Children of Earth: Ideology and Literary Form in Ancient Greece*. Ithaca, NY: Cornell University Press.

Rose, Peter 1995. "Historicizing Sophocles' *Ajax*." In Goff 1995: 59–90.

Rose, Peter 1997. "Ideology in the *Iliad*: Polis, *Basileus, Theoi*." *Arethusa* 30: 151–99.

Rose, Peter 1999. "Theorizing Athenian Imperialism and the Athenian State." In Thomas Falkner, Nancy Felson, and David Konstan (eds.), *Contextualizing Classics: Ideology, Performance, Dialogue*, 19–39. Lanham, MD: Rowman and Littlefield.

Rose, Peter 2006. "Divorcing Ideology from Marxism and Marxism from Ideology: Some Problems." *Arethusa* 39: 101–36.

Rosen, F. 1994. "Did Protagoras Justify Democracy?" *Polis* 13: 12–30.

Rosenberger, Veit 2003. "Reisen zum Orakel. Griechen, Lyder und Perser als Klienten hellenischer Orakelstätten." In M. Witte and S. Alkier (eds), *Die Griechen und der Vordere Orient*, 25–58. Freiburg, Switzerland: Universitätsverlag.

Rosenbloom, D. 1995. "Myth, History, and Hegemony in Aeschylus." In Goff 1995: 91–130.

Rosenbloom, D. 2006. "Empire and its Discontents: *Trojan Women, Birds*, and the Symbolic Economy of Athenian Imperialism." In Davidson et al. 2006: 245–71.

Rosenstein, N. 2004. *Rome at War: Farms, Families, and Death in the Middle Republic*. Chapel Hill: University of North Carolina Press.

Rosivach, V. 1987. "Autochthony and the Athenians." *Classical Quarterly* 37: 294–306.

Roskam, G. 2007. *Live Unnoticed: On the Vicissitudes of an Epicurean Doctrine*. Leiden: Brill.

Ross, Shawn A. 2005. "*Barbarophonos*: Language and Panhellenism in the *Iliad*." *Classical Philology* 100: 299–316.

Ross, W. D. 1957. *Aristotelis. Politica*. Oxford: Clarendon Press.

Roth, Martha T. 1995. *Law Collections from Mesopotamia and Asia Minor*. Atlanta: Scholars Press. (2nd edn 1997.)

Rowe, C. 1995. *Plato's* Statesman. Warminster: Aris and Phillips.

Rowe, C. 2000a. "The *Politicus* and Other Dialogues." In C. Rowe and Schofield 2000: 244–51.

Rowe, C. 2000b. "Aristotelian Constitutions." In C. Rowe and Schofield 2000: 366–89.

Rowe, C. and Schofield, M. (eds) 2000. *The Cambridge History of Greek and Roman Political Thought*. Cambridge: Cambridge University Press.

Rowe, Greg 2002. *Princes and Political Cultures: The New Tiberian Senatorial Decrees*. Ann Arbor: University of Michigan Press.

Roy, J. 1998. "The Masculinity of the Hellenistic King." In L. Foxhall and J. Salmon (eds), *When Men Were Men: Masculinity, Power and Identity in Classical Antiquity*, 111–35. London: Routledge.

Ruokanen, Mikka 1993. *Theology of Social Life in Augustine's De civitate Dei*. Göttingen: Vandenhoeck and Ruprecht.

Ruschenbusch, E. 1966. *Solonos Nomoi. Die Fragmente des solonischen Gesetzeswerkes mit einer Text- und Überlieferungsgeschichte*. Wiesbaden: Steiner.

Ruschenbusch, E. 1983. "Tribut und Bürgerzahl im ersten athenischen Seebund." *Zeitschrift für Papyrologie und Epigraphik* 53: 125–43.

Ruschenbusch, E. 1985. "Die Zahl der griechischen Staaten, und Arealgrösse und Burgerzahl der 'Normalpolis.' " *Zeitschrift für Papyrologie und Epigraphik* 59: 253–63.

Russell, D. A. and Wilson, N. G. (ed. and trans.) 1981. *Menander Rhetor*. Oxford: Clarendon Press.

Rutherford, R. B. 1996. *Homer*. Greece and Rome New Surveys in the Classics 26. Oxford: Oxford University Press.

Ryberg, I. S. 1955. *Rites of the State Religion in Roman Art*. Memoirs of the American Academy in Rome 22. Rome: American Academy in Rome.

Sachs, J. 2002. "Wholes and Parts in Human Character." *St John's Review* 46.3: 5–27.

Sagan, E. 1991. *The Honey and the Hemlock: Democracy and Paranoia in Ancient Athens and Modern America*. Princeton: Princeton University Press.

Salkever, S. 1990. *Finding the Mean: Theory and Practice in Aristotelian Political Philosophy*. Princeton: Princeton University Press.

Salkever, S. 1991. "Women, Soldiers, Citizens: Plato and Aristotle on the Politics of Virility." In C. Lord and D. K. O'Connor (eds), *Essays on the Foundations of Aristotelian Political Science*, 165–90. Berkeley: University of California Press.

Saller, Richard 1982. *Personal Patronage under the Early Empire*. Cambridge: Cambridge University Press.

Salmon, John 1999. "The Economic Role of the Greek City." *Greece and Rome* 46: 147–67.

Samons, L. J. 2004. *What's Wrong with Democracy? From Athenian Practice to American Worship*. Berkeley: University of California Press.

Samons, L. J. (ed.) 2007. *The Cambridge Companion to the Age of Pericles*. Cambridge: Cambridge University Press.

Sancisi-Weerdenburg, H. (ed.) 2000. *Peisistratos and the Tyranny: A Reappraisal of the Evidence*. Amsterdam: J. C. Gieben.

Sancisi-Weerdenburg, H. 2001. "*Yaunā* by the Sea and across the Sea." In I. Malkin (ed.), *Ancient Perceptions of Greek Ethnicity*, 323–46. Washington, DC: Center for Hellenic Studies.

Sandbach, F. H. 1985. *Aristotle and the Stoics*. Cambridge: Cambridge Philological Society.

Sandberg, Kaj 2000. "Tribunician and Non-Tribunician Legislation in Mid-Republican Rome." In C. Bruun (ed.), *The Roman Middle Republic: Politics, Religion, and Historiography, c. 400–133 BC*, 121–40. Rome: Institutum Romanum Finlandiae.

Sandel, M. J. 1982. *Liberalism and the Limits of Justice*. New York: Cambridge University Press.

Sandel, M. J. 1996. *Democracy's Discontent: America in Search of a Public Philosophy*. Cambridge, MA: Harvard University Press.

Sandel, M. J. 1998. "Reply to Critics." In A. L. Allen and M. C. Regan, Jr (eds), *Debating Democracy's Discontent: Essays on American Politics, Law, and Public Philosophy*, 319–35. Oxford: Oxford University Press.

Saunders, T. J. (reviser) 1981. *Aristotle. Politics*, trans. T. A. Sinclair. Harmondsworth: Penguin.

Saunders, T. J. (trans.) 1984. *Plato. The Laws*. Harmondsworth: Penguin.

Saunders, T. J. 1991. *Plato's Penal Code*. Oxford: Clarendon Press.

Saunders, T. J. 1995. *Aristotle. Politics: Books I and II*. Oxford: Clarendon Press.

Savonarola, G. 2006. *Selected Writings of Girolamo Savonarola: Religion and Politics, 1490–1498*, trans. and ed. A. Borelli and M. P. Pasaro. New Haven, CT: Yale University Press.

Savunen, Liisa 1995. "Women and Elections in Pompeii." In R. Hawley and B. Levick (eds), *Women in Antiquity*, 194–206. London: Routledge.

Saxonhouse, A. 1978. "Comedy in Callipolis: Animal Imagery in the *Republic*." *American Political Science Review* 72: 888–901.

Saxonhouse, A. 1980. "Men, Women, War, and Politics: Family and Polis in Aristophanes and Euripides." *Political Theory* 8.1: 65–81.

Saxonhouse, A. 1983. "An Unspoken Theme in Plato's *Gorgias*: War." *Interpretation* 11: 139–69.

Saxonhouse, A. 1985. *Women in the History of Political Thought: Ancient Greece to Machiavelli*. New York: Praeger.

Saxonhouse, A. 1986. "Myths and the Origins of Cities: Reflections on the Autochthony Theme in Euripides' *Ion*." In Euben 1986: 252–73.

Saxonhouse, A. 1992. *Fear of Diversity: The Birth of Political Science in Ancient Greek Thought*. Chicago: University of Chicago Press.

Saxonhouse, A. 1996. *Athenian Democracy: Modern Mythmakers and Ancient Theorists*. Notre Dame, IN: University of Notre Dame Press.

Saxonhouse, A. 2004. "Democratic Deliberation and the Historian's Trade: The Case of Thucydides." In Fontana, Nederman, and Remer 2004: 57–86.

Saxonhouse, A. 2006. *Free Speech and Democracy in Ancient Athens*. Cambridge: Cambridge University Press.

Scafuro, A. 1994. "Introduction: Bifurcations and Intersections." In Boegehold and Scafuro 1994: 1–20.

Scaltsas, T. and Mason, A. (eds) 2002. *The Philosophy of Zeno*. Larnaca: Pierides Foundation.

Scheffler, S. 1999. "Conceptions of Cosmopolitanism." *Utilitas* 11: 255–76.

Schmitt-Pantel, P. 1990. "Collective Activities and the Political in the Greek City." In O. Murray and Price 1990: 199–213.

Schmitz, W. 2004. *Nachbarschaft und Dorfgemeinschaft im archaischen und klassischen Griechenland.* Berlin: Akademie.

Schofield, M. 1990. "Ideology and Philosophy in Aristotle's Theory of Slavery." In Patzig 1990: 1–27.

Schofield, M. 1991. *The Stoic Idea of the City.* Cambridge: Cambridge University Press.

Schofield, M. 1995. "Cicero's Definition of *Res Publica*." In J. G. F. Powell (ed.), *Cicero the Philosopher: Twelve Papers*, 63–83. Oxford: Clarendon Press.

Schofield, M. 1999. *Saving the City: Philosopher-Kings and Other Classical Paradigms.* London: Routledge.

Schofield, M. 2002a. "Cicero, Zeno of Citium, and the Vocabulary of Philosophy." In M. Canto-Sperber and P. Pellegrin (eds), *Le style de la pensée. Recueils de textes en homage à Jacques Brunschwig*, 412–28. Paris: Belles Lettres.

Schofield, M. 2002b. "'Impossible Hypotheses': Was Zeno's *Republic* Utopian?" In Scaltsas and Mason 2002: 309–23.

Schofield, M. 2006. *Plato: Political Philosophy.* Oxford: Oxford University Press.

Schofield, M. forthcoming. "The Fourth Virtue." In W. Nicgorski (ed.), *Cicero's Practical Philosophy.* Notre Dame, IN: University of Notre Dame Press.

Scholten, J. B. 1999. *The Politics of Plunder: The Aetolians and Their Koinon in the Early Hellenistic Era, 279–219 BC.* Berkeley: University of California Press.

Schulz, Fritz 1936. *Principles of Roman Law*, trans. M. Wolff. Oxford: Clarendon Press.

Schulz, Fritz 1951. *Classical Roman Law.* Oxford: Clarendon Press.

Schumpeter, J. A. 1951. *Imperialism and Social Classes.* New York: Augustus M. Kelley.

Schütrumpf, E. 1991–2005. *Aristoteles. Politik.* 4 vols. Berlin: Akademie.

Schwartzberg, Melissa 2007. *Democracy and Legal Change.* Cambridge: Cambridge University Press.

Scullard, H. H. 1973. *Roman Politics, 220–150 BC.* 2nd edn. Oxford: Oxford University Press.

Seaford, R. 1994. *Reciprocity and Ritual: Homer and Tragedy in the Developing City-State.* Oxford: Oxford University Press.

Seaford, R. 1995. "Historicizing Tragic Ambivalence: The Vote of Athena." In Goff 1995: 202–21.

Seaford, R. 2000. "The Social Function of Attic Tragedy: A Response to Jasper Griffin." *Classical Quarterly* 50: 30–44.

Seaford, R. 2003. "Tragic Tyranny." In Morgan 2003: 95–115.

Seager, R. 1984. "Some Imperial Virtues in the Latin Prose Panegyrics: The Demands of Propaganda and the Dynamics of Literary Composition." *Papers of the Liverpool Latin Seminar* 4 (1983): 129–65.

Seager. R. forthcoming. "Polybius' Distortions of the Roman 'Constitution': A Simpl(istic) Explanation." In T. Harrison and B. Gibson (eds), *The World of Polybius: Essays in Honour of F. W. Walbank.*

Sealey, R. 1987. *The Athenian Republic: Democracy or the Rule of Law?* University Park: Pennsylvania State University Press.

Sealey, R. 1994. *The Justice of the Greeks.* Ann Arbor: University of Michigan Press.

Searle, John R. 1995. *The Construction of Social Reality.* New York: Free Press.

Segal, Charles 1986. *Interpreting Greek Tragedy: Myth, Poetry, Text.* Ithaca, NY: Cornell University Press.

Sellers, M. N. S. 1994. *American Republicanism: Roman Ideology in the United States Constitution.* New York: New York University Press.

Sen, A. 1982. "Rights and Agency." *Philosophy and Public Affairs* 11: 3–39.

Sen, A. 1999. *Development as Freedom*. Oxford: Oxford University Press.

Seybold, K. and Ungern-Sternberg, J. von 1993. "Amos und Hesiod. Aspekte eines Vergleichs." In Raaflaub and Müller-Luckner 1993: 215–39.

Seybold, K. and Ungern-Sternberg, J. von 2007. "Zwei Reformer: Josia und Solon." In Burckhardt, Seybold, and Ungern-Sternberg 2007: 103–61.

Shackleton Bailey, D. R. 1991. *Cicero, Back from Exile: Six Speeches on His Return*. American Philological Association Classical Resources Series 4. Atlanta: Scholars Press.

Shapiro, H. A. 1989. *Art and Cult under the Tyrants in Athens*. Mainz am Rhein: Philipp von Zabern.

Shapiro, H. A. 1993. *Personifications in Greek Art: The Representations of Abstract Concepts 600–400 BC*. Kilchberg: Akanthus.

Sherwin-White, A. N. 1973. *The Roman Citizenship*. 2nd edn. Oxford: Oxford University Press.

Shipley, G. 1987. *A History of Samos, 800–188 BC*. Oxford: Clarendon Press.

Shipley, G. 2000. *The Greek World after Alexander, 323–30 BC*. London: Routledge.

Shklar, J. 1987. "Political Theory and the Rule of Law." In Hutchinson and Monahan (eds), *The Rule of Law: Ideal or Ideology*, 1–16. Toronto: Carswell.

Shrimpton, G. S. 1991. *Theopompus the Historian*. Montreal: McGill-Queen's University Press.

Simpson, P. 1998. *A Philosophical Commentary on the Politics of Aristotle*. Chapel Hill: University of North Carolina Press.

Sinclair, R. 1988. *Democracy and Participation in Athens*. Cambridge: Cambridge University Press.

Sinclair, T. A. 1951. *A History of Greek Political Thought*. London: Routledge and Kegan Paul. (2nd edn 1967.)

Sinos, Rebecca 1998. "Divine Selection: Epiphany and Politics in Archaic Greece." In Dougherty and Kurke 1998: 73–91.

Sissa, G. 1990. "Philosophies du genre. Platon, Aristote et la différence sexuelle." In G. Duby and M. Perrot (eds), *Histoire des femmes*, vol. 1: *L'antiquité*, ed. P. Schmitt Pantel. Paris: Éditions du Seuil.

Sissa, G. 1997. *Greek Virginity* trans. A. Goldhammer. Cambridge, MA: Harvard University Press.

Sissa, G. 2000. "Sexual Bodybuilding: Aeschines against Timarchus." In J. Porter (ed.), *The Construction of the Classical Body* 147–168. Ann Arbor: University of Michigan Press.

Sissa, G. 2008. *Sex and Sensuality in the Ancient World*. London: Yale University Press.

Skinner, Marilyn 1997. "*Ego mulier*: The Construction of Male Sexuality in Catullus." In J. Hallett and M. Skinner (eds), *Roman Sexualities*, 129–50. Princeton: Princeton University Press.

Skinner, Q. 1974. "Some Problems in the Analysis of Political Thought and Action." *Political Theory* 2: 227–303.

Skinner, Q. 1978. *The Foundations of Modern Political Thought*. 2 vols. Cambridge: Cambridge University Press.

Skinner, Q. 1984. "The Idea of Negative Liberty: Philosophical and Historical Perspectives." In R. Rorty, J. B. Schneewind, and Q. Skinner (eds), *Philosophy in History*, 193–221. Cambridge: Cambridge University Press.

Skinner, Q. 1986. "The Paradoxes of Political Liberty." In S. M. McMurrin (ed.), *The Tanner Lectures on Human Values* VII, 225–50. 2nd edn. Salt Lake City: University of Utah Press.

Skinner, Q. 1990. "The Republican Idea of Political Liberty." In G. Bok, Q. Skinner, and M. Viroli (eds), *Machiavelli and Republicanism*, 293–309. Cambridge: Cambridge University Press.

Skinner, Q. 1991. "The Paradoxes of Political Liberty." In D. Miller (ed.), *Liberty*. Oxford: Oxford University Press.

Skinner, Q. 1992. "The Italian City-Republics." In J. Dunn (ed.), *Democracy: The Unfinished Journey, 508 BC–AD 1993,* 57–69. Oxford: Oxford University Press.

Skinner, Q. 1998. *Liberty before Liberalism.* Cambridge: Cambridge University Press.

Skinner, Q. 2001. "A Third Concept of Liberty." *Proceedings of the British Academy* 119: 237–68.

Skinner, Q. 2002a. "Introduction: Seeing Things Their Way." In Skinner, *Visions of Politics,* vol. 1: *Regarding Method,* 1–7. Cambridge: Cambridge University Press.

Skinner, Q. 2002b. "Interpretation and the Understanding of Speech Acts." In Skinner, *Visions of Politics,* vol. 1: *Regarding Method,* 103–27. Cambridge: Cambridge University Press.

Skinner, Q. 2002c "Machiavelli on *Virtù* and the Maintenance of Liberty." In Skinner, *Visions of Politics,* vol. 2: 160–85. Cambridge: Cambridge University Press.

Skinner, Q. 2002d. "Classical Liberty and the Coming of the English Civil War." In Q. Skinner and M. Van Geldren (eds), *Republicanism: A Shared European Heritage,* 9–28. Cambridge: Cambridge University Press.

Skinner, Q. 2003. "States and the Freedom of Citizens." In Q. Skinner and B. Stråth (eds), *States and Citizens: History, Theory, Prospects,* 11–27. Cambridge: Cambridge University Press.

Slater, W. (ed.) 1996. *Roman Theater and Society.* E. Togo Salmon Papers. Ann Arbor: University of Michigan Press.

Slater, W. 2002. *Spectator Politics: Metatheatre and Performance in Aristophanes.* Philadelphia: University of Pennsylvania Press.

Sluiter, I. and Rosen, R. M. (eds) 2004. *Free Speech in Classical Antiquity.* Leiden: Brill.

Smith, H. H. H. 1988. *Hellenistic Royal Portraits.* Oxford: Clarendon Press.

Smith, S. 2006. *Reading Leo Strauss.* Chicago: University of Chicago Press.

Snell, D. C. 2001. *Flight and Freedom in the Ancient Near East.* Leiden: Brill.

Snell, D. C. (ed.) 2005. *A Companion to the Ancient Near East.* Oxford: Blackwell.

Snodgrass, A. 1980. *Archaic Greece: The Age of Experiment.* Berkeley: University of California Press.

Snodgrass, A. M. 1990. "Survey Archaeology and the Rural Landscape of the Greek City." In O. Murray and Price 1990: 113–36.

Sommerstein, A. 1989. *Aeschylus. Eumenides.* Cambridge: Cambridge University Press.

Sommerstein, A. 1996a. "How to Avoid Being a Komodoumenos." *Classical Quarterly* 46: 327–56.

Sommerstein, A. 1996b. *Aeschylean Tragedy.* Bari: Levante Editori.

Sommerstein, A. (ed. and trans.) 1996c. *Aristophanes. Frogs.* Warminster: Aris and Phillips.

Sommerstein, A. 1997. "The Theatre Audience, the *Demos,* and the *Suppliants* of Aeschylus." In Pelling 1997: 63–79.

Sommerstein, A. 2004. "Harassing the Satirist: The Alleged Attempts to Prosecute Aristophanes." In Sluiter and Rosen 2004: 145–74.

Sommerstein, A. 2005. "*Nephelokokkygia* and *Gynaikopolis*: Aristophanes' Dream Cities." In Hansen 2005b: 73–99.

Sommerstein, A. et al. (eds) 1993. *Tragedy, Comedy and the Polis.* Bari: Levante Editori.

Sourvinou-Inwood, Christiane 1990. "What is Polis Religion?" In O. Murray and Price 1990: 295–322.

Spawforth, A. J. S. 2006. *The Complete Greek Temples.* London: Thames and Hudson.

Spoerri, W. 1988. "Hekataios von Abdera." *Reallexikon für Antike und Christentum* 14: 275–310. Stuttgart: Hiersemann.

Stahl, Michael 1987. *Aristokraten und Tyrannen im archaischen Athen.* Stuttgart: Franz Steiner.

Stalley, R. F. 1983. *An Introduction to Plato's Laws.* Oxford: Blackwell.

Stalley, R. F. 1994. "Persuasion in Plato's *Laws.*" *History of Political Thought* 15: 157–77.

Stalley, R. F. 1995a. "Punishment in Plato's *Laws*." *History of Political Thought* 16: 469–87.

Stalley, R. F. (reviser) 1995b. *Aristotle. Politics*, trans. E. Barker. Oxford: Oxford University Press.

Stalley, R. F. 2007. "Platonic Philosophy of Law." In F. Miller and C. Biondi (eds), *A History of the Philosophy of Law from the Ancient Greeks to the Scholastics*. Dordrecht: Springer.

Stampolidis, N. and Kotsonas, A. 2006. "Phoenicians in Crete." In S. Deger-Jalkotzy and I. S. Lemos (eds), *Ancient Greece: From the Mycenaean Palaces to the Age of Homer*, 337–60. Edinburgh: Edinburgh University Press.

Stanton, G. R. 1968. "The Cosmopolitan Ideas of Epictetus and Marcus Aurelius." *Phronesis* 13: 183–95.

Stärk, E. 2000. "Politische Anspielungen in der römischen Tragödie und der Einfluß der Schauspieler." In G. Manuwald (ed.), *Identität und Alterität in der frührömischen Tragödie*, 123–33. Würzburg: Egon.

Starke, F. 2005–6. "Los hititas y su Imperio. Constitución, federalismo y pensamiento polít-ico." *Revista del Instituto de Historia Antigua Oriental*, 3rd ser. 12–13: 189–303.

Stauffer, D. 2006. *The Unity of Plato's "Gorgias."* Cambridge: Cambridge University Press.

Steel, C. E. W. 2005. *Reading Cicero: Genre and Performance in Late Republican Rome*. London: Duckworth.

Stehle, Eva 1997. *Performance and Gender in Ancient Greece*. Princeton: Princeton University Press.

Steiner, Deborah 1998. "Moving Images: Fifth-Century Victory Monuments and the Athlete's Allure." *Classical Antiquity* 17: 123–49.

Stein-Hölkeskamp, Elke 1989. *Adelskultur und Polisgesellschaft. Studien zum griechischen Adel in archaischer und klassischer Zeit*. Stuttgart: Franz Steiner.

Sterling, R. W. 1974. *Macropolitics: International Security in a Global Society*. New York: Knopf.

Steve, M.-J. 1974. "Inscriptions des Achéménides à Suse (suite)." *Studia Iranica* 3: 135–69.

Stevenson, J. (ed.) 1989. *Creeds, Councils, and Controversies: Documents Illustrating the History of the Church AD 337–461* [1966]. 2nd, rev. edn. 1989. London: SPCK.

Stewart, A. 1993. *Faces of Power: Alexander's Image and Hellenistic Politics*. Berkeley: University of California Press.

Stewart, A. 1997. *Art, Desire, and the Body in Ancient Greece*. Cambridge: Cambridge University Press.

Stockton, David 1990. *The Classical Athenian Democracy*. Oxford: Oxford University Press.

Stone, I. F. 1988. *The Trial of Socrates*. New York: Little, Brown.

Storey, I. C. and Allan, A. 2005. *A Guide to Ancient Greek Drama*. Oxford: Blackwell.

Straus, E. W. 1966. "Shame as a Historiological Problem." In *Phenomenological Psychology: The Selected Papers of Erwin W. Straus*, trans. (in part) E. Eng, 217–24. New York: Basic Books.

Strauss, B. 1986. *Athens after the Peloponnesian War*. Ithaca, NY: Cornell University Press.

Strauss, L. 1945. "Farabi's Plato." In S. Lieberman, S. Spiegel, S. Zeitlin, and A. Marx (eds), *Louis Ginzburg Jubilee Volume*, 359–83. New York: American Academy for Jewish Research.

Strauss, L. 1953. *Natural Right and History*. Chicago: University of Chicago Press.

Strauss, L. 1964. *The City and Man*. Chicago: University of Chicago Press.

Strauss, L. 1966. *Socrates and Aristophanes*. New York: Basic Books.

Strauss, L. 1968. *Liberalism: Ancient and Modern*. New York: Basic Books.

Strauss, L. 1970. *Xenophon's Socratic Discourse*. Ithaca, NY: Cornell University Press.

Strauss, L. 1973. *Xenophon's Socrates*. Ithaca, NY: Cornell University Press.

Strauss, L. 1978. "An Unspoken Prologue to a Public Lecture at St John's College in Honor of Jacob Klein." *Interpretation: A Journal of Political Philosophy* 7.3: 1–3.

Strauss, L. 1983. *Studies in Platonic Political Philosophy.* Chicago: University of Chicago Press.

Strauss, L. 1988. "Letter to Karl Loewith, June 23, 1935." *Independent Journal of Philosophy* 5/6: 182–5.

Strauss, L. 1989a. *An Introduction to Political Philosophy: Ten Essays by Leo Strauss*, ed. H. Gildin. Detroit: Wayne State University Press.

Strauss, L. 1989b. *The Rebirth of Classical Political Rationalism: An Introduction to the Thought of Leo Strauss.* Chicago: University of Chicago Press.

Strauss, L. 1991. *On Tyranny*, ed. V. Gourevitch and M. Roth. New York: Free Press.

Strauss, L. 1995. *Philosophy and Law* [1935], trans. E. Adler. Albany: State University of New York Press.

Strauss, L. 1997. *Spinoza's Critique of Religion.* Chicago: University of Chicago Press.

Striker, G. 2006. "Aristotle's Ethics as Political Science." In B. Reis (ed.), *The Virtuous Life in Greek Ethics*, 127–41. Cambridge: Cambridge University Press.

Stroud, R. 1979. *The Axones and Kyrbeis of Drakon and Solon.* Berkeley: University of California Press.

Sullivan, F. A. 1941. "Cicero and Glory." *Transactions of the American Philological Association* 72: 382–91.

Susemihl, F. and Hicks, R. 1984. *The* Politics *of Aristotle.* London: Macmillan.

Swain, S. 1996. *Hellenism and Empire.* Oxford: Oxford University Press.

Swift, L. J. 1966. "The Anonymous Encomium of Philip the Arab." *Greek, Roman, and Byzantine Studies* 7.3: 267–89.

Syme, R. 1939. *The Roman Revolution.* Oxford: Oxford University Press.

Syme, R. 1958. *Tacitus.* Oxford: Clarendon Press.

Syme, R. 1977. "Liberty in Classical Antiquity." *Memoirs of the American Philosophical Society* 118: 8–15 = Syme, *Roman Papers* 3: 962–8. Oxford: Oxford University Press.

Szegedy-Maszak, A. 1978. "Legends of the Greek Lawgivers." *Greek, Roman, and Byzantine Studies* 19: 199–209.

Szlechter, Émile 1952. "L'affranchissement en droit suméro-babylonien." *Revue Internationale des Droits de l'Antiquité* 1: 125–95.

Talbert, Richard 1984. *The Senate of Imperial Rome.* Princeton: Princeton University Press.

Tandy, David 1997. *Warriors into Traders: The Power of the Market in Early Greece.* Berkeley: University of California Press.

Taplin, O. P. 1992. *Homeric Soundings: The Shaping of the* Iliad. Oxford: Clarendon Press.

Taplin, O. 1999. "Spreading the Word through Performance." In Goldhill and Osborne 1999: 33–57.

Tarn, W. W. 1913. *Antigonos Gonatas.* Oxford: Oxford University Press.

Tatum, J. 1989. *Xenophon's Imperial Fiction: On the Education of Cyrus.* Princeton: Princeton University Press.

Tatum, W. J. 1999. *The Patrician Tribune: Publius Clodius Pulcher.* Chapel Hill, NC: University of North Carolina Press.

Tatum, W. J. 2007. "*Alterum est tamen boni viri, alterum boni petitoris*: The Good Man Canvasses." *Phoenix* 61: 109–35.

Taylor, C. 1994. *Multiculturalism: Examining the Politics of Recognition*, ed. A. Gutmann. Princeton: Princeton University Press.

Taylor, C. 2001. "Bribery in Athenian Politics, part 1: Accusations, Allegations and Slander." *Greece and Rome* 48: 53–66.

Taylor, C. 2007a. "From the Whole Citizen Body? The Sociology of Election and Lot in the Athenian Democracy." *Hesperia* 76: 323–45.

Taylor, C. 2007b. "A New Political World." In Osborne 2007: 72–90.

Taylor, G. 2006. *Deadly Vices*. Oxford: Oxford University Press.

Taylor, John Hammond (ed. and trans.) 1982. *The Literal Meaning of Genesis / St. Augustine*. 2 vols. Ancient Christian Writers Series 41–2. New York: Newman Press.

Taylor, L. R. 1949. *Party Politics in the Age of Caesar*. Berkeley: University of California Press.

Taylor, R. 1985. *Ethics, Faith and Reason*. Englewood Cliffs, NJ: Prentice Hall.

Taylor, R. 2002. *Virtue Ethics: An Introduction*. Amherst, NY: Prometheus Lecture Series.

Tessitore, A. (ed.) 2002. *Aristotle and Modern Politics: The Persistence of Political Philosophy*. Notre Dame, IN: University of Notre Dame Press.

Thacker, Andrew 1993. "Foucault's Aesthetics of Existence." *Radical Philosophy* 63: 13–21.

Thalmann, W. 1998. *The Swineherd and the Bow: Representations of Class in the Odyssey*. Ithaca, NY: Cornell University Press.

Thalmann, W. G. 2005. "'The Most Divinely Approved and Political Discord': Thinking about Conflict in the Developing Polis." *Classical Antiquity* 23.2: 359–99.

Théodoridès, A. 1967. "A propos de la loi dans l'Egypte pharaonique." *Revue Internationale des Droits de l'Antiquité*, 3rd ser. 14: 107–52.

Théodoridès, A. 1971. "The Concept of Law in Ancient Egypt." In J. R. Harris (ed.), *The Legacy of Egypt*, 291–322. 2nd edn. Oxford: Clarendon Press.

Théodoridès, A. 1995. *Vivre de Maât. Travaux sur le droit égyptien ancien*, ed. J.-M. Kruchten. 2 vols. Brussels: Société Belge d'Études Orientales.

Thesleff, H. 1965. *The Pythagorean Texts of the Hellenistic Period*. Turku: Abo Akademi.

Thesleff, H. 1967. *Studies in the Styles of Plato*. Acta Philosophica Fennica. Helsinki: Suomalaisen Kirjallisuuden Kirjapaino.

Thomas, J.-F. 1994. "Un groupe sémantique: *gloria, laus, decus*." In C. Moussy (ed.), *Les problèmes de la synonomie en latin*, 91–100. Paris: Presses de l'Université de Paris-Sorbonne.

Thomas, R. 1989. *Oral Tradition and Written Record*. Cambridge: Cambridge University Press.

Thomas, R. 1996. "Written in Stone? Liberty, Equality, Orality, and the Codification of Law." In L. Foxhall and A. D. E. Lewis (eds), *Greek Law in Its Political Setting: Justifications Not Justice*, 9–31. Oxford: Clarendon Press.

Thomas, R. 2000. *Herodotus in Context: Ethnography, Science, and the Art of Persuasion*. Cambridge: Cambridge University Press.

Thompson, N. 1996. *Herodotus and the Origins of the Political Community: Arion's Leap*. London: Yale University Press.

Thomsen, R. 1980. *King Servius Tullius: A Historical Synthesis*. Copenhagen: Gyldendal.

Thornton, Bruce 1991. "Idolon Theatri: Foucault and the Classicists." *Classical and Modern Literature* 12: 81–100.

Tierney, Brian 1964. *The Crisis of Church and State, 1050–1300*. Englewood Cliffs, NJ: Prentice Hall.

Todd, S. 1990. "Lady Chatterley's Lover and the Attic Orators." *Journal of Hellenic Studies* 110: 146–73.

Todd, S. 1993. *The Shape of Athenian Law*. Oxford: Clarendon Press.

Tondriau, J. 1948. "La tryphè, philosophie royale ptolemaique." *Revue des Études Anciennes* 50: 49–54.

Trédé, M. et al. (eds) 1998. *Le rire des anciens*. Paris: École Normale Supérieure.

Trompf, G. W. 1979. *The Idea of Historical Recurrence in Western Thought*. Berkeley: University of California Press.

Tuck, R. 1979. *Natural Rights Theories*. Cambridge: Cambridge University Press.

Tully, J. (ed.) 1988. *Meaning and Context: Quentin Skinner and His Critics.* Princeton: Princeton University Press.

Tully, J. 1993. *An Approach to Political Philosophy: Locke in Contexts.* Cambridge: Cambridge University Press.

Turner, E. 1984. "Ptolemaic Egypt." In F. W. Walbank et al. (eds), *The Cambridge Ancient History*, vol. 7· part 1, 101–74. 2nd edn. Cambridge: Cambridge University Press.

Turner, F. 1981. *The Greek Heritage in Victorian Britain.* New Haven, CT: Yale University Press.

Ungern-Sternberg, J. von. 1970. *Untersuchungen zum spätrepublikanischen Notstandsrecht. Senatusconsultum ultimum und hostis-Erklärung.* Vestigia 11. Munich: Beck.

Urbinati, N. 2002. *Mill on Democracy: From the Athenian Polis to Representative Government.* Chicago: University of Chicago Press.

Van de Mieroop, M. 2004. *A History of the Ancient Near East, ca. 3000–323 BC.* Oxford: Blackwell.

Van de Mieroop, M. 2005. *King Hammurabi of Babylon.* Oxford: Blackwell.

Vanderbroeck, P. J. 1987. *Popular Leadership and Collective Behavior in the Late Roman Republic (ca. 80–50 BC).* Dutch Monographs on Ancient History and Archaeology 3. Amsterdam: J. C. Gieben.

Vanderspoel, John 1995. *Themistius and the Imperial Court: Oratory, Civic Duty, and Paideia from Constantius to Theodosius.* Ann Arbor: University of Michigan Press.

Van Effenterre, H. and Ruzé, F. 1994–5. *Nomima. Recueil d'inscriptions politiques et juridiques de l'archaïsme grec.* 2 vols. Rome: École Française de Rome.

Van Oort, J. 1991. *Jerusalem and Babylon: A Study into Augustine's* City of God *and the Sources of His Doctrine of the Two Cities.* New York: E. J. Brill.

Van Straten, F. T. 1992. "Votives and Votaries in Greek Sanctuaries." In A. Schachter (ed.), *Le sanctuaire grec*, 247–84. Entretiens Fondation Hardt 37. Geneva: Fondation Hardt. (Repr. in R. Buxton (ed.), *Oxford Readings in Greek Religion*, 191–223. Oxford: Oxford University Press, 2000.)

Van Straten, F. T. 1995. *Hiera Kala: Images of Animal Sacrifice in Archaic and Classical Greece.* Leiden: Brill.

Van Wees, H. (ed.) 2000. *War and Violence in Ancient Greece.* London: Duckworth/Classical Press of Wales.

Van Wees, H. 2004. *Greek Warfare: Myths and Realities.* London: Duckworth.

Van Wees, Hans 2006. "Mass and Elite in Solon's Athens: The Property Classes Revisited." In Blok and Lardinois 2006: 351–89.

Vasaly, Ann 1993. *Representation: Images of the World in Ciceronian Oratory.* Berkeley: University of California Press.

Veenhof, K. R. 1995. " 'In Accordance with the Words of the Stele.' Evidence for Old Assyrian Legislation." *Chicago-Kent Law Review* 70: 1717–44.

Vernant, J.-P. (ed.) 1968. *Problèmes de la guerre en Grèce ancienne.* Paris: EHESS.

Vernant, J.-P. 1976. "Remarks on the Class Struggle in Ancient Greece," trans. R. Archer and S. C. Humphreys. *Critique of Anthropology* 7: 67–81.

Vernant, J.-P. 1980. *Myth and Society in Ancient Greece,* trans. J. Lloyd. Brighton: Harvester Press.

Vernant, J.-P. 1982. *The Origins of Greek Thought.* Ithaca, NY: Cornell University Press.

Vernant, J.-P. 1988. "The Historical Moment of Tragedy in Greece: Some of the Social and Psychological Conditions." In Vernant and Vidal-Naquet 1988: 23–8.

Vernant, J.-P. 1989. *L'individu, la mort, l'amour. Soi-même et l'autre en Grèce ancienne.* Paris: Gallimard.

Vernant, J.-P. and Vidal-Naquet, P. 1988. *Myth and Tragedy in Ancient Greece*, trans. J. Lloyd. New York: Zone. (French original 1972.)

Vessey, Mark et al. (eds) 1999. *History, Apocalypse and the Secular Imagination: New Essays on Augustine's* City of God. Bowling Green: Philosophy Documentation Center.

Veyne, P. 1975. "Y-a-t-il eu un impérialisme romain?" *Mélanges de l'École Française de Rome* 87: 793–855.

Vidal-Naquet, P. 1997. "The Place and Status of Foreigners in Athenian Tragedy." In Pelling 1997: 109–19.

Villa, D. 1996. *Arendt and Heidegger*. Princeton: Princeton University Press.

Villa, D. (ed.) 2000. *The Cambridge Companion to Hannah Arendt*. Cambridge: Cambridge University Press.

Villa, D. 2001. *Socratic Citizenship*. Princeton: Princeton University Press.

Viroli, Maurizio 2002. *Republicanism*. New York: Hill and Wang.

Vishnia, Rachel 1996. *State, Society, and Popular Leaders in Mid-Republican Rome, 241–167 BC*. London: Routledge.

Vlastos, G. 1983. "The Historical Socrates and Athenian Democracy." *Political Theory* 11: 495–516.

Vlastos, G. 1989. "Socratic Piety." *Proceedings of the Boston Area Colloquium in Ancient Philosophy* 5: 213–38.

Vlastos, G. 1991. *Socrates, Ironist and Moral Philosopher*. Ithaca, NY: Cornell University Press.

Vlastos, G. 1994a. *Socratic Studies*, ed. M. Burnyeat. Cambridge: Cambridge University Press.

Vlastos, G. 1994b. "Socrates and Vietnam." In Vlastos 1994a: 127–33.

Volkmann, H. 1967. "Die Basileia als Endoxos Douleia." *Hermes* 16: 155–61.

Volterra, E. 1937. *Diritto Romano e diritti orientali*. Bologna: Nicola Zanichelli. (Repr. Naples: Jovane, 1983).

von Fritz, K. 1958. *Aristotle's Contribution to the Practice and Theory of Historiography*. Berkeley: University of California Press.

von Fritz, K. 1975. *The Theory of the Mixed Constitution in Antiquity: A Critical Analysis of Polybius' Political Ideas* [1954]. New York: Columbia University Press.

von Heyking, John 2001. *Augustine and Politics as Longing in the World*. Columbia: University of Missouri Press.

von Reden, Sitta. 1995. *Exchange in Ancient Greece*. London: Duckworth.

Vos, Harm de 1956. *Themis*. Assen: Van Gorcum. (Repr. New York: Arno Press, 1979.)

Wade-Gery, H. T. 1932. "Thucydides the Son of Melesias: A Study of Periklean Policy." *Journal of Hellenic Studies* 52: 205–27.

Wagenvoort, H. 1980. "Pietas." In Wagenvoort, *Pietas: Selected Studies in Roman Religion*, 1–20. Leiden: Brill.

Walbank, F. W. 1933. *Aratos of Sicyon*. Cambridge: Cambridge University Press.

Walbank, F. W. 1967. *A Historical Commentary on Polybius*, vol. 1. Oxford: Clarendon Press.

Walbank, F. W. 1972. *Polybius*. Berkeley: University of California Press.

Walbank, F. W. 1979. *A Historical Commentary on Polybius*, vol. 3. Oxford: Oxford University Press.

Walbank, F. W. 1984. "Monarchy and Monarchical Ideas." In F. W. Walbank et al. (eds), *The Cambridge Ancient History*, vol. 7: part 1, 62–100. 2nd edn. Cambridge: Cambridge University Press.

Walbank, F. W. 1993. "*Hē Tōn Holōn Elpis* and the Antigonids." *Ancient Macedonia* 5: 1721–30.

Walbank, F. W. 2002. *Polybius, Rome and the Hellenistic World*. Cambridge: Cambridge University Press.

Waldron, J. (ed.) 1984. *Theories of Rights*. Oxford: Oxford University Press.

Waldron, J. 1993. "Rights." In P. Pettit and R. E. Goodin (eds), *A Companion to Contemporary Political Philosophy*, 575–85. Oxford: Blackwell.

Waldron, J. 2000. "What is Cosmopolitan?" *Journal of Political Philosophy* 8: 227–43.

Walker, L. J. 2002. "Moral Exemplarity." In W. Damon (ed.), *Bringing in a New Era in Character Education*, 65–83. Stanford: Stanford University Press.

Wallace, R. W. 1983. "The Date of Solon's Reforms." *American Journal of Ancient History* 8: 81–95.

Wallace, R. W. 1994. "Private Lives and Public Enemies: Freedom of Thought in Classical Athens." In Boegehold and Scafuro 1994: 205–38.

Wallace, R. W. 1995. "On Not Legislating Sexual Conduct in Fourth-Century Athens." In G. Thür and J. Vélissaropoulos-Karakostas (eds), *Symposion 1993, Vorträge zur griechischen und hellenistichen Reschtsgeschichte*, 151–66. Vienna: Böhlau.

Wallace, R. W. 2004. "The Power to Speak – and Not to Listen – in Ancient Athens." In R. Rosen and I. Sluiter (eds), *Freedom of Speech in Ancient Athens*, 221–32. Leiden: Brill.

Wallace, R. W. 2005. "Law, Attic Comedy, and the Regulation of Comic Speech." In M. Gagarin and D. Cohen (eds), *The Cambridge Companion to Greek Law*, 357–73. Cambridge: Cambridge University Press.

Wallace, R. W. 2007a. "Law's Enemies in Ancient Athens." In E. Cantarella (ed.), *Symposion 2005, Vorträge zur griechischen und hellenistichen Reschtsgeschichte*, 183–96. Vienna: Austrian Academy of Sciences.

Wallace, R. W. 2007b. "Revolutions and a New Order in Solonian Athens and Archaic Greece." In Raaflaub, Ober, and Wallace 2007: 49–82.

Wallace, R. W. forthcoming a. "Thucydides as Historian: Facts and Judgments." In A. Pierris (ed.), *Mind, Money, and Might*. Patras: Center for Philosophical Research.

Wallace, R. W. forthcoming b. "Tyrants, Lawgivers, Sages." In Raaflaub and van Wees forthcoming.

Wallace-Hadrill, A. 1982. "Civilis Princeps: Between Citizen and King." *Journal of Roman Studies* 72: 32–48.

Wallace-Hadrill, A. 1983. *Suetonius: The Scholar and His Caesars*. New Haven, CT: Yale University Press.

Wallace-Hadrill, A. 1997. "*Mutatio Morum*: The Idea of a Cultural Revolution." In T. Habinek and A. Schiesaro (eds), *The Roman Cultural Revolution*, 3–22. Cambridge: Cambridge University Press.

Wallach, J. 1994. "Two Democracies and Virtue." In Euben, Wallach, and Ober 1994a: 319–40.

Wallach, J. 2001. *The Platonic Political Art: A Study of Critical Reason and Democracy*. University Park: Pennsylvania State University Press.

Walsh, G. B. 1978. "The Rhetoric of Birthright and Race in Euripides' *Ion*." *Hermes* 106: 301–15.

Walsh, P. G. 1963. *Livy: His Historical Aims and Methods*. Cambridge: Cambridge University Press.

Waltz, K. N. 1959. *Man, the State and War: A Theoretical Analysis*. New York: Columbia University Press.

Waltz, K. N. 1979. *Theory of International Politics*. Boston: McGraw-Hill.

Waltz, K. N. 1988. "The Origins of War in Neorealist Theory." *Journal of Interdisciplinary History* 18: 615–28.

Walzer, M. 1983. *Spheres of Justice*. New York: Basic Books.

Walzer, M. 2004. *Politics and Passion: Toward a More Egalitarian Liberalism*. New Haven, CT: Yale University Press.

Warmington, E. H. (ed. and trans.) 1935. *Remains of Old Latin I: Ennius, Caecilius*. Cambridge, MA: Harvard University Press.

Warner, R. (trans.) 1971. *Thucydides. The History of the Peloponnesian War*. Harmondsworth: Penguin.

Waters, K. H. 1971. *Herodotos on Tyrants and Despots: A Study in Objectivity*. Wiesbaden: F. Steiner.

Waters, K. H. 1972. "Herodotus and Politics." *Greece and Rome*, n.s. 19.2: 136–50.

Watson, Alan 1975. *Rome of the Twelve Tables*. Princeton: Princeton University Press.

Weber, Gregor and Zimmermann, Martin (eds) 2003. *Propaganda – Selbstdarstellung – Repräsentation im römischen Kaiserreich des 1. Jhs. n. Chr*. Stuttgart: Franz Steiner.

Weber, Max 1958. "Politics as a Vocation." In *From Max Weber: Essays in Sociology*, ed. and trans. H. H. Gerth and C. Wright Mills, 77–128. New York: Galaxy.

Weber, Max 1978. *Economy and Society*, ed. G. Roth and C. Wittich. Berkeley: University of California Press.

Weiler, I. 2004. "Sklaverei in der homerischen und altorientalischen Welt. Vergleichende Betrachtungen." In Rollinger and Ulf 2004a: 270–91.

Weinstein, Donald 1970. *Savonarola and Florence: Prophecy and Patriotism in the Renaissance*. Princeton: Princeton University Press.

Weiss, R. 1998. *Socrates Dissatisfied: An Analysis of Plato's Crito*. New York: Oxford University Press.

Weithman, Paul 1992. "Augustine and Aquinas on Original Sin and the Purposes of Political Authority." *Journal of the History of Philosophy* 30: 353–76.

Welles, C. B. 1934. *Royal Correspondence in the Hellenistic Period: A Study in Greek Epigraphy*. New Haven, CT: Yale University Press.

Welles, C. B. 1965. "Alexander's Historical Achievement." *Greece and Rome* 12: 216–28.

Wells, B. 2005. "Law and Practice." In Snell 2005: 183–95.

Welwei, K.-H. 1963. "Könige und Königtum im Urteil des Polybios." Diss., Cologne.

West, M. L. (ed.) 1966. *Hesiod. Theogony*, with Prolegomena and Commentary. Oxford: Clarendon Press.

West, M. L. 1971. *Early Greek Philosophy and the Orient*. Oxford: Clarendon Press.

West, M. L. 1993. *Greek Lyric Poetry*. Oxford: Clarendon Press.

West, M. L. 1997. *The East Face of Helicon: West Asiatic Elements in Greek Poetry and Myth*. Oxford: Clarendon Press.

Westbrook, R. 1988. "The Nature and Origins of the Twelve Tables." *Zeitschrift für Rechtsgeschichte, Rom. Abt.* 105: 74–121.

Westbrook, R. 1989. "Cuneiform Law Codes and the Origins of Legislation." *Zeitschrift für Assyriologie* 79: 201–22.

Westbrook, R. (ed.) 2003. *A History of Ancient Near Eastern Law*. 2 vols. Leiden: Brill.

Westbrook, R. forthcoming. "Drakon's Homicide Law." In *Symposion 2007: Vorträge zur griechischen und hellenistischen Rechtsgeschichte*.

Wetzel, James 1992. *Augustine and the Limits of Virtue*. New York: Cambridge University Press.

Whitley, J. 1998. "Literacy and Law-Making: The Case of Archaic Crete." In N. Fisher and H. van Wees (eds), *Archaic Greece: New Approaches and New Evidence*, 311–31. London: Duckworth/Classical Press of Wales.

Whitmarsh, T. 2002. "Alexander's Hellenism and Plutarch's Textualism." *Classical Quarterly*, n.s. 52.1: 174–92.

Whitmarsh, T. 2006. *The Second Sophistic.* Cambridge: Cambridge University Press.

Wieacker, F. 1967. "Die XII Tafeln in ihrem Jahrhundert." In *Les Origines de la république romaine*, 291–359. Geneva: Fondation Hardt.

Wieacker, F. 1988. *Römische Rechtsgeschichte*, vol. I, Munich: Beck.

Wiesehöfer, J. 1996. " 'King of Kings' and 'Philhellên': Kingship in Arsacid Iran." In Bilde et al. 1996a: 55–66.

Wiesehöfer, J. 2004. " 'Persien, der faszinierende Feind der Griechen.' Güteraustausch und Kulturtransfer in achaimenidischer Zeit." In Rollinger and Ulf 2004a: 295–310.

Wilcke, C. 1993. "Politik im Spiegel der Literatur, Literatur als Mittel der Politik im älteren Babylonien." In Raaflaub and Müller-Luckner 1993: 29–75.

Wilcken, U. 1967. *Alexander the Great.* New York: Norton.

Wilkinson, D. 1999. "Unipolarity without Hegemony." *International Studies Review* 1: 142–72.

Will, E. 1982. *Histoire politique du monde hellénistique*, vol. 2. 2nd edn. Nancy: Presses Universitaires de Nancy.

Willetts, R. F. 1955. *Aristocratic Society in Ancient Crete.* London: Routledge and Kegan Paul. (Repr. Westport, CT: Greenwood Press, 1980.)

Willetts, R. F. 1965. *Ancient Crete: A Social History from Early Times until the Roman Occupation.* London: Routledge.

Willetts, R. F. 1967. *The Law Code of Gortyn*, ed. with introd., trans., and a commentary. Berlin: De Gruyter.

Williams, B. 1981. "Internal and External Reasons." In Williams, *Moral Luck*, 101–13. Cambridge: Cambridge University Press.

Williams, B. 1985. *Ethics and the Limits of Philosophy.* London: Harmondsworth.

Williams, B. 1993. *Shame and Necessity.* Sather Classical Lectures, vol. 57. Berkeley: University of California Press.

Williams, B. 2002. *Truth and Truthfulness.* Princeton: Princeton University Press.

Williams, B. 2006a. "Acting as a Virtuous Person Acts." In Williams, *The Sense of the Past: Essays in the History of Philosophy*, ed. M. F. Burnyeat, 189–97. Princeton: Princeton University Press.

Williams, B. 2006b. "Hylomorphism." In Williams, *The Sense of the Past: Essays in the History of Philosophy*, ed. M. F. Burnyeat, 218–30. Princeton: Princeton University Press.

Williamson, Callie 2005. *The Laws of the Roman People: Public Law in the Expansion and Decline of the Roman Republic.* Ann Arbor: University of Michigan Press.

Winkler, John 1990. *The Constraints of Desire: The Anthropology of Sex and Gender in Ancient Greece.* New York: Routledge.

Winkler, J. J. and Zeitlin, F. I. (eds) 1990. *Nothing to Do with Dionysos? Athenian Drama in Its Social Context.* Princeton: Princeton University Press.

Winton, R. 2000. "Herodotus, Thucydides and the Sophists." In C. Rowe and Schofield 2000: 89–121.

Wiredu, K. 1996. *Cultural Universals and Particulars: An African Perspective.* Indianapolis: Indiana University Press.

Wiredu, K. 2001. "Society and Democracy in Africa." In T. Kiros (ed.), *Explorations in African Political Thought*, 171–84. New York: Routledge.

Wirszubski, C. 1950. *Libertas as a Political Idea at Rome during the Late Republic and Early Principate.* Cambridge: Cambridge University Press.

Wiseman, T. P. 1971. *New Men in the Roman Senate 139 BC–AD 14.* Oxford: Oxford University Press.

Wiseman, T. P. 1994a. "The Senate and the Populares, 69–60 BC." In J. A. Crook et al. (eds), *The Cambridge Ancient History,* vol. 9: 327–67. 2nd edn. Cambridge: Cambridge University Press.

Wiseman, T. P. 1994b. "Caesar, Pompey and Rome, 59–50 BC." In J. A. Crook et al. (eds), *The Cambridge Ancient History,* vol. 9: 368–423. 2nd edn. Cambridge: Cambridge University Press.

Wiseman, T. P. 1995. *Remus: A Roman Myth.* Cambridge: Cambridge University Press.

Wiseman, T. P. (ed.) 2002. *Classics in Progress: Essays on Ancient Greece and Rome.* Oxford: British Academy.

Wiseman, T. P. 2004. *The Myths of Rome.* Exeter: University of Exeter Press.

Wohl, V. 1998. *Intimate Commerce: Exchange, Gender, and Subjectivity in Greek Tragedy.* Austin: University of Texas Press.

Wohl, V. 2002. *Love Among the Ruins: The Erotics of Democracy in Classical Athens.* Princeton: Princeton University Press.

Wolff, J. and de-Shalit, A. 2007. *Disadvantage.* Oxford: Oxford University Press.

Wolin, S. 2004. *Politics and Vision.* Princeton: Princeton University Press.

Wollheim, R. 1990. *Sigmund Freud.* Cambridge: Cambridge University Press.

Wood, E. M. 1988. *Peasant-Citizen and Slave: The Foundations of Athenian Democracy.* London: Verso.

Wood, E. M. 1994. "Democracy: An Idea of Ambiguous Ancestry." In Euben, Wallach, and Ober 1994a: 59–80.

Wood, E. M. 1996. "Demos vs. 'We, the People': Freedom and Democracy Ancient and Modern." In Ober and Hedrick 1996: 121–37.

Wood, Ellen, and Wood, Neal. 1978. *Class Ideology and Ancient Political Theory: Socrates, Plato, and Aristotle in Social Context.* Oxford: Basil Blackwell.

Woodruff, P. 2005. *First Democracy: The Challenge of an Ancient Idea.* Oxford: Oxford University Press.

Woozley, A. D. 1979. *Law and Obedience: The Arguments of Plato's Crito.* Chapel Hill: University of North Carolina Press.

Wray, David 2001. *Catullus and the Poetics of Roman Manhood.* Cambridge: Cambridge University Press.

Wright, M. R. 1988. "The Origins of Political Theory." *Polis* 7.2: 75–104.

Yack, B. 1993. *The Problems of a Political Animal: Community, Justice, and Conflict in Aristotelian Political Thought.* Berkeley: University of California Press.

Yakobson, Alexander 1999. *Elections and Electioneering in Rome: A Study in the Political System of the Late Republic.* Stuttgart: Franz Steiner.

Yamauchi, E. M. 1980. "Two Reformers Compared: Solon of Athens and Nehemiah of Jerusalem." In G. Rendsburg et al. (eds), *The Bible World: Essays in Honor of Cyrus H. Gordon,* 269–92. New York: Institute of Hebrew Culture and Education of New York University.

Yaron, R. 1993. "Social Problems and Policies in the Ancient Near East." In B. Halpern and D. Hobson (eds), *Law, Politics and Society in the Ancient Mediterranean World,* 19–41. Sheffield: Sheffield Academic Press.

Young, C. 1988. "Aristotle on Temperance." *Philosophical Review* 97: 521–42.

Yunis, H. 1996. *Taming Democracy: Models of Political Rhetoric in Classical Athens.* Ithaca, NY: Cornell University Press.

Zacharia, K. 2003. *Converging Truths: Euripides' Ion and the Athenian Quest for Self-Definition.* Leiden: Brill.

Zanker, Paul 1988. *The Power of Images in the Age of Augustus,* trans. A. Shapiro. Ann Arbor: University of Michigan Press.

Zeitlin, F. I. 1990. "Thebes: Theater of Self and Society in Athenian Drama." In Winkler and Zeitlin 1990: 130–67. (Earlier version in Euben 1986: 101–41.)

Zeitlin, F. I. 1996. *Playing the Other: Gender and Society in Classical Greek Literature.* Chicago: University of Chicago Press.

Zetzel, J. E. G. (ed. and trans.) 1995. *Cicero De Re Publica: Selections.* Cambridge: Cambridge University Press.

Zetzel, J. E. G. (ed. and trans.) 1999. *Cicero: On the Commonwealth and On the Laws.* Cambridge: Cambridge University Press.

Zhmud, L. 1996. *Wissenschaft, Philosophie und Religion im frühen Pythagoreismus.* Berlin: Akademie.

Zuckert, C. and Zuckert, M. 2006. *The Truth about Leo Strauss.* Chicago: University of Chicago Press.

Zuckert, M. 1998. *Natural Rights and the New Republicanism.* Princeton: Princeton University Press.

Index of Subjects

A Companion to Greek and Roman Political Thought, First Edition. Edited by Ryan K. Balot.
© 2013 Blackwell Publishing Ltd. Published 2013 by Blackwell Publishing Ltd.

imports, cultural, Greece 38–41
incentive problems 70–1
  Aristotle 81, 82, 83
  in Greek literature 72–3
  Plato 79–80
income declaration, law on 40–1
individuals
  Arendt 546–8
  happiness of 399–400
  one job for 355–6
  personal freedom 164–77
  in political context 31–2
  relationship with communities 172,
    173–4, 391
  rights 149–63, 169
  self-interest 70–84, 310–13, 318, 530–2
  as self-sufficient 389
influences, outside, on Greek political
    thought 37–56
information, and public action 74, 75–6, 78,
    81
injustice 286
  and anger 298
  equated with vice 425
innovation, and public action 76–8
insects, social, as political animals 402
institutional setting, drama 442–3
institutions
  Aristotle 407–12
  checks on 339–40, 351
  democratic 138–40, 223
  to encourage public action 80
  foreign influences 39
  as ideological state apparatus 27
  interplay with structural conditions 27–8
  of mixed constitutions 532–3
  in modern political philosophy 554
  for political participation 532
  politics as formalized 21–3
  separation of powers 538–9, 540
insults, public 164
intellectual life *see* contemplation,
    philosophical
intellectuals 415
intelligence, in good governance 182–4
international relations
  hellenistic monarchies 256–7
  Rome 94
international relations theory, use of
    vocabulary of 8
international trade, and self-sufficiency 389

international treaties, Greek 44
intuitions, moral, Aristotle 406
Ionian Greeks 64, 91–2
  in drama 450–1
irony, Aristophanes 448–9
isēgoria 75, 107, 136, 236–7, 531
Islamic political philosophy, and Strauss
    549–51
Isocrates 244, 253, 345
  biographies 421–2, 427, 431
  character of political leaders 457
  education of rulers 241, 242
  withdrawal from politics 496
isogonia 136
isokratia 107, 236–7
isonomia 107, 134, 236–7, 239
isopoliteia 67
isopsēphia 154
Italy, northern, republicanism 534, 535

Jefferson, Thomas 529, 539–40
Jerusalem 502, 503, 516, 519, 522
Jewish political philosophy, and Strauss
    549–51
Jews 515–16, 518, 520
jobs
  one for each individual 355–6
  see also labor; work; workers
Judaism, relationship of Romans to 129
judges 46–7
  supplication before 314
jurors
  Greece 65, 66, 139, 140–1, 142, 330
  in Greek drama 448
  payment for 139, 142, 330
  Rome 68
justice
  Aristotle 400–1
  Augustine 507
  Callipolis 354–5
  Greek 41, 52
  by ideal rulers 254
  and knowledge 327–8
  and *magnitudo animi* 209
  and minding one's own business
    489–90
  in mixed constitutions 533–4
  natural 358–9
  and public action 78, 79–80, 81, 82
  and religion 120–1, 122
  as royal virtue 269, 273–4, 276

Stoics (*cont'd*)
  education 494
  engagement in politics 497
  libertas 176
  mixed constitution 190
  monarchs 274
  theology 121–3
  virtues 201–2, 203, 204–5, 207, 210
  and withdrawal from politics 492
stories, traditional 86
stratēgoi 107
Strauss, Leo
  background 542–3
  and Platonic political philosophy 543,
    549–55
street theatre, recall of Cicero 315–17, 318
strife *see* conflict, civil
strong, power of 358–9, 361–3
structure, political, Greece 22–3
structures, interplay with institutions 27–8
subjects, ethical and political, Foucault 31–2
succession, hereditary, rulers 192
Suetonius, royal vices 275
Sulla 460–1, 466, 467
  charismatic authority of 28
  Plutarch on 469
summons, Socrates 324–5
superior, rule by 342–3, 350–1, 358–9,
    362–3, 533
supernaturalism 382
supplication 313–16
symbolic violence, Bourdieu 30
sympoliteia 67
synoecism 64

Tacitus 277
  character of German tribes 458
  citizenship 93
  on Roman character 462–4, 469
taxation, in hellenistic monarchies 255
technē
  as profession 345–6
  and virtue 424–5
technology, Marx 549
teleology 426
  Aristotle 402, 406, 409
temperance, as royal virtue 275, 276
Themistius, Roman universalism 482
Theodorus 497
Theognis of Megara, good and bad rule 234–5
theologies, doctrine of three 122

theology 119–23
  civic 122, 123, 126
  mythical 122–3, 126
  natural 122, 123, 126
  philosophical 122
  traditional 119–21
Theophrastus 491
Theopompos, biography 431
theory, and practice 543, 549, 554, 555
thetes 138–9
Thirty Tyrants 241, 325–6, 334, 349, 495
Thrasea Paetus 464
Thrasymachus 348, 351, 356–7, 430
  expert knowledge 346–7
  law 371
Thucydides
  on Alcibiades 166
  collective deliberation 289
  constitutional debate 343
  democracy 135, 239–40
  history 429
  immigration to Athens 91
  innovation and learning 76–8
  mixed constitutions 178–80, 196, 197
  monarchy 240–1
  passions 294–6, 297–8
  personal freedom 167–8, 173
  political participation 137–8
  politics 390
  tyranny 364
  virtue 422–3, 430–1, 432
  see also Pericles
thumos see spiritedness
Tiberius, character of 462–4
tolerance 168
topical approach, described 15–16
totalitarian regimes 544
  Arendt 543
  and leaders 554–5
  Strauss 543
totalitarianism, and ethical education 433
trade, international 389
  and self-sufficiency 389
tradition
  and cosmopolitanism 474
  prestige of 428
tragedies, Greek
  barbarism in 478–9
  and political thought 440, 442, 443,
    445–8, 450–1
  see also specific authors

Index Locorum

Note: References to ancient texts are in **bold** print.

A Companion to Greek and Roman Political Thought, First Edition. Edited by Ryan K. Balot.
© 2013 Blackwell Publishing Ltd. Published 2013 by Blackwell Publishing Ltd.